THE POSITION OF THE GERMAN LANGUAGE IN THE WORLD

The Position of the German Language in the World focuses on the global position of German and the factors which work towards sustaining its use and utility for international communication.

From the perspective of the global language constellation, the detailed data analysis of this substantial research project depicts German as an example of a second-rank language. The book also provides a model for analysis and description of international languages other than English. It offers a framework for strengthening the position of languages such as Arabic, Chinese, French, Portuguese, Spanish and others and for countering exaggerated claims about the global monopoly position of English. This comprehensive handbook of the state of the German language in the world was originally published in 2015 by Walter de Gruyter in German and has been critically acclaimed.

Suitable for scholars and researchers of the German language, the handbook shows in detail how intricately and thoroughly German and other second-rank languages are tied up with a great number of societies and how these statistics support or weaken the languages' functions and maintenance.

Ulrich Ammon was Professor of German Linguistics with sociolinguistics at the University of Duisburg-Essen. He taught at universities all over the world, including: The University of North Carolina, Chapel Hill, USA; in Australia at the University of Sydney, Australian National University in Canberra; in Japan at Dokkyo University, Soka; and in Austria at Vienna University. Ammon was a member of several scientific organisations and was President of the International Association of Applied Linguistics (GAL) from 2003–2006. He was involved in many third-party projects funded by the German Research Foundation, the Volkswagen Foundation, the Fritz Thyssen Foundation, the European Union and the German Academic Exchange Service. His main research interests were sociolinguistics, language policy, international language research, variation linguistics and dialectology.

THE POSITION OF THE GERMAN LANGUAGE IN THE WORLD

Ulrich Ammon

TRANSLATED BY DAVID CHARLSTON

Routledge
Taylor & Francis Group

LONDON AND NEW YORK

First published 2020
by Routledge
2 Park Square, Milton Park, Abingdon, Oxon OX14 4RN

and by Routledge
605 Third Avenue, New York, NY 10017

First issued in paperback 2022

Routledge is an imprint of the Taylor & Francis Group, an informa business

© 2020 Ulrich Ammon
Translated by David Charlston

Ammon, Ulrich: *Die Stellung der deutschen Sprache in der Welt*

Original Edition © Walter de Gruyter GmbH Berlin Boston. All rights
reserved

"The translation of this work was funded by Geisteswissenschaften
International – Translation Funding for Work in the Humanities and Social
Sciences from Germany, a joint initiative of the Fritz Thyssen Foundation,
the German Federal Foreign Office, the collecting society VG WORT
and the Börsenverein des Deutschen Buchhandels (German Publishers &
Booksellers Association) Translation"

Publisher's Note
The publisher has gone to great lengths to ensure the quality of this reprint but
points out that some imperfections in the original copies may be apparent.

British Library Cataloguing-in-Publication Data
A catalogue record for this book is available from the British Library

Library of Congress Cataloging-in-Publication Data
A catalog record for this book has been requested

ISBN: 978–1–03–240126–3 (pbk)
ISBN: 978–1–138–71765–7 (hbk)
ISBN: 978–1–315–15787–0 (ebk)

DOI: 10.4324/9781315157870

Typeset in Bembo
by Apex CoVantage, LLC

CONTENTS

Contents

Contents

TABLES

FIGURES

MAPS

FOREWORD

The Position of the German Language in the World is related to the previous books and articles I have written but goes considerably beyond them thematically and methodologically. Mindful of the comprehensive sweep of its title, I have tried at least to point towards the need for further research whenever I became aware of any gaps. Apart from those attributable to my personal shortcomings, these derive, on the one hand, from institutional separation between the relevant disciplines (especially linguistics, sociology, economics and political science) and, on the other hand, from continuing compartmentalisation of research – despite globalisation – among different major language communities. I recognise, however, that to complain about this last point is hardly compatible with the theme of the book.

In many places, readers will be aware that I have drawn – out of necessity – on a range of outside information providers using diverse media, especially the Internet, including Wikipedia, to which I resorted in the absence of a more robust resource. Generous assistance received from the rich network of colleagues and students at my disposal has been an invaluable and more reliable source. In every case, I have endeavoured to name these sources at the appropriate place in the book. Although I shall not mention them all individually here, I take this opportunity to thank them once again very warmly.

Moreover, I would like to express my personal, and belated thanks to Professor Hermann Bausinger (University of Tübingen), who guided my academic interests towards the topic of the present book at a decisive phase of my studies. I am very grateful to David Charlston, the translator of this book from German into English, and to Martin Durrell who introduced us. David Charlston (Honorary Research Fellow, University of Manchester, Centre for Translation and Intercultural Studies) has been in regular communication with me throughout the translation process and has produced an excellent translation. The English version of the book has been slightly abridged by comparison with the German original. I would also like to thank the devoted members of my doctoral studies group warmly for their many comments and suggestions. I am indebted to the research funding organisations, especially the German Research Foundation (*Deutsche Forschungsgemeinschaft*), for their support of my projects over many years, and to the German Publishers and Booksellers Association (*Börsenverein des Deutschen Buchhandels*), which generously financed the translation of this book. Thank you also to Birte Kellermeier-Rehbein, for her substantial support on the index and manuscript preparation.

Special thanks are due to Walter de Gruyter for publishing the German version of this book on which this translation is based as well as previous books of mine, especially to their conscientious reader, Daniel Gietz. I also express my gratitude to Routledge for publishing the English translation, especially to their helpful and considerate reader, Andrea Hartill.

Ulrike Schulz, my secretary for many years, who meticulously prepared the original German-language manuscript for publication, also deserves heartfelt thanks for her indispensable assistance. Finally, I must gratefully acknowledge that, even with all this help, the present book could not have been completed without the support of my wife and family.

Duisburg, Summer 2019
Ulrich Ammon

PREFACE

Sadly, Ulrich Ammon passed away on 3 May 2019 at the age of 75, just before the typeset proofs of this translation became available, and so he did not have the pleasure of seeing the publication of this translation of his book, which he was very much looking forward to. Ulrich Ammon was one of the pioneers of modern sociolinguistics in Germany, beginning with his Tübingen doctoral thesis on the social status of standard language and dialect in Germany, and in the years following, he gained recognition as one of the leading scholars in the field of German sociolinguistics, being appointed in 1980 as Chair of German Linguistics at the University of Duisburg, where he remained until his retirement. He built a notable international reputation through his many publications in German and English (14 books and more than 300 articles). He also played a leading role in a number of academic bodies, including a term as President of the German Association of Applied Linguistics (GAL) and held visiting professorships in more than a dozen countries worldwide.

Over the years, his interest turned to more general issues of language policy; in particular, the nature and status of standard languages, especially the various national varieties of German, which was the subject of a comprehensive survey co-edited by him and a number of colleagues and which has now appeared in a second edition. The present work, documenting in detail the position and status of German as a world language, was published in Germany in 2015 and was immediately acclaimed as a major contribution to scholarship. He was delighted that this work, the result of a lifetime's intensive study of one of the major European languages in all its facets, would appear in English, and he was especially pleased that David Charlston, an experienced translator with specialised subject knowledge, was able to undertake the task of translation. This meant that his work would be accessible to a much larger international community than only specialists in Linguistics, since it is written for a wider public, and it is thus a matter of deepest regret that he was, ultimately, not able to see it in print.

Martin Durrell
Emeritus Professsor of German
School of Arts, Languages & Cultures
University of Manchester

A
THE GERMAN LANGUAGE BETWEEN NATIONAL INTERESTS AND GLOBAL COMMUNICATION

Terminology and theory

1. Speakers' interests in a language with a strong global positioning

Regular viewers of foreign news on German or Austrian television will probably have noticed that reporters in different countries have little difficulty finding German-speaking respondents. Occasionally, interpreters have to be used, which makes the conversation more awkward and less authentic. Companies from German-speaking countries (Ch. B.4) seeking business links with foreign enterprises also often express relief at finding colleagues who can communicate in written or spoken German. These are among the advantages derived from the *position* of German in the world, which forms the subject matter of this book. People who enjoy such advantages, especially derived from the international position of German (Ch. A.3), have an interest in preserving or strengthening this position.

The advantages in the two examples mentioned above benefit primarily *native speakers* of German and – more generally – German-speaking countries. But these advantages also extend to non-German partners and contacts. Thus, speakers of German as a foreign language (*German FL speakers*) – who have learnt German in addition to their native language – also benefit from the global position of German. These include young people in China, Cameroon and other countries who learn German in their home country as a foreign language, so that they can then study or work in a German-speaking country for a time; and foreign entrepreneurs who, because of their knowledge of German (as a foreign language), gain easier access to German-speaking countries: Germany, Austria, German-speaking Switzerland, Liechtenstein, Luxembourg (where German is one of three official languages), the Italian province of Bolzano in South Tyrol and German-speaking eastern Belgium (Ch. D). Such advantages are enjoyed by native speakers and German FL-speakers because of the *international position* of German. An important factor in this global position is therefore the learning of German outside German-speaking countries (see Kloss 1974b). In the case of languages of a lower international position or none at all, such as Finnish, Greek, Czech and many other languages, opportunities for learning these languages abroad are more restricted, which makes contact between foreigners and native speakers of these languages more difficult, at least in linguistic terms.

Knowledge of an international language is advantageous for native speakers and for those who use it as a foreign language. In the long term, if knowledge of German was not advantageous for German FL-speakers, very few people would bother to learn German. Indeed, there is hardly a set of knowledge or skills more complex and more effort-intensive than learning a language, its *system* (grammar, vocabulary, pronunciation, spelling) and its situationally appropriate use or *pragmatics*. This applies especially to high-level linguistic *competence*, which is much more difficult to achieve in a foreign language than in one's native language. To some extent, the native language or languages (some people have two or even three) can be acquired naturally, through contact, imitation, abstraction of rules, correction and constant use. As a result, people hardly notice the complexity of their own language. By contrast, learners of a foreign language tend to be more conscious of its complexity, especially in the context of controlled acquisition, for example, in school, but also for adult learners in cases of uncontrolled acquisition.

Accordingly, FL speakers are often more consciously interested than native speakers in benefiting from their language skills. On one hand, the benefits are never secure, because, in many cases, language skills are not used after they have been acquired. On the other hand, foreign-language speakers experience their use of that language as a more conscious decision, even if the choice was made not by themselves but rather by their parents, or if there was no choice, because the school offered no other option. By contrast, native speakers take the benefits of knowing their language for granted, because it is constantly reinforced through communication with the social environment.

In general, the advantage of knowing a language is gained primarily through the possibilities for communication it opens. A foreign language increases these possibilities beyond the native language, but there are other advantages. The cognitive enrichment associated with additional language skills is one obvious advantage, but this is a difficult question which I will address later (although even in Ch. G.6 – a complete answer will not be possible). Additional vocabulary and the associated meanings can open new insights. Even teaching materials initiate an easily recognisable widening of learners' horizons by providing knowledge of the native speakers' different culture. Learning foreign languages thus increases learners' understanding and the possibility for knowledge.

Other obvious advantages of language skills – especially foreign-language skills, but also a good knowledge of the native language – include an improvement of professional qualifications. This may also be associated with increased personal prestige which is not necessarily directly associated with better qualifications. This advantage often comes with studying classical languages. But learning German as a foreign language can also enhance learners' personal prestige, especially as it allows direct access to classic scientific and philosophical texts (Ch. G.1). Students of linguistics, for whom knowledge of languages can be advantageous without the communicative function, enjoy a further special interest.

Nevertheless, the possibility of communication with contemporary people and institutions represents the most important basis for an interest in language skills. In fact, this defines the instrumental value of a language. For example, *communication potential* or *communicative range* is measured with reference to the people who can communicate in the language. On one hand, this relates to number: the more speakers a language has or the greater its *numerical strength*, the greater its communication potential will be (Ch. A.7). However, the type of speaker (especially whether they are native speakers or FL speakers) and their competence will also play a role, because the possibilities for communication also depend upon this factor (for other speaker types, such *as Second-Language Speakers (SL speakers)*, see Ch. A.3).

The *socio-economic range of a language* – its distribution among speakers of given social status, in institutions and across geographical regions – is also significant with regard to interest in knowing a language. This includes the legal anchoring of the language in *language policies* or *language regimes* of organisations or national governments, for example, its *status* as an *official language*, which also influences its communication potential. The special focus of the present book is on the *geographical communication potential* of a language, its distribution among regions and states or groups of states (for example, the EU; cf. Stickel 2007a for language interests in Europe, or the website "Language Policy in the EU: shared values versus particular interests": www.goethe.de/ges/spa/pan/spw/de4782810.htm). The focus on states or groups of states allows comparison of key aspects of communication potential. If all languages in such a region or political unit (for example in Germany, the German-speaking countries, the EU, the whole world) are included, reference can be made to the *language constellation* within the given frame (cf. Ch. A.7). In such a constellation, the position of one language is determined with reference to the other languages. For German, it is obviously different in Germany, in the EU and in the (entire) world. The topic of the present book repeatedly refocuses attention on the global language constellation which is sometimes also called the *global language system*. Instead of *communication potential* or *communicative range* of a language (*within a nation, the whole world* etc.), I sometimes also refer to its *distribution* or its *position* (Ch. A.3).

Interest in knowing a language, the core of its instrumental value, is measured largely against its communication potential. The more speakers there are in more positions of power, in more countries, distributed over larger areas of the world's surface, and the higher the legal status of the language, the greater its instrumental value, and therefore interest in knowing it, will be. However, this quantifying perspective does not exclude other reasons behind the value of knowing languages. For instance, just consider the possibility of communicating with highly respected individuals or having access to a few very interesting texts or to cultures with a small population. In view of such possibilities, there may also be a specialist interest in languages with low communication potential. However, it is the potential for communication, for broadening contacts and gaining information provided by a language which underpins any of these advantages and anyone's interest in learning it.

For that reason, also, the *spread* of a language, the expansion of its communication potential is relevant to its speakers. Its *contraction*, the shrinking of its communication potential, runs counter to their interests. Many speakers are not fully aware of these interests, but their behaviour in certain situations often reveals an underlying sense. For instance, German-speakers usually express satisfaction when they hear that more German is being learnt somewhere and respond negatively to reports of declining numbers of learners. The intensity of such responses also tends to correlate with the benefits of the German language for the respondents' own occupation. Maximum intensity is presumably reached in German teachers, or even teachers of German as a foreign language (Ch. K.3.5). For them, the general interest of all German speakers in a broad global distribution of German is distilled down to a question of professional survival.

Ultimately, it is all German-speakers, native speakers and FL speakers, who are affected, not just German teachers. But this also includes all German-speaking regions and nations (*native countries*) and their populations, because, for all these people, the potential for communication depends upon the global distribution of German. This potential is greater the more people there are in influential positions in large areas of the world who speak German. By contrast, wherever such language skills terminate, communication must take place via a foreign language or via translation and interpreting services, which is more effort-intensive, cost-intensive and susceptible to error.

Indeed, the advantages of a broad distribution of a language are not limited to its communication potential alone. On the contrary, native speakers and their nations additionally profit from

3

the fact that speakers who have learnt the language as a foreign language generally maintain special relationships with the native countries of this language. For instance, FL learners and FL speakers of German favour German-speaking countries, their populations and institutions for economic, academic, political and – in the broadest sense – cultural contacts. With regard to the shortfall in skilled workers in Germany, it has often been diagnosed that the number of overseas applicants would increase if knowledge of German were distributed more widely in the world: "Many applicants do have the requisite occupational skills, but without German language things become difficult [...]" ("Germany invites applicants from debtor countries/ *Deutschland umwirbt Fachkräfte aus Schuldenländern*", *Welt Online* 18 July 2011).

Furthermore, foreigners with German-language skills act as multipliers for a differentiated and generally positive image of German-speaking countries, their inhabitants and their culture. The reverse is an exception rather than the rule, but not impossible in principle, for example, because of experiences of xenophobia, not infrequent in Germany, or cultural differences between country of origin and country of residence, suffered by Chinese students in Germany before WWI (also in the USA – both referenced in Harnisch 1999: 18, note 5; 2000: 24–28). Nevertheless, relevant research generally shows a positive account for host countries, that is, the native countries of the foreign language. In an overview of German student courses and visits to Germany by Chinese citizens "the German side [...] achieved positive results, because many former students expressed their attachment to the German culture by trying to promote mutual understanding between China and Germany through translations and other publications. Their focus was on mediating German thought in China" (Harnisch 1999: 490).

When speakers of languages other than German learn German as a foreign language, this has more far-reaching benefits for all German-speakers and German-speaking countries than just improving communication. Conversely, a decline in the learning of German as a foreign language is accompanied by more serious disadvantages than linguistic communication. In fact, with the current state of knowledge, it is difficult to assess the advantages and disadvantages. Like many of the questions addressed in the present book, this opens a broad and hitherto under-investigated field of research.

The same applies for the advantages and disadvantages drawn by FL speakers and their countries from the acquisition of a foreign language, in the present case, German as a foreign language. They resemble the advantages and disadvantages for native speakers but are easier to understand. FL speakers gain for themselves access to the native speakers and their countries and therefore create commercial, academic, political and cultural contacts. It is these opportunities which motivate them to learn the language – and the motivation sometimes endures even if the value of the contacts has diminished, because their home culture has overtaken the FL culture in key civilisational developments. The advantage may even be reversed if native speakers begin to profit from relationships with the FL speakers of their language and with their countries because they can communicate with them in their own language.

But even without this reversal, native speakers' access to countries in which their language is learnt as a foreign language can be associated with advantages. One example is those countries with whose businesses German businesses can communicate – at least in part – in German. This occurs quite specifically in countries in which German is often learnt as a foreign language (Chamber of Commerce Hamburg 1989, 2005, Ch. F.3). Given otherwise similar conditions, it can be assumed that German businesses will give preference to commercial contacts with these countries. Looked at in this way, the benefits to both sides seem to balance out. Nevertheless, in many respects, they are greater for the native speakers. I emphasise this point, because the advantages to native speakers have traditionally remained out of view (Ammon 2009a: 116).

More of the native speakers' culture and history is communicated to FL speakers than vice versa. This represents an asymmetry in cultural distribution or at least mutual recognition of culture (Ch. A.9). It is determined by the fact that FL speakers receive more of the native speakers' texts than vice versa. This occurs even during language learning, because the texts used contain primarily information about the native speakers' culture and society. Furthermore, FL speakers author fewer texts in this language over which they have limited mastery, or such texts are hardly acknowledged by native speakers, in any case, less than the native-speaker-authored texts are acknowledged by FL speakers. One need only think of knowledge about German writers in Japan or Korea – both countries with a long tradition of German learning (Ammon 1994d; Ammon/Chong 2003) – by contrast with the lack of knowledge about Japanese or Korean poets in Germany. In general, knowledge about culture, way of life and probably also ideologies, is asymmetrical: FL speakers learn more about native speakers than vice versa. Occasional efforts to counter this tendency fail to achieve real symmetry because a relatively small number of native countries is faced with a much larger number of countries in which their language is learnt as a foreign language, so that the native-country population could not possibly achieve an overview.

Added to this is the asymmetry in the distribution of products in the "language industry" (compare Edwards/ Kingscott 1997; McCallen 1989) from the native-country to FL speakers and their countries. This involves not only teaching materials, but also other goods associated with language, such as books, TV series, films, Internet content and similar. This form of distribution is often associated with commercial advantages. In fact, with languages such as German, which enjoy only sluggish demand, these gains are held in check, because export of such materials is subsidised by the native-country population. The same applies to language tuition, for example, the courses offered by the Goethe Institute or the Austrian Institute (Ch. K.3.3).

Another asymmetry to the benefit of native speakers deserves consideration. This relates to the function of native language as a symbol of nationality. European national languages and official national languages have achieved this function in recent history, on one hand, because dialects have been combined through a standard variety to form a single language (Ch. B.1; B.2) and, on the other hand, because minority languages have been suppressed (compare Anderson 1983; Barbour 2004; Gellner 1983; Wright 2000). For Germans in particular, *their* language achieved this function through the arduous formation of the German nation state and has preserved it up to the present day (Ammon 1995a: 18–34). This is borne out by recent efforts, though yet unsuccessful, to enshrine German in the German Basic Law as the official state language but also in feelings of resistance to *superfluous* anglicisms in German (also in academic guise, as in Bartzsch/ Pogarell/ Schröder 2003). The underlying attitude emerges as pride in the strong positioning of one's own language in the world – although less pronounced among Germans than among the French, for whom it has become part of a stereotype. Strengthening national identity through the positioning of the native language in the world benefits only native speakers but not FL speakers. As a result, conflicts between native speakers and FL speakers can also arise. I experienced this in 2000 at the World Congress of the International Association for German Studies (IVG) in Vienna, when I delivered a petition to the governments of the German-speaking countries, which I had written – at the request of Peter Wiesinger – for the promotion of the German language in the world. As I recall, the content was condemned by Italian Germanists for having injured their pride in their own language. Indeed, it is often difficult to keep national pride and linguistic interests apart, primarily when countries are competing for the positioning of their languages in the world.

Table A.1–1 Advantages of a strong position of a language in the world for native speakers and foreign-
language speakers

---

(1) Easier communication with speakers of other languages and foreign contacts;

(2) Closer relations between native countries and FL speakers and their countries (trade; corporate
subsidiaries; outsourcing; earning *human capital*; academic, political and cultural contacts; tourism);

(3) Mutual image enhancement, removal of prejudices (more positive image of language communities,
their countries and citizens);

(4) Better understanding of values and culture, also further dissemination (reception of texts from the
native countries, acknowledgement of contents and appropriation of values);

(5) Additional employment opportunities through language skills, both for native speakers (in foreign
countries) and for FL speakers (in FL countries and native countries);

(6) Financial gains of native countries from the language industry (sales of teaching materials, tuition,
language-related goods, such as books and other media);

(7) Increase in communication potential and therefore instrumental value of the language through
additional speakers, and therefore increase in motivation to learn the language;

(8) Strengthening of pride in language and national identity of native speakers.

However, there is no doubt that FL speakers, who invest time and money in learning a language, do have an interest in its stable, global position. Especially in their own countries, they
often act as lobbyists for this language, not least in discussions about its positioning in school and
university curricula (Ch. K.3.5). Table A.1–1 summarises the most important advantages of the
strong global positioning of a language for native speakers and FL speakers, where 4) and 8) in
Table A.1–1 benefit primarily the native speakers.

These considerations frame the relevance of the topic dealt with in the present book, especially for all German-speakers, native speakers and FL speakers, for German-speaking countries
and also countries where German is learnt as a foreign language. It is tempting to stretch its
relevance further, for example, to include mutual understanding between peoples and the promotion of peace through improved linguistic knowledge, especially between native speakers and
FL speakers. But in former times, such *elevated* advantages were, in part, ideologically distorted
as one-sided advantages for FL speakers (Ammon 2009a: 116). By contrast, this book brings
forward the advantages for native speakers as well as for FL speakers, thereby exposing complex
tensions between German and other languages and the conflicts (or convergences) of interest
between language communities and their countries.

In view of the current global position of the English language, such tensions often arise
from the relationship between German or the German-speaking countries and English or the
Anglophone countries (compare Ch. A.2; A.7; A.8). When concerns about the dominant position of their own language are occasionally raised from within the English-speaking countries
themselves, it is generally by language professionals, such as language teachers, translators and
interpreters who have a professional interest in the long-term international position of languages other than English. If everyone spoke English, English teachers and interpreters would
lose their clients. Otherwise, the English-speaking countries generally welcome the global position of their language.

Many linguistics scholars, whose interests may also be involved, have even expressed approval
of a future, with a) English for international communication and as a symbol of cosmopolitanism and b) other languages restricted to communication with their own language community,
as symbols of national or ethnic identity. The appeal for linguistics scholars in this context is

in preserving linguistic diversity. But I have some doubts concerning the survival of linguistic diversity. For example, David Crystal's (1997: 19) vision of the ideal speaker of the future who is bilingual with English + local language:

> It is perfectly possible to develop a situation in which intelligibility and identity happily co-exist. This situation is the familiar one of bilingualism – but a bilingualism where one of the languages of a speaker is the global language, providing access to the world community, and the other is a regional language, providing access to a local community. The two functions can be seen as complementary, responding to different needs. And it is because the functions are so different that a world of linguistic diversity can in principle continue to exist in a world united by a common language.

In this world, there would be no space for other international languages, including those in the second rank (Ch. A.3; A.7; critical of this view: Mühleisen 2003). This position is supported by those who stress the load in learning and communication attached to multiple international languages (for example, Wright 2009: 118f.). It is primarily language communities in which the academics have already largely adopted English as the single international language, for example, in the Netherlands, which tend towards this view (compare van Parijs 2011: 48f.; van Els 2003, 2005a, b, 2007; critical of this position: Ammon 2006g). Attractive as their argument seems, it underestimates the fact that English provides only restricted access to language communities and speakers whose knowledge of English is still inadequate – or who refuse to communicate in English. Young people from Mediterranean countries who recently sought access to the employment market in Germany were painfully disappointed that a knowledge of English alone was insufficient. Indeed, there remains the question of how long this language barrier in the non-Anglophone countries which are striving worldwide to improve their English skills, will continue. And also, for whom, and in precisely which respect, the magical monopoly of English, conjured up as the only international, i.e. *global language*, might be advantageous or disadvantageous. Such questions, including occasional visions of the future, are recurring themes throughout the present book.

2. German-speakers in the conflict of interests between German and English

The *international position of a language* (further details in Ch. A.3) is an important component of its position in the world. For the present chapter, an adequate working definition is that the international position of a language is determined by how frequently it is used between people of different nationality and different native language. So, for example, German has a higher international position than Hungarian, and English has a higher position than German.

It also follows from this definition of the term that every international use of a language strengthens its international position, and every avoidance of such use where it might have been possible weakens this position (Ch. A.6). For example, if a German person speaks German to non-German-speakers, the international position of German is strengthened and otherwise it is weakened – although this choice exists only if the other speakers have an adequate command of German (as a foreign language). So, it is in the linguistic interests of all German-speakers to use their own language internationally wherever possible.

However, there are numerous communicative situations in which the use of one's own language limits the *communicative range*, and switching to another language increases it. Here, the rules of politeness, which can also complicate the choice of one's own language (Ch. A.6; F.2), are not taken into account. The following points relate primarily to communicative range – in other words – to the number and power of people and institutions within the range of a language.

Many people find themselves in situations which give rise to the following conflict of interests:

(1) On the one hand, they want a maximum range for their communication, which they can achieve less with their own language, German, than with a foreign language, generally English;
(2) On the other hand, it is in their interests to strengthen the international position of their own language, German, which seems more likely by using German instead of English.

To understand this dilemma better, we need to grasp the primary motivating interests of such people in each situation. There are often economic reasons, the push for professional success, possibly together with other needs, like optimising holiday plans. The primary communicative purpose for a business person might be to close a successful deal, for an academic to disseminate knowledge quickly, for a diplomat to achieve political goals, for an international broadcaster to reach large numbers of listeners/viewers outside its national language region, or for holidaymakers to make themselves understood on the spot. Often, communicative goals such as these can be achieved less effectively with one's own language, e.g. German, than with a foreign language. Using, for example, English therefore serves such people's primary interest more effectively than using their own language.

We should also bear in mind that these people – motivated by business, academic, diplomatic, journalistic interests – are in competition with other people involved in the same *field of action* (for the term see Ch. F.1). Academics, for example, need to disseminate their own ideas as widely and quickly as possible through publications, for which English is the most suitable language. It is also essential for academics in almost every discipline to read specialist literature and attend conferences, where more extensive information is available in English than in any other language. The disadvantages for non-Anglophone academics have been pointed out by Harold Schiffman (2009) in his critique of one of my joint publications (Carli/ Ammon 2007).

A governmental international broadcaster tasked with disseminating news worldwide is placed under similar pressures, because this will be more successful in English than in German. Again, the broadcaster faces competition from international broadcasters in other countries which also use English. The business community faces similar pressures. And diplomats must communicate with as many diplomats from other countries as possible in order to influence decisions in the interests of their own country. In brief, choosing another language, usually English, is often a better way of achieving one's primary goal than insisting on one's own language. The people affected must decide between success in the business, academic or diplomatic community, or *loyalty to their own language* (for critical comment on *language loyalty*, see Hoberg 2013, also Ch. E.2).

People facing such a choice of language find themselves in the *prisoner dilemma* modelled in game theory (en.wikipedia.org/wiki/Prisoner%27s_dilemma). In the same way that the two prisoners cannot speak to one another, such people are not able to communicate with their competitors. At least, reliable discussion about a solution which would be optimal for all competitors trapped in the dilemma, is often impossible. Instead, only the second-best solution is available – at least by the rules of rational-choice theory (en.wikipedia.org/wiki/Rational_choice_theory). Otherwise, the risk would be too great.

This can be explained by considering competing companies which offer goods of the same type and quality. Let us assume that, in the long term, a consistent use of German and accordingly a reinforcement of its international position would bring most advantages to both parties. But because they cannot agree in general to trust this procedure, they choose the safer option and use English. Otherwise – this is their worry – the competition will do so, thereby gaining communicative and commercial advantages. In this instance, the competitors fail to strengthen the international position of German; in fact, they weaken it and further reinforce the international position of English. Other things being equal, the same applies for academics, diplomats and so on.

The prisoner dilemma illustrates the situation with reference to two prisoners (A and B) who have committed a serious crime but have not been proven guilty. They are kept apart so that they cannot communicate or cooperate. In strict isolation from one another, the court makes them both the following offer:

- If neither confesses: two years prison for both (for the minor offences for which they have already been convicted);
- If both confess: four years prison for both;
- If A confesses and B does not: only one year prison for A (reduction of sentence under rules for Queen's evidence), but six years for B (reversed if B confesses and A does not).

A (or B) therefore has to choose between one year or four years in prison if he confesses, and two years or six years if he does not confess. The temptation to own up – i. e. *betrayal*, as it is called in game theory, is obviously great. Because both think this way, both will in the end receive four years prison, a total of eight years. If neither had confessed, they would have got away with just two years each, a total of just four years. But this optimum solution would require a reliable agreement to ensure one prisoner does not betray the other, hoping for Queen's evidence of just a one-year sentence.

For serious competitors, an agreement of this kind is difficult especially, for example, for rival companies, academics, politicians, journalists and the like. For German-speakers or groups of speakers, the situation regarding the use and promotion of German is more complex, but it still has much in common with this dilemma. This applies especially for the difficulty of reaching an agreement on which all players can really rely. Agreements about the use of German and the promotion of its international position can be difficult, because they do not guarantee the maximum direct advantage for the individuals (corresponding to the two-year prison sentence each in the prisoner dilemma, instead of only one year in the case of a betrayal). The example explains why it is more attractive to outdo the competition by using English than to join forces and strengthen the position of German. This occurs, for instance, when choosing the language for business contacts or languages required in job specifications. In the short term at least, the player who puts English first and holds back on German has the upper hand in terms of successful communication with business partners or larger numbers of applicants for posts advertised.

A unified strategy on using German or on preference for German is difficult to establish because of uncertainty about whether this will significantly increase the position of German in reality. However, if all companies from German-speaking countries operating internationally were to promote German as much as possible, for example, through a clear preference for job applicants with a knowledge of German, this would presumably increase motivation to learn German in many regions. Over time, this would benefit all companies from German-speaking countries. There would be a larger number of employees with the double advantage of useful language skills, on the basis of which they could communicate with domestic venues, and also increased loyalty to their company. Loyalty would be established through appropriate language qualifications and built up simply by learning the language and the generally positive attitude towards people in the native country. If promoting the learning of German was successful, parent companies in the German-speaking countries would enjoy the additional advantage of having a larger reservoir of qualified personnel from overseas at their disposal.

Such considerations, including the consequences drawn from the prisoner dilemma, are important, but they only account for a presumably small proportion of the interests involved and people's perception of them. Possibly the most important objection is derived from classical liberal economics in the tradition of Adam Smith ([1776] 2003). In essence, it is that in their economic activities, individuals generally pursue only their individual interests, but that precisely this is often of the greatest advantage to the society or nation as a whole. Adam Smith visualised this unintentional beneficial effect of individualistic economic behaviour on the community through the metaphor of the *invisible hand*. In his extensive works, he mentions it only once, but it has been taken up by numerous followers. Cut down to basics, the relevant extract reads as follows: "every individual [. . .] intends only his own gain, and he is in this, as in many other cases, led by an invisible hand to promote an end which was no part of his intention. Nor is it always the worse for the society that it was no part of. By pursuing his own interest he frequently promotes that of the society more effectually than when he really intends to promote it" (Smith 2003: 572) Transferring this assumption to our present problem, it would be more useful for the German-language community as a whole if German companies overseas abandoned the use of their own language in favour of English.

This relates, first of all, to economic usefulness, because businesses are perhaps more likely to succeed in English than in German. But it could also apply – indirectly – to the position of the German language in the world. Initially, the individualistic use of English by academics, diplomats and so on could in the end be more advantageous for society as a whole than clinging to German, because they might achieve their actual objective more successfully as a result. These successes could then improve the academic or respectively political prestige of the German-speaking countries in the world. And this prestige could contribute to an increase in the learning of German in the world and then perhaps – in the sense of the invisible hand – strengthen the international position of German more sustainably than doggedly insisting on the use of German.

A combined effect of this kind is well illustrated with the example from academia. Here, renouncing the use of English as a language of publication can lead to the loss of potential prestige outside the German language region. I have begun to investigate this question (Ammon 2012c), but further research is required. Accordingly, significant contributions to knowledge have reached the world community either with a delay or not at all because they did not become available in English for a long time. One example is the book by Jürgen Habermas which appeared in 1962 with the German title *Strukturwandel der Öffentlichkeit* but was not published in English until 1989 (*The Structural Transformation of the Public Sphere*, translated by Thomas Burger and Frederick Lawrence). Earlier publication would certainly have contributed to the prestige of German research especially in the humanities. The same possibly applies for French in the case of Claude Truchot's book *L'anglais dans le monde contemporain* (1990), which remained largely unknown outside the French-speaking world and was not even mentioned in subsequent English books on the same topic (Crystal 1997, 2003; Graddol 1997, 2006) because of the lack of an English translation.

Those who insist loudly on an increase in the use of German might do well to consider the potential consequences of a failure to use English and the dilemma facing the business community, academics, diplomats and others. However, the above quotation from Adam Smith about the invisible hand should not be misunderstood – like a caricature of economic liberalism – as a ban on state intervention. On the contrary, Smith decisively demands such intervention, if the powerful are manipulating the invisible hand to their own advantage against the socially disadvantaged (see Alan B. Krueger in the "Introduction" to Smith 2003: xi–xxiii). By way of clarification, every individualistic use of English does not necessarily serve the common good of one's own society, nor need state intervention in promoting the native language necessarily be condemned, even from a liberal perspective.

3. The term *international position of a language* and related terms

My earlier volume covering a similar topic was entitled *The International Position of the German Language* (Ammon 1991a). Although the present book is considerably more comprehensive in scope, the *term international position of a language* remains key. It can be defined in different ways (e.g. different approaches in Kloss 1974b). One possible sense, which I explain in this chapter, is the scope of international communication in the relevant language. A language is therefore more international the more often it is used for communication between different nations. Other possible senses, which will be discussed in later chapters, are the distribution of the language among different nations, e.g. as an official national language (Ch. D) or as a native language (Ch. E), or being learnt as a foreign language (Ch. J). These terms can also diverge extensionally. For example, as an official language, Japanese is entirely restricted to a single country (Japan); as a native language, it is largely limited to Japan. It is learned as a foreign language in many countries and is therefore also used internationally.

Explanatory definition of *international communication* requires clear understanding of the term *nation*. Any serious concept of *nation* implies a – usually large – group of people, but to specify the term further, at least the following three conceptual variants (cf. Fishman 1972a) should be considered. For the present book, I have settled on variant (1).

(1) A *nation* in this sense comprises "all subjects of an individual (sovereign) state" (*state nation*). The term *state nation* is not well established in English but is useful to denote the difference from the following two concepts (2 and 3) of a *nation*. The United Nations Organisation also works with this concept in counting or acknowledging its members as "nations", and the UK, Switzerland or Belgium are salient examples of such *nations* with each comprising several "nations" in sense (2) described below (*ethnicity* or *nationality*). The underlying concept of *state nations* can, at least indirectly, be traced back to Ernest Renan's idea of *nations* formed by a people's will to live together in a single state (especially Renan 1882). For our purposes such a state nation includes all the citizens of the state, but under some circumstances also other people with a (unrestricted) permit of residence. Such state nations can overlap, to some extent, with regard to their subjects (in the case of individuals' multiple state citizenship), in which case uncertainties can arise in classifying acts of communication as international or not, for example, between individuals with dual Turkish and German citizenship communicating between Turkey and Germany, as to whether they should be counted as international or not. However, such cases rarely seriously affect the figures provided in this book.

Nevertheless, a clear statement of what counts as a (sovereign) state is essential. The appropriate criterion here is recognition by the (UNO). Accordingly, there were 196 states, that is, 196 "nations" (i.e. state nations) in the world in 2012 (*Fischer Weltalmanach* 2013: 578). For the period before 1945, that is, before the foundation of the UNO, other definitions may have been applied.

The term and concept *state nation* is not compatible with the term *divided nation* which is or was used by specific groups to refer to pairs of states like the People's Republic of China and Taiwan, South and North Korea and the former "two Germanies" (FRG and GDR, 1949–1989). In this context, classification as a single nation has been founded on history or on the following sense (2) of a *nation*, which I do not share.

(2) Nation as *ethnicity* or, synonymously *nationality* (for the latter terms see Ch. B.3). Such a nation would include all people of the same *ethnicity* or membership of the same *group of people* or *nationality*. In this sense Belgium or Switzerland would stretch over several *nations*. Such nations' coherence can be based on the belief in a shared history, language, culture or religion. But the term *belief* is crucial here, because it generally only approximates the reality of the situation (Heckmann 1997). Such beliefs are typically supported by historical myths which emphasise connections and ignore divisions. The German *Volk* (ethnicity) was founded primarily with reference to a common language (e.g. by Jakob Grimm), the most conspicuous or expressive symbol of an allegedly shared culture (Ammon 1995a: 18–30). Terms such as *language nation* or *cultural nation* often correspond with this conceptualisation of nation, which is sometimes seen as typically German (Ammon 1995a: 25–34, 2010a).

In spite of difficulties with classification and demarcation, the existence of ethnicities cannot be seriously doubted (for details, see Fishman/ Garcia 2010). This also applies to the existence of a *German ethnicity* or *German people* (Ch. B.3) – who should not be simply equated with the citizens of specific *German-speaking countries* (Ch. D). One need only consider German(-speaking) minorities (Ch. E).

(3) Combining (1) and (2) leads to the idea of a *nation* as a *nation state*, i.e. a state which comprises precisely one ethnicity, all of it and it only. This idea is in conflict with and, in fact, a counter-project to ideas of the French Revolution and has been criticized sharply by various sides, e.g. by F. Gross 1998 as a *tribal state* in contrast with a *civic state*. The discrepancies between idea and reality have led to calamitous campaigns for annexation or autonomy – a problem which is widely recognised today but has still not been resolved (cf. Anderson 1983; Gellner 1983; Coulmas 1985: 41–58; Ammon 1995a: 18–34; Hobsbawm 1996). However, *civic* (or *constitutional*) *states* also often tend towards the national state by exerting pressure on the entire population to assimilate to the majority ethnicity, often the *titular ethnicity* after which the state is named. Such linguistic pressure has typically been based on the idea that linguistic assimilation would gradually come to entail ethnic assimilation (cf. with reference to France, e.g. Laponce 1987a; Ammon 2000a).

In the present book, I link the term *nation* firmly with sense (1), that is, the *state nation*. However, this term is insufficient for the differentiation necessitated by *international communication*, in the *broad* and *narrow senses* of this term. For this purpose, reference must also be made to the term *native language*, which is associated, in turn, with the term *ethnicity* in sense (2), primarily understood in terms of a *language community*. I understand a language community in the sense of all people with the same native language, who are then generally also classified with the same ethnicity. However, like different states, different language communities can overlap. In the same way that there are people with multiple nationalities, there are also those with multiple native languages.

With regard to international communication, it is expedient to make a distinction between *people of the same/ different nationality* and *people of the same/ different native language*. This allows a differentiation, for example, in the communication between Germans and Austrians and between Germans and Czechs. In the first case, communication between people with the same native language taking place in this language, is designated *intra-lingual*, and the second, between people with different native languages, *interlingual*.

Between people with the same native language, the choice of this language is the default choice. This also applies for people of different nationality, that is, for international communication. Such communication (in the common native language between people from different state nations), will only be designated *international communication in the broader sense*. However, my primary interest is in *international communication in the narrower sense*. This is, in fact, not only international, but also interlingual. Accordingly, the people communicating do not have a shared native language or, if they do have a shared native language, they are not using it to communicate. In this case, at least one person must be communicating in a foreign language. These terms therefore touch on the structure of the *global language constellation* which will be described in detail in chapter A.7. With groups of participants, this definition which refers initially only to pairs of communicating parties can be classified by degree of interlingualism or respectively internationality.

Regarding the obvious difficulties for empirical application, I mention only a small subset here. One such difficulty is derived from the term *Muttersprache* (English: *mother tongue* or *native language*; in this regard, e.g. A. Davies 2003; Skutnabb-Kangas/ Phillipson 1989; Dietrich 2004a; also Ch. J.1). Especially in Germany, it is already loaded because of its misuse for evil, nationalistic purposes (Ahlzweig 1989). However, it is possible to shake off this ideological ballast. Showing up linguistic variation in a language community (Ch. B1; B.2) relativises the linguistic *community*, and references to mother-tongue multilingualism or to the fact that the shared standard variety tends to be learnt in school rather than from one's mother, argue against ideas of an unbreakable bond with the native language.

Moving beyond this, the term *native language* can be specified more closely as the language which a) one learnt first (*first language* – the most usual synonym for *native language*), with which one b) (at present) identifies (identification language; Hüllen 1992), c) which one uses (at present) most frequently in the family (*family language* or *home language*) or which one d) masters best (*best-mastered language*) (Skutnabb-Kangas/ Phillipson 1989; Knipf-Komlósi 2008: 311). For various reasons, simply asking people for a declaration of their native language is not always reliable, but then assessment is also often too labour-intensive. Furthermore, it is often unclear whether terminological variants are synonyms, for example, in German *Muttersprache* and *Erstsprache* or in English *mother tongue* and *native language*, or whether they can be accurately translated into other languages. The complementary terms *second language* and *foreign language* (Dietrich 2004b) are not necessarily any clearer. However, for the present book, they are similarly indispensable, because speaker numbers are often based on them (compare Ch. C). In the sense shared by myself, a *second language* differs from a *native language* with reference to the chronology of language acquisition, and from a *foreign language* through regular use in the native language community in which the second-language users live or have temporarily lived, in contrast with FL speakers.

Continuing this series of terms allows a differentiation between *speakers* (*native speakers*, *SL speakers* and *FL speakers*) and *non-speakers* of a language. It is also less trivial than it initially appears. For example, learners and speakers (who can communicate in the language) should not simply be equated. The transition from non-speakers to speakers is fluid, as suggested by the ascending levels of competence of the *Common European Framework of Reference* (www.coe.int/t/dg4/linguistic/Source/Framework_EN.pdf). The demarcation between speakers and non-speakers is specified differently according to purpose. Regarding the immigration of spouses into Germany, the German government requires only elementary level A1 of the Framework; B1 for citizenship (see Li 2014) and B2 or preferably C1 for study at a university. In fact, for the present book, the demarcation between *speakers* and *non-speakers* is not generally specified more precisely, but the underlying terminological distinction is indispensable for many questions (e.g. Figure A.3–2 contains only speakers).

Finally, a distinction must be made between *learners* and *non-learners* because the number of FL learners provides a readily accessible but not always unproblematic indicator for the

Speakers and non-speakers of a language

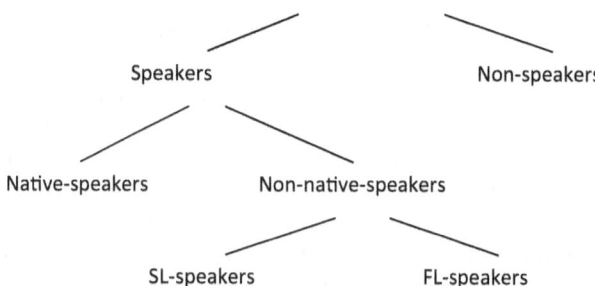

Figure A.3–1   Terminology for *native language – second language – foreign language*

international position of languages. It should be noted in this context that *learning* can be given a more precise time index than *competence*, which, once achieved, does not decline so quickly. By contrast, *current learners* can easily be distinguished from *former learners*, but sometimes, both are differentiated from people who have never learnt the language (*never-yet learners*). Figure A.3–1 shows the most important conceptual classifications so far (without learners).

Sometimes, even coarser classifications are expedient, and the terms vary dependent upon context, e.g. in the following cases, between (1) and (2):

- *Speakers of L_a = L_a-speakers* (e.g. German-speakers) for (1) *native-language speakers of the language L_a* or for (2) *any speaker type of L_a* (native speakers ∪ SL speakers ∪ FL speakers)';
- *Non-native speakers of L_a* for SL speakers ∪ FL speakers of L_a;
- *Speakers of languages other than L_a* for (1) non-speakers of L_a or for (2) SL speakers ∪ FL speakers ∪ non-speakers of L_a;
- Special terms not applicable for all languages include *(non-)Anglophone/Francophone* and similar for *(non-)native speakers of English/French* and so on.

These elementary terms and concepts are necessary for specification of the terms *interlingual communication* and *international communication in the narrower sense* (cf. Figure A.3–2) which are needed for defining *international position of a language*. In the case of *interlingual communication*, the language used is the native language of none of the communicating parties. However, if it is the native language of at least one but not all communicating parties, I designate the language choice *asymmetrical* (or also *non-genuine lingua franca communication*). The native language used is then used in an *(asymmetrically) dominating* manner, while the native languages not used are *(asymmetrically) dominated*. For example, the use of German in communication between German speakers and Polish speakers would be asymmetrical with dominating use of German and domination of Polish.

By contrast, if a language used interlingually is the native language of none of the communicating parties, its use is *symmetrical* (or a *genuine lingua franca*), because it is a foreign language for everyone. At present, English functions most frequently worldwide as a genuine or as a non-genuine lingua franca. In the case of second languages, the degree of domination is attenuated, that is, weaker than with FL speakers. Occasionally, a special type of *symmetrical use* of different native languages is observed, for which the term *polyglot dialogue* coined by Roland Posner (1991a, b, 1992) can be used (synonymous with *passive multilingualism* or *passive bilingualism*). In this case, the communicating parties each use their own native language actively (productively, encoding)

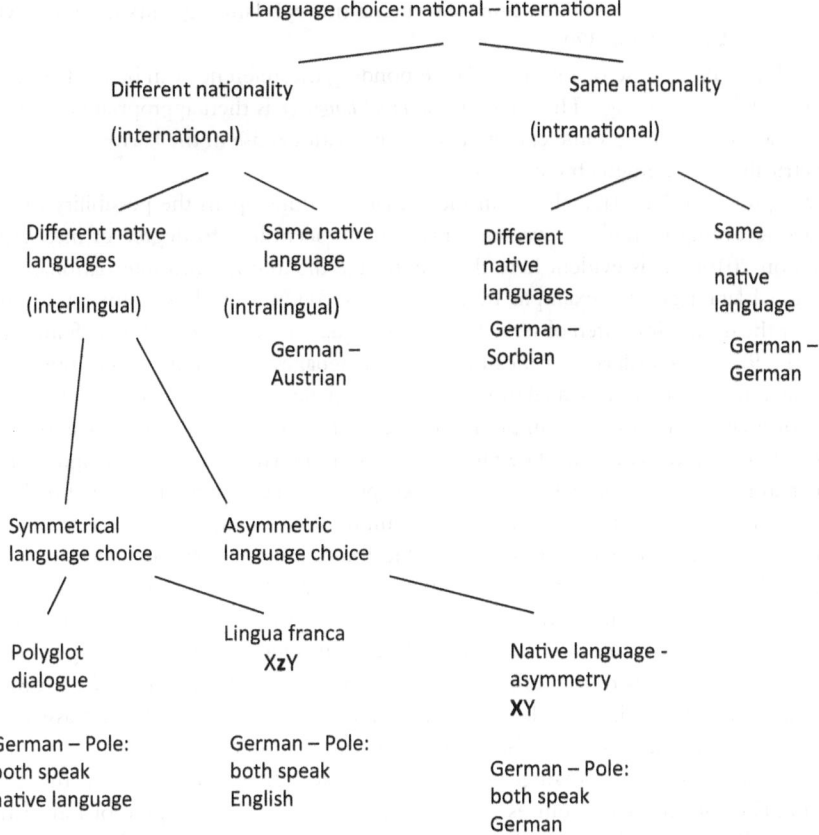

Figure A.3–2 Terminology field for "international communication" uppercase = native language, lowercase = foreign language, bold = language used; with the use of abbreviations such as G/g = German, P/p = Polish, E/e = English, S/s = Sorbian, the relevant combinations can also be symbolised as follows (from left to right): GP, GeP, GgP, GG etc.

and the native language of the other communicating parties passively (receptively, decoding). For example, German-speakers speak German with Polish-speakers, who, conversely, speak Polish. However, this choice of languages occurs only rarely and almost only in the case of linguistically similar languages (cf. Ch. B.1; B.2), e.g. German and Dutch. To a certain degree, people are evidently predisposed towards *monoglot dialogue* – either through conditioning or even genetically. However, this disposition is not insurmountable, even with linguistically remote languages.

It should be noted that Figure A.3–2 relates to a single situation (*asymmetric use, lingua-franca use* of the relevant language) and says nothing about the frequency of such use. Corresponding regular use is often ascribed as a property to the language, which then counts e.g. as a lingua franca. Where misunderstandings are likely, I shall speak of *use* or *communication* with reference to individual situations (*lingua-franca use* or *lingua-franca communication*); when I only refer to a lingua franca, this means a language which is regularly or frequently used as a lingua franca. In German, the term *Verkehrssprache* [language of communication] (Born/ Stickel 1993) has about the same meaning. The original meaning of the term *lingua franca*, probably "franconian language", corresponds with what is meant in this context only to a limited extent. It was the name for a language of communication which came into being through language mixing in the Mediterranean region (Vikør 2004: 329).

Accordingly, in the case of a frequent corresponding use, reference can be made to an (*asymmetrically*) *dominating language*. The term *international language* is then appropriate as a hypernym for a language of which, to some extent, regular international use in the narrower sense is made, asymmetrically or as a lingua franca.

This approach to language choice in individual situations opens the possibility of ordering languages according to rank or even measuring them according to degree of internationality (cf. Ammon 2010c). It is evident here that the simple dichotomy into international and non-international languages, for example, by Braga (1979: 31), is a crude simplification. The same applies for the distinction often observed between lingua francas and non-lingua francas (e.g. Van Parijs 2011: 9). A rank ordering or measurement of languages according to their internationality can be based upon use in individual situations and frequency of use. Such a use is also possible in the case of small languages, for example, if they are learnt as foreign languages by enthusiasts and occasionally used internationally. The rank or degree of internationality of a language increases with increasing frequency of such use. The highest possible degree would be used for all international communication, so that international communication would not take place in any other language. However, this seems almost impossible for as long as there are different languages. Such considerations lead away from the classificatory term *international language* (international – non-international) to a comparative (less or more international) and finally to a metrical term (to what extent international?) (see Hempel 1952 with reference to terminological types). In statistics, this corresponds to the difference between *nominal*, *rank* and *ratio scales*. However, the development of empirically reliable, practically usable scales of this kind is a massive research undertaking which can presumably be achieved only to a limited extent.

One proposal by Gerd Grözinger/ Wenzel Matiaske (2008) for measuring the degree of internationality of university courses points towards measuring the degree of internationality of languages. Translating this to the internationality of languages, what is relevant is how many international communicative acts with the language L_a (native speakers of L_a) are made with how many other languages (people with different native languages). The larger this number, the greater the degree of internationality of L_a. A mathematical approach is offered by the Herfindahl(-Hirschman)-index (en.wikipedia.org/wiki/Herfindahl-Index). However, this initially measures the opposite of the parameter desired, namely, non-internationality. It was developed by economists to measure the monopoly status of suppliers or, more generally, the degree of concentration of a property in one position. To measure the degree of internationality of languages, the inverse is required, the degree of disparity. The more native languages included in the communicative act by means of L_a, the greater the internationality of L_a. In order to calculate the concentration, the "sum of the squares of participants [here, international communicative acts by means of L_a relative to languages L_a, L_b, L_c and so on! U.A.] is divided by the square of all participants [all communicative acts by means of L_a! U.A.]". For the inverse, that is, the disparity or respectively the degree of internationality of L_a, what is required is "to subtract this value from 1" (based on Grözinger/ Matiaske 2008: 316).

Let us assume that a (random) sample has been taken for three languages in every 1,000 communicative acts, more precisely, for every 1,000 native speakers of the languages L_a, L_b and L_c. To simplify calculations, only those communicative acts are included which are either (a) both intra-national and also intra-lingual or (b) international in the narrower sense (that is, international and interlingual); accordingly, communicative acts which are (c) intra-national and at the same time interlingual or which are (d) international only in the broader sense (international and intra-lingual) are not included. Moreover, with regard to the native languages, I assume continuous disjointedness, i.e. {native speakers of L_a} $\cap$ {native speakers of L_b} $\cap$ {native speakers of L_c} and so on = $\varnothing$. This dramatic simplification in contrast with reality gives an idea of the difficulty of representative and precise measurements of the internationality of languages. In the case of L_a, all 1,000 communicative acts would again take place only with L_a, so that – according to definition – L_a would exhibit no internationality. In the case of L_b, 500 would take place with L_b and 500 with L_d. Finally, in the case of L_c, 250 would take place with L_c, 250 with L_d, 250 with L_e and 250 with L_f. This would lead to the following degrees of internationality (I):

$$IL_a = 1 - (1,000^2 : 1,000^2) = 1{-}1 = 0$$
$$IL_b = 1 - ((500^2 + 500^2) : 1,000^2) = 1{-}0.5 = 0.5$$
$$IL_c = 1 - ((250^2 + 250^2 + 250^2 + 250^2) : 1,000^2) = 1{-}0.25 = 0.75$$

The measurement remains within the limit values $0 \leq 1$. The findings are in agreement with our intuition to the extent that the degree of internationality of L_a = 0 (= no internationality) and of $L_b < L_c$. However, one might expect the degree of internationality of L_c proportionally to L_b to be somewhat higher, since the international communication includes three times as many other languages, which should image a ratio scale. Admittedly, in this case, it would not be possible to specify an upper maximum value (as here with 1), which, however, other ratio scales, for example, for length or for temperature (Kelvin scale) also lack. Alongside lack of proportionality, another defect of the measurement outlined here is that it is restricted to relative instead of absolute internationality. Internationality is measured only relative to the total number of communicative acts taking place within one language. As a result, a language with few speakers or communicative acts easily reaches a higher degree of internationality than one with a large number of speakers. For instance, Esperanto – which is also counted among the questionable category of languages because it does have (a small number of) native speakers – would then presumably rank above the *world language* English. However, a closer approximation to our intuition is achieved if the relative degree of internationality is multiplied by the total number of speech acts (or speakers).

One basic problem is the – sufficiently precise – definition (operationalising) of communicative situations (communicative acts or events), which would have to be counted in a valid and reliable measurement. In this context, the communicative use of the languages (e.g. international in the narrower sense), the scope of the communication (e.g. short conversation, lecture) and the number of participants must also be taken into consideration (e.g. dialogue, mass communication). Furthermore, different media (e.g. verbal, written, electronic or especially Twitter, Facebook and so on – Ch. I.1.4, especially I.1.4.2). Aspects which have hitherto not been discussed, such as the geography of the language region (distribution/scattering) or the linguistic distance between the native languages of the communicative participants (compare Ch. B.1; B.2) deserve special consideration. Unambiguous definition of the languages – which has already appeared in the encyclopaedias relevant to the present book – can also be a problem. One example is the *Ethnologue*, the most comprehensive inventory of all languages in the world with speaker numbers, which also happily lists dialects as "languages" (Ch. B.1). Finally, there remain language mixtures (accumulations of transferences or code switching) where there are doubts about whether these should be allocated, for example, to the German or Turkish language. This multiplicity of unanswered questions, which makes a precise measurement of the internationality of languages seem almost impossible, should be borne in mind when using this term.

Instead of directly determined degrees of internationality of communicative acts and languages, I am therefore forced by necessity to employ – sometimes very indirect – indicators, which often provide a scientific expedient. Even the natural sciences seldom rely on directly observed *phenomena*, but rather on indirect *data* relating to these (e.g. mean-values of measurements) (Bogen/ Woodward 1988). However, their constructs are generally secured through known causal connections (e.g. thermometer readings for temperatures, oscillograms for sound characteristics) and mathematical operations (e.g. arithmetic mean with confidence interval). In contrast, social-science data are often based only on dubious hypotheses or connections and questionable measurements. So far as I can see, especially in the case of the present topic, valid and reliable indicators are in short supply. Careful, thematically applied constructs, which are initially promising, often prove less useful when transferred to the present topic (e.g. measuring the degree of internationality of company supervisory boards in Schmid/ Daniel 2006). Devising and seriously testing my own constructs was not possible in view of the cost. As a result, improving and securing the indicators employed is still an urgent but also enormous research undertaking. So far, they have relied largely on plausible but not fully tested assumptions, such as (high) positive correlations:

• Between scope and distribution of the learning of a language as a foreign language and scope and distribution of its competence and scope of its use for international communication (in the narrower sense) – where it is evident that learning is a prerequisite for competence, and competence is a prerequisite for use, but learning does not guarantee competence nor does competence guarantee use;
• Between frequency of scholarly publications in a language and frequency of adoption in periodical, scholarly bibliographies and frequency of international reception of publications in this language (international reception in the sense of international communication in the narrower sense) – where these correlations are not guaranteed.

In spite of such reservations and in view of the diversity of aspects and data, I stake the claim that the present book gives a picture of the internationality of the German language which tends towards correctness. This, in turn, is an important part of its aim of providing a comprehensive picture of the position of German in the world. It is rounded off with a differentiation of international communication according to the fields of economics, academic research, diplomacy, media and literature (Ch. F – I) and supplemented by speaker numbers for German and the economic strength of its speakers (Ch. C), the distribution of the language as an official national language (Ch. D) and as a minority language (Ch. E), the scope of learning German as a foreign language (Ch. I) and its promotion, above all, in the context of international cultural policy (Ch. K).

4. German as a lingua franca, alongside English?

At present, German would hardly be described as a lingua franca, although this characterisation is typical for English, for example, when Philippe Van Parijs (2011: 9) describes "English as Europe's lingua franca". He defines the term as "any language widely used for communication between people with different mother tongues [. . .]". But he does leave room for other lingua francas: "A lingua franca, so defined, does not need to be known by all members of the communities it links. Nor does there need to be only one lingua franca at a time. Spanish, for example, can operate as a lingua franca in this sense within Spain, while English operates as a lingua franca within Europe, Spain included".

From the function of Spanish as a lingua franca in Spain, it can be inferred that Van Parijs understands the term in the comprehensive sense, including choice of their own language by native speakers toward FL speakers, that is, not restricted to genuine lingua-franca communication (see Ch. A.3 for the distinction between genuine and non-genuine lingua franca). The German term *Verkehrssprache* [language of communication] is also used in this comprehensive sense.

It is in this sense that German is also often used as a lingua franca – at least in the German-speaking countries (Ch. B.4): as a non-genuine lingua franca between the German-speaking majority and minorities with other native languages (such as indigenous Sorbs, Danes, Romani or non-indigenous immigrants and migrants from Turkey, Greece, Korea and so on), and as a genuine lingua franca between these groups. The same applies to a lesser extent in the regions extending beyond the German-speaking countries with German as the official state language (Ch. D) or in isolated cases even in residential areas of other German-speaking minorities (Ch. E).

On closer inspection, the territorial assignment of lingua francas applied by Van Parijs to Spain and Europe, to which I now add the German-speaking countries and regions, raises some questions. The complexity of the relationship between languages and territories is dealt with in detail by Jean A. Laponce in his book "Languages and their Territories" (1987b). I limit myself here to the question of German as a potential and actual lingua franca. In an earlier book, I reported on personal research, according to which, around 1990, German expanded in east-central Europe and even became a genuine lingua franca (Ammon 1991a: 121–149, especially 137). However, in this function, it was not only limited territorially (to east-central Europe) but also to the older generation. Younger people tended to choose Russian and, even at that time, English. Nowadays, as over most of the rest of the world, English is the first lingua franca in east-central Europe, in some regions, alongside Russian and also, to a very limited extent, with German exclusively in the older generation.

However, this does not mean that, as a lingua franca, German is entirely limited to the German-speaking countries and regions. On the contrary, the distinction between *genuine lingua franca communication* (symmetrical) and *non-genuine lingua-franca communication* (asymmetric) allows a more differentiated view. Nowadays, German is hardly ever learnt with the intention of using it as a genuine lingua franca. Learners of German primarily want to communicate with the German-speaking countries and their inhabitants (Ch. B.4). However, language skills acquired for this purpose also create the possibility of genuine lingua-franca communication in German. For example, Hungarians or Chinese people who have learnt German as a foreign language can also communicate in German with each other, not only with Germans. This can be observed, e.g. at international conferences, especially German-teaching and German-studies conferences, but also between non-Germans at German universities. The same applies for all languages which are learnt to some extent as foreign languages. Like asymmetric communication, such lingua-franca communication occurs less often in other languages than it does in English.

At least potentially, German connects a considerably larger number of countries through lingua-franca communication than through asymmetric communication. In six countries or parts of countries, German is the predominant native language – in all these, where it is also the official state language, except in Luxembourg (Ch. D), and in a series of other countries, there are German-speaking minorities with German as the native language (Ch. E). Just how many is effectively a question of definition (of *native language* and *minority*) but, for the present, let us assume provisionally around 20 such countries. German is also learnt as a foreign language in some 100 countries (Ch. J.7), where at least some learners also achieve a level of competence sufficient for communication. These successful learners can then communicate asymmetrically in German with native speakers in 26 countries (with German as the native language of at least one minority) and in genuine lingua-franca communication with each other. Considering the combinations possible here indicates the diversity of potential international contacts (between different countries) in German. The number of possible pairs of asymmetric contacts runs to 1300 (26x100 : 2), the number of possible pairs of genuine lingua-franca contacts runs to 4950

(100x99 : 2). That makes 6,250 possible pairs of contacts with international communication (see Ch. A.3). Dividing by 2 neutralises the sequence, i.e. (contact state A ➔ state B) = (contact state B ➔ state A); combinations of identical elements count as the same contact regardless of the sequence of elements.

However, one must not be deceived by the large number of possible lingua-franca combinations. At the same time, the generally very small proportion of German-speakers in the total population of the countries must be considered. For example, a recent survey of the entire People's Republic of China showed only 41,900 learners of German (Ch. J.9.13 – meanwhile the figure has more than doubled). It is not possible to infer from this how many German-speakers with adequate communicative competence there are in China, but we are presumably close to the order of magnitude if we assume, as an unsupported speculation, around 65,000 (consider, on one side, the generations of previous learners and, on the other, subsequent forgetting). Only the approximate order of magnitude is relevant here. This would represent just 0.005% of the entire population of approximately 1.3 billion. The probability of a random encounter with a German-speaking Chinese person is therefore vanishingly small at ≈ 1 : 20,000 (p = 0.00005). German is therefore hardly likely to be considered as a lingua franca or language of communication for German-Chinese relations. For English, the divergence from German in this respect is enormous and continues to grow, because English has been a compulsory school subject in China for many years. In Ch. J.9.13, I estimate, on the basis of the present rough data, that for every individual German learner in China there are approximately 7,000 English learners (with 300 million English learners in total). With the same proportion of learners to speakers as in German, this would amount to 474 million English-speakers (300 million x 1.58; 65,000 : 41,900 = 1.58). The probability of meeting an English-speaker in China is correspondingly greater, namely 1 : 2.74 (p = 0.36).

On the basis of proportions alone, also by comparison with English, many Germans might consider the use of German in China (or elsewhere) hopeless from the start. The proportions described contribute to an evaluation of English as the default choice. This evaluation is actualised in the attitudes of speakers, who are then predisposed to choose English for international communication. Deciding to opt for another language (apart from Chinese) requires special reasons or circumstances. For many reasons, these are not always perceived or judged correctly and, even when entirely appropriate circumstances are present, English is still spoken instead of German (see Ch. A.6; F.2; F.5).

Above all, it is easy to overlook the fact that the German learners and German-speakers are concentrated in given places and situations. To stay with the example of China, there are sometimes up to 15,000 learner/speakers at the Tongji University in Shanghai, where almost half of all students regularly learn German as a foreign language, generally as a subsidiary subject, with comparatively fewer actual Germanists (communication from the former Dean of the German Department, Jianhua Zhu). It was therefore a questionable decision for speakers from Germany to speak exclusively English at the 100-year celebration of Tongji University in 2007 (report from the former President of the Society for German Language, Armin Burkhardt), especially as the German-studies department would gladly have provided simultaneous interpreters free of charge. A very accurate specification of regions, towns, fields of action and situations (domains) in which German-speakers are concentrated, could represent an important guide for an appropriate language choice. In such locations, German can indeed serve as a lingua franca. Prime examples include international German-studies or German-teaching conferences. But further opportunities are offered by guest-speaker visits from German-speaking countries to German-studies departments or schools, but also through contact with humanities subjects or in corporate branches employing people with German-language skills.

Lingua franca communication through German, which has become easier anyway through contemporary transport arrangements, no longer requires face-to-face contact. Cost-favourable voice and text media are now widely accessible, primarily via the Internet (e.g. Skype, email and also telephone). Indeed, an interesting research topic, which has so far received little attention, would be international, asymmetric and lingua-franca communication via the Internet using German (Ch. I.1.4.1; I.1.4.2). At a conference, a Brazilian student once told me he was interested in this topic and planned to write his MA dissertation on language choice in international Internet communication between German-speakers and non-German-speakers, primarily through personal rather than just commercial contacts. Unfortunately, I have lost contact with him.

Finally, a modification of the distinction proposed by Werner Hüllen (1992) between native languages as "languages of identification" and lingua francas as "languages of communication" is relevant here. As Jennifer Jenkins (2007: 197–235) has explained with the example of English, a lingua franca can, indeed, also serve as a symbol for group membership, even if it is obvious that it is not the native language (accent, differences from native-language grammar, lexis, idioms or pragmatics). Accordingly, people communicating in the lingua franca may feel that they are members of a language community, e.g. in the case of English, proud to participate in globalisation. This attitude can become part of their social identity. What might seem to be merely a language of communication then becomes a language of identification. Correspondingly, people communicating in non-native-speaker German might feel membership and pride, based on a variety of reasons, within the international community of German-speakers. Presumably such a self-understanding remains largely unconscious, but can still form a facet of social identity for these people (for "identity", see also Ch. B.3; E.1; E.2). Further research on this question is long overdue.

5. Complementary national and international positioning of languages?

The relatively low position of German in the world is often attributed to neglect of the German language in the German-speaking countries themselves, which is assumed to have favoured a move away from German in foreign countries. This theme fuels not only people and organisations inclined towards linguistic purism, such as the "*Verein Deutsche Sprache*" [Society for German Language] (Ch. L.3.4) and the ADAWIS working group on "German as a Language of Science and Scholarship", but also resonates with many language-critical comments. One example is the book by former president of the Goethe-Institut, Jutta Limbach, "Is there a Future for German?" (2008: 25–30) which has been taken up by the media but, in fact, clearly distances itself from linguistic purism (ibid: 30–33). Although the relationship between the national and international position of languages is obvious here and also recurs throughout the present book, explicit reasons are seldom articulated. The relationship between valuation and use of German in German-speaking countries and valuation and use outside seems so obvious to many that they consider more detailed analysis or explanation superfluous. To me, however, this seems a worthwhile undertaking.

In this regard, two factors are particularly significant:

(1) The rise in position of other languages, primarily English, within the German-speaking countries; and
(2) The growing number of borrowings from English into German.

I will now examine both factors, which overlap to some extent, with regard to their connection with the position of German in the world.

With reference to factor (1), inside German-speaking countries, other languages are now used alongside German more than hitherto (Ch. A.8: *Linguistic Hyper-diversity*). This includes not only the languages of indigenous minorities (in Germany, e.g. Sorbian or Romani), which are protected in all German-speaking countries by the *European Charter for Regional or Minority Languages* (conventions.coe.int/treaty/Commun/ChercheSig.asp?NT=148&CM=&DF=&CL=GER). In addition, the many languages of immigrants and migrants (Turkish, Polish etc.) now receive greater support than previously, although the need for a knowledge of German has recently been emphasised and required for citizenship (Li 2014). Finally, foreign languages, primarily English, are used more widely in education and science, especially in private schools and universities, particularly during lessons (Ch. G.8; Ammon 1998; Oberreuter/ Krull/ Meyer/ Ehlich 2012).

It might be considered that the use of minority languages does not influence the position of German if the minorities also learn and use German, and it becomes their second language or even second native language (Ch. A.3). However, if one considers why non-German-speakers learn German, this view requires modification. The central motive is certainly to communicate with German-speaking countries, their population and institutions. But if communication is possible in another language, this motive is weakened. This applies primarily with relatively large minorities, for whom it is possible to communicate in their own language. Accordingly, many Turkish people in Germany avoid learning German because they have almost exclusive contact with other Turkish speakers. As a result, some Turkish people in Turkey believe there are already sufficient Turkish-speakers in the German-speaking countries. The same applies – to a lesser extent – for other minorities. Although there have been isolated comments on this subject, comprehensive investigations into this "other side" of the preservation of immigrant languages are in short supply.

In fact, all indigenous minorities have good German skills and, as a result of integration laws, so have a growing number of non-indigenous minorities. However, preserving languages of origin is a decisive factor in weakening the motivation to learn German. And preservation is desirable for other reasons. These even include the material interests of German-speaking countries, because non-indigenous minority languages are an economic resource in the sense that they facilitate commercial contacts with the countries of origin (see e.g. Brizic 2009; Krumm 2008: 7f.).

This exposes a dilemma facing commercially motivated language policy: on one hand, preserving immigrant languages improves foreign contacts for German-speaking countries; on the other hand, it undermines the position of German in the world. The first point serves the German-speaking countries economically; the second damages them (Ch. F.1). Such dilemmas also occur in differently determined cases of a decline in the position of the German language (see e.g. Ch. A.6) and can hamper counteractive language policies.

However, beyond the merely economic, there are more comprehensive reasons for preserving immigrant languages: they facilitate every kind of international relationship. An ethical factor also applies here, which becomes evident through a different bundle of reasons for language preservation, as explained by Hans-Jürgen Krumm (e.g. 2008, 2011). A policy of non-recognition of languages of origin can lead to disruption of families and to challenges to individual identity – similar to the damaging consequences associated with *language death*. But to expand on this exceeds our present purpose. What must be shown here is only that the preservation of minority languages (desired for good reasons) can be detrimental to the position of German in the world. This is a correlation between the position of German in and outside the German-speaking countries which has hitherto hardly been considered, although an accurate investigation is vital to a balanced language policy.

It now seems appropriate to discuss the question whether preserving immigrant languages in non-German-speaking countries can be detrimental to the position of German in the world. The effect is more difficult to detect than preservation inside the German-speaking countries, but it can be shown with the example of Sweden. There, e.g. Turkish immigrants can preserve knowledge of their native language in so-called *hemspråksklasser* (native-language classes) (Belke 2011). Furthermore, as the language of instruction, Swedish is the second language for these pupils. A genuine foreign language comes in only after this as a school subject (not language of instruction), which is therefore a third language for the students. For most, this is English. The same applies for other countries with similar rulings on immigrant languages. In this context, it remains open whether English is compulsory – as in an increasing number of countries – or optional because, in the latter case, it is chosen by almost all students anyway. German and other foreign languages are relegated to fourth place, and generally only as one element in a bundle of foreign languages, as an optional or – more rarely – elective subject. For many students, the fourth language is not available because of excessive demand or over-stretching. If the immigrant's language was not a school language, languages like German would remain in third place and would therefore be a more realistic teaching goal. In this way, the preservation of immigrant languages even in non-German-speaking countries can indirectly restrict the learning of German or other languages and therefore their position in the world. Ultimately, therefore, even the overarching reason for preserving immigrant languages, namely, ensuring the undeniably valuable multilingualism, becomes doubtful. I have already mentioned that there are equally good reasons for such a preservation policy and explained the dilemma of opposing such a policy, which could be motivated, for example, by efforts to strengthen the position of German in the world.

I continue the discussion of the non-German-speaking countries with the question of whether preserving indigenous minority languages or also additional official state languages is detrimental to the position of languages like German. In fact, these languages are demoted in the rank-ordering of school languages, at best to fourth place, generally as one of several languages available as options. For example, for Basque people in Spain, the rank-order of school languages is: Basque – Spanish – English – X, or for Friesians in the Netherlands: (West) Friesian – Dutch – English – X (with German X), where, for many students, X does not even come into consideration. More generally, therefore, preserving minority languages or additional official state languages tightens the restriction to English as the only foreign language, thereby eliminating other foreign languages (on this question, compare Ammon 2009b: 24–27, 2010d: 18f.). At the same time, however, any arguments against multiple official state languages or against the preservation of minority languages would be directed against German, because, in four countries, German is one of several official languages (Ch. D) and also a minority language (Ch. E) in a relatively large number of countries. Moreover, there are overarching reasons, not least the ethical reasons mentioned, against such a restrictive policy.

A closer look at the non-German-speaking countries shows that boosting foreign languages in school, which has often been implemented in this context, also acts against German as a foreign language (GFL). This refers primarily to Asian languages such as Chinese or Japanese. However, the establishment of English as the first foreign language, whether compulsory or as an elective subject, which is taking place worldwide, is even more detrimental to GFL.

The observation that preference for English does not remain limited to school leads us back to the loss of position of German inside the German-speaking countries and the associated effect on its position in the world. In addition to the minority languages, international foreign languages (cf. Ch. A.3; A.7) are also learnt in the German-speaking countries and used, albeit only in niches. As everywhere in the world, only English is present in diverse form – (with reference to Germany, see Hüllen 2007). Native German-speakers also often speak and write English even within the German-speaking countries, primarily in the following situations:

- On public transport in announcements, on long-distance rail and air travel;
- In popular music, on stage and in the media, especially radio (Ch. I.2.3);
- In tourist areas, especially on road signs, brochures, notice boards (e.g. in museums), menus and by tourist guides;
- In advertising, not only in individual words and phrases, but also longer utterances;
- In job advertisements, also in longer utterances.

Extensive use of English in the following, less public domains is less overt:

- In large companies as corporate language (cf. Ch. F.7), where foreign supervisory-board members often hardly speak German; in smaller businesses as a negotiating language;
- In university publications, at conferences and in teaching situations; in the increasing number of private universities, teaching in English is widespread (cf. Ch. G.3–G.8);
- In private schools as the language of instruction, in some subjects;
- In politics at international conferences, meetings and visits, when foreign politicians are present: in public addresses, lectures and consultations (cf. Ch. H.5.1);
- In towns and cities during organised visits by foreigners, e.g. from twin-towns or schools;
- In cultural programmes, in films, theatres and lectures;
- For information, in meetings, order confirmations, in restaurants, shops, by police and other authorities, in doctors' surgeries, hospitals and similar, although often with linguistic difficulty;
- In media contacts with foreign countries, via email, Facebook, Twitter or Internet telephony (Skype) (Ch. I.1.4.2).

The trivially obvious reverse side of these uses of English is the less frequent use of German in such situations, which can be detrimental not only to the position of German but even to its structure and vocabulary. As an inverse conclusion, this follows from the fact that diverse use of a language enriches its expressiveness, because, by contrast with other consumables which lose value through usage, languages are not worn out by use.

> *La langue [. . .] au contraire [. . .] se valorise d'autant plus qu'elle est plus utilisée. Pour dire les choses simplement, plus une voiture roule et plus elle perd de sa valeur (une voiture d'occasion se vend moins cher qu'une voiture neuve [. . .]), alors que [. . .] plus une langue sert et plus elle se valorise.*
> *(Calvet 1999: 12)*

[On the contrary, . . . language increases in value the more it is used. Put simply, the more a car is driven, the more it loses value (a second-hand car is sold for less than a new one [. . .], while [. . .] the more a language is used, the greater its value becomes.]

Some of the situations named are particularly relevant for the *elaboration* [*Ausbau*] (Ch. G.11) of vocabulary, terminology and metaphors, e.g. research and teaching at universities or negotiations in business and politics. But even in less suspect situations, e.g. in popular music, expressiveness can be impoverished if more and more texts are written in English. An impoverishment of expressiveness could make GFL less attractive, particularly when German is learnt mainly for *cultural* motives, e.g., in Japan (Ch. J.9 14) or Australia (G. Schmid 2011; Ch. J.9.15). However, this entire complex of questions still requires scholarly investigation and was unfortunately not addressed in the *First Report on the Situation of the German Language* (Deutsche Akademie für Sprache und Dichtung 2013).

Damage to the position of German in the world from the use of English in German-speaking countries is more obvious, because as a result, less German penetrates to the outside. This occurs in popular music with the increasing use of English texts and, for example, in the *Eurovision Song Contest*, where German participants sing exclusively in English, and in 2010, Lena won the contest with the completely English-language song "Satellite" (Ch. I.2.2). Even bands which are supposed to motivate the learning of German generally sing in English when on tour, e.g. *Tokio Hotel*.

Ultimately, the use of English in German-speaking countries damages the positioning of German in the world for the same reason as the preservation of immigrant languages by making German seem unnecessary for communication (Hoberg 2004: 94; H. Wagener 2012). This potential effect – more hypothesized than reliably corroborated – is presumably a deeper reason for the bitterness of many critics of the "flooding" of Germany by English and its development into a "lingua-franca country" (Weinrich 2000/ 2001). It is one of the most consequential effects of the global lingua franca on the learning of foreign languages worldwide.

Use of English in German-speaking countries is supported by an expansion in the learning of English, for which there is a considerable appetite in parts of the population (see Quetz 2010 for the situation in Germany). This begins in primary school and even kindergarten and creates the impression that, in future, foreigners will be able to communicate with all German people in English. The only obstacle is offered by those who refuse to cooperate and insist on using German. But this demands tenacious linguistic or national identity and can conflict with elementary rules of politeness (Ch. F.2).

Even today, foreigners in German-speaking countries no longer absolutely require a knowledge of German. Above all, in universities and in business, they can operate successfully exclusively in English. Limitations arise only in cultural life and possibly also in personal contacts – that is, if English-speakers do not, in fact, gain advantages of prestige in this context, because they possess *transnational linguistic capital* and belong to the *transnational [social] class* (Gerhardt 2010: 54).

The image of German-speaking countries accessible without a knowledge of German is reminiscent of the historical attitude of Germans towards smaller neighbouring language communities. Germans had grown accustomed to the fact that people there all spoke German. However, young people today increasingly try to communicate in English. Motivating them to learn German somewhat resembles the call to German-speakers to learn their neighbours' languages (e.g. "German language expert presents the case for learning neighbours' languages" *Der Standard* 19 July 2011; Raasch/ Cuny/ Bühler/ Magar 1992). The debate continues on both sides.

The Netherlands and Scandinavian countries provide good examples of the influence of a comprehensive knowledge of foreign languages in a population on the learning of their home language as a foreign language. Knowing such languages comes to seem largely superfluous. German-speaking countries have not travelled quite so far along this road. This is corroborated by a comparison of students attending English-speaking university courses in Denmark and Germany. With study visits of equal length, knowledge of German achieved in Germany was significantly higher than the knowledge of Danish achieved in Denmark. This was reported to me by Frauke Priegnitz on the basis of her comparative investigation (email: 12 October 2011; see also Priegnitz 2015). She explained, "Of course, the German language still has quite a different status from Danish. But, the Danish did advertise a purely English-speaking way of life in Denmark. Nevertheless, I had not imagined this level [of use of English! U.A.]!" However, this could reinforce the impression that it is also possible to live in Germany without knowing German, which would further undermine people's interest in learning German (cf. He 2013). So much for the effect of factor (1) of the positional gain of English in German-speaking countries, on the position of German in the world.

We turn now to factor (2), the increased borrowing from other languages, once again, primarily from English, on the position of German in the world. This effect is less complicated. The *linguistic landscape*, a concept which has become fashionable in sociolinguistics (e.g. Shohamy/ Gorter 2009), provides a variegated picture in German-speaking countries, partly with regard to immigrant languages, but again, predominantly English. Borrowing, primarily of words and phrases, begins with *transferences* from the language of origin. Through habituation and ultimately acceptance, these become components of the recipient language, that is, German. Acceptance is eventually almost complete when borrowings are codified in reference works, e.g. the Duden dictionaries, as correct German (for examples of linguistic standardisation including model writers/speakers and model texts, language codex, language experts, linguistic-standardisation authorities and their interaction, see Ammon 1995a: 73–82; for borrowings into German, see Eisenberg 2011).

English is preferred in situations which exude cosmopolitanism or scientific and technical progress. This prestige often makes anglicisms seem more attractive than traditional loanwords from Latin or French. In word-pairs such as: *shorts – kurze Hosen, boots – Stiefel, tracking bag – Rucksack, shoppen – einkaufen, sale – Schlussverkauf, pets – Streicheltiere* etc., the borrowing from English enjoys higher prestige than its German equivalent. The first variant tends to be used by businesses, and *Dinner* or *Hangover* seems more refined than *(festliches) Abendessen* or *Kater*. The traditional German variants have a provincial feel.

I am not linking these points with any purist agenda, because a preference for anglicisms can originate from attitudes such as cosmopolitanism, which I share. Furthermore, anglicisms enrich the German language with additional expressiveness. But they can also impair the prestige of German, and this can dampen foreigners' motivation to learn GFL, in other words, it can have a negative influence on the position of German in the world. This is how I explain the widespread rejection of anglicisms by GFL teachers and learners which I have encountered, for example, in the publication of books about the German language in Japan, Korea, China and Russia (Ammon 1994d; Ammon/ Chong 2003; Ammon/ Reinbothe/ Zhu 2007; Ammon/ Kemper 2011). One indicator for the rejection of anglicisms is the fact that many GFL teachers and learners turn to the *Verein Deutsche* Sprache (VDS) [Society for German Language] (Ch. K.3.4), which is known for taking a position against anglicisms, with its campaign expressions such as *unnecessary anglicisms* or *Denglisch* (= German with an inflationary number of anglicisms) (Bartzsch/ Pogarell/ Schröder [1999] 2003; Zabel [2001] 2003).

One government measure against the neglect of German in German-speaking countries is the recent legislation on integration. Regarding the immigration of spouses, the new German Residence Law stipulates a knowledge of German, so that "the spouse can communicate, at least simply, in German" (Residence Law § 30, see Uhl n.y.: 1). However, for this, knowledge level A1 of the *Common European Reference Framework* is sufficient. The new Citizenship Law for naturalisation in Germany stipulates more stringent requirements, generally, a knowledge of German at level B1 of the Reference Framework (see e.g.; criticised by Li 2014 as still inadequate). The many German courses established for this purpose – and because of the refugee crisis – have given momentum to the teaching of German as a second language (GSL) and act against the avoidance of learning German – but without removing the ongoing effect of factors (1) and (2).

6. Language choice and its influence on the international positioning of languages

A group of English pupils who had been studying German at school had a disappointing experience during a recent visit to a German grammar school in Duisburg-Rheinhausen. They hardly managed to speak a word of German and did not improve their language skills, which was the primary purpose of their visit. Their German counterparts were much too eager to practise their English, which – as their English teacher proudly reported in the newspaper – was better than the English pupils' command of German anyway (*Rheinische Post* 27 March 2009).

When former German Foreign Minister, Guido Westerwelle, was asked a question in English by a British journalist at a press conference in Berlin, he refused to answer in English, explaining that the event had been arranged in Germany for German citizens ("Discrimination against German in the EU?" *Welt Online* 25 February 2010).

It is easy to imagine the influence of these examples of language choice in international communication on the position of German in the world. While individual incidents have a minimal effect, this cannot be maintained in the case of regular occurrences. Accordingly, the motivation of students visiting Germany to learn German who are hardly allowed to use their German-language skills during the visit is hardly reinforced by this experience. The same applies for foreign journalists if German politicians regularly answer their questions in English. It is therefore remarkable that many in the German press criticised Westerwelle's behaviour as inappropriate for a German Foreign Minister instead of commenting on the inappropriateness of the British journalist's choice of English. Their response evidently corresponds with widespread opinions among Germans about the appropriate choice of language when speaking to foreigners. Harald Weydt (2004) cites numerous examples of such language choices which undermine the speaking and learning of German by foreigners – and therefore ultimately weaken the position of German in the world (see Ch. H.5.3; Ammon "Appropriate language choice for international communication", www.goethe.de/ges/pra/prj/sog/fst/ de4622069.htm).

The topic of "language choice" is complex (cf. Coulmas 2005a; Ch. F.2). Joshua Fishman (1965) formulated it neatly in a now famous question, "Who speaks which language to whom, when (in which situation) and why?". The present chapter focuses on the types of language choice which can be advantageous or detrimental to the position of languages in the world, and, for this purpose, makes a distinction between the following, sometimes overlapping, types of language choice:

i)   For communication in individual situations, between individuals or larger groups: (a) for genuine communication, (b) with symbolic purposes, (c) for learning and practice;
ii)   For regular communication in the family, therefore, basically, the native language(s);
iii) For learning as foreign language(s);
iv)   For communication in institutions and organisations, that is, working languages or official languages of associations, authorities, governments or international organisations.

In this context, all four types of language choice may be controlled by superordinate bodies, even in contexts which seem purely private, for example, within families, under pressure from wider policies of language preservation or *revival*. The following factors are particularly relevant.

Rules for social behaviour, including, for example, polite social interaction, often influence language choice. The politest choice is often the native language of the person to whom one is speaking, who, as a result, is allowed to *preserve face* with maximum certainty. Erving Goffman ([1959] 2003) derived this terminology from the idiomatic expression of *losing face*. It was then taken up by Penelope Brown and Stephen C. Levinson ([1978] 1987; Brown 2005) in their politeness theory. This is based on two basic human needs, namely the preservation of *negative face* (personal freedom and *territory*) and *positive face* (respect from other people). In the present context, only the latter is relevant: politeness as a testimony of acknowledgement. Here, the choice of the native language of the person one is speaking to is most appropriate, even if the effect is only symbolic and not related to the goal of actual communication. Examples of such language choice in international communication often occur in political settings, for instance, as reported during a visit by the Prince of Monaco to southern Germany. "Prince Albert delivers the first sentence of his speech with a perfect German accent: *'Es ist eine Grosse Freude für uns, hier in Stuttgart zu sein. Danke'*" ("Mit Öko-Antrieb", *FAZ* 11 July 2012: 7). The Prince then switched back into his native French, and an interpreter was provided. Sometimes, however, the choice of one's own language can be polite if the people addressed have learnt it as a foreign language and want to use it to practise their language skills – like the English pupils at the start of this chapter. The choice of this language then indicates an acknowledgement of their learning or a desire to help them practise instead of their using the advantage of native language to gain communicative superiority.

In addition to politeness, people also tend towards linguistic *accommodation* of their communication partners to achieve communication (Giles 1977). This corresponds with the *principle of cooperation* proposed by conversation theorist Paul Grice ([1975] 1989). Added to this are *power relations*, which favour the language of the more powerful communication partner (Ammon 2009d). Rules for language choice in given situations can thus result from a combination of politeness, efforts to achieve communication and power relationships. Under some circumstances, these factors become fixed as norms, the observation of which is reinforced through sanctions. Such norms can become involuntary *motives* for action and constituents of *personal identity*, for example, if children in the family (language-choice type ii above) – are motivated to speak language A with their father and language B with their mother. Norms differ from mere *prescriptions* because of their internalisation. They are evident in the expectations of *norm authorities* (persons or groups) that the people subjected to the norm (*norm subjects*) will act according to the norm. These expectations depend upon the social position of the people involved (e.g. children, people with a certain official status etc.).

As a result of such expectations, the occupiers of a given position become carriers of *social roles* (the role of child, official-status holder). In this way, theories about norms engage with theories about social roles. However, role carriers still have room to act according to their own *values* (Dahrendorf 1965). Ultimately, individuals associate themselves with given groups, e.g. social groupings, ethnicities or nationalities, as a component of their *social identity* (Tajfel 1974; Edwards 2009). Group membership of this kind can also be a factor in language choice, for example, when a French person speaks French even though they can also speak English and their communication partner has a poor command of French. All these factors influence the choice of languages which individuals make in order to communicate in specific situations and they therefore ultimately influence the position of languages in the world. Under some circumstances, these are combined with other motives including cultural and economic factors. For communication in the family, ethnic identity is an important factor, to which Fishman drew attention in his numerous investigations of language preservation or revival (e.g. Fishman 1966, 1991a, b; Fishman/ Nahirni et al. 1966). Examples are also to be found in German-speaking minorities who have preserved their German for centuries in *language islands* surrounded by other languages (Mattheier 1994; Berend/ Knipf-Komlósi 2006; Ch. E.1; E.2). Language of origin is thus a symbolic expression of continuing identification with German ethnicity (Ch. B.3).

However, Bengt-Arne Wickström (2005) generally assumes additional motives for language choice, such as the prestige of the language or economic relations with German-speaking countries. Choice of a foreign language to learn (language-choice type iii) is also often influenced by economic motives. Even the tendency for small language communities to prefer learning the languages of large language communities rather than vice versa may be guided by cost-benefit factors, without this necessarily being a conscious factor. A larger language community generally promises increased economic advantages. However, its total wealth is probably a more important factor. This explains, e.g. the fact that Japanese is learnt more frequently as a foreign language than Bengali, which has almost double the number of speakers (Ch. C.4), or also the fact that Japanese and Chinese flourished as foreign languages only after the economic upturn in their home countries (see Coulmas 1989 for Japanese).

Motives for choice of a foreign language originating from such considerations are designated as *instrumental* (Ch. J.8). These are distinguished from *integrative motives* which are typical for a second language (by contrast with a foreign language; cf. Ch. A.3 for this term). They are often found in the case of immigrants, e.g. who learn German in order to integrate linguistically in Germany, Austria or German-speaking Switzerland. The distinction between instrumental and integrative motives was suggested by the Canadian psycholinguists Robert C. Gardner/Wallace Lambert (1959, 1972; also, Gardner 2001). However, not all motives for learning a language fit the rough dichotomy between instrumental and integrative, e.g. the *cultural motive* mentioned in surveys, that is, the interest in the culture of the relevant language community, which Gabriele Schmidt (2011) found predominantly in cases of German learning at universities in Australia (Ch. J.9.15). The same applies for learning the language of one's ancestors, often found in the case of emigrants who turn back to their long-lost language of origin (with regard to Australia, see Ammon 1991b: 73–111).

The following list draws together the points made so far by re-naming the most important factors in such a language choice, which can influence the position of languages in the world, in some cases, from different perspectives. They can, to some extent, be correlated with the four types of language choice differentiated at the beginning of the chapter: (i) for communication between individuals or larger groups, (ii) in families, (iii) for learning as a foreign language and (iv) communication in institutions and organisations.

(1) *Legal regulation* is an important factor for institutions, with specification of official languages and working languages in *language regimes*. The choice of languages to be learnt is also often legally stipulated in school curricula. A distinction must be made between custom and codification, e.g. in the statutes of organisations;

(2) *Existing language skills* are a trivial factor which limits the choice of language, with opportunities for expansion through translation or interpreting;

(3) *Power* can act as a further factor, in that the language of the more powerful tends to be selected – according to Max Weber's ([1922] 1972: 28) concept of power as "the chance to assert one's own will within a social relationship even against resistance, regardless of what this chance is based upon". One fictional example, which is typical for the period of colonialism, is the language choice between Robinson and Friday in Daniel Defoe's famous novel. Robinson's superior power supported by the flintlock and a sense of cultural superiority leaves no choice other than English – both for learning and for communication. There are many examples showing that power relations have been decisive in the choice of an official language or treaty language: after WWI, the assertion by Great Britain and the USA (against resistance from France) of English (alongside French) as the negotiating language, the language of the Treaty of Versailles and the official language of the League of Nations, with the exclusion of German from all three functions (Ostrower 1965: 360–371; Rudolph 1972: 93–96; Ch. H.1); the compulsory and exclusive use of German by the Nazis as treaty language between Germany and other countries for as long as they had power to assert this (Ch. H.2); and finally, a preference for the language of hierarchical superiors in institutions of the European Union (Haselhuber 2012: 69–80);

(4) *Politeness* can have the effect of restricting power. Even the powerful sometimes choose the language preferred by the less powerful in order to strengthen the *positive face* of the latter (Brown/ Levinson [1978] 1987: 62);

(5) *Attitudes* towards and *evaluations* of languages, on whatever basis, represent a further considerable factor. In this context, attitudes towards speakers are often transferred to languages. For example, for a considerable time, German was vilified as the Nazi language, e.g. in Great Britain through continuing television programmes about the Nazi period (Jurgen Trabant "The barked language", *FAZ* 28 September 2007: 40). However, the image of Germany in the world has recently improved (compare e.g. "Goodbye to the ugly Germans. According to a BBC survey, our country now enjoys maximum prestige worldwide [. . .]", *Welt am Sonntag* 13 March 2001: 16). This enhanced image presumably also influences attitudes towards the German language.

(6) *Identity: national, ethnic, linguistic (language community), transnational:* this complex factor marks a special attitude, which deserves separate treatment, namely, people's attitude towards themselves and their own grouping. By choosing their own language, speakers can express identification with their country, ethnicity or language community (linguistic identity) – including their affiliation with the rising *transnational social class* of world citizens (examples in O'Driscoll 2001a, b; on the transnational social class, Gerhards 2010: 54). Language choice of this kind can run counter to the rules of politeness. The French and Flemish-speaking Belgians (Flemish) are sometimes accused of a correspondingly obstinate insistence on their own language. By contrast, Germans tend to suppress their own language even if their conversation partners speak German well (Ch. H.5.3). This is often attributed to a damaged national identity in consequence of Nazism or to *linguistic disloyalty*, a term presumably introduced into sociolinguistics by Joshua Fishman (Fishman/Nahirny et al. 1966). For instance, the *Verein Deutsche Sprache (VDS)* [Society for German Language] sees in the general trend towards English "a shocking disloyalty to the German language" (cf. "Nominated language desecrator of the year", *DPA-News* 17 May 2009).

(7) *Self-presentation* as another factor in language choice is guided by the effort to boost, or less frequently sometimes to lower, one's own self-esteem, as in "The presentation of self in everyday life", to which Erving Goffman ([1959] 2003) has drawn attention. It can become a motive for choosing a foreign language, even if the native language would serve the purpose of communication better. Image boosting and showing-off cannot always be excluded, e.g. when Germans communicate in English even if there are only Germans present, as already referenced with regard to academic conferences, seminar events and laboratory discussions (Mocikat 2006: 4).

(8) A *desire to learn* can also be a factor in language choice, with a view to improving competence in the relevant language. This is presumably also sometimes a motive for German academics choosing to speak English.

(9) *Facilitation of subsequent communication* sometimes also plays a part when the content of the discussion or text is to be transferred to other people or institutions in a multi-stage communication. The choice of language is then guided by the language known by the recipients, also often English, in order to avoid errors and translation costs.

(10) *Personal acquaintance of communication partners* can, finally, overpower other factors, leaving the field open for language choice. One signal for social proximity among German-speakers is still the use of the familiar second-person *du* pronoun (instead of the formal *Sie*), which generally allows greater variation in conversation, regarding the associated social distance and proximity, in other words, *power* and *solidarity* (see e.g. Brown/ Gilman 1960).

This list of factors, which are, admittedly, not always clearly distinguishable, is no doubt still incomplete and needs to be reformulated more precisely and systematically – thereby opening a broad area of research relevant to the topic of this book.

Research is required primarily into language choice in relatively large groups. In this context, Philippe Van Parijs claims to have established what he calls the "minim*ex* rule", which should not be confused with the "minim*ax* rule" from game theory. The abbreviation suggests a "minimisation of ex": in other words, no one should be excluded. The language of choice is "the language of minimum exclusion (or minim*ex*), i.e. the language best known by the participant who knows it least" (Van Parijs 2007b: 39, 2011: 13–17; also "maxi-min criterion" 2011: 19–21). Reference can be made to the "minim*ex* language" (for the given situation). This means that, whether spontaneous or permanent, groups tend to choose the language common to all members (or to the largest proportion of them), even if a few individuals do not know this language well. Such a distribution of knowledge is preferred to one in which some of the group members know the language very well, but some not at all. In the case of a minim*ex* language choice, the person in the weakest position is still better off than the weakest person if another language were to be chosen, who would then possibly be entirely excluded from the communication. In this manner, on one hand, the minim*ex* rule fulfils the minimum requirements for common communication. On the other hand, it conforms with ideas about fairness from the discourse on social inequality, to the extent that the difference between *poor* (knowledge level still > 0) and *rich* (knowledge level 1), is, at least in mathematical terms, not infinitely large (∞), as between *penniless* (knowledge level 0) and *not without means* (knowledge level >0). However, the minim*ex* rule has, to my knowledge, still not been tested empirically. It can be assumed that its use varies dependent upon situation, region, linguistic and national composition of participants.

With regard to foreign-language skills in the contemporary world, the minim*ex* rule leads, in most situations, to the choice of English. Accordingly, to preserve the international position of German, strategies with which this rule can be overcome if desirable would be significant, e.g. *chuchotage* (whispered interpreting) for people with no German. In this context, a decision may have to be made between (a) discussion at a higher linguistic level in German in a subgroup with only indirect participation of group members with no knowledge of German (e.g. by means of *chuchotage*) versus (b) discussion at a lower linguistic level in English with direct participation of all group members. However, for a consistent language choice of German, a self-assured attitude would be required of German-speaking participants, native speakers and FL speakers. Primarily for native speakers, this requires a relatively intact national or linguistic-community identity. But, as already mentioned, the citizens of the largest German-speaking country are often associated with a damaged national identity which motivates them to relinquish their own language. However, exaggerated resistance of this tendency has a detrimental effect on the position of German in the world, primarily if it goes against the basic rules of politeness and fairness – as does, vice versa, the notorious use of German with conversational partners who do not want to communicate in German in the specific situation.

7. The global language constellation

Prompted by concepts and theories of globalisation, the interaction between languages in the world is increasingly regarded as a totality. Uncontested pioneer of this view is Abram de Swaan who developed through numerous publications a now widely acknowledged model of the *global language system*. The initial publication was "Notes on the Emerging Global Language System: Regional, National and Supernational" (1991); a more developed version of this model was presented in his book *Words of the World: The Global Language System* (2001a). The discussion which follows concentrates on this later version.

By contrast with my earlier discussions of de Swaan's theory, I now prefer the designation *global language constellation* because it leaves the character of the system more open. Although de Swaan also uses this term (2001: 14 and passim), in some places with the attribute "coherent", and alternates it with the term *global language system* (ibid: 2), he emphasises the interconnection between all languages in the form of a single *system*, or at least developments in this direction, as a part of globalisation. However, doubts have been expressed about this overall interconnectedness, e.g. by Douglas A. Kibbee (2003: 52) "Can we claim, as does Abram de Swaan, that the languages of the world together constitute a single, evolving 'global system'? [. . .]. In a system, one change entails others. Did the death of the last speaker of Dalmatian influence Croatian? Or influence other Romance languages along the Adriatic? Or bring about the loss of the language faculty of others living in this region?". Such scepticism raises questions about the elements of the system and the relationships between them – and, in fact, also about the rigour of the concept of *system* (comprehensive or partial connection between elements).

As a sociologist, de Swaan was evidently inspired by system theories from the social sciences, above all by Immanuel Wallerstein's *capitalist global system* (Wallerstein 1974, 1998), to which he also expressly refers (de Swaan 2001: 18, 195, Note 30). De Swaan sees the global *system of languages* as an *integral part* of the globalised world which is also said to comprise the following further global systems:

- *Political system* (approximately 200 nations of the world and the network of international organisations which holds them together);
- *Economic system* (worldwide linking of markets and business organisations);
- *Cultural system* (linked primarily by electronic media);
- *Ecological system* (humanity's "metabolism with nature"; 2001a: 1).

Considerable scholarly attention has been given to these systems.

> However, the fact that humanity, divided by a multitude of languages, but connected by a lattice of multilingual speakers, also constitutes a coherent language constellation, as one more dimension of the world system, has so far remained unnoticed. Yet, as soon it has been pointed out, the observation seems obvious.
>
> *(Ibid: 1f.)*

This global constellation is constituted in that "[m]utually unintelligible languages are connected by multilingual speakers" (including bilingual speakers). The connection between languages occurs "not at all in random fashion", but in "a strongly ordered, hierarchical pattern" (ibid: 4).

The shape of this system resembles a galaxy in which de Swaan makes a metaphorical distinction between the following four language types – in ascending order (astronomical correspondence in brackets):

(1) *Peripheral languages* (world);
(2) *Central languages* (planets);
(3) *Supercentral languages* (suns); and
(4) A single, *hypercentral language* (possibly, by definition only one?): "so to speak at the centre [. . .], the hub of the linguistic galaxy" (ibid: 6). The hypercentral language – English, of

course – thus corresponds to the centre of the galaxy – thereby giving the metaphor ominous undertones. Consider, for example, a black hole and its enormous force of absorption as the centre of the galaxy. However, de Swaan is careful to avoid such suggestions about the relationship of English to other languages.

Perhaps the concept of de Swaan's system would be more understandable if he had started with *language communities* and referred to languages only afterwards, through the language communities; in every case, however, he points towards the connection through multilingual speakers. Indeed, the concept relates directly and exclusively to multilingual speakers participating in interlingual acts of communication (Ch. A.3), but where those who do not use their multilingualism represent an additional potential. In fact, all language communities in the modern world are connected to one another through the mediation of multilingual speakers, because there is no longer even a single community in existence with which at least *one* multilingual speaker could not communicate verbally. Accordingly, de Swaan's *language system* does not refer to a *linguistic* system in the sense of linguistics but to a *social* system, of which the elements (the language communities) are interconnected through knowledge and use of language. I use the term *interconnected* to suggest that not all language communities are connected to one another directly, but in some cases only indirectly through the mediation of other languages. Accordingly, there may be no direct connection between the German or, even more likely, the Sorbian language community and a small indigenous community on the Amazon, but there are certainly interconnections such as, Sorbian <-> German <-> Portuguese (perhaps more directly: Sorbian <-> Portuguese) <-> indigenous language, even if there is just one of these indigenous people who knows (some) Portuguese alongside the native language. Kibbee's scepticism possibly originates from a misunderstanding of de Swaan's *systems*, because, in his critical question, Kibbee (2003: 52) is evidently referring to Dalmatian, Croatian, etc., as linguistic systems, not as sociological language communities.

For the purposes of the present book, it is primarily the supercentral languages which are of interest. In de Swaan's (alphabetical) ordering, these are (ibid: 5): Arabic, Chinese, English (the hypercentral language which de Swaan lists again with the supercentral languages), French, German, Hindi, Japanese, Malay, Portuguese, Russian, Spanish and Swahili – a total of 12 languages. For German, and also for Japanese and Russian, he introduces the limitation that, because of recent speaker losses, they are "nowadays barely supercentral languages, confined as they are to the remaining state territories" (ibid: 12). However, greater clarity about this limitation would be desirable. What kind of "confinement" is meant, e.g. by comparison with Hindi, Malay or Swahili? At least as foreign languages, German, Japanese and Russian are learnt worldwide with a much greater extension than these languages, and are presumably also used in international communication (for this concept see Ch. A.3). The question about the essential difference is even more pressing, because de Swaan subsequently gives special weight to distribution as a foreign language for the positioning of a language in the world.

In explaining the reasons for his rank ordering, he assumes that languages are goods of a special kind (ibid: 27–33; compare also Ch. A.1). Initially, he distinguishes between goods of limited access – which are acquired through exchange or purchase (e.g. bicycles) and could be called "personal goods" – and generally accessible goods – which can be called "collective goods, e.g. the air (for breathing)". Languages belong to the latter category to the extent that, disregarding the special case of secret languages, no one is prevented from acquiring, learning and using them. However, beyond this, de Swaan claims that languages can be described by a concept and term which he has introduced especially for this purpose: "hypercollective goods". These are characterised in that their owners either have, or with a correct assessment of their interests, should have, an interest in other people acquiring them. In the case of hypercollective goods (e.g. computer operating systems), the utility value increases with the number of owners. By contrast, with merely collective goods, this is not the case, because, for example, in the case of air, the utility value does not increase when more people breathe it (the typical form of acquisition of this good). With languages, the utility value is increased by additional learners and speakers (the typical forms of acquisition for languages), who augment the *communication potential* of these languages, i.e. the group of people, institutions etc. with which they allow communication. Languages are hypercollective goods especially because of this *communication value* which grows with increasing *acquisition*. Under some circumstances, greater communication potential can lead to wider distribution through the media (books, films, Internet and so on) with greater diversity, higher productivity and therefore more favourable prices. Added to this are secondary advantages for the language community, such as the distribution of teaching materials etc. Greater communication potential not only makes the language more desirable as a foreign language, but also strengthens its preservation as a native language and gives people improved reasons for switching to it. Incidentally, this consideration provides a more plausible explanation for the current "stampede towards English" (ibid: 171) than the metaphor of the *Catherine wheel* suggested by Miquel Strubell (1997, 2001) and recently revived with a more specialist reference by Clive W. Earls (2013a).

On the basis of his specification of languages as hypercollective goods, de Swaan (ibid: 33–40) then defines the status of a language La in a society S as follows, where S can refer to communities of different magnitude or structure (the whole world, a group of nations, one nation etc.). First, he distinguishes between "prevalence" and "centrality" of La in S. The "communication value", "Q-value", also referred to as "communication potential", in S is composed of these two parameters (ibid: 33f.). The *prevalence* of La in S is the numerical proportion of native speakers of La in the population of S (quotient of "number of La native speakers in S" : "population of S"). The definition of *centrality$_1$* of La in S (with index because it seems to me that two readings are possible here) is the numerical proportion of non-native speakers of La in the population of S (quotient of "number of non-native speakers of La in the population of S" : "population of S"). Another definition which, in my opinion, is even closer to de Swaan's formulation, *centrality$_2$*, relates only to the population with knowledge of at least one foreign language rather than to the entire population: "the 'centrality', c_2, of a language l_i is accordingly defined by the proportion of *multilingual* speakers that are competent in l_i" (Ibid: 33 – emphasis in the original. Please do not be irritated by the Greek symbol for a language!). Presumably, de Swaan would not include among the "multilingual speakers" people who have more than one native language, but no foreign language or second language (compare Ch. A.3). This centrality (centrality$_2$), to which I have added a different index, 2, would then be defined as the quotient of "number of non-native La speakers in S" : "number of multilingual speakers in S".

However, in the remainder of his book, de Swaan generally refers to centrality$_1$. The reference to the total population of S, which is essential to this definition, is also analogous to the prevalence. Above all, it is more practicable for empirical investigations because appropriate data for this parameter is much more readily available. For many Ss, the numbers of native speakers and FL speakers are registered at reasonably regular intervals; numbers of multilingual speakers are recorded much less frequently. However, figures from which both sets of data can be derived – if not absolutely directly – are available for the EU (published regularly in the *Eurobarometer*). De Swaan is familiar with the EU figures, and he is possibly thinking of these in the following reference, which presumably relates to centrality$_2$: "In those cases where reliable data on mother-tongue and second-language skills [which I take here to be foreign-language skills! U.A.] are available, the Q-value yields results that correspond with an informed assessment of the constellation" (ibid: 34). However, sets of worldwide data on centrality$_2$ are not available with any certainty; and only with gaps for centrality$_1$. The same applies even for supercentral languages, and these figures generally relate only to FL learners and not people with FL competence, which is relevant here. In fact, level of competence would also be important for an accurate picture.

As already mentioned, prevalence and centrality of La together give the *communication value* or the *communication potential* of La, which de Swaan (2001: 34) defines as the product of both values. De Swaan possibly refers to "Q-value" to indicate that what is involved here is just one of various possibilities for operationalising the more general concept of "communication potential". In the following, I also use the term *communication potential* in the sense of de Swaan's Q-value provided it is clear from the context what is meant. But, in line with the two readings of centrality, two understandings are possible:

Communication potential$_1$ = prevalence x centrality$_1$ and
Communication potential$_2$ = prevalence x centrality$_2$.

They are significantly different and can lead to strongly divergent figures. Since a larger number can never be obtained for centrality$_1$ than for centrality$_2$ (at most, an equal value in extreme cases), communication potential$_1$ is almost always smaller than communication potential$_2$.

It is problematic that – in both cases – for languages without native speakers or without FL speakers in S, that is, with prevalence 0 or respectively centrality 0 (centrality$_1$ or centrality$_2$) in S, a communication potential 0 is obtained (factor 0 → product 0). This possibility is in no sense impossible, e.g. for Esperanto (no native speakers) or for many minority languages (no FL speakers). However, it is counter-intuitive to deny such languages any *communication potential* in the relevant society, at least where there is more than one speaker. De Swaan possibly uses the term "Q-value" instead of "communication potential" to protect himself from this objection.

However, this problem also detracts from the Q-value as a theoretical concept, which de Swaan sees primarily in the fact that the Q-value explains the choice of foreign languages, and their rise and fall. As already mentioned, de Swaan believes that, in choosing a foreign language, FL learners are guided by the Q-value (communication potential) of the language. Although I share this view to a considerable extent, I would wish to relativize it. De Swaan takes the Q-value as the most important factor, giving the impression that it is the only factor in the choice of foreign languages. Accordingly, languages with Q-value 0, that is, without native speakers or without FL speakers, would have no chance as foreign languages. But this is difficult to reconcile with facts such as the learning of Esperanto, which is not at all rare, and the rise of previously neglected languages to desirable foreign languages. I wonder whether this problem with the Q-value as an explanatory, theoretical concept could not be remedied if prevalence and centrality were to be added instead of multiplied. I must confess, though, that this apparently straightforward solution may still have disadvantages.

Abram de Swaan's analytical approach and conceptual suggestions have quite rightly been taken up with interest and generally positively by the scholarly community. Their special advantage is that they are based on linguistic action or linguistic communication, i.e. what people can do to their advantage and disadvantage with differently distributed languages. On this basis, they prompt explanations of language choice, loyalty, switching, preservation and loss. My criticisms are not intended to question these advantages. The following points are not meant to be fundamental criticisms but rather to provide a stimulus towards possible improvements.

De Swaan's Q-value relates globally to S, that is, the specific society for which the positioning of the language La is to be determined, e.g. with reference to the whole world, a group of nations (e.g. EU), one nation etc. However, this approach suggests subdividing large Ss into smaller Ss contained within them and then considering in greater detail the distribution of languages in these Ss. For example, the whole world can be subdivided into nations, large nations into regions or (autonomous) provinces/Cantons etc. ($S = \{S_1, S_2, \ldots, S_n\}$).

The uniformity or skewness in the distribution of prevalences, centralities and communication potentials of a language in these Ss can then be expressed numerically. For example, the mean value (arithmetic mean) of all Ss can be calculated first, and then the scatter (standard deviation) around this mean value, in each case, for prevalence, centrality and communication potential. The standard deviation rises in proportion with the skewness (imbalance) of the distribution and falls with increasing uniformity (balance) of distribution, ultimately up to the extreme value 0. In this manner, given the available data, the uniformity or skewness in the distribution of native speakers (prevalence), FL speakers (centrality) and communication potential of languages could be measured over larger territories, nations or the entire world. In this respect, it can be assumed, for example, that the native speakers of Spanish (Castilian) in Spain are more uniformly distributed over the different provinces of the whole nation than the native speakers of Basque, Galician or Catalan, or that the FL speakers of English are distributed more uniformly over all nations in the world, that is, globally, than the FL speakers of any other language, including German (compare Ch. K.7). Similarly, for both cases, a higher mean value can be anticipated for centrality and therefore presumably also communication potential. For English, its status as a *hypercentral language* in the world would be numerically demonstrated.

I turn now to my own assessment of the Q-value as a factor (or indicator) of the attractiveness of a language as a foreign language. In de Swaan's words (2001: 39): "The Q-value is an indicator of the communication value of a language. But it also purports to reconstruct the 'value' that speakers attribute to that language, an evaluation that guides their choices of foreign languages to learn". In my opinion, de Swaan overvalues this factor, which is limited entirely to speaker numbers. He names no other, accompanying factors. It is beyond doubt that speaker numbers play a role in cost-benefit assessments for foreign-language choice, but there are certainly other important factors. One of these is the economic weight of the language communities. The increasing demand for Japanese as a foreign language in the 1980s (Coulmas 1989) or of Chinese in recent years could not be explained otherwise. However, the number of native speakers of these languages has hardly grown during this period. By contrast, Bengali experienced a considerable growth in speaker numbers (estimated speaker numbers in 1964: 85 million; 1999: 211 million – S.H. Muller 1964 and *Ethnologue* 2000: 392), but its desirability as a foreign language has hardly risen. The obvious difference is the considerably more powerful economic growth of Japan and China (with consequences for technology, science and other fields) than in Bangladesh. William Mackey's (1976, 1989) more complex concept of the "status of a language" ("*status des langues*") takes this factor of the economic power of a language community for the choice of foreign languages into consideration more effectively than de Swaan's Q-value. However, I prefer the term *position of a language*, because *status* could be misunderstood as having a meaning specified in law.

One final point is again not intended as a criticism of de Swaan, who is certainly aware of it. His prevalence, centrality and Q-value ultimately have the form of ratio scales. This renders questionable the subdivision into precisely four ranges (or types) of language, which – it seems to me – the astronomical metaphor mistakenly suggests. If this metaphor were to be removed, the continuous transitions between ranges could be observed more clearly. The ranges could then possibly be reconstructed in the form of clusters – if possible with different boundaries and associations. However, such a process has not so far been feasible because of lack of data. Nevertheless, de Swaan is planning a research programme which he will apply to a series of societies (individual nations, groups of nations, confederations of nations): India and Indonesia, three constellations each in Francophone and Anglophone Africa, South Africa and the European Union.

An attempt to bring the *supercentral* languages (naturally including German) into a rank ordering on the global scale according to prevalence, centrality and communication potential, or even better, to plot them on a ratio scale (see Ammon 2010c) would be even more relevant to the topic of the present book.

The same 12 languages which de Swaan calls supercentral are selected – without explicit reference to de Swaan – by David Dalby as *megalanguages*, "spoken by an estimated 100 million voices or more" (1999/2000, 2000, Vol. 1:291). They are a subset of the 28 *arterial languages*, which are spoken by at least 1% of the world population (or at least 60 million people). Dalby understands the interrelation between all languages in the world by analogy with biology and ecology: "Just as 'biosphere' denotes the terrestrial mantle of living organisms, so the term 'linguasphere' may be usefully employed to describe the mantle of communication gradually extended around the planet by humankind" (ibid: 295).

De Swaan's position (1993) is expressly opposed by Louis-Jean Calvet (1999: 75–99) in *Pour une écologie des langues du monde* with his "galaxy of languages". However, he names only nine supercentral languages (understandably without English), but indicates the possibility of other languages with ellipses at the end of his list: Arabic, Russian, Swahili, French, Hindi, Malay, Spanish, Portuguese and Chinese. . . (his sequence). For our topic, it is particularly relevant that he expressly excludes German and also Japanese, which de Swaan (2001: 12) also relegates to a marginal position in this category. It remains open which other languages are suggested by the ellipses. Calvet gives no reason for excluding German and Japanese and relegating them to the merely central languages. He characterises the supercentral languages as those with the most speakers, but he clearly means native speakers here. He then limits this defining feature for German and Japanese: "The important number of speakers is not sufficient to confer the status of supercentral language: for example, German and Japanese which exceed 100 million speakers do not fulfil this role" (Calvet 1999: 78f.). It is regrettable that he does not give detailed reasons for relegating German and Japanese.

I am tempted to suspect prejudice against languages competing with his own language, French, is at least one of the reasons for their relegation. There are indeed indications of such a tendency in France, e.g. inscriptions on tourist attractions, where German is often absent even when many other languages are included. This makes possible the following experience by one museum visitor: "The tour guide answered my almost embarrassed question [about the absence of a German inscription U.A.] in a loud and irritated voice: 'Because German is not a world language'" (*FAZ* 23 December 2013: 8). It is also puzzling why Calvet ranks Swahili and Malay higher than German and Japanese, although these languages are considerably more widely distributed in the world, at least as foreign languages (Ch. J.7). Calvet's additional comment that the speakers of supercentral languages only learn English or a language of the same rank as their own, as a foreign language, is simply not true. In fact, the French, whose language he classifies as supercentral, do also learn German, which, in his opinion, is of a lower rank, albeit with a declining trend (as is the case with Germans learning French) (Ch. J.9.2). More generally, there is the question of whether Germans and Japanese differ fundamentally from French people in their preferences for foreign languages.

8. Linguistic superdiversity, world-empires, globalisation and the post-national constellation

Linguistic superdiversity is the latest buzzword in sociolinguistics. Jan Blommaert (2010: 8–13, 2013), who possibly coined the term, relates it primarily to the linguistic landscapes (Ch. A.5) which occur in the immigrant quarters of large cities. Incomers with diverse native languages often communicate using different "truncated languages" which can become dominant lingua francas. In Antwerp, where Blommaert lives and conducts much of his research, these include French, Dutch and German – alongside English (ibid: 8). Linguistic superdiversity exists in many cities throughout the world, such as Essen in Germany where school-age respondents named 122 different home languages (Baur/ Chlosta/ Claus/ Schroeder 2004). Residential areas of this kind differ from traditional immigrant communities in that they are often in a state of constant change, so that linguistic superdiversity becomes a permanent condition. The role played by truncated German in different cities appears not to have been investigated so far.

A special subset of linguistic superdiversity is to be found in the case of foreign visits by business people. For the topic of the present book, it is particularly relevant that such trips are becoming increasingly short and presumably occur in countries with increasing linguistic diversity. This tendency may be even more influential than urban immigrant communities on the global positioning of supercentral languages (Ch.A.7), including German. In fact, short visits to different linguistic regions hinder linguistic distribution. Figure A.8–1 shows the increase in "short-term assignments", as these are called in the source. The cutting edge of this development is North America because people believe their trips require no linguistic preparation, as English is the world lingua franca. Business trips to and from German-speaking countries are often very short, which also promotes the use of English.

Modern transport and media have a similar effect by allowing more diverse international contacts. David Crystal (2003: 13) illustrates this with fictional but still realistic examples of meetings arranged by the boss of a Japanese company with German and Saudi-Arabian partners in a hotel in Singapore, and an Internet conference between Swedish, Italian and Indian physicists. In both cases, the easiest form of communication is "to make use of the same language", which is nowadays almost always English. Numerous publications, not least by Crystal himself (2003), but also by Graddol (2000, 2006) and Phillipson (1992, 2006b), have explained why the choice falls on English. However, I would now like to turn to some different aspects of this question.

In this context, I assume that the economic power of native speakers can be an important factor and a useful indicator for the position and distribution of a language in a community (end of Ch.A.7; Ch. C.4; C.5). However, the position can persist after the downfall of the native country, as in the case of Latin after the downfall of the Roman Empire. This has been explained with

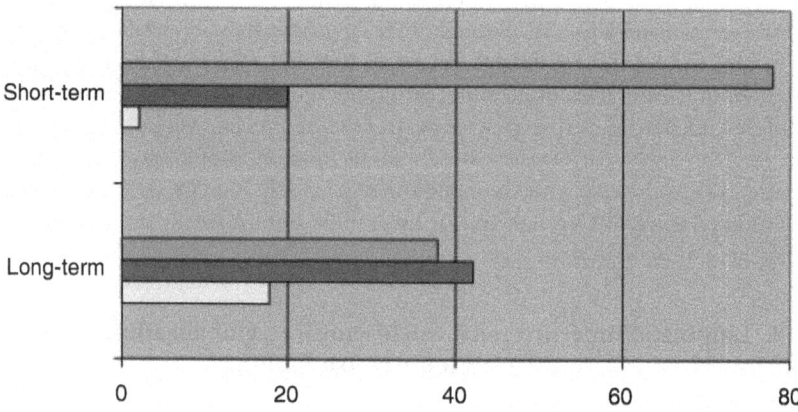

Figure A.8–1   Increase in short-term assignments abroad (light grey = increase, dark grey = no change, white = decrease)

reference to a general rule on *inertia in the position of a language* (de Swaan 1993: 222; Ammon 1998: 192–194), because learning and switching to another language are effort intensive. Opposing factors can, however, also hinder the distribution of languages in economically strong countries. In the case of China, which was by far the most powerful economic power in the world in the period from approximately 1000 to 1500 CE (Maddison 2007: 157–165), its language was not widely distributed because of China's policy of isolation. The situation was different in European colonial countries in subsequent centuries. With modern, global communications, the economic power of a country generally strengthens the position of its language, both within the country and also worldwide. This occurs through the markets opened by the language and through access to science, technology and culture.

However, from an economic perspective, the supremacy of English does not have a very long history. Evidence for this is provided by Immanuel Wallerstein's analysis of the *world-system of nations* (also Shannon 1996), which identifies a total of three economically hegemonic nations in recent history. He refers not only to economic power, but also to global economic engagement. "The first was the United Provinces (today called the Netherlands) in the mid-seventeenth century" (Wallerstein 2004: 57). This nomination may surprise many who would perhaps have placed Spain in first position, especially in the sixteenth century. It has also been largely forgotten that Dutch, the language of that once prominent economic power, once enjoyed a considerable international position (van der Sijs/ Willemyns 2009: 122–149; Willemyns 2013: 181–233), which extended far into the nineteenth century in East Asia, as the first German teachers in Japan were to discover (Naka 1994: 237f.). Only after the downfall of the Dutch Empire, from the middle of the nineteenth century, did the British Empire become dominant worldwide (Wallerstein 2004: 57). This was followed by the third, and so far, last hegemony since the middle of the twentieth century, that of the USA. The global position of English is based upon these last two empires. Wallerstein does not consider the rise of China in recent history.

Angus Maddison's (2007) research on technological leadership as a basis for economic success fits with this economic succession of dominant nations. He distinguishes between technological *lead countries* and technological *follower countries* and proposes the following sequence: "Since 1500 there have been four leading countries, northern Italy in the sixteenth century, the Netherlands from the sixteenth century until the Napoleonic wars, when the UK took over. The British lead lasted until around 1890, and the US has been the leader since then" (Ibid: 304). No mention of a German-speaking country! But there is also no mention of France, for which a similar economic and technological ranking might have been expected as for Britain, at least at the time of Napoleon, i.e. at the end of the eighteenth and the beginning of the nineteenth centuries. In fact, according to Wallerstein and Madison, Britain's economic and technological supremacy does not reach further back than the nineteenth century. Towards the end of the nineteenth century, the USA overtook Britain and also Germany, which was growing stronger since the foundation of the German Empire in 1871 and catching up with Britain in economic and technological terms by the turn of the nineteenth century.

The almost uncontested rise of English as the dominant, worldwide lingua franca began only after WWI. America's national economy, which had grown to match the economies of Europe as a whole by the middle of the twentieth century, formed the basis for change. This driving force of the economy was supported by policies for the global spread of English pursued primarily by Britain but more discreetly also by the USA (Phillipson 1992). The assertion of English alongside French as the language for the Treaty of Versailles after WWI (1914–1918) and as official language of the League of Nations is symptomatic for this trend (end of Ch. H.1; H.2).

While Wallerstein (2004: 58) believes that, so far, no state had succeeded in extending its economic hegemony to include political hegemony ("transforming the world-economy into a world-Empire was never possible"), other theoreticians do regard the USA as a global, political hegemonic power in the second half of the twentieth century. In their bestseller *Empire*, Michael Hart and Antonio Negri (2000: xiiif.) reference this widely accepted view, but they reject it themselves, allowing the USA only a "privileged position" in the world. Their term *Empire* relates to the structure of the world as a whole and not to the dominance of a single nation (ibid: 9).

Indeed, the decisive factor for the relationship between economic power and the position of a language is not a single nation, but the totality of all nations using that language. Taken together, all English-speaking nations, with the emphasis on the USA, have enjoyed by far the strongest economy of all language communities (compare Ch. C.4; C.5), and also the greatest political and military power, for at least 150 years, with a sharp rise after both world wars. Their global influence was often boosted by close cooperation with "inner circle" nations (Kachru 1982, 1986): USA, Britain, Canada, Australia, New Zealand and Ireland. No other language is based on a group of nations with approximately comparable economic and political strength. It would thus be astonishing if another language were to be the global lingua franca.

The economic power of the English-speaking countries does in fact form the basis for the global position of their language, but this has been promoted by other factors often referenced with the term *globalisation* (e.g. Beck 1997, see also "Globalisierung" in German Wikipedia). It seems almost trivial to list the relevant technologies, such as air travel, telephone, satellite communication, digitisation and the Internet, with their diverse opportunities for travel and communication now available to billions of people. As a result, political borders have become more porous, contributing substantially to the growth of international and worldwide movements of people, capital, goods and services. Finally, worldwide political and economic cooperation has been secured and institutionalised in the United Nations with its numerous sub-organisations and through other governmental and non-governmental organisations, global corporations and their interconnections.

It is of primary importance for our question that countless networks (Habermas 1998a: 102) and short-term contacts have been and continue to be established as a result of these changes. They often connect people and organisations from different nations and linguistic communities by means of *interlingual communication* (for the term see Ch. A.3). Added to this is the frequent switching of communication partners, in the face of which even the most diligent language learning can no longer respond adequately. The options of translation and interpreting have, at least so far, failed to offer a fully satisfactory alternative (Ch. A.10). The simplest solution is still to choose a common language as the lingua franca, where a single language is often more economical than several (Ch. G.12). Indeed, English has established itself as such a lingua franca. As the most widely learnt and best mastered foreign language in the world, it enjoys the *hypercentral* position (de Swaan 2001: 33–40; also, Ch. A.7; K.7). In the case of subordinate, to use de Swaan's terminology, merely *supercentral languages*, including German among the dozen or so listed, the limits of communication are reached more quickly.

An additional reason for the general trend towards a global lingua franca can be seen in the deep socio-economic transformation into a *post-national constellation* diagnosed and named by Jürgen Habermas (1998a): break-up of the national structure of the world; loosening of bonds tying citizens or inhabitants to national states; and consequent changes in social identity. These are side-effects or even constituents of globalisation (ibid: 101–110). Its cutting edge is formed by members of the *transnational class*, which exists in almost all countries, as referenced by Jürgen Gerhards (2010: 54f.). Because these privileged individuals "act transnationally and are integrated in transnational networks, their ties to the nation state are broken" (ibid). Perhaps we should refer more cautiously only to a *loosening* of ties, because this weaker sense also includes those integrated less intensively into the processes of globalisation. In Gerhards' view (alluding to Pierre Bourdieu), this new social class welcomes the global lingua franca as *transnational linguistic capital*, beyond this, as a *common symbol* (for their social class), making it into a component of their *social identity*. This weakens the national symbolism of their own language: the symbolism of German for the Germans, French for the French and so on. As a result, the choice not to use one's own language in favour of the world lingua franca is easier to make – a point which resonates or is articulated throughout this book. It goes without saying that this attitude weakens the global position of languages such as German.

9. International position of languages and cultural influence

Could a decline in the learning of German or negative changes in the position of German in the world also lead to loss of influence and knowledge of German culture? I mean by this knowledge of the culture created in German-speaking countries or in the German-language community (Ch. B.4). A typology of cultural goods according to relative linguistic content provides a useful basis for investigating the relationship between language and culture (in general, see Risager 2000), and especially their distribution outside their own language region. In fact, the extent to which a knowledge of language, in the present case, primarily German, is necessary for reception or consumption of cultural goods depends on this typology.

Cultural goods can be subdivided by linguistic content roughly as follows:

(1) Non-linguistic cultural goods, which have no substantial linguistic content. They can be received without knowledge of a given language and can therefore be exported independently of existing language skills (e.g. paintings, instrumental music, architecture, ceramics, porcelain arts, physical performance arts);

(2) Cultural goods with both substantial linguistic and substantial non-linguistic content. Without knowledge of the relevant language, only the non-linguistic content can be received. Options for distribution of such cultural goods are correspondingly limited. To make the linguistic content accessible to people without relevant language skills, they must be translated or interpreted, which can make distribution cost-intensive (e.g. comic strips, vocal music);

(3) Linguistic cultural goods which are entirely language-bound, that is, they have no substantially non-linguistic content. Without knowledge of the language in which they are written, not even parts can be received; these cultural goods therefore require translation or interpreting (texts of any kind, e.g. literature, technical literature, academic texts).

This typology shows very simply that, on one hand, there are non-linguistic cultural goods (Type 1), the distribution of which does not depend on a knowledge of German, at least not directly; and, on the other hand, language-bound goods, the distribution which depends on such knowledge. However, there are also transitional types of which, for the sake of simplicity, I name only a few. For example, academic texts which are largely written in a universal symbolic language and are sufficiently intelligible without verbal-linguistic components are placed in the transitional region between Type 2 and Type 3 (specialist mathematical texts, chemistry, physics etc.). Special ways of responding to cultural goods can also build bridges between the three types, e.g. listening to music with lyrics as if it were instrumental music, as with rap. Instances of Type 3 can thus be received as if they were Type 2 or even 1.

Type 3 and, in part, also Type 2 can also be differentiated by degree of translatability. For example, scientific texts (Type 3) are more completely translatable than literature; within classical literature, prose texts are more completely translatable than poetry. In my opinion, scientific texts, or at least their essential scientific contents, are completely translatable (Ch. G.6). However, this presupposes that the target language has been sufficiently *elaborated* (German: *ausgebaut*), that is, has the requisite terminologies and textual conventions at its disposal (Ch. G.11).

By contrast, literary texts seem to me never to be completely translatable, because the content of the text and details of linguistic expression, which are inevitably changed through translation, are both essential. This would therefore include polysemy in the translation of metaphors: literal meaning (source) as well as figurative meaning (target). For example, translating the metaphor *alte Schachtel* [old box] (deprecating for a woman) as *old trout* triggers different figurative meanings or connotations (literal meaning 'fish' instead of 'box'). The same applies for idiomatic expressions such as *hinter dem Mond leben* [to live behind the moon] – *to be way behind the times*; *nicht hinter dem Berg halten mit etwas* [not to stay behind the mountain with something] – *to make no bones about something*. The "translation" of poetry into different languages requires special creativity to preserve the sense of the text as well as its beauty to some extent.

Type 2 cultural goods, with substantial linguistic content and substantial non-linguistic content, can be distributed more independently of linguistic knowledge than Type 3. With some popular music, such as Nena's song "*99 Luftballons*" [*99 Air Balloons*] which attracted many listeners with no knowledge of German, this is clearly evident. The same applies for bands, such as *Silbermond* and *Tokio Hotel* (both from Germany), which even seem to have motivated foreign teenagers to learn German.

Examples of successful distribution of Type 2 cultural goods because of the appeal of the non-linguistic content include choral music, such as Bach's Cantatas, or Schubert's *Lieder*, which have worldwide audiences with no knowledge of German. However, with no understanding of the text, cultural distribution is limited, e.g. if German texts are sung without a knowledge of German. The many performances of the 4th movement of Beethoven's Ninth Symphony in Japan during Advent exemplify this. Singers in the large amateur choirs often have no German and only a general knowledge of the text (J. Ziegler 1994). I found an even clearer example of limitations on cultural distribution because of lack of linguistic knowledge in German Christmas carols played to encourage Christmas shoppers in Japanese department stores. In the 1990s, during a visit to a Tokyo department store while a recording of "*Stille Nacht*" was playing, I asked customers where this song originally came from (I emphasised "originally"). Of the 20 people I questioned, 19 said "USA" and only one "Germany" (not Austria). Because of my inadequate knowledge of Japanese, the questions were in English, and the song was also sung in English ("*Silent Night*"). Although clearly not representative, these findings fit the supposition that people preferentially link a foreign culture with countries whose language they have learnt or encountered frequently. German cultural goods are thus happily allocated to English-speaking countries, generally the USA or Britain. German teachers from Brazil have told me that many people there believe that Grimms' fairy tales originated in England. This kind of confusion is even more likely with cultural goods without linguistic content (Type 1).

Sometimes, Germans have even preferred an incorrect association, suppressing the country of origin for fear of losing sales because of anti-German feelings. This would explain an interpretation of the company name BMW as "British Motor Works", which I once heard in England. Germanisation of the names of foreign companies or their products after a German takeover is possibly avoided for the same reason. The US truck company "Freightliner" purchased by Daimler-Benz in a 100% takeover in 1981 provides an appropriate example.

Apart from such special effects of German history, promoting exports and economic advantage have long been cited as motives for a policy of expansion of the German language (Ch. K.1; Ammon 2009a: passim). One of many examples is when Ulrich Braess, former director of the Goethe Institute in Washington DC, said in an interview "anyone who learns German also buys German and anyone who is friendly towards Germany is a good customer for export-orientated trade in Germany" (www.business-on.de/muenchen/wer-deutsch-spricht-kauft-deutsch_id3464.html). Barthold Witte, former director of the Cultural Division of the German Foreign Office, has made similar statements (1985c, 1987).

A positive image for German-speaking countries is generally spread by the learning of German. Interest in German culture may develop from learning the language and this can stimulate further language learning. Cultural goods of Type 2 and especially Type 3, with linguistic content, are often present in teaching materials. Strengthening the worldwide position of a language increases the cultural influence of its native speakers. The blurb on the cover of the journal *Kulturaustausch* (Vol. 1, 2010) asks "What explains their 'cultural advantage'?" – referring to the UK, whose massive cultural export this issue investigates. The answer (which the issue fails to divulge) could be: The position of their language in the world. Or at least, that global linguistic position is an important factor.

10. Cognitive limits of multilingualism and attempts to overcome them

If people had a considerably higher-performance brain, there would be no need for lingua francas because every language could be learnt rapidly on demand. However, to achieve this, the brain would require an unimaginable memory capacity – more than ever imagined in previous utopias of future species (Homo sapiens sapiens *sapiens*). I doubt whether enhancing the performance of the brain through technical means (implants or exo-prostheses) will ever meet this demand – in spite of Stephen Hawking's bold vision: "neuronal implants will ensure improved memory performance and the storage of complete information packages, for example, for the perfect learning of a language [. . .] within the space of a minute" (Hawking 2001: 175; in greater detail, ibid: Ch. 6). If Hawking were right, the languages required for international communication could be learnt "perfectly" at lightning speed. It would become part of our normal preparations for a journey, like packing a suitcase.

In the absence of such fantastic possibilities for interlingual communication in human history so far, international languages have been selected and learnt – generally with considerable effort. At present, these include around ten languages (Ch. A.7), with English uncontested at the top of the list. But even this number exceeds most people's learning capacity. Otherwise, the position of these international languages, including German, would be less disputed and threatened.

As everyone today knows, learning a single foreign language requires a considerable time commitment. Evening classes for one semester are often only sufficient to enable simple everyday communication. By contrast, the types of communication referred to in subsequent chapters F, G and H require considerably more effort-intensive competences: for formulating business agreements, scientific communication, negotiating international treaties etc. Regarding the amount of learning required for basic foreign-language skills, expert Esperantist and psychologist Claude Piron (Switzerland) once explained to me the quintessence of his research: "Most people whose foreign language was very good had had a few years of study in a university of the relevant country, or had worked at a rather high level in such a country. They had at least 10,000 hours of language exposure". However, for less gifted individuals, often "blue-collar workers", he claimed that: "Even after 10 years of working in the relevant linguistic setting, the language level was rather poor in most cases [. . .] compared with the language of their counterparts speaking their mother tongue" (Piron's letter to me 6 January 2000; publication 2001: 95).

In this context, one should bear in mind that 10,000 hours is almost five years with a 40-hour week.

In fact, the effort required to learn foreign languages varies according to individual disposition and the following general conditions:

(1) Linguistic distance between starting language and target language;
(2) Sequence of learning (in the case of several foreign languages);
(3) Intended level of competence;
(4) Method of teaching and teacher commitment;
(5) Learner's strength of motivation and learning method.

I will briefly discuss here the factors (or independent variables) (1) to (3) whose influence on learning effort can be explained easily, at least roughly. The explanation is more difficult with factors (4) and (5) if trivialities are to be avoided.

With reference to the *Common European Framework of Reference* for Languages (CEFR; www. goethe.de/Z50/commeuro/), Andreas Guder (2005) explains that the time required to achieve the foreign-language competence level for university admission can diverge considerably depending on starting language and target language. He references a publication by the Goethe Institute which refers only to teaching time, without home-learning time (ibid: 70, Note 4) and differentiates this only according to target languages and not according to starting languages: "For German, it is assumed that language skills required for university admission (Level C1) can be achieved within 700 to 1,000 teaching units, while for Chinese the teaching plan [. . .] stipulates approximately 1,600 teaching units". This approximate doubling of the learning time for Chinese is evidently based – tacitly – on Indo-European starting languages, although this is not stated explicitly. However, the learning effort would be considerably reduced with a linguistically-related starting language, e.g. Cantonese.

An overview of the wide divergence in learning effort between different starting languages and target languages, which is based on empirical investigation, is provided by Chong Si-Ho (2003c: 306–308). In each case, to achieve the same competence level in Germanic or Romance languages, such as German, Dutch, French or Spanish, US Americans – the respondents were diplomats – required only 575–600 hours, while 2,200 hours were required for Arabic, Chinese, Korean or Japanese (ibid: 306).

However, the large number of hours needed for languages at a large linguistic distance from German only apply for the first foreign language. Factor (2) above, the sequence of learning in the case of several foreign languages, plays a part here. Accordingly, before learning German, all Chinese students learn English, a language at a short linguistic distance from German. They are therefore already familiar with the Latin alphabet and, for German, only need to learn the Umlaut letters (ä/Ä, ö/Ö, ü/Ü) and the letter ß. Other similarities between the two languages also allow relatively rapid learning. By contrast, previous learning of English hardly helps Germans if they then begin to learn Chinese. Independently of their particular difficulties, e.g. German grammar for the Chinese, or Chinese script and pronunciation (tones) for Germans, the sequence of languages therefore makes a difference.

Beyond this, it goes without saying that the effort of learning a foreign language depends upon the intended level of knowledge, which brings us to factor (3). The general assumption above that the competence levels of the GER, C1 for German and B2 for Chinese, is therefore relevant here and also for subsequent chapters of this book. However, according to my own experience and reports from colleagues, these represent only a minimum for successful study. For example, for Chinese students with C1 competence in German, lectures in German are indeed partially understandable. However, because of phonetic differences between the two languages, listening comprehension is particularly difficult. But in the other language skills also, with the possible exception of reading, competence level C1 is still below the level really required for university study. It is therefore all the more admirable that, in spite of this, Chinese students show the lowest dropout rate of all foreign students, only 20% (Heublein/ Richter/ Schmelzer/ Sommer 2012: 36–38 – reference to Jun He; see also He 2013: 155–184).

Maintaining the level of competence reached in a foreign language is also effort-intensive. During visits to Germany, Chinese students often lose some of their initial German skills because they take English-speaking courses and hardly have contact with Germans (Chen 2012; on English-speaking courses in German universities, Ch. G.8). Maintaining required foreign-language competence also requires considerable effort for managers, academics and diplomats, especially when high-level communication essential for professional activities is required. This leads to selection pressures on the international languages, which can push some languages out of this category.

Without a technical solution for this problem – where the possibility of expanding the capacity of the brain considered at the start of this chapter will presumably remain utopian for a considerable time – translation and interpreting technology offers a more realistic alternative. Practicable solutions for written translation, such as those available on the Internet, e.g. from Microsoft (www.bing.com/translator) or from Google (translate. Google.de/#auto/en/), seem to be within range. Any required link to a website written in a foreign language can be entered, and a translated version is returned. However, there are still linguistic errors in lexical choices, syntax and style, which can limit understanding of the text. Jonathan Pool (2010: 148) has shown such defects with the example of widely divergent translations of the same English sentence into French from nine different machine translation systems, which, admittedly almost ten years ago, "have produced results far inferior to expert human translations" (ibid: 147).

Machine interpreting (spoken) is even more difficult. David Crystal (2003: 27) describes a desideratum inspired by Douglas Adams' novel *The Hitch-Hikers Guide to the Galaxy* (London: Pan 1979: Ch. 6): "The Babel Fish, inserted into the ear, thus making all spoken languages (in the galaxy) intelligible [. . .]". For our purposes, it need not include all languages; the ten international languages would be quite sufficient. Even in the title of one of his programmatic essays, physicist Wolfgang Hilberg is optimistic for an imminent technical solution: "The Babel of languages will be sorted – with technology, not the diktat of one-language-fits-all! (Hilberg 2000a, 2000b). He accordingly advises speech recognition and learning without explicit grammatical analysis, by analysing complete text components as networks, – in his opinion, in the same way as children learn linguistic expressions. On this basis, interpreting machines, which he calls "translation machines", could be built rapidly and cost effectively "so that they could perhaps be dialled and hired through telephone networks. You could speak into a microphone in Germany, and your business partner in Japan could hear what you said on his phone in Japanese. Conversely, the Japanese person speaks their native language and the German listener can listen in German", furthermore, "such technology will be available in the relatively near future". "The nanoelectronics to be used could even make the "futuristic 'ear fish' [mentioned above; Crystal's 'Babel fish' U.A.] commercially available within a few decades" (Hilberg 2000a: 307). I have corresponded with Hilberg about this vision but I must confess that, while I cannot follow it, neither can I refute it. To my knowledge, Hilberg's and similar visions have, so far, not yet been realised. Even his most recent book (2008) fails to convince me that the road to realisation is open. Some time ago, Christa Hauenschild (2004: 765) saw the most important "impulse from machine interpreting" in the fact that it leads "to greater awareness of problems and reality". She evaluates it "initially as a hopelessly unrealistic undertaking". This assessment is shared by

PhilippeVan Parijs (2011: 38f.).To all appearances, humanity will not be able to do without FL learning in the foreseeable future, and accordingly, pressure on the international languages and competition over their position is likely to continue.

11. Historical outline of the international position of the German language

Preliminaries

Unlike most language histories, the relevant point here is not change in the linguistic structure of German but, rather, its position in the world, either as a native language (GNL), a foreign-language (GFL) or with reference to its official embedding. I have limited the present outline to brief remarks because a detailed discussion will be provided in later chapters.Among the many histories of the German language, the three-volume work by Peter von Polenz (1994–2000) is the most prominent. Relevant specifics in the history of German are also discussed with reference to GFL by Helmut Glück (2002: Middle Ages to Baroque; 2013: Enlightenment, Classical and Romantic); for individual countries or language regions, by Lévy (1950/52: France), Ort-manns (1993: Britain), Ammon (1994: Japan), by Ammon/ Chong (2003: Korea), by Ammon/ Reinbothe/ Zhu (2007: China), by Ammon/ Kemper (2011: Russia); and comprehensively, by Helbig/ Götze/ Henrici/ Krumm (2001, Vol. 2, Chapter XXIII); Krumm/ Fandrych/ Hufeisen/ Riemer (2010,Vol., 2, Chapter XIX) and in the *Jahrbuch für Internationale Germanistik* (2002–2007).

The period up to the Peace of Westphalia (1648)

The early history of German with the politics of the Franconian Empire, its tripartition and the formation of the Eastern Empire of Ludwig the German (Regency 843–876) are skipped over here. However, the early expansion of the German-language region through colonisation from the eighth to fourteenth centuries, towards the east, beyond the Elbe and Saale, and to the north, across the Danube as far as eastern Prussia, Silesia and into present-day Slovakia deserve men-tion. At this time, the indigenous Slavic population was largely linguistically assimilated, while German-speaking people migrating further to the east often formed *language islands* (Ch. E.1).

Delays in forming the nation had serious consequences for the positioning of German in the world, primarily by comparison with France and England (Plessner 1974), which also hindered the institutionalisation of German as an official state language and its development as a language of science.To some extent, these delays were determined by the multilingualism of the *Holy Roman Empire* (962–1806, from the fifteenth century, with the addition: *of the German Nation*). Indeed, the latter extended far beyond the German language region. Under Kaiser Karl IV, for example, who was emperor from 1355–1378, Italian and Czech were official languages of the Empire alongside German. But above all, Latin (von Polenz 2000: 280) retained this function in some places until the beginning of the twentieth century (Ammon 2015: 3–5). Late develop-ment into a nation state was also determined by the territorialisation of the Empire.This repre-sents a disadvantage of the weak centralisation of imperial power resulting from the fact that the role was elected rather than inherited.The Elector Princes (originally seven, later eight, of which three bishops, ofTrier, Cologne and Mainz, and the temporal rulers of Bohemia, Bavaria, Saxony, Brandenburg and the Palatinate).These *Kurfürsten* also secured their prerogatives in treaties, e.g. against Emperors Friedrich II who lived in Sicily ("*Statutum in favorem principum*", 1231) and Karl IV (*Goldene Bulle*, 1355) (overview: https://de.Wikipedia.orf/territorialisation).

A powerful strengthening of the German language is generally attributed to the Protestant Reformation – which officially began in 1517 with the presumed posting of Luther's 95 theses on the door of Wittenberg church – because of Luther's linguistic creativity and the effects of distribution through printing. However, our focus on the position of German in the world also suggests an inverse effect. The strengthening effect of Reformation literature on the standardisation of the language remains unaffected, as indeed does its orientation towards eastern-central German, because of Luther's adoption of Saxon chancellery language. The same applies for the position of German by comparison with Latin; the effect of Luther's pushing high German towards low German reduced the latter to the level of a dialect; and finally, also the spread of German as a foreign language in all Lutheran-reformed countries, especially all of the Scandinavian countries.

In spite of this undisputed strengthening of German as a result of the Lutheran Reformation, it also had a long-term weakening effect on the position of German. Indeed, it secured and deepened territorialisation of the Empire and thus contributed to the complete fragmentation of the German-language region into a patchwork of small *duodecimo princedoms*. One enduring step in this direction was the Religious Peace of Augsburg (1555) which granted territorial regents power over their subjects' religious confession (*cuius regio eius religio*). In this way, it secured the autonomy of the territories – but failed to resolve long-standing confessional conflicts between territories and also with the Emperor, as originally intended. Instead, these conflicts ultimately ignited in the Thirty Years' War (1618–1648), which decimated the German-language region, ruined it economically and fragmented it into more than 300 separate administrative regions. Moreover, the Peace of Westphalia, which ended this war in 1648, reduced the size of the German-language region, among other factors, by enshrining in a treaty the loss of Alsace-Lorraine to France, although it must be admitted that a full switch to the French language occurred only after 1945 (Ch. E.4.3).

Because of the weakness of all the German-speaking countries at that time, none could participate in colonialism, which was gathering momentum. They were not therefore morally burdened with this policy, but, as a result, the spread of German remained (largely) restricted to Europe. In this respect, the current position of German differs markedly and unfavourably from that of Spanish, Portuguese, French, also Russian, Dutch, and, of course, English (minor exceptions, see Ch. E). Viewed from this perspective, it is questionable (and certainly worth asking) whether, all in all, Luther's Reformation did strengthen the position of German in the world or in fact weaken it – although a reliable answer to this question seems ultimately beyond reach. Indeed, the evaluation of other historical events can also change correspondingly, if one's focus is shifted from the structure of a language to its global position. One comparatively small-scale example is the recent German spelling reform (1996 ff). Not only was the thinking behind this based only on structure rather than position, it left out teaching resources and other materials (e.g. bilingual dictionaries) for GFL in foreign countries, failing to consider that these must still be used even if they contain the old spelling, which could be detrimental to the teaching of GFL.

Although German-speaking countries did not participate in colonialism because of their economic backwardness and repressive internal politics, at least not in its most expansive phase, they did contribute significantly to emigration from Europe to overseas territories. This emigration began in the sixteenth century and increased from the seventeenth century onwards. Initially, it led to North America, but later also to South and Central America, Australia and Southern/South-West Africa. In most cases, the immigrants became linguistically assimilated, but, in some cases, they also formed language minorities (Ch. E).

For a long time, GFL was learnt very rarely and in an uncontrolled way. However, from the seventeenth century, controlled private tuition began. Indicators for this are grammar books and dictionaries, e.g. in France (Daniel Martin 1635, *Acheminement à la langue allemande* [. . .], see Lévy 1950: 93) or in England (1680, *High Dutch Minerva à la Mode*, subtitled: "[to] learn the Neatest Dialect of the German Mother-Language", see Van der Lubbe 2007). The motives were economic, religious (Luther's writings) or scientific, e.g. Russian Enlightenment thinker Michael W. Lomonossov (1711–1765), who studied in Marburg and Freiberg. In Russia, German became the lingua franca in many places (Glück 2002: 283).

Up to the foundation of the Empire (1871)

The fragmented German-language region also lingered economically and culturally behind the unified western nations of Europe, especially France, whose influence led to the broad acceptance of the French language in the courts and cultivated classes throughout Europe. The most notable example in the German-language region was Prussia, whose King Friedrich II accorded the French language and culture considerably greater esteem than German which, as Voltaire reported from Berlin, was spoken only to the horses (Ammon 2015: 7).

However, German was, of course, also the language of the King's subjects. It was therefore fully in harmony with Friedrich's esteem for French that he asserted German as the language of education in the previously Polish-speaking regions of Silesia (Fischel 1910: XXXII) after he had taken them from Austria (finally, in the Seven Years' War, 1756–63). German was also asserted by Austria in the regions of Poland which fell to it after it was divided between Prussia, Austria and Russia, 1772, 1793 and 1795. These divisions were lifted only after WWI.

A further attempt at expanding the German-language region was made when Austrian Kaiser Joseph II declared German the official language of all Habsburg countries (during his sole monarchy from 1780–1790, not the preceding dual monarchy with his mother, Maria Theresia). In fact, he had to repeal the decree on his deathbed because of Hungarian protests (Fischel 1910: XXXII–XLIV), but it did strengthen the position of German in the long term. Such attempts at language expansion sometimes humiliated the non-German-speaking population which, over time, weakened the position of German, with an impact possibly extending to the present (Grucza 1995: 718f.).

Despite enthusiasm for French, primarily in the courts, cultivation of the German language among the gradually expanding urban middle-class began during the sixteenth and seventeenth centuries with a flourishing literature, including poetry and fiction (*German Classic* 1790–1930) but also academic writing, especially in the humanities and philosophy. Napoleon's conquests (1799–1815) of Prussia and Austria (1806, 1809) provided a lasting incentive to overcome national divisions. He ultimately not only annexed the entire region to the left of the Rhine but also declared French as the official language in large parts of the western and northern German-language region (see von Polenz 1999: 10–37, 108–111). Via numerous hesitations and acts of violence, the associated *German nationalist movement* led – to the *German Empire* [*Deutsches Reich*] dominated by Prussia in 1871.

Up to the present

This most recent period need only be outlined here. It will be explained in greater detail in subsequent chapters (especially, German as international language of science Ch. G.1 and of diplomacy Ch. H.1, promotion of German in the world K.2).

After the founding of the Empire, the German-language region achieved its largest extension in history. It was the official language in the extensive Empire, even in marginal regions with other native languages, such as Polish in the East. In the vast Danube monarchy also, German was the official language in most areas and the dominant lingua franca throughout.

However, large parts of these territories were lost after the Treaty of Versailles in 1919 and especially after the destruction of national socialism (*Nazism*] in 1945. At the same time, the German language lost its former position. Attempts by the German Empire to catch up with colonialism ended in a similar way. With the loss of all colonies after WWI, the German language also disappeared to a considerable extent, leaving conspicuous traces of its former position only in Namibia (Ch. E.4.9).

In the period after 1871, German became a language of science of similar rank to English and French. But it largely lost this position again during the twentieth century as a result of the two world wars and Nazism (Ammon 1998: 1–15; Gordin 2015: 23–185 passim).

After 1871, Bismarck also attempted, with a certain degree of success, to strengthen the position of German in international politics. However, after WWI, German was excluded from the official languages of the League of Nations and, after WWII, of the United Nations (UN). In the European Union (EU) also, German has not achieved the position of English or French.

Following the foundation of the Empire, GFL experienced a powerful boost supported by language policy. German was the most learnt foreign language in the USA and France and an important foreign language in Japan (Ch. J.9.2, J.9.10, J.9.14). However, during the twentieth century, it lost this preferential position to a considerable extent. The German Empire promoted the spread of German in the world, and this policy was continued in the Weimar Republic (1919–1933), not least through institutions such as the Goethe Institute, founded specially for this purpose in 1932. Since more recent times, especially after the reunification of Germany in 1990, all German-speaking countries or subnational regions have participated increasingly in promoting German worldwide (Ch. K.3.6). This has certainly contributed to the fact that German continues to be among the most widely learnt foreign languages in the world (Ch. K.7).

B

"GERMAN LANGUAGE", "GERMAN-LANGUAGE TERRITORY"

What these terms include and exclude, and the question of a German ethnic group

1. Disputed varieties and allocating them to the German language

To determine the position of German in the world or in a specific region with any precision requires careful definition of the term *German language*. In fact, there is no consensus about the scope and content of the term, either in general or among experts. Mindful of the complexity of this topic, I shall defer it until the next chapter. Firstly, I consider disputed varieties and their association with German, thereby introducing criteria which, in my opinion, justify or preclude allocating them to the German language. For this purpose, I use short text samples, followed, at the end of the chapter, by somewhat longer samples. In the second chapter, I explain the relevant terms in detail and justify the criteria for applying them to other languages.

One initial difficulty in defining the term *German language* is the ambiguity of the term *language*. For example, we often hear statements such as, "The *language* of the people of Cologne is a kind of singsong" or "The German *language* has many dialects" (both authentic quotations from everyday communication) or "Many people only realise what a unique *language* their dialect is when they read dialect poetry" (Swiss German, emphasis U.A.; Lötscher 1983: 75). In the present context, the second example, which distinguishes between "language" and "dialect", is more important. "Written German", "specialist German medical language" etc. also stand in the same quantitative relationship with "the (whole) German language". For brevity, I designate all such sub-categories of languages with the widely used term *varieties* (of a language) or *language varieties* (compare e.g. Ammon 1987, 2004b), which contrast with a (*whole, autonomous*) *language*. German is such a whole, autonomous language – for which the adjectival specification can be dropped if the intended meaning is clear. By contrast, dialects such as Saxon or Swabian are "only" varieties and not (independent) languages. The same applies for *Hochdeutsch* [literally "High German"], in the sense approximately synonymous with (*Deutsche*) *Hochsprache* [(German) high language], *Schriftsprache* [written language], *Literatursprache* [literary language], *Einheitssprache* [unified language] or *Standardsprache* [standard language], which each express a different aspect. It is also only a variety, but somebody who is learning "the German language" can easily forget this. Presumably, nobody has yet attempted to learn the entire German language, i.e. all its varieties. I will refer to the variety often called "*Hochdeutsch*" as *Standard German*.

But I will also show that this German, which is generally considered the most correct, can still be subdivided into further varieties.

It should by now be clear that I understand German, and indeed, every other language, as a set of varieties. This can be explained using the conventional mathematical notation of writing sets in upper case and their elements in lower case (or with only initial capitals), e.g. GERMAN LANGUAGE = {Swabian, Bavarian, Standard German, . . .}. The ellipse indicates that German has many further varieties. By contrast, smaller languages (see Haarmann 2001a), with fewer speakers mostly have fewer varieties. Languages (L) with only a single variety (V) are also conceivable: $L_a = \{V_a\}$. In terms of set-element relations, such languages *contain* the variety, that is, – expressed in more technical terms – they are indeed extensionally identical with it, but not intentionally (same conceptual scope, but different conceptual content).

At the opposite extreme of larger languages, including German (compare Ch. C), relations are additionally complicated by the fact that many varieties found in the first subdivision can be further subdivided, i.e. they can also be taken as sets, e.g. SWABIAN = {West Swabian, Middle-Swabian, . . .}, STANDARD GERMAN = {Austrian Standard German, Swiss Standard German, . . .}.

For certain purposes, it may be instructive to continue with the analysis referring to individual "varieties" only when further subdivision is no longer possible, but otherwise referring to "sets of varieties". Only such individual varieties are, strictly, also systems in the sense of structural linguistics. However, a more inclusive concept of variety which also includes sets of varieties is sufficient for our purposes provided they are not whole languages. Swabian and Standard German are thus also varieties, although they can be subdivided into subvarieties if required.

One difficult question, which I do not discuss here, is the allocation of individual expressions to varieties. The occurrence of mixed expressions (e.g. partially Swabian, partially Bavarian or even partially Alsatian dialect, and partially French) exemplifies this complexity. This is a topic within the micro-perspective which contrasts with the macro-perspective generally adopted in this book. I treat the term "variety" as a primitive notion (or concept) not specified in microperspectival terms. Most expressions can be intuitively assigned to given varieties reasonably reliably.

The distinction between "variety" and "language" is intended to guarantee that, on one hand, German is considered as comprehensively as possible as a whole language (with all varieties), but, on the other hand, remains intrinsically limited as a single language (only included varieties). In earlier periods characterised by nationalism or imperialism, there was a trend towards expansion. Historical German dialectology maps often showed such a trend by allowing "German" dialects to extend into Dutch-language regions (e.g. Bach, even in 1950: 8). More recently, this trend has been reversed, magnanimously releasing disputed varieties from subordination to German and allowing them to stand as independent languages. One example, to which I will return, is the Low German dialects.

Discussion of whether a variety or a whole language is involved also requires a term which can reference both concepts, i.e. a hypernym. The term "language system" is suitable for this when used in an imprecise manner. With reference to Heinz Kloss (e.g. [1952] 1978: 23), the term "idiom" seems possible, but also has the meaning of "conventional locution or form of speech". If the criteria to be elaborated are to allow a precise definition of the term "German language", every relevant language system must be identified as a variety or a language, and all varieties must be allocated to German or to another language. A comprehensive goal would be a taxonomy of all language systems in the world with reference to languages and all the associated varieties (compare Ch. B.2).

Moreover, the desired allocation of varieties to languages also requires identification and distinction between two types of variety: "standard varieties" and "non-standard varieties". A brief explanation will suffice here because further details are given in Ch. B.2. Standard varieties are identified e.g. by the existence of valid reference works for them: (language) codices, e.g. the Duden series for the standard variety of German in Germany, where *validity* is taken to mean that justifiable reference can be made to these volumes. Such codices serve to justify linguistic corrections and to guide "correct" usage of the codified variety. Codification of a variety is an important step towards standardisation and transforms it – to put it briefly – from a non-standard variety to a standard variety. In fact, there are detailed linguistic descriptions of non-standard varieties, e.g. dialects; but these are not used for language correction, for which reason I do not classify them as codices. By contrast, language codices for standard varieties serve to guide non-standard speaking and writing towards the standard variety. One central institution, alongside others, is schooling, where pupils are instructed by teachers (mostly subordinated to institutional superiors) that the standard variety is the more correct form of their language, at least for public use, than any non-standard varieties. To the extent that this succeeds, the non-standard varieties are "roofed" [German *überdacht*] by the relevant standard variety, using terminology introduced by Heinz Kloss (1978: 60; Muljačić 1989). For example, the Swabian dialect predominant in one part of south-west Germany is roofed by Standard German, or more precisely by Germany's Standard German.

In the further discussion, I assume that, on one hand, only standard varieties are capable of roofing but cannot be roofed themselves, and on the other hand, only non-standard varieties can be roofed but cannot themselves roof. I take these properties to be essential for both types of variety. "Roofing" is therefore a strictly asymmetric relation of standard varieties relative to non-standard varieties. In principle, this does not preclude competitive roofing by several standard varieties of the same non-standard variety (multiple roofing), and the roofing of several non-standard varieties by a single standard variety is, in fact, normal (Ammon 1995a: 73–88). Now, "roofing" provides one of the required criteria for allocating varieties to languages.

However, it is not sufficient for reliable classification. As a second criterion, the degree of linguistic similarity, or conversely, the linguistic distance between varieties, must also be considered. This criterion may even be more basic because it is more resistant to change than roofing, which can be susceptible to political upheavals, such as regional annexation. By contrast, changes in linguistic similarity or distance tend to extend over generations. Indeed, after such transformations, the respective varieties may no longer be considered the same. It is counterintuitive to allocate varieties which are not recognisable as at least remotely similar to the same language. The functional reason for this is that communication is still possible – albeit perhaps with great difficulty – only if there is recognisable similarity between different varieties. Only then can the people affected by roofing accept that both varieties belong to the same language.

Instead of criteria, it is also possible to specify factors for allocating varieties to languages which act on speakers' consciousness, so that they accept or reject the allocation of two varieties to the same language. It will be rejected in the absence of linguistic similarity. Conversely, roofing is not necessary for allocation to the same language if two varieties are very similar to one another, so that communication between them is possible without difficulty. Roofing becomes more significant if similarity is reduced. However, as already mentioned, for allocation to the same language, similarity must still be recognisable. I am referring here to moderate similarity (between high and absent similarity/ dissimilarity). This moderate degree of similarity exists between standard German and many German dialects. Speakers of Standard German experience this in communication with speakers of German dialects, which may be difficult but, with a positive attitude, is still possible. Because of the interplay between at least moderate linguistic similarity and roofing, speakers become aware that their varieties are associated with the same language and often take this for granted. This attitude is typical for speakers of dialects which are roofed by the same standard variety, which has at least moderate similarity to their dialect. As a result, the standard variety becomes a kind of central variety of the language.

This does not preclude the existence of several standard varieties of a single language. However, they must exhibit high, not merely moderate similarity with one another, if they are to be allocated to the same language, because – unlike dialects – they lack the cohesion of a common roofing variety. These relationships apply especially to German, since Austria, Germany and Switzerland have different but mutually very similar standard varieties. Languages with several standard varieties are designated pluricentral languages (Ammon 1995a; Ammon/ Bickel/ Ebner et al. 2004; Ammon/ Bickel/ Lenz 2013/16; Schmidlin 2011).

By contrast, standard varieties of lower, only moderate similarity are allocated to different languages – because of the absence of roofing. One example is standard Luxembourgish/ Letzeburgisch relative to the standard varieties of German, Austrian or Swiss German, which is accordingly not allocated to the German language.

Finally, if there is no similarity recognisable (to non-experts) between two varieties, they cannot be allocated to the same language by roofing. Association with the same language simply cannot be communicated to the speakers. For example, the Alsatian dialects lack the requisite similarity with standard French, for which reason they are not varieties of French.

The following criteria are thus obtained for allocating varieties to languages, especially to German:

(I)   Linguistic similarity with a standard variety – of German: (1) high, (2) moderate ((1) and (2) = similarity is present), (3)) absent (no similarity);

(II) Roofing by a standard variety – of German: (1) present, (2) absent (none).

Relying on these two criteria, I turn now to the allocation of some disputed varieties of German in order to explain the scope of the concept of "German language" on which this book is based. The discussion of each variety begins with a short text sample, followed by the allocation to German and the associated justification. Longer text samples are provided at the end of the chapter. The texts are printed in alphabetic rather than phonetic script to facilitate access to readers not trained in linguistics. Pronunciation can be inferred approximately from the spelling. The starting point is a (constructed) text in German Standard German, from which translations have been made as literally as possible. The assessment of similarity can therefore be based on correspondence between word pairs.

The differences between the following four German standard varieties are underlined, but not all the differences of the first three by comparison with the fourth.

German Standard German

Wäre ich Abstinenzler, dann wäre mir das nicht passiert. Nach dem Abendessen – Rinderbraten mit Bratkartoffeln und Rotkohl – trank ich noch ein Viertel [different measurement] *Weißwein.*

[English translation

If I were a teetotaller, that would not have happened to me. After dinner – roast beef with roast potatoes and red cabbage – I drank another large glass [different measurement] of white wine.]

Austrian Standard German

Wäre ich abstinent, dann wäre mir das nicht passiert. Nach dem Nachtmahl – Rindsbraten mit Gerösteten und Blaukraut – trank ich noch ein Viertel [different measurement] *Weißwein.*

Swiss Standard German (*Schweizerhochdeutsch*)

Wäre ich abstinent, dann wäre mir das nicht passiert. Nach dem Nachtessen – Rindsbraten mit Brat-
kartoffeln und Rotkabis – trank ich noch einen Dreier [different measurement] *Weisswein.*

Mennonite High-German (from the Chaco in Paraguay)

Würde ich nicht Alkohol trinken, dann wäre mir das nicht passiert. Nach dem Abendessen – Asado
mit gebratene_ Papas und Rotkohl – trank ich noch ein Viertel Glas [different measurement]
Weißwein. (*Asado* "Roast", *Papas* "potatoes", both Spanish)

All four varieties are allocated to the German language as per criteria I.1 and I.2.

These standard varieties, especially the first three, are possibly the least disputed varieties allocated to German. Their high mutual linguistic similarity, also with the standard variety named in fourth place, guarantees their allocation to the same language, even in the absence of roofing (since standard varieties cannot be roofed by definition). The text samples given here show a cluster of differences (underlined forms); many other text samples of the same length – at least when reproduced in alphabetical script – would show fewer or even no differences.

Swabian (Germany: Middle-Swabian)

Wär i Abschdinenzler, no wär mr des ned bassierd. Noch m Obadessa – Rendsbroda mid Brägela on
Blaugraud – hao e no a Virdalle Weißwai drongga.

Bavarian (Germany: Freising, Upper Bavaria)

Boi i a Abstinenla waar, na waar ma dees ned passiad. Noochm Omdessn – Rindsbroon mit gräste
Kadoffe und Blaugraud – howe no a Scheppal Weißwei drunga.

Both varieties are allocated to German as per criteria I.2 and II.1.

The spelling varies between text samples because dialects are not standardised. However, it is evident that differences from the roofing German Standard German are greater than between the four standard German varieties. Conversely, a moderate similarity with the roofing standard, in this case of German Standard German, is also evident. This can also be heard in speech, at least after brief habituation. With regard to the Swabian region, I am not aware of any serious claims to linguistic independence of Swabian, that is to non-allocation to German. Furthermore, the *Ethnologue*, presumably the largest collection of languages and varieties in the world, does not distinguish, at least not strictly, between varieties and whole languages and treats all the varieties discussed here as "languages" (Swabian e.g. in *Ethnologue* 2005: 538; see also Ammon 2015: 116).

Evaluating Bavarian as an independent language is less far-fetched than would be Swabian but could be based on statements from the German Federal State of Bavaria. Examples are provided by the *Förderverein Bairische Sprache und Dialekte e. V.* [Society for the Promotion of Bavarian Language and Dialects, Registered Society]; even its title suggests this perspective. However, the Society informed me that it still takes Bavarian to be a part of the German language. This corresponds with our criteria: moderate similarity with German Standard German (criterion I.2) and roofed by the latter (criterion II.1).

Basler Dialekt (Switzerland)

Wäär ych abschtinänt, so wäär mir das nit passiert. Noon em Nachtässe – Rindsbroote mit Broothärdöp-
fel und Rootkrut – hanni noon e Dreyerli Wysse drungge.

Senslerdialekt (Switzerland)

Weren i abstinent, de we mer das nit passiert. Nam Znacht – Ründsbrate mit pratete Häpperlini u
blauem Chabis – han i no as Dryerli Wiissa truche.

Both varieties are allocated to German as per criteria I.2 and II.1.

Here also, on one hand, the differences from Standard German, even Swiss Standard German, are significantly greater than between the four standard German varieties, and, on the other hand, the similarity with the roofing Swiss Standard German is unmistakable. This similarity can also be heard in speech after brief habituation. Both non-standard varieties are classified among the Alemannic dialects, which should not be confused, because of their frequent designation as "Swiss German", with "Swiss High-German", the Standard German of Switzerland.

In fact, among experts, they are predominantly classified as dialects (of German), but designation as a "language" is quite frequent. One example is provided in the subtitle of the monumental dictionary which catalogues it: *Schweizerisches Idiotikon: Wörterbuch der schweizerdeutschen Sprache* (Antiquarische Gesellschaft, published by Frauenfeld Huber from 1881 onwards; so far, 16 of the planned 17 volumes have appeared). The ubiquitous use of dialect in Switzerland, even in public life, reinforces the impression of an independent language. In the 1930s, the "*Schwyzer Schproch-Biwegig*" attempted to develop an independent language "*Alemannic*" to distance the country linguistically from Nazi Germany (Baer 1936; Ammon 1995a: 239f. 296). However, in view of our criteria of moderate similarity with a standard variety of German (Swiss High-German; criterion I.2) and its being roofed by it (criterion II.1), I allocate the Alemannic dialects of Switzerland to the German language. The corresponding allocation can be generalised to all Upper and Middle-German dialects which are roofed by standard German varieties.

Elsässischer Dialekt (Strassburg, Low-Alemannic with Rhine-Franconian features)
Wenn i nix trinke dät, no wärd mr au nix pàssiert. Nooch m Znààchtesse – mr hàn Rindsbroote mit gebrädelte Grumbeere un Rotkrüt ghet – haw i noch e Viertele Wisser getrunke.

Allocated to German as per criterion I.2 with reference to Standard German and criterion I.3 with reference to Standard French.

Here also, moderate linguistic similarity with the German standard varieties is present, in the same manner as with the largely identical, neighbouring German dialects on the east of the Rhine. However, Alsatian dialect is roofed by Standard French, at least primarily. Circumstances for the Lorraine varieties are similar. There is possibly also a weak roofing from German Standard German (possibly also Swiss Standard German) (compare Ch. E.4.3; also, Ammon 2007c), primarily because of bilingual schools with German as the language of teaching (alongside French). Allocation to French is, however, precluded despite roofing because of absence of similarity (criterion I.3). The sample sentence in French illustrates the lack of similarity here.

Si j'étais abstinent, alors cela ne me serait pas arrivé. Après le dîner, un rôti de bœuf avec pommes de terre sautées et chou rouge, je bus encore un quart de vin blanc.

If we disregard the (weak) roofing by standard German, the allocation of Alsatian and Lorraine varieties to one language demands an expansion of our criteria. However, we still maintain that absence of linguistic similarity precludes allocation to the same language. There are then only two possibilities for varieties such as Alsatian and Lorrainian: either to allocate them to the language with the standard variety of which they still show moderate linguistic similarity, even if they are not roofed by it, or to evaluate them as independent languages. The first option seems more appropriate simply to prevent too much glottotomy (language fragmentation). Heinz Kloss, who designates such varieties as "roofless or non-roofed external dialects", without expressly explaining their allocation to languages, also tends in this direction (1978: 60–63). Further details in Ch. B.2.

French language policy has repeatedly avoided allocating the Alsace and Lorraine varieties to the German language. This applies especially to previous French-government pronouncements (Born/ Dickgiesser 1989: 89) which sometimes refer only to the *dialecte* (without reference to a language), *dialecte alsacien* or *dialecte lorrain* (Born/ Dickgiesser 1989: 89; see also Grossmann 1999), or often just to *alsacien* or *lorrain*, thereby suggesting independent languages. The more current expression "Alsatian dialect, of which the nearest cultural language or *langue de référence* is standard German" (Morgen 2007: 66), also avoids explicit inclusion (in the sense of an element-set relationship) within the German language. However, even Alsatian linguists do not shy away from such allocation, e.g. Frédéric Hartweg (1988) and Daniel Morgen (2003), who refer to "*dialecte allemand*" or respectively "*dialectes de l'allemand*". Purely based on linguistic similarity, allocation to the Luxembourgish language would also be conceivable, but not plausible because of the complete absence of roofing by standard Luxembourgish.

Standardletzeburgisch
Wier ech Abstinenzler, da wier mer dat net passéiert. No dem Owesiessen – Rëndsbrot, gebrode Grom-peren a roude Kabes – hunn ech nach e Véierel wäisse Wäi gedronk.

Not allocated to German as per criteria I.2 and II.2, in each case relative to Standard German.

Here also, there is moderate similarity with Standard German varieties, but roofing is absent, because Standard Luxembourgish is itself a standard variety, which – as per the terminological specification above – cannot be roofed. Standard Luxembourgish has its own codification (primarily, its own orthography, but also the *Luxemburger Wörterbuch* 1950–1975/1977), and its status as the standard variety of a separate standard language is supported by the fact that Luxembourgish is the official and national language of Luxembourg (see Ch. D.2.5). Because of the still moderate linguistic distance, i.e. not high similarity, Standard Luxembourgish is not allocated to German, nor are the dialects roofed by standard Luxembourgish. Like Kloss (1978: 113), experts today overwhelmingly classify Luxembourgish as an autonomous language.

Niederdeutscher *Dialekt* [Low German Dialect] (Mecklenburg-Vorpommern)
Wenn ik nich so giern een' drinken dee, denn wür dat nich passiert. Nå denn Åbendäten – dat geef Rinnerbråden mit Bråttüffel un Rotkohl – heff ik noch'n poor Glas witten Wien drunken.
Niederdeutscher *Dialekt* [Low German Dialect] (Segeberg in Holstein)
Wenn ik een enthoolsame Minsch weer, denn weer mi dat nich passeert. Nah dat Avendeten – Rindsbraden mit Bratkatüffeln un Rotkohl – drunk ik noch een Viddel Wittwien.

Both varieties are allocated to German as per criteria I.2 and II.1.

In fact, the Low German dialects are linguistically less similar to Standard German – especially German Standard German, by which they are roofed – than most of the varieties discussed so far. However, the similarity is unmistakable. Traditional German dialectologists have therefore presumably felt justified in allocating the Low German dialects to German, as is evident from the dialect maps of the *Deutscher Sprachatlass* [German Language Atlas] (1927–1956). Jan Goossens (1977: 48–50) also expressly supports this classification.

However, there is an older tradition of separating the two different languages, e.g. in the *Deutsches Wörterbuch* by the Grimm brothers. It prevents them, "as anyone can see, from including Low German words in a dictionary of German [...]" (Grimm/ Grimm 1854: XV). Classification as an independent language is also suggested by the once important function of Low German even in international communication in northern Europe at the time of the Hanseatic League in the fourteenth and fifteenth centuries. Furthermore, the German government included Low

German in the "minority languages" according to the *European Charter for Regional or Minority Languages of the European Council* (German ratification with effect from 1 January 1999; conventions.coe.int/treaty/Commun/QueVoulezVous.asp?CL=GER &NT=148; cf. Ch. E.2). As a result, even the constitutions of several Federal States of Germany are translated into Low German varieties (Bremen, Hamburg, Lower Saxony, Schleswig-Holstein and Mecklenburg-Vorpommern). There is, however, no standard variety of Low German, but it is roofed by (High German) German Standard German. Attempts to establish a "Low German written language" have so far been unsuccessful (Elmentaler 2009b: 41–43). Because of its linguistic similarity, i.e. moderate similarity, with German Standard German, which is recognisable even by non-experts, Low German is therefore included within the German language according to our criteria.

> Plautdietsch [Low German] (of the "Russian-Mennonites" in North and South America. See also Ch. E.4.11)
> *Wan etj enn enthoolsame Mensch wea, dan wea mie daut nijch passeat. Noh de Owendkost – Rindsbrohden mett jebrohdne Eadschocke enn rote Komst – drunk etj noch een Veadel Wittwien.*

Allocated to the German language as per criteria (1.2) and (2.1).

This variety is roofed by Mennonite High German, which is very similar to the other German standard varieties, as demonstrated above; Plautdietsch exhibits approximately the same linguistic distance from them as do the other Low German varieties from German Standard German.

> *Saterfriesisch* [Sater Friesian] (Saterland community, Cloppenburg district, Lower Saxony)
> *Waas iek aan Woaterdrinker, dan waas mie dät nit geböard. Ätter't Äiwendieten – Bäisteflaask mäd brätte Tuwwelke un Roodkool – droank iek noch een Fjondel Wietwien.*
> *Nordfriesisch* [North Friesian] (*Bökingharder Dialekt*, Germany)
> *Wus ik foonouf e brâmen, dan wus me dåt ai schänj. Eefter e nåchtert – bäistebroos ma brooskantüfle än rüüdjküülj – drunk ik nuch en gou glees witwin.*

Neither of these varieties is allocated to German as per criteria I.3 and to some extent II.2.

In some cases, the Friesian varieties have such low mutual linguistic similarity that they are taken as three separate languages. The two presented here are spoken in Germany; a third – West Friesian, with by far the most speakers – is spoken in Groningen province in the Netherlands. Our text samples indicate that especially the linguistic similarity of Sater Friesian and North Friesian to German Standard German is lower than that of Low German. Whether this means that it no longer fulfils our criterion of moderate similarity remains unresolved at the present state of research. I am not aware of any well-founded, precise demarcation for this criterion (cf. Ch. B2). Accordingly, there is hardly another option but to join the majority of experts in no longer including the Friesian varieties within the German language. The most prominent expert in recent times to argue for inclusion within German is Jan Goossens (1977: 50). The only decisive factor for exclusion from the German language is the considerable linguistic distance from standard German. Sater Friesian and North Friesian do not in fact have their own standard variety (cf. Munske 2001; Walker 1983; Fort 2001). There is a West Friesian standard variety (Kloss 1978: 165–171; Gorter 2008: 337–344), but this does not roof Sater Friesian and North Friesian.

> Standard West Friesian (translated by Durk Gorter)
> *As ik hielûnthâlder wêze soe dan wie der neat bard. Nei it jûnsiten – rosbyf mei earpels en reade koal – dronk ik noch in fearn wite wyn.*

The translation of this sample into standard West Friesian indicates the considerable linguistic distance from Sater Friesian and North Friesian, which precludes allocation to the same language.

Standard Dutch

Was ik geheelonthouder, dan zou mij dat niet overkomen zijn. Na het avondeten – rundsgebraad met gebakken aardappels en rode kool – dronk ik een vierde liter witte wijn.

Standard Afrikaans

As ek 'n geheelonthouer was, sou dit nie met my gebeur het nie. Na aandete – beesbraaivleis met gebakte aartappels en rooikool – het ek nog 'n kwartbottel witwyn gedrink.

Standard Yiddish (*Ostjiddisch*)

Volt ikh geven a ti-touteler, volt dos nisht hobn getrofn mit mir. Nochn vetshere – rinderbrotn mit gebrotene kartofl un roytkroyt – ob ikh getrunken noch a fertl wayswayn.

None of these three varieties is allocated to German as per criteria I.2 and II.2.

All three varieties are standardised, i.e. cannot be roofed, not by Standard German either, and have at most moderate (not high) similarity to any standard German variety. As a result, allocation to German is precluded for all three varieties. This applies equally to all varieties roofed by these standard varieties, which thus belong either to the Dutch, the Afrikaans or the Yiddish language (for Yiddish, see Biehl 2008).

The somewhat longer text samples for the varieties discussed are now shown in the form of a text translated as literally as possible with the same meaning (fuller versions in Ammon 2015: 125–131). The names of the translators, to whom I am particularly grateful, are added in brackets. The differences between the first three German standard varieties are underlined; as are all differences of the fourth (Mennonite High German) by comparison with the first three.

German Standard German (Ulrich Ammon)

Wäre ich Abstinenzler, dann wäre mir das nicht passiert. Nach dem Abendessen – Rinderbraten mit Bratkartoffeln und Rotkohl – trank ich noch ein Viertel [different measurement] Weißwein. Dann schwang ich mich auf mein Fahrrad, um zu meiner Wohnung zu fahren, die in einem alten Fachwerkhaus innerhalb der Stadtmauer liegt. Mir wurde plötzlich so schwindelig, dass ich die Kontrolle verlor und zuerst einen Omnibus streifte und dann auf ein Auto auffuhr, das gerade an der Ampel wartete.

English translation

If I were a teetotaller, that would not have happened to me. After dinner – roast beef with roast potatoes and red cabbage – I drank another large glass [different measurement] of white wine. Then I jumped on my bike to cycle to my flat which is in an old, timber-framed building inside the town wall. I suddenly became so dizzy that I lost control and first clipped a bus and then ran into a car which was waiting at the traffic lights.

Austrian Standard German (Herbert Tatzreiter)

Wäre ich abstinent, dann wäre mir das nicht passiert. Nach dem Nachtmahl – Rindsbraten mit Gerösteten und Blaukraut – trank ich noch ein Viertel [different measurement] Weißwein. Dann schwang ich mich auf mein Fahrrad, um zu meiner Wohnung zu fahren, die in einem alten Fachwerkhaus innerhalb der Stadtmauer liegt. Mir wurde plötzlich so schwindlig, dass ich die Kontrolle verlor und zuerst einen Bus streifte und dann auf ein Auto auffuhr, das gerade vor der Ampel wartete.

Swiss Standard German/ *Schweizerhochdeutsch* (Walter Haas)

Wäre ich abstinent, dann wäre mir das nicht passiert. Nach dem Nachtessen – Rindsbraten mit Bratkartoffeln und Rotkabis – trank ich noch einen Dreier [different measurement] Weisswein. Dann schwang ich mich auf mein Velo, um zu meiner Wohnung zu fahren, die in einem alten Riegelhaus innert der Stadtmauer liegt. Mir wurde plötzlich so schwindlig, dass ich die Kontrolle verlor und zuerst einen Autocar streifte und dann in ein Auto hinein fuhr, das gerade vor dem Lichtsignal wartete.

Mennonite High German (from Chaco in Paraguay; Joachim Steffen)

Würde ich nicht Alkohol trinken, dann wäre mir das nicht passiert. Nach dem Abendessen – Asado mit gebratene_ Papas und Rotkohl – trank ich noch ein Viertel [different measurement] Glas Weißwein. Dann nahm ich mein Fahrrad, um zu meiner Wohnung zu fahren, die in einem alten Fachwerkhaus innerhalb der Stadtmauer liegt. Mir wurde plötzlich dieslich, dass ich die Kontrolle verlor und_erst einen Omnibus streifte und dann gegen ein Auto prallte, das gerade an der Semáforo anhielt.

(*Asado* 'roast', *Semáforo* 'traffic lights', from Spanish; *Papas* 'potatoes', from Quechua; Notes: Bettina Thode)

Schwäbisch [Swabian] (*Mittelschwäbisch*; Ulrich Ammon)

Wär i Abschdinenzler, no wär mr des ned bassierd. Noch m Obadessa – Rendsbroda mid Brägela on Blaugraud – hao e no a Virdalle Weißwai droṅgga. No ben uf mei Fahrrad khopfd, om zo meire Wohnung z fahra, wo em a alda Fachwerkhaus ennerhalb va dr Stadmauer leid. Mir isch bletzlich ganz durmelich worra, dass e d Kondrall vrlaora hao on zaerscht an Omnibus gsdroefd hao on no uf a Audo nufgfahre be, wo grad an arra Ambl gwarded had.

Bairisch [Bavarian] (Freising, Oberbayern; Ludwig Zehetner)

Boi i a Abstinenla waar, na waar ma dees ned passiad. Noochm Omdessn – Rindsbroon mit gräste Kadoffe und Blaugraud – howe no a Scheppal Weißwei drunga. Na howa me auf mei Raadl gschwunga und wäi zu meina Wohnung fahrn. De is in an oidn Fachwerkhaus glei hinta da Stoodmaua. Auf oamoi is ma so schwindle woan, daas i s nimma darissn hob und zeascht an Omnibus gstroafft hob, und nachad bin i auf a Auto grumped. Des hood grod an da Ampe gwart.

Basler Dialekt (Switzerland; Simone Ueberwasser)

Wäär ych abschtinänt, so wäär mir das nit passiert. Noon em Nachtässe – Rindsbroote mit Broothärdöpfel und Rootkrut – hanni noon e Dreyerli Wysse drungge. Denn han ych mii ufs Velo gschwunge, zem zue myynere Wohnig z fahre, wo im ene alte Riigelhuus innerhalb vo dr Stadtmuure liggt. Mir isch plötzlig so sturm worde, ass ych d Kontrolle verloore und zerscht e Bus gstreift ha und denn in en Auti gfahre bi, wo grad am Liechtsignal gwaartet het.

Sensler Dialekt (Switzerland, Kanton Fribourg; Raphael Berthele)

Weren i abstinent, de we mer das nit passiert. Nam Znacht – Ründsbrate mit pratete Häpperlini u blauem Chabis – han i no as Dryerli Wiissa truche. Näi han i mier uf ds Wölo gschwunge fur zu mir Wonig z faare, wo im ena aute Riguhuus innerhaub va de Stadtmuur ligt. Mier isch plötzlich schwindlig cho, ass i d Kontrola verlore ha u zersch a Car gstreift ha u näi in as Outo ychigfaare bü, wa grad vor um Liechtsignaau gwaartet het.

Elsässisch [Alsatian] (Strassburg: Low Alemannic, Rhine-Franconian features; Dominique Huck)

Wenn i nix trinke dät, no wärd mr au nix pàssiert. Nooch m Znààchtesse – mr hàn Rindsbroote mit gebrädelte Grumbeere un Rotkrüt ghet – haw i noch e Viertele Wisser getrunke. Dann hàw i mi uf s Vélo gschwunge fir haamzefàhre. Ich hàb e Wohnung im e àlte Fachwerickhüs, wo innerhàlb von de Stàdtmüre steht. Mir isch s uf aamol so schwindli worre, àss i nix meh im Griff hàb ghet: zerscht hàw i e Autobüs [otobys] gstreift un bin dànn geje e Auto gfàhre, wo gràd àm rote Licht gewàrt het.

Standardlëtzebuergesch [Standard Luxembourgish] (Fernand Hoffmann, revised by Peter Gilles)

Wier ech Abstinenzler, da wier mer dat net passéiert. No dem Owesiessen – Rëndsbrot, gebrode Gromperen a roude Kabes – hunn ech nach e Véierel wäisse Wäi gedronk. Du hunn ech mech op mäi Vëlo geschwong fir a meng Wunneng ze fueren, déi an engem ale Fachwierkhaus bannent der Stadmauer läit. Et ass mir op eemol esou schëmmeleg ginn, datt ech d'Kontroll verluer hunn a fir d'éischt en Omnibus gesträift hunn an du an en Auto geknuppt sinn, dee grad bei der Verkéierslucht gewaart huet.

Niederdeutsch [Low German] (Mecklenburg-Vorpommern; Renate Herrmann-Winter)
Wenn ik nich so giern een' drinken dee, denn wür dat nich passiert. Nå denn Åbendäten – dat geef
Rinnerbråden mit Bråttüffel un Rotkohl – heff ik noch'n poor Glas witten Wien drunken. Denn
heff ik mi up mien Fohrrad sett' un bün to mi Nåhus führt. Ik wåhn in een' ollen Fachwarkhus,
dat innerhalf de Stadtmuer licht. Mit eis wür mi so schwummerich, dat ik nich mihr fohren künn
un tauierst een Bus anrammeln dee un denn up een' Auto rupfuhr, wat grå an'e Ampel töben dee.

Niederdeutsch [Low German] (Segeberg district in Holstein; Joachim Steffen)
Wenn ik een enthoolsame Minsch weer, denn weer mi dat nich passeert. Nah dat Avendeten – Rinds-
braden mit Bratkatüffeln un Rotkohl – drunk ik noch een Viddel Wittwien. Denn swung ik mi op
mien Fohrrad, üm to miene Wahnung to fohrn, de in een oolet Fachwarkhuus binnen de Stadtsmuur
liggt. Mi wor miteens so swindelig, dat ik de Kuntrull verleer un toeerst een Bus striepen dee un denn
op een Auto ropfohr, dat grad bi eene Ampel töv.

Plautdietsch [Low German] (Russian-Mennonite dialect, Brazil; Joachim Steffen)
Wan etj enn enthoolsame Mensch wea, dan wea mie daut nijch passeat. Noh de Owendkost –
Rindsbrohden mett jebrohdne Eadschocke enn rote Komst – drunk etj noch een Veadel Wittwien.
Dan schwung etj mie opp mien Foahraud, om to mien Wohninj to foahre, de ennerhaulf fonn de
Staudtsmie liedjt. Mie woa platzlijch soo dieslijch, daut etj de Kontroll veloah, enn toeascht eene Bos
striepje deed enn dan opp eene Koah noppfoah, de jrods aun de Ampel wachten deed.

Saterfriesisch [Sater Friesian] (Gretchen Grosser, submitted by Pyt Kramer)
Waas iek aan Woaterdrinker, dan waas mie dät nit geböard. Ätter't Äiwendieten – Bäisteflaask mäd
brätte Tuuwelke un Roodkool – droank iek noch een Fjondel Wietwien. Dan smeet iek mie ap mien
Rääd, uum ätter mien Woonenge tou fiehren, ju in een oold Fäkwierkhuus binnen fon ju Muure
fonne Stääd lait. Toumoal wuud mie so duusich, dät iek ju Kontrolle ferloos un toueerst an Omnibus
tou nai koom un dan ap een Auto apfiehrde, dät juust an een Ampel täiwde.

Nordfriesisch [North Friesian] (Mooringer Mundart, Bökingharder Dialekt; Uwe Johannsen,
    submitted by Alastair Walker)
Wus ik foonouf e bråmen, dan wus me dåt ai schänj. Eefter e nåchtert – bäistebroos ma brooskantüfle
än rüüdjküülj – drunk ik nuch en gou glees witwin. Dan stäk ik aw min fiilj, am tu min boog tu
käären, dåt lait önj en üülj fäägehüs baner e stäasmööre. Aw iinjtooch wörd me sü swöömi, dåt ik e
balangse ferlüüs än tujarst en bus straife däi än dan iinj en auto kjard, wat jüst bai rüüdj hül.

Standardniederländisch [Standard Dutch] (Sonja Vandermeeren)
Was ik geheelonthouder, dan zou mij dat niet overkomen zijn. Na het avondeten – rundsgebraad met
gebakken aardappels en rode kool – dronk ik een vierde liter witte wijn. Dan sprong ik op mijn fiets,
om naar mijn woning te rijden, die in een oud vakwerkhuis binnen de stadsmuren gelegen is. Ik werd
ineens zo duizelig, dat ik de controle over het stuur verloor, eerst een omnibus raakte en dan op een
auto inreed, die net aan de verkeerslichten wachtte.

Standardafrikaans [Standard Afrikaans] (Riana Roos)
As ek 'n geheelonthouer was, sou dit nie met my gebeur het nie. Na aandete – beesbraaivleis met gebakte
aartappels en rooikool – het ek nog 'n kwartbottel witwyn gedrink. Toe het ek op my fiets gespring
om na my woonstel, wat in 'n ou vakwerkhuis binne die stadsmuur gelê is, te ry. Ek het plotseling
so duiselig geword dat ek beheer verloor het en eers teen 'n bus geskurr en toe teen 'n motor wat by
die verkeerslig gewag het, vasgery het.

Standardjiddisch [Standard Yiddish] (Ostjiddisch [East Yiddish]; Jürgen Biehl)
Volt ikh geven a ti-touteler, volt dos nisht hobn getrofn mit mir. Nochn vetshere – rinderbrotn mit gebrotene
kartofl un roytkroyt – ob ikh getrunkn noch a fertl wayswayn. Noch dem hob ikh sikh gevorfn af rnayn
velosiped, keday zu forn zu mayn woynung in a halb-gehiltsten hoyz, wos iz gelegn ineweynik fun
der shtotmoyer. Plutsim iz mir gevorn azoy shvindldik, az ikh hob farloyren dem control. Ersht hob
ikh fartshepet an oytobus un noch dem bin ikh arayngeforn in an oyto, wos hot gewart far a trafik fayer.

2. General rules for allocating varieties to languages

This chapter deepens and sharpens the rules for allocating varieties to (whole) languages. However, the rules are still limited to the two criteria identified in Ch. B.1:

(1) Linguistic distance (the converse of linguistic similarity), with three degrees: low (high), moderate (moderate) and high (low);
(2) Roofing: present, absent.

Both criteria or groups of criteria refer to relationships between two varieties (V) each, on the basis of which these varieties must be allocated to the same language or different languages. Where they distinguish consistently between varieties and languages at all, most proposals for allocating varieties to languages introduce further criteria, such as subjective allocation by speakers (of the varieties themselves: *emic* or speakers of other varieties: *etic*) – or historical connections between varieties. But such additions make it harder to reach an unambiguous decision about allocation; limitation to our two criteria makes matters simpler.

However, limiting the criteria to just one of the two is insufficient. This even applies to the enticing criterion of linguistic distance, which, in fact, fails in the case of continua of distance between several varieties, such as the *dialect continua*. One example is the West Germanic dialect continuum, which extends from South Tyrol to the North Sea coast of the Netherlands. With such dialect continua, adjacent varieties would have to be allocated to the same language because of the low linguistic distance. But with increasing geographical distance, the linguistic distances become additive, so that the distant varieties (according to linguistic distance) would be allocated to different languages (Chambers/ Trudgill: 1980: 10–14; Ammon 1989b: 31–47). More generally, the failure of the linguistic-distance criterion can be explained by the fact that it is not transitive. If there is high similarity between V_a and V_b and also between V_b and V_c, it does not follow that there is also high similarity between V_a and V_c.

With dialect continua, the second criterion of roofing releases us from this difficulty in the presence of standard varieties. However, the criterion of roofing is not available for allocating different standard varieties. It was established and justified in Ch. B.1 that standard varieties cannot be roofed. Here, therefore, we must make do with the criterion of linguistic distance for them. In this context, all relevant standard varieties must be compared with one another and must exhibit low linguistic distance from one another (high similarity) if allocated to the same language. With n standard varieties, this requires n-1 comparisons. For the four standard varieties of German (Germany, Austria, Switzerland and Mennonite settlements; Ch. B.1), distances must be determined in three directions to justify the allocation to languages. Regarding linguistic distances, I therefore work intuitively throughout the book, without serious measurements. But with the standard varieties of German, there is no doubt about high linguistic similarity. This may be different with languages with more potential varieties, e.g. English.

Our rules for allocating varieties to languages are limited to languages with standard varieties, which I call standard languages, and are inadequate for non-standard languages (vernacular languages) in the absence of a standard variety. The extent to which the rules are even insufficient for standard languages must be determined in future research (preliminary work: Ammon 1991a: 19–31; 1995a: 1–9). The allocations made by speakers themselves are not explicitly components of our rules, but these rules are conceived with reference to assumptions (hypotheses) about how speakers – generally unconsciously – tend to allocate varieties to the same or different languages and thus conceptualise linguistic communities.

First, the rules for allocating different standard varieties (cf. Ammon 1995a):

(i)   Two standard varieties, SV_a and SV_b belong to the same or different languages under the following conditions:
(ia)   If the linguistic similarity between SV_a and SV_b is high, both belong to the same language;
(ib)   If the linguistic similarity between SV_a and SV_b is only moderate or low, both belong to different languages.

Rule (ia) ensures that different (national or regional) standard varieties are allocated to the same "pluricentral" language. For German, this refers to the varieties named above. The text samples at the end of Ch. B.1 show their high linguistic similarity.

Rule (ib) ensures that autonomous languages, linguistically close to German are not incorporated into the German language, especially not their standard varieties. The text samples at the end of Ch. B.1 also show such cases of only moderate and low linguistic similarity with standard German. This is recognisable even with standard Luxembourgish, in which – despite some similarity – numerous forms differ from any standard German variety. With standard Dutch, standard Afrikaans and standard Yiddish, the similarity with any standard German variety is even lower. According to rule (ib), therefore, none of these standard varieties is allocated to German – but form the cores, so to speak, of separate languages.

Turning now to the question of how non-standard varieties of the same or different languages should be allocated, the two subordinated rules of (ii), (iia) and (iib) are distinguished by somewhat detailed specifications.

(ii)   A standard variety SV_a and a non-standard variety NSV_b belong to the same or different languages under the following conditions:
(iia) If SV_a roofs NSV_b and, at the same time, the linguistic similarity between the two is at least moderate (moderate or high), both belong to the same language. This also applies if NSV_b is linguistically more similar to another standard variety SV_c than to SV_a, but not roofed by SV_c. The meaning of roofing was explained provisionally in Ch. B.1 and further details are given in the second part of this chapter.

The relationship addressed in (iia) exists between a standard variety and the dialects or other non-standard varieties it roofs. Ch. B.1 contains samples of dialects which are roofed by German or Swiss Standard German, such as Swabian and Bavarian or respectively *Basler Dialekt* and *Sensler Dialekt*. Similarity with the relevant standard varieties is recognisably only moderate, not high, as between the standard variety of Germany and Standard Luxembourgish. But by contrast with standard Luxembourgish, these dialects belong to German because they are roofed by varieties of standard German.

The second sentence in rule (iia) precludes the possibility that, e.g. the Mosel-Franconian dialect on the German side, which resembles Standard Luxembourgish more than German Standard German, is allocated to Luxembourgish. In fact, it is roofed not by standard Luxembourgish, but by German Standard German. By contrast, the almost identical Mosel-Franconian dialect varieties in Luxembourg belong to Luxembourgish, because they are roofed by Standard Luxembourgish. Allocation to different languages on either side of the border thus occurs not only because of linguistic considerations but also political and sociological conditions.

In the absence of linguistic similarity between SV_a and NSV_b, the following rule applies:

(iib) If the linguistic distance between a standard variety SV_a and a non-standard variety NSV_b is high (non-similar), then SV_a and NSV_b belong to different languages. Here, the criterion of roofing becomes irrelevant. If there is another standard variety SV_c, which exhibits at least moderate similarity to (at most, moderate distance from) NSV_b, then NSV_b belongs to the same language as SV_c, even if NSV_b is not roofed by SV_c. Otherwise, NSV_b belongs to a completely different language, without standard variety, i.e. a non-standard language (*vernacular language*), possibly with still more non-standard varieties.

Rule (iib) explains e.g. why the Alemannic and Rhine-Franconian dialects in Alsace and Lorraine do not belong to French but to German, although they are roofed by French Standard French. However, if there were no standard variety of at least moderate similarity with these varieties, they would belong to a third language, possibly "Alsatian".

Figure B.2–1 visualises these rules by allocating the varieties to languages presented in Ch. B.1.

Regardless of their logical agreement, all the rules (ia) to (iib) remain somewhat vague because essential terms remain insufficiently operationalised. But sufficient operationalisation proves to be so complex that I can only outline it roughly here. Regarding linguistic distance or its converse, linguistic similarity, the outline remains especially rudimentary. For rule (ia), the linguistic distance within a language – which will then be pluricentric – must be very low between all standard varieties, that is less than moderate, and for rules (iia) and (iib), it must be at most moderate, that is not high, between every non-standard variety and the standard variety roofing it. The following approach is thus obtained for linguistic distance within a single language, which can be expanded as required for more standard and non-standard varieties:

moderate + low + moderate = low +2 x moderate (NSV_1 – moderate – \{SV_1 – ... Low... – SV_m\} – moderate – NSV_n)
(Example: High Alemannic – moderate – Swiss Standard German – low – German Standard German – moderate – Low German).

The methods available for measuring linguistic distance are very diverse and often complicated to use. For rough access, texts in the relevant varieties, which have been translated word for word (while retaining grammatical correctness), can be compared by number of word pairs whose paired formal similarity is recognised even by linguistic non-experts – while the representativeness of the texts for each variety must be guaranteed. Preparing such texts raises a multitude of questions: whether they are spoken or written, orthographic or phonetic script and so on.

Instead of complete texts, comparison of word pairs alone is more manageable, as used in "lexical statistics" or "glottochronology" as reference points for time periods at which previously unified varieties or languages have presumably split, e.g. Latin into the Romance languages (Swadesh 1955, 1972). For this purpose, words with meanings distributed in as many language communities as possible are required (basic vocabulary). This method, which was originally conceived diachronically (historically), is transferable for synchronic similarity measurements. In principle, "dialectometry" also proceeds in this manner to determine the geographical distribution of individual dialect features and boundaries (isoglosses), where the linguistic distance usually rises with the geographical distance from the starting point of the measurement (see Goebl 1984). In this context, all structural features, especially phonetic-phonological, morphological and lexical, are often given the same weighting, because weightings are difficult to justify in purely linguistic terms, and different results are obtained with different grammatical theories (W. Klein 1974: 142–148).

Instead of purely linguistic measurements, it is often preferable to measure the distance between varieties by mutual intelligibility. However, this is not only a shift from objective to

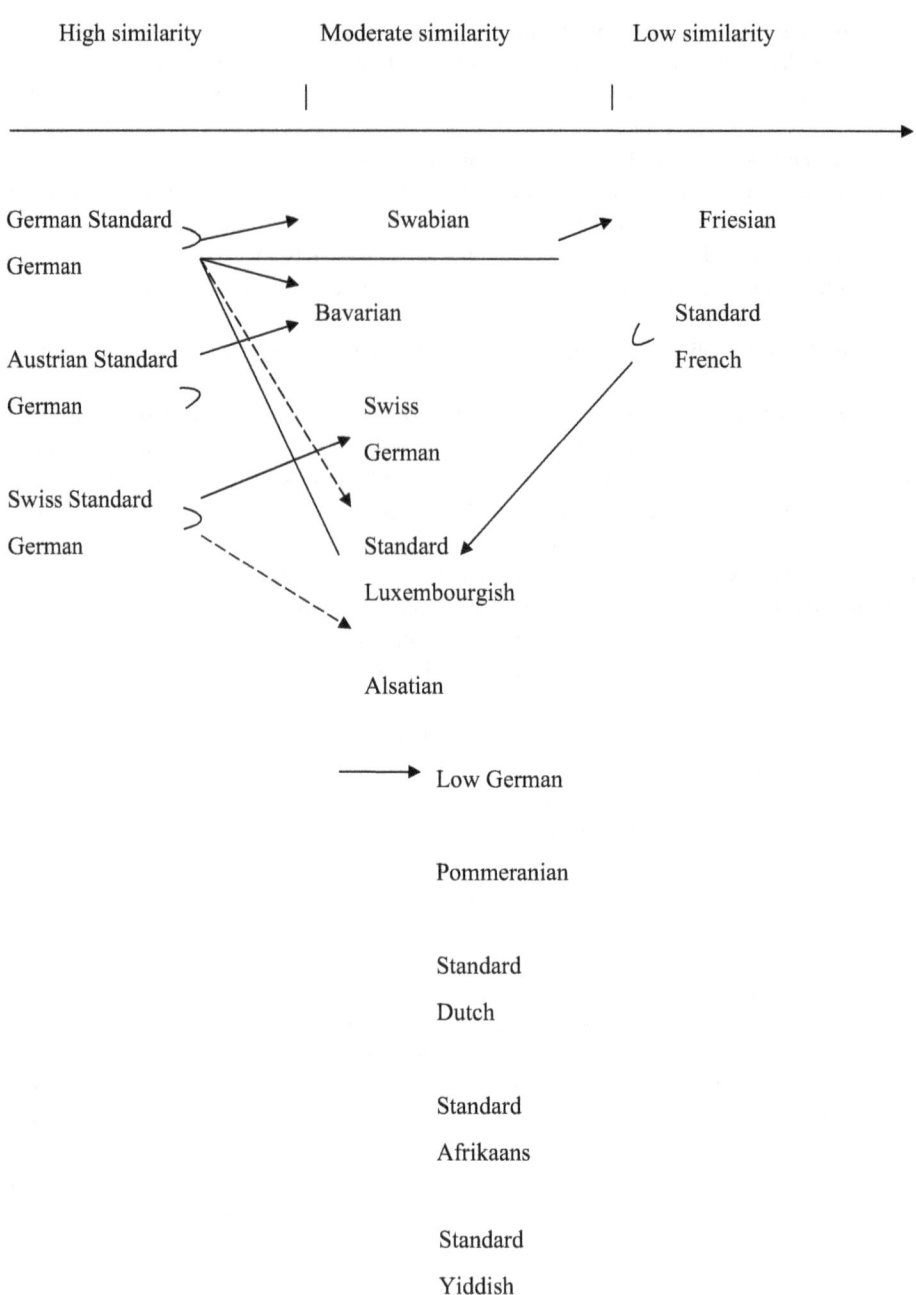

Figure B.2–1 Roofing ([Insert 15031-3015-Icon-001 Here]) and relevant degrees of linguistic similarity (→) for allocating varieties to languages (based on the example of German)

subjective level, but also from direct to indirect measurement – intelligibility as an indicator of linguistic distance. With reference to linguistics, there are often marked differences in the effect of different semiotic or grammatical levels on intelligibility (of writing/ orthography, phonetics, lexis etc.). For example, in tests carried out by Charlotte Gooskens (2007), intelligibility correlated in an approximately linear manner with degree and number of phonetic differences, while it fluctuated erratically in the case of lexical differences. Gooskens (2007: 461) distinguishes between "cognate words" and "non-cognate words": "One single non-cognate word in a sentence or even a larger part of text can lower intelligibility considerably if the non-cognate word is a central concept. On the other hand, if the non-cognate words in a text have little semantic content, intelligibility is less heavily influenced". However formal similarity is more relevant than etymological relatedness of words; Charles Ferguson (1966: 320) stressed the priority "not of genetic relationship, but of some measure of similarity" for intelligibility. Gooskens (2007) and Gooskens/ Heringa (2004; referenced by Marian Sloboda) use an algorithm for distance measurement developed by Vladimir I. Levenshtein, which measures only the perceived, not the objective linguistic distance ("perceived dialect distance measurement"). I limit myself here to referencing this method, which places considerable demands on users; further details would be too great a digression (introduction: de.wikipedia.org/wiki/ Levenshtein-distance).

All measurements of linguistic distance relying on subjective judgement have the basic problem that the two measurement directions are not absolutely symmetrical. Similarity from V_a to V_b is only of the same magnitude as similarity from V_b to V_a in objective, generally linguistic, measurements. The problem is damaging in the case of a limitation to degree of intelligibility as an indicator of linguistic distance. This limitation has been conventional for a long time, and measurements are therefore generally made in both directions (*mutual intelligibility*). Its application often serves to create a common written form for adjacent varieties which are so far without a written form, with the goal of developing them into a standard language. Efforts in this direction have been guided by the *Summer Institute of Linguistics*, since renamed as *SIL International* (en.wikipedia.org/wiki/SIL-International; for the method of measuring intelligibility see Casad 2005: 1267f). The method has the primary advantage of feasibility. Native speakers of variety V_a are accordingly played series of sentences or complete texts (sentence test or text test) of variety V_b, and native speakers of V_b are played sentences or texts of V_a. Degree of understanding is determined by questions about the meaning of what has been heard. Trial participants include only people who have no prior knowledge of the other variety. Symmetry in the degree of understanding in both directions may be impaired primarily by different attitudes towards the varieties. Since the famous investigation by Wolff (1959), it is now known that sympathies or antipathies can influence readiness to understand.

Key distances for linking varieties are not rigidly specified. In the planning of new languages, speaker attitudes and political circumstances also play a role alongside mutual intelligibility. While the particularly important, moderate linguistic distance is often considerably extended for large European languages, and many dialects are thus incorporated, the SIL tends towards a narrower limitation. Primarily African-language researchers have commented critically on this (e.g. Prah 2004) and located the resulting glottotomy (language fragmentation) in the tradition of colonialism with its slogan of "divide and conquer". This also seems to have influenced the fragmentation of languages in *Ethnologue* which is administered by SIL. If the dimensions of the major European languages had been used for orientation, a clearer overview of the languages of Africa would have been achieved.

Turning now to the criterion of *roofing*, it was explained in Ch. B.1 that standard varieties incorporate non-standard varieties (e.g. dialects) into the same language through roofing. Furthermore, only standard varieties are capable of roofing but cannot be roofed themselves, and only non-standard varieties can be roofed, but are not capable of roofing themselves (asymmetry of the roofing relationship). Roofing occurs essentially through the speakers of the non-standard varieties being corrected in the direction towards the standard variety, so that the attitude that both varieties belong to the same language is communicated to them (which succeeds only

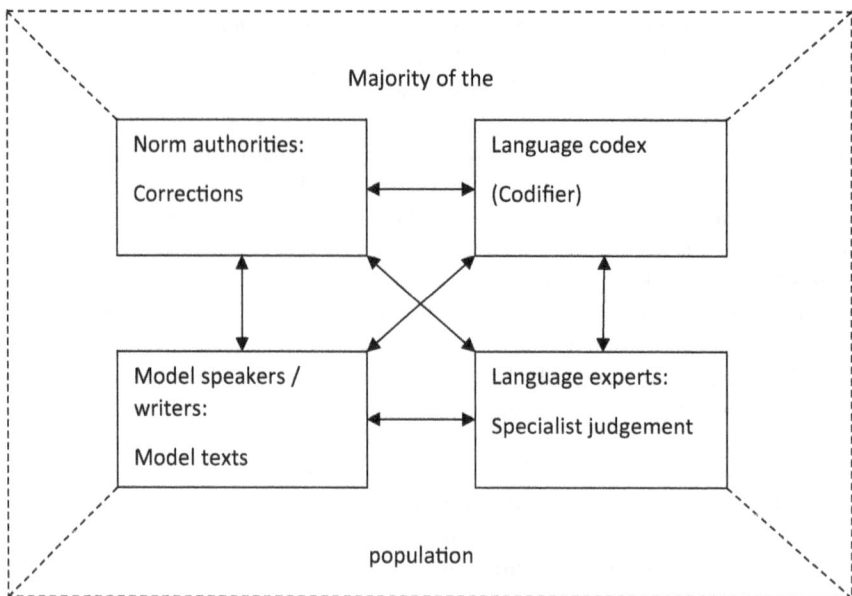

Figure B.2–2   Key social factors determining a standard variety

if the linguistic distance between two varieties is at most moderate). Finally, codification, the existence of reference works which can be used (prescriptively) to establish "correct" language usage (of the standard variety), was identified as a characteristic of standard varieties, while, for non-standard varieties, only scientific descriptions are available, which are not used to correct language usage (descriptive). These factors will now be justified and differentiated.

In this context, it is important to bear in mind that standard varieties differ from non-standard varieties not only through codification but also through the participation of other social factors on their formation. These factors, including their interaction, are shown in Figure B.2–2 (see Ammon 1995a: 73–88; 2005b; 2017).

A language codex is a reference work giving the correct forms of a standard variety. Its "validity" is guaranteed by a hierarchy of norm authorities, which generally extends as far as the state leadership, e.g. when, in cases of doubt, the cultural bureaucracy determines which reference books should be used as a basis for teaching materials in schools. For German Standard German, the Duden dictionaries form the central components of the codex, for Austria, the *Österreichisches Wörterbuch*, and for Switzerland, possibly the *Schweizer Wörterbuch* (K Meyer 2006). However, this is never explicitly stipulated; it is demonstrated only in conflicts over linguistic correctness. In Switzerland, the *Duden Spelling Dictionary* is also an acknowledged reference work, although it is not clear whether this applies only for spelling or also for vocabulary. Vague demarcation is typical for language codices, as indeed for the other three social factors shown in Figure B.2–2. But this does not mean that such factors do not exist or have no influence on specifying the form of each standard variety.

In practice, language codices can never contain all forms of a standard variety, because this would make changes of the standard variety between editions of the codex impossible. A key role in these changes is played by model speakers and writers. These are people whose language use is taken as exemplary, regardless of whether it is based on the codex. The central position within this group is occupied by professional speakers and writers, nowadays, primarily news presenters of nationwide mass media and journalists of nationwide newspapers. Historically, it was mainly actors in large theatres or authors primarily of non-fiction books rather than fictional, because fictional writers are known for their often deliberate use of non-standard forms. Model speakers and writers are the harbingers of standard-language neologisms which will be adopted into the next edition of the codex if they have achieved sufficient familiarity.

The double arrows in Fig.B.2–2 indicate the interaction between all four social factors: model speakers are educated on the basis of the language codex (e.g. in Germany, news presenters of ZDF in Mainz on the basis of the *Duden Pronunciation Dictionary*, and even in school – though less precisely – on the basis of teaching materials written to conform with the codex). But in professional life, they develop linguistic peculiarities which may then be adopted in the language codex. The relationship between model writers and codifiers is similar. Both sides therefore influence each other – in the direction of the arrows. Model speakers and writers also take their bearings from changing language use among the majority of the population; however, this language use – as indicated by the missing arrows in Figure B.2–2 – does not act directly on the forms of the standard variety.

Language norm authorities are people professionally obliged to correct the language use of norm subjects – who are subordinate to them in this respect – in the direction towards the standard variety. The most important group of language norm authorities are teachers who correct their pupils accordingly; they are obliged to provide such correction in the direction towards the standard variety and may certainly not simply dispense with corrections or base them on arbitrary varieties, e.g. their favourite dialect. Publishers' readers or copyeditors are also among the language norm authorities and, historically, also printers, about whose textual interventions even Martin Luther is believed to have complained in vain. The language norm authorities can also influence the form of the standard variety in different ways, for example, via their associations, although their principal function is the distribution (*promulgation*) of the standard variety.

Finally, there are the language experts, primarily linguists who act on the form of the standard variety by critiquing the codex or the language use of model speakers and writers, or even the customs of correction by the language norm authorities. But this group does not include the codifiers, although they too are linguists, because their opportunity for acting on the form of the standard variety is quite different. The two groups cannot be kept strictly apart in terms of persons but only functionally (by role rather than person), because many people exercise both functions side-by-side, for example, as a university teacher of linguistics and as a collaborator on the language codex. The same applies for the personal union between language experts and language norm authorities, and model writers or speakers.

The social factors outlined here and their interaction in the formation of a standard variety can also be grounded in norm theory. Of the norm theories known to me, Henrik von Wright (1963) seems the most suitable; but important insights are also provided by Renate Bartsch (1985) and Klaus Gloy (1975). I will mention a few points, mainly with reference to von Wright. Of the nine types of norm distinguished by von Wright – without claiming completeness or precision in demarcation – standard varieties are closest to *"prescriptions"* – by contrast with non-standard varieties which are closer to *"customs"* (von Wright 1963: 7–9). Customs are not issued by personal norm authorities and often not communicated in language let alone in writing, but form part of the way of life of groups of people, which are learnt by imitation. The consequence of not following them tends to be exclusion from the group rather than more specialised sanctions (penalties) – as in the case of prescriptions. This characterisation of customs fits with the acquisition and use of traditional dialects. By contrast, prescriptions are communicated in language or even in writing (in the case of standard varieties via codification, von Wright 1963: 95), issued by personal norm authorities (e.g. teachers) and failure to follow them is punished by special sanctions (e.g. poor grades at school, difficulty in social advancement). The additions in brackets are my own; von Wright does not consider standard and non-standard varieties.

Von Wright's distinction between "categorical" and "hypothetical norms" is also illuminating (ibid: 129f., 168–171). The former applies absolutely; the latter only in given situations or "conditions of application". Standard varieties evidently belong to the latter, because their use is in no sense prescribed in all situations. In keeping with the main reason for the development of standard varieties from dialects and their most important function, their use is prescribed primarily, or in fact only, for public situations. School prepares pupils for this as the classroom represents a kind of public space. The prescription to use the standard variety generally applies only in the classroom, not in the playground. This prescription is most clearly evident in native-language tuition, in our case, in German lessons. Prescription outside school is correspondingly graded according to how public the occasion is. At a community or regional level, only partial approximation to the standard variety is required by contrast with the national level (e.g. in Germany, representative public bodies at community, state and federal level).

Von Wright's reference to the hierarchy of norm authorities, according to which lower ranking authorities are obliged or empowered by higher authorities to issue prescriptions (ibid: 189–207), is also helpful. In fact, prescriptions already exist when they are issued by norm authorities, if these have the power to assert them with credible sanctions; but they only become "valid" if issuing them is required or permitted by a higher authority. This is reminiscent of standard varieties, the acquisition and use of which, e.g. in school, is prescribed not by the teacher alone, but by the cultural bureaucracy disposed above the teacher. As suggested, with standard varieties, the hierarchy of norm authorities often reaches as far as state leadership level.

Finally, von Wright points out that norm systems are often not closed (ibid: 85–90). Accordingly, he distinguishes between "strong" and "weak permission" for actions (ibid: 86). Being permitted to use a specific norm content is strong; e.g. in the case of our topic, the use of a given word. By contrast, all actions which are not expressly prohibited exhibit weak permission. This corresponds more to the type of prescriptions for standard varieties, especially their constant transformation. Codifications are therefore, in principle, incomplete. Teachers comply with this, or at least should, by tolerating or even rewarding the not-yet-codified language use of model speakers and writers.

The norm-theoretical understanding of standard varieties as roofing non-standard varieties explains, with clear demarcation, the subdivision of dialect continua into languages or – in the case of pluricentric languages – into "language centres" (Ammon 1995a; Schmidlin 2011; Ammon/ Bickel/ Lenz 2013/16). Viewed in norm-theoretical terms, the roofing ceases geographically, where – primarily in schools – corrections are made in the direction towards different standard varieties of at least moderate linguistic distance. In many cases, this is a national border.

The specification of standard varieties and non-standard varieties as "autonomous" and "heterogenous" proposed by J.K. Chambers and Peter Trudgill (1980: 10–14) tends in a similar direction but with less clarity. Taken literally, it explains whole languages rather than standard varieties as "autonomous". Demarcation on the theoretical basis of the "development" of varieties into languages, in the sense of usage in domains with high linguistic demands, e.g. in universities or in science, as suggested by followers of Kloss (1978: 23–60; see Muljačić 1989; Ammon 1989b: 78–82; Haarmann 2004) is also too vague. However, even in these attempts, the standard variety appears crucial for subdividing dialect continua into languages with several varieties. Otherwise, one would be faced with a problem formally similar to the classification of lifeforms into species, as visualised by Dawkins (2011: 38–42): with historical hindsight, where does our own species, homo sapiens, begin? Between parents and children there is always an extremely small – in this case genetic – distance, which guarantees shared reproductive capacity – crucial for allocation to the same species (disregarding the problem of inbreeding). As a result, a subdivision into species cannot be made at any point in the sequence of generations. The genetic distance required for a separation into different species is created only when numerous intermediate stages are overridden. The shared reproductive capacity, which is then broken, corresponds to the linguistic distance of an order of magnitude which makes mutual intelligibility impossible. With languages, such distances can arise through migrations or isolation of populations. The opposite case of subdivision of dialect continua into languages, which has no analogy in biology, splits dialect continua and bridges moderate linguistic distances through roofing by standard varieties developed from the dialects.

Psychological securing of a standard variety as a roofing of the non-standard varieties begins in young children at school, almost as a kind of brainwashing. It continues in numerous, often subtle forms in many situations. As a result, standard and non-standard varieties are rigidly linked in speakers' minds. Evaluating the standard variety as the "correct" form of one's own language becomes part of the linguistic identity of all speakers of the relevant language. This gives rise to a larger "language community" of speakers of all the non-standard varieties, encompassing different varieties roofed by the same standard variety. In this context, speakers generally also internalise the standard variety as their "native language", although possibly with traces of internal distance. This function of standard varieties, which forms identity and therefore language community in the narrower sense referenced by Renate Bartsch (1985: 254), is an important consequence of the formation of languages through roofing described here (for the political connection with the formation of nations, see e.g. Anderson 1983; Ahlzweig 1989; Ch. B.3).

3. The difficult concept of a "German ethnic group"

The concept of a "German ethnic group" [*Ethnie*] is used here in the context of German minorities (Ch. E) and occasionally elsewhere (see also Ch. A.3). The terms *deutsche Sprachnation* and *deutsche Kulturnation*, which, in their determinative parts, express what the exponents of these concepts take as constitutive of a German *ethnic group*, have approximately the same conceptual scope. Ernst M. Arndt (in his song *Des Deutschen Vaterland*, 1813) and Jacob and Wilhelm Grimm (*Deutsches Wörterbuch*, vol. 1, 1854: *Foreword*, Jacob Grimm [1848], 1868) were prominent exponents of the concept of a German *language nation*, while Friedrich Meinecke ([1907] 1969: 12; further details in Ammon 1995a: 18–30) conceptualised the German *cultural nation*. I must, however, reject both terms as designations for the German ethnic group: not because of their reference to language and culture, but because I limit the term *nation* to states, i.e. the "state nation" (Ch. A.3). By contrast, the term *German Volk* has largely the same semantic scope as *German ethnic group*; but I shall also avoid this as far as possible because of its conservative connotations. The terms German *Volksgruppe* and German *Nationalität* tend to designate only subsets of the German ethnic group, mostly outside the German-speaking countries (Ch. B.4), e.g. the German *ethnic group* or *nationality in Hungary*.

While most of these terms refer to groups, German *nationality* can also designate the attribute of a person: A *has* German *nationality* is synonymous with A *is of* German *nationality*. The adjectival term corresponding to ethnic group [*Ethnie*] is *ethnicity*: *has German ethnicity/is of German ethnicity/is an ethnic German, is ethnically German*. Accordingly, in the present book, I use the term *ethnic group* for whole groups and *ethnicity* for individuals, regarding their association with their ethnic group. I use the other terms mentioned in quotations or where conventional in context. Joshua Fishman (2010: xxv–xxvii) points to the historical pedigree of *ethnic-group* terminology, with Herder as the *presiding spirit* of Fishman's own understanding of this sense (ibid: xxx–xxxi).

It is easier to demarcate the term *ethnic group* from terms with which it could be confused than to frame it positively. Primarily, it must not be confused with "national citizenship", i.e. the legal relationship between citizens and state nations. Similarly, legal definitions of ethnic groups or ethnicity by individual states must not be equated with the superordinate, universal term. For example, German Federal Refugee Law § 6 (1) defines as "*deutsche Volkszugehörige*" [members of the German people], people who, "in their homeland [outside Germany U.A.], have declared themselves members of the German people [Volkstum], provided their declaration is confirmed by attributes such as family origin, language, education, culture".

> People born after 31st of December 1923 are thus members of the German people, if they are descendants of a member of the German state nation or German people and, until leaving the emigration territories, have exclusively declared their member-ship of the German people, through a corresponding declaration of nationality or in a comparable manner, or have been assigned German nationality according to the law of their country of origin. The declaration of membership of the German people or legal assignment of German nationality must be confirmed through mediation of the German language in the family.
>
> *(§ 6 (2); www.gesetze-im-internet.de/bundesrecht/bvfg/gesamt.pdf)*

As might be imagined, this "membership of the German people" is formulated more narrowly than "descendant of members of the German people" in order to restrict claims. However, the more broadly formulated concept of "German ethnicity (membership of people/nationality)" seems more appropriate for many purposes, as does the definition based on a person's declara-tion of such membership.

We can therefore state that an ethnic group is a relatively large group of people who are not defined in terms of national citizenship or according to laws of individual states and who believe in their shared history, language, culture or religion (Bergem 2000; Fishman 1972a; also Ch. A.3). Their belief is thus the ultimately decisive factor. This must not disagree entirely with the facts, but anything irreconcilable with the content of beliefs generally tends to be suppressed and transformed by historical myth. Because of this priority of belief in the community over its reality, declaration of membership of an ethnic group is also the appropriate criterion for membership. Hermann Bausinger (2000: 103–111) portrays the typical historical narrative of the German people as a steady compression from broadly defined precursors of the Germanic tribes (with Hermann the Cherusker) via an ethnic group of narrower conceptual scope (Ger-man language or cultural "nation" – victory over Napoleon) towards the condensed German state nation (with the three Kaisers, primarily Wilhelm I and II).

In this context also, overlapping occurs because of multiple associations. I know German citizens who feel they are members of both the German and Turkish "peoples". Such double ethnicity (German + x) or "floating ethnicity" (Born/ Dickgiesser 1989: 164) is encountered throughout the world, especially in German or German-speaking minorities, e.g. Romanian + German, Russian + German etc. Although not identical, this duplicity is related to the vagueness and vacillation of the term *ethnic group* referenced by Kathleen N. Conzen (1986: 149, 151) with the example of Germans in the USA.

The meaning of German *ethnic group/ ethnicity* also varies between different territories and nations. In part, this is linked with difficulties in distinguishing German citizenship, e.g. in the case of Swiss German-speakers, who do not like to be called "Germans" by other ethnic groups in their country but prefer "German-speaking Swiss". In Switzerland, it is mostly inhabitants of Germany who are called "Germans". The same or similar dynamics are found in Austria (emails from Hans Bickel, Switzerland, and Rudolf de Cillia, Austria, 14 May 2013), also for minorities outside their own country, which can only be understood ethnically, e.g. the "German Slovenians" (*Der Kärntner* 92 (2011): 12). Correspondingly, in many minorities, self-designation or designation by others as *Ungarndeutsche* [Hungarian Germans], *Rumäniendeutsche* [Romanian Germans], *Russlanddeutsche* [Russian Germans] etc. is taken for granted in context (Ch. E.4.6; E.4.7; E.4.8). Differently named ethnic groups which are considered parts of the German ethnic group e.g. *Swabians* in Hungary or *Hunsrücker* in Brazil must also be mentioned (Ch. E.4.6; E.4.10). These groups, traditionally speakers of German dialects, are also generally self-classified and classified by others as ethnic Germans. The classifications correspond broadly to those in Germany.

Other ethnic specifications must be regarded as more ambiguous, special cases of the German ethnic group, e.g. the Alsatians, at least to the extent that they still speak the traditional dialect. Referring to this group, Alsatian cabaret artist Roger Siffer once said: "A good Alsatian is a Frenchman! And a very good Alsatian is half Swabian" (*"Zwischen Erbfreunden"*, *FAZ* 4 August 2013: 3). One wonders if many would admit a trace of German ethnicity in addition to the French (Ch. E.4.3). Similar confusion is found with "Silesians" in present-day Poland, not only with German but also Polish Silesians, whom many Polish nationals suspect of clandestine ethnic self-classification with the Germans (Ch. E.4.4). By contrast, the Amish people in North America are nowadays hardly suspected of self-classifying with the German ethnic group, although they are sometimes seen in this light by outsiders (Ch. E.4.11). Indeed, in the case of the German-speaking South Tyroleans, there is no doubt about self-allocation, and allocation by outsiders, of German as their native language rather than Italian, although in some cases, they may tend towards double ethnicity German + Italian (Ch. D.3.2; Grote 2009).

Identity, a term which I have so far avoided, is almost essential for explaining the concepts of "ethnic group" and "ethnicity". A person's "ethnic identity" is one facet of their often extremely diverse *social* identity, and more specifically, their *group* identity, by contrast with their *role* identity, which relates to their social position within groups (group theory, e.g. Homans 1991; role theory, e.g. Dahrendorf 1965). The richly faceted nature of group identity is explained by the possibility of simultaneous membership of such diverse groupings as gender, social class, profession, political party, club etc. – and ethnic group, in the case of dual ethnicity, two ethnic groups. According to the currently dominant view, people are genetically predisposed to membership in groups. They have historically only been able to survive in groups, so that the life of a Robinson Crusoe has never been realistic (Dobelli 2012: 157). For this reason, people often take the slightest shared interest as an opportunity for forming a group and identifying with its members. Henri Tajfel has become famous for his experimental demonstrations of this phenomenon (1974, 1978; also, Gerhards 2010: 37–44; Pinker 2013: 772f). Ethnic groups and language communities are groups in this sense, whose members feel connected with one another. However, "identity" theories are an almost unfathomable topic (e.g. Krappmann 2004), and a plethora of publications on nation state and ethnic identity, and their connection with language, already exists (e.g. in chronological order of publication: Isajiw 1990; Hobsbawm 1996; Myhill 1999; Pedersen 2000; Riehl 2000; S. Wolff 2000; Ammon 2003b; Wodak/ de Cillia 2006; Gerner 2006; Carl/ Stevenson 2009; Edwards 2009, 2010; Grote 2009; Gilles/ Seela/ Sieburg/ Wagner 2010; Krumm 2011).

Within the framework of this book, I always understand identity as a property of an individual, in the case of group identity, as an attitude (Spitzley 2003) towards the groups with which individuals identify. Accordingly, "ethnic identity" is the attitude towards an ethnic group, in the case of double ethnicity, two ethnic groups, with which a person identifies. I distinguish this from "national identity", which can refer to several state nations (multiple citizenship) (Ch. A.3). With ethnic groups, membership criteria can diverge, especially in the case of the German ethnic group, the scope of which is sometimes limited to Germany, but often extends far beyond.

Ideas about typical "German" attributes, which have been discussed in numerous publications, vary widely (e.g. Bausinger 2000; Asserate 2013). Such variability is also evident in historical overviews (e.g. Wiegrefe/ Pieper 2007).

What is required for ethnic identity is an often diffuse belief in a shared history, family origin, language, culture and possibly also religion, or parts of it. Like other attitudes, ethnic identity can also be analysed into cognitive components (belief in ethnic-group membership), evaluative (positive, negative or neutral evaluation of this membership), affective/emotional (strong or weak feelings about membership) and finally practical (readiness to act), especially with regard to ethnic-group membership, relative to members of the ethnic group and to the ethnic group as a collective (for components of attitudes: Gardner 1972; Lasagabaster 2004; Garrett 2005; Garrett/ Coupland/ Williams 2003; on readiness to act: Pinker 2013: 826–830). Particularly relevant for the present context is the attitude of people of German ethnicity towards the most frequently named, shared feature of the German ethnic group: the German language and its varieties (Ch. B.1; B.2). Is their attitude positive, indifferent or negative, and what kinds of readiness to act or concrete actions are derived from it? These questions will be addressed several times throughout the book, especially in Ch. E on German-(speaking) minorities.

4. "German-speaking countries", "German-language territory" and related terms

This chapter serves primarily to clarify concepts and the definition of terms used throughout the book. For further clarification of terms used in these definitions, it may occasionally be helpful to refer to the chapters indicated, e.g. for the term *official language* (see Ch. D; also Map D.1–1).

I turn first to compounds with the terms *state* or *country*. These include, on one hand *states (countries) with German as national official language* (Ch. D.1; D.2), namely, Germany, Austria, Switzerland, Liechtenstein and Luxembourg (n= 5), and, on the other hand, *states (countries) with German as a regional official language* (Ch. D.1; D.3), namely, Belgium and Italy (n= 2). *States (countries) with German as official language* (without adjectival specification) thus comprise all states with German as national or regional official language (n= 7). Of these, the *German-speaking countries (states)* are only a subset, namely, those in which German is both national official language and also native language of the majority of the population. These are all states with German as national official language apart from Luxembourg, where Luxembourgish is the native language of the majority of the population (which the majority declare as their native language; Ch. D.2.5). The *German-speaking countries (states)* accordingly comprise Germany, Austria, Switzerland and Liechtenstein (n= 4). A minor distinction should be made between *countries (states) with German as a national language*. These are the four German-speaking countries and also – albeit in a restricted sense – Namibia (Ch. E.4.9) (n=5). In general, a language is considered the national language of a country (state) when it is the native language of the majority of the population or of a traditionally important part of the population declaring membership of the country – where this addition allows room for different specifications. However, this explanation of terms, does explain why, despite being a national official language, German is not a national language of Luxembourg (because only a few Luxembourgers declare it as their native language), and why German is not a national language of Belgium or Italy (in each case it is only a regional official language and – because of the annexation after WWI – has no significant tradition for the country as a whole; Ch. D.3.1; D.3.2). It may seem obvious to specify the term *German-speaking states* with a different, more specialised meaning than *German-speaking countries*, and, in fact, most likely as a short form for *states with German as the national official language*. Apart from the German-speaking countries, this would also include Luxembourg. However, the two terms are often misunderstood as synonymous, for which reason I have opted to use them synonymously.

Turning now to compounds with the terms *territory*, *region* and *area*, in addition to which the terms *district* and *space* are also conventionally used as synonyms. For instance, the latter terms are used in various contributions in the *Handbuch Deutsch als Fremd- und Zweitsprache* (Krumm/ Fandrych/ Hufeisen/ Riemer 2010). I also use the five terms synonymously, the last two rarely. All five terms can be referenced to the term *official language*, but also occur without this reference. The *German official language territory* (*German official language region*) includes the territories of the states with German as the national official language, that is, the entire regions of Germany, Austria, Liechtenstein and Luxembourg (Ch. D.2.1–D.2.3; D.2.5), but only the German official-language sub-region of Switzerland defined according to the territoriality principle is included (also, *territorial principle*) (Ch. D.2.4). Furthermore, the sub-regions of Belgium and Italy with German as a regional official language, that is, the German official-language regions in East Belgium and South Tyrol are included (Ch. D.3.1; D.3.2).

This must be distinguished from the *contiguous German-language territory (in central Europe)*. Synonymous with this, and possibly more current, is the term *coherent German-language territory* which, however, seems likely to be misunderstood because of discussions in the EU about border crossings and freedom of establishment, and which I therefore avoid. The conventional addition *in central Europe* can be dispensed with because there is no correspondingly coherent German-language territory anywhere else. It therefore seems most expedient to specify the term *coherent German-language territory* in such a manner that it extends not only over the entire German official language territory, but also beyond it to the adjacent – but only the adjacent – territories of German-speaking minorities, namely, in France, Denmark, Poland, Czech Republic and Hungary. However, this expansion makes precise demarcation more difficult (Ch. E.4.2–E4.6). To distinguish more clearly from the term *German official language territory*, more explicit reference can also be made to the *coherent German-language territory including adjacent minority territories*. Finally, the *German-language territory* includes the *coherent German-language territory* and the *territories of all German-speaking minorities* (Ch. E), where precise specification exposes numerous difficulties.

C

SPEAKER NUMBERS AND ECONOMIC STRENGTH OF GERMAN

1. Current speaker numbers (numerical strength) of German

Speaker numbers, or the "numerical strength" of languages, are generally cited as a parameter for measuring "large" or "small" languages. For many experts, e.g. Abram de Swaan (2001: 27–33), they represent a key factor and a significant indicator for the global position of languages. Opportunities for contact with a language increase in proportion with rising speaker numbers. Especially in the case of international contacts, experiencing the "communication potential" of a language (Ch. A.7), can motivate people to learn it, thereby further boosting opportunities for use.

However, as Heinz Kloss noted (1974b; also Lieberson 1982), the number of speakers, especially native speakers, is not a reliable indicator for the international or interlingual use of a language (Ch. A.3). This is evident from the relatively weak international position of many numerically strong languages, e.g. Bengali with considerably more than 200 m native speakers (211 m, including second-language speakers, according to *Ethnologue* 2005: 320). However, the existence of a positive correlation between the rank ordering of languages by speaker number and their ranking as international languages is beyond doubt, at least with numerically strong languages. The only notable exception is the constructed language Esperanto (Sakaguchi 1987, 1989). It has very few speakers, but they often communicate internationally. Estimates of the speaker number, including the very few native speakers, vary from 500,000 to 2 m (de.wikipedia.org/wiki/Esperanto).

When considering speaker numbers, it is therefore expedient to distinguish between speaker types: primarily, native speakers, second-language speakers (SL speakers) and foreign-language speakers (FL speakers). The latter have learnt the language outside its language territory and can still speak it (Ch. A.3). In the statistics, it is often unclear whether only native speakers have been included or SL speakers as well; FL speakers are generally not included.

Apart from constructed languages, native speakers represent the starting capital for the development of a language into an international language. Other factors being equal, a high native-speaker number motivates people to learn the language as a foreign language. For example, compare the larger European languages (English, French, German, etc.) with the smaller languages (e.g. Czech, Danish, Greek, etc.). With larger languages, learning is more "worthwhile" in cost-benefit terms and because of the increased communication potential. Additional SL- or FL speakers therefore boost development into an international language. FL speakers may, in fact, be crucial for its international position. For example, English enjoys a dominant international position in the EU, although it has fewer native speakers than German, and in the world, in spite of its smaller number of native speakers than Chinese (Graddol 1999, 2006). Such examples confirm the different relevance of native speakers, SL speakers and FL speakers and the need to keep these figures separate. Mere FL learners of a language should be included, not only because it is difficult to distinguish them from real FL speakers, but because "mere" learners can motivate non-learners to learn, even if they themselves do not have and may never reach useful language competence.

However, it is easier to define speaker and learner types than it is to register them statistically. Uncertainties arise from the almost unavoidable reliance on self-assessment, or whether a subsequently learned language which is now mastered better than the native language should be counted as a native language, perhaps a second native language, or even as the only actually mastered language. Difficulties also occur with self-assessment of competence levels as a means for distinguishing genuine FL speakers from mere learners. Collections of data in different regions can also present different problems. For example, for learners of German, some reliable worldwide data is available (e.g. Netzwerk Deutsch 2010; Foreign Office, Bulletin 610, 2015); Ch. L.3.2); but, for German-speakers, similarly reliable data is only available for limited regions, such as the EU and adjoining countries (defined by self-assessment of ability to converse in German; e.g. the *Eurobarometers special*); also Ch. H.4.4). Native speakers and SL speakers can be determined with reasonable accuracy in the official-language territory of German (Ch. D), but this is not so easy for German (speaking) minorities (Ch. E), not to mention the small groups distributed worldwide, the "German diaspora" (Kloss 1935; Ammon 1991a: 91). It is therefore expedient to estimate total speaker numbers for the German language subdivided into the following three groups:

(i)   German native speakers and German SL speakers in the official-language territory of German (in central Europe) (Ch. B.4 and D);
(ii) German native speakers and if possible German SL speakers in the German (speaking) minorities outside the official-language territory of German (Ch. E);
(iii) German FL speakers including all German learners worldwide, former and current, with useful competence level (Ch. C.1, end) – although distinguishing "competent speakers" from mere learners is an almost impossible task.

Turning first to (i): German native speakers and SL speakers in the official-language territory of German. Even registering these figures can become flawed with errors in validity and reliability (Crystal 1985; Graddol 1999; Haarmann 2002a: 21–29; Coulmas 2005a: 151–157). Census figures with representative data provide a reference point, but it is often precisely speaker numbers which are missing, not to mention data differentiated by speaker type. In 1872, the first International Statistical Congress in St Petersburg recommended that censuses should register at least the "language spoken in normal conversation" as one of the 12 significant features of the population (no. 8 of the list; de.wikipedia.org/wiki/Volksz%C3%A4hlung). However, in many censuses, language is not even mentioned or the questions are formulated vaguely and vary between time periods and countries, which hampers comparison. Limitations on validity and reliability of data because of self-assessment are an additional factor (de Vries 2005).

Censuses in the German-speaking countries and the German-language territory (Ch. B.4) also suffer from these defects. The 2011 census for Germany contains not even one explicit question about language. The evaluation of this census therefore also contained no relevant information. Census information from other states with German as the official language differs with regard to knowledge of German. To achieve an overview, it would be advisable to divide the population comprehensively into citizens, naturalised foreigners and non-naturalised foreigners with a "permanent residence permit" – as provided in Germany under the Residence Act of 1 January 2005 for citizens from non-EU states; EU citizens have this permanent permit anyway (www.bundesauslaenderbeauftragte.de/aufenthaltsberechtigung.html). In the following, I refer more generally, not only with reference to Germany, to foreigners with a permanent residence permit. It is often only foreigners defined in this or in a similar way who are included in censuses.

For simplicity, in states or parts of states with German as the sole official language (e.g. the Sorbian area), I count all citizens as German-speakers and even as German native speakers. I also assume that in minority regions, in which German is an official language alongside the minority language, all minority-language speakers will also classify as German-speakers, – possibly with German as a second native language. By way of partial compensation, I count all foreigners as non-native speakers, with the larger fraction (according to the criteria explained below) as SL speakers of German and the smaller as non-German-speakers. The distinction between German speakers and non-speakers also remains unspecified because of lack of data. It is only relevant for SL speakers who might achieve competence level B1 of the Common European Reference Framework as a minimum level for German-speakers ("can converse simply and coherently about familiar topics and areas of personal interest" – as stated in the summary). This is often required in Germany for naturalisation (for criticism, see Li 2014).

The following considerations relate initially to Germany (Ch. D.2.1), then to the other states and parts of states with German as the national official language (Ch. D.2.2–D.3.2), and finally to the German (speaking) minorities without official status of their language (Ch. E). Before going any further, I must say that the findings on foreigners' knowledge of German do not entirely agree with the numerous, alarmist claims; on the contrary, they are largely positive. "Second-generation immigrants almost all have a good knowledge of German" (W. Werner 2005: 11). "Competent use of their German skills in different everyday situations [. . .] is relatively unproblematic for most migrant groups" (Haug 2008: 6). According to one representative telephone survey (n = 1000) in North-Rhine Westphalia in 2011, 98.9% of third-generation Turkish (im)migrants classify their knowledge of German as very good or good; even in the second generation, the figure is 86.3%. The figures for first-generation migrants, who arrived during their lifetime, are lower (43.6%), but the high figures for those who have grown up in Germany indicate an upward trend (Sauer 2012: 5). In this context, Turkish migrants are among the most integration-resistant (Haug 2008: 6). However, most have come to realise that success at school correlates very positively with knowledge of German, especially with German as family language, and this is confirmed by the "Second Integration Report of the Federal Office for Migration, Refugees and Integration" (Engels/ Köller/ Koopmans/ Höhne 2011: 157–159).

Based on these findings, at least the majority of foreigners with a permanent residence permit can be classified as SL speakers of German. For Germany, I have estimated a somewhat optimistic proportion of 90% of foreigners (still with a permanent residence permit) as SL speakers of German. A figure of 95% for Turkish people may apply to the next generation but would be an overestimate for the present generation; however, other foreigners are often more prepared to integrate. Accordingly, if 100% of citizens are counted as German native speakers, and 90% of foreigners as SL speakers of German, the total number of people with a knowledge of German in Germany is calculated as: Σ German-speakers = 100% citizens +90% foreigners.

I am also guided by this formula for the other states and parts of states with German as the predominant native language and sole national or regional official language – i.e. Austria,

Liechtenstein and East Belgium. In states or parts of states with German as the widespread native language and one of several official languages, I adopt the same approach, allocating the foreigners in proportion to the German native speakers (Switzerland, South Tyrol).

For Germany (Ch. D), the following figures were derived from information from the Federal Office for Statistics at the end of 2011: a total population of 81,843,743, of which 7,409,753 foreigners, i.e. 74,433,990 citizens. According to the considerations above, the latter count as German native speakers. 90% of the foreigners, i.e. 6,668,778 people count as German SL speakers (the proportion of foreigners with a permanent residence permit still unclear). Native speakers + SL speakers then amount to 81,102,768 German-speakers (www.destatis.de/DE/Publika tionen/Thematisch/Bevoelkerung/Bevoelkerungstand/VorlBevoelkerungsfortschreibung 5124103119004.pdf?).

For Austria (Ch. D.2.2), the available data justify the assumption that around 90% of foreigners have knowledge of German. This has been described as "certainly a very cautious estimate" (Rudolf de Cillia, email, 28 August 2012). In the 2001 census, only 2.8% of the Austrian population indicated that they speak no German in daily communication; by contrast, 88.6% speak only German, and 8.6% German together with one other language (de Cillia 2012). The proportion of foreigners in Austria in 2012 was around 11.5% of the population (Statistik Austria *inter alia* 2012: www.integrationsfonds.at/zahlen_und_fakten/statistisches_jahrbuch_2012). In fact, the 2.8% non-users of German constitute 24% of the foreigners, so that only 76% of foreigners would be German users; however, the proportion of potential German users, probably even in 2001 and certainly today, may be estimated as higher. At the end of 2011, the total population of Austria was around 8,420,900 (www.statistik.at/web_de/statistiken/bevoelkerung/index.html). With the percentages named for 2012, that would be 7,452,497 citizens and German native speakers, and 868,403 foreigners and 781,563 German SL speakers.

The Statistics Office in Liechtenstein (Ch. D.2.3) quoted a total population of 36,476 (2010: 36,149) with a proportion of foreigners of 33.3% (www.llv.li/pdf-llv-as-bevoelkerungsstatistik_vorlaeufige_ergebnisse_31.12.2011). For 2010, it is claimed that the "one third of the population [...] of foreign nationality" are "predominantly Swiss, Austrian and German nationals" (Regional Administration Principality of Liechtenstein: www.llv.li/llv-as-bevoelkerung). I therefore classify 90% of the total population as German native speakers (32,824 people), and of the assumed 10% of foreigners from non-German-speaking countries, 90% as German SL speakers (3,283 people).

The German-speaking community in East Belgium (Ch. D.3.1) had a total population of 73,119 people in 2006. Of these, 80.9% were Belgians and 14.9% immigrant Germans, but only 4.3% were foreigners from other countries (www.kathonrw.de/uploads/media/7._Die_Deutschsprachige_Gemeinschaft_Belgiens.pdf). Since German is the sole official language, the Belgians, like the immigrant Germans, can also be counted as German native speakers (95.8% = 70,048 people), and 90% of the other foreigners (3,144) as German SL speakers (2,830 people). This gives a total of 72,878 German-speakers.

For Switzerland (Ch. D.2.4), I am grateful to Christoph Freymond (Deputy Sectional Director in the Regional Federal Office for Statistics) for figures according to which, in the last census of 2010, 65.6% of the population declared German as the "main language", and a further 6.9% declared German as the language which they speak "at home and at work/in education". Clarifying terms, Freymond explained, "In normal speech, the main language [...] is what we call our native language". Accordingly, at least 72.5% of the Swiss population speak German, of which 65.6% can be counted as native speakers and 6.9% as SL speakers (1.3% of the native speakers do not use German in the named situations). The continuous resident population of Switzerland in 2010 was 7,870,134 (Federal Office for Statistics: Leporello_Bevölkerung_2010_D_web.de).

Of these, as per the data, 5,705,847 were German-speakers with 5,162,808 native speakers and 543,039 SL speakers.

For Bolzano, South Tyrol in Italy (Ch. D.3.2), the Regional Institute for Statistics gives the total population for year-end 2011 as 51,750, with 8.7% foreigners (www.provinz.bz.it/astat/news/news_d.asp?cate_id=9737). Of these, 467,228 are citizens and 44,522 foreigners. Among the citizens, language groups are subdivided as follows: German native speakers 69.41% (324,303 people), Italian native speakers 26.06% (121,760) and Ladin native speakers 4.3% (30,091) (de.wikipedia.org/wiki/Ethnischer_Proporz_%28S%C3%BCdtirol%29). The Italian and Ladin native speakers learn German as a school subject. However, it is not known how many of these can subsequently speak and use German, so I have no option but to estimate 50% in each case as SL speakers. This would amount to 75,926 people. Regarding the foreigners, as for the other regions, I assume 90% knowledge of at least one of the three languages and subdivide this between the native-speaker proportions. This gives, for German: 37,812 SL speakers and, together with the SL speakers among the 75,926 Italian and Ladin native speakers, a total of 113,738 German SL speakers. Together with the 324,303 German native speakers, that makes 438,041 German-speakers.

For Luxembourg (Ch. D.2.5), the "Institut national de la statistique" gives a (rounded) total resident population for 2011 of 511,800, of which 221,300 foreigners and of these, in turn, 12,100 are Germans, that is, 290,500 citizens (www.statistiques.public.lu/catalogue-publications/luxembourg-en-chiffres/Luxemburg-zahlen.pdf). All the citizens can be considered German SL speakers. Of the foreigners (minus Germans), I again, out of necessity, count half as German SL speakers, i.e. 104,600, which gives 395,100 German SL speakers with the 12,100 Germans as German native speakers. All in all, this amounts to 407,200 German-speakers.

Table C.1–1 provides an overview of the findings so far.

By contrast with previous alarmist warnings, the outlook for the future seems more like limited growth rather than a decline. However, the proportion of German native speakers may decrease while the proportion of German SL speakers may increase, because in all the states or parts of states considered here, the birth-rate for the citizen population has been falling while immigration is increasing, so that immigration now exceeds the decline in population (caused by falling birth rates) in all states with German as the national official language.

Whether the number of German-speakers will rise in the longer term depends on the power of linguistic integration in the receiving language communities. It is possible that linguistic integration will be weakened as postnational tendencies and globalisation are intensified (compare Ch. A.8). Immigrants may increasingly retain English as a lingua franca, and

Table C.1–1 German (native and SL) speakers in the official-language territory of German

	Native speakers	SL speakers	German speakers total
Germany	74,433,990	6,668,778	81,102,768
Austria	7,452,497	781,563	8,234,060
Liechtenstein	32,824	3,283	36,107
Switzerland	5,162,808	543,039	5,705,847
Italy (Bolzano, South Tyrol)	324,303	113,738	438,041
Belgium (German-speaking community)	70,048	2,830	72,878
Luxembourg	12,100	395,100	407,200
Total	87,488,570	8,508,331	95,956,901 (≈96 m)

this could succeed in line with the citizen population acquiring ever more comprehensive knowledge of English (Ch. A.5; Wagener 2012). 4.1% of the stable resident population of Switzerland currently speaks English at home ([Swiss] Federal Office for Statistics: media bulletin 19 June 2012).

Turning now to the next part of our inventory (ii): German native speakers and possibly SL speakers outside the official-language territory of German (compare Ch. E). SL speakers can always be incorporated within reasonably intact native-speaker networks. Gauging such networks by identifying and counting the actual German-speakers worldwide would, however, be a major research project because the methodological problems named previously even for the official-language territory of German would increase exponentially. With language minorities outside the German official-language territory, speaker numbers may be subject to interest-dependent distortions, because funding by the home government or the German-speaking countries is often dependent on size. Anyone who has ever visited "German" minorities – as I have e.g. in Pennsylvania (USA: Amish), in Rio Grande do Sul (Southern Brazil) and in the Kaliningrad region (Oblast Kaliningrad in Russia) will know how difficult it is to identify real speakers of German. However, I have at my disposal only the available numerical data, much of which is presumably inflated.

The data listed includes only nations in which German is not a national official language (Ch. D). Moreover, the following data sources were removed:

*   From Born/ Dickgiesser 1989: Soviet Union and Czechoslovakia, because of dissolution of these states;
*   From "Deutsche Sprache" [German language] in Wikipedia: Greece, Britain, ("United Kingdom"), Ireland, Netherlands, Spain, Thailand and Turkey, and from *Ethnologue* 2009: Mozambique, Philippines, Puerto Rico and United Arab Emirates, because there were no real minorities (for this term see Ch. E.1), but rather expatriates (contract Germans) or seasonal or border dwellers.

The varieties of Hutterite, Pennsylvanian and Mennonite German, Silesian and "*Unserdeutsch*" (Rabaul Creole German), the latter, with only about 100 speakers, being named for Australia and Papua New Guinea (*Ethnologue* 2009: 581, 640), are included in the figures for German. The total in the last column (7.493 m) must not be understood as an average of the three totals before it in the same row, otherwise its value would be lower. Instead, the averages from all rows were totalled and averaged and, in fact, on the assumption that each of the three sources has overlooked one or other minority but not added any.

The uncertainty of numerical estimates of German minorities is clearly articulated in the Born/Dickgiesser text, which discusses the diversity of the sources on which it is based. This can be seen especially in the numerical ranges for many states, e.g. Brazil or Hungary. Born/ Dickgiesser had no figures for German native speakers in Poland (1989: 161f.), but only for people recognised by the Polish government as "indigenous" and by the Federal Government at the time as German citizens (former Germans). Born/ Dickgiesser expressly relate the figures for Canada, Mexico (and the Soviet Union at that time) only to German native speakers (1989: 15f). The naming of their other categories varies according to source: "German speakers" (Argentina, Belize, Bolivia, Chile, Denmark, Namibia, Paraguay, Uruguay and Venezuela), "German-speaking" (Peru), "speakers of German" (Brazil), "German as home language" (Australia, USA), "German as home or conversational language" (South Africa), "passive knowledge of German" (France), "German national/naturalised of German-speaking origin", "from Germany and Austria", "German" and "of German nationality" (Ecuador, Israel, Colombia, Romania,

Table C.1–2 Native- and SL speakers of German outside official-language territory of German in m

	Born/Dick-giesser 1989	Ethnologue 2009	"Deutsche Sprache" in Wikipedia	Average
Argentina	0.300	0.400	0.330–0.350	0.347
Australia	0.109	0.135	0.200	0.148
Belize	0.003	0.069	n.d.	0.036
Bolivia	0.011	0.160	n.d.	0.086
Bosnia and Herzegovina	-	Named, n.f.	n.d.	-
Brazil	0.500–1.500	1.506	0.850–0.900	1.127
Chile	0.020–0.035	0.035	0.020	0.028
Denmark	0.020	0.026	0.020	0.022
Dominican Republic	n.d.	n.d.	0.030	0.030
Ecuador	0.002–0.003	0.032	n.d.	0.018
Estonia	-	0.001	0.002	0.002
France (Alsace-Lorraine)	1.200	1.500	1.200	1.300
Israel	0.096	0.200	0.200	0.165
Canada	0.439	0.641	0.438	0.506
Kazakhstan	-	0.050	0.358	0.204
Kyrgyzstan	-	0.101	0.020	0.061
Croatia	-	0.003	0.003	0.003
Columbia	0.010–0.012	n.d.	n.d.	0.011
Latvia	-	n.d.	0.003	0.003
Lithuania	-	n.d.	0.003	0.003
Mexico	0.050	0.040	0.080–0.090	0.058
Moldavia	-	0.007	n.d.	0.007
Namibia	0.020	0.023	0.030	0.024
Paraguay	0.125	0.038	0.166	0.110
Peru	0.005	n.d.	n.d.	0.005
Philippines	n.d.	0.001	n.d.	0.001
Poland	1.100	0.523	0.150	0.591
Puerto Rico	n.d.	0.001	n.d.	0.001
Rumania	0.200–0.220	0.045	0.045	0.100
Russia	-	0.647	0.862	0.756
Serbia	-	n.d.	0.005	0.005
Slovakia	-	0.005	0.006	0.006
Slovenia	-	0.002	0.002	0.002
South Africa	0.041	0.012	0.300–0.500	0.151
Tajikistan	-	Named, n.f.	n.d.	-
Czech Republic	-	0.039	0.030	0.035
Ukraine	-	0.038	0.035	0.037
Hungary	0.220	0.033–0.088	0.035–0.200	0.133
Uruguay	0.008–0.009	0.029	n.d.	0.019
USA	1.610	1.488	1.100	1.395
Uzbekistan	-	0.040	n.d.	0.040
Venezuela	0.025	Named, n.f.	n.d.	0.025
Totals	6.114–7.153	7.870–7.925	6.523–6.968	7.493

Note: "n.d." = no data; "n.f." = no figures

(*Sources*: Born/ Dickgiesser 1989; *Ethnologue* 2009; "Deutsche Sprache" in Wikipedia: de.wikipedia.org/wiki/Deutsche Sprache: 17f.)

Czechoslovakia, Hungary). My reinterpretation into German-speakers probably leads to an overestimate of the figures, primarily in the last-named categories. It should also be noted that there are smaller groups of native speakers of German in other countries ("*Streudeutschtum*" [scattered German (ethnicity)]; Kloss 1935), which are not included here.

The estimated total number of native speakers and SL speakers of German of 103.5 m is obtained by adding the figures from Tables C.1–1 and C.1–2 (96 m in the official-language territory of German +7.5 m outside).

In the often cited sources for corresponding figures, the data are somewhat lower, – at least for the most recent period, perhaps even too low – e.g. for the total number of German native speakers: around 92 m (*Fischer Weltalmanach* 1990: 758; Finkenstaedt/ Schröder 1990: 14); 100, 95 and 90 m (*Ethnologue* 2000, 2005 and 2009), and 101 m (Haarmann 2002a: 33). Haarmann presumably includes SL speakers, at least for Germany (ibid: 74). In *Ethnologue* (2000, 2005, 2009), figures for German SL speakers are also named expressly, and in fact in all three editions at a consistent 28 m. Accordingly, the figures for native speaker + SL speakers add up to, respectively, 128, 123 and 118 m. All in all, this results in a declining trend in view of the shrinking number of native speakers.

It is difficult enough to determine figures for native speakers and SL speakers of languages, especially large languages. However, the difficulties are considerably greater in the case of FL speakers. As suggested at the start of the chapter, this does not mean FL learners. On the contrary, it is those people who have learnt the language as a foreign language and a) still master it, but b) have not become SL speakers or native speakers. To explain b) with an example: a Turkish woman who learnt German as a foreign language (GFL) as a child in Turkey and now lives in Germany, is no longer counted in the group of German FL speakers but is a German SL speaker. She will also be registered as such through our data collection method in the separate data for the official-language territory of Germany.

It is much harder to deal with criterion a) of adequate competence in German, on the basis of which German-speakers could be distinguished from non-speakers of German. This demarcation by specifying a minimum competence, is therefore even more urgent than in the case of SL speakers, because considerably larger numbers and corresponding possibilities for distortion are involved. For the dichotomy into speakers and non-speakers, with regard to SL speakers, I have already suggested competence level B1 of the Common European Reference Framework ("can converse simply and coherently on familiar topics and areas of personal interest"). To avoid inconsistency, this same competence level should also be used to define FL speakers. I shall resist giving further details, which are not relevant for the present, practical purpose of counting speakers. Regarding the worldwide figures, which concern us here, it is not currently possible to determine representative levels of competence of German FL (GFL) learners, especially former learners.

The following overall figures are totalled from all states offering GFL tuition. Since they often originate from official school and university statistics, they can, cautiously, be evaluated as reliable (for data quality, see also Ch. K.7).

Figures for GFL learners worldwide are available for the following years:

- 1982/ 83: around 16.8 m (precisely 16,836,172 = total of the columns for the different types of learners in *Report* 1985: 46f);
- 1995: 17.5 m (precisely 17,476,665 = total of the columns for the different types of learners in the Goethe Institute 2000: last page, no page numbers);
- 2000: around 20.2 m (precisely 20,167,616; StADaF 2005: 15);
- 2005: around 16.7 m (precisely 16,718,701; StADaF 2005: 15);

- 2010: around 14.5 m (precisely 14,500,940) (Netzwerk Deutsch + supplements shown to me by the Goethe Institute);
- 2015: 15,455,452 (Foreign Office, Bulletin 6010:16).

A helpful reference point for actual GFL speakers (from competence level B1 of the Common European Reference Framework) could be provided by estimates of how many current or former GFL learners use German regularly to any extent. But, to my knowledge, the only estimate was made many years ago. It is based on annual reports from overseas branches of the Federal Republic of Germany in 1982/ 83. Its reliability is doubtful because of lack of information on the method of data collection. The figure cited is around 40 m (*Report* 1985: 47; see also Witte 8 July 1987).

The upper limit for the required overall figure of GFL speakers is derived from the global sum of current GFL learners and former GFL learners who are still alive today. On one hand, one could start with an estimated average life expectancy, say 65 years (in 2008, the average life expectancy worldwide was around 68.9 years: de.Wikipedia.org/wiki/Lebenserwartung). On the other hand, the average start of learning should perhaps be set at 15 years of age, providing a period of 50 years for the totality of GFL learners to be included, extending from 1965 to 2015. From the learner figures named above, a yearly average of around 17 m learners would thus be obtained for this period (assuming learner figures similar to 1982/ 83 dating back to 1965). Now, what is still required is an average learning period, which could perhaps be set at around three years, so that the period of 50 years would accommodate around 17 generations of learners. With 17 generations, we would have a total figure of approximately 289 m former and current GFL learners still living today (with 25 generations: 425 m learners). If a certain reality value for today can still be ascribed to the earlier estimated figure for users, and therefore speakers, of German of 40 m, and if this is assumed to be a lower limit because of the subsequent, higher learner figures, the numerical ranges for worldwide GFL speakers – which are now fictional rather than speculative – would be:

40–145 m (taking half of the 289 m learners as speakers); or
40–289 m (quite unrealistically taking all learners as speakers).

If the numbers of native speakers estimated in this manner, including SL speakers (Table C.2–1), and our speculative figures for GFL speakers (40–145 m) are added, the following total figure for speakers of German (native speakers, SL speakers and FL speakers) is obtained as ranging from 143.5 to 248.5 m.

In this context, the total number of learners is not included. However, "mere" GFL learners, who are not German-speakers, because they have never reached an adequate level of competence or have lost it again, should also be considered. In fact, these are people who have become more familiar with German-speaking countries, their language and culture than people who have never learnt German. They thus represent a certain potential for international contact which could be worth investigating for German-speaking countries and their inhabitants. An order of magnitude of around 300 m still-living former + current learners is therefore not unreasonable. Thinking about these people, who have already had contact with German language and culture, and at least selectively considering them where possible, also falls within the sustainable promotion of the global position of German (Ch. K).

2. Speaker numbers of German compared with other languages

The following comparison is based on existing data. Ch. C.1 showed how difficult it is to determine speaker numbers, especially with larger languages. The total figures for German, which

Table C.2–1 Speaker numbers for German compared with other languages (in m)

Muller 1964			Culbert 1977		Ethnologue 1984		Comrie 1987	
1.	Chinese	515	Chinese	821	Chinese	700	Chinese	11,000
2.	English	265	English	369	English	391	English	300
3.	Hindi+Urdu	185	Hindi+Urdu	278	Spanish	211	Spanish	280
4.	Spanish	145	Russian	246	Hindi+Urdu	194	Russian	215
5.	Russian	135	Spanish	225	Russian	154	Hindi+Urdu	200
6.	German	100	Arabic	134	Portuguese	120	Indonesian	200
7.	Japanese	95	Portuguese	133	German	119	Arabic	150
8.	Arabic	90	Bengali	131	Arabic	117	Portuguese	150
9.	Bengali	85	German	120	Japanese	117	Bengali	145
10.	Portuguese	85	Japanese	113	Indonesian	110	Japanese	115
11.	French	65	Indonesian	101	Bengali	102	German	103
12.	Italian	55	French	95	French	63	French	68

Dalby 1999/2000			Ethnologue 2005			Ethnologue 2009	
1.	Chinese	1,000	Chinese	873	1,051	Chinese	845.+178
2.	English	1,000	Hindi+Urdu	425	588	Spanish	329 (+60)
3.	Hindi+Urdu	900	English	309	508	English	328 (+?)
4.	Spanish	450	Spanish	322	382	Hindi+Urdu	243 (+224)
5.	Russian	320	Russian	145	255	Arabic	221 (+246)
6.	Arabic	250	Arabic	206	246	Bengali	181 (+69)
7.	Bengali	250	Bengali	171	211	Portuguese	178 (+15)
8.	Portuguese	200	Portuguese	177	192	Russian	144 (+110)
9.	Japanese	130	Indonesian	23	163	Japanese	122 (+1)
10.	German	125	Japanese	122	123	German	90 (+28)
11.	French	125	German	95	123	French	68 (+50)
12.	Italian	70	French	65	115	Italian	62 (+?)

I collated from previous research, agree approximately with other sources. But for the other languages included in this chapter, especially for Spanish and French, the figures often diverge widely. In this context, very high figures often originate from sources with vested language-policy interests. Native countries of languages, the associated institutions and individuals tend to exaggerate because large speaker numbers motivate continued learning of the language and support claims for an advantaged position of the language, e.g. in international organisations or school curricula. To limit distortions which might privilege individual languages, I have limited myself to sources which supply figures for all languages relevant to our context not just individual languages. But even this limitation does not guarantee a neutral perspective and certainly does not guarantee uniform methods of data collection.

In many cases, the speaker number for a language refers only to the number of native speakers, without this always being derivable from the sources, but this may explain some of the low figures, especially for English, French and to some extent German. If SL speakers had been included, the figures would have to be higher. The inclusion of SL speakers in Table C.2–1 is only certain in the case of Dalby (1999/ 2000), *Ethnologue* (2005, column 2), at least in part in *Ethnologue* (1984; e.g. 315: "probably includes second-language speakers and Low German)" and in *Ethnologue* (2009). For some languages, Comrie (1987) gives figures only for individual regions which I have added to the named total speaker numbers.

Ethnologue, which is the most comprehensive inventory of languages in the world, tends towards language splitting (glottotomy). For example, German dialects are shown as independent languages. Alongside disputable cases such as "German, Swiss" or "Saxon, Low" (compare Ch. B.1), these include "Bavarian", "Saxon, Upper", "*Kölsch*", "*Mainfränkisch*", "*Pfaelzisch*" and "Swabian" (*Ethnologue* 2009: 553–555). To counteract this splitting, I have taken comprehensive data for all varieties where indicated, but otherwise, figures for the standard variety. Accordingly, for Arabic, e.g. in *Ethnologue* (1984), I have added figures for "Eastern Colloquial Arabic", "North Eastern Colloquial Arabic", "Western Colloquial Arabic", "Sudanese Arabic" and "Egyptian"; however, from *Ethnologue* 2005 (page 508) onwards, figures were available for "Arabic Standard". Throughout, I have also combined figures for Hindi and Urdu (language: Hindi-Urdu). In *Ethnologue* 2009, there are no data for "L2 speakers" (SL speakers) of English and Italian. With some other languages, the figures for the standard variety differ from those for the totality of varieties. For instance, for "Chinese, Mandarin", there are 845,456,760 "L1 speakers" (native speakers), with the addition of 178 m "L2 speakers" (ibid: 339), however, 1.213 m for all varieties of "Chinese", which seems to refer to native speakers (ibid: 20). Presumably, the large figure includes those "varieties" which would be evaluated orally according to linguistic distance as different languages, but which are mutually intelligible in writing because of the same (ideographic) writing system (compare Ch. B.1). For "Arabic, Standard", there are 206 m "L1 speakers" (ibid: 523); but for "Arabic" in the sense of all Arabic varieties, 221 m and 246 m L2 speakers of all Arabic varieties" (ibid: 21, 523). For Bengali, without distinguishing between standard and other varieties, there are 181,272,900 "L1 speakers" and, "including L2 speakers", 250 m (ibid: 21, 328). Because of the incomplete data on SL speakers, *Ethnologue* does not allow a comprehensive comparison of languages. Relevant data in Table C.2–1 (last column) are shown in brackets; the unbracketed data relate only to native speakers.

According to these findings, based on the number of native speakers, German moves between positions six and 11 of all languages in the world. With the inclusion of SL speakers, French was recently neck and neck with German (*Ethnologue* 2009), and in fact in position ten, which German had previously shared with Japanese (*Ethnologue* 2005). However, there are many much higher figures for French, which evidently include FL speakers (Ch. A.3) or even FL learners. By all accounts, Chinese, English, Hindi-Urdu (also only Hindi), Spanish and Russian are ahead of German; in some cases, their speaker number is many times greater than that of German. Arabic, Portuguese, Bengali and Japanese are only ahead of German according to some of the sources, but these are the more recent ones. The long-term trend gives an impression that German is dropping back in rank position; this question will be taken up again in Ch. C.3. However, the long-term trend does not explain all fluctuations in speaker numbers; short-term fluctuations are presumably determined by differences in the inclusion of SL-speakers or the projection of older figures.

Comparing the languages named in Table C.2–1 with the very high-ranking international languages (Ch. A.7; F.1; G.1; H.1) reveals the following correlation: internationally important languages simultaneously belong to the group of the numerically strongest languages. Languages which play a leading role in international economic, academic or diplomatic communication are all among the 12 numerically strongest languages in the world. It should be borne in mind that at least 2,500 languages are currently still spoken in the world (Ch. A.7). However, there are also marked discrepancies between numerical strength (based on native speakers and SL-speakers) and international rank. On one hand, the numerically strong languages Hindi-Urdu and Bengali hardly play a role in international communication (Ch. A.3). Conversely, English and French are considerably more important than several numerically stronger languages. In this respect, English surpasses all other languages, and French possibly all apart from English.

A closer correlation between international importance and numerical strength could be secured if numerical strength including FL speakers could be determined. However, figures for different languages are not available for this comparison. I have only been able to estimate approximately the number of current FL learners, as per Table J.7–3 (Ch. J.7; also Ammon 2010c: 105). Many of these figures may have been overtaken already or will be in the near future. Caution is therefore required with regard to inflated expectations relating to vested interests. For example, it may be questioned whether the Chinese-government prognosis (2006: 63) that the learner number for Chinese as a foreign language "[will] rise to around 100 m in the next few years", will be fulfilled. Above all, learner numbers must on no account be equated with the numbers of actual FL-speakers (Ch. A.3; C.1).

3. Long-term development of speaker numbers of large European languages

Disregarding fluctuations, Table C.2–1 shows significant changes over time. In the 45 years registered, the speaker numbers of Chinese, Arabic, Bengali, Hindi-Urdu, Portuguese and Spanish have grown more than those of German and Japanese. This corresponds to population growth in the native-speaker and official-language territories of these languages. The distance between those languages and German has thus continued to increase, e.g. for Spanish, it has more than doubled from 1:1.45 to 1:3.66; for Chinese, it increased by 40%, from 1:5.15 to 1:8.67 (in each case *Ethnologue* 2009 compared with Muller 1964). This lag in the development of German is also evident in world population and presumably began towards the end of the nineteenth century. Its course is approximately proportional to global population which grows more strongly in developing countries than industrial countries. The numerical proportion of German native speakers and SL speakers to the world population in 1925 was still around 5% (1:20; Winkler 1927: 26) and is currently just under 1.5% (Ch. C.1: 103.5 m by comparison with more than 7 bn). Analysis of longer term development requires: 1) speaker numbers of German relative to other languages; 2) speaker numbers of German relative to world population. For 1), I only have figures for six European languages, i.e. not for all the current international languages (cf. Ch. A.7). For Portuguese and all non-European languages, older figures are not available. Figure C.3–1 shows the development of six European languages since 1500.

Regrettably, Jespersen does not indicate sources – apart from Tesnière (1928) for 1926 (Jespersen 1933: 229, Note 1). It is also unclear whether he means only native speakers. In Figure C.3–1, the highest numbers named by Jespersen are given in brackets, the lowest without brackets. Similar figures occur in Burney (1966: 67).

It is faintly evident from Figure C.3–1 and Table C.3–1 that German had high speaker numbers at two periods: around 1500, level with French; and, around 1800, as the numerically strongest language. In the intervening period, it was surpassed by French and then by English (Table C.3–1). Might it be possible to show a causal connection between the larger reservoir of German native speakers and the cultural flourishing in the German-language territory? Around 1500, this would mean the humanism inspired by the Italian Renaissance and the Reformation; and around 1800, German Classicism. Moreover, Goethe, an exponent of German Classicism, emphasised the international position and cultural standing of his language which was perhaps apprehended even at the start of the nineteenth century. Around 1825, he welcomed an English "engineering officer" on a visit to Weimar saying, "you have done well [. . .] coming over to us to learn German [. . .]". The visitor told Goethe that, in England, interest in German had become so great "that there is hardly a young English gentleman of good family who is not learning German". Goethe replied, "If someone understands German well, he can do

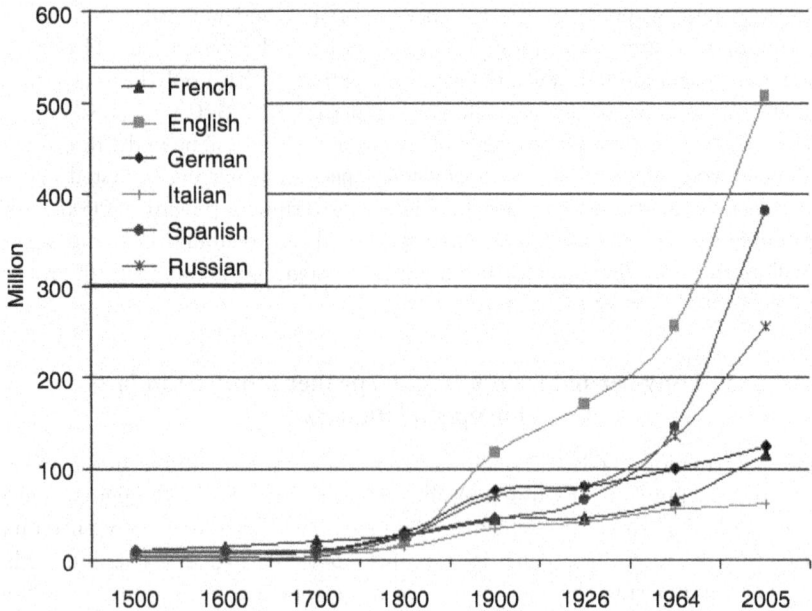

Figure C.3–1 Numbers of speakers of major European Languages over time
(*Sources:* Jespersen 1933; Muller 1964; *Ethnologue* 2005)

Table C.3–1 Long-term development of speaker numbers of six European languages in millions

Language Year	English	German	Russian	French	Spanish	Italian
1500	4 (5)	**10**	3	10 (12)	8.5	9.5
1600	6	10	3	14	8.5	9.5
1700	8.5	10	3 (15)	20	8.5	9.5 (11)
1800	20 (40)	**30** (33)	25 (31)	27 (31)	26	14 (15)
1900	116 (123)	75 (80)	70 (85)	45 (52)	44 (58)	34 (54)
1926	170	80	80	45	65	41

(*Source:* after Jespersen 1933: 229)

without many other languages", because "we can now "read the most excellent works [. . .] in good German translations". Goethe expressly stated that only French could not be replaced by German, because it "is the language of commerce and is especially indispensable on journeys" (*Eckermann's Conversations with Goethe*, 1825, Geiger, L. (ed.) (1902) Leipzig: Hesse, 101f). Other historical contemporaries confirm this interest in German among the British. For example, reporting on an English travel company on the Lower Rhine in the 1820s, Johanna Schopenhauer (1828: 128) describes "children whose education is to be completed on tour. Because learning German is now the fashion in England; in Godesberg I saw a family with three or four boys and girls who wanted to spend the next winter in Innsbruck to have their children tutored in German".

Table C.3–2 Long-term development of speaker numbers of German in proportion to world population

1500	2%	10:	500 m
1800	3%	30:	1000 m
1927	4%	80:	2000 m
1960	3.3%	100:	3000 m
1987	2.7%	133:	5000 m
1999	2.1%	125:	6000 m
2011	1.5%	104:	7000 m

Note: German native speakers as percentage of world population, speaker numbers 1500 to 1926

(*Sources*: after Jespersen 1933: 229; from 1964, after Muller 1964, for 1987, after *Ethnologue* 1984, for 1999, after Dalby 1999/2000, for 2011, as per Ch. C.1 end)

By contrast, the high speaker numbers for French and English (Table C.3–1) each correlate positively – at least roughly – with phases of political dominance of the native countries. Second position, behind each of the numerically strongest European languages, is typical for German. The previously low figures for Russian and English are also remarkable. For Jespersen, Portuguese was not worth mentioning because, in his day, colonial activities of native countries hardly impacted on the speaker numbers of their languages.

The speaker numbers for German during the approximately 500-year period initially rose relative to world population and then, from around the middle of the twentieth century, declined again. This relative decline is likely to continue in future decades. Around 1500, the world population was some 500 m (UN estimate); it only "surpassed 1 billion people [. . .] in 1804". During the twentieth century, the global population almost quadrupled. 1927: 2 bn, 1960: 3 bn, 1974: 4 bn, 1987: 5 bn, 1999: 6 bn, 2011: 7 bn. "With a mean projection up to 2025, the UNO anticipates [. . .] 8.17 billion, and 10.9 billion by 2100" (de.wikipedia.org/wiki/Weltv%C3%B6lkerung). The sequence of proportions shown in Table C.3–2 is derived from Tables C.2–1 and C.3–1, without the – uncertain – prognoses for future decades.

4. Comparing the economic strength of language communities

In addition to speaker numbers, the economic strength (GNP) of a language is a significant factor for global position. As with numerical strength, this refers, more precisely, to the economic strength of the speakers or language community. The term "numerical and economic strength of a language" is used for short. International contacts with a language community – commercial, academic, diplomatic and so on – tend to be more intensive if it has greater economic strength at its disposal.

Table C.4–1 gives an overview of existing data and figures collected specially for this book (Mackey 1976; Ammon 1991a: 49, also for 2005 and 2009). The figures are not comparable throughout. Mackey (1976: 199–220) is not primarily concerned with the ten economically strongest language communities in the world at his time because Japanese is missing, and several numerically strong languages (Chinese, Hindi-Urdu, Bengali and Portuguese) are not included. Moreover, Mackey's figures relate to the purchasing power of speakers, while the subsequent figures relate to their gross national product (GNP). These were based on *Ethnologue* (1984, 2005, 2009), which gives speaker numbers for languages in every state in the world. The gross national product for the states was taken from the *Fischer Weltalmanach* 1990, 2007 and 2012; for individual, small states, the gross domestic product was used by way of assistance. Since the

Table C.4–1 Development of economic strength of economically strongest language communities in recent years

c	1975		1984		2005		2009	
1.	English	944	English	4,271	English	12.717	English	14,187
2.	Russian	266	Japanese	1,277	Japanese	4.598	Chinese	5,379
3.	German	204	German	1,090	German	3.450	Japanese	5,029
4.	French	141	Russian	801	Spanish	3.204	Spanish	5,001
5.	Spanish	88	Spanish	738	Chinese	2.399	German	4,257
6.	Italian	78	French	669	French	2.215	French	3,109
7.	Dutch	37	Chinese	448	Italian	1.207	Portuguese	1,866
8.	Arabic	26	Arabic	359	Arabic	985	Arabic	1,703
9.			Italian	302	Portuguese	872	Italian	1,687
10.			Portuguese	234	Russian	584	Russian	1,185
11.			Dutch	203	Hindi-Urdu	215		
12.			Hindi-Urdu	102	Bengali	113		

(*Sources*: Mackey 1976; *Ethnologue* 1984 and Fischer Weltalmanach 1990; *Ethnologue* 2005 and Fischer Weltalmanach 2007; *Ethnologue* 2009 and Fischer Weltalmanach 2012)

data in the *Fischer Weltalmanach* show a delay, they were matched as accurately as possible to the publication year of *Ethnologue*. For each state, the gross national product per head of population was calculated (total GNP: population) and then multiplied by the speaker numbers of the respective language in the relevant state (= economic strength of the language community in the relevant state). Finally, all values determined for each language across all the states in the world were added (= economic strength of the language in total). It can be assumed that Graddol (1997: 28f.) calculated the economic strength of languages in about the same manner for 1994, but without specifying sources and method.

Regarding changes over the 34-year period, which I mention here only for the higher-ranking languages, the enduring stability of German in position 3 is particularly noticeable (1984 to 2005). German has only recently been relegated from this "customary" position, very evidently by Chinese and to a lesser extent by Spanish. Relegation by Chinese is hardly surprising given China's rise to a world economic power of currently similar rank to the USA. Its economic advantage over German (2009 approximately 21%) has become even greater since 2009. However, it may be exaggerated for 2009, because the calculation was based not only on speaker numbers for Mandarin, but also for all varieties of Chinese (1,213 m by comparison with 845 m native speakers +178 m SL-speakers; cf. Ch. C.2). The fact that German has also been economically overtaken by Spanish – although not to such a great extent – is perhaps more surprising in view of recent reports on economic weaknesses of Spain and Latin American countries. Maybe these weaknesses have been compensated by population growth in the Latin-American countries (see Ch. C.5), which could mean that the rising popularity of Spanish as a foreign language (Ch. J.7) stands on a more stable foundation than flamenco and beach holidays.

5. Comparison of economic strength with numerical strength

As suggested in Ch. C.4, the ranking of language communities according to economic strength (GNP) does not coincide with ranking by numerical strength (speaker numbers). This is shown by comparison of Table C.2–1 with Table C.4–1 (Ch. C.2; C.4). Figures C.5–1 and C.5–2

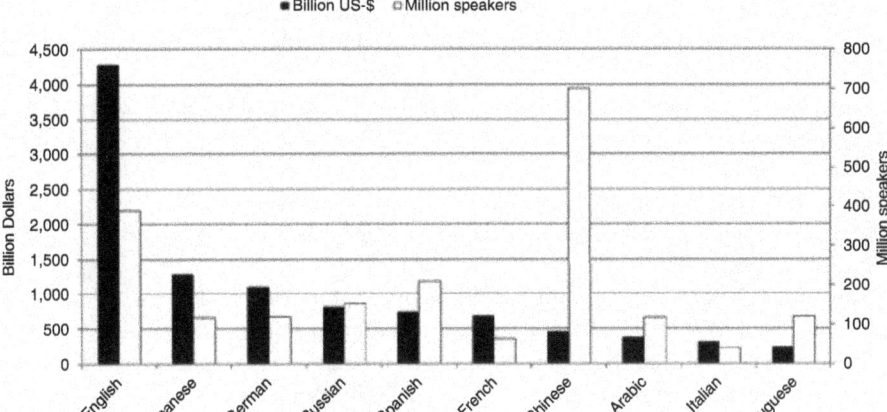

Figure C.5–1 Economic strength of German-language community compared with other language communities around 1984 in billion US $

(*Sources: Ethnologue* 1984 and Fischer Weltalmanach 1990)

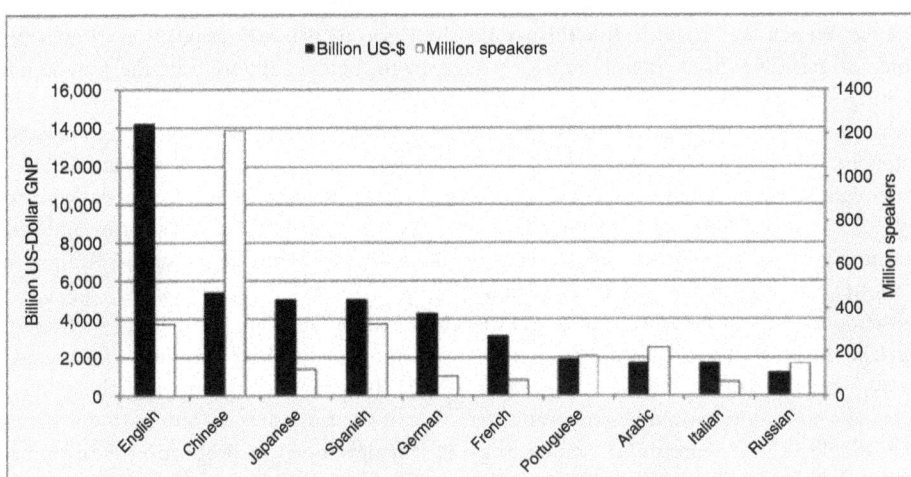

Figure C.5–2 Economic strength of German-language community compared with other language communities around 2009 in billion US $

(*Sources: Ethnologue* 2009 and Fischer Weltalmanach 2012)

illustrate the comparison for the two years included, with data for economic and numerical strength.

Of particular relevance here is the decline in economic strength of the German-language community from position 3 to position 5. A simultaneous decline in speaker numbers from position 7 to 10 is relevant to this explanation. The parallelism suggests that the decline in economic ranking is determined by the decline in numerical ranking which may even be the principal factor. In the period from 1984 to 2009, German lagged economically behind Chinese and, albeit slightly, behind Spanish, which it still outranked in 1984 – and even in 2005 (cf. Table C.4–1).

In detail, in the period 1984–2009, the proportions varied as follows (cf. C.2–1, C.4–1 – data less rounded here).

Chinese: German;

Numerical 13.5 (2009) : 6.9 (1984) (growth quota of proportions 1.9);

Economic 1.3 (2009 : 0.4 (1984) growth quota of proportions 3.3);

Spanish: German;

Numerical 3.7 (2009) : 1.8 (1984) (growth quota of proportions 2.1);

Economic 1.2 (2009) : 0.7 (1984) (growth quota of proportions 1.7).

The figures suggest that the Chinese-language community overtook German in economic terms primarily through stronger economic growth (GNP). With Spanish, however, it was primarily through stronger numerical growth (speaker numbers). In this period, the Chinese-language community grew economically stronger than the German, while Spanish grew primarily in terms of population/speaker numbers.

The difference between the Chinese- and the English-language communities is also evident. With Chinese, numerical ranking far exceeds economic; for English, this is reversed. But with the German-language community, economic position is stronger than numerical, and the same applies for Japanese, German, French and – to a lesser extent – also Spanish. This finding suggests that the Chinese-language community has greater economic growth potential than the English, Japanese, French and Spanish. But this would always occur if future population growth were subject to narrower limits than pure economic growth. This is supported by the now familiar warnings about global overpopulation, which seem better founded than the equally familiar warnings about continuing economic growth, as the associated ecological damage may ultimately be controllable with new technologies. Moreover, population growth has flattened in the more highly developed countries, so that additional economic growth is unlikely (de.wikipedia. org/wiki/Bev%C3%B6lkerungsexplosion). This applies primarily for the countries under discussion here: the English-speaking, German-speaking, Japanese-speaking, French-speaking, and to a lesser extent Spanish-speaking countries.

Various indicators have even suggested that the Chinese-language community will one day overtake the entire English-language community economically. This possibility is illustrated by the two pairs of bars in Figures C.5–1 and C.5–2. The economic strength of the Chinese-language community would be far greater than that of the English – according to our data for 2009 (Table C.2–1) – around 3.7 times as great, if it developed in proportion with numerical strength. During the period between the two Figs., i.e. within 25 years, the proportions have declined from 9.6:1 to 2.6:1. Recent economic-growth data suggest that this decline will continue. However, a linear projection would be dubious. Above all, it must therefore be assumed – as has been routinely observed during the "maturing" of underdeveloped economies into developed economies – that the economic growth rate of Chinese will decline over time. One notable example is Japan, whose economic growth, as it approached the technological level of competitor states, also slowed down to their rate of growth. Instead of linear modelling, a logarithmic modelling with a flattening course would presumably be closer to reality.

An ultimately even more serious objection to the present prognosis can be constructed if our previous scale for the economic strength of a language or language community is seen as being limited to native speakers and SL speakers (Ch. C.4). If FL-speakers were included, English could not even be approached by Chinese. Learners and speakers of English as a foreign language far exceed FL speakers of Chinese, even including native and SL speakers and show a tendency to expand further in the direction of the total world population (cf. Ch. A.7; Graddol 2000, 2006; Crystal 2003). If its economic potential is included in the measurement of economic strength, English will remain – so far as can be estimated at present – the economically strongest language with a strong lead for an undefined period. But the relationship between economic strength and language communities no longer fits so neatly, unless the concept of language community is expressly expanded to include FL speakers. Then the terms "economic strength of *language X*" and "economic strength of *speakers of language X*" (including FL speakers) would be synonymous and probably clearer.

D

GERMAN AS THE OFFICIAL LANGUAGE OF STATE

1. Explanation of terms and overview of countries with German as an official language of state

As with speaker numbers and economic strength (Ch. C), the number and size of countries in which a language is the official language of state can also be used for characterisation or as an indicator of global position (e.g. Conrad/ Fishman 1977: 7–13; Haut Conseil 1986: 14f.; Jernudd 1987). In the case of several countries with the same official language, this will be preferred for "international communication in the wider sense" (internationally, but not interlingually; Ch. A.3). With otherwise identical conditions, this also increases the probability that others will have contact with this language and experience its communication potential, which can therefore motivate learning of the language (Ch. A.7). Anchorage within several states is thus a potentially position-strengthening factor. It can play a part in guaranteeing a privileged position in international organisations or conferences (Ch. H.3). It can also influence curriculum decisions on foreign languages to be learnt. Every state also grants protection and promotion to its official languages, not least through the associated preferential position within the school system (Kloss 1969b: 549). These factors can all strengthen the global position of the language and also its survival chances in each country. Only languages which are not official languages of state anywhere are seriously threatened with "extinction" by falling completely out of use (Ch. E).

Useful definitions of the term "official language of state" are to be found in Conrad/ Fishman (1977: 7–13) and in Korkisch (1978). For example, the status of official language of state may be *declared* or not. In this context, it is significant in which laws an official language of state is declared (e.g. in the constitution or only in lower-ranking provisions). Official-language status can also be restricted to given domains. However, unless more narrowly defined, it generally includes government and parliament, state administration, legal system, executive (police) and military, which are therefore sometimes designated as *official domains*. In almost all cases, the official state language is also the language of instruction in school or at least an obligatory school subject, at least in state schools. But status as an official language regulates only official, formal use in the relevant domains, not private, informal communication.

A declared official language can be determined more readily than a merely functional (de facto) official language, which may require more detailed empirical investigation. Function need not necessarily be declared, but is generally sufficiently clear, so that this difference can mostly be ignored in counts of official languages, as here in Ch. D.4. This is also true of the terminological contrast between *(official) status* (declared) and *official function* (de facto) (Conrad/ Fishman 1977: 8; Fasold 1984: 20, 72). Occasionally, a distinction is made between "official languages" and "working languages", where the latter have only the relevant function, without needing to be correspondingly declared, or special functions, for which they are also declared. Such demarcations are found primarily in international organisations or in the institutions of groups of states like the EU (Ch. H.3; H.4.2).

Accordingly, there are at least three combinations of official status and official function – where official status in the complete absence of official function hardly ever occurs:

(i) Official status with subordinate official function (e.g. Swahili in Kenya; *inter alia*, all parliamentary resolutions must be formulated in English; Ogechi 2003: 287);
(ii) Official function without official status (e.g. English in Malaysia, subsidiary alongside dominant Malayan);
(iii) Official status and full official function (e.g. English in Canada).

In the case of a single official language, it can be specified as *sole-official* by contrast with *co-official*, or more precisely, also as *co-official with one other language, co-official with two other languages* etc. A state with official language La can also be designated as an *official-language state of La* – terminologically not yet current. However, further differentiation of this term with reference to sole-official and co-official status is awkward. Unless greater precision is required, all states with La as official language can be subsumed under the term *official-language states of La*, whether sole-official or co-official. For example, for German, Switzerland is then also included alongside Germany. If required, a further differentiation can be made to the effect that, for German, there are three *sole-official* and four *co-official-language states* (Germany, Austria, Liechtenstein and respectively Switzerland, Luxembourg, Italy, Belgium). However, on one hand, such formulations lead to terminological confusion and, on the other hand, they do not take the important distinction into account.

I refer here to the difference between *national* and *regional official language*. This difference must not be confused with the difference between "sole-official and co-official". For example, German is the national official language in Germany, Austria and Luxembourg, but, in Austria, it is sole-official and in Luxembourg co-official (Ch. D.2.2; D.2.5); in Belgium and Italy, by contrast, German is a regional official language, but in Belgium (in the German-speaking community), it is sole-official and, in Italy (in the province of South Tyrol), it is co-official (Ch. D.3.1; D.3.2). The situation in Switzerland is more complicated, where German is, in fact, co-official but still a national official language; however, the "territoriality principle" restricts its use regionally (Ch. D.2.4). It is national official language on the basis of status and function in the government and in the federal parliament (in Bern), and indeed for the whole of Switzerland; and it is regionally restricted to German-speaking Switzerland for the other official domains and language of instruction in school.

Before 21 March 1990, German also had an official status in Namibia, for which I have previously also used the term *regional official language* (Ammon 1991a: 75–80). In fact, when granted, reference was made to the "territory of the whites", to which this status – with racist overtones evidently influenced by the South African policy of *apartheid* – was restricted. However, this "territory" lacked the clear definition generally required for the term *regional official language*. When Namibia achieved full national independence after the victory of the *South West Africa People's Organisation* (SWAPO) (21 March 1990, Declaration of Independence), German lost that official status. However, in Namibia, German still has the declared status of a *national language*, in acknowledgement that its speakers (native speakers) represent a significant, indigenous ethnic group, i.e. people already settled there before the foundation of the state (Ch. E.4.9).

It is important to distinguish the term *national language* from the term *official language* and, for the next chapter, Ch. E, also from the term *minority language*. Its essential feature is its symbolism for the nation (see Ch. A.3). One prerequisite is generally that the relevant language is the native language of an "important" part of the national population. In this context, importance does not necessarily require a high speaker number (numerical strength), but, rather, importance for the history of the nation state. Another prerequisite is indigenousness, generally taken to mean presence before the foundation of the state (Ch. E.1). This is the case with German in Namibia. A national language can therefore be a majority or a minority language. Furthermore, by analogy with an official language, it may be declared as such or not (*declared* versus *de facto* national language, also *de-jure* versus *de facto national language*), where a reliable specification of the non-declared bare fact is often more difficult here than for official languages. A national language can be, but need not be, a national or regional official language at the same time (Heine 1979: 15–18). In Luxembourg, for example, Luxembourgish is both the declared national language and also the declared national official language, while German and French are only the latter. They are used only for official communication, but are not national symbols for Luxembourg (Ch. D.2.5).

Luxembourg is the only state in which German is the national official language but neither a national language nor the native language of a significant part of the population, held to be important for the history of the country. Conrad and Fishman (1977: 6) proposed the number of such countries (in which a language is a national official language but not a national or important native language) as a possible indicator, alongside others, for the degree of internationalism of a language. According to this criterion, German would evidently not have a high-ranking.

In every state (apart from Luxembourg) in which it is the national official language, German is also the national language, at least de facto (not necessarily declared as such); i.e. it is the native language of an important, indigenous part of the population; in fact, this is always the majority of the population. However, in the case of official-language status at merely regional level, its position as a national language often remains doubtful. This is true for German in Belgium and also in Italy.

Finally, with regard to terminology, it must be added that, in German, *Staatssprache* [language of state] is also used synonymously with *nationale Amtssprache* [national official language] (Glück 2010: 665). But I do not usually use these terms except in quotations (the latter, e.g. for Austria and Liechtenstein; Ch. D.2.2, D.2.3). I proceed in a similar manner with the term *Landessprache*, which is sometimes encountered instead of *national language* or instead of *regional official language*.

These terms allow the following overview of all states in which German has a special status (apart from that of a foreign language or the German diaspora). The names of states are always given in alphabetical order:

National official language, sole-official:

- Austria, Germany, Liechtenstein (Ch. D.2.1–D.2.3);

National official language, co-official:

- Luxembourg (with French, Luxembourgish), Switzerland (with French, Italian, Romansch) (Ch. D.2.4; D.2.5);

Regional official language, sole-official:

- Belgium (German-speaking community) (Ch. D.3.1);

Regional official language, co-official:

- Italy (Province of South Tyrol, with Italian) (Ch. D.3.2);

National language:

- Austria, (Belgium?), Germany, (Italy?), Liechtenstein, Namibia, Switzerland (Ch. D.2.1–D.3.2);

Minority language, but not official language of state:

- Argentina, Australia, Belize, Bolivia, Bosnia and Herzegovina, Brazil, Canada, Chile, Croatia, Columbia, Denmark, Dominican Republic, Ecuador, Estonia, France (Alsace-Lorraine), Hungary, Israel, Kazakhstan, Kyrgyzstan, Latvia, Lithuania, Mexico, Moldavia, Namibia, Paraguay, Peru, Philippines, Poland, Puerto Rico, Rumania, Russia, Serbia, Slovakia, Slovenia, South Africa, Tajikistan, Czech Republic, Ukraine, Uruguay, USA, Uzbekistan, Venezuela (Ch. E; cf. also Ch. C.1 Table C.1–2).

Terms such as *states with German as official language* or *official-language states of German* generally mean the seven states with national or regional official language, i.e. (in alphabetical order) *Austria, Belgium, Germany, Italy, Liechtenstein, Luxembourg, Switzerland.* However, they are usually named in the sequence national > regional official language, larger > smaller speaker number, national language > not national language: *Germany, Austria, Switzerland, Liechtenstein, Luxembourg, Italy, Belgium.* The *German official-language territory* is then the entire territory of these states, or the respective parts, in which German is the official language of state – taking into consideration the territoriality principle and regional restrictions. In general, and also in the present book, unless specified otherwise, *German-speaking states* or, more often, *German-speaking countries*, include those with German as both national official language and also national language (distributed native language), i.e. *Austria, Germany, Liechtenstein and Switzerland* (also Ch. B.4). Map D.1–1 gives an overview of the national territories with German as an official language of the state.

2. German as a national official language

2.1 Germany

("Federal Republic of Germany; approximately 82 m inhabitants, of which 75 m German (91%) and 7 m foreigners (9%), with Turkish people as the largest group, 1.63 m": de.wikipedia.org/wiki/Deutschland.)

Before the reunification of Germany on 3 October 1990, German was the national official language in the territory of present-day Germany in three states or state-like political entities: The Federal Republic of Germany (FRG), The German Democratic Republic (GDR) and semi-independent West Berlin. A narrow-minded numerical approach might interpret reunification as a loss of national-official linguistic capital and therefore as a weakening of one of the pillars of the international position of German (Ch. D.1). But it is hardly necessary to point out the short-sightedness of this view, which ignores the economic, scientific, technical and political weight of the countries. However, the mere number of states in which a language has national official status can be relevant for language policy decisions, e.g. as an official language of the United Nations (Ch. H.3), as it happened in the case of Spanish and Arabic. Every member state of the United Nations participates in its decisions, as Article 18.1 of the charter rules: "Each member state of the General Assembly shall have one vote" (www.un.org/en/sections/un-charter/un-charter-full-text/).

German as an Official Language of the State

National official language

Regional official language

0   200 km

Cartography: Harald Krähe

Map D.1–1   German as the official language of state

In Germany – officially, *The Federal Republic of Germany*, because the former GDR joined the former FRG after reunification – German is the sole national official language. As the native language of the overwhelming majority (Ch. C.1), it is also the national language of Germany (Ch. D.1). Moreover, Germany is the only state, of which the name – or more precisely, the defining element of the name – coincides with the name of the language. To this extent, the position of *German* as national official language of state and also as national language in fact goes without saying. This is certainly a substantial reason why, in the "Basic Law of the Federal Republic of Germany", which serves as the constitution, there is no corresponding declaration. There are only various more specific provisions which regulate the official use of German:

Administrative Procedure Act (VwVfG), §23, and the 10th Social Code Book (SGB X), §19, respectively as the official language; the Notarisation Act, §5, as the language for notarial documents, and the Courts Constitution Act, §184, as the language of the court (de.wikipedia.org/wiki/Deutsche_Sprache#Deutschland).

However, for several years, the certainty which led the authors of the Basic Law to consider a Language Article in favour of German to be superfluous, has been undermined. Several events have presumably contributed: the spread of English as a lingua franca, in Europe and worldwide, as well as increasing use of English in Germany (H. Wagener 2012); the numerous migrants into the German-speaking states and their sometimes hesitant adoption of German; the language policy of France and its constitutional supplement through the addition of Paragraph 2 in 1992: "The language of the Republic is French" (www.culture.gouv.fr/culture/dglf/ressources/dates. htm); finally, the campaign in the USA for a "Constitutional Amendment" with a constitutional paragraph which was to declare English as the national official language. While the language paragraph in France is directed primarily against the regional languages and English, the corresponding campaign in the USA was an attempt to defend the English language against the Spanish imported by Latin American immigrants, but failed to secure a sufficient majority.

Even in Germany, concerns about the position of German are not just imaginary. The status of German as the national official language of state has not prevented German from coming under pressure from English in prestigious institutions or domains. This applies especially to universities, especially research communication, but also teaching (cf. Ch. G.1; G.3; G.8). Private sector research is also affected, with international companies or *Global Players* generally using English as the dominant language for communication, and – at least to some extent – in board meetings (Ch. F.7). Even in courts of law in Germany, English has recently been admitted as the language of negotiation, at least in commercial procedures in which non-German-speaking parties are present (*SZ* 27.01. 2010: 6; *FAZ* 10 February 2010: 19; 17 November 2010: 21; 9 January 2011. For English in Germany see also Hüllen 2007). Similar developments are evident in all states with Germany as an official language of state.

In view of such developments, demands have been voiced in Germany to amend the Basic Law with an article stating that: "The language of the Federal Republic of Germany is German". Such calls have possibly aroused interest in the German language and language generally among the population. Broad interest is evident from surveys (cf. Hoberg/ Eichhoff-Cyrus/ Schulz 2008: 41–43; Projektgruppe Spracheinstellungen 2011: 7–11, 47–49). Controversy about the amendment to the Basic Law raged among those committed to language even in the highest ranks of the political class. For example, in October 2010, a CDU party conference voted with a large majority for the language article in the Basic Law, while the party president and Federal Chancellor, Angela Merkel, opposed it: "I personally do not find it good to write everything into the Basic Law" (www.sueddeutsche.de/politik/cdu-vorstoss-aergert-merkel-deutsch-ins-grundgesetz-1.372377). The President of the Bundestag, Norbert Lammert, was an eloquent supporter, while the former president of the Federal Constitutional Court and subsequent president of the Goethe Institute, Jutta Limbach, decisively rejected the idea: "the proposed article in the constitution testifies only to narrowmindedness. It incorporates doubt into our most important constitutional document. Even the hoped-for symbolic function is unlikely to influence social behaviour" (Limbach 2008: 35, in-depth 34–38). So far, the Basic-Law amendment has not been resolved.

In Germany, agreement between the name of the country and the name of the language has presumably contributed to general self-assurance about German, also in the sense that, to some extent, this country holds dominion over the German language. This self-assurance in Germany has been and still is strengthened by the difference in size compared with the other

German-speaking countries. However, the attitude to the German language found in Germany is sometimes interpreted as arrogant. One aspect of this attitude is the opinion that the kind of German which is "correct" in Germany (Standard German, "*Hochdeutsch*") is considered, even if not current, then at least correct in all German-speaking countries. However, this judgement is false. It does apply for the spelling, to the extent that forms accepted in Germany are also acknowledged as correct in the other German-speaking countries; however, even in spelling, Austria and Switzerland have their own additional forms which each count as correct (e.g. *Kücken* alongside *Küken* in Austria, or generally *ss* instead of *ß* in Switzerland). Especially, in vocabulary, all German-speaking countries have national, in some cases also internal, regional (e.g. North German – South German) peculiarities in their standard German: so-called *national* and *regional variants*. These standard German peculiarities are "correct" German in the respective country or region. Germans are not generally aware of the peculiarities in their standard German, but words like *Abitur* [high school graduation], *Apfelsine* [orange], *Sonnabend* [Saturday] and many others are current only in Germany (details in Ammon/ Bickel/ Lenz 2013/16). In sociolinguistics, linguistic features which betray someone's group membership without the speakers themselves realising it are known as "shibboleths" – after an episode in the Bible, in which the victorious people of Gilead identified the conquered Ephraimites through their pronunciation of the word *shibboleth* (Hebrew for 'ear of wheat'). If they said [s] instead of [ʃ], they were taken for Ephraimites and executed (*Book of Judges* 12, 5–6).

In principle, the fact that one language has a monopoly as the national official language of a country does not exclude the possibility that other languages have an official status at lower, regional or communal levels. In large regions of Germany, primarily Low German and Sorbian enjoy declared official status at community level alongside German, to which they are, however, subordinate especially for contact with national institutions. Low German translations of the constitutions of some federal states are also available: for Mecklenburg-Pomerania, Brandenburg, Schleswig-Holstein, Hamburg and Bremen – but this does not imply an official status. Low German enjoys (limited) official status only in Schleswig-Holstein where local authorities must prepare and reply to enquiries and applications in Low German (de.wikipedia.org/wiki/Niederdeutsche_Sprache). However, Low German is not the regular language of instruction in any ordinary schools, which distinguishes it from a regional official language in the sense of Ch. D.1.

The situation is different in the case of Sorbian, which comprises two languages: Upper and Lower Sorbian, which are not considered varieties of the same language because of their mutual linguistic distance (moderate, not low) and the absence of a common standard variety (cf. Ch. B.1; B.2). Their official status in Lusatia, in the territories around Bautzen (Upper Lusatia with Upper Sorbian) and Cottbus (Lower Lusatia with Lower Sorbian), was guaranteed by Article 40 of the GDR constitution. In reunified Germany, its former status is anchored indirectly "in Article 35 of the Unification Treaty [...] of 1990; it is anchored explicitly in the constitutions of the federal states of Brandenburg and Saxony. The German Code on Court Constitution (§184, GVG) guarantees the right "to speak Sorbian before the court in the home areas of the Sorbian population" (de.wikipedia.org/wiki/Sorbische_Sprachen). Furthermore, the two Sorbian languages are languages of instruction in bilingual general education (Sorbian/German); for Upper Sorbian, in the Sorbian Gymnasium in Bautzen, this even applies up to university matriculation level (*Abitur*).

Finally, Danish is also an official language in Germany alongside German in the communities of the Danish-minority region in southern Schleswig. There are 48 Danish schools, two with grammar-school sixth forms, offering Danish as the language of instruction (alongside predominantly German) in at least one subject at native-language level (details of community-official and minority languages in Germany: www.bmi.bund.de/SharedDocs/Downloads/

DE/Broschuren/2008/Regional_und_Minderheitensprachen.pdf. For Danish, ibid: 8–16; de.wikipedia.org/wiki/D%C3%A4nischer_Schulverein_f%C3%BCr_S% C3%BCd schleswig).

2.2 Austria

("Republic of Austria; approximately 8.44 m inhabitants. The proportion of foreigners at the start of 2016 was around 1.268 m, 14.6% of the population. The largest group of foreigners are the Serbs, followed by Montenegrins and Germans": de.wikipedia.org/wiki/%C3%96sterreich).

German is also the national official language of Austria (additional information gratefully received from Rudolf de Cillia). Moreover, as native language of the majority of the population or of an important indigenous part of the population (Ch. D.1), it is a national language corresponding to our definition of the term. However, in the case of Austria, the agreement between name of language and country is not present, which has presumably motivated the declaration of German as the "language of state". German is the sole language with this declared status and is also the only national official language. The declaration goes back to 1920, when the Republic of Austria, reduced after WWI to the German-speaking territory, received a new constitution (Federal Constitution), which has subsequently been renewed several times. The language article, 8 (1), which is still in force, reads: "regardless of the rights furnished according to the Federal Law for Linguistic Minorities, the German language is the language of state of the Republic" (www.wienkonkret.at/politik/gesetz/bundesverfassung; Wodak/ de Cillia 2006: 21–23). All the federal states of Austria with the exception of Vienna also expressly declare in their constitutions that German is the "language of state" (therefore also a regional official language) or also "Landessprache" or "administrative language of the authorities and offices" (Veiter 1970: 462–471).

After WWII, the experience of National Socialism and "Annexation" to Germany (1938–1945), many groups in Austria were reluctant to declare German as the national official or national language, which was expressed, e.g. by renaming native-language school teaching as "the language of instruction". However, as early as 1952, the subject was renamed as "German language of instruction" and in 1955 simply as "German". However, Austria then gave symbolic expression to its national independence through government promotion of national peculiarities of the German language: by fostering an Austrian national variety which is also supported by a government-financed *Österreichisches Wörterbuch* [Austrian Dictionary] (first edition 1951; 42nd edition 2012) (Ammon 1995a: 126–136). The seriousness of this nurturing of an independent national variety of the German language was also evident in Austria's insistence on official recognition of Austrianisms at the time of joining the EU (ibid: 201–213; de Cillia 1997, 1998). Austrian Standard German exhibits a considerable number of peculiarities at all linguistic levels (Ebner [1969] 2009; Ammon/ Bickel/ Lenz 2013/16).

Alongside German, several minority languages also have official status in Austria in communities in several regions: Slovenian in southern Carinthia and in small parts of Styria, and Croatian and Hungarian in parts of Burgenland. The legal bases for these are to be found in the Austrian Independence Treaty of 15 May 1955, Art. 7, and in the Ethnic Groups Act, 1976, in the version of 20 July 2011 (www.sochorek.cz/de/pr/blog/1147731529-regionale-amtsprachen-in-osterreich.htm; Wodak/ de Cillia 2006: 44–52).

2.3 Liechtenstein

("Principality of Liechtenstein; approximately 36,500 inhabitants, of which 24,000 native Liechtensteiner (65.8%) and 12,500 immigrants (34.2%), with 11% Swiss, 6% Austrians and 3.4% Germans as the largest groups": de.wikipedia.org/wiki/Liechtenstein).

In the small country of Liechtenstein, there is no other language than German with an official position (status or function), not even at community level. This is therefore the only officially purely German-speaking country. Moreover, this position of German is not questioned by the large proportion of foreigners, who represent one third of the resident population, but who originate largely from the German-speaking countries. German is declared as the national official language of Liechtenstein in the constitution of the principality of 5 October 1921, Art. 6, which is still in force today: "the German language is the national and official language". This formulation emphasises its status as the national official language.

Because of the large majority of citizens with German as their native language, German is, at the same time, the national language. The title of the most widely read daily newspaper "Liechtensteiner Vaterland" [sic! U. A.] – with both parts of the name in different font size on the cover page – possibly symbolises the predominantly positive attitude towards German as the native language. The commitment to promoting the German language, which is astonishing for this small country, points in a similar direction, e.g. in the case of the – vain – attempt to achieve the status of official language of the European Council for German (Ch. H.4.6). Liechtenstein Standard German coincides largely with Swiss High German, but has a few peculiarities in vocabulary (Ammon/ Bickel/ Lenz 2013/16).

2.4 Switzerland

("Schweizerische Eidgenossenschaft, Swiss Confederation, Confédération Suisse (French), Confederazione Svizzera (Italian), Confederation svizra (Romansh), Confoederatio Helvetica (CH) (Latin); approximately 8.041 million inhabitants, of which 6.190 million national citizens (77%) and 1.851 million foreigners (23%); German-speaking (resident in German-speaking territory) 72.5% of citizens or respectively 63.7% of the total population, French-speaking 21.0% of citizens or respectively 20.4% of the total population, Italian-speaking 6.5% of citizens or respectively 4.3% of the total population and Romansch-speakers 0.6% of citizens or respectively 0.5% of the total population; of the 1.851 million foreigners, Italians form the largest group (16.3% of foreigners), followed by Germans (14.9%) and Portuguese (12%)": de.wikipedia.org/wiki/Schweiz).

In Switzerland, German is a national official language as in Luxembourg (Ch. D.2.5), but not sole-official, as in Germany, Austria and Liechtenstein, but co-official with other national official languages. Sharing the status as the national official language with other languages indicates a restriction of status, which also depends on the balance of this sharing. Among the possible imbalances, speaker numbers and size of the regions are clearly relevant to the topic of the present book, but the choice of the various co-official languages in cases of contact between citizens, between foreigners with an unlimited residence permit (see Ch. C.1) and between citizens and foreigners with an unlimited residence permit is also of particular relevance. However, useful data on these aspects is not readily available for Switzerland or indeed for Luxembourg.

In Switzerland (information gratefully received from Hans Bickel), Art. 4 of the Federal Constitution of the Confederation of Switzerland of 18 April 1999 specifies, by way of continuation of earlier rulings, that "[T]he regional languages are German, French, Italian and Romansh". While these "regional languages" could also be designated national languages in our terminology (cf. Ch. D.1), Art. 70 continues:

(1) "The official languages of the Federation are German, French and Italian. In communication with speakers of the Romansh language, Romansh is also an official language of the Federation". Accordingly, German, French and Italian are unrestricted national official

languages of Switzerland, while Romansh is restricted. The following data on regional language rights also apply;

(2) "The Cantons shall determine their official languages. To preserve agreement between language communities, they shall take into consideration the traditional linguistic composition of the territories with due consideration for hereditary linguistic minorities" (www.admin.ch/ ch/d/sr/1/101.de.pdf).

The Cantons' right to decide on their official languages underlies the so-called "territoriality principle" (Altermatt 1995: 46–48; Haas 2006: 1775f.), according to which the national official languages (of the Federation) are cantonal official languages only in those Cantons which have specified this (based on Art. 4 (2) of the Federal Constitution). In this context, the territoriality principle takes priority over the "persons principle", which would allow freedom of choice of language to every individual. The official languages of the Cantons specified in this sense are also the languages of instruction in schools in the Cantons, of which most are monolingual in this sense, but a few are multilingual. An overview of the language territories specified in this manner and the breakdown of Cantons is shown in Map D.2.4–1.

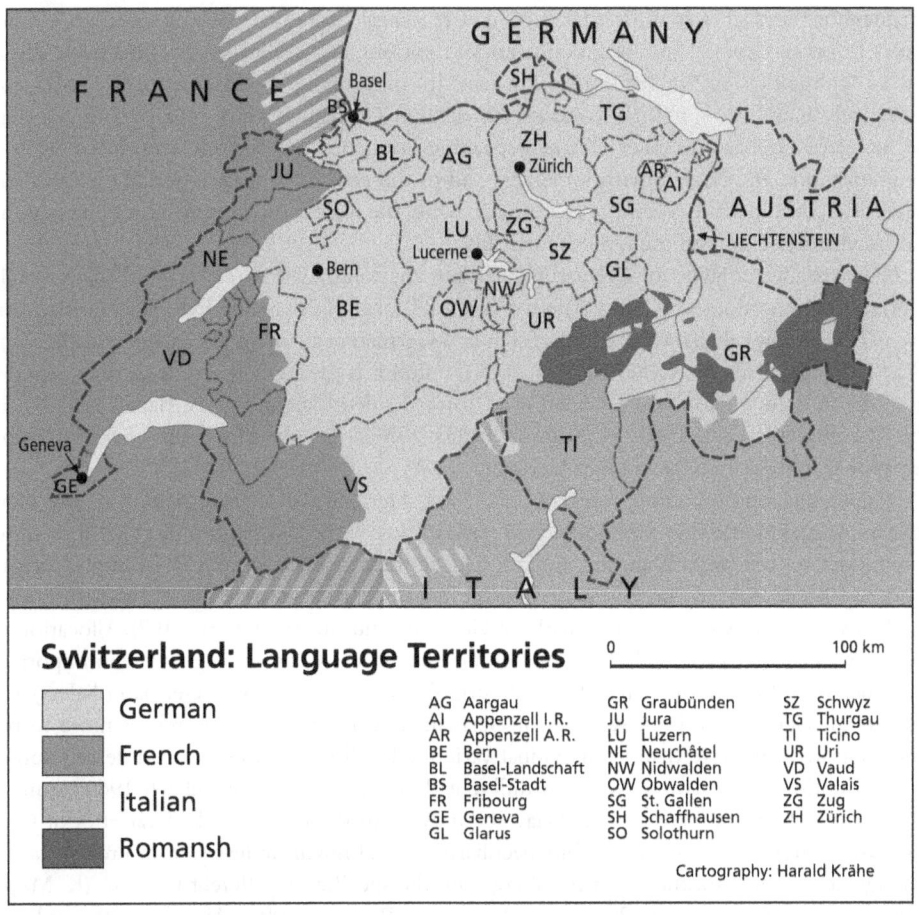

Map D.2.4–1 Language territories and Cantons of Switzerland

The map shows that of the total of 26 Cantons, 17 are entirely German-speaking and four partially. In three of the partially German-speaking Cantons, French is an additional official language (Bern, [this Canton should not be confused with the Federal City of the same name], Freiburg, Wallis) and in one, additionally, Romansh and Italian (Graubünden). Four Cantons are completely French-speaking (Neuenburg, Geneva, Jura, Waadt), and one is completely Italian-speaking (Tessin/Ticino). In the "Federal City of Bern", which is not constituted as a Canton, this official name avoiding the designation "capital city", German is also the sole official language (apart from the multilingual rulings for the organs of the Federation).

A much-discussed peculiarity in German-speaking Switzerland (generally designated as *Deutschschweiz* in Switzerland) is "diglossia" with the two language varieties Swiss German (*Schwyzertüütsch*) and Swiss High German (*Schweizerhochdeutsch*).

The spelling of *Schwyzertüütsch* varies. Specification as "Swiss High German", not simply "High German" or "Standard German", highlights its numerous peculiarities, primarily in pronunciation and vocabulary, but also in spelling, grammar and phraseology (Ammon/Bickel/ Lenz 2013/16).

One essential aspect of diglossia in German Switzerland is that all social classes of the indigenous population also speak dialect (Swiss German). Furthermore, speaking dialect is conventional into the highest ranks of the public domain, also in the mass media. Because of the openness of the dialect towards education and technical expressions, which exists to a lesser extent in other German-speaking countries and regions, Swiss German has also been designated a "cultural dialect" or "educational dialect" (terms proposed by Haarmann 1973a: 33, and respectively Kloss 1978: 58). By contrast, Swiss High German is more restricted in use than the Standard German in other German-speaking countries and regions, namely to written communication and contact with foreigners and to the public domains, especially schools and universities, in some cases even the parliament, while the dialect is also spoken in churches and mass media depending on the level of formality.

The avoidance of Standard German by German-speaking Swiss wherever possible, especially in private conversations, can be interpreted as a mild form of distancing from the German language. The occasional characterisation of standard German as a "foreign language" has the same effect (A. Baur 1983: 10; Ammon 1995a: 298f.), unless it is meant only in jest, as does, in most cases, the insistence that Swiss German is an "(independent) language" (A. Baur 1983: 37–41; critical comment Rupp 1983: 36; Ammon 1995a: 295–297), especially if this characterisation also applies to their own Swiss High German.

Despite this attitude among speakers, the Swiss German dialects still belong to the German language, because they are roofed by a standard variety of German from which they show only moderate (not large) linguistic distance. The roofing standard variety, Swiss High German is beyond doubt part of the German language because of its great similarity with the other standard varieties of German, particularly of Germany and Austria (Ch. B.1; B.2). Allocation of the Swiss German dialects and of Swiss High German to the German language is an important difference from Luxembourgish in Luxembourg (Ch. D.2.5). Since Swiss German (dialect) and Swiss High German are both varieties of German, and the present book relates more to the whole German language than to individual varieties, I will forgo more detailed description of the distribution of the two varieties in different domains (see Schwarzenbach 1969; Ammon 1995a: 283–300; Rash 1998: 49–72; Haas 2006). As with the other standard varieties of German, Swiss High German also exhibits peculiarities at all linguistic levels, from pronunciation to pragmatics, in administrative terminology, even the specifics in different Cantons (K. Meyer 2006; Ammon/ Bickel/ Lenz 2013/16; Dürscheid/ Businger 2006). An increasing tendency to use English noted by various studies (Dürmüller 1986, 1991, 1994, 2001, 2002; Murray/

Wegmüller/ Kan 2000; Murray/ Dingwall 2001; Watts/ Murray 2001) also betrays a certain distancing of German-speaking Switzerland from the German language. However, in this regard, there is a lack of comparative research with other German-speaking countries.

2.5 Luxembourg

("Groussherzogtum Lëtzebuerg (letzebuergisch), Großherzogtum Luxemburg (German), Grand-Duché de Luxembourg (French); approximately 524,800 inhabitants, of which 298,100 indigenous (57%) and 226,700 foreigners (43%), with the Portuguese (81,800 ≈ 16% of the total population), French (30,950 ≈ 6% of the total population) and Italians (19,900 ≈ 4% of the total population) as the largest groups": de.wikipedia.org/wiki/Luxemburg).

We now come to the fifth and last state with German as a national official language: Luxembourg (information received with thanks from Peter Gilles). Here also, German is co-official, together with the other two national official languages, French and Letzebuergisch. However, by contrast with Switzerland, simply because of the small overall size of the national territory, there is no territoriality principle in Luxembourg. In consequence, the distribution of the three co-official languages between domains in the same territory is more complicated than in Switzerland (Fehlen 2009; Gilles 2009; Gilles/ Moulin 2009; Gilles/ Seela/ Sieburg/ Wagner 2010). One significant difference compared with Germany, Austria, Liechtenstein and German-speaking Switzerland is that the people of Luxembourg certainly do not regard German as their native language. Their native language is *Letzebuergesch* (in German also *Luxemburgisch*, in Luxembourgish: *Lëtzebuergisch* – the term I use is based on this and was used by Heinz Kloss 1952: 239; Fehlen 2009: 11, Note 2). Since German is not the native language, Luxembourg is not counted as a German-speaking country or German-speaking state, either in general or in this book (Ch. B.4). The Luxembourg government occasionally stresses this distance, e.g. through their express non-participation in the recent German spelling reform (Fehlen 2009: 46).

However, all three languages, German, French and Letzebuergisch, are declared as national official languages. The revised constitution of 1948, Art. 29, initially only provided that the administrative language of state was to be specified by law ("*L'emploi de la langue d'administration sera réglé par la loi*"; Kramer 1984: 186). Fernand Hoffmann (1979: 34) has explained the absence of an explicit ruling at that time with reference to the short time after national socialism, under which Luxembourg suffered not only the normal repressive measures, but also was liquidated as an independent state and incorporated into the German Empire (occupation 1940–1945, declared part of the "Great German Empire" in August 1942; see also Ch. K.2). As a result, the German language was completely spoilt for the people of Luxembourg. On 10 October 1941, an "inventory of personnel" in the form of a public survey required people to declare German as their native language. In the accompanying propaganda, their own language was described as a mere "dialect", like "*Plattdeutsch*" and was thus disqualified as a native language. This opinion poll was clearly intended to legitimate the annexation of the country by Nazi Germany. However, the results were not evaluated because, with an overwhelming majority, the population declared Letzebuergisch and not German as their native language (Fehlen 2009: 31f.; Newton 1987: 164, 170; Ammon 1995a: 398f). "After liberation, hatred of the Germans is greater than ever. [. . .] Luxembourgish has replaced German in parliamentary debates, and official documents are published only in French" (Fehlen 2009: 33). To some extent, this narrative presumably continues today in the negative evaluation of German by the majority of the population as ugly (*laid*) or uncultivated/brutal (*brutal*) and similar – at least by comparison with Letzebuergisch, French or English (ibid: 45, 195).

The relationship between official languages was only finally regulated in a special Language Act on 24 February 1984 (Hoffmann 1989). Accordingly, Letzebuergisch received a – not previously furnished – official status which stabilised it as an independent language. While Kloss (1978: 23–37, 105–116) has previously justified the linguistic independence of Letzebuergish with reference to its "elaboration (*Ausbau*)", in my view, its standardisation is the decisive factor: the creation of an independent standard variety which has an adequate, i.e. not only small but moderate, linguistic distance from the standard varieties of the nearest linguistic neighbour, German (Ch. B.1; B.2). A standard variety with such a considerable linguistic distance from the standard varieties of Germany and Austria is not present in German Switzerland (Ch. D.2.4). Above all, the orthography of Letzebuergisch (latest reform 1999) has been provided with clear differences from all standard varieties of German: with its own letter ë, French accented characters and a choice of orthography meticulously faithful to the pronunciation (see text sample of standard Letzebuergisch in Ch. B.1). Apart from its declared status, the official position of Letzebuergisch is based on its corresponding function, including its written function (Hoffmann 1989: 48–50), which requires a standard variety.

The new Language Act gives priority to French as the language of legislation. Art. 2: "*Langue de la législation: Les actes législatifs et leur règlement d'exécution sont rédigés en français. Lorsque les actes législatifs et réglementaires sont accompagnés d'une traduction, seul le texte français fait foi*" (*Mémorial, Remeil de Législation*, A-No 16: 27 February 1984: 196).

However, alongside French and Letzebuergisch, German is admitted for administration and case law (Article 3), especially for enquiries to the administration (Art. 4). These must be answered in one of the three official languages in which they were asked, but only "as far as possible" ("*dans la mesure du possible*").

Art. 3: "*Langues administratives et judiciaires: En matière administrative, contentieuse ou non contentieuse, et en matière judiciaire, il peut être fait usage des langues* française, allemande *ou* luxembourgeoise, *sans préjudice des dispositions spéciales concernant certaines matières*".

Art. 4: "*Requêtes administratives: Lorsqu'une requête est rédigée en luxembourgeois, en français ou en allemand, l'administration doit se servir, dans la mesure du possible, pour sa réponse de la langue choisie par le requérant*" (*Mémorial* 27 February 1984: 197).

It is also significant that this Act declares Letzebuergisch as the only national language of Luxembourg, which it is *de facto* as the native language of the majority of the population (Ch. D.1).

Art. 1: "*Langue nationale: La langue nationale des Luxembourgeois est le luxembourgeois*" (*Mémorial* 27 February 1984: 196). Positioning as a national language relates to national symbolism, with symbols of sovereignty, national hymn etc. (Gilles/ Moulin 2009: 184f.)

Compared with the two other official languages, German is therefore downgraded: by comparison with Letzebuergisch as a non-native and non-national language and, by comparison with French, it is not a language of legislation. This difference in ranking is also evident in road signs, where French is always printed at the top, i.e. in first position, with Letzebuergisch below it but without German. Elsewhere on public notices, i.e. in the "linguistic landscape" of Luxembourg, German is placed in the background, primarily behind French (Gilles/ Seela/ Sieburg/ Wagner 2010: 91–101).

In parliamentary debates after WWII, Letzebuergisch took the place of German which, like French, now plays a minimal role in that context. French has the advantage over German that the President of the Parliament speaks French, and, for some time, written summaries of parliamentary debates have been published, in print and also online (www.chd.lu) in French, with the title *Compte rendu des séances publiques*. For a considerable time after WWII, they were still written in German as *Analytische Kammerberichte* and distributed free of charge to households.

Communication between various instances of the court is also almost exclusively in French. Judgements used to be announced in German (Hoffmann 1979: 51f.); nowadays, this occurs only rarely, if Germans, i.e. non-Luxembourgers, are involved. German plays almost no role in military life. French also serves as the command language for communication between officers, while Letzebuergisch is generally spoken in teams. In business communication, French is more important than German, and Letzebuergisch is gaining in importance. This is evident from the choice of language in job advertisements, even in the mostly German-speaking newspaper *Luxemburger Wort*, and in language skills required in tenders (Pigeroth-Piroth/ Fehlen 2005: 15f).

School education aims at trilingualism for the entire population (Kramer 1986), but this is often only partially successful. Pre-schooling is primarily in Letzebuergisch (three years; compulsory schooling from age four), which is provided as "language of care" (Gilles/ Moulin 2009: 187). In the subsequent six years of primary schooling, reading and writing are learnt in German (literacy), but Letzebuergisch is still spoken in lessons. From the second year of primary school, French is added as a language of instruction and then takes priority in secondary school, where it becomes "sole language of instruction in higher classes, except in the subjects German and English" (Fehlen 2009: 51). Secondary schooling comprises two alternative branches: general-level *Lyceum*, for three years, i.e. until the end of compulsory schooling, or *Vocational Lyceum*, three to five years, depending on subjects taken (Horner/ Weber 2008: 87–89; Davis 1989: 158f).

Because of the numerous immigrants from romance-language countries, sociolinguists have recommended switching literacy from German to French or at least subdividing it between these two languages (e.g. J. Weber 2009; Horner/ Weber 2008: 87–89). This seems to have been proposed after change of government at the end of 2013, because the new social-democrat dominated government of Luxembourg provides "that children of immigrants from southern European countries, e.g. Portugal, can in future opt for schooling in French instead of German" ("Agreement in Luxembourg on the 'Gambia' coalition", *FAZ* 2 December 2013: 6). However, an extension of this ruling to include the Letzebuergisch-speaking majority of the population is not expected. Literacy in two different languages could lead to linguistic "fragmentation" of the population (Gilles/ Moulin 2009: 187) and may set a precedent for the impact of massive immigration in a small country on the language of schooling.

In line with the general avoidance of German in public language usage, Luxembourg has advertised the multilingual University of Luxembourg as the "*Université du Luxembourg*" since 2003. It has three faculties: (1) Communication, Science and Technology; (2), Economics, Finance and Law; and (3) Arts, Education, Humanities, Languages and Literature. The languages of instruction are English, French and German, with Letzebuergisch only in the subject Letzebuergisch.

Before WWII, the non-Latin components of liturgical language in Catholic Luxembourg were in German. Since the war, they have been largely Letzebuergisch. This trend was reinforced after Vatican Council II (1962–1965) which recommended the use of vernacular languages. However, German is often still used during masses, primarily in the liturgy.

In the oral mass media, German plays a subordinate role alongside French and Letzebuergisch. The situation is different in the newspapers. "If you disregard newspapers targeting foreign residents, Luxembourg newspapers and magazines are published primarily in German" (Fehlen 2009: 45). However, there are items in French and, in the local section, in Letzebuergisch, although rather seldom (Berg 1993: 41). In descending order of circulation, the four daily newspapers are: *Luxemburger Wort*, *Tageblatt*, *Lëtzeburger Journal* and *Zeitung fir d'lëtzeburger Vollek*. With reference to fiction and poetry, Hoffmann (1979: 65–111) acknowledges the existence of literature in the three languages – German, Letzebuergisch and French – in this order. The

German-speaking literature (cf. Hoffmann 1988b) is more widely distributed than the rather high-brow French-speaking literature.

Luxembourg German also has some lexical peculiarities, primarily borrowings from French, Letzebuergish and also English (Ammon/ Bickel/ Lenz 2013/16). Finally, it must be stressed that Luxembourg is the only country in which German is a national (not only regional) official language without, at the same time, being the native language of the majority of the population. In general, and in this book, Luxembourg is therefore not counted among the "German-speaking states (or countries)".

3. German as a regional official language

3.1 The German-speaking community in Belgium

("75,700 inhabitants, approximately 0.7% of the Belgian population (almost 11 million); small group of French-speaking Belgians in the northern communities of Kelmis, Lontzen and Eupen": de: wikipedia.org/wiki/Deutschsprachige_Gemeinschaft_Belgiens).

Position as a regional official language can differ significantly from that of a national official language because living together in a shared national framework compels speakers of merely regional official languages to learn and use the language/s of the majority. The pressure is generally greater than in the case of co-official but national official languages. In spite of currently generous language rights, this situation applies for German-speaking Belgians and Italians. In this respect, there are in fact similarities between regional official languages and many minority languages without official status (Chapter E).

The current position of German as a regional official language in Belgium and Italy, which brings advantages but is, at the same time, precarious, becomes comprehensible with regard to its history. The two German-speaking regions only acquired their current status as nations after WWI – through annexation – and, it must be assumed, against the will of the majority of their population. In Italy, there was no attempt at a referendum, and in Belgium, only the possibility for individual written protests to the Belgian authorities, of which only a very small minority (271 people) made use of. In view of the unlikeliness of success, because of far greater Belgian territorial demands, this was predictable (Pabst 1997: 26). Both cessions of territory were incompatible with the right of political self-determination for ethnic groups suggested by US President Wilson's 14-point plan for shaping the peace after WWI. In both regions, annexation led to protracted conflicts between the German-speaking population, central governments and national majority population, which were broadly resolved only decades after WWII with the formation and consolidation of the European Union.

The Belgian territory with German as an official language comprises the eastern part of the region allocated to Belgium in the Peace of Versailles with effect from 10 January 1920. Prior to this, it was part of the larger territory of Eupen-Malmedy belonging to the German Empire. While the surrender of French-speaking towns Malmedy and Waimes and surrounding regions to Belgium corresponded to the spirit of Wilson's 14-point plan, different reasons, relating to reparation for the enormous destruction caused by the German attack on this neutral country, were given for the secession of the German-speaking regions (history: Rosensträter 1985; Brüll 2005; Berge/ Grasse 2003: 168–172; also Rosensträter, 3 vols. 1985; Nelde 1979b; Hinderdael/ Nelde 1996; Jenniges 2001 (419 68–72); Darquennes 2004, 2013; language rights: Pan/ Pfeil 2006: 42–58).

The official German-speaking territory of Belgium, the *German-Speaking Community* [*Deutschsprachige Gemeinschaft*], is divided – by a corridor around Malmedy and Waimes running from west to east – into a northern half (with Eupen as capital of the whole community) and a southern half (with smaller town St Vith). In the north, it borders the Netherlands, in the south, Luxembourg, and in the east, Germany (Map D.1–1, Ch. D.1). According to the law of 30 July 1963, it comprises the following nine communities realigned by territorial reform (from south to north): Burg-Reuland, Sankt Vith, Amel, Büllingen, Bütgenbach, Eupen, Raeren, Lontzen and Kelmis (Council of the German Cultural Community 1978: 10–14).

The German-speaking community should not be confused with the formerly also German-speaking territory around the town of Arlon (in German also "*Areler Land*"), situated to the west and south, which was already Belgian before WWI ("*Alt-Belgien*"). German is not an official language there, and the indigenous dialects exist only as vestiges, without standard-German roofing (Nelde 1987: 11; 1979a, b; Darquennes 2011a; b; 2013). The dialects could equally be allocated to Letzeburgisch or German.

Since 1963, a legal distinction exists between different language territories in Belgium, including the German-speaking territory (Verdoodt 1968: 33). Distinguishing these language territories, which are known as *Communities* since the constitutional reform of 1978, from the *Regions*, is important for understanding the political structure of Belgium. Added to these are a further ten *Provinces* (since 1994, previously nine), which play a subordinate role because of their more restricted powers. The loose incorporation into the European region *Euroregio Maas-Rhein* (*Maas-Rijn/Meuse-Rhin*) in the Belgium/Germany/Netherlands border region is also relevant here (de.wikipedia.org/wiki/Liste_der_Europaregionen).

The official-language German-speaking territory in fact forms its own "community" (*Deutschsprachige Gemeinschaft*, alongside the Dutch-speaking community in Flanders (*Vlaamse Gemeenschap*) and the French-speaking community in Wallonia (*Fédération Wallonie-Bruxelles*) (a total of three communities). It is not an independent "region", but part of the region of Wallonia, existing alongside the regions Flanders and Brussels City (a total of three regions). The central government is still superordinate over the communities, regions and provinces; at state level, German has only a rudimentary official-language function, primarily in the form of German versions of basic laws (Christen 2005; Henkes 2005; Berge/ Grasse 2003: 196). The new King Philippe (since 21 July 2013) recently added German to his addresses to the nation when he gave his Christmas address "completely in German" alongside French and Dutch" (*FAZ* 27 December 2013: 9). However, in central government and parliament, German is not spoken because of its proportion in the population. With 75,000 to 80,000 members (depending on source), the German-speaking community amounts to only around 0.7% of the total population of the country.

The constitutional amendment of 1988/89 significantly strengthened the communities. In particular, they were given power over cultural matters and education including languages used (*Blick auf den Bundesstaat Belgien* 1989). Every community has its own government with its own parliament as legislature. The seat of government of the German-speaking community is in Eupen and comprises four ministers, one of whom is prime minister. The parliament, the *Council* of the German-speaking community, which was installed on 30 January 1984, also based in Eupen, has 25 MPs. German is used universally in parliament, government and administration for the nine communities. Since the language laws of 1963 (Art. 10, 13), German has been provided exclusively for internal administrative communication or documents relating to private individuals, while external written communication is bilingual (German and French) (Art. 11, 14; Verdoodt 1968: 34). In principle, the administration is in contact with the population bilingually; however, forms are distributed in French only "on request" (Council of the German-speaking Community 1989: 6). All laws and *decrees* in the German-speaking community are also bilingual. Internal posts in the administration of the German-speaking community may be occupied "only by candidates who can demonstrate the necessary knowledge of German" (Council of the German-speaking Community 1989: 6). Court proceedings normally take place in German since the German-speaking community has had its own court in Eupen since 1988 (Henkes 2005: 179–188; Berge/ Grasse 2003: 197).

In schools in the German-Speaking Community, German is the language of instruction generally and as a school subject, from kindergarten to the end of secondary education (details in Darquennes 2004). However, French is added as a subject in primary school, at the latest from the third year of schooling, and in secondary school, it is the language of instruction in some subjects. This even goes so far that "contrary to the provisions of the (Language) Act [. . .], independent French sections exist in many individual schools" (Berge/Grasse 2003: 199f). This shows that the maintenance of language requires constant effort, not only in the case of minorities without official status of their language (Ch. E), but also in the case of merely regional official languages and applies even in the case of apparent linguistic stability – e.g. for South Tyrol (Ch. D.3.2). In these cases, native speakers stand behind the language – in contrast with Luxembourg, where they are absent. This possibly explains why less resistance is shown to the weakening of the position of German in Luxembourg in spite of its national official language status. Because of its small size, the German-Speaking Community in Belgium does not have its own university. However, it does have the – rather small – private *Autonome Hochschule in der Deutschsprachigen Gemeinschaft* (AHS) in Eupen, "the only German-speaking college in Belgium", which originated from the two teacher training seminars for primary and kindergarten teachers. Church language for the almost consistently catholic German-speaking community is exclusively German. By contrast, French and Dutch predominate in the Belgian army; but the entrance examination for an army career can be taken in German (Berge/ Grasse 2003: 196f).

Since 1961, there has been a German-speaking radio broadcaster, and since 2001, the public-sector *Belgische Rundfunk* (*BRF*) has broadcast a 24-hour German channel to Eupen, St Vith, Lontzen, Liège and Brussels. There are also private-sector, German-speaking broadcasters in Eupen, St Vith, Kelmis and Raeren, and independent TV in the form of the news magazine *BRF-blickpunkt*, broadcast from Eupen every hour from Monday to Friday, with "items from around the region" and "Regional News in German" (www.dglive.de/desktopdefault.aspx/tabid-112/414_read-17005; brf.be/tv/blickpunkt/). Alongside various periodicals, including church newsletters, the daily newspaper *GrenzEcho* has been published since 1927 in Eupen (circulation approximately 13,000; de.wikipedia.org/wiki/Grenz-Echo). Newspapers and magazines are also imported from Germany, above all the *Aachener Volkszeitung*. Popular books on the region are published regularly, primarily by *Grenz-Echo Verlag* (GEV). As part of the "linguistic landscape", road signs have been monolingual German since 1977. A strong flow of shoppers and tourists come in from Germany, while many thousands of East Belgians work in Germany (Berge/ Grasse 2003: 181–183). However, in supermarkets, which are often branches of chains operating throughout Belgium, French predominates, and items are often labelled only in French (ibid: 200).

The German dialect (in the north, Lower Franconian and Ripuarian, and in the south Ripuarian and Mosel-Franconian) is still in use among the older generation, but younger people prefer Standard German. This exhibits some Belgian lexical peculiarities, primarily borrowings from French (Ammon/ Bickel/ Lenz 2013/16). German and French bilingualism, which facilitates upward professional mobility, is increasingly predominant among the population. By contrast, in the French-speaking and Dutch-speaking majority population of Belgium, only a small proportion, primarily in the younger generation, can speak German, which increases motivation to choose English for interlingual contact. This asymmetry of language skills, including the choice of English for interlingual contact, is typical in the case of regional official languages and has been criticised from several perspectives.

3.2 The autonomous province of South Tyrol in Italy

("*Autonome Provinz Bozen-Südtirol* (also simply *Südtirol*), *Provincia autonoma di Bolzano Alto Adige* (Italian), *Provinzia Autonoma de Balsan-Südtirol* (Gadertalish Ladin) or Provinzia Autonoma de Bulsan-Südtirol (Grödnerish Ladin). Total population 511,750, of which 467,400 indigenous and 44,350 foreign (8.7% of the population, with Albanians (5560 people), Germans (4680) and Moroccans (3570) as the largest groups. Among the indigenous population, the 3 acknowledged language groups are subdivided as follows: German-speaking 324,380 (69.4%), Italian speaking 122,000 (26.1%) and Ladin-speaking 21,030 (4.5%)": de.wikipedia.org/wiki/S%C3%BCdtirol).

Numerous publications have described the linguistic circumstances in South Tyrol (additional information gratefully received from Franz Lanthaler). Details of the history of South Tyrol since annexation by Italy are provided by Georg Grote (2009) and Michael Gehler (2008); Ruth Volgger describes the official function of German in South Tyrol (2008: 95–148); and Peter Hilpold the relevant minority rights (2001, 2009; briefly Pan/ Pfeil 2006: 219–241). Overviews of the linguistic situation are offered by Voltmer/ Lanthaler/ Abel/ Oberhammer (2007), Lanthaler (2012a) and Ludwig Eichinger (1996). In the autonomous province of South Tyrol in Italy, German is a regional official language of state alongside Italian and, in some valleys, alongside Ladin; the position of German is therefore co-official (Map D.1–1). South Tyrol borders Austria and belongs to the Italian region of Trentino South Tyrol. Nowadays, "belong" means relatively little but makes it part of the loose regional grouping of the *Arbeitsgemeinschaft Alpenländer* (*ARGE ALP*) [Working Community of Alpine Regions], which also includes the Austrian Federal States of Tyrol and Vorarlberg, the Swiss Cantons of Graubünden, St Gallen and Tessin and the German federal states of Baden-Württemberg and Bavaria (Grote 2009: 225–249).

Until the end of WWI, South Tyrol belonged to Austria. It was allocated to Italy by the Allies in 1919 without referendum. In a sense, this was Italy's reward for siding with the Allies and for joining the war against the Central Powers; a pseudo-scientific justification by Italian politician and subsequent fascist Ettore Tolomei was used to give the appearance of legitimacy (ibid: 43–47, 49–58).

Annexation was followed by a long policy of suppression of German; from 1925, also strict prohibition as a language of instruction, supported by an organised resettlement of southern Italians and siting of major Italian companies, primarily in the urban centre of Bolzano. The climax of this policy was ultimately reached on 22 June 1939 in an agreement between Hitler and Mussolini whose support Hitler needed for his military plans, which aimed at the complete ethnic and linguistic Italianisation of South Tyrol. For this purpose, the South Tyroleans were given a choice of emigrating to the German Empire (including Austria, which had been annexed in 1938 with the approval of Mussolini) or remaining in the Italian national territory and allowing themselves to be fully linguistically assimilated. Faced with this "option without option" (Grote 2009: 103–140), 86% of South Tyrol people had opted for emigration to the German Empire by the end of 1939. In spite of the confusion of the war, 37% (75,000) carried out this plan, of whom approximately 25,000 returned to South Tyrol after WWII – i.e. a migration loss of approximately 50,000 (ibid: 137).

The policy of suppression certainly contributed to the commitment of the German linguistic group to their ethnic and linguistic identity, which was supported by the Austrian state, acknowledged by the UN as a "protective power" for the rights of the South Tyroleans. The language rights of South Tyroleans had been prepared in the Gruber-De Gasperi Treaty between Austria and Italy on 9 May 1946 (named after the Austrian Foreign Minister Gruber and the Italian Prime Minister De Gasperi), which was ultimately expanded into the "Statute of Autonomy" of 1972. Granting independence to the province of South Tyrol from the majority Italian-speaking

Table D.3.2–1 Development in the proportion of the three language groups in South Tyrol 1981–2011

	1981	1991	2001	2011
German	66.43	67.99	69.15	69.41
Italian	29.38	27.65	26.47	26.06
Ladin	4.20	4.36	4.37	4.53

Note: percentages, in each case relative to all three language groups, together = 100%

region Trentino South Tyrol was important in this context. The *Südtiroler Volkspartei* played a significant part as the most influential political representative for German-speaking and also Ladin-speaking South Tyroleans.

The Statute of Autonomy forms the basis for the current equality of rights of the German and Italian linguistic group and also the rights of the Ladin language group (Egger 1990: 79f.), with the following guarantees:

(1) Proportion of the three language groups in public administration

Within 30 years (from 1972), public administrative offices should be staffed in proportion to the numerical strength of the linguistic groups – the Italian-speaking group had previously held a disproportionate share. Numerical strength was to be monitored every ten years in censuses, in fact, by self-allocation (declaration rather than determination). Table D.3.2–1 shows that the proportions between the three language groups have shifted slightly over time in favour of the German and Ladin-speaking groups. Part of this shift may be attributable to changes in declarations rather than actual growth, motivated by differences in access to public office – as a result of the proportion aimed at in view of the former bias towards the Italian-speaking population (Tyroller 1986: 21; Lüsebrink 1986: 75). In recent times, the set proportions have been loosened because of political tensions but also because an adequate number of applicants was not always available from each language group.

(2) A requirement for all administrative offices to demonstrate oral and written knowledge in both languages, and in Ladin in certain regions

This means that all administrative officers must present appropriate certificates or pass language examinations.

(3) Official usage of these language skills

In fact, "documents with legal force" and texts for nationwide circulation are formulated in the national official language, i.e. "the wording in Italian shall be binding" (§ 99 of the Statute of Autonomy of 1972). However, German and, in some regions Ladin, may also be used at all official levels within the province. The only domain reserved exclusively for Italian is the military, especially as the command language (§ 100).

(4) Equality of rights of German and Italian, also including Ladin, in schools

This provision presumably has the most sustainable language-maintenance effect (overview of school policy in S. Baur/ Mezzalira/ Pichler 2009). Independent school boards have been set up for both larger language groups, including Ladin in certain regions. Language groups were allocated to separate schools. In the respective schools, German or, respectively, Italian are the sole language of instruction, from kindergarten to the end of secondary schooling. In the first year of primary school, German is added as a compulsory subject in the Italian-speaking schools, and Italian is added in the German-speaking schools, in each case as a compulsory subject, which it remains until the end of secondary schooling. Lessons are taught by native speakers. By contrast, in the Ladin schools, Ladin is only a school subject, and the other subjects are taught half in German and half in Italian (Wehrmann 1988: 24).

Earlier reports suggest that bilingualism and even trilingualism through to the end of schooling are generally achieved (Lüsebrink 1986: 74; Egger 1977: 117–122). But there are indications of an asymmetry in language skills in favour of the national official language, Italian. Many German-speaking and Ladin-speaking school leavers evidently have good knowledge of Italian; the Ladin-speakers also have reasonable knowledge of German; however, knowledge of German among Italian-speaking school leavers is often poor (Egger/ Heller 1997: 1352). This contributes to the fact that "interlingual contact" (Ch. A.3) is predominantly in Italian. South Tyrolean German-speakers occasionally protest against this asymmetry, but so far without effect. As in Belgium (cf. Ch. D.3.1), the national official language is also ultimately dominant in South Tyrol. This can be taken as a sign that – in spite of generous language rights – the maintenance of German in South Tyrol requires continuing effort.

The domain of education was expanded to the highest level through the foundation of the Free University of Bolzano in 1977 (S. Baur 2009: 391–394; www.unibz.it/de/public/university/default.html). The university comprises five faculties: Arts and Design, Economics, Education, Informatics and Sciences. An additional Language Research Centre performs academic and consultative functions. The languages of instruction are German, Italian and English, but not to the same extent in all faculties. For example, English predominates in economics and informatics, while German and Italian are dominant in education.

Outside government and community administration, German has equal status with Italian in provincial government. It is admitted without restriction in the South Tyrolean Regional Parliament with its 35 MPs: in parliamentary debates, committees and administration. Since 2008, the provincial government comprises nine Regional Councils/*Assessori* (ministers), including the Head of Regional Government/*Presidente* (Prime Minister). The South Tyrolean People's Party has regularly been the strongest party since 1945 and has also consistently appointed the Head of Regional Government (Prime Minister). It represents cultural autonomy in the sense of the rights granted in 1972. At national level, in parliament and government in Rome, German is not admitted as a working language. In religious institutions, German almost has a monopoly in the German language group. According to the principle that religion should be offered in the native language, each language group holds services in its own language.

Through its multiple functions, Standard German is well established in South Tyrol and roofs the dialect which is still spoken there, primarily Southern Bavarian with transitions to Alemannic in the West (Egger/ Lanthaler 2001; Lanthaler 2012a). South Tyrol Standard German is largely congruent with Austrian Standard German, but also German Standard German. But it also has lexical peculiarities, primarily borrowings from Italian (Abfalterer 2007; Ammon/ Bickel/ Lenz 2013/16). Frequent contact with German-speaking tourists, mostly from Germany, is presumably an important factor for the maintenance of German. The German-speaking population is dominant in rural areas. By contrast, Italian speakers are concentrated in the cities as a result of the settlement policy.

Italian-language and German-language TV and radio broadcasts can be received throughout the province. A range of local German-speaking radio stations includes *Radio Holiday* and

Südtirol 1. German-language broadcasts are preferred by German-speaking South Tyroleans, with TV primarily from the broadcaster *RAI Bozen*. One exception is the Italian TV sports broadcasts (Dolde et al. 1988: 75f). The leading German-language daily *Dolomiten* is published by the long-standing publisher *Athesia* in Bolzano; the *Neue Südtiroler Tageszeitung* is also published in Bolzano (circulation approximately 56,300 and 16,000 respectively), alongside various church and weekly newspapers. Furthermore, South Tyrol has a surprising wealth of German-language fiction and poetry, some of which is published by Athesia but some also in Austria (Gruber 1989; Riedmann 1984). Institutions promoting culture and language, primarily the South Tyrolean Cultural Institute in Bolzano (www.kulturinstitut.org/), further strengthen the collective identity of the German-speaking South Tyroleans. As a part of the linguistic landscape, road signs are bilingual: Italian and German (the language of the local majority population is placed at the top in each case). In the Ladin valleys, they are trilingual. However, lasting peace has not yet been secured in the linguistic landscape. For example, recent attempts to print road signs in rural areas exclusively in German – on the basis of tradition – have provoked violent protest from Rome (*FAZ* 31 July 2010).

4. Worldwide language comparison according to distribution as an official language of state

The position of languages as an official language of state is relevant to the topic of the present book. The foregoing detailed description of the anchoring of German in its own official-language territory is now followed by a considerably less detailed comparison with other international languages. As explained in Ch. D.1, the anchoring of languages as an official language of state can be taken as a factor or indicator for their position in the world – even if this raises some doubts about weighting and reliability. What is particularly important is that position depends not only on the mere number of states but also on their other properties. However, there is no unified measure and there is also a lack of corresponding data to ensure a well-founded comparison of all international languages (Ch. A.3; A.7). The following dimensions would need to be considered:

(1) The number of states in which the languages are an official language of state;
(2) The size of the territories of the states;
(3) The geographical distribution of these territories;
(4) The speaker numbers of the states;
(5) The economic power of the states;
(6) Whether the language is a national or only regional official language of state.

Since the book has already given details of speaker numbers and economic power of language communities (Ch. C), and comprehensive data for dimension (6) are unavailable, I will limit myself here to dimensions (1), (2) and (3).

Unfortunately, these dimensions are only suitable as indicators for the position of languages in the world to a limited extent. According to (1), e.g. Greek or Swedish (in each case with two "official-language states": Greece, Cyprus and respectively Sweden, Finland) and certainly Dutch (with three official-language states: Netherlands, Belgium, Suriname) would be positioned globally higher than Japanese (with only one official-language state: Japan). Even (2) and (3) do not converge on the global position of the languages. According to (2), languages such as German, Japanese and Italian would be positioned far behind Russian, and according to (2) and (3), behind Portuguese; but this does not agree with other criteria, such as global figures for FL learners (Ch. J.7). In spite of these limitations, the three dimensions do at least provide a rough guide to the position of the languages in the world.

It must be borne in mind that quite a few (independent) states do not enjoy a very stable existence, but arise and disappear in relatively short periods of time. Moreover, at hardly any time is there a consensus about which political units can be considered as independent states in the first place. Relatively recent examples are provided by the fluctuations following the dissolution of the Soviet Union and Yugoslavia, which, even now, may not yet have stabilised. Furthermore, there are divergences in the acknowledgement of independent states. One example is Chinese. In the sources named in Table D.4–1, Taiwan is consistently considered an independent state, but it is no longer in the current list of states recognised by the UN (de.wikipedia.org/wiki/Liste_der_Staaten_der_Erde). In the case of German, the number of official-language states was reduced by two recent political developments. One was German reunification in October 1990. Before this, Banks (1987) counted West Berlin as a separate political unit, a kind of independent state (probably because of the Four-Powers Statute). The second political development affecting German occurred in 1990 in Namibia. When Namibia was constituted as an independent state, German lost its status as an official language of state (but this was limited in a racist manner to the "white population"; Ch. E.4.9). Both events reduced the number of states with German as an official language of state, as shown by comparing 1987 with 2007 in Table D.4–1. The most legitimate basis for counting independent states is their recognition by the UN. At the time of writing (2013, 2017), the grand total was 193. "However, 11 other states, nations, countries or territories, in which either their identity as a state is disputed or they are disposed in free association with other states", must be added to these (de.wikipedia.org/wiki/Liste_der_Staaten_der_Erde).

In view of fluctuations in the preceding period, counts from previous years have been superseded. However, I have included them in Table D.4–1. I have also added the figures for "official languages of all states according to continents" prepared by Ernst Kausen (2013, accessible at: de.wikipedia.org/wiki/Liste_der_Amtssprachen). Compared with other Internet data, this list seemed relatively reliable and representative – although the author relativised his assessment in an email: "The list is already quite old but should still hold to a large extent [. . .]" (Kausen 26 February 2013). By contrast, the Wikipedia "List of Official Languages" seemed unsuitable, because it is based upon a considerably broader concept of "official language" than my specification of an "official language of state" (Ch. D.1).

Table D.4–1 The six most frequent official languages of state in the world according to number of states (ranking after Kausen 2013). In brackets: first, the number of states in which the relevant language is sole-official; second, the number of states in which it is co-official; Portuguese before German because of greater frequency as sole-official than co-official

	Banks 1987	Fischer Weltalmanach 1987	Banks 2007	Fischer Weltalmanach 2007	Kausen 2013
1. English	63 (19 + 44)	59 (30 + 29)	53	50	49 (26 + 23)
2. French	34 (11 + 23)	27 (15 + 12)	26	29	29 (11 + 18)
3. Arabic	22 (14 + 2)	23 (18 + 5)	23	22	24 (19 + 5)
4. Spanish	23 (15 + 8)	21 (17 + 4)	21	21	21 (16 + 5)
5. Portuguese	7 (6 + 1)	7 (7 + 0)	6	7	7 (7 + 0)
6. German	8 (4 + 4)	9 (4 + 5)	7	7	7 (3 + 4)

The following languages, which are relevant to the present book because of their global position, must be added to the figures in Table D.4–1: 7. Italian (four states: 1 + 3, i.e. next ranking language after German according to number of official-language states), 8. Chinese (three states: 2 + 1), 9. Russian (two states: 1 + 1), 10. Japanese (one state: 1 + 0). These figures are the same in Banks 2007, *Fischer Weltalmanach* 2007 and Kausen 2013. Dutch and Tamil, which are of the same rank as Chinese (2 + 1) according to the number of official-language states, are also worth mentioning. I have already mentioned that other languages have two official-language states. These are Greek, Swedish, Malayan, Quechua, Swahili, Turkish, Hungarian and Urdu (all according to Kausen 2013).

Table D.4–1 does distinguish between sole and co-official position, at least for some of the years registered, but not between national and regional official language of state. This distinction was not made consistently in the sources and I could not establish it reliably. Accordingly, in Kausen's list (2013), the specification of German as only a regional official language in Belgium is not given. Where more than one language is named for one state, I have classified all languages as co-official regardless of any specification as regional.

Despite deficiencies of the mere number of official-language states as an indicator for the international ranking of a language, this number is not entirely meaningless (Ch. D.1). Indeed, official-language states occasionally cooperate effectively to strengthen the position of their language. In many international organisations or conferences, each member or participant state has one vote regardless of number of inhabitants or economic power, so that even small states have some weight. This applies primarily in the UN and the EU (cf. Ch. H.3; H.4.2–H.4.6). This circumstance was pointed out by Heinz Kloss (1974b: 46, 26f.): "In the age of the UN and its egalitarian one-country-one-vote principle [. . .], seven small states induced by sociocultural emancipation to combine into a large federal-state would lose considerable international influence – especially with regard to their languages". But states with great economic power naturally have more effective means for strengthening the position of their own language. Map D.4–1 provides an overview of territories of the international languages (as per Ch. A.3), geographical size and distribution.

To rely on a determination of the exact size of official-language territories would be to overestimate the information value of this dimension, at least as an indicator for the global position of languages. However, the difference between languages with relatively large and those with relatively small official-language territories is remarkable. The first category includes (in alphabetical order): Arabic, Chinese, English, French, Portuguese, Russian and Spanish; and the second includes German, Italian and Japanese.

As for distribution among the continents, the following ranking by number of continents is obtained:

1. English 5 (Africa, America, Asia, Europe, Oceania including Australia);
2. French 4 (Africa, America, Europe, Oceania including Australia);
3. Portuguese, Spanish 3 (Africa, America, Europe);
4. Arabic, Russian 2 (Asia, Europe);
5. German, Italian (Europe), Chinese, Japanese (Asia) 1.

This overview of size and worldwide distribution of official-language territories of the international languages seems to project the history of the "native countries" onto the present: on one side, the successful colonial powers (Great Britain, France, Portugal, Spain, "Arabia", Russia and China), on the other, those whose colonial ambitions failed (Germany, Italy and Japan). The second group also became involved in colonial politics according to their power; but they came

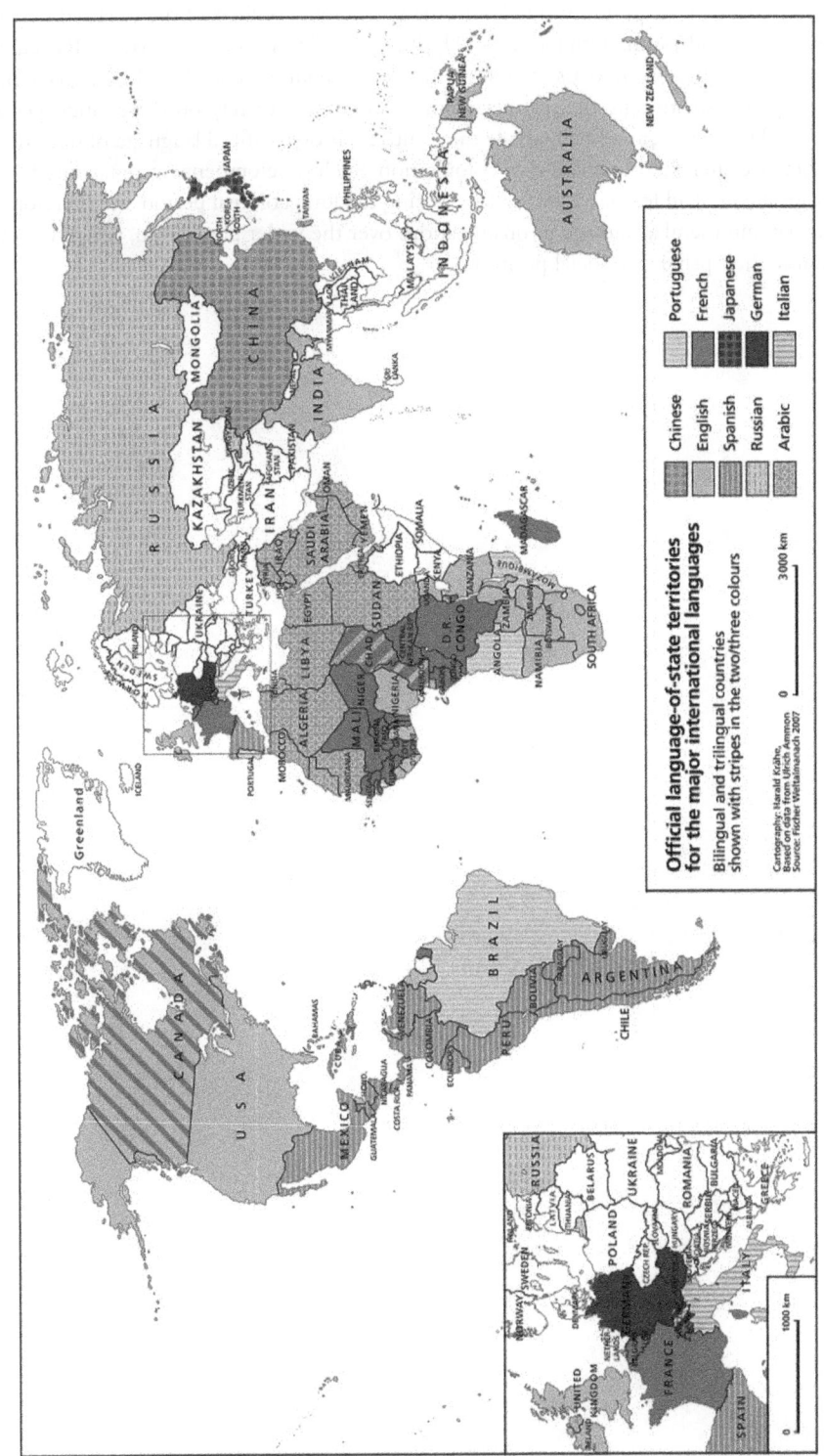

Map D.4-1 Official language territories of the ten most important international languages

too late and lost their acquisitions quickly in the belligerent conflicts of the twentieth century. Andrew Conrad and Joshua Fishman (1977; Fishman 1977b; Fishman/ Cooper/ Rosenbaum 1977) have shown that many years of colonial rule were required to anchor the language of the colonising power so strongly that former colonies continued to rely on these languages after achieving independence, and finally made them into their own official language of state, despite their reluctance after the humiliation of colonisation. Such developments were favoured by the fact that local elites had learned the language during the long colonial period and therefore had a spectacular and useful advantage in qualifications over the wider population, which they used to legitimise their privileged social position.

E

GERMAN AS A MINORITY LANGUAGE, BUT NOT AN OFFICIAL LANGUAGE OF STATE

1. General characterisation of German-speaking minorities today

Many people with German as their native language live outside the territories in which German is an official language of state (Ch. D). The present chapter defines these people as speakers of German as a minority language. German-speaking minorities are relevant to the global position of German whenever they use German with German-speaking people in other countries. In such contexts, communication is international in the broader sense, because it is between native speakers. (In the case of German as a foreign language (GFL), it is international communication in the narrower sense; Ch. A.3.) But German-speaking minorities also strengthen the position of German for other reasons, e.g. if they have schools with German as a language of instruction or at least as a school subject, and media, societies or clubs. This can bring non-German-speakers into contact with German language and culture and motivate them to learn German. There are remarkable examples in Hungary, Romania and Namibia (Ch. E.4.6; E.4.7; E.4.9). German-speaking minorities also contribute to securing GFL in the school curricula in their countries.

Apart from such effects, the chapter is also concerned with the *maintenance* of German within the minorities by passing it on to subsequent generations and using it in different domains. However, structural details of the respective German, which have been the focus of previous research on minorities, and the allocation of varieties to the German language (Ch. B.1; B.2) are less relevant to the present topic. The opposite of language maintenance is *language shift* or *language loss*, an enduring phenomenon which must be distinguished from situational *code switching*. I prefer these terms to metaphors with biological connotations (e.g. *language death*). For the inverse process, I use *reversal of language shift* instead of the familiar *language revival*.

In the minorities under discussion, the "German ethnic group (ethnicity or nationality)" (Ch. B.3) is also relevant, alongside "German as native language". Accordingly, none of the conceivable combinations of a) "German as native language" and b) "German ethnicity" can be excluded. We are likely to encounter i) a with b, ii) a without b, iii) b without a. The total scope of the minority is therefore the unitary set of all people with the feature combinations {i}∪{ii}∪{iii}. In this context, the term "German ethnicity" should be understood broadly as corresponding to the origin of the people or their ancestors in any part of the German-speaking territory and their distribution before the start of the German Empire.

For the minorities under discussion, the question of a bottom limit, especially the corresponding minimum size, must also be addressed. Heinz Kloss used the term "scattered German"

[*Streudeutschtum*], without negative connotations (1935; Ammon 1991a: 91), to refer to German-speaking individuals, families and small groups which exist worldwide in almost all countries. Although only to a minimal extent, they can also influence the global position of German, e.g. by motivating neighbours to learn German or visit a German-speaking country. For reasons of scale, I have limited myself to larger groups, especially those which are *institutionalised* as a group through their own institutions. Such institutions include schools, religious organisations, media and societies with different purposes, such as sport, music, theatre, dance, gastronomy, commercial art, language maintenance, social games or enacting German *Gemütlichkeit* [friendliness and good cheer]. I was, however, not able to include all such German(-speaking) groups and have limited myself to the most well-known based on recent research (Born/ Dickgießer (1989); especially, Born/ Jakob 1990).

The present focus is therefore on *indigenous* (or *autochthonous*) minorities. *Exogenous* (*allochthonous*, recently formed) minorities, which have so far hardly been researched, will not be considered until Ch. E.5. Indigenousness is often taken as a criterion for granting minority rights. The *European Charter for Regional or Minority Languages* only applies to minority languages which are "*traditionally* used in a given region of the country by citizens of this country [. . .]" (Art. 1.a, 1.i; emphasis U.A.). The Charter was proposed by the European Council, adopted by the EU and recommended to member states (conventions.coe.int/Treaty/ Commun/QueVoulezVous. asp?CL=GER&NT=148). It gives no further explanation of "indigenousness" other than that it apparently relates to "regional or minority languages which have *grown historically*" (Preamble: § 2 – emphasis U.A.). The languages of more recent immigrants do not receive funding on the same scale, because immigration, which is unrestricted within the EU, should not "disadvantage the official languages [. . .]" (Preamble: § 5). Otherwise, immigrants could ultimately dominate small member states linguistically. I am not aware of a generally accepted, clear definition of "indigenousness (of a minority or language)". Definitions based on absolute duration of existence or number of previous generations are problematic. The following suggestion by Paul Philippi (2009: 33) seems more likely to achieve consensus: "Minority groups are indigenous in every case if their existence is older than the state to which they currently belong. Above all, older than the state, which, on the basis of the majority of one of the ethnic groups present in the territory, has declared itself as the nation state of precisely this one ethnic group". I agree with this definition. However, Philippi's definition is formulated narrowly. It specifies that these minorities are "at least" indigenous (ibid). However, groups previously recognised as linguistic minorities can also be included, after their resettlement in other countries, e.g. the Mennonites, who emigrated from Russia and further to North America (Ch. E.4.11). This broadening of the term "indigenousness" corresponds to its current usage. However, the following – allochthonous/exogenous – persons or groups are, with respect to German(-speaking) minorities, excluded from my understanding of indigenousness:

- People who have recently migrated from German-speaking countries to states with other languages, unless they join groups which are indigenous according to Philippi's criterion;
- *Expatriates* sent by companies in German-speaking countries (Ch. E.5; Ch. F) or scientists from German-speaking countries working abroad (Ch. G), who are not naturalised there;
- People ordered abroad by governments or authorities of German-speaking countries (Ch. H);
- Holiday or retirement colonies from German-speaking countries, e.g. in Spain (Ch. E.5).

Indigenous German(-speaking) minorities specified in this manner have a range of shared properties which distinguish them from other linguistic minorities and which are significant for their continued existence. To my knowledge, comprehensive typologies of linguistic minorities which are compatible with all research interests are so far unavailable. Corresponding attempts have generally ended in collections of dimensions or factors, or lists of open questions which require further differentiation and operationalisation. One example, which is no longer new, but still worthy of note, was provided by John Edwards (1992). With regard to this and more recent typological proposals, I have identified and partially operationalised 47 factors (possible causes) (Ammon 2011a), which can influence the language maintenance of minorities. Subjecting them to serious, empirical assessment, primarily with reference to weighting and interaction, will be a task for the future. Apart from the volume of work required, this will be possible only with severe restrictions because of the very small number of comparable minorities. However, in the next chapter, E.2, I shall outline this list of factors to introduce the possible causes for language maintenance or language shift in a comprehensive manner.

According to my assessment, the following eight features are a) generally valid for German-speaking minorities (i.e. they apply – with certain restrictions – to all), b) specific (taken together, they generally apply only to them) and c) relevant for the maintenance of German. 1) and 2) tend to promote language maintenance, while 3) to 8) are detrimental to it.

1) German-speaking minorities have an international language at their disposal (Ch. A.3; A.7)

As with all international languages (except Esperanto), German is a numerically strong language with over 100 million native and SL speakers, and FL speakers also approaching the millions (Ch. C.1; C.2; J.7). Furthermore, German-speakers (native and SL-speakers) form one of the economically strongest language communities in the world (ranking 4 or 5; Ch. C.4). In this respect, German-speaking minorities differ very significantly from minorities with small or economically weak language communities. German is only a second-rank international language, positioned far behind English (Ch. A.7), but its global position is stronger than the languages of many other minorities.

Language communities with very small speaker numbers are often associated with minorities without a majority or official-language state. Edwards (2010: 69f.) speaks of "small and stateless language communities", whose speakers often have little opportunity but to shift to a higher-ranking language, because the communication potential and utility of their own language are too low (Ch. A.7). Their function is limited to symbolising the social identity of their speakers. Questions about the maintenance of such languages "touch essentially upon identity" (Edwards 2010: 14). By contrast, language maintenance in German-speaking minorities can have additional advantages, because German has official-language states with majorities of native speakers (Ch. D). The prospects for communicating and cooperating with them can strengthen language-maintenance efforts by German-speaking minorities. Even the existence of other German-speaking minorities can act in this manner. Especially, the religious German-speaking minorities are often interlinked over great distances. They form "language archipelagos" (Ch. E.4.11; Steffen/ Altenhofen 2014). In this case, German acts as a native-language bridge over foreign-language territories (not to be confused with a lingua franca, which bridges different native languages as a foreign language; Ch. A.3).

The most obvious motivation for maintaining a language with international position and economically strong majority territories is derived from cost-benefit considerations: the prospect of markets, employment and education opportunities. The appeal by Peter Clever of the Federal Union of German Employer Associations (*BDA*) to school leavers from German schools abroad also applies to German-speaking minorities. For many applicants, "it is, first and foremost, language [. . .] which represents a major hurdle on the road to Germany". But he added, that for the school leavers present, there were apparently "concrete prospects [. . .] for professional training in a German company or studying in a German university [...] via practical placements" (*Begegnung. Deutsche Arbeit im Ausland* 33 (4), 2012: 9–11). The same applies to German-speaking minorities, provided they hold firm to the German language. There may even be vocational prospects in their own country in corporate branches from German-speaking countries (e.g. Romania, Ch. E.4.7). This gives rise to an "instrumental motivation" for language maintenance, to use the term introduced by Robert Gardner and Wallace Lambert (1959: 267f.) for language learning undertaken for career advantages (Ch. J. 8). This differs from the "integrative motivation", striving for integration in a group (G. Schmid 2011: 51–53), which relates to social identity. Efforts towards language maintenance thus become "acts of (social) identity" (Le Page/ Tabouret-Keller 1985), towards integration in a group of which the language is an essential symbol or "core value" (Smolicz 1980a; b; 1981). Both motivational complexes, instrumental and integrative (or identificational), are relevant for language maintenance.

2) *Language maintenance in the German-speaking minorities may be promoted by German-speaking states*

This correlates with the preceding feature. The German-speaking states have the necessary economic resources to support the German-speaking minorities in maintaining their language. This differs from minorities without a majority-language state or with only a small official-language state. Moreover, in the case of German-speaking minorities, language maintenance is advantageous for the German-speaking states themselves because it strengthens the international position of German. One special advantage is the potential function of the German-speaking minorities as regional door-openers. They also constitute potential "human capital", especially for skilled workers who are in great demand in the German-speaking states. As a result, promoting their language maintenance is worthwhile. Such promotion is part of the foreign cultural policy (*AKP*) of the German-speaking countries, especially Germany and Austria (details in Ch. K). One example is the promotion of East-Central European German-speaking minorities by the "Institute for Foreign Relations" (*Institut für Auslandbeziehungen, ifa*) in Stuttgart, which is co-financed by the German Foreign Office (Ch. K.3.3). This funding is directed primarily to young people and the media. The leading German AKP Institute is also committed in the same way. "For more than 10 years, the Goethe Institute has been funding German minorities in Central Europe, Eastern Europe and Central Asia on behalf of the Foreign Office" (www.goethe.de/ Ihr/prj/dtm/deindex.htm). Austria, Switzerland, Liechtenstein and occasionally South Tyrol and East Belgium also participate to a limited extent in such funding of minorities (but not Luxembourg). It can be assumed that this funding contributes towards the language maintenance of the German-speaking minorities.

3) *For the German-speaking minorities, German is only one of two, usually three languages*

Nowadays, German-speaking minorities must also always learn and use the majority language e.g. Romanian, for the German-speaking minority in Romania, or Portuguese, for the German-speaking minority in Brazil (Ch. E.4.7; E.4.10). "Linguistic islands" which are (largely) cut off from the surrounding linguistic majority, no longer exist (e.g. Berend/ Knipf-Komlósi 2006; Eichinger/ Plewnia/ Riehl 2008). Even "religious isolationists" acknowledge the need to open towards the majority society and their language. The largest of such German-speaking groups are the Amish people, the Mennonites and the Hutterites in various states of Anglo-and Ibero-America (Ch. E.4.11).

Bilingualism is unavoidable for almost every member of a German-speaking minority. The importance of this fact for language maintenance is captured by the suggestion that the proportion of monolingual members of minorities can be used as an indicator for secure language maintenance (Grin 1992: 73). In the contrasting case of bilingualism or multilingualism of the entire minority, maintenance of the minority language is endangered. For German-speaking minorities, bilingualism is often a minimum for language skills and language use. It is generally sufficient only if the surrounding majority language is English. With every other majority language, the German-speaking minorities sense that, like every other language apart from English, German is limited in its international position, and much international and especially global communication is successful only in English (Ch. A.2). Additionally required languages often hamper the maintenance of German even further.

4) For the German-speaking minorities, German is often only a "nearby language"

The vocational usefulness of German often remains more of a hope than a practical reality. Even in German companies abroad, communication may seldom take place in German (Ch. F.5; F.7). The public use of German in residential areas of the minority is generally quite restricted. Public debates or contacts with government offices, hospitals, businesses, etc. take place largely in the majority language. German therefore functions only as a "nearby language" (*Nähesprache*; Koch/ Oesterreicher 1985), with use in informal domains such as family, friends, pub and selected minority events (festivities and gatherings). As a result, German is strengthened as a language of emotion and group identity, but impaired in prestige. By contrast, the competing "distance language" gains in prestige, which it gathers from the domains in which it predominates. Above all, German-speaking minorities experience the subordination of their own language to the majority language as the official language of state and dominant language at school and work. This applies especially if German is not a language of instruction in schools but only a school subject, or not even this. As a result, pressure is exerted within the families to use the majority language to prepare children for school, which limits German even as a nearby language and can easily lead to a complete language shift. The use of German in school as language of instruction and not just as a school subject is an important prerequisite for language maintenance. However, this is often the main stumbling block. Use of German in kindergarten or pre-school would be important for securing linguistic competence and symbolism for social identity (Cummins 1995), but it is very seldom available. Even university courses with German as the language of instruction are often missing; there is often only the subject of German or German Studies. It was again Heinz Kloss (1927) who first pointed out the importance of German-speaking universities and courses for securing self-respect and thus linguistic and cultural maintenance of minorities.

5) The German-speaking minorities are numerically weak

In his overview of the successful reversal of language shift in the French language community in Québec (Canada), Richard Bourhis (2001: 102–106) highlighted the importance of "demographic variables". This factor of the numerical strength of the minority was extremely important for reversing the shift back to more French. Indeed, when this reversal of language shift was gathering momentum at the start of the 1970s, approximately 7 million people, more than 80% of the population of Québec, named French as their native language. In general, a large speaker number is considered a good basis for a successful language-maintenance policy (ibid: 105).

However, the German-speaking minorities are numerically considerably smaller than those for French in Québec, which therefore hampers language maintenance.

6) The German-speaking minorities are widely scattered without linguistically homogeneous settlement territories

The members of German-speaking minorities seldom live together in large numbers and they have neighbours who speak other languages. Entire localities with exclusively German speakers exist only in religiously motivated groups (Amish, Mennonites, Hutterites; Ch. E.4.11). However, *linguistic homogeneity* of the place of residence or "cohesiveness" (Edwards 1992: 39f.) is understood to strengthen language maintenance, especially in conjunction with compactness or density of settlement as opposed to living far apart (Ammon 2011a: 52). With linguistically mixed settlements, it is not generally possible to realise the territoriality principle which, unlike the identity principle (Myhill 1999; Ch. D.2.4), secures language maintenance well because the territoriality principle enforces the use of the language in important institutions. By contrast, in the case of mixed settlement, the usefulness of the language is restricted in proportion with the number of speakers of other languages. Mixed settlement also favours linguistic exogamy, i.e. marriage between speakers of other languages, mostly the majority language. It is frequent among German-speaking minorities. With linguistic exogamy, the family usually becomes bilingual. Under pressure from school, "subtractive bilingualism" then readily occurs to the detriment of the minority language, i.e. German is pushed into the background. The consequence is that the native language is not passed on to the next generation, and there is a shift to the majority language (de Vries 1992: 220).

7) All German-speaking minorities have experienced traumatic ethnic and linguistic discrimination with after effects and, in many places, continuation – albeit in attenuated form

Mentioning this feature is not an attempt to transfer blame. Negative experiences of the German-speaking minorities are largely the consequence of devastating policies of the largest German-speaking state, Germany. However, at times these have been intensified by local politics, e.g. Stalinist policies in the Soviet Union, which extended across Eastern European states, and the nationalist policies of the *Estado Novo* under President Getúlio Vargas (1930–45) in Brazil (Ch. E.4.8; E.4.10). Without exception, all the German-speaking minorities described in greater detail here experienced suppression and discrimination against the language during the twentieth century, including complete prohibition of use, at least in public. Today, resentment against "Germans" or Germany in consequence of wars and national socialism seems to be disappearing. But, in many places, the memory still characterises attitudes towards Germany. This can continue to hamper language maintenance of German-speaking minorities, perhaps less through the surrounding language majorities than inside the minorities themselves. Importing trauma from the German-speaking countries into the minorities also possibly plays a part, because – given the enduring, no doubt justified memory of German crimes – a comprehensively positive attitude towards their own national identity and language is difficult even for Germans. All actors in the maintenance of language – the minorities themselves, the surrounding linguistic majorities and the populations and governments of the German-speaking countries – must cope with attitudes of reservation towards everything German, including the language. As a result, such attitudes can impair maintenance or promotion of the minority language, which makes it difficult for German-speakers to stand up for their own language and easier for others to reject their claims.

8) The German-speaking minorities tend towards language shift: away from the native language, or in some cases reversing the shift to German as a foreign language (GFL)

More clearly than any other feature, this also has an impact on linguistic-structure. Features 3) to 7) combine in the direction of subtractive bilingualism at the expense of German and in favour of a language shift to the majority language. This development is shown in numerous borrowings and transferences from the majority language, the "Contact German" (*Kontaktdeutsch*) specified and described by Czaba Földes (2005: 68–209), and in *language attrition* of German, especially, reduced vocabulary and simplified morphology (Schwartzkopff 1987; R. Born 1995, 2003; Riehl 2004: 74–77). These are a consequence of the restricted use of German even as a nearby language (feature 4)). Parents give their children only an impoverished language input, and, because of the resulting limits on self-expression, the children shift to the majority language. This varies depending on factors such as ethnic German identity (Ch. B.3), level of education, frequency of contact with the German language and vocational advantages of language maintenance. Whether the next generation will return to German as a kind of foreign language, a second language in sequence and type of learning (only in school), which they perhaps declare as their second (or even genuine) native language, will probably depend most strongly on their preservation of ethnic German identity and vocational opportunities based on the knowledge of German.

2. Causes (factors) for language maintenance and language shift

Investigating the causes for language maintenance and shift in linguistic minorities can lead to the mistaken view that only a single factor is relevant. In my own unrepresentative experience, many people engaged with this question take the key factor to be the minorities having their own schools in which German is the language of instruction and not only a school subject. According to this view, the language of instruction in dedicated schools would guarantee language maintenance for the minority. However, this kind of reduction to a single dominant or salient cause often falls into the frequently encountered "fallacy of the single cause" (Dobelli 2012: 201–203). It is evident that dedicated schools are of little help if the pupils have no interest in German, possibly because a knowledge of German will not be useful to them later in life (lack of instrumental motivation) or because their parents have only a weak linguistic or ethnic German identity, so that German is hardly spoken in the family. Moreover, dedicated schools depend on other factors, such as the numerical strength of the minority, the homogeneity and compactness of their settlements, language rights in the respective state and so on. In brief, the "single cause" is a fallacy which frequently occurs when people are looking for the "true reason" for a development or trying to "get to the bottom of it". To avoid this error, the following descriptions of German-speaking minorities (Ch. E.4.2–E.5) include a considerable number of factors which I consider relevant for language maintenance or shift on the basis of the available theoretical research and empirical investigations on language minorities, as well as personal visits to German-speaking minorities. However, at the present level of research, I can only assess their weighting and interconnections subjectively, on a case-by-case basis. As Schiffman (1987) explains with regard to language shift among American-Germans, German as a language of school instruction certainly seems to be a very important factor, but its effect is linked with other factors which I also include.

Disregarding early essays on "language maintenance", such as those of Heinz Kloss (1927), Joshua A. Fishman (1964, 1965) can be regarded as the founder of language-maintenance research. The book *Language Loyalty in the United States: The Maintenance and Perpetuation of Non-English Mother Tongues by American Ethnic and Religious Groups* (Fishman/ Nahirny/ Hofmann/ Hayden 1966) published under his supervision provides a broad and detailed overview of relevant questions. Apart from looking for causes, Fishman was also engaged in the practice of language maintenance, especially for his own native language, Yiddish. In the US-American context, he experienced difficulties in putting theory into practice in his own family. His and other investigations have shown that the conditions for language maintenance and language shift cannot be understood fully without reference to political history. Regarding Yiddish and German minorities, one need only think of the Holocaust and Nazism. Accordingly, each of the following presentations of German-speaking minorities (Ch. E.4.2–E.4.11, but not E.5) begins with a brief historical summary.

However, influential factors, interwoven in a complicated manner as already suggested, may also be found in the present. In trying to identify and evaluate their effect, the following difficulties rapidly occur:

- Many factors depend upon others or influence each other and are therefore intensified or attenuated in their effect. Many can be specified or operationalised only with difficulty in isolation, and definitions may not overlap. Sometimes, "deeper causes", which go beyond the horizon of my knowledge, lurk behind them;
- The weighting of factors varies between language minorities and changes over time, e.g. depending on political circumstances or technical innovation. As a result, but also because of lack of research, it is difficult to estimate weightings from case to case;
- With imprecise knowledge of their individual effect, the plurality of factors involved makes it difficult to assess the combined effect and therefore to formulate superordinate regularities of language maintenance and/or language shift. Longer term prognoses for individual language minorities are therefore extremely uncertain, especially if the empirical data are incomplete
(Popper 1975; Dobelli 2011: 165–167).

The extremely large number of factors can be explained by the fact that objective factors may correlate with subjective factors; in particular, with suppositions by members of the minorities about the objective factors. Such suppositions can themselves act as factors of language maintenance or language shift. For example, the "speaker number of a minority", the "vocational opportunities for members of minorities with knowledge of the minority language" or the "promotion of the minority by countries in which the minority language is an official language or majority language" are objective (potentially effective) language-maintenance factors. But suppositions by members of the minorities about these objective factors can influence language maintenance or language shift. In fact, they can strengthen or weaken the will of members of minorities to maintain their language, which in turn influences language maintenance in the manner of a self-fulfilling prophecy. On the basis of such considerations, Bourhis, Giles and Rosenthal (1981) developed a "subjective vitality questionnaire" as a research instrument, which they proposed and used as an indicator for the "vitality" of the minority language and its chances of being maintained. However, the combination of subjective correlations with the objective factors increases the number of factors. Adding one subjective factor to every objective factor doubles the number. In the following, I will therefore limit myself largely to objective factors, apart from attitudes towards language and language maintenance. In addition to my own previous work (Ammon 1991a: 105–114; 2007c; 2011a), I shall rely mainly on the following publications: Born/ Dickgießer 1989; Bourhis 2001; Bourhis/ Giles/ Rosenthal 1981; Bourhis/ Lepicq 2004; Clyne 2001; Darquennes 2005, 2011a, b; Edwards 1992; Ehala 2009; Fishman 1991a,

2001a; Fishman/ Nahirny/ Hoffman/ Hayden 1966; Giles/ Bourhis/ Taylor 1977; Grenoble/ Whaley 1998b; Haarmann 1986; Harwood/ Giles/ Bourhis 1994; Hyltenstam/ Stroud 1996; Johnson/ Doucet 2006; G. Kaufmann 2006; Kloss 1927, 1966; Mattheier 1994, 1996; McConnell 1996; Riehl 2004; 166f.; P. Rosenberg 1994, 2003a, b; Sasse 1992; Wiesinger 1980: 495f).

Contrary to my reservations about generalisation and interdependence of factor weighting and, in view of current research, many theoretical proposals on language maintenance and shift still do suggest such generalisations. In fact, Fishman's "stages of reversing language shift" (2001a, 2001c: 466) – an introduction to the reversal of language shift, no doubt strongly influenced by the success of Israel with Hebrew (Ivrit) – provides one well-known example. But, at the same time, it is based on general assumptions about language-maintenance factors and their interdependence. Successful reversal of language shift is said to begin with the linguistic reconstruction of the language (primarily, building up of vocabulary, grammar and corresponding codification), a step which can be skipped for the shift or reversal towards German. This is continued through learning of the language by adults; followed by introduction into family communication; socialisation of children in their language; and its consequent establishment as a native language. From this basis, anchoring in public domains then occurs, e.g. with high importance, schools and media (a total of eight major steps or actually nine, because one step is subdivided into a) and b).

This model suggests the three domains, family, school and media, and regular use of the language there, as the decisive supports for language maintenance. However, emphasising such anchors for language maintenance prompts the counter question of how the language could have lost these in the first place, and therefore also, how they are to be recovered. To me, the logical answer seems to be, precisely through other factors which have been ignored, – because this certainly does not happen of its own accord! This answer applies to every step of Fishman's sequence and, with further consistent and robust analysis, it ultimately leads to the unfathomable diversity of language-maintenance factors. In the following, I have singled out and explained those which seem particularly important for German-speaking minorities.

Analogous questions are raised by all the attempts at dramatic reduction of factors known to me, which are typical, e.g. in the case of proposed definitions of threshold values or handy indicators for language maintenance (e.g. Grin 1992; McConnell 1996; overview of indicators in Castonguay 2005). The factors highlighted only bring further factors into view. In one case, charismatic speakers and writers are suddenly shown to be important for language maintenance: "presence and quality of leaders who can head the formal and informal institutions representing the ethnolinguistic group [. . .]", "activists and proto-elites who succeed in mobilising ethnolinguistic groups [. . .] (Harwood/ Giles/ Bourhis 1994: 170; see 2) (factor cluster X, below). Another case is Gorter's (2001: 216 f.) criticism of Fishman (2001a) which ignores transnational factors acting on language maintenance. One example of these is the *European Charter for Regional or Minority Languages*, by means of which the European Council and the EU exert pressure on member states to promote language maintenance in linguistic minorities (see 1) in factor cluster XIII below). Such factors go beyond Fishman's approach which remains within a national framework.

Another question is the grouping (classification) of factors. Bourhis/ Giles/ Rosenthal (1981; also Bourhis 2001: 103) suggest a three-way division into "Demographic Factors", "Institutional Support and Control Factors" and "Status Factors". But this seems too coarse-grained because the diversity of individual factors which must then be subsumed becomes overwhelming. For such reasons, even at the upper level of classification, I have opted for a more detailed subdivision into 12 groups (classes) of moderate differentiation. In principle, the UNESCO Ad Hoc Expert Group (2003) proceeds in a similar manner but limits itself to language minorities without majority or official-language states of their own language, so that the languages readily fall out of use ("die out"). Johnson/ Doucet (2006) are also wary of a coarse-grained classification and therefore offer a useful starting point.

At the same time, the following factors are potential indicators of language maintenance or should be taken into consideration when constructing such indicators. Introducing them and reiterating them in summary in Ch. E.4.1 is intended primarily as a checklist for descriptions of language minorities with regard to their chances of language maintenance. These factors are suitable for minorities, such as the German-speaking minorities (Ch. E.4.2–E.5), with a (native) language which is counted among the international languages (below the level of English; Ch. A.7), which is a national official language of state in at least one country (Ch. D) and has an economically and numerically strong language community (Ch. C). The list allows room for further factors, different factor weightings and operationalisations. Its use is, of course, dependent on available data.

I. Identification of the minority

For the purpose of this book, German-speaking minorities are defined as having members whose native language is German. The criterion can be considered as corroborated if they declare German as their native language. In general, allocation to German is unambiguous because the declaration refers either directly to German or to a dialect which, when asked, respondents acknowledge as a German dialect (dialect of the German language). But self-allocation can be doubtful if many members of the minority fail to perform or refuse this allocation, and only a small proportion, typically functionaries of the minority or intellectuals, accept it (e.g. possibly with the Amish people, Ch. E.4.11). In such rare cases, allocation to German is guided by the criteria specified in chapters B.1 and B.2 of at least moderate linguistic similarity of the dialect to the roofing variety, and, at the same time, high linguistic similarity of this roofing variety to one of the undoubted standard varieties of German, or at least moderate similarity of the dialect to any of the standard varieties of German in the absence of being roofed by a standard variety of another language with equal or greater linguistic similarity to the dialect (e.g. Alsace, Ch. E.4.3).

Ethnic allocation of the minority is less certain. Peter Rosenberg (1994: 158) and Harald Weydt (Rosenberg/ Weydt 1992) pointed out, "that there is an ever-growing proportion of Germans in the CIS [Community of Independent States! U.A.], who understand themselves as 'German', without speaking German". The same can be shown for other relevant minorities, e.g. the "Germans of Hungary" (Ch. E.4.6). When there are no longer any native speakers of German, this minority ceases to correspond according to the initial definition with the object of the present study. However, merely ethnic Germans (Ch. B.3) who allocate themselves to the linguistic minority are also included. They can be important for language maintenance by supporting language-maintenance efforts and e.g. sending their children to German-speaking schools. They often have a combined ethnic identity (German-Russian, Hungarian-German or similar). In empirical investigations, it should be noted that their "German" ethnicity possibly has a larger extension than that of every contemporary German-speaking state, because it is rooted in an earlier time. Furthermore, in the case of ethnic allocation, it is important to distinguish as clearly as possible between "ethnic group or nationality" and "state", i.e. ethnicity and citizenship respectively (Ch. B.3). The simplest investigative method, which is also possibly the most superficial, is through questionnaires. But statements by spokespeople or reports and commentaries in the media can also be revealing. What is important is to assess their representativeness for the population as a whole. The following aspects must be considered in research.

(1)   Native-speaker status of the minority variety;
(2)   Self-designation of the minority variety and linguistic self-allocation;

(3) Designation of the respective variety and linguistic allocation by the majority;
(4) Ethnic self-designation and ethnic self-allocation;
(5) Ethnic designation and ethnic allocation by the majority.

II. Demography of the linguistic minority

Quantifying linguistic and ethnic allocations points towards the demography of the linguistic minority, whose significance for language maintenance is beyond doubt. A small speaker number makes language maintenance difficult. However, multilingualism is also possible instead of language shift. Corresponding to the specifications under I., the demography of a minority also includes people who have shifted language, but still allocate themselves to the relevant German ethnic group, possibly because they are prepared to reverse the shift or motivate other people to learn German. The following classification is therefore appropriate for the demography of a language minority.

(1) *Numerical strength* – a) of the ethnic group ("Germans"), b) of the speakers of the minority language (German), c) of monolingual German-speakers, d) of multilingual German-speakers (German and majority language): d.α) primarily German-speaking, d.β) equal ranking with majority language, d.γ) lower ranking German-speaking (down to rudimentary knowledge).

The data for a), sometimes also b) to d) can often be acquired from censuses, but this is based on the declaration principle (self-allocation by respondents). Differentiations from d.α) to d.γ) generally require additional research and appropriate demarcation of speakers from non-speakers. In censuses, the ethnicity (nationality) "German" (*German, Nemtzki, Alemán* etc.) generally also includes Austrian, German Swiss and other German-speaking origins.

The following factors provide information about developmental trends:

(2) *Birth rate*, differentiated at least according to (1)a) and (1)b);
(3) *Immigration and emigration rate*, again differentiated according to (1)a) and (1)b).

Immigration of speakers of the minority language strengthens language maintenance and, conversely, emigration weakens it. Recent immigrants increase the speaker number and, under some circumstances, also modernise the respective variety. They intensify internal group communication for as long as they lack knowledge of the majority language.

III. Geography of the linguistic minority

In spite of modern communication and transport media, possibilities for contact still depend on geographical distance from states in which the language is a majority language or official language of state. One simplified classification is that between border minorities and language islands, corresponding to the presence or absence of borders with German-speaking countries. The following breakdown provides greater differentiation.

1) Geographical distance from German-speaking states: a) border minorities, b) minorities close to borders, c) remote minorities

One practicable distinction between German-speaking minorities still "close to the border" and those which are already "remote" is their position "inside" and "outside the EU".

Apart from geographical distance, other aspects of the geography of linguistic minorities are relevant for language maintenance (Edwards 1992), such as:

2) Linguistic homogeneity of the settlement region

This means that all the inhabitants of this region speak the same native language, although possibly with different varieties (dialects). Linguistic homogeneity used to be typical for language islands and favoured language maintenance (Mattheier 1994: 334). But nowadays, it is still found in "religious isolationists", such as the Amish people, Mennonites, Hutterites and possibly Templers (Ch. E.4.11). The modified Simpson index (also "Gibbs-Martin-index") has been suggested as a measure for linguistic homogeneity of the settlement region (Ammon 2011a: 51f). In fact, it measures the opposite of homogeneity, namely, diversity (D), which ranges between extreme values 0 (minimum) and 1 (maximum) (*wikipedia.org/wiki/Diversity_index*). This can easily be converted into a measurement for homogeneity (H) (minimum 0, maximum 1) through the following transformation, in which I classify the minority according to factor cluster 1) as specified under II. above (II.1.a, II.1.b, . . .):

$$D = 1 - \Sigma\, n_i(n_i - 1) : N(N - 1) \rightarrow H = \Sigma\, n_i(n_i - 1) : N(N - 1).$$

Illustrative sample calculation:

N = total population (of the defined territory)
n_i = number of individuals in each category $(n_1, n_2, \ldots, n_k)$
Categories: M (member of minority = II.1.a or II.1.b or II.1.c or II.1.d),
Non-M (non-member of minority = neither II.1.a nor II.1.b nor II.1.c nor II.1.d).
Assumed total population: 10,000.
Example 1: 5,000 M and 5,000 non-M.
Degree of homogeneity of territory = 0.5
((5,000 4,999 + 5,000 4,999) : (10,000 9,999)) = (49,990,000 : 99,990,000);
Example 2: 8,000 M and 2,000 non-M.
Degree of homogeneity of territory ≈ 0.74
((8,000 7,999 + 2,000 1,999) : (10,000 9,999)) = (73,991,000 : 99,990,000).

The difference between the two examples corresponds to our intuition, according to which the homogeneity in the second example must be greater than in the first (see also Van Parijs 2007b).

In my earlier experiments for the identification of language-maintenance factors, I also proposed the *density of the settlement* (Ammon 1991a: 106f., 2011a: 52). Relatively simple measurements are available for this, such as the quotient of "number of members of minority : area of minority territory" (which, however, presupposes the not always unproblematic demarcation of the two parameters). However, this potential factor for language maintenance in German-speaking minorities now seems of subordinate significance.

The following feature correlates with the attitude of members of the minority to their language, but also with the tolerance of the linguistic majority towards its use, and could also be allocated to feature group X.

3) Linguistic landscape in the minority language

Linguistic landscape (Shohamy/ Gorter 2009) refers to lettering on notices, posters, graffiti and similar, referring to shops, restaurants, museums or places of assembly and expressing political statements. Town names and road signs can also be considered part of the linguistic landscape. A rich linguistic landscape in the minority language also motivates towards further use of the language and therefore secures maintenance. For researchers of minorities, it also acts as an index for the pulsating "vitality" of the language community (Landry/ Bourghis 1997).

IV. Contacts with the linguistic majority and other-language minorities within the country of settlement

External contacts between members of the minority and the linguistic majority, and with other-language minorities in the country of settlement are also significant for language maintenance. Mixed settlement, which prevails in most German-speaking minorities, makes contact with the linguistic majority and other linguistic groups unavoidable. In this context, the social character of these contacts (private – business); their frequency and the choice of language; above all, the potential for choosing their own minority language, which comes into consideration as a possible indicator for strong language maintenance, are significant. Particularly intensive contact occurs in linguistically and ethnically mixed marriages, which are generally frequent. The following would therefore need to be registered:

1) *Contacts with the linguistic majority within the country of settlement*: a) business/public-services, α) frequent, β) rare; b) private, α) frequent, β) rare;
2) *Frequency of linguistic exogamy*.

A further relevant language-maintenance factor, which has been investigated by Göz Kaufmann (1997) and Johanna Bottesch (2008), following Lesley Milroy (1980), is that of linguistic networks, primarily, their proportions of minority and majority members, and their language choice.

V. Economic strength and social structure of the linguistic minority

With reference to the socio-economic structure of the minority, different language-maintenance factors can be conceived, depending on perspective. The following points are significant:

1) Economic strength of the minority as a whole

Which resources does the minority have at its disposal for language-maintenance measures, e.g. setting up and maintaining its own schools, including appointment of qualified teachers, financing its own media, identity-strengthening cultural events etc.?

2) Economic prosperity by comparison with the linguistic majority

Economic prosperity strengthens the prestige and self-confidence of a group. In general, language maintenance is more likely to succeed in minorities whose material welfare is higher than that of the majority population. A useful measurement would be the average gross domestic product or gross national product per person in the linguistic minority compared with that of the linguistic majority (measured as a median, if possible, to avoid distortion of the extremes). However, figures allowing such a comparison are seldom available which forces researchers to make do with other reference points.

3) Presence of all social strata

A comprehensive social structure of the minority is also relevant, in which the educated stratum in particular should not be under-represented. With most East-European German-speaking minorities, members of this group have often emigrated in recent history. As a result, experienced organisers and effective public speakers and advocates for language maintenance, as well as model speakers and writers for "correct" language use (Ch. B.2) are absent. Indeed, serious gaps in the social structure can undermine prestige and self-esteem of the minority and impair the will for language maintenance.

VI. Use of the minority language in the totality of domains

Any attempt at a comprehensive, generalisable typology of domains quickly encounters the problem of the wide potential for differentiation, which can broaden into an insurmountable number of domains. For a coarse-grained classification, even recent research (e.g. Werlen 2004: 336) often refers back to Georg Schmidt-Rohr (1932: 183). Fishman also refers to his work (1964, 1965, 1972b). Schmidt-Rohr's "types of multilingualism" (1932: 183, 1933: 179), the term he uses for domains, comprise "family, playground, street, language of instruction, school subject, play-times and language of conversation, church, literature, newspaper, army, court, administration". In broad terms, this classification is still useful today. Schmidt-Rohr's strong weighting of school (with three domains) is remarkable. The playground can provide valuable insights, e.g. after WWII, speaking *"le dialecte"* was strictly forbidden in Alsace, primarily as a deliberate prohibition of German. The example also shows that different domains become significant within a single life, for which reason the following subdivision of the life cycle into three parts should be considered as a minimum: a) life before working life, b) during working life (including working at home) and c) after working life.

In this context, the following classification of domains, which are generally restricted to those domains in which a use of the minority language is possible at all, seems useful for investigating linguistic minorities: family, friends (private networks), schools (school levels and types, language of instruction, school subject), religion (primarily in services), legal matters (solicitors offices, court proceedings), authorities (town halls, other offices), health matters (GP surgeries, hospitals), old people's homes, banks, insurance, restaurants and hotels, shops (supermarkets, specialist shops), media (newspapers, radio, TV, Internet: own and visited websites, social media), festivals and cultural events. In principle, language maintenance is more likely to be successful if the language is used regularly in more domains. However, family, school and media are particularly important, making the following classification expedient.

1) *In families*: a) with grandparents, b) between grandparents and parents, c) between parents, d) between parents and children, e) between children – in each case subdivided into α) exclusive use, β) use alongside one or more other languages, γ) no use;
2) *In schools*, differentiated into the most important school levels and types: a) as language of instruction, subdivided into α) exclusive use, β) use alongside one or more other languages, γ) no use, b) as school subject;
3) *In the media*: a) newspaper/magazines, b) radio, c) television, d) mobile and smart phone (social media), e) Internet (website access), once again, subdivided into α) exclusive use, β) use alongside one or more other languages, γ) no use.

The choice of language between grandparents, parents and children in 1) is an indicator for the particularly significant language-maintenance factor of "inter-generational continuity and maintenance" (Bourhis 2001: 110). At the same time, this relates to a differentiation of factor cluster II "demography of the minority".

VII. Rights of the minority relevant to language maintenance in the country of settlement

The use of the minority language is regulated by law in many domains. For example, the use of German in newspapers in Alsace after WWII was severely restricted by law for a considerable time; after the independence of Namibia in 1990, German was permitted as a language of instruction in state schools only up to the third year of schooling (Ch. E.4.3; E.4.9). Only the choice of language in the private sphere (family, friends, private networks) is generally immune from direct legal provisions (for legal questions for minorities, see Pan/ Pfeil 2006; Hilpold 2001, 2009; Heintze 1998; de Varennes 1996).

References to possible legal rulings are provided e.g. in the *European Charter for Regional or Minority Languages* of the European Council and the EU (47 or respectively 28 member states in 2014; conventions.coe.int/Treaty/Commun/QueVoulezVous.asp?CL=GER&NT=148). The charter covers the domain complexes "education" (Art. 8), "legal authorities" (Art. 9), "administrative authorities and public services" (Art. 10), "media" (Art. 11), "cultural activities and facilities" (Art. 12), "economic and social life" (Art. 13) and "cross-border exchange" (Art. 14). The charter therefore also includes cross-border contacts between "states [. . .] in which the same language is used in the same or similar form [. . .]".

The rights of a minority to engage in political activities are also significant, primarily:

1) *Right of the minority to its own interest group;*
2) *Right of the minority to its own representation, generally through the interest group, in community administration or regional or national government.*

VIII. Support for maintenance of the minority language from outside the home country

The *European Charter for Regional or Minority Languages* referenced above is an example of support of minorities in language maintenance from outside their country of settlement. The European Council and EU also provide PR work against the suppression of minority languages, e.g. in the diverse events within the *European Year of Languages* (2001). Such ideological support is also provided by the UN, especially UNESCO, which promotes language maintenance for minorities by recommending appropriate policies. For governments acting against them, such recommendations can cause difficulties of legitimation.

German-speaking minorities receive more substantial external assistance from German-speaking states and private organisations, primarily charity organisations. Germany, Austria and Switzerland (within the scope of its potential as a multilingual state) promote the global position of German in many different ways (Ch. K.3; K.4). Such external promotion may consist, e.g. in the supply of schoolbooks, teachers, media resources or financial support to the interest groups of the minority. However, there is a lack of effective preliminary work for a systematic description of language-maintenance assistance from outside the country of settlement. The following classification may assist orientation:

1) *Non-material support* from a) the UN, b) other international government and non-government organisations (GOs and NGOs), c) the EU, d) individual states or sub-state divisions of German majority or official language countries (Germany etc.);
2) *Material benefits* from the states or sub-state divisions of German majority or official-language countries, for a) regional cultural institutes, b) schools, c) media, d) cultural purposes, e) other.

IX. Contacts of the linguistic minority with states and regions with German language

Support and contributions from outside must be distinguished from contacts from and towards the outside, the most significant of which for German-speaking minorities are contact with German-speaking states. In fact, there are also contacts with other German-speaking minorities and with GFL learners, but these often play a marginal role because they are small in scale. Language archipelagos (see 9) below) form one exception, but contacts with German-speaking states are potentially significant language-maintenance factors. An important factor and indicator is double or multiple citizenship, including a German-speaking state. The following aspects may be relevant:

1) *Number of members of the minority with double citizenship including a German-speaking state:* a) absolute number, b) relative number;
   Among contacts with German-speaking states, the following deserve special consideration:
2) *Contacts via branches of companies from German-speaking states:* a) local employment, b) work or placement at head office or in branches in German-speaking states (see Ch. F.7);
3) *Contacts via schools or universities:* a) locally, e.g. German schools abroad (Ch. J.3), b) school/ university visits in German-speaking countries;
4) *Contacts via tourism:* a) from German-speaking states, b) to the latter (Ammon 2015: 833–864);
5) *Contacts by means of media, mass media and private media, primarily from and to German-speaking states:* a) newspapers/magazines, b) radio, c) TV, d) Internet, e) mobile and smart phone, f) email, g) Facebook and similar (Ch. I.1). Especially in the case of e–f, communication from the minority to the German-speaking states, i.e. reverse direction, can secure the maintenance of German in the minority (Ch. I.1.4);
6) *Contacts via cultural institutes of German-speaking states,* e.g. the Austrian Institute (*Österreich Institut*; Ch. K.3.3; K.4);
7) *Other cultural contacts:* a) visits, e.g. by artists from German-speaking countries, b) visits e.g. of home artists to German-speaking countries. It should be specified whether the communication takes place a) predominantly in German or b) predominantly in another language;
8) *Sports contacts:* a) visits from German-speaking countries, b) visits to German-speaking countries;
9) *Contacts via language archipelagos* (Ch. E1: 1; E.4.11).

X. Attitudes towards the ethnic group and language of the minority in the minority itself and in the majority

Maintenance of a minority's own language is more likely to be successful with a strong will to maintain the language, at least in parts of the minority. Maintenance of the minority language also requires tolerance if not support from the majority population. Especially in linguistically mixed marriages, passing the minority language to children depends on the "ethnolinguistic" attitude of the parents. In this respect, a conservative attitude (in the literal sense) corresponds to Uriel Weinreich's ([1953] 1974: 100) "language loyalty". According to Jerzy J. Smolicz (1980a, b, 1981), it can also form a "core value" for the relevant group. This means that – as the native language of its members – the ethnic group is existentially linked with the respective language, so that it is dissolved if they shift to another language. Regarding one's own language as an important symbol of *group identity*, especially *ethnolinguistic identity*, is similar (Tajfel 1978). Through this symbolic function, the common language strengthens group cohesion. Like all attitudes, identification with one's own language community or ethnic group – conceived from various perspectives – also has cognitive, affective and pragmatic components. Individuals allocate themselves to the group, develop a feeling of "We" and are disposed to act towards group cohesion. Such an attitude generally also secures language maintenance (Giles/ Bourhis/ Taylor 1977). The following factors can be distinguished:

1) *Attitude of the minority towards their own language*: a) positive, b) negative, c) indifferent;
2) *Attitude of the minority towards their own ethnic group*: a) positive, b) negative, c) indifferent;
3) *Attitude of the majority (or also of other minorities) to the minority language*: a) positive, b) negative, c) indifferent;
4) *Attitude of the majority (or other minorities) to the minority ethnic group*: a) positive, b) negative, c) indifferent;

As explained in Ch. E.1 (7), there are historical reasons for an insecure or shaky ethnic identity in German minorities. This can perhaps be best understood as a combination of strongly positive and strongly negative evaluations of one's own ethnic group. Attitudes of the majority may show a similar disparity, presumably with stronger marking of the negative evaluation. Indices for a positive attitude to one's own ethnic group and language are:

5) *Internal representation of the interests of the minority* in the form of an organisation;
6) *Language-policy goals for maintenance of own language;*
7) *Committed leaders of own organisation;*
8) *Committed spokespeople for language maintenance.*

XI. Position of minority language and majority language in the global language constellation (Ch. A.7) and linguistic distance from one another (Ch. B.2)

The sociolinguistic relationship between minority and majority language can also influence language maintenance and shift in the minority. Language maintenance is more likely if the minority language has a significantly higher comparative global ranking than the majority language, especially as an international language by comparison with a local language, or as a numerically strong language (with many speakers) by comparison with a numerically weak language, or if it has higher prestige for other reasons than the majority language, e.g. traditional function as an academic language. This assessment corresponds to Uriel Weinreich's view that "'prestige' had better be restricted to a language's value in social advance, or dispensed with altogether as too imprecise" (1974: 79, Note 34).

The following language-maintenance factors result from these considerations:

1) *International position and prestige of minority language and majority language*: a) degree of internationality, b) numerical strength, c) other prestige, e.g. as an academic language;

In all these respects, English is ranked above German, which acts in favour of a language shift towards English, especially in English-speaking countries with German as a minority language. With most East European languages, the prestige relationship with German is reversed.

A great linguistic distance (structural dissimilarity) of the minority language from the majority language makes shifting more difficult and can therefore favour language maintenance, while linguistic similarity favours shifting and consequently makes language maintenance more difficult (Clyne 2001; de Bot 1996. For "linguistic distance" see Ch. B.2).

2)   *Linguistic distance between minority language and majority language.*

In this respect also, English makes the language shift from German easier, while Slavic languages and especially Hungarian obstruct shifting for German-speakers and therefore motivate towards maintenance.

XII. Competence of the minority in their own language

The traditional internal means of communication of the minorities relevant here is generally a dialect of German. If competence in the traditional minority variety is limited, this is often an indicator for language shift to the majority language and therefore hampers the maintenance of German. This applies especially if the minority is affected in its entirety, that is, even speakers relatively well-versed in the minority variety exhibit weaknesses in competence. Such "language attrition" may be apparent in grammar, especially word-level grammar (e.g. noun gender), morphology (e.g. case endings, inflection of strong verbs), in vocabulary (over-generalisation of word meanings, transference from the majority language) or in pragmatics (especially speech-act transference) (e.g. Schwartzkopff 1987; Keel 2003; Born 1995, 2003; Riehl 2000: 74–77; overview in Földes 2005: 68–209). Code-switching is often also an indicator for incipient language shift (Rindler-Schjerve 1998; Földes 2005: 230–239). Relevant language-maintenance factors include:

1)   Competence in the dialect: a) absolute number of members of the minority, b) relative number – with α) full competence, β) restricted competence, γ) no competence;
2)   *Competence in standard German*: a) absolute number of members of the minority, b) relative number – with α) full competence, β) restricted competence, γ) no competence.

This completes my overview of language-maintenance factors relevant to the German-speaking minorities. It is conceived primarily as the basis for a checklist (Ch. E.4.1) for the description of language-maintenance opportunities.

3. Overview of the German-speaking minorities

Joachim Born and Sylvia Dickgießer (1989) have described German-speaking minorities in 25 states in which German is not an official language of state (and additionally in East Belgium and the province of Bolzano South Tyrol in Italy, in each case with German as a regional official language of state; Ch. D.3.1; D.3.2). At that time, the Soviet Union, Yugoslavia and Czechoslovakia had not been dissolved and were separate states. The bibliography of this global inventory, which is the most comprehensive to date, has been supplemented by Born/ Jakob in 1990. Their findings are included in Tables E.3–1 and E.3–2 as far as possible (references also in Wiesinger 1980, 1983b). I have also considered three later sources from the time since the dissolution of the Soviet Union (in 1991), Yugoslavia and Czechoslovakia (both in 1992): *Ethnologue* 2005 and *Ethnologue* 2009, which name 34 and respectively 36 states without German as an official language of state but with German-speaking minorities (in each case, under "Germany" or under the individual states), and the Wikipedia website "Deutsche Sprache", with 29 such states (de. wikipedia.org/wiki/Deutsche Sprache 17f).

Table E.3–1 States named in all four referenced sources with German as a minority language but not an official language of state

Argentina, Australia, Belize (b,9), Bolivia (b,5,9), Bosnia and Herzegovina (5,9), *Brazil, Canada, Chile,* Czech Republic (5,9,w), *Denmark,* Dominican Republic (w), Ecuador (b,5,9), Estonia (5,9,w), Finland (5), *France, Hungary, Israel,* Kazakhstan (5,9,w), Kyrgyzstan (5,9,w), Mexico (b,9,w), Moldavia (5), *Namibia, Paraguay,* Peru (b), Philippines (5,9), *Poland,* Puerto Rico (5,9), *Romania,* Russia (5,9,w), Serbia (w), Slovakia (5,9,w), Slovenia (5,9,w), *South Africa,* Tajikistan (5,9), Ukraine (5, 9,w), Uruguay (b,5,9) *USA,* Uzbekistan (5,9),Venezuela (b,5,9), United Arab Emirates (5).

Table E.3–2 States named in at least three of four sources (except Belize named only in two) with German as a minority language but not an official language of state (italics if named in four sources, otherwise sources in brackets)

Argentina	Estonia (5,9,w)	*Romania*
Australia	*France*	Russia (5,9,w)
Belize (5,9)	*Hungary*	Slovakia (5,9,w)
Bolivia (b,5,9)	*Israel*	Slovenia (5,9,w)
Brazil	Kazakhstan (5,9,w)	*South Africa*
Canada	Kyrgyzstan (5,9,w)	Ukraine (5,9,w)
Chile	Mexico (b,9,w)	Uruguay (b,5,9)
Czech Republic (5,9,w)	*Namibia*	*USA*
Denmark	*Paraguay*	Venezuela (b,5,9)
Ecuador (b,5,9)	*Poland*	

Table E.3–1 names all the corresponding states referenced in these sources in alphabetical order, distinguished as follows:

- States named in all sources are printed in italics and not marked otherwise;
- States registered only in some of the sources are printed in plain (non-italic) text, indicating the sources in brackets (b = Born/ Dickgießer, 5 = *Ethnologue* 2005, 9 = *Ethnologue* 2009 and w = Wikipedia website "Deutsche Sprache").

On this basis, I define states named in at least three sources as the core inventory, a total of 28 (Table E.3–2). For reasons to be explained, Belize is included although only named in two sources.

The following states from Table E.3–2 are named in fewer than three sources and are therefore not included in the table (apart from Belize): Bosnia and Herzegovina, Dominican Republic, Finland, Moldavia, Peru, Philippines, Puerto Rico, Serbia, Tajikistan, Uzbekistan, United Arab Emirates. Checking showed that all these minorities are very small or not indigenous. Checking was based primarily on the following three sources (additionally to those for Tables E.3–1 and E.3–2):

- *Sprachen-Almanach* by Harald Haarmann (2002a): for individual states;
- *Fischer Weltalmanach 2013*: for individual states under the headings "official language(s)" and "population [. . .] languages";
- *Wikipedia* (German): on the websites for the individual states, under the headings "languages" and "ethnic groups".

In detail, the descriptions are as follows (alphabetical order of relevant states):

- *Sprachen-Almanach* by Harald Haarmann (2002a), in each case under the heading "Deutsch":

  Belize "(*Plattdeutsch, Mennonitendeutsch*)" 5–10,000;
  Finland 1–3,000;
  Puerto Rico 1–3,000;
  Tajikistan 20–50,000;
  Uzbekistan 20–50,000.

- *Fischer Weltalmanach 2013* (single nomination of German in doubtful states):

  Belize "languages: [. . .] German dialect (Mennonites)".

- *Wikipedia* (in each case, website for relevant state):

  Belize: "*Plautdietsch*. Especially in the case of Low German-speaking Mennonites, Standard German is used in religious services and instruction. In many (Mennonite) colonies, *Pennsylvania German* is used additionally";
  Tajikistan: "German minority[.] In Tajikistan, there is still a small minority of people of German origin. Their number has declined strongly, especially after the breakup of the Soviet Union. The Germans are now in the poorest stratum of the population [. . .]";
  Uzbekistan: No reference to the German language, only under "ethnic groups [. . .] In 2001, there were still 24,000 Germans in Uzbekistan. In the 1940s, Stalin deported around 40,000 Volga Germans to Tashkent";
  United Arab Emirates: only listed under "Foreigners: [. . .] Germany: 8,000".

Of the remaining 29 states (Table E.3–2) only a limited selection will be described in greater detail for reasons of space and effort. The following list contains 19 minorities; 10 minorities from Table E.3–2, with features which are not clearly characterised, have been omitted. The minorities described in greater detail in Ch. E.4.2 to E.4.11 (three in E.4.11) are marked with an asterisk.

- Border and close-to-border minorities (*Czech Republic, *Denmark, *France, *Poland, Slovakia, Slovenia, *Hungary);
- One minority from the colonial period: *Namibia;
- Former language islands: *Brazil, *Romania, *Russia;
- Minorities with religious identity: Australia (Templers), *Belize, Bolivia, Ecuador, *Mexico, *Paraguay, Uruguay (in each case Mennonites), *Canada (Hutterites), *USA (Amish, Mennonites). The description in Ch. E.4.11 includes Mennonites, Amish and Hutterites, in some cases in several states.

Ch. E.5 gives an overview of allochthonous German-speaking minorities which are hardly considered in the sources named above.

4. Selected German-speaking minorities in greater detail

4.1 Overview of descriptions

The next 11 chapters E.4.2–E.4.11 and also E.5 give brief descriptions of a range of German(-speaking) minorities. The description follows the factors or indicators for language maintenance explained in Ch. E.2, which allow an assessment of opportunities and promotional possibilities for maintenance of German. For all 11 descriptions, I have received significant support from outstanding colleagues in the field, whom I name at the start of each chapter. I must also acknowledge the specialist competence of many others. Each of the following descriptions begins with the (recent) history of the minority. The other descriptions are based on the aspects developed in Ch. E.2 and summarised below in the form of a list. However, numbering is not provided in the descriptions themselves, and the sequence and weighting of aspects may vary depending on the presumed significance for language maintenance in the relevant minority. The frequently used bracketing "German(-speaking)" is intended to connect linguistic and ethnic contexts (German-language community and ethnic group of Germans in the wider sense), which are both relevant for the self-understanding and definition of the minority. The aspects of the descriptions are as follows:

I.   *Identification of the minority*

1) Ethnic self-designation and ethnic self-allocation;
2) Ethnic designation and ethnic allocation by the majority;
3) Self-designation of the minority variety and linguistic self-allocation;
4) Designation of the minority variety and linguistic allocation by the majority;
5) Native-language status of the defined variety.

II. *Demography of the minority*

1) Numerical strength of the ethnic group;
2) Numerical strength of speakers a) native speakers, b) non-native speakers;
3) Rate of immigration and emigration.

III. *Geography of the linguistic minority*

1) Geographical distance from German-speaking states;
2) Linguistic homogeneity of the settlement territory;
3) Linguistic landscape in the minority language.

IV. *Contacts with linguistic majority and other-language minorities in the country of settlement*

1) Contacts with linguistic majority in country of settlement;
2) Frequency of linguistic exogamy;
3) Linguistic composition of social networks.

V. *Economic strength and social structure of the linguistic minority*

1) Economic strength of the minority as a whole;
2) Material prosperity by comparison with linguistic majority;
3) Presence of all social strata.

VI. *Use of the minority language in the totality of domains*

1) Families;
2) Schools and universities;
3) Media: mass media, personal media;
4) Religious domain;
5) Cultural events.

VII. Important rights for language maintenance of the minority in the home country

1) Guarantees and rulings in language laws;
2) Own interest group;
3) Own representation at community, regional, national government level.

VIII. Support for maintenance of the minority language from outside the home country

1) Political and non-material support;
2) Material benefits.

IX. Contacts of the linguistic minority with German-language states and regions

1) Number of members of the minority with double citizenship;
2) Contacts via corporate branches;
3) Through schools or universities;
4) Through tourism;
5) Through media: mass media, personal media;
6) Through cultural institutes;
7) Other cultural or sports contacts;
8) Language archipelagos.

X. Attitudes towards the ethnic group and language of the minority, of the minority itself and of the majority

1) Attitudes of the minority to their own language;
2) Attitudes of the minority to their own ethnic group;
3) Attitudes of the majority to the minority language;
4) Attitudes of the majority to the minority ethnic group;
5) Own organisations of the minority;
6) Language-policy goals for maintenance of own language;
7) Committed leaders within own organisations;
8) Committed spokespeople for language maintenance.

XI. Position of minority language and majority language in the global language constellation and linguistic distance between them

1) International position and prestige of minority language and majority language;
2) Linguistic distance between minority language and majority language.

XII. Competence of the minority in their own language

1) In the dialect;
2) In Standard German.

4.2 Denmark

In 1920, following the Treaty of Versailles, North-Schleswig, in Southern Denmark, was restored to Denmark after a referendum. Denmark had lost the whole of Schleswig-Holstein through a war of conquest between Austria and Prussia (1864), firstly to Prussia (1867) and then to Germany (1871) (Pedersen 1996: 39–41; 2000: 16–18). The subdivision of Schleswig in 1920 was probably the only German frontier change following the two world wars to be regarded as fair by both sides. One reason for the absence of conflict was that the separation of North-Schleswig had never been questioned even by Nazi Germany, so that Denmark had no concerns about territorial claims of Germany or doubts about the loyalty of its German minority. In this respect, Denmark differed substantially from France (Alsace and Lorraine), Poland and the Czech Republic (Ch. E.4.3–E.4.5). However, the memory of National Socialism is still alive today, especially the occupation by German troops in 1940–1945. I am grateful to Karen Margrethe Pedersen (see also Pedersen 1996, 2000, 2005; Byram 1986; also www.agdm.fuen.org/land/ dk.html; de.wikipedia.org/wiki/Deutsche_Minderheit_inD%C3%A4nemark).

The German ethnic group in North-Schleswig in Denmark – *Die deutsche Volksgruppe* as it is known officially – comprises between 10,000 and 20,000 people (10–15,000 after Pedersen 2000: 18; approx. 15,000 after Pedersen 1996: 33; also according to the *Bund der Nordschleswiger:* www.bdn.dk/; 20,000 according to de.wikipedia.org/wiki/ Deutsche_Minderheit_in_D%C3%A4nemark; 25,900 after *Ethnologue* 2009: 549) – with a total population of 250,000 in North-Schleswig and 5,574,000 in Denmark as a whole (*Fischer Weltalmanach* 2013: 94). It is the only recognised indigenous minority in Denmark. Officially, its members call themselves *deutsche Nordschleswiger* and unofficially just *Nordschleswiger;* young people use the term *deutsche Südjüten.* As suggested by official and self-designation, they presumably consider themselves as primarily ethnic Germans, but also have a strong relationship with the German language which would justify the designation of a German-speaking minority. However, only one third have German as their actual native language. Danish censuses do not register the numerical strength because they are not allowed to ask about ethnicity, native language or similar details. The numerical strength has remained relatively stable for several years. In a complementary manner to the German minority in Denmark, approximately 50,000 Danish(-speaking) citizens of Germany live in the north of Germany, in South Schleswig (self-designation *Südjüten* rather than *dänische Südschleswiger*) (on reciprocity between the two minorities, see Ipsen 1997).

Membership of the German minority is based on self-allocation, generally family tradition. Their relationship with the German language is complicated, because primary socialisation takes place less frequently in Standard German than in a dialect, *Sønderjysk* (*Südjütisch*), which, according to linguistic distance, belongs to Danish rather than German. German – in the form of Standard German with a North-German colouring – is learnt only in secondary socialisation, but as early as kindergarten. However, the relationship with German is not as a foreign language but rather as a "second native language". In fact, the German language is a substantial symbol of membership of the German ethnic group.

The settlement territory of the German-speaking minority begins at the border with Germany, with decreasing settlement density the greater the distance northwards from the border. It is concentrated in the communities of Hoyer (*Højer*), Tondern (*Tønder*), Tingleff (*Tinglev*), Sonderburg (*Sønderborg*) – the four towns on the border – and Lügumkloster (*Løgumkloster*) Rothenkrug (*Rødekro*), Apenrade (*Aabenraa*) and Hadersleben (*Haderseu*) (Danish names in brackets; detailed maps in Pedersen 1996: 29, 33). The German(-speaking) population is not the majority in any of these localities and is not even noticeably concentrated in neighbourhoods. But, even in the case of remote settlement, they do not lose contact with their own language group and have not therefore become a German diaspora. Linguistic exogamy is not unusual, but hardly ever causes a complete shift to Danish. Lack of German linguistic landscape, of which there is some evidence in Apenrade, also has a limited effect in favour of language shift. All town signs are monolingual Danish; only direction signs for minority institutions are in German. The otherwise tolerant attitude of the Danish majority seems to end at bilingual town signs. For example, a 2007 proposal by the minority to introduce bilingual town signs was rejected. The reasons included a reminder to the German minority that the horrors of the Nazi period have still not been forgotten in Denmark, and harmony between the two ethnic groups cannot be taken for granted (see, Peter Hoop's select bibliography on the history of the German minority in Denmark including the Nazi period: www.akens.org/akens/lit/Nationale %20Minderheiten.pdf).

The residential territory of the German minority is predominantly rural in structure. Economic conditions and living standards correspond to those of the Danish majority. All social strata are also represented. Despite the dialect dominating in family communication, acquisition of basic knowledge of Standard German is secured for all members of the minority. The German minority has an exemplary system of kindergartens and schools with German as the language of instruction, which is readily accessible to people living at a distance through free transport. The schools include all levels of schooling, but there is no university because of the low numerical strength of the minority. In 2013, there were 22 kindergartens, 14 schools for the middle age group (primary and secondary I) of which nine extended over eight school years and five over 11 school years, and, in Apenrade, a type of grammar school up to *Abitur* (university-entrance) level (www.deutschesgym.dk/) (total school students: 1,247, grammar school 160, Tingleff FE College 178. Information from Pedersen). A fraction of the grammar-school curriculum, only in maths, is also delivered in Danish, which is supposed not to impair pupils' knowledge of German (Pedersen 1996: 43–48, see 48). Of course, Danish is also an important school subject in all schools. All university-entrance certificates are recognised in Germany and Denmark. More than half the teachers in the minority schools come from Germany and form the majority of immigrants (Pedersen 2000: 19). Approximately two-thirds of school leavers with *Abitur* study in Denmark; one-third in Germany. Religious practice (services, religious festivals and ceremonies) is consistently in Standard German, with most clergy originating from Germany or having been trained there.

Language maintenance is favoured by multiple access to German-speaking media, also from Germany. The locally published daily newspaper *Der Nordschleswiger* (circulation approximately 4,000) with the online edition, is prominent. On work days, editors of *Der Nordschleswiger* also produce daily bulletins in German which are broadcast via the private *Radio Mojn* and accessible via the Internet (www.radio700.de and www.radio-flensburg.de). However, there is no internal TV channel. The minority enjoys generous rights from the Danish state, primarily based on the "Bonn-Copenhagen Declarations" of 1955 (Declaration by Denmark and Germany; Pedersen 2005). Declaration of membership of the respective minority is therefore free to all and may not be questioned (www.wahlrecht.de/doku/doku19550329.htm). Like the Danish minority in Germany, the German minority in Denmark has the right to its own interest groups. The most important is the *Bund Deutscher Nordschleswiger*. Other significant interest groups include *die Schleswige Partei* and various youth, sporting and church associations, including the dialect-preservation society *Æ Synnejysk Forening*, in which German- and Danish-speakers meet and often speak *Südjütisch*. In fact, German is not an official language of administration in town halls, but minority members in the localities named above are served in German. However, German plays no role in public political life (Pedersen 1996: 54).

Another support for the German minority is promotion from outside Denmark, non-materially from the European Council and the EU of which Denmark is a member. Denmark also ratified the *Charter for Regional or Minority Languages European* (conventions.coe.int/treaty/ger/ Treaties/html/148.htm) (08.09.2000, enactment 1 January 2001). Furthermore, the minority receives significant assistance from Germany: apart from the provision of teachers and clergy, further resources, especially from the Federal State of Schleswig-Holstein (approximately 2 million EUR annually ("German Minority Receives Cash", *Kieler Nachrichten* 28 November 2012). The money goes primarily to the education sector. By contrast, branches of companies from German-speaking countries, which are not common, and border traffic provide no significant assistance (information: Pedersen). The idea that German is a significant foreign language certainly also plays a part, and as a result, by contrast with Danish in Germany, German is also used in families of the minority (Pedersen 1996: 48, 55f). The German minority occasionally also experiences an influx "of people who originally belonged to the Danish majority but have come to identify with German culture, eventually choosing to be a member of the minority even if they were born in Copenhagen" (Pedersen 2000: 19).

All in all, the maintenance of German in the German minority in Denmark seems to be secure for the foreseeable future, in fact, in stable bilingualism with Danish and German. However, speaking dialect has declined slightly, and Standard German is more common even in families. German also has some competition through the increase of English as the language of commerce and in academia, which could destabilise the German–Danish bilingualism in the long run. For example, in Danish schools, German is now only an optional subject; even in the minority region, English is the dominant language of business (information: Pedersen; also Ch. F.6).

4.3 France

Alsace (Elsass) and Lorraine (Lothringen) are in the East of France and have borders with South Germany to the west and Switzerland to the south. In the Peace of Westphalia of 1648, a large part of the territory fell to France, which also annexed Strasbourg (Strassburg); in 1766, this was followed by Lorraine through inheritance from the estate of King Leszczynski of Poland, and in 1798, by autonomous resolution, the city of Mulhouse (Mülhausen) in Alsace joined revolutionary France. In 1871, the newly formed German Empire annexed a large, generally the Germanophone, part of this territory, which fell to France again in 1918, through the Treaty of Versailles after WWI. Nazi Germany occupied the territory from 1940–1944 without formal annexation and forced the population into military service. Apart from the independent decision by Mulhouse, there has never been an autonomous decision by the population about membership of a state. However, a language policy of assimilation to the respective national official language was adopted very early and has been reinforced since the French Revolution. This has continued in a milder form up to the present (Petit 1997: 1224–1235; Bister-Broosen 1998: 19–35; Broadbridge 2000: 52–55; Verdoodt 1968: 71–79).

In recent history, repressive language policies imposed by the side in possession in each case have corresponded with concomitant territorial claims. In this respect, conditions in France, Poland and the Czech Republic differ significantly from those in Denmark (Ch. E.4.2; E.4.4; E.4.5). Even today, the historical and contemporary language situation and language policy in Alsace and Lorraine are sometimes judged differently as an after effect of opposing national interests of Germany and France, which have since developed more friendly relations, but sometimes also because of different interests of the inhabitants themselves. Examples of internal differences in judgement can be found in Robert Grossmann (supporting French language domination; 1999) and Pierre Klein (supporting maintenance of German dialects; 2007). A balanced presentation is accordingly difficult (see, e.g., Hartweg 1988; Bothorel-Witz 2001; Huck 2007). Informative accounts are provided in Hartweg 1981, 1983, 1997; Harnisch 1996; Petit 1997; Bister-Broosen 1998; Broadbridge 2000; Bothorel-Witz 2001; Huck 1999; Huck/ Botherel-Witz/ Geiger-Jaillet 2007; and Verdoodt 1968: 58–132. I am grateful to Dominique Huck for additional information.

In identifying the minority relevant to this chapter, it must be borne in mind that, after each of the recent annexations, immigration from the new occupying state was promoted, i.e. migration from Germany after 1871 and from France after 1918 and again after 1945, as well as emigration in the reverse direction. Immigrants from inside France are not among the minority relevant here, because they are neither German-speaking nor ethnically German in the broad sense. Even with indigenous Alsatians, a corresponding allocation is not obvious; only French citizenship is beyond doubt. Regarding allocation to an ethnic group, I assume that hardly any indigenous Alsatians would still allocate themselves even to a broadly defined German ethnic group (*Volk*, nationality; Ch. B.3); but many would acknowledge cultural proximity. If asked about their native language, they would presumably answer "*l'alsacien*" or just "*le dialecte*". However, very few would allocate this dialect to the French language – but also not to German without some reluctance. This is suggested by spot findings, e.g. responses in a single village, Zillisheim (8.6% allocation of the dialect to French, 60.1% "no opinion", 37.3% refuse to answer the question of allocation to German; Broadbridge 2000: 56). Changing the perspective, I myself allocate the indigenous dialects of Alsace and Lorraine, which are classified in traditional dialectology as Alemanic or Rhine-Franconian, to the German language. The reasons for this (Ch. B.1; B.2) relate absolutely to the current circumstances: only moderate (not large) linguistic distance of the dialects from Standard German and roofing by standard French, from which, however, the linguistic distance is too great for allocation to the same language.

The regions of Alsace and especially Eastern Lorraine (*Lorraine thioise*), which are relevant here, belong to the French *Département Haut-Rhin* (Upper Alsace), *Bas-Rhin* (Lower Alsace) and *Moselle* (Eastern Lorraine) (detailed map in Petit 1997: 1223). Uncertain ethnic and linguistic allocations limit, however, the quantitative data on this minority. They also betray opposing linguistic interests between France and Germany, which has no difficulty allocating the dialects to German (see, e.g. Botherel-Witz 2001). In France, people tend to speak only of *dialecte* ("*dialecte alscacien*" or "*dialecte lorrain*"), without reference to a language, or just of *alscacien* or *lorrain*, which suggests an independent language. This corresponds with a clear rejection of the ethnic allocation "German" and acceptance of *Elsässisch* or *Lothringisch*. The speaker numbers for the indigenous dialect in Alsace is often set at approximately 1.2 million well into the 1990s (e.g. Petit 1997: 1224; in *Euromosaic* 1996: [68] even 1.8 million). However, it is evident from Wolfgang Ladin's provocative investigation (1980, 1982) that this number has been overestimated. Tables E.4.3–1 and E.4.3–2 show the development of the figures.

Table E.4.3–1 Percentage of adult Alsatians between 1962–1998, who could speak dialect according to self-assessment

	1962	*1979*	*1986*	*1991*	*1998*
19 to 24-year-olds	82.4	65.5	52.2	40	37
65 and above	94.6	88.3	90.7	n.d.	84

(*Source*: Huck/ Botherel-Witz/ Geiger-Jaillet 2007: 30, excerpt from table)

Table E.4.3–2 Use and knowledge of dialect in adult Alsatians 1998, self-assessment, as percentage

1998	*Speak often/fluently* "*couramment*"	*Speak occasionally*	*Understand, but do not speak*	*Do not understand and do not speak*
18 to 24-year-olds	22	15	24	39
65-year-old and above	79	5	10	6

(*Source*: Huck/ Bothorel-Witz/ Geiger-Jaillet 2007: 30, excerpt from table)

The decline in dialect speaking is unmistakable and influences use and competence, primarily in the younger generation. Young people also confirm this development themselves (Bister-Broosen 1998: 153–169). The generational difference cannot be explained away just on the basis of a life cycle, according to which older people tend to use the dialect more than younger people. The move away from dialect in cities by comparison with the countryside is as pronounced as that between the younger and older generation (Huck/ Botherel-Witz/ Geiger-Jaillet 2007: 31). Dialect is now spoken almost exclusively by older people in the country. However, the shift from the dialect is not in the direction towards Standard German but towards French, but the French is still coloured by the dialect. In both regions, the shift is evident in families. Through lack of use, the dialect is passed on to a maximum of 10% of children – by comparison with 80% in the 1960s (Huck/ Botherel-Witz/ Geiger-Jaillet 2007: 31, also 32f). Language shift is therefore taking place according to the "third generation rule": parents still speak the dialect natively (active use); the children still understand it (passive use), but not the grandchildren (neither active nor passive use) (Petit 1997: 1234). According to the dominant view in France, the Alsatians achieved this language shift largely voluntarily and judge it satisfactory. However, isolated investigations, such as those of Bister-Broosen (1998: 160–163) on attitudes among young people in Colmar indicate a degree of dissatisfaction: the dialect should not disappear; speaking dialect is fun; all Alsatians should at least understand dialect; the state should promote maintenance. This is also held by non-dialect speakers, though less so than by dialect speakers.

There is still some memory of the several-years' prohibition of German, including the dialect, in school, which was energetically asserted even in the playground. The official ban on German teaching in primary schools in fact only lasted from 1945 to 1952 but its effects linger on. The ban included the media. For example, in the press, only French was allowed for topics of special interest to young people, such as sports; in radio and television, dialect was permitted but not Standard German (Petit 1997: 1234). This ruling contributed to the closure of some German-speaking newspapers for a time (UA has left something out here. It is safer to leave out this entire reference to avoid confusion Huck/ Botherel-Witz/ Geiger-Jaillet 2007: 34–38; the article "*Das Elsass spricht Französisch*" 6 June 2012 about the end of the last German-speaking daily, *Dernières Nouvelles D'Alsace* in the follow-on publication *Forum*, which appears only weekly). However, dialect is now heard regularly on the radio, e.g. daily in *Radio France Bleu Elsass*. Of course, German-speaking newspapers, radio and television are accessible from Germany or Switzerland. Continuing negative judgements, according to which French is more "chic" than German, which still shows traces of the "*langue des nazis*" (Huck/ Botherel-Witz/ Geiger-Jaillet 2007: 29) are probably more influential than the historical banning of German. Under such conditions, the development of a linguistic landscape in German was inconceivable. One exception is the town names, which are still written in German for smaller towns, but generally in dialect rather than Standard German, and without special German characters (Umlaut, *ß*). Larger towns have only French names.

Faced with such strong aversion to the German language, the attitude of restraint and non-criticism adopted by the German-speaking states, especially Germany, is remarkable. The underlying attitude is presumably not to ruffle German-French friendship. In France, it seems not to be enough that the national official language, French, is firmly anchored in the entire population, nationwide and in all domains, but that no other language is allowed even a remotely comparable position alongside it. The resolution by the French Constitutional Court to declare the *European Charter for Regional or Minority Languages* incompatible with the French Constitution can be understood in this sense (judgement of the *Conseil Constitutionnel* of 15 June 1999; see also Ammon 2007c: 110; legal background in Pan 2006). Added to this, German as a native language is treated with special suspicion. In this respect, linguistic competition with Germany within the EU is therefore possibly replacing history, the influence of which is gradually diminishing. For France, this is occasionally apparent when Germany makes a claim for German as an EU working language, alongside French and of course English (see Ammon 2007c: 112–115). At present, it seems that the dialects in Alsace and Lorraine have only a residual or folkloristic function. However, even this could strengthen the motivation to learn Standard German. A start has been made by the bilingual schools which have arisen since 1991 with German as a language of instruction, of course, alongside predominantly French. But hopes for *"une renaissance du fr.-ald"* associated with this by many observers are probably exaggerated (Petit 1997: 1239; fr. = (langue) française, ald. = (langue) allemande). Details, including on the status of bilingual schools over time, have been published in Huck 1995a, b; Huck/ Bothorel-Witz/ Geiger-Jaillet 2007: 57–85; Morgen 2004, 2006, 2007; Geiger-Jaillet 2004, 2010. Several such schools are now well established, but further development seems to be stagnating. Among state schools in Alsace for the school year 2008/9, there were, 143 pre-schools, 125 primary schools, 41 *collèges* and 11 *lycées* (grammar schools), with a total of approximately 17,500 pupils, which corresponded to 10% of the total pupil number for the region – more recent figures were not available. Added to this were ten private schools with 54 classes and approximately 1,100 pupils, eight of which were in Alsace and two in Lorraine, which were funded by the *Association pour le Bilingualisme en Class dès la Maternelle – bilingualism (ABCM Bilingualism)* (www.fvfz.de/formulare.html). Additional funding for the bilingual schools came from the EU Commission and from private sources in Germany such as the "Robert Bosch Foundation" and the *Förderverein für die Zweisprachigkeit im Elsaß und im Moseldepartment e.V* (based in Duisburg).

Advantages derived from a knowledge of German have been spelt out from different perspectives for a considerable time. They can easily be imagined in view of the considerable number of commuters to Germany and Switzerland; in 1999, there were 36,606 and 33,224 respectively (Huck/ Bothorel-Witz/ Geiger-Jaillet 2007: 89). There are also company branches from Germany and Switzerland in Alsace and Lorraine – which value a knowledge of German at least by some of their employees (Ch. F.6). German skills are also advantageous with regard to tourism primarily from Germany. However, the outlook for German in Alsace and Lorraine is still uncertain. As in the rest of France, English is the most popular foreign language (Ch. J.9.2) and is often used in contact with Germans, even between neighbours.

4.4 Poland

The history of a minority can hardly be more tragic than the topic of this chapter, except in the case of complete physical destruction as with the Jews in the Nazi period. The German(-speaking) minority in Poland comprises substantially those "Germans" and their descendants who did not flee and were able to escape the expulsion of Germans from the territory of present-day Poland after WWII and then declared themselves to be "German". Unless otherwise specified, "German" refers here to the ethnic allocation ("ethnic group/nationality") of Polish citizens. Their expulsion was part of the displacement of Poland to the West by the Soviet Union. The territory of Poland east of the Curzon line established after WWI was annexed by Russia, for which, by way of reparation, Poland received the former German territories of South East Prussia, East Pomerania (Hinterpommern), East Brandenburg and Lower and Upper Silesia (maps in Panzer 1997; Lasatowicz/ Weger 2008: 145; de.wikipedia.org/wiki/Deutsche_Minderheit_in_Polen; de.wikipedia.org/wiki/Polen). A majority of the Polish population from former Eastern Poland were settled there. This displacement of territory and population to the west was a consequence of the war sparked by Germany, which caused Poland enormous suffering, mainly because "under German occupation more than 2 million non-Jewish Polish civilians were killed" ("*Gefangen in einer ausweglosen Hölle*" [Trapped in an inescapable hell], *FAZ*

7 May 2013: 30). During the entire period of German occupation (1939–1945, the use of Polish was also strictly forbidden (Kneip 1999: 145–155; Urban 2000: 46–49). Prussian language policy for the Polish-speaking population had been repressive even before WWI (Glück 1979), and Prussia contributed significantly to all three partitions of Poland in 1772, 1793 and 1795 (together with Russia and Austria). Apart from a brief interlude from 1807–1815, Poland was eliminated as a state as a consequence of these partitions, and only restored in 1918. Concerns about German attempts at revision still resonate in Poland's language policy towards the German minority – but confidence has grown thanks to common ties within the EU. An overview of the topic of the present chapter, including further details, can be found in Kneip 1999; Urban 2000; Lawatowicz/ Weger 2008, 2009; Kamusella 2009: 573–644; European Council 2011 (www. ostdeutschesforum.net/EUFV/PDF/Uebersetzung-Bericht-Europarat.pdf) and in the named Wikipedia articles; I am grateful to Maria K. Lasatowicz, Werner Jost and Karina Schneider-Wiejowksi for additional information.

Designation of the minority as "German" here refers to the allocation to an ethnic group, generally through self-allocation by members. Even if they declare German as their native language, only a small proportion are really German-speakers, and even fewer have full competence in the language. One substantial reason for the lack of German skills is the long-standing ban on speaking German after WWII, not only in public, but also in private, which prevented the learning of German by subsequent generations. Even if only parts of the German minority (GM) are de facto native speakers of German (NSG), everyone who declares German their native language can still be counted among the German minority (GM $\supset$ NSG; see Ch. A.3; B.3). Furthermore, some of the members of the minority are among the GFL learners, of whom there are more in Poland than in any other state in the world (Ch. J.9.5). Quantification of the German minority is further complicated because the self-allocation "Silesian", often coupled with "German", intended in an ethnic sense, has become popular in recent years. According to Lasatowicz/ Weger (2008: 149), there were still 147,094 Germans and 173,148 Silesians, and in the named article: de.wikipedia.org/wiki/Deutsche_Minderheit_in_Polen, the total number of people who declare themselves "German" (including dual ethnicity), was reckoned at 148,000 in 2011 – so that it would have remained stable over the last decade.

However many ethnic Germans there might be today, they are distributed mainly in the south-west and north-east of Poland, the former Upper Silesia, to the south of Wroclaw (*Breslau*), and East Prussia, especially Mazury (*Masuren*), to the south of Olsztyn (*Allenstein*) (map in Duschanek 1997b; Lasatowicz/ Weger 2008: 145). In this context, the first group, primarily in the administrative district ("Wojewodschaft" or "Woiwodschaft") Opole (*Oppeln*). represents the main focus. In fact, this territory is close to the border, but has no direct border with Germany. The fact that the ethnic Germans in Poland do not form the majority in any region, not even in the Opole Woiwodschaft, is more unfavourable for language maintenance than the absence of a border with the German-speaking state. Even in the territory with the greatest concentration, the proportion within the Woiwodschaft hardly reaches 10% of the inhabitants. However, in 28 communities of the Opole Woiwodschaft, the proportion is above 20% (de.wikipedia.org/wiki/ Deutsche_Minderheit_in_Polen: 5). As a result of this scatter and low numbers, frequent contact with the ethnically Polish, i.e. the Polish-speaking majority is unavoidable. Mixed marriages are also frequent (ethnic exogamy). Both factors favour language shift to the majority language (Polish). Furthermore, the economic position of the German minority does not support language maintenance. Its standard of living or economic strength does not differ substantially from that of the Polish majority. The fact that the educated stratum is under-represented because of disproportionate emigration to Germany could be disadvantageous for language maintenance. But members of the German minority (all social strata) have gained economic advantages through easy economic migration into German-speaking countries over more than 20 years. Dual citizenship granted to 288,000 Polish citizens by 2005 (Lasatowicz/ Weger 2008: 154) forms a basis for this (de.wikipedia.org/wiki/Deutsche_Minderheit_in_Polen: 11). This economic migration secures and motivates the acquisition of German-language skills.

The continuing ban on speaking German after the war (Kneip 1999: 156–247; Urban 2000: 67–100) meant that most families spoke only Polish. As a result, transfer of German and German-language skills largely followed the three-generations law: active use in the older generation, only passive in the middle and not at all in subsequent generations. Restrictions on teaching German in school, even German as a foreign language – which was completely banned, especially in Upper Silesia, until around 1990 – has had an enduring influence in favour of language shift. The trade-union movement *Solidarność* contributed greatly to subsequent political change, and personalities such as the first non-communist prime minister, Tadeusz Mazowiecki, promoted rapprochement with Germany (Kneip 1999: 256). A further step was the *Treaty between the Republic of Poland and the Federal Republic of Germany Consolidating their Border* (14 November 1990; Kneip 1999: 262). This was followed by the broader legal basis of the *Treaty between the Federal Republic of Germany and the Republic of Poland on Neighbourly and Friendly Collaboration of 1991* (Lasatowicz/ Weger 2008: 157). It allows public and private use of German and also German first names and family names, including the reversal of Polonisation (Kneip 1999: 264f). The *European Charter for Regional or Minority Languages*, which Poland joined, was then directed more specifically towards the minorities (ratification 12 February 2009, enactment 1 June 2009. See conventions.coe.int/Treaty/ Commun/ChercheSig.asp?NT=148& CM =&DF=&CL=GER).

The teaching of native-speaker German has been permitted since the early 1990s, as has the teaching of GFL throughout Poland – even in Upper Silesia. German-language religious practice is also permitted. However, up to the present, almost all German teaching has remained de facto GFL teaching, with only three hours per week in most cases (Kneip 1999: 270–272; Urban 2000: 154–158). This should be noted when the official statistics are interpreted. According to the Central Statistics Office, there were 299 primary schools with 24,756 pupils in Poland for the school year 2011/12, 84 secondary level I schools with 5,566 pupils and seven secondary II schools with 126 pupils, in which German was taught (Główny Urząd 2012: 147f). This notice is to be found under the provisions for "national and ethnic minorities" (official English translation). The *Deutsche Bildungsgesellschaft* [German Education Association], an institution of the German minority in Poland sent me the following figures for schools with native-speaker German teaching (email: Martyna Halek, 4 June 2013): in the Opele Wojewodschaft 148 kindergartens, 202 primary schools, 56 grammar schools, two FE colleges, one Lyceum, one Technical College; in Śląskie (Silesia), 28 kindergartens, 101 primary schools, 26 grammar schools; with smaller numbers in Lubuskie (*Lublin*), Warmińsko-mazuskie (*Ermland-Masuren*) and Pomorskie (*Pommern*). But these figures do not always refer to native-speaker teaching, because, according to the ruling from the Education Ministry, tuition comprises only three hours per week language, with an additional 30 hours of history, culture and geography of Germany in the fifth year of schooling. According to Martin Chichon (email 3 June 2013), who wrote the curriculum plans for this additional course, many pupils who are not members of the German minority participate because parents anticipate improved job prospects for their children. Poor language skills among pupils make German as a language of instruction impracticable – but a really good knowledge of German is ideally achieved on the basis of a language of instruction across different subjects. However, there is a marked absence of appropriate bilingual schools. For example, in 2013, there was only a single Polish–German bilingual kindergarten in the whole of Poland (Opole Woiwodschaft) and a single bilingual primary school (Woiwodschaft Śląskie) – both funded from Germany. At secondary level, German was not the language of instruction anywhere; it was only a school subject with just three hours per week. The European Council criticised this provision as not compatible with the *European Charter for Regional or Minority Languages* (Kneip 1999: 283–289).

German is the continuous language of instruction only in the single German School Abroad in Poland, the Willy-Brandt School in Warsaw, but this is located too far from the settlement area of the German minority. It teaches from kindergarten (approximately 75 pupils) to completion of secondary level II (approximately 180 pupils) and also has a Polish branch, in which "by the start of the 10th class, pupils must have reached the linguistic level of German native speakers if they are to join pupils in the German-speaking branch for German lessons in the 10th class" (www.wbs.pl/). German-speaking courses at Polish universities are also not intended primarily for the German minority (www.studieren-in-polen.de/132,1,sprache.html). But Maria Lasato-wicz informed me (email 28 May 2013) that, in the German-Studies Institute at the University of Opole, which was founded in 1990, "around 2000 graduates have now completed the five-year German programme".

However, the institutions of the German minority are still modest, especially the provision of media (Kneip 1999: 279–283). Above all, there is no daily newspaper – but only the bilin-gual *Wochenblatt.pl*, with the inserts *Schlesisches Wochenblatt* and *Oberschlesische Stimme*, and the supplement *Heimat* in the weekly newspaper *Nowa Trybuna Opolska*, all of which are published in Opole. The radio has a single, short time window in German, including *Schlesien Aktuell* (Mondays to Fridays, 15 minutes); another on television: *Schlesien Journal* (twice weekly, 11 minutes in each case) (figures for 2013 from Werner Jost). It is also remarkable that, since 2012, German has sometimes had the status of a local official language. This is reported by 22 localities, which have been declared bilingual because the German proportion of the popu-lation reached at least 20% (e.g. Biala/ Zülz, . . . Walce/ Walzen – beginning and end of the alphabetical list). German-speaking personnel and forms in German are provided for town halls there (Steinbach: *Polens Regierung macht Hausaufgaben nicht* [Poland's government is not doing its homework], *RP* 14 November 2012). A German-speaking landscape is also taking shape tentatively, at least in the form of bilingual town signs, now in 19 communities (Pol-ish at the top, German beneath in the same-sized lettering). However, some German town names have become contentious, because they only originated in the Nazi period through Germanisation of Slavonic names (see Urban 2000: 159–163 for the dispute about town and street names). The limited reintroduction of German would not have been possible without political representation of the German minority. For the Sejm, the national parliament, one MP is guaranteed, thereby overriding the 5% minimum-vote clause (Urban 2000: 121–128). Furthermore, the German minority appoints 24 town mayors and is represented in 278 com-munity administrations (information: Werner Jost). Added to this, there are numerous internal interest groups, which combined in 1991 to form the "Association of German Socio-cultural societies in Poland (VdG)", with around 200,000 members (de.wikipedia.org/wiki/Verband_der_deutschen_sozialkulturellen_Gesellschaften_in_Polen). Contacts with Germany and Austria through economic migration, study visits and placements, contacts with friends and relatives who have emigrated are particularly important for language maintenance. By con-trast, tourism has not developed greatly in either direction. So far, there are few German or Austrian company branches in the minority regions.

Under these circumstances, shift reversal to German as a second native language, while retaining Polish, remains difficult. A return to the traditional dialect is highly unlikely because it offers no practical utility for contacts with German-speaking states which use Standard German – even as "Contact German" with transferences from Polish (Földes 2005). Weakening of the international position of German by making English more attractive for globally orientated

Polish citizens, may also be detrimental. Maria Lasatowicz wrote: "[F]ewer and fewer children want to learn German, English is preferred, and bilingual classes in the upper school are being closed down" (email 28 May 2013). Under these conditions, shift reversal to German as actual family language (alongside Polish) remains a challenge (cf. Fishman 2001c: 466). It will require a more comprehensive school provision than hitherto, with German as a language of instruction.

4.5 Czech Republic

As with Poland, the history of the German(-speaking) minority in the Czech Republic has been unimaginably tragic. From German and Austrian perspectives, the German language has enjoyed an illustrious history, with highlights including: the Prague Chancellery German of Charles IV (1316–1378; Roman-German King from 1346; Holy Roman Emperor 1355–1365); Prague as the oldest German-speaking university (founded 1348); and world-famous authors such as Franz Kafka (1883–1924). From the Czech perspective, however, it seems more like a history of German linguistic dominance which was contested from the earliest times, but more decisively since the nineteenth century. As a result of this resistance, Czechoslovakia was formed as an independent state after WWI. It included a large German-speaking minority, primarily the "Sudeten Germans" in the West, but also German-speakers in the North in the *Iser, Riesengebirge* and *Adlergebirge* mountains, where integration proved difficult. The German-speaking western part of Czechoslovakia was annexed in 1938, and then the entire state was occupied by Nazi Germany, with the humiliating imposition of the German language (Scholten 2000a: 134–200; 2000b; Ch. K.2). After the war, the tide turned with the expulsion of all German(speaker)s, apart from anti-fascists, partners in ethnically mixed marriages and some skilled employees (Tišerová 2008: 179–189; Stevenson/ Carl 2010: 50–66). In a similar manner to Poland and to some extent to France (Ch. E.4.4; E.4.3), language policy in the Czech Republic was characterised by concerns about claims from Germany, in this case also from Austria, which declined only as a result of partnership in the EU. Overviews including more specialised presentations can be found in Tišerová 2008, the main support for the following description; Povejšil 1997; Nekvapil 1997a, 2000, 2003a, b; Nekvapil/ Neustupný 1998: 123f; Stevenson 2000a: 118–121; Goethe-Institut Prague 2001; Zich 2001; Wassertheurer 2003; Dovalil 2006; Kamusella 2009: 714–802; Stevenson/Carl 2010; https://dewikipedia.org/wiki/ Deutsche_Minderheit_in_Tschechien. For additional information, I am grateful to Viték Dovalil.

Some members of the German(-speaking) minority are ethnic Germans (German nationality) and some are German-speakers – and today, of course, consistently citizens of the Czech Republic. Before WWII, all ethnic Germans were German-speakers (native speakers), and many with native-language Czech also spoke German. Now, however (according to declaration or passport entry), many ethnic Germans hardly speak German even if they have declared German their native language. Based on language autobiographies, Stevenson/ Carl (2010: 200) refer to the "wider cultural identification with the 'German-speaking world' following the 1989 *Wende*". Of the approximately three million (ethnic) Germans (all with German as their native language), who lived in the Czechoslovakia of around 1938, only about 180,000 remained in 1947 as a result of compulsory expulsions. This number declined further, primarily through emigration to Germany, but also reversals of declared ethnic group, to just 62,000 in 1980. In the census of 2001, 41,328 declared their "first language" as German, and 39,106 declared "German nationality"; in the census of 2011, only 14,148 declared first-language German, and 18,658 German nationality. Accordingly, the number of German(speaker)s today is below 20,000 (information: Dovalil). Reversal of the numerical ratio "speakers – members of nationality" reveals language shifting from native-language German to native-language Czech. Regarding the decline in the

1990s, the secession of Slovakia in 1992 must be taken into account, with a German minority of approximately 6,000, among whom language shifting to Slovakian is in progress (www.czso.cz/ csu/2008edicniplan.nsf/engt/24003E05E7/$File/403 2080117.pdf; also Plewnia/ Weger 2008; (www.europeonline-magazine.eu/deutsche-sprache-kaempft-in-der-slowakei-ums-ueber-leben_277261.html; Plewnia/ Weger 2008. Tišerová 2008: 176f., 196, 241). However, a positive attitude towards German predominates in the minority remaining in the Czech Republic (Tišerová 2008: 219–229).

The settlement territory of the minority in the Czech Republic borders Germany: in the northern Egerland, around Sokolov (*Falkenau*), in the wider region of Karlovy Vary (*Karlsbad*) and around Ústi nad Labem (*Aussig an der Elbe*), and with Poland around Liberec (*Reichenberg*) and Ostrava (*Ostrau*). However, there is no coherent settlement region (maps in Duschanek 1997a; Tišerová 2008: 171). Even in the region of greatest concentration, the proportion of the population does not reach 5% in any district (ibid: 178f.); in 18 very small towns, it is above 10% (https://de.wikipedia.org/wiki/Deutsche_Minderheit_in_Tschechien). As a result, contact with the Czech majority is intensive and ethnic-linguistic exogamy is frequent. There is also no linguistic landscape in German, nor any bilingual town signs, and all formerly German-language town names have been officially shifted to Czech.

The fact that the minority ranks lower economically than the Czech majority is also unfavourable for the promotion of German. Most people are workers; the educated elite is underrepresented, primarily as a result of emigration in 1968, at the time of the "Prague Spring", and after 1989 (Tišerová 2008: 177–179). The language shift to Czech occurred in families after the war according to the three-generations law: for those born up to 1938, German was the main family language; those born after 1939 could still understand it; but it was no longer taught to those born after 1980 – although some learnt it in school as a kind of foreign language (ibid: 203). For a long time, there was a generally clear attitude of enmity towards everything German including the language among the ethnic Czech population. Its use in public was banned and is still limited to minority events with symbolic rather than truly communicative functions.

The minority only has a very limited number of its own schools, although German has been permitted as a language of instruction since 1968. A bilingual class with German and Czech was not established until 1991, in a state primary school in Český Krumlov (*Krummau*), which was then followed by isolated primary schools. The barrier for setting up these schools was set very high with a required number of 30 pupils (Stevenson/ Carl 2010: 65; Neustupný/ Nekvapil 2003), but this was lowered to eight pupils for kindergarten; ten for primary schools and 12 for middle schools, in the new Schools Act (No. 561/2004 SL, § 14 (2) and (3)). Since 1991, there has been a small private German-Czech primary school in Prague, but less for the minority than for German expatriates. The same applies for the Thomas-Mann High School in Prague, with approximately 150 pupils, where German is the first foreign language and "some subjects, such as maths, geography, biology, German history, German literature and art history, are taught partly in German" (www.pasch-net.de/par/spo/eur/tcr/de3348851.htm; Tišerová 2008: 197f). The *Deutsche Schule Prag* with just under 450 students, which was founded in 1989 by the GDR and adopted by the reunified Germany, has the same clientele. It is a "German School Abroad" (cf. Ch. J.3) in the form of a German-Czech "Contact School", with German as a language of instruction but also with a Czech-speaking branch, and German as a compulsory school subject (www.dsp-praha.org/die-schule-stellt-sich-vor/). The Austrian High School in Prague (Ch. K.4), with 200 students, is also not intended for the German minority. The weekly *Prager Zeitung* (circulation 15,000) and the fortnightly *Landes Zeitung der Deutschen in der Tschechischen Republik* (circulation 2,500), which addresses the minority specifically, are among the German-speaking media (www.pragerzeitung.cz/; www.landeszeitung.cz/).

For the rights of the minority, it is important that the Czech Republic has ratified and enforced the *European Charter for Regional or Minority Languages* (15 November 2006 and 1 March 2007. See conventions.coe.int/Treaty/Commun/ChercheSig.asp?NT=148&CM=&DF=&CL=GER; for other rights of the minority: Dovalil 2006; Stevenson/ Carl 2010: 68–74). The minority also has its own interest group. After the former Czechoslovakia acknowledged the existence of the German minority in 1968, the *Kulturverband der Bürger Deutscher Nationalität in der ČSSR* [Cultural Association of Citizens of German Nationality in the CSSR], in which use of the native language is also permitted, was formed in 1969. This was followed in 1989 by regional associations; in 1990, the *Verband der Deutschen* as an umbrella organisation (successor of the Cultural Association); and, additionally, in 1993, after the secession of Slovakia, the *Landesversammlung der Deutschen in Böhmen, Mähren and Schlesien* [regional Assembly of Germans in Bohemia, Moravia and Silesia]. There are therefore currently two umbrella associations and several regional associations with a total of around 8,500 members. Their work is promoted by funding from Germany and Austria, not least via "Contact Centres" (Tišerová 2008: 191–194). The Goethe-Institut participates in this funding with a full institute in Prague and in cooperation with various partner libraries (in Plzeň (*Pilsen*), Olomouc (*Ölmütz*), Brno (*Brünn*), Liberec (*Reichenberg*) and Ostrava (*Ostrau*); www.goethe.de/ins/cz/pra/net/dis/deindex.htm, and also the Institute for Foreign Affairs (ifa) (www.ifa.de/ foerderung/integration-und-medien/foerdern-durch-projekte/ foerderschwerpunkte.html). Significant tourism from Germany and Austria also supports the German language, as do student visits, employment opportunities in German-speaking states and joint ventures or local branches of German companies, e.g. Škoda with parent company *Volkswagen*. A knowledge of German is valued here, but the Czech side resists a dominant position of German on Czech soil (Höhne/ Nekula 1997; Möller/ Nekula 2002; Nekula 2002; Nekula/ Šichová 2004; Nekula/ Nekvapil/ Šichová 2005a, b; Nekula/ Marx/ Šichová 2009). Although a knowledge of German is judged useful, English has now become a more important foreign language in the Czech Republic; but German still occupies second place on the basis of the total number of learners in the Czech Republic (Dovalil 2006: 113f). The extent to which German can be re-established, alongside Czech, of course, as a family language and therefore native language, remains uncertain – however it will not be in the form of the traditional dialect, which is of limited practical utility.

4.6 Hungary

The history of the German(-speaking) minority in Hungary resembles both the proud tradition and also more recent, difficult developments in other German minorities of Eastern and Central Europe (detailed discussion in Seewann 2012, Vol. 1: *Vom Frühmittelalter bis 1860*, Vol. 2: *1860–2006*). In fact, the settlement in the Pannonian lowlands (Carpathian Basin) reaches back into the Middle Ages, but the majority of Germans did not migrate to present-day Hungary until the eighteenth century. Even in the nineteenth century, they were subjected to strong Magyarisation pressures, and some of the urban educated elite shifted to Hungarian as their family and native language. But the larger part, primarily farming communities, became ethnically and linguistically stabilised. After WWI, their enclosed settlements endured in a Hungary divided by the Treaty of Trianon (1920). However, there were serious setbacks after WWII, mostly as a result of widespread expulsions (Knipf-Komlósi 2008: 270–277; Stevenson/ Carl 2010: 50–66). This affected people who had declared German nationality or native language in the 1941 census (Stevenson/ Carl 2010: 52), or had reversed the Magyarisation of their name, or belonged to an armed German unit during the war. The census of 1941 registers 477,000 people with German native language, of which 300,000 declared German nationality. After the war, approximately

130,000 were expelled to the West and 50,000 to East Germany (de.wikipedia.org/wiki/ Ungarndeutsche). Overviews are provided in Knipf-Komlósi 1988, 2001, 2003, 2006, 2008; Hutterer 1991;Wild 1985, 1992 (German teaching); Seewann 1994, 2012; Eichinger 1995; Erb 1994, 1995, 2010; Erb/ Knipf-Komlósi; Hessky 1995; Manherz 1998; Bradean-Ebinger 1999; Fenyvesi 1998; Földes 2001a, b; 2004b; Kern 1999a, b; Deminger 2004; Gerner 2006; Kontra 2006; Kamusella 2009: 645–713; Maitz/ Sándor 2009; Stevenson/ Carl 2010; Müller 2010a, b; 2012; de.wikipedia.org/wiki/Ungarndeutsche. I am grateful to Elisabeth Knipf-Komlósi and Marta Müller for further information.

Self-designation as "Hungarian Germans" with variants such as "Germans in Hungary" reveals ethnic identity (Gerner 2006). More specialised self-designations, e.g. primarily, *Schwaben* [Swabians] (*Donauschwaben* is only used abroad), are hyponyms (for subordinate terms), but with undoubted allocation to the German ethnic group. This allocation is also used by the majority of the population, the titular nation of Hungarians. People from the area surrounding the *Schwaben* are also often allocated to this group (Seewann 2012,Vol. 2: 411). Many of those born between 1950 and 1980 have limited mastery of a variety of German, and only a minority declared German as their native language, even if they classify their knowledge of German as "quite good" or "moderate" (ibid: 409). But knowledge of German has recently improved, although the use of German has declined (ibid: 411). In cases of obvious Hungarian citizenship, many are still uncertain about their ethnic allocation ("floating" identity; Ch. B.3) or declare dual identity (German + Hungarian). As a result, even a declaration of German native language can be combined with non-declaration of German ethnic group (on identity uncertainties, see Gerner 2006: 157–161). In recent history, a declaration of membership of the German ethnic group was politically sensitive, and the figures registered fluctuate considerably (e.g. 1960: 8,640–2001:62,233–2011:131,951). Censuses have been anonymous only since 2001 (Knipf-Komlósi 2008: 269f). Of the approximately 132,000 (declared) ethnic Germans in 2011, 62,233 declared German as their native language. Around 32,000 ethnic Hungarians also declared this, but not membership of the German ethnic group. As a result, native speakers of German ran to around 94,000 and the total number of Hungarian Germans to approximately 164,000 (132,000 ethnic +32,000 only native language).

The settlement territory is widely distributed over 13 of the 19 administrative districts (*Komitate*) (Wild 1985), but concentrated in the west around the cities of Sopron/ *Ödenburg* and Györ/ Raab, Szombathely/ *Steinamanger*, in each case on the Austrian border, around Veszprém/ *Vesprim*, to the north of Lake Balaton/ *Plattensee* and Budapest and around Pécs/ *Fünfkirchen* (Swabian Turkey) and Baja/ *Frankenstadt* (Batschka) (Knipf-Komlósi 2008: 268; maps: Duschanek 1997b; Knipf-Komlósi 2008: 265). In none of these localities do the Hungarian Germans come close to forming a majority. Historical scattering was intensified after WWII by the expulsions and restructuring into agricultural production cooperatives. This has made constant contact with the linguistic majority unavoidable and, combined with frequent exogamy, supports language shifting to the majority language, Hungarian (Seewann 2012,Vol. 2: 413). This also largely explains the absence of linguistic landscape in German, apart from tourist notices. However, all villages with Hungarian Germans have bilingual Hungarian-German town names. Reinstated German town names are used consistently in the German-speaking media in Hungary (Knipf-Komlósi 2008: 281). In Sopron/ *Ödenburg* and Pilösvörsvár/ *Werischwar* with officially 3.5% and 23.7% Hungarian Germans respectively), there are also bilingual road signs and road names. The social structure of the Hungarian Germans has been weakened since the nineteenth century by erosion of the educated stratum: relocation into cities and higher than average emigration. There are no longer any monolingual, German-speaking, Hungarian Germans, and until recently, most families are tending towards a complete shift to Hungarian (Knipf-Komlósi 2008: 281–283, 303–307).

However, this tendency has been slowed and, in one form, even reversed through new developments, especially a remarkable school provision. In this respect, there are parallels with Romania (Ch. E.4.7). Since the end of the 1970s and then in consequence of the Minorities and Education Acts (No. LXXVII and LXXIX, both in 1993), a school system which fosters the maintenance of German has evolved. In this context, German is designated as a "minority language", "nationality language" or "second language" (in the sense of a second native language) and taught with explicit reference to the ethnic identity and history of the Hungarian Germans. In bilingual minority schools, at least 50% of school subjects are taught in German: German language and literature, history, minority culture, geography and sometimes even biology and mathematics (Müller 2010b: 104f). German is taught to an even greater extent as a foreign language, surpassed only by English. Within this framework, allocations and forms of learning as a minority and a foreign language overlap. The decisive factor is that German is not only a school subject, but – in bilingual schools – it is also a language of instruction, alongside Hungarian. This school provision extends from kindergarten through to university. For the year 2000, Knipf-Komlósi (2008: 280) reports 284 *Schulen* with 45,240 pupils/students, approximately 250 kindergartens, 13 bilingual grammar schools and five universities with teacher-training courses for these schools (for the Hungarian school system, see Müller 2010a, b). The German School Abroad in the Hungarian German Cultural Centre Baja/ *Frankenstadt* is also designed for the German (-speaking) minority. University applicants wishing to study "German as a minority language" can choose between four courses as follows:

1) Kindergarten-teacher training in five universities and colleges;
2) Primary-teacher training in eight universities and colleges;
3) German studies/German as native language (BA) in three universities and colleges; and
4) German studies/German as native language (MA) in two universities (Muller 2012: 108f).

By contrast, other German-language training and academic courses in Hungary are not intended for Hungarian Germans: the German School Budapest, the Andrássy Gyula German-Language University in Budapest (since 2002) and German-speaking courses in eight other universities (www.studieren_in_ungarn.de/486,1,studiengaenge_auf_deutsch.html). German-speaking media for the Hungarian Germans include the weekly *Neue Zeitung* and the *Sonntagsblatt* which appears every two months – whereas the *Budapester Zeitung* and *Balaton-Zeitung* are aimed at expatriates and tourists (www.press-guide.com/hungary.htm). Furthermore, *Radio Pécs/ Funkhaus Fünfkirchen* broadcasts in German to Hungarian Germans for two hours daily. There is also the full range of media from Germany and Austria.

Efforts towards language maintenance find support in minority rights. The first Minorities Act was amended in 1993 and 2011. The minority's own association is now fully institutionalised. It was founded in 1955 as the *Kulturverband der Deutschen Werktätigen in Ungarn* [Cultural Association of German Employees in Hungary], renamed in 1969 as *Demokratischer Verband Ungarnländischer Deutscher*, and in 1978 as *Demokratischer Verband der Ungarndeutschen* and finally in 1989 as *Verband der Ungarndeutschen* (Kerekes 2010: 153). The *Landesverwaltung der Ungarndeutschen (LdU)* has existed since 1993 (www.ldu.hu/menu/1) as an umbrella organisation for 378 local minority, self-administrative groups (Seewann 2012, Vol. 2: 403–406). Further support is provided by the *European Charter for Regional or Minority Languages* of the European Council and EU, which was promptly ratified and enforced by Hungary (26 April 1995 and 1 March 1998: conventions. coe.int/Treaty/Commun/ChercheSig.asp?NT=148&CM=&DF=&CL=GER). Since 1990, there have been minority community councils, which existed in 321 localities in 1997 and formed the community administration in 38. However, the minority has no representation in the national parliament (Knipf-Komlósi 2008: 2007).

Another form of support, which must not be underestimated, is aid from outside, primarily from Germany and Austria. This includes guest teachers sent to the minority schools (Knipf-Komlósi 2008: 280). The Goethe-Institut, the Institute for Foreign Affairs (ifa) and private associations such as the *Donauschwäbische Kulturstiftung* (Stuttgart) participate in promoting the minority. They also support cultural associations such as the *Verband Ungardeutscher Autoren und Künstler (VUdAK)*, within which a German-speaking literature is again beginning to develop (see: kulturportal-west-ost.eu/institutions/verband-ungarndeutscher-autoren-und-kunstler-vudak/). The position of the German language is also strengthened by possibilities for locating company branches from German-speaking countries and by training, study and employment in Germany and Austria. By contrast, contacts between German departments in universities and German companies or their associations are less developed. In individual cases, the various connections can even motivate a shift reversal to German as family language and native language, alongside Hungarian, which would continue as the dominant language. However, this development is hampered by the fact that English is now learnt more frequently as a foreign language than German, primarily in the east of the country.

4.7 Romania

The recent history of the Romanian Germans has been as dramatic as in the other eastern-central European, German(-speaking) minorities, but with some striking differences. The Romanian Germans are more clearly classifiable into different groups. For example, Johanna Bottesch (2008: 333–344) distinguishes the following eight groups by settlement territory and history: **Siebenbürger Sachsen,* *Sathmarer Schwaben*, *Banater Berglanddeutsche*, **Banater Schwaben*, *Landler*, *Zipser*, *Buchenlanddeutsche* and *Dobrudschadeutsche* (similar in Baier et al. 2011: 19–36). Only the groups marked with an asterisk here are still represented in significant numbers; the largest groups are marked with a double asterisk. The root names ("*Sachsen*", "*Schwaben*") should not be taken literally, because their actual origin is not unified. In some cases, the settlement goes back to the twelfth century, with the *Siebenbürger Sachsen* as the oldest immigrants. In fact, territorial variation in the Romanian state between the end of WWI and WWII also influenced German nationality; but the expulsion of the Dobrudscha, Bessarabien and Bukovina Germans, and the flight of large numbers of North-Siebenbürger and Banater Germans to Germany and Austria as a result of Romania's changing alliances was even more serious. Added to these effects were the occasional land alienation and collectivisation under Soviet influence of those who remained. In view of such oppression, a total of 226,654 Romanian Germans decided to emigrate to Germany in the period 1967–1989 ("bought out" by the Federal Republic of Germany; Baier et al. 2011: 114); the total loss for the period 1950–1989 ran to 242,320 (ibid: 115). After the collapse of the Ceaușescu regime, a further 111,150 Romanian Germans left the country in 1989. Their number in Romania declined from more than half a million to just 36,900 today. In the 2011 census, only 27,019 Romanian citizens declared German as their native language. 120,000 people had declared German nationality in the 1992 census; in 2002 only 59,764 (Lăzărescu 2013: 375f.: Note 15; older figures in Dingeldein 2006: 68; both texts give historical overviews). Other important sources of information include Baier et al. 2011; Lăzărescu 2005, 2011; Scheuringer 2008; Dingeldein 2004; M. Bottesch 1997; M. Bottesch/ Grieshofer/ Schabus 2002; U.-P. Wagner 2002; Gadeanu 1998; Gündisch 1998; Kroner 1998; Rein 1997; Sundhausen 1992; McArthur 1990; E. Wagner 1990; Gabanyi 1988; Steinke 1979; Barcan/ Millitz 1977. I am grateful to Ioan Lăzărescu for additional information.

The relevant minority in this chapter refers to themselves as "Romanian Germans (*Rumänien-deutsche*)", subdivided into "*Siebenburger Sachsen*", *Sathmarer Schwaben*", "*Banater Schwaben*", "*Banater Berglanddeutsche*" and "*Landler*", i.e. with ethnic rather than linguistic reference (hardly ever as "German-speaking Romanians"). These designations are also used by the linguistic majority in Romania and by the German-speaking countries. Of course, all have Romanian citizenship, but often dual citizenship with a German-speaking country which is readily available (www.siebenbuerger.de/zeitung/pdfarchiv/suche/doppelte%20staatsb%FCrgerschaft/). As with most German(-speaking) minorities, surrounding a core of competent German native speakers (dialect or Standard German), there is a group who have shifted to the majority language, Romanian, but still allocate themselves to the German minority. Lack of clear allocation at the defining margins makes it difficult to specify accurate numerical data and demands caution even with recently registered figures. In fact, massive emigration since WWII has dramatically reduced the number; but this decline has evidently not continued. Conversely, neither has there been a sometimes-hoped-for major re-immigration, but instead, a seasonal return of "summer Romanians" to visit friends, relatives or properties they still own.

Geographically, the present-day German minority is concentrated, on the one hand, in the centre of Romania, in *Siebenbürgen* (or "Transylvania"), to the north of Sibiu/ Hermannstadt and to the east by Braşov/ Kronstadt; on the other hand, in the West in Banat, around the cities of Temeschwar/ Timişoara (the German name is also preferred in the Romanian media) and Reşiţa/ Reschitza, in smaller territories in the north-west around Satu Mare/Sathmar and in the north. Within the minority, German town names are still used, but orally rather than in writing (Bottesch 2008: 365). In its charter (§25), the most important organisation of the German minority, *Das Demokratische Forum der Deutschen in Rumänien*, defines and explains the subdivision into five regions, for which regional associations are responsible: "Siebenbürgen = Siebenbürger Sachsen, Landler; Nordsiebenbürgen = Sathmarer Schwaben, Zipser; Banat – Banater Schwaben, Berglanddeutsche; Bukovina = Buchenlanddeutsche; Bukarest = Germans from the 'Altreich'" (www.fdgr.ro/de/statutul_organizatiei/5.html). The city of Cluj-Napoca/ Klausenburg also plays an important role as a kind of cultural centre for the German minority, with respected German-speaking courses at the University (Ch. J.6; territorial maps: Steinke 1997; Bottesch 2008: 329; Dingeldein 2006: 75). Even in the capital Bucureşti/ Bukarest, there are scattered members of the minority and, as elsewhere in many places, traces of a German-speaking past and provenance (Scheuringer 2008; Herta/ Jung 2011).

Since the distance from German-speaking countries is not great, it is possible to undertake visits in private vehicles. But, to some extent, distance does obstruct reception of electronic media and delivery of printed media. In the country itself, contacts between German minority and the titular nation, the Romanians, are intensive; in the west of the state, this includes the Hungarian minority, which is today much larger than the German (6.7% by comparison with 0.3% of the total population). As a result, Hungarian is also a regional official language rather than German. In practically all localities, the Romanian-speaking population is in the majority; except Hungarian-speakers in some regions. Towns with a German-speaking majority are a thing of the past. Linguistic exogamy is frequent, and the maintenance of purely German-speaking social networks is almost impossible. As a result, almost all members of the German minority are at least bilingual, and Romanian is the dominant day-to-day language. Social contacts are limited for many members of the German minority who, apart from cases of agricultural self-sufficiency, are no longer at work because of their age. Ageing in the German minority weakens the maintenance of German, especially as a native language. In the absence of a next-generation, there is often no question of passing on their knowledge and use of German to children and grandchildren, which, in any case, cannot be taken for granted. In many families, Romanian is the dominant language of communication and a more firmly anchored native language – although German often functions as a symbol of identity and is named as the native language.

Mass migration has also reshaped the social structure of the minority. The distribution of the social strata is not balanced, which further obstructs the use of German in domains outside the family, e.g. shopping, medical appointments, legal information or local administration. In most domains, members of the German minority capable of communicating in German are to be found only sporadically, but this is more likely in Siebenbürgen and Banat than in the smaller German settlement regions. Based on a questionnaire with 33 respondents in Siebenbürgen, Johanna Bottesch (ibid: 371–381) has given details of the possible German networks. As a result of emigration, primarily from rural regions, "with only a few exceptions, a German community [. . .] is only possible today in urban settings" (Baier et al. 2011: 116). Because of low speaker numbers in the population, German is not a local official language in any locality, at least not in terms of status; in practice, it may have this function just because of the personnel available – but there are training courses for administrative German in contact centres (Bottesch 2008: 379). The linguistic landscape, meaning the presence of public notices in German, is modest. In fact, town signs in languages of minorities with at least 20% of the inhabitants are provided by law; but the German minority never reaches this proportion (Bottesch 2008: 348). However, there are isolated bilingual town signs in traditional centres with the German name at the bottom of the sign in smaller lettering, e.g. "Municipiul Sibiu/Hermannstadt". In the religious domain, German still plays a role, primarily in church services. The evangelical church (Augsburg Confession), to which approximately one third of Romanian Germans belong, also contributes to the maintenance of a German-speaking infrastructure (Dingeldein 2006: 68f). Several theatres and research institutes also use German (Bottesch 2008: 345). Regarding internal media, works in print must be highlighted, including – more than in other east-central and eastern German minorities – highbrow literature, fiction and poetry. The Wikipedia article "Romanian-German Literature" mentions 26 distinguished modern Romanian German authors (de.wikipedia.org/wiki/Rum%3C%A4niendeutsche_Literatur), however, also including emigrants who maintain contact with their country of origin, such as Nobel Prize winner Herta Müller. The Romanian-German publishing house Kriterion (*Editura Kriterion*) has an established tradition (new titles at: www.siebenbuerger.de/suche/alle/kriterion%20verlag/). Periodical publications include the *Allgemeine Deutsche Zeitung für Rumänien*, which appears daily apart from Sundays (www.adz.ro) and is published by the most important minority association, *Das Demokratische Forum der Deutschen in Rumänien*, with financial support from the Romanian state (circulation 3,000). It contains the *Karpatenrundschau* and the *Banater Zeitung* as weekly supplements. There is also the weekly *Hermannstädter Zeitung* and a relatively large number of specialist periodicals, primarily for German Studies, church and association news. No less than six Romanian radio broadcasters run German-language programmes between one hour per day and one hour per week. State television broadcasts by TVR1 and TVR2 are broadcast between 30 minutes and 90 minutes weekly (Bottesch 2008: 346).

The most spectacular linguistic success for the Romanian Germans is their school system. What Hungarian Germans are striving for (Ch. E.4.6), the Romanian Germans have realised in a sustainable manner, namely, that schools previously attended by the German minority are now attended primarily by the majority population and in some cases also by other minorities, with tuition in German, in a few cases alongside their own language. Dingeldein (2006: 69–72) outlines the situation appropriately as follows: "educational facilities have been transformed from 'schools of the German minority' to 'schools in the language of the German minority'" (ibid: 71). In the school year 1993/94, of the 21,000 pupils in German-speaking kindergartens and schools, 60 to 80% had no parent of German nationality. Lăzărescu (2013: 384, also, note 44) refers to statistics from the Regional Schools Commission, according to which, in the school year 2012/13, tuition was given in German in 196 facilities below university level, with a total of 14,296 pupils. These facilities comprise 59 schools from classes I – VIII, 26 grammar schools (*Lyzeen*), five of which have exclusively German as the language of instruction, and 111 kindergartens. This school system is academically and pedagogically well secured with training institutes at universities and colleges in which qualified staff are trained in German as native language and foreign language, and in the teaching of school subjects. Teacher shortage presents some difficulties which are mitigated to some extent by personnel from German-speaking countries. Bottesch (2008: 383) sees the influx of Romanians into the German-speaking schools as "instrumentally" motivated (Ch. E.2) by a "cost-benefit calculation" with regard to job prospects. It is evident that motivation among Romanians – by contrast with Romanian Germans – is not "integrative" (the contrary term) because, for them, German generally remains a "work language" and not "language of everyday use" or "family language" (Bottesch 2008: 383f). As a result, speakers' relationship with German is more susceptible to economic recession than if it were anchored as the native language. After WWII, the German minority in Romania received comprehensive language rights earlier than other German minorities in central eastern and eastern Europe. These rights have been broadened in recent history, in part through the *European Charter for Regional or Minority Languages* (ratified by Romania 29 January 2008, enforced 1 May 2008. See: conventions.coe.int/Treaty/Commun/ChercheSig.asp?NT=148&CM=&DF=&CL=GER). Language rights support the school system and allow the establishment of internal associations, the most important of which, *Das Demokratische Forum der Deutschen in Rumänien*, was mentioned above. It is often abbreviated as *Deutsches Forum* and – with government aid – supports contact centres, cultural associations and events and the daily newspaper.

As already suggested, relations between the German minority and German-speaking countries, especially Germany and Austria, are close (Bottesch 2008: 380). Apart from government funding, primarily via cultural institutes and quangos, which supply and to some extent finance teachers and lecturers (e.g. *DAAD-Lektoren*), commercial contacts are particularly important. They form a substantial basis for the instrumental motivation for attending German schools. On the Internet, there is no shortage of reports with headings like the following: "With big-name German companies like Continental, Siemens, Marquardt and Metro, the Hermannstadt Business Park has plenty to boast about. German firms currently provide 55% of all jobs in the Sibiu district" (www.reporterreisen.com/zehn-tage-siebenbuergen/reportagen/fast-made-in-germany/). Apart from local jobs, there are placements and employment opportunities in the German-speaking countries themselves. Provided this situation is maintained, a knowledge of German is relevant to Romanians, and supports the maintenance of German.

However, the prospects for maintaining the dialect, even in minority families, are slim, because it is of little use for most practical communication (Bottesch 2008: 372f). But the spoken Standard German coloured by the dialect is still a regional identity symbol for the various Romanian German groups (ibid: 386). Their Standard German is still influenced by Austrian German, but the details are limited to vocabulary e.g. *Titularisierung* for "*Verbeamtung*" [appointment as a government official], *ultrazentral* for "very central (residential)" (2013: 381f). Such national variants ("Romanianisms") are codified and thus acknowledged as Romanian Standard German (cf. Ch. B.2) in the *Variantenwörterbuch des Deutschen* (Ammon/ Bickel/ Lenz 2013/16; also Lăzărescu 2013, 2011, 2006). However, not all German teachers and their trainers are inclined to accept them, especially not borrowings from Romanian (M. Bottesch 1997: 9–21). In spite of these encouraging signs, German is still only ranked as the third foreign language in Romania, behind French (because of the linguistic similarity with Romanian and traditional relations with France, currently via the *Francophonie* organisation). German is positioned even further behind English.

Johanna Bottesch (2008: 379) has noted the trend for young people to watch TV in English. If German companies communicate in English, as they do in some other regions of the world (Ch. F.5; F.7), or are satisfied with Romanian employees with a knowledge of English, this could be detrimental to the learning of German.

4.8 Russia

The "Russian Germans" include descendants of former German-speaking agricultural colon-isers and immigrants from subsequent periods. At the time of the Soviet Union, large numbers were resettled in the territories of the present CIS states (Community of Independent States with 11 member states including Russia, officially the "Russian Federation"). Compulsory resettlement almost eliminated the Russian Germans (Berend 1994; Risse/ Roll 1997; Eisfeld 1999: 165–174; FAZ 1 August 1998: 10), but they look back over a respectable history. After an initial wave of immigration in earlier centuries, the first major influx occurred as a result of generous promises by Czarina Katherina II (1763–96), forming the well-known Rus-sian-German "language islands" (Berend/ Mattheier 1994; Berend 2011; Rosenberg 2003a: 199–201; Detlef Brandes, in Eisfeld 1999: 12–44). Under Czar Alexander III (1865–81), the Russian government's attitude hardened, and they lost some of their privileges. In particular, their schools were forced to shift from German to Russian as the compulsory language of instruction, because of the growth of capitalist forms of economy and possibly also as a reac-tion against the formation of the German Empire (1871), which was perceived as a threat. This caused one group of Mennonites (Ch. E.11) to emigrate. Towards the end of the 1920s, they were followed by other groups in the wake of the collectivisation of agriculture. After the October Revolution (1917), the circumstances of Russian Germans initially improved when, in 1924, they were even allowed to found the *Autonomous Socialist Soviet Republic of Volga Germans* (ASSRdWD) in their principal settlement territory, following Lenin's national-ity policy (Dubinin 2011; Eisfeld 1999: 120–134). However, the situation worsened again in the 1930s when Stalin restricted their rights and finally liquidated the Autonomous Republic on 28 August 1941 following the Nazi German attack on the Soviet Union. This liquidation was associated with complete dispossession and deportation of all the approximately 377,000 "German" inhabitants of that republic. Russian Germans from other territories of the Soviet Union were also forced to resettle, bringing the number of deportees to almost 700,000. They were redistributed in Central Asia and Siberia; most died under forced labour (Eisfeld 1999: 125). After the war, they were prevented from returning to their former territories, and re-formation of the Autonomous Volga Republic proved impossible (ibid: 165). Even an official amnesty for Russian Germans in 1955 failed to include a restoration of rights which would have been significant for language maintenance, especially the right to schools with German as a language of instruction. In the aftermath of the war, there was a general avoidance of the German language in public and private domains (Stricker 2000). Under these condi-tions, Russian Germans' attitude to their own ethnic group shifted from pride (coupled with loyalty to the Russian state), through anxieties and feelings of shame, to a tentative revival in the period since glasnost (Najdič 1997: 198). Even today, the term "Russian Germans" still includes people who emigrated to Germany (seldom to other German-speaking countries) (Eisfeld 1999: 188–197), who have since become more numerous than those who remained in the CIS states, primarily Russia. The term "ethnic" in this context should be understood "to depend crucially on the 'nationality' entry in the Russian passport rather than an actual association with German culture or mastery of the German language" (de.wikipedia.org/ wiki/Russlanddeutsche). Since this is generally taken as a sufficient criterion, the entry is particularly important. It can be assumed that some of the Russian Germans only remain in the CIS states today because, in the absence of this entry and with inadequate knowledge of German, they were unable to emigrate to Germany or another German-speaking country (Eisfeld 1999: 172). Various accounts are provided in Berend 1994, 2006, 2011; Klaube 1994, 1997; Krindac 1997; Risse/ Roll 1997; Barbasina 1999; Eisfeld 1999; Stricker 2000; Bruhl 2003; Rosenberg 2003a, b; Dubinin 2005, 2011; Berend/ Riehl 2008; Blankenhorn 2008; Riehl 2008; Schirokich 2008; Damus 2011; Djatlova 2011; Troshina 2004, 2010, 2011, 2013; de.wikipedia.org/wiki/Russlanddeutsche). I am grateful to Nina Berend and Sergej I. Dubinin for additional information.

The present settlement territories of the Russian Germans in Russia are mainly in Siberia, in the region surrounding Omsk and Novosibirsk (*Nowosibirsk*) in Western Siberia and Ekaterinburg (*Jekaterinburg*) in the Urals, and – as a result of more recent influx – in the territory of the former Autonomous Volga Republic and to a lesser extent around Kaliningrad (formerly *Königsberg*) (map in Berend/ Riehl 2008: 17). An itemised listing of residential regions is provided in de.wikipedia.org/wiki/Russlanddeutsche. Two references are important: "Most of the Germans living in the Altai region have emigrated, but a group of German nationals is living here again now". And "in 2010, Russian Germans still represented only the largest *minority* in the Altai region and the Novosibirsk territory" [italics U.A.]. But even here, Russians were more numerous. Nowhere else were the Russian Germans even the largest minority. The current total number of Russian Germans in Russia can only be roughly estimated. Once again, de.wikipedia.org/wiki/Russlanddeutsche claims that "today, around 800,000 Russian Germans still live in the Russian Federation [. . .]". But, diverging somewhat from this: "The last census (2002) gives a total number of 597,212 Germans, of which 350,000 in Siberia". The census of 1989 found 842,295 Russian Germans in Russia (data also in Berend/ Riehl 2008: 20; for associated problems, see Bruhl 2003, vol. 2: 469f). Presumably the total number in Russia is less than 500,000, with the majority in Siberia. Only a small proportion can still speak German to some extent. German has no official status at state level (Ch. D.1), except in two "German national regions" (districts), in fact, since 1991, in the *Halbstadt* district near the town of Slavgorod in the Altai region (details in Klaube 1997; also, Bruhl 2003, vol. 2: 430–443, 450–460) and since 1992 in the *Asovo* district in the region (*Oblast*) near Omsk (Berend/ Riehl 2008: 25; Bruhl 2003, vol. 2: 443–450), both close to the north-eastern frontier with Kazakhstan. The scale can be imagined from the fact that Halbstadt, the local centre of the district, is a village with only 1,750 inhabitants, and the town of Slavgorod, which serves as an orientation point in geographical descriptions, has less than 33,000 inhabitants. Asovo is also a village with almost 6,000 inhabitants; but there are now supposed to be only 5,000 Russian Germans in the entire Asovo district, who therefore form only a significant minority of 24% of the inhabitants, even in their own district (de.wikipedia.org/wiki/Nationalkreis_Asowo). The formation of networks within the national group is hampered by scattered settlement. Only a few small villages of Mennonites in Siberia and in the Orenburg region, who did not emigrate and whose conservative lifestyle contributes to language maintenance, form a relatively greater density of German-speakers (Berend 2006: 85). The remaining Russian Germans live mainly in the countryside. Those who have migrated into the towns have generally been linguistically and ethnically assimilated. But most of the others have also shifted to Russian, even in the German districts. "For many representatives of the older and middle generation, discrimination based on ethnicity was a significant cause for their speaking less German with the children, and many representatives of the middle generation have entirely stopped speaking German with their children and even with their parents" (Djatlova 2011: 400f.). Most of the children can no longer speak German at all (for Siberia, see Blankenhorn

2008; for Baschkiria, see Schirokich 2008: 72). German is almost non-existent in the linguistic landscape of the German districts. Even German town names are absent. In most institutions, primarily government offices, the use of German is extremely limited, despite its explicit legal authorisation. German is spoken much less frequently between colleagues at work and neighbours [...], even in the Altai villages. In public contexts, such as local politics or when shopping in the village, Russian is generally used [...]" (Damus 2011: 34).

School provision is particularly important for the future. In fact, bilingual Russian/German schools are legally provided for Russian Germans living in compact settlements of more than 2,000 people (Berend/ Riehl 2008: 26f). However, these provisions have, so far, hardly been realised. A serious start was made only in isolated cases for German as a foreign language (GFL), but this was not continued (Baur/ Chlosta/ Wenderoff 2000; Baur/ Mamporija/ Schymiczek 2011a). The outlook for native-language tuition initially seemed favourable because, after the amnesty of 1955, the government had already "made arrangements for the school year 1957/58 [...] from the second class upwards in territories with a high concentration of German population" (Eisfeld 1999: 137f). However, implementation failed to meet expectations. It is also unfavourable that Russia lagged behind other member states of the European Council (of which it is a member) with regard to minority rights, and had not ratified the *European Charter for Regional or Minority Languages* (at least not by July 2015 – conventions.coe.int/Treaty/ Commun/ChergeSig.asp?NT=14&&CM=&DF=&CL=GER). At present, if Russian Germans learn German at all in school, it is almost always only as GFL (Berend/Riehl 2008: 27f.; Berend 2006: 86) – which does, however, correspond with their previous knowledge. The same applies for the German national districts in which German is "learned as a compulsory foreign language" (Damus 2011: 34), and, in fact, by all inhabitants. In Russia, GFL can also be chosen as an alternative to English as the first foreign language, i.e. it is not necessarily only the second foreign language (Ch. J.9.6).

The situation is somewhat different for extramural German tuition which takes place primarily in German-Russian centres and meeting rooms (for the situation around 2003, see Berend/ Riehl 2008: 28). For example, the Education and Information Centre (BIZ) in the German-Russian Centre in Moscow lists its own "German courses, also for language teachers, youth and training projects", and support for "13 meeting rooms in Neudorf (Strelna), Murmansk, Novodvinsk, Petrosavodsk, Pskov, Severodvinsk, Tosno, Kotlas, Koplino, Kirischi, Gatschina, Vyborg, Volchov", which also offer German courses (www.ornis-press.de/deutsch-rissisches-begegnungszentrum-an-der-petrikirche-st-petersburg.676.0.html). German-Russian centres which still provide German courses also exist "in the Russian cities of Kaliningrad, Moscow, Novosibirsk, Tomsk, Smolensk and Barnaul [...]", with "branches in the respective regional units (the Russian Obslasts)". These centres are also "important meeting places for Russian Germans" and "contribute to maintaining the cultural identity of Russian Germans" – or at least have this as a goal (de.wikipedia.org/wiki/Deutsch-Russisches_Haus). According to Dubinin's estimate, the entire language-teaching provision still available for Russian Germans ultimately depends on the Goethe-Institut. As with other GFL learners in Russia, it can be assumed that learning German among Russian Germans relies on vocational and economic rather than traditional or ethnic motives. In one extensive survey of German school pupils and students (n = 732 completed questionnaires), 92.7% declared the most important motive for choice of language as "Knowledge of German will secure me a good job" (Voronina 2011: 280; also, Radschenko 2011a). Since the amnesty of 1955, German-speaking media are again provided in Russia (Eisfeld 1999: 137). A series of newspapers is still in existence, but they are published only weekly or monthly with small circulation: *Neues Leben* (Moscow), formerly important, but now appearing only sporadically; the *Zeitung für Dich* (Altai region, monthly insert in *Altajskaja Prawda*), *Ihre*

Zeitung (German district of Asovo, bilingual weekly), *Königsberger Express* (Kaliningrad, monthly 5,000), *Moskauer Deutsche Zeitung* (bilingual, fortnightly, 25,000). There are also community newsletters and specialist journals. However, the fact that such data (e.g. in Akstinat 2012/13: 227–236) are subject to frequent variations betrays the precarious situation. From 1957, there was also German-speaking radio in the Orenburg, Omsk and Novosibirsk regions (Eisfeld 1999: 137), but this is evidently no longer the case (Dubinin). There is certainly no German-speaking television. However, newspapers, other print media, radio and television from German-speaking countries are accessible via the Internet, and German-speaking radio broadcasts via the Russian foreign broadcaster *Stimme Russlands* (www.press-guide.com/Radio-Russland.htm). Galina Woronenkowa (2011: 251) considers the "basic media provision in German and from Germany to be secured by the Internet [...]". In general, however, contacts with German-speaking countries are more difficult than within the EU, both for political reasons relating to the difficulty of border crossing, and also because of the geographical distances, e.g. 4,000 km to the German districts. As a result, such contacts are largely a privilege for organisational leaders and functionaries. Contact with companies from German-speaking countries, represented in great numbers elsewhere in Russia (Martynova 2010, 2011), hardly play a role for Russian Germans. For this, they would have to move to the city.

However, contact with German-speaking countries does exist through the support they provide. This was and continues to be considerable in economic and political terms, especially from Germany (Bruhl 2003, vol. 2:450–452, 461–468; Berend/ Riehl 2008: 24f.; Eisfeld 1999: 156–174 passim). Since glasnost and perestroika, funding opportunities have been available, e.g. in the case of ultimately unsuccessful efforts to restore the Autonomous Volga Republic, but also in the foundation and care of the German district of Asovo and Halbstadt. Bruhl (2003, vol. 2) references considerable financial aid from Germany, e.g. 90 m DM for the Halbstadt district from 1991 to 1996 (ibid: 452) and 200 m DM for the Asovo district from 1993 to 2000 (ibid: 461). Some of this support has been wasted, e.g. on oversized private housing (ibid: 463f). Even today, Russian Germans receive generous funding from Germany, e.g. through German tuition via the Goethe-Institut and the German-Russian centres and meeting rooms, as already mentioned. The German Association for Technical Collaboration (GTZ) also expressly declares its funding for the Education and Information Centre (BIZ) of the German-Russian Centre in Moscow as "aid for the German minority in Russia, Ukraine and Central Asia" (www. giz.de/Themen/en/dokumente/BIZ-de.pdf). Further support, also from private foundations and international cultural societies, could be added to this (e.g. *Ost-West-Gesellschaft Baden-Württemberg*, with funding for Samara). Town twinning also plays a part. Where it is still provided, such support very probably contributes to the maintenance of German. An important mediating role is played by the associations of Russian Germans which were formed after the 1955 amnesty (Guseynova 2011; Belobratow 2011). However, alongside organisational difficulties, one further problem is that management personnel now tend to live in Germany rather than in Russia, so that the "educated stratum [. . .], which is already thin, is further weakened by emigration" (Eisfeld 1999: 173f). The *Wiedergeburt* society founded in 1989 played an important part until attempts to re-establish the Autonomous Volga Republic failed. The *Verband der Deutschen in der UdSSR* broke away from this group in 1991. After a period of renaming and conflicts, the *Internationaler Verband der deutschen Kultur (IVDK)* is now the most influential organisation: "The principal aim of the association is to maintain the cultural identity and community of Russian Germans" (www. Rusdeutsch.eu/?menu00 = 6). Operating alongside and in conjunction with the IVDK is the "Federal-National Cultural Autonomy of Russian Germans (FNKA)", with the principal aim of "strengthening the legal status of the German minority (continuation of legal rehabilitation of Russian Germans)" (de.wikipedia.

org/wiki/F%C3%B6derale_Nationale_Kulturautonomie_der_Russlanddeutschen). It remains uncertain whether the German language or only ethnic identity is maintained among those who have not yet given it up (Risse/ Roll: 213f).

4.9 Namibia

Namibia is the only state having developed from a former German colony with a German(-speaking) minority which corresponds to the criteria designed for the present book (Ch. E.3). All the other former German colonies now show only traces or memories of historical colonial domination (see e.g. Mühlhäusler 1977, 1979, 1980; research group "Colonial Linguistics" at the Institute for German Language in Mannheim: de.wikipedia.org/wiki/Koloniallinguistik). Walter Wentenschuh (1995) provides a balanced overview of the history of the Germans in Namibia until shortly before independence and is also critical of colonialism. Namibia's relationship with the "mother country" can be characterised with reference to its favourable climate, size, small population and its relatively short distance from Germany, making it the favoured "settlement colony" by contrast with the other "exploitation colonies" (chronological details in Kube/ Kotze 2002). With its cruelties to the black, indigenous population, the colonial period is an enduring moral burden for Germany and the German Namibians. From 1884 to 1915, the territory of the present Namibia was a German colony known as German-South West Africa; in 1920, it was mandated by the League of Nations to British-controlled South Africa. Most of the German settlers were initially expelled but called back again to boost the proportion of Europeans in the population (Interest Group of German-speaking South-Westerners 1980; references also in Hess/ Becker 2002). With reduced numbers, this influx of Germans has continued until the present. Based on an understanding between German settlers and South Africa, which included support for the apartheid policy, German once again became the official language of state of Namibia in 1983 but limited to the "Territory of the Whites" and alongside the unrestricted official languages of Afrikaans and English (Ammon 1991a: 75–80). The Official Gazette was also published in German and, for the "Regional Parliament of the Whites", it was stipulated that documents must be published in all three languages: "*dat proklamasies, ordonnansies, regulasies en kennisgewings [. . .] in die Afrikaanse, Duitse en Engelse taal moet geskied*" (Minutes of the Regional Parliament Session of 9 November 1983). However, like Afrikaans, German lost its official status when Namibia gained independence on 21 March 1990, and English was retained as the sole official language of state. Despite minimal anchoring within the population, English owed this preferential status to its global position and its function as a lingua franca in the *South-West Africa People's Organisation of Namibia* (SWAPO), which fought for Namibian independence, but also to the fact that it was less implicated than Afrikaans and German with racist apartheid policies. But German has retained the status of a "national language" of Namibia and therefore as a recognised, minority language, together with Afrikaans and six languages of the indigenous black population, which previously had no recognised status (Khoekhoegowab, OshiKwanyama, Oshindonga, Otjiherero, RuKwangali, Silozi). This status as a national language is not anchored in the constitution but only declared in subordinate decrees (see *Language Policy for Schools in Namibia Discussion Document,* January 2003; language policy for schools 1992–1996 and beyond: www.nied.edu.na/images/Language%20Policy%20For%20schools%20 1992_1996%20and%20be-yond.pdf).

It is also worth mentioning the maintenance of German among the *DDR-Kinder,* 425 Namibian children sent to the GDR during the war of independence 1979–1985, who returned to Namibia in 1990 with an excellent knowledge of German (Engombe 2004, timeline 378f). Detailed, specialist accounts of German in Namibia are provided in *Interessengemeinschaft*

Deutschsprachiger Südwester 1980; Esslinger 1985, 1990, 2002; M. Pütz 1991, 1992, 1995, 2007; Junge/ Tötemeyer/ Zappen-Thomson 1993; Worbs 1993a, b; Gretschel 1994, 1995; von Nahmen 2001; Hess/ Becker 2002 (containing: Düxmann; Esslinger; Hofmann; Kube/ Kotze; Weck/ Glaue; Weitzel/ Nöckler/ Crüsemann-Brockmann; von Wietersheim/ Grellmann; Zappen-Thomson 2002a); Zappen-Thomson 2002b, 2012; Bohm 2003: 518–578; Ammon 2012a; Klinner 2012; Lipp 2012; Kellermeier-Rehbein 2014; de.wikipedia.org/wiki/Deutsche_Sprache_in_Namibia; de.wikipedia.org/wiki/Deutschnamibier. I am grateful to Dieter Esslinger and Marianne Zappen-Thomson for further information.

Although their politically correct designation is *Deutschnamibier*, the people often refer to themselves simply as *Deutsche* – by contrast with inhabitants of Germany who are known in Namibia as *Deutschländer*. When compared with Germans, they proudly call themselves *Namibier* and are, of course, Namibian citizens; however, some have dual citizenship in addition to German citizenship, primarily because it is more convenient when travelling and allows children easier access to schools or universities in Germany. The German Namibians also identify more strongly than many other German(-speaking) minorities with German as their native language, although most can also speak Afrikaans as the continuing lingua franca (Böhm 2003: 530f.), and especially English, as the current, sole official language of state. The strong position of these two languages obstructs the maintenance of German, for which the small number of German Namibians is also unfavourable. Figures between 20,000 and 25,000 – or 1% of the population of 2.324 m are current (*Fischer Weltalmanach* 2013: 325), so that there would be approximately 23,240 German Namibians.

Regardless of the small number of speakers, the presence of German in Namibia is remarkable. The settlement territory of the German Namibians extends over almost the entire national territory, concentrated on focal points such as the capital Windhoek (*Windhuk* in the traditional spelling of the German Foreign Office), the towns of Swakopmund, Omaruru, Karibib, Otavi, Otjiwarongo and Grootfontein and the many farms still owned by German Namibians. With regard to education and also property, German Namibians are unmistakably among the privileged stratum of the population, which facilitates the formation of networks and maintenance of German. However, for contacts with the majority population, apart from their own employees and many Hereros or Damaras who can often speak German, they must generally rely on Afrikaans or English. In mixed-language marriages (exogamies), often with Afrikaans speakers, the choice of language varies, or German is relegated. However, the public presence of German in the linguistic landscape is considerable. German place names are clearly in evidence, such as the relatively large *Mariental* and smaller towns or even just railway stations e.g. *Altenstein, Aus, Bethanien, Bodenhausen, Brandberg, Grünau, Grünental, Halb, Helmeringhausen, Hochfeld, Kalkfeld, Klein, Aub, Kolmannskuppe, Königstein, Maltahöhe, Sooheim, Steinhausen, Teufelsbach, Uhlenhorst, Warmbad, Wilhelmstal* and *Witputz* (map in commons.wikimedia.org/wiki/File:NamibiaDetailFinal.jpg). Signs for shops, tourist attractions and street names are also often in German, especially in larger towns such as Windhoek or Swakopmund and in tourist hotspots. However, after independence, many streets were renamed in English (e.g. in Windhoek, "*Kaiserstraße*" became "Independence Avenue" in 1990; in Swakopmund, "*Kaiser-Wilhelm-Straße*" became "Sam Nujoma Avenue" in 2001). Reaction against colonialism is also evident in the renaming of German town and regional names, such as the town "Lüderitz" (after the founder of the German colony) which became "Naminüs" or the region "Caprivi" after the former Imperial Chancellor" which became "Sambesi". There are also individual cases of anglicisation of the root word of street names (e.g. "*Uhlandstraße*" in Windhoek became "Uhlandstreet"). But it is still possible to communicate in German in many shops, restaurants, tourist hotels and attractions. Religious life, which is symbolised for German Namibians by the Evangelical Lutheran *Christuskirche*, built on a hill overlooking the city of Windhoek, also takes place primarily in German, in Evangelical and also Roman Catholic services (Kuntze 2002; Wolf 2002).

Schools are particularly important for language maintenance (Esslinger 1985, 1990, 2002; Zappen-Thomson 2002a, b, 2012). There is, in fact, broad provision in German, but with remarkable weaknesses. It is problematic that German is permitted as a language of instruction only in private schools in any school year (Esslinger 2002). A prominent example is the *Deutsche Höhere Privatschule (DHPS)* in Windhoek, which takes around 1,200 pupils, not exclusively German Namibians, through to the German *Abitur*, giving access to universities in Namibia and South Africa. As a German School Abroad, it awards the *Deutsches Sprachdiplom* (see Weitzel/ Nöckler/ Crüsemann-Brockmann 2002; de.wikipedia.org/wiki/Deutsche_H%C3%B6here_ Privatschule_Windhoek). There are other German-Namibian private schools in Grootfontein, Omaruru, Otavi, Otjiwarongo and Swakopmund. Windhoek also has several German-speaking kindergartens. But German is not the sole language of instruction in any of these schools; even the DHPS has an English-speaking branch, which, however, includes German as a compulsory subject (Lipp 2012). Moreover, the number of pupils in German private schools has increased steadily in recent years, from a total of 3,702 in 2005 to 4,758 in 2013 (information from Monika Hoffmann, Director of the Working Group of German School Associations/AGDS). In state schools, German is allowed as a language of instruction without restriction only in the first three school years. English is introduced stepwise from the fourth school year as a compulsory language of instruction. From the fifth school year, other languages, such as German, are taught only as a school subject. This provision of German is certainly inadequate for the acquisition of basic German skills. However, as a school subject, German does transfer German skills to Namibians who speak other languages (Zappen-Thomson 2002, 2012).

A substantial improvement would be state schools with German as a language of instruction at all levels of schooling, or at least a German-speaking track. In fact, the Namibian government does seem to be listening to this view. One conference, which took place from 18–20 June 2013, developed a proposal for expanding tuition in native languages up to and including the seventh school year; however, the government must still endorse this (email from Marianne Zappen-Thomson 3 July 2013). But another problem in schools is the lack of German teachers, no doubt because of poor teacher pay (Worbs 1993b: 9). Teachers sent from Germany provide assistance only in the private schools, primarily the DHPS. The University of Namibia in Windhoek founded in 1992 has a German Studies department which also trains German teachers (Zappen-Thomson 2012). However, German is the language of instruction only in this subject; otherwise exclusively English. As a result, specialist German terminology remains alien to students, even in professions with considerable contact with the population, such as doctors and teachers (apart from German teachers). Many Namibians studying in South Africa use English or Afrikaans, but a considerable number also study in German-speaking countries.

The provision of media for German Namibians is robust given their numerical weakness (von Nahmen 2001; Hofmann 2002). With its 100-year tradition, The *Allgemeine Zeitung* (founded in 1916, current circulation 5,000–6,000) takes pride of place. It appears every day except Saturday and Sunday. There are also newspapers financed by advertising, literary and specialist journals (e.g. *Felsgraffiti*) and publications by clubs, schools and churches. German-speaking radio from Namibia Broadcasting Corporation (Herma-Herrle 2002) broadcasts local and international news and entertainment 24 hours daily (de.wikipedia.org/wiki/NBC_ Deutsches_H%C%B6rfunkprogram). However, German-speaking TV is available only via satellite from Germany.

In fact, German Namibians have no special political rights, e.g. no guaranteed seats in the Namibian parliament, but – even by tradition – they are well organised in terms of civil society and are not hindered in this respect. The *Arbeitsgemeinschaft Deutscher Schulvereine* (AGDS) (Kreutz-berger/ Springer 2002), the *Namibia Wissenschaftliche Gesellschaft* (NWG) (Gühring 2002) and the *Namibisch-Deutsche Stiftung für kulturelle Zusammenarbeit* (NaDS) are all significant for lan-guage maintenance. They organise teacher conferences and cultural festivals, and offer grants. On the one hand, the function of the German language as a symbol of ethnic identity for German Namibians is important for the language's maintenance (Junge/ Tötemeyer/ Zappen-Thomson 1993); on the other hand, it offers benefits in education and employment. In findings based on a questionnaire presented to companies in Namibia (all branches and countries of origin), which has since become somewhat dated, Worbs (1993a), found that 19% expected a good knowledge and 30% basic knowledge of German at management level; 8% expected good knowledge and 24% basic knowledge of German at "middle-management" level (but no knowledge at "lower" levels). Various accounts emphasise that German can be a considerable vocational qualification, even as a foreign language (Gretschel 1994, 1995; Zappen-Thomson 2002a, b), and stress the economic benefits of maintenance as a native language (Zappen-Thomson 2012). However, the economic advantage in tourism, including big-game hunting is even more evident (Weck/ Glaue 2002; von Weitersheim/ Grellmann 2002). The proportion of tourists from the German-speaking countries is far higher than from all other countries (apart from neighbouring African countries), e.g. 2011: 87,072, followed by Britain 25,717, USA 17,826 (www.namibiatourismus. com.na/uploads/file_uploads/Tourists_Arrival_Statistics_Report_MET_2011.pdf). Tourists from Germany would be considerably less numerous if they were not greeted almost every-where – as a matter of course – in German (Ammon 2012a). Tourist numbers also point towards the special relationship between German Namibians and the German-speaking countries, pri-marily Germany (see also www.deutschinnamibia.org). Support is provided through the supply of teachers already mentioned. German Namibians studying in Germany are also supported by grants, but only for postgraduates. Added to this is the regular supply of a *DAAD-Lektor* to the German Department in the University of Namibia. The long-promised upgrading of the for-mer Goethe Centre into a full Goethe-Institut in Windhoek in 2015 is a further important step. Various associations of German Namibians derive funds from Germany. However, a stronger participation of the German economy which, for understandable economic reasons, shows more interest in South Africa and even Angola, would be particularly welcome for the maintenance of German. If more companies from German-speaking countries were to open branches in Namibia which rewarded and promoted a knowledge of German (alongside English naturally), language maintenance would perhaps be better served than by any other means.

The German Namibians have developed their own special forms of German. Alongside col-loquial peculiarities (e.g. in Joe Pütz 2001), many specific vocabulary items have become stand-ardised and therefore represent national variants. They are used in "model texts" (cf. Ch. B.2), e.g. in the *Allgemeine Zeitung* and accepted as correct by teachers. Often these are borrowings from Afrikaans or English, e.g. *Ram*, pl/ *-en*, "male sheep", *Veld*, no pl. "open grassland (by contrast with a managed agricultural area)", also words for specific physical objects which do not exist in the German-speaking countries, like *(das) Rivier*, pl. *-e* "dry riverbed". These are codified and thus acknowledged as Namibian Standard German (cf. Ch. B.2) in the *Variantenwörterbuch des Deutschen* (Ammon/ Bickel/ Lenz 2013/16).

4.10 *Brazil* – Hunsrücker

It would be possible to consider German(-speaking) minorities in several countries in America: in the Anglophone regions of Canada and the USA; and in Latin America (from north to south) in Mexico, Belize, Venezuela, Colombia, Ecuador, Peru, Brazil, Bolivia, Paraguay, Uruguay,

Argentina and Chile (Born/ Dickgießer 1989; Ammon 1991a: 86–114). However, the following chapters give only a selection covering the non-religiously constituted group of *"Hunsrücker"* in Brazil (this chapter) and the religiously constituted groups of Mennonites (as a focus), Amish and Hutterites (Ch. E.4.11). This selection allows a representative characterisation. In fact, the consistent feature of the *Hunsrücker* is the linguistic variety, not religion; but religion does play a part in language maintenance and ethnic identity (Diel 2001). After isolated, earlier arrivals from German-speaking countries, the Brazilian colonisation law of 1820 and the constitution of 1824 allowed a broader influx by admitting non-Catholic immigrants. The group of German speakers who arrived in 1824 in the region of the subsequent city of São Leopoldo (founded 1846) can be regarded as a spearhead. This first colony was then expanded (Altenhofen 1996: 76f.; Damke 1997: 30–32) with further immigrants, to include larger parts of the climatically moderate southern Brazilian federal states of Rio Grande do Sul, Santa Catarina, Paraná and Espirito Santo. However, alongside German(-speaking) colonists, there were also Portuguese as well as other colonists, especially from Italy. The Brazilian government, at least the republican government from 1889, operated a targeted policy of ethnically mixed settlements to promote the linguistic shift towards Portuguese (Altenhofen 1996: 68f). However, many German-speakers were able to maintain their own language through their largely isolated way of life (Altenhofen 2013: [6]). Developmental disturbances led to the Heydt Decree of 1859 in Prussia (named after the Finance Minister August von der Heydt), which put a stop to emigration from Prussia, but this was repealed in 1896 for southern Brazil; and to a ban on German-speaking associations and publications in Brazil after the declaration of war with Germany in 1917, which was also lifted after the war. Rigorous limitations on the use of any languages other than Portuguese in school and public life at the time of the nationalist President Getúlio Vargas (governed 1930–1945), who conceived of Brazil strictly as a nation state, were more enduring. In 1938 (according to many sources, as early as 1937), at the start of the policy of *Estado Novo*, which lasted officially until 1945, approximately 1,300 German private schools, 2,000 associations, 70 newspapers and periodicals and any form of German tuition were banned throughout Brazil (for education and press, see Ilg 1979: 233–238). These prohibitions were softened after WWII, and in 1961, German was readmitted as a foreign language in schools; individual private schools with German as a language of instruction were also authorised, but the former level of German-speaking institutions has never been restored. For example, in 1930 in Rio Grande do Sul, 937 schools and 36,933 pupils with German as a language of instruction were recorded; by contrast, in 1994, there were only 114 schools and approximately 17,000 pupils with German, but only as a school subject (Altenhofen 2013: [20]; the differentiation between a language of instruction and school subject is my own addition). At present, there may be around 250 schools (email from Altenhofen 10 July 2013). Such school bans primarily hamper the learning of standard German and favour a restriction to the Hunsrück dialect, which is increasingly stigmatised as a sign of poor education (Altenhofen 1996: 69–72). The damaging effect of this development on the maintenance of German is obvious. By contrast with South Tyrol (cf. Ch. D.3.2), repressive nationalist policy in Brazil has not provoked a will to maintain the language by way of resistance. On the contrary, social and technical developments, such as industrialisation, urbanisation and better transport facilities have widened the opening towards Portuguese as the official language of state. In contrast, the comprehensive siting of branches of German companies in Brazil, primarily in the cities, especially São Paulo, but also in the south of the country, in the federal states preferred by the German-speaking settlers, has acted to promote the maintenance of German (historical and more extensive overviews are provided in Oberacker 1979; Ilg 1979; Fröschle 1979b: timeline 1494–1977; Damke 1997: 5–42; Tornquist 1997: 2–12. Various accounts can be found in Born 1995: 141–148; Altenhofen 1996, 2013; Rosenberg 2003a, b; Steffen 2006;

Steffen/ Altenhofen 2014; Koch 1996; A. Ziegler 1996; Dahme-Zachos 2001; Diel 2001; Kaestner 2003; de.wikipedia.org/wiki/Riograndenser_Huns%C3%BCckisch; de.wikipedia.org/wiki/Deutschbrasilianer. Additional information gratefully received from Cleo V. Altenhofen and Joachim Steffen.

I use the designation *Hunsrücker*, or more specifically *Riograndenser Hunsrücker*, as a *pars pro toto* term for the autochthonous (indigenous) German (speaker)s in southern Brazil, based on the previously familiar, colloquial designation for their way of speaking as *Hunsrückisch*, which, as far as I can see, has been adopted as a scientific term by Altenhofen (1996: 4–8). My choice of this designation is intended to demarcate this group from the Mennonites (Ch. E.4.11), who are also German-speakers but differ with regard to language variety and lifestyle. The object of discussion here is not the dialect spoken in the *Hunsrück* district of Germany (Altenhofen 1996: 16–24), but only the Brazilian *Hunsrückisch* (described in detail in Altenhofen 1996: 24–27, 127–346), a mixed dialect developed by diverse German-speaking immigrants which predominates and to some extent functions as a lingua franca among German-speakers in southern Brazil (Damke 1997: 46; Altenhofen 2013: [13]). Other dialects, primarily Swabian-Alemannic, Bavarian-Austrian and Westphalian, exist alongside it, but their speakers drift towards *Hunsrückisch*. Self-designation is generally as *Daitsch(e)* or *Taitsch(e)* (Altenhofen 2013: [7]; 1996: 5; and respectively Damke 1997: 46), with unrounded diphthong. This is how they identify themselves, even if they hardly speak German any longer. They are known to other Brazilians as *alemão*. The distance from the German-language territory in Europe and its inhabitants is greater, not only geographically but also in terms of solidarity, than in the case of European and Central-Asian German(-speaking) minorities. It is symptomatic that the idea of dual citizenship (with a German-speaking country) is virtually non-existent.

At present, the main settlement territory for the *Hunsrücker* (Altenhofen 2013: [3–6]) is still in the federal states of Rio Grande do Sul, Santa Catarina, Paraná and Espirito Santo. However, it also extends up to the north-eastern province of Misiones in Argentina and regions of eastern Paraguay, which I will not consider here. Individual *Hunsrücker* have also relocated to urban centres in other federal states of Brazil, São Paulo or Rio de Janeiro, where they have often become linguistically assimilated. By contrast, in the four preferred federal states, many have maintained their German, which is also evident from the linguistic landscape there. It must be admitted that iconic, folklore symbols outside restaurants with Bavarian-Tyrolean figures wearing a traditional felt hat and holding a beer mug are more noticeable than linguistic features. But some German place names have been maintained (e.g. *Blumenthal, Harmonia* (pronounced like *Harmonie*) and *Selbach*). German settlements often have their own unofficial German name alongside the Portuguese (e.g. *Neuschneis – Linha Nova, Kaffeschneis – Picada Café* etc.). Many *Hunsrücker* live in villages which are relatively compact but do not form a homogeneous or coherent settlement territory. However, the villages are connected in the form of "language archipelagos" (Steffen/ Altenhofen 2014), as with the Mennonites (Ch. E.4.11), over relatively large distances. Maps of the settlement territory in Rio Grande do Sul, Santa Catarina, Paraná and Espirito Santo are to be found in Born/ Dickgießer 1989: 61–63; only for Rio Grande do Sul in Altenhofen 1996: 52f., Appendix – also included in Tornquist 1997: Appendix.

Numerical data for native German-speakers in Brazil as a whole, of which the *Hunsrücker* form the majority, range between 600,000 and 1.5 m, and for "people of German origin" or ethnic Germans, between 2 and 5 m (de.wikipedia.org/wiki/Deutschlandbrasilianer); the lower numbers are more realistic (see also Table C.1–2, Ch. C.1). In an email (10 July 2013), Altenhofen reminded me that all official figures, in which the last relevant poll of 1950 is merely updated, are questionable (see Roche 1959). Speakers, or those who declare German as their native language, are largely a subset of those who declare themselves as ethnic Germans. Their numerical strength, or rather weakness, depends more on linguistic and ethnic shifts within Brazil than on an influx from German-speaking countries. The shift to Portuguese is determined by migration into the cities with subsequent assimilation, and also by the scattering and mixing of settlements. This favours linguistic and ethnic exogamy, which makes it difficult to maintain German as a family language. Even in ethnically homogeneous families, Portuguese is often spoken with the children, because of language requirements in schools, TV-viewing habits or language choice with people of the same age outside the family. In one investigation (small sample, n = 30), Tornquist (1997: 45) found that adults communicated entirely in German among themselves or spoke German with their grandchildren only in one third of the families. Altenhofen (2013: [22]) observed in language interviews that "in the middle of the interview, which was held in *Hunsrückisch*, the respondents chatted with the children in Portuguese". Tornquist (1997: 101–141) noted the absence of any will among *Hunsrücker* to maintain their language. However, for remote towns and villages in Paraná, Damke (1997: 56) has confirmed "the use of HR [Hunsrückisch! U.A.] in most inter-family situations and situations perceived as familiar [. . .]".

As with most linguistic minorities, schools are very important for the maintenance of German. In this context, however, German-Brazilian schools and German or Swiss Schools Abroad (Ch. J.3; K.4) are less significant. In Brazil, especially in the federal states of the *Hunsrücker*, there are several of these, the number fluctuating depending on classification (16 according to: www.brasil.diplo.de/Vertretun/brasilien/de/09_Kultur/Deutsch_lernen/D_Schule.html, and "22 private schools, of which four are German Schools Abroad and 18 Sprachdiplomschulen", according to the Federal Administration Office 2013a: 23). But their clientele is generally different from the minorities. Of the total number of approximately 250 local schools directly accessible to the *Hunsrücker*, hardly any provide German as the language of instruction. Individual experiments were reported in presentations at the second German Teaching Congress of the Mercosul in São Leopoldo in 2002, but these reports were not published in the conference proceedings (Kaufmann/ Bredemeier/ Volkmann 2003). When German is provided in school, it is generally only as a school subject and without any clear distinction whether it is for native speakers or FL speakers. My principal impression after visiting a lesson in Missal, a village in Paraná, in 2007 (kindly arranged by Ciro Damke) was an undisguised lack of interest among many students despite full teacher commitment, but at the same time, with a generally reasonable standard of German. According to Altenhofen (email 10 July 2013), German is still more popular than other settler and foreign languages, but government support leaves much to be desired. In fact, the provision of training for German teachers is good in the *Hunsrücker* territories, with no less than five universities (four in Rio Grande do Sul and one in Paraná). But the indifference I noticed among students invites questions about the motivation to learn and maintain German and about opportunities for use and advantages to the *Hunsrücker*. The declining traditional, identity-related motivation to use German in families has been compensated only to a limited extent by its practical usefulness in the local setting: in community councils, shops, with doctors or in hospital, because Portuguese is almost always spoken in preference to German. However, during my visit to the region around Missal (Paraná) in 2007, speaking German in the town halls presented no problems and was encouraged by – admittedly not always youthful – conversational partners over a friendly cup of *maté*.

In the church domain, which is important for many members of minorities, services only rarely take place in German, sometimes because local priests or vicars do not consider their standard German (*Hochdaitsch*) adequate and do not wish to preach in *Hunsrückisch* (information from Altenhofen). Even in the 1960s, church reports in Germany stressed that a good knowledge of Portuguese was required for clergy sent to Brazil because parishioners apparently understood less and less German (Ammon 1991a: 518f).

With regard to the media, which are so important for language maintenance, the *Hunsrücker* receive only a modest provision. Online access has become easier and is also used by the older generation. Otherwise, there is no daily newspaper or even a weekly, but only community newsletters published monthly or at even longer intervals. Regarding printed periodicals for Rio Grande do Sul, Altenhofen 2013 [20f.] confirms that there are now only three church newsletters (breakdown of figures ibid: [21]). Must it therefore be assumed that the *Hunsrücker* still speak but now hardly read German? In every case, comparison with German-language print media from earlier times suggests a dramatic decline in the reading culture (historical review in Tornquist 1997: 144–146; Born/ Dickgießer 1989: 59; Oberacker 1979: 237f.; Ilg 1979: 277). The same evidently applies for German-language fiction and poetry of the *Hunsrücker* which has a notable history (Ilg 1979: 249–251). According to Born (1995: 146), by the start of the 1990s, "it had largely died out, [. . .] either through poor language skills or lack of reader interest. As Althofen explains "the younger generation shows great difficulty in reading the German text, but, conversely, considerable fluency when reading Portuguese" (2013: [18]).

Cultural events, especially festivals such as the "German Immigration Day", which has been held in São Leopoldo on 25 July every year since 1924, are well attended, but they do more to strengthen ethnic identity than to maintain the language. This also applies for the cross-regional events such as the *Kartoffelfest, Früchtefest, Mai-Fest, September-Fest* and *November-Fest*. Clubs and societies, some of which are still thriving, especially, as in other German(-speaking) minorities, the amateur choirs, seem to be more effective at promoting the language (cf. Ammon 1991a: 418–420; on the tradition, Oberacker 1979: 254). All four villages I visited in 2007 in Paraná had local choirs which entertained me superbly not only with German folk songs but also with richly varied conversation in German. However, there is a shortage of inter-group contact between societies which support German, so that the language archipelago continues to function largely at a private level.

Political associations do not exist at all, and there is no question of political representation in Brazilian regional governments. The *Hunsrücker* are only represented at local level in the town halls but without integration into an association as they could be considering their proportion of the population. There is also a lack of prominent opinion role models who could promote inter-regional coherence. I was also aware of the minimal contact between the *Hunsrücker* and the German-speaking countries. Notice of my arrival went through the villages as if I was an extra-terrestrial being: "*Do is enne von driebe*" [Here is someone from "over there"]. Exchange visits between *Hunsrücker* and European German-speakers are rare and generally limited to a few functionaries, such as the festival committee of São Leopoldo, who travelled to the Hunsrück in Germany in 2004 to mark the 180th anniversary of German immigration (www.brasilien-freunde.de/Archiv/Jahr%202004.htm). In general, tourism from Germany to Brazil is minimal and tends to bypass the *Hunsrücker*, who are hardly known in Germany and possibly associated with Nazis on the run. In the other direction, there is almost no tourism. This lack of contact is linked with the fact that most family relationships have been broken by the long time interval since migration and the geographical distance.

However, new contacts have been made in recent years. For example, I have met an increasing number of people whose relatives have married in Germany, leading to mutual visits, or family-history enthusiasts who have established links between Germany and Brazil. I have also read of active town-twinning arrangements (e.g. St Wendel – São Vendelino or Simmern – Igrejinha). Study and work visits which entice young Brazilians to Germany, primarily in the horticultural and agricultural industries are even more promising, e.g. when participants happily declare on their return that they have now realised that a knowledge of German "might have a value" (*en Weat honn*; information from Cléo Altenhofen). Appropriate involvement of the German economy in Brazil would no doubt offer special opportunities for the maintenance of German. In this context, the following account by the *Federal Association of German Industry (BDI)* is relevant: "Even today, Brazil is Germany's most important economic partner in Latin America. German companies are closely linked with the Brazilian economy. The contribution of German companies to industrial production in Brazil is around 16%. The potential for further growth of economic cooperation between the two countries is considerable" (www.bdi.eu/DBWT2012. htm). But German companies are concentrated in major cities, with a focus on São Paulo, about which it has been said: "Germany's largest industrial city is in Brazil" (www.brasilieninitiative. de/index.php?option=com_content&view=article&id=18%3Awirtschaftsstandord-sao-paulo- &Itemid=50). In fact, they are also well represented in the *Hunsrücker* federal states. For example, in an announcement around 2010, the "German-Brazilian Chamber of Commerce in Porto Alegre" listed a series of major German companies in Rio Grande do Sul (www.bitkom.org/ files/documents/Deutsche_Investitionen_im_Sueden_Brasiliens.pdf). There are hints of economic benefits associated with a knowledge of German to be derived from these companies, which could be developed through contacts with schools or universities in the region which teach or research German. Funding from German-speaking countries is less than in the case of the German(-speaking) minorities in Eastern Europe. Nonetheless, two of the six Goethe Institutes and two of the ten DAAD lektorships in Brazil are in the territory of the *Hunsrücker*: respectively in Porto Alegre (Rio Grande do Sul) and in Curitiba (Paraná) (www.goethe.de/ins/ br/lp/lrn/wdl/wls/goe/deindex.htm and www.daad.org.br/de/18304/index.html).

One difficulty for language maintenance could also be the insecurity of the *Hunsrücker* regarding their traditional German: an apparently deep-rooted impression about the inferiority of their dialect. Language teaching must give maximum possible consideration to this issue (see Földes 1995). It is helpful, in this context, to spell out that even in the German-speaking countries, many dialects are spoken, especially in southern Germany which has recently shown economic leadership, and no one should therefore feel ashamed. Ultimately, however, maintaining the dialect seems less promising than closing the gap with Standard German – by all means, while retaining a local dialect colouring.

4.11 Mennonites, Amish and Hutterites

The three groups described here are Baptist groups (*Täufer/Wiedertäufer/Anabaptisten* – *adult-baptists* would probably be accurate) which originated at the time of the Protestant Reformation in Europe. Their history has been driven by essentially religious motives (de.wikipedia. org/wikiT%C3%A4ufer). The description in this chapter is structured somewhat differently from the discussion of the other minorities (Ch. E.4.2–4.10). The introductory historical sketch describes the three groups separately and in order of size: Mennonites, Amish, Hutterites; the first description also contains information relevant to language maintenance. At the end of each of these sketches, I list the most important specialist literature and experts who have kindly provided additional information.

I begin with the *Mennonites*, named after the theologian Menno Simons (1496–1561) who originally came from Dutch Friesland. They resemble the Amish and the Hutterites in that their roots go back to the Reformation but also because of their strict pacifism, which has brought them into frequent conflict with their countries of residence. Moreover, like the two other groups, they live relatively cut-off from the surrounding society, as "religious isolationists". Their isolation seems to be motivated, amongst other factors, by their belief that their central dogmas are threatened by modern science (e.g. theory of evolution, history of the universe). The Mennonites have a dual origin, on the one hand, the "Swiss Brethren", from whom the Amish also subsequently broke away, and the Russian Mennonites, as I call them here (prompted by Mark Louden). Like the Amish, the Swiss-origin Mennonites came fairly directly, with one intermediate stop in the Palatinate, to North America, where they often live as neighbours to the Amish. I shall mention this Mennonite group again in the paragraphs about the Amish. By contrast, the "Russian Mennonites" on whom the present description focuses, only reached their present homes after a long journey, especially through Russia. The two groups of Mennonites also speak different varieties: Swiss-origin Mennonites speak Pennsylvania German and Russian Mennonites speak *Plautdietsch*. Finally, the Hutterites arose, with and against one another, in parallel with the Swiss-origin Mennonites. The history of the Russian Mennonites is described in detail by G. Kaufmann (1997: 59–62) and Steffen (2006: 14–22) who refer back to C. Dyck (1993) and respectively Penner (1972). To avoid religious persecution, these Mennonites migrated from their home territories in Dutch Flanders and Friesland around the middle of the sixteenth century to the Vistula delta on the Baltic. In contact with the linguistic environment there, they developed their own Low German dialect *Plautdietsch* (Siemens 2012), which is still spoken today by many in this group. Alongside this, the conservative groups used and still use an archaic sounding Standard German, Mennonite High German (Ch. B.1) which they themselves call *Hüagdietsch* (Kaufmann 1997: 65). When they were threatened with military service after the annexation of the region by Prussia (see "divisions of Poland" Ch. E.4.4), most of them moved on into the Ukraine, which belonged to Russia at that time, where they founded two major settlements (*Chortitza* and *Molotschna*) and developed a form of economy based on agriculture, which still predominates today. When Russian was to be imposed on them as a language of instruction, and they were to be forced into military service, some of the group emigrated from 1873 to North America, where there are still significant colonies in central Canada and north-central USA. But because English was then prescribed as the language of instruction, and they were disliked as Germans during WWI, some of this group migrated to Latin America, initially Mexico and Paraguay, and from there some continued to Belize and Bolivia. Around 1930, others came from the Soviet Union to Brazil and, after WWII, from the former Western Prussia and Danzig to Uruguay, amongst other reasons because of the socialist restructuring of agriculture. This latter group does not speak *Plautdietsch* but High German with Low German colouring. There are now Mennonite groups all around the world. At the World Mennonite Conference in 2009, their number was estimated at around 1.6 m (oldsite.mwc-cmm.org/en15/index. php?option=com_content&view=article&id=384:08-oct-2009–2009-new-global-map-locates-16-million-anabaptists). However, these have been largely converted and do not speak *Plautdietsch*. The description below is restricted to descendants of the Russian Mennonites in Paraguay, Brazil and above all Mexico, from where they also travelled to Belize and Texas (USA) (Steffen 2006: 19–22; Kaufmann 1997: 70f). As with the two other groups, there are significant differences between orthodox and modern traditions among the Mennonites (see Huffines 1980, 1989; Louden 2003). The following discussion relates primarily to the former, with the "Old Order Mennonites" as the most conservative. Relevant accounts, generally also of linguistic relationships, include Penner 1972; Moelleken 1987 (Canada, Mexico); Klassen 1988 (Paraguay); 1995, 1998 both Brazil); Rohkohl 1993; Brandt 1992 (Mexico); C. J. Dyck 1993; G. Kaufmann 1997 (Mexico, USA); 2004a, 2004c (both Brazil, Paraguay); Steffen 2006 (Belize); Steffen/ Altenhofen 2014 (Brazil); Dück 2011 (Brazil); *Mennonitsches Lexikon* (1913–1967); de.wikipedia.org/wiki/Mennoniten). I am grateful for further information from Göz Kaufmann and Joachim Steffen.

In 1693, the *Amish* broke away from the Swiss-origin Mennonites. Initially, they were based outside Switzerland in Alsace and also in the Palatinate, of which the dialect most strongly influenced their way of speaking. They are named after the Swiss Jakob Ammann, who demanded a very strict segregation from the rest of the world and a frugal lifestyle also to be expressed in clothing and hair style. Soon after their foundation, to avoid persecution in Europe, most of the Amish migrated to North America, where they are still settled. Between 1736 and 1770, the first settlers colonised the region of the subsequent USA known as Lancaster County in Pennsylvania, which guaranteed them generous religious freedoms. A second wave of immigration from 1815 to 1860 distributed them over the federal states of Illinois, Indiana, Iowa and Ohio and Ontario in Canada. Their principal residential territory still includes all these regions. In 2010, it included 427 colonies in 28 federal states of the USA, primarily Pennsylvania and Indiana (each approximately 50,000), and the federal state of Ontario in Canada (de.wikipedia. org/wiki/Amische). Their total number is more than 250,000 – and continues to grow because of their rejection of birth control. The Amish lifestyle is directed, even more strongly than that of the Mennonites, towards agriculture. Refusal of technical innovations is symbolised by their use of horse-drawn carriages instead of motor vehicles. However, differences of opinion, also about modernisation, have led to a splitting, on the one hand, into the conservative "Old Order Amish" (*amische Leit*), who form the principal focus here, and, on the other hand, more modern groups, e.g. the "Beachy Amish". Only the first subgroup still speaks the mixed dialect of Pennsylvania-*Deitsch*, with Palatinate influence, which originated in America, and for which there are two names in English: "Pennsylvania German" and "Pennsylvania Dutch". The latter name owes its origins more to the formerly broader meaning of Dutch, which included "*Deutsch*" than to the phonetic similarity between *Deutsch* (or *Deitsch*) and *Dutch*. However, at times of anti-German attitudes in North America, during both world wars, such confusion was welcomed by speakers (Louden 2006: 91, note 4; Yoder 1980). Alongside Pennsylvania German, an archaic Standard German, similar to that of the Mennonites, is also in use for religious services, hymns and religious instruction. Relevant accounts, including linguistic relationships, are provided in Huffines 1980, 1989, 1994; Langin 1996; Louden 2003, 2006a, b; Raith 1991, 2004; Johnson-Weiner 1992, 1999; Hostetler 2008; Langwasser 2008; de.wikipedia.org/wiki/Amische. I am grateful to Mark L. Louden and Michael Werner for additional information.

The *Hutterites*, who refer to themselves as "Hutterite brethren" (Rein 1994: 249), owe their name to their founder Jakob Hutter (also *Huter* or *Hueter*, meaning "hat maker") (for their history, including analysis of origins of the dialect in structural-linguistic terms, Rein 1977: 216–267). Hutter came from Pustertal in South Tyrol, and his model was the original Christian community in Jerusalem. When Emperor Karl V. banned all Anabaptist movements in 1529, Hutter's followers began to emigrate. Hutter himself was executed in Innsbruck in 1536. The Hutterites migrated, via various destinations, to Russia, which, like the Mennonites, they left again because of changes in schooling laws in 1874 and the introduction of military service, heading first to South Dakota in the USA. Because of discrimination against "Germans" during WWI, they migrated to Canada, but some returned to the USA. Their total number today is around 50,000, of whom three-quarters live in Canada (in British Columbia, Alberta, Manitoba, Saskatchewan) and one-quarter live in the USA (Washington, Oregon, Montana, North Dakota, South Dakota and Minnesota). They are distributed among some 465 *Bruder-Höfe*, each with between 60 and 150 inhabitants (de.wikipedia.org/wiki/Hutterer). Despite some differences regarding the degree of openness to the majority society, they still all live in isolation (see Schabus 2007) and still all speak *das Hutterische* or, as they call it themselves, *das Tyrolische* (Rein 1984: 250), a mixed dialect with Carinthian features (ibid:253; Rein 1977: 265). They additionally use Standard German varieties, such as *das Predigerhutterische* [preacher Hutterite] (Rein

1977: 279; 1984: 253), similar to the Standard German of the Mennonites and Amish. Relevant accounts are provided in Hostetler 1974; Rein 1977, 1979, 1984; Längin 1996; Brednich 1998; Allert 2006; Kirkby 2007; Wikipedia "Hutterer": de.wikipedia.org/wiki/Hutterer. I am grateful to Kurt Rein for further information.

The social identity of the three groups is primarily religious. The extent to which a kind of German ethnicity exists (not restricted to a reference to Germany; Ch. B.3) is less clear. Kaufmann (2006c: 257) reports self-allocations of Mennonites in Paraguay and Brazil (Rio Grande do Sul), of which in each case, 13% describe themselves as "German" and "German Paraguayan" (in each case 5 of 38; $\Sigma = 26\%$) and respectively 28% as "German" (*Dietsche*) and 17% as "German Brazilian" (13 and 8 of 47; $\Sigma = 47\%$), where the designation as German did not refer to Germany. The others only declared the nationality of their country of settlement, i.e. as Paraguayans or Brazilians. This finding suggests that some of the Mennonites have a German ethnic identity; but Kaufmann (email 11 July 2013) believes that the declaration is intended only in the sense of a German-*speaking* identity (German as native language; Ch. A.3). In the case of the Hutterites, Rein (verbal communication) assumes at least an awareness of their German linguistic-cultural origin. By contrast, the Amish are evidently further removed from both ethnic German and also German-speaking identity, partly because of the longer separation from German-speaking countries. However, there is a need for a comparative investigation of the three groups. Among US academics, the allocation of Anabaptists to German ethnicity is variable. Don Yoder (1986) leaves the question open whether "Pennsylvania-German identity" is a special case of German ethnicity. For him, the core is formed by "the Mennonites, the Amish and the 'brethren' (*Tunker*)" (ibid: 69) – from *tunken* "to immerse (completely)" at baptism, are a linguistically assimilated, pietist group (see M. Meier 2008; de.wikipedia.org/wiki/Schwarzenau_Brethren). Other US researchers, e.g. Kathleen N. Conzen (1986), do not mention the Anabaptists at all in accounts of "German Americans", but include only other German-speaking immigrants, whose ethnic German symbols (from Kant to *Biergarten*) are also hardly compatible with those of the Anabaptists. According to Michael Werner (personal communication), these are the "New Germans", the later, not primarily religiously motivated immigrants.

With the groups under discussion here, what seems immediately evident is a German-*speaking* identity rather than German ethnicity; but even this is not certain. With reference to "Pennsylvania Germans", Amish and Mennonites, Mark Louden (2008: 92) considers that "Pennsylvania Germans as a group have never viewed themselves as Germans in America, or even German Americans, but simply as Americans, albeit a minority group within American society. "Regardless of the label that one attaches to Pennsylvania German, the crucial fact remains that its speakers have formed a sociolinguistic identity independent of any association with German (dialect) speakers in Europe or elsewhere". However, I question this because, in conversation with Amish people in Lancaster County in Pennsylvania, I not only found no rejection of the "label" "Pennsylvania *German*", but, when I spoke Swabian (dialect), I was told that it was similar to this and readily comprehensible. Additional information from Louden (ibid: 95) suggests allocation to the German language, namely that "there is a strong connection perceived between using Pennsylvania German and Standard German in worship services, and Pennsylvania German in other intragroup settings", and especially the following statement by an Amish man quoted by Louden (ibid: 98) about the appropriate relationship between English and German: "[I]t would be wrong not to make an effort to express ourselves better in the English language. But it would be just as wrong to fail to keep and pass on the German to our children – that rich language our forebears left for us". All of this sounds like German-speaking identity, i.e. self-allocation to the German-language community. The same applies for the self-designation of their way of speaking as *Pennsilfaanisch-Deitsch* (Enninger 1983: 351). However,

Michael Werner assumes the allocation to the German-language community mainly among the 10% of educated and religious function holders, but not among the great majority. Presumably, the relevant allocation among the Russian Mennonites and Hutterites is better established.

However, in none of the three groups is the allocation of their everyday variety to the German language taken for granted. Having said this, the allocation also seems justified according to the reasons given in chapters B.1 and B.2, albeit with restrictions. In fact, it can be argued that, on the one hand, the everyday dialect is at least partially roofed by a standard variety, from which the linguistic distance is not excessively great for allocation to the same language, and, on the other hand, this roofing variety still shows such close linguistic similarity to the other Standard German varieties, especially those in the German-speaking countries (Ch. D) that it can justifiably be allocated to the same language as these, i.e. German. This applies even in the case of the Amish, whose High German and the Standard German of the German-speaking countries are mutually intelligible (linguistic similarity), if one disregards the Gothic script of the Amish High German. Especially in Mexico and Paraguay, the Mennonites also use many books from Germany in addition to their own Standard German, so that the partial overarching of their *Plautdietsch* even by German Standard German is self-evident. Furthermore, they have access via electronic media to modern German, which is often added in brackets to the texts of their newspapers, e.g. the *Deutsch-Mexikanische Rundschau*, and these newspapers are also read by the conservative Mennonites (email Steffen 21 July 2013). For these reasons, I consider allocating the varieties of the religious minorities described here to the German language to be justified (for the linguistic similarity between each standard variety and the standard varieties of the German-speaking countries, see also Rohkohl 1993; Brandt 1992: 11–23, 27). In the case of the Hutterites, the linguistic similarity of their Standard German to that of the German-speaking countries is also obvious. In agreement with the self-allocation by the speakers, experts on these circumstances also generally unreservedly allocate the Hutterite varieties to German, e.g. Rein (1984: 269), who counts the Hutterites among "the hardest core of German speakers in America" (ibid: 249). Among the Amish, the functional restriction of the standard variety seems considerable, and among the Mennonites, the linguistic distance from the everyday Low German *Plautdietsch* seems great. But in both cases, I see no doubt about the allocation to the German language, even disregarding the dialect designation *Hüagdietsch* for the Mennonite Standard German (Kaufmann 1997: 65 and passim). Its lexical peculiarities are codified in the *Variantenwörterbuch des Deutschen* (Ammon/ Bickel/ Lenz 2013/16). Examples include *Angedenk* "memento", *Graduation* "completion of schooling", *Hochweg* "motorway/highway" or *Ohm* "(Mennonite) preacher".

However, it is also evident that such a codification and linguistic allocation cannot secure the maintenance of German. One warning sign is the obvious openness among all three groups towards the majority community, to learning and using their language, albeit alongside their own rather than instead of it. Despite constant shifting of small numbers into the majority community, the numerical strength of the group is maintained because they reject birth control. In fact, whole groups, e.g. the "Beachy Amish" in the USA, mentioned above, have also broken away and shifted completely to English. This kind of dropping out of the group is determined by the restrictive lifestyle rules. At the time of their baptism, young people decide whether to remain within the group, which, e.g. in the case of the Old Order Amish in Lancaster County, around 85% do (de.wikipedia.org/wiki/Amische). In all three groups, growth exceeds the dropout rate. Group isolation is also preserved through the observance of endogamy.

Despite the large geographical distances between "colonies", there is lively, international exchange between them. In this way, colonists can remain among their own kind. The role played by modern media here does not seem to have been investigated so far. There are likely to be considerable differences between colonies, e.g. openness in Paraguay and large parts of Mexico contrasted with isolation in Mexico, in the *Kleine Gemeinde* and the *Konferenzgemeinde*, or in Belize. The newspaper *Mennonitische Post* is available via Facebook, so that at least the groups distributed around America have a common platform. Readers' letters from throughout America are published in the print version. Closer contacts are formed through travel, including international visits. When national boundaries are breached in this way, international communication in the broader sense takes place (Ch. A.3). For the topic of the present book, it is important that, in the case of the Mennonites, this communication takes place – at least partially – in *Plautdietsch*. Accordingly, *Plautdietsch* is not a lingua franca in the normal sense, because it is not a foreign language by means of which people with different native languages communicate with each other (Ch. A.3). Rather, the common native language bridges different national official languages. It could therefore be described as a "native-language bridging language" in order to avoid confusion with a genuine lingua franca. The geography of such communication is well visualised by the term "language archipelago" which has so far not been widely used, but which Joachim Steffen (2006) adopted in the title of his dissertation to illustrate the example of the Mennonites in Belize. He found "the metaphor of an archipelago of similar islands, between which linguistic contact exists in a sea of indigenous languages, justified [. . .]" (ibid: 41; in Steffen/ Altenhofen 2014). Presumably, such language archipelagos contribute to the maintenance of the everyday German in the religious minorities, especially *Plautdietsch*. However, language maintenance among Mennonites, is not necessarily stronger than among the Amish or the Hutterites. For example, Kaufmann (2004c: 272) considered the Mennonites in Brazil to be at the centre of "continuing language change [= language shift! U.A.] from *Plattdeutsch* [=*Plautdietsch*! U.A.] to the majority language, Portuguese [. . .]" (also, Dück 2011). By contrast, the Mennonites in Paraguay were not inclined to shift to the national official language, Spanish (Kaufmann 2004c: 278). Among the causes, Kaufmann mentions that, on the one hand, by contrast with Brazil, there have never been repressive measures against the use of German, and on the other hand, there has been assistance from Germany in questions of schooling. I shall return to this presently. Restrictive measures against German were applied not only in Brazil (see Ch. E.4.10) but also in the USA and Canada (Ch. K.2). These were certainly detrimental to the maintenance of German, but especially the Amish avoided anti-German repression through the alias "Pennsylvania *Dutch*". Like the conservative, Old Order Mennonites and the Hutterites, group solidarity assisted the maintenance of the dialect. Louden explains (2006: 106) the stable bilingualism in the interplay with English as follows: "Stable and active use of both Pennsylvania German and English by Old Order Amish and Mennonites is the norm [. . .]. The health of Pennsylvania German today is a direct consequence of the stability of the Old Order spiritual communities [. . .]".

Most groups show specific weaknesses for the maintenance of German in the underdeveloped schools with significantly shorter compulsory schooling compared with the majority community. Apart from the Mennonites in Spanish-speaking countries, the respective national official language, i.e. English and respectively Portuguese, is the main language of instruction (for Hutterites, see Rein 1977: 282f). German is taught only as a school subject and for religious education. This is often archaic German and is mediated largely only by reading, occasional copying out and rote learning (on the Hutterites, Rein 1977: 279, 1984: 259; Moelleken on the Old Order Mennonites 1986: 69). As a result, skills often remain rudimentary (on the Mennonites, Brandt 1991: 16) and the "functions [. . .] are increasingly transferred from English" (Rein 1977: 280). The standard minority variety has almost become a hagiolect, only for religious purposes, which is barely understood by some in the language community, almost like Latin in the Roman Catholic Church. However, this characterisation applies more to the Amish and the Hutterites than to the Mennonites. For example, reporting on the Mennonites in Mexico, Brandt (1991: 17) explains that "[a]rithmetic [. . .], as an additional subject in school, was also taught in High German", which would certainly not be possible exclusively in archaic German. According to Kaufmann (1997: 64), many colonies, such as the *Kleine Gemeinde* in Mexico, no longer teach "Hüagdietsch only from traditional primers and religious writings, but use relatively modern teaching materials". In primary grade (primaria), some subjects were taught in *Hüagdietsch*; but in the secondary grade (secundaria) it was still only a school subject (ibid: 66).

By contrast with Anglo-American countries, the stronger language maintenance in Latin-American countries is remarkable. For example, Kaufmann (1997) found significant differences between the Mennonites in Mexico and USA (Texas). *Hüagdietsch* was a language of instruction in Mexico, but only a school subject in Texas. This corresponded with a different degree of language maintenance. "In Mexico, Hüagdietsch can still be regarded as a roofing standard with regard to competence, because it is positioned slightly ahead of Spanish, while, in the USA, it must be regarded as almost lost, because it has been overtaken by English" (ibid: 73). The everyday *Plautdietsch* has also lost ground more significantly in Texas than in Mexico (ibid: 140). The difference between Mexico and the USA is not sufficiently explained by reference to different attitudes, which must in turn be explained as being determined by two factors: different economic power of the environment and different prestige of the majority language. In both respects, Mexico offers the typical basis for a "language-island mentality" (Mattheier 1994: 335): the Mennonite colonies are economically healthier than the surrounding majority society, and their language, German, has a higher rather than a lower prestige – which is shown, among other things, in that especially women showed no interest in knowledge of the majority language, Spanish, which was "largely taboo" for them (Kaufmann 1997: 144). The situation in Texas is reversed, although the Mennonites have become more economically equal with their surroundings over time; above all, however, English has significantly greater prestige than German.

Because they are less isolated, the Mennonites' maintenance of German also benefits from support from Germany, primarily its colonies, e.g. Fernheim in Paraguay (details, Rohkohl 1993), in fact by sending teachers and advisers (see also www.auslandschulwesen.de/nn_2143686/ Auslandschulwesen/NeuesausderZfA/2013/VillBallesterAustauschParaguay.html). The Hutterites and especially the Amish do not enjoy such support because they shun "outside intervention". In general, religious groups are less interested in outside contacts than other minorities (Ch. E.4.2–E.4.10), the more fundamental their religious views are. They fear the introduction of ideas which might undermine their faith. Steffen believes that "the Mennonite colonies also achieve their language-archipelago character deliberately with the intention of keeping away external influences on their community" (2006: 57f). However, their most likely way of making contact with German-speaking countries is through visits. This is probably because, especially in recent decades since WWII and the opening of the Iron Curtain, there are large numbers of Mennonites in German-speaking countries, who have migrated from Eastern Europe. In Germany alone, there are around 40,000 (www.mennoniten.de/deutschland.html), whose *Plautdietsch*, as a variety of Low German is then protected by the German government within the framework of the *European Charter for Regional and Minority Languages*.

The Amish and the Hutterites receive only minimal cultural tourism from the German-speaking countries and occasionally advertise, e.g. in a full-page newspaper article about "Amish in Ohio" where "visitors [. . .] will be welcome". The article also mentions that they are "in the eighth generation since migration"; they speak German; and English is learnt "only as a foreign language in the village school"; but this article fails to point out the community's special attractiveness as a travel destination for German-speakers ("*Leben wie vor 250 Jahren*" [Life as it was 250 years ago], *WAZ* 13 July 2013: travel section). There are, however, some flourishing, individual research contacts between Amish, Hutterites and German-speakers in Europe, and tentative efforts to support language-maintenance. One example is the *German-Pennsylvanian Association* founded in 2003, with the participation of German scholars, which, amongst other things, sets up Internet contacts, produces the monthly newsletter *Deutsch-Pennsylvanisches Echo* (PDF), lobbies for the installation of bilingual, English/Pennsylvania German town signs in the residential territory and, since 1996, has published the half-yearly Pennsylvanian German newspaper *Hiwwe wie Driwwe* [Here as well as There] (edited by Michael Werner, University of Mannheim; dpak.wordpress.com/2012/12/). Skills in German could presumably be secured through relationships with company branches from German-speaking countries or longer stays in the German-language territory in Europe, in the form of school visits, study trips or placements. Indeed, these would offer an economically based, instrumental motivation for maintaining German in the longer term. To some extent, such opportunities are sought by parts of the religious minorities, primarily in Brazil. However, the conservative groups have difficulties with this. It is questionable whether their fundamentalist religious identification and motivation can guarantee long-term maintenance of German.

5. Emigrants, remigrants, expatriates and retirement colonies

The discussion so far has been exclusively about *autochthonous* (indigenous) minorities who are long-term residents in their country of residence and are also widely recognised as indigenous minorities – although this does not necessarily mean they are granted any special minority rights. In this final chapter I turn to the *allochthonous* German(-speaking) groups in countries in which German is not an official language of state to point out their relevance for the global position of German. *Allochthonous* (non-indigenous) groups are not generally considered in research on minorities, even research on German(-speaking) minorities, and not thematised in relevant monographs or edited volumes (e.g. Hinderling 2006; S. Wolff 2000; Eichinger/ Plewnia/ Riehl 2008).

The allochthonous German(-speaking) groups outside countries with German as an official language include "normal" emigrants from German-speaking countries or from German(-speaking) minority regions when they are not considered indigenous in the destination country and when they have retained German language or ethnicity (in the sense defined in Ch. B.3). Emigrants who live permanently in the destination country and possibly adopt its citizenship tend to integrate rapidly and often shift completely to the local language, generally the official language of state (linguistic assimilation). After leaving the German-language community, they may seem irrelevant to research and policy-making concerned with the German language. However, many, including those who have made a complete language shift, still foster a special relationship with their country of origin. In this respect, they may indeed be relevant to this book. This applies particularly at the present time, in which modern communications media offer unprecedented opportunities for maintaining contacts, so that, essentially, all emigrants could be relevant for the global position of German. Another relevant group includes migrants who are not seeking permanent residence. Many could have become the focus of migrant research, although this hardly seems to have occurred, and never with reference to the aspects relevant to the present book. Migrants from German-speaking countries lack the properties typical of "guest workers", to describe them with a term which has become politically incorrect but is perhaps still the clearest designation. However, jobseekers from the new Federal States of reunited Germany, who work primarily in Switzerland and Austria, might be included in this group, but hardly suffer the typical language difficulties. German-speakers therefore hardly appear in research on economic-migrants in non-German-speaking countries (see e.g.

Bernhard 2008; V. Edwards 2008; Extra 2008; Gadet 2008; J. Edwards 1984). Even recent migration linguistics in those countries shows little interest in them, although they could at least be a focus for migration sociolinguistics. Regarding migration linguistics in the German-speaking countries themselves, this tends to focus on immigrants (including refugees and asylum seekers) rather than emigrants, because the problems of immigrants are more urgent. *Remigrants* (returning "guest workers") from the German-speaking countries are indeed a topic for migration research, but hardly with reference to language – but, in fact, they are of obvious interest for the global position of German.

Research in linguistics (including sociolinguistics) possibly shows even greater reluctance about the two other groups considered here: *expatriates*, company employees or diplomats posted abroad from German-speaking countries, and *retirement colonies*, typically located in holiday regions but also originating from German-speaking countries. Investigating these groups in linguistic terms may seem superfluous because of their apparent privileges. However, they are important for the global position of German. My discussion of all these allochthonous, German(-speaking) groups outside the German-speaking countries must be limited to sporadic data and the demonstration of gaps in research, either because of the lack of previous research or my inability to find more data. What is relevant here is primarily the relationship of these people to the German language – with regard to its global position, but also with a view to international language policies of the German-speaking countries (Ch. K).

Emigrants from the German-speaking countries are people who want to live permanently abroad. In every case, most of them are or were previously driven by integrative, linguistic-cultural motives (Gardner 2001; also Ch. J.8), i.e. they were prepared to adapt to the destination country, which usually led to a complete language shift, generally completed at the latest in their grandchildren ("three-generations law"; Ch. E.1; E.2). Such people can no longer form a linguistic minority and therefore differ in principle from the indigenous minorities discussed in Ch. E.4.2–E.4.11. The total number of emigrants from German-speaking countries throughout history far exceeds 10 m. According to passenger lists, around 7 million people emigrated from *Bremerhafen* alone between 1830 and 1974, the date of the last emigration vessel. More than 90% travelled to the USA (www.deutsche-auswanderer-datenbank.de/index.php?id=478). Emigration from German-speaking countries continues to this day and, in fact, intensified temporarily, especially from Germany after reunification, as a result of the increase in unemployment. Emigration from Germany has declined in recent years because of improved economic conditions and is currently numerically below immigration ("immigration into Germany 2012 at a record level", *FAZ* 08 May 2013: 1; "New statistics: immigration no longer as high as 20 years ago", *Spiegel online* 05 January 2014). But emigration from all German-speaking countries continues.

As already suggested, most former emigrants have become linguistically assimilated in their destination countries (for USA, see e.g. Eichhoff 1986) – apart from exceptions, as described in Ch. E.4.2–E.4.11, and smaller groups not referenced in the present book. The language shifts and many unsuccessful attempts at language maintenance are well documented, especially for North America (e.g. Huffines 1986; Schiffman 1987; Schwarzkopff 1987; most contributions in Auburger/ Kloss 1977; Auburger/ Kloss 1979; Auburger/ Kloss/ Rupp 1979; Kloss 1985). There are also various accounts of cultural continuity in the form of ethnic folklorism (ibid; several contributions in Trommler 1986).

However, there is still a lack of research on continuing relationships between linguistically assimilated emigrants and their countries of origin. Some evidently do still foster, or have recently revived, such relationships. One example is the growth in interest over many years now in family-history research. Researching one's own origins is often linked with travel and longer stays in countries of origin. Such experiences strengthen awareness and occasionally motivate people to learn German. Parents and grandparents can influence children and grandchildren to learn GFL or to take courses in German studies (e.g. for Australia, see Ammon 1991b: 80–90). But here also, there is a lack of representative, convincing data, especially on the broader question of other relationships between linguistically assimilated emigrants and their German-speaking countries of origin and with the German language.

Technical innovations and improved opportunities for contact between emigrants and their countries of origin do seem to have changed emigrants' attitudes about the finality and depth of separation from their country of origin. Readiness to separate is presumably more limited in the case of destination countries which do not promise a higher standard of living than the country of origin. Emigrants are also hesitant about linguistic assimilation, i.e. complete language shift, to destination languages of lower prestige or lower international position than German. But even with countries which are attractive economically and regarding the international position of their language, linguistic assimilation is now no longer taken for granted. At least, this applies for all of the dozen or so of my acquaintances who have emigrated over the last 50 years from Germany to the USA or Australia. All of them maintain contact with Germany and diligently foster their own and their children's knowledge of German, even if they are not considering returning. For present day emigrants, especially from the German-speaking countries, it seems quite typical to avoid a final break with the country of origin.

This attitude can also strengthen the local position of German, as suggested by many activities, such as participation at events, perhaps in a local university, which are held in German or refer to German; supporting German language courses and involving children; motivating children to contact speakers of German; and subscribing to and circulating German newspapers, magazines and other media contacts (further details below, with reference to expatriates). Documentation can be found in numerous sources, such as the yearbooks or periodicals of the Goethe-Institut (G-I), the Institut für Auslandbeziehungen (ifa), the Zentralstelle für das Auslandschulwesen (ZfA), the Pädagogischer Austauschdienst (PAD), the Auswärtiges Amt (AA) or the Verein für Deutsche Kulturbeziehungen im Ausland (VDA). In this context, collecting and researching activities developed by emigrants from German-speaking countries to strengthen the German language locally could bring into the limelight this deserving and effective support for the position of German in the world.

Remigrants, i.e. people from German-speaking countries returning to their countries of origin – not to be confused with people returning to German-speaking countries from emigration – are also of considerable importance and should not be underestimated. The largest group includes former "guest workers", to describe them as unambiguously as possible, using a politically incorrect term, as mentioned above. Former asylum seekers would also be worth investigating, but, in general, it is the "guest workers" who have become more thoroughly familiar with the German language. The contribution of these remigrants to the global position of German has so far also received inadequate scholarly attention. In an account about German in Turkey, Nilüfer Tapan (2002: 29; also Ch. J.9.7) pointed out that "almost 3 m Turkish citizens [...] live in the German-speaking region of Europe", but that also, "around 5 m [...] have returned home from there", a fact which is less widely acknowledged in the German-speaking countries. This comment has fallen on deaf ears in the research community, at least in linguistics research. My lecture at the University of Oldenburg entitled "The position of German in remigration countries: neither national language nor lingua franca", which engaged with the same topic suffered a similar fate, as did my claim that "it is an enormous advantage for the German-language community, if people who have learnt German retain these language skills", and accordingly, it is "actually a task for German language policy to maintain German-language skills and to promote their acquisition everywhere in the world" (Ammon 2004c: 39). In fact, at that time, I possibly underestimated German politicians' interest in promoting German abroad. In the lecture, I spelt out the shortcomings in detail for the parties represented in the Bundestag (ibid: 41f.); but, with reference to remigrants, these criticisms were and are still justified. Even today, the linguistic aspect of remigration arouses little interest in the academy and among politicians. It therefore seems worthwhile to me to investigate just how remigrants, who are concentrated in various Mediterranean coastal states, can support the position of German. I know a great many people personally in such regions who work as school or university teachers of German or German Studies, or who work at least partially in German in tourism or as journalists, or who foster relationships with German-speaking countries in local or foreign companies because of their own knowledge of German. It is also remarkable that many contemporary remigrants seek or already have dual citizenship. This wish alone indicates that they do not want to break off relations with the German-speaking countries and want to retain their German-language skills (e.g. www. dw.de/doppelpass-pl%C3%A4ne-als-signal-f%C3%BCr-einwanderer/a-16947081). In individual cases, there are lasting relationships between remigrants and former German friends and acquaintances, which are maintained using modern communications media. In this context and in mutual visits, German is generally used, sometimes in addition to the remigrants' language. In town-twinning partnerships, remigrants often play an important role as interpreters.

The extent to which such remigrants are committed to German, is shown by comments I received from Jenin Dahinden (email 18 July 2013) based on research for her book *Prishtina – Schlieren. Albanian Migration Networks in the Transnational Space* (2005). The remigrant women she describes include former guest workers as well as asylum seekers:

> For women returning to Kosovo, the German language was often a symbol of distinction but also of identity. For example, one woman who'd returned from Germany just watched German TV all day. This connected her with her German friends, who had an important identity function for her. Because, after her return, – and, as she repeatedly emphasised, she returned voluntarily – this interviewee felt like a 'foreigner' in Kosovo and couldn't find access to local women's networks. She often kept in touch with women friends from Germany; they also came to visit. The situation at that time was sometimes dramatic, especially for returning children, because so far, the children had spent the majority of their life, especially their school life, in a German-speaking space and therefore couldn't really speak Albanian when they returned. I was often told that these children and young people spoke German to each other in the playground and, here again, German was not only a language of identification but also a symbol of distinction from the 'others'.

Another under-researched, *allochthonous* German-speaking group which is important for the global position of German, are the *expatriates*. This term generally relates to company employees who work abroad for a limited time, but it can also be used in a broader sense to include especially diplomats working abroad. In this context, of course, the focus is on employees and diplomats from German-speaking countries. But it should be mentioned, incidentally, that expatriates from other countries who work in German-speaking countries can also contribute to strengthening the position of German if they improve their knowledge of German during their stays and perhaps go on to use it elsewhere – so that, in a sense, they resemble the remigrants. An investigation of expatriates from German-speaking countries in Kuala Lumpur, the capital of Malaysia, was carried out by Miroslava Majtanova (2015). Majtanova explains the activity of these expatriates primarily based on their national and language-community identity (Ch. E.1; E.2). However, her observations also confirm an instrumental motivation based on the usefulness of a knowledge of German. Expatriates from German-speaking countries in Kuala Lumpur have organised themselves into various associations, which have English-language names (corresponding to the local priority of English as the language of business and science, if not actually the official language of state of Malaysia): "The Malaysian-German Society", "The Swiss Club of Malaysia" (dissolved in 2007), "German Language Association of Malaysia" and "German Alumni Association Kuala Lumpur". The "Malaysian-German Chamber of Commerce and Industry", the "Swiss-Malaysian Business Association" and various Christian communities, in which Catholics and Protestants work together, can be added to this list (Majtanova 2015: Ch. B.2). In all these organisations, people communicate at least partially in German. Many even run German courses for locals, contributing to an increasing interest in learning German. The local Goethe-Institut is ready to satisfy this rising demand. Although the contacts are often quite loose, all these organisations are in contact with one another and together help to strengthen knowledge about German and therefore the position of the German language. Despite many other examples throughout the world, there is still a shortage of individual investigations as well as a general overview.

The final allochthonous group of German-speakers outside the German-speaking countries is the *retirement colonies* (Ammon 2015: 844–864). These are concentrated groups of people from German-speaking countries who have settled permanently or for longer periods and who form a kind of German-speaking community, including German-speaking institutions and businesses – but all with a holiday ambience. They are found primarily in Turkey and Spain, especially Mallorca, but also in other Mediterranean countries. A typical example is outlined in a *Spiegel* report (10 December 2006) entitled "Turkish Riviera: a colony of fair-skinned, blond-haired people" as follows: "More than 10,000 Germans live in Alanya. They have left their homes as pensioners or unemployed people to try their luck with a new life on the Turkish Riviera". That is why, readers learn, the local Turkish people have renamed the town "Alemania". The Germans arrived at the start of the 1980s, "initially as holidaymakers, but then as long-term holidaymakers". "Alanya has 99 German shops, 2446 Germans have unlimited residence permits and almost 3000 own an apartment". "They came because, with their small pensions, they were nobody in Germany". "Nowadays, everyone speaks German in Alanya" (www.spiegel.de/reise/fernweh/tuerkische-riviera-die-kolonie-der-blassen-blonden-menschen-a-453538.html). Similar colonies exist in Romania, Bulgaria and especially Spain. In 1997, "the German *Wurstkönig* [sausage king], Horst Abel, 58, wanted to form a political party *Deutsche Freunde in Spanien* to defend German interests in Mallorca", but he gave up the idea because of strong resistance from the locals. In many regions, economically weak countries try to attract German-speaking settlers, so that more retirement colonies will be formed. For example, Portugal advertises not only the advantages of the Mediterranean climate and the beauty of the Algarve coast, but also offers taxation advantages (e.g. *auslandsjournal* ZDF, 10 July 2013: 22.25–22.55). In typical colonies of this kind, it is possible to communicate almost exclusively in German. Apart from German-speaking shops, restaurants and various services, there are radio programmes and print media in German, e.g. the fortnightly *Mallorca Zeitung* or the magazine *Mallorca und die Deutschen*. When they do have contact with German-speaking settlers, the local inhabitants can also communicate adequately in German. But their relationship with foreign settlers is occasionally tense, whenever they feel ostracised or relegated to a servant status. The extent to which such colonies arouse a deeper or broader interest in the German language, which radiates into the surroundings or to other regions, must remain an open question. However, they do deserve to be investigated with regard to their effect on the global position of German.

F

GERMAN IN INTERNATIONAL BUSINESS COMMUNICATION

1. Language and the economics of international and global business

The focus of this book so far has been on the speakers of German (compared with other languages), on their numerical and economic strength, and their distribution between nations and regions. Our attention now moves over to individual, large-scale subdivisions or sectors of society, which I shall call (social) action fields. They are broader than the "domains" familiar in sociolinguistics (Ch. E.2:VI), which refer to narrower situational types, such as family, friends, school, workplace and similar. These are relevant in sociolinguistics and especially for the present book in so far as they are associated with specific linguistic expectations or norms, including the choice of languages and varieties (Fishman 1972b; Ammon 1989b: 70–78; Werlen 2004). By contrast, the broader action fields can cover several domains and therefore also include different types of language choice; but all these domains are interconnected by common social purposes, goals and values of the individuals acting in them; they may also be linked by specific legal provisions. Action fields include e.g. business economics, science, politics, art (or different branches of art subdivided by media), sport and tourism. For example, the action field of business economics, includes extremely diverse institutions (production, trading, banks etc.), in each case with different domains (e.g. manufacturing, distribution, management etc.). "Action fields are interconnected complexes of purposes with action situations relevant to vocational, personal and social life. They are always multidimensional because they link together vocational, social and individual problems" (www.wikipedia.de: *Handlungsfeld*). It is difficult to provide a more precise, general definition because of overlapping, e.g. if some of the domains and actions attributable to action field A can, at the same time, be allocated to action field B, and others to action field C etc. The examples, such as, economics, science, diplomacy (politics) (Ch. F; G; H) etc. also overlap to some extent but they must suffice for our present purpose. At any rate, I was not able to find a disjoint system and shall therefore concentrate on those action fields which seemed particularly relevant to the global position of languages.

It is widely agreed that the action field of business economics provides an important incentive for internationalisation and globalisation. Of course, its development requires appropriate political framework conditions, and these have been significantly expanded by the collapse of the Soviet Union and the opening of China. Modern transport and communications media have created conditions essential for development. The action fields of diplomacy (politics) and science and technology (Ch. G; H) also play a crucial role. Without their contribution, the global movement of people, capital, goods (products) and services, could not have developed to their present scale.

In view of its acknowledged role as a driving force, I turn first to the action field of business economics. My discussion selects from a vast complex of topics subsumed under the heading "language and business" only those aspects essential to the book (overviews: e.g. Vaillancour 1985; Grin/ Vaillancour 1997; Coulmas 1992a, b; 2005b). As for the other action fields, the main question here is: what role does German, compared with other languages, play in international communication, i.e. between German-speakers and speakers of other languages (in asymmetric communication) and between non-German-speakers with different native languages (as a lingua franca; Ch. A.3; A.4)? The question covers use of German – and languages other than German, primarily English – outside and, in some respects, also inside the German-language territory. An explanatory sub-question would interrogate the extent that the position of German (in single countries, groups of countries or worldwide) interrelates with the position of other languages, especially English. A further question would investigate the extent to which changes in the position of languages are determined by globalisation and have a retroactive effect on it.

The economic power of the German-speaking community is fundamental to the role of German in international business communication. As referenced in Ch. C.4, based on its economic power (gross national product), the German-language community occupies fifth or possibly fourth position of all language communities in the world, behind English, Chinese, Japanese and possibly also Spanish. However, it can be assumed that the participation of German-speaking countries (with German as the national official language and most frequent native language; Ch. B.4) in international trade has had an even more direct effect on the position of German in international business communication. In this respect also, German-speaking countries are among the most prominent global players. This applies especially to Germany – including the FRG before unification, which has been a leader in global trade for many years. Table F.1–1

Table F.1–1 The world's top trading nations: export and import of goods and services in 2011

Commercial goods				Services			
Export		Import		Export		Import	
China	10.4	USA	12.3	USA	13.9	USA	10.0
USA	8.1	China	9.5	UK	6.6	Germany	7.3
Germany	8.1	Germany	6.8	Germany	6.1	China	6.0
Japan	4.5	Japan	4.6	China	4.4	UK	4.3
Netherlands	3.6	France	3.9	France	4.0	Japan	4.2
France	3.3	UK	3.5	Japan	3.4	France	3.5
South Korea	3.0	Netherlands	3.2	Spain	3.4	India	3.1
Italy	2.9	Italy	3.0	India	3.3	Netherlands	3.0
Russia	2.9	South Korea	2.8	Netherlands	3.2	Ireland	2.9
Belgium	2.6	China Hong Kong	2.8	Singapore	3.1	Italy	2.9
UK–	2.6	Canada	2.5	China Hong Kong	2.9	Singapore	2.9
China Hong Kong	2.5	India	2.5	Ireland	2.6	Canada	2.5

Note: global proportions as percentage; data from WTO

(*Source*: www.wto.org/english/res_e/statis_e/its2012_e/its12_world_trade_dev_e.htm)

gives an overview of recent figures (2011) for the strongest trading countries in the world. For a time (from 2003 to 2007), Germany occupied first position in the export of goods, but not services. I will discuss this point later, but Germany's stronger position in total exports by comparison with total imports seems to be a permanent condition.

The other two major German-speaking countries (Austria, Switzerland) are also high on the scale in their proportion of world trade, as shown by the national rankings for 2011 (same source as Table F.1–1). Commercial goods: Export: Switzerland position 23, Austria 29; Import: Switzerland 23, Austria 26; Services: Export: Switzerland position 14, Austria 21; Import: Switzerland 25, Austria 27. The former GDR was also a major trading partner, at least within the Comecon block.

But does this high ranking of the German-speaking countries in world trade necessarily secure a strong position for the German language in international business communication? Also, does this position strengthen German as a foreign language because of the associated economic value of speaking German? These assumptions are supported by various findings, such as the spread of Japanese as a foreign language in the 1980s, which can hardly be explained other than with reference to the apparently unstoppable economic growth of Japan, its role in world trade and the promise of its market (cf. Coulmas 1989). With reference to German and Japanese, Gage (1986: 374; tr. U.A.) has noted that it is their importance in international trade which gives these languages international significance. The recent spread of Chinese as a foreign language can be explained on the same model (figures for FL learning in Ch. J.7). However, a language's attractiveness as a foreign language also depends on factors other than the role of associated countries in international trade. Indeed, the influence of this factor in the German-speaking countries is limited by the preponderance of exports over imports, already referred to in the comment on Table F.1–1. The long-term export surplus is presumably economically advantageous but may involve disadvantages for the position of German in international trade and its attractiveness as a foreign language. It has been known since Adam Smith ([1776] 2003: 79–83) that this occurs if the supply of goods is greater than the demand, i.e. in the present context, if exporters are competing to sell their goods. Indeed, in the contemporary global market, and presumably almost everywhere in the market for goods, this situation prevails. In most cases, there is strong competition between different exporters. Almost the only exception is with monopolies, e.g. for goods with a cult value (such as tablet computers, iPhones) or scarce raw materials (such as rare earths), but these are not generally among the goods exported from German-speaking countries. In the prevailing competitive situation, exporters (sellers) have less power than importers and must woo them according to the exaggerated slogan: "The customer is king (always right)" (see also Ch. F.2; A.2). But such courtship demands maximum possible politeness. And this also applies to the choice of language for communication between exporter and importer. In this scenario, choosing the native language of the importer or the official language of the importer's country conforms best with the dictates of politeness.

The overall effect of this asymmetric power relationship may be that the languages of major import countries tend to be learnt as foreign languages in preference to those of major export countries, at least, if this asymmetry endures for long periods, as in the present case. For German-speaking countries, this suggests that, their economically possibly more favourable dependence on exports in world trade does not necessarily strengthen the international position of German; an economically less favourable dependence on imports might be more advantageous in this respect. The effect is prominent in English-speaking countries; at least in the largest, the USA, it has become notorious in recent years. Its influence is not balanced by export strength in services, especially since monopolies do sometimes exist in this context (which do not require linguistic concessions by the exporter). Contrasting with its economic disadvantage, this dependence on imports is a factor – although perhaps not especially weighty – which additionally strengthens the international position of English. In fact, the global position of English depends on more important factors, which have been influential for longer (Ch. A.7; Graddol 2000, 2006; de Swaan 2001; Crystal 2003), but dependence on imports is a possible contributory factor.

It should be added that, for "native countries" and official-language states, a strong global position of their own language represents an economic advantage per se (Grin 2000, 2001). Economic advantages of a language with a strong position are obvious in the case of English. But by implication, the weaker global position of German compared with English represents an economic handicap and any strengthening in the position of German represents an economic gain for the German-speaking countries. Some of the economic advantages of English-speaking countries and their businesses associated with the global position of their language (Ch. A.7), and the corresponding disadvantage to countries of any other languages, are also obvious. They can be most clearly formulated as competitive economic advantages (or disadvantages). One such advantage for English-speaking countries is smoother business relationships with countries in the "outer circle of the English language", especially former British colonies – or more precisely, former "exploitation colonies". By contrast, the "settlement colonies", which include the USA, Canada, Australia and New Zealand, and the "native country", Great Britain, as well as Ireland, all belong to the "inner circle" (six nations in total; Kachru 1982, 1986); apart from Ireland, all these also belong to the "Five-eyes Club", whose secret services collaborate closely with one another ("'Five Eyes': the exclusive espionage club", *Die Presse* 06 July 2013). Bernhard Steinrücke, Director of the German Chamber of Commerce Abroad in India, addressed the comparatively language-related, economic disadvantages of non-English-speaking countries as follows: "If you tell a medium-sized German entrepreneur [. . .], that to conduct business [in India! U. A.] in English, it is likely to fall on deaf ears. Thanks to their language and their proportionally high Indian-origin population, the Americans are noticeably more relaxed ("Do not underestimate the risks in India", *FAZ*, 25 August 2006: 13). Generalising from this and other references, it can be inferred that access to all former British colonies is easier in English than in German. Having said this, other previously successful colonial countries enjoy similar advantages with the Spanish, French and Portuguese languages. However, beyond this, English offers easy access to practically all countries in the world, because English is learnt more frequently worldwide as a foreign language and is mastered better than any other languages – including German (J.7; J.9.2–J.9.14). Unfortunately, it is not easy to measure the scale of this economic advantage for English-speaking countries. The principle is sometimes questioned with reference to the export successes of Germany, Japan and more recently China, but it can be argued that their export success would be even greater without their linguistic handicap. There can be little doubt that easier linguistic communication is a catalyst for business contacts and success. Occasionally, however, the linguistic superiority of English-speakers can become a handicap if it is perceived as arrogant or acts as a reminder of the colonial era. The complex web of factors suggested here does not appear to have been adequately disentangled so far. Above all, the relative weighting of linguistic communication relative to the attractiveness of the goods offered remains unclear. *The Economist* ("Chasing an elephant", 20 January 2007: 39f.) ran a report on unsatisfactory British business with India, even despite excellent linguistic conditions. The article explains that, on one hand, "India's elite speaks impeccable English", but complains that, on the other hand, "the House of Commons select committee on trade and industry recently declared that British business has been left behind. Exports [to India! U. A.] have grown slowly compared with those from other big economies" – no doubt including Germany.

Britain's deficit, bemoaned in this article, certainly impacts on goods more than services, which are more strongly bound to language. The export of services is facilitated to a high degree by a common language and hampered by language difference. This assumption is borne out by the leadership of English-speaking countries in the export of services. The situation, according to which, in addition to the USA and UK, Ireland is also numbered among the ten leading countries, is shown in Table F.1–1. Even India and Singapore, which belong to the "outer circle" of English-speaking countries (Kachru 1982, 1986), are close to the top. The dominance of the English-speaking world in developing and exporting services has existed for decades – and is not likely to be challenged in the foreseeable future. In the service sector, a shared language significantly facilitates cooperation. The direct access to cost-favourable "human capital" in emerging and developed countries enjoyed by English-speaking countries, primarily the USA and UK, also offers an important competitive advantage. This applies to the production and distribution of goods to a reduced extent. Especially for small and medium-sized companies in the non-English-speaking countries, i.e. including German-speaking countries, considerable additional costs, known as "transaction costs", can be incurred from foreign-language requirements (Ch. F.7). From the opposite perspective, by comparison with otherwise comparable countries with different languages, the English-speaking developing and emerging countries also gain advantages from their linguistic orientation. India, where knowledge of English dating back to the colonial period has supported the country's transformation into one of the global leaders in software manufacture, again provides a prime example (Zingel 2002). Such cases also motivate other countries to invest more intensively in building on their own knowledge of English. The best example is China, which, like many other countries, has made English into the only compulsory foreign language in all its schools, which are also all state-run anyway (Ch. J.9.13).

These considerations also raise the question of how far the prominent economic position of English-speaking capital cities has been boosted by the global position of the English language and by their global provision of services, especially in the banking trade. One example is London, especially the London Stock Exchange, which occupies a key position not only in Europe but also globally. This has been achieved even though Britain is not first in Europe in terms of overall economic performance but comes behind Germany and France. A further advantage for the English-speaking countries is their more direct access to "human capital". Poor knowledge of German worldwide explains why the German-speaking countries find it so much more difficult to recruit urgently needed specialist employees.

While economic effects in the sense addressed so far have often been relativized or questioned, no one seriously doubts the wide divergence in opportunities for the "language industry" as such. These depend substantially on the global position of each language. The language industry comprises the business of language tuition and goods directly related to language, such as printed items, films and other media (McCallen 1989; J.A. Edwards/ Kingscott 1997). In this context, the dominance of the English-speaking countries is overwhelming, and the reasons are self-explanatory. Throughout the world, it is evident on a day-to-day basis that people want to learn the "world language" (supply and demand for language tuition, language trips, language in mass culture, such as pop music and so on; see also Grin 1999a). There is no need here for detailed evidence or explanations as this topic will be considered later, e.g. with reference to the action fields of the media and linguistic arts (Ch. I.1.4; I.2) and FL learning (Ch. J.7).

Although important investigations and surveys on the languages of international business communication have been implemented in recent years, considerable gaps still exist in the knowledge available. There is a shortage of direct observations, rather than generalised information and reports, about language choice in international business contacts. The data available on language choice at corporate-leadership level, e.g. in board meetings, is sporadic. The same is true for data about the German-language skills of board members in global organisations with head offices in a German-speaking country. Even when the official language of the organisation is known, actual language choices generally remain obscure. Unfortunately, this is also the case in the discussion below. The following aspects relevant to the topic of the book will therefore be addressed in the next chapters:

- Size of organisations, e.g. large – medium-sized – small enterprises; and opportunities for internal language services or provision of FL skills;
- International structure of organisations, e.g. geocentric – ethnocentric; influence on language of the organisation and local, site-specific languages;
- Siting of components of the organisation and their official languages of state or predominant native languages; influence on corporate language and local site-specific languages;
- Head offices or traditional seat of organisations and the international position of local official languages of state; choice of language for external contacts;
- Type of business relationships between organisations, as seller/supplier or buyer/purchaser; influence on language choice.

2. Principles of language choice for international business contacts

International business contacts can be structured in many different ways. The choice of language is necessarily subject to various conditions, but for the present, one specific configuration, that between sellers (or exporters) and buyers (importers), will be considered in greater detail. It is frequently encountered; it is particularly relevant for the choice of German; and it has already been addressed in Ch. F.1 with reference to the "dependence on exports" of the German-speaking countries. As the following considerations show, factors influencing language choice in business communication are extremely complex. For example, it might be assumed that the question of language choice arises only for communication partners with different languages (native languages or official languages). But in some circumstances, even communication partners with the same language must consider the possibility of future recipients (listeners or readers). In business, this may be required primarily for documented, generally written texts. Sometimes, even amongst themselves, German-speaking communication partners therefore choose English rather than German to ensure future linguistic accessibility.

Language learning and communication must be considered separately as conditions for language choice. To communicate, participants can only choose from languages which they already know – unless they resort to language services (translation, interpreting); but other options are available for language learning. Here also, however, the choice is limited, e.g. for children, by the languages offered at school or their parents' financial situation. The following considerations refer directly only to language choice for communication, but they are sometimes transferable to language learning. For example, rules of politeness generally apply to language choices for communication, especially between exporters and importers. In this context, provided the requisite language skills are available, it is generally considered polite to accommodate linguistically to suit one's partner. This rule for communication can be transferred to the context of language learning as a trend. The degree of politeness seems greater in this case because of the considerable increase in effort, e.g. when employees of a company learn their business partners' language, the official language of their country or their native language, to accommodate them linguistically. In the following section, such parallels between language choice for communication and for learning will not always be mentioned. Similarly, trivial marginal conditions, such as restrictions on language choice for communication and/or learning because of available language skills or opportunities, will not always be addressed.

Many discussions of language choice, which are also relevant for language choice in business, have been published in recent years (overview, e.g. Coulmas 2005). I will therefore focus on factors identified in that context. One such factor is social identity. Accordingly, it is assumed that a communicating person (*communicant*) expresses a given social identity through the choice of a given language, although with different degrees of clarity, because of the involvement of other factors. The most general identity a person can express through language choice is membership of the relevant language community (Ch. B.3). This applies not only to the choice of one's own native language, but also to foreign languages, where the choice expresses membership of the group of FL speakers of the respective language (e.g. speakers of German as a foreign language, "GFL speakers"). However, to the extent that a person's native language is anchored more deeply in their psyche, this choice expresses a more fundamental group identity, membership of the native speakers of that language.

In the absence of foreign-language skills, the "choice" of the speaker's native language is the unavoidable "default choice", unless translation services are used. But if a choice is possible, it can demonstrate group identity in a targeted manner, e.g. when communicants choose their own native language even though their language skills allow the choice of another language which their partner might understand better. Membership of a group, e.g. German native speakers, overarches situational considerations, and this must be distinguished from social roles they play in different situations (e.g. seller, personal friend etc.; see Dahrendorf 1965). Accordingly, role identity can be expressed or manifested through communication. It is sometimes difficult to distinguish between group and role identity, e.g. in the case of a "cosmopolitan identity" expressed through the choice of English as a foreign language or by using "international English" or non-native-speaker English (Jenkins 2007: 197–235, 1997; Seidlhofer 2005a, b; 2011). This language choice can signal a cosmopolitan role, membership of the vast group of non-native speakers, or even all speakers of English. By contrast, for people with a leadership function in a specialist discussion, the same language choice may instead express this social role.

The other key factor for language choice mentioned above was politeness, which often interacts with other factors in international contacts (Ch. A.6). Jim O'Driscoll (2001a, b) has addressed the interplay between politeness and identity, especially *ethnic* (or *national*) and *cosmopolitan identity* (as two forms of group identity). He distinguishes *politeness* from its negation (lack of politeness) and especially from its opposite (rudeness). In O'Driscoll's terminology – borrowed from Erving Goffman – communication partners show a different "face": "ethnic" or "cosmopolitan", "polite", "not polite (neutral)" or "rude". I shall refrain from using the term face with reference to these two factors but use it in its more conventional sense in sociolinguistics only with reference to politeness (Brown/ Levinson 1987; Brown 2005). O'Driscoll represents the plausible view that a national (or ethnic) identity is clearly signalled through the choice of distinctly non-international, i.e. only ethnic (or national) languages; but a cosmopolitan identity is expressed through the choice of the "lingua franca", by which he means primarily the "world language", English. To provide a ranking scale from ethnic to cosmopolitan identity, his view can also be formulated as follows: an ethnic (or national) identity is expressed more clearly the lower the international position of the language selected (e.g. Czech rather than German); and a cosmopolitan identity is expressed more clearly the higher its international position (e.g. English rather than German; see Ch. A.3). In fact, linguistic politeness is always shown by accommodating to the language of the conversational partner (their native language or official language), and this must involve a foreign language for the person accommodating (otherwise it makes no sense to speak of accommodation). However, accommodating to a language which is only ethnic or national is generally perceived as politer than accommodating to an international language or to the "world language". For example, accommodating to Czech is generally more polite than accommodating to German, and in turn, accommodating to German is more polite than accommodating to English.

Explaining such politeness differences in communication, seems to me to require an investigation of the motives for language choice in the context of FL learning. In fact, evaluating the choice of language to learn merges with the evaluation of language choice in communication. This suggests, in turn, that learning an international language need not be motivated by a special interest in a communication partner's group, because an international language is characterised precisely by more comprehensive opportunities for communication. To some extent, this possible comprehensive motivation for learning dilutes the element of politeness in the choice of an international language. By contrast, someone who has learnt as a foreign language a language which is only ethnic or national and demonstrates this through their language choice in communication demonstrates to their communication partner undiluted politeness towards that ethnic or national group.

Studying the conditions for linguistic accommodation to a communication partner has been a respected research field in sociolinguistics for several decades. The field was probably opened by Howard Giles (Giles 1977; Giles/ Bourhis/ Taylor 1973, 1977). Linguistic accommodation is accordingly considered a basic need of human communication, required to guarantee understanding (Grice [1975] 1989), and could ultimately have a genetic basis (Burgoon/ Stern/ Dillman 1995). As an indicator, it is sometimes pointed out that "polyglot dialogue" (Posner 1991b), based on passive bi- or multilingualism, in which different languages are used alternately, is widely considered highly unnatural. Polyglot dialogue is a conversation between people with different native languages who each speak their own native language and understand the other language or languages (Ch. A.3). Having said this, the un-naturalness of a polyglot dialogue can be overcome to some extent through training and practice.

However, the need for linguistic accommodation does not specify who accommodates to whom or who expresses which identity or is more polite. This depends primarily on power relations between communication partners. One important aspect of power relations in business communication, which is characteristic for modern market economies, is expressed in the popular slogan "the customer is king (always right)". In contemporary market economies, there is a surplus for most goods and services, which places the supplier (seller) in a weaker position than the recipient (customer, buyer); the same applies for exporters and importers. Buyers are generally the "economically dominant business partners" (Bungarten 2001: 31). Suppliers must make a greater effort than buyers to make a deal. This asymmetry in the market economy means that suppliers are generally more polite to buyers than vice versa. In the case of a shortage of goods, the reverse applies. This often occurs in planned economies or by the owners of rare goods or important suppliers (e.g. some suppliers from Germany in Alsace in Bothorel-Witz/ Choremi 2009: 126). Alongside others, one component of such politeness is the seller's linguistic accommodation to the buyer. "[W]henever he or she is able to do so, the merchant speaks the customer's language" (Coulmas 1992b: 166. Cf. also the title of Bowen 1980: "Death of a monoglot salesman" or books about language learning for business, such as "The Customer's Language" (*Die Sprache des Kunden*; Beneke/ Freudenstein 1994). Long-term market relationships of this kind also provide a motive for corresponding language learning. It can be assumed that sellers are inclined to acquire the relevant language skills primarily if the anticipated advantage (revenue from sales) exceeds the additional costs (effort of learning). This will apply more strongly the greater the purchasing power of the potential sales market, i.e. the relevant language community. With approximately equal economic development, purchasing power is approximately proportional to the numerical strength of the language community. This explains in economic terms why large (numerically strong) languages tend to be learnt as foreign languages more than small languages and – everything else being equal – thus generally have a higher international position (Ch. A.7).

The fact that sellers in modern goods economy are more likely to accommodate linguistically to buyers than vice versa can be explained, on the one hand, by the market structure, based on which sellers must make more effort than buyers but, on the other hand, because of the effort involved in learning and using foreign languages, which must be undertaken by the weaker communication partner to spare the stronger one this effort. More recent politeness theories have deepened this explanation. They assume two basic needs of every person: the need for recognition and for freedom of action, a protected space or "own territory" (details cf. Brown/ Levinson 1987). The need for recognition can also be described in terms of "preserving positive face", alluding to the expression "losing face". The need for freedom of action then corresponds – although not entirely without the possibility for misunderstanding – to "preserving negative face". Accordingly, acts towards another person can be "face saving" (polite) or "face damaging" (rude), so that it is possible to distinguish two types of politeness and two types of rudeness: preserving positive face (recognition) and negative face (opening a space for action), and respectively damaging positive face (disparagement) and negative face (restriction of action). The sense of "positive" and "negative" is more easily understood with reference to the associated attentiveness: registering recognition, or respectively non-attentiveness: allowing space for action. But in the present context, negative face hardly plays a role, and the following discussion can be narrowed down to positive face. However, the choice of a customer's language (native or national official language) is more polite with reference to both types of face. On the one hand, it allows customers more room for manoeuvre (preserving negative face), because customers are still free to choose the supplier's native language, if they speak it. On the other hand, choosing their own native language allows customers a communicative advantage (native-language advantage) and therefore also a feeling of superiority; suppliers place themselves in the communicatively weaker position by accepting the "foreign-language disadvantage". Indeed, taken by itself and regardless of communicative advantages or disadvantages, this language choice can be understood as an acknowledgement of the customer's language and culture. So, it acts to preserve the customer's positive face in a double sense.

Sharon Miller and Astrid Jensen (2009: 100) quote accounts by Danish business people of experiences of this kind, e.g. "I think you experience no matter what country you come to that if you try to use the local language, perhaps with the exception of France, you get some kind of goodwill for it. That you bother to try in that broken Spanish even if it definitely sounds like something any professor at a Spanish University would be horrified at". According to this informant, France is an exception because only good French is valued, not "broken" French. This account also betrays that it only relates to language choice in initial contacts (language of encounter), but not business agreements (language of negotiation). Guaranteeing the communicative advantage for business negotiations generally requires even greater politeness. But the fact that a choice of the native language in an initial encounter serves as a sign of respectful recognition, can also be explained with reference to identity theory. Instead of operating with the vague term "linguistic identity", I prefer to draw on the function of the native language as an expression of a communicant's ethnic or national identity discussed at the start of this chapter (and Ch. E.1). In fact, the choice of a person's native language for communication does not necessarily signal respect, e.g. in the case of a generally unfavourable image of that language group. For example, the choice of a low-prestige dialect and therefore the demonstrative relegation of the communicant to the group in question can act as a malicious disparagement. But, such interpretations are remote from most business situations. Here, the choice of the customer's native language generally serves as a respectful recognition of their ethnic or national group. Such types of language choice are often used as paradigm cases in research on the linguistics of politeness (e.g. Ide 1982: 367). They are also recommended by sales strategists: "Customers consider it a courtesy to be addressed by a foreign supplier in their own language" (*Hopper* 5, September/October 1988: 16). The supplier's effort to show linguistic respect is confirmed in one survey of foreign suppliers and German buyers (n = 1300). In this context, Italian suppliers recorded comprehension difficulties (79% of respondents), French suppliers (50%) and English (49%); the figure for Swedish suppliers was significantly less (20%). It can be assumed that the Swedish suppliers had the best skills in German. The fact that they perceived fewer language difficulties than their partners suggests that the German buyers were less inclined towards linguistic accommodation than the foreign suppliers: faced with Italian suppliers, only 29% of German buyers recorded problems (vice versa 79%), with French suppliers 44% (vice versa 59%), with English buyers 27% (vice versa 49%) and with Swedish buyers 7% (vice versa 20%) (Kutscher/ Kirsch 1979: 98–100).

In principle, the choice of a lingua franca is also more polite than choosing one's own language, because both speakers relinquish their native-speaker advantage and therefore preserve their partner's positive face – although to a reduced extent. However, preserving face succeeds only if the person addressed masters the lingua franca adequately. Initially, the international ranking of this lingua franca plays no part. But, with a higher-ranking international language, shared language skills are more likely, especially with English. To some extent, therefore, English is the default choice. However, the value of a choice of English by its native speakers is changing correspondingly. On the one hand, this choice, and therefore the native-speaker advantage, is expected of them, because a knowledge of English is already almost taken for granted. On the other hand, however, such an unadorned assumption can also be perceived as arrogant and rude. If such marginal cases are disregarded, the more significant the international position of a language is, the more normal (or natural), and therefore also more acceptable, a choice of that language for international contacts will be. This applies even for the least polite variant in language choice, namely, the choice of one's own native language. If this assessment is correct, many German business people apparently evaluate the international position of German as rather low. At least, this is the inference drawn in Marina Vollstedt's (2005: 266) summary of her survey of small and medium-sized firms in Schleswig-Holstein: "The majority of respondents evidently do not consider German [. . .] a serious option in international business communication. One respondent even claimed, 'German is not a language you can use for public appearance, not even as a buyer'". However, some indications suggest that German is given a lower status by Germans than by foreign partners. Carola Bleich's findings in a survey of language choice in German-Swedish business contacts (2005: 281f.) can be interpreted in this way: "for all activities, the Swedish firms always rated a knowledge of German as more important than the German firms [. . .]".

In general, for international (and interlingual) contacts, the following language choices comply, in descending order, with the simplified, overarching rule suggested by the slogan "the customer is king (always right)":

1) Most completely, the customer's native language;
2) Somewhat less, a lingua franca;
3) Even less, the supplier's native language.

As already suggested, even politeness rules depend on market conditions, on the relationship between supply and demand. This can vary from plentiful supply of goods and competition between suppliers (rule of maximum politeness) to scarcity of goods in demand and competition between buyers (rule of minimal politeness). In the latter case, the suppliers' linguistic politeness seldom extends further than the lingua franca: "To be sure, there are also markets in which a lingua franca is used by all participants, especially oligopolistic markets such as the crude-oil or grain markets" (Coulmas 1992: 166). With a scarcity of goods, the rule of politeness between suppliers and customers can be reversed: the suppliers are always right, and the customers treat them with politeness.

A distinction must also be made between at least two phases of the contact: a) the encounter, in which knowledge of languages is first disclosed; b) the negotiation, in which the actual deal is made. Greater sensitivity towards identity and politeness generally applies in the encounter than in the negotiation. For this reason, greater attention is given to the symbolic choice of a partner's language at the time of greetings and other contact conventions (apologies, saying "cheers" etc.). By contrast, in the working phase, the use of the language best mastered by both sides, or in which both sides are at least confident, is not subject to such constraints.

Even if the choice of a language with a stronger international position is initially more natural than a lower-ranking language, exceptional cases also deserve consideration. These include business partners, including customers, who have made a special effort to acquire knowledge of a less widely distributed language, of which they are rightly proud and would like to cultivate. It can be established in the encounter phase whether this is the case, and it may be more polite to choose this diligently learnt language than to choose any other language, because it entails the maximum possible degree of recognition through language choice (preserving positive face) and additionally allows that partner to build on their special qualification or, to use Bourdieu's term, "cultural capital". In the case of German, such opportunities are evidently often forgotten. Harald Weyth (2004) and Si-Ho CHONG (2006) give accounts of German-speakers' refusing to speak German, and this included leading German business people and top politicians. Their refusal was perceived by speakers and learners of German as a foreign language (GFL) not only as discouraging but as directly offensive. However, this sensitivity tends to be felt most strongly not between business partners but rather by teachers and lecturers of GFL, whose professional reputation is at stake.

3. Correspondence languages in German business

In some countries, country-specific conventions have developed for their companies' choice of languages in external contacts. These can become established as expectations or norms, so that, even if it is a foreign language for the buyer, a choice of the supplier's own language is not perceived as arrogant. This often occurs with the choice of English by English-speaking companies. This is not problematic if the business contacted already has the relevant language skills at its disposal. Otherwise, there are various options. Firms can acquire the relevant foreign-language skills – depending on the presumed duration of the business relationship – by appointing staff with language skills, by training staff or by purchasing language services. But they can also resort to a lingua franca, generally English, or reply – somewhat brusquely and rudely – in their own language. The Hamburg Chamber of Commerce has occasionally investigated the relevance of these conventions to German companies. Their published findings are useful to internationally operating German businesses and provide pointers for appropriate language choice. The "correspondence languages" are particularly important for business contacts, alongside country-specific language regulations for marking goods, guarantee certificates and texts on packaging. Correspondence languages relate primarily to written correspondence but, in some cases, also to spoken communication between German companies and foreign partners and are listed for 180 countries (including Germany) in the *Export-Nachschlagewerk "K und M" – Konsulats- und Mustervorschriften* ([Export-Directory] Hamburg Chamber of Commerce 2005). I am grateful to Ulrich Baar from the Hamburg Chamber of Commerce for information on key aspects of definition and data acquisition. (Unless indicated otherwise, all the following quotations are also derived from him.) The correspondence languages operate in both directions, i.e. firms from the respective country also "generally" choose these languages in contact with German partners.

According to Baar's assessment, "German is chosen less frequently by foreign partners than by German-speakers". But this position contradicts the findings from Sonja Vandermeeren's questionnaire with inverse frequency (1998; Ch. F.5). The foreign companies may have overestimated the frequency of their choice of German to Vandermeeren, or the German companies understated the frequency of their choice of foreign languages, or the frequencies found by Vandermeeren are correct and were therefore registered incorrectly by the Hamburg Chamber of Commerce. However, according to Baar, "these correspondence languages are used regardless of whether you want to *sell* or *buy*" (emphasis U.A.). In turn, this finding is not compatible with the greater readiness of suppliers to accommodate linguistically to purchasers, which has been shown to be theoretically plausible and confirmed in empirical investigations (Ch. F.2).

With several correspondence languages, these are generally, but not always, arranged in alphabetical order in the *Export-Nachschlagewerk "K und M"* (Hamburg Chamber of Commerce 2005). Alphabetical ordering does not necessarily imply equal ranking, and "a sequence other than alphabetical denotes a corresponding ranking (position 1 = most appropriate language etc.)". The country-specific, different weighting of languages displayed individually in the directory has not been adopted in Tables F.3–1 and F.3–2. Regarding the correspondence languages in Edition 36 (2005) used here, it is claimed that they are never a mere "update of the data from the preceding edition" and have been newly registered for each country. However, the sources were not "firms with experience of the respective country", but rather the "German Chamber of Commerce Abroad". These sources were supplemented by questionnaires issued to "embassies, consulates and business associations; in some cases, national data (evaluation of [...] available specifications, e.g. for the marking of goods)"; and the "evaluation of various publications, e.g. the monthly periodicals of the Chambers of Commerce Abroad. Laws on the use of indigenous languages (Arabic, Polish, French etc.) must also be considered. For the marking of goods, guarantee certificates and packaging, the language to be used is determined independently of the correspondence language". I have not evaluated these last-named legal provisions in detail.

Table F.3–1 shows all countries (a total of 37) with whose business enterprises German firms can correspond in German. German is the sole correspondence language only in Austria. I refer to this as a *sole-correspondence language*, contrasting with a *co-correspondence language*. Liechtenstein,

Table F.3–1 Countries with German as the correspondence language for German trade in 2005 and 1989

Europe			Outside Europe
Albania	(Yugoslavia)	Sweden	America
*Andorra	*Croatia	Switzerland	Chile ("poss.")
*Armenia	*Latvia	*Serbia and Montenegro	Africa
*Belarus	*Lithuania	*Slovakia	Namibia
Belgium	Luxembourg	*Slovenia	Middle East
*Bosnia and Herzegovina	*Macedonia	*Czech Republic	(Israel)
Bulgaria	*Moldavia	(Czechoslovakia)	Asiaand
Denmark	Netherlands	(USSR)	Oceania
*Estonia	Norway	*Ukraine	(Afghanistan)
Finland	Austria	Hungary	*Azerbaijan
Greece	Poland	(Turkey)	*Kazakhstan
(Iceland)	Romania		Mongolia
Italy	*Russia		

* = new, not named in 1989; (. . .) = deleted, still named in 1989

(*Source*: according to Hamburg Chamber of Commerce 2005, 1989)

for which German is certainly also a sole-correspondence language, is absent from this source, as are many other small countries. Any amendments relative to the previous edition (1989) have been shown. The number of countries with German has risen by ten since the 1989 edition, but this is attributable exclusively to the formation of new states in eastern and southern Europe, which were formerly parts of the USSR, Yugoslavia or Czechoslovakia. In reality, the territory for the use of German has shrunk somewhat, because Iceland, Israel, Turkey and Afghanistan have dropped out. In view of the total number of countries accessible to German, this loss seems small, but still amounts to 10% of the countries (starting from 40 as a basis for the percentage). Moreover, the countries lost are not insignificant, either because of the traditionally close economic and political relations with Germany (all three) or their size (Turkey), apart from one special case (Afghanistan). Some of the countries named are linked with sad memories, such as Israel because of the historical context, and Iceland, because of the closure of the Goethe-Institut there in 1998 and then the Goethe Centre in 2006. However, they are all aligned with a development which threatens the long-term international position of German, namely, the replacement of German with English or the local official language for international communication. In all four cases, English is named as the correspondence language for German business, with the addition of their own languages in Iceland (Icelandic) and Turkey (Turkish).

Expansion of the correspondence languages of German business through the addition of these and numerous other languages – a total of 17 in the 16 years between the two editions (Table F.3–2) – reflects an aspect of language policy for the German business economy which is emphasised even by the title of an investigation by the Institute of German Business "Head Start through Foreign-Language Training" [*Vorsprung durch Fremdsprachentraining*] (Schöpper-Grabe/Weiß 1998 – see Ch. F.5). One key finding was that German firms are expanding their foreign-language skills to improve access to markets. However, these efforts can indirectly weaken the international position of German – a side effect which is undesirable and may not have been considered. To the extent that German firms accommodate to their partners' languages or resort to English, the use of German becomes superfluous.

Otherwise, the distribution of German as a correspondence language has not changed much by comparison with the previous edition (1989), taking into account the formation of new countries in place of the former USSR and Yugoslavia. It is remarkable that German can still be used almost universally in eastern and south-eastern Europe, and in northern Asia (but, see Ch. F.5), but also that this marks the limit of its range. According to this source, the major non-European economic centres of North America, eastern and southern Asia are not accessible with German. Throughout Africa, only Namibia, and in the whole of Latin America, only Chile are marked with the condition "possible". Even in Europe, Germany is not a correspondence language for such economically important nations as France, UK and Spain. Map F.3–1 gives a worldwide overview.

For evaluation, it should be remembered that these data are published specifically as a guideline for German business. Presumably, e.g. a British firm can easily correspond with an Austrian firm in English, even as the supplier, although the *Export-Nachschlagewerk* (2005) names German as the sole correspondence language for Austria – which is generally the appropriate language choice for companies from Germany. The extent to which the correspondence languages indicated refer specifically to Germany could only be determined by including corresponding sources for other countries. However, a comprehensive analysis of this kind for the relationship between German and other languages would presumably not show a very different picture. This assumption is reasonable, because, for many countries, the available source, names languages which only play a peripheral role in contacts with German companies (targeted by the source), e.g. for Albania, apart from English and German, also Italian and French (not Albanian!); or for Lithuania, apart from English, Lithuanian and German,

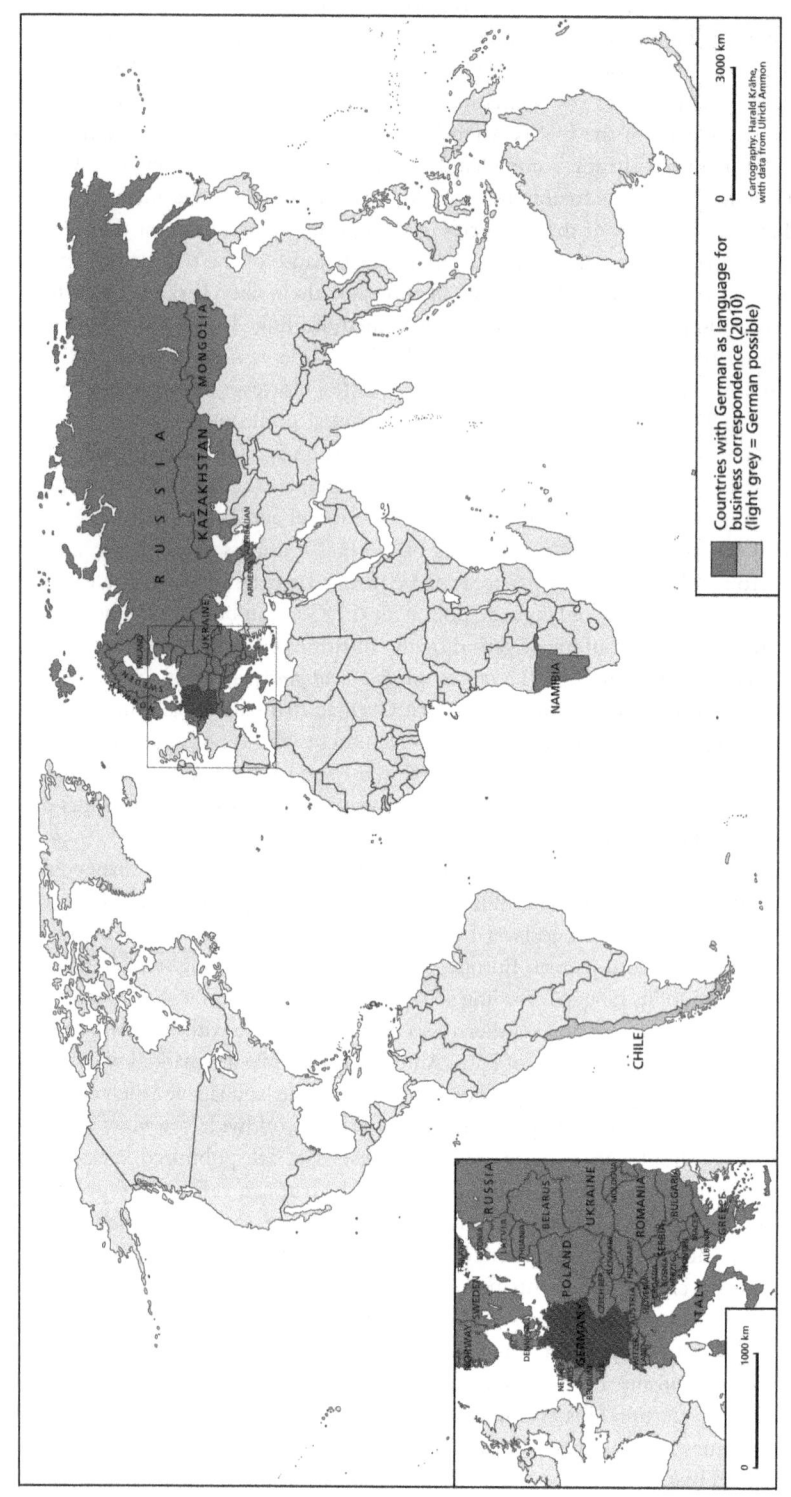

Map F.3–1 Countries with German as a language for business correspondence 2005

(*Source*: after Hamburg Chamber of Commerce 2005)

Table F.3–2 Correspondence languages for German firms with number of countries 2005 outside brackets, and 1989 in brackets

	Sole- or co-correspondence-language	Sole-correspondence-language	Co-Correspondence-language
1. English	137 (122)	52 (64)	85 (58)
2. French	58 (57)	18 (25)	40 (32)
3. German	37 (26)	1 (1)	36 (25)
4. Spanish	28 (26)	16 (17)	12 (9)
5. Russian	23 (1)	0 (0)	23 (1)
6. Arabic	17 (12)	0 (0)	17 (12)
7. Portuguese	13 (8)	0 (0)	13
8. Italian	9 (4)	0 (0)	9 (4)
9. Dutch	7 (8)	0 (0)	7 (8)
10. *Chinese	3	0	3
11. *Croatian	2	0	2
12. Bahasa Indonesia, Czech, Danish, Finnish, Norwegian, Polish, Slovenian, *Swedish	1 (1)	0 (0)	1 (1)
*Belarusian, *Estonian, *Filipino, *Georgian, *Greek, *Hungarian, *Icelandic, *Latvian, *Lithuanian, *Malayan, *Persian, *Romanian, *Slovakian, *Turkish, *Ukrainian, *Uzbek	1	0	1

* = new; Figures from 1989 in brackets

(*Source*: according to Hamburg Chamber of Commerce 2005, 1989)

also Russian. Such data shows the effort to present comprehensive information rather than only data relevant to German companies.

Having said this, the data in the *Export-Nachschlagewerk* should not be taken as absolute. In many countries for which German is not named as a correspondence language, there are certainly also enterprises with which German firms can still correspond in German, and, even in countries with German as a correspondence language, many German firms prefer to use English (Ch. F.5). It would, in fact, be worth investigating language shifts currently in progress, because there are presumably still German companies in a situation similar to the *Handelsunternehmen für Kosmetik und Lebensmittel KMS GmbH* [trading company for cosmetics and foodstuffs] around 1990 (Mönchengladbach, 90 employees at that time). English would have been welcome as a correspondence language with its Polish business partner (150 employees) if this company had not readily accepted German. The managing director of KMS, Werner Scholten (who kindly provided this information) wrote to me in 1990, "It would certainly have been more sensible [on the part of the Polish partner! U.A.] to appoint an English-speaking correspondent; but our business partner had already appointed a German-speaker". In fact, KMS already had correspondence capability in English which was used in business relations with "EC countries, Hong Kong, Korea, Taiwan, Japan, USA, Sweden [. . .] (spoken and in writing)". The decisive factor for the linguistic encounter with the Polish partner was no doubt that, at the time of making the contact, they [the Polish Partner] had no foreign-language correspondence capability at all, not even English, and that, for KMS, "initial contact with the Polish partner was in German". The Polish firm initially had to reply in Polish, for which KMS was not prepared. "So, our middleman in Poland recommended our new business partner to appoint a German-speaker". In this way, German was initially the only foreign language available to the Polish firm, which it then presumably tried to use elsewhere. This example also shows how crucial language choice can be at the time of the first contact.

Table F.3–2 shows all correspondence languages for the German business economy arranged according to frequency of countries. Compared with 1989, the number has almost doubled, from 18 to 35. For more than two-thirds of these (24), only a single country is named, for which reason there are only 12 ranked positions. English, and – with a significant interval – French and Spanish, are clearly ahead of all other languages. By contrast, with languages of equal numerical strength, Russian, Arabic and Portuguese, they are also often sole-correspondence languages. Firms which have business relationships with the relevant countries cannot therefore resort to other languages – at least, one might assume, not if they are in the role of supplier. English presumably has even greater weighting than shown in Table F.3–2, because it is sole-correspondence language for the economic giants, USA and Japan, but also for UK and India, and co-correspondence language for China. It can also be assumed that English is used very intensively as co-correspondence language, and it is also often a lingua franca, i.e. a foreign language for both sides, but then generally only a co-correspondence language. It is surprising that English is also sole-correspondence language for Japan, and that Japan's language is absent from the correspondence languages of the German economy (Hamburg Chamber of Commerce 2005: 285), although Japanese is now often studied at German universities and even schools. By contrast, the fact that languages such as Estonian or Uzbek are numbered among the correspondence languages of the German economy does not seem to be adequately explained by lack of English skills, local rejection of Russian or lack of Russian skills on the German side. French is significantly sole-correspondence language for France, a particularly important business partner of Germany (ranking position one for exports from Germany, three for imports to Germany in 2011; *Fischer Weltalmanach* 2013: 97). However, by contrast with English, it is noticeable that French is only sole-correspondence language when it is, at the same time, national official language and dominant native language, at least for the leadership stratum of the country. It is therefore a genuine lingua franca to a lesser extent than English. In this respect, Spanish and German resemble French. Because of the present focus on Germany, the extent to which German has been overestimated in the ranking as an international language of business correspondence must remain an open question.

4. Languages of the German Chambers of Commerce Abroad

Foreign relationships in the business economy of the German-speaking countries are mediated to a considerable extent by the German Chambers of Commerce Abroad. In 1871, the first such chamber of a German-speaking country was formed as the Austro-Hungarian Chamber of Commerce in Constantinople. In 1894, the first German-Imperial Chamber of Commerce Abroad was founded in Brussels (*Der Große Brockhaus*, 1954, vol. 5:670). It was quickly followed by others. Present-day German Chambers of Commerce Abroad stand in the same tradition. In 2006, the year to which the figures in this chapter refer, German Chambers of Commerce Abroad and offices for delegates and representatives existed in 90 countries, including groups of countries (e.g. Central America, Southern Africa), with four of these countries being served via neighbouring states (e.g. Luxembourg via Belgium, Sudan via Egypt). This covered almost the entire world. Large gaps existed only in Sub-Saharan Africa, where there were only three German Chambers of Commerce Abroad (Nigeria, South Africa, West Africa), to which a further three had been added by 2013 (Angola, Ghana, Kenya) (ahk.de/ahk-standorte). Then there was a slightly different distribution from 2006: "120 sites in 80 countries". In northern, Arabic-speaking Africa, there were still six Chambers of Commerce Abroad in 2006 (Algeria, Egypt, Libya, Morocco, Sudan – via Egypt, Tunisia), which were joined by other Arabic states in the Middle East. By comparison with the period before the collapse of the USSR and Yugoslavia, new chambers were established in almost all the succession states and also in China (representation in four cities) and Vietnam (two cities). Otherwise, there were generally branches in several cities in large countries (Brazil three, USA four). Provision was at its densest in Western Europe. The Chambers of Commerce Abroad and delegate offices received specialist support from a dedicated department of the German Federation of Chambers of Industry and Trade (DIHT), the umbrella organisation for the 81 German Chambers of Industry and Trade, which had around 3.6 m corporate members in 2006. The Chambers of Commerce Abroad advise German firms on their foreign contacts, especially small and medium-sized firms which cannot support their own foreign subsidiaries, providing them with information and establishing contacts with business associations and foreign organisations. Conversely, they provide corresponding services to foreign firms in the respective country about their contacts with Germany (www.dihk. de/inhalt/diht/ index.html). Numerous portals and links are accessible from this website (e.g. www.e-trade-center.com), with information and offers of support for business contacts between German and foreign companies. Like the former periodicals, these webpages are predominantly bilingual or multilingual – in German and the national official language of the respective country or a lingua franca/language of communication (e.g. English for China and Korea, French for Algeria). In some cases, the same information was communicated in the various languages, in other cases different information – depending on addressees and interested parties. Advertisements are mostly published in one of the languages relevant to specific addressees; they are seldom published in parallel in several languages. Table F.4–1 gives an overview of the languages in the country-specific webpages.

It is not clear why the websites were only in German in some countries where extensive knowledge of German cannot be taken for granted (Bosnia and Herzegovina, Serbia and Montenegro, El Salvador). What is remarkable in this context is that the use of German (as an additional language) extends far beyond the territory of correspondence languages (according to Hamburg Chamber of Commerce 2005; Ch. F.3) and includes almost the whole of America, Asia and Oceania. Presumably, the websites are used primarily by German business people and firms, while information relevant for the foreign webpage is available in the respective national official language or a language of communication. The only foreign language necessary for German firms to obtain the information provided for them by the German Chamber of Commerce Abroad is English. For most countries, information is also provided in German, but for a total of 11 countries including China, information is provided only in English. In 2006, 33 different languages were used on the webpages. By contrast, in 1988, only 12 languages were used in the Chambers' magazines (Ammon 1991a: 174). The Chambers of Commerce Abroad have therefore considerably expanded their repertoire of foreign languages – and, surprisingly, at the same time as restricting the use of English. In 1988, English was represented in 34% of the Chambers' magazines, but, in 2006, only in 28% of webpages. The German Chambers of Commerce Abroad were, and still are, evidently trying to address foreign business partners in their own languages. Beyond this, they often also offer German, in 73% of webpages. This expansion is compatible with the finding that German firms have recently expanded their knowledge of foreign languages (Schöpper-Grabe/ Weiß 1998). But, because of the more comprehensive use of German, this does not necessarily support the more extensive use of foreign languages. It would require an additional investigation to determine the extent to which texts in languages other than German or English are used by German firms.

Table F.4–1 Languages of country-specific websites of German Chambers of Commerce Abroad, delegates and representatives of the German economy

Albania ?	El Salvador G	Lithuania G/Es/La/Li	Sweden Sw/G/E
Algeria G/F	Estonia G/Es/Le/Li	Luxembourg (see	Switzerland G
Argentina G/S	Finland Fi/G/E/Sw	Belgium)	Serbia and
Australia E	France F/G	Malaysia E/G	Montenegro G
Austria G	Greece Gr/G	Morocco F/G	Singapore E
Belgium G/Ni/F	Guatemala G/S	Macedonia ?	Slovakia Sk/G
Bolivia S/G	Honduras S/G	Mexico S/G	Slovenia Sn/G
Bosnia-Herzegovina G	Hungary Hu/G	New Zealand E/G	Spanish G/S
Brazil P/G	India E	Netherlands Ni/G	South Africa E
Bulgaria G/Bu	Indonesia In/G/E	Nicaragua S/G	Sudan (see Egypt)
Canada E/F/G	Iran Fa/G	Nigeria E	Taiwan Ch/G
Central-America S/G	Ireland E/G	Norway G/No	Thailand E
Chile G/S	Iceland G/Is	Oman see UAE	Tunisia F/G
China E	Israel He/G	Palestinian Territories	Turkey G/Tr
Colombia S/G	Italy I/G	G/E/A	Ukraine G/Uk
Costa Rica S/G	Japan J/G	Panama G/S	United Arab Emirates
Croatia Cr/G	Kazakhstan ?	Paraguay S/G	E/D
Czech Republic Cz/G	Korea E	Peru S/G	United Kingdom D/E
Denmark G/Da	Kosovo ?	Philippines E	USA D/E
Dominican Republic G/S	Latvia G/Es/ La/Li	Poland Po/G	Uruguay S/D
Ecuador G/S	Lebanon E	Portugal P/G	Venezuela S/D
Egypt E	Libya (see Egypt)	Romania Rm/G	Vietnam E/D
		Russian Federation R/G	White Russia R/D
		Saudi Arabia G/E	Western Africa E

Note: ? = No website, A = Arabic, Bu = Bulgarian, Cr = Croatian, Cz = Czech, Da = Danish, Du = Dutch, E = English, Es = Estonian, F = French, Fa = Farsi (Persian), Fi = Finnish, G = German, Gr = Greek, He = Hebrew, Hu = Hungarian, Ic = Icelandic, I = Italian, In = Indonesian, J = Japanese, La = Latvian, Li = Lithuanian, No = Norwegian, Po = Polish, P = Portuguese, Ro = Romanian, R = Russian, Sk = Slovakian, Sn = Slovenian, Sw = Swedish, S = Spanish, Tr = Turkish, Uk = Ukrainian

(*Source:* www.ahk.de)

5. Language choice between businesses in German-speaking and non-German-speaking countries

Business contacts between German-speaking and non-German-speaking countries and regions exist on many levels. It will be important to distinguish between such levels if we are to understand how they interact. This chapter concentrates on communication between firms based in German-speaking countries and those with their head office in a non-German-speaking country. Communication between head offices in German-speaking countries and subsidiaries abroad (see Ch. F.6), communication between head offices outside German-speaking countries with subsidiaries in German-speaking countries and those in countries with the same language will not be considered. Language choices in such "external business contacts" depend on a multiplicity of circumstances. Legal regulations may be relevant (Bungarten 2001: 28), such as the rigorous provisions on the use of French based on *Loi 101* in Québec (Much 2008: 28). But to some extent, merely practical conditions, such as the availability of language skills, also play a role. For example, if both sides speak the national official language of one partner but not of the other, this language will generally be chosen. The approximate distribution of such language skills can be inferred from the statistics for foreign language learning in individual countries (see *Sociolinguistica 24* (2010)). This also influences the "traditional language choice in mutual relationships" established between countries (Bungarten 2001: 31) which impact on the current "correspondence languages" (Ch. F.3). Added to these factors are the potential market roles of participants (supplier/seller – consumer/buyer; Ch. F.2), which, as has often been emphasised, are significant for language choice: "If you wish to buy from us, there is no need to speak German. But if you wish to sell to us [...]" (German Trade Minister) (Lo Bianco 1987: 53). However, the data for actual language choices in international business contacts do not fit seamlessly with these hypotheses, possibly because they occasionally act in opposite directions. For example, foreign-language skills may contradict the distribution of market roles. Imagine the case in which language Lb (of country B) is not learnt in country A, but language La (of country A) is learnt there, however, firms from A export (sell) more to B than vice versa. A rough guide is provided by the results from a questionnaire on foreign-language needs of small and medium-sized companies in 29 European countries, mostly in the EU, implemented by *ELAN* (2006) on behalf of the European Commission. The report also gives pointers relating to language choice, according to which English is used "for trade in more than 20 different markets, including the four English-speaking countries UK, USA, Canada and Ireland. German is used for export in 15 markets (including Germany and Austria); Russian is used for trade with the Baltic states, Poland and Bulgaria; and French in 8 markets, including France, Belgium and Luxembourg". The reason given for English not enjoying the absolute domination which might be expected is that "wherever possible companies tend to use the home language of the export market" (ibid: 23. Further details on *ELAN* in Ch. F.6).

However, one investigation by Sonja Vandermeeren (1998) which distinguishes between three strategies for international business contacts is more informative on the questions underlying this chapter (ibid: 36–47; in greater detail 1999): 1) "adaptation": use of the language (native language or official language of state) of the respective business partner; 2) "standardisation": exclusive use of a single language as lingua franca, generally English and 3) "non-adaptation": exclusive use of one's own language. With firms in English-speaking countries, standardisation and non-adaptation generally overlap – this is often diagnosed as "a lack of foreign-language skills" and considered obstructive to sales or the conclusion of business (e.g. *ELAN* 2006). But Vandermeeren's findings also point to other factors relevant for language choice. These are derived from a questionnaire, supplemented by interviews, on the use of German between firms from Germany and firms from different, non-German-speaking countries (1,611 questionnaires issued, between 25% and 31% returned from each country (Vandermeeren 1998: 142–144). The question (in the respective questionnaire language) was: "How often does your firm use the named languages in business contacts with the following countries? Please circle for each country and each language: 0 = never, 1 = seldom, 2 = regularly, 3 = always". The specified responses were: "language of the country", "English", "German" – with no other responses possible (ibid: 295).

The most important findings from this questionnaire are shown in Figure F.5–1. They do not correspond exactly with expectations. The most surprising result is the frequent use of German, which does not agree with the "correspondence languages" of the German business economy registered by the Hamburg Chamber of Commerce (2005, also 1989) (Ch. F.3; Map F.3–1). According to the sources, firms in Germany should not have used German with firms from Italy, France, Spain and Portugal, and firms from France and Portugal should not have used German with firms in Germany. Presumably, companies in the non-German-speaking countries considered themselves in the role of supplier rather than buyer. This would also explain the more frequent use of German with German companies than vice versa in the comparison between the two communication directions for the Netherlands, Hungary, France and Portugal.

Firms from Germany in contacts with firms in non-German-speaking countries

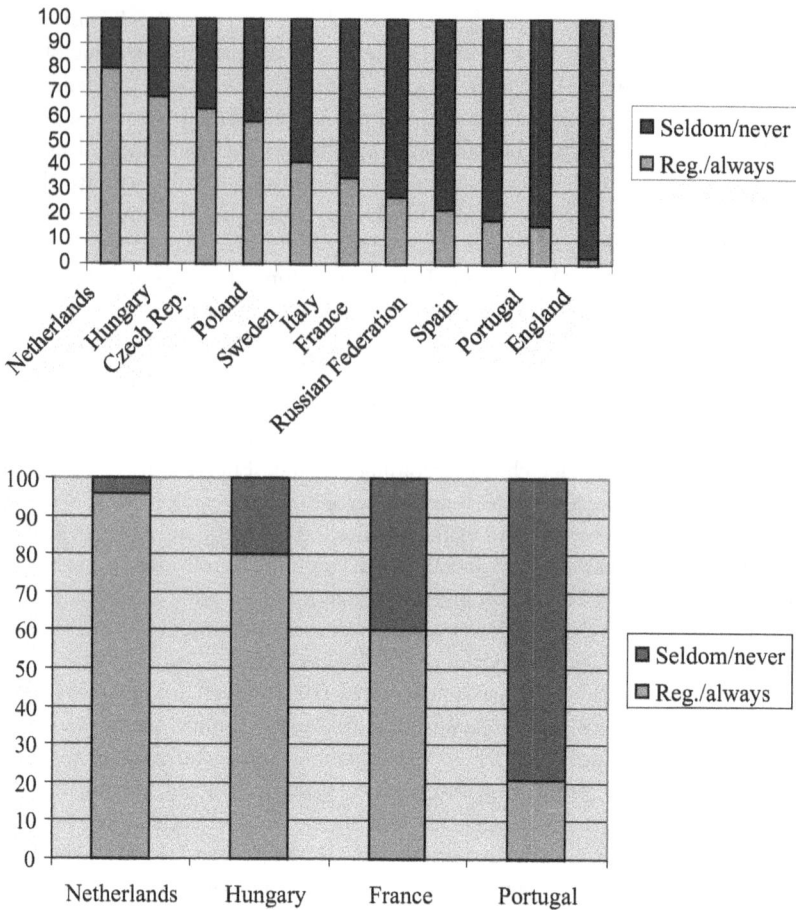

Figure F.5–1 Use of German between firms from Germany and various non-German-speaking countries in Europe

(*Source*: based on questionnaire; Vandermeeren 1998: 242f)

Firms from non-German-speaking countries in contacts with firms in Germany

Vandermeeren (e.g. 1999) is surprised that, "[A]ccording to respondents' reports, the type of business relationship (buying or selling) appears to have only a minor influence (only 5 to 15%). This contradicts the repeatedly voiced opinion that firms tend to use the national language of their business partner when the latter is in the role of buyer" (ibid: 129). However, the results also suggest that, with companies from Germany, firms from non-German-speaking countries tend to choose German as follows:

a) If their own language has a relatively weak international position (the Netherlands, Hungary compared with France, Portugal);

b) If their country is geographically closer to Germany (France compared with Portugal);

c) If their own language is structurally close or related to German (the Netherlands compared with Hungary).

Similarly, for the choice of German by German firms, the findings show that they tend to choose German with firms from countries:

a) Whose language has a weak international position (the Netherlands, Hungary, Czech Republic, Poland, Sweden by comparison with England, Portugal, Spain, Russian Federation, France or Italy);
b) Which are geographically closer to Germany (e.g. France compared with Portugal, Spain);
c) Whose language is structurally close or related to German (the Netherlands compared with Hungary, also Czech Republic, Poland).

Beyond this, other factors are suggested, such as the tradition of language choice between the countries; degree of acceptance of English as absolutely dominant international business language; and, trivially, the scope of German-language skills in the population (e.g. percentage of population, ≥ 15-year-olds who can converse German in 2005: the Netherlands 66, Czech Republic 31, Sweden 28, Poland 19, Hungary 16, France 7, UK 6, Italy 4%, Portugal and Spain both <0.5 – no figures for Russia: europa.eu.int/comm/public_opinion/archives/ebs/ebs_237. en.pdf: 4). Accordingly, at least the following factors for language choice between firms in countries with different languages deserve closer investigation:

i)   Relationship between business roles (supplier–buyer);
ii)   International position of both languages;
iii) Geographical distance between the two countries;
iv)   Linguistic similarity (relatedness) of the two languages
v)   Degree of acceptance of English in the two countries;
vi)   Historical language-policy relationships between the two countries;
vii) Scope of knowledge of the other language in each case in the two countries.

If we consider more closely individual countries and the language choices of their companies in contacts with firms from German-speaking countries, geographical proximity initially seems to be a relevant factor – as suggested by the correspondence languages in the German business economy (Ch. F.3; Map F.3–1). One of many possible examples is the frequent use of German in the border regions between the Czech Republic and Germany since the fall of the Iron Curtain (Zich 2001: 33). Another example relates to the Netherlands: a high demand for German was found "in the German-Netherlands border region" (see Ch. F.6) (Frietman/ Buis/ Broekhoven/ Busse 2001), which also suggests corresponding use: 91% of Dutch companies in this region had a demand for German-language skills. However, the effect of geographical proximity also acts in the opposite direction, influencing the demand for Dutch-language skills on the German side, which "at 32%, is neck and neck with demand for French-language skills" (ibid: 33), and therefore considerably greater than elsewhere in Germany. Geographical proximity to Germany also promotes the learning of German and use of German in Alsace differently from the interior of France, although historical reasons must also be taken into consideration (Ch. E.4.3): "*Cette incitation à l'apprentissage de l'allemand est motivée par le souci de la direction de pouvoir rivaliser avec les concurrents allemands ou s'adapter à la langue des fournisseurs [. . .]*" (Bothorel-Witz/ Choremi 2009: 126). There is therefore a desire to retain linguistic competitiveness with nearby rivals.

The notion that greater geographical distance acts in an inverted direction is also supported by many findings. For example, South Korean and German firms hardly ever communicate in German but almost exclusively in English (KIM 2003). The non-use of German is also typical for German-Japanese business contacts, although Japan looks back on a long tradition of German learning (Ammon 1994d; Ch. F.9.14). The non-use of German can be assumed because of the meagre market demand for German-language skills in the Japanese employment market (Ammon/ Kato 1994c) or the minimal proportion of German in Japanese translation offices (Yamashita 1994). The results from one questionnaire issued to 120 branches of German companies points in the same direction (returns n = 77; 64%): "German business people in Japan speak German amongst themselves, but it does not play any significant role in the conduct of business". Not only do German business people prefer to speak English on location in Japan, but "in many cases, the use of German is discouraged" or "English is preferred although the use of German would be possible" (Coulmas 1994: 80f). The non-use of German between German and Japanese firms also suggests that Japanese firms based in Germany carry out successful business entirely without the use of German (Ch. F.8).

The use of German in bilateral contacts with companies from German-speaking countries is less clear in the enormous market of China. In view of the size difference between the countries and the comparatively modest tradition of learning German in China (Ammon/ Reinbothe/ ZHU 2007), the fact that German is also used is, in fact, surprising but is presumably a reflection of the late economic development of China and the fact that its position as a rising technological country has not yet been fully secured. Accordingly, based on a rigorous survey, Jin ZHAO (1999) reports widespread use of German in German firms based in China. However, more medium-sized firms than large firms (55.9% by comparison with 44.1%) participated in this survey (ibid: 584). Having said this, the following total frequencies for use of German were still identified: "as language of oral communication": "almost always" (20% of firms), "a large number" (14.3%) and "in some cases" (42.9%). The extent to which German firms use German especially in contact with Chinese firms remains an open question. Furthermore, in ZHAO's investigation, German firms in fact registered the frequency of use of English as higher than German (54.3%, 22.9%, 22.9%) (ibid: 586; further details in Ch. F.6). Yuqing WEI (2007) and Hans-Werner Hess (1992) recorded a decidedly low use of German between firms in China and Germany. Hess (2007: 340) summarises his – admittedly subjective – assessment as follows: "Internally or with Chinese partners, even German firms [in China! U.A.] tend to communicate mostly in English".

Higher expectations for the use of German in Russia may be justified because of the position of German as a correspondence language there (Ch. F.3; Map F.3–1). Olga Martynova (2010, 2011) questioned 108 German firms and 36 Russian firms; there were more German firms because of ease of access (although, as a Russian native speaker, she used both languages in her investigation). She found that German firms do communicate in German with firms in Russia, but they do so more often with their own subsidiaries than with purely Russian firms. Corresponding with Ch. F.2, she also confirmed that firms from Russia which export to Germany use German more often than German firms exporting to Russia (22.2% by comparison with 12.3%; Martynova 2011: 295; 210:147–150). However, her finding that larger German firms use more German than smaller firms (> 200 employees 39.9%, ≤ 200 only 18.6%; Martynova 2011: 295) does not agree with more general assessments. There are also peculiarities, such as a more frequent use of English in chemicals firms (69.2%; ibid: 296) and variable language choice in different situations (Martynova 2010: 152–168). Overall, and by comparison with Russian firms, German companies use more English and more Russian than German, primarily for contracts (ibid: 160). It is therefore not for nothing that German is only a *co*-correspondence language for all countries apart from Austria (Ch. F.3; Table F.3–2). Even for internal language tuition in German firms in Russia, German is not always ranked first. Although "Russian respondents [. . .] [would] actually prefer German", "English courses are provided more frequently than German

Table F.5–1 Frequency of use: "almost always/often" among the Finns responsible for German-Finnish trade in corporate subsidiaries in Finland and Germany

	Oral communication in Finland	*Oral communication in Germany*	*Written communication in Finland*	*Written communication in Germany*
German	76.4/6.7	93.8/2.1	73.6/11.3	97.9/1.0
English	12.0/11.0	1.0/6.3	12.6/15.3	1.0/7.3

(*Source*: percentage of respondents; Müntzel/ Tiittula 1995: 137–139)

courses by some [. . . German! U.A.] firms in their Russian branches". This is explained with reference to the value of a unified language of communication for the entire, international organisation (Martynova 2011: 299f.; also Ch. F.7).

A questionnaire on language choice in German-Finnish business contacts, carried out in 1994 by Ute Müntzel and Liisa Tiittula (1995: 126), was aimed at the "target group of [the] Finns in Finland and Germany responsible for Finnish-German trade". It included 326, primarily small, firms in Finland (744 issued, 44% returns) and 111 in Germany (322 issued, 34% returns) which were distributed in most industrial sectors. The findings are restricted to Finns, and do not include Germans. They indicate that "in all communicative situations, German is used most often, somewhat more in oral communication than in written communication". Alongside German, only English played a part, more often in Finland than in Germany, but Finnish and Swedish played almost no role (Table F.5–1).

Findings from an investigation by Ewald Reuter and Eila Minkkinen (2003) implemented in 2001 with 326 Finnish and 96 German firms are also significant here (ibid: 38f). Quite predominantly, these firms use German less in speech than in writing – according to size differences of the firms, this was the case in approximately one third of the small companies (≤ 9 employees), three fifths of the medium-sized firms (50–249 employees) and three quarters of the large firms (≥ 250 employees – the gap between small and medium-sized firms is presumably based on *de facto* employee numbers). With small companies, use [of German] in speaking was more frequent than in writing. However, there were signs of a decline in written use [of German]. By comparison with an earlier investigation "writing [in German! U.A.] seems to be perceived as problematic by a growing number of people". At least, only 32.5% of respondents found it problematic in Müntzel/ Tiittula (1995: 217), but in Reuter/ Minkkinen, the figure was already 45.6% (2003: 39). By contrast, there was no decline in competence in reading and text comprehension.

My own investigation in 1989 (Ammon 1991a: 155–162) provided a broader, but less clear picture of the situation 35 years ago. Primarily, it shows that, even at that time, German only played a subordinate role in international business contacts, and this was thought to be declining. Through the *Bundesverband der Deutschen Industrie* (BDI – Confederation of German Industry) and six of its member associations, I contacted 27 firms with strong international involvement, from which 15 usable responses were received. The report from the *Hauptverband der Deutschen Bauindustrie*, the National Confederation of the German Construction Industry (29 August 1989) was particularly informative, as the following excerpts show:

> Among the international organisations and associations with which we are in constant contact, English unambiguously plays the most important role. [. . .] Within Europe, French takes second place behind English. [. . .] In general, English-speaking and French-speaking decision makers are often inclined to think that other European

languages do not enjoy the same rights. For example, international documents produced under the leadership of an English-speaking or French-speaking decision maker are sometimes available only in these languages or, after a delay, in an [. . . often] very poor translation. [. . .] [Neglect of other languages – U.A.] is sometimes based on a reluctance by many decision makers to take the trouble to learn and work in a foreign language. However, competition certainly also plays an important part, because an intensified flow of information achieved through the medium of language also guarantees greater freedom for action. The possibility of constraining such rivals achieves a genuine competitive and active advantage for one side.

The firms questioned reported changes over recent decades in the language choices between German head offices and their foreign subsidiaries: nine shifted to English, 0 shifted to German, three no change (two no response). Two of the nine firms which reported a shift to English also reported shifts to other foreign languages, including 12 to French. However, one response considered that not only German, but also "French [has been] strongly pushed out" by the advance of English. Two companies indicated that communication with subsidiaries in the Far East and in Brazil was primarily in English – not Chinese, Japanese or Portuguese. A shift to German was not reported by any organisation.

Overall, these findings confirm a growing effort by German firms to equip themselves with foreign-language skills. At least, this tendency was found by Sigrid Schöpper-Grabe and Reinhold Weiß (1998) in a representative survey of German firms (663 responses from 5,089 questionnaires issued: return 13%; ibid: 28, 30, 35; also, Schöpper-Grabe 2009). 69.1% of firms reported a demand for – a total of 28 – foreign languages: from English to Romanian (Schöpper-Grabe/ Weiß 1998: 47). The demand was most urgent (and presumably also most comprehensive in terms of knowledge) in the fields of management, export, import, logistics and engineering (ibid: 54; for the term "foreign-language requirement" Ch. F.6). The most important measure for the fulfilment of this demand was the diverse internal provision of foreign-language tuition for employees (ibid: 61, 65, 71, 76, 86), followed by increases in the appointment of employees qualified in foreign languages (ibid: 76). Almost 50% of firms shared employees' costs for further foreign-language training (ibid: 91, 93). There was no significant difference between large and small firms in their effort to provide internal foreign-language skills (ibid: 125). It can be assumed that this trend will continue, that German firms will develop their foreign-language skills further and that their readiness to accommodate business partners in their own language will grow. Presumably, these developments would contribute to business success. However, the assumption that they could also be detrimental to the position of the German language is self-evident. Having said this, the possibility of a positive effect is not necessarily precluded. For example, better skills and increased use of foreign languages could lead to improved business success for German firms, so that their prestige, and therefore also that of their country and its language, would increase. In turn, this could motivate more people to learn German. I must, however, admit that the likelihood of such an effect seems slim.

To consider one further German-speaking country, recent investigations in Austria show a similar picture to Germany, if not entirely comparable. A survey by Sabine Archan and Helmut Dornmayr (2006) of 26,817 firms received responses from 2,017 (returns 7.5%; ibid: 39–41). Table F.5–2 gives an overview of responses to the question: "which language is used primarily for communication with non-German-speaking countries in existing business relationships?". The relatively frequent use of German, primarily in contact with Eastern Central Europe, corresponds approximately with the geography of German as the correspondence language for Germany (Ch. F.3; Map F.3–1).

Table F.5–2 Language choice of Austrian firms with business partners in non-German-speaking countries

	German	English	National language	Other language
USA	2	98	–	–
UK	3	97	–	–
China	5	92	3	1
Portugal	8	84	7	2
Russia	8	79	11	2
Latin America	6	75	17	2
Spain	8	21	20	1
Poland	24	67	8	1
B&H, Cr, S&M	29	59	11	1
France	12	54	31	3
Slovakia	37	54	8	1
Slovenia	39	53	8	1
Czech Republic	40	51	9	1
Italy	25	49	25	2
Hungary	47	45	8	1
Other countries	18	71	10	1

Note: B&H = Bosnia and Herzegovina; Cr = Croatia; S&M = Serbia and Montenegro; UK, USA: National language = English

(*Source*: Archan/ Dornmayr 2006: 51)

6. Demand for German-language skills in firms in non-German-speaking countries

Language planning and sociolinguistics do not generally use the terminology and concepts of classical market economics in the tradition of Adam Smith ([1776] 2003: Book 1), according to which the present chapter ought to evolve from the interplay between "supply" and "demand". More specifically, it would refer to a supply by companies of positions for which German-language skills are desired or required, and a market demand for such posts by people with corresponding skills who are prepared to work. In this context, the following basic rule applies: if the supply of posts is greater than the market demand from appropriate applicants, wages will increase because businesses will be competing for the applicants; by contrast, if fewer posts are offered than there are applicants in the market, wages will fall. Instead of basing the chapter on this approach, which would certainly allow many aspects of the topic to emerge more clearly, I shall adhere to the terminology used in existing investigations, which is conventional in socio-linguistics. According to this model, use of and demand for languages in the business economy are compared, but, even in empirical investigations, these are not always clearly distinguished from one another, and they do, in fact, correlate, which sometimes leads to an overlap with the preceding chapter F.5. Especially for foreign languages, use and demand are informative indicators for the position of languages in international business relationships. In this context, the objective "demand" (by firms) must not be confused with the subjective "need" (of individuals) to learn the language. Sometimes, the number of people who would like to learn a language exceeds the demand for knowledge of this language in firms or in society. Christ (1987: 213f.) further distinguishes the "need to learn" from the – once again objective – "market demand for learning" based on actual decisions to learn, which may correspond approximately with the supply of learning opportunities, primarily in schools. The business demand for a language is shown primarily in the posts (job opportunities) in firms, for which knowledge of the relevant language is desired or required. One indicator for this is e.g. the skills in the language required or desired in job advertisements. The present chapter relates primarily to jobs in the business economy (more than e.g. by government authorities) – but investigations of job advertisements are not generally consistent in this respect. They also generally fail to distinguish whether the jobs are offered by firms in the relevant country or by branches of foreign firms, e.g. in German-speaking countries. One parameter which is significant in this context is the "available knowledge of the relevant language" in the respective society (examples in Ch. J.9.2–J.9.15). Where discrepancies occur, it is possible to speak of a *knowledge surplus* or *unsatisfied demand*.

The question under discussion here relates primarily to the demand for foreign-language skills, in fact, for languages different from the respective official language of state or widely distributed native languages. For the remainder of the book, I shall therefore speak of *foreign-language demand*, the primary interest being in knowledge of German. Unfortunately, older research, e.g. in the Dutch tradition of Theo van Els and Maria Oud-de Glas (1983; also, Claessen/ van Galen/ Oud-de Glas 1978, 1979), has not been continued in recent decades, so it will not be possible to pursue historical developments fully here. However, even such historical investigations leave no doubt that English has been the globally dominant language for international business contacts for a considerable time. As revealed by job advertisements (e.g. Glück 1992; Ammon with KATO 1994; Augustin 2003c), the demand for a knowledge of English is correspondingly greater than for other languages. But it is not possible to infer from the available investigations whether this demand, based on the ubiquitous learning of English (Ch. J.7), can be satisfied more readily than the smaller demand for other foreign languages, because the figures are not appropriately differentiated.

One analysis of job advertisements by Helmut Glück (1992) gives a somewhat dated overview of the foreign-language demand in several European states. Since this study was about the international position of German, German-speaking countries are not considered. A total of 10,000 job advertisements with foreign-language requirements from the most representative newspapers were investigated (Table F.6–1). English is already clearly dominant everywhere except Hungary. There, as in Poland, there are impressive figures for German, as presumably also in large parts of Eastern Central Europe at that time, although these have now declined everywhere, falling far behind English. At least, this can be assumed, based on the general decline in the position of German in this region (Földes 2001a, b, 2002, 2004b).

A somewhat more recent overview of foreign-language demand in the European economy is given in the *ELAN* study (2006: "Impact of lack of foreign-language skills in companies on

Table F.6–1 The four foreign languages with highest demand in newspaper job advertisements in six European countries around 1990

	English	*French*	*German*	*Spanish*
UK	–	15.3	6.9	5.6
France	71.1	–	10.7	5.4
Italy	68.8	9.4	6.2	2.3
Spain	60.1	21.0	7.5	–
Hungary	36.7	3.4	40.0	0.0
Poland	46.4	6.6	25.6	0.8

Note: percentages by country

(*Source*: after Glück 1992)

the European economy"; summarised in Hagen 2010). The questionnaire included small and medium-sized enterprises (SMEs) in 29 European countries, mostly in the EU, but including e.g. Turkey. The return from 1,989 firms seems impressive but was proportionally modest: between 5.5% from Spain and 0.4% from the Netherlands (ibid: 74). Doubts about the representativeness of the findings imply doubts about the validity of the conclusions, primarily the level of economic damage caused by lack of foreign-language skills. I mention these doubts here, because they relate to an aspect of insufficient foreign-language demand, which is ignored in most investigations. My doubts about the damage assessment are twofold. Firstly, the survey question: "Is there a possibility that your company has ever lost an opportunity to secure an export order because of lack of foreign-language skills?" (ibid: 20), which is so suggestive that it seems almost impossible to answer in the negative. And yet it was affirmed by only 11% of firms. Secondly, the validity of the inference from the 11% affirmative responses is doubtful. These 11% are in fact related to the total exports of all companies of the relevant type (SME) in the EU and then registered as 11% losses. According to the inference drawn here, "the total losses for the EU economy caused by lack of foreign-language skills in the SME sector runs to approximately €100 bn per year" (ibid: 21). Apart from the 11% which was presumably exaggerated by the question, it has not been taken into account that the orders lost may have been taken over by competitor companies also in the EU and would therefore not be losses for the EU economy.

These conclusions do provide a stimulus for follow-on investigations, as does the differentiation into functions of use (Table F.6–2). It remains open whether what is involved here is an unsatisfied demand, which might be presumed in the case of the high figures for German and French (compared with English), because knowledge of them is not so widely distributed.

It is understandable that there is a greater demand for German in correspondence and for French in negotiations. But the demand for German skills in response to the question about languages "which firms must acquire in the next three years" is remarkable. The following percentages of firms named the following languages in this context: English 25.8%, German 17.8%, French 13.2%, Russian 11.7%, Spanish 6.6%, Italian 4.7%, Chinese 4.1%, Polish 2.7%, Arabic 1.8% and other diminishing percentages (ibid: 45; Hagen 2010: 27). The high figures for German and French by comparison with English suggest that what was expressed here was also unsatisfied demand. The reason proposed by *ELAN* is "that English is not distributed more widely" (demand and use), that firms are inclined, wherever possible, to use the home language of the export market, and if not, one of the leading European languages such as German or French" (ibid: 23).

The following overview of countries extends, as far as possible, around the world, taking into account considerable gaps in the data in some cases. There is a lack of comparative data for historical discussion (compare Ammon 1991a: 182–195) because many investigations, primarily of relatively small language communities, are published in languages to which I have no access.

Table F.6–2 Percentage of orders lost through inadequate knowledge of relevant languages in the named situations in SMEs in the EU

	English	*German*	*French*	*Italian*	*Russian*	*Chinese*
Negotiations	11	5	8	3	3	3
Correspondence	8	11	7	–	–	–
At trade fairs	–	–	3	–	–	–

(*Source*: after *ELAN* 2006: 22f.)

European countries frequently report a discrepancy between low learner or student numbers for German and relatively high market demand for knowledge of German in the economy. Outside Europe, the reverse is often the case.

In the **UK**, there have been complaints for decades about the greater demand for foreign languages than language skills sought by school pupils. The opinion-leading newspaper in this context is the *Guardian* (relevant article: www.scoop.it/t/language-teaching-and-learning-in-higher-education. I am grateful to Martin Durrell (email 6 September 2013) for this reference and must also thank Teresa Tinsley (2013) for the report on "demand and supply" of foreign languages in the UK, which paints a gloomy overall picture (ibid: 9 – emphasis in the original has been removed):

> There is strong evidence that the UK is suffering from a growing deficit in foreign-language skills at a time when globally, the demand for language skills is expanding. The range and nature of languages being taught is insufficient to meet current and future demand. Language skills are needed at all levels in the workforce, and not simply by an internationally-mobile elite. A weak supply of language skills is pushing down demand and creating a vicious circle of monolingualism. Languages spoken by British schoolchildren, in addition to English, represent a valuable future source of supply – if these skills can be developed appropriately.

Among the many findings in the report, the following is particularly interesting: "French and German are the two languages which are currently most sought-after, in some cases in combination with each other. In the more recent survey 15% of employers requested both French and German" (ibid: 57; similarly, 16%, in Mulkerne/ Graham 2011: 3). This finding is surprising in view of the regular media reports about Spanish as the preferred foreign language, with increasing learner numbers, whereas learner numbers for German and French have been on the decline for a long time, followed more recently by the figures for Japanese and Chinese (Coleman 2012). Interest in Spanish is often associated by the British press with holidays and South American lifestyle. By contrast, vocational benefits hardly play a role in British schoolchildren's foreign-language choices. In view of the earning potential for foreign-language skills in Great Britain, this motivation is not particularly surprising. Language skills clearly bring hardly any financial advantage: "The bad news for British graduates is that 'only in the UK is there apparently no income return to using a second language on-the-job'" (Williams 2011: 388, quoted in Coleman 2012: 14). This – evidently seriously investigated – finding also arouses scepticism about reports of damage allegedly caused to the British economy by a lack of foreign-language skills. Responding to the impression that English is the "world language", British schoolchildren seem to have lost sight of the practical purposes of foreign-language learning. In fact, this is based on an oversimplified view of the world, but critics tend towards the opposite exaggeration that "English-only" will rapidly encounter limits to communication outside the English-speaking world. These limits no doubt exist, but it is surprising how far it is possible to travel with only a knowledge of English (see Ch. F.8). In the past, Durrell (2004a: 29) noted excellent employment opportunities for people with a knowledge of German but he has recently corrected this with reference to Coleman (2012) (email 1 January 2013): the data, "which showed a very high employability for German, were unfortunately flawed for a number of reasons. In practice [. . .], the employability of modern-languages graduates is no better and no worse than that for other subjects".

Valuable information on the economic demand for German in **France** and conversely, the demand for French in Germany, is provided in an investigation by Christof Römer, Sigrid

Schöpper-Grabe, Anne Wegner and Reinhold Weiß (2004, also: www.europrofession.de/uploads/media/bilateraler_Fremdsprachenbedarf.pdf). It draws attention to one important finding: "The demand for a knowledge of French/German cannot be derived directly from the scope of customer relations. [. . .] Paradoxically, the demand for French skills turns out to be higher, the weaker business relationships with France are, because companies with a large share of the market in France can process customer business largely via their branches or subsidiaries abroad" (ibid: 36). The same applies for French companies and knowledge of German. On the French side, 35 of the largest companies were recruited for a telephone survey (of 55 companies contacted; returns: 64%); on the German side, 42 (of 50; returns: 71%). The most interesting finding here was: "for French firms [. . .], English is unambiguously the most important foreign language. [. . .] All the companies considered English to be very important [. . .]. This was followed by Spanish, which was classified, on average, as important to less important. German was classified as the third most important language, i.e. as less important" (ibid: 74). The "firms which considered German important pointed out that the 'German-speaking territory is the most important market [. . . for them! U.A.]'". Corresponding to the less pronounced demand, "only five companies [14%! U.A.] considered it necessary for senior employees to speak German" (ibid: 74f.). But eight of the French companies [23%! U.A.] recorded language-related "problems", and one company even spoke of "major problems" in contacts with German business partners (ibid: 76). A knowledge of German was required most by "head secretaries", "industrial management assistants", [. . .], "male and female sales staff in the divisions of communication/public relations" and "employees travelling to the two head offices" (ibid: 77). But most French firms found cultural differences more important and more difficult than purely linguistic differences (ibid: 80f.). However, more recent figures from France point towards a strengthening demand for German (received from Odile Schneider-Mizony, email 17 September 2013). The author is Frédéric Auria, president of the ADEAF (Association for the Development of German Teaching in France), who would perhaps also be seeking to promote the learning of German. Table F.6–3 lists the four most frequently "demanded" (*demandées*) foreign languages.

Recent, relevant data for **Italy** is not available (confirmed by Sandro Moraldo, email 31 August 2013). However, Goranko Rocco (email 10 October 2013) has given me references containing indirect pointers. Accordingly, Italian firms do not name a knowledge of German as a factor for their success in the German market. It remains an open question whether knowledge of German is so obvious to them that it does not deserve mention, or whether they manage (largely) without German, presumably using English as a lingua franca. In one report of a survey of 146 small and medium-sized Italian enterprises in 2008 and 2009, only the following sales-relevant factors were named, in this order: quality of products and services, meeting of deadlines, customer service and competitive price (German-Italian Chamber of Commerce 2010: 11).

I was unable to find any relevant investigations for **Spain**, not even through colleagues, the cultural officer for the German Embassy in Madrid, Max Meier, or the director of Personnel Service and Education of the German Chamber of Commerce for Spain, Marcelo Scocco (emails 10 October and 15 October 2013). Scocco added the following comment to his email,

Table F.6–3 The four foreign languages most frequently demanded in job advertisements in France

English	German	Italian	Spanish
29,430 (72%)	4,907 (12%)	3,468 (9%)	2,980 (7%)

Note: timespan 1 January–12 December 2012; percentages based on the four languages

"In enquiries from firms in Germany about the recruitment of specialist personnel from Spain, the topic of language is always important. They always expect candidates to speak German, which is unrealistic in most cases. Compromises are generally made, and many firms also accept that the candidates are prepared to learn German". However, this relates to a question which goes beyond the scope of the present chapter.

For the **Netherlands**, Kees de Bot and Theo van Els (emails: 10 September 2013 and September 2013) explained to me the low scholarly interest in the demand for foreign languages today by comparison with the grand tradition mentioned above (e.g. van Els/ Maria Oud-de Glas 1983). However, one relevant survey was carried out by local German representatives in 36 "employment and personnel agencies" (Schirbel et al. 2005). It showed the following proportions for the most frequently desired or required foreign-language skills: English 80.6%, German 13.9% and French 3%. Additionally, 44% of respondents claimed, "that knowledge of German is an advantage for jobseekers", and 34% claimed that they were "fully in agreement" and 90% "in agreement" with the statement: "Is it difficult today to find people who have adequate German-language skills?". In this context, the demand for German-language skills was assumed primarily in the fields of "engineering" (30.6% of respondents) and "purchasing and logistics" (25%) (ibid: 23–25). But this relatively high demand is reported less by Dutch people than by Germans. The survey can be described as among the attempts from Germany to promote the learning of German, as shown by the following appeal to the Dutch people: "As a Chamber of Commerce, we have received reports from firms for many years complaining about the lack of German-speaking personnel. That is why we now call upon Dutch schoolchildren to start learning German again, seriously and in the interests of the Dutch economy [. . .]" (www.dradio.de/dlf/sendungen/europaheute/1672011). The "start learning German *again*" is a reminder of better days in the past. Nowadays, most communication takes place in English instead of German or less frequently through polyglot dialogue, where both sides speak their own language and understand the other. It should not be forgotten that, for the Netherlands, Germany is by far the most important export market (24% of exports, ahead of Belgium with 12% and France 9% – in 2011. *Fischer Weltalmanach* 2013: 332). An investigation by Frietman/ Buis/ Broekhoven/ Busse (2001; see Ch. F.5) in the German-Netherlands border region also deserves further mention here: 91% of Dutch businesses reported a demand for German-language skills (ibid: 33), considerably higher than the demand for German elsewhere in the Netherlands. But by contrast with earlier times, a clear shift away from German towards English can now be assumed. For example, in the Netherlands in 1985, German-language skills were desired in 21.8% of job advertisements and English-language skills only in 30.2% (after Beermans 1987: 36), and, in 1983, 74% of Dutch managers questioned named German as "one of the two most important negotiating languages" (English 95%) and 95% "one of the three most important negotiating languages" (English also 95%) (Ulijn/ Gorter 1989). Contemporary surveys would certainly show considerably higher figures for English.

For **Belgium** as a whole, there are no recent investigations on the demand for foreign languages (email from Jeroen Darquennes 31 August 2013), apart from one not particularly informative study relating to Brussels (Mettewie/ van Mensel 2009). Firms in Brussels (sample n = 595) reported no demand whatsoever for German alone, only in combination with French, Dutch and English, i.e. one of four languages, and, in fact, only in two firms (0.3%). Having said this, there was also no reported demand for English alone, only in combination with at least French and Dutch, and only by 43 firms (7.2%) (ibid: 141). German was the only explicitly named foreign language alongside English, because French and Dutch are not considered foreign languages in bilingual Brussels. Moreover, a considerable number of firms reported the *de facto* use of German: 38.4% "using it outside the company and 27% inside [. . .], due to the importance of the markets located in Germany and Eastern Europe". 85.4% of companies reported the use of English; 16.8% Spanish and 8.7% Italian (ibid: 138). These findings suggest that, on the one hand, German cannot be replaced by English, but on the other hand, current demand is largely covered by existing skills. It is evident that German is still an important foreign language for the Belgian economy in view of its position as a regional official language of state (compare Ch. D.3.1) and because Germany is the most important export market (18% of exports, but closely followed by France with 17%, for 2011. *Fischer Weltalmanach 2013*: 58). The following comment by the investigators is also interesting, "Strikingly neither fashionable business languages such as Chinese, nor migrant languages do significantly appear in the companies' practices, contrary to neighbouring languages such as German" (ibid: 147). For these languages also, no demand was reported. Once again, individual pointers suggest an overall shift towards English. In the early 1980s, firms in Brussels still considered German of equal importance to English (Verdoodt/ Sente 1983: 278).

In **Norway**, there are indications of an economic demand for German skills at the same time as a declining interest in learning German. One example is the "two-year course in *Business German and International Commerce* in Halden, which offered 40 places in 1995 but only 15 in 2002". By contrast, there is very clearly an economic demand for German-language skills, "English has not pushed German out; German skills are still required in professional life". Enquiries at the local "Employment Office (AETAT) in February 2001 showed that the daily requirement for German is high: on average, there are 220 posts in which German-language skills are explicitly required in some form. There is therefore a clear discrepancy between the demand for German skills in job advertisements and the demand for places on German language courses [. . .]" (Kvam 2003: 73). There do not appear to be any more recent data.

The situation in **Iceland** is similar. For example, Oddny Sverrisdóttir (2003: 92–94; also 2005; Ögmundarson 2002), emphasises that, in view of intensive Icelandic business relations with Germany (e.g. 16.4% of Icelandic foreign trade in 2000), primarily based on the export of fish, trained personnel with German-language skills are "very much in demand" in Icelandic firms, but the supply is apparently insufficient. Intense frustration was therefore felt in Iceland about the closure, first, of the local Goethe-Institut in 1998 and then also of the trimmed-down Goethe Centre in 2006.

There may be differences in **Denmark** where, according to Martin Nielsen (2003: 105), people are aware of the limited size of their own language community (approximately 5.5 m speakers). "Spoken and written business communication with non-Danish speakers is therefore still conducted almost exclusively in the language of each respective communication partner". As a result, the introductory and advanced university courses "in business communication in German were renewed and adapted to the demands of modern corporate business in 1993 and 1996 respectively". In fact, it seems as if learning German is largely in agreement with requirements and market demand for German in the Danish economy. At least, the relatively high level of German skills in firms, which can be inferred from the figures for use of German, support this assessment. In a representative survey in the period 2006–2011, the following numbers of firms questioned confirmed their daily use of languages as follows: 169 English (42%), 134 German (34%), 72 French (18%) and 23 Spanish (6%) (Miller/ Jensen 2009: 90 – errors in percentages have been corrected here). These companies reported the greatest communication difficulties with French and Spanish, which they explain with reference to the fact that the French- and Spanish-speaking countries, especially Western Africa and Latin America respectively, lack English-language skills (ibid: 99–102). This suggests that a great deal of communication takes place in English, by far the preferred business language in Denmark, even with firms from German-speaking countries – and perhaps for this reason, the demand for a knowledge of German does not seem urgent. For example, Charlotte Rønhof (2010: 63) reports an "electronic questionnaire action" in conjunction with *Dansk Industri* carried out in autumn 2007: "English is the language that basically all enterprises use when they communicate and trade at the international market". Of 312 responding firms (return 32.6%), 267 (85.6%) had international business relationships. The most important findings for the present chapter are summarised below (report from Verstraete-Hansen 2008: 74f.; Summary 2010):

- "Small and medium-sized enterprises need primarily English (26.2%), followed by German (19.4%), Nordic languages (14.1%) and French (13.6%). 11.2% and respectively 10.7% indicate a demand for Chinese and Russian".
- "Large enterprises (with more than 250 employees) record a large future demand for Russian (21.3%), followed by Chinese (13.1%). English is indicated by 11.5% of respondents, while French (6.6%), Spanish (4.9%) and especially German (3.3%) are less strongly represented".
- "Almost 60% of the firms questioned (59.7% of the small and medium-sized enterprises and 57.4% of the large enterprises) use exclusively English in communication with their foreign trading partners [. . .]".
- "In total, 31.5% of the firms questioned (33.5% of the small and medium-sized enterprises and 24.6% of the large enterprises) report that lack of foreign-language skills has hampered international corporate activities. [. . .]".
- "Danish firms encounter language-related difficulties most frequently in China, followed by France, Germany and Russia".
- "In total, 41.4% of the firms questioned (41.3% of the small and medium-sized enterprises and 42.6% of the large enterprises) experience problems which they ascribe to lack of foreign-language competence among their foreign trading partners. [. . .].Inadequate or non-existent knowledge of English by foreign business partners is very frequently indicated as a reason [. . .]".
- "The firms questioned [. . .] consider foreign languages other than English the least necessary employee competence in international trading relations".
- "By contrast with technical, scientific, economic and legal knowledge, knowledge of languages is not considered sufficiently profitable to invest in".

Presumably, communication difficulties with German business partners are often ascribed to their inadequate knowledge of English (cf. for broken English in German business e.g. "Hallo, sis is Dieter koling"; "I understand only railway station", *FAZ* 12/13 October 2013: C1 and respectively 6 November 2013: 7). Accordingly, Danish firms often communicate with German firms in English, although sometimes with difficulty (see also Pogarell 2007). Comparison with earlier findings (e.g. Ammon 1991a: 186–188) indicates an increase in the use of English and therefore probably a decline in the demand for German.

There are no specific investigations on the demand for German-language skills for business in **Poland** (information from Ulrike Würz and Michael Falz, Goethe-Institut, Warsaw). However, Maciej Mackiewicz (email: 22 November 2013) found an analysis of language requirements in job advertisements on the Polish Job Portal <pracui/pl>, but only for the short timeframe from 1 January – 24 February 2013. The language skills required were distributed among the jobs advertised as follows: English 57.6%, German 12.2%, French 4.2%, Russian 2.0%, Spanish 1.9%, Italian 1.7%, Czech 0.8% and Swedish 0.5%. Here at least, German was in second position. Its importance for Poland can also be seen in the fact that Poland is now the country with the highest learner figures for German as a foreign language (2,345,480 or 2,288,125 in total, according

Table F.6–4 Language skills required in job advertisements in the Czech Republic 1997–2007

	Czech	English	German	French	Polish
1997	78	18	3	1	–
2002	75	24	1	–	–
2007	86	13	0.7	–	0.3

(*Source*: Nekula/Marx/Šichová 2009: 74)

to Netzwerk Deutsch 2010: 10 and respectively Auswärtiges Amt 2015: 14). The strong position of German is also evident in Mackiewicz's (2013) evaluation of the *Deutsch-Wagen-Tour* organised by the Goethe-Institut in Warsaw to promote the learning of German.

For the **Czech Republic**, there is one investigation on language skills required in job advertisements by Marek Nekula, Christoph Marx and Kateřina Šichová (2009: 73–82). It is based on an investigation by Nekula (2004), updated to 2,230 advertisements in total, all from the business magazine *Hospodářské noviny*. Since this is a panel survey, it also shows changes over time. The local official language was included in the evaluation (Table F.6–4).

The proportion of German is very low and declining, which the authors attribute partly to the fact that the magazine targets "white-collar" professions. In newspapers "with a stronger focus on 'practical' jobs or jobs without university qualifications and responsibility for personnel", there would apparently be a "stronger demand for German" (ibid: 78). This might be expected because of the strong "presence of German-Czech companies with German or German and English as company languages". "On the other hand, German-Czech firms can hardly break away from English as the lingua franca of a globalising economy [...]" (ibid: 80f). This was confirmed by Silke Gester (2011: 85) primarily for large firms. By contrast, a survey of German-Czech Chambers of Industry and Trade in February 2010 showed that "in small and medium-sized firms with German or Austrian participation" in the Czech Republic, "German-language skills were classified as more important than English skills" and "[t]hree quarters of the firms questioned" regarded "a knowledge of German among their employees" as a "very important qualification", contrasted with only 40% for a knowledge of English (ibid: 86).

The investigation by Ute Müntzel and Liisa Tiittula (1995, already referenced in Ch. F.5) on the *use* of German between **Finland** and Germany says relatively little about the *demand* for German skills in Finnish business – because the sole "target group was Finns in Finland and Germany responsible for Finnish-German trade" (ibid: 126). However, it is worth mentioning that the traditional dichotomy of business communication into correspondence and negotiations has been blurred by the new media, because even correspondence, via email and smart phone, is increasingly carried out by management personnel instead of secretaries. The respondents, who were mostly management personnel (managing directors, directors), generally had and needed German-language skills. For the specialist group investigated, it was found that "German is most often used in all communication situations, in spoken communication somewhat more than in written communication" – ahead of English, Finnish and Swedish, in this order (Table F.6–5). However, employees working in Finland also use English significantly more often than those who work in Germany.

For **Estonia**, Viktoria Umborg (2003: 127) obtained the following percentages for foreign-language skills required in newspaper job advertisements in: English 62, Russian 38, German 15, Finnish 9, Swedish 1. Based on a questionnaire, she also investigated the frequency of use of foreign languages in Estonian firms (Table F.6–6). This gives the impression that – at least at the

Table F.6–5 Frequency of use "almost always" by Finns responsible for German-Finnish trade in corporate branches in Finland and Germany

	German	English	Finnish	Swedish
Oral communication in Finland	76.4	12.0	4.3	0.9
Oral communication in Germany	93.8	1.0	2.1	–
Written communication in Finland	73.6	12.6	3.1	0.9
Written communication in Germany	97.9	1.0	2.1	2.1

(*Source*: percentage respondents; after Müntzel/ Tiittula 1995: 137–139)

Table F.6–6 Number of firms questioned in Estonia with relevant foreign-language use

	English	German	Russian	Other
As main foreign language	63	20	8	0
As additional foreign language	95	66	71	13

(*Source*: after Umborg 2003: 133)

time of the investigation – adequate German-language skills were available in firms, because use is proportionally higher than requirements and market demand. Presumably, a relatively large number of German-speakers are still available from the Soviet period with its comprehensive learning of German, so that the current demand is covered. This may change in future.

For **Russia**, the only relevant data are sketchy, unrepresentative and merely give a vague idea of the economic demand for German-language skills. In her questionnaire of 108 German and 38 Russian firms, Olga Martynova (2011; also 2010) found a clear preference for English over German. This occurs primarily in negotiations and agreements "for reasons of legal security: the INCOTERMS definitions and rules (*International Commercial Terms*) are apparently relied upon, so that, instead of two versions of the contract (one column in Russian, one in German), for which translators are needed, a unified, English version, is provided, which, in the opinion of these companies, excludes legal misunderstandings" (Martynova 2011: 298). The priority of English over German is also likely to be maintained in future. German firms predict that English will be used approximately three times as often in German-Russian business contacts as German or Russian; and Russian companies predict that English will be used approximately 2.4 times as often as German and 5 times as often as Russian (ibid: 299: Table 2). The account by Natalia Troshina (2011: 227f.), which emphasises that "business English courses are prescribed and generally also paid for by the company, especially for Russian specialist personnel employed in major internationally active German, Austrian and Swiss firms". "However, a knowledge of German is also an important prerequisite for further promotion" (similarly Troshina 2013: 484–486). The recommended "spectrum of activities" for German learners at the Moscow State University for Linguistics (MGLU) also suggests this rank ordering of languages and therefore also the demand in business (although German is a special focus of teaching and research at the MGLU). In this context, Olga Titkova (2011: 2008): writes "Students are prepared [...] to begin with English, but also hope to be able to use German in their work". In part-time work, alongside their studies, "85.5% of students in the higher semester [...] use English", and "30% use German". Finally, Oleg Radschenko (2011a: 288), emphasises that future Russian bank managers, whose training is financially funded by German businesses, are trained at the "Frankfurt School of Finance and

Management predominantly using English [. . .] – as might be assumed, based on the demand for this knowledge of language in German-Russian business contacts".

For **China**, Jun HE (email: 17 November 2013) reported a lack of "studies with secure and wide-ranging data" on foreign-language demand in business. If the "number of foreign-language departments in Chinese universities" is taken as an indicator, the following "approximate top-5 list is obtained for foreign-language demand in China [. . .]: 1. English 2. Japanese 3. French 4. German 5. Spanish". I believe the correctness in positioning French ahead of German, especially for business, should be checked. This is not impossible if one thinks beyond Europe to the countries with French as an official language, for example, Québec or Western Africa, and the Chinese interests there. But, the stronger position of French over German is primarily in diplomacy (Ch. H.3; H.4.2). HE added that he:

> presumes [. . .] a knowledge of French is rewarded more by French firms than a knowledge of German by German firms. To my knowledge, Chinese employees in French firms tend to enjoy language training after their start of employment, so that they can use French in future, e.g. on a business trip to France, because it is well known that, when faced with non-native speakers, French people do not like to resort directly to English. By contrast, in international communication, Germans are much more prepared to make the language shift from German to English.

The investigation by Jin ZHAO (1999 – see Ch. F.5) which is, however, limited to German firms in China, including participations in Chinese firms, provides the most likely pointers towards the demand for German in China. Of the 70 mostly small and medium-sized firms addressed, 35 responded to the questionnaire (return 50%; ibid: 584), but demand can only be inferred conditionally from the *de facto* use reported in the questionnaire. German is used more in speech than in writing, primarily in "informal meetings" (40% of companies), "negotiations" (24.3%), "discussions" (26.8%) and "telephone calls" (29.3%). However, for all communication situations, English was named significantly more often (56.1%–62.2%); the difference was slight only in the case of informal meetings (English 43.8%). English was especially dominant in "corporate representations" and "product presentations": 71.9% and 78.6% of the situations while only in 15.6% or respectively 10.7% German. Chinese was used, in general, less often than German (but most often in discussions: 17.1%; ibid: 587). In writing, English was even more prominent than in speech ("almost always" 54.3%, "a great deal" 25.7% of firms – by comparison with German 14.3%, 17.1% and Chinese 5.7%, 11.4%; ibid: 588). However, there does seem to be a demand for German, to the extent that it is possible to infer demand from use. This applies especially in respect of the firms' specific "business area" (ibid: 590f). Having said this, the companies emphasise that there is virtually no demand for an exclusive knowledge of German or German Studies; at the very least, business management and a basic knowledge of economics are said to be additionally required (ibid: 593).

The priority position of English applies even more strongly in **Japan** (Coulmas 1994; Ch. F.5). In 1991/92, with the support of Noaki KATO, I analysed 6,836 job advertisements in the *Japan Times* (Ammon with KATO 1994c: 106–112). However, the proportion of English in this English-language newspaper was presumably especially high (Table F.6–7).

Even with the help of colleagues in Japan, I was not able to find any more recent investigations. However, all colleagues I contacted agreed that the demand and scope for the learning of Chinese has subsequently risen, moving to the second position. The learning of Spanish has apparently also increased, while French and German have declined – without any clear changes in demand. Shinishi Sambe (email: 02 October 2010) wrote to me that the current need for foreign-language skills is not considered "a serious question in Japan, but, [. . .], it is simply that

Table F.6–7 Required or desired foreign-language skills in job advertisements of the *Japan Times* 1991–1992

English	French	German	Spanish	Italian	Chinese
90.36	3.19	2.95	1.45	0.73	0.53

Korean	Russian	Portuguese	Cantonese	Thai
0.36	0.34	0.15	0.10	0.10

(*Source*: percentage in advertisements with foreign-language requirements; after Ammon with KATO 1994c: 108f)

Table F.6–8 Required or desired foreign-language skills in job advertisements in South Korea, in the news-paper *Chosun Ilbo* in 2000 and in the Internet 2000 and 2001

	English	Japanese	Chinese	German	French	Spanish	Russian
Chosun Ilbo 2000	69.9	20.8	6.0	1.5	1.1	07	–
Internet 2000–2001	70.7	23.8	3.6	0.7	0.7	0.2	0.2

(*Source*: percentage in advertisements with foreign-language requirements; after Augustin 2003c: 150f)

no language other than English is useful in the field of business". "Subsidiaries of German firms in Japan are also only very slightly interested in job applicants' German-language skills. For example, in the branch offices of Lufthansa or Daimler-Benz in Tokyo, there is only a single post, for which very good knowledge of German is required, namely, the secretary of the German director. As a result, professional opportunities for successful learners are also very slight". "Hardly anybody in Japan learns German for business reasons. German tends to be learned as a language of culture. In fact, that is the weakness and the strength of German teaching in Japan". The absence of relevant investigations, in which anyway "English would be the only winner", has been confirmed for Japan by Fumiya HIRATAKA (email: 08 November 2013). But I am assuming that there is also an economic demand for Chinese.

For **South Korea**, Matthias Augustin (2003b) carried out an analysis of job advertisements based on the methodology of Ammon with KATO (1994c), with samples from the newspapers *Korea Times* and *Chosun Ilbo* from 1996–2000 and from the Internet in 2000 and 2001. From his many tables, I have selected two typical findings for Table F.6–8, the content of which diverges only slightly.

According to various sources, the proportion of Chinese has also recently grown in South Korea. It now ranks ahead of Japanese but remains clearly behind English. German and French have lost ground – to the extent that this was still possible.

To jump now to the **USA** in North America, only relatively old statements and requirements are available on the topic of "foreign-language demand in the economy" but no investigations. For example, a call for foreign-language learning from 1992 by Geoffrey M. Voght and Ray Schaub entitled "Foreign Language Needs in Today's Business World" gave the following advice: "Although English is widely used in European business, it is still not seen [as] a totally international language. In France and Germany, for example, it is necessary to use French and German. In a survey of leading executives in European countries, only 31% reported using English for professional purposes. Increasingly, English alone cannot be used to penetrate the non-English speaking markets" (voices.yahoo.com/foreign-language-needs-todays-business-world-312373. html). But the "increasingly" is questionable here, because there are few signs that English is in the process of relinquishing its aptitude for opening European markets.

The lack of recent, relevant investigations for the USA has been confirmed by colleagues (emails: Herbert Arnold 31 August 2013; Tom Lovik 2 September 2013). In a similar vein, Helga Bister-Broosen (email: 05 September 2013) added "that everywhere, foreign-language programs are being reduced, combined with other programs or completely abolished", which suggests that there is no significant demand. However, learning German as a foreign language has stabilised (Ch. J.9.10). According to José Camacho (oral communication 25 September 2013), the dominant view in the USA is that the economic demand for foreign-language skills takes care of itself and therefore does not merit scholarly investigation; the trend is rather towards investigating foreign-language demands for military purposes. Although Spanish is by far the foreign-language learnt most in the USA, discussions of demand in the business economy focus almost exclusively on Chinese.

In Latin America also, there are apparently no investigations of foreign-language demand, at least not in the major countries. This was confirmed for **Mexico** by Rainer E. Hamel, whose investigations have ranged widely (email: 17 October 2013). The same applies to Joachim Steffen's work (emails: 14 and 22 October 2013) in **Brazil**, which includes information from the Chamber of Commerce Abroad (AHK, Martin Gebhard) and the Goethe-Institut in Porto Alegre (Adrian Kissmann) and São Paulo (Eva Fiedler). Further evidence for the low level of interest in German for business in Brazil is the fact that in recent years, the Goethe-Institut in Porto Alegre has offered courses in business German three times, for which there was not a single applicant. Such an extremely low learning need suggests with some certainty a lack of demand. However, this is compatible with the fact that the market demand for other forms of German learning has recently risen (Ch. J.9.11).

The situation in **India** is similar (cf. Ch. J.9.12). After concluding my own research without results, I addressed the following question to colleagues at the University of Pune: "Do you know of any recent investigations on foreign-language demand in India? Which foreign languages are especially important for Indian business? Some indications might be found e.g. in analyses of job advertisements with requirements/desire for foreign-language skills – but also, of course, in surveys of companies". In general, the answers amounted to "As far as I can see, there has not been a study about the question you asked either by the IGCC [Indo-German Chamber of Commerce! U.A.] in Pune or by any other Germanists". Anja Hallacker agreed with this message from Swati Acharya (both emails: 11 October 2013) and added by way of explanation: "for large firms such as BASF and Siemens, the company language, even in Germany, is English. For medium-sized enterprises, the company language at home is, in fact, German, but the interfaces between parent companies and subsidiaries in Pune are few and far between and are generally processed solely by the German director. Big firms like Volkswagen, where the company language at home is German, provide in-house training in German for qualified employees in Pune".

In the Pacific region also, there seem to be no recent investigations on foreign-language demand. For **Australia**, this was confirmed by Gabriele Schmidt (email: 02 September 2013). The lack is presumably attributable "to the fact that [. . .] 'the rest of the world speaks English'" – at least, this view is widespread "down under". At all events, "official government guidelines [. . .] have underlined the importance of Asiatic languages". One example is the document published under the leadership of the former prime minister, Kevin M. Rudd: *Asian Languages and Australia's Economic Future. A Report Prepared for the Council of Australian Governments on a Proposed National Asian Languages/Studies Strategy for Australian Schools* (February 1994: Queensland Government Printer). The "White Paper" published in 2012 emphasises the benefits of Asiatic languages in similarly strong tones (asiancentury.dpmc.gov.au/white-paper). However, there is a lack of academic evidence on the demand for Asiatic languages here as elsewhere (email: Brian Taylor 18 September 2013).

The same applies for **New Zealand**, from where Kristina McGuinness-King (email 9 September 2013), who could also find no recent investigations of demand, sent me the following assessment by Judith Geare, language officer at the Goethe-Institut in Wellington: "I cannot (alas) think of any study since Geoffrey Waite's *Aoteareo: Speaking for ourselves*. There is a definite push from somewhere for Chinese and Spanish, but I don't think it is based on any academic research, rather the number of speakers and NZ's position in the Pacific with South America to the right and China to the left (geographically speaking!). ILEAP in Auckland (International Languages Exchanges [&] Pathways [a language-advisory institution financed by the government! U.A.]) has a broader focus, and there are still advisers in the 5 key languages: Chinese, French, German, Japanese, Spanish [. . .]". The study by Waite (1992) is concerned primarily with language problems of the Maori.

Despite its incompleteness, this overview of countries around the world reveals some overarching trends. While a business demand for German-language skills appears in the geographical proximity to the German-speaking countries, it loses significance at greater distance. Just compare the UK or even Russia with Japan or Australia. The difference is also apparent in the motivation to learn German. For instance, Galina Voronina in Russia found that the motive "Knowledge of German will secure good employment for me" was ranked at the top with a safe margin" and – not quite in agreement with other findings (e.g. Radschenko 2011a: 289) – "100% of respondents" in the same investigation, will find "good employment [t]hanks to their knowledge of German [. . .]" (Voronina 2011: 280 and respectively 283f). By contrast, in Japan (email: Sambe 02 October 2010) or Australia (G. Schmidt 2011), employment prospects play virtually no role – while "cultural interests" – however these are understood – are clearly in the foreground (see also Ch. J.9.14; J.9.15). Moreover, regardless of geographical distance from the German-speaking countries, vocational aspects of learning German hardly play a role in English-speaking countries because of the widespread belief that English can always be used everywhere. The fact that this belief is exaggerated, is revealed by the – albeit limited – demand in the British economy. Other findings show that the tendency towards communication in English in firms in German-speaking countries restricts the demand for a knowledge of German. Conversely, inadequate knowledge of English in German firms (or even lack of readiness to communicate in a foreign language) does occasionally hamper their communication with foreign companies. As a result, a split can appear in the demand for German skills, which is shown e.g. in Denmark (see above), but presumably also elsewhere. The actual situation is often unclear, because investigations do not distinguish between the "total demand for German skills in business" and the "unsatisfied demand (caused by lack of German-language skills)". German firms increasingly accommodate foreign business linguistically by providing themselves with skills in their partners' languages (Schöpper-Grabe/ Weiß 1998, 2000), but also by making English into the company language (Vollstedt 2002; Hauschildt/ Vollstedt 2002; Much 2008). The next chapter addresses this last tendency, which is motivated and determined more generally by the globalisation of the world economy.

7. Language planning and internal communication in German firms

This chapter investigates developments in internal business communication resulting from the expansion of businesses abroad – especially into non-German-speaking regions. Internationalisation of business is one component of "globalisation" (see e.g. Beck 1997). Companies involved in this development quickly experience the limitations of the official language of their own country. Even firms of English-speaking countries may find that their "world language" has not reached everywhere yet (Crystal 2003; Graddol 2006). However, countries of second-rank international languages (Ch. A.7), including German, suffer the geographical limitation more painfully, and it is felt more acutely still by countries with smaller language communities. In this context, an effect described in general terms by Theo Bungarten (2001: 24f.) occurs:

> Language and its targeted, instrumental use in communicative actions is an economic cost factor in the business economy, just like raw materials, production, distribution and transport costs, and the cost of services. We describe these costs as communication costs. [...] Economic partners who can use their native language in business exchanges therefore need to meet smaller communication costs than trading partners for whom the trading language is a foreign language (training costs for acquisition of the foreign language, ongoing language-training costs, operational costs for translators and interpreters, or the appointment of employees with foreign-language competence [and!] costs for delay in the transfer of information relevant to the business [...]).

Such costs are incurred through internal as well as external business communication, especially in the case of corporate sections in foreign-language speaking countries. They form part of the "transaction costs" which are "significantly lower in national than in international enterprises" (Hausschildt/ Vollstedt 2002: 175). These costs are among the "frictional losses" of commerce (Picot 1993: 4194f.), which can be minimised by the planning of company languages, often through the addition of English or a shift towards English.

The urgency for language-planning provisions also depends upon corporate structure. In this context, the distinction between large, medium-sized and small enterprises is important. According to the definition of the European Union in 2005, businesses which employ up to 250 people with an annual turnover not exceeding €50 million are considered medium-sized by contrast with large enterprises; small enterprises employ up to 50 people with a turnover of €10 million (www.hk24.de/standortpolitik/mittelstandspolitik/367862/mittelstand_definitionen.html). In an online survey of such medium-sized enterprises in Germany in autumn 2008/spring 2009 (effective sample n = 79), Strobel/ Hoberg/ Vogt (2009) found that a high value was placed on language skills: 95% placed "very high value on good German skills" among their personnel; only 24% on corresponding skills in English (ibid: 180). However, for the question, "which languages will play an important role in your own firm in the foreseeable future, firms gave approximately equal importance to English (45%) and German (43%) (ibid: 182). Since 31% saw "certainly no disadvantage" and 43% saw "no real disadvantage [...] by comparison with firms from English-speaking countries", i.e. a total of 74% (ibid: 184), only a minority, it seems, felt the need to introduce English as their company language. The preference for German is confirmed by branches of medium-sized enterprises in German-speaking countries abroad. A corresponding survey "in small and medium-sized enterprises with German or Austrian participation" in the Czech Republic in February 2010 "even showed that knowledge of German was classified as more important than knowledge of English" (Gester 2011: 86; Ch. F.6). The situation in large enterprises is different: "For a long time now, powerful global players like Siemens or Continental have agreed [...] on English as the language [even! U.A.] for internal corporate communication" (ibid: 85).

For these large firms also, the extent to which English is used depends upon corporate structure. Inspired by Howard Perlmutter (1969), Marina Vollstedt (2002: 108–120) has proposed distinct corporate types as a basis for understanding this correlation. This typology is based on the relationship between the parent company and subsidiaries abroad, the focus of interest here being parent companies in German-speaking countries or regions with subsidiaries in non-German-speaking regions abroad. The typology rises from the lowest level of internationalism of companies to the highest. An "ethnocentric" corporate structure is accordingly orientated entirely towards the parent company which has exclusive responsibility for strategic planning. In this context, subsidiaries abroad hardly have any contact with one another. This structure is typical for small to medium-sized enterprises which operate only distribution companies abroad but not production facilities. Communication between the parent company and subsidiaries abroad is almost exclusively in the "language of the parent company". This can lead to local communication difficulties if there are no well-qualified, on-site bilingual mediators (Vollstedt 2002: 111f). Such difficulties are reduced in a "polycentric" corporate structure, where subsidiaries abroad have greater autonomy and management personnel who know the local "on-site language" but generally also the language of the parent company. Accordingly, the parent company must also have knowledge of the on-site languages at its disposal, especially if subsidiary production companies attain an important position in the firm. By contrast, in an ethnocentric corporate structure, "only a small number of employees participate in international communication", which remains orientated towards the head office (ibid: 113–116). Polycentric structures can be further differentiated into "region-centric" or "geocentric" structures. Region-centric structures extend across international regions, while geocentric structures extend around the globe (ibid: 116–119). Within this framework, there are also gradations and fluid transitions.

But the company language is also influenced by other factors, e.g. legal provisions in individual countries (e.g. compulsory French in Québec) or by resistance from personnel for reasons of linguistic pride, because their own language is an identity symbol (Bungarten 2001: 32f.; also, end of this chapter). Having said this, there is still an overarching tendency for the languages of the head office to lose importance as internal company languages gradually, in the sequence (rank ordering) of the typology outlined above. With an ethnocentric structure, the language of the head office is still completely satisfactory for internal corporate communication, although other languages become necessary for foreign contacts (cf. Ch. F.2). This also applies at the lowest level of the region-centric structure, provided the subsidiaries remain entirely orientated towards the head office. But with the loosening of the head office-orientated structure and especially in the case of a geocentric structure with growing autonomy of corporate elements abroad, this all changes. If the language of the head office is English, it may still be adequate, but a second-rank international language, such as German (Ch. A.7) can no longer meet the requirements. In general, English then tends to be adopted as the company language and is sometimes even declared the sole language throughout the company. With growing autonomy of corporate elements, management positions in the individual sites are occupied by local employees, because "having locals in top jobs can be a boon in foreign markets" (*The Economist* 24 June 2006: 73–76, see 74). They are more familiar with conditions in the local market, and through them, the local languages in the subsidiaries gain importance. Under some circumstances, a knowledge of German is then no longer required for all employees, not even in job advertisements, because this expectation may scare off well-qualified applicants who have no German.

For many firms, the language question is a problem laden with conflict. Thomas Much (2008: 58; in more detail 58–60) found that "most of the firms contacted in the region of Essen and Düsseldorf" were already "reluctant from the start" about an investigation of their company languages and language planning. The potential disclosure of language or communication difficulties could create a negative image, as would the discovery of inadequate knowledge of English among leading employees. "Since language skills – at least a knowledge of English – nowadays constitute an indispensable additional qualification for specialist and management employees, no one is prepared to admit to problems in this respect. Consequently, the topic is taboo in many companies, and no active attempts are made to resolve it" (Vollstedt 2002: 55). Rulings intended to strengthen English could also come into the crossfire of language-preservation activists, e.g.

the *Verein Deutsche Sprache* (VDS) (Ch. K.3.4), which has an influential media presence. Possibly because of such concerns, existing studies of these problems have been unsatisfactory. For example, I was not able to gain a reliable overview of company languages in Germany. Individual reports, such as that the major book publisher "Bertelsmann AG has published an increasing number of English books since 1999" and has thus "made English the official corporate language" or that after the "merger of the HypoVereinsbank with a major Italian bank Unicredito in November 2005, English has become the official language of communication" (www.dw.de/ herausforderung-englisch-als-unternehmenssprache/a-1805008, 11.12.2005) do not provide an adequate basis.

One specialist magazine recently published an overview of "corporate languages" – as described here – in firms listed in the German share index *DAX*. It contains other interesting references to the topic 'English in German businesses" (*Handelsblatt* No. 227, 24/25/26 November 2017: 58f). Unfortunately, the method of data acquisition for the magazine's "own research" remains obscure; it is probably safe to assume a questionnaire, possibly supplemented with additional research.

Many firms seem reticent about declaring their company languages. For instance, on questioning 20 firms in Germany (admittedly, not all with head offices in Germany), Vollstedt (2002: 51f.) found only a single firm, Bayer AG, in which "the group languages [= corporate languages! U.A.] [...] were specified in the guidelines", in this case, German and English; "concrete details on usage, e.g. use in given communication situations or types of text, were not given". Apart from Bayer, the following firms were also sent questionnaires: Alcatel, Aslthom, BASF, Bertelsmann, BMW, Boehringer Ingelheim, DaimlerChrysler, Danisco, Continental, Drägerwerk, Heidelberg Prepess, Hugo Boss, MaK, Porsche, Rheinmetall, Schering, Siemens, Unilever and VW. At Bertelsmann, DaimlerChrysler, Danisco and Siemens "the company languages [German and English respectively! U.A.] were not officially specified. But they were known, because reference was regularly made to this fact in employee magazines and further training courses". "By contrast, most companies reacted with incomprehension to the question about an official language for internal communication. Respondents claimed that choice of language was made pragmatically".

In view of a similar lack of comprehension during initial enquiries while I was preparing my own survey of firms (see Ch. F.5, towards the end), I omitted the question about declared company languages from the start (which I have subsequently come to regret). In my telephone enquiry to the North-Rhine Chamber of Industry and Trade in Duisburg (21 August 2013), during which I was connected to various offices, no one was aware of any source which might provide information about the declared languages of large firms in Germany, and even Reiner Pogarell (email: 23 August 2013), Director of the Institute for Business Linguistics in Paderborn, answered my question in the negative: "I do not believe there is such a list [declared company languages of firms in Germany! U.A.]", he added: "Even if there was such a list, its information value would be zero". Pogarell justified this comment by explaining that there would be a wide gap between what was declared and actual language use. Hauschild/ Vollstedt (2002: 174) comment on the survey by Vollstedt mentioned above (2002: 51–53), explaining that six of the 20 firms questioned "decided in favour of a radical introduction of English as the company language [...]", of which, however, there were "three subsidiaries of foreign parent companies". "In 11 of the 20 firms, English is accepted and fostered alongside German as the corporate language, but this has not been introduced as a compulsory measure" and is therefore certainly not declared as such. "Only in two companies was a conscious decision made against English and in favour of retaining German – for the present". (One firm did not respond.)

Volkswagen (VW) used to be known for its perseverance towards the maintenance of German (but, for the shift to English, see Table F.7–1 and the article from the *Handelsblatt* named

Table F.7–1 Company languages in the largest German firms

English: generally, and on the board	n = 14
(Adidas, Allianz, Bayer, Beiersdorf, Continental, Deutsche Telekom, Fresenius, Fresenius Medical Care, Heidelberg Zement, Linde, Merck, SAP, Siemens, Volkswagen)	
English: generally, for board, no response	n = 1
(Daimler)	
English: generally, on the board	n = 3
(Eon, RWE, Thyssen-Krupp)	
German and English: generally, English on the board	n = 5
(BASF, Deutsche Bank, Deutsche Börse, Henkel, Lufthansa)	
German and English: generally, German on the board	n = 2
(Commerzbank, Infineon)	
German: generally, and on the board	n = 3
(BMW, Pro Sieben Sat 1, Vonovia)	
German: generally, for board, no response	n = 1
(Munich Re)	
No response: generally, and on the board	n = 1
(Deutsche Post)	
Totals: English (+ x) = 25, German (+ x) = 14, English + German = 10	

(*Source*: *Handelsblatt* 24/25/26 November 2017: 58f.)

there). I therefore wrote to the "Head of Communications of the Volkswagen Group India", Alexander Skibbe about this corporate maintenance of German; to which he replied with "14 reasons" (email 29 January 2013). I reproduce three of these here:

> 1. Despite globalisation, German is still the main language of all multinationals with head offices in Germany. 2. Discussions involving international participation are indeed held in English, but sometimes commented on in German. With a knowledge of German, it is also possible to understand the comments and information 'between the lines'. 3. Small talk opens many doors. If you chat with Germans in their native language, they usually open up more rapidly than in English.

By contrast, many companies emphasise the advantages of English as the company language (see Hauschild/Vollstedt 2002). There is presumably considerable uncertainty on all sides, which explains why companies are reluctant to provide unambiguous answers and decisions: "most respondents [. . .] explained that language choice tends to be handled pragmatically. It is always important to avoid confronting employees with bureaucratic regulations". Based on this kind of uncertainty, it can be assumed that planning and decisions about language policy for further company languages or the replacement of an existing company language with another language, generally English, might be superfluous or even counter-productive. However, a permanent language shift (by contrast with situation-specific code switching) represents a profound change with far-reaching consequences. It is therefore not surprising that it has often been an important, even indispensable strategic objective for management, which can succeed only with careful planning (Vollstedt 2002; Hauschildt/Vollstedt 2002; Much 2008).

One fundamental question is the profitability of the language shift, which can be presented in the form of a cost-benefit analysis: in financial terms, do its economic benefits exceed the costs ultimately incurred? And which approaches to language shift might minimise costs and max-imise benefits? Coulmas (1992b: 132–138) outlines the costs and economic benefits of various language-policy measures ("payoff"; ibid: 138–152). In this context, he also considers the prob-lem of the accuracy of such cost-benefit analyses. Inaccuracy can be registered in terms of how far subsequent costs exceed predictions. In fact, costs can be calculated more readily than the benefits, which are generally felt in the distant future. Accordingly, "the calculation of benefits [is] often characterised by a high degree of uncertainty" (ibid: 140). Coulmas explains the uncer-tainties of language-policy measures with reference to attempts to strengthen the international position of German or French ("language export promotion"), to promote foreign-language teaching in US schools, to replace Russian with English as the first foreign language in eastern central European countries, to introduce English as a university teaching language in the Neth-erlands, and regarding Irish language policy. Despite the uncertainty of cost-benefit analyses for language planning, they are still helpful for organising priorities and assessing measures required for the intended goals (ibid: 150). This also applies for the shift to other company languages, but the point is not addressed by Coulmas. Attempting a cost-benefit analysis generally also reveals factors not easily calculated in financial terms which may be important under some circum-stances, especially "where a language is subject to strong emotional attachment, or closely linked to other social attributes". "Cost-benefit analysis can only reckon with factors which can be operationalised by means of economic value assessment" (ibid: 150 and 152).

In the event of a shift between company languages, it is not always possible to predict all relevant factors, even if attempts are made to consider them under overarching aspects, such as "prestige planning and policy" and "acceptance planning and policy", which I shall address shortly. In general, when a shift is made to a different company language, language planning, as developed in sociolinguistics, also plays a key role (Vollstedt 2002; Hauschildt/ Vollstedt 2002; Much 2008). The various directions conceived by Heinz Kloss (e.g. 1927, 1969a), Einar Hau-gen (e.g. 1966, 1987), Joshua Fishman (e.g. 1974) and others are generally used nowadays in the abridged and supplemented version by Robert Cooper (1989). Specifically, he added the concept of "acquisition planning" to the previously limited distinction between "status plan-ning" and "corpus planning". However, for the planning of company languages, this term can be particularly confusing, "because it is semantically referenced in business economics as the acquisition of entire companies". Accordingly, it has been replaced by Hauschildt/ Vollstedt (2002: 177) with the term "language-acquisition planning". Vollstedt (2002: 215–223) adds the term "prestige planning" (Ammon 2012b) suggested by Haarmann (1984a, 1990), which can also be designated – from a more specialised perspective – as "acceptance planning" (cf. Vollstedt 2002: 216f., 222f). In this context, status planning and corpus planning have a somewhat strate-gic character, while language-acquisition planning, prestige planning and acceptance planning, which are associated with "implementation", have a more operational character (Hauschildt/ Vollstedt 2002: 176). All these aspects have been formulated in planning proposals by Vollstedt (2002: 98–223) and Hauschildt/ Vollstedt (2002: 176–182).

Status planning focuses on which people (in which positions or functions) within the com-pany should use the language in which communication situations and text types (and conse-quently have corresponding skills at their disposal). Often, use of the new language is restricted to corporate management or research and development departments. Corpus planning relates to the speech forms to be used, especially centralised technical terms, image-forming and iden-tity-forming keywords and formulas, as well as linguistic style (e.g. informal/formal, simple/ elaborate). The modifier *corpus-* is derived from the idea of a "linguistic body" and should be understood approximately in the sense of "linguistic structure"; it is therefore distinct from the sense of "corpus linguistics". By contrast and with less likelihood of misunderstanding, the term language-acquisition planning expresses that what is meant here is who should learn which languages or which components of languages, up to which level, in which manner and within which time span. Finally, prestige planning is ultimately supposed to justify the value of the new company language or languages, present them and communicate them to the workforce, motivating them to accept the innovation (acceptance planning). It goes without saying, that, in the case of English, which is generally involved here, this is achieved primarily by emphasising its global position and its communicative advantages.

Despite companies' reservations about investigations into their language planning and policies, several detailed inventories of language shifts are now available. Vollstedt (2002: 46–97) describes the communication situation, motives for language planning, goals, implementation and reaction of employees for three companies. However, instead of naming the companies, she merely characterises them – abbreviated here as: 1) company in the chemicals industry in the Rhine-Main region with 18,000 employees and 60 production sites in 20 countries; 2) 100% subsidiary of a US mineral-oil company with almost 20,000 employees in Germany, with openly region-centric or even geocentric structure ("managed by regional managers"); 3) mixed company with head office in the Rhine-Main region with more than 170 of its own companies in 48 countries and its own production sites in 25 countries (ibid: 56, 69f., 80). The consistently high degree of internationalisation is obvious. A similar description by Hauschildt/ Vollstedt (2002) is available regarding the special-glass company Schott with approximately 10,000 employees in Germany and the same number again in production sites in 20 countries and distribution companies in a further almost 20 countries. Furthermore, Much (2008: 58–82) reports on the language shift in the TÜV Rheinland Group, which has a total of 12,500 employees and 360 subsidiaries in 62 countries.

A comprehensive account of these various language plans and implementations would be excessive here. Instead, I shall restrict myself to a few comments on their success, which, as will be shown, depends to a large extent on the planning of prestige and acceptance. The problems emerging from this discussion anticipate the topic of Ch. F.8. One important condition for the success of language shifts in German companies, especially the inclusion of English or even the replacement of German with English, is the consideration shown for identity and linguistic pride which go beyond the merely communicative function of language.

Prestige and acceptance planning can therefore be taken as indispensable. On the one hand, it is essential for "the local language, including German, still to be respected", and, on the other hand, for the new language, generally English, to satisfy emotional needs in addition to its communicative advantages. The shift must contribute to "presenting the company as globally open and innovative and should communicate an improved image". Furthermore, with the new language, which includes all corporate elements, "the feeling of belonging between all employees should be strengthened, and a unified corporate culture should be developed worldwide" (Hauschildt/ Vollstedt 2002: 174). This emotional goal attempts to overcome the opposition between "language of identification" and "language of communication" (on this opposition, see Hüllen 1992). If it is to be successful, a language-shift policy must combine both language functions and ensure that the shift is "also emotionally 'accepted' by the language community", which, here, means the corporate employees. This is facilitated, if it is regarded as "especially prestige-enhancing" (Vollstedt 2002: 215, 217).

Language planning of this kind also highlights the connection between language and culture. However, this can become confusing because of different conceptualisations of "culture", e.g. in a broad sense which includes language, as opposed to a narrower sense, according to which language and culture are separate (Risager 2000). Vollstedt (2002: 27) does not address this question, but she understands company languages as important corporate symbols, which she allocates to two groups. She distinguishes between interactional symbols (which also include rites, rituals, ceremonies and festivals) and objectified symbols (such as logos, flags, gifts, documents, clothing and awards). The symbolism of company languages has also been recognised by business consultants and the advertising industry. Furthermore, Vollstedt touches on potential problems in the shift from German to English, which can arise from differences in symbolism between the two languages and associated identity conflicts. For example, German tends to express a certain national identity or belonging, particularly to the German-language community; by contrast, English expresses a more cosmopolitan identity, membership of the global community (Ch. E.1; E.2; F.2). But English can also symbolise membership of one of the English-speaking nations. With reference to this point, German-speakers possibly judge the shift from German to English as an unfair game in which they, as foreign-language speakers, are supposed to compete with native speakers.

Language shift can also influence social relationships within the company. One catalyst for this change may be the different forms of address, especially the use of pronouns in German and English, which signal a different social distance. The formal second-person [*Sie* as opposed to the informal *Du*] is not available in English, and the use of first names is extended to include a wider group. Other English modes of expression for social distance and formality are also incongruent with German and not nearly so easy to handle as simply using the *Sie* form. Furthermore, relevant text types are structured differently in the two languages. For example, academic texts in English are structured in a more linear manner (fewer digressions), less explicitly (no excursus), closer to orality (fewer markers for written style), and more personal than in German (Clyne 1984, 1987; House 2002a, 2003b). There are corresponding divergences in commercial texts, which also express different attitudes or social relations between writers and readers.

All these differences must be taken into consideration, but not exaggerated. To some extent, similar differences exist within the German-language territory, between north and south Germany, Austria and Switzerland, and between the old and new federal states, and even within the same region, between social strata. Moreover, the English language is not necessarily associated with a homogenous culture, but rather with a cultural mix including the USA, the UK, South Africa, Australia, India, Singapore and so on. Finally, for decades now, German culture has been widely influenced by English-language culture, primarily from the USA. But the linguistic shift is not a purely cognitive and rational undertaking; it also involves the emotional agreement of employees. For their sake, diverse methods and means are used, such as consistent, exemplary language choices by corporate management, e.g. by using the new language as a language of instruction in language courses and in corporate magazines, and including all kinds of gimmicks, such as humorous newsletters and promotional gifts (Vollstedt 2002: 219–223). It goes without saying that successes in this context are uncertain (ibid: 68f., 79., 90). "It will take several years for TÜV Rheinland to evaluate whether internal communication [between branches in the various countries! U.A.] is actually running more smoothly and in a goal-orientated manner" (Much 2008: 80). To achieve sustainable results, a major shift implemented in a single powerful move is not sufficient; what is required is continuous "language management" by corporate leaders (Hauschildt/ Vollstedt 2002: 182; Coulmas 1992b: 152; Neustupný/ Nakvapil 2003; Neustupný/ Nekula 2006; more generally, Spolsky 2009).

8. Successful business in Germany without using the German language

It is tempting to think that firms in Germany cannot do business without using German and certainly cannot be successfully managed by people who have no knowledge of German. The example of the collapse of Walmart in Germany gave a relevant warning. As *The Economist* explained (5 August 2006: 54): "The first error was to appoint a boss for Germany who spoke no German". But the article also mentions other reasons for the complete withdrawal of the US supermarket chain from Germany (details in Knorr/ Arndt 2003; Pogarell 2007: 19–26). Apart from a few bad investments, the corporate culture was entirely inappropriate. It lacked linguistic and cultural knowledge at all levels through to customer contact. It is no coincidence that Walmart also failed in South Korea. By contrast, the use of English within limits inside the head offices of German firms does not necessarily seem harmful to business. It is often a matter of course. For example, former CEO of Deutsche Post AG, Klaus Zumwinkel, explained that "in communication with our customers and in controlling a growing corporate group, the English language is one of the everyday tools used by our management team" (*Bild am Sonntag* 5 December 1999: 4) Especially in the case of bilingualism, i.e. the ability to switch to German if required, this seems unproblematic. However, a lack of German skills still represents a weakness. The new head of department store Karstadt was prepared to make the effort: "'I'm learning German', she said – clearly distinguishing herself from the previous British manager who could only communicate with the majority of his employees through interpreters [. . .]" ("*Karstadt gibt sich bodenständig* [Karstadt still proud of its roots]). New boss, Eva-Lotta Sjostedt, wants to outdo her predecessor in more ways than one [. . .]", *WAZ* 4 January 2014).

At the same time, many management and supervisory boards in German head offices also have members with no knowledge of German. For example, Deutsche Bank and Allianz des Deutschen have appointed board members with no knowledge of German ("Radical restructuring for Allianz", *Die Welt* 13 September 2005), so that English has become not the only working language but the dominant operational language at the head of the company, even in Germany. Of course, this is not a problem provided it only relates to internal company communication. But difficulties can arise in contacts with the German public or the company's own staff. One example was provided by the doll manufacturer Zapf Creation – a significant name in this context – when it organised its AGM in Coburg in English, because three Spanish directors on the board did not have adequate knowledge of German. Despite simultaneous interpreting, there was violent protest from the German Shareholders' Association, which described this language choice as "extremely shareholder-unfriendly". One newspaper (*FAZ* 23 August 2006: 15) commented: "In fact, there are foreign CEOs in many [German! U.A.] firms, but, in shareholder meetings, they are generally represented by a German-speaking member as the leader of the meeting". For German company chiefs appearing in public in Germany, ignorance of the German language is considered a weakness. But poor German is still acceptable if it is intelligible and the terminology is correct. The Swedish press officer of MAN, Håkan Samuelssen, regularly stepped forward in this way at shareholders' meetings (e.g. on 21 February 2006). Knowledge of German was also a condition for the appointment of Marijn Dekkers, who is Dutch, as CEO of Bayer AG: "Without these language skills, he would not have become the boss of Bayer" (*RP* 16 September 2009: C2). In line with the rules for politeness in the market which govern language choice to accommodate to the customer (Ch. F.2), a knowledge of German is required, especially for communicating with German-speaking customers.

Faced with all these circumstances, it is surprising that there are foreign companies which have been trading successfully in Germany for decades even though their top executives have no German-language skills. But this takes place in an environment in which they can use their own language for most day-to-day needs. It could almost be described as a kind of ghetto, provided this is not seen as suggesting pressure from the surrounding majority; because such an extensive limitation to their own language – and their own culture – is completely self-imposed. This description applies to around 530 Japanese companies in Düsseldorf and the surrounding area, in the *Stadmitte* business and cultural centre of the city and key settlement areas in the *Oberkassel* and *Niederkassel* districts (details in: de.wikipedia.org/wiki/Japaner_in_Düsseldorf).This *Nippon am Rhein*, as it is sometimes called locally, as an alternative to "Japan town", is generally highly respected and receives prominent visits, e.g. from the Japanese imperial couple, Akihito and Michiko in 1993.

However, Japanese firms in Düsseldorf cannot do business exclusively in Japanese. Instead of German, they generally use the foreign language with which they are most familiar: English (Ch. J.9.14). As the preferred foreign language in Japanese schools and universities since the end of WWII (Hirataka 1994) English is regarded as the main reason for Japanese companies' long-term preference for sites in the UK rather than on the European mainland. "The English language, which is still most convenient for Japanese managers, has contributed [. . .] to their almost exclusive choice of the island kingdom at the edge of Europe" ("*Immer mehr Japaner wollen in Europa Autos bauen*" [More and more Japanese want to build cars in Europe], *WAZ* 13 October 1989). Other, "harder" economic factors, such as lower wages and tax incentives may also have played a part. But over time, the hard factor of rental costs, which are much higher in London than in Düsseldorf, has begun to make its mark. An excellent infrastructure, developed by the more than 8,000 Japanese residents, has further contributed to the rising value of Düsseldorf. This guarantees that day-to-day and especially essential tasks can all be carried out in Japanese. The Hotel Nikko, which also houses the Japanese Chamber of Commerce and the Central Japanese Consulate, provides an impressive centre point. The infrastructure comprises (in 2013) around 30 Japanese restaurants, two supermarkets, ten food stores, two bakeries, various photo and electronics stores, six hairdressing salons, 18 haulage firms and – more importantly – three kindergartens, a Japanese International School up to the end of Secondary Level I (www.jisd. de/about_jisd/deutsch/charakter_der_schule.html), a Buddhist Church, the EKO-Haus (www. trinosophie.info/zeitgeschehen/ekohaus-duesseldorf-buddhistischer-kraftort-der-stille)   and several associations. There are also daily newspapers and magazines, video-rental stores, film shows and satellite TV. It is difficult to give exact figures because many resources are in a mixture of Japanese and German (information gratefully received from Yasuo Inadome, Spokesperson of the Japanese Club Düsseldorf). Finally, the University of Düsseldorf offers a course on "Modern Japan". Against this background, every member of the family can thrive in Japanese, apart for special needs, such as visits to specialist doctors.

Some time ago, Emi Morita (1989) issued a questionnaire on day-to-day conditions in "Nippon am Rhein" (sample: 84 Japanese men and women, all married and with children). The result was that, contrary to widespread opinion and despite access to everything required for day-to-day life through Japanese, the majority still acquired a knowledge of German during their stay in Düsseldorf. This included a larger proportion (95%) of those not in paid employment, mostly women, than of those in employment (88%). In a follow-on investigation, Kaori Okamoto (1991) found that most Japanese women learnt German at least to the level of day-to-day functional communication. There are no indications that this has changed. But knowledge of German is more important for day-to-day living away from the workplace than for professional life.

A knowledge of German in working life in Düsseldorf is therefore less urgent because communication in Japanese firms between Japanese and German people takes place mostly in English. 55% of Japanese questioned by Morita (1989) indicated that, in the workplace, they speak only English, 19% only German and 26% German and English. Communication with the head office in Japan does not require knowledge of English and certainly not German, because it takes place largely in Japanese. German managers are generally used for operational business, including other Europeans for areas such as sales, logistics and finance. Knowledge of German plays almost no role in the selection of employees from Japan (Merz 1987: 263–268). There is not even a requirement to learn German during their stay in Düsseldorf. Learning German is undertaken voluntarily and leads to widely varying levels of knowledge. Extensive avoidance of German in the workplace has two advantages for the Japanese, which may not be entirely intentional. Firstly, it withholds communicative superiority from the Germans, which would conflict with the Germans' relatively lower position in the company hierarchy; secondly, it excludes Germans from important communication (e.g. with the head office). Such communication takes place in Japanese, which, apart from a few exceptions, is not understood by the Germans. Conversely, for German employees, German unavoidably constitutes a kind of secret language. Such a division of language and communication between components of the workforce can also be disturbing and lead to misunderstandings which may damage the working atmosphere and, despite the provision of mediating services, can also have detrimental effects on marketing. Osamu Watanabe, a member of the Supervisory Board of the Bank of Tokyo has drawn attention to this point (1989).

Communication does not always run smoothly, because English-language skills on both sides often fall short of the ideal. This was the opinion of some respondents who were reluctant to be named. Not only the Japanese, but also the Germans bring their English skills from school and, at least to a certain degree, also their willingness to communicate English – in the middle of Germany. Their ability and their willingness to use English are a consequence of the overarching international position of English and its prioritisation in foreign-language curricula – but also of the omnipresence of English in the public sphere in Germany (Ch. F.9). By contrast, in the UK, it would be impossible to communicate with British employees predominantly in German. For good or ill, Japanese employees there are compelled to concede the native-speaker advantage to the English. Perhaps this linguistic inferiority of the Japanese in the UK has contributed, albeit slightly, to the trend towards Germany mentioned above. But this is pure speculation. The example of the Japanese who can do business in Germany largely without the use of German is symptomatic on the one hand for the modest international position of German and on the other hand for the formidable position of English in Germany (Ammon 2006f; Hüllen 2007). In the sense described by Braj Kachru (1986), Germany does not belong to the "outer circle" of the English language, but rather to the "expanding circle". With Japanese alone, the Japanese would not cope; they need their own knowledge of English, and they can also expect a knowledge of English from the Germans. This knowledge also allows them to communicate beyond the German-language territory with partners in the other European states.

9. Advertising in German outside the German-language territory

Inside German-speaking countries, languages other than German are often used for commercial advertising. Some examples will be discussed below. However, for the topic of the book, it is the use of German for advertising outside the German-speaking countries and regions which is of primary interest. A more detailed discussion will therefore be provided on this aspect. It hardly needs to be mentioned that, for advertising as well as other fields inside the German-speaking countries, English is the dominant foreign language. It is omnipresent on advertising pillars in the streets, on TV and radio, in newspaper advertisements, in seminars and on the Internet. English appears in writing and in speech, for foreign and German-made products, in product names, slogans and longer advertising texts. In Germany, even German companies advertise in English alongside German, like Daimler in car advertisements (e.g. "Intelligent Drive"), and French companies, such as Renault (e.g. "Drive the Change") – to name only two of numerous examples. Companies from English-speaking countries adopt this approach to an even greater extent (e.g. Coca-Cola on the football World Cup 2006 in Germany: "It's your Heimspiel [home game] !"). These companies and/or their advertising agencies must be convinced that English-language advertising appeals to consumers in German-speaking countries, possibly no less than German. English-language names for German companies, even parts of names or parodistic names, are less frequent, e.g. "ThyssenKrupp Steel", "Douglas", "Jack Wolfskin" or "Tom Tailor" and "Symrise". Such companies often advertise in English in Germany, e.g. Douglas with "YOUR PARTNER IN BEAUTY". They probably mean to signal their international or global orientation, perhaps also their modernity. Alongside other frequent occurrences of English, e.g. in academia and science or pop music, this use of English in the business economy contributes to the familiarisation of the German population with the English language and their acceptance of its use in public (Ammon 2006f; Hüllen 2007).

By comparison with English, the French, Italian and other foreign languages nowadays play only a modest role in the public use of language, the "linguistic landscape" of the German-speaking countries. In advertising, they serve primarily as symbols of authenticity for products from the respective "native countries". Accordingly, foreign companies display names or product designations in their own language, even with Chinese or Japanese characters, which German consumers can neither read nor pronounce. For some of their own products and in some cases even for the company name itself, individual German companies have adopted names in languages of which the native country symbolises the quality or elegance of the relevant products, especially France and Italy. One example of a name for a company and its products is "Montblanc" (writing goods). Examples of products include "(Karmann) Ghia" and "(VW) Scirocco" (car). Added to these are specific items from the native countries, occasionally also with partially Germanised original names, such as the familiar "*Cognac*", "*Pommes frites*", "*Spaghetti*", "*Campari*" and more recently "*Cidre*", "*Baguette*", "*Panettone*", "*Cannelloni*" etc. Traces of the traditional dominance of French in the courts of Europe and as the preferred foreign language are evident here. In recent history, German alternatives or variants for French words were created and, after the foundation of the German Empire (1871), these were disseminated through the "*Verdeutschungsbücher des Allgemeinen Sprachvereins*" [Germanisation handbooks of the General Society for German Language], e.g. in the volume *Deutsche Speisekarte* [German menu] (1911).

Correspondingly, the use of German for commercial advertising in non-German-speaking countries often relates to specifically German products, relying on the positive image of products manufactured in Germany, which has been described sympathetically by Asfa-Wossen Asserate in his book *Deutsche Tugenden* [German virtues] (2013: 35f). The advertising therefore draws on values associated with the mark "Made in Germany". This was introduced in 1887 by the British government for goods from Germany. "At the time, this was thought to be an effective means of scaring off customers and inducing them to buy British goods". But, "[t]hings turned out differently". German companies concentrated on improving quality, and "Made in Germany" became "a worldwide seal of quality [. . .], a status it has retained up to the present day" (historical background: www.process.vogel.de/index.cfm?pid=2995&title-Made_in_Germany).

Before turning to German-language advertising for German products in the non-German-speaking countries, I would like to add a brief comment on the function of the quality seal. The purchase of German goods by foreign companies is based partly on the background to the values associated with "Made in Germany". Now, as we read regularly in German newspapers, Chinese companies have recently become active in this context. Even the names of German companies are also sometimes sought after, as suggested by newspaper headlines: "German company names attract investors" (*Handelsblatt* 11 August 2012). "A medium-sized Italian company buys German company names because of their good reputation. A German name can boost access to the world market". Gianluigi Nova, CEO of "Tenova", an "Italian manufacturer of furnaces and machines for the steel industry and mining, explains that 'in the world market, it's a great help if you can step forward with a German company name and a visiting card with German names'" (www.handelsblatt.com/unternehmen/mittelstand/uebernahmen-deutsche-firmennamen-locken-investoren/6968450.html). The creation of a German-language brand name in Russia is framed somewhat differently below:

> 'Erich Krause' is a Russian trademark for writing goods, which are mostly manufactured in Southeast Asia and distributed in Russia. The owner is the Russian firm 'Office Premier', which was founded in 1994 in Moscow by the Russian entrepreneur Dmitrij Beloglasov. The brand name was developed by the advertising agency 'Megapro'. This marketing concept is associated with the traditional consumer belief that German writing goods are particularly reliable.
>
> *(Natalia Troshina, email: 30 January 2013)*

One curious example is reported from India: "KÖNIG – WORLD's #1 IN OFFSHORE TRAINING" (# = number; the Ö in the name is filled in colour):

> An Indian company based in Delhi with a German name? No problem, [. . .] and what was the Indians' motivation? My father started a manufacturing business in India in the 1960s for import substitute electromechanical components such as microswitches. German and Japanese were held in high esteem so [. . .] [t]his time he chose Koenig, and Koenig Electronics was born. [. . .] Koenig is difficult to pronounce, and marketeers say it is not a good choice [. . .]. But it has proven lucky for us.
>
> *(www.werner-brandl.de/wordpress/tag/indien/)*

Compared with other languages – such as English, of course, but also French, Italian and Chinese – German-language expressions are relatively rare in the public sphere in non-German-speaking countries. However, there is a lack of comparative studies covering a range of countries and cities. In Tokyo, to cite one example, Peter Backhaus (2007: 71) found the following proportions of public inscriptions. For German, they are pitiful even if you take the geographical distance into account: English 2,266, Chinese 62, Korean 40, French 20, Portuguese 12, Spanish 8, Latin 6, Thai 5, Italian 4, German 2. This scarcity may be an after-effect of German history, which, even today, still inhibits Germans from appearing in public. But considering the esteem currently enjoyed by Germany worldwide, there is no reason for this: "In a survey [commissioned by the BBC! U.A.] every year in 24 countries, Germany is still the country whose 'influence on the course of events in the world' was judged best, even in 2014". Many similar findings have been published in preceding years (www.auswaertiges-amt.de/DE/Aussenpolitik/AktuelleArtikel/140604 – GlobeScan-Umfrage.html). Presumably, one of the more important reasons relates to the goods predominantly manufactured in Germany, with a high proportion of investment goods, which are generally advertised less strongly in public than luxury consumer goods and fashion articles, which tend to come from France or Italy. However, even foreign firms use German-language names for their products. For example, a chocolate egg manufactured by the Italian company Ferrero filled with miniature toys, which is also sold outside Italy is named, "*Kinder ÜBERRASCHUNG* [childrens' surprise]". The names of beers, such as *Steinbräu* (Wuhan, China) or *Rheingold* (USA), provide further examples, the latter also being the name of the company. But, in proportion with the reputation of German beer, German-language beer names are not exactly frequent. Sometimes there are modifications of names which suggest a German connection to the local population – but are not necessarily understood in this way by German-speakers themselves. For example, Tom Lovik (email 28 October 2013) drew my attention to the name "Uberon", a beer brewed by Bells Brewery in Kalamazoo MI (USA), "a mixture of a beer called 'Oberon' and the popular German prefix 'über' [. . .]. As you probably know, the preposition 'über' is very popular in English and very productive" [more on this below with reference to South Africa! U.A.]. The preposition "*über*" is indicated to customers in the USA by the 'U'. "The Umlaut has no significance for American marketing people". Having said this, Volkswagen ran a campaign in the 1990s in the USA with "*Fahrvergnügen*. It's what makes a car Volkswagen", with the Umlaut in spelling and pronunciation. Sometimes, products from other foreign companies are not in fact named as German but advertised using the German language, as described here:

> French manufacturer Renault has even started using the German language in France. French-manufactured cars are marketed in German-French gobbledygook, and this is in a country obsessed with resisting language invasion, for example, by warding off 'anglicisms'. But a friendly Frenchman is now on TV screens all over France praising the virtues of the new Mégane 3 in half-German/half-French, with French subtitles. The climax of the ad is when he says: *Isch bin ein Berliner. La berline, das ist das französische Wort für Limousine. Es geht um Qualität auf französische Art.* [*La berline*, that is the French word for limousine. It's all about quality French style.]

It is less surprising that German companies also advertise their products in German abroad. "Over the last year, the team from Rüsselsheim [site of the Opel car company! U.A.] has been broadcasting entire German-language advertisements in France" (*SZ* 22 October 2011). I have also read reports about this kind of advertising in Italy and the Czech Republic: "*Opel – Wir leben Autos* [*leben* 'to live' is here associated with *lieben* 'to love']" (Sandro Moraldo, Marie Vachkova, emails: 6 November 2013). The reference below is also relevant to motor-vehicle advertising:

> German suppliers using their language of origin abroad has become almost a tradition. Some time ago, VW launched the untranslated concept of '*Fahrvergnügen*' [joy of driving] in the USA. For a long time, the Wolfsburg team have been marketing '*Das Auto*' [the car] worldwide as if there was only one, the one made by Volkswagen. And corporate subsidiary Audi proudly boasts its slogan '*Vorsprung* [head start] *durch Technik*', using German language to sell far away from home.
>
> *(www.sueddeutsche.de/wirtschaft/renault-und-opel-werben-in-frankreich-auf-deutsch-isch-bin-ein-berliner-1.1172245)*

I have reports about this kind of German-language advertising by Volkswagen from several countries, e.g. Italy: "Golf. *Das Auto*" (Sandro Moraldo, email 27 October 2013); Czech Republic and Malaysia "Volkswagen. *Das Auto*" (Marie Vachkova, Miroslava Majtanova, emails 6 November 2012 and 28 October 2013); China: "Regardless of the type or model, advertisements by VW always end with the German words '*Das Auto*', not just as a subtitle but also actually spoken in German" (Jun HE, email: 28 October 2013); similarly, USA (Tom Lovik, email: 28 October 2013), Argentina (Joachim Steffen, email: 29 October 2013), Russia (Dirk Kemper, email 29 October 2013), Finland (Jarmo Korhonen, email 9 November 2013) and Japan, where Audi also advertises with the traditional slogan "*Vorsprung durch Technik*" (Hitoshi YAMASHITA, email: 6 November 2013). It is obvious that Volkswagen is the leading German company – when it comes to advertising in German. But medium-sized companies with head offices in Germany also advertise worldwide in German. For example, Grohe, the bathroom-fittings manufacturer, advertises with the slogan "*Pure Freude am Wasser*" [The pure joy of water], underlined in the soundtrack with Beethoven's "*Ode to Joy*'". David Haines, the British-born CEO explains that this underscores the quality of the products ("Grohe is proud to show its German cultural roots", *FAZ* 13 March 2013: 25). Miele, the white-goods manufacturer, advertises in Australia with the slogan "*IMMER BESSER*" [Better and better] (Brian Taylor, email 3 November 2013).

In South Africa, in 2013, VW also advertised on radio with: "'Wunder-bar' in the sense of a bar for the upper cost limit for financing the car by the month, i.e. low-cost – and the spot ends with 'isn't this wundervoll?'" (Kirsten Mbohwa-Pagels, Goethe-Institut Johannesburg, email: 28 October 2013). Matthias Jakus (Goethe-Institut Johannesburg, email: 28 October 2013) also reported the over-worked word "*über*": "[O]ne widely used and currently popular term in advertising language (and in the creative scene) is the adverbial adjunct 'über', which, interestingly, is not used that way in German at all. Something which is 'über' stands out and is simply the best. You can buy an 'über luxury penthouse', Audi makes 'über offers' and restaurants advertise 'über starters' and 'über pasta'". The word "*über*" should probably be adopted into the next edition of the book *Ausgewanderte Wörter* [*Emigré* words] (Limbach 2007). From Russia, I have examples of advertising using German wordplay for foodstuffs imported from Germany: "Very nice too: Ritter Sport-Schokolade. All the text on the packaging is in Russian/cyrillic, with only one line in bold typeface in German/Latin: '**Quadratisch. Praktisch. Gut**'" (Dirk Kemper, email: 29 October 2013). "The slogan for Media-Markt [in Russia! U.A.] is: '*Fantastisch Markt! Media-Markt!*' This grammatical error ("*fantastisch*" instead of "*fantastischer*") is intended to trigger an association with the slogan of 'Ritter Sport'. So, this creates a morphological advertising context" (Natalia Troshina, email: 30 October 2013). "Sometimes, the strategy is attempted in a bizarre manner, e.g. in Australia, ALDI collaborated with a car showroom, advertising on large street-side posters with the slogan 'Learning to Speak German': '*SEI KEINE DUMME WURST!*' [Don't be a stupid sausage!] over the image of a German sausage with a hat and a moustache" (Gabriele Schmidt, email: 13 November 2013).

Advertising in German close to the settlement regions of German(-speaking) minorities (Ch. E) represents a special case. For example, Joachim Steffen (email: 28 October 2013) reports from Brazil (Ch. E.4.10): "[I]n Chihuahua, there is a great deal of advertising (also) in German on placards by the roadside". Non-German-speakers also advertise in German alongside the local language, Portuguese, e.g. one doctor wrote: "*Untersuchungen vom Körper mit Computer und 'Rayon X'* [Physical examinations of the body with computer and x-ray]".

Details about the spread or decline of German-language advertising outside German-speaking countries would require panel surveys over a longer period, and these are not available so far. But the many German-language names for products from Japanese companies, found by Harald Haarmann in the early 1980s in Japan, suggest that there may have been a decline. Haarmann gives the following examples (1984: 36f., 1989: 30f.): "*Mein Knäcke*" (crispbread), "*Alpen Weiss*" (sweets), "*Auslese*" (hair tonic), "*Märchen*" (deodorant scent package), "*Sahne*" (skin cream), "*Märzen*" (beer), "*Alpen Horn*" (type of cheese) and "Brigitte" (clock); and also – though only rarely – product characterisations such as "*schick*" (instead of the French *chic*) for a Japanese car, and even entire slogans such as "*ich hab' Märzen* [a type of beer! U.A.] *als Sommergeschenk bekommen*", with enclosed Japanese translation [I was given *Märzen* as a summer gift]. At that time, Haarmann found German in third position in a ranking of foreign languages according to frequency of use in advertising, a long way behind English and also behind French, but approximately neck-and-neck with Italian and Spanish. By contrast, the position of German in the linguistic landscape of Tokyo described above lags a long way behind. In Haarmann's assessment (1984: 35), English symbolised the international standing of a product, while the other languages stood for more specific qualities or matched the stereotype of each language community. For example, German-language advertising matched the stereotype of the industrious, correct or *gemütliche*, jolly Germans.

10. German business economics between global communication and language maintenance

It is also possible to portray businesses in the German-speaking countries as faced with a dilemma (see Ch. B.2). Depending on their interests, they must pursue two goals at the same time: 1) strengthen their capability for international or even global action and 2) maintain solidarity with their own language community and nation. Both goals have economic advantages: 1) the advantage of an unrestricted market and respectively 2) the advantage of a good reputation ("Made in Germany") and a reliable production base. Goal 1) requires a capability for international communication and therefore the English language; goal 2) requires a capability for communication in their own German language. But the two goals are not easily combined. At first glance, they might seem incompatible: success with the one goal seems to preclude success with the other. However, this is not an aporia in the sense of an unsolvable logical contradiction, as if e.g. someone wanted to increase and reduce their body weight at the same time. Combining the two goals requires special care as well as a reformulation of the goals, along the following lines: 1') increased international business activity, improved knowledge of English and more frequent use of English; alongside 2') continuing solidarity with their own language community, maintenance of the knowledge of German and also – as far as possible – use of German for international communication (Ch. A.3). Even efforts to strengthen the international position of German are not strictly incompatible with goal 1) or 1'). But the same balancing act will also be required for the other action fields discussed in this book, and for the associated agents, the German academics and scientists (Ch. G), the diplomats and the politicians (Ch. H). To this extent, therefore, the considerations discussed below are, at least partially transferable. Speakers of all international languages (apart from English) are faced with an essentially similar situation (Ch. A.3; A.7).

To understand this situation better, we can assume that the actors are all trying to play their specific role as successfully as possible: as entrepreneurs, academics etc. For the action field of the present chapter, this means conducting business as successfully as possible. Even a glance at the more than 100,000 Google hits for the search term "successful business", shows that successful business is less about short-term profit and more about sustainable profitability (for your own business), and that this depends on a multiplicity of factors. I am not an expert in this action field but, based on examples, I hope to shed light on key aspects relevant to the topic of this book.

A German company could shift its company language entirely to English to save transaction costs and – at least linguistically – to develop a unified corporate culture (Ch. F.7). By abandoning German as company language, it may even hope to achieve greater employee identification with the company. But it is precisely this hope which may be shattered. The choice of English as the company language is the least specific choice possible because it is most widely distributed in the world. This may limit its power to bind people through identification (Ch. E.2: X). By contrast, as the company language, German is more specific and therefore also a more powerful symbol for the company. In terms of practical communication, English is virtually indispensable for companies operating internationally. But limiting communication to English can undermine employee identification with the company. For companies from the German-speaking countries, it must be assumed that this applies especially to subsidiaries outside the German-language territory. With German as the corporate language, Chinese, Indians, Chileans and other people presumably develop a stronger identification with the company than with English as the corporate language. If they have learnt German – up to a certain level of communicative competence – they will have gained the "Plus" in the slogan introduced by Jutta Limbach for the Goethe-Institut, "*Englisch ist ein Muss, Deutsch ist ein Plus*" [English is a must, German is a plus]. Knowledge of German is a valuable qualification and, as a symbol for the company, the German language constitutes something specific which can strengthen the bond between company and employees on both sides. Quite apart from any emotional aspects, just consider the costs, above all, the amount of time required to learn German. Employees are sure to be reluctant to surrender this asset, e.g. by moving to a company where it is worth nothing. German companies should also realise that, with German as the company language, even in branches in non-German-speaking countries, the learning of German will be promoted in those regions – precisely because there are improved job prospects to be obtained through a knowledge of German, particularly through employment in the relevant companies.

German skills of this kind, which may be acquired in school, can then further benefit the company, even indirectly benefiting head offices in German-speaking countries (Ch. K.8). Recall here the long-term complaint, especially in Germany, about a lack of skilled employees. Time and again, the lack of German-language skills abroad has been diagnosed as a serious obstacle to the employment of migrants. The immigration of skilled employees from EU countries is also hampered: "[T]he numbers of newcomers from the euro crisis countries increased most [. . .]. But the absolute numbers [. . .] are still modest. [. . .] That is mainly because of language". In fact, there are other difficulties in Germany, "but the language is 'the hardest part'" ("More southern Europeans are going where the jobs are. But not enough", *The Economist* 26 February 2012). More unemployed people from Mediterranean countries headed to the UK even though there were fewer job opportunities there. Corresponding reports can be found everywhere in the German press (e.g. "Well, where are you then?", *Welt am Sonntag* 24 June 2012: 31). In fact, the Goethe-Institut also reported a surge of southern Europeans (e.g. "Thousands of Italians are swotting up on their German", *Spiegel Online* 28 October 2012); but German skills already acquired at school would have opened access to jobs in Germany much faster. German as an additional company language, even in non-German-speaking countries, could ultimately also motivate increased learning of German in-school, especially if a knowledge of German were to be rewarded in the appointment. Inadequate knowledge of German has also hampered the German "Green card" programme, the "fast-track for covering the demand for IT specialists" which existed between 2000 and the end of 2004 [. . .]. During this period, 17,931 IT experts came to Germany through the Green card scheme" (de.wikipedia.org/wiki/ Greencard_%28Deutschland%29). But the big surge never came; not even all the 20,000 Green cards were claimed. Demand for the "Blue card", which followed the Green card, was also less than expected, even though conditions, such as providing evidence of secure employment, were softened. "Language, eating habits and cultural differences" were enduring barriers. [. . .] "English-speaking countries are most popular" ("*Zuwanderung von IT Fachkräften Deutschland? Muss nicht sein*" [Migration of IT experts to Germany? May not be needed], *Spiegel Online* and *Manager Magazin Online* 11 May 2012).

A more consistent adoption of German as the company language would certainly not lead to a broad increase in the learning of German as a foreign language; but it may strengthen motivation to learn German slightly. The associated strengthening of the global position of German would, in turn, benefit companies in German-speaking countries and their business. But this would not mean that English could simply be dispensed with as *de facto*, if not unconditionally declared, a supplementary company language. Use of English in German-speaking countries would continue regardless. For German companies, it may still be essential in some cases, "to accept English-speaking applicants or to offer the employment contract in English", as a sign of friendly welcome ("*Wir brauchen mehr Willkommenskultur*" [We need a more welcoming culture], *FAZ* 3/4 November 2012: C12).

The difficulty of keeping English out of German-speaking countries is highlighted by one legal proposal in Germany: "English as the language of German courts". Pressure is being applied from a number of directions, including the following: "It is precisely the most interesting cases – and the most lucrative cases for treasury and lawyers – with German companies participating as plaintiff or defendant, which are generally dealt with by English-speaking or private courts of arbitration at the request of foreign business partners. [...] 'Germany as a court location suffers from the fact that the German Code on Court Constitution stipulates German as the language of the court'", claimed former North-Rhine Westphalian Justice Minister, Roswitha Müller-Piepenkötter, an advocate for the corresponding amendment to the Code on Court Constitution ("German courts now also work in English", *FAZ* 9 January 2010: 11). The request was accepted with a large majority by an expert hearing in the Bundestag (www.bundestag.de/dokumente/textarchiv/2011/36400205_kw45_pa_recht/). Allaying fears about language difficulties for German judges, it was claimed that judges increasingly acquire an adequate knowledge of English in international law firms or on supplementary "Master of Laws" courses. Otherwise, in actions between companies, English has already been used for some time at the Supreme Regional Court in Cologne, although legal documents and judgements must be formulated in German. At all events, the introduction of English into German legal life seems unavoidable at least for commercial cases.

It may be asked whether the position of English in Germany and other German-speaking countries, its omnipresence and institutional anchoring are simply analogous to the position of French in the eighteenth century. But this parallel has also been framed somewhat differently, e.g. by Werner Hüllen (2007: 19): "A summing up of these observations leads to the view that, in the historical perspective, the modern presence of English in Germany (and in Europe) is nothing extraordinary. It can even be regarded as a return to the past before linguistic nationalism was popular, i.e. before the French Revolution and the Napoleonic wars". However, to me, this parallel between present-day English and historical French seems out of true. By contrast with French at that time, English is here to stay – and will even strengthen its position. The only means of resisting it would demand technologies hitherto deemed utopian, but which would allow a radically different way of handling languages (see Ch. A.10). To struggle against the rise of English in the German-speaking countries – which is a marginal phenomenon anyway – is a quixotic undertaking. Instead of this conflict, a mutually acceptable balance between German, English and other foreign languages must be striven for to secure long-term benefits, not only for the German-language community but, wherever possible, also for the other language communities cooperating with it.

G

GERMAN FOR INTERNATIONAL SCIENTIFIC AND ACADEMIC COMMUNICATION

1. From world academic language to niche language: stages and causes of change

In the action field of academic communication, there is ample evidence of how the historical German-language community made the gradual transition to using its own language. The transition to German as an academic language was a protracted process which began in the late Middle Ages with the turn away from Latin, occasionally interrupted by intermediate turns, primarily towards French in the seventeenth and eighteenth centuries (cf. Pörksen 1983, 1986, 1989; Schiewe 1991, 1996) and which was completed only in the second half of the nineteenth century (for an overview, see Skudlik 1988, 1990: 4–24). This progression can be explained with reference to the formation of nations in Europe. With all its diversions and delays, German history follows substantially the same principles as that of other European nations (Andersen 1983; Gellner 1983). In synoptic form, typical features were the development of roofing written varieties based on a continuum of dialects; emerging from this, a standard variety, or rather several of them, largely unified the language with reference to regions (cf. Ch. B.1; B.2); followed, then, by the large-scale shift in the German-language community from academic communication in foreign languages (Latin, French) to communication in German. In parallel with the formation of standard German varieties, a community for communication in German was also secured beyond state and national boundaries, especially between Germany, Austria and Switzerland. Based on the economic power and performance of its academic institutions and industrial research, this German communicative community represented one of the three globally leading academic centres, alongside the French-speaking and English-speaking communities. During these developments, German ultimately became one of the three internationally dominant languages for academic and scientific communication, alongside English and French. The German communicative community expanded to include foreign-language speakers in many countries. Along with the internationalism of scientific languages, communicative communities made up of native speakers and foreign-language speakers arose, but, because of the extensive multilingualism among the individuals participating, these communities overlapped and were not separate. Alongside the three most important academic centres, other, smaller centres were formed, e.g. with the Italian and Dutch languages.

I described the recent history of German as an international academic language in my book *Ist Deutsch noch internationale Wissenschaftssprache?* [Is German still an international scientific language?] (1998: Ch. A.1), to which I refer in some cases in the present chapter. *Scientific Babel* by Michael D. Gordin (2015) covers a significant part of the history of the major scientific languages in recent times, with copious data and rigorous explanations. It concentrates on the changing scientific languages of chemistry, primarily, although not restricted to, French, German, Esperanto, Russian and English, and explains their development, in each case from the scientific, economic/political and sociolinguistic perspective.

WWI, National Socialism and WWII, with all their consequences, destroyed the fragile equilibrium between the three most important centres of scholarship at that time. Led by the USA, the English-language community became the dominant global economic centre (Wallerstein 1974, 1980, 1983, 1998, 2004; Ch. A.8) and – associated with this – also the dominant centre of science and scholarship in the world (on the relationship between economic power and scientific performance, see de Solla Price 1986). Consequences for the position of the languages of scholarship appeared only with a delay because of the inertia of entrenched language customs and knowledge (Ammon 1998: 192–194), but, by the last third of the twentieth century, the consequences became manifest notwithstanding the complexity of their development. Their development is also linked with globalisation and the loosening of national structures in the evolving "post-national constellation" (Habermas 1998; Ch. A.8). One component of globalisation which is particularly important in the present context is the occurrence of a global communicative community with a single, global language (English), leaving behind all other international languages, including German and French. Loosening of national ties promotes the shift towards English for international communication and acceptance of its priority among speakers of other languages, even their native speakers. Attitudes corresponding to the post-national constellation therefore provide the social-psychological foundation for the global communicative community and its language. Despite this simplification of historical facts, such a synoptic view seems appropriate as a basis for a rough explanation of the large-scale context. In fact, developments were less linear and considerably more complex, as the following description attempts to show (see also Ammon 1998: 1–15; 1999, 2000b; Reinbothe 2006: 23–30, 2013).

For academic communication, the German-language community limited itself predominantly to its own language only during the relatively short period from about the middle of the nineteenth century to about the middle of the twentieth century. This was possible at this time more than ever before or after because German was an international academic language. Its use for academic communication was not restricted to native speakers; other language communities also used German especially for reading texts written in German. In fact, the same applies for the other international languages of science, English and French, but for German, its prominent position in science and scholarship was more characteristic, while French dominated diplomacy and English international trade (Ammon 1991a: Ch. 7 – Ch. 9). "Global status is attributed to German predominantly in the field of science and technology" (Zabrocki 1978: 184f.). Indeed, this or a similar reason is given whenever German is numbered among the significant international languages or even "world languages" (Braga 1979: 39f.; Ostrower 1965: 148). For a time, German enjoyed world leadership in science: "indeed at one time it was almost true to say that the language of science was the language of Heidelberg and Göttingen" (Savory 1953: 152). But German never occupied a monopoly position, as Savory seems to suggest, because English and French were positioned on a par, although with differences depending on scientific disciplines. German universities were respected abroad even in Napoleonic times but were then considered primarily "speculative" or theoretical. For example, Germaine de Staël found the Protestant North Germany "*rempli d'universités les plus savantes de l'Europe*" [full of the most knowledgeable universities in Europe], but with the limitation that "*tout s'y passe en théorie*" [everything happens in theory](de Staël [1810] 1968: 137). Only during the further course of the nineteenth century, did they turn towards empirical, primarily scientific research where they established an international reputation based on scientifically grounded knowledge. To gain access to this knowledge, scientists with other native languages learnt German, thereby making it into an international language of science.

There is considerable evidence for the global position of German as an academic language. For example, the British biologist Allan Savory quoted above (1953: 152) recalls the "advice that at one time was commonly given to young scientists, given with every desire to be helpful. It was that they should learn to read German". He refers to a bibliography on the biology of spiders, compiled by himself, among the titles of which "almost exactly [...] one third were German", and continues: "Many scientists will agree that in the first 40 years of the present century [20th century. U.A.] it was if not impossible at least exceedingly difficult to keep abreast of any branch of biology or medical science if one did not read German". In fact, a brief look at any representative bibliography of specialist literature in the natural sciences from the second half of the nineteenth to the first half of the twentieth century will show an impressive proportion of German-language titles. For example, the US-American periodical *Biological Abstracts* (1926ff.), primarily in the 1920s, contains not only a high proportion of German-language publications, but also Russian and Japanese titles "with German résumé" (e.g. in Vol. 1, 1926/1927, title nos. 32 and 74) and German-language contributions by Japanese authors, which had been published in Japanese periodicals with German titles (ibid, no. 104 in the periodical *Berichte des Ohara Instituts für Landwirtschaftliche Biologie Okayama Universitaet*) and similar. In the British *Zoological Record* (1864ff.) from the period before WWI, not only are, on average, more than one third of the titles published in German, but German also often functions as a lingua franca, i.e. for zoology, since e.g. Russian or Norwegian titles are made accessible by means of German translations rather than English translations as might be expected (1910: no. 42, 50, 132; details in Ammon 2015: 523f.). The position of German in chemistry was even more significant than in biology (Hopf 2011; Gordin 2015). As with the other natural sciences, similarly large proportions of German-language publications can easily be found for chemistry. One indicator for the significance of German in chemistry, even outside the German-speaking countries, is its distribution as a compulsory university course component. In many places, at least a reading knowledge in German was considered indispensable, e.g. in the USA (Sheppard 1935); German-language textbooks for chemistry were also used in US universities in the 1930s (Ray 1963: 54). But the significance of German extended far beyond the natural sciences: "until the Second World War, German was a language requirement for all psychology students in the USA [...]" (Heckhausen 1986: 32).

German was a particularly important academic language in the smaller countries adjacent to the German-language territory: in Scandinavia (Wiggen 1995a: 73; Saari 2000), the Netherlands and the central and eastern European countries, including the Baltic states and former Yugoslavia. In Portugal, German was a compulsory course component for law students (W. Ross 1967: 221, 1972). Accordingly, "German science and scholarship occupied a leading position in Europe" where "German could be read without difficulty in academic circles" relatively independently of discipline (Hagège 1996: 76). German also played an important role in countries remote from the German-language territory, e.g. in Japan, again in medicine (KAKINUMA 1994); in Korea (CHONG 2003a); also, in jurisprudence in Japan (MORI 1994; MURAKAMI 1989); and in other disciplines (cf. contributions in Ammon 1994d). In medicine, German terminology was current, and practising doctors kept their medical records in German (DOI 1982: 20; KAKINUMA 1994). There are numerous accounts of the high prestige accorded to German as an academic language in Japan.

The first volume of the *Zeitschrift für Deutsche Sprache* (p. 1) published in Tokyo from 1898 suggests a reason for the introduction of German as a foreign language: the already established knowledge of English apparently no longer corresponded with current needs:

> we outline here [...] some of the most prominent advantages of the German language, especially in the field of science, indicating the high standard of all academic work among the Germans and the respect consequently shown to this nation by the other peoples of Europe and the Americas.
>
> Germany now has the reputation of being the most advanced country in the sciences, and this is justified, because students eager to learn travel there from all over the world to pursue further research on German soil, in all branches of science and scholarship. After they have completed their courses at our own university, the most able of our own students are generally sent to Germany [...]

During the Meiji period (1868–1912), Japan was interested in scientific and technical knowledge from the German-speaking countries for its own programme of modernisation (additional political motives in NAKA 1994; for learning German in Japan, see also Ammon 1992a, 1994d). Evidently, interest in the German language developed significantly in response to the academic performance of German-speaking countries in different disciplines.

Respect for the language corresponds perfectly with demonstrable academic achievement. For instance, Shigeru NAKAYAMA (1981: 48) has shown that orientation towards Germany was expedient for medicine in Japan. In a statistical evaluation of the medical history of Fielding H. Garrison (1924), he concluded that, during the period from 1830 until around 1910, the German-speaking countries had contributed most to discoveries in this discipline. In the first decade of the twentieth century, five of the total of ten Nobel prizes awarded for chemistry went to Germany (Gordin 2015), and in the second decade, three of the eight Nobel prizes awarded (Skudlik 1990: 22; Hermann et al. 1978). Physics is another of the sciences in which German-speaking countries enjoyed leadership for a time, especially in the first third of the twentieth century (Hermann 2000). The fact that this influenced the language choices of non-German-speaking scientists is supported by the example of the Japanese Nobel Prize winner of 1965, TOMONAGA. He spent the period from 1937–1939 in Leipzig, and the list of his publications up to 1942 contains primarily German-language publications (Skudlik 1980: 180). From the present day perspective, one further indicator for the scientific status of German is particularly moving: in 1913, the planning committee of the Jewish Institute of Technical Education in Haifa, the *Technion*, which was one of the most important educational institutions in the resurgent state of Israel, chose German as – the sole – language of instruction (I. Cohen 1918: 12f.; communication by Bernard Spolsky). However, the foreign policy of the German Empire, which sought to strengthen German influence in the Middle East against British and French ambitions, also influenced this decision (Sadmon 1994), and the German-speaking religious group of Templers, who had migrated from Württemberg and settled in Haifa, may also have played a part (Carmel 1973). In fact, there were demonstrations against this role for German, but only by advocates of Hebrew; other foreign languages, such as English or French, were not under discussion. Of course, future political developments – WWI and especially Nazism – then made any significant role for German impossible.

Numerous visits by non-German-speaking students and researchers (Weinrich 1986: 190) testify to the prestige accorded to scholarship in the German-speaking countries, especially in the natural sciences. The following comment applies far beyond the USA: "[U]p to the First World War most American Scientists did their graduate work in Europe, particularly in

Germany". The attractiveness of Germany was maintained for a time after the WWI, e.g. in physics, as the following quotation shows: "The Rockefeller-supported International Education Board's programme of post-doctoral fellowships allowed promising Americans to absorb the newest approaches in and around Germany" (both quotations from Hoch/ Platt 1993: 136). The biographies of Nobel Prize winners in science reveal that German-speaking countries were key to their training and specialist commitment. For example, an overview of Nobel Prize winners up to 1937 by T.W.Mac Callum/ Stephen Taylor (1938) gives the following numbers of prize winners in natural sciences from non-German-speaking countries, who were active in German universities (one also in Vienna) during their training or research: chemistry seven, physics six and medicine eight (details in Ammon 2015: 527f.; see also Martin 1985). However, most of these also had contact with other countries, especially France, Britain or the USA. Furthermore, bearing in mind the element of randomness in the awards, the Nobel Prize should not be overestimated as an indicator of academic achievement in this context (cf. Küppers/ Weingart/ Ulitzka 1982; Wilhelm 1983: 39–50). But other pointers are also problematic or would require excessive effort in the present context. At least, the Nobel Prize promotes an image of leadership in scientific research and may therefore ultimately strengthen the position of the prize winners' language as a scientific language. It must be added that academics from German-speaking countries who had moved to live abroad often did not shift linguistically or at least continue to publish in German. One of presumably many examples is the chemist Hans von Euler-Chelpin, who taught in Stockholm from 1898 onwards (Nobel prize 1929. Examples of his German-language publications after 1898: *Die qualitative chemische Analyse* 1907; *Grundlagen und Ergebnisse der Pflanzenchemie* 1908/09; *Chemie der Enzyme* 1910; *Chemie der Hefe und der alkoholischen Gärung* 1915. Mac Callum/ Taylor 1938: 153).

By the middle of the nineteenth century at the latest, German, alongside French and English, was also a language used by scholars with other native languages to distribute their findings and increase their status. For example, Russian chemist Alexander Butlerov valued the fact that his *Lehrbuch der Organischen Chemie* was translated into German (Leipzig: Quandt & Händel 1868) because it helped him to make a name for himself internationally. The now world-famous Russian chemist Dmitri Mendeleyev had his *Grundlagen der Chemie* translated into German (St Petersburg 1890), but then also into French and English, to underline his priority claim for the discovery of the periodic system at an international level, especially against his rival for this award, Lothar Meyer from Tübingen. "Russian counted for less than German", explains Michael Gordin (2012: 94) regarding this language choice, and he lists further Russian examples and their background (for details of Mendeleyev, see Meyer in Gordin 2015: 51–78). Furthermore, publishing in German was not unusual for non-German-speaking scholars, even if they were working outside the German-language territory. One example is the ground-breaking treatise by Russian Nobel Prize winner in medicine Ilya Metchnikoff: *Die Lehre von den Phagozyten und deren experimentellen Grundlagen* (1913; Mac Callum/ Taylor 1938: 192). The advantages of this language choice are revealed by the following reference to the seminal publication by the Russian founder of behaviourism, Ivan P. Pavlov: "It was only when, in 1899, his book [. . .], 'The Activity of the Digestive Glands' was translated into German that his reputation as a physiologist became international". In the 1920s, other works by Pavlov were published directly in German (Mac Callum/ Taylor 1938: 178; also, Wickler 1986: 30). German-language periodicals appeared in several non-German-speaking countries. Examples from medicine – before WWI and in some cases after – include:

• In Russia: the *St Petersburger medicinische Wochenschrift* and the *Pharmaceutische Zeitschrift für Russland*;

- In Hungary: the *Pester medizinisch-chirurgische Presse* and the *Homöopathische Blätter*;
- In Czechoslovakia: the *Prager medicinische Wochenschrift* and the *Verhandlungen des naturforschenden Vereins in Brünn;* and
- In Japan: the *Archiv für Japanische Chirurgie* (Lippert 1986: 40f).

Before WWI, presentations were often given in German at international conferences. Max Weber lectured in German at the international "Congress of Arts and Science" in St. Louis (USA) (Scaff 2011: 60). The same can be assumed of other German conference participants from different disciplines, e.g. Werner Sombart, Ferdinand Tönnies, Johannes Conrad, Paul Hensel, Wilhelm Ostwald and certainly also the theologian Adolf von Hartnack (ibid: 54–66), who declined the offer of becoming German Ambassador in Washington after WWI because of his lack of English.

Until WWI, the bibliographies, referencing and abstracting services, or to put it in more contemporary language, bibliographical data banks, strengthened the position of German as an international academic language. They were the leaders in important disciplines, so that academics worldwide had to refer to them – and they were published in German. John E. Flynn, chief editor of the American *Biological Abstracts* for many years, begins his autobiographical *résumé* as follows: "Up to 1914 American biologists relied mainly on German abstracting periodicals – the botanists on Botanisches Zentralblatt, Just's Botanisches Jahresbericht, Hedwigia and the Zeitschrift für Pflanzenkrankheiten; zoologists on Zoologischer Bericht and Berichte über Wissenschaftliche Biologie; bacteriologists on the Zentralblatt für Bakteriologie, etc." (Flynn 1951: 1; similarly, Davis 1987: 3; Davis/ Schmidt 1995: 5). Finally, the numerous textbooks of scientific German, which have been re-issued many times, especially since the second half of the nineteenth century, also reveal the international position of German as an academic language (e.g. Hodges 1880; Gore [1891] 1893; Phillips [1913, 1915] 1924).

However, at the latest, since WWI, there are signs of a loss of position for German. Important abstracting services, e.g. the *Zentralblatt für Zoologie* (1894–1918) collapsed at around this time. Flynn's review touches on some of these changes:

> After the outbreak of World War I these German abstracting agencies were no longer available to American scholars. The lack of abstracting service was so keenly felt that the Botanical Society of America and the Society of American Bacteriologists decided to provide abstracts in English, covering the respective fields. Botanical Abstracts, under the auspices of the Botanical Society of America, and Abstracts of Bacteriology, under the auspices of the Society of American Bacteriologists, were thus established, and began publication in 1917 and 1918, respectively.
>
> *(Flynn 1951: 1f.; also, Steere et al. 1976)*

Construing WWI as a turning point is presumably an oversimplification. In fact, initial signs of minor damage to the position of German are already evident shortly before or at least around the start of the war. For example, as a source of citations from US publications in chemistry, the US periodical *Journal of the Chemical Society* outranked all German-speaking chemical periodicals between 1911 and 1915, while it was still in second place from 1906–1910 behind *Berichte der deutschen chemischen Gesellschaft* and in 1886–90 was still only in fourth place, behind *Liebigs Annalen der Chemie* and the *Zeitschrift für physikalischen Chemie* (Ammon 1998: 43 – based on Gross/ Gross 1927; for details of Gross/ Gross, see Ch. G.3). The background to this development was the rise of the USA to the strongest economic power in the world even before WWI, thereby forcing the German Empire from the leadership position previously occupied by Great

Britain. Despite the risk of overstating the role of WWI as a turning point, it is associated with various events which were seriously damaging to the position of German as an international academic language, or as an international language at all. This is not to deny that many disciplines remained predominantly German speaking even after WWI, especially some newer developments. For example, "[i]n its early stages, behavioural research [. . .] was a German or German-speaking discipline. At that time [between the world wars! U.A.], German was initially dominant at international conferences. This was not because of the overwhelming number of German participants, but simply because the terminology and key works were all published in German" (contribution by Wickler to the discussion in Kalverkämper/ Weinrich 1986: 80). Having said this, there were of course also founding figures with other native languages, e.g. Frenchman, Jean-Henri C. Fabre (1823–1915).

For all this, it is still difficult to differentiate mere indicators from causative factors influencing the position of German as an international academic language. In fact, the same events can often be regarded both as indicators of position and as factors acting on its development. For example, on the one hand, availability via internationally leading periodical bibliographies or databanks can be an indicator of the strong position of the relevant language as well as a factor which motivates towards its increased use. On the other hand, provided they promote scholarship in the relevant language communities or favour the language, economic and political developments are less ambiguous factors. It is therefore important to look even further back in history to recall briefly at least the most influential events. These include: the Thirty Years' War, which brought lasting devastation to the German-speaking countries; perhaps also the Seven Years' War, which strengthened the position of Great Britain as a colonial power and therefore also strengthened the English language; the Napoleonic Wars and France's loss of equality with the English-speaking world as a colonial power and loss of clear hegemony in the European continent; the rise of the German-speaking countries in economic and political power during the nineteenth century; the formation of the German Empire and its policy of world power; WWI and its consequences (including the economic collapse of Germany and Austria, the dissolution of the Habsburg monarchy and loss of German colonies); Nazism and WWII with its consequences; the creation of the European Union; and finally the formation of the newly unified Germany as a medium-sized power (within the circle of established and rising major powers). Although these major events are seminal factors with an enduring effect on the position of the German language in the world and as an academic or scientific language, they can only be mentioned in passing here (a more systematic discussion is given in Ch. A.8; A.11).

Relevant consequences of WWI include the events grouped under the heading of the "language boycott". This refers to the organised exclusion of the German language from international academic communication which was perpetrated by academics among the victorious powers for several years after WWI. The following report draws on archival research by Roswitha Reinbothe (2006), who investigated this development based on accounts of the underlying processes (Schröder-Gudehus 1966: 111–120; Schröder-Gudehus 1973, 1990; Kevles 1971; Weindling 1996; Ammon 2000b: 68–72). As already mentioned, the spread of German as an international academic language had been supported by the establishment of comprehensive bibliographies and abstracting services in Germany. It was also promoted by collaboration in foreign projects, primarily the *International Catalogue of Scientific Literature*, which appeared in England (1902–1914), and to which German-language publications were diligently contributed from Germany (Reinbothe 2006: 30–36). The influential position of German academics in international academic associations, some of which had been founded in Germany – e.g. the *Internationale Assoziation der Akademien* (from 1899 onwards) (Reinbothe 2006: 23–110, especially 37–41; Ammon 2000b: 68f.), was also significant. An international network of German academics institutionalised in this way was torn apart by WWI, and the use of German for international academic communication was consciously prohibited. During the war, this was initially prompted by Germans, but later in the war and after the war, primarily by the Allies. The underlying reason was the effort by some groups within the victorious powers to enforce restrictions on the Germans, not only militarily but also academically and linguistically. Having said this, it was the "*Aufruf an die Kulturwelt!*" [appeal to the cultural world] (Kellermann 1915), in which 93 prominent German academics and artists addressed the public on 4 October 1914, i.e. shortly after the outbreak of the war, to justify the war from the perspective of the Central Powers, which provided the foundations for the boycott of German and its legitimation. It was followed on 16 October by a declaration of similar content "*Erklärung der Hochschullehrer des Deutschen Reiches*" [declaration of the German Empire's university teachers], with no less than 3,000 signatures (Reinbothe 2006: 96–110, especially 97–100). German academics thus stepped onto the world stage in great solidarity as uncritical deniers of German co-responsibility for the outbreak of the war and the cruelties of the battlefield. What is more, they expressed themselves in an openly racist manner about the "disgraceful spectacle" of the Allies "arousing hatred against the white race among Mongolians and Negroes" (Kellermann 1915: 65). Furthermore, even during the war, academic boycott measures originated from Germany itself. For example, the Germans withdrew their collaboration from the *International Catalogue of Scientific Literature*, which brought about its collapse in 1914 (Reinbothe 2006: 113). Beyond this, the German government banned not only the distribution of texts containing information relevant to the war, but also issued a temporary, general "ban on the sale of academic books and periodicals, not only to enemy countries but also to their allies and neutral countries abroad", even for specialist medical literature (ibid: 116). Because of their uncritical attitude, German academics therefore cast themselves in an unfavourable light by comparison with the French, who resisted distribution bans, at least for specialist medical literature (ibid: 126, comprehensively 111–127).

However, such humanitarianism did not prevent French scholars from implementing a comprehensive boycott, especially against academics from Germany and Austria, or from excluding the German language from all international academic communication. With support from Belgium, they gained the – admittedly, sometimes reluctant – cooperation of academics from the other victorious powers and neutral states. The most effective measures of this boycott included the foundation of new, international academic associations, excluding German and Austrian academics and excluding German as a language of the association, conference language and publication language. These measures extended to almost all natural-science disciplines. German was also extensively excluded from the humanities by the new *Union académique internationale*, which limited its official language to French (ibid: 164). Reinbothe (2006) gives details of the "exclusion of the German language" from academic associations (ibid: 149–163), the "criticism, condemnation and suppression of German as an international language of academic publication" (ibid: 165–201) and the "elimination of German as an international conference language" (ibid: 202–243).

But the boycott did not prevent individual, prominent German scientists from giving lectures abroad in German, e.g. Albert Einstein in England in 1921 and in Japan in 1922 (Neffe 2005: 300f. and 141). Finally, in 1926, advocates of the boycott signalled a relaxation of their measures, partly in connection with Germany's joining the League of Nations. But now, German academics proved to be recalcitrant and insisted on the full restoration of German for all academic communication. Reinbothe (2006: 345–363) assesses these demands as "exaggerated" and even speaks of a "counter boycott" (also, Ammon 2000b: 71f.). Brigitte Schröder-Gudehus (1966: 181–211) has presented important findings on the power politics behind this conflict. In the end, however, the German side failed to achieve either personal or linguistic equality (Reinbothe 2006: 345–397). The result of all the German efforts in the second half of the twentieth century was "[t]he dominance of French and English and the decline of the German language" (Reinbothe's chapter heading: 399–424). Moreover, France's ambitions for its language as holding a prominent academic position have endured into more recent history. One example is the EC project *CERN*, which was founded in the 1950s primarily between France and the then Federal Republic of Germany and situated – at the insistence of France – on French-speaking soil in Meyrin near Geneva: the project runs without German as an official language, but with English continuing to gain ground alongside French. The acronym *CERN* stands for "*Conseil Européenne pour la Recherche Nucléaire*" (Hermann 2000: 226f.). The role model for limiting the association and conference languages to English and French here was the League of Nations, recently founded through the Treaty of Versailles, which was restricted to these two official languages (Ch. H.3). Following this, opinions about rejecting German as a third academic language of equal status, differed (Reinbothe 2006: passim). But the organisers of the language boycott were careful not to advertise this fact. Accordingly, the boycott was concealed even from contemporary researchers of international academic communication, e.g. US researchers P.L. and E.M. Gross (1927) and Herbert N. Shenton (1933), who, at least, make no mention of it in relevant publications.

In their analysis of citations for the year 1926, Gross and Gross (1927) did not find a significant decline in the use of German-language chemical periodicals by US scientists, but, as mentioned, an increase in the use of one – naturally English-language – US periodical (details in Ch. G.3). By contrast, Shenton's investigations did suggest the decline of German. After a larger scale overview of scientific abstracting services originating in the 1920s in the USA for an increasing number of disciplines, Shenton evaluated their significance for the future of scientific languages as follows: "Yet when all the work is done in these digests, information is only available to the scientists who know English". Even at that time, he considered the corresponding services in German to be comparatively small scale: "A minor service of similar sort in the field of Economics is rendered by the Jahrbücher für Nationalökonomie und Statistik [. . .]" (Shenton/ Sapir/Jespersen 1931: 31). In a worldwide investigation, carried out at the end of the 1920s, Shenton confirms German as the third most important language at international conferences, but significantly behind French and English (Shenton 1933: 223, 229; Ammon 1991a: 242–245). The use of German among academics in the smaller states neighbouring Germany could evidently no longer be taken for granted even in the 1920s. For example, before his lecture in Copenhagen, Werner Heisenberg was advised by Niels Bohr that it was "taken for granted that we will speak English" (Hermann 2000: 220).

The collapse of commercial life in Germany and Austria during WWI, because of which their academic communities lost their economic foundation, was a stronger influence than any of the boycott measures. Even the most prominent research organisation in Germany, the *Kaiser-Wilhelm Gesellschaft*, forerunner of the present Max-Planck Institute needed financial support from Japanese sponsors (Friese 1990: 811–827). By contrast, the USA gathered strength from the war and succeeded in developing its academic institutions sustainably (Ch. G.9). The subsequent, even profounder self-destruction of German and Austrian academic life and language as a result of Nazism is almost beyond comprehension. On one hand, there were mass expulsions and murder of their own, especially Jewish academics. Even by 1936, 1,617 German, not only Jewish, university teachers had been driven overseas, of whom 1,160 migrated to English-speaking countries, 825 to the USA (Kröner 1983: 13; also, Löffelholz/ Trendelenburg 2008). Many in fact still spoke German but mostly in private. In their academic activities, they made every effort to use English, although this was often not easy for them – as the example of Einstein, who largely continued relying on German, shows (Hermann 2000: 224; Neffe 2005: 410). The emigrants generally preferred English for written communication. Many consciously turned away from German, especially refugees from Central Eastern Europe, as Paul Weindling has described (1996: 218). It is particularly difficult to imagine the loss of prestige of German academics and scientists, also because many German academics supported Nazism (Weinreich [1946] 1999). In particular, the perversion of science known as "eugenics" contributed to an extensive loss of prestige. This led not only to now infamous murderous consequences (ibid: 35f.), but also to an evaluation of academic performance according to the "race" of the author rather than quality of scholarship; it even included the retrospective stripping of doctoral titles from Jews. For example, at the University of Cologne, from 1933 to 1945 alone, 65 doctorates were withdrawn – and only re-granted in 2005 (Szöllösi-Janze/ Freitäger 2005). Added to this was the isolation, enforced by the regime, of academics who had not emigrated. The ban on the acceptance of Nobel prizes imposed by Hitler in 1937 after the award of the peace prize to Carl von Ossietzky, was symptomatic (Beyerchen 1982: 217). In an offensive letter obviously vetted by Hitler himself, three German academics had to decline Nobel Prizes they were offered in 1939. After this, no more prizes were offered to Germans until the end of the war ("*Sie sollen sich dies hier abholen. Als Hitler den Chemie-Nobelpreis stahl* [. . .]" [They should come and collect this. When Hitler stole the Nobel Prize]; *FAZ* 28 September 2004: 44). As a result of such self-destructive policies, German achievements began to decline even in disciplines such as physics which can be important for war, which by the way has awakened the doubtful delusion that German scientists tried to deny Hitler the atom bomb. For the position of German as an international language of scholarship and science, an equally unfavourable but less harmful consequence of Nazism was the collapse of other German referencing services such as the *Zoologischer Bericht* (1922–1943/44).

After WWII, German had largely relinquished the basis of its international position as an academic language, even though this did not become particularly evident for several decades. In fact, such a position of the language tends to persevere because of the widely branching language skills associated with it. For example, comments praising the international standing of German as an academic language are still to be found some time after the political-economic catastrophe (e.g. Ross 1972; with further examples). But there are also more realistic assessments, e.g. in a comparison of languages by US Esperantist Mario Pei. Towards the end of the 1950s, he discussed languages which could be considered world languages at that time. German was characterised as follows: "You are, despite your extent, a highly localised language. What overseas possibilities you once had you have lost. [. . .] Your former scientific appeal is waning [. . .]. You are a tongue of the past, not of the future" (Pei 1958: 228f.). The reference to "overseas" relates to the loss of German colonies after WWI. However, in the reference to science as the pillar of its world status, there is also perhaps an allusion to the damage done to German by the Nazis. But, contrary to the weakness of German diagnosed by Pei, there are still some encouraging accounts. For example, referring to the worldwide proportion of publications on food science and technology, Wilson O. Aiyepeki (1973: 53) explains "that approximately 40% of the papers were in English, 20% in German, 14% in Russian, 6% in French, 4% in Italian and 2% in Spanish", adding that, "[t]his shows quite convincingly that any researcher in this field must be familiar with at least English and German to cover about 60% of the literature". Another indicator for the continuing respect for German even after Nazism is that a reading knowledge in German remained a compulsory component for PhD programmes in various disciplines in US universities (cf. e.g. F.X. Braun 1954). Only at the end of the 1960s, was this questioned in the USA for students of science, as indeed were all foreign language requirements (discussion in the periodical *Science*: Ross/ Shilling 1966; Wren 1966; Hartman 1967; Di Pietro 1967; Andmussen 1967; Stern/ Rudowski 1968; de Santi/ Huber/ Pearce 1972). The academic advantages were brought into doubt: "It is not surprising that language requirements have come under mounting criticism as being of doubtful utility [. . .]" (Wiltsey 1972, Part 1:7). In this context, opponents to dropping the language requirement referred specifically to science in the German-speaking countries. Three German Nobel Prize winners (Rudolf Mössbauer, Karl Ziegler, Feodor Lynen) were cited with the comment that, "the majority of important German scientific works are neither translated into English in their entirety nor in the form of comprehensive digests" (Stern/ Rudowski 1968: 432). The abolition of the "foreign-language requirements" in US universities which followed anyway was not only an indicator but also an additional causative factor for further decline in the position of German. Since US scientists now hardly learnt German, the language became less suitable for communication with the dominant centre of the scientific world. German-language publications were also consulted less, and German academic publishers had to shift to English to survive in the dominant English-language market. At the latest by the 1980s, there was a serious decline in the learning of German for scientific purposes. At the same time, publication of textbooks for scientific German in the English-speaking world had largely ceased. In May 1997, the last title recorded in the *WORLDCAT*, at that time the world's largest online library, was *Readings in Scientific German* (1983). Somewhat later and less consistently, universities and academics in other countries either shifted from German to English as a means of communication or continued for reasons of tradition (cf. for Japan and Korea, contributions in Ammon 1994c; Ammon/ CHONG 2003). Exceptions and enduring "niches" for German as an international academic language will be described in chapters G.6 and G.7.

2. Differences between disciplines, types of academic communication and availability of data

The shift from German to English as an international academic language did not happen concurrently or equally consistently in all disciplines. Differences were initially identified in Kalverkämper/ Weinrich (1986) and with greater clarity in Skudlik (1990: e.g. 215f.), Debus/ Kollmann/ Pörksen (2000) and Ammon (1991a: 230f, 1998: 38f). Attempts at differentiation between disciplines initially followed the traditional classification into natural sciences, social sciences and humanities, with the structural sciences (logic, mathematics) allocated to the first of these groups. Skudlik drew attention to the differences between theoretical and applied sciences – and to the possibility of "niche disciplines" for German as an academic language, presumably inspired by Weinrich (Deutscher Bundestag 1986: 196). Accurate allocation of disciplines is often difficult because of increasing interdisciplinarity. However, I have based the following discussion on the classification of disciplines sketched above:

(1)   Theoretical (also "pure") natural sciences including structural sciences (Ch. G.3);
(2)   Applied sciences (Ch. G.4), especially applied natural sciences and technologies, by contrast with (1);
(3)   Social sciences (Ch. G.5);
(4)   Humanities (Ch. G.6);
(5)   (Humanities) niche disciplines (Ch. G.7).

This classification is motivated by hypotheses about differences in the international position of German and English; in some cases, these are empirically supported but require further testing. Similar reservations apply to the following assumptions about groups of disciplines.

a) Global versus national relevance of content

The theoretical natural sciences focus primarily on universal laws. Since these are generally of global interest, they also tend to be communicated worldwide. Because of its global position,

English is therefore the most appropriate language. By contrast, research questions in applied sciences, social sciences and especially in the humanities often focus on a specific language community or nation, so that their own official language of state or native language is often more appropriate for people specifically interested.

b) High versus low degree of disciplinary specialisation and cooperation within groups

Disciplinary specialisation has progressed further in the natural sciences than in the social sciences and humanities. Professorships in the social sciences and especially the humanities are thus more likely to cover "the full breadth" of a discipline. With increased disciplinary specialisation, there are only a few specialist representatives within individual language communities, so that partners for an exchange of ideas must be sought outside or even worldwide. In the natural sciences and in some cases in the social sciences, "invisible colleges" have therefore been formed (de Solla Price 1974: 74–102). These are groups of academics within the same specialist field; membership is often international, and the groups (rarely more than 100 members) cooperate internationally. In "science", the opinion is widespread that with group cooperation, "knowledge can grow more rapidly than any individual can move by himself [sic]. The humanities, by resting with the capability of the individual, eschew this growth rate and certainty" (de Solla Price 1970: 6). In view of this social structure within research, the use of English in the natural sciences is therefore more likely than in the humanities because of its worldwide distribution.

c) Difficult versus easy access for non-experts

In the natural sciences, the gulf between experts and non-experts is greater than in the applied sciences, social sciences and the humanities. Regarding intelligibility by non-experts, the theoretical natural sciences, including the structural sciences, are quite strictly confined to the proverbial ivory tower. By contrast, widespread criticism, e.g. of "sociological gobbledygook" implies an expectation that the social sciences and the humanities should be widely intelligible. Nobody even considers this in the case of the theoretical natural sciences. Their expert languages, including higher mathematics, are only accessible to experts anyway. Accordingly, the shift to a foreign language does not involve any significant increase in difficulty of understanding for society at large. By all accounts, it does further symbolise the ivory tower to which people have become accustomed, at a further level of symbolism. By contrast, in the applied sciences, the shift to a foreign language can introduce a considerable interference factor for communication – whenever that language is inadequately known. This is presumably also the case with English in the German-language territory, even among academics (Haße 2002: 4; also, Ammon 1991a: 269–277; Ch. G.10).

d) Easy versus difficult translatability into a foreign language

In the natural sciences, the structure of the specialist language facilitates the shift to a foreign language, i.e. English. Formulas, graphic and other visual representations play a major role, reducing the significance of verbal components of the text. Such formal or symbolic languages are largely universal, not only in mathematics, but also in other specialist subjects e.g. chemistry (cf. titles such as Wendy Warr's (1988) *Structures: The International Language of Chemistry*). By contrast, formal languages play a reduced role in the social sciences and almost none in typical humanities subjects. Furthermore, the terminology in the natural sciences is based more consistently on Greek or Latin roots, and such "internationalisms" are almost interchangeable between languages. In contrast, the social sciences and especially the humanities make extensive use of ordinary language, including a rich array of stylistic variation (Oskaar/ Skudlik von Stackelberg 1988). Their terms interlock more strongly with ordinary language, so that entire word fields must often be matched in translations. Sometimes, even aesthetic standards are applied to their texts (cf. Ch. G.6: beginning). In the humanities, textual structures are also more variable and therefore more difficult to capture, whereas they tend to follow internationally unified patterns in the natural sciences (to simplify: theory, hypotheses, testing of hypotheses, discussion of findings). In view of such linguistic and textual norms, academics in the humanities prefer to stay within their own native languages or official languages of state rather than to shift to a foreign language.

e) Non-agreement between academic language (metalanguage) and object language

This factor generally applies to the enduring international position of the German language in the discipline of German Studies (*Germanistik*), which apparently depends upon "the nature of the objects of study" (e.g. Council of Science and the Humanities 2006: 16; Ch. G.7). What is meant here is that when German is the object language (the language of the object under investigation), this also seems to secure the position of German as an academic language (metalanguage), i.e. it hinders the shift towards English as an academic language. Although this factor seems plausible, its significance should not be overestimated and requires testing. It should be borne in mind that, in subjects such as Finno-Ugric Studies and parts of Slavic Studies, German sometimes enjoyed a more prominent international position than the languages in question, and that, in German Studies, languages other than German, i.e. foreign languages, are increasingly used for academic communication (Ch. G.7). In German Studies, factor e) "metalanguage = object language" is only more noticeable but not necessarily more important than factors a) to d), which correlate with the fact that it is a humanities subject.

In light of these considerations, groups of subjects can be now listed in an – at least partial – rank ordering according to the presumed proportion of English and German in the associated academic communication (starting from the German-language territory). The proportion of German (in an average of the subjects contained within the subject groups) would increase from (1) to (5) and that of English would decrease. This rank order – which must be subjected to further empirical testing – is also suggested for languages other than German relative to English, e.g. French, Italian or Dutch. Accordingly, with the five subject groups, corresponding to their numbering at the start of the chapter, the proportion of German in academic communication can be represented schematically as follows. If we designate a higher proportion of German (or other languages of similar international position) in subject group x than in subject group y as "x>y", the following applies: $(5)>(4)>(3)\approx(2)>(1)$. The difference in rank ordering for (3) and (2), i.e. social sciences and applied sciences, is questionable.

Alongside the warnings already mentioned about the imprecise demarcation between the subject groups (1) to (5) and the across-the-board formulation of factors a) to e), it is also important to note the constraint that English-language and German-language communication of German academics must not simply be assumed to be on a par with international or intranational communication (corresponding to Ch. A.3). For example, English-language communication can, of course, also take place between native speakers of German. Wolfgang Klein (2000: 289) has even stated that his English-language publications were "received more strongly" than those in German "even in Germany".

Regarding the preferences within certain disciplines for German or English and the degree of internationalism in communication, it is only possible to achieve any degree of precision for specific communication situations. The discussion will therefore focus primarily on the following communication situations facing university teachers:

- Reading of specialist literature;
- Use of bibliometric resources, such as bibliographic data banks and citation indexes;
- Written publication;
- Spoken presentations at conferences;
- Informal discussions in research, especially laboratory discussions;
- University teaching.

Meaningful data for other communication situations were not available (e.g. subject-related or social email communication, academic exams, consultations, communication with university administration). This also applies for subject-specific communication in "Research and Development (R&D)" within companies. For almost all the situations addressed in the following discussion, the data hardly meet the quality criteria for empirical research, such as validity or reliability, especially not the latter. For example, the language proportions of publications, primarily for German, in bibliographical data banks with a global orientation, have been used as indicators for the actual language proportions in worldwide publications. But these databanks are nowadays produced: a) predominantly in English-speaking or Anglophile countries (e.g. USA or the Netherlands) and are therefore presumably skewed in favour of English-language titles, and b) they never register all the actual worldwide publications within a discipline, often not even approximately. Nevertheless, from the proportions of German-language publications included in such databanks, I have inferred the scope of international communication in German. In the absence of parameters such as standard deviation, I was not even able to indicate confidence margins. Accordingly, there is still considerable room for further work on verification. Citation frequency seems to be useful, at least as an indicator of receptive language choice for the reading of academic publications. But the major citation indexes (*Science Citation Index, Social Sciences Citation Index, Arts and Humanities Citation Index*) are probably also skewed in favour of English – as the language policy of their founder, Eugene Garfield, might suggest (Garfield 1977b; Ammon 1998: 34). In some cases, this has been demonstrated (Sandelin/ Sarafoglou 2004). I have tried to avoid this skewing in my own investigations (supported by Stefan Michels), which cover only the period from 1920 to 1990.

Direct and reliable assessment of international communication is effort intensive, and representative data are in short supply. Only informal reports appear to be available, especially for language choice in laboratories with international personnel, which are highly important in the sciences. Information about language choice at international conferences is similarly unrepresentative. Available information about the official languages of international academic associations, which are generally also accepted as conference languages, says little about actual language choices at conferences. But, perhaps informal and even anecdotal information should be granted a certain validity, if it points in a coherent direction. In the following discussion at least, I have often felt myself having to rely on this stopgap solution.

3. Theoretical natural sciences and structural sciences

In the subject group of "theoretical" (or "pure") natural sciences, I include primarily biology, chemistry, physics and (human) medicine (excluding clinical medicine). Other conceivable candidates, such as geology, have been omitted because of difficulties obtaining data. But the structural science mathematics is included because it has been part of previous research and because of the similarities in international communication conditions and language choice. Among the various academic communication situations (Ch. G.2 towards the end), representative data for written publications are most readily accessible. This preference also responds to the fact that the international position of German as an academic language has always been based primarily on written publications. And for this reason, the learning of German by foreign academics has concentrated on reading comprehension (Ch. G.1). The most basic relevant data are the German-language proportions by comparison with other languages in the global total for publications in the natural sciences. Presumably, the scope of international communication (Ch. A.3) through these texts (reading and other uses by non-German-speakers) is approximately proportional to its proportion worldwide and is therefore an appropriate, if rough, indicator for the international position of the language (in the relevant discipline). This assumption still requires checking, which has not been possible within the present framework. However, further data presented throughout this chapter, e.g. on the citation frequency of German-language texts (citation analyses), provide supporting indicators.

The most representative data on frequency of publication can be taken from periodic bibliographical databanks which claim global coverage. But these are susceptible to skewing in favour of their home language and culture, e.g. the more recent bibliographical databanks produced predominantly by English-speaking or Anglophile states (e.g. USA or the Netherlands) with their over-representation of English-language titles. Large bibliographies were also previously located in other language territories. Increasing concentration in English-speaking countries is itself an – indirect – indicator for the prioritisation of English as *the* international academic language and the loss of position of other languages. In fact, former, leading German periodical bibliographies have been replaced or absorbed by English-language bibliographies (for the rise of *Biological Abstracts*, see Ch. G.1). For example, the *Chemisches Zentralblatt* (which had existed since 1830) merged with *Chemical Abstracts* in 1969, and *Physikalische Berichte* (which had been published since 1845) – after renaming as *Physics Briefs* in 1979, and after a period of decline – was taken over by *Physics Abstracts* in 1995 (Ammon 1998: 141). There are various indicators for skewing in favour of the home language. For the period between 1890 and 1980, I compared the language proportions of the largest natural-science periodical bibliographies from Germany, France, Russia and the USA with the language proportions of exclusively US databanks (data from TSUNODA 1983). In this context, the proportion of English in an average of all databanks (all four countries) remained behind that of the US databanks; in the final year of the evaluation, 1980, almost 10% (64.1% by comparison with 73.6%). But, based on these findings, it is also important not to overestimate the national or language-community-specific skewing. The arithmetic mean for all databanks in fact showed a continuous rise in English-language publications and a decline for all other languages, similar to that for the US databanks taken by themselves (Ammon 1991a: 219–222, 253f.). If an underestimate of the proportion of English in non-US databanks approximately equals the overestimate in the US databanks, the skewing amounts to less than 3% (relative to the arithmetic mean of three non-US databanks and the US data bank combined). For 1980, this would still give a corrected proportion of English-language publications above 70%. It should also be borne in mind that databanks should heed a relatively balanced representativeness across countries and languages in order to preserve valuation and prestige, especially in view of the recent growth in critical monitoring. However, control investigations have demonstrated some skewing in favour of English, e.g. for the medical databank *Medline* (Guardiolo/ Banos 1993; see also Navarro 1996a: 1564). Conversely, a comparative investigation I carried out myself, although only on a small subset, produced contrary results. On comparison of the two largest bibliographical databanks for mathematics: *Mathematical Reviews* (USA) – *Zentralblatt für Mathematik* (Germany), the proportion of English-language publications in the German databank proved to be higher. In all four years under comparison, 1980–1983, it exceeded the English-language proportion in the US databank, in fact by 3.9% to 11% (Ammon 1998: 144, 150). Accordingly, not only the English-language databanks seem to be skewed in favour of English. And it would be completely misleading to explain the "dominance" of English as an academic language as a mere *"fata morgana"* of bibliographical databanks.

The most balanced findings on language proportions in worldwide publications can presumably be obtained from databanks claiming or offering global coverage, which have been produced in countries with different languages. However, for this purpose, the appropriate breadth is available only for earlier historical periods, for over half of the earlier part of the period between 1890 and 1980 which I have covered here, relying on data from TSUNODA (1983). In this context, all values were averaged twice (in each case, unweighted arithmetic mean): initially, for all subjects within every country (or every language community) and then for all countries (Ammon 1991a: 219–222, 254). By contrast, for the period from 1981 to 2005, I had to rely completely on databanks from English-speaking or Anglophile countries (USA and the Netherlands). It was not possible to include the *Zentralblatt der Mathematik* because of the impossibility of computerised analysis of language proportions. For the most recent years, it was no longer possible to consider mathematics at all, because *Mathematical Reviews* no longer allows language proportions to be counted – as if they considered this superfluous, because of the hegemony of English. Otherwise, the most representative databank for the subject globally was included in each case. As Figure G.3–1 shows, the proportions for almost all languages apart from English

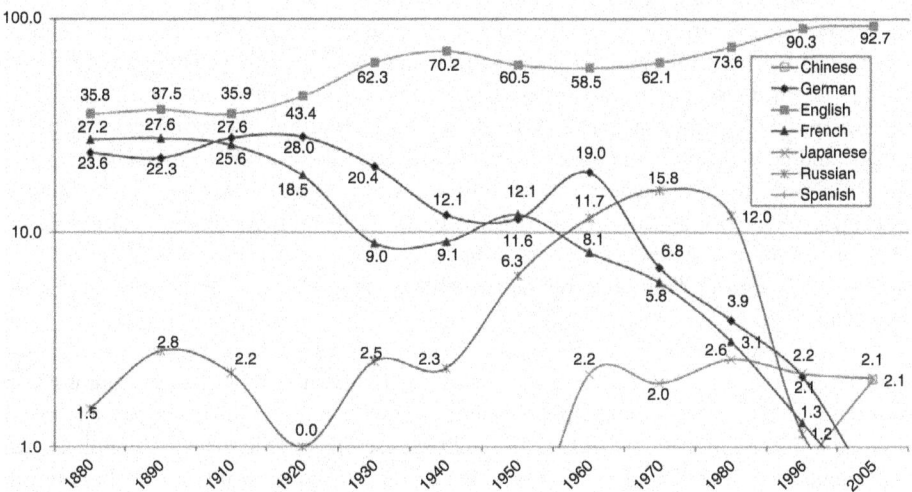

Figure G.3–1   Language proportions of publications in biology, chemistry, physics, medicine and mathematics worldwide 1880–2005

Note: arithmetic means from databanks in different countries as percentages, logarithmised for differentiation in lower percentage ranges

(*Source:* older figures based on TSUNODA 1983, more recent, after Ammon 1998: 146–151 and later. *Biological Abstracts* (biology, only up to 2004), *Chemical Abstracts* (chemistry), *Medline* (medicine), *INSPEC* (physics) and *Mathematical Reviews* (mathematics, only up to 1996))

(2005: 92.7%) have declined continuously over time. German, French and Russian even fall below 1% (2005: 0.6% in each case). In the case of Russian, which recorded considerable proportions around 1970 (20.5%), the losses are dramatic. The proportions for all languages not included were consistently below 1%.

Only Japanese has remained relatively stable, although at a low level (2005: 2.1%). Chinese, which joined only recently, is the only language with a growing proportion, but with a large gap behind English (2005: also 2.1%). Chinese reached 1% only in 1999, but this has been entered in 1996 for the sake of visual clarity. The ordinate scale was also logarithmised for the sake of visual clarity, so that the scale for 1–10% is the same size as for 10–100%; values <1% have not been included. Apart from the possible skewing in favour of English in recent times, the curve for the first decades of the twentieth century suggests skewing in favour of German. This could have arisen through an overzealous supply of German bibliographical data to the *International Catalogue of Scientific Literature* (suggestion from Roswitha Reinbothe; also, Ch. G.1) or the over-weighting of German titles in German databanks during the war years.

For one process which is very significant for our topic and for which there is evidence in much of the individual data, namely, the shift by many academics from German to English as their language of publication, this curve offers no clear pointers. A kink in the curve which might have been expected has presumably been smoothed because the language shift took place at different times in different disciplines. The largest shift in mathematics, e.g. (based on figures from the *Mathematical Reviews*), took place in the early 1980s; in biology (based on *Biological Abstracts*), not until the 1990s. Accordingly, the proportion of authors from Germany among the English-language titles in mathematics rose between 1980 and 1985 from 6.0% to 12.2%, while it hardly changed in biology during this period, but then, between 1988 and 1995, it rose from 3.1% (1991, only 1.4%) to 5.3%. By contrast, in mathematics, the proportion of authors from Germany among the German-language titles jumped, between 1980 and 1985 from 2.1% to 38.3%, and in biology, between 1988 and 1995, from 26.7% (1992, only 10.7%) to 77.2%. The rise in the proportions of German academics among the English-language titles can only be explained by their shifting to English as their academic language; but the rise in their proportions among German-language titles must be explained by the "flight from German" by academic speakers of other languages. As the figures show, this movement of flight is particularly dramatic and has led to the consequence that German-speaking academics remain increasingly linguistically isolated, i.e. German has relinquished its international position. In mathematics, this language shift occurs around ten years earlier than in biology (details in Ammon 1998: 154f.). In view of such differences between disciplines, Figure G.3–1 creates the false impression that German lost ground continuously rather than abruptly – before stabilising somewhat at its present low level.

Unfortunately, even this finer differentiation does not fully reflect the international use of the languages (Ch. A.3). In fact, the proportions of publications are relatively uninformative about the number of readers, and especially about the spoken use of the languages. The recently considerably higher proportions of Japanese and Chinese suggest that the non-English-language publications may be read largely only within their own language communities, because these languages are still far from being learnt worldwide as foreign languages (Ch. J.9.13; J.9.14). The sometimes desperate efforts by Chinese and Japanese researchers to publish in English support this assumption (Flowerdew 2007; Ammon 2012c). They also suggest that the proportion of the native languages of these scientists among the total of academic publications will not rise very far, at least in the foreseeable future. As Figure G.3–1 shows, the proportion of Japanese has declined somewhat after a brief rise. In the meantime, many reports indicate that, English has achieved a virtual monopoly position as the international academic language, especially in the theoretical natural sciences, which also effects the reception of written publications. Sabine Skudlik (1990: 114f.) has described the theoretical natural sciences as "anglophone sciences" and as the "Nobel Prize sciences". Perhaps with somewhat provocative intent, she attributes "a perfect mastery of English" even to the non-anglophone academics in these disciplines, which has, however, "been purchased with an exclusive bilingualism", i.e. at the expense of other foreign languages.

Another indicator, the frequency with which publications from different languages are cited, brings us closer to the reality of international communication than the mere publication figures (Ammon 1998: 31–89). Admittedly, even citations do not guarantee actual reading; they may mask "second-hand" origins or be no more than the mention of a title, but this tends to be the exception rather than the rule. The most representative data on citations are obtainable from the three citation indexes by the *Thomson Reuters Corporation* (formerly *Institute for Scientific Communication* in Philadelphia, USA): *Science Citation Index, Social Sciences Citation Index* and *Arts & Humanities Citation Index*. However, these are all susceptible to skewing in favour of English – because of the open advocacy by their founder Eugene Garfield (e.g. 1977b) of English as the sole academic language, just because it is allegedly already dominant. Bo Sandelin and Nikias Sarafoglou (2004) have, in fact, demonstrated the unilateral preference for English-language texts. Control calculations by a US research group on the *Impact-Factors* named by Thomson Reuters (the current publisher of the citation indexes) point in the same direction of a distortion in favour of English (Rossner/ van Epps/ Hill 2007; on the Impact-Factor, see, e.g. Ammon 1998: 36–38; Winkmann/ Schlutius/ Schweim 2002a: 132, 2002b: 139).

But, for our purpose, there is no doubt about the usefulness of citation analyses. One example from the 1920s is provided by P.L.K. Gross and E.M. Gross (1927; see also de Solla Price 1986: 72 and 280, note 15). To assist purchasing in university libraries, they investigated the most-cited chemistry periodicals in the USA. For this purpose, they registered all citations (apart from self-citations of the periodical) in the year 1926 from The *Journal of the American Chemical Society*; at that time, the most prestigious US periodical for chemistry (not to be confused with the British *Journal of the Chemical Society*). The citation sources (from 247 different periodicals) for the total of 3,633 citations were arranged chronologically by languages. Among the four most frequently cited periodicals (43% of all citations), three were from German-speaking countries. Furthermore, with a considerable margin, German was the most frequent language of all citation sources (Tables G.3–1 and G.3–2). The investigators drew the following relevant conclusion: "Certainly it should be insisted that a reading knowledge of German be required of every

Table G.3–1 Number of citations from the four most-cited periodicals in *The Journal of the American Chemical Society* in 1926

	1871 – 1875	1876 – 1880	1881 – 1885	1886 – 1890	1891 – 1895	1896 – 1900	1901 – 1905	1906 – 1910	1911 – 1915	1916 – 1920	1921 – 1925	Total
Berichte der deutschen chemischen Gesellschaft	33	44	53	56	60	64	79	115	67	30	78	668
Journal of the Chemical Society	-	1	2	5	20	21	47	45	60	37	122	390
Liebigs Annalen der Chemie	-	13	18	19	21	22	23	33	37	8	26	278
Zeitschrift für Physikalische Chemie	-	-	-	6	16	28	19	29	21	6	53	191

(*Source*: after Gross/ Gross 1927)

Table G.3–2 Language proportions of all non-American citation sources in *The Journal of the American Chemical Society* 1926

	Number of citations	Percentage
German	1,667	53
English	1,557	35
French	300	9
Other	87	3

(*Source*: after Gross/ Gross 1927)

student majoring in chemistry in college. French can hardly be accepted as a substitute [. . .]" (Gross/ Gross 1927: 388).

The decline of German is evident from Table G.3–1, primarily from the development of the figures for the *Berichte der deutschen chemischen Gesellschaft* by comparison with the British *Journal of the Chemical Society*. The fact that *Liebigs Annalen* and *Zeitschrift für Physikalische Chemie* remain behind the British *Journal* also suggests a loss of position even before WWI – by contrast with the widely accepted assumption that German-language publications only lost position in or after the war. Arnold Thackray et al. (1985: 160) also noted "the decline in the importance of German chemistry since 1890" in a subsequent long-term analysis of citation frequencies of American, British and German periodicals. But the decline after the war, the "*Urkatastrophe*" of the twentieth century (Mommsen 2002), is beyond doubt (Ch. G.1). Its causes are also largely known: annihilation of economic and scientific resources in Germany and Austria (Ammon 1998: 183f., 2000b: 68–71), boycott against German as an international academic language (Reinbothe 2006) and condemnation of German cultural goods in the broadest sense, including language, in the English-speaking world (Finkelmann 1993; Schiffmann 1987).

My own citation analysis of chemistry periodicals, based on preliminary work by Stefan Michels, shows developments in the period between 1920 and 1990 (Ammon 1998: 46–56). In each case, the most important chemistry periodicals from six countries were evaluated at ten-year intervals. According to the *Science Citation Index 1990* (1991), *Journal Citation Reports* and the view of local experts, these were, for the USA: *Journal of the American Chemical Society*; *Chemical Reviews*; for the Soviet Union: *Schurnal Obtschschei Chimii/Journal of General Chemistry*; *Uspechi Chimii* [Successes in Chemistry]; France: *Bulletin de la Société Chimique*; *Biochimie*; the Netherlands: *Receuil des travaux chimique des Pays-Bas*; *Analytica Chimica Acta*; Poland: *Przeyst chemiczny* [Chemical Economy]; *Chemia analityczna* [Analytical Chemistry]); Hungary: *Acta Chimica Hungaria*. Since this was an investigation of the international position of German, no periodicals from German-speaking countries were included. Accordingly, for English, the figures for US periodicals and for France, the figures for French periodicals, were removed. The proportion of citations for the languages (titles in these languages) were averaged without weighting, first for both periodicals of the relevant country (where two were available) and then for the various countries. It was shown that, as languages from which the citations were drawn, only German, English and French occurred throughout. Russian was not represented everywhere and not for the entire period but followed in fourth place based on frequency. Japanese appeared only in more recent years, but with a slightly rising trend. Otherwise, citations from the following languages were found sporadically (rank ordering according to number of periodicals with citations): Italian, Spanish, Polish, Chinese, Czech and Dutch.

As Table G.3–3 shows, the proportion of German-language citations at the beginning of the period of investigation was high, which corresponds with the prominent position of German

Table G.3–3 Proportions of German, French and English-language citations in chemical periodicals 1920–1990

	1920	1930	1940	1950	1960	1970	1980	1990
German	50.5	36,9	30.6	26.5	21.2	15.1	11.9	10.7
English	14.3	17.0	23.9	29.8	38.2	45.8	53.4	57.6
French	10.0	8.0	11.7	8.8	7.2	5.9	3.4	3.2

(*Source*: percentages; after Ammon 1998: 53)

as an academic language for chemistry at that time (Ch. G.1), but it declines continuously over time. This applies for all the periodicals analysed, where the proportion of citations in countries adjacent to the German-language territory, especially in Hungary, remains higher than in distant countries (USA; Soviet Union). The English-language proportion develops in the reverse direction to the German-language proportion, growing continuously. It is below the German-language proportion only at the start, in conformity with the findings by Gross/ Gross (1927). Around 1920, German was presumably still an internationally higher-ranking academic language for chemistry than English (Ammon 1991a: 251–256). However, English gradually gains a more dominant advantage than German ever had. According to informal data, English-language periodicals in the natural sciences today cite practically only English-language literature (for developments in psychology see Finison/ Whittemore 1975; Traxel 1975; also, Braun/ Glänzel/ Schubert 1987; Braun et al. 1994; Louttit 1957). During the period under investigation, French proves to be the third most important language for chemistry, but with a trend in the same direction as German. But by contrast with German, the proportion of French remains more stable beyond WWII. The stabilisation may be explained as a flight from the German, without leading directly to English.

More recent, representative citation analyses do not seem to be available, but they would presumably confirm the increased dominance of English – despite widespread criticism of "monolingualism in the sciences" (cf. end of this chapter; Ch. G.10–G.13). A sustainable move away from English is unlikely and seems impossible at least for the foreseeable future.

Continuing German-language titles for academic associations in Germany, Austria and German-speaking Switzerland possibly betray a certain nostalgia for German. For each of the following natural-science disciplines, a sample title is given with the number of the German title referenced against the total number of associations in brackets:

Biology – Germany: *Gesellschaft für Biologische Systematik* (10 of 14), Austria: *Vereinigung Österreichischer Biologen* (3 of 4), Switzerland: (0 of 2);

Chemistry – Germany: *Gesellschaft Deutscher Chemiker* (7 of 10), Austria: *Gesellschaft österreichischer Chemiker* (8 of 10), Switzerland: *Schweizerische Chemische Gesellschaft* (3 of 7);

Physics: Germany: *Deutsche Physikalische Gesellschaft* (4 of 9), Austria: *Österreichische Physikalische Gesellschaft* (5 of 5), Switzerland: *Schweizerische Physikalische Gesellschaft* (1 of 1);

Medicine: Germany: *Internationale Forschungsgemeinschaft für Bioelektronische Funktionsdiagnostik und Therapie* (50 of 61), Austria: *Österreichische Gesellschaft für Anästhesiologie, Reanimation und Intensivmedizin* (20 of 23). Switzerland: *Schweizerische Gesellschaft für Allgemeine Medizin* (9 of 13, 2 French) (Kirchner 2006: 545f., 551f., 614, 594–597).

The four disciplines named as examples are given a narrow definition in the data source used *World Guide to Scientific Associations and Learned Societies* (Kirchner 2006) and are not representative for the theoretical sciences in general. A look at the many sub-disciplines and inter-disciplines ("Biochemistry", "Biophysics" etc.) and their numerous associations shows their still largely German-language titles, including French-language titles in Switzerland. But it is not possible to infer the use of these languages for international communication, e.g. in conferences, from the language of the official title of the associations.

Abstracts of current research in the theoretical natural sciences are evidently now published worldwide almost exclusively in English. Almost everywhere, periodicals are also published in English (Michels 1991). In the German-speaking countries, they have often shifted so far towards English that contributions in other languages, including German, are no longer accepted. Even the titles of the periodicals have also generally been anglicised, sometimes in intermediate stages or with Latin titles, or with a temporary acceptance of other publication languages. Examples (already named in Lippert 1986 and Karger 1986) which have shifted to English and some of which have also been taken over by publishers outside the German-speaking countries, include the following:

- Germany: *Archiv für Kreislaufforschung > Basic Research in Cardiology; Zeitschrift für Kinderheilkunde > European Journal of Pediatrics; Zeitschrift für Tierpsychologie > Ethology;*
- Austria: *Österreichische Botanische Zeitschrift > Plant Systematics and Evolution;*
- Switzerland: *Archiv für Verdauungskrankheiten > Gastroenterologia > Digestion; Radiologische Rundschau > Radiologia Clinica > Diagnostic Imaging.*

No new periodicals with German-language titles or German-language contributions have been founded in the theoretical sciences. But it must be noted that Anglicisation in the applied sciences has occurred to a lesser extent (Ch. G.4). For example, in clinical medicine, by contrast with theoretical medicine, there are still several predominantly German-language periodicals (*Deutsche Medizinische Wochenschrift; Der Chirurg* and others). In manuals and reference books, the language shift from German to English has taken place as in the case of periodicals. One example is the long-established *Beilsteins Handbuch der organischen Chemie*, with the following history: "The basis for the current Beilstein System was developed in 1907 by B. Prager and P. Jacobson. [...] The effort of producing a new edition was then made only one more time by Beilstein. The fourth edition has been published since 1918; with the fifth Supplement, comprising literature from 1960 to 1979, only in English, appearing since 1984": *Beilstein. Handbook of Organic Chemistry* (www.tu-harburg.de/b/hapke/beilst.html#Beilstein). In the relevant publishing houses in German-speaking countries, the entire production process has gradually shifted from German to English (Ch. G.10). As early as 1989, (Julius) Springer, the largest German academic publisher, estimated that 70% of their publications were in English, with 35% of authors from German-speaking countries – by contrast with 1927: 0.5% English-language publications and 90% authors from German-speaking countries (information from Bernhard Lewerich, Springer Verlag).

At international conferences in theoretical sciences, the relationship between the three languages German, English and French has developed in the same way as for publications and citations. Before WWI, all three languages ranked approximately equally. After the war, English and French played a somewhat more significant role than German. At least, this is what Herbert N. Shenton (1933) has shown for the period from 1923 to 1929 (details in Ammon 1991a: 243–245; also, Thierfelder 1933: 299–303). However, Shenton's investigation was not limited to academic organisations; his findings show no significant differences between academic and other organisations. He classified the total of 298 organisations, which gave information on 1,088 international conferences, into 14 fields. For the field of art/science, the frequencies of different functions for the languages occurring were obtained as shown in Table G.3–4.

Table G.3–4 Frequency of languages according to functions in international conferences in the field of art/science in the 1920s

	Official	*Translation*	*Accepted*
1. French	31	4	23
2. English	21	4	25
3. German	15	4	25
4. Italian	5	2	25
5. Spanish	2	2	23

(*Source*: Shenton 1933: 241–243)

To my knowledge, there is no comparable, comprehensive investigation of language choice at academic conferences in recent history. One investigation by Roswitha Reinbothe entitled "Multilingualism at international academic conferences" was interested less in quantification than in the organisational background to the conferences (Reinbothe 2013). According to this research, German scientists were still excluded from significant overarching international academic associations until long after WWII. Moreover, even after the war, they were often not admitted to international conferences (especially in chemistry, physics, zoology and surgery, but more readily admitted in mathematics and the humanities). Furthermore, major conferences were generally held in the USA and the UK, so that even the French, who were committed to the inclusion of their own language, were rarely able to assert themselves, not to mention the Germans. Isolated cases, such as the International Chemistry Congress held in Munich in 1959, where more presentations were in German than in English, remained exceptions which were not repeated (ibid: 7f.). The fact that English increasingly became the exclusive conference language in theoretical sciences is also shown in a questionnaire study by Skudlik (1990; 326, question 11); but, once again, this is less pronounced in the applied sciences (details in Ammon 1991a: 246f.). Even inside the German-speaking countries, at international conferences in the theoretical sciences, German is generally not accepted for written communication (papers, conference reports) or oral presentations (lectures, discussion). Even conferences with exclusively German-speaking participants are often restricted to the use of English. Similarly, English predominates in laboratory discussions in German-speaking countries (as early as Markl 1986: 21f.; contribution to discussion by Markl in Kalverkämper/ Weinrich 1986: 60), and German is hardly used internationally, i.e. by non-German-speaking participants. English is often spoken and minuted between German-speakers. "Even if they [foreign guests at German universities! U.A.] have learnt German, spent several years in Germany and would like to use their knowledge of languages, they are often required by their German colleagues to use only English" (Mocikat 2006: 12f.; www.goethe.de/Ihr/prj/mac/mac/spb/de4244182.htm). However, as in the case of conferences with only German-speaking participants, the use of English may have different motives which may be entirely understandable: because of available English-language specialist literature, to facilitate external communication (further distribution of papers and findings to speakers of other languages) or simply to practise English. Having said this, such uses of English tend to strengthen the norm for language choice, so that observing this norm then becomes expected even if it is not communicatively expedient (for rules on language choice, see Ch. A.6). In extreme cases, German scientific research institutes even address English to the German public (e.g. the spokesperson for the Institute of Primate Research at the University of Leipzig in a TV interview – with interpreting for German TV viewers in "*heute-journal*" 8 June 2009).

It is therefore not surprising that some people rebel against such tendencies, e.g. the *Arbeitskreis Deutsch als Wissenschaftssprache. ADAWiS* (www.adawis.de). Demonstrative refusals to use English presumably also sometimes occur: the obstinate use of German even when it is not communicatively functional. The Germanisation of English-language terminology routinely demanded by the *Verein Deutsche Sprache/VDS* to compensate the "modernization deficit" of the German language represents a component of such protests (for terms and content, see Ammon 1991a: 277–288). However, there is a need for further clarification about whether and in precisely which respect scientific communication is hampered by anglicisation; whether it is possibly more efficient; and which realistic alternatives there may be (cf. Ch. G.11; G.13).

4. Applied sciences

While the theoretical sciences tend strongly towards English as their academic language of choice (Ch. G.3), the opposite pole to this "anglophone" group of disciplines is formed by the "national-language-orientated" social sciences and especially the humanities, which adhere most firmly to German. These designations and specifications originate from Sabine Skudlik (1990: 98f., 214–216), who also positions the "anglophone-orientated disciplines" between the two groups mentioned. Of these, I focus on the "applied sciences" in this chapter (Ammon 1991a: 233–235). The overarching feature of this heterogenous group is given by its own special communication conditions: the relationship with users of the respective knowledge (Ch. G.2), which places a limit on the use of a foreign language, i.e. English. But differences between a more applied and a more theoretical orientation also exist within the social sciences and even the humanities. For example, among the economic sciences, business graduates [*Diplomkauffrauen/-männer*] see themselves as more application-orientated than business economists and especially political economists, so that it is no coincidence that business graduates resist attempts at anglicisation more decisively, adhering to the German-language academic title ("*Diplom-Kaufmann/-frau*") and to German as the language of university teaching ("Teach it in German, please", *FAZ* 8/9 May 2010; Ch. G.8). The difference between theoretical and applied orientations is also evident from a survey of German-speaking economists, in which English-language periodicals were shown to be more theory-orientated, while German-language periodicals were more application-orientated and of greater "relevance (to their own work)" (Bräuninger/ Haucap/ Muck 2011: 1). Among "periodicals from the German-speaking territory", the majority were in German or at least had a German title (19 of the 30 most relevant). The survey included 2,991 members of the *Verein für Sozialpolitik*, who were asked to evaluate the "up to 150 selected specialist economics periodicals" (response 909 = 30.4%). Another example of the distinction between theoretical and applied orientation is provided by linguistics, which – by way of distinction from its primarily theoretical orientation – also comprises "applied linguistics", with the German association, the *Gesellschaft für Angewandte Linguistik (GAL)* and the world association, the *Association Internationale de Linguistique Appliquée (AILA)*. Philosophy has also recently shown signs of a similar differentiation. For example, there are now professorships at the University of Duisburg-Essen with a focus on "Practical Philosophy", and even literary science, exemplified by the German professorship in "*Angewandte Literaturwissenschaft*" at the Gerhardt-Mercator University in Duisburg since the 1970s. However, the contrast between theoretical and applied disciplines seems more pronounced in the natural sciences than in the social sciences and especially than in the humanities. I shall therefore concentrate here on the applied natural sciences including their technologies.

Even so, the demarcation is often blurred in different directions, and signs for the difficulty of differentiating are evident from bibliometric analyses, such as *Global Research Report Materials*

Science and Technology by Thomson Reuters, which refers to the contrast between "more funda-mental research of universities" and "more application-oriented research of national laboratories" and therefore highlights the balancing act in this group of disciplines between theoretical and applied approaches (researchanalytics.thomsonreuters.com/ m/pdfs/grr-materialscience.pdf: 6). This report also gives an impression of the enormous size of the applied sciences, because even the applied section of Materials Science and Technology comprises approximately 30,000 pub-lications per year (if the total of 60,000 is divided into theoretical and applied, where the latter represents only 2.5% (half of the total of 5%) of the titles indicated in the *Web of Science* for this group of disciplines) (ibid: 4). By contrast, the engineering sciences, which can be classified *en bloc* among the applied sciences, amount to a proportion of 9% and therefore – in the sense of the present rough estimate – approximately 108,000 indexed titles yearly. In this context, "indexed" means 'included in *Web of Science*', where the number of titles not included remains obscure. An approximate overview of the vast field of applied sciences is provided by bibliographical data banks, such as *Applied Science & Technology Abstracts*, which are published in the USA (H.W. Wilson Company). They include no less than 71 "subjects", the scope of which can be imag-ined even by non-experts: alphabetically, from "Acoustics, Aeronautics, Applied Mathematics, Artificial Intelligence", Other Industrial & Mechanical Artsto "Space Science, Textile Industry and Fabrics, Transportation, and Waste Management". Indeed, such databanks seem sufficiently representative for the analysis of language proportions. But, by contrast with the databanks used in Ch. G.3 for the theoretical natural sciences, all those I have considered show clearly that they are not concerned with achieving an equal balance of languages but instead exhibit a unilateral preference for English. Explanations such as the following are typical: "English-language peri-odicals published in the United States and elsewhere are covered; non-English-language articles are included if English abstracts are provided" (www.hwwilson.com/newdds/aa.cfm). It is not possible to estimate how many non-English-speaking titles have been ignored due to a lack of English-language abstract. This linguistic imbalance may perhaps be taken as providing a certain confirmation of our test hypothesis. In fact, it may have been determined differently from the theoretical natural sciences (see also Winkmann/ Schlutius/ Schweim 2002a, b; Blümle/ Antes 2006), because, in this case, English is the "home" language of the databank and, at the same time, the official language of state of its home in the USA – which supports our hypothesis about preference for the home language in the applied sciences. It would be no coincidence that I found no globally representative bibliographical databank with correspondingly balanced proportions of languages for this group of disciplines.

These provisional findings are not supposed to serve as a verification of our hypothesis, but a serious attempt at falsification proves difficult. To repeat the hypothesis: the applied natural sci-ences can be regarded rather more as national than international disciplines or – with the two languages of primary interest here – they are more German-language disciplines than English-language disciplines by comparison with the theoretical natural sciences. The explanation is that the theoretical natural sciences primarily interest expert scientists – in their proverbial ivory tower – and can therefore use a foreign language, English, in the German-language territory; by contrast, the applied sciences must remain open to users who may be non-experts, so that the language of the surrounding society – generally the national official language, in our case German – is indispensable (Ch. G.2). In the German-language territory, this difference ought to be discernible from the language proportions in academic publications. The proportion of Ger-man in the applied sciences ought to be greater, and the proportion of English less than in the theoretical natural sciences. Of all hypotheses on language choice between groups of disciplines, this is, so far, possibly the least well tested empirically. It is significant that Skudlik's evaluation of annual bibliographies from universities in Munich in 1972 and 1982 and Heidelberg in 1982

(Skudlik 1990: 73–75, 87–91 and 269f., Tables 9 and 10) is still counted among the relevant data. Although these figures are dated and show gaps, they still confirm the difference in question and, in fact, regarding the following two more specific hypotheses:

1) In the applied sciences (e.g. forestry, veterinary medicine), the number of scientists publishing in German is relatively greater than in the thematically related theoretical sciences (e.g. biology, (theoretical) human medicine), where the number of scientists publishing in English is relatively higher (ibid: 269, Table 9);
2) In the applied sciences, the proportion of German-language publications among the total number of publications is greater than in the thematically related theoretical sciences (ibid: 270, Table 10).

The two hypotheses are coherent regarding content, although it is not strictly possible to derive one logically from the other. Table G.4–1 contrasts sciences which are clearly comparable with reference to theoretical and applied orientation (data from ibid: 262–266), by connecting the comparable disciplines with identical (superscript) index numbers. Skudlik considers "*Geowissenschaft*" to be an applied discipline, in the same way as does the databank *Applied Science & Technology Abstracts* cited above by including "geology". The figures in Table G.4–1 are arithmetic means taken from the annual bibliographies for 1982 at the universities of Munich and Heidelberg; but statistical validity is seriously restricted because of gaps in the data and, in some cases, very small samples, not to mention the lack of significance tests. However, even with these restrictions, the findings confirm the two hypotheses 1) and 2).

Language differences between applied and theoretical sciences are further substantiated by the language choices of publishers. Especially in the applied sciences, periodicals and reference works have shifted less consistently from German to English. However, there are also complete shifts, e.g. the traditional reference work *Ullmann's Enzyklopädie der technischen Chemie* (1914–1922): the fourth edition was the last in German 1972 > *Ullmann's Encyclopaedia of Industrial Chemistry* (1996; seventh edition 2010 online, 2011, print). There is also a full series of

Table G.4–1 Proportion of publications in German and/or English in applied sciences by comparison with theoretical natural sciences

	Proportion of scientists publishing in German or also in German	Proportion of scientists publishing in English or also in English	Proportion of publications in in German	Proportion of publications in in English
Applied Sciences				
Geoscience[1]	98.5	97.0	72.5	26.0
Forestry[2]	100	95.0	N.d.	N.d.
Clinical medicine[3]	n.d.	n.d.	78.6	20.0
Theoretical Sciences				
Mathematics	84.5	100	30.5	67.5
Physics[1]	73.5	98.5	18.0	81.0
Chemistry[1]	86.5	96.5	47.5	51.5
Biology[2]	84.5	97.5	12.0	88.0
Human medicine[3]	97.0	97.0	34.2	74.2
	(Human medicine total)		(Theoretical human medicine)	

(*Source*: percentages; based on Skudlik 1990: 269f., Tables 9 and 10)

other English-language reference works for applied sciences, e.g. *Encyclopaedia of Computational Mechanics, Encyclopaedia of Software Engineering, Springer Handbook of Robotics*, 15 in total (accessed: 7 May 2011 in the catalogue at the University Library of Stuttgart: www.uni-stuttgart.de/suche/ebooks/uebersicht01.phtml). But, significantly in line with our hypothesis, directly adjacent to this list is the note: "a list of approximately 1000 German-language titles published by Springer-Verlag between 2005–2010 is also available. This series also includes titles published by Teubner and Vieweg and is continuously updated with new 2010 titles". I did not find notes of this kind anywhere for the theoretical natural sciences. Furthermore, in the applied sciences, when English is introduced into German-language reference books, German is not always completely abandoned. For example, in many encyclopaedias of clinical medicine and dentistry, German terms are glossed with English equivalents, but the German-language texts are retained. Friedbichler/ Friedbichler/ Türp (2008a: 795) cite the example of *Pschyrembel. Klinisches Wörterbuch* (2007, 261st edition, Berlin: de Gruyter) and *Roche Lexikon Medizin* (1998, 4th edition, Munich: Urban & Schwarzenberg).

A corresponding difference is found among the periodicals. For example, in the theoretical natural sciences, periodicals previously in German have almost completely shifted to English as the sole publication language (cf. Ch. G.3). By contrast, in the applied sciences, a range of German-language periodicals have been retained, e.g. in medicine, *Zeitschrift für Orthopädie und Unfallchirurgie; Medizinisches Wochenblatt; Zentralblatt für Chirurgie; Der Chirurg*, or continue to accept German-language contributions alongside submissions in English. A twin-track approach is also familiar in periodicals: German-language articles alongside articles in English. The periodical *Angewandte Chemie* (founded 1887) has adopted this approach since 1962. The English-language version enjoys a reputation as one of the world's leading periodicals within its discipline: "*Angewandte Chemie, International Edition*, with its excellent Impact Factor of 11.829 (2009) strengthens its leading position among general chemistry journals. It is one of the foremost chemistry journals in the world, with an Impact Factor higher than those of comparable journals" (www.wiley-vch.de/publish/en/journals/alphabeticIndex/2001/). In 2008, the bulletin of the *Bundesärztekammer* and the *Kassenärztliche Bundesvereinigung*, the *Deutsches Ärzteblatt* (founded 1872), supplemented its printed German-language version with an online English-language version (www.aertzteblatt.de/int/; Baethge 2008, 2011). Multilingual periodicals are also a relatively frequent occurrence, e.g. the *Schweizer Monatschrift für Zahnmedizin/ Revue mensuelle suisse d'odontostomatologie/ Revista mensile svizzera di odontologia e stomatologia*. Entire language shifts from German to English tend to be unusual in the applied sciences. However, one example is the *Schweizerische Medizinische Wochenschrift* > *Swiss Medical Weekly*, whose website announces: "[W]e have switched from our multilingual tradition to an English-only journal" (www.vet-magazin.com). All in all, the data indicate unequivocally that the German language plays a more important role in applied sciences than in theoretical sciences, but this is still not an exclusive role.

On closer inspection, the stronger adherence to German in applied sciences by comparison with theoretical sciences seems to be based only on contact with the users, but not on a stronger international position of German in these disciplines. This view is supported by the lower Impact-Factor and smaller circulation of German-language versions by comparison with English-language versions of the same periodicals and corresponds to the more restricted market of the German-language community by comparison with the more global context of English. Accordingly, the Impact-Factor of the German-language periodical *Der Chirurg* is lower (0.539 in 2007) than that of the English-language *Langenbeck's Archives of Surgery* (1.533 in 2007; Hasse/ Fischer 2010: 362; also: www.springer.com/medicine/surgery/journal/423), even though both periodicals have a similar orientation and are published by the same publisher (Julius) Springer).

Der Chirurg certainly has a smaller circulation (5,480 copies sold and 5,700 "distributed" in 2010 (www.fachzeitungen.de.seite/p/titel/titelid/1002640376) than *Langenbeck's Archives of Surgery*, which, according to the website, "belongs in the top 10 journals in general and GI-tract surgery worldwide" (www.springerlink.com/content/3k9exwek3uyw923n/). Accordingly, German-language periodical versions are certainly not used by English-speaking surgeons, the number of whom in the USA and the UK alone is 2.6 times as large as in all German-speaking countries together (Hasse/ Fischer 2010: 363); they are also presumably hardly read by surgeons in other non-German-speaking countries. The fact that German-language publications in dentistry, especially clinical studies, are only included sporadically in the US databank *Medline*: depending on orientation, only half or at most three-quarters (Türp/ Schulte/ Antes 2002; Blümle/ Antes 2006; "*Schieflage. Deutsche Publikationen in Datenbanken unterschlagen* [Skewing the data. German publications misappropriated in databanks]", *FAZ* 16 Februaray 2005: N1) also suggests a low international distribution of German-language "applied" publications. By contrast, the lack of German-language titles in the theoretical natural sciences in US databanks may be determined only by their *de facto* smaller numbers. In the applied sciences, other causes, such as lack of linguistic knowledge among possible recipients, are presumably more important. However, caution is required when assessing the function of German internally within the language community as irrelevant to the international position of German (cf. Ch. A.5), because, in every case, learners of German gain a potential benefit, e.g. if they want to study or work in a German-speaking country (see the end of this chapter).

By contrast with the communicative reasons emphasised in this chapter so far, Skudlik (1990: 215) considers adherence to German in the "national-language-orientated" disciplines to be more fundamentally determined, namely "as causally intertwined with the language in which their knowledge is formulated", in other words, as cognitively determined (language "as an instrument of cognition"). This also explains Skudlik's restriction of these disciplines to the humanities (Ch. G.6; G.7). By contrast, I see the most important reason relating to the applied sciences in more banal terms in the lack of foreign-language skills or even the refusal to use English by the clientele (see also Ch. G.10). This reason would diminish if the entire population were to acquire an adequate knowledge of English – a goal towards which the education policy of all German-speaking countries is working intensively (Germany, see Quetz 2010; H. Wagener 2012; Austria, see de Cillia/ Krumm 2010). However, acceptance of the use of English, which is associated with the linguistic and national identity of the clientele, would also have to be considered (Ch. B.3). This obstacle does not seem insurmountable if one bears in mind the openness of the German-speaking population towards anglicisms and the ubiquity of English-language advertising and pop music. By contrast, if the factors mentioned above have been correctly diagnosed, German seems more firmly anchored in the humanities (Ch. G.6). Perhaps opponents to anglicisation in academic life in Germany suspect a greater susceptibility to English in the applied sciences, because medical doctors, who, even with their interest in theory, are certainly also concerned with applications, are prominent among them. For example, professor of medicine and doctor Wolfgang Hasse (Berlin) is co-founder of the "*Arbeitskreis Deutsche Sprache in der Chirurgie* (ADSiC)" [Working Party on German Language in Surgery] and also active in the "*Arbeitskreis Deutsch als Wissenschaftssprache* (ADAWIS)" [Working Party on German as a Scientific Language], whose president, Ralph Mocikat (Munich), is also a professor of medicine. Both have been committed to the maintenance and strengthening of German as an academic language for years (e.g. Mocikat 2006, 2007, 2010; Hasse et al. 2007; Hasse/ Fischer 2010). In this context, their commitment is directed primarily towards German in internal German communication; they do not dispute the justification for English in international communication. However, apart from the reference to practice, they also emphasise what they consider to be the epistemological function of the (native) language, but without making a serious effort to prove this – given my understanding of serious. Perhaps this anchoring in applied medicine is less secure than in the humanities, but could still explain the admittedly slow spread of English in applied medicine, or at least in the associated publications. Yet in the three most important German-language periodicals for dentistry, the proportion of English-language citations in the period from 1970 to 2005 has grown steadily (Reinhöfer 2009: 11f., 19–25), in *Deutsche Zahnärztliche Zeitschrift*; *Deutsche Stomatologie/ Stomatologie der DDR, Österreichische Zeitschrift für Stomatologie*). The list of traditional anglicisms has been regularly supplemented since 1995, especially "to designate new methods and materials" (ibid: 38; list of anglicisms 39–41).

Patents deserve special mention here as a commercially important form of publication in the applied sciences. Patent applications are generally filed at official patent offices in the national official language i.e. in German, in the German-speaking countries, e.g. at the German Patent and Trademark Office (in Munich, Jena and Berlin). The European Patent Office (Munich), where patents can be filed in German, English or French, is also significant for the international position of German. For many years, there has been a struggle over which languages are to be admitted. Italy and Spain declared their resistance to the final agreement between 12 member states on the three patent languages: German, English and French ("Breakthrough for the EU Patent Office", *FAZ* 25 May 2011: 9). On the global scale, China recently attained a leading position in patent applications, toppling Japan from first place in chemistry in 2008; it should be noted that this was in applied chemistry, especially pharmacy ("China Leads All Nations in Publication of Chemical Patents"; www.cas.org/newsevents/releases/chinesepatents 112309.html). So far as I know, Chinese patents are formulated in Chinese and English. But it would be premature to infer from their availability in English that they are irrelevant for the global position of Chinese. The fact that there are Chinese-language versions offers an advantage to learners of Chinese – however slight this factor may be for the international position of Chinese, by comparison with other factors deriving from the rise of China to a world power. Correspondingly, the accessibility of patents in German is also not entirely without significance for the global position of German. Indeed "[regarding] patent applications, Germany is in fourth place in the world" – 7.4% of all applications in 2008 (www.ip-notiz.de/was-die-zahl-der-patentanmeldungen-uns-sagen-kann /2008/09/30/, *FAZ* supplement 17 September 2008). Similarly, even if it is primarily motivated by concerns internal to the language community, adhering to German in periodicals, reference works and other specialist texts strengthens the international position of German to a certain extent. As a result, tuition in universities and further training in companies can, in fact, be based on German texts. Accordingly, a knowledge of German among foreign guests in the German-speaking countries becomes a recognisable advantage, which can strengthen the motivation to learn German. By contrast, knowledge of German in the theoretical natural sciences has now forfeited this advantage. Accordingly, non-German-speaking applied scientists possibly learn German more often than theoretical scientists. This assumption seems plausible if one considers the popularity of "German as an applied subject" for technological modernisation, e.g. in countries like China (J. ZHU 2007; Hess 2007).

5. Social sciences

Comparing overviews of the social sciences quickly reveals uncertainties in the allocation of disciplines, e.g. in databanks such as the *International Bibliography of the Social Sciences* (IBSS) (www.proquest.co.uk/en-UK/catalogs/databases/detail/ibss-set-c.shtml), *Sociological Abstracts* (www.

csa.com/factsheets/socioabs-set-c.php) and even in Wikipedia with the appropriate search term. Wikipedia names 20 disciplines, from "*Anthropologie* (social and cultural anthropology); *Demografie* (population science)" to "*Soziologie; Sportwissenschaft; Wirtschaftswissenschaften* (business studies and economics)" (de.wikipedia.org/wiki/Sozialwissenschaft). Overlapping occurs especially in the humanities (Ch. G.6). One clear example is "*Rechtswissenschaft* (law, jurisprudence)", which Wikipedia ascribes to the social sciences, as did Rottleuthner: *Rechtswissenschaft als Sozialwissenschaft* (1973), but which is grouped among the humanities in the present book (Ch. G.6), with reference to Kretschmer: *Rechts- als Geisteswissenschaft* (2007).

The classification of psychology, which is sometimes subdivided into individual psychology (as a natural science) and social psychology (as a social science), shows a similar ambivalence. This last classification occurs in Wikipedia, where the designation does not suggest a dichotomy but, rather, a focus: "psychology, especially social psychology". By contrast, psychology in total is listed in the *International Bibliography of the Social Sciences* (IBSS) among the social sciences. As such, in its undivided form, the associated language choice has recently been intensively investigated and discussed by German subject specialists (Ammon 1998: 16–18). The incentive was provided by an observation in the 1970s that German-language publications were hardly considered any more outside the German-language territory, and even journals published in the home country promoted English-language submissions. In this context, Werner Traxel (1975, 1979) argued that German-speaking psychologists should retain German as the language of publication, because – according to his principal argument – they could never compete seriously with their English-speaking colleagues in a foreign language. However, his colleague within the discipline, Gustav A. Lienert (1977), encouraged German-speaking psychologists to turn towards English to regain their international impact. Among the numerous statements around this dispute, most chose a middle path or tended towards Traxel (Reinhardt 1979; Eysenck 1980; Süllwold 1980; Marx 1989; R.J. Smith 1981; Roth 1989; A.F. Sanders 1989; Weingart 1989; but Freeman 1976; Heckhausen 1986). The *Recommendations of the Board of the German Association for Psychology* (1985) resolved to retain German as the exclusive language of publication for "German-language psychology periodicals" but recommended English-language abstracts. Joachim H. Becker (1980, 1994a) demonstrated that German-speaking psychologists were publishing increasingly in English and that US psychology periodicals were cited much more frequently than German periodicals. Even for the most widely distributed German journal, *Zeitschrift für Sozialpsychologie*, "reception was minimal or non-existent [...] not only in the US but in other countries geographically closer to us" (Becker 1981: 334). Other investigations also confirm that German-language publications are hardly considered outside the German-speaking countries (Schoepflin 1989; Montada et al. 1995; Markovich 1996; Strack 1996; Wolke 1996; Montada/ Schoepflin/ Baltes 1996; Frese 1990; Keul/ Gigerenzer/ Stroebe 1993). By contrast, older investigations by US researcher S.W. Fernberger (1917, 1926, 1936, 1946, 1956) show that, before WWI, German had a greater proportion of worldwide publications in psychology than any other language (30–55%, English 25–30%), so that a reading knowledge of German was considered indispensable for US psychologists. However, the proportion of German-language publications began to dwindle after the war: ultimately to just 4–7% in the 1980s, while the proportion of English-language publications had grown to approximately 90% by that time. Becker (1994b) also found that publications in English by German psychologists were received better in prestigious international periodicals than their work in German, but that the international reception of the German periodical *Psychological Research* had not intensified even four years after the complete shift to English in 1974 (previously *Psychologische Forschung*). Merely shifting language was thus no guarantee to help periodicals, at least not quickly.

These developments in psychology evidently parallel those in the theoretical natural sciences (Ch. G.3), possibly because, regarding methods and knowledge to be gained, psychology ought to be classified with the natural sciences rather than the social sciences. But this fails to consider the different communication conditions in the social sciences, which would motivate towards a stronger retention of German (cf. Ch. G.2):

a) Topics relating more to the internal language community and therefore of greater interest to this group, for which a foreign language would be impracticable;
b) Because of reduced formalisation of the specialist language, easier accessibility of the texts to non-experts, which would be restricted by a foreign language;
c) Increased difficulty of translation of texts in a foreign language because of the use of every-day or conversational language with its stylistic nuances.

Once again, language proportions in global publications allow a rough comparison with the theoretical natural sciences. But bibliographical databanks for the social sciences seem less representative worldwide than for the natural sciences. Possible bibliographies include the *International Bibliography of the Social Sciences (IBSS)* and *Sociological Abstracts*. At the time of the investigation, both were owned by the company ProQuest based in Cambridge (UK). The *International Bibliography of the Social Sciences* (IBSS) was in fact orientated more strongly towards Europe because its publishing office was originally in France (Paris; founded 1951) before relocating to the UK in 1989. It serves here as the primary source for the analysis not only for this reason but also because of the longer time span of the available data. Figure G.5–1 shows the development of

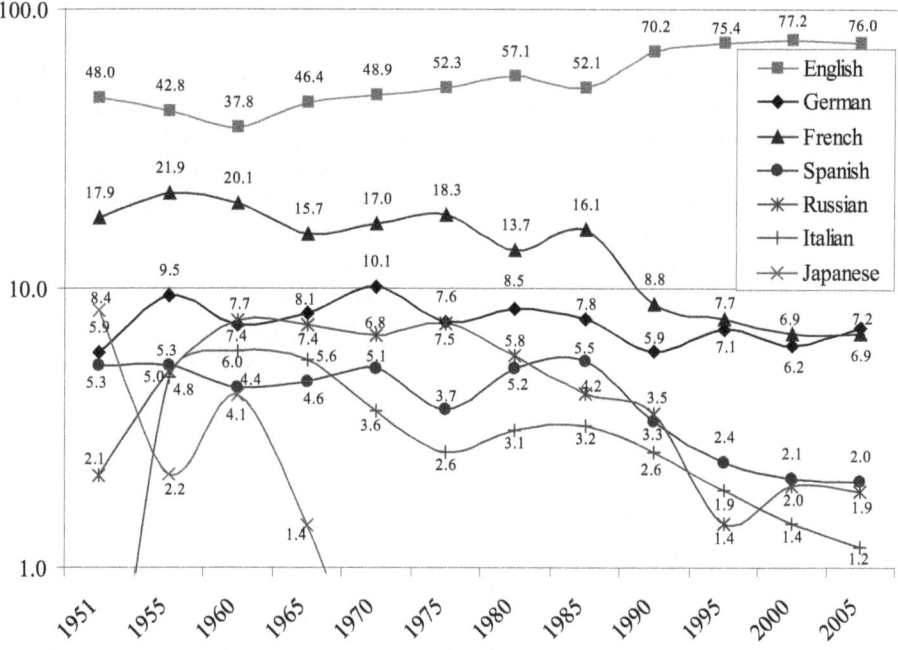

Figure G.5–1 Percentage shares of major languages in social-science publications worldwide *Note*: ordinate logarithmised; proportions of other languages always < 1%; rank order following 2005

(*Source*: International Bibliography of the Social Sciences (IBSS))

language proportions in the period from 1951 to 2005. Once again, the ordinate was logarithmised to make the proportions of languages other than English more clearly visible – though it can disguise the wide gap from English. The advance of English evidently grows in the period under investigation, from 48% in 1951 to 76% in 2005. However, this is considerably lower than in the theoretical natural sciences, with 92.7% in 2005 (cf. Figure G.3–1), which is important for our hypothesis. In the social sciences, German and French retain significant proportions (7.2% and respectively 6.9% in 2005) – after a considerable proportional loss of French between 1985 (16.1%) and 1990 (8.8 %).

Sociological Abstracts, for which figures were accessible only for 1974–2006, was evidently orientated more strongly than *IBSS* towards the USA. The advantage for English over all other languages is similar in magnitude to that of *IBSS* but remains relatively constant (1974: 75.7% and 2006: 70.7%, with several intermediate peaks of > 80%). The most noticeable difference in the case of German by comparison with *IBSS* is its falling behind Spanish since 2000 (2006: French 5.9%, Spanish 3.9%, German 3.0% – in the period before 2000, German was still ahead of Spanish). Presumably the reversal of proportions is determined by the different geographical focus of the two databanks (*Sociological Abstracts*: USA – *IBSS*: Europe). In the USA, Spanish is widely distributed as an immigrant language and as the most learnt foreign language with a considerable margin (Ch. I.9.10). The position of Spanish may also have been favoured by the raising of Spanish to the official language of the *International Sociological Association* (*ISA*) at the World Congress in 1982 in Mexico City (under pressure from a student revolt against the *gringos*. See Ammon in *Die Welt* 20 October 1988: 10). Below the 1% threshold, it is evident that Chinese is gradually gaining in importance. Its proportion in *Sociological Abstracts* grew from 0.04% at its first appearance in 1995 to 0.7% in 2006, with an upward trend. Apart from Spanish, Chinese is the only language with an increasing proportion.

As with the natural sciences, in addition to global publication proportions, the citation frequencies of German-language sources are also relevant in the social sciences, and the relevant data are available, but not for the most recent period. These data indicate the international use of a language more directly than merely the quantity of publications. For my own citation analysis, I selected the "economic sciences" as representative for the social sciences, which, based on their methods as well as other considerations, occupy a midway position between the "hard" natural sciences and the "soft" humanities (see de Solla Price 1986: 155–179, 1970), and which therefore fit appropriately into the triad of natural sciences, social sciences and humanities. The following citation analysis is limited to the branch of "Economics" and does not therefore consider the branch "Business & Finance" (details in Ammon 1998: 56–66). As for chemistry (Ch. G.3), the most important specialist periodicals were included, determined according to their Impact-Factor (as per *Social Sciences Citation Index 1990* (1991) *Journal Citation Reports*) or, where the factor was not available, based on assessment by local experts. On this basis, the following periodicals were selected: USA *(American Economic Review* and *The Journal of Political Economy); Soviet Union (Voprosy ekonomiki* [questions of economy]) and *Mirovaja ekonomika i meschunarodnyje otnoschenija* [global economy and international relations]); France (*Revue économique Française* and *Revue économique*); the Netherlands (*De Economist* and *Journal of International Economics*); Poland (*Ekonomista* and *Gospodarka planowa* [planned economy]); Hungary (*Acta Oeconomica* [economic proceedings]). Since it was the international position of German which was of relevance here, no periodicals from German-speaking countries were included. For purposes of comparison, figures for the US periodicals were then removed in the case of English and for French periodicals in the case of French. The citation proportions for the languages, i.e. of titles in the relevant language, were averaged without weighting, in the first step for both periodicals of the relevant country (where two were available) and, in the second step, for the different countries.

Citations originated consistently only from German, English and French. However, other languages did play a part as sources of citations, in the following rank ordering (based on the number of periodicals with citations from the languages): Russian, Italian, Spanish, Polish, Dutch = Swedish = Czech, Danish = Finnish = Norwegian = Portuguese = Serbo-Croatian = Hungarian. The direction of development of the proportions of the German-language and English-language citations is the same as those for chemistry (cf. Table G.3–3), insofar as the overarching trend for German is downwards and for English upwards.

As with chemistry, English can be seen on closer inspection to have absolute dominance in the US periodicals in more recent history, and this is also true of the Dutch periodicals, whereas, in the eastern European periodicals, English does not achieve such a prominent advantage – but this may have changed in the period since the dissolution of the Soviet Union. Furthermore, periodicals from countries closer to the German-language territory have more German-language citations, at least during earlier periods, than those from further afield. Overall, German shows a somewhat larger proportion than French. After French, Russian is the most important citation language. As one might imagine, it is dominant in USSR periodicals, though the difference from English has dwindled in recent history (1960: 73% and 1990: 42%, by comparison with English 23% and respectively also 42%). Russian is also approximately equal with German and French in Polish periodicals (1960: Russian 4% and 1990: 0%, German 11% and respectively 1%, French 2% and respectively 3%). However, the importance of Russian from 1980 to 1990 falls noticeably everywhere – presumably even more distinctly after the dissolution of the Soviet Union. By contrast with the chemistry periodicals, in the economic sciences, Japanese and Chinese play no part as citation sources, at least not during the period of investigation.

However, for the question addressed here, the decisive finding is that the citation proportion from German-language texts is not higher than in the theoretical science, chemistry, but in fact lower (3.1% in the economic sciences compared with 10.7% in chemistry periodicals in 1990; Table G.5–1; Table G.3–3). Accordingly, the data falsify our overarching hypothesis that German has kept a higher international position in the social sciences than in the theoretical natural sciences. The following reference may arouse the suspicion that the falsified hypothesis is now to be rescued by a "conventionalist turn", against which Karl Popper ([1934] 1973: 47–52) warned: in this case, through retrospective questioning of the test method. Regarding the risk of this suspicion, I would still maintain that the choice of "economics" now seems less representative for the social sciences as a whole, at least less representative than chemistry was for the theoretical natural sciences (Ch. G.3). Unfortunately, I must concede that I realised too late that the German-language contribution to economics has been disproportionately low. One indicator – although a weak one – is the meagre proportion of academics from German-speaking countries among the Nobel prizes for economics, in fact, only a single one, and this was a shared prize in 1994, awarded to the German, Reinhard Selten. A second prize winner Friedrich A. von Hayek, 1974, in fact originated from Austria; he taught in Freiburg in Breisgau

Table G.5–1 Proportions of German, French and English-language citations in economics periodicals 1920–1990

	1920	1930	1940	1950	1960	1970	1980	1990
German	9.8	14.6	10.6	4.1	8.9	3.8	3.4	3.1
English	12.5	17.7	25.7	22.7	31.4	40.0	44.3	57.7
French	3.0	5.3	2.8	2.3	2.6	7.0	2.0	1.6

in the 1960s, but at the time of the award, he was a citizen of the UK and also worked primarily there and in the USA. The most important representatives of the "Austrian School" associated with Carl Menger, Eugen von Bohm-Baweck, Friedrich von Wieser and Ludwig von Mises, which was crushed under Nazism, also emigrated to the English-speaking world (Magill 1991: 101–106). The same applies to John von Neumann, founder of game theory, in whose footsteps Reinhard Selten followed.

Even if the citations do not substantiate our hypothesis, it is supported by the global publication proportions, because, in recent history, as in the case of the applied sciences, these have remained higher for the social sciences than for the natural sciences (cf. Figures G.5–1 and G.3–1: 7.2% compared with <1% in 2005). This corresponds with Skudlik's results (1990: 149) for the FRG in the 1980s, that natural scientists tended towards greater reception of English-language specialist literature than German-language specialist literature. "In economics" by contrast, "the programme of reading was distributed approximately equally between specialist literature in German and English; in the humanities, German-language reading predominated". However, the greater adherence to German indicates its stronger international position in the relevant discipline only if the German-language publications are also received more strongly by scientists who are speakers of other languages. The figures in Table G.5–1 still suggest this, but developments in psychology (start of this chapter) to a lesser extent. At least this report does not exclude the possibility that the reception of German-language texts by non-German-speakers is still more extensive than in the theoretical natural sciences.

One example from sociology spotlights the former significance of German and German-language contributions to this discipline. In a worldwide survey, the *International Sociological Association (ISA)* investigated the ten sociological books from the twentieth century which, in the assessment of its members, had exerted the strongest influence on the discipline. Table G.5–2 shows the findings which were presented at the ISA World Congress in Montréal in 1998. The underlining, which I have added, marks titles originally written in German which were subsequently all translated into English. Berger and Luckmann were German-speakers but, even at the time of publication in 1966, they wrote in English. These findings motivated the president of the *ISA*, Immanuel Wallerstein, to commit himself publicly, in Montréal, in support of German

Table G.5–2 Books from the twentieth century with the greatest influence on sociology, based on a worldwide survey by the *ISA* in 1998

In 1997 the *ISA* program committee surveyed members to identify the ten books published in the twentieth century that respondents considered to be the most influential for sociologists. This produced a 16% response rate and the list of books below

Max Weber, *Economy and Society*
C. Wright Mills, *The Sociological Imagination*
Robert K. Merton, *Social Theory and Social Structure*
Max Weber, *The Protestant Ethic and the Spirit of Capitalism*
Peter Berger and Thomas Luckmann, *The Social Construction of Reality*
Pierre Bourdieu, *Distinction: A Social Critique of the Judgment of Taste*
Norbert Elias, *The Civilizing Process: Power and Civility*
Jürgen Habermas, *The Theory of Communicative Action*
Talcott Parsons, *The Structure of Social Action*
Erving Goffman, *The Presentation of Self in Everyday Life*

Note: titles originally written in German underlined by U.A.

(*Source*: www.isa-sociology.org/bookswww.isa-sociology.org/books)

as a further official language of the world association, especially since Spanish had been added to the original official languages, English and French, at the World Congress in Mexico City in 1982 – following student protests against the linguistic dominance of the *gringos*.

However, German-speaking sociologists lacked commitment to Wallerstein's efforts, which consequently dissipated (see Ammon "Many speakers do not make a science. People need to understand the classics: how the reputation of German could be restored in sociology", *Die Welt* 20 October 1998: 11). This episode invites questions about the possibility and desirability of a targeted strengthening of the international position of languages like German – especially in academia (Ch. G.13). It is possible that – like the applied scientists – German-speaking social scientists do adhere more strongly to their own language than natural scientists, but that this does not help strengthen the international position of German. This would occur because the frequency of reception of German-language publications by speakers of other languages had not increased. Because of the associated reduction of communication in English, German-speaking social scientists would be even more strongly isolated internationally, not to say more provincialized, than the natural scientists who are apparently able to participate more intensively in global communication through English.

Finally, therefore, as in the case of the theoretical natural sciences, we come to the titles of academic associations in German-speaking countries which still provide an indicator for the tradition of German as an academic language in this context, but no longer relate to current language use. Here also, I have restricted myself to the economic sciences. Once again, an example of a title is indicated along with the number of German-speaking titles relative to the total number of associations, added in brackets (after Kirchner 2006):

Economics – Germany: *Deutsche Weltwirtschaftliche Gesellschaft* (33 of 38), Austria: *Volkswirtschaftliche Gesellschaft Österreich* (13 of 17), Switzerland: *Forschungsgemeinschaft für Nationalökonomie* (5 of 7–1 French);

Business Administration, Management – German: *Deutsche Gesellschaft für Personalführung* (21 of 23), Austria: *Österreichisches Produktivitäts- und Wirtschaftlichkeits-Zentrum* (3 of 3), Switzerland: *Schweizerische Management Gesellschaft* (5 of 6);

Marketing – Germany: *Gesellschaft für Konsum-, Markt- und Absatzforschung* (3 of 3), Austria: *Verband der Marktforscher Österreichs* (1 of 1), Switzerland: *Schweizerische Gesellschaft für Marketing* (2 of 3–1 French).

6. Humanities

There is broad consensus among experts in the present field that the humanities [*Geisteswissenschaften*] are intimately connected with the German language (e.g. Oksaar/ Skudlik/ Stackelberg 1988; Ammon 1998: 162–170). This view is also evident from the recommendations by the German Council of Science and the Humanities [Wissenschaftsrat] (2006: 15f.) on the development of the humanities in Germany. Humanities are contrasted in a triadic model with social sciences and natural sciences. With reference to Wilhelm Windelband's ([1894] 1904) Strasbourg Inaugural Lecture, the humanities are also sometimes juxtaposed with the natural sciences as ideographic rather than nomothetic, i.e. more historically descriptive than seeking law-like principles. But, when defining his concept of *Kulturwissenschaften*, which broadly corresponds with the humanities, Heinrich Rickert (1899) emphasised that this description should be abstracted towards culturally significant aspects. Having said this, I share the general view that, if events can be derived from universal principles as empirical "marginal conditions" – using corresponding inferential methods, including statistical methods (according to the

Hempel-Oppenheim scheme for scientific explanation), historical description and explanation need not stand in opposition to one another. From a different perspective, the humanities are concerned principally with "understanding" by contrast with "explanation", and, in fact, with reference to texts or other artefacts. Hermeneutics is accepted as an appropriate method in this context, although – by way of difference from the more strongly objectivised methods of other empirical research, especially formal logic and mathematics – the knowledge acquired remains ultimately subjective. One questionable legitimation for this, which is occasionally still referenced, is to appeal to the speech delivered by Jacob Grimm at the first Germanists' conference in Frankfurt in 1846: "On the value of the inexact sciences" (Grimm 1884). Demarcation from the social sciences is difficult, as shown by the example of law or legal studies (= *Jura, Jurisprudenz* in Germany – *Jus* in Austria and Switzerland; the plural *Rechtswissenschaften* [Legal Studies] is also found) (Ch. G.4, beginning; also, the end of the present chapter). The Council of Science and the Humanities (2006: 17) does not include these in its recommendations for the development of the humanities in Germany, "although, in systematic approaches to science/ scholarship, they are often allocated to the humanities". Instead, the Council includes philosophy, linguistics and literary studies, history, regional studies, religious studies, ethnology, media studies, art, theatre and music studies" under the rubric of the humanities. Its detailed "Overview of disciplines within the humanities according to the system of the Federal Office for Statistics [of Germany! U.A.]" comprises two groups of disciplines: "language and cultural studies" and "art, art studies", with 12 and respectively five (i.e. a total of 17) "fields of study", and with 66 and respectively 30 (i.e. a total of 96) disciplines (Council of Science and the Humanities 2006: 122; for diversity and system of disciplines, see also ibid: 64–70; Behrens/ Fischer/ Minks/ Rösler 2010: 4–7). In English, the *Geisteswissenschaften* correspond with the *Arts and Humanities*, generally incorporated into the triad of disciplines mentioned at the start of this chapter. This model is also followed in the citation indexes: *Arts & Humanities Citation Index*, *Social Sciences Citation Index* and *Science Citation Index*.

The connection with the *Arts* expressed in the English designation is typical for the humanities. This can even extend to similarities in language usage, which have been characterised by Theodor Berchem (2003: 26) as follows: "In the exact sciences [*Naturwissenschaften*], it may be less important to exploit all the nuances of a language". By contrast, in disciplines such as "rhetoric, philosophy or literature" it is "not 'what' is said but 'how' it is put [. . .] which forms an essential part of the message [. . .]". As a result, it becomes difficult to find the appropriate expression – especially in a foreign language. "If this [. . .] is true of the mother tongue, how much more true must it be for everything expressed in a foreign language". In a similar manner, Carl F. Gethmann (2011: 61) stresses the difficulty of "a translation adequate to the level of language" necessary in humanities texts – in my terms, "a stylistically equivalent translation", from German into English.

The difficulty of finding an equivalent expression is one of the reasons for humanities scholars distancing themselves from the foreign language, English, more than scholars in the natural sciences. Other reasons for the greater distance from English include the dominant thematic reference to scholars' home-language community and therefore to "fellow language users", including non-experts, as the main recipients interested in knowledge derived from the humanities. However, I am sceptical about attributing greater value to the "how" than the "what" of statements in academic disciplines, including the humanities, and about blurring the boundaries with the artistic. By contrast, I share the view of Hans Martin Gauger (2000: 36) about the relationship between all academic disciplines and the linguistic means of expression: "[T]he contents of academic discourse are detachable [. . .] from the language in which they have been formulated. It is this which characterises academic content as such, the fact that it can be expressed [. . .] in infinitely many *other* languages [. . .]. Accordingly – and it must be stated with this degree of clarity – if it could be maintained that a given content could only be expressed [. . .] through the medium of *this* language, this content would be scientifically insignificant". In this sense, Gauger distances himself fundamentally from the Humboldt-Sapir-Whorf hypothesis, at least from its radical interpretation, according to which languages can form barriers to knowledge because of their specific structure. I share Gauger's view that languages can be released from such barriers – at least through appropriate "development (or modernisation)" [*Ausbau*], especially of terminology (for the term *Ausbau*, see Kloss 1978: 37–63; Ammon 1989b: 78–82; Ch. G.11). In my opinion, this also applies to the frequently quoted examples about the un-translatability of German philosophers, especially Hegel and Heidegger (Gethmann 2001: 61). The problem here relates to the polysemy of certain terms (e.g. *aufheben* in Hegel and *zuhanden* in Heidegger), for which, e.g. in English, several meaning variants must be considered as possible interpretations. Solving such problems can be effort intensive, e.g. in private law, if the terms relate to different legal systems (Hermann 2011). But even then, what is meant can ultimately be formulated in an intelligible manner in English – if the meaning in the original is clear (for a polemic account, see Florian Coulmas *Unsinn redet deutsch* (Nonsense speaks German), *SZ* 17 March 2003: 31). To me, it also seems that those philosophers tended to obscure their thoughts by means of the German language rather than to illuminate them. Accordingly, Heidegger exploits the mixing of etymological and current meanings of words or the separate, literal meaning of parts of composites which have been absorbed into the current, overall meaning. For me (in contrast to Jürgen Trabant 2003: 318–322), these techniques do not disclose any "deep insight". Having said this, the fact that the epistemological barriers of individual languages can be overcome in this manner does not preclude the possibility that language A discloses certain academic knowledge more readily than language B, in purely heuristic terms (because of syntax, word semantics, idiomatics, metaphor or pragmatics). This is how I understand Peter Eisenberg's reference (2012: 53) to the rich possibilities for the "formation of composite nouns or of complex verb roots" in German, "so that conceptual structures [can be] constructed, which are transparent, semantically watertight/ rigorous and can be connected back to everyday language if required" – and which may also trigger the occasional flash of inspiration. This heuristic function can be reconciled with research findings on "linguistic relativity" (Werlen 1989, 2002, 2005; see also Biere/ Liebert 1997; Kuhn 1993; Ch. G.11), even with John H. McWhorter's spirited polemic against the "language hoax" of "linguistic relativity" (2014), but it must not be overestimated.

These considerations certainly do not mean that the humanities are "immune" from anglicisation, especially given the high level of development of English, in which the potential for expression can be spontaneously expanded through circumlocutions and neologisms. Indeed, work on foreign cultures in the humanities is also published in German and the study of German abroad [*Auslandsgermanistik*] provide respectable contributions to humanities research through German as a foreign language. Language difficulties are an important factor in distancing the humanities from English, but other reasons relating to national and linguistic identity must also be considered (Stukenbrock 2005; Ammon 1995). The unavoidable inclusion in many humanities texts of stylistically nuanced ordinary language presents significant difficulties in a foreign language. Texts are often intended not only for the expansion of knowledge but also for "edification". The linguistic knowledge required for this purpose can often only be acquired through extended periods of residence abroad in the "inner circle" of the English-speaking countries: USA, UK, Ireland, Canada, Australia or New Zealand (Kachru 1986; Crystal 2003). In a telephone survey I conducted in 1990 with 20 university English lecturers in Germany, 19 declared that they rely on stylistic assistance from native speakers when preparing texts for publication; only one disputed this (Ammon 1991a: 273). It is no doubt language difficulties of this kind which led Gauger (2000: 35) to the negative prognosis: "Under conditions as they are at present, anglicisation in the humanities is not possible. It simply will not happen. At least not in a whole range of humanities disciplines". I am not so certain of this myself.

At this point, we should ask, to what extent do German-speaking academics in the humanities consciously adhere to German as an academic language? And do academic speakers of other languages within the humanities still use German more than in the natural sciences or the social sciences, at least receptively? As for the other disciplines (Ch. G.3–G.5), the proportion of German in worldwide publications provides an indicator, but only a weak indicator. This allows comparison of the humanities with the social sciences and natural sciences. However, the use of this indicator is limited because there are no genuinely interdisciplinary databanks for the humanities. As a discipline which is to some extent typical for the humanities, I have chosen philosophy, with the bibliographical databank *The Philosopher's Index*, which also includes theology and religious studies. In interpreting the findings tabulated in Table G.6-1 below, it should be considered that this databank is produced in the USA (at the Philosopher's Information Center at Bowling Green State University, OH), and that, in the USA, Spanish is widely distributed as an immigrant language and a foreign language alongside English as the official language. Regarding *Sociological Abstracts* (Ch. G.5), which is orientated towards the USA, the suspicion that Spanish is treated preferentially has already been mentioned. The high proportion of Spanish in the *Philosopher's Index* (6.4% in 2006) also suggests this. The proportion of German ranks second among the languages other than English (3.3%), closely followed by Italian (3%), which is, surprisingly, ahead of French (2%). But the proportions of all languages are modest by comparison with English; apart from those included here, no language reached above 1% during the entire period.

As with the natural sciences and social sciences (Ch. G.3, G.5), we turn now to the somewhat more reliable indicator for the international position of languages, in which an inference is drawn from frequency of citation to the frequency of reception of texts in the respective languages. However, once again, the available citation analysis does not extend up to the most recent period. It also relates to a different, but similarly typical humanities discipline, history. The contribution of German-speaking countries to this discipline is less widely known than for philosophy, so that a brief explanation is appropriate here. The fact that German-speaking academics have also made a considerable contribution to history [*Geschichtswissenschaft*] is supported by international reference works, e.g. by comments such as the following:

> [H]istorical study as one of the most important methods available to the human mind was begun by Edmund Burke and German writers like Herder and Wilhelm von Humboldt [. . .]. The work of Ranke placed German historians in the vanguard and, particularly after the establishment of the German Empire in 1871, historians in many countries modelled themselves upon German methods.
>
> *(Cannon et al. 1988: 193)*

Table G.6–1 Language proportions in publications in philosophy worldwide 1970–2006

	1970	1980	1990	2000	2006
German	11.9	4.6	4.1	4.0	3.3
English	72.7	75.2	80.1	77.2	77.6
French	7.1	5.5	4.3	2.0	2.0
Spanish	2.5	3.7	4.8	6.6	6.4
Italian	3.8	3.2	3.1	3.4	3.0

(*Source*: percentage; based on *The Philosopher's Index*)

Similar comments about history as an academic subject occur elsewhere:

Inaugurated in German universities in the 18th century [. . .]. In 1800, there were a dozen chairs in German universities, but none in France. By 1900, there were 175 in Germany and 71 in France, while the number of university professors of history in the United States rose in a single decade, 1884–1894, from 20 to 100.

And then, "Leopold von Ranke [. . .] emerged as the most highly regarded and influential historian of the 19th century" (Boia et al. 1991: X). Both works name other historians from German-speaking countries whose influence has extended beyond the German-language territory, e.g. Jakob Burkhardt from Switzerland, and the German historians, Friedrich Meinecke, Georg Waltz and Heinrich Schliemann, as well as ground-breaking philosophers of history such as Georg F.W. Hegel, Karl Marx, Friedrich Engels, Wilhelm Windelband, Heinrich Rickert and Wilhelm C.L. Dilthey. From a global perspective Lucian Boia et al. (1991) discuss a larger number of historians from Germany, a total of 51, than from any other country apart from the USA (USA 52, Italy 46, France 43, UK 29). An additional indicator for the international prestige of German historiography is provided by reprints and reissues of works abroad, e.g. the *Lehrbuch der historischen Methode und der Geschichtsphilosophie* by Ernst Bernheim [1914] in the USA (1960).

As with the other disciplines already considered, history can also be divided into sub-disciplines. *Historical Abstracts* (Vol. 47, 1996) differentiates between (1) themes ("General", "International Relations", "Wars and Military History" etc.); (2) Regions and Countries ("Africa and the Middle East", "Asia and the Pacific Area", [. . .] "Europe" etc.) and (3) historical eras ("Modern History", "Twentieth Century" etc.). Staying with my general assumptions about the humanities mentioned above, this subdivision might suggest a focus of history in German-speaking countries on their home territory and on Europe, and a corresponding distribution of citations from German-language history books. This regional focus can be assumed to apply more strongly for history than for economics (Ch. G.5) and especially chemistry (Ch. G.3). When explaining the findings, it should be borne in mind if they are not addressed more fully because of lack of clear indicators (for details of the following investigation, see Ammon 1998: 66–77). For the citation analysis, periodicals were generally selected according to the recommendation of local experts, because there were no *Journal Citation Reports* for the *Arts & Humanities Citation Index* which was most relevant to this discipline. They were as follows: for the USA: *American Historical Review*; *The Journal of American History*; Soviet Union: *Istoritscheskij schurnal/ Istorija* [Historical Journal/ History]; *Voprosy Istorii* [Questions of History]; France: *Revue Historique*; *Annales Historiques de la Révolution Française* [Historical Review; Annals of the History of the French Revolution]; the Netherlands: *Tijdschrift voor Gescheidenis* [Journal for History]; *International Review of Social History*; Poland: *Polska/Polska i swiat wspó łczesny* [Poland and Modern World]/ *Acta Poloniae Historica*; *Wiadomości historyczne* [Historical News]; Hungary: *Acta Antiqua Academica Scientarum Hungaricae* [Science in Ancient Academic History]; *Acta Historiae Artium Academiae Scientarum Hungaricae* Historical Arts in Ancient Academic History]. Because the focus of the investigation was on the international position of German, periodicals from German-speaking countries were not included. Accordingly, in the case of English, the figures for US periodicals and in the case of French, periodicals from France, were excluded. The proportion of citations for each language, i.e. titles in each language, were otherwise averaged without weighting, in the first step, for both periodicals of the relevant country, and in the second step, for the various countries. Table G.6–2 gives an overview of the results. As for chemistry (Ch. G.3) and economics (Ch. G.5), German, English and French were the only languages consistently above 1% as citation sources. But more or less sporadic citations from the following languages also occurred, ranked according to

Table G.6–2 Proportion of German, French and English-language citations in history periodicals 1920–1990

	1920	1930	1940	1950	1960	1970	1980	1990
German	21.0	20.0	12.2	15.3	12.9	18.6	10.4	12.5
English	12.3	10.0	17.4	16.2	19.0	18.2	25.0	23.7
French	9.0	19.0	13.3	17.1	12.0	8.7	10.0	9.0

(*Source*: percentage; after Ammon 1998: 75)

citation frequency (number of periodicals with citations from these languages): Italian = Russian, Spanish = Dutch = Polish = Czech = Hungarian; Arabic = Latin = Portuguese = Romanian; Japanese = Lithuanian = Swedish = Serbo-Croatian = Slovakian = Turkish = Ukrainian; Afrikaans = Armenian = Bulgarian = Chinese = Estonian = Finnish = Georgian = Greek = Hebrew = Yiddish = Macedonian = Norwegian = Persian = Urdu.

German was therefore still a significant citation language in the recent past, which allows tentative inferences to be drawn about the associated reception of German-language texts by non-German-speaking academics. It is also evident that German was not dominant as an academic language at any phase of the period under investigation by comparison with the two other languages; however, as might be expected, it did have a certain priority position at the beginning of the twentieth century. English gained leadership only recently, but considerably less so than in the natural sciences (Table G.3–3); but, the detailed investigation shows a strong rise in the Netherlands. It also shows that French ranked above German in Poland before and even after WWII and only recently declined. Otherwise, the countries neighbouring the German-language territory cite more from German-language texts than remote countries (USA, USSR). France forms an exception with relatively few German-language citations. This trend and, in part, the other variations in German-language proportions in the neighbouring countries, can be explained by political circumstances. In general, the German-language citation proportion is in decline, even in the neighbouring countries. But German and French have retained a level of international position – with particularly fierce competition (outside the USA) in the Netherlands. It is noticeable that Japanese and Chinese play virtually no part in the period under investigation.

Our findings for history agree substantially with the results of a more recent citation analysis for "history, classics, linguistics, and philosophy" (Kellsey/ Knievel 2004), which its authors consider representative for the "humanities" as a whole. In this study, the language proportions of citations in one periodical were analysed for each of these disciplines, in 1962, 1972, 1982, 1992 and 2002 respectively. Alongside other less relevant points, the authors stress that: "Another interesting result of the study is the finding that German and French remain the most important non-English languages of scholarship for the humanities. As with the citation analysis in the Hutchins, Pargeter and Saunders study, this study found that German was more cited than French" (ibid: 202); but the investigation by Hutchins/ Pargeter/ Saunders (1971) is considerably older. Unfortunately, Kellsey/ Knievel (2004) show the language proportions in the citations only in combination for all the years, as follows: English 78.8%, German 7.8%, French 5.7%, Italian 2%, Latin 1.2% and Spanish 0.6% (ibid: 201). Without giving numerical data, they point out that the proportions of German and French have remained relatively constant over this period, but with a declining trend compared with English. Furthermore, they complain of "the decline in the study of German in the United States" which is "worrisome" because it has unfavourable consequences on the "cataloguing and collection development needs in US research libraries" (ibid: 202). They therefore presumably regard the prospects for German as an international academic language less favourably than for French and indeed Spanish.

Finally, I briefly consider jurisprudence or the study of law (*Rechtswissenschaft* and *Rechtswissenschaften* in the plural – also sub-disciplines, such as legal history, philosophy of law, legal theory, sociology of law, legal dogmatics and methodology [*Rechtsdogmatik* und *Methodenlehre*]). Law which, together with other norms and customs, regulates how people live together in a community, is strongly language-orientated. This applies not only to the codified law but also common law via court decisions. It is therefore plausible to allocate jurisprudence to the humanities. Its methods of text analysis (exegesis, interpretation) are reminiscent of literary studies or source analysis in history, e.g. the "Canones" by Friedrich Carl von Savigny (1779–1861), which differentiate between grammatical, historical, systematic and teleological aspects, and hermeneutics. However, to the extent that the law is also always characterised by the social structure and culture of the associated community, the study of law also belongs to the social sciences, especially the sub-discipline of sociology of law (see Ch. G.5 beginning).

In the German-speaking countries, jurisprudence continues to be studied predominantly in German. But, given its orientation towards the German language, to what extent does it reach out into countries with other languages? Perhaps the most notable case is Japan (MORI 1994). Faced with modernisation after the fall of the Shogunate, during the Meiji-period (1868–1912), Japan orientated itself towards Western legal systems and, after an initial turn towards France, adopted major components of its law from the recently formed German Empire: especially commercial law, civil process law, court constitutional law and parts of penal law. In 1889, Japan announced "the constitution of the Japanese Empire (*Dai-Nihon-Teikoku-Kenpô*) according to the Prussian model" (ibid: 53). As a political model, the German Empire seemed more appropriate than the Western democracies for the authoritarian Tenno state (NAKA 1994). "As can easily be imagined, a dependence of Japanese jurisprudence upon the German model arose from this" (MORI 1994: 53), which was consolidated by the subsequent proximity to Nazi Germany and the Anti-Comintern Pact in 1936. However, this earlier role model was crushed by history, especially the joint defeat in WWII. The turn towards the USA and its jurisprudence began after the war, and is still in process today, as is the absolute preference for English as the primary foreign language taught in schools (HIRATAKA 1994; Ch. I.9.14). According to Isamu MORI's assessment of the future "[things] are hardly likely to progress so far that people in Japan abandon their consideration of the law and jurisprudence of that country on which the law and jurisprudence of Japan have relied for so long". In view of the "major collections of German legal literature" in Japanese university libraries" MORI comments (1994: 57): "[A]s a result, the German language will also remain important for Japanese legal scholars, so that in future it will continue to be considered as a foreign language which must be studied intensively". However, the following addition to his statement seems incongruous: "Students' readiness to learn German is gradually declining [. . .]. The neglect of German in general education [. . .] will mean that, with increasing frequency, graduates from legal faculties will have only a poor knowledge of German if they have any at all" (ibid: 59f.). Regarding Korea, to which Japan exported German law, German jurisprudence and German language during its colonial rule (1910–1945), Soon-Im KIM (2003) paints a similar picture, suggesting an even stronger decline of the German language.

The adoption of elements of English-language law in more recent times is not restricted to Japan and Korea but has also reached the German-speaking countries, primarily, e.g. in the German economy, where companies increasingly agree on "a foreign court of jurisdiction" and "formulate entire agreements in English" ("*Das deutsche Recht hat an Boden verloren*" [German law has lost ground] and "*Prozesse auf Englisch*" [Court cases in English], *FAZ* 27 December 2008: 12 and respectively 17 November 2010: 21; and even as early as Berns 1992). By contrast, a new interest in German law and associated with this also in the German language has taken root in some EU member states. This is evident from university course descriptions at German universities, e.g. at the University of Bonn: "in the framework of the course 'German as a foreign language', the law faculty offers foreign students the possibility to familiarise themselves with German legal terminology in various modules" (www.jura.uni-bonn.de/index.php?id=4486). The present chapter has provided evidence of a stronger, although limited adherence to the German language in the humanities than in the previously discussed disciplines. The next chapter relates to the "niche disciplines" in the humanities, in which an even more significant, even international position for German is presumed to exist.

7. Niche disciplines for German as an international academic language?

German-speaking academics in the humanities generally tend more towards German and less towards English than those in the social sciences and especially in the natural sciences (cf. Ch. G.6, G.3), but with differences between individual disciplines, e.g. *Germanistik* [German Studies] (trend towards German) and *Anglistik* [English Studies] (trend towards English). This chapter investigates disciplines within the humanities in which German still has a significant international position. Harald Weinrich (Deutscher Bundestag 1986: 196) coined the term "niche disciplines (for German)" to describe these disciplines. For 30 years or so, they have been widely referenced as – possibly the last – bastions of German as an international academic language. However, there is a lack of methodical identification and investigation of these disciplines which still hampers the present discussion, in which the niche disciplines will be identified and ranked according to their international position and prospects. In one early investigation, Sabine Skudlik (1990: 216) named the following seven disciplines: theology, archaeology, classical philology, Finno-Ugric studies, Assyriology, Slavic studies and Indo-Germanic studies. In my own survey of German publishers in the humanities in 1997 (of which seven responded), the following 12 niche disciplines were named (number of nominations in brackets): classical archaeology (five), classical philology, protestant (Christian) theology, musicology, theology unspecified (three in each case), philosophy (two), Egyptology, Near-Eastern archaeology, prehistory and early history, art history, Jewish studies, oriental studies (one in each case; Ammon 1998: 176). Harrassowitz, the leading German exporting publisher for academic literature, named 13 almost identical niche disciplines (email from director Knut Dorn, 19 January 2009) in a rank ordering of three groups according to the position of German as language of publication: 1) "home [German-language! U.A.] literature, and associated home, German-language, criticism and analysis"; 2) "archaeology, religious history, theology, philosophy, classical antiquities, music, art"; 3) "Oriental studies, Slavic studies, Jewish studies, Egyptology, Indo-Germanic studies". In my email survey of relevantly qualified German-studies professors outside the German-language territory in 2009 (one expert in each of: Australia, Brazil, Finland, France, UK, Italy, Japan, Turkey and USA), I asked the question: "In which disciplines are academic publications still received in German, from your perspective and in your country?". The following 23 disciplines were named (frequency in brackets; disciplines separated by commas, variant names after stroke): German studies, history/ historical studies (seven each), philosophy (six), music/ musicology, theology (four each), jurisprudence, ancient history (three each), general linguistics/ linguistics, classical philology, archaeology, art history, literary studies, sociology (two each), hermeneutics, Indology,

Iranistics, Islamic studies, cultural studies, multicultural studies, philology of Middle-Eastern and Far-Eastern languages, political studies, theatre studies and terminological studies (one each). A more recent survey of a different kind on the "international position of the humanities in Germany" identified the following nine disciplines: African studies, Egyptology, Islamic studies and Arabic studies, German studies, history, communication and media studies, art history, music or musicology, religious studies (Behrens/ Fischer/ Minks/ Rösler 2010: 5). Although the term was not used, what was meant here was doubtless the niche disciplines (for German as an international academic language); their choice was influenced by the German Council for Science and the Humanities (*Wissenschaftsrat*). The authors refer to its *Recommendations for the Development and Promotion of the Humanities in Germany* (ibid: 5; *Wissenschaftsrat* 2006). According to this Council (2006: 15 f.), "German scholarship and language represent key reference points and enjoy high prestige worldwide" and are "even today, international conference languages" in the disciplines of classical antiquities, Egyptology, Classical Oriental studies, German studies and philosophy. Table G.7–1 gives an overview of all the disciplines named so far, including investigations and frequencies of nomination. In individual cases, discipline titles have been abbreviated (e.g. "Islam/Arab" For "Islamic and Arabic studies"), and there are certain interdisciplinary overlaps. However, the 14 multiple nominations can be taken as a core inventory for these niche disciplines, i.e. German studies, (classical) archaeology, Egyptology, music(ology), philosophy, theology (four nominations each, n=6), ancient history, art history, (Classical) Oriental studies, classical philology (three each, n=4), history, Islamic studies, Jewish studies, Slavic studies (two each, n=4).

Many of the smaller disciplines can be combined, giving the following five larger disciplines: *German studies, musicology, (ancient) history* (including archaeology, Egyptology, classical antiquities, art history, Classical Oriental history, classical philology), *philosophy* and *theology* (including Islamic studies, Jewish studies). Some of these data have been confirmed by other findings from the online survey included in Table G.7–1 (Behrens/ Fischer/ Minks/ Rösler 2010; www.his. de/publikation/bericht; summary Fischer/ Minks 2010), in which 1,030 academics in Germany (response 22%) and 181 in Australia, UK and USA (response 14%) took part (Behrens/ Fischer/ Minks/ Rösler 2010: 4f.). 6Six of the nine disciplines included belong within the core inventory of 14 disciplines listed above, namely German studies, Egyptology, history, art history, musicology, Islamic studies. For statistical reasons, responses by academics from Australia, UK and USA were not differentiated according to discipline in Behrens/ Fischer/ Minks/ Rösler (2010). For the nine combined disciplines, the following proportions were obtained for "*foreign* languages, in which academics in the humanities from Australia, UK and USA most frequently read academic publications (responses from the three English-speaking countries given as %)": French 69, German 59, Italian 21, Spanish 17, Dutch 12 (ibid: 32). However, more than half (59%) named German, which therefore ranks behind French (69%) but ahead of all other foreign languages. Accordingly, German is still widely distributed as an academic reading language in the "inner circle" of English-speaking countries (Kachru 1986; Crystal 2003), close behind French and with a significant margin ahead of Italian, Spanish and Dutch. Unfortunately, a subdivision into individual disciplines is not given. Responses from academics in Germany to the same question, regarding "foreign languages" in which they "most frequently read academic publications (responses from Germany as %)" show substantially the same languages – except for the world lingua franca, in first place: English 97%, French 65%, Italian 32%, Spanish 17% and Dutch 14% (Behrens/ Fischer/ Minks/ Rösler 2010: 32).

Academics from Germany allocated a different international position to their own language, German, from discipline to discipline. The response "only relevant in the German-language territory" may be interpreted as a denial of any international position. It must be borne in mind

Table G.7–1 Niche disciplines for German as an international academic language based on various investigations and sources

	Skudlik 1990	Publishers 1997	Science Council 2006	Harrassowitz 2009	Experts 2009	Behrens/ Fischer/ Minks/ Rösler 2010	n
Archaeology (Classical)	x	x		x	x		4
Egyptology		x	x	x		x	4
German studies			x	x	x	x	4
Music(ology)		x		x	x	x	4
Philosophy		x	x	x	x		4
Theology	x	x		x	x		4
Art history		x			x	x	3
Classical philology	x	x			x		3
Classical studies			x	x	x		3
Oriental studies (ancient)		x	x	x			3
History					x	x	2
Islam/ Arabic					x	x	2
Jewish studies		x		x			2
Slavic studies	x			x			2
African studies						x	1
Art				x			1
Assyriology	x						1
Communication/ Media studies						x	1
Cultural studies					x		1
Evangelical Theology		x					1
Finno-Ugric studies	x						1
Hermeneutics					x		1
Indo-Germanic studies				x			1
Indology					x		1
Iranian studies					x		1
Linguistics					x		1
Literary studies					x		1
Middle-Eastern/Far-Eastern philology					x		1
Multicultural studies					x		1
Near-Easternarchaeology		x					1
Political studies					x		1
Law					x		1
Prehistory/ Early history		x					1
Religious studies						x	1
Sociology					x		1
Theatre studies					x		1
Terminological studies					x		1

Note: ranked according to total frequency of nomination; alphabetical within the same total frequency

that this question was not restricted to reading. Table G.7–2 shows the findings in the summary of disciplines by Behrens/ Fischer/ Minks/ Rösler (2010: 33) in a rank ordering (produced by myself) based on the sum of the first two columns. Apart from German studies, respondents found a significant international position for German in musicology, history and art history.

Largely compatible findings were obtained for the three English-speaking countries (Australia, UK and USA) – again without differentiation of disciplines (Table G.7–3).

Additional individual responses from the qualitative interviews fit the same picture, with one representative for each of the nine disciplines in the three English-speaking countries, and one representative each from Japan for five of the disciplines. For instance, a musicologist from the USA commented: "Every serious American and British musicologist has to learn German" (ibid: 39). Furthermore, Fischer/ Minks (2010: 10f.) have determined that knowledge of German tends to be more necessary in "Islamic mysticism" and "Bible studies" than "for other areas of religious studies" and summarise their findings to the effect that "reading competence in German is still indispensable in many fields", namely for "Egyptology, Arabic studies/Islamic studies, art history, musicology, theology and, of course, German studies". In my own survey of experts, respondents also confirmed the need for a reading knowledge of German for essentially the same disciplines, e.g. in Australia: "At our institute [University of Sydney! U.A.], courses in reading German for academics have been available for years. The courses are attended by colleagues especially from archaeology, ancient history, Islamic studies, Indology, Iranian studies, history, who, as always, claim that translated scholarly literature is not available, so that it is essential

Table G.7–2 Position of German as an international academic language in various disciplines based on expert assessment in Germany; percentages

	Lingua franca	*Equivalent with other academic languages*	*Less important than other academic languages*	*Important only in the German-language territory*
German studies	66	13	5	16
Music(ology)	9	51	23	17
History	5	38	28	29
Art history	6	29	45	20
African studies/Arabic studies/ Islamic studies/Egyptology	–	28	42	30
Communication/Media studies	1	9	24	66
Total	24	28	22	26

(*Source*: after Behrens/ Fischer/ Minks/ Rösler 2010: 33)

Table G.7–3 Position of German as an international academic language in eight or nine humanities disciplines based on expert assessment in Australia, UK and USA, percentages

	Lingua franca	*Equivalent with other academic languages*	*Less important than other academic languages*	*Important only in the German-language territory*
Total excl. German studies	1	31	37	31
Total	8	32	33	27

(*Source*: Behrens/ Fischer/ Minks/ Rösler 2010: 33)

just to be able to read it in German" (DAAD lecturer Andreas Jäger, email 21 January 2009). Professor Brian Taylor, who led the reading courses, summed up the views of PhD graduates in "classical archaeology, Roman history and mediaeval history" as follows: "There's a huge body of literature on all aspects of my thesis topic in German" (email 24 March 2010).

Library catalogues in non-German speaking universities also offer pointers towards the niche disciplines for German under investigation here. One potential indicator is given by the languages of periodicals subscribed to. But, for this purpose, I have at my disposal only (out)dated data from the University of North Carolina, Chapel Hill (USA), and this applies only to two groups of disciplines: classical archaeology and classical philology/ classical history combined. In cases of doubt, allocation to languages was based on the subtitle of the periodicals, e.g. *Akroterion. Quarterly for the Classics in South Africa* → English, *Germania. Anzeiger der Römisch-Germanischen Kommission des Deutschen Archäologischen Instituts* → German (Table G.7–4). However, periodicals with German-language titles also contained contributions in other languages, especially English. The same applies for periodicals with French or Italian titles. By contrast, periodicals with English titles hardly ever contained contributions in other languages.

In my effort to find representative information about libraries outside the German-language territory, I returned to US university libraries, on one hand, to guarantee stringent test conditions (because the USA has a reputation for neglecting languages other than English) and, on the other hand, to achieve global representativeness (because the USA is regarded as the academic centre for the contemporary world; cf. Ch. G.1 towards the end). In this context, ideas about a balanced catalogue published in the guidelines for US university libraries seemed more informative than the library catalogues themselves. The most famous of such guidelines are Sheehy (1976/80/82) and Balay (1996) – the latter was also the most up-to-date in 2012. "Reference works" for potential niche disciplines for German should provide pointers towards the international position of German. In the case of Sheehy, the analysis had to be restricted to four selected disciplines for reasons of operational capacity. I chose Lutheran theology, archaeology, classical philology and musicology (details in Ammon 1998: 171–175).

Lutheran theology is reached via → humanities → religion → Christianity → Protestantism → "Lutheran" (1 of 13 protestant denominations). The search path reveals the small size of this niche in which there was nevertheless not a single German-language title – despite the German-speaking founder, Martin Luther, who is also a national symbol for Germany and is considered a pioneer of contemporary standard German. However, the more comprehensive search via theology, did lead to German-language works, where German was at least represented under "General works" and "Christianity" with 24 titles among a total of 257 (9%). The proportion of French was of a similar size, while titles in English were predominant, as expected.

Table G.7–4 Language proportions of periodicals for classical archaeology and classical philology/classical history combined in the library of the University of North Carolina, Chapel Hill, in 1996

	Classical archaeology	*Classical philology and Classical history*
English	39	207
German	22	104
French	17	105
Italian	17	70
Other languages	13	144

(*Source*: based on *Classical Periodicals in Davis Library* 1996; subject allocation by Gerhard Koeppel)

Theology – although not especially Lutheran theology – was therefore confirmed as a niche for German as an international academic language, but with meagre representation.

Starting from "History and area studies", archaeology is accessed via several steps, under "Archaeology and prehistory" and "Classical antiquities". Of the total of 71 titles, 15 (21%) were in German (43 English, seven French, three Russian, two Spanish and one Hungarian) (Sheehy 1976: 603f.). Archaeology is therefore a solidly confirmed niche for German as an international academic language. Closer consideration of the German-language titles shows that German is largely restricted to the region of the Mediterranean and the Near East. However, the associated classical archaeology has strongly influenced other archaeologies theoretically and methodologically and, in many Western countries still forms the core of the entire discipline.

The best match for classical philology in Sheehy (1976/80/82) seems to be the so-called "Classical languages", which are found under "Literature" rather than "Linguistics". Of the total of 68 titles named here, 9 (13%) are in German, i.e., a relatively larger proportion than in theology, but smaller than in archaeology. Once again, the proportion of French is of a similar size, but the largest proportion is English. German is therefore also confirmed as an international academic language for classical philology. In many countries, a reading knowledge of German is still compulsory or is at least recommended, alongside a similar knowledge of French and relevant classical languages, for the study of classical archaeology and classical philology, at least for higher degrees. Especially in the USA, these language skills are often inadequately provided but certified anyway (communication by Gerhard Koeppel, Archaeology, University of North Carolina, Chapel Hill).

Finally, in "Music", only 7% of titles are in German (25 of 356); but the proportion under the heading of "Bibliography" is higher (22%; 11 of 49 titles). Music is suggested as a niche for German because of the worldwide distribution of classical music from German-speaking countries (J. Ziegler 1994), the associated practical training and many references to the importance of a knowledge of German for the study of music (Ammon 1991a: 411–420). Accordingly, a similarly dated survey of foreign-language skills required for PhD research in the USA (around 1970) showed a preference for German in the natural sciences and for French in the social sciences and humanities, but this was for the humanities "except music, which had a higher percentage using German". The same investigation also points out that music departments in US universities often resisted the abandonment of "foreign-language requirements" for PhD researchers and insisted on foreign-language skills, which must therefore have meant a knowledge of German (Wiltsey 1972, Part I: 55, 72; 41).

I analysed Balay/ Carrington/ Martin (1996) using the same method as for Sheehy but included more disciplines. Table G.7–5 gives an overview of the proportions of German among reference works for all disciplines considered (original English designations). The percentages allow a comparison with Sheehy, whose figures have been added in square brackets. In fact, the comparison shows a decline in more disciplines (three) than an increase (one), but the disciplines have possibly not been defined sufficiently accurately. As in the case of Sheehy, there were again errors regarding Lutheran theology.

In general, these additional analyses confirm the 14 niche disciplines for German as an international academic language shown in Table G.7–1. However, there are still some discrepancies. For example, there is a significant gap in the data on actual language usage, especially regarding permitted and *de facto* language choice at international conferences. Prognoses about the linguistic future of the – inadequately identified – niche disciplines for German are correspondingly doubtful. Can we anticipate the maintenance of German as an international academic language for these disciplines or must we expect a broad language shift towards English, as for most other disciplines? Individual responses in Behrens/ Fischer/ Minks/ Rösler (2010), which

Table G.7–5 Niche disciplines for German based on proportions of basic works

	Religion				Language, Linguistics, Philology	
	General works	The Bible	Christianity/ Lutheran	Lutheran	Slavic Language	Iranian/Indo-European Languages
English	90 (81)	93 (106)	86 (214)	100 (6)	43 (6)	71 (5)
German	4 (4)	2 (2)	4; Σ = 8 [9] (11)	- [-]	21 (3)	29 (2)
French	2 (2)	2 (2)	4 (11)	-	-	-
Spanish	-	-	-	-	-	-
Italian	-	-	2 (4)	-	-	-
Russian	1 (1)	-	-	-	21 (3)	-
Other	2 (2)	4 (4)	4 (9)	-	14 (2)	-

	Music	General History		
		Archaeology and Ancient History		
		General works	Classical studies	Ancient Egypt
English	83 (330)	74 (23)	83 (25)	83 (5)
German	8 [7] (31)	19 (6)	10 [13] (3)	17 [21] (1)
French	5 (18)	3 (1)	3 (1)	-
Spanish	2 (7)	-	3 (1)	-
Italian	1 (4)	-	-	-
Russian	1 (2)	3 (1)	-	-
Other	2 (6)	-	-	-

(*Source*: percentage, absolute numbers in brackets, after Balay/ Carrington/ Martin 1996. Percentages for German in Sheehy in square brackets; sum of "general works" and "Christianity" under "religion")

retrospectively relativize an initially claimed international position of German, suggest the latter outcome. For example, for history in the USA: "German is a very important language for European historians because so much high-quality work is written in German [. . .]. On the other hand [. . .], English has obviously become the international language" (Fischer/ Minks 2010: 11). A more sceptical view was expressed by one musicologist, also in the USA: "I think a German musicologist who does not read English cannot be internationally competitive" (Behrens/ Fischer/ Minks/ Rösler 2010: 39). A similar view was expressed by a British Islamicist: "I suspect that German is beginning to slip quite seriously in the field, and increasingly German colleagues will just write in English because they are [...] much more likely to have an impact if they write in English than if they still write in German" (ibid: 35). Other responses reveal the loss of position already suffered by German, e.g. the criticism by one German Egyptologist about the lack of readiness to learn German abroad: "I do absolutely criticise one or more of my foreign colleagues for their reluctance to learn, because German is well established as an academic language" (ibid: 36).

My own survey of professors of German studies and German as a foreign language produced similarly pessimistic results, e.g.

- From Italy: "In Italy, the situation [position of German as an academic language! U.A.] out-side German studies seems rather gloomy. Traditional disciplines such as classical antiquities and philosophy may still be an exception in some cases, but not really in the long term" (Sandro Moraldo, email 02 January 2009);
- From Brazil: "As an academic and cultural language, German is still found in the humani-ties, but not very often [...], it is really only among people who have done their training in Germany" (Cleo V. Altenhofen, email 22 January 2009);
- From France: "Among scholars in German studies, the idea of at least occasionally includ-ing an English-language article among their 'international' publications is beginning to take root" (Odile Schneider-Mizony, email 15 January 2009);
- From Turkey: "However, in recent years [even in German Studies! U.A.], there has been a slight tendency to lecture in Turkish. The reason is the steady decline in German-language skills among students" (Nilüfer Tapan, email 11 January 2009).

So, even German Studies is not immune from the loss of position of German. In fact, here also, German never really had a monopoly as a language of publication. But the increase in English-language publications is a new phenomenon. It is found especially in the linguistics of German but to a lesser extent also in the study of German literature. In the mid-1990s, the proportion of English among German-studies publications was higher than all other foreign languages together: German 80%, English 12.8%, French 3.3%, Italian and Russian 1% each (sum of the last three: 7.2%. Collins/ Rutledge 1996: 76f.; cf. also Detering 2000). My question to German publishers in 1997 expressly interrogated the chances of maintaining German: "What is the developmental trend for the international position of German in the most important niche disciplines?"

Table G.7-6 shows the developmental trend for the international position of German in niche disciplines for German:

Table G.7–6 Outlook for German as an international academic language in niche disciplines for German based on assessment by German specialist publishers

Rising trend	Relatively stable	Falling trend
–	4	2

Risk of loss of position of German in niche disciplines:

No loss	Loss in the long-term	Loss in the medium-term	Imminent loss
3	2	1	
No risk	Lowrisk	Moderate risk	Highrisk
3	–	3	–

None of the publishers see the international use of German as a "rising trend". At conferences on the topic, representatives of niche disciplines have also confirmed losses of position for German, including the fact that German-language texts tend to be read less frequently by academic speakers of other languages, e.g. at the conference "*Deutsch in der Wissenschaft*" (Tutzing, 10–12 January 2011) or the open forum "Have we gambled away our inheritance? German humanities in the world context" (Bonn, 24 February 2010).

Tension between stability and the decline of German into the niche disciplines is reflected in the history and language choice of major reference works. German historian of antiquity Hartmut Leppin (email 19 January 2011) gave me the titles of seminal works and projects in his discipline,

which necessarily presuppose [. . .] a knowledge of German:

- *Altägyptisches Wörterbuch*: also contains French and does not avoid English on principle, but the core is exclusively German;
- *Reallexikon für Antike und Christentum*: exclusively in German, even when English native-speaker authors are writing;
- *Augustinus-Lexikon*: German, English and French articles side-by-side; the user must know all three languages;
- Editing and revising sources of Byzantine law.

Conversely, the tradition-rich, multi-volume reference work *Paulys Realencyclopädie der classischen Altertumswissenschaften* (founded in 1837) has recently appeared in English translation as *BRILL'S New Pauly*, which, according to the publisher's blurb, is "the English edition of the authoritative DER NEUE PAULY published by Verlag J. B. Metzler since 1996". It is now available online as *New Pauly Online: Encyclopaedia of the Ancient World*. Similarly, for some time, the *Lexikon der Ägyptologie* has been published in California, in English with the title *The UCLA Encyclopedia of Egyptology*. The current editors explain the linguistic shift as follows: "For an English reading public, the LÄ [Lexikon der Ägyptologie! U.A.] poses a number of problems. For example, most of the texts and all entry titles are in German [. . .]" (www.egyptology.ucla.edu/pagefiles/encyclopedia-info.html). These examples relativize the statement by the German Council for Science and the Humanities (2010: 16), that, in general, "specialist literature in Classical Oriental studies and Egyptology [. . .] is apparently not translated into other languages".

Another indicator for the turnaway from German by the USA, as the current centre of world scholarship, is the staffing policy of German university libraries, which James Campbell (Librarian for German at the University of Virginia Library, Charlottesville) described as follows (email 03 January 2011):

The truly interesting thing is that people [. . .], who selected books in German for many subject areas, are retiring and they are not being replaced. Our *Fachreferenten* are typically monoglots – or perhaps know a little of one European language. They will buy the occasional German book if a professor or graduate student specifically asks for it, but have neither the linguistic ability nor the knowledge of German scholarship and publishing to build collections.

This has been true for many years at less well-funded libraries, but recently has affected even elite institutions. Yale and Chicago used to have 2–3 *Referenten* for European literatures. This last year after a retirement and a resignation they decided to make do with one person *(in neither case a* Germanist *as it happens)*.

The worsening decline in the position of German as an international academic language associated with such staffing policies also influences the niche disciplines. They too slide into the global communication network. Even the titles of many German research centres reveal this trend, e.g. the "Dahlem Humanities Center" in Berlin, which is described as follows: It "bundles the Germany-wide unique breadth of humanities research at the Free University of Berlin. [. . .] But existing collaborations with Humanities Centers at prominent American and European universities [. . .] underline the clear international orientation of the Center" (www.fu-berlin.de/sites/dhc/). In the global communication network, even in the niche disciplines, German-speaking academics are, on the one hand, becoming a minority and, on the other hand, possibly losing their leadership of scholarly opinion. In the words of one Italian philosopher: "I believe the trend of reading German philosophy in German will be retained at our university; the only problem is that the hegemony of German philosophy is gradually declining" (Gian Franco Frigo, University of Padua, email 11 January 2011).

The position of German as an international academic language may be unshakable only in German studies – because, according to the German Council for Science and the Humanities (2006: 16), it is "in the nature of the subject matter", that "outstanding research cannot be achieved without a knowledge of German-language research literature". For German studies, German seems as "natural" as the language of scholarship as English does for English studies or French for French studies. However, warnings, such as the "outcry" by Austrian Romance studies expert Hans Goebl (2010) at the increasing use of English at romance-languages conferences, must not be ignored. The "nature of the subject matter" does not seem to provide protection here. Indeed, the nature of the subject matter has not prevented the rise of German as the foremost academic language for Finno-Ugric studies or Slavic studies. The fact that such a "natural" connection does not constitute a necessary connection becomes clearer if a distinction is made between "object language" and "metalanguage". The academic metalanguage need not be identical with the object language; e.g. English is in no sense precluded as a metalanguage for the object language French; nor is German precluded as a metalanguage for Finnish. But it is never possible to do without a knowledge of the object language – at least not beyond a limitation of the study to aspects which are not bound to the object language. "German Studies" in the USA have become infamous in this respect; some forms of comparative literary studies which "make do" with translations instead of original texts also fall into this category. By contrast, a metalanguage different from the object language is indispensable if the object language is not terminologically elaborated and does not satisfy academic requirements. It follows from these considerations that no disciplinary subject matter (object) can reliably protect the position of German as an international academic language "by its very nature".

Better protection may be provided by the interests of the home language community and government support associated with these interests (Ch. K.3.3; K.3.4). Another significant cause for the resilience of German is to be found "in the history" [in the sense of tradition! U.A.] of the respective disciplines. The German Council for Science and the Humanities (2006: 16) assumes that this is the case for "Classical studies"; other niche disciplines can be added to the list. For German studies, tradition also has a stabilising effect. But the – sometimes only imagined – commercial insignificance of many niche disciplines, or of the entire humanities, is not an advantage. Despite all the evidence to the contrary – not wishing to end e.g. in the "year of the humanities" in Germany, 2007 – the financing of the humanities still lags far behind that of the natural sciences, and their low commercial value therefore also reduces their prestige. Another handicap is the small scale of many niche disciplines – with the exception of German studies and possibly theology. Such small disciplines are seriously pressured by regulations for university study, recently, by the "Bologna reform". In this context, see e.g. Fischer/Minks (2010: 2) or "Are the experts dying out? Professors in smaller disciplines are weakened by the Bologna reform" (*Welt am Sonntag* 12 December 2010: NRW 10). Regarding the identification of small disciplines, see *Potsdamer Arbeitsstelle Kleine* Fächer (www.kleinefaecher.de).

8. University teaching

The analyses presented so far have related essentially to communication in the context of research, i.e. between academics, which is primarily written communication. But research constitutes an inner core of the ivory tower of university life which is relatively inaccessible to non-experts and to the general public; the transition to a foreign language, English, is accordingly not particularly noticeable. By contrast, university teaching, the subject of the present chapter, is less detached from the surrounding society. University administration will not be addressed in detail in this book. Relevant pointers for the openness of university teaching towards society are provided by students from schools at the start of their degree programmes and overseas students, the number of whom has increased in German-speaking countries in recent decades. Links with universities are also established through academic journalism. In this context, Hubert Markl, president of the German Research Foundation (*DFG*) for many years, drew a parallel between university teaching and public life when he addressed the question of German or English in academia. On one hand, he strongly defended the use of English in publications, especially for the natural sciences, but on the other hand, for German-speaking academics, he recommended "the undeniable obligation to do everything, through textbooks, popular academic writing, through all available media and through intensive, open and patient collaboration with academic journalists, to make scholarship [. . .], in all its diversity, informative value and beauty, accessible to everyone prepared to receive it, *not only in German but in the best possible German*" (Markl 1986: 24 – emphasis U.A.). Markl's recommendation of German-language textbooks here was a reference to the increasing use of English-language teaching materials even in the 1980s. Having said this, oral teaching in the German-speaking countries generally continued to be delivered in German apart from foreign-language disciplines or in the case of guest visits by foreign academics.

But this situation began to change with the introduction of "international degree programmes" which will now be considered in greater detail. The most relevant types of such courses are not defined by their international content, but rather by their international participants (Hellmann/ Patzold 2005: 19–22). In the present context, what is characteristic and especially interesting about these courses is that at least some of the teaching is delivered in English, partly out of consideration for the international participants. By way of generalisation, I shall therefore refer to "degree programmes in English" although at least some parts of the teaching are often delivered in German and, in isolated cases, also in other foreign languages, especially French. These degree programmes in English began in Germany in the winter semester 1997/98 in 18 universities, for undergraduates, in nine universities and for graduates, in 16, at both levels, in seven universities (Ammon 1998: 227–252; Ammon/ McConnell 2002; Motz 2005a). They were financed by the Federal Ministry for Education, Science, Research and Technology and administered centrally by the German Academic Exchange Service (DAAD). To begin with, they aroused largely positive reactions from the German press (e.g. "*Studium in English: Visionär*", *Die Zeit* 9 May 1997: 17). They were more noticeable than the preceding anglicisation of research and written teaching materials. But initial approval was soon followed by harsh criticism (e.g. Ehlich 2002, 2004). As the planning documents betrayed, the prime motive for introducing degree programmes in English was not the establishment of linguistic unity between research and teaching for German students, but the opening of German universities to students from non-German-speaking countries ("foreign students"). In fact, despite a growth in student numbers worldwide, fewer and fewer students were coming to Germany from high-tech countries, such as the USA and Japan, and from emerging countries. Most of these students were attracted to countries in the "inner English-speaking circle" (Kachru 1986; Crystal 2003). The trend became glaringly obvious because German politicians had only recently been looking for ways to limit "the large influx of applications to German universities from foreign students" (German Bundestag 1981: 41). Very different complaints were now heard e.g. from development minister Carl-Dieter Spranger: "The number of students from Asia has been declining for five years now [. . .], while thousands are flooding into the USA". This soon began to impinge on research and to worry research-funding bodies,

> such as the Alexander von Humboldt Foundation [Ch. K.3.3 U.A.]. Because many who are applying for a grant have already been students in Germany and have therefore learnt some German. Without this background, the tendency to prefer going directly to the USA is strengthened. At the time, the Foundation observed this especially in Asian countries.
>
> *("Die Humboldt-Mafia", Die Zeit 4 July 1997: 17)*

One significant cause for this problem was often diagnosed as the dwindling knowledge of the German language abroad (Ch. K.2; K.4; K.7). It was hoped that the resulting "language barrier" could be overcome by teaching in English, which would make access to German universities easier for foreign students. The dominance of English as an academic language remained in the background as an argument for teaching in English but was certainly an additional factor in the view that German students should be included, especially in postgraduate courses. Greater familiarity with English would make them better equipped for global academic competition. Finally, researchers and teachers could perfect their English by means of the new courses.

The number of degree programmes in English has now grown enormously. At approximately the same time as they were introduced in Germany, similar courses were also launched not only in all German-speaking countries, but almost everywhere in Europe and beyond the boundaries of the EU (Ammon/ McConnell 2002; Maiworm/ Wächter 2002; Wächter/ Maiworm 2008, 2014). They have now been extended to a large number of disciplines, among which isolated disciplines in the humanities, especially niche disciplines for German (Ch. G.7), form the only exceptions. In the winter semester 2011/12, the total number of degree programmes in English in Germany was 733, which corresponded only to 5.2% of the total of 14,133 degree programmes (Foundation for Promoting the German Rectors' Conference: www.hochschulkompass.de). However, the proportion continued to grow, so that by the academic year 2013/14, it had reached 5.9% of degree programmes in Germany, 9.4% in Austria and 13.9% in Switzerland. But the proportion of these students among the total number of students remained relatively low, in the academic year 2013/14: 1% in Germany, 1.8% in Austria and 2.1% in Switzerland (Wächter/ Maiworm 2014: 40).

Courses in English are not *per se* detrimental to the international position of German, especially as an academic language. They may even draw new learners and speakers to the German language by facilitating access to Germany for foreigners. But this would depend upon the condition that foreign students familiarise themselves with German during their degree programme. One possibility would be accompanying, possibly compulsory, German-language courses which lead to advanced language skills. Levels B2 or C1 of the Common European Framework of Reference (CEFR) might be appropriate (Quetz 2002), although it must be remembered that the reference framework relates to ordinary language rather than specifically academic language. Encouraging students and possibly future academics to participate in German-language teaching events may therefore be more expedient. However, this goal only seems realistic if the entire degree programme, including introductory courses, were to take place in Germany or a German-speaking country, rather than being limited to short visits. The fact that foreign students' interests might diverge would have to be taken into account. Presumably, only some of them would be interested in acquiring a knowledge of German in the first place, and, for most, training in their chosen discipline would take priority over learning German, so that conflicts between aims like those experienced by German students and academics with reference to their own language and English may arise (Ch. A.2).

Examination of the representative 110 bachelor programmes for the winter semester 2011/12 named by the German University Rectors' Conference [*Hochschulrektorenkonferenz*] (www. hochschulkompass.de) shows a marked propensity towards *application-orientated* natural sciences and economics (e.g. *Biochemical Engineering, Computer Engineering, Engineering Physics*, and *Business Administration, International Management, Shipping* and *Ship Finance*). It is particularly noticeable here that the *theoretical* natural-science and structural-science disciplines: biology, chemistry, physics, medicine and mathematics, are hardly represented. This is especially surprising because it is precisely these disciplines which have shifted fundamentally to English in research (Ch. G.3). The humanities are also largely absent – with the less surprising exception of English studies and American studies. If the total of 20 associated degree programmes are removed, only five courses within the broad definition of humanities remain: *Intercultural Relations and Behaviour, International Politics and History, Literatur- und Kulturwissenschaften (angewandte), Bachelor-Studiengang im englischen und deutschen Recht, Sprachwissenschaften (angewandte)* – where the three German-language titles indicate that the course is held at least partly in German.

The distribution of degree programmes among university types is as unilateral as the distribution of disciplines. Private universities, which have existed in Germany only for a few decades, are clearly dominant; they are generally small and primarily orientated towards teaching rather than research. Only 14 (12.7%) of the 110 degree programmes were taught at state-run colleges or universities. Such figures for degree programmes in English are achieved by some of the private universities by themselves. The lead is taken by Jacobs University Bremen (20 courses in English), followed by Hochschule Rhein-Waal (in Kleve – 13). In this kind of university, all teaching is generally in English. But potential explanations for the asymmetrical distribution are unfortunately speculative. The abstinence of the theoretical natural-sciences and of state-run universities is presumably at least partly determined by capacity. However, the theoretical disciplines in Germany may no longer be as secure in their international image as they were, especially compared with the English-speaking "elite universities", and, for this reason also, they may shy away from teaching in English. By contrast, the application-orientated disciplines may feel more secure in attracting foreign students in view of the "Made in Germany" factor (Ch. F.9). In traditional universities, there is possibly also a broader language-policy interest in maintaining the position of German in academia, corresponding to the interest in the country as a whole. This may be a reason for preserving a distance from English in university teaching, while the newer private colleges and universities are more concerned about international competitiveness, including linguistic competitiveness.

Due consideration of the students, especially the foreign students, taking part in degree programmes in English is also relevant. A distinction must be made between "educational residents", who have already completed school education in a German-speaking country but who do not yet have the appropriate citizenship, and "educational foreigners" who received their schooling abroad. The educational residents retain the status of foreigners until they become German citizens. However, for the topic of the present book, it is the educational foreigners who are of particular interest. Figures have been recorded since 1993. There were 74,612 in 1993; 100,033 in 1997; and another five years later, in 2002, there were already 142,786. Accordingly, in the five years after the introduction of degree programmes in English (in the winter semester 1997/98), the growth was steeper than in the five years before (43% compared with 34%), and since their introduction, the number has multiplied more than threefold. In the winter semester 2009/10, there were 181,249 and in 2016, as many as 251,000 ("*So viele Studenten aus dem Ausland wie nie*" [More students from abroad than ever], *FAZ* 19/20 July 2014: C.1). It certainly looks as if the degree programmes in English have attracted additional foreign students.

This could create the possibility of attracting new learners and speakers of German. But the full potential of this opportunity has evidently not been realised, especially not by the private universities. For example, Klaus and Mandy Boehnke (2007: 177) found that the Jacobs University in Bremen "is doing too little to improve their students' knowledge of German". Courses in German are offered, but they are not compulsory. Perhaps the university is afraid that if they were to introduce compulsory German courses, they would lose students who "are not particularly interested in Germany or the German language" (ibid: 178). Such considerations seem legitimate in the case of fee-paying students, especially since the university relies on them financially. By contrast, in state-run universities, in which foreign students' degree programmes are also strongly subsidised, an interest in the language of the host country might be more robustly expected of students, and attendance at courses in German might even be made compulsory. However, even at private universities, a knowledge of German would serve the interests of many students, at least in social terms. A distinction should be made between social interests and disciplinary or academic interests. The latter are linked with an instrumental motivation to learn foreign languages, while the former are associated with an integrative motivation (Ch. I.8). Instrumental motivation is orientated towards profession and career prospects; integrative motivation towards social life and integration in groups (Ch. K.8). For example, on the campus of the Jacobs University, students can "muddle through" their degree programme without a knowledge of German (Boehnke/ Boehnke 2007: 177), but – it must be assumed – they can only establish social contacts which go beyond the campus, not to mention integration into German society for a longer term stay, subject to considerable limitations. To some extent, the prestige associated with their knowledge of English may be an asset, but their chances would be improved by additional knowledge of German. The level of German which might be appropriate for this seems, so far, not to have been determined with any certainty. Liudmilla Li (2012) considers B1 of the Common European Framework of Reference to be insufficient for the level of integration for which it is generally intended. Similar considerations would also apply for work-related visits after students have completed their degree programme. Students with this kind of plan in mind are certainly interested in the associated knowledge of German, or they ought to be if they have understood their interests correctly.

In interviews conducted by Clive W. Earls (2013b: 200–210) with 42 students in international degree programmes at three German universities (which he does not name for reasons of data protection), many foreign students did express a wish for better knowledge of German to establish social contacts and for integration. For them, German counted as a "prestige language" in relationships with German students (ibid: 212, 215). Findings by Katja Petereit and Elke Spielmanns-Rome (2010: 172) with foreign students on degree programmes in English in Germany point in the same direction. Their wishes are summarised as follows: "Speak German with us! Foreign students on degree programmes in English want to learn more German". This investigation was limited to masters' courses. But the desire expressed might be especially expected of students on bachelors' programmes or long-term courses with a longer stay in Germany. According to Petereit/ Spielmanns-Rome (2010: 172), a lack of German-language skills "spoils the overall impression and satisfaction with the international course". This assessment presumably includes the programme itself and therefore also the instrumental motivation. The findings of Marcus Motz (2005b: 134) give an even clearer indication that many students on international courses would like to learn German in addition to English because they anticipate improved employment opportunities as a result. Perhaps unsatisfactory opportunities for learning German are among several reasons for the frequent dropout rate especially by foreign students. "Germany is popular with foreign students. But half of them cannot cope and drop out of the course" ("Live here? No thanks", *FAZ* 13 September 2009: 14). Poor prospects for integration after the course because of inadequate knowledge of German possibly have a demotivating influence on student participation in the programme itself. Warning signs suggesting inadequate opportunities for learning German have been widely recognised. For example, Yu Chen (2012) has shown that, during a period of study in Germany, initial knowledge of German deteriorates instead of improving.

In their investigation of postgraduate "courses primarily or predominantly in English" at German universities, Christian Fandrych and Betina Sedlaczek (2012) also received a sobering impression of the German-language skills of foreign students on international degree programmes. A small selection of their findings is sufficiently informative for our purposes. Among participants in three masters' programmes (Humboldt University Berlin, University of Stuttgart, Technical University Dresden; n = 48), most had very poor knowledge of German: neither "an appropriate productive competence in everyday language" nor "a basic receptive competence in academic German" (ibid: 24). 95.5% failed to achieve level B1 in active vocabulary and 93% in receptive vocabulary of the Common European Reference Frame (ibid: 23f.). However, experts consider at least level B2 or preferably C1 necessary for study at a German university, and university entrance tests are orientated towards this level (www.testdaf-pruefungszentrum.de). Furthermore, level B2 was not achieved by 90.5% in writing, in which test participants did best (Fandrych/ Sedlaczek 2012: 24). Accordingly, the students were not only linguistically hampered in their social contacts, but also incapable of studying in the German-language components of the course. The language test used by Fandrych/ Sedlaczek included not only ordinary language but also the competence in German required for a degree programme.

A different aspect of such findings, which has already been alluded to above, is also problematic from the German perspective. One investigation by Ammon/ McConnell (2002: 148f.) showed that considerable numbers of foreign students on courses delivered in English considered their course in Germany only as a transitory phase and were not interested in continuing contact with Germany after the course. Table G.8–1 shows the proportions in courses at the universities of Duisburg-Essen and Aachen (n=70, 31 Duisburg-Essen, 39 Aachen), who wanted subsequent employment in Germany or respectively in an English-speaking country (USA, UK, Australia, Canada) (see also Ammon "The Green Card is not enough. Contrary to reason, we are training foreign students primarily for the USA", *Die Welt* 1 December 2000: 11).

In Fandrych/ Sedlaczek (2012: 39), only 27% (n for this question = 83) of foreign students sought future employment "in a German-speaking country"; 32% "in an English-speaking

Table G. 8–1 Countries preferred by foreign students at German universities for future employment (%)

Preferred countries for future employment	First preference	Second preference	Third preference
Germany	27.5	12.1	19.5
English-speaking country	34.7	34.1	24.4

(*Source*: Ammon/ McConnell 2002: 148f.)

country" and 18% "in another country" (remainder: no response). Other reports confirm the low interest in remaining: "there are many foreign students in Germany, but only a few want to stay in the long term" (*"Ein Umzug für immer"* [A Permanent Move], *FAZ* 17/18 May 2014: C1). However, there have recently been signs of a change, partly because the employment market in Germany has improved, and bureaucratic obstacles to remaining have been removed. Thus in Earls' interviews, 57% of foreign students on full-time degree programmes claimed, "that they intend to remain in Germany beyond their current degree programme, while 14% are undecided between Germany and another non-English speaking country. The remaining 39% of permanent international students intend on working or studying further in an English-speaking country, predominantly the US [. . .]" (Earls 2013b: 236). But this still does not represent a "brain gain" for Germany from the international degree programmes, because the gain in foreign students is counterbalanced by a loss of home students, who also participate in these degree programmes: "61.6% of all German students surveyed intend leaving Germany upon completion of their bachelor degree programme". "26.8% rank studying further, while 34.8% rank working in an English-speaking country as their top choice under future plans as opposed to 17% and 21.4% for Germany respectively" (ibid: 231). On the German side, the international degree programmes are certainly not conceived as aids to emigration – especially not for the much-needed supply of qualified personnel. But the students surveyed possibly only envisage temporary visits abroad. Despite the growth in interest, it is still difficult for foreigners to settle in Germany. When efforts are made within the German business economy to attract qualified foreign employees, inadequate knowledge of German is a recurring topic: "Many applicants do have the specialist subject qualifications, but without a knowledge of German, things become difficult" (*"Deutschland umwirbt Fachkräfte aus den Schuldenländern"*, *Welt Online* 18 July 2011). The difficulty often arises through degree programmes in English. Some time ago, Gunde Kurz (2000: 585 and 585, Note 1) explained that, for foreign students in Germany, "language requirements [. . .] vary considerably". Sometimes, "the DSH [German-language test for university access! U.A.] is required as a matter of principle (if a student wants to leave university with a degree), in other cases, the DSH or an appropriate proof of knowledge of German is 'at last' no longer required for the short-sighted reason that 'everything is in English'".

On one hand, insufficient attention is paid to foreign students' learning of German, but on the other hand, efforts are being made to improve their knowledge of English. Knowledge of English is seldom tested at the start of the degree programme, but Fandrych/ Sedlaczek (2012: 26) found that English-language skills were often inadequate. "Overall, based on language-test results for the various skills, it is evident that international students not only have quite alarming difficulties with German, but also show significant problems with English". Anja Soltau (2008a, b) found that the testing of English-language skills is inconsistent and often inadequate. Instead, German universities often provide English-language courses alongside degree programmes (information from Hans Wagener, who was responsible for such courses at the University of Duisburg-Essen). This effectively thwarts one of the language-policy opportunities of these degree programmes. They no longer serve – at least no longer exclusively – to allow foreign students easier access to the degree programme through the provision of English; they also provide foreign students with an improved knowledge of English. As a result, Germany is participating directly in the spread of the English language. This also makes it easier for foreign students to succeed without learning German, because their contacts in German universities are also equipped with a knowledge of English. Such courses are hosted, for example, by the DAAD, or more precisely, the International DAAD Academy, which offers courses in "English in International Academic Relations" (*DAAD Seminars and Workshops, Seminar 1*, 2008: 10), "English for

Lecturers" or "English for Tutors" (12/22 September 2010 and 23/24 August 2010 – emails to the universities on 12 July 2010, boeker@daad.de and 4 August 2010).

German-Chinese degree programmes also send out warning signals about the damage caused by degree programmes in English to the learning of German as a foreign language: "[B]ecause of the possibility of also studying English during a stay in Germany, the desire to acquire German has declined considerably, according to one university [in China! U.A.]" (Rogler 2005: 140 – however, relativising this position, see also He 2012). Any further lowering of the German-language skills required for degree programmes in English would intensify this trend. This change of direction is exemplified in a ruling by the Federal State of North-Rhine-Westphalia which switches the levels of knowledge of German and English previously required for "International Degree Programmes ": previously, German C1 and English B1 of the Common European Framework of Reference were required, but this has been reversed, so that now only spoken German is tested: "In preparation for degree programmes which are held partly or entirely in English, the assessment test can be taken in English. In this case, the subject English is tested instead of the subject German" (Examination regulations of 2010, §2: recht. nrw.de/lmi/owa/br_vbl_detail_text?anw_nr=6&vd_id=11990&ver=8&val=11990&menu=1 &vd_back=N). In fact, these rulings hardly seem compatible with the "Framework Regulation for German Language Examinations for Degree Programmes at German universities", which was resolved in 2004 by the German University Rectors' Conference and Conference of Culture Ministers (www.fh-kiel.de/fileadmin/data/studium/ Studienangebot/Rahmenordnung_ Sprachnachweis.pdf). In this context, for students at German universities, "German-language skills are required, which give students the competence to study at a university (competence to study)" (§2 (1)). However, even this Framework Regulation allows "[d]ifferentiated linguistic entry conditions" and reduced conditions if advanced language courses accompanying the degree programme" are completed and certified (§1 (4), (5)). Besides, certification of language testing in German is only required for university access to a full degree programme (including bachelor-level degree programmes): the DSH (*Deutsche Sprachprüfung für den Hochschulzugang*, the TestDaF (*Test Deutsch als Fremdsprache*) or the DSD (*Deutsches Sprachdiplom der Kultusministerkonferenz II*, which can be obtained at German Schools Abroad and *Sprachdiplomschulen* (Ch. I.3). In the case of higher degrees, when a first degree has been completed abroad, but especially a master's degree or PhD, all requirements for knowledge of German are generally waived (see Fandrych/ Sedlaczek 2012). This waiver also represents an indirect promotion of English and therefore – indirectly and certainly unintentionally – has the effect of further undermining the international position of German (cf. Ch.A.4; A.5). In view of such considerations, even foreign experts (e.g. Durrell 2013) have concluded that international degree programmes in Germany do not fulfil the expectations placed on them. Susanne Hilgendorf (2005: 64) considers that Germany is moving upwards within Braj Kachru's (1986) three stages in the spread of English as a world language: from the "outer circle" to the "expanding circle" and therefore closer to the "inner circle" (similar views in Erling 2004; Erling/ Hilgendorf 2006a, b; Berns 1995a, b).

However, before prematurely condemning degree programmes in English, we should be reminded of the different interests associated with them: on one hand, promoting scholarship in Germany and, on the other hand, strengthening the international position of German (Ch. K.3.2). For universities and academics, and for many mediating organisations supporting them (Ch. K.3.3), the promotion of scholarship takes precedence. The global expansion of university and academic contacts are more important for them than strengthening the international position of their own language. Furthermore, the linguistic consequences of these degree programmes cannot be estimated with certainty. Perhaps the gain in learners of German ultimately outweighs the loss. At least, abandoning degree courses in English would be academically detrimental to

German universities and academics (see Wächter/ Maiworm 2007; Soltau 2008a). It is therefore important to keep both goals and interests in mind: the internationalisation of scholarship in the German-speaking countries and the strengthening or at least the maintenance of the international position of German (Ch. A.5). There are also recognisable efforts to combine these two goals, as explained by the Vice-President of the Technical University of Munich, Liqui Meng. On one hand, teaching in English should favour the internationalisation of German scholarship by making it easier for foreigners to gain access to degree programmes and possibly even "giving German students a head-start with English". On the other hand, it is important to maintain German as an academic language: "But the examination should be in German again. The German language is part of our academic culture" ("*Deutsch ist das Problem*", *Die Zeit* 30 April 2009: 73). Other observers have stressed even more emphatically that, without questioning the inclusion of English in principle, German is indispensable: "Ultimately, German must be established as a trademark in academia and as a component of international degree programmes, multilingualism must be accepted as a substantial feature of the qualification if Germany is to be established as an academic site in the long-term and as an attractive option in the 'university market'" (Fandrych/ Sedlaczek 2012: 147). The German Academic Exchange Service (DAAD) combined these two linguistic goals even in the title of its "Memorandum on German as Academic Language" in 2010: "*Offen für English, Einsatz für Deutsch*" [Open for English, committed to German] (www.daad.de/portrait/presse/pressemitteilungen/2010/13058.dehtm). The memorandum claims that "while, on one hand, the worldwide communicative competence of research must be guaranteed [by means of English! U.A.], on the other hand, German academics must retain the possibility of targeting and mediating their knowledge in their own native language [. . .]". Other mediating organisations have also spoken out in favour of multilingualism. Their view is summarised in the "Common Declaration by the Presidents of the Alexander von Humboldt Stiftung, DAAD, Goethe-Institut and HRK [German Rectors' Conference]", which want to "secure a sustainable future for German as an academic and cultural language with the concept of multilingualism [. . .] realised through their activities" (announced in 2009: www.goethe.de/Ihr/prj/diw/dos/de7753902.htm; see Ch. K.3.3).

Nevertheless, the maintenance of German is still no longer guaranteed in all international degree programmes, although English is firmly anchored in many courses at private universities. Recently, schools in the German-speaking countries have begun to prepare the ground for the English-language entry of home students into university degree programmes in their own country. For this reason and others, English teaching has been expanded in recent years compared with other foreign languages (Quetz 2010). In many places, specialist English tuition has been introduced ("*Sachfachunterricht*"), once again, especially in expanding, private schools but also in state schools. Added to this are the increasing private school visits to English-speaking countries, especially the UK and the USA by children of the globally active, privileged classes in the German-speaking countries – Jürgen Gerhards (2010: 54) speaks of a "transnational class" (top entrepreneurs, managers, politicians and similar). In fact, specialist English-language tuition is not yet compulsory in ordinary schools in German-speaking countries as it is in many developing and emerging countries (e.g. for Malaysia, see Gill 2004, 2007 – withdrawn; for Singapore: Pakir 2004). But the current trend may one day lead to an extensive abandonment of German as the language of higher-level school education and university teaching in non-humanities subjects.

Although the "cascade model" designed by the *Verein Deutsche Sprache* (Figure G.8–1 by Heino Jückstock, email 13 May 2012) engenders panic about possible future developments, it does deserve serious consideration. The diagram visualises how elementary educational institutions could prepare for the higher levels. If knowledge of English is required in universities or

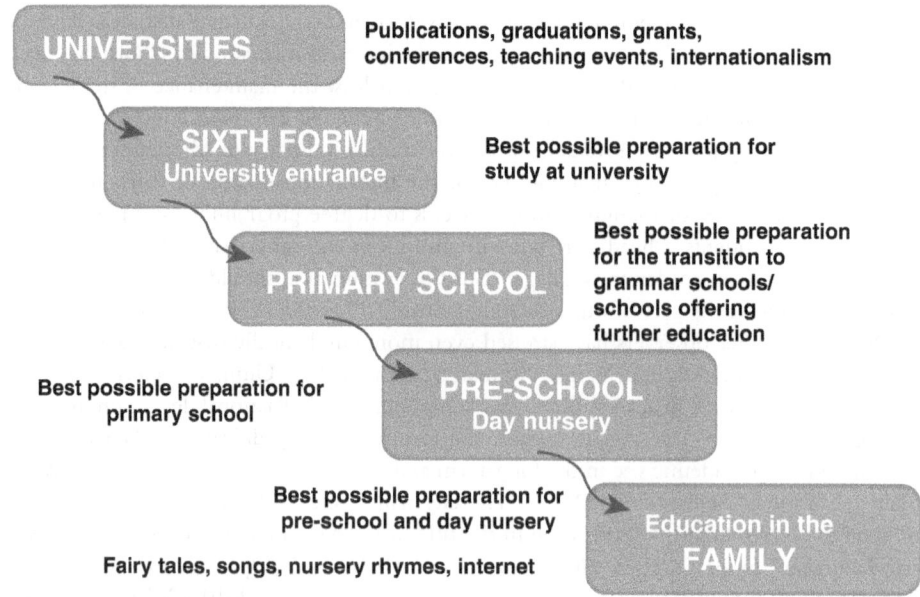

Figure G.8–1 Cascade model for the introduction of English in the German-language territory (Design: Heino Jückstock, production: Lucie Eschricht)

is advantageous there, the higher-level schools will soon be preparing for it and so on – until ultimately down to kindergarten level and even into the family. This development had historical precedents in the spread of standard German relative to the dialects, starting from requirements in school and extending down to the family (Ammon 1973). As in this case, social differences and linguistic disadvantages must be also anticipated for English: the educated classes adjust more rapidly to new linguistic requirements than classes more distant from education, which lag behind in the competition for a good education. Although this perspective may seem speculative at present, it is not perverse. Especially because the spread of English is also promoted by other action fields, especially the economy, politics and social media (cf. Ch. F.7; H.4.6; I.1.4.2).

9. Is the loss of position of language and scholarship linked?

Another idea which deserves consideration here is that German has lost its position as an international academic language because of a decline in the academic ranking of German-speaking countries compared with countries with other languages, or at least that this decline in ranking represents a significant factor in a more complex interplay of effects. Comparison with the English-speaking countries is of primary interest here. Decline in the ranking of German-speaking countries may relate to actual academic performance compared with countries with other languages or to the evaluation of academic performance or to both. Standards for academic performance of countries are difficult to establish or of doubtful validity and reliability. For reasons of scale, I therefore limit myself here to indirect indicators for academic performance. In fact, regarding performance capacity, I limit the discussion primarily to the economic basis for academic scholarship in the German-speaking countries by comparison with the English-speaking countries. I then turn to the evaluation of the academic performance of German-speaking countries and English-speaking countries. Once again, the model of *academic centres* (cf. Ch.

A.8; Gizycyi 1973) provides appropriate global orientation. The historical events which have characterised contemporary history become most evident if we look back before WWI. With reference to Ben-David Joseph (1977), Bernhardt vom Brocke (1996: 5) comments as follows on this period: "In the 19th century, Germany overtook the older 'world centres' for science and scholarship – England in the 17th century and France in the 18th" (similarly, Gizycki 1973; Alter 1987: 89–137). It must be added to this that, during the twentieth century, Germany was overtaken as a world centre for science and scholarship by the USA. By way of expansion, one could substitute the "German-speaking countries" for "Germany" and the "English-speaking countries" or their "inner circle" (Kachru 1986; Crystal 2003) instead of the "USA". In fact, this perspective oversimplifies the circumstances, because the "ousted" centres have maintained considerable importance; but the simplification does sharpen the focus on key aspects of this development.

Academic centres are defined in that they show leadership in academic performance as well as in terms of evaluation. A rough indicator for the academic performance, or more specifically performance capacity, of countries or language communities is given by the financial resources available to academia, because successful scholarship requires adequate financing (Ammon 1998: 186–188). Resources were available in the German-speaking countries before WWI, especially in the German Empire, of which the government, including Kaiser Wilhelm II himself, understood scholarship as a form of power. According to the sources known to me, German-speaking countries at that time could bear comparison in academic funding with the English-speaking countries, and even more so with countries with other languages (Kroll 2003: 60f.; vom Brocke 2005). However, WWI brought about a serious decline, which endured to the extent that the shortfall, gaping after the loss of the war compared with the English-speaking countries whose leadership had now been taken over by the USA, was never subsequently overcome. On the contrary, for 100 years without interruption, the English-speaking countries have had more financial resources at their disposal for academia than the German-speaking countries, with particularly wide differences during and after the two world wars. Figures for the present, which will be indicated shortly, give an idea of the scale. As Max Planck's statement in November 1918 suggests, funding does not directly determine academic performance or its evaluation: "[O]ne thing, however, no external or internal enemy has taken from us: that is the standing enjoyed by German science in the world" (quotation from vom Brocke 1990: 203). The large number of natural-science Nobel prizes for Germany even after WWI also seems to confirm Germany's continuing high status (ibid). But in the long-term, sustained under-financing does influence academic performance and, ultimately, the associated evaluation. This generally occurs with a delay for as long as academics and institutions can survive on skills and resources already acquired. The financial crisis after WWI must have awoken doubts about the sustainability of German leadership. It even shook the most prominent government research institution, the *Kaiser-Wilhelm Gesellschaft* (vom Brocke 1990: 227–238) and – as suggested in the relevant chapter heading by Eberhard Friese (1990: 811–827) – could only be mitigated through "Japanese financial assistance to German scholarship" (see also, Ch. G.1 towards the end). A brief financial recovery was followed by a dramatic shortage of funds in the world economic crisis 1929–1932 (vom Brocke 1990: 330–335). After this, National Socialism siphoned the available resources unilaterally into armaments and other fields relevant to ideology, thereby neglecting basic and more specialist research (vom Brocke 1996: 11; Kriekhaus 2005: 232). Added to these factors were the mass murder and expulsion especially of Jewish but also non-Jewish, politically unpopular academics (Beyerchen 1982; Kröner 1983; Ammon 2000b: 68–73) and the loss of prestige of German universities and scholarship, because so many of their representatives had placed themselves at the service of National Socialism (compare Weinreich [1946] 1999). For the discipline of physics, Armin Hermann (2000: 223–226) has shown how, through Nazi policies, Germany completely lost its leadership role, which had already been weakened in the Weimar Republic. Michael Gordin (2015: Ch. 7:"Unspeakable") gives details of similar developments in chemistry. The economic ruin of Germany resulting from Nazi politics and a war which contributed to the continuing brain-drain after the war, and to a lesser extent, up to the present. Despite the post-war "economic miracle" and the successful rebuilding of Germany and Austria, academic funding never even approximately reached the level of the English-speaking countries led by the USA; presumably, this gap has widened over time.

The current proportions are shown in Table G.9–1 with reference to the total expenditure on R&D of the 20 global leading nations. The largest German-speaking countries, Germany, Austria and German-speaking Switzerland, together account for only a fraction of the expenditure for the largest English-speaking countries USA, UK, English-speaking Canada and Australia. If 64% of the resources for Switzerland and respectively 77% of the resources for Canada are included, corresponding to the German-speaking and English-speaking proportion of inhabitants, the German-speaking countries offer US$ 82.6 bn per year compared with US$ 478.3 bn in the English-speaking countries (ratio 1:5.8), so that the USA alone delivers almost five times the total funding for the three German-speaking countries.

It could be argued that a considerable part of the US spending flows into "big science" (Weinberg 1961; de Solla Price 1963) and especially military research; however, this presumably also promotes academic performance, at least in the natural sciences and their technical applications. An institutional structure in the German-speaking countries, e.g. combining the research and teaching in universities shaped by Wilhelm von Humboldt with government research institutes, such as the former *Kaiser-Wilhelm Gesellschaft* and the present *Max-Planck Gesellschaft*, would also be conceivable and more conducive to research. However, especially the USA has adopted and further improved substantial elements of this structure, especially the combination of research and teaching in graduate studies at university (Ben-David 1977: 93–126). It is therefore improbable that the German-speaking countries will be able to compensate their economic inferiority through structural advantages. Instead, if we assume, realistically, that the English-speaking countries operate with similar efficiency in academic terms, their academic performance capacity and actual performance can also be reckoned as a multiple of those achieved in the German-speaking countries.

Table G.9–1 Spending on R&D by the 20 global leading countries in 2011 (US$ bn, by purchasing power parity/PPP and proportion of gross national product/GNP)

Rank	Country	US$bn	% GNP	Rank	Country	US$bn	% GNP
1	USA	405.3	2.7%	11	Brazil	19.4	0.9%
2	China	153.7	1.4%	12	Italy	19.0	1.1%
3	Japan	144.1	3.3%	13	Taiwan	19.0	2.3%
4	Germany	69.5	2.3%	14	Spain	17.2	1.3%
5	South Korea	44.8	3.0%	15	Australia	15.9	1.7%
6	France	42.2	1.9%	16	Sweden	11.9	3.3%
7	UK	38.4	1.7%	17	Netherlands	10.8	1.6%
8	India	36.1	0.9%	18	Israel	9.4	4.2%
9	Canada	24.3	1.8%	19	Austria	8.3	2.5%
10	Russia	23.1	1.0%	20	Switzerland	7.5	2.3%

(*Source*: en.wikipedia.org/wiki/List_of_countries_by_research_and_ development_ spending: www.battelle.org/aboutus/rd/2011.pdf, after www.reporter.ir/ archives/89/10/006635.php)

Having said this, the German-speaking countries are, even today, still significant global players in the academic field. There are numerous indicators for their continuing performance, e.g.
in the reports by the Thomson-Reuter media group, which is familiar to academics because
of its citation indexes. According to these reports, Germany is in the front row for academic
publications, e.g. in the *Global Research Report Materials Science and Technology* in the 2006–2011
evaluation phase, based on the total number of registered publications, in fourth position of all
nations. Germany: 16,832 came in behind China: 55,003, USA: 38,189 and Japan: 25,473, but
ahead of South Korea: 15,261, India: 12,693, France: 12,344 and the UK: 11,611 (researchana-
lytics.thomsonreuters.com/m/pdfs/grr-materialscience.pdf: 5f.). At the same time, these figures
suggest other strong players alongside the English-speaking countries. But mere frequencies of
publications do not necessarily correspond to academic significance. The impact of citations, for
which the most current measurement is the citation frequency in the form of the *Impact-Factor*,
is more informative (see Ammon 1998: 36–38; Winkmann/ Schlutius/ Schweim 2002a: 132;
2002b: 139). Unfortunately, the available report does not provide data on the impact-factor for
Germany or the German-speaking countries, but only for the EU-15 (i.e. the European Union
before the 2004 expansion). In this context, the ranking is: USA: 5.53, EU-15: 4.07, Japan: 3.37,
Taiwan: 3.14, South Korea: 3.10 and China: 2.61 (researchanalytics.thomsonreuters.com/m/
pdfs/grr-materialscience.pdf: 6). The fact that no single EU state (i.e. including Germany) is
considered in isolation suggests that Thomson Reuters considers these nations as less promising
aspirants to global academic leadership. This could also mean a limited evaluation of Germany's
academic potential and – because of the size relationship of Germany – of the potential of the
German-speaking nations together. Regarding the individual institutions (rather than whole
countries) with the greatest impact-factor, the dominance of the USA and therefore of the
English-speaking countries is even more evident. The first ten ranked positions are occupied by
US universities, the same applies to positions 12–17. But Germany's *Max-Planck Gesellschaft* is
ranked between these blocks in eleventh position (ibid: 6), i.e. ahead of all institutions in other
countries. Although this position is noteworthy, it also betrays the proportions involved here,
because the *Max-Planck Gesellschaft* achieves a higher performance than any single German
university, none of which appear in this rank ordering. This fact resonates with the decline in
German-language science and social-science publications during the twentieth century (Ch.
G.3; G.5). However, what we are concerned with here is not German-language publications
themselves, but those originating in Germany or German-speaking countries – of which today,
many are in English, especially in the disciplines included here. And English-language publications are presumably more significant than German-language publications for the academic
performance of German-speaking countries or at least for the evaluation of performance.

The reported findings and similar findings do seem to show that scholarship in Germany
and the other German-speaking countries has recovered to some extent from the enormous
losses associated with the war and National Socialism but has not reached the same level as the
English-speaking countries. A former major centre has become a sub-centre alongside others;
what was once large has become medium-sized, admittedly achieving peak performance, but
publishing primarily in the humanities, in German (Ch. G.6; G.7). However, even in the humanities, where it is difficult to preserve the distinction between actual performance and evaluation
of performance, there are signs of loss of position. For example, Wolfgang Klein (1985) sees
a lack of originality as one substantial reason for the loss of influence of contemporary German linguistics by comparison with the nineteenth century. The book *"Grimm's Grandchildren"*
published by English-speaking authors also indirectly ascribes a smaller scale to the present
representatives of linguistics in Germany than to their famous forebears (Jacob Grimm) of the
nineteenth century (Herbst/ Heath/ Dederding 1980; especially in the *Preface*). One example

from the social sciences: in criticising a German colleague's work in social anthropology, US author T.O. Beidelmann (1986: 663f.) emphasises the historical, ground-breaking performance of German theoreticians such as Max Weber, Georg Simmel, Alfred Schutz, Werner Sombart and Karl Marx, but is disappointed by the "relative theoretical barrenness of many German anthropological writings" in the contemporary scene. It is significant in the present context that he sees this as justifying corresponding language preferences: "Most senior American and British social anthropology professors tend to suggest French, Russian, Spanish, or even Arabic, Japanese or Chinese as more useful linguistic priorities for new graduate students".

Similar references to losses in performance and evaluation are also evident beyond the humanities and social sciences. For example, based on statistical evaluations of the history of medicine by H.F. Garrison (1929), Japanese author Shigeru Nakayama (1981: 48) finds that the German-speaking countries contributed most to discoveries in medicine in the period from approximately 1830 to 1910. After that, the USA apparently assumed leadership in medical research. For the most recent period, another Japanese author Toshio Aoki (1989: 69) has passed the following dismissive judgement, which he also extends to the German language: "German medicine and German law which have always been our role models since the Meiji period [1868–1912! U.A.], no longer fulfil this role. American science has stepped into this role instead. In a word [. . .], German has lost its intellectual attractiveness". But such judgements are dated and – based on my findings – no longer expressed quite so harshly.

A rough, but presumably valid indicator for global evaluation and possibly also for the actual level of academic performance is provided by the Nobel prizes for science. At the very least, these influence the academic prestige of nations and language communities. Accordingly, developments in the proportion of German-speaking countries among Nobel prizes are relevant – and sobering. One example is the Humboldt University in Berlin. The university foyer is decorated with representations of the 29 Nobel Prize winners associated with this alma mater. But the most recent prize was awarded to Erwin Schrödinger in 1933 when the university was still known as the Friedrich-Wilhelm University, before the name change in 1946. This chronology is also a consequence of the partition of Germany. While the Humboldt University belonged to the GDR, West German academics and academics from other German-speaking countries certainly won Nobel prizes. So, the division of Germany constituted yet another academic weakening, already shaped by the economic failure of the GDR.

A more representative picture of the allocation of prizes can be obtained from the overall statistics from the start of the award scheme up to the present. I shall limit myself to prizes for natural sciences because the prize for economics was first awarded in 1969, and prizes for literature and peace are in a different category. For reasons of labour-saving, my data up to 1986 are based on figures obtained by Sabine Skudlik and retain the grouping of countries used by Skudlik, which erroneously includes the whole of Switzerland (Skudlik 1990: 319, Table 34 – for the inclusion of Austria and Switzerland, ibid: 177). Since many Nobel Prize winners are academic migrants, their nationality at the time of the award was taken as the standard for the allocation; in the case of dual citizenship of a prize winner at the time of the award, a half prize was assigned to each country. Table G.9–2 shows that up to the start of WWII, the German-speaking countries represented around one third of all Nobel prizes for science. Until 1920, the proportion is higher than all English-speaking countries included, and from 1921–1930, the proportion is the same. After that, however, it declined dramatically, while the English-speaking countries, with a clear dominance of the USA, massively boosted their share.

The French-speaking countries (including the Netherlands – according to Skudlik's classification!) show a similar proportional decline to that in the German-speaking countries, but it begins even earlier. What is remarkable with both groups of countries is the – admittedly

Table G.9–2 National origins of Nobel Prize winners for science (physics, chemistry, medicine – %)

	Germany Austria Switzerland	USA	UK Ireland Canada	France Belgium Netherlands	Other countries	Total prize-winners
1901–1910	36.1	2.8	13.9	27.8	19.5	36
1911–1920	33.3	4.2	12.5	33.3	16.7	24
1921–1930	33.3	6.1	27.3	15.2	18.2	33
1931–1940	37.1	25.7	20.0	11.4	5.8	35
1941–1950	19.4	41.7	19.4	0.0	19.5	36
1951–1960	5.8	51.9	21.2	1.9	19.2	52
1961–1970	8.5	45.8	20.3	8.5	17.0	59
1971–1980	9.0	58.2	19.4	6.0	7.5	67
1981–1990	16.8	51.0	11.1	2.8	18.3	64
1991–2000	13.9	53.9	8.0	12.2	11.9	62
2001–2010	9.7	48.6	13.6	6.1	21.9	76

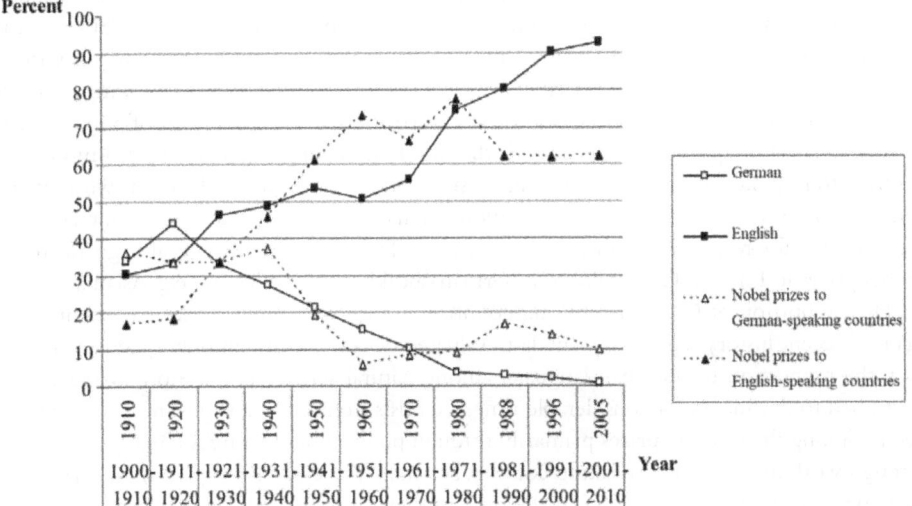

Figure G.9–1 Proportion of German and English scientific publications worldwide and German-speaking and English-speaking countries awarded Nobel Prizes for science

moderate – recovery in recent history. I shall return to this point later. The recent increase of the "other countries", which resonates with the proportion of Asian states (Japan, China, South Korea) mentioned above in the research report from Thomson Reuters (researchanalytics.thomsonreuters.com/m/pdfs/grr-materialscience.pdf: 6) is especially noteworthy.

Considering the proportion of German-speaking countries among Nobel prizes for science as an indicator for their academic prestige, and possibly also their academic performance, invites the question of the extent to which the international position of German as an academic language correlates with this. This question is answered – at least in part – by Figure G.9–1 which compares the development of Nobel prize proportions with the development of language proportions in global science publications, as reported in Ch. G.3 (for the period 1880–2005;

Figure G.3–1). The course of the graph (Figure G.9–1) leaves no doubt that there is a strong positive correlation.

Just as the German proportions for both parameters fall, the English-speaking proportions rise, although without complete parallelism in the proportions of prizes and languages. But a closer correlation of the two parameters could not have been anticipated. Apart from the inaccuracy already mentioned regarding Nobel prizes as an indicator for academic prestige let alone for actual academic performance, the two parameters respond with a delay. Nobel prizes are generally awarded long after the performance to which they relate, and an academic language is maintained for a considerable time after the loss of its basis, namely the academic performance of the associated language community, because academics continue to use the language skills previously acquired and only shift gradually to a new language. This is confirmed by well-known examples: "Einstein stayed [after his emigration to the USA! U.A.] with the German language, because he could no longer learn the new language properly" (Hermann 2000: 224; also, Ammon 1998: 192–194). Language shifts often occur only in a subsequent generation.

As the example of mediaeval Latin shows, an academic language can even gather momentum contrary to its political or social basis (Roman Empire) and contrary to its native-language anchoring (Latin as a native language). This possibility cues an explanation of the differences shown in Figure G.9–1 between the proportions of publications in the respective languages and the proportions of the associated countries among Nobel prizes since the 1980s. With the English-speaking countries, the proportion of Nobel prizes declines by comparison with the proportion of publications in their language, and conversely, for German-speaking countries, the proportion of Nobel prizes increases by comparison with the proportion of publications in their language. One possible explanation is that the English language has gathered momentum contrary to its political and native-language basis. Even for academics and nations with different languages, English has become the publication language (in addition to their home language), the language for research and in part for teaching. These academics then also go on to win Nobel prizes in English. This applies for German-speaking academics and e.g. Asian academics.

The proportion of German-speaking countries among the Nobel prizes has begun to rise again in recent history (apart from the last evaluated decade), although only gradually; by contrast, the proportion for German language among natural-science publications worldwide has continued to decline. For a considerable time, scientists from German-speaking countries have been winning their Nobel prizes primarily through publications in English; many of them also through work in an English-speaking country, generally the USA. Examples of German Nobel Prize winners working in the USA at the time of their award include:

*   Johann Deisendorfer, physics, 1988;
*   Hans G. Dehmelt, physics, 1989 (German and US citizenship);
*   Horst L. Störmer, physics, 1998;
*   Günter Blobel, physiology/medicine, 1999 (German and US citizenship);
*   Herbert Kroemer, physics, 2000;
*   Wolfgang Ketterle, physics, 2001.

In total, during the period of the awards from 1988–2010, the following numbers of academics were working in the USA: 33.3% (6 of 18) of prize winners from Germany, 100% (2) of those from Austria and 20% (1 of 5) of those from German-speaking Switzerland. The same applies in effect for academics with other native languages, e.g. French speakers. Comparison of Table G.9–2 with Figure G.3–1 in Ch. G.3 provides appropriate pointers. Complacency about the rise in the proportion of Nobel prizes by German-speaking academics or countries would therefore be out of place. The question of whether academic successes have been achieved through or despite the shift to English remains so far unanswered. But the fact that they have been achieved is generally ignored in polemics against English as the lingua franca of science (e.g. in S. Klein 2007), as is the collaboration with English-speaking colleagues and institutions, which, in general, is certainly academically conducive. As a result, such polemic sometimes appears grotesque, even if the language difficulties of non-native speakers about which they complain are undeniable (Ch. G.10).

10. Language problems and loss of impact by academics and publishers

With English as the dominant international academic language, German-speaking academics can still think themselves lucky. After all, English is so closely related to German that even disgruntled German colleagues can usually see the joke that English is merely a dialect of their own language as just an over-exaggeration rather than downright nonsense. In fact, the effort required to learn English as a German-speaker is considerably less than for speakers of structurally more remote languages, e.g. Chinese, Japanese or Korean (see Chong 2003b: 306–308). Nevertheless, the groan emanating from German academics is not entirely groundless. The global position of English was attained at the cost of the international position of German and, indeed, of other languages, although "competition between language communities" is not a zero-sum game without remainder (Ch. A.2; A.7).

German-speaking academics create problems for themselves if they try to resist the temptations offered by the – possibly illusory – ease of learning of English and adhere strictly to German as their academic language. In effect, they are cutting themselves off from international communication – to a different extent depending on the discipline: more so in the natural sciences than in the humanities, least of all in German studies (Ch. G.3–G.7). Their publications may hardly be noticed outside the German-language community and – even with ground-breaking innovations – may be noticed only after a considerable delay. For example, according to Wolfgang Gerok (2000: 235), the invention of the cardiac catheter by Werner Forßmann remained "completely unknown" internationally because it was published only in the German-language *Klinische Wochenschrift*, and the inventor eventually received the Nobel prize for medicine only some 30 years later. To stay with medicine, Winkmann/ Schlutius/ Schweim (2000b: 138, 141) found that German-language contributions to periodicals are in fact cited in English-language articles, but "64% of the English-language articles citing them had institutional addresses in the German-language territory; 13.5% in the USA". At the very least therefore, academics who restrict themselves to German as their sole language of publication risk reduced international recognition. At the same time, they largely bar themselves from collaboration with internationally distributed periodicals, because nowadays, these are generally in English for most disciplines. They can neither publish nor collaborate in that context. Nor can they act as editor or on the editorial board or as a reviewer of submissions. Similarly, their collaboration in many international research groups is precluded, both in terms of research and writing reviews; at best, this is possible in bilateral or possibly trilateral groups (e.g. German – French or German – Italian – Spanish). Under some circumstances, they may also be hampered in their reception of innovations within the discipline. Added to this are restrictions on research funding. In fact, applications in German are accepted by many international funding institutions, e.g. by the European Science Foundation, but the response is often delayed – as might easily be understood from a glance at the list of referees. One obstacle to the international distribution of publications in German, which has been discussed from various perspectives, is the lack of attention paid by the English-speaking world. For example, Wolfgang Klein (1985) and Peter Eisenberg (1987) found that German-language research in linguistics is completely ignored in the USA (see also Georgas/ Cullars 2006). The unilateral preference for English-language publications in bibliographical databanks in English-speaking countries has multiple consequences. The Senckenberg Research Institute in Frankfurt am Main identified approximately 75,000 German-language book and periodical publications in biology for the years 1970–1996, which were absent from the relevant databank *Biological Abstracts*, which is produced in the USA and claims global representativeness (biolis.ub.uni-frankfurt.de/about.html#zugang). Neglect of non-English-language research in English-language publications is sometimes complained about even by English-speakers, for example, in the review of a book by Robert Bickers entitled "The '*Scramble For China*' [London: Allen Lane! U.A.] is based largely on English-language sources, which leaves the reader sometimes yearning for more insight from other actors: the Germans and the Russians [. . .]" (*The Economist* 19 February 2011: 76).

The market-leading citation indexes (*Science Citation Index, Social Sciences Citation Index* and *Arts & Humanities Citation Index*) which were founded by Eugene Garfield and are now incorporated in the Thomson Reuters services group, presumably play a central role in blocking non-English-speaking academic literature. They have considerable influence on the worldwide distribution and evaluation of academic publications and favour English-language publications – simply because they concentrate on the most-cited publications. Their primary measuring instrument is the impact-factor, routinely published in the *Journal Citation Reports* (explanation in Ammon 1998: 36–38; Winkmann/ Schlutius/ Schweim 2000a: 132). The citation frequency measured with this instrument also influences university rankings (Tonkin 2008). Many governments award overseas grants only to universities at the top of such university rankings. Universities in English-speaking countries have an advantage in these rankings and can therefore also command high tuition fees, which, in turn, benefits their quality ("America profits from foreign students", *FAZ* 20 November 2007: 12; "Arrogant Brits", *Die Zeit* 12 May 2010: 75). In many countries, the citation frequency of publications according to the impact-factor also serves as an appointment criterion for university academics, especially in the natural sciences. For German university teachers, courses in English as an academic language are in great demand despite the costs involved (e.g. www.karriere-und-berufung. de/cms/index.php?id=226).

Citation frequency is a reasonably useful indicator for the international distribution of publications and the international range of communication by academics and institutions. But its validity as a standard for academic quality is less certain. It is especially unfair because it disadvantages non-English speaking academics; a point to which I will return shortly. Moreover, however outrageous it might appear at first glance, even taking the publication language English as an indicator for the academic quality of publications is not entirely misguided. For example, English-language publications, especially articles in periodicals, are cited more often than those in German (e.g. for medicine Winkmann/ Schlutius/ Schweim 2001a: 136, 2001b; Ch. G.4), for which reason they are presumably also received more frequently. But being received and cited more frequently means that academics prefer to publish in such periodicals (with a high impact-factor). Because of this and the additional attraction of increased circulation, these periodicals receive a broader range of submissions, which are also qualitatively superior at the top end. Wolfgang Gerok has explained this feedback mechanism (citation frequency – distribution – quality – citation frequency. . .) for medicine and supports his findings with figures reproduced in Table G.10–1. "The wide circulation of English-language periodicals allows their editors to apply particularly high critical standards in selecting from submissions; the quota of rejected submissions, i.e. not accepted for publication, is higher in English-language periodicals

Table G.10–1 Number of subscribers and rejection quota for submissions to English-language and German-language periodicals

Title of periodical	Subscribers	Rejection quota %
Deutsche Medizinische Wochenschrift	17,500	40
Medizinische Klinik	6,000	30
Journal of the American Medical Association	360,000	84
New England Journal of Medicine	240,000	90
Zeitschrift für Kardiologie	2,500	30
Cardiovascular Research	29,000	65
Zeitschrift für Gastroenterologie	4,000	50
Gastroenterology	15,000	75

(*Source*: after Gerok 2000: 235)

than in comparable German-language periodicals. As a result, the attractiveness and quality of the periodical increases at the same time" (Gerok 2000: 234).

Criticism of these conditions has concentrated primarily on the impact-factor as an indicator for the distribution and associated evaluation of academic performance. In fact, the original intentions of its inventor, Eugene Garfield, have been perverted by its use for measuring academic performance. His primary concern was to make academic publications rapidly known and widely accessible. But the neglect of rarely cited texts is immanent within this goal (Finzen 1998; Wiese 2006). The global position of English acts as an intensifying factor for this distortion by giving additional prestige to publications in this language (Ammon 1998: 194–197). Some time ago, J.P.Vanderbroucke (1989: 1461) wrote about this problem with reference to dissertations in medicine: "By the language a thesis is written in you immediately judge its quality". This statement referred to the relationship between English and Dutch; but it applies – to a different extent for all languages relative to English (cf. Ch. A.7 for the global language constellation). Charles Durand (2006) wrote a related article from the French perspective entitled: "If it's not in English, it's not worth reading!". The influence of language choice on the evaluation of academic quality of content was demonstrated in comparative tests in Scandinavia. For texts with the same content and the same academic quality written in different languages, "the majority of different aspects of scientific content was assessed to be better in English than in the national language version" (Nyllenna/ Riis/ Karlsson 1994: 151). The existence of such evaluations of texts according to their language choice shows the need for great caution in judging academic quality. But these are not necessary refutations of statistical inferences based on the assumption of a positive correlation in the sense of the context indicated by Table G.10–1. It might therefore be tempting to answer the question, "Is the 'impact-factor' killing the German language?" (Haller/ Hepp/ Reinold [1998] 1999) in the affirmative. However, it would have to be added that the impact-factor owes this effect to the global position of the English language. Having said this, neither the impact-factor nor the world language English will "kill" the German language, they will only continue to undermine its international position, especially as an academic language. There may possibly be no loss-free way out of this predicament (cf. Ch. G.13).

All non-English-speaking language communities find themselves in this situation. The obvious solution is a language shift towards English, especially as language of publication. Indeed, this solution might appear easy for German academics by comparison with Eastern Asians (cf. beginning of this chapter). But on closer consideration, it turns out to be quite difficult (see Ammon 1991a: 266–277). To give one relevant example, the former editor of the *Journal of*

Pragmatics, Jacob Mey, told me that he had often returned texts submitted by German linguists for correction because of deficiencies in language. Then again, a renowned German science journalist once admitted that while he could read texts in English, "I'm afraid I have considerable problems with speaking and listening comprehension". Especially, "expressing myself in a sufficiently differentiated manner in English, in discussions and as a presenter [. . .]" (Hoimar von Ditfurth (1989) *Innenansichten eines Artgenossen*. Düsseldorf: Claassen: 26). In Sabine Skudlik's (1990) survey of academics from Munich and Bielefeld, 11% of respondents admitted that they did not have full competence in English (= reading, writing, listening comprehension and speaking); in law and literary studies, the proportion was 15%, and in philosophy 25% – which corresponds to the different trend towards English in the various disciplines (Ch. G.3–G.7). When evaluating such surveys, the tendency not to admit the full extent of weaknesses must be borne in mind. In one questionnaire I issued to academics at the University of Duisburg and at two large companies with intensive research facilities (Ammon 1990c, 1991a: 272–277), 25% admitted to problems with reading English, 38% in listening comprehension and as many as 57% in writing. Furthermore, 19% confessed that the need to use English had at least occasionally prevented them from attending conferences. This finding fuels the suspicion that German-speaking academics are sometimes under-represented at international conferences with English as the conference language – which is confirmed by individual observations and surveys, although this has not been checked empirically. One third (33%) of respondents would even occasionally refrain from publishing if it had to be in English. In this context, the deficits in English among academics in the humanities are worse in every respect than in the natural sciences (statistically significant difference based on χ^2 tests).

Regarding the dates of the investigations by Skudlik and me at the end of the 1980s, such findings could easily be dismissed as relating to "times past". Indeed, Skudlik (1990: 306, Table 24) found a better knowledge of English in younger academics than among older colleagues. But the fact that this problem continues is still evident. For example, in my doctoral-research seminar at the University of Duisburg-Essen, I offer special sessions in which English-language texts are discussed exclusively in English; I have always detected a quantitative and qualitative deterioration in the academic performance compared with sessions in German, usually accompanied by complaints from participants about the time requirement, difficulties in understanding the readings and problems of articulation in discussion. Dirk Scholten, linguistics lecturer at the University of Wuppertal, sent me a series of anonymised letters of apology from seminar participants who had withdrawn from presentations on English-language texts. A typical example began as follows: "I must confess that my knowledge of English is not particularly outstanding [. . .]. And academic texts are generally complicated". During my time as President of the *Gesellschaft für Angewandte Linguistik* (*GAL*, 2003–2006), several section leaders and representatives from disciplines other than English studies withdrew their active participation at the world conference of the umbrella organisation, the *Association of Applied Linguistics* (AILA) in Madison/WISC (24–29 July 2005) referring to their "rusty" English; other members of the Association declined to give their own papers at the subsequent world conference in Essen (24–29 August 2008). These certainly included representatives of the most recent generation of university lecturers. From among many individual complaints by scientists about inadequate knowledge of English in the younger generation, I cite only the Director of the Institute for Virology at the University of Bonn, Christian Drosten, who complained in the periodical of the German Association of Professors and Lecturers, that he often feels as if he is an "English teacher" and sees "the inadequate linguistic knowledge of many students of medicine and biology as a genuine problem" ("*Zu Ende gedacht*", *Forschung & Lehre* 2017, 10:944). Lara Kopriviza (2010) distributed a questionnaire to academics in North-Rhine Westphalia on "attitudes [. . .] towards English as the predominant international academic language", in which she also asked for knowledge of languages and for language-associated difficulties (questionnaires returned n = 90, response 30%). The survey included all age groups, natural scientists, social scientists and colleagues in the humanities; however, a neat comparison between groups was not possible because of the uneven distribution. For the whole cohort, the most relevant results were as follows (missing values are either negative or missing responses): 90% admitted that "their ability to express themselves in English was limited" (ibid: 67). In presentations, they saw their principal difficulties in pronunciation (6% frequently, 54% sometimes), and in discussion (9% frequently, 54% sometimes) (ibid: 71f.). 14% indicated that papers submitted for publication in English had generally been returned for language corrections (ibid: 77f.). The additional time requirement for preparing a text in English was rated by 6% at more than 100%, by 21% at 50–100%, by 30% at 25–50%, and by 33% at less than 25% (ibid: 79). Some 38% found it "difficult for reasons of language [. . .] to publish in English-language periodicals (ibid: 81f.). 26% responded in the affirmative to the question whether they felt at a disadvantage compared with English-speaking academics, and 40% answered "occasionally" (83). In response to the question whether they wished "that German academics should receive more support to improve their knowledge of English", 20% answered "yes, it is necessary", 49% answered "yes, it would be advantageous" (ibid: 84f.). 13% answered "yes" to the question "Are academics in the international scene ignored if they have poor English?", 63% answered that "Such a tendency exists" (ibid: 89). Unsurprisingly, the difficulties are or seem greater in productive than in receptive communication and cause most difficulty when authoring written texts for publication.

Perhaps such language difficulties do not weigh so heavily on natural scientists because – as Wolfgang Klein (2000: 290) claims with obvious exaggeration – in their work, "the linking text between the formulas could probably be left out if required". By contrast, social scientists and writers in the humanities feel exposed to almost unattainable normative claims on the texts they write, so that even in English studies, German-speaking authors generally have their texts revised for publication by native speakers (Ammon 1991a: 273; Ch. G.6). Requirements for correctness in spoken communication are less rigorous, but this point is often implied or hidden in warnings about the "bad English", "pidgin English" or even "globalese" which is gaining ground as a global academic language. Such warnings create the false impression that noticeably poor English might still be acceptable for international academic communication.

The fact that German academics have difficulty especially with written texts can be inferred from the existence of entire companies which thrive on providing the associated support services. Indeed, I have regularly received email offers of language correction services. The following is one response to my enquiry about costs: "Thank you for requesting price information for optimal English text presentation. [. . .] We will send you a definitive price quotation from us once we have received your draft, which we will treat as absolutely confidential at all times. After the price has been agreed, the turnaround time for delivery of the corrected text is very short". Life Science Editorial limited, UK, July 23, 2011". Numerous similar examples can be found without difficulty. The English-language problems experienced by German academics are therefore also a source of income for the "language industry" in the English-speaking countries (Burrough-Boenisch 2006; Edwards/ Kingscott [1994] 1997). Similar difficulties are experienced by all non-English-speaking academics, although the extent of the problem diverges broadly depending on linguistic distance and socio-economic conditions. Examples of non-German-speakers, generally also with variable perspectives, can be found in Durand 2001 (French speakers); Medgyes/ Laszlo 2001 (Hungarians); Carli/ Calaresu 2003 (Italians); Flowerdew 1999, 2000, 2001, 2007 (Hong Kong Chinese); G. Ferguson/ Perez-Llantada/ Plo 2011; Hamel 2006b, 2007; Vasconcelos et al. 2008; Thode 2011 (Spanish speakers); G. Ferguson 2007;

Meneghini/ Packer 2007; Salager-Meyer 2008; Stolerman/ Stenius 2008 (all the latter, more than one language).

In describing linguistic diversity as an obstacle to science, British biologist Theodore H. Savory (1953: 154f.) placed himself in the Enlightenment tradition, for which the elementary problem is that "[T]he time spent on languages is time lost to science" (cf. also Ch. G.12). However, he added: "[I]t must not be forgotten that other languages than English are in fact also used by many scientists". Even in the 1950s, he considered this warning appropriate for British scientists, and for them it might still be necessary today. But German academics would find warnings of this kind ridiculous; for them it is only too clear that they must learn foreign languages: at the very least, and for most disciplines, English. As a result, the time available to them for science is inevitably reduced by the time required for this language learning. However, whether learning foreign languages, especially English, impairs their performance capacity because it is time consuming is a topic of considerable complexity, which I can address here only through a few pointers. Most commentators seem to adopt the contrary view. But in any case, English-speaking scientists enjoy the privilege of having the choice to opt for or against learning foreign languages (on the abandonment of *foreign-language requirements* in US universities, see Ch. G.1, towards the end). They can also choose between different foreign languages – which may all be similarly unimportant for them. By contrast, non-English-speaking academics have no choice about learning foreign languages, especially about learning English.

Arguments stressing the advantage of learning foreign languages are often based on the Humbolt-Sapir-Whorf hypothesis, according to which every language contains a special, unique cognitive potential, so that learning each language is accompanied by a cognitive gain (see Ch. G.6; G.12; Trabant 2003, 2011; also, Thielmann 2009, 2010). To me, the possibility of heuristic cognitive stimulation based on semantic, including metaphorical, grammatical-syntactic and pragmatic peculiarities, seems plausible (regarding metaphor, see Drewer 2003; Liebert 1997), but not the exaggerated view that linguistic structures determine or unavoidably limit cognitive options (for arguments against, see Gerhards 2010: 75–79; McWhorter 2014). This applies especially to the relationship between German and English. Expressive and epistemological barriers can, in fact, be overcome through "elaboration" (German *Ausbau*) of the language (Kloss 1978: 37–63; Ammon 1989b: 78–82; Ch. G.11). Such elaboration is orientated towards the language which is better developed (or judged to be better developed) in the relevant discipline. Fumio Inoue (2001) has shown how Japanese has been elaborated for modern science and technology through orientation towards English. By the same token, English can also always be expanded by reference to other languages. German academics do not therefore need to worry about being restricted or deflected in undesirable directions in their expressive or cognitive options through terminological gaps or grave divergences in relation to English. Such worries have been expressed e.g. by Helmut Hesse (2000: 280): "Anyone who writes in English subjects themselves to English-language terminological specifications, questions and research methods. Much is lost in this process. German economists often speak of '*Staatstätigkeit*' and '*Staatsausgaben*'. A translation for the term '*Staatstätigkeit*' is not to be found in any English dictionary". Against this view, it can be objected that neologisms can be coined for this purpose, or expressions missing in English can be borrowed from German, as in the case of *Zeitgeist*, *Leitmotif* etc. "Subjection" to the cognitive traditions predominating in the other language is not necessary for this. Accordingly, Abram de Swaan (2001b), who also sees terminological gaps in English from the Dutch perspective (ibid: 76), argues for the further elaboration of English (he does not use the term elaboration) and joins Pierre Bourdieu's appeal: "'*Il faut désangliciser l'anglais*' [. . .]: English should be released from the English!" (ibid: 79). Ultimately, this demand leads to the creation of a global academic language without restrictions on its expressive potential.

While the purely cognitive gain for academics of learning English or, more generally, of learning foreign languages, remains doubtful, there is no need to list the communicative advantages of learning English. They have already been presented in detail in Ch. G.1–G.10 and form the obvious primary motivation for learning and use. By contrast, for English-speaking academics, even the communicative advantages of learning foreign languages, and in fact for all foreign languages, are doubtful. Many disciplines hardly require foreign-language skills, because, regardless of their linguistic origins, academics nowadays either know English sufficiently well, or this is expected of them, and because the quantity and originality of academic publications in other languages is modest by comparison with English, or at least appears so.

The effort of learning, a still inadequate knowledge of the target language, i.e. loss of time in reading and preparation of texts, and communicative deficits in impact, are therefore all undoubted disadvantages for German-speaking academics compared with their English-speaking colleagues. As Gethman (2011: 62f.) suggests with reference to many, if not all FL speakers, "Language competence in a language acquired as a second language is limited in all dimensions: lexis, connotations, linguistic style, allocation to linguistic register, neologisms etc. by contrast with a language acquired as a first language". Beyond the narrowly defined linguistic rankings and levels (phonetics, orthography, grammar, lexis), these difficulties also extend to pragmatics, discourse and textual features (Clyne 1984a, 1987b; House 2003b; Thielmann 2010).

So far, German academics have not shifted to the global academic language, English, as fully as Dutch and Scandinavian academics. This also applies to academic publishers. Publishers in the Netherlands are almost on a par with those in English-speaking countries. By contrast, the role of German-language academic publishers is more modest, especially in view of their tradition and the size of the language community. For the sake of simplicity, I have called the academic publishers in the German-language territory "German-language publishers" – even if they do not publish exclusively in German. The fundamental shift to English as the preferred academic language worldwide has caused the market for German-language publications to shrink. In consequence, German-language academic publishers feel compelled to follow the trend towards English. In natural-science periodicals, the shift to English was unavoidable (Ch. G.3, towards the end). In public libraries outside the German-language territory, whenever savings must be made, periodicals in other foreign languages tend to be dropped rather than those in English. Sales opportunities and securing famous authors drive the shift towards English. As already explained, many authors prefer to publish in English-language periodicals because of their wider distribution and because writing in English is generally easier for non-German-speaking authors than writing in German (this was pointed out long ago, e.g. by Schwabl 1986). For the shift towards English, publishers require English-speaking staff, also in their editorial teams. This often means additional costs not incurred by English-speaking publishers. Despite the language shift, access to the English-speaking market and other non-German-speaking markets is still difficult for German-language publishers, in terms of sale of publications as well as acquisition of authors. Among the ten or so academic publishers (owners/employees) I asked informally, all agreed that, given the choice, many authors prefer publishers in the USA or UK. None envisaged a broad return to German as a publication language.

I conclude this chapter with the disadvantages for the entire German-language community, the German-speaking countries and their citizens caused by the loss of position of German as an international academic language. In the past, when numerous non-German-speaking academics spoke and wrote in German, German functioned as a conveyor belt for academic knowledge between other language communities. Direct importation of knowledge was especially valuable, e.g. when Russian scientists Pavlov and Mendeleyev published their ground-breaking theories, on behaviourism and respectively the periodic system of the chemical elements, in German immediately after Russian (Ch. G.1). Moreover, in the opposite direction, German allowed rapid exportation of knowledge. This increased the prestige of the German-speaking countries abroad and boosted interest among foreigners in working academically, studying and establishing contacts in a German-speaking country. Today, this conveyor belt has largely worn out. As a result, a strong motive for learning German as a foreign language (GFL) has been lost, which, in turn, damages GFL departments abroad. This is one of the causes for the global decline in GFL learners in recent decades – from approximately 20 million in 2000 to approximately 14.5 million in 2010, with a slight resurgence to 15.4 million in 2015 (Ch. I.7). This decline in learners has led to dwindling opportunities for international communication with German-speaking countries and evaporation of the reservoir of linguistically qualified employees abroad, which the German economy urgently requires.

I have explained the disadvantages of the loss of position of German as an international academic language more fully elsewhere (Ammon 1998: 252–286). The most important aspects are summarised here:

- Deterioration in the quality of university teaching through teaching in English, unless a knowledge of English by lecturers and students which is equivalent to their knowledge of German can be guaranteed;
- Obstruction of communication between academics and non-experts, and the associated "ivory-tower" isolation of universities from the home community, unless the entire population of the German-speaking countries have good English-language skills at their disposal;
- Decline in the prestige of the German language even within German-speaking countries, and therefore loss of a national symbol (the value of which is admittedly difficult to estimate). The German language was a substantial orientational parameter for German nationalism in the nineteenth century (Ammon 1995a: 18–34; Stukenbrock 2005: 298–305). Even today, it is an expression of national identity for many Germans. Just try to imagine "real" Germans without a knowledge of German.

11. Is German less "elaborated" than English?

In simple terms, the "elaboration" of a language ensures that it is possible to express all thoughts, especially modern ideas, through that language, and to speak and write freely about all kinds of knowledge and subject matters. The term and the initial definition of the concept of "elaboration" (*Ausbau*) originated from Heinz Kloss (1952: 24–37; 1978: 23–60) and is now considered among the basics of sociolinguistic knowledge (Haarmann 2004; Ammon 1989a, 2004). From a different perspective, the elaboration of a language designates an expansion of its expressive means (especially words and their meanings, syntax and textual forms), especially for use in given domains, e.g. in elementary education, in academic work or, at a higher level, in the most advanced research in certain disciplines. By analogy with language planning, it is also possible to speak of *corpus elaboration* (or *structural elaboration*) and to distinguish this from *status elaboration* (also *functional elaboration*), which relates to the external conditions for use of the language in the relevant domains (legal, institutional, economic and personal circumstances). In language planning, a distinction is made between *corpus planning* and *status planning*. This distinction also originates from Kloss (1952: 24–31; 1978 37–63) and not – as often erroneously claimed – from Einar Haugen, although it was disseminated primarily in his English-language adaptation ("status planning"/"corpus planning") (e.g. Haugen 1987). The present chapter is primarily concerned with corpus elaboration in the "most advanced" domains of the action field of academic work, primarily in research, i.e. with terms (words and word combinations) and their components, and, less frequently, with grammar and academic text forms. This context raises the question of whether German shows a deficit compared with English.

Chapters G.1 to G.10 have demonstrated what might be called a *status deficit* of German compared with English in different respects within the academic action field. The titles of various publications suggest such a deficit in the contemporary context: either because they see a "domain loss" for languages like German (e.g. G. Ferguson 2007); or at least a subordinate position on the research front; some even suggest the relegation of German, as, e.g. the much cited title by Hubert Markl (1986/2011) "*Die Spitzenforschung spricht englisch*" [cutting-edge research speaks English] (similarly, Schwabl 1986); and possibly consider the "vitality" of the language as a whole to be under threat (Carli 2009). The fact that, even within German-speaking countries, English is dominant, and German is marginalised in publications, especially in theoretical natural sciences, hardly leaves any doubt about this. In fact, this is not so certain for spoken language use, i.e. regarding whether English is predominantly spoken and German is avoided even in the German-speaking countries, especially in "cutting-edge research" in the natural sciences. But such views have been expressed, e.g. by Ralph Mocikat, who claims that in Germany, "often, at conferences without any international participants, in internal seminars or in day-to-day laboratory discussions, only English is spoken [. . .], even if there is nobody present who does not speak German" ("*Die deutsche Sprache in den Naturwissenschaften*", www.goethe.de/Ihr/prj/mac/mac/spd/de4244182.htm). So, is German still used at all to speak about the most advanced research topics in German-speaking countries? It certainly is in the humanities, presumably also in the social sciences. But what about the theoretical natural sciences? These questions have still not been adequately researched, especially not with reference to different situations and staffing configurations.

Restricting the discussion to corpus elaboration – the structure rather than the function of language – is directly suggested by the term *elaboration deficit*, and, anyway, the term *corpus elaboration* also suggests primarily the creation of a terminology for science and for communication via the most advanced research. This kind of elaboration is possible through the home language (*indigenous* elaboration) or by borrowing from *other*, "foreign" languages (*exogenous* elaboration). Indeed, since the historical period of humanism, German academics have borrowed many terms or their component parts from Latin, ancient Greek, and subsequently from Italian and especially from French; English has now become the primary donor language. However, often in parallel with this, there has also been an indigenous elaboration, perhaps even linguistic purism, where "foreign words" have been Germanised, initially during the humanist era and then more intensively since the anti-Napoleonic, German-nationalist movement far into the twentieth century (von Polenz 1999: 264–293). Examples of Germanisation include *Universum* > *Weltall* (Philipp von Zesen, seventeenth -century), *fundamentum* > *Grundlage* (Christian Wolff, seventeenth/ eighteenth centuries) or *Avancement* > *Beförderung* (official-language Germanisation in the Wilhelmine Empire). Indigenous elaboration also includes loan translations (English: *calque*) (e.g. *black hole* > *Schwarzes Loch* or *fuzzy logic* > *unscharfe Logik*). The following features can also be attributed to indigenous elaboration in the broad sense: the re-use of word components which originate from another language but are already integrated in the receiving language (e.g. the originally Latin verb suffix -*ieren*: *konnotieren*, *kommutieren* etc. which are already current in German, but were previously borrowed from the French). The conventional term nowadays for this process is "loan-word formation" (von Polenz 1999: 395–398). For the lexical inventory in the final volume of *Deutsches Fremdwörterbuch* (1913–1988, before it was revised by the *Institut für Deutsche Sprache*), it was established that more than one third of the lemmas (35.1%) had not been adopted into German as whole words but built up from previously borrowed components (Best 2001: 14). Such loan-word formation for academic terminology occurs widely in many languages, including English, especially by drawing on components of ancient Greek or Latin origin. The same applies for German, even in the "Golden Age" of German as an academic language towards the end of the nineteenth and the beginning of the twentieth centuries, when there was no elaboration deficit relative to other languages. Loan-word formations are therefore not a sign of elaboration deficit; otherwise English would also be massively affected.

However, "genuine foreign words" are generally evaluated differently. They generally also include "false borrowings", i.e. words are made up from foreign-language components, generally English, which do not exist as whole words, or exist only with another meaning, in the relevant foreign language, i.e. English. Examples in everyday German include *Handy* or *Beamer* (English *mobile (phone)* or *cellular (phone)* and respectively *(powerpoint) projector*. The many anglicisms in modern German, including everyday language, which is often perceived as "over-foreignised", also presumably intensify the impression of an elaboration deficit in academic language. Among the approximately 20 colleagues I asked informally whether "German has an elaboration deficit as an academic language compared with English", almost all answered in the affirmative. In this context, I explained "elaboration deficit" with the sense that appropriate technical expressions or terms for scientific innovations are occasionally not available. According to individual conversations, the view that German has an elaboration deficit compared with English seems to be based on two assumptions: 1) anglicisms (borrowings from English) occur more frequently in the language use of German-speaking scientists than Germanisms (borrowings from German) occur in the language use of English-speaking scientists or in scientific/academic texts; 2) that, on average, German-speaking scientists have terms for scientific innovations at their disposal later than English-speaking scholars. This last point almost implies – admittedly, not in a strictly logical sense – that German-speaking scholars are generally limping along behind their English-speaking colleagues.

In a previous book, I also squarely judged the frequent occurrence of anglicisms in German (compared with the scarcity of Germanisms in English) as an indicator for the elaboration deficit compared with English (Ammon 1991a: 277–281; similarly, in Zimmer 1997: 213). It seems that linguists who otherwise stress the continuing richness of the German language, e.g. Peter Eisenberg (2012: 53), still tend towards this view: "Domain loss necessarily means that given terms or entire conceptual frameworks [according to my own understanding 'expressive frameworks'! U.A.] no longer exist in German, and the vocabulary shows gaps compared with that of English. There can be no doubt that there are developments in this direction". If the lack of indigenous word-formation and especially terminology-formation from indigenous (German) components is judged as a corresponding number of gaps, then all languages nowadays show an elaboration deficit relative to English. It is in this sense that Grypdonck (1985: 17) refers to a "lexical menopause" of all languages apart from English. According to this view, anglicisms are taken as an entirely valid criterion for an elaboration deficit. But is this correct? Even if they are "adopted" as fully valid components of the receiving language by the associated language community? Manfred Görlach (2001, 2002a) has documented this phenomenon for many languages throughout Europe. They resemble immigrants with citizenship in their new home, whose foreign origin can still be recognised but who are otherwise fully integrated. Many anglicisms are used without difficulty in this way in speech or in texts. They then receive semi-official recognition of their belonging to the German language through codification (Ch. B.2), i.e. adoption in reference works for the German language, in the present context, in specialist academic glossaries or dictionaries. For everyday language, there is an intermediate stage of codification in dictionaries of "foreign words". The following abridged excerpt (from Ammon 1991a: 278f) addresses the question, with slightly "updated" examples (according to *Duden*, "*upgedatet*" [updated] is now a component of the German language). At the same time, the excerpt exemplifies the wide use of anglicisms nowadays. But inverted commas and lower case spellings of nouns reveal limitations in the integration of these terms into German.

Through computer technology, anglicisms have already penetrated all disciplines. The word "Computer" itself, with its English spelling (C) and pronunciation [. . . pju. . .], exemplifies the phenomenon alongside *Hard Disc, Double Density, Desk Info, Byte, Return-Taste* [key] etc. But specialist languages in individual disciplines are also adopting more and more English terms in an un-Germanised form, even in the humanities, social sciences and applied sciences. The following examples appeared in a randomly chosen issue of a chemical-technology periodical, i.e. applied chemistry: *Dead End Filtration, Cross Flow Microfiltration, Bio Process, Protein Engineering, Protein Design* and so on (*Nachrichten aus Chemie, Technik und Laboratorium* 37 (12) 1989: passim).

These considerations provide a start for what I consider to be a desirable narrowing and specification of the term "elaboration deficit". One appropriate criterion is given by the integration of the anglicisms into the receiving language. Indicators of an incomplete integration are precisely markings such as quotation marks or lower case spellings (other possible meanings must be taken into consideration, such as quotation or metalinguistic use), whereas the absence of such marking reveals integration or belonging to the language, at least according to the respective author. This specification agrees with the definition of "foreign words" based on use rather than linguistic structure, which has been suggested by various authors for some time now (e.g. von Polenz 1999: 298). Accordingly, e.g. words such as *Baby* or *Computer* are no longer foreign words in German although their origin from English is still evident, or more generally: designating a word as an anglicism, a gallicism or similar based on its form is entirely compatible with its unlimited acceptance as a component of the German language. Immediately evident criteria for this include a high degree of currency, which is admittedly not always easy to measure, and codification in reference works, including specialist dictionaries, which is less doubtful, but possibly over-restrictive. Accordingly, a long-term *borrowing* is completed, which contrasts with a merely situational or ephemeral *transference*. This therefore provides a rough definition for "elaboration deficit", especially for scientific *terms*, but the definition still requires polishing, through the addition of at least three conditions. Two of these are: an elaboration deficit of language L_a (e.g. German) relative to language L_b (e.g. English) is only present with reference to a specific term if: a) the foreign (not current/integrated) term in L_a is current in L_b (in the case of an elaboration deficit relative to L_b), and b) if no synonym for this term is available in L_a (I am not addressing questions about grammatical or pragmatic equivalence here, i.e. possibilities for collocation, textual integration or substitutability according to stylistic level). The third condition which relates to entire languages (rather than just individual terms) is: by comparison with L_b, language L_a exhibits elaboration deficits in its entirety if: c) the number of terms in L_a with elaboration deficit relative to L_b is larger than the number of terms in L_b with elaboration deficit relative to L_a. The criterion therefore could be expanded beyond terminology to include grammar and text forms).

It follows from this definition that the elaboration deficit of L_a relative to L_b declines with every borrowing (in the sense of linguistic integration) of a term from L_b into L_a. But the definition does not exclude elaboration deficits of a language L_b relative to L_a *in parts*, even if L_b is more elaborated than L_a as a whole. Accordingly, there are indications of a partial elaboration deficit of English relative to German. For example, Lawrence Scaff (2011) occasionally uses italicised German terms inserted into the English text when reproducing the content of German texts, especially in the work of Max Weber. He either suggests the meaning directly in English or relies on context to suggest it, e.g. "'spirit, the *Geist* of capitalism" (p. 21, "*Wirklichkeitswissenschaft* – that is, an experimental enquiry into the phenomena and actualities of the world" (p. 58) or "*Volkslied*" (p. 48), "*Geisteswissenschaften*" (p. 55,) "*Drang*" (p. 56). Various references have been made to terminological gaps in English, especially for governmental, social or economic structures or even legal systems. For example, there is allegedly no equivalence for the terms *Staatstätigkeit, Staatsausgaben* or *Mittelstand*, which are current among German authors in politics and economics (Hesse 2000: 280; examples from Dutch in de Swaan 2001: 76) or terms for distinguishing between *soziale Schicht* [social stratum] and *soziale Klasse* [social class] (Ammon 2010b: 155). The extent to which the German terms are familiar to English-speaking specialists would have to be tested here to determine whether they could be considered as borrowings in English. Demonstrating elaboration deficits accurately may therefore require effort-intensive investigations. However, based on the findings of the preceding sections of Ch. G, it seems obvious to me that quantitative research would establish an elaboration deficit of German relative to English as a whole, although this may be reversed in individual humanities disciplines. From the German perspective, a race to catch up presumably often develops from such elaboration deficits, nowadays, especially through the borrowing of anglicisms.

These are often only adapted to German linguistic structures in a makeshift manner, especially in terms of spelling (*Galaxie ie* instead of *y*) and grammar (e.g. allocation to a different gender, such as feminine for *Scientific Community* instead of neuter; cf. Eisenberg 1998: 337f., 1999: 421). Hybrids are also frequent, e.g. *Pivot-Grammatik* in linguistics (relates to two-word utterances by infants; Bußmann 1990: 588) or *patch-clamp-Technik* in medicine (Gerok 2000: 236; a "measurement method in electro-physiology, with which the current through a single ion channel in the cell membrane of a cell can be demonstrated"; de.wikipedia.org/wiki/Patch-Clamp-Technik). Even among scientists, there are divergences in the evaluation of such structural anglicisation of scientific German. Wholesale dismissal of these processes as "*Denglisch*", "restricted Lingua franca" and similar do not help, because they suggest a categorical abandonment of anglicisms or English as an academic language for non-English-speakers, which seems unrealistic. Contrasting opinions overwhelmingly affirm the use of terminology borrowed from English or English as an academic language, e.g. the medical writer Wolfgang Gerok (2000: 236): "Anyone who translates German scientific texts into English realises that a good English translation is just as accurate but generally significantly shorter than the original German text. There are many English specialist expressions which are hardly translatable into German, e.g. *Clearance, patch-clamp-Technik, enhancer, Splicing, Capping*. For scientists, the imagery of these expressions is helpful, informative and memorable".

However, difficulties of translation and brevity of expression seem to me to provide an inadequate basis for a generally positive evaluation. This would have to refer to advantages or disadvantages for German-speaking academics and the entire German-language community. Presumably, serious attempts at Germanisation are not often made, because it is assumed that present-day German academics will welcome Germanisations (declared attitude) but then not use them in practice – which is the only way they could become established components of German. The adoption of structurally Germanised terms cannot be reliably determined merely from declarations, such as the rejection of English as an "internal German" publication language or conference language, as claimed in surveys of medical professionals (Haße/ Fischer 2003; Haße et al. 2007). Attitude researchers therefore distinguish between expressed evaluation and a commitment to act accordingly. Discrepancies may also be explainable because the users of terminology attach greater value to the international usefulness of anglicisms than to the more congenial German-language forms. They possibly find the "costs" of structurally German-language terms greater than the benefits, as they would have to be nurtured alongside the anglicisms (additional learning effort, double communication). Having said this, the minimal Germanising impact achieved by criticisms of the anglicisation of German scientific terminology, which have been voiced with considerable emphasis among medical circles (e.g. Haße 2002; Mocikat 2006,

2007), is remarkable. Medical writers also play an important part in the *Arbeitskreis Deutsch als Wissenschaftssprache* (*ADAWIS*) [working group on German as an academic language], which demands that "newly discovered elements of content should be provided with native-language designations, established German-language terms should not be replaced with English terms, and the specialist associations should engage with questions about German terminology and appeal for people to use the terms found" (Guidelines of the *ADAWIS*, Berlin, June 2007). The reasoning behind this demand is at least partly based on the Humboldt-Sapir-Whorf hypothesis. Links between anglicised terminology and the replacement of the entire language are implied: "Every language models reality in its own unique way. As a result, banishing a language from entire scientific disciplines represents an intellectual impoverishment [. . .]" (ibid). However, by themselves, the terms do not imply any intellectual impoverishment, because borrowings can be linked with meanings ("concepts", in the linguistic sense) just as rich as the German terms. The idea that German scientists might lose the ability to connect English-language terms with complex concepts is inconceivable. Peter Eisenberg (2012: 53) considers it unlikely "that German will lose the ability to form such concepts in the foreseeable future", and this also applies especially to borrowings from English. Moreover, the diversity of word formation in German will not be damaged. "Such anxieties are implausible, and there are no more signs justifying them than there are for an impoverishment of German syntax". A more plausible worry would be that communication with the surrounding society and with other disciplines might be made more difficult: "Ordinary-language users in the social environment will lose weight in the communication and in the discussion of new knowledge, and this will make the formulation and answering of interdisciplinary and transdisciplinary questions considerably more difficult even within the respective discipline" (ibid). This argument, which I share (Ammon 1998: 273 f.), relates especially to a wholesale shift to English as the academic language in German-speaking countries. Otherwise, in view of present trends in foreign-language learning, English terminology is generally more comprehensible than Greco-Latin terminology (Quetz 2010). However, even for specialists, frequently occurring – ordinary-language as well as scientific – acronyms are difficult to decipher (e.g. *AIDS = Acquired Immune Deficiency Syndrome* and *WIMPS = Weakly Interacting Massive Particles*, which are relevant for astrophysicists researching "dark matter").

But critics of the anglicisation of German scientific language are not only "concerned" on practical grounds relating to communication and knowledge. For example, regarding German speakers' abandonment of their own language (ibid, June 2007), the warning in the *ADAWIS* "Guidelines" about "speakers' commitment to themselves" is evidently concerned more with preserving linguistic identity or linguistically supported national identity (Ch. B.3). In this context, I have referred to the pathos of "worries about the dissolution of the 'German-language national group'" (Ammon 1998: 257–261). This clearly ideologically laden motive should not simply be dismissed as antiquated or dangerous; it deserves careful analysis and evaluation. Blatantly lagging behind the English-language world is likely to injure national as well as linguistic pride. Previous investigations of Germans' attitudes to their language have only partially registered this kind of resentment (Hoberg/ Eichhoff-Cyrus/ Schulz 2008; Eichinger/ Plewnia/ Schoel/ Stahlberg 2012). Accurate understanding of such resentment, including peaks and troughs against time, would provide an important basis for dealing with it appropriately. The extent to which English serves as a "language of identification" and not only a "language of communication" would need to be assessed (Hüllen 1992). This would clearly not relate to national identity, but – with a longer view – to European and/or global identity, including its role as a lingua franca and non-native language (Crystal 2005: 172–177; Seidlhofer 2005a, b).

On closer consideration, many apparently minor problems relating to the anglicisation of German academic language prove to be more than trivial. This would apply to many of the "false friends", linguistic expressions with considerable expressive similarity but different in meaning in both languages. One familiar example is the introduction of the meaning of "*Begriff*" translating the English word *concept* as a new meaning for the German word *Konzept*. Previously, *Konzept* had the two meanings: a "sketched draft, rough version of a text" and a "clearly delineated plan for a project" (*Duden – Das grosse Wörterbuch der deutschen Sprache*, Vol. 8, 1994: 1957). The addition of the meaning "*Begriff*" for *Konzept* was associated with a shift in the meaning of the expression *Begriff* in German, which is now used with the meaning of a "(linguistic) expression". As a result, a *Begriff* now has a meaning which was previously reserved for the linguistic *expression*, e.g. the word. A sound tradition in German terminology has therefore been destroyed. How should the content [*Inhalt*] and scope [*Umfang*], the traditional German-language terms for "intention" and "extension", of a concept [*Begriff*], be understood now? How should the student's famous objection to Mephisto in Goethe's *Faust* be interpreted "*Doch ein Begriff muss bei dem Worte sein*" [But there must be a concept behind the word]? Words (in linguistic terminology "lexical items") are a specific type of linguistic expression alongside others such as word groups, clauses etc. The fact that linguists have joined in with this terminological confusion (Vater 2000) and possibly even promoted it is a matter for laughter as well as despair. But this "accident" is not typical for the anglicisation of terminology; indeed, elaboration based on English is communicatively less disturbing to the younger generation than elaboration based on Latin and Greek – and most of the borrowings from English are based on Latin and Greek origins anyway.

Finally, the elaboration of a language for science and scholarship includes the appropriate stylistic and textual forms. In this regard, a call to improve the clarity and readability of German-(language) academic texts has often been heard, especially from the English-speaking territory. The problem is suggested by the title of Claudia Kalensky's dissertation (2009), admittedly qualified with a question mark: *Kompliziert – Komplizierter – Wissenschaftsdeutsch?* The motto of a relevant article by Clyne/ Hoeks/ Kreutz (1988: 457 – a quotation from Mary E. Wildner-Bassett) voices the same idea: "For readers not extremely well-versed in German academic prose, the structure of the work limits its readability: chapter introductions and summaries as well as both an explicit cohesive element among the sub-chapters can be sought in vain". The extent to which this really is the typical "German academic style" (ibid: passim) and to which it has possibly been changed in recent history by the influence of the English language, does not so far appear to have been scientifically verified. In comparative investigations of German and English academic texts, Juliane House (2002a: 204–209; also, 2003a: 173–177) did not find any such crude differences, although the texts translated from English into German contain surprisingly few transferences of discursive and textual structures: "Cultural filtering is still operative, i.e. German textual norms are maintained" (House 2002a: 204). What was remarkable, was the rather didactic perspective of the German texts, which anticipated and answered readers' questions more than the English originals. In fact, this contradicts the infamous incomprehensibility of German academic prose. There is clearly a need for further investigation of typical structural features of English-language academic texts compared with German academic texts (see Thielmann 2009). The findings of Michael Clyne (1984a, 1987b, 1991) – according to which English texts are distinguished from German texts by a preceding explanation of the aims of the presentation (what is to be proved or refuted), a more linear development of ideas (avoidance of far-flung digressions), a limitation of impersonal and passive constructions and a concluding summary and discussion of results – have received wide circulation. Macro structural features such as a preceding abstract and limitation of footnotes are also considered typical for English-language texts. I am convinced that German academic texts are also tending in this direction nowadays. If the English-speaking world has been the driving force behind this change, I would not see this as a sacrifice of German academic culture, but rather as a welcome elaboration of German (in a sense which includes textual structures) through borrowing from English.

12. For and against: one international academic language or more than one?

From the sixteenth/seventeenth centuries onwards, after the replacement of mediaeval Latin as the academic lingua franca throughout Europe, especially by the larger languages, such as French, Italian, English, Spanish and German (Ch. G.1: beginning), scepticism began to arise about linguistic diversity and the associated additional burden of learning. In an infamous complaint voiced in the co-editor's preface to Diderot's Enlightenment encyclopaedia, Jean D'Alembert claims that the spread of his language, French, over the whole of Europe now means, "*qu'il etoit tems de la substituer à la Langue latine, qui depuis la renaissance des Lettres étoit celle de nos Savans*" [. . . it is time to substitute French for Latin which has been the language of academics since the Renaissance]. In fact, this may have contributed to the spread of the Enlightenment, but it also led to imitation in other countries:

> *L'Angleterre nous a donc imité; l'Allemagne, où le Latin sembloit s'être refugié, commence insensiblement à en perdre l'usage: je ne doute pas q'elle ne soit bien-tôt suivie par le Suédois, les Danois, & les Russiens. Ainsi, avant la fin du dix-huitieme siecle, un Philosophe qui voudra s'instruire à fond des découvertes des ses prédécesseurs, sera contraint de charger sa mémoire de sept à huit Langues différentes; & après avoir consumé à les appredre le tems le plus précieux de sa vie, il mourra avant de commencer à s'instruiere.*

> [England has followed our lead; in Germany, where Latin seemed to have fled, Latin is also beginning to lose ground: I am sure the same will happen with Swedish, Danish and Russian. By the end of the 18th century, a philosopher who wants a grounding in the work of his predecessors will have to load down his memory with seven or eight different languages and, having used up the best years of his life, he will die before even starting to learn anything new. . .]

D'Alembert therefore fears that academics will die just from having to learn – as he imagines, seven to eight – academic languages, before they can begin with their actual research ("*Discours préliminaire*" 1749: 39f., in *L'Encyclopédie ou Dictionnaire raisonné des sciences, des arts et des métiers*, http://gallica.bnf. fr/ark:/12148/bpt6k75325s/f2.image.r=grande+encyclop%EF%BF%BDdie.langFR.swf).

From the time of the Enlightenment, suggestions for a single academic lingua franca began to be voiced, somewhat later, in conjunction with plans for an artificial, global lingua franca. These reached their climax in a request to the League of Nations in 1921 to assess the prospects for the artificial language Esperanto. It seems surprising today that this request was filed by the *British* and *American Association for the Advancement of Science* (*Report of the Committee* [. . .] 1922). Under significant pressure from France, the plans were dropped (see end of this chapter). Such efforts found no special resonance in the German-language territory. On one hand, German reluctance may have been influenced by "romantic ideas", including Wilhelm von Humboldt's espousal of linguistic diversity as a source of knowledge, but on the other hand, by the international position acquired by German as an academic language in the nineteenth century (Ch. G.1). Unlike speakers of smaller languages, German-speaking academics experienced the constraints of linguistic diversity only to a limited extent, because of their own language's strong position.

This linguistic advantage of German-speaking academics in the second half of the nineteenth century to the middle of the twentieth century comes to the surface in individual observations, but there is a lack of comprehensive research. One example relates to a visit to the USA by German sociologist Max Weber in 1904. Weber gave his talk without difficulty in German at the World Congress in St. Louis. Lawrence A. Scaff (2011), who has published a book about Weber's trip, corresponded with me about US sociologists' knowledge of German at that time: "among Weber's colleagues Du Bois, Seligman, and Hollander all knew German, for example, they would have had no difficulty following Weber's lecture or conversing with him in German". So, Weber hardly experienced the constraints of linguistic diversity. Having said this, Scaff did, however, suggest that a knowledge of German could not be taken for granted among US academics at that time, but he unfortunately lacked the necessary "biographical information", which would require "a lengthy and time-consuming process" to gather reliable data (email from Scaff, 15 September 2011).

Priority of rank and approximate parity between the three academic languages English, French and German did not mean that all academics knew all three languages. German-speaking academics sometimes also experienced this. Armin Hermann (2000) offers details such as the following: "In 1905, Austrian physicist Ludwig Boltzmann was invited to Berkeley as a visiting professor, where he gave lectures in English, which he had struggled to learn" (ibid: 210). He would presumably have spared himself the trouble if all his listeners had understood German. Einstein often spoke German in his lectures abroad in 1921/22. "In the USA, in England and in Japan, many vice chancellors would introduce Einstein with an opening address in German. However, newspaper reporters have spread doubts about how many listeners might have understood Einstein's German". In Paris and Jerusalem, he spoke French (ibid: 218).

In Japan, Einstein's presentations were also sometimes translated; a Japanese caricature of one of his lectures shows him by the side of poet and physicist Jun Ishihara who served as his interpreter (Friese 1990: 809). Brigitte Schroeder-Gudehus (1990: 875) describes a lecture by German chemistry Nobel Prize winner Fritz Haber in Paris in 1927. Haber spoke in French, but – as suggested in brackets – not without difficulty: "His forceful (but linguistically not exactly slick) commitment to working together for progress [...]". In Paris, Haber was therefore evidently not expecting a widespread knowledge of German, but, for his own part, neither was he completely secure in French. Somewhat later, a German Nobel Prize winner for physics also reached the limits of his linguistic skills: "For his first research visit in Copenhagen in winter 1924/25, Werner Heisenberg learnt Danish and English at the same time". After he had prepared his colloquium presentation in Danish, the event organiser, Niels Bohr explained to him, "half an hour before the talk" [...]: 'It goes without saying that we will speak English'" (Hermann 2000: 220). On one hand, Heisenberg did not want to rely on his knowledge of German abroad but, on the other hand, even at that time, he was confronted by the strong position of English as an international academic language, even in a country neighbouring Germany, with a traditional tendency to learn German as a foreign language. It should be borne in mind, that Bohr had worked for many years in England, and that a knowledge of English was not widespread among German scientists at the time. When he emigrated to the USA in 1933, Einstein knew no English and was never to achieve perfection in this language (ibid: 224). His colleague Leopold Infeld reported that, during a visit by the Italian mathematician Tullio Levi-Civita "the two of them spoke in a language which they took to be English". "As collaborators, he [accepted] only German-speaking assistants [...]". "He could not pronounce the English 'th' [according to his successor Banesh Hoffmann]" and "reproducing German syntax he [would utter] comical-sounding sentences, such as 'I will little tink'" or in "English tinged with Swabian dialect [...] 'Oh, he is a very good formula'". In a TV address against the hydrogen bomb, "he spoke such an incomprehensible gobbledygook that English subtitles [had to be] provided for viewers" (Neffe 2005: 410f.).

These examples suggest that assessing the advantages of a single international academic language compared with more than one international academic language will require an investigation of the effort (cost and difficulty) of learning foreign languages and using them in an academic context. By contrast, assessing the advantages of more than one international academic language compared with a single language, will require evidence of any accompanying gain in resources. According to the Humbolt-Sapir-Whorf hypothesis (Ch. G.6), such gains are supposed to include the fact that (provided they do not coincide), the cognitive potentials of the different languages are added, and that native-language access to science and scholarship releases more creativity than through the use of a foreign language. In the case of several languages (L_a, L_b, . . .), more academics have access to science directly through their own native language than in the case of a single language (L_a), so that more knowledge could be attained. Special advantages of native speakers of the academic language(s) or respectively disadvantages of the FL speakers are added/subtracted. However, it is extremely difficult to weigh these advantages and disadvantages reliably against one another. Above all, the cognitive resources of multilingualism have so far not been fully explained (Ch. G.6). In all the work known to me which articulates worries about a single academic language with reference to the cognitive resources of multilingualism, even the work of eloquent advocates like Jürgen Trabant (2003, 2011, 2014), I detect an absence of careful analysis and lack of empirical evidence. It is important to ask: do the potential cognitive advantages gained by carrying out academic work in the native language counterbalance the difficulties encountered through the use of an international language for wider communication?

The following discussion provides preliminary evidence for the claim that the total effort of learning and working in several international academic languages is greater than with a single language. This generally also applies to linguistically included academics, not only to linguistically excluded academics. I designate academics as "linguistically included" and respectively "linguistically excluded" if their native language either is or is not, at the same time, an international academic language, that is, if their native language either is or is not counted among the international academic languages. Linguistically included academics can engage in international communication in their native language without learning effort and, at the same time, they can communicate nationally and internationally. Their international academic communication is directly linguistically accessible to their own language community, so that the ivory tower-effect is less than if international communication is conducted in a foreign language. Having said this, in the case of a single international academic language, these academics would lose the cognitive advantage of multilingualism. But widespread complaints about the disadvantages of non-English-speaking academics compared with English-speaking academics create a strong impression that multilingual academics do not rate their cognitive advantage very highly (cf. Ammon 2001a, 2007d; Carli/ Ammon 2007; La Madeleine 2007). With several international academic languages, all linguistically included academics (native speakers of one of these international academic languages) would indeed have the advantage of multilingualism, but they would still have to learn the other international academic languages in order to participate fully in international academic communication; however, they would require only passive (receptive) skills in the other academic languages. Their learning effort would therefore still be less than for the linguistically completely excluded academics.

Learning effort differs depending on the linguistic distance between languages, including writing systems (ideographic scripts, e.g. in Chinese and Japanese, contrasted with alphabetic scripts). In simple terms, learning the scripts of Chinese and Japanese provide special difficulties for speakers of Indo-European languages, while speakers of Chinese and Japanese find the grammar of the other languages difficult to learn (Chong 2003). Above all, the acquisition of active (productive) language skills is more effort-intensive than for passive (receptive) skills. All non-English-speaking academics are faced with this challenge. The greatest difficulty is generally writing to a publishable standard, because written publications are subject to particularly rigorous language norms (Ch. G.10). Indications from historical periods of presumed problem-free academic multilingualism give a sense of these difficulties. For example, reports by reviewers and editors of submissions received, such as the report by German physicist Max Planck in 1909 on a manuscript submitted by Dutch physicist Cornelis J. Bakker to the periodical *Annalen der Physik*: "In its present form, it can on no account be printed, because it is full of linguistic errors and foreign turns of phrase [...]" (Hermann: 212). And this was a scientist from a language community which was not only open to foreign languages but also a linguistic and geographical neighbour! In this context, the linguistic standards for humanities texts are even higher than for texts in the natural sciences. I refer to my survey of 20 university English-studies lecturers in Germany, all of whom relied on help from native speakers when authoring English-language publications (Ch. G.6; Ammon 1991a: 273).

Conversely, the disadvantages of linguistically excluded academics correspond to advantages for linguistically included colleagues: the ability to write linguistically correct texts more rapidly and the possibility of direct financial gains from the linguistic correction of academic texts, for which the linguistically excluded pay (Ch. G.10; Ammon 2001a, 2003c, 2006d, 2007d, 2010b). I have personal experience as an editor of the enormous difficulties faced by non-native speakers in writing academic texts in a foreign language, in this case German (GFL), especially in the humanities and social sciences (in the yearbook *Sociolinguistica* and in Ammon 1994d; Ammon/ Chong 2003; Ammon/ Reinbothe/ Zhu 2007; Ammon/ Kemper 2011; Ammon/ Dittmar/ Mattheier 1987/88; Ammon/ Dittmar/ Mattheier/ Trudgill 2004–06). Even professors of German studies and GFL encountered untold problems. Except for the case of ideographic writing systems, it is generally reading skills which provide least difficulty. By contrast, Eastern Asian, and more recently especially Chinese visiting students and PhD researchers have admitted that they often have difficulty understanding spoken German, despite the fact that they have previously passed examinations in German. It is evident from German professors' lecturing style that they are seldom aware of these difficulties. There is a lack of knowledge about the difference in time needed to acquire passive linguistic skills rather than active linguistic skills – in each case, for successful academic communication. However, this question exceeds the frame of reference for the present book (see Quetz 2002; Quetz/ Vogt 2009).

One further question must be addressed: Which would be more effort-intensive for some academics or for all academics worldwide: a single academic language or more than one? Working towards an answer, I feel compelled to resort to a simple model which can, however, be translated by analogy to cover more complex relationships. For this purpose, let us start with five equally sized groups of academics, each comprising ten people with different native languages (L1, L2, ... L5), and let us assume that all languages would require equal effort to learn for all participants. Let us also assume that – for circumstances similar to the present day, with globalisation and interdisciplinarity – all academics would have to learn all international languages. In this context, I distinguish between a) the effort for individuals and b) the effort for entire groups of speakers and c) the total effort for everyone (n = 50).

Model I (without differentiation of active and passive skills)

Case 1: Let only 1 language L (say, L1) be an (international) academic language. The speakers (native speakers) of L1 do not therefore need to learn any L: 0 language-learning processes per individual, 0 for the group (10 x 0). The speakers of L2, L3, L4 and L5 must learn 1 L (L1):

1 learning process per individual, 40 for the group (40 x 1). In total therefore, there are 40 language-learning processes (0 + 40);

Case 2: Let 2 L (L1 and L2) be academic languages. The speakers of L1 and L2 must then each learn 1 L (L2 or respectively L1): 1 language-learning process per individual, 20 for the group (20 x 1). The speakers of L3, L4 and L5 must each learn 2 L (L1 and L2): 2 per individual, 60 for the group (30 x 2). In total, that makes 80 language-learning processes (20 + 60);

Case 3: Let 3 L (L1, L2 and L3) be academic languages. The speakers of L1, L2 and L3 must then each learn 2 L (L2 and L3 or respectively L1 and L3 or respectively L1 and L2): 2 learning processes per individual, 60 for the group (30 x 2). The speakers of L4 and L5 must each learn 3 L (L1, L2 and L3): 3 per individual, 60 for the group (20 x 3). In total, that makes 120 language-learning processes (60 + 60);

Case 4: Let 4 L (L1, L2, L3 and L4) be academic languages. The speakers of L1, L2, L3 and L4 must then each learn 3 L (L2, L3 and L4 or respectively L1, L3 and L4 and so on): 3 learning processes per individual, 120 for the group (40 x 3). Furthermore, the speakers of L5 must learn 4 L (L1, L2, L3 and L4): 4 per individual, 40 for the group (10 x 4). In total, that makes 160 language-learning processes (120 + 40);

Finally, Case 5: Let all 5 L be academic languages. All 50 speakers must then each learn 4 L (all apart from their own): 4 per individual, 200 for the group (50 x 4). In total, there are also 200 language-learning processes (50 x 4).

The total learning effort therefore grows steadily with the number of academic languages. For individuals, the learning effort also rises, but not constantly for everyone. For speakers of L5, the effort rises no further at the transition from case 4 to case 5. Furthermore, in case 5, but only in case 5, the asymmetry between groups disappears. These trends will occur by analogy for larger numbers of speakers and languages.

The model becomes more realistic if a distinction is introduced between merely passive use of language and active use (active ≠ passive). All academics then require active skill in (at least) one of the academic languages, but only passive skill in the others. This presupposes the capability for "polyglot dialogue" (Posner 1991b; Ch. A.3), in which one side uses a language actively and the other passively. As mentioned above, since no generally valid quantification is available for how much smaller the learning effort for passive skills is than for active skills, I have applied two possibilities randomly: a 0.5 fraction and a 0.8 fraction of the effort for the acquisition of active skills – in the following, the data are separated by a stroke (0.5/0.8).

Model II (with differentiation of active and passive skills)

Case 1': Let only 1 L (L1) be an (international) academic language. This case remains unaffected by the distinction between active and passive. Once again, speakers (native speakers) of L1 do not need to learn any L: 0 language-learning processes per individual, 0 for the group (10 x 0), and speakers of L2, L3, L4 and L5 must each actively use (learn active use of) 1 L (L1): 1 learning process per individual, 40 for the group (40 x 1). In total, that also makes 40 language-learning processes (0 + 40);

Case 2': Let 2 L (L1 and L2) be academic languages, of which everyone must use one actively and one passively, where both parameters for the effort for passive use: 0.5/0.8 are applied. Speakers of L1 must use L2 passively, and speakers of L2 must use L1 passively: 0.5/0.8 language-learning processes per individual, 10/16 for the group (20 x 0.5/0.8). The speakers of L3, L4 and L5 must each use one of the 2 L (L1 or L2) actively and the other passively: 1.5/1.8 per individual, 45/54 for the group (30 x 1.5/1.8). In total, that makes 55/70 language-learning processes (10/16 + 45/54);

Case 3': Let 3 L (L1, L2 and L3) be academic languages, of which all academics must use 1 actively and 2 passively. Speakers of L1, L2 and L3 must use 2 L passively: 1/1.6 per individual,

30/48 for the group (30 x 1/1.6) speakers of L4 and L5 must use 1 L actively and 2 passively: 2/2.6 per individual, 40/52 for the group (20 x 2/2.6) in total, that makes 70/100 language-learning processes (30/48 + 40/52);

Case 4': Let 4 L (L1, L2, L3 and L4) be academic languages, of which all academics must use 1 actively and 3 passively. Speakers of L1, L2, L3 and L4 must use 3 L passively: 1.5/2.4 per individual, 60/96 for the group (40 x 1.5/2.4). Speakers of L5 must use 1 L actively and 3 passively: 2.5/3.4 per individual, 25/34 for the group (10 x 2.5/3.4). In total, that makes 85/130 language-learning processes (60/96 + 25/34);

Case 5': Let all 5 L be academic languages, of which now, all academics must use 4 passively: 2/3.2 per individual, 100/160 for the group (50 x 2/3.2). In total, that also makes 100/160 language-learning processes (50 x 2/3.2).

The total effort for merely passive use is less than in Model I, but it also rises steadily in line with the number of academic languages. Once again, for speakers of L5, the effort increases no further at the transition from case 4' to case 5', and, similarly, the asymmetry between the groups disappears in case 5', but only in case 5'. Here also, the trends apply by analogy for larger numbers of speakers and languages.

It can be seen that the learning effort for individuals, groups and the totality is lowest in each case with only one international academic language and rises steadily with a growing number of international academic languages. This is presumably an essential – if also obvious – driving force behind the *de facto* trend in this direction, with English as the single "world language". But apart from the economy of the solutions, their symmetry or asymmetry is also significant. The most economic case (1 equals 1'), with the smallest effort for all participants, is in no sense symmetrical. Because of its asymmetry, it is unfair to the extent that the effort of foreign-language learning is unevenly distributed. The same applies for all other cases – apart from 5 and 5'. They are all unfair because of their asymmetry. Symmetry and fairness would require all native languages to be international academic languages (case 5 and 5'). Obviously, this is not possible, because the number of languages is too large.

A feasible, fair and, at the same time, economical solution would require a completely different approach – tending towards historically familiar paths: the international academic language ought to be no one's native language. For this, there are two options:

1) A "dead" language which has fallen out of use, possibly a classical language; or
2) A newly created, "artificial" or planned language.

Only a language which is foreign to everyone would also be a genuine lingua franca (Ch. A.3). Neither suggestion is new, and the most frequently proposed candidates are Latin (classical language) and respectively Esperanto (planned language). All academics would then have to learn the relevant language and could limit themselves to this language for international communication. As a result, an identical learning effort and a fair distribution of the burden would be guaranteed (if the diverging difficulties of learning resulting from different linguistic distances between starting languages are disregarded).

As mentioned at the beginning of the chapter, the option of a planned language as the (sole) world academic language still seemed realistic less than 100 years ago, when it was proposed to the League of Nations in 1921 by 12 nations, based on an initiative by the *British* and *American Association for the Advancement of Science*. The recommendation was for the "International Auxiliary Language" Esperanto, subject to assessment, with the justification that, "The acceptance of any modern national language would confer undue advantages and excite jealousy. [...] Therefore an invented language is best" (*Report of the Committee* [...] 1922). At that time, French was more prominent than English, for which reason France blocked the initiative; it harboured corresponding ambitions for its own language (cf. Ammon 1975: 140; also, Lins 1988: 54–61). Today, France would probably prefer an invented language rather than English. But the realisation of such a proposal seems impossible today. Prejudices against (artificial) languages, fuelled for a long time by opponents, would presumably be a minor obstacle (Ammon 1975: 140); even political resistance by the English-speaking world, which would lose its linguistic advantage, would probably not be decisive. By contrast, the enormous investments channelled into the learning and use of English, and to a lesser extent other "living" foreign languages, represent a considerably larger inertia. These investments would have to be written off. But that is not all: millions of English teachers and other FL teachers and professors, as well as translators and interpreters would lose their source of income. Shifting to a completely different, possibly artificial global academic language or even a world language would be accompanied by unimaginable economic consequences – and cannot be expected in the present age of long-term economic crises.

On the other hand, the asymmetry in favour of English makes it harder for other language communities to give up any vestiges of the former position of their language as an international academic language. To give up their language seems like a complete betrayal of the prestige and status of their own language to the English-speaking world. So long as scholarship is still carried out in German, e.g. in the German-speaking countries, and so long as non-German-speaking students and academics study or work here, German can be maintained as an international academic language (at least in vestigial form). There is also considerable interest in this project in the German-speaking countries (Ch. A.1; G.13). If all scholarship in the German-speaking countries in which non-German-speakers participate were to be conducted in English or in another foreign-language, and the German-language skills of foreigners (non-German-speakers) were to be limited to everyday communication for the purpose of "guest integration", German would, in effect, have entirely relinquished its position as an international academic language.

Considering all these findings, it seems an almost idle question to ask whether the language difficulties of international academic communication are greater with only a single international academic language or with several. However, this question deserves even more precise investigation than I have outlined provisionally here. One answer tailored for English-speaking academics is given by Scott L. Montgomery (2013) in a book, the title of which articulates the fundamental question: "Does Science Need a Global Language?". As might be expected, his answer is decidedly in the affirmative. But, at the same time, he warns his English-language comrades not to become complacent about their own language, because "[e]ven if that single tongue is global in extent. A native English-speaker who can read material in another language of science – Chinese, Spanish, Russian, Portuguese, German, French, or Japanese – is in a much superior position to a monolingual speaker" (ibid: 185). Having said this, it seems to me that this warning, tailored as it is for contemporary circumstances, contains a hidden conditional: so long as important scientific innovations are published in other languages and not always immediately translated into the same language, scientific monolingualism also contains disadvantages for every individual, even for scientists of the dominant academic language. And it therefore seems important to investigate the extent to which this still applies today.

13. Promotion of German as an international academic language?

The best way to promote German as an international academic language would be for the German-speaking countries to demonstrate outstanding scholarly performance. This is a widely accepted view which has been reiterated by Wolfgang Klein (2000: 290f.): "If the best experimental physics, the most innovative molecular biology, the most interesting cognitive psychology in the world were to be achieved by the University of Göttingen, even for a few years, people would read the corresponding papers [. . .] regardless of the language they were published in – perhaps not overnight, but very quickly". It should be added that the promotion of German as an international academic language would be best served if this outstanding scholarly research were published in German, even exclusively in German. But Klein doubts the possibility of such outstanding German performance and linguistic choice, which would have to continue for a certain duration to take effect. In fact, the findings reported in Ch. G.9 do not give much support to this hope, despite the "excellence initiatives" currently implemented in German universities. Limiting the language of publication to German also seems unlikely. Academics would be reluctant because of the uncertainty of such a language policy and the risk of being received with a delay outside the German-language territory. This point should sensitise us to the fact that promotional measures for German as an international academic language may have undesirable side effects, which must be carefully assessed and averted as required. Lack of appropriate awareness, not to mention appropriate assessment measures, are shortcomings of many promotional proposals. Potentially undesirable side effects introduce the need to draw a difficult dividing line between intended outcomes and undesired consequences. My warning here is not intended as an outright rejection of the following proposals, but rather as an appeal for caution. From among many proposals, I have selected a few which seem particularly relevant (further reference to this topic in Ch. K.3.2).

Proposals for strengthening the position of German as an (international) academic language are almost more strongly focussed on improving perceptions of scholarly performance outside the German-language territory than on improving performance itself. One example is the European citation index or "European citation bank" which was brought into play some time ago, having been demanded e.g. by the *ADAWIS* (*Guidelines of the Working Group on German as an Academic Language*: indent 7). The *HRK* [German University Rectors' Conference] has intensified this demand: "[A]t European level, an alternative [should] be established to the currently used bibliometric instruments, which gives intensified consideration to native-language publications. [. . .] Alternative European methods should also be developed to the English-language approach of measuring research performance based on citation frequencies" (*Recommendation "Language Policy in German Universities"* 12 November 2011: 3.1. Research: Publishing). What is being suggested here, is an alternative to the Thomson-Reuters citation indexes, which have been justifiably accused of giving precedence to English-language titles (Ch. G.3). The goal is therefore to create broader attention for other academic languages, including German. But for this purpose, publications written in these languages must be correspondingly cited, because a citation index cannot ignore citation frequency. Furthermore, the Thomson-Reuters indexes are now established worldwide and, despite considerable criticism, enjoy high prestige – which filters through to the academics whose publications are named in them. Apart from the doubtless considerable cost of alternative citation indexes, they would have to be prepared to endure long periods of low prestige before they could possibly catch up with the "establishment". It is even possible that being named in such indexes could be detrimental to an academic's reputation if they were not also named in the more established indexes. In view of the widespread belief that "cutting-edge research speaks English" (Markl 1986), this anxiety which accompanies a focus on non-English-speaking publications is certainly not delusional. The new indexes would therefore either have to contain the established ones or to be marketed as supplements, which may foster the idea that the entries are second rate. It is therefore no wonder that – so far as I know – this plan has not been taken up seriously.

A more realistic measure for broadening the perception of German scholarship outside the German-language territory is to have prominent works, especially in the humanities, translated.

Since 2008, translation has been funded especially by the *Börsenverein des deutschen Buchandels*. "The goal of funding translation from German is to contribute to worldwide distribution of research findings in the humanities from Germany and, at the same time, to maintain German as an academic language and as the language of initial publication of works in the humanities" (www.boersenverein.de/de/portal/Uebersetzungsfoerderung/186810). This measure seems appropriate as a means of supporting the existing, albeit modest international position of German in the humanities (Ch. G.6; G.7). I gratefully acknowledge that the translation of the present book has also been funded within this programme. However, it must also be stated – through whatever accompanying communication required – that the works translated represent only a small selection from a larger pool of valuable works which are still accessible only by reading them in German. This should prevent the false impression that all genuinely valuable publications will, in future, be translated into English anyway, so that readers can spare themselves the trouble of learning German and of reading the German-language texts.

Misunderstanding of English-language reports about research in German-speaking countries which have obviously been developed more from the English-language perspective than by German-speakers can also have a detrimental impact. On one hand, they serve to inform especially English-speaking academics who shy away from foreign languages and, on the other hand, they are no doubt also a response to complaints from non-English-speaking academics that their research has been unjustifiably ignored by the English-speaking world as well as globally (see Durand 2001, 2006; Ammon 2001a, b; 2003c, 2007d, 2010b; Carli/ Ammon 2007). One example is the periodical *Language Teaching: Surveys and Studies* (Cambridge University Press), which reports on non-English-language research in its field. The editor, Graeme Porte, wrote to me as follows (email 20 January 2011): "[W]e feel that too much L2 published research is L2 English focused and that there is very often an implied assumption in the papers that one-size-fits-all in methodological terms for all languages, when this is clearly not the case". "This cyclical series has been welcomed by our readers and began with a review of L2 French and continued with L2 German, L2 Spanish and Italian [L2 = second or foreign language! U.A.]". It would therefore be possible to report on non-English-speaking research, including German-language research in other disciplines. Perhaps this could also become an ultimately economically rewarding project for publishers in German-speaking countries. However, here again, there is a risk associated with the misunderstanding that readers are being informed about what is outstandingly important and can therefore save themselves the effort of reading the original texts, which would weaken the position of German as an international academic language.

International degree programmes in German universities (Ch. G.8) create a completely different opportunity for strengthening German as an international academic language. The idea of strengthening the global position of German by means of these degree programmes is generally obscured by concerns that they may be detrimental to the position of German. These programmes are delivered largely in English and are supposed to make German universities more easily accessible to foreigners and to boost the international competence of German academics, students and researchers. However, in view of the increased popularity among foreigners for studying in Germany or in the German-speaking countries, these programmes could also generate new learners of German, thereby strengthening the global position of German. This would happen if the foreigners attracted to Germany were to learn German during their stay in Germany. If this was not limited to everyday German for social integration but included academic German, it could also strengthen German as an international academic language. There is no doubt about the growth in the number of foreign students and academics (Ch. G.8), or indeed about the rise in the number of "academics of foreign origin" appointed in German universities – who are certainly associated with these degree programmes. The number for 2012 was

estimated at "around 35,000", with a rise of approximately 60% compared with 2006" (www.
bmbf.de/press/3611.php). However, their acquisition and use of German as an academic language remains uncertain. Some findings about the students are sobering (Fandrych/ Sedlaczek
2012;Ammon/ McConnell 2002: 137–170). I do not have data relating to teachers and researchers. The extent to which the corresponding German-language requirements frighten foreign
students and academics away from German universities but would attract precisely highly motivated and highly performing individuals requires further investigation. With their high student
fees, private universities can hardly even entertain language requirements. But at least the offer of
skills in German, if only for social integration though not for academic communication, would
hardly be detrimental to these universities. This could also promote the spread of German as a
foreign language (GFL) and therefore its global position.

Another possibility for promoting German as an international academic language with which
I conclude this topic, is provided by the German and German-speaking universities or degree
programmes recently springing to life in non-German-speaking countries (Ch. I.6; K.3.2). In
2014, with the title "Transnational Education", the *DAAD* funded a total of 55 "projects for
German universities abroad" (information from Roman Luckscheiter, *DAAD*). German was
the sole teaching language in three of these universities and German together with one or two
other languages in 23 universities. But in 24 cases, German was not a language of teaching at
all. 22 were exclusively English-language, and in 37, English was present as a language of teaching. Having said this, in a good half of the cooperations or foundations of German universities
funded by the *DAAD*, German was indeed the language of teaching and was therefore also
promoted as an academic language. But English played a significantly more important role. In
many cases, though, without being named in the *DAAD* documentation, learning German as a
subsidiary subject was in fact compulsory, but generally only up to the elementary level A1 or
A2 of the Common European Reference Framework (Quetz 2002). Such projects do open a
door to study in Germany and, to that extent, also provide potential support – via the possibility
of further local developments – for German as an international academic language.

Exceptional cases, such as the following, also deserve mention: the *Deutsch-Französische
Hochschule (DFH)/ Université franco-allemand (UFA)*, with its administrative headquarters in Saar-
brucken:"an association of 169 partner universities from Germany, France and – in the case
of tri-national degree programmes – other European countries [. . .]", for "bi-national degree
programmes with double-diploma degree and structured bi-national doctoral programmes and
network formation for early-career academics" and "tri-national degree programmes in other
European countries (Bulgaria, Canada, Spain, Luxembourg, the Netherlands, Poland, UK, Russia and Switzerland [. . .])" (de.wikipedia.org/wiki/Deutsch-Franz%C3%B6sische_Hochschule).
The position of German as an international academic language is no doubt also promoted by
such projects, although to an extent not yet fully understood.

H

GERMAN IN DIPLOMACY AND THE EUROPEAN UNION (EU)

1. History of German as a language of diplomacy

"Diplomacy is the art and praxis of negotiating between authorised representatives of different groups or nations (diplomats). The concept generally relates to international diplomacy, i.e. fostering cross-national or supra-national relationships by discussing matters such as the securing of peace, culture, the economy, trade and conflict" (de.wikipedia.org/wiki/Diplomatie; similar in Ostrower 1965: 99–107). In this sense, diplomacy is evidently an international action field *par excellence*, in which language choice impacts on the global position of languages. This involves the legal status of languages as well as their function, language choice in international organisations and diplomatic contacts, especially between nations with different official languages and native languages. These factors therefore offer valid indicators for the position of languages in the action field of diplomacy.

The conceptual differences introduced in Ch. A.3 are again appropriate for analysis of this kind of language choice. Countries with the same official language of state generally use their own language among themselves. This *international communication in the wider sense* (international and intra-lingual) is less relevant to the present book than communication between two countries with different official languages of state, which then relates to *international communication in the narrow sense* (international and interlingual). This can be further subdivided into *asymmetrical dominant* and *symmetrical*, and the latter can be further subdivided into *lingua-franca communication* and *polyglot dialogue* (or *passive bilingualism* or *multilingualism*). In the latter case, which occurs rather rarely, partners use their own language actively and their partner's language passively. The choice of a language for international communication in the narrow sense indicates and strengthens its international position. In this context, there is a correlation between the named types of language choice and the degree of internationalism of the languages. It is based on the following rank ordering of these types of language choice (1 = highest rank, ... 4 = lowest rank; e.g. German compared with other languages):

1. Lingua franca (*German* between Czechs and Hungarians);
2. Asymmetric dominance (*German* between Germans and Hungarians);
3. Polyglot dialogue (*German and Dutch* between Germans and Dutch people);
4. Non-use (*no German* between Germans and British people).

The more frequently a language is used in the higher-ranking type of language choice, the higher its international position.

The international position of a language in different action fields does correlate but not so closely that it can be inferred from one action field to the other. Especially not from business economics or academic language to diplomacy. The relative independence of these action fields is suggested by the once familiar topos that German used to be the language of science (Ch. G), English the language of trade (Ch. F) and French the language of diplomacy (e.g. Scott 1924; Braga 1979: 39f.; Ostrower 1965: 148). In fact, English is now the preferred language for international communication in all three action fields; but, in diplomacy, French continues to play a significant role. The international position of German in diplomacy is the topic of this chapter, which begins, as for the previous action fields, with a look back at history.

During the long period from the Roman Empire into the seventeenth century, Latin was the dominant language for diplomacy throughout Europe (Scott 1924; Ostrower 1965; Gerbore 1964: 114f.; Rudolph 1972). However, the "vernaculars", which, by contrast with later Latin, were "living" languages, with native speakers, played a limited but persistent role in diplomacy. This also applied to German, presumably at the latest since Emperor Karl IV of the *Holy Roman Empire* (reign 1355–1378). The efforts of the French King François I (reign 1515–1547) to strengthen the position of French, also, at least provisionally, with diplomacy in mind, are well known (Knecht 1994). But until the middle of the seventeenth century, Latin remained the dominant language in this action field throughout Europe.

Since that time, French diplomats, encouraged by successes in power politics and culture, have fought an increasingly tough battle to replace Latin with French. It must be remembered that, even in mediaeval times, French had been a prestigious language of culture. After François I made it into the sole national official language, it became the dominant language for diplomacy in Europe, at the latest under Louis XIV (1643–1715) (four stages of development, see Ostrower 1965: 288–319). In the negotiations for the Peace of Westphalia in Münster (1647/48), French negotiators notoriously used French instead of Latin, which would have been more appropriate given the linguistic diversity of the participants. But the other negotiating partners managed to ensure that the treaty itself was formulated in Latin. During negotiations in Mainz in 1682, following the annexation of Strasbourg by Louis XIV, French ambassadors insisted on the right to formulate their treaties in French. However, they did not demand an asymmetrical dominant use of French but suggested the use of German instead of Latin to the German-speaking representatives of the Holy Roman Empire (of the German Nation) (Rudolph 1972: 24). The authoritative (legally binding) versions of the treaty were to be in French and German, with Latin translation by way of assistance. The Treaty of Rastatt, signed by Prince Eugen on behalf of the Emperor, Karl VI, with the French Duke of Villars, in 1714, was formulated exclusively in French, although the Prince had initially insisted on Latin (Ostrower 1965: 293). "The transition to the 18th-century marks the approximate date from which French became dominant" (Rudolph 1972: 25).

By contrast with French, German was hardly protected by its regents. For the Holy Roman Empire, Latin remained the uncontested language of diplomacy, which is partly explainable because of internal and external opposition, but also especially because of the multilingual structure of the state. "The main reason for the failure of German as a language of political importance was the international organisation of the Holy Roman Empire, which strove to create the appearance of political continuity with the Ancient Empire of Rome. The official language of the Empire was Latin, and German linguistic advancement in international relations consequently suffered" (Ostrower: 145f.). In the Viennese Court, which followed the tradition of the Holy Roman Empire most closely, Latin remained the official language of correspondence up to WWI (Rudolph 1972: 24). Other reasons for reticence in the use of German include personal preferences for French, e.g. in the case of Friedrich II of Prussia.

Initially, even military victories over France did not destabilise the priority of French as the language of diplomacy in Europe. For instance, at the Congress of Vienna (1814/15), despite Napoleon's defeat, negotiations were held exclusively in French, and the treaty itself was for-mulated in French. The principal reason was that the languages of the victorious countries, German, English and Russian, were not known by all delegations. The fact that two of the four victorious powers (Austria and Prussia) and the meeting place, Vienna, were German-speaking, was not sufficient to secure a choice of German. But, then again, none of the German-speaking negotiating parties appears to have argued for the use of their own language. They were still far removed from the national(ist) sentiments of the ensuing "freedom fighters". Only when victorious powers began to think of themselves more in national terms, did they regard their own language as a national symbol and try to strengthen its position relative to other languages.

Provisional moves in this direction were made during the reign of Emperor Josef II (1765–1790), who declared German the official language throughout his multilingual empire in 1784 (see Ch. K.2; Stark 2002: 92). Because of resistance from other language groups, especially the Hungarians, he annulled this language decree on his deathbed.

Further significant government attempts to strengthen the position of German were not made until Bismarck, who saw the potential of language choice in diplomacy as an instrument of power. The following anecdote is informative: "In 1888, Bismarck was apparently asked what he considered the decisive factor in modern history. His laconic answer was that the North Americans speak English". The story has often been told as if it were a fact (e.g. by Limbach 2008: 66 or Van Parijs 2011: 217) But even Bismarck could only weaken the priority of French in diplomacy by attrition. For instance, the Versailles Peace Treaty in 1871 following the defeat of France by Prussia/Germany, was formulated monolingually in French. For a considerable time, German-speaking countries issued instructions for reports sent by their own foreign mis-sions to the government to be written in French. However, in 1862, having previously had to report in French while he was Prussian ambassador in St Petersburg (Zechlin 1960: 179, 194), Bismarck introduced German as the reporting language for Prussia. He also insisted on rigor-ous observance of the use of German in the Parliament of the German Empire, the *Reichstag* (Nass 1978: 14f.). His subsequent efforts also to use German in communication with foreign missions in Berlin had only limited success. "When the Foreign Office in Berlin attempted to correspond with diplomatic representatives there in German, they also replied in their own language" (Rudolph 1972: 27; Gerbore 1964: 116). "Bismarck instructed the Foreign Office in Berlin that replies must be made in German, if other states write in their own language, but that French should be used as a diplomatic mediating language for countries which wrote in French". Other languages were not accepted as lingua francas. But with France itself, equality of rights was robustly asserted. "Replies to France were to be written in German" (Rudolph 1972: 28). France adhered rigidly to its own language. Bismarck was said to have recommended the following rule for identifying the French ambassador in Berlin: "You wish to recognise the French ambassador? He is the only member of the diplomatic corps who only speaks French" (Gerbore 1964: 118).

In the Wilhelmine period, various attempts were made to strengthen German in diplomacy, not least as an international treaty language. Initial efforts strove to use German at least sym-metrically in treaty texts, including treaties with Britain, which, for its part, was confronting the predominance of French (e.g. Treaty with Samoa 1899, Yangtze Agreement 1900). Later, the German Empire even favoured dominant asymmetric treaties (with German as the domi-nant language), but these could only be asserted in the case of non-French speaking partners.

For example, the Treaty of Björkö with Russia (1905) was formulated in German as well as in French, but not in Russian. A similar procedure was adopted during WWI towards several allies (Treaties of Alliance, Germany–Turkey 1914, Germany–Bulgaria 1914). During the Wilhelmine period, there were however no exclusively German-language treaties with non-German-speaking partners, and less so during the Weimar Republic.

The prospects for further strengthening of German in diplomacy worsened after WWI. For example, German was excluded from significant new institutions for international diplomacy which adopted English alongside French (Ch. H.3). The Versailles Treaty negotiations, for which German and, for different reasons, Russian were not even considered, played a significant part: "Russia was in a state of revolutionary turmoil and the Germans were defeated in the field of battle, thus the Russian and German languages were out of contest" (Ostrower 1965: 360). At the insistence of British negotiator Lloyd George and American President Wilson, the *de facto* winners of the war, and against fierce resistance from France, English became the second negotiating language of Versailles (Ostrower 1965: 360–371; Rudolph 1972: 93–96). Britain and the USA had already tried to undermine the supremacy of French in diplomacy, admittedly without convincing success (details in Ostrower 1965: 347–359). Only the position of strength attained by both countries after WWI opened their approach to this goal: English became a negotiating language in Versailles, and the Treaty itself was formulated in English as well as French.

The fact that the first 26 articles of the treaty at the same time formed the constitution of the newly founded League of Nations (headquarters in Geneva, active from 1920) was of great importance for the future position of these two languages in diplomacy. French and English also became its official languages and working languages (Art. 10, 11 and 16), a status which they retained exclusively throughout its existence until 1945, when the UN was founded as successor organisation (Ostrower 1965: 365; Rudolph 1972: 34f.). German was never considered an official language of the League of Nations, especially since Germany was only admitted in 1926 and left again in 1933 under Nazism. Incidentally, a larger number of working languages would have been a hindrance at that time, because only consecutive interpreting was available but not simultaneous interpreting. This only became possible later, in the UN. With two languages, the time required for speeches and contributions to discussions was therefore doubled, with three languages, it was tripled and so on. This is certainly one of the reasons why efforts to introduce Spanish as a third working language for the League of Nations ultimately failed.

The rise of English to become a language of diplomacy even more important than French can be explained partly with reference to the economic and military power of the English-speaking world, especially the USA, but it was also promoted by support from other countries in which English was neither the official language nor a widespread native language. For example, Japan and Greece voted against France in favour of English alongside French as an official language and working language of the Permanent Court of International Justice, which was founded in 1920 as a component of the Versailles Treaty (Article 14) with headquarters in The Hague (Ostrower 1965: 367f.). Support from third parties (without official status of the language or large numbers of native speakers) is an important factor for the spread of languages (Lieberson 1982). German lacked this support which it would have needed to establish itself as a language of diplomacy.

Through the loss of all German colonies after WWI, an important base for wider international influence was also removed from the German language. Conrad/ Fishman (1977) have shown that, outside its native country, English became an official language especially in nations which had previously been colonies of the native country or colonies of a former colony of the native country, namely the USA. The same applies for French, Spanish and Portuguese. A long period of colonial dominance was crucial for anchoring as an official language. This never existed in the German colonies, and German has not been maintained in any of them – with the possible exception of Namibia (cf. Ch. E.4.9).

During the Weimar Republic (1918–1933), it was not possible to strengthen the position of German in diplomacy. In the subsequent period of "National Socialism" (1933–1945), some expansion was achieved through brute violence, but this was completely unsustainable. For example, only the German text of the Munich Agreement of 1938 between Germany, Britain, France and Italy was authoritative, although there were translations into English, French and Italian; and the German-French armistice agreement of Compiègne in 1940 was formulated only in German. But to secure a language in an action field or a domain, it is necessary for its corresponding use not only to be *accepted* as a necessity based on power relations but ultimately to be *adopted*, i.e. internalised in the full sense of a norm (see Bartsch 1985: 218). Nothing could have been more obstructive to such an adoption of German for diplomacy than the behaviour of Nazi Germany.

Immediately following this period, German was universally rejected by other nations. It had no supporters at the time of foundation of the UN (1945), when significant guidelines for languages in international diplomacy were set out (Ch. H.3). It seemed unlikely that German could ever recover a position it had not managed to achieve during a period of power, as Ostrower (1965: 148) emphasises with subliminal derision: "German [. . .] never acquired the position of a diplomatic form of linguistic expression, even under the Kaiser Wilhelm II or Hitler, the most steadfast champions of the German idiom". The present situation is also often summarised approximately as follows: "Today, English and French are accepted (as they have been for centuries) as worldwide languages of diplomacy. Both are the exclusive working languages of the UN. They are also the official languages of numerous international organisations (e.g. UNESCO, NATO, the International Olympic Committee, International Red Cross)" (de.wikipedia. org/wiki/Diplomatie; original emphasis removed). However, in terms of practical language use, French has now fallen far behind English. Alongside the various reasons associated with globalisation (cf. De Swaan 2001; Crystal 2003; Graddol 2006; Ch. A.7), the growing importance of informal consultation also supports the dominance of English. According to Stephen B. Pearl (1996: 33), "a rise in the practice of informal consultation" almost always leads to the choice of English as a lingua franca, for example, in nine of the ten informal consultations he observed in the UN, in which native speakers of other UN official languages, Arabic, Chinese, Russian, Spanish "and even French" were participants. The minimex rule, according to which, if possible, no participants should be entirely excluded from the communication (minimisation of the "ex"), evidently comes into play here, so that the language chosen is one which everyone knows at least a little – in most situations today, this is English (Van Parijs 2007b: 39; 2011: 13–17; Ch. A.6). The dominance of English in diplomacy is also served by the fact that, when communicating with heads of governments of other countries, American presidents are distinguished by the fact that they do not speak any foreign languages. Franklin D. Roosevelt was evidently the last US president able to speak a language other than his own (en.wikipedia.org/wiki/List_of_multilingual_Presidents_of_the_United_States). The next chapter is devoted to the history of German as a cross-national treaty language, and the chapter after that to international organisations.

2. German as a cross-national treaty language

The available data allow statistical underpinning of the historical sketch above, especially regarding international treaties. For the period 1492–1963, the *Vertrags-Plötz* (Vols. 3, 4a, 4b; Rönnefart/ Euler 1958, 1959, 1963) gives a relatively complete overview of cross-national treaties, including treaty date, states participating and generally also treaty languages. Of course, it would

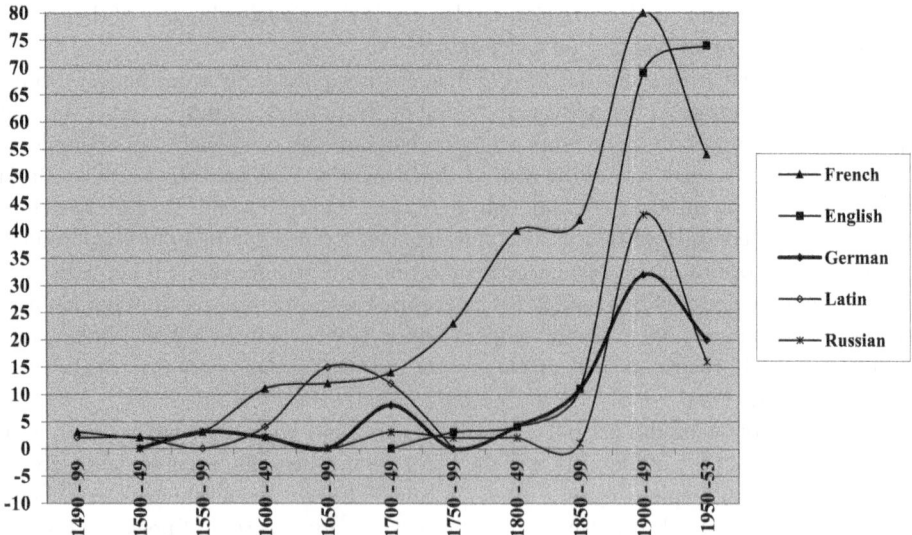

Figure H.2–1 Total frequency of the five most frequently used languages in cross-national treaties 1492–1963

(*Source*: based on Rönnefart/ Euler 1958, 1959, 1963)

be desirable to continue this analysis up to the most recent history. Figure H.2–1 shows the periods and frequencies in which German, English, French, Latin and Russian have been used (total frequency). The figures relate to the languages most frequently used for cross-national treaties in the respective period.

If the period up to 1550 is disregarded because of the small number of treaties, it is evident that Latin was still being used as a treaty language as often as French around 1700. Only after this does French start to gain a significant lead, which it retains for a long time until the period 1900–1949. French then loses this lead to English only after 1950.

In the period 1850–1899, and especially 1900–1949, the number of treaties formulated in German and in Russian also increases. Even since the middle of the sixteenth century, German plays a role, albeit a modest role with interruptions, into the second half of the seventeenth and eighteenth centuries. The German involved here is High German (as always in this book when the term *German* is used without further specification), not Low German. The figures for the final, short time interval (13 years) are as follows: English 74, French 54, German 20, Russian 10. It is remarkable that Arabic, with 22 treaties, scores higher than German, and that other languages also score relatively high values (Chinese 15, Spanish 14, Portuguese 6). However, these languages have not been included in the diagram because they are not among the five most frequent languages in the period overall.

A fuller picture of the international treaty languages is provided by considering (asymmetric) dominant use (Ch.A.3). In this context, one language is considered dominant if the language of at least one treaty partner in the treaty is not used (where the "language of the treaty partner" is a language which is both the native language of a considerable part of the population of that country and is also the official language of state). In the case of multilateral treaties, there can also be several dominant languages (provided the language of at least one partner is still excluded). Figure H.2–2 gives an overview of the most frequent dominant languages in the total period:

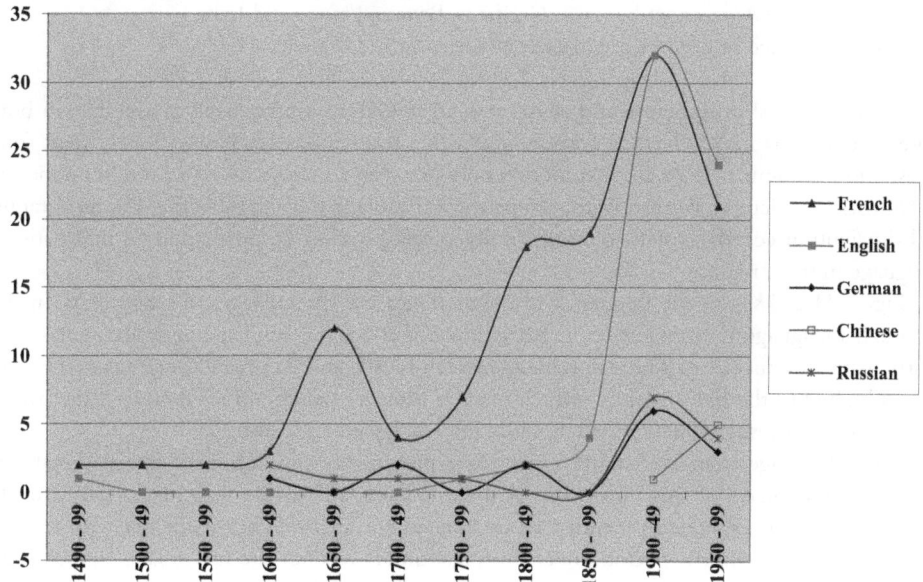

Figure H.2–2 Frequency of the five most frequent (asymmetric) dominant languages in cross-national treaties 1492–1963

(*Source*: based on Rönnefart/ Euler 1958, 1959, 1963)

Chinese, German, English, French and Russian. Latin is not included, because it is not the native language of a considerable part of the population of any treaty partner.

In general, dominance exhibits a similar characteristic to that of total frequency. However, English overtakes French even in the period 1900–1949, and Chinese outstrips German in the most recent period. Conversely, the figures in the most recent period show a general decline, including English. One reason for this – alongside the relatively short time interval – is certainly a growing aversion to any symbolic inequality between states. The asymmetric dominance of languages in treaties symbolizes political dominance and is generally avoided today (Rudolph 1972: 40, 54f.). It will thus be worthwhile to consider treaties with a dominance of German (other dominant languages in brackets):

1629 Peace of Lübeck: Kaiser Ferdinand II and Denmark;
1719 Peace of Stockholm: Sweden and Hanover;
1720 Peace of Stockholm: Sweden and Prussia;
1805 Treaty of Potsdam: Czar Alexander I of Russia and King Friedrich Wilhelm III of Prussia;
1812 Convention of Tauroggen: Russia and Prussia;
1905 Treaty of Björkö: Russia and Germany (also French);
1914 Treaty of Alliance between Germany and Turkey (also French);
1915 Treaty of Friendship and Alliance between Germany and Bulgaria (also French);
1915 Military Convention between Germany, Austro-Hungary and Bulgaria (also French);
1920 Peace Treaty of Trianon between Austria, the Allies and Hungary (also French, English and Italian);
1922 Treaty of Rapallo between Germany and the Soviet Union (also French);

1938 Munich Agreement between Germany, Britain, France and Italy;
1940 Armistice of Compiègne between Germany and France.

Events in WWI, shortly before and at the start of WWII are immediately noticeable; in both cases, the dominance of German corresponds with a relatively crude power policy. Apart from these cases, a dominance of German occurs only between German-speaking and Scandinavian (Denmark, Sweden) or Eastern European partners (Russia, Hungary, Bulgaria). This geographical distribution correlates with the historically strong position of German as an international language in these regions.

Figure H.2–3 shows the frequency of lingua franca use of languages in treaty texts. In this context, a language is considered a lingua franca if it is not the language of at least one of the participating partners, e.g. if French is used between Russia and Germany. Once again, the analysis is limited to the five languages which serve as most frequently lingua francas in the overall period under investigation: German, English, French, Italian and Latin.

Three languages stand out here, which were presumably the dominant international languages of diplomacy at this time. One of these is Latin, still acting as a lingua franca up to the middle of the eighteenth century; its frequency as a lingua franca coincides with its total frequency because (in the period under investigation), it was not the native language of a significant part of the population of any country. From the middle of the eighteenth century until the middle of the twentieth century, French was the most important lingua franca, but English rises in the middle of the nineteenth century and overtakes French in the most recent period after 1949.

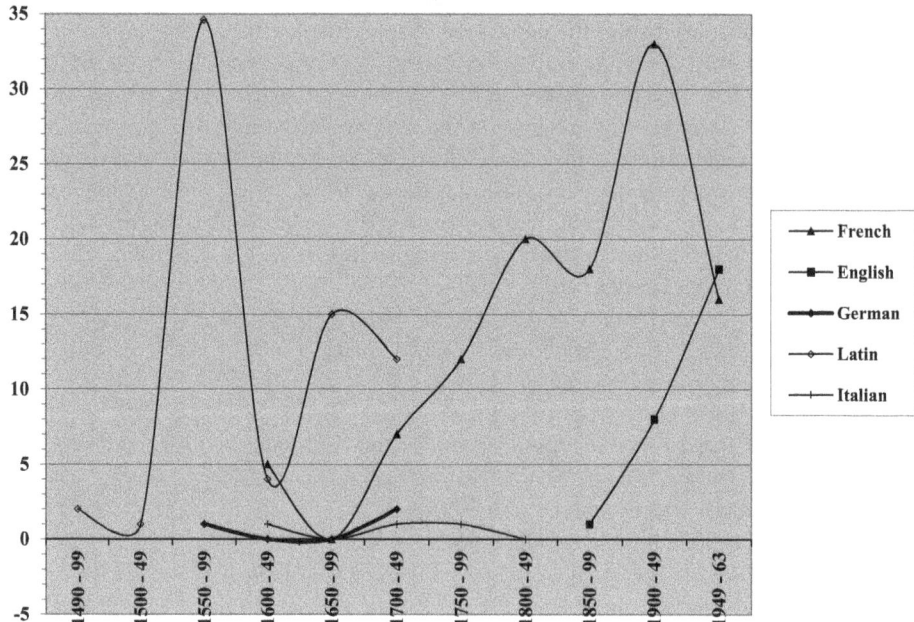

Figure H.2–3   Frequency of the five languages most frequently used as lingua francas in cross-national treaties between 1492–1963

(*Source*: based on Rönnefart/ Euler 1958, 1959, 1963)

By contrast, German was hardly ever a treaty lingua franca, apart from the following three treaties:

1570 Peace of Stettin: Denmark and Sweden;
1720 Peace of Friedrichsburg: Denmark and Sweden;
1720 Peace of Nystad: Russia and Sweden.

These treaties fit with the geography of dominant use of German mentioned above. If anywhere, German played a dominant role as a language of diplomacy in Scandinavia and Eastern Europe, and, in fact, before the middle of the eighteenth century, before French also became the dominant language there. Ostrower describes this situation and establishes that, "German language and political thought predominated there" for the period of Czar Peter the Great (1696–1725). The after-effects were evident in the foreign languages taught at the Military Academy of St Petersburg, e.g. in the figures for 1731, when German was chosen by 237 students compared with 51 for French and 15 for Latin. Although Peter's daughter, Czarina Elizabeth, tried to oust German with French, which was successfully used in Western Europe, German retained a strong position in the Russian court alongside French. Still at the time of Czar Alexander I, at the start of the nineteenth century, the British Ambassador to the Russian Court, Lord George Forbes, complained about "the German linguistic claims in Russia which forced him, at his age, to study that language". However, Alexander I expressly stipulated French as the official language of the Russian Foreign Ministry (Ostrower 1965: 448f.). The delayed dominance of French as the language of diplomacy in Russia and Scandinavia was also associated with the geographical situation in these regions. German was never completely ousted by French as the language of diplomacy, only perhaps more recently by English. Otherwise, from the seventeenth century onwards, French was predominant in treaties between German-speaking and non-German-speaking states. However, for treaties between German-speaking states themselves, it remained the exception. In the middle of the eighteenth century, German is, remarkably, only found in the following cases, always with Prussia as one of the treaty partners:

1742 Preliminary Peace Treaty of Breslau: Prussia and Austria;
1745 Peace of Dresden: Prussia and Austria or respectively Prussia and Saxony;
1779 Peace of Teschen: Prussia and Austria.

These treaties dominated by Prussian power politics confirm the well-known preference for French in the court of Frederick the Great (reign 1740–86). But in relationships with German-speaking states, Prussia did not retain this preference for French for long. Even in 1785, still under the reign of Friedrich II, Prussia resolved the "League of German Princes" with Hanover and Saxony in German. Apart from the Prussian treaties in the middle of the eighteenth century, French was clearly the treaty language between German-speaking states only in one case, the "Treaty of Ried" in 1813, between Austria and Bavaria. At this time, Napoleon I dominated all the German-speaking countries and made French into the official language in the German-speaking Rhineland (von Polenz 1994: 73; Pabst 1997). Otherwise, French was the cross-national treaty language for German-speaking countries only with non-German-speaking treaty partners. Through its use in treaties, especially between German-speaking states, German also became terminologically elaborated for international treaties.

However, into the last quarter of the nineteenth century, most treaties between German-speaking and non-German-speaking states are not formulated in German but in French or respectively, in earlier periods, in Latin. Bilateral treaties with France were always in French, as was the Preliminary Peace of Versailles of 1871 and the Peace Treaty of Frankfurt, signed in the same year – in spite of the Prussian–German victory over France. Only towards the end of the nineteenth century were treaties with non-German-speaking states increasingly formulated in German, together with the language of the treaty partner, even between the German Empire and Britain, e.g.

1898: Angola Treaty;
1899: Samoa Treaty;
1900: Yangtze Agreement.

What is expressed here is that Britain, the USA and the German Empire, which was behaving in an increasingly imperialist manner, no longer fully accepted the linguistic priority of French in diplomacy. Ultimately, the German Empire no longer accepted the dominance of French even in relations with France. The Morocco Agreement of 1909 between France and Germany is formulated in French and German, both versions being equally binding. In the Wilhelmine period therefore, German "emancipated" itself from French as a treaty language. This remained the case after WWI, as confirmed by a list of languages in treaties in the 1920s (Hudson 1932).

Changes in the choice of treaty languages around the turn-of-the-century are associated with two trends:

(1) Attempts to make the national/home language the dominant language of diplomacy; therefore, also isolated cases of asymmetric dominant use of German in conjunction with Germany's power-political ambitions;
(2) Efforts to guarantee all treaty partners a version in their own language, especially when only a few parties were involved, e.g. in bilateral or trilateral treaties (Hudson 1932: 372).

These trends can be designated (1) the *dominance principle*, (2) the *equality principle*. The dominance principle was certainly crucial in ensuring that the Armistice of Compiègne in 1918 was formulated only in French, and the Peace Treaty of Versailles of 1919 was formulated only in French and English. The equality principle came into play later, after WWI, when, in bilateral treaties with the victorious powers, Germany was again respected as a treaty partner (e.g. the Peace of Berlin of 1921 between the USA and Germany: German and English). After WWII, the equality principle was generally also asserted in the global context of decolonisation. In recent history, there have been no treaties with German-speaking states in which German is not a treaty language.

3 Official languages and working languages of international organisations

The present book has shown repeatedly that it is advantageous for individuals, institutions and nations to use their own language (native language or official language of state) for international contacts (Ch. A.3). They not only have communicative and emotional (psychological) advantages but also financial gains by avoiding the costs for translation and interpreting. Under present circumstances, English-speaking diplomats manage without interpreters much more frequently than diplomats from other language communities. Powerful states have therefore repeatedly tried to establish their own language for diplomatic communication. France has been particularly persistent and successful (Ostrower 1965: 267–319; Rudolph 1972: 23–28; Ch. H.1; H.2). But success for such nations is accompanied by corresponding disadvantages for countries less successful in their language policy. Non-French-speaking diplomats have often been reluctant to accept French as the sole language of diplomacy, questioning its future use in treaties by means of proviso clauses e.g. in the Peace of Rastatt 1714 between France and the Holy Roman Empire (Ostrower 1965: 293) or the Vienna Congress Acts 1815 (Gerbore 1964: 116; in general, see Ostrower 1965: Ch. 11 and 13). As a result, the priority of one language in diplomacy has remained a convention with a doubtful legal basis. Greater stability is guaranteed by international political organisations agreed upon by different states. Within them, preferred languages are specified with legal force by means of statutes (Tavernier 1988) which are difficult to revise. The statutory provisions in international political organisations also strengthen the position of languages elsewhere in diplomacy, which, in turn, further strengthens their position in the organisations through feedback mechanisms. For German, it was certainly disadvantageous that the two most important international political organisations in earlier history were founded at times of evident weakness of the German-speaking countries: the League of Nations after WWI and the United Nations (UN) after WWII (for the correlation with the international position of German, see Ammon 1991d).

The League of Nations resulted from the Treaty of Versailles of 1919 (Ch. H.1), the first 26 articles of which simultaneously formed the constitution of the League of Nations. Articles 10, 11 and 16 specified French and English, the languages of the victorious powers of WWI, as the sole official languages of the League of Nations. When Ostrower (1965: 360) points out that German and Russian were not considered because of their defeat in the war and the confusion of revolution in their countries, this might suggest that they may have been considered as official languages of the League of Nations under different political conditions. The fact that Russian attained the status of an official language and subsequently also a working language of the UN after WWII is also significant in this respect. It further supports the suggestion in Ostrower's account that languages of victorious nations have a better chance of achieving official status in an international organisation than languages of defeated nations. This certainly applies for the two international political organisations founded immediately after the world wars. After WWII, it was important for France to be recognised as a victorious power. Of course, other factors were involved. For example, at the time of foundation of the League of Nations and the UN, French had a much stronger tradition as a language of diplomacy than German – and also than English, although, by contrast, French enjoyed a smaller global distribution and had a weaker numerical and economic basis (Ch. D.4 and respectively C.2 and C.4).

The prestige of German was more seriously damaged after WWII than after WWI. But the number of candidate languages for official status was now greater than previously in the League of Nations. At the foundation conference in San Francisco in 1945, a distinction was made for reasons of expediency between *working languages* and *official-only languages*. I have introduced the term official-only languages as an ancillary term to refer to a more limited status. By contrast with official-only languages, more explicit reference can be made to *full-official languages*, which are also working languages.

No explicit reference is made to the official status of languages in the founding treaty of the UN, but the original five official languages are identifiable from the fact that the treaty is formulated in all five. From the outset, it was understood that all five languages could be used without restriction, but that it would not always be required to translate or interpret into all of them. However, directly from 1945 onwards, translation and interpreting would be provided from all official languages into English, French and, from 1948, also into Spanish – only into these three languages. In this sense, these three languages were therefore working languages – by contrast with Chinese and Russian which remained official-only languages for a considerable time, despite insistence to the contrary by the Soviet Union and China (Ostrower 1965: 407–421,

422–427). In 1973, Arabic was added as a sixth official-only language, initially only for the General Assembly and its six principal committees, with financing by the Arab states for the first two years. However, the difference between working languages and official-only languages became blurred over time. For example, especially at the General Assembly and in the Security Council, "the official languages [= official-only! U.A.] and working languages have since been merged, so that interpreting is provided from every language into every language, and all documents appear in all languages [the six official languages! U.A.]" (Paqué 1980: 165). Beyond this, however, the distinction no longer exists (for a more detailed, but still valid overview, see Tabory 1980: 7–20; more up-to-date, but less detailed, see Unser 2004: 185–187; Wu 2005: 47–50).

To attribute the non-adoption of German among the UN official languages exclusively to Nazism and its consequences would be an oversimplification. This is evident from the criteria for the five original official languages, which were, in fact, not presented explicitly, but can be plausibly reconstructed. At the time, they could not have included the German language without difficulty, and possibly could not do so today. Deeper causes for this deficit must be sought in the history of the German-speaking countries. I note here only a few of the more striking instances (see also Ch. H.1). One such cause with a long history is the sustained national territorialism within the German-language region; with further fragmentation through religious, confessional conflicts, such as the Thirty Years' War (1618–1648); delayed formation of a nation state compared with France or Britain (German Empire 1871); and the correspondingly short-lived period of colonialism (1884–1918), so that, as an official language of state, German was restricted to Central Europe. Added to this are the exclusion of Germany from the League of Nations until 1926 and its rapid withdrawal in 1933. National Socialism (1933–1945) then destroyed any chance of rehabilitation of German as a language of diplomacy.

Alexander Ostrower has summarised the significant reasons for adoption as a UN official language as he sees them (Table H.3–1).

For Arabic, which was adopted in 1973, the same reason applies (language of numerous states in the Middle East, official language of 22 states at that time, 23 today, according to Banks/ Muller/ Overstreet 2007, or 26, according to *Fischer Weltalmanach 2007*) as for Spanish. Accordingly, German is outscored by the UN official languages: either because of the number of states (English, French, Spanish, Arabic) in which it is an official language of state or because of the number of speakers (English, Spanish, Russian, Chinese, Arabic) or because of both (English, Spanish, Arabic). According to these criteria, it would be legitimate for German to be excluded. But factors in favour of German include the economic power of the German-speaking countries, which have also given considerable financial contributions to the UN since their joining (Austria 1955, FRG and GDR 1973, Liechtenstein 1990, Switzerland 2002); the wide global

Table H.3–1 Reasons for adoption as official languages of the UN

Languages	Reasons for adoption
French and English	"two international languages with a distinguished record of past performance in diplomacy"
Spanish	"language of [. . .] Central and South-American countries"; "better choice [than Portuguese]"
Russian	"the language of one of the two dominant powers"
Chinese	"the idiom of the largest and most populous power on the Asiatic mainland"

(*Source*: Ostrower 1965: 406)

distribution of German as a foreign language (Ch. I.7); and – at least in the 1970s, when joining the UN seemed conceivable – the significant tradition of German as an international academic language, though it was already beginning to decline at that time (Ch. G.1). However, there are no criteria for the official status of languages in the UN, at least no criteria recognised by the majority, which relate to this.

Having a large number of states with the same official language of state not only guarantees votes for adoption as a UN official language, but also allows "deals based on reciprocity", e.g. between Spanish-speaking and Arabic-speaking states (Ostrower 1965: 412f.). When the Spanish-speaking states were struggling to increase the status of Spanish to a working language, they were supported by the Arabic states with the clear expectation that they would support the Arabic states regarding the Arabic language when the time came, and it did. Such "collaboration" was not available to the German-speaking states if only because of their small number and late joining. Austria joined in 1955, the FRG and the GDR in 1973; Liechtenstein and Switzerland even later (1990 and 2002 respectively).

Nevertheless, there are indications that the UN anticipated a request for official status of the German language when the FRG and GDR joined the UN (Tabory 1980: 43), especially since Arabic became a UN official language in the same year. However, the German faction did not file a request. This received wide criticism, including my own (e.g. Ammon 2005c: 92; 2009a: 122; 2010a: 98), as a missed opportunity for German language policy abroad – with serious consequences difficult to assess. A request may in fact have been hopeless, perhaps even damaging to the prestige of the requester, because, in view of the appalling history of Germany, it might have been interpreted as a lack of sensitivity or sense of proportion. But there is still a need for clarification here, and a research project investigating the circumstances at the time and providing a well-founded assessment seem worthwhile.

It is indeed difficult to imagine the extent to which the lack of official status in the UN has impacted negatively on the global position of German, especially in the action field of diplomacy. Knowledge of the UN official languages is expected of diplomats worldwide. For the German Foreign Service, a sound knowledge of "two official languages of the UN is a prerequisite" (Bernhard E. Hauer, AA, email 22 November 2010). By contrast, outside Germany, there is a lack of training in German for diplomats even in universities with a special focus on German as a foreign language; e.g. at the National Linguistic University in Moscow, there are only "courses for UN interpreters/translators in the UN languages English, French and Spanish" (Alekseeva 2011: 131). Absence of the German language from UN communications distributed worldwide is detrimental to the prestige and therefore also the international position of German. The existence of this problem is suggested indirectly by the fact that it is so surprising when German is used, as the following notice in the British press confirms: "In New York last week, German Foreign Minister Joschka Fischer delivered a speech to the United Nations General Assembly. It wasn't the first time the statesman had done so, but until now, he's always spoken in English, without exception. This time he made his first official speech abroad in German" (www.dw.world.de/dw/article/0,1546,13454740,00.html). But such "appearances" of the German language on the world diplomatic stage are rare exceptions.

By contrast, there was an extremely modest gain in prestige when, one year after the joining of the FRG and the GDR, in 1974, German became a *document language* of the UN at the request of German-speaking members at the time (FRG, GDR, Austria) (Resolution 3355. XXIX of the General Assembly of 18 December 1974), with effect from 01 July 1975 (I am grateful to Volker Weyel, Chief Editor of the periodical *Vereinte Nationen*, and Ruprecht Paqué, first director of the German UN Translation Service, for this and other relevant information on German in the UN). As a document language, the most important documents of the General

Assembly and the resolutions of the Security Council and the Economic and Social Council are translated into German, and a German Translation Service was established for this purpose. However, the condition was that, in the long term, the costs must be borne entirely by the German-speaking countries – while, for the official languages, the UN pays for all translation and interpreting costs. In the case of Arabic, the UN bore the costs even during its time as a document language (1955–1973). Germany, Austria, Switzerland and Liechtenstein shared the costs for German as document language in proportion to their size. The term *document language*, which has become institutionalised, but does not occur in the formulation of the UN resolution, expresses the fact that translation into German will only be in writing and that (oral) interpreting is not to be provided (details in Jaschek 1977; Paqué 1980). Only the most important documents are translated, not all documents; this accounts for the designation *semi-document language* which is sometimes used (reference R. Paqué).

Despite the scale of the difference between a document language and an official language of the UN, informed observers believed that it could be overcome. At least, this was the view held by Mala Tabory (1980), who, as a teacher at the University of Tel Aviv (at the time of publication of her book), was beyond suspicion of representing the interests of the German-speaking countries:

> The process for the addition of German to the roster of United Nations languages has already begun. [. . .] However, based on the experience with Arabic, such a measure may be only the first step in the process of eventually adopting still another official and working language of the General Assembly. The delegations supporting the decision to translate documents into Arabic did not believe that it would establish a precedent for the addition of other languages, but those who warned that the precedent based on Arabic would be difficult to ignore in the future may be proven to be correct.
>
> *(Tabory 1980: 43)*

However, the anticipated boost to the status of German has not happened because there was no drive for it from German-speaking UN Member States.

In some of the other special organisations of the UN, German has a status similar to that in the General Assembly, the Security Council and the Economic and Social Council of the UN, as a kind of document language: namely, in the *World Post Union* (Tavernier 1988), the *Food and Agriculture Organisation* (Federal Government Report 1985: 85), the *International Labour Organisation*, the *World Health Organisation* and in the *World Bank* (Paqué 1980: 170) and the *World Organisation for Intellectual Property*, where patent applications can be filed in German (Tavernier 1988; de.wikipedia.org/wiki/Sonderorganisationen_der_Vereinten_Nationen). By contrast, in other sub-organisations of the UN, German does not enjoy any preferential status, not even in UNESCO (United Nations Educational and Cultural Organisation). This omission has sometimes been interpreted as serious discrimination (e.g. by Kloss 1974b: 36), especially because Italian and Hindi do enjoy a special status in this institution – alongside the six UN official languages. German outscores Italian in both the criteria relevant for the UN official languages (Table H.3–1): speaker numbers and number of states with official language, and for the latter criterion also outscores Hindi. Contrary to many Germans' self-image as the "*Volk der Dichter und Denker*" [people of poets and thinkers], factors, such as German political history before 1945 and an undervaluing of German culture, may have been involved here.

But the non-official status of German in other international political organisations, especially those with regional focus outside Europe, but also e.g. NATO, is hardly surprising. In the case of NATO, this is evidently a consequence of the wars and the fact that no German-speaking

Table H.3–2 Rank ordering of languages according to status in international political organisations

	Working language 1987	Working language 2007	Official language 1987	Official language 2007	Working or official language 2007
1. English	16	18	35	39	57
2. French	12	12	37	38	50
3. Spanish	9	10	19	23	33
4. Arabic	2	6	5	17	23
5. Chinese	5	5	10	8	13
6. Russian	1	5	4	8	13
7. Portuguese	0	2	3	9	11
8. German	1	1	3	4	5
9. Italian	0	0	2	3	3
10. Dutch	1	1	2	2	3
11. Kiswaheli	–	2	–	0	2
12. Danish	0	0	2	2	2
13. Swedish	–	0	–	2	2
14. Estonian	–	0	–	1	1
15. Finnish	–	0	–	1	1
16. Greek	–	0	–	1	1
17. Latvian	–	0	–	1	1
18. Lithuanian	–	0	–	1	1
19. Maltese	–	0	–	1	1
20. Norwegian	–	0	–	1	1
21. Polish	–	0	–	1	1
22. Slovakian	–	0	–	1	1
23. Slovenian	–	0	–	1	1
24. Czech	–	0	–	1	1
25. Hungarian	–	0	–	1	1

(*Sources*: Banks/ Muller 1987 and Banks/ Muller/ Overstreet 2007)

country is a nuclear power (cf. for the language regulations of various international organisations also Haselhuber 2012: 12–14).

Other possible data sources would also show the same weak position of German in international political organisations as noted in Table H.3–2, especially compared with English, French and Spanish. It is evident that precisely the six UN official languages are ranked at the top and that Portuguese is still ahead of German. This suggests that official status in the UN not only facilitates access to other international political organisations but also broad distribution as an official language of state, possibly across several continents. For example, Portuguese is an official language of state outside Europe, in South America and Africa, so that it reaches into international political organisations with a focus on these continents. For German, Banks/ Muller/ Overstreet (2007) indicate an official status only in European international political organisations, or in those with headquarters in Europe (official languages other than German added in brackets):

(1) Bank for International Settlements (headquarters in Basel, also English, French, Italian);
(2) Council of Europe (also Italian, Russian – and English, French as higher-ranking "official languages", to use the terminology of the Council of Europe (see below!);

(3) European Union (EU) (also 23 other official languages, since 1 July 2013);

(4) European Organisation for the Safety of Air Navigation (EUROCONTROL) (also English, French, Dutch, Portuguese);

(5) Food and Agriculture Organisation (FAO, special organisation of the UN, headquarters in Rome: also, the six UN official languages).

The details given in Banks/ Muller/ Overstreet (2007) are not always accurate (detailed criticism in Ammon 2015: 727f.). This applies e.g. to the designation of German as an official-only language in the EU instead of the correct indication as a working language. German has this status especially in the EU Commission, although it is positioned far behind English and French in *de facto* use (see Ch. H.4.2; H.4.6). Furthermore, the characterisation of the EU as an "international organisation" in Banks/ Muller/ Overstreet (2007) is questionable. Their data also ignore the fact that, compared with normal usage, the terminology of the Council of Europe reverses the use of "official languages" and "working languages". For example, in the Council of Europe, the status of German is called, a "working language", as for Italian and Russian, but, it is used *de facto* as an official-only language. The real working languages (= full-official languages) of the Council of Europe are English and French (based on Resolution 52 of the Council of Europe of 11 December 1970), but these are referred to in the Council as "official languages". Accordingly, the use of German, Italian and Russian is restricted compared with English and French (details in During 1995). For example, in the Parliamentary Assembly and the Committee of Ministers, resolution reports are formulated only in English and French (Rule 22, rules of court 2 March 1971).

The lower status of German compared with English and French in the Council of Europe (47 Member States in 2012) means that German cannot be a working language in the European Court of Human Rights or in the European Foreign Language Centre in Graz, both of which are institutions of the Council of Europe. It also means that, at the European College in Bruges (Belgium) and Natolin (Poland), where around 400 Europe experts are trained every year, German is not a teaching language or at least not a full teaching language, except in training for the language services – but it is a subject within individual degree programmes, especially for the diplomatic service.

A request by German-speaking and other Member States of the Council of Europe for German as "official language" (i.e. *de facto* working language) failed in 1994, as did various subsequent attempts. The best-known reason for this failure is probably: "So far, this has been unsuccessful because of lack of funds in the Council of Europe" (*Das Parlament* 11 May 2001: 17; Merker 2006: 66f.). But the German-speaking Member States contribute more to the budget of the Council of Europe than the French-speaking or English-speaking Member States. Perhaps this failure by the German-speaking states can provide a lesson about lack of diplomatic skill (regarding the failed language policies of Germany in the Council of Europe, see also Ch. H.4.6: paragraph 4). It also shows how difficult it is to introduce a language as an official language long after the foundation of the organisation (although the Arab states were successful in the UN). None of the German-speaking states were among the founding states of the Council of Europe on 5 May 1949. The FRG was the first German-speaking state to join on 2 May 1951; a request by the German-speaking states for official-language status for German was not made until 40 years later. But this example also reveals the consequences of "false economy", a charge which may be levelled against Germany. In the early 1990s, Liechtenstein was especially committed to the official-language status of German. This attempt may have been successful if Germany had accepted its fair share of the costs, which were in the range of the low single-figure millions. Austria and Liechtenstein were prepared to pay their share (Merker 2006: 58f.).

A comment made by one employee of the German delegation of the Council of Europe in a telephone conversation typifies the casual German attitude, at that time and later, which seems to be based on ignorance of the consequences: "It is not bad that German is not an official language. Everything is interpreted anyway". Stefanie Merker (2006: 54), who researched this question, adds the following: "This view seems to be shared by many delegates". She is referring here to Germany's delegates to the Council of Europe. Admittedly, the full details behind Germany's reticence will not be available for inspection until 2024, after the 30-year document-blocking period. But Germany's language policy towards the EU does not create an impression of clear diplomatic vision and skill (see Ch. H.4.6).

4. German in the European Union (EU)

4.1 Goals and history of the EU

When faced with the topic "German in the EU", German-speakers tend to think about the negative consequences for the position German in the EU and in the world. References to such negative consequences, including consequences for other languages, receive a different focus in each case, e.g. Phillipson (2003); Lohse (2004); Ginsburgh et al. 2005; Ehlich (2010); Haselhuber (2012) and Kruse (2012), as well as my own discussion of this topic (e.g. Ammon 2006g, 2007b, 2009b, 2009c). But this sense of dissatisfaction seldom goes so far as to doubt the advantages of the EU, which promises much more than mere problems of language. If doubts do arise, the EU would be seen as the greater good compared with a strong global position for the German language. Distilled down to its most important goal, the EU came into being to make war between Member States virtually impossible. So far, it has achieved this goal. In view of the history of Europe, whose negative course has been substantially shaped in recent history precisely by Germany, the priority of this goal seems beyond question. But the significance of language in the EU should not be underestimated, because it must be assumed that, in the long term, citizens will be satisfied with the community only under rules which are acceptable both to the majority and to language-sensitive minorities. Politicians and theoreticians in the EU have been aware of the challenge since the start, but with variable intensity.

The EU is neither an international organisation nor a state. Its position between the two categories has been described as a "confederation of states" and more recently an "association of states". The possibility of its developing into a federation has also often been raised as a realistic but not necessary possibility (e.g. report "Debate on federal Europe – Sigmar Gabriel (SPD) pushes for 'political union' [...] in the spirit of Helmut Kohl." EurAktiv.de 27 December 2001). However, all the Member States and ethnic groups in the EU look back over a long history of political or at least cultural and linguistic autonomy, which has left indelible traces in the identity of members and citizens – a fact which any EU language policy must consider (Coulmas 1991b; Haselhuber 2012: 228–232). The fact that the EU has managed this so far reveals its cautious, sometimes almost whimsical handling of linguistic diversity in the community. A sketch of the most important stages will suffice here as a historical overview, provided it sheds light on the relevant language rulings and conditions (details in Coulmas 1991b; Schloßmacher ([1994b] 1997: 7–11); A. Ross (2003: 15–20); Schreiner 2006a, 2006b; Haselhuber 2012: 6–12).

The beginnings of the EU were commercial mergers, initially the *European Community for Coal and Steel* (ECCS) founded in 1951 at the instigation of French foreign minister Robert Schuman. It established legally binding rights for the founding states: Belgium, Federal Republic of Germany, France, Italy, Luxembourg and the Netherlands. The *European Atomic Community* (EURATOM) and *European Economic Community* (EEC), which were orientated towards closer economic cooperation, were founded in 1957. All three European Communities were linked through the Treaties of Rome. In 1967, the three communities (ECCS, EEC and EURATOM) merged to form the *European Community* (EC), and established a joint *Council* and a joint *Commission*. From 1968 onwards, trade tariffs between the Member States were abolished in favour of a common external tariff. The *European Union* (EU) was then formed through the Maastricht Treaty which entered into force in 1993.

From the outset, the French government openly attempted to make French the sole official language of the institutions, but this was rejected by the other Member States. The precise background details still require further clarification. According to one commentator, the German government opposed the prioritisation of French – even if only statutory – and demanded parity for the German language: "*Dès le départ, les délégués allemands surprennent par la fermeté de leur propos concernant le régime linguistique. Ils exigent – sans compromis possible – que la langue allemande soit mise sur le même pied que la langue française. On envisage par conséquent quatre langues officielles* [. . .]" (Hemblenne 1992: 112; Stark 2000b: 96). According to other accounts, Belgium was – presumably unexpectedly – strongly opposed, because "the sensitive equilibrium inside Belgium was not compatible with a preference for one language, even at supra-national level [. . .]" (A. Ross 2003: 16). In any case (with the exception of Luxembourg), all national official languages of state of the six founding states became formally equal, official languages of the new community: German, French, Italian and Dutch. However, a French claim to "linguistic priority" – albeit largely latent – continued to exist and was also conceded in *de facto* language use (Haarmann 1973b: 122–130; cf. also, the language regimes considered in Haarmann 1974). But German also seems to have played a considerable role (K. Muller 2002: 46). Only after the subsequent inclusion of English did French lose its priority and German was pushed aside (cf. Ch. H.4.2; H.4.6). The overall language regime was established in 1958, in Regulation 1/58 of the legislative body, the Council. This also formed the basis for the inclusion of languages of subsequent Member States and is still in force today, as is the provision that any amendment shall require unanimous agreement of all Member States (Ch. H.4.2).

When the UK, Ireland and Denmark joined in 1973, the number of Member States rose to nine, and the number of the EU official languages rose to six (with the addition of Danish and English). Greece followed in 1981 with Portugal and Spain in 1986, increasing the number of Member States to 12 and the EU official languages to nine (Greek, Portuguese and Spanish added). Reunification of Germany in 1990 added the population and territory of the GDR to the EU. In 1995, Finland, Austria and Sweden joined, further increasing the number of Member States to 15 and the EU official languages to 11 (Finnish and Swedish added). This was followed, in 2004, by expansion to the east and south-east with the addition of ten states: Estonia, Latvia, Lithuania, Malta, Poland, Slovakia, Slovenia, Czech Republic, Hungary and Cyprus (Greek part), making a total of 25 Member States and 20 EU official languages (Estonian, Latvian, Lithuanian, Maltese, Polish, Slovakian, Slovenian, Czech and Hungarian added). After the adoption of Maltese (despite Maltese familiarity with English), Ireland also insisted on the status of an EU official language for its national language Irish (Gaelic), increasing the total to 21. In 2007, Bulgaria and Romania joined (27 Member States and 23 EU official languages). Finally, in 2013, Croatia joined (28 Member States and 24 EU languages). Other potential new Member States with new official languages are in preparation, primarily in the Western Balkans (Montenegro, Serbia, Bosnia and Herzegovina, Kosovo and Albania). However, the prospects for Turkey have worsened. Other European countries which would be welcome, such as the EFTA states, Norway, Liechtenstein and Switzerland, and the small states such as Andorra and San Marino, have shown no interest (de.wikipedia.org/wiki/Beitrittskandidaten_der_Europ%C3%A4ischen_ Union). There has also recently been a setback which would have been unimaginable even a

Table H.4.1–1 Development of the EU – arranged by entries and exits of Member States

1952/58	Belgium, Germany, France, Italy, Luxembourg, the Netherlands
1973	Denmark, Great Britain and Northern Ireland, Ireland
1981	Greece
1986	Portugal, Spain
1995	Finland, Austria, Sweden
2004	Estonia, Latvia, Lithuania, Malta, Poland, Slovakia, Slovenia, Czech Republic, Hungary, Cyprus
2007	Bulgaria, Romania
2013	Croatia
2019	Brexit (the planned exit by Britain and Northern Ireland)

few years ago: Brexit (British + exit),[1] the leaving of the EU by Britain and Northern Ireland which was decided in a referendum on 23 June 2016 by 51.89% of voters and is supposed to come into force on 29 March 2019 at 23:00 British time (https://de.wikipedia.org/wiki/EUAustritt_des_Vereinigten_K%C3%B6nigreichs). This brings the number of Member States back down to 27 – but the future position of English remains to be clarified. It will then only be a co-official language of the Member State Ireland (alongside Irish). Table H.4.1–1 summarises these developments.

With its future number of only 27 Member States, the EU will still have a population of approximately 450 million and an economic power of a similar order of magnitude to the USA or China (depending on the scale used). However, the EU lacks the cohesion of a unified state, so that economic and political differences between Member States are more sharply delineated. Because of the introduction of the Euro (€) in 1999, a currency gap has occurred between the 19 states which were members after the joining of Estonia in 2011 and Latvia in 2014 and the other nine, or in future eight, states. Since 1 January 2015, Austria, Belgium, Cyprus, Estonia, Finland, France, Germany, Greece, Ireland, Italy, Latvia, Lithuania, Luxembourg, Malta, the Netherlands, Portugal, Slovakia, Slovenia and Spain belong to the Eurozone.

Border crossings have been facilitated, especially by the *Schengen Agreement* initiated by a core group of Member States in 1985. This was expanded to 30 states in 2014, including – with partially restricted application – the non-EU states of Iceland, Liechtenstein, Norway and Switzerland. All new EU Member States were to be included automatically. Only Britain with Northern Ireland remained outside, but they will be leaving the EU anyway. The Schengen Agreement entails the abolition or restriction of border controls and cross-border collaboration of authorities and police. The easing of border crossings is associated with multiple consequences at a micro-level, e.g. the revival of neighbour-language programmes (Raasch/ Cuny/ Bühler/ Magar 1992; Raasch 2002).

Continuing development of central EU institutions, still with head offices in Brussels, Luxembourg and Strasbourg – predominantly in the French official-language territory – is more spectacular and possibly more consequential for the linguistic future of the EU (overview in the "*Das Portal der Europäischen Union*": europa.eu/about-eu/institutions-bodies/index_de.htm). The following institutions are of primary political significance (key functions in brackets): Council of Europe (issuing directives), Council of Ministers (legislation), European Parliament (legislation and control of the Commission), Commission (executive and legal initiative)

---

1 At the time of publication in summer 2019, the original date set for Brexit had been extended, and protracted renegotiation of the "Brexit deal" was taking place.

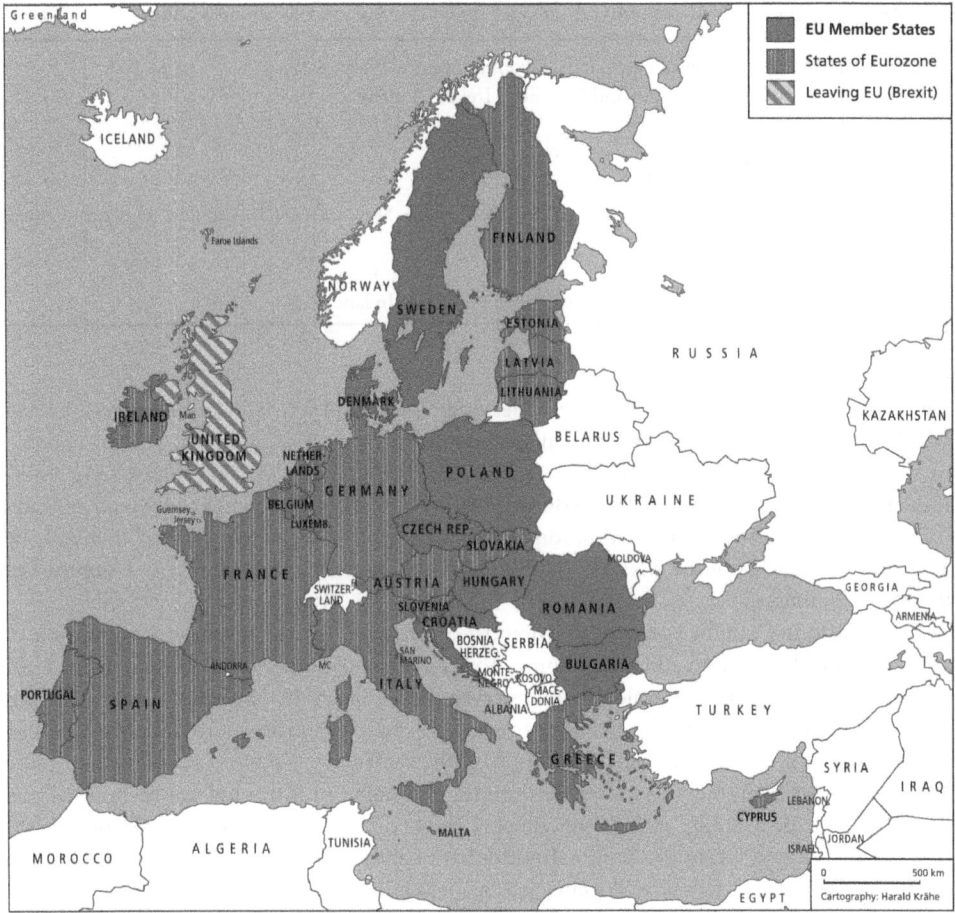

Map H.4.1–1   The European Union and the Eurozone in March 2018

and European Central Bank (headquarters in Frankfurt am Main, i.e. in the German official-language territory; Ch. D.1). At the time of its foundation in 1998, the ECB was not yet an institution of the EU and only became an institution in 2007 through the Treaty of Lisbon. The European Patent Organisation (headquarters in Munich, in the German official-language territory; 38 Member States in 2017) is not an EU institution.

To some extent, the Treaty of Lisbon in 2007 secured the EU as a substitute for the EU constitution which was rejected in referenda by France and the Netherlands and could not be enforced. The Treaty strengthened EU external policy which had been brought to life in 1986 in the "Unified European Act" and then defined more precisely in the Maastricht Treaty of 1993. The Lisbon Treaty and the preceding, rejected draft constitution, contain no statements on official languages or working languages of the institutions, despite pressure from linguists for a declaration on multilingualism (see Ammon 2005a: 196; Kruse 2012). However, the principle that amendments to the content of Council Regulation 1/58 on the language question in the EU shall be possible only by unanimous agreement has been retained, i.e. they can be blocked by a single veto of any individual Member State (cf. Ch. H.4.2).

4.2 Language rulings and language choice in the EU institutions

Many investigations have been carried out on the language situation in the EU institutions, on legal rulings and language praxis. The following titles are referenced in various parts of Ch. H.4: Haarmann 1973b, 1974; Coulmas 1991c; Mamadouh 1995; Schloßmacher 1994a, 1997; Bruha/ Seeler 1998; Oppermann 2001; de Swaan 2001: Ch. 8; Phillipson 2003; A. Ross 2003; Lohse 2004; Ginsburgh/ Weber 2005; Wu 2005; Ehlich 2010; Kruse 2012; Ammon 2012e; Haselhuber 2012. From the outset, the importance of the language question for EU policy is evident from the fact that the Council of the European Economic Community addressed this question immediately, in its first Regulation. Council Regulation 1/58 applied to the European Communities in their entirety and still applies in all its points to the entire EU today. A further 20 languages have been added to the original four EU official languages to reach the present total of 24 (since 2013, joining of Croatia). Even after Brexit (the planned exit by Britain and Northern Ireland), which will come into force in 2019, English will still be included (among other reasons because it is the co-official language of Ireland, alongside Irish; Ch. H.4.1). Council Regulation 1/58 is part of the "secondary legislation", not the "primary legislation" provided in the treaties between Member States. For this Regulation, by contrast with other secondary legislation, there is no majority decision, but instead: "the ruling of the language question for the institutions of the Community shall be taken unanimously by the Council regardless of the statute of the Court of Justice" (Art. 290 Treaty of Nice, 2003, based on Art. 217 of the Treaty of Amsterdam: eur-lex.europa.eu/de/treaties/dat/12001C/pdf/12001C_DE.pdf). The requirement for unanimity in case of amendment has been reconfirmed in the Treaty of Lisbon, which entered into force in 2009 (see also Ginsburgh/ Weber 2011: 181). This also shows the continuing importance of the language question for Member States. Jürgen Gerhards (2010: 137f. – Italic text ibid) speaks of "*interpreted* 'high politics'", the approval of importance similar to the "core areas of the state" (security, resources and similar). So long as there is no prospect of amendments to the applicable rulings, any discussion of improved language regimes for the EU must remain a sand-table exercise (e.g. Pool 1996; van Els 2001, 2003, 2005a, b; Grin 2004b; Gazzola 2006a, b; Ammon 2002, 2005a, 2006g, 2007b; Voslamber 2006). The same applies for any proposals regarding a language article in a future EU constitution, such as: "Languages – English, French and German shall have equal standing as the sole official languages of the Union institutions" ("A Constitution for the European Union", *The Economist* 28 October 2000: 22). Table H.4.2–1 shows the version applicable since 2013 (in Google, under "Regulation Number 1 of the Council of 1958 on the regulation of the language question").

Article 1 names all the EU official languages stipulated by this regulation, which represent only a small fraction of the languages spoken in the EU. These are only the national official languages of the Member States, not the regional languages, even if they are numerically strong like Catalan (which is the *national* official language only in Andorra, which is not a member of the EU – compare the difference between national and regional official languages Ch. D.1). Mere minority languages are certainly not included, whether they are autochthonous [indigenous] or allochthonous [non-indigenous]. However, even after Brexit, English will remain on the list, on one hand as a national co-official language of Ireland (alongside Irish), and on the other hand certainly because of its overarching function as a working language. All national official languages of Member States have now been adopted in Article 1 apart from Luxembourgish (see Ch. D.2.5), but this country waived its inclusion because it is already represented with its two national official languages, French and German. By contrast, Malta insisted on the inclusion of Maltese even though English is also an official language (co-official with Maltese) and almost all Maltese citizens (approximately 95%) speak English – in consequence of many years of British

Table H.4.2–1 Based on Council Regulation 1/58 (European Economic Community) for the regulation of the language question, in the version applicable in 2016

The Council of the European Economic Community has enacted the following regulation:

Article 1 The official languages and the working languages of the institutions of the Community shall be Bulgarian, Croatian, Czech, Danish, Dutch, English, Estonian, Finnish, French, German, Greek, Hungarian, Irish, Italian, Latvian, Lithuanian, Maltese, Polish, Portuguese, Romanian, Slovakian, Slovenian, Swedish and Spanish;

Article 2 Documents which a Member State or a person subject to the jurisdiction of a Member State sends to institutions of the Community may be drafted in any one of the official languages selected by the sender. The reply shall be drafted in the same language;

Article 3 Documents which an institution of the Community sends to a Member State or to a person subject to the jurisdiction of a Member State shall be drafted in the language of such State;

Article 4 Regulations and other documents of general application shall be drafted in the official languages;

Article 5 The Official Journal of the Community shall be published in the official languages;

Article 6 The institutions of the Community may stipulate in their rules of procedure which of the languages are to be used in specific cases;

Article 7 The languages to be used in the proceedings of the Court of Justice shall be laid down in its rules of procedure;

Article 8 If a Member State has more than one official language, the language to be used shall, at the request of such State, be governed by the general rules of its law.

This Regulation shall be binding in its entirety and directly applicable in all Member States.

colonial rule. Following this, Ireland also requested and received EU official-language status for Irish (Gaelic), although English is not only a co-official language in Ireland, but the Irish also speak it better than they do Irish. Of the 13 members in the EU parliament, only four spoke Irish at the time of the request, so that the EU financed tuition in their own "native language" for the other nine (Gerhards 2010: 137). This kind of multiplication of EU official languages serves primarily nationalistic language needs rather than communicative requirements. Furthermore, it arouses corresponding wishes among sub-national ethnic groups. For example, the Spanish government felt compelled to accept the regional official languages of the country at EU level in certain situations and to finance interpreting. Moreover, the multiplication of EU official languages increases the demand for a lingua franca and therefore the dominance of English – corresponding to the warning by Abram de Swaan: "The more languages the more English!" (2001a: Ch. 8; cf. also Ch. H.4.3). By contrast, Regulation 1/58 is intended primarily to allow communication between EU institutions and EU Member States, which is largely guaranteed by the national official languages.

Having said this, Article 6 deserves special attention because it opens broad differences in status and function between the EU official languages, which are referred to in Article 1 as "[t]he official languages and the working languages". This wording leaves it unclear whether what is meant is a unified concept (which could be expressed less ambiguously by the designation "official and working languages") or two different concepts (official languages ≠ working languages). Article 6 allows the latter interpretation and accordingly provides the individual institutions with a right to select working languages for their specialist requirements. Within the EU institutions, they are generally referred to as "procedural languages", presumably also as a means of avoiding the possible misunderstanding based on Article 1. The choice of these languages is one of the most vehemently disputed points in EU language policy and is especially relevant for German (see Ch. H.4.5 and the rest of this chapter). In the following discussion,

I use the term more current in language policy "working language" rather than "procedural language". This is a subset of the languages named in Article 1 (Regulation 1/58), which I refer to simply as "(EU-) official languages". The fact that Article 7 still furnishes for the Court of Justice of the EU (CJEU) the highest judicial body of the EU (headquarters in Luxembourg), the power to regulate its own procedural languages is almost a redundant point (for the CJEU, compare Alber 2004 – the CJEU must not be confused with the European Court of Justice for Human Rights (ECHR) of the Council of Europe, with head office in Strasbourg.).

Council Regulation 1/58 regulates primarily written correspondence between EU institutions and Member States and their citizens. Enormous translation services – the largest in the world – ensure that this can take place in all official languages, but these still hardly manage to translate all relevant documents into all official languages. For example, even the German Bundestag receives texts "relevant for discussion" from the EU Commission which are written in English rather than German (for details Kruse 2013; Kruse/ Ammon 2013; Ammon/ Kruse 2013). Presumably, only the UK and Ireland receive all texts from the EU institutions in their own national official language, English.

However, the functional differences between EU official languages relating to oral language use allowed by Article 6, are still more far-reaching. They vary between individual institutions, which I will present initially as an overview (see also EU website under "institutions" (www. google.com/?gws_rd=ssl#q=Portal+der+Europäischen+union). The institutions which are particularly relevant or remarkable in the context of language regulations, and which I refer to in the further discussion, are listed in Table H.4.2–2, with brief notes in brackets on the working languages; other institutions grouped together at the end.

Table H.4.2–2 Overview of important EU institutions with their working languages

---

- *Council of Europe*: establishes the general policy direction of the EU. Members are the heads of state and heads of government of the Member States and the President of the Commission. The President of the Council presides for a period of office of 2.5 years (all 24 EU official languages);
- *European Parliament*: adopts legal provisions. Elected directly by citizens for a five-year period of office (all 24 EU official languages);
- *Council* (also Council of Ministers) of the European Union: adopts legal provisions. Representation of the governments of all Member States. Presided over by the Member States in turn (all 24 EU official languages; English and French predominant);
- *European Commission*: legislative initiative and control of the implementation of law in the Member States. Represents the interests of the entire EU. The Commission President presides for a five-year period of office (English and French predominant, German);
- *European External Action Service (EEAS)*: for a five-year period of office, the president is the supreme representative for foreign policy and security (English, French);
- *Court of Justice of the EU (CJEU)*: ensures the observance of EU law (French);
- *European Central Bank (ECB)*: responsible for currency policy (English);
- *Office for Harmonisation in the Internal Market*: responsible for the registration of community trademarks and community designs (German, English, French, Italian, Spanish).

Court of Auditors: audits EU expenditure; *European Economic and Social Committee*: represents employers and employees; *Committee of the Regions*: represents regional and local authorities; *European Investment Bank*: finances investment projects and supports small enterprises; *European Ombudsman*: investigates grievances in administration and institutions; *European Data Protection Supervisor*: protects personal data for citizens; *Publications Office*: publishes information about the EU; *Personnel Selection Office*: acquires personnel for the EU institutions; *European Academy of Management*: organises further training for employees, amongst other responsibilities.

In the formal sessions of the Council of Europe and the Council of Ministers, all EU official languages are admitted, and simultaneous interpreting is provided if required. The possibility for comprehensive simultaneous interpreting is also available in the Council of Ministers but, *de facto*, French, and increasingly English, have a privileged position. In this context, Germany and Austria resolutely resisted the demotion of German in 1999 when Finland no longer wanted German in informal sessions of the Council of Ministers (Kelletat 2001a – Ch. H.4.6). At their most unrestricted, in public debates of the European Parliament, all EU official languages also function as working languages. For example, the procedural rules provide that: "MEPs have the right to express themselves in an official language of their choice, while the right to speak and the time of speaking are strictly regulated" (europa.eu/legislation_summaries/justice_free dom_security/citizenship_of_the_union/o10000_de.htm). This is supplemented by the following in the version dated January 2007, Article 2: "Statements in one of the official languages are translated [interpreted! U.A.] simultaneously into all other official languages and into every other language considered necessary by the presidium".

With 24 official languages, 552 combinations of language pairs are possible (n x (n-1), n = 24). This number of interpreters would be required if all were to interpret only from one foreign language into their own native language. However, the number of interpreters is dramatically reduced by a series of measures described in detail on the website of the "European Commission Interpretation" (ec.europa.eu/dgs/scic/index_en. htm). As per the section "Asymmetric", the number of interpreters can be reduced by means of various techniques: "A team [of interpreters! U.A.] interpreting back-and-forth between the current official languages requires 69 or more interpreters, but if you limit the active languages to 3, you can get by with only a dozen or so interpreters" (ec.europa.eu/dgs/scic/what-is-conference-interpreting/asymmetric/index_en.htm). The effort and difficulty of full interpreting has already generated much thought and many jokes (see also Kelletat 2004a; b; Neff 2001, 2006). For example, relay interpreting, i.e. interpreting indirectly via a third, relay language, e.g. Greek → English (relay language) → Finnish, is particularly problematic. Relay interpreting further intensifies the inequality between official languages, because it unavoidably prioritises languages which are already international languages – although German is one of the relay languages. Furthermore, it motivates the speakers of smaller languages to speak directly in one of the international languages, increasingly in English, which is already determined by the schooling policies of the EU Member States (cf. *Sociolinguistica* 23 (2009); H. Wagener 2012).

Differences in position between EU official languages in which the statutes of the institutions themselves restrict the number of working languages, are more conspicuous. This is exemplified by the Court of Justice of the EU (CJEU), which Article 7 of the Regulation 1/58 authorises for separate language regulation, according to which internal consultation by judges takes place exclusively in French, and the other EU official languages are admitted only for negotiations. The other language-restricting institution (in fact, of the Eurozone rather than the EU) is the European Central Bank (ECB). It has chosen English as the sole working language despite the fact that its headquarters is in the German official-language territory (in Frankfurt am Main). In all EU institutions, German has a *de facto* inferior function to English and French. However, for the EU Commission, one of the most important EU institutions, there is an explicit declaration of parity by decree of the former Commission President Jacques Delors, at the insistence of the then German Federal Chancellor Helmut Kohl. It is worded as follows: "If documents are presented for internal use by the Commission, they shall be formulated in the working languages German, English and French" (*EC Bulletin* 34, 6 September 1993: 4). This regulation was also adopted in the procedural rules of the Commission, which is accordingly available in these three languages (*Manuel des procédures [. . .] de la Commission: Exigences linguistiques en fonction de la procédure d'adoption*:Art. 1 – resolution of 20 July 2005). However, this only specifies the language choice of the documents but not the language in which they are to be processed. In practice, German serves predominantly only as a written language. As a spoken, working language, it has always ranked behind French, even in the Commission, as in other institutions, and English is becoming increasingly important. After working as an official in the Commission for 13 years, Johannes Wachter (email 23 April 2008) described the situation to me as follows, explaining that a knowledge of German is advantageous but not necessary: "Without a working knowledge of either English or French, it is, in practice, impossible to 'survive' in the Commission; anyone who does not know both languages is at a clear disadvantage". One indicator for the continuing loss of function of German is provided by the figures for original texts presented for translation to the Directorate General for Translation of the Commission in 2002 and 2006 (Table H.4.2–3). The author of these figures, who was language coordinator for German for many years in the Directorate General of the Commission, Reinhard Hoheisel, explained the crucial reason for the weakness of German as a working language as follows:

> For a multilingual organisation, the languages best suited as languages of communication are those which are known adequately by most participants either as a native language or a foreign language. In the European Commission, these are English and French. German does not fulfil this functional condition for a language of communication in the European Commission. Optimists estimate that only a third of the officials speak or understand German adequately. In consequence, it plays only a subordinate role as a language in which texts are prepared and published.
>
> *(Hoheisel 2004: 79)*

According to this account, the roots of the problem are therefore in the language requirements for job appointments which are not orientated towards parity between working languages (cf. Ch. H.4.6: paragraph 7).

The gap between official-only languages and the real working languages widens in the numerous committees and working groups of the institutions, where interpreting is not provided. Presumably, the minimex rule ("minimising exclusion") strengthens the use of English because of the knowledge of foreign languages already laid down in school education (Quetz 2010). According to this rule – generally followed unconsciously – wherever possible, no member of the group is completely excluded from communication because of lack of language skills (Ch. A.6; Van Parijs 2007b: 39; 2011: 13–17).

However, not all working groups need to manage without interpreting. In the preparatory working groups of the European Parliament and the Council of Ministers, interpreting is provided, although not always. The same or similar applies in the *Committee of Permanent*

Table H.4.2–3 Proportions of languages among original texts prepared in the EU Commission

	2002	2006
1) English	57.4 %	72%
2) French	29.1 %	14.4%
3) German	4.6 %	2.8%
4) Italian	2.1 %	n.d.
5) Spanish	2.0 %	n.d.

(*Source*: Hoheisel 2004: 81; presentation by Hoheisel 2007, communicated by Dietrich Voslamber)

Representatives of the Member States (COREPER = Comité des représentants permanents), in a sense, ambassadors to the Member States, who vote on their interests among themselves and with the Parliament and the Commission. However, from May 2004, to limit interpreting costs, "interpreting-on-demand" was introduced. This guarantees an annual amount for interpreting of equal magnitude (approximately €2.5m per language) for every EU official language from EU funds. Requests for interpreting which go beyond this must be financed by the Member States themselves, which widens the gap between large and small languages. The large languages, English, French, German, Italian and Spanish, are backed by Member States which can finance general interpreting, which is hardly possible for the states associated with the smaller languages. However, this hardly favours bringing German closer to the position of French or even English as desired by the German government. The special position of the five languages, English, French, German, Italian and Spanish, is also institutionalised in a single, although not particularly important EU institution: The *Office for Harmonisation in the Internal Market* – which I have included in the list of EU institutions (H.4.2–2). Since this institution has its headquarters in Alicante in Spain, Spain insisted on Spanish as one of the working languages. Following this, Italy also demanded this status for Italian, because Italian has more speakers in the EU and Spanish. Both these demands were granted. The Netherlands requested the inclusion of Dutch, which was rejected. The Netherlands then filed a case with the CJEU which subsequently failed (Kürten 2004: 103–119). Regarding the position of their language in the EU, the Dutch saw their language as next in rank behind the five chosen working languages, so that this exclusion was frustrating for them (for the principles behind this kind of language choice, see Ch. H.4.5).

Corresponding attitudes and principles also underlay various demands by Italy and Spain to gain the same status for their languages as German. A more recent example is the rejection of the "European Patent" (of the EU) because of its restriction to German, English and French, where Spain showed itself to be less prepared to compromise than Italy (www.finanzen.ch/nachrichten/aktien/EU-Bewegung-im-Streit-um EU-Patent-Italien-zieht-mit-58964). However, these objections were unsuccessful. Conflicts of this kind can lead to cooperation between excluded parties with a similar ranking. This was experienced by the former Vice-President of the EU Commission, Neil Kinnock, incidentally also an English-speaker, when he suggested presenting the consultation documents for the Commission only in English to save translation costs. France and Germany united in opposing Kinnock's suggestion, which was therefore defeated (Ammon 2010e: 1; "Fischer and Védrine against more English", *FAZ* 10 January 2001; "Kinnock accused of trying to force English in Europe", *The Daily Telegraph* 15 August 2001 – information from Robert Phillipson). The quasi contractual deal of the "Joint German-French Language Directive" (June 2000) originated from experiences of this kind; the two states promised mutual support in the event of attempts at discrimination against their languages. However, this has hardly ever been applied (Ammon 2009a: 124). One example of a previous lack of cooperation between Germany and France is the *European Central Bank* (ECB) with English as the sole working language. Admittedly, it originated before the Joint Language Directive (in 1998, but only became an institution of the EU in 2007); however, a subsequent amendment of its language regime may have been possible. The monopoly position of English was presumably accepted because of the assumption of greater efficiency in view of the dominance of English in international business. Germany's readiness to give up on its own language despite the fact that the head office is in the German official-language territory may be explained by the satisfaction of having won the bid for this location.

One striking failure of German EU language policy is the *European External Action Service* (EEAS), which has restricted its working languages almost entirely to English, and occasionally French – at least in practical terms, if not by statute. In this context, there were several attempts from the German side to have German included, which seemed to gain force from the economic power of Germany. The former German Foreign Minister, Guido Westerwelle was a prominent advocate for the case for German to become a working language (www.euractiv. de/globales-europa/artikel/deutsch-im-ead-westerwelle-frchtet-verfestigung-003838), as were several Bundestag members through direct questions to the Commission and, to some extent, to the first divisional chief, EU Minister for Foreign Affairs, Baroness Ashton. However, it quickly became evident that job advertisements for the EEAS required only a knowledge of English and French, and the homepage was published only in these two languages ("Discrimination against the German language", *FAZ* 13 December 2010). Furthermore, it became known that Germany was more poorly considered than other, even small, Member States, also for the appointment of key posts in the EEAS. For example, in September 2011, only seven of the total of 136 newly nominated EU ambassadors at that time were from Germany, with 15 from France, 14 from Italy, 14 from Belgium, 11 from Spain and nine from the UK (*EurActiv.de* 29 September 2011).

Indeed, there is no doubt that English and French have a considerably stronger position in international diplomacy than German, even in the UN and in the Council of Europe (Ch. H.3). German has never played a significant role in the external relations of the EU (Haselhuber 2012: 56–59), not even in relations with central European countries, despite their considerable tradition of using and learning German. Even in their applications to join the EU, it was a matter of "Whoever wants to negotiate with the EU had to speak and understand English [. . .]" (ibid: 57). It was also taken for granted that "Correspondence of the Commission with the African, Caribbean and Pacific (ACP) states [associated developing countries! U.A.] shall take place in the language of the former colonial rulers of the respective country: Spanish, Portuguese, Dutch, English and French" (ibid: 56). Incidentally, these ACP states are not insignificant; there are 79 states which include large parts of Africa and extend to the Caribbean and Pacific regions; most are former colonies of Britain and France (de.wikipedia.org/wiki/AKP-Staaten). With these countries in mind, the claim to position as an EEAS working language would be more likely to be granted to EU official languages other than German, especially Spanish. The decision here evidently depends on whether the position of the language inside or outside the EU is rated higher.

For all that, the German government does not recognise the priority of English and French in the EU, at least not explicitly. A new regulation on the promotion of officials, which was adopted some time ago, is sometimes seen as one of several attempts to achieve greater parity for German. Accordingly, EU officials, "whose first promotion comes into effect after 30.04.2006", can achieve further promotion only if they know three EU official languages: "Within the framework of reform for the status [of officials in the EU institutions! U.A.], the Council has resolved that, in future, every official shall be capable of working in a third language. For the implementation of the resolution, according to Article 45 (2) of the statute, a first promotion after appointment is linked directly with evidence that the applicant can work in a third language" (eur-lex. europa.eu/LexUriServ/LexUriServ.do? uri=COM:2011:0042:FIN:DE:HTML). However, it is sobering to consider this ruling with regard to strengthening the position of German. It can be assumed that all officials already know one EU official language, namely their own (Bulgarians know Bulgarian, Danish people know Danish etc.). Those from EU Member States with German as their official language (n=3, including Luxembourg) choose English and French in addition to their own language. Those from English-speaking or French-speaking countries (n=5, including Belgium and Luxembourg) choose French or respectively English + {Bulgarian$_1$, Danish$_2$, German$_3$, . . . Hungarian$_{22}$}, i.e. one item from this set of 22 languages, in which German is almost lost. Those who do not come from English-speaking, French-speaking or German-speaking countries (n=21 = 28–7: UK, Ireland, France, Belgium, Luxembourg, Germany, Austria), choose English and French. Everyone chooses these two languages because knowing them is indispensable. By contrast, a knowledge of German is dispensable, although less so than knowing smaller languages such as Danish, Greek etc. But Italian, Spanish, Portuguese and Dutch are far from useless. This new regulation therefore only strengthens the case for German as a working language to a limited extent, presumably less than it promotes French alongside English, which already predominates anyway.

4.3 EU language policy: German eclipsed by plurilingualism and the lingua franca

An overview of the language policy claimed and implemented by EU institutions would seem to suggest that the overriding aim is to maintain and even increase linguistic diversity in the EU; all other language-policy objectives are subordinate to or intended to serve this aim. However, it is equally obvious that actual developments often run counter to this (e.g. Ammon 2007b, 2009b; Ehlich 2010). Chapter H.4.2 demonstrated this in the opposition between the diversity of EU official languages emphasised in Council Regulation 1/58 and the trend towards monolingual or bilingual communication in the EU institutions, which is – unobtrusively – acknowledged in Articles 6 and 7 of the Regulation. Looking beyond the institutions shows a similar picture: an invocation of plurilingualism in tandem with a *de facto* trend towards overarching monolingualism or bilingualism, which is not without consequences for German and other languages. The EU Council, Commission and Parliament have designed numerous regulations and programmes, also in conjunction with the Council of Europe, to strengthen multilingualism or plurilingualism in the EU. Table H.4.3–1 gives a selection of particularly relevant examples.

The aim of all these plans and measures, alongside other goals in some cases, was to maintain or to promote multilingualism or plurilingualism in the EU, i.e. *social* plurilingualism in

Table H.4.3–1 Programmes and measures of the EU for the promotion of multilingualism

- Council Regulation 1, since 1958, guaranteeing a plurality of EU official languages (cf. Ch. H.4.2);
- "European Charter for Regional or Minority Languages", since 1992, protecting the indigenous minority languages (cf. Ch. E.1);
- "Lingua", since 1990: programme for development of FL teachers and teaching materials (within a programme for lifelong learning);
- "European Year of Languages", 2001, with the aim of maintaining linguistic and cultural diversity in Europe;
- "Action plan for the 'Promotion of Language Learning and Linguistic Diversity'", 2004–2006 (details in Commission Bulletin: "The SOCRATES and LEONARDO DA VINCI programmes together invest more than €30 million per year in measures with the specific aim of acquiring foreign languages (ec.europa.eu/education/doc/official/keydoc/actlang/act_lang_de.pdf);
- Establishment of an area of responsibility for "Multilingualism", 2004–2006 and again from 2010, in the Commissariat "General and Vocational Education and Culture";
- Establishment of a special commissariat for "Multilingualism", 2007–2009 (see: "The commissioner, the Romanian, Leonard Orban, has constantly reaffirmed the Commission's unequivocal support for multilingualism". S. Wright 2009: 96);
- Convening of the "High Level Group on Multilingualism", 2006–2007, of the Commissariat for "General and Vocational Education and Culture" (final report: ec.europa.eu/education/policies/lang/doc/multireport_en.pdf);
- Research projects of the EU Commission "Languages in a Network of European Excellence (LINEE)", 2006–2010, and *"Dynamique des langues et gestion de la diversité* (DYLAN)", 2007–2011 – both of which are to show the advantages of multilingualism based on a comprehensive investigation.

residential areas and domains and *individual* multilingualism in EU citizens and residents. The goal of individual multilingualism was expressed through the formula "M+2" with the intention that, in future, as many EU citizens as possible should know at least three languages: mother-tongue +2 foreign languages (details in Kruse 2012).

This M+2 goal is declared e.g. in the *Action Plan* (2004–2006: paragraph 1.1) under the heading "Mother-tongue +2 other languages: from the earliest years of childhood", and is specified as follows:

> Overall, the plan should include the 'smaller' European languages as well as the 'larger' languages; regional languages, majority languages and migrant languages; vernaculars and the languages of our most important trading partners worldwide. The proposed expansion of the EU will be accompanied by many additional languages from different language families; it will require special effort to ensure that the languages of the new Member States are learned more comprehensively [than previously! U.A.] in other countries.
>
> *(ec.europa.eu/education/doc/official/keydoc/actlang/act_lang_de.pdf)*

Regarding the German language, it is significant that not only EU official languages and the languages of the most important trading partners worldwide are included, but – contrary to the tradition of FL learning – "also the 'smaller' European languages". This implies an orientation of FL learning towards "regional, minority and migrant languages". Other projects and measures also suggest this, including the *European Charter for Regional or Minority Languages* (1992):

> Within the field of education, with reference to regions other than their own in which the regional or minority languages are traditionally used, the parties to the agreement undertake to allow tuition of the regional or minority language or tuition in this language at all educational levels, to encourage or to offer this tuition [. . .]
>
> *(conventions.coe.int/Treaty/ger/Treaties/Html/148.htm: Article 8 paragraph 2)*

In fact, the context here suggests that this tuition should be understood as native-language tuition; however, it is not explicitly restricted to this. FL teaching is in no sense precluded. On one hand, this may mean large languages which are learnt as foreign languages in the minority regions (e.g. German in German schools in the German minority region, for example, in Romania; Ch. E.4.7), but, on the other hand, it may also refer to small minority languages, e.g. Friesian in the Netherlands or Welsh in the UK.

This interpretation which includes the learning of small languages as foreign languages is suggested more clearly in other EU bulletins. One example was when the President of the "High-Level Group on 'Multilingualism'" of the EU Commission, Amin Malouf, stated that as many EU citizens as possible should select one of the languages in the EU as a "personal adoptive language" and should acquire it as a foreign language; if possible, this should be one of the smaller languages not included in the school curriculum. This suggestion resonated with the planners of the EU language policy and other prominent personalities, such as the then president of the Goethe-Institut, Jutta Limbach (2008: 80–83). In presenting this proposal, the EU Commissioner for multilingualism especially supported the focus on smaller languages: "This adoptive language would not be the language which is normally used for international communication" (europa.eu/rapid/pressReleasesAction.do?reference=IP/08/129&format=HTML &aged=1&language=DE&guiLanguage=en).

However, the idea of the adoptive language was not taken up in the final report of the High-Level Group, presumably because it was immediately criticised as unrealistic (e.g. Ammon 2009c). The final report is differentiated and balanced but in German translation it is only available in an abridged form (ec.europa.eu/languages/documents/multi short_de.pdf; English: ec.europa.eu/education/policies/lang/doc/multireport_ en.pdf). In fact, the content relevant in the present context is included in this abridged version, but I shall refer to the full English version. The report stresses the importance of the small languages: "Regional or minority languages are constituent elements of Europe's linguistic and cultural diversity and wealth" (ibid: 18, in Ch. VI (1) "Regional and minority languages"). However, it also contains clear pointers, generally watered down in official EU statements of language policy, to the "elephant in the room", as Sue Wright (2009) titled her courageous essay on this topic. The reference here is to the progressive spread of English as the dominant lingua franca in the EU (cf. Ch. H.4.4). Although the final report of the High-Level Group does not contain a specific section on this topic, it is mentioned at various points, for example, "[I]t may well be possible to recognise the role of a quasi *lingua franca* for European integration, while at the same time stressing the importance of multilingual competence" (ibid: 7). The qualification with "quasi" is intended not so much as a doubt about the existence of this lingua franca as a defence against any possibly associated objections to the demand for multilingualism for all EU citizens, which the report emphatically maintains.

Apart from the ultimately inevitable lingua franca, which languages should be components of the multilingualism envisaged for future EU citizens? The report divides them into two categories: languages with "community value", namely "regional or minority languages" – presumably meaning primarily but not explicitly only the native languages; and languages with "global value", of which the following are explicitly named: "Bengali, English [again, in this category! U.A.], Hindi, Japanese, Mandarin Chinese, Portuguese, Russian and Spanish" (ibid: 7). This is a curious list, because the "global value" of Bengali or Hindi is doubtful, and because French and – possibly less surprisingly – German and Italian are missing. Added to this, neither French nor German are mentioned in the text at all, and Italian is not referenced anywhere as a "value" but only as a media application which has been successful as "edutainment", e.g. in Finland (ibid: 11).

Regarding the questions relevant to the present book, EU language policy seems, on one hand, to be making an effort towards greater parity between smaller and larger EU languages but, on the other hand, it reluctantly acknowledges the one lingua franca overarching all other languages. Both views fail to notice the traditional school foreign languages of Europe, which include German alongside French, Italian and Spanish (cf. Ammon 2009b, 2009c). This neglect of the large EU languages (apart from English, which cannot be ignored) can perhaps be explained by the fact that ethnic or national identities are given highest priority. Their high-ranking in EU language policy is presumably rooted in the – certainly not incorrect – judgement that these identities represent a time-bomb for the continued existence of the EU. At any event, this has been the lesson taught by the history of Europe up to and including the conflicts in the Balkans and more recently Ukraine/Russia. The correlation between linguistic and national identity and their conflict-causing potential have been convincingly investigated in many studies of language policy (e.g. Coulmas 1991b; S. Wright 2000; Anderson 1983). Despite its obvious necessity, securing communication within the EU has seemed less urgent for EU politicians by comparison, at least in the recent past and up to the present. One indicator for this is the fact that they have ultimately accepted the defects in the translation and interpreting services of the institutions as unalterable (compare Ch. H.4.2). Another is that while they do not deny the growing pre-eminence of English and its increasing function as a lingua franca, they also fail to see the value of a thorough investigation of its possible advantages, at least to the same extent as for plurilingualism. The topic of English as a lingua franca in EU institutions has been discussed openly only in recent years (cf. Ch. H.4.4). To all appearances – after the adoption of Council Regulation 1/58 and the establishment of procedural rules for the institutions based upon it – EU policy for securing communication in the EU is tending towards a *laissez-faire* of market and political forces (see K. Muller 2002).

4.4 Democracy and cohesion in the EU based on a single lingua franca?

The question of whether one lingua franca is appropriate for the whole of the EU has been under intensive discussion for some time, even in the EU institutions themselves, although still with a certain time-delay (z.B. European Commission 2011, *Lingua franca: Chimera or Reality?* Ec.europa.eu/dgs/translation/publications/studies/lingua_franca_en.pdf). For reasons of expediency, I shall focus my discussion on the relevance of this question to political developments in the EU, especially its democratic structures and its cohesion either as a loose "group/ (con) federation of states" or as a more rigidly integrated federal-state. Sue Wright (2009) touches on the subject of an EU lingua franca by criticising the way EU language policy is fixated on promoting plurilingualism and multilingualism (cf. Ch. H.4.3) but neglects the development of a "community of communication". Only within such a community, for which social plurilingualism would be an obstacle rather than an advantage could EU citizens discuss important political questions among themselves and with the EU government. I would add to this that this obstacle becomes even clearer if it is framed as "language difference" instead of plurilingualism. By contrast, Wright believes that a communicative community needs a common language, and, in the absence of a common native language, it needs a lingua franca which is known by all EU citizens. She adds with apparent regret the all-too obvious inference that only English (which happens to be Wright's own native language) can be considered for this role which it is already beginning to adopt. In this framework, the further spread of this lingua franca becomes the key language-policy aim for the EU, which must be supplemented by measures mitigating the disadvantages to non-English-speaking inhabitants.

For our central topic, "the position of German in the world", it is significant that Wright is strongly in favour of a single lingua franca. She rejects the option of several lingua francas – such as the "three large languages" English, French and German – because of the learning load for non-native speakers: "Seen from the viewpoint of speakers of languages other than the 'big three', it must appear more burdensome [than just one lingua franca! U.A.]. To participate in flows, exchanges and networks, which may take place in any one of three languages that is not one's native language, represents an enormous language-acquisition load".

Wright's question: "Who benefits from a plurality of lingua francas? We should keep asking this question", is recognisably rhetorical. But having said this, other lingua francas (in addition to English), e.g. French or German, would be advantageous for the respective native speakers, but would still be a burden for everyone else (Wright 2009: 109). Philipp Van Parijs (2011: 46–49, also, 221: note 65) considers a plurality of lingua francas to be a greater learning load than just one lingua franca even for native speakers. This question has already been discussed in Ch. G.12. From three languages upwards, the learning load becomes greater than with one lingua franca, with differences depending on linguistic distance and active or passive use. Beyond the learning load, Wright and Van Parijs see further disadvantages for non-native speakers, especially in the preparation of texts and communicative impact (see Ch. G.10). These also grow with the number of lingua francas and additionally justify a limitation to one lingua franca. However, Wright and Van Parijs may be underestimating native speakers' motivation to accept additional burdens for a strong position of their language, and the associated resistance to "English-only" by the French or German language communities (Ch. A.1). Wright justifies her demand for one lingua franca for the EU essentially based on the "common public sphere", which is required by a democracy. In this respect, she is following an idea proposed by Jürgen Habermas ([1962] 1990), according to which such a sphere is required to discuss publicly the political problems of the community. However, more strongly than Habermas, Wright emphasises the *linguistic* accessibility of this sphere, which, to her, seems to be guaranteed most comprehensively by one lingua franca (see also Gerhards 2010 and Bourdieu et al. 2001). By contrast, Habermas (2001: 121f., 2006) skims over the language question as if it were not a serious problem and only mentions English in passing as a possible common language for the EU (for a criticism of Habermas' neglect of the language question, see, Gerhards 2010: 56–59; also, Kraus: 142).

Since the historical rise of the bourgeoisie originally addressed by Habermas (1962), political and technical conditions have changed irreversibly. However, social media (Ch. I.1.4) does not exhibit an adequate degree of publicness [*Öffentlichkeit*], and even the EU mass media lack general accessibility. Hitherto, they have generally been restricted to Member States of the same language. Parallel media or programmes in different languages, such as *Euronews* (headquarters in Lyon), which, at least in spring 2018, was broadcasting in eight EU official languages (https:// en.wikipedia.org/wiki/Euronews), are severely restricted in terms of programme breadth and viewer numbers. There is accordingly a lack of a lingua franca readily available to all EU citizens, and for this reason, all attempts at EU-wide newspapers, radio and TV broadcasts have so far failed or remained in their pilot stage (A. Ross 2003: 110f., 121–123; Beierwaltes 2001: 20–25). Having said this, popular music represents a niche of its own: "With the significant exception of music there is no European market for mass media content in any single language" (Berns/ de Bot/ Hasebrink 2007: 117). EU-wide reception is possible because even vocal music does not require an accurate understanding of the text (see Ammon 1991a: 413–417; Ch. I.2.3). However, vocal music is only a marginal phenomenon relative to the political public sphere (for a limiting comment, see Pennycook 1994). Other public forms are more politically relevant, such as "event-publicness" or informal "encounter publicness" (Beierwaltes 2000; A. Ross 2003: 118). Event publicness includes conferences, announcements, demonstrations, ceremonies and festivals as well as cooperation between parties and associations; encounter publicness includes town-twinning visits and random encounters, such as on trains or air travel. At least linguistically, these would all be less restricted with one lingua franca. The realisation of a "voluntary year of Europe for everyone" proposed by Ulrich Beck and Daniel Cohn-Bendit, in which as many EU citizens as possible are supposed to live in another EU country for a relatively long period, would also be facilitated by one lingua franca (www.euractiv.de/wahlen-und-macht/artikel/ wir-sind-europa-00626). Finally, a lingua franca would contribute to the development of the "four freedoms": unrestricted border crossings between EU Member States of "goods, persons, services and capital". This is guaranteed in the EU treaties (e.g. Article 95, "Harmonisation rule", of the "Founding Treaty the European Community (EGV)": eur-lex.europa.eu/de/treaties/dat /12002E/pdf/12002E_DE.pdf). The four freedoms are not only highly economically significant, they also help promote the development of a common political sphere.

Communication between EU institutions including the EU government and EU citizens provides a centre for the EU-wide, common public sphere. Access for citizens to key Commission press conferences is restricted by language difference. In fact, they are addressed only to journalists who understand the predominant English and French and publish through translations (Ross 2003: 125). But with one lingua franca, EU citizens could take part directly (via appropriate media such as radio, TV, Internet), which may enhance their political maturity. Debates in the European Parliament are even more important in this respect. They are basically accessible to all EU citizens via a transmission website, where interpreting into the relevant official language can be selected via the abbreviation for the country – e.g. "de" for Germany (www.europarl.europa.eu/ep-live/NL/schedule/live-broadcast. Link can be selected as a country abbreviation). However, by comparison with national parliaments, communication is impaired by interpreting. In fact, crude interpreting errors are rare, although they are sometimes publicised with great mirth. But some rhetorical finesse is inevitably lost through interpreting, and this often detracts from the impact of speeches.

The idea of extending an EU lingua franca to the EU official languages and working languages is therefore obvious but would presuppose the cancellation of the Council Regulation 1/58 (Ch. H.4.2). For some time now, Theo van Els (2003, 2005a, b, 2007) has campaigned for one, single EU working language, English, of course. The reasons he gives are like those given by Wright and Van Parijs, namely, more efficient communication and increased linguistic fairness between language communities. It could be added that this would also serve democratic progress. All EU officials and politicians could develop comprehensive skills in the single working language, so that English native speakers would lose their linguistic superiority. Over time, the non-native speakers could even assert their own linguistic and communicative norms. Of course, all communication by EU institutions with the Member States and citizens could then take place in this language. The social consequences for the language services – the "supply" of numerous translators and interpreters – would then, of course, need to be clarified, but this goes beyond van Els' proposal. And his deliberations are more compelling because developments are already moving in the direction he describes (see, e.g., de Swaan 2001: 144–175; Van Parijs 2011: 6–9; H. Wagener 2012; for the increasing proportion of English-language communication between Commission and German Bundestag, see Ammon/ Kruse 2013; Kruse/ Ammon 2013; Kruse 2013).

However, there is so far a lack of thorough investigations into the weaknesses of the proposal in favour of a single lingua franca. The possibilities for communication would clearly be limited by the degree of skill attained by citizens, which, for many, would probably remain limited for a considerable time. Van Parijs (2011: 30) takes this circumstance into account but avoids the objection to the EU lingua franca by seeking refuge in an elitist model of society. Van Parijs considers inadequate skills in the lingua franca only to be a problem in the case of *active* participation in political discussion: "The average citizen only feels comfortable debating political issues in their mother tongue" (here, Van Parijs quotes with approval a statement by Will Kymlicka 1999: 121). As a non-native language, the lingua franca would therefore only hinder "ordinary citizens" (ibid: 31). But, we must ask, would not this also be detrimental to democracy or at least an obstacle to its further development? Van Parijs' comment, which is presumably intended to be calming, seems frivolous to me "[G]iven appropriate socio-linguistic conditions, they ['ordinary people' U.A.] can also quickly feel comfortable enough debating in a language distinct from their mother tongue" (ibid: 31). However, these "appropriate sociolinguistic conditions" are not specified here. One key statement by Van Parijs (2011: 31) is that the common lingua franca "creates and expands a transnational demos, by facilitating direct communication, live or online, without the cumbersome and expensive mediation of interpretation and translation". But whether this would be equivalent to an expansion of the "transnational demos" is still doubtful unless it is supplemented by political discussion in the respective native languages in which the citizens have good language skills. By way of explanation, it should be added here, that there is a broad consensus that the EU cannot become a unified *ethnos* (ethnic group, *Volk* or people) but at best a – politically connected – *demos* (Grimm 1995; Habermas 1995; Ross 2003: 101f.). In fact, national states do not contain an ethnic group precisely (all its members and only them), but, all the same, they often do so extensively enough to construct an illusion of ethnic unity (cf. Ch. B.3). The most prominent symbol of this is then the common language, which simultaneously acts as the native language of all citizens (Ch. A.3; B.3; Anderson 1983; Gellner 1983; Wright 2000; Ammon 2010a). But a correspondence of this kind is not in view for the EU: unless it is a native language, a lingua franca is unsuitable as a constitutive symbol of ethnicity.

The political interconnection of the Member States of the EU and all the EU citizens to form a single demos is based on its founding treaties. A constitution (Grimm 1995; Habermas 1995) – and the treaties of Nice (resolved 2000, enforced 2003) and Lisbon (2009) already approximately correspond to such a constitution – would be even more binding. These are based on common values, interests and political "issues", which are distributed in numerous networks and translated into various languages EU-wide. Viviane Manz (2002: 197–213) also considers Switzerland, to which no one would deny democratic qualities, to be a community of fundamentally identical values, interests and problems, but without a common language, mediated in this manner (through multilingualism and translation). In the case of the EU, Manz does not see the admittedly greater linguistic diversity as necessarily an obstacle to developments in a similar direction, including emotional cohesion – which would require patience and time (for a more sceptical view of the comparison between the EU and Switzerland, see Altermatt 1995).

To achieve legitimacy, a targeted policy for promoting an EU lingua franca or an EU working language would need to be accepted by a majority of EU citizens. Regarding the EU, Fritz W. Scharpf (1999) has made a distinction between "input-orientated" and "output-orientated legitimation" (ibid: 16–28; also, Ross 2003: 98f., 141). Input-orientated legitimation emphasises authority *through* the citizens ("*demos*"), whose (majority) "authentic preferences" must be reflected in government decisions. By contrast, output-orientated legitimation emphasises authority *for* the citizens, so that the government decisions recognisably promote the benefit of the community and are based on the majority interests of the citizens (Scharpf 1999: 21). EU policy attempts to do justice to both dimensions of legitimation. By comparison with nation states, this is more difficult in the case of input-orientated legitimation, because of the additional level of government above the Member States and because of linguistic diversity (Kraus 2008: 37–75).

One decidedly input-orientated solution to the language question (the question of only one EU lingua franca or EU working language) would be a referendum of EU citizens. This ensures the maximum possible degree of democratic legitimation ("On democracy in Europe. The legitimating power of the democratic act of voting has not been reached [. . .]", *FAZ* 9 February 2012: 7), but citizens would not simply be trusted to vote on complex questions, the consequences of which may be difficult to assess. However, based primarily on questions of principle, there are opinions in favour of this. One advocate, especially in the context of the EU, is the former Vice-President of the Federal Constitutional Court, Ferdinand Kirchhof, who reasons as follows: "Direct democracy is appropriate wherever fundamental decisions have to be made by the citizens of the union. These include, for example, treaties and the euro" ("Direct democracy in the EU. Constitutional judge: the people should vote on the euro", *FOCUS* 6 December 2012; also www.focus.de/finanzen/news/staatsverschuldung/direkte-demokratie-in-der-eu-verfassungsrichter-volk-soll-ueber-euro-abstimmen_aid_711262.html). So, why not hold a referendum on the question of a single EU lingua franca or working language? There have already been opinion polls with this focus, but no referenda. In 1997, a representative survey was carried out in eight Member States (total respondents 7,515). Although this did not relate to a single EU lingua franca, but to the EU official languages, many respondents may have had a single EU lingua franca in mind. Anyway, 48% (unweighted arithmetic mean of all eight states) voted in favour of a single language, with the highest percentage (72%) in

Italy and – surprisingly – the lowest (31%) in the UK. Perhaps the British were afraid that this single language might be French. In all states, a majority also voted in favour of a referendum on this question (mean 64%) – apart from the Netherlands (52% against), possibly anxious that a referendum might slow down the trend towards a single EU official language and lingua franca (English). The preferred languages were English (86% of all respondents), French (65%), German (47%), Spanish (30%) and Italian (21%) (Roemen 1998).

At that time, there were more specific opinion polls among EU interns regarding EU working languages, with a surprising rejection of a single language. The combination of English + French (38%) was preferred, followed – with a gap – by English + French + German (24%); only 17% voted for only one working language, English (Quell 1997: 67). In a representative survey carried out in Germany, 78% voted against a "common language [. . .]" in the EU, and 53% for "a stronger use of the German language in the EU" (Hoberg/ Eichhoff-Cyrus/ Schulz 2008: 42f.). It can therefore be assumed that they were also against a single language in the EU institutions. Younger respondents (16 to 19-year-olds) were less definitely against a "common language" (73%) than older respondents (≥ 60-year-olds: 81%) (ibid: 43). But this is only an *apparent* change of attitude, as sociolinguists say, which proves to be *real* only if the young people retain their attitude when they become older. Other representative surveys were carried out in 2005 and 2012 in all the 25 or respectively 27 EU Member States (*Eurobarometer Spezial 243* (2006); *Eurobarometer Spezial 386* (2012)). Only EU citizens (not other inhabitants) were questioned. The percentages named in Table H.4.4–1 agreed with the following statements:

1) "Everyone in the Union (or 'in the EU') should be capable of speaking a common language" (*Eurobarometer Spezial* 243:55 and *Eurobarometer Spezial* 386:131, 136f.);
2) "The European institutions should agree on one language in which they communicate with European citizens" or "the European institutions should agree on a single common language for communication with citizens" (*Eurobarometer Spezial* 243:55 and *Eurobarometer Spezial* 386:131f.).

Virtually everyone had English in mind as the lingua franca for all citizens (question 1). The language for communication with EU institutions (question 2) would also have to be a lingua franca for the citizens; it would have to be known by everyone and would also be English. However, it is remarkable that agreement with question 2) is weaker than for question 1). Perhaps concern about linguistic dictatorship by the institutions motivated this reticence, or simply the correlation with political power. Such concerns would certainly be reduced for internal communication within the institutions, where the restriction to a single EU working language would presumably meet with reduced resistance. However, this raises the serious question of whether a monolingual internal communication could remain limited to the EU institutions or whether it would unavoidably spill over into other areas of life in the EU.

Table H.4.4–1 Agreement by EU citizens on a single lingua franca for citizens and for communication by EU institutions with citizens (percentage of respondents)

Date of survey	2005	2012
Lingua franca among EU citizens	58	69
Lingua franca between EU institutions and citizens	55	53

Table H.4.4–2 Percentage of EU citizens with native language and FL-knowledge

	English 2005–2012	German 2005–2012	French 2005–2012	Italian 2005–2012	Spanish 2005–2012
Native language	13–13	18–16	12–12	13–13	9–8
Foreign language	38–38	14–11	14–12	3–3	6–7
Combined	51–51	32–27	26–24	16–16	15–15

(*Sources: Eurobarometer Spezial* 243 (2005): 8, 13; *Eurobarometer Spezial* 386 (2012): 12, 22)

The question of restriction to a single language must therefore be directed towards three domains or functions: a) internal communication in the EU institutions (EU working language), b) communication between EU institutions and EU citizens (EU official language) and c) communication between citizens (EU lingua franca). This complexity would necessitate careful preparation for a referendum on any corresponding language policy based on detailed public debate to minimise the chances for populist fudging tactics. Many EU citizens would certainly have difficulty assessing the consequences of such a language policy, especially since – so far as I can see – these have not been explained satisfactorily even in academia. Added to this may be the problem that citizens are not interested in this group of complex questions which, compared with the "more tangible" economic problems, might seem trivial.

Another question deserving discussion in this context is whether excluding the language with most native speakers in the EU from the functions of lingua franca and working language would be fair. Although it has lost a little ground in recent years, this language is still German. Table H.4.4–2 shows the percentage of EU citizens who, in 2005 and 2012, declared themselves speakers of the respective languages: i) as their native language, ii) as a foreign language in which they could hold a conversation.

Among native languages, Polish, with 8%, is also important, and, among foreign languages, Russian, with 6%; but, in each case, the percentages for the other category are vanishingly small. There are no data for 2005 for Spanish as native language, but they can be estimated to the value indicated (*Fischer Weltalmanach* 2009: 442; *Fischer Weltalmanach* 2007: 556). Italian as a foreign language can be estimated, for example, from *Eurobarometer 54 Spezial* (2001: 2) and *Eurobarometer Spezial* 386, at 3%. The numerical loss for German in the period from 2005 to 2012 may possibly be explained with reference to the expansion of the EU by two Member States which was associated with a relative reduction in the number of native speakers and FL speakers of German. Other possible factors will be discussed in Ch. H.4.6.

4.5 Language interests of German and other language communities in the EU

In a relevant article, Gerhard Stickel (2007a: 134–137) distinguishes two kinds of interest in a language: 1) raising awareness of it or enhancing its attractiveness; 2) a desire to use or maintain it. The present book is about both, but especially about interest in the position of a language: within its community or in the world (see also Ch. A.1). This interest also entails the motivation to commit oneself to maintaining or strengthening the position of the language. It may be supported by knowledge of the advantages of a strong position and the disadvantages of a weak position of languages for their speakers and their language community. Such an interest in language may be subordinate or superordinate to other interests (Ch. A.2), e.g. academic interests, so that *priorities* or *hierarchies* of *interests* are formed. Initially, this relates to a property (attitude) of individuals, which can diverge within collectives, e.g. groups.

Interest in a strong global position of German can therefore diverge widely among different members of the German-language community. For certain questions, it may be important to distinguish between subjective (conscious) interests and objective interests, the latter with the meaning that they are given for certain individuals; the former with the meaning that one might be more or less aware of these objective interests. In my opinion, a strong position of the German language is in the objective interest of all members of the German-language community, some of whom may be more or less aware of this. A differentiated awareness of one's own interests includes not only the most correct (possible) assessment of one's own interests, but also awareness of the interests of others. In the case of interests in language, this relates especially to the members of other language communities, whose objective interest is directed correspondingly to the maintenance and strengthening of their own language. Only with such a comprehensive view is it possible to speak appropriately of a "well understood interest". In turn, this is initially a property of individuals, with different emphasis on different individuals, distributed differently in different collectives, where regional governments can be seen as collectives particularly relevant to language policy. Every language policy, especially a language policy directed towards the EU with its diverse contexts, should consider this diversity of interests.

Corresponding with the title of the book, the present chapter (Ch. H) is concerned primarily with an interest in a strong or weak position of German in the EU and its institutions (see also Ammon 2006g, 2007b, 2010e). The advantages for every language community of a strong position of their own language in the EU are rather obvious, while significant disadvantages are hardly imaginable (Ch. A.1). What is particularly relevant for German is its position (status and function) as an EU working language. As already mentioned, the position of German is precarious. A language policy which aims to maintain or strengthen the position of its own language, must not only assess accurately the chances of success per se, but also any advantages associated with possible successes and disadvantages associated with failures. By contrast with its position as an EU working language, the position of German as an EU official language is secure, for the time being, and therefore less in need of investigation. The position of German as a minority language in some EU Member States, which is supported by the EU, together with the Council of Europe based on the *European Charter for Regional or Minority Languages*, operates at another level (see Ch. E).

The direct advantage of German as an EU working language can be seen in that it ensures more efficient communication by the German-speaking countries and by all German-speaking individuals with the EU institutions and facilitates the work of German-speaking EU officials and MEPs. However, for the topic of the present book, a less prominent, indirect advantage may be even more significant. This is based on what seems to me a plausible assumption that, over time, the EU will develop into a kind of federation (Habermas 2001/2006: 98–103, 124–129; also Ch. H.4.1; H.4.4) and that the EU working languages will become the predominant languages for the centralised government of this state and its parliament. Although development towards this point is uncertain, it has been affirmed many times in the very recent past and may become more attractive in future. If German were not to be one of the working languages in the government of a future EU federation, its international function in diplomacy would become completely redundant. Exclusion of German from the working languages of the federation would further weaken its position in the EU. Indeed, the government languages would gain an increasing proportion of the communication between central government and the federal states. Current trends already point in this direction, e.g. the fact that the EU Commission already sends documents relevant for consultation to the German Bundestag entirely in English, which is, in fact, incompatible with Council Regulation 1/58, Article 3 (Ch. H.4.2, also Ch. H.4.6; Ammon/ Kruse 2013; Kruse/ Ammon 2013). Habituation of the Bundestag and the Federal German Government to English-language texts will make it easier for other countries inside and outside the EU to shift their contacts with Germany to English.

A further consequence of such a development is that German may be further reduced in school foreign-language curricula in many countries, so that many students' readiness to learn German is further eroded. Loss of position as an EU government language would presumably have an impact beyond the EU, where the respective language would also become less interesting. The more effortlessly relationships with the EU and with Member States could be fostered exclusively in the EU government languages, the more strongly this would apply. The tendency, already noticeable today, to limit communication with the EU and learning of European foreign languages to English, may also be intensified (cf. Ch. H.4.4; Quetz 2010; H. Wagener 2012). In consequence, German would lose considerable regions of its global distribution as a foreign language (GFL). Motivation to learn German would be weakened in substantial pragmatic components (the need to know German for direct contact with the German-speaking countries and their citizens) and would be largely reduced to merely "cultural interests" – as is already the case today in many English-speaking countries (G. Schmidt 2011: 153–155; Ch. J.9.15).

To assess the prospects of deflecting such developments, it is important to realise that the language interests of EU Member States and their citizens are different. By way of simplification, they can be described as follows. All Member States and their citizens would be interested in ensuring that their own language, "their" EU official language, should also become an EU working language. But for most languages this is delusional because the number of EU working languages must be narrowly restricted for pragmatic reasons. The "small languages" therefore have no chance to position their language as an EU working language. Although it is not possible to classify them with any accuracy, only the large languages, especially English, French, German, Italian and Spanish come under consideration (Ch. H.4.4: Table H.4.4–2). English is the only uncontested EU working language; the position of all other languages as working languages is under threat, although to a different extent in each case.

Having said this, all countries with "large languages" set their hopes on the position of their language as an EU working language and prefer corresponding working-language regimes. And all states have an additional interest in preventing the number of working languages from becoming too large, so that the learning and communication load can be kept within limits. For countries and their citizens which have no prospect of working-language position for their own language, a single EU working language would be most economical – and English is the only candidate. Of course, this would also be the most convenient solution for Member States with English as their official language – after Brexit, Ireland and Malta (with English alongside Irish and Maltese respectively as their official language of state). By contrast, for the other countries with large languages, a single working language would be disadvantageous because this ruling would exclude their own language. But if their hopes for working-language position for their own language were not to be fulfilled, a single EU working language would also be the lesser evil for them (compared with several working languages excluding their own). On one hand, therefore there is an interest that one's own language is among the working languages, and, on the other hand, that the number of working languages is kept as small as possible. Apart from this objective interest, other factors may be relevant for the subjective interest of citizens or decision-makers and may influence their behaviour in referenda or elections.

At the very least, language policymakers should be aware of the objective interests described and take their possible effects into account. They can have a considerable influence on people's subjective interest, especially against a background of skillful agitation. The objective interests of

Table H.4.5–1 Preference table for EU working languages (with equal weighting of Member States: 1. = 1st preference, 2. = 2nd preference and so on). Underlying assumptions: preferred language regimes a) contain the country's own language, and b) have the minimum possible number of languages

Member States (N)	Working-language regime			
	E	E&F	E&F&G	E&F&G&I&S
UK, Ireland, Malta (3)	1.	2.	3.	4.
France, Belgium (2)	4. (2.)	1.	2. (3.)	3. (4.)
Germany, Austria (2)	3. (2.)	4. (3.)	1.	2. (4.)
Italy, Spain (2)	2. (1.)	3. (2.)	4. (3.)	1. (4.)
Luxembourg (1)	4. (3.)	1.	2.	3. (4.)
Others (18)	1.	2.	3.	4.
N Countries with first preference	21	2	3	2 ($\Sigma = 7$)

Note: G = German, E = English, F = French, I = Italian, S = Spanish

Member States can be visualised in the form of "preference tables", as I prefer to describe these models. Abram de Swaan (1998: 23), from whom I have adopted this idea, uses the term "voting cycles" instead, suggesting the correlation with actual voting behaviour. But since other subjective factors can also flow into voting behaviour, I refer, more cautiously, to "preference" rather than "voting". The preference can switch if circumstances change, e.g. through the leaving or joining of Member States, so that cycles are no longer present. I have renamed de Swaan's model and modified it for the EU in 2015 (Table H.4.5–1). The possible language regime English and German (E&G) has not been considered here; it seems unrealistic to me because of the traditional priority of French as an EU working language ahead of German (Ch. H.4.2; H.4.6). Based on this analysis, it is evident that only a total of seven EU Member States are interested in more than one working language (English), and then only with a large number of five working languages (E&F&G&I&S). However, Table H.4.5–1 does not consider the size of the countries. Five of the seven countries interested in more than one language are large states of the EU; the UK is the only country interested in a single language but, after Brexit, it will no longer be a member.

Because of the approximate balance between countries interested in only one working language and those interested in more than one (many small countries versus a few large countries), consistent implementation of one of the two solutions: single language versus multiple languages – seems difficult. It is not clear how the two assumptions from which the interests have been derived are weighted relative to one another. This depends on how far inclusion of the country's own language relieves the burden created by additional working languages. However, for countries and their citizens, there are other reasons, beyond difficulties of learning and communication, for being committed to the position of their own language as an EU working language, especially when it is their native language. This is shown e.g. in the struggle by Italy and Spain for their languages to be included among the EU working languages even though five languages (E&F&G&I&S) would also require more effort from them than limiting the regime to English (cf. Working-language regime of the EU *Office for Harmonisation in the Internal Market* in Alicante in Spain, Ch. H.4.2). In Table H.4.5–1, figures added in brackets indicate fluctuating preferences based on possible factors other than learning load. A five-language regime is unrewarding for any side based simply on economy of learning and communication; it must offer other advantages.

For German, it can be assumed that global position depends upon its position as an EU working language. Being excluded from the EU working languages would diminish both its practical benefits for international communication and its prestige. As political and economic integration of the EU Member States progresses, a growing part of the communication relevant for the German-speaking countries takes place via the EU institutions. This could take place largely without German if German were not one of the EU working languages. In this case, German would lose a considerable portion of its practical value. This would also permanently damage its attractiveness as a foreign language. Exclusion from the EU working languages hits German harder than other large EU languages, because German is restricted – as an official language of state entirely, and as a native language largely (apart from language minorities) – to Europe. Among the large EU languages, only Italian is in a similar situation (see Map D.4–1, Ch. D.4). In this context, I refer again to the advantages of the international position of a language described at the beginning of the book (Ch. A.1; also, 2007b: 102). It should by now be clear that it is in the interests of the German-speaking countries and of all speakers of German to maintain and even strengthen these advantages, wherever they still exist. The position of German as an EU working language could contribute to its maintenance and stability. To refer to the beginning of the present chapter, it almost goes without saying that every policy for maintaining or strengthening the position of a country's own language should also consider corresponding interests of other language communities (see also Ch. K).

4.6 Unifying Europe at the cost of the international position of German?

In the founding phase of the EU, the German-speaking countries were in a politically extremely weak position. Germany was divided, militarily conquered, its cities had been bombed and – even more seriously – morally discredited through Nazi crimes and war. The other German-speaking countries remained at a distance from the new association of countries, Switzerland up to the present and Austria until 1995. By contrast, France was a victorious power, a founding member of the UN and a permanent member of its Security Council; it was also morally respectable – because, so far as they were known at all, the deeds of the Vichy regime could be attributed to Nazi Germany. At that time, Belgium, still a predominantly French country, was also a founding member, and Luxembourg was inclined towards the UN and NATO (Ch. H.3). With hindsight, it almost seems surprising that France's original attempt to make French into the sole EU official language and working language was rejected by the other founding members (Stark 2002: 207; Hemblenne 1992: 112). Perhaps France acquiesced on the assumption that the priority or monopoly position of its language would develop of its own accord without a corresponding ruling.

The ground already seemed prepared for this by the siting of all institutions of the new association of countries in the French official-language territory (Brussels, Luxembourg, Strasbourg) – although they were at the geographical periphery of the French language territory, which softened the impression of a planned linguistic domination. Another step towards mitigating the impression of linguistic domination was the nomination of a German, Walter Hallstein, to be the first President of the Commission. He was in office from 1958–1967 (cf. Haselhuber: 26, note 44). But Hallstein was hardly less inclined towards the French language than a French person. Not only did he speak French on almost every occasion; he also accepted its priority for official use, as far as permitted by Council Regulation 1/58 (Ch. H.4.2).

Immediate, initial prioritisation of French laid the foundations for its continued linguistic position in the community. In the long term, the position of languages in institutions or states is generally characterised by initial circumstances. One example is the League of Nations, in which the official languages (English and French) retained their official status without question in the successor organisation, the UN (Ch. H.3). Other examples include the Spanish, Portuguese, French and British colonies, where the initially established languages (Spanish, Portuguese, French, English) generally retained their position over any subsequent influx of other languages. This resilience is determined by the effort required for an institutional language shift and the difficulty of language shifting for individuals who must acquire new language skills. Specification of official languages requires both the appointment of correspondingly linguistically qualified staff and the preparation of documents in these languages. The resulting "inertia of an already existing language regime" (Ammon 1998: 192–194) can only be overcome with difficulty. A further example is therefore the dominance of French in the EU institutions challenged by the superior "battalions" of English.

The forces standing behind the German language, including its economic preponderance even in the FRG and then in the united Germany, were never sufficient to threaten the priority of French in the EU institutions. Lack of anchoring of the German language in countries outside Europe was a limiting factor (not an official language in UN or NATO), and the weaker position of Germany compared with France in international organisations (e.g. no permanent seat on the UN Security Council).

One obstacle to a commitment to German language interests and their implementation was, and still is, a lingering mistrust of Germany by neighbouring countries; this relates back to the Nazi period and is reflected in widespread attitudes within the German-speaking countries. The continued existence of these attitudes is exposed time and again in conflicts between Germany and other countries, e.g. Greece and Turkey, where German politicians have been caricatured as Nazis. The title of a British newspaper article characterises the mood appropriately: "Only now is Europe learning to stop fearing the Germans" (*Financial Times* 17 July 2007: 9). Former German Federal Chancellor, Helmut Schmidt (2008), who was intimately familiar with German post-war politics, linked these attitudes to the political priority of France in the EU and beyond:

> It will take several generations before the terrible memories of German conquest and occupation fade from the minds of our neighbours. [. . .] We should on no account create an impression [. . .], that Germany might be trying to use its large, high-performance economy to gain leadership of the EU. (p. 95) [. . .] Of all our European neighbours, France was the first country to offer us Germans collaboration and – later – reconciliation after Hitler's world war. European integration also emanated from France, time and again, the crucial momentum originated in France. (p. 97) [. . .] [O]nly France [has] the possibility of playing a leadership role in Europe. In this context, France's position in the UN Security Council and its nuclear arsenal are likely to retain great importance into the foreseeable future. However, within the EU, France will continue to seem a *primus inter pares*.
>
> (p. 101f.)

This kind of assessment has presumably characterised Germany's EU policies, including language policy, up to the present. Justified though this may seem, it still raises questions about the degree of reticence in language policy which might once have been appropriate and whether it is still appropriate today. This policy has no effect on former perpetrators but only current and future Germans and inhabitants of other German-speaking countries and regions, and ultimately even teachers and learners of German as a foreign language anywhere in the world.

There have been several remarkable cases of language-policy reticence by Germany since 1945. The following list of failed attempts to assert German linguistic interests, including those outside the EU, is unfortunately still incomplete. Full details about circumstances and impact on the position of German in the EU are also unavailable. The list, which is subdivided by headings (in italics), reaches back to the foundation of the EU, but is not arranged in strict chronological order or with any kind of ranking.

1) Accepting the location of all EU institutions in the French official-language territory

As already explained, in the founding phase of the EU, the siting of EU institutions in the German-language territory was presumably inconceivable. But the sites were very close to the German-language territory or had historical relations with the German language: Strasbourg is in traditionally German-speaking Alsace (Ch. E.4.3); German became one of three official languages in Luxembourg (Ch. D.2.5).

2) The German, first President of the Commission supporting the establishment of French as the main EU working language

There is no doubt that the first President of the Commission, Walter Hallstein, acknowledged and implemented the prioritisation of French as a working language for the EU Commission although he was himself a German (Stark discusses limits on this, 2002: 207). Presumably he had no other choice.

3) Failing to apply for the status of an official language of the UN

Was this reticence motivated by considerations of power politics, and were the actors aware of the possible consequences for the global position of German? In 1973, the FRG and the GDR joined the UN following Austria, which had joined in 1955 (Ch. H.3). An application to the UN for official-language status for German was evidently anticipated (Tabory 1980: 43) but never filed. In view of the efforts made for Arabic, which became a UN official language in 1974, an application for German would have been taken for granted. Perhaps the UN would then have made both languages, Arabic and German, into official languages. In fact, German was anchored in fewer states than Arabic and in none of the oil-producing states (there was an oil crisis at the time); instead, German had a traditional reputation – still intact at that time – as an international academic language (Ch. G.1, end), and German was learnt as a foreign language worldwide. This "failure" of German language policy abroad was widely criticised (Ammon 2005c: 92; 2009a: 122). The negative consequences of this lack of UN official-language status for German may be important, but they are difficult to assess accurately. In 1975, at the request of the FRG, GDR and Austria, German was given the limited status of a UN document language. The German-speaking countries did not attempt to improve that status – although the Arabic countries managed to upgrade their language from a UN document language (1955–1973) to a UN official language in 1974.

4) Waiving "official-language status" (in fact, working-language status) in the Council of Europe

In the Council of Europe, an "official language" has a higher status, enjoyed only by English and French (all functions), than a "working language", which has lower status (fewer functions). The meaning is therefore reversed by comparison with the EU (Ch. H.3, towards the end).

German, Italian and Russian have this lower status. As in the case of the EU, the starting conditions were unfavourable for German. Added to the historical burden was the fact that no German-speaking country was among the founding states of the Council of Europe (founded 5 May 1949). The FRG only joined two years after foundation, as the first German-speaking country (2 May 1951). Some 40 years then passed before Germany, Liechtenstein and Austria, in association with some non-German-speaking Member States, filed an application for German as an "official language" (in fact, a working language). This was rejected in 1994, as were several other attempts. "So far it has failed because of lack of funding in the Council of Europe" (*Das Parlament* 11 May 2001: 17). This is often cited as a justification for the repeated rejection – although the German-speaking countries routinely contribute more to the budget of the Council of Europe than French-speaking or English-speaking states. The application to boost the status of German was driven more by Liechtenstein than by Germany and may have been successful if Germany had not refused to accept a fair proportion of the costs (proportional to the number of inhabitants), which amounted to a figure in the low, single-figure millions (Merker 2006: 58f.) and would presumably have been taken over by the organisation itself after some time. In view of other massive expenditures, this refusal seems incomprehensible nowadays. Statements, such as the following comment by one employee of the German Council of Europe delegation in Strasbourg that "[i]t is not bad that Germany is not an official language. Everything is interpreted anyway" (Merker 2006: 54), suggest the naivety of the language policy adopted by German actors in this context. However, this second-rate status of German in the Council of Europe means that German is also not a working language in its institutions: neither in the European Court of Justice for Human Rights (Strasbourg) nor in the European Foreign Language Centre (Graz), and German is not a full teaching language at the European College of the Council of Europe in Bruges (Belgium) and Natolin (Poland), where approximately 400 Europe experts are trained every year. German is only a teaching language there in individual degree programmes for the language services and the diplomatic service.

5) Waiving the German-language requirement for English-speaking EU officials

Among EU officials, it is widely known that, during the British joining negotiations for the EU in 1971, French President Pompidou coaxed from British Prime Minister Edward Heath a promise that "all members of community institutions sent from the UK 'must speak the French language'" (Stark 2002: 210; Décsy 1973: 242). France is said to have dropped its resistance to the membership of the UK only after this promise had been made. From the German side, there was no such attempt to secure a knowledge of German by EU officials, which would have been significant for German as an EU working language, at this time or at the time of any other EU expansion. In fact, it is doubtful whether the FRG at that time even heard about the agreement between Pompidou and Heath. According to a detailed investigation by Katrin Ruecker-Guitelmacher, giving a good insight into power relationships in the EU at that time (2009 – information from Wilfried Loth), during the membership negotiations with the UK, the FRG was limited to receiving filtered information about the discussions. The German ambassador in Paris, Hans Hellmuth Ruete, "*n'a été que brièvement et très sommairement informé de la rencontre franco-britannique* [. . .]". He could only speculate about what Pompidou and Heath were discussing: "*Ruete pense que les deux chefs d'Etat et de gouvernement se sont entretenus sur l'avenir de l'Europe et son rôle dans le monde, la forme de l'Europe élargie, l'UEM, les accords de Yaoundé, les problèmes néo-zélandais, l'avenir de la langue française à Bruxelles ainsi que la défense nucléaire future des deux pays*" (ibid: 335). However, in the preparations for the face-to-face talks, it became clear why the language question was important to Pompidou:

> *Georges Pompidou [. . .] juge [. . .] important certaines questions qui n'ont à priori rien à voir avec des directives communautaires. Parmi ces questions, il y a celle de la langue. Le Président français veut préserver la prédominance de la langue française au sein du marché commun élargi. Selon lui, 'il faudra en tout cas, dans la pratique être farouche ['inflexible'! U.A.]. Non seulement ne jamais parler anglais, mais exiger que toute intervention en anglais soit traduite. Je [=Pompidou! U.A.] ne crois pas à une négociation dans ce domaine.*
>
> *(Ibid: 298)*

However, in the 12-hour talks held on 20/21 May 1971 in Paris, with only the heads of state and two interpreters (ibid: 453), Pompidou touched on the language question very skillfully, only in passing. Heath then responded nonchalantly with his own meaning:

> *En ce qui concerne la langue française, de facto langue de travail dominante dans les instances communautaires, Pompidou y attache une certaine importance pour des raisons intellectuelles, nationales et européennes. Au-delà de l'élargissement du marché commun, la sauvegarde du français face à l'anglais est en effet l'une des préoccupations du Président de la République. Aussi Heath, pour apparemment faire plaisir à Pompidou, assure-t-il d'envoyer des fonctionnaires capables de travailler en français à Bruxelles.*
>
> *(Ibid: 464)*

In this context, both sides underlined the close relationship between France and the UK, for example, Heath pointed out, "*la communauté du passé français et britannique commun comme celui d'anciennes puissances impériales, et la communauté de leur présent en tant que puissances européennes* [. . .]" (ibid: 460). But Heath's promise did not prevent British EU officials from drawing attention to themselves soon afterwards by notoriously using their own language. For example, the General Secretary of the Council of Ministers commented as early as 1973 on the "*bad habit* taken up by some UK representatives at General Affairs meetings to intervene in their own language, when it is *accepted practice* not to provide interpreting services at these meetings; the practice is accepted by all eight language groups, except for the UK" (Lenaerts 2001: 236). Anyway, over the years, the Heath–Pompidou agreement may have supported the position of French in the EU institutions at the expense of German.

6) Call to waive language-policy claims by Foreign Office Language Services

One indication for the readiness of German politicians to waive language policy claims to the EU was a "call for pragmatism" by Hermann Kusterer (1980), head of the Foreign Office Language Services of the FRG and chief interpreter for several Federal Chancellors (see also Kelletat 2001a: 56f.). Kusterer expressly suggested to the German public and politicians that they should give up German as an EU working language and accept the restriction to English and French. It can only be assumed that this corresponded with the then predominant mood in the Foreign Office – although it was not in the interests of their own staff, because it would reduce the demand for interpreters and translators. This was in the days of Helmut Schmidt's chancellorship (1974–1982) with Foreign Minister Hans-Dietrich Genscher (1974–1992), a point which links back to the start of this chapter. At an international conference on EU language policy in 1989 in Bad Homburg, which I attended, Kusterer's plea was cited several times and acknowledged almost incredulously by non-German participants (cf. Coulmas 1991c, b). The attitude of the German Foreign Office and of the Chancellor's Office, which was largely in agreement with this call, was therefore entirely compatible with the Pompidou-Heath agreement – but it was certainly not beneficial to the position of German in the EU institutions.

7) Failure to insist on realisation of working-language status of German in the EU Commission

The attitude of self-denial changed under the chancellorship of Helmut Kohl (1982–98), who announced directly in his first government statement (4 March 1983): "We will renew our efforts towards spread of the German language abroad" (Ammon 1989c: 254; 1991a: 542). Very soon afterwards, and more intensively after German reunification, Helmut Kohl's demands were also directed towards the position of German in the EU institutions. Finally, Jacques Delors, President of the Commission, gave way to his insistence and declared German a working language of the EU Commission in 1993 (Ch. H.4.2). His ruling was that "Whenever documents are presented for internal use by the Commission, they shall be formulated in the working languages German, English and French" (*EG-Nachrichten* 34, 6 September 1993: 4), and this is still among the procedural rules of the EU Commission today. However, it does not contain any provisions on the use of German as an oral working language. On the contrary, Delors' regulation and the Commission agenda are satisfied if documents prepared in English or French are then translated into German by the Translation Service. This possibility and its consequences were not realised by the German side for a long time. The relevant provision does not suggest the oral use of German or the knowledge of German which officials would require for this purpose – so that, now, "optimists estimate that only around one third of officials (of the EU Commission! U.A.] speak or understand German sufficiently well" (Hoheisel 2004: 79). Table H.4.6–1 shows a random but presumably typical example for language requirements in EU job advertisements, with the requirements for the Commission in brackets. The linguistic knowledge of Commission Presidents, who always knew French and, since EU membership of the UK also always knew English, but seldom German, fit into this overall picture. The same applies for the language

Table H.4.6–1 Frequency of required and desirable language skills in job advertisements for EU institutions (figures for EU Commission in brackets)

Language	Total	Required	Desirable
English	89 (13)	85 (12)	4 (1)
French	42 (9)	28 (4)	14 (5)
German	15 (1)	5 (1)	10
Spanish	4 (2)	2 (2)	2
Portuguese	2	0	2
Greek	1	1	0
Italian	1	1	0
Maltese	1	1	0
Dutch	1	1	0
EU official language, unspecified	78 (5)	50 (4)	28 (1)
Non-European language	4 (3)	4 (3)	0

(*Source*: www.europa-kontakt.de/index.html?www.europa-kontakt.de/AD_stellen.html)

skills of commissioners, e.g. in 2011: of 27 commissioners, 25 could speak English, 23 French and only 14 German (Ammon/ Kruse 2011).

8) Accepting the non-use of German in the CEE entry negotiations

A strengthening in the position of German in the EU, including the EU institutions, was widely anticipated from the expansion of the EU towards Central and Eastern Europe (CEE). France was concerned about the priority position of its language and strove to secure French in the new Member States. One of its successes was to include all Central and Eastern European states, including even Austria, into *La Francophonie* – at least with observer status, but without voting rights and with recognition and promotion of the French language (de.wikipedia.org/wiki/Frankophonie; Map-Francophonie organisation 2005. png). At the time of the collapse of the Soviet Union, German was the second most frequently learnt foreign language after Russian, in many CEE states (Ammon 1991a: 121–149), and the lingua franca among the older generation (ibid: 137).

Although it is true that English was making headway, the older, German-speaking generation played a significant part in the EU entry negotiations. Nevertheless, the German language was largely excluded from negotiations, which took place almost exclusively in English and still in French if necessary – although the German Commissioner Günter Verheugen was responsible for EU expansion in the crucial period between 1999–2004. With reference to these negotiations, German TV journalist Franz Stark (2002: 212f.) wrote that, in contacts with the EU, politicians of the CEE states quickly noticed:

> that 'nothing could be achieved' in Brussels without using English and French. During the 1990s, this led to a recognisable loss in the status and prestige of German in Central and Eastern Europe. [. . .]. Ignoring the actual distribution of foreign languages in the country, internal job advertisements of the EU Commission for the newly established representations of the former East Bloc required on principle only a knowledge of English and French, but not German. [. . .] One attentive observer of these events, the former Brussels correspondent of the *Süddeutsche Zeitung*, Winfried Münster, noted in a TV interview in 1992: 'Latvians, Estonians and Russians, Poles and Hungarians would like to speak (to the EU) in German. But from here [Brussels! U.A.], attempts are being made, especially by the Commission, to undermine this, to suppress it. [. . .] Once again, the Federal German Government and most German officials in Brussels have done nothing significant to defend themselves from these events [. . .]'.
>
> *(p. 213 – paragraph images removed! U.A.)*

Similarly, the training of German interpreters in CEE states was ignored by the German side (Kelletat 2004a, b). It is possible that this kind of negligence originated from excessive self-confidence by German politicians, which many CEE politicians had instilled into them. "The Germans should not be worried on that count", quoted in a *FAZ* article ("Language is Power", 15 June 2004) with one Hungarian politician agreeing: "That will come of its own accord" – meaning that German in Brussels would allegedly be a matter of course.

9) Failure to insist on interpreting for German in informal EU Council sessions

The biggest scandal so far about German as an EU working language occurred in 1999 around the interpreting of informal EU Council sessions (details in Kelletat 2001a; also "*Deutsch hat ein Potential für internationale Kontakte*", *Die Welt* 9 July 1999: 13). When Finland took over the half-yearly rotating EU presidency, it refused to interpret German for informal Council sessions in favour of exclusively English, French and its own language. But under Chancellor Gerhard Schröder and Foreign Minister Joschka Fischer, Germany demanded interpreting for German, invoking a custom – which had in fact not been practised consistently, and which was opposed by Spain and Italy (Kelletat 2001a: 62). Mindful of the regular, maximum payment contributions to the EU budget by Germany, the German government possibly felt that Finland's justification regarding costs was an additional provocation. When Finland proved to be inflexible, Germany and Austria boycotted the informal EU Council sessions. After several boycotted sessions, Finland gave way (ibid: 63, also 64). But Germany did not consistently pursue a relentless policy of claiming German as a working language of the Council of Ministers. On the contrary, during the subsequent Council presidencies of Denmark (2002) and Greece (2003), Germany accepted setbacks for German, albeit under protest (Wu 2005: 65). This has contributed to the fact that English and French are now the only real working languages of the Council of Ministers – where full interpreting of all EU official languages already applies for formal sessions. The fact that the German media criticised the attitude of Schröder's government towards Finland as non-conciliatory – compared with previous examples of conciliation, e.g. under Chancellor Helmut Schmidt (point 6 above), may have contributed significantly to Germany's giving way. "Precisely in 'government-friendly', left-liberal newspapers such as the *Süddeutsche Zeitung* and *Die Zeit*, there was little understanding for the Federal Chancellor's actions". On the contrary, they were interpreted as an ominous sign of Euro-scepticism. *Die Zeit* (no. 28, 8 July 1999) called this attitude "*linguistic-de-Gaullism*", which, to EU partners, seemed like "a re-run of the Wilhelmine era", and Helmut Schmidt himself, as co-editor of the newspaper, once again demanded recognition of the leading role of France in Europe (Kelletat 2001: 31).

10) Abandonment of German as a working language of the European Central Bank (ECB)

Despite the location of its headquarters in Frankfurt am Main, the European Central Bank, which was opened in 1998 and achieved the status of an institution of the EU in the Treaty of Lisbon of 2007, has only one working language, English. For most EU institutions, the local official language of state is also their working language, at least in the case of the large EU languages. One example is the Harmonisation Office for the Internal Market in Alicante in Spain, where Spanish is one of the working languages, but also – because of an objection by Italy – Italian, alongside English, French and German. Perhaps Germany wanted to avoid endangering the bid for the German location by making additional demands about language. However, this acceptance without argument fits seamlessly into the long history of abandonment of the German language.

11) Abandonment of German as a working language of the European External Action Service (EEAS)

When the European External Action Service was established (EEAS; based on the Treaty of Lisbon 2007 and an organisational stipulation of 2010), it seemed as if the German Government was at last insisting on German as a working language, alongside English and French. At least, this is what German Foreign Minister Guido Westerwelle emphatically demanded ("*Westerwelle will Deutsch retten*" [*Westerwelle wants to save German*], taz 23 March 2010; www.taz.de/!50139/), but the first "High Representative", in a sense, Foreign Minister of the EU, Lady Catherine

Ashton (UK), admitted that she had completely forgotten the German she had once learnt and "apart from a few scraps of French, I have no knowledge of foreign languages" ("Catherine Ashton – Pale Baroness", *Financial Times Deutschland* 5 December 2010). "[A]t the fringes of an event in the German Society for Foreign Policy (DGAP) in Berlin", Westerwelle stated that, "[h]e had 'discussed the topic of the German language several times with Cathy Ashton. I have also obtained the corresponding promises. But if this has not been adopted by organisational units to the extent which was agreed politically [. . .] between the two of us, we will follow up on it immediately'" (26 October 2010; www.euractiv.de/globales-europa/artikel /deutsch-im-ead-westerwelle-frchtet-verfestigung-003838). However, these efforts did not bear fruit. One account from the same year affirms that, "[A]lthough Catherine Ashton [. . .] gave an assurance [. . .] to Foreign Minister Westerwelle that German would receive due consideration in the European External Action Service (EEAS), the facts tell a different story: the (provisional) homepage of the EEAS is not available in German, and job advertisements for first appointments require only a knowledge of English and French, not German" ("Discrimination against the German language", *FAZ* 13 December 2010: 13). And to all appearances, German foreign policy has – yet again – accepted the marginal position of German in the European External Action Service. The situation has not improved just because there are now some webpages at least partially in German (eeas.europa.eu/index_de.htm).

12) Acceptance of communication in English between EU institutions and German Bundestag

In recent years, it has become taken for granted that EU institutions communicate with the German Bundestag in English (Ammon/ Kruse 2013; Kruse/ Ammon 2013). Experts estimate the proportion of documents transferred by the EU Commission to the Bundestag for discussion at around 25%. In fact, the president of the Bundestag sends a proportion of these back under protest and demands versions in German, as stipulated by Article 3 of the Council Regulation 1/58 ("documents addressed by an institution of the Community to a Member State or to a person subject to the national jurisdiction of a Member State shall be drafted in the language of the state"). However, urgency and importance are invoked to justify deviations from this norm. Subsequent presidents of the Bundestag may not continue to stand up for German as robustly as Norbert Lammert has so far. The language choice of the EU Commission towards the German Bundestag also shows that the EU working languages have an impact inside the Member States. The choice of English undermines the position of German in the German parliament in the sense that a knowledge of German is no longer adequate or sufficient for the work there. It is remarkable that individual parliamentarians have admitted that they have difficulty understanding English but – contradicting this position – have also claimed that they can still complete their work as MPs correctly (Ammon/ Kruse 2013; Kruse/ Ammon 2013). Does this open the gates for unrestricted future communication in English with the German Bundestag, and with the German Government as well?

Individual experiences strongly suggest that it is not impossible to influence language choice in the EU institutions. For example, Dietrich Voslamber, a member of the board of the *Verein Deutsche Sprache (VDS)* has achieved remarkable changes by writing letters. He gave documentary evidence of this during a lecture at the University of Hamburg on 9 May 2012:

- After Voslamber's request, internal administrative communication in the EU institutions was also produced in German, alongside English and French, but this has since been completely abandoned (all language versions);

- In response to his request, German was included in the EU Internet presence;
- At his request, German was, in fact, not added to the text banner for press conferences of the Council of Europe, but English and French were also removed. German was therefore no longer demoted.

However, because of lack of sustained pressure, these changes have been withdrawn. Voslamber justified his demands with reference to the numbers of speakers of German, but also partly based on the contribution made by Germany to the EU budget, and the fact that – at least so far – there is no legal basis for demoting German to being behind English and French.

All of the above points raise the question of why the German Government is so unsuccessful in its language policy in the EU. Many readers might remember announcements at the time of the reunification of Germany to the effect that the German language would achieve an outstanding position in Europe in future and along with this a strengthening of its position worldwide (e.g. Davidheiser 1993). I witnessed an example of this in Singapore, shortly after Goh Chok Tong took up office as Prime Minister on 26 November 1990. A new book on overseas advertising for the city state was presented on TV; it was published in three languages, English, Chinese and German. The German version was explicitly justified with the reason that, after reunification, German would become a very important language in Europe. Why was this prediction not fulfilled in reality? Could it be that integration of Germany and Austria in the EU did not strengthen the position of German in the world but weakened it instead? However delusional this suggestion might seem, it deserves closer consideration, which will be provided in the next chapter. But I would first like to avert any misunderstanding: the advantages of the EU and of European integration for German-speaking countries and other Member States are far more important than any presumed linguistic disadvantages – even if these have been confirmed by thorough investigations. In my opinion, a plausible rejection of the EU cannot be based on such disadvantages because the EU has given Europeans an unprecedented level of peace, welfare and freedom.

4.7 Potential solution including German as an EU working language?

To begin with, it should be noted that the probable development of the EU into a federal state could be taken up differently from the way envisaged in chapters H.4.5 and H.4.6 to strengthen German as an EU working language, although this would only be possible in the long term. The EU would no longer be able to brand itself, as it occasionally does today, as a kind of international organisation. Arguments in favour of English and French as the uncontested working languages of international organisations (cf. Ch. H.1; H.3), which are sometimes heard in the context of language policy, would be jettisoned, because different rules apply to international organisations and states. It would be less easy to justify a situation in which the language with the second largest number of speakers (native speakers + FL speakers) can rank, as a working language, far behind the language with the third largest number of speakers (Ch. H.4.4, towards the end; *Eurobarometer Spezial* 386 (2012): 12, 22). But continuing strong pressure for English as the sole EU working language would still have to be anticipated. According to Theo van Els (2003, 2005a, b, 2007) and Philippe Van Parijs (2011), the restriction to English would be the most practicable and also the fairest solution for EU working languages within an association of states. However, other proposals are possible in this context (Ammon 2002: 32–35, 2005c: 94, 2005e: 321–324, 2007b: 104–108; Haselhuber 2012: 389–401; Ginsburgh/Weber 2011). Having said this, any new ruling on EU working languages would require an amendment of Council Regulation 1/58 – which is hardly possible while it still requires unanimity (ratified in 2003 in the Treaty of Nice, Article 290, and in 2009 in the Treaty of Lisbon – see Ginsburgh/ Weber 2011: 181; also Ch. H.4.2).

Jakob Haselhuber (2012) designed a "language bundle" based on ten criteria and including five EU working languages, English, German, French, Spanish and Russian, "which includes all the large language families represented in the EU, "Russian for the Slavic language family" (ibid: 397). Now, on one hand, the inclusion of Russian is questionable, because it is not one of the EU official languages, and, on the other hand, Italian is missing. Haselhuber's criteria for EU working languages are as follows (Haselhuber 2012: 390–392, italics as in the original):

1) "*only languages* [...] *which are native to a (present or future) EU-MS* [EU Member State! U.A.]";
2) "*the number of native speakers*";
3) "*the number of states in the EU in which the individual languages are native languages*";
4) "*The large European language families,* i.e. Romance, Germanic and Slavic languages, should be represented [...], *which are most widely distributed as native languages in one or more EU-MS and as language of communication beyond the linguistic boundaries and beyond the EU*";
5) "*distribution and use of the languages as foreign languages*";
6) "*the position of the languages in international organisations*";
7) "*acceptance* [of the languages! U.A.] *by citizens*";
8) "*the respective financial contribution of the EU-MS to the budget of the EU*";
9) the ruling should "*prevent any politicisation of the language* [...]";
10) the ruling should contribute to the "*avoidance of unrestrained competition*" between languages.

This list of criteria has the advantage of richness, but it also contains some obscure points. For example: is Russian "native" to the EU or will it ever be? (criterion 1), and is "the distribution and use of the languages as foreign languages" concerned with the EU or worldwide? The weighting of the criteria relative to one another is particularly difficult and is not addressed by Haselhuber; this remains unclear in other proposals, including my own (at the end of this chapter).

The proposal by Victor Ginsburgh and Shlomo Weber (2011) introduces the readiness of Member States to accept their own 'linguistic disenfranchisement' ("sensitivity towards language disenfranchisement"). The authors consider this sensitivity to be greater the more prepared the states are to accept a working-language regime which does not contain their own language (own EU official language). Their second relevant criterion is the "degree of comprehensiveness" of the language regime throughout the EU (ibid: 179). They only touch on other criteria briefly, apparently without considering them equally relevant. They measure readiness to accept one's own "language disenfranchisement" by percentage of citizens of the EU Member States who answer the following question in the affirmative: "Should European institutions agree on a language in which they communicate with the citizens of Europe?". They therefore evaluate readiness to accept a lingua franca for the EU as an indicator. In 2005, this readiness showed the following levels among the inhabitants of the largest states with the most important languages: Germans: 62% answers in the affirmative, French: 51% and British: 48% (*Eurobarometer Spezial* 2006: 55 – the relevant figures are given in the present book in Ch. H.4.4: Table H.4.4–1). Ginsburgh/ Weber measure the weighting of this readiness (r) of every Member State (k) within the EU according to its population (p_k) relative to the population of the total EU (p), that is, $r_k = p_k : p$ (sum of all $p_k = 1$). But it is questionable whether the respondent's answers to that question can in fact be interpreted as a readiness to relinquish their own language as an EU working language. At least, it is doubtful if the result would turn out the same if the people questioned were made aware of the possible consequences of this relinquishment (cf. Ch. H.4.4, towards the end). The possibility that with greater *reliability* of measurement (corresponding to the operationalisation of the concept), the *validity* of the results would still leave much to be desired, cannot be ruled out.

Moreover, it is not clear how Ginsburgh/ Weber intend to determine the degree of comprehensiveness of the EU working-language regime in the EU; their discussion remains somewhat vague. One possibility, which they do not exploit, would be to base measurements on the number of EU citizens who understand the languages included in the various working-language regimes, where speaker numbers per language registered would provide pointers. If native speakers and FL speakers are combined, the following percentages of EU citizens would understand the respective languages within the period registered by Ginsburgh/ Weber: English 51%, German 32%, French 26%, Italian and Spanish 15% each (*Eurobarometer Spezial* 2006: 8, 13). But these figures cannot simply be added to achieve the degree of comprehensiveness of the language regime, because there are non-empty overlaps the magnitude of which is not known (people who speak English and German, German and French and so on). However, it can be assumed that the comprehensiveness of the language regime grows approximately proportionally to the percentages named, that is, e.g. more for German than for French (32% compared with 26%). I fail to understand why Ginsburgh/ Weber ignore such considerations. Instead, they calculate the votes which might be expected in the case of a majority voting right on the language question – but this is neither available nor likely. Accordingly, from different perspectives, they arrive at between two and 11 EU working languages. In view of the speculative character of the associated, very complex deliberations, I can only refer interested readers to the original text (ibid: 181–187).

What is important, however, is Ginsburgh/ Weber's idea that the EU Member States and citizens excluded from the EU working languages should receive compensation. Once again, their calculations here are speculative and susceptible to variation (Ginsburgh/Weber 187–199). But their idea that the excluded states should not be provided with such – financial – compensation entirely according to their own evaluation (ibid: 200) seems worth considering in greater detail. My own proposal, which I shall include below, also suggests that the Member States excluded from the working languages could promote their own language from the financial compensation granted to them. I present this proposal by way of conclusion here (cf. Ammon 2007b: 104–108, from which the following paragraphs are derived, although I have not marked them as a citation). Accordingly, the question of implementation within applicable law remains open, because for the moment – because of the need for unanimity between Member States required for any amendment of Council Regulation 1/58 – it remains unlikely. I therefore limit myself to the question of what a legitimate ruling might be and the reasons behind it. As already explained in Ch. H.4.4 (towards the end), an EU-wide referendum could give legitimacy to a new ruling. Prior to this, and if necessary, even instead of it, reasons would have to be discussed, but I shall limit myself here to an evaluation of such reasons. It seems to me that they ought to be compatible with principles and values which could be assumed to be acceptable to most EU Member States and citizens and which also reflect the various interests of the EU Member States.

I do not know of any systematic approach to such principles, values and interests. At best, I am aware of demands aligned in this direction (e.g. Philipson 2003: passim) and suggestions which correspond with rather specific interests. I have not included the proposal, which is sometimes heard, that all three major language families, Germanic, Romance and Slavic, must be represented, because it seems of minor relevance for the requirements of an EU language regime as I understand it. I shall begin by naming some principles which – corresponding to the topic of the present book – would support the inclusion of German in an EU working-language regime. I then consider those which do so to a lesser extent. Principle A, which is superordinate to the choice of specific working languages, already provides support for German.

Principle A: Multilingualism is preferable to monolingualism even in the case of working languages. This principle agrees with the official EU affirmation of individual multilingualism and societal poly-lingualism in the EU, which is considered, amongst other factors, as an expression of cultural diversity (cf. Ch. H.4.3; Kruse 2012; Lammert 2006: 171). The principle is further bolstered by the assumption that the internal working languages cannot be cordoned off from the surrounding EU society in the long term, and that monolingualism would permeate the entire EU, far beyond the EU institutions. This is also supported by other indicators, e.g. that EU institutions already communicate with the Member States partly in English and publish important texts exclusively or mostly in the working languages (Ammon/ Kruse 2013; Kruse/ Ammon 2013; Lammert 2006: 173f.).

Principle B: The languages with most speakers in the EU (the numerically strongest languages) should be among the working languages. This principle corresponds with considerations of comprehensiveness (cf. Ginsburgh/ Weber above) and with democratic principles – corresponding to the number of possible users of the languages and citizens identifying with them. Even if there is no majority of EU Member States or EU citizens behind the German language, as the language with the second largest number of speakers after English in total, it should not be excluded from the EU working languages (German has most native speakers and third largest number of FL speakers (Ch. H.4.4: Table H.4.4–2), at least not from a working-language regime with two or more languages (reasons based on Principle A).

Principle C: The languages of the economically strongest language communities in the EU should be among the working languages. It could be added that the languages whose Member States or speakers make the largest contribution to the EU budget should be among the EU working languages. This principle is often dismissed as despicable or something similar but seems justified to me. It would, of course, support German as a working language, because the German-speaking countries, especially Germany, have always made the largest net contribution to the EU budget with a considerable margin.

Principle D: It is more important for the language of a geographically central territory to be among the working languages than the language of a geographically peripheral territory. In my view, this principle carries more weight than the previous principle. But a central geographical position is otherwise also a relevant perspective in linguistic and language planning, e.g. in the choice of a standard variety for a language. Because of its central location, German has more possibilities for contact and more neighbouring languages than any other EU official language.

While the preceding principles support the inclusion of German in the EU working-language regime, this applies less for the next principles.

Principle E: The EU working languages should offer wide international distribution. This facilitates external communication for the EU and therefore corresponds with considerations of use. Accordingly, not only English, but also French and Spanish – and even Portuguese, although it is not in the closest circle of potential EU working languages for other reasons – would take priority over German.

Principle F: The EU working languages should be associated with a respected culture and political history. This applies especially to the consideration that these languages could become the future governmental languages of a federal EU if this continues to develop towards a sovereign state (Ch. H.4.4; H.4.5). The principle can be justified based on whether the languages are acceptable to EU citizens as a symbolic expression of European identity. But the use of this principle, especially the establishment of a corresponding rank ordering of languages, is more problematic.

Nazism and the militarism of the Wilhelmine period count against German; this may also be true of the day-to-day culture of the largest German-speaking country (lifestyle, culinary and clothing considerations). For example, individual preferences among Germans, such as the preferences of the once legendary "Tuscany set" among German politicians, sometimes show signs of disdain for their own day-to-day culture.

In several published articles, I have distilled these principles down to two, which seem the most important for the choice of EU working languages. These are Principle B (number of speakers in the EU) and Principle E (international position of the language) (e.g. Ammon 2006g: 336 – with different numbering of the principles; agreement Göttert 2013: 281–284). Because of difficulties in operationalisation (demarcation of languages based on B, measurement of E, cf. C.2 and A.3 in the present book), a limitation to a simple ranking scale seems appropriate (3 levels: 1 = highest level etc.). This would give the following rank ordering of working languages (for a similar approach limited to three working languages, see A. Ross 2003: 145f.):

1. English (B: 1, E: 1; Σ = 2);
2. German (B: 1, E: 3; Σ = 4) = French (B: 2, E: 2; Σ = 4);
3. Spanish (B: 3, E: 2; Σ = 5) = Italian (B: 2, E: 3; Σ = 5).

The finding that, according to this model, German is ranked at the same level as French, i.e. German would be better positioned than in the current working-language situation (cf. Ch. H.4.2) is especially remarkable. This would certainly be a point of dispute with this proposal; it could be objected against its rank ordering that, compared with German, the degree of internationalism of French is relatively higher than the number of speakers of German in the EU compared with French. The dispute over the difference in ranking between these two languages might become more embittered if it turned out that a working-language regime with two languages was considerably more practicable than with three languages, because EU officials can reasonably be expected to learn two foreign languages (one active and the other passive), but three would hardly be possible (cf. Ch. H.4.6; "German as the third EC language?" *FAZ* 8 July 1991; Nass 1999; "Why not German?" *FAZ* 9 July 1999: 12). This difficulty would affect all EU officials whose own language was not one of the working languages. It could also be a substantial reason for the *de facto* neglect of German, even in the Commission, although, according to the procedural rules, it is a working language ("procedural language") alongside English and French.

This consideration leads to a fundamental question about whether working-language multilingualism is compatible with communicative efficiency. The fact that several working languages are less efficient than one working language can hardly be denied (cf. arguments in favour of an EU lingua franca in Ch. H.4.3). But, as explained above and in the preceding chapters, the Member States and citizens of the French, German, Spanish and Italian languages have a legitimate interest in the inclusion of their languages in an EU working-language regime. In the long term, however, the working-language multilingualism required for this can only be maintained at considerable cost. To ensure success, interested states would have to fulfil at least the following conditions:

a) To agree on a gradation of working languages according to rank and distribution of tasks and to accept these universally (cf. "graded working-language model", A. Ross 2003: 145f.);
b) To cooperate reliably on this basis;
c) To accept full costs for losses in efficiency caused by the working-language multilingualism (graded according to their economic power), especially costs for language services;

d) To agree on and to observe a code of behaviour which reduces their native-language advantage, e.g. because it would be considered as quite unacceptable to speak only one's native language in EU work;

e) To secure the necessary language skills among their officials;

f) To motivate English-speaking Member States to cooperate in good faith (after Brexit, Ireland and Malta); they could refuse, arguing that it is impossible without English, and that they should therefore also not have to pay any compensation for the position and function of English as a working language;

g) To guarantee the technical preconditions for functional working-language multilingualism.

Condition g) is a topic by itself. The technical preconditions include comprehensive availability of interpreters, even for informal meetings, because otherwise, the working groups will often simply resort to English as the sole lingua franca. Regarding e), it must be pointed out that language skills must be distributed proportionally in the institutions. For example, in the case of three or five working languages of equal status within one institution, each language would have to be known by at least two thirds or respectively two fifths of the officials, if knowledge of at least two working languages were to be demanded of all officials. Only then could working groups be formed with corresponding language skills. Regarding f), it would have to be made clear that other Member States must be prepared to make payments beyond the extent necessary for them, e.g. Germany, through its financial contribution to the EU budget, and that this readiness to contribute is indispensable for the formation and cohesion of such a community.

However, these points already suggest that the maintenance of working-language multilingualism exerts enormous demands, thereby striking a pessimistic note for the chances of its realisation. This would apply especially for the EU schooling policy required in preparation for such a plan. At present, schooling policy in all Member States is orientated towards an absolute preference for English with the neglect of all other foreign languages (*Sociolinguistica* 24, 2010). Faced with the consequences of such a schooling policy, any rescue attempts for working-language multilingualism may be in vain.

5. Language choice in diplomatic contacts

5.1 Visits, face-to-face meetings and public speeches by German politicians abroad

Which languages do German or German-speaking politicians use in contact with foreign politicians who speak other languages, and which languages do these politicians use with German-speaking politicians? There has evidently been no systematic research on this question so far, despite my having urged for it a considerable time ago (e.g. in Ammon 1991a: 315–322). At this point, I can therefore only give a few relevant pointers and suggestions. Theoretical considerations and individual observations suggest that language choice in international, diplomatic contacts depend on a large plurality of factors. The factors listed below deserve special consideration:

I) Location of meeting

In location 1), in the home country (e.g. a German diplomat meets a foreign diplomat in Germany), different rules apply from location 2), in a foreign country. A further distinction must be made between a) the country of the foreign diplomat (e.g. German diplomat meets French diplomat in France), b) a third country (e.g. German diplomat meets French diplomat in Italy) and

c) transnational communication via media (e.g. German diplomat telephones from Germany to a French diplomat in France or vice versa).

II) Permanent residence compared with short visit

Expectations about language differ for people who are permanently resident, e.g. embassy staff, compared with short-term visitors, because of the different possibilities available for linguistic preparation and adaptation. The location of a meeting can also play a part (e.g. German ambassador/foreign minister in Buenos Aires – Budapest).

III) Global position of each language, especially in diplomacy

Less linguistic accommodation is expected of diplomats 1) from an English-speaking country (because English is a "world language") than from diplomats 2) from a country with another language, and possibly also less of diplomats a) from a country with an international language (Ch. A.7) than b) from a country with a language without an international position.

IV) Formal versus informal communication

In situation 1), informal contacts, such as small talk, there is generally more freedom of language choice than in 2) formal communication, for which further distinctions are required: a) public speech, b) negotiation, c) personal exchange of ideas.

V) Institutional specifications

The working languages and official languages specified according to statute or custom for given institutions allow only limited room for language choices in formal communication (working languages in the UN, Council of Europe, NATO, EU institutions etc. Ch. H.3; H.4.2).

Beyond this, other principles or rules for language choice may apply. For example, by contrast with individual meetings, groups tend towards the "minimex" rule (=maxi-min), i.e. the choice of the language, "which [. . .] is best known by the member of your audience who knows it least well. This language I shall call the maxi-min language – the language of maximal minimal competence". This is the language which is known at least a little by a large number of participants – instead of the language which is known by fewer participants, even if they may know it better (Van Parijs 2011: 14; Ch. A.6). Especially in groups of two or another small number, the effects of personal acquaintance or language skills of the diplomats, political relations between their countries, such as permanent or temporary power relations, and the rules of politeness in language choice otherwise applicable in international contacts (transferable *mutatis mutandis* from Ch. F.2) may also apply.

This web of potentially active factors, which I have introduced lightly here, should be borne in mind throughout the following discussion. In the absence of a systematic framework, the discussion will be limited to individual examples, with warnings about overly hasty generalisations and pointers for desirable further research. Any attempt to explain and interpret individual observations must also consider the circumstances of the conversational situation. For example, from the fact that a German politician is greeted in German abroad, as sometimes shown on TV, it can on no account be inferred that German will be spoken in subsequent situations, such as negotiations, after-dinner speeches, press interviews and conferences, addresses to the parliament, assemblies and – even less frequently – to the general public. After an initial greeting, it is not unusual to switch entirely to the language of the host country or to a lingua franca (generally English). For example, if a Polish diplomat greets a German diplomat in German when she arrives in Poland, this may reveal a corresponding asymmetry in the language-choice conventions and language skills, but in no sense precludes the possibility that German will not be spoken in any other situation during this visit, but that both sides will each speak their own language, with the help of interpreters, or use English as a lingua franca. A German diplomat seldom speaks Polish.

Based on my own observations and reports received, German is still used more frequently than the other language in diplomatic contacts with countries of relatively small language communities surrounding the German-language territory. This applies for contacts with the Benelux countries, Central and Eastern European and to some extent also Scandinavian countries. Numerous instances are given in Ammon 1991a (316f.), to which I will now add further examples. One German newspaper gave the title "*Arbeitssprache Deutsch*" to a report about former Federal President Horst Köhler's visit to the Netherlands and explained "that, at the suggestion of the Dutch, the working language for the state visit was to be German" (*FAZ* 12 October 2007: 12). *The Economist* (22 December 2007: 44) reported that the Polish Prime Minister Donald Tusk spoke to Angela Merkel "not only in her own language, but even using the intimate *Du* form". Another report about a visit by the president of the Czech Republic, Václav Klaus, to Germany showed images of his notepad with German keywords ("*nach der Verleihung*" [after the award], "*Umweltschutz*" [environmental protection], and it was clear from the context that German was also spoken (*RP* 18 January 2008: A6). In Berlin, German Minister for Foreign Affairs, Frank-Walter Steinmeier, also delivered a speech entitled "*Die Welt im Umbruch – wo steht Europa?*" [Global turmoil – where does it leave Europe?] in German, without difficulty in the presence of the Minister of Foreign Affairs of the Czech Republic, Karel Schwarzenberg (email circular from the German Foreign Office 25 January 2009). These examples suggest that for countries neighbouring Germany, there is still a traditional language asymmetry in favour of German. Proportionally more citizens of the Central and Eastern European, Scandinavian and Benelux countries still learn German than Germans learn their languages. However, the figures for learners of German in these countries have been declining for a long time (Ch. J.2, towards the end; Netzwerk Deutsch 2010: 12). Many indicators also show that knowledge of German is more limited among younger diplomats than among their older colleagues there. By contrast, a good knowledge of English is increasingly taken for granted everywhere. This also applies for German diplomats, who can generally be addressed in English without communication difficulties. But prominent exceptions, especially among the older generation or those socialised in the former GDR, should not blind us to the facts, e.g. the former Federal Chancellor, Helmut Kohl never used foreign languages in any situation. Federal Chancellor Merkel probably speaks Russian better than English. "Frau Merkel never makes speeches in English but often chats in English with other politicians" (Gunnar Hille, Language Services of the German Federal Foreign Office, email 15 July 2014). All foreign and German diplomats are certainly aware of the spread of English as a lingua franca and of the loss of international position of German. Awareness of this shift in the position of languages and the declining knowledge of German among foreign diplomats further contributes to the unabashed use of English. Accordingly, "a trend towards the use of English in international politics has been identifiable over recent years or even decades. Former Federal Chancellors Helmut Kohl and his successor Gerhard Schröder were the last to limit themselves to German, asking for everything to be interpreted. Since Hans-Dietrich Genscher's time, foreign ministers have tended to use English for small talk" (Gunnar Hille, email 11 July 2014).

Presumably, many foreign diplomats whose own languages are among the international languages (Ch. A.3) now see themselves as linguistic "climbers" compared with German and are showing increasing linguistic self-confidence. Nevertheless, there are some who still choose German in some situations, based on tradition, politeness or even to demonstrate their knowledge of foreign languages. The speech by Russian president Vladimir Putin before the German Bundestag on 25 January 2001 is well known (www.bundestag.de/kulturundgeschichte/geschichte /gastredner/putin/putin_wort/244966). But, more often, only greetings or short statements are spoken in German, even in countries with higher ranking languages. For example, there are reports from China of Federal Chancellor Schröder's visit there after the accidental NATO bombardment of the Chinese embassy in Belgrade: "Tension is released when Jiang Zemin speaks German", or the excellent German-language skills of Chinese Minister for Science and Technology, Wan Gang: "A 'German' in the Cabinet in Beijing" (*FAZ* 14 May 1999: 4 and 25 August 2007: 6). But there is no doubt about the growth in linguistic self-confidence, especially among politicians with languages such as Chinese or Spanish, and to a lesser extent also Russian, Portuguese, Japanese and Arabic. With French, the sense of linguistic superiority has a long tradition, while for English, it tends to be taken for granted (Ch. H.4.6). Admittedly, this does not preclude the possibility that German is sometimes spoken, or that politicians with a knowledge of German are specifically appointed to foster special relations. Examples include the former French Secretary of State for European Affairs "with his faultless knowledge of German" (*"Ein Glücksgriff"* [Perfect for the job], *FAZ* 23 January 2009: 10) or Jean-Marc Ayrault, a former German teacher appointed as Prime Minister by French President François Hollande when he was elected in 2012, a fact which the German media found newsworthy. But Hollande also appointed sinologist Paul Jean-Ortiz, who is a fluent Chinese speaker, as a consultant.

One significant reason for the fact that English is spoken much more frequently than German between English-speaking and German-speaking politicians is the wide gulf in language skills. Isolated exceptions are even more remarkable, e.g. the American, Henry Kissinger, who was born in Fürth in Germany. He had no trouble with the German language and did not shy away from using it with German-speaking politicians. In general, however, German politicians hardly ever expect a knowledge of German from English-speaking politicians and they are glad to accept "broken German" from them. One example was supplied by John Kornblum. He was associated with Germany in various capacities and was US ambassador in Berlin from 1997 to 2001. With grammatically idiosyncratic but fluent German, he coped well from the start and was subsequently able to perfect his German. Even US President John F. Kennedy's famous statement *"Ich bin ein Berliner"* (on 26 June 1963) during his visit to Berlin was substantially more effective because, to everyone's surprise, he said it in German (background details in Eichhoff 1993). Speakers of prominent languages can always get speakers of a less prominent language onto their side by using the less prominent language, if only with a greeting or a single statement (cf. Ch. F.2; H.5.3). In contacts between German-speaking and French speaking politicians, more French is presumably used than German. However, relationships here are more ambiguous than with English, which is an indication that French is no longer the prominent language of diplomacy that it once was. In the nineteenth century and even in the first half of the twentieth century, the asymmetrical dominance of French in contacts with German was still no doubt accepted (Ch. H.1). Nowadays, symmetry dominates language choices in German—French diplomatic contacts. Interpreters are generally used between top politicians. For example, in sealing and fostering the German–French friendships between de Gaulle and Adenauer and between Mitterand and Kohl. I have also been told by an insider who did not wish to be named that Federal Chancellor Angela Merkel has also been able to communicate linguistically with French presidents. In the televised walks she made with former President Nicolas Sarkozy, interpreters were apparently kept at a distance. Conversely, I was assured that they also both resorted to English. A temporary removal of interpreters was also reported in the case of Merkel's conversations with Prime Minister Wen Jiabao in China: "Protocol had even driven away the two interpreters to create a face-to-face impression on camera" ("Close, one-to-one conversation with feelings expressed", *FAZ* 28 July 2007: 2).

In passing, it casts significant light on the now more than 50-year-old friendship between France and Germany (or on the unimportance of a shared language?), that hardly any of the top politicians has ever been able to speak the language of the other country. In a follow-on meeting between the two former foreign ministers, Joschka Fischer and Hubert Védrine, "both statesmen were equipped with simultaneous-interpreting headphones" ("*Am Küchentisch*", *FAZ* 14 May 2012: 29). English also plays a significant role between German and French politicians as a lingua franca, although it is accepted reluctantly by the French. One example involves Federal Chancellor Helmut Schmidt and French President Valéry Giscard d'Estaing, who had befriended him, although the French President was chided for this by the French public. Both forms of communication, interpreting and English as a lingua franca, also generally serve for oral communication between German-speaking diplomats and Spanish-speaking, Italian-speaking and Portuguese-speaking diplomats. In every case, asymmetry in favour of one language or the other is also uncommon.

To find out whether there are guidelines for German diplomats regarding language choice during visitor contacts, and to gain insights into the actual language choices made, I addressed the following questions to the German Foreign Office, initially for an earlier book (Ammon 1991a) in Bonn (on 4 January 1988), and then for the present book in Berlin (25 May 2012):

a) Are there any guidelines/recommendations for diplomats of the Federal Republic of Germany in contacts/ discussions with non-German-speaking foreign countries regarding the use of the German language in given situations, or is the choice of language always made entirely at the discretion of the diplomats or depending on their knowledge of languages?
b) If so, to which diplomats do these recommendations/ guidelines apply and under which conditions?
c) What is the wording of these guidelines/ recommendations, and how binding are they?
d) From which partners in non-German-speaking countries and at which level of diplomacy can a knowledge of German be expected?
e) If interpreters/ translators are required, are the provided by the host country, or do they accompany the German diplomats? Is this regulated in a unified manner or does it differ from country to country, and what are the differences here between target countries?

The responses from the Foreign Office in Bonn (13 January 1988) showed that there were no rulings for the use of given languages in such visitor contacts. German was apparently prescribed only for contacts with the foreign missions in the Federal Republic of Germany and the EU. "Beyond this, unless otherwise provided in individual cases, procedure is guided by the following pragmatic principles: with conversation partners who speak German well or when addressing a public which understands German (e.g. German teachers, Germanists), German is spoken; this is also a rule of politeness towards German-speaking foreign partners". This ruling still applies, as the Foreign Office in Berlin subsequently confirmed: "The perspective of the Foreign Office on the language question in visitor contacts by German diplomats has not changed since 1988" (Frank Werner, Dept. E01, email 5 July 2012). According to a more recent report from the Language Services of the Foreign Office, the Foreign Office now recommends the use of German more clearly than previously, wherever possible (Gunnar Hille, email 11 July 2014).

However, there are recurring problems with language choice in the case of public speeches by German politicians abroad, because the audiences often contain many more learners and teachers of German and people with a knowledge of German than in the overall population – who, understandably, may prefer to listen to the speech in German. It also seems important to these individuals to show their own politicians and business people that German is valid on such occasions and should therefore not be neglected in education policy. Furthermore, local university departments for German as a Foreign Language (GFL) or German Studies almost always offer simultaneous interpreting free of charge, both into the local language and into English. It is difficult to describe the bitter disappointment felt by local learners, speakers and teachers of German when their wishes are disregarded, as reported to me by various correspondents. Even when requests to speak German are explicitly voiced by the public, politicians from Germany often turn a deaf ear and continue in English. For example, in a lecture to the German Teachers' Congress in Korea in 1999, former Federal Chancellor Helmut Schmidt openly limited himself exclusively to English (Trabant 2008: 2012). In March 2012, former German Foreign Minister Guido Westerwelle gave a lecture at the State Ivane Javakhishvili University in Tblisi, Georgia, entirely in English and also replied in English to questions asked in German. He later apologised as follows: "That was the protocol" (report from Eka Narsia, Ivane Javakhishvili University). However, "diplomatic protocol" can probably not forbid a minister from speaking in German, especially not for at least part of the speech or when answering questions. The choice of language during foreign visits is "clarified between the ministerial office and the language services [Dept. 105 of the Foreign Office! U.A.] which then also provides "the necessary interpreters". "The call from the Language Services to the ministerial office [is generally along the following lines! U.A.]: please carry out the discussions in German, we have interpreters for every language" (email Gunnar Hille 11 July 2014). Added to this, the Javakhishvili University offered interpreting free of charge. In an earlier letter, the Foreign Office informed me that, "There is no ruling which prescribes the use of a given language in oral contacts. The Language Services of the Foreign Office have at their disposal interpreters for 15 languages; their services are used during various trips" (email Frank Werner, Dept. E01, 5 July 2012). Besides, the "rule of politeness" to speak German with "German-speaking foreign partners" applies especially to learners, teachers and students of German.

Language choice is often difficult when faced with a public which is mixed in its knowledge and preferences for languages. It may be helpful for orientation and evaluation to imagine a corresponding situation in the case of visits to Germany by foreign politicians. For instance, would it be welcome, in Germany, if the Chinese or Japanese head of government were to deliver a speech at the Free University or the Humboldt University in Berlin in Chinese or Japanese, with simultaneous interpreting into German and English, possibly provided by the local university department of Chinese or Japanese – and to voice implied criticisms of the policies of the German government? Well, a similar approach was adopted by German Chancellor Angela Merkel on 8 July 2014 at the Tsinghua-University in Beijing ("Merkel calls on Chinese students to think critically", *Zeit Online* 8 July 2014). From the German perspective, this was evidently taken for granted – but what might the opinion of the Chinese government have been?

Having said this, learners and teachers of German should probably not be thrown into one basket with diplomats. Even with a knowledge of German, diplomats presumably often find it appropriate when they are approached in English, interpreting this as linguistic accommodation, and an effort towards fairness by relinquishing the native language advantage. Perhaps, using German without an initial apology seems rude to them even if German is widely known, especially in smaller neighbouring countries, where assertive use of German can arouse bad memories. In the language choice between diplomats, smooth communication, which is dependent on available language skills and/or interpreting options, is presumably of substantial importance. This would correspond with the "pragmatic" approach explained to me by government officials in Bonn in

1988: "For operational, oral communication with foreigners, the language used is generally the language in which accurate communication can be achieved most quickly and with least effort, except in individual cases in which the diplomat is accompanied by an interpreter for linguistic reasons or other more important reasons. [. . .] Each diplomat is generally accompanied by their own interpreter. If this is not possible or, by joint agreement, not required, a pragmatic approach is adopted". This probably means that communication is achieved using languages which guarantee understanding or for which interpreters are available. Regarding interpreting, it would be interesting for the international position of languages to know which governments have how many interpreters at their disposal for which languages. This would provide an indicator for the international position of languages in diplomacy. Only very incomplete responses were returned from an earlier survey of foreign embassies in the former German capital Bonn (1989). The findings can be roughly summarised to the effect that the diplomats of all countries are trained mainly in the official languages of the UN (Ammon 1991a: 321f.). Roudybush's list (1972: 3) of "diplomatic languages", which also includes Portuguese, gives a similar impression.

5.2 Communicating with foreign representations in Bonn and Berlin

The German Foreign Office considers it valuable for communication, at least for written communication, between foreign missions in the German capital and the Federal Government to be carried out in German. In response to my question, the Foreign Office in Berlin described the ruling as follows:

> The supplementary procedural order of the Foreign Office regarding the Joint Procedural Order of the Federal Ministries stipulates that written communication by the Foreign Office with diplomatic missions in Germany shall be conducted exclusively in German. German foreign representatives shall adapt their written communication with authorities in the host country to local conditions. If German is chosen, a politeness translation [presumably what is meant here is into the language of the respective country or into English! U.A.] is appended.
>
> *(email Frank Werner, Dept. E01, 5 July 2012)*

It is only written communication which is regulated fairly strictly here, i.e. the exchange of "notes", as written documents are designated in diplomacy (for details of the form of such notes, see Zechlin 1960: 169–180). Greater flexibility is required for oral communication. The current ruling from the German authorities stands in a long tradition which harks back to Bismarck's efforts to introduce German in Berlin for written communication with foreign representations there (Ch. H.1). Admittedly, even Bismarck had difficulties with implementation. Many missions responded to German-language notes in their own language or in the lingua franca of diplomacy at that time, French. So, it does not necessarily follow from the stipulation for German offices in Berlin that the other side will use the same language. In the former FRG, German-language notes from foreign missions were unusual for a considerable time. After WWII, German was therefore a completely dominated language in diplomacy (terminology, Ch. A.3):

> The [. . .] foreign missions in Bonn [generally write U.A.] in their own languages, usually accompanied by a translation, possibly in English or French, if less well-known languages are involved. [. . .] Overseas, a German diplomat will use the language of the host country in written communication with representatives of other countries – apart from representatives of German-speaking countries; because if the diplomat were to

use his own language, he would have to be prepared, according to the principle of reciprocity, to be answered in a language with which he is not familiar and for which he possibly has no ancillary resources at his disposal.

(Zechlin 1960: 180f.)

Faced with patchy information, I undertook to investigate further the language choices between foreign embassies in Germany and German Government offices. To a certain extent, this indicates how far they recognise German as a language of diplomacy – or more precisely as an international language of diplomacy, because German is used here between diplomats of different nations (Ch. A.3). Accordingly, in autumn 2009, I addressed the same questions, which I had sent to Bonn in 1989 and received unsatisfactory responses, to 16 foreign embassies in Berlin (Ammon 1991a: 321f.). This time they were answered by nine of the 16 embassies approached. The questions related to knowledge of German among embassy staff and to written and oral communication with German offices in Berlin. The responses were as follows:

Question 1a): "Is it correct to assume that at least some of your embassy staff have good oral and written *German-language skills?*"

"Yes", all 9.

Question 1b): "Are good oral and written German-language skills among the requirements for appointment of at least some of your embassy staff?"

"Yes", all 9 – but Mexico added a limitation that "German-language skills are indispensable for local staff, not for the diplomats".

Question 1c): "Are these members of staff given corresponding linguistic training *already in their home country*, or is training given only after arrival in the Federal Republic?"

"Mostly in the home country" 5 (France, Italy, Japan, Canada, South Africa), "Both at home and in the FRG" 2 (Australia, the Netherlands), 2 "Not at all [by the embassy country U.A.]" (Mexico: "Some diplomats prepare themselves for service in Germany by taking language courses. But there are no general training courses", Spain: "Diplomatic staff are not given training in the German language in Spain; each diplomat is personally responsible for acquisition of German-language skills").

Question 2a): "Which part of the embassy staff requires no German-language skills whatsoever?"

"All require German language skills" 3 (the Netherlands, Spain, South Africa), "All require a minimum" 2 (Japan, Mexico), "5–15% require no German-language skills" 3 (France, Italy, Canada), No response 1 (Australia). Some individual responses seem inconsistent, e.g. South Africa, which translated all questions into English and responded only in English – at the same time as stressing the generally compulsory knowledge of German. But the answer to Question 2a) was: "None, German language training is compulsory to all South African diplomats posted in Germany". The apparent contradiction is resolved if one considers the restriction to diplomats; there are other embassy staff members in addition to diplomats.

Question 2b): "Which part of the embassy staff requires *no oral German-language skills?*"

Same answers as for Question 2a) – apart from France, which indicates 10% for 2a) by contrast with 15% for 2b), and Canada, which specifies people who require no German-language skills as: "A small number of diplomats in purely technical and administrative departments".

Question 2c): "Which part of the embassy staff requires *no written German-language skills?*"

Same answers as for Questions 2a) and 2b) – apart from France: 30%, Canada, same as 2b), Mexico: "The diplomats do not necessarily need written German-language skills", the Netherlands: "A small number of embassy staff require no written German-language skills, depending on their post". Accordingly, there is a tendency to require written German-language skills from a smaller proportion of the staff than oral language skills.

Question 3a): "Does oral contact with German politicians or authorities take place predominantly in German, predominantly in English or in another language, and if so, which?" "Only in German" 3 (Italy, Japan, South Africa – Italy, more precisely: "Contact is taken up only in German"), "Predominantly in German" 2 (the Netherlands, Spain), "Predominantly in German, but also in [. . .]" 3 (France: "Seldom in French", Canada: "Partly in English", Mexico: "Partly in English, partly also in Spanish, because many of the representatives responsible for Latin America in authorities and ministries speak Spanish"), "In German or [. . .]" 1 (Australia: "English"). If it is assumed that the responses "Only in German" – many say simply "In German" – could be exaggerated (cf. the addition in the case of Italy!), then "Predominantly in German" is by far the most prevalent. Only the response from Australia sounds like an equal frequency of English. However, all the relatively larger languages are also used; Spanish with the justification of widespread knowledge of Spanish by Germans.

Question 3b): "Does *written communication* with German politicians or authorities take place predominantly in German, predominantly in English or in another language, and if so, which?"

"Only in German" 5 (Italy, Japan, the Netherlands, Spain, South Africa), "Predominantly in German" 4 (Australia: "Written communication is predominantly in German", France: "Predominantly in German, rarely in French", Canada: "Quite predominantly in German", Mexico: "Practically exclusively in German").

Question 4a): "Does it ever happen that the ambassador her/himself does not have good German-language skills *upon arrival* in the Federal Republic of Germany?"

"No" 5 (Australia, France, Italy, Japan, Canada), "Yes" 4 (Mexico, Spain, the Netherlands: "Yes, unfortunately", South Africa: "It is likely, but all are required to acquire German language proficiency within a given time (2 years)".

Question 4b): "Does it ever happen that the ambassador herself/himself does not acquire good German-language skills *during their period of office* in the FRG?"

"No" 8 (Australia, France, Italy, Japan, Canada, Mexico, the Netherlands, Spain), "Most unlikely" 1 South Africa.

Question 5a):	*Question 5b):*	*Question 5c):*
"*How many* different ambassadors has your country sent to Germany so far?"	"*How many* of the ambassadors had a good knowledge of German when they *arrived?*"	"*How many* of the ambassadors had a good knowledge of German when they *left* Germany?"
Australia: no response	All	All
France: 15	All (recent decades)	All
Italy: after German reunification: 6	All	All

Question 5a):	Question 5b):	Question 5c):
Japan: since 1949: 21	No data	No data
Canada: no data	No data	No data
Mexico: since 1952: 19	Half	Half
Netherlands: 1948–99: 9	No response	No response
Spain: since 1949: 13	Not known	Different levels
South Africa: Not known	Not known	Not known

John B. Emerson, the US ambassador residing in Berlin since August 2013, has "German roots" through his grandparents and learnt German at school, but when he took up office, he described his knowledge of German as "a little rusty" ("*Deutsche Wurzeln*", *FAZ* 27 August 2013) and he limited himself almost completely to English in public statements in Germany. Perhaps qualities other than language skills are sometimes more important for ambassadors themselves nowadays.

Question 6): "Has the *language choice* between your embassy and German politicians and authorities changed since the reunification of Germany?" "If so, to what extent?"

"No" 7 (Italy, Japan, France, Canada, Mexico, the Netherlands, Spain), "Yes, to a certain extent" 1 (South Africa: "Oral communication can be in English, but written communication remains in German"), "Yes, with the new Federal States" 1 (Australia: "With the inclusion of the new Federal States [. . .], new contacts have been made in which German or English is used in the communication corresponding to the language skills of the respective German conversation partner"). Language choice has evidently remained generally unchanged. However, South Africa has allowed more room for English in oral communication. Australia also uses English, also primarily orally, provided language skills on the German side allow this.

Question 7): "Have the *linguistic requirements or preparations* of your embassy staff *changed since the reunification of Germany?*" "If so, to what extent?"

"No" 6 (Australia (implied), Italy, Japan, Mexico, the Netherlands, Spain), "Yes" 3 (France: "Language training in German has been further intensified", Canada: "Since 1992, there is the CSFI [presumably what is meant is the online dictionary, also referred to as "csfi" <www.linguee.de/englisch-deutsch/uebersetzung /csfi. html> U.A.], but no connection with reunification", South Africa: "It has now become compulsory to learn German language" [sic! U.A.]). Especially France and South Africa now place greater value on German-language skills than previously, although South Africa uses English at the same time (Question 6).

Altogether, these results indicate that between the Federal Government and the foreign missions in the German capital, German is the preferred language. However, the findings cannot be generalised because of lack of representativeness of the sample. Embassies of smaller countries which cannot afford such good language training for their staff possibly use other languages, no doubt generally English, more frequently. It can be assumed that, alongside staff with a knowledge of German, there are also staff in most embassies with minimal or no knowledge of German, especially staff designated in many responses as "technical". The ambassadors themselves need not necessarily be familiar with German. The days of Charles Martens' *Guide Diplomatique* (fifth edition Leipzig 1866) are evidently remote history. Martens placed a knowledge of the language of the country first among the skills required by an envoy or ambassador. How else was he supposed to follow debates in parliament, read the newspapers "study the national character" or "form intimate relations in the city of his residence"? (Gerbore 1964: 76). Gerbore (ibid: 119) also suggests how modern ambassadors manage without a knowledge of the local language: "This is possible because the professional interpreter, the occidental dragoman has now materialised as the diplomat's constant companion". I should add that contemporary options for Internet translation are also relevant here – the shortcomings become evident as soon as they are tested – and they are even less adequate for oral communication than for written communication (Ch. A.10).

5.3 Position-strengthening language choices in diplomacy?

For diplomats, the language in which they communicate is of secondary importance. Their priority is to achieve the actual – political – goal, in the same way that business people or academics are primarily concerned with commercial or academic goals (Ch. A.2). Marcell von Donat (1999: 22), who worked in the European Community for Coal and Steel from 1958 onwards and in the EU Commission from 1968 to 1997, has commented on this priority. In his view, when faced with the question of whether they should speak German in the EU institutions or not, German-speaking diplomats should be guided exclusively (or at least principally) by the goal of convincing their addressees about matters of content in the best possible manner. Doing without the use of German is often, he claims, "more expedient for the matter in hand", and the notorious choice of German seems more about the "self-realisation" of the speaker than anything else. The point seems important and is transferrable – *mutatis mutandis* – to language choice in other international contacts, especially in business economics and academia (cf. Ch. F.10; G.13).

However, I believe that neglecting language choice and failing to give due attention to potentially negative consequences (I am not accusing von Donat of these failings) can be problematic. In fact, concentrating on core objectives generally does lead to their achievement, but mindlessly ignoring the use and promotion of one's own language undermines its position in the respective domain and therefore also in the entire action field. Ultimately, this is also detrimental – although possibly very indirectly – to the politics, business economics and scholarship of the German-speaking countries (Ch. A.1). What is at stake here is therefore to fulfil the one goal without failing to consider the other, where core objectives clearly generally deserve priority. Such prioritisation is generally appropriate unless it is absolutised. And it is ultimately advantageous for social groups represented by the individuals involved; for the entire German-language community; and for maintaining the position of the German language, because diplomatic, commercial and academic consequences also – indirectly – strengthen the position of the relevant language. By implication, dramatic examples of this are provided by the failures in German diplomacy which led to WWI and WWII and subsequently brought about devastating losses for the global position of German in recent history. Accordingly, any criticisms about abandoning the speaking of German, generally in favour of English, must always keep in mind the core objectives of the people involved. This kind of circumspection is often absent from superficial criticisms against the use of English by German diplomats, business people or academics, who then become scapegoats for every loss in the international position of German.

Having said this, not all criticisms of the language choices of German diplomats are unjustified (and this also applies for business people and academics; see Ch. F and G). The now almost stereotypical image of the German diplomat (manager or academic) nonchalantly switching to the foreign language, generally English, is not entirely unrealistic. Examples of suspected heedless language choices have already been mentioned in Ch. H.5.1. Further examples can be found on a website which I set up for the Goethe-Institut on the question of appropriate language choice in international contacts (www.goethe.de/ges /spa/prj/sog/fst/de4622069.htm). I note some further examples here, some of which I observed in the context of German diplomacy:

- At the World Congress of Sociology in New Delhi in 1986, the German ambassador surprised the approximately 100 sociology professors from Germany he had invited to his residence for dinner by delivering a speech entirely in English. I was present. Later, by way of justification for this language choice, it was whispered that one British guest had also been expected – but had not in fact arrived;
- Si-Ho Chong, who was president of the Korean Society for German as a Foreign Language for many years, told me about the society's ten-year jubilee in 2005. After the meal, the German ambassador in Seoul delivered a 15-minute speech to the assembled German teachers and learners, "but surprisingly in English! At the beginning, the ambassador pointed out that the president [of the University at which the conference was taking place! U.A.] was the only person who could understand no German. It was therefore entirely appropriate to speak for a few minutes in English. But he continued to speak only in English. One German participant shouted out loudly: "*Bitte, nicht mehr auf Englisch!*" [Please, no more English]. But the ambassador continued in English. Finally, the leader of the symposium again politely pointed out that all the attendees were Germanists and asked if it would therefore be possible to speak only German. Nevertheless, the ambassador spoke to the end of his speech only in English" ("*Dolchstoß aus Deutschland*" [A stab-in-the-back from Germany], *Sprachnachrichten* 01/ 2006: 29);
- After stepping down as Defence Minister (accusations of plagiarism in his doctoral thesis), Karl-Theodor zu Guttenberg introduced himself at a press conference in Brussels as a future adviser to the EU Commissioner Neelie Kroes. "He announced all of this in English, even when journalists asked questions in German. Only when Mrs Kroes answered a question from the Netherlands in Dutch was Guttenberg prepared to utter a few words in German" ("*Der talentierte Herr Guttenberg*", *FAZ* 13 December 2001: 2). It should be borne in mind that – by contrast with Dutch – German is a declared working language of the EU Commission (Ch. H.4.2);
- Finally, the language choice (experienced by myself) of a diplomat in the broader sense, which is intended to generate reflection rather than criticism. At a conference in the Goethe-Institut in Paris in 2004, organised by the GI with a French partner organisation, the director of the Institute welcomed guests entirely in French; less surprisingly, the French partner did the same. When I asked the director of the Institute privately after the event whether an address half in German and half in French might have been more appropriate, she agreed without hesitation – and added that language choice is often difficult, but there are *no* practical guidelines available.

Perhaps blunders, as in the first three examples, or difficulties, as in the last case, have become less frequent. One collection of examples of unfortunate language choices in international contacts – not just by diplomats – with critical comments on the failure to speak German, is provided by Harald Weydt (2004; cf. also Ch. A.6). In recent years, the topic has been discussed more openly, especially by some of the recently founded, German-language-promoting societies (Ch. K.3.4). However, making the appropriate language choice in international contacts will always be difficult even for diplomats aware of the problems and, correspondingly, also for academics and business people. Attempts to make the right language choice sometimes seem like navigating Scylla and Charybdis, between fulfilment of the core objective and promoting one's own language. On one hand, it is obvious that the almost proverbial German "linguistic subservience", that automatic switch to English or the language of the others, is detrimental to the global position of German. On the other hand, obstinate insistence on one's own language can obstruct the achievement of core objectives, the diplomatic goal, the distribution of academic knowledge etc. This kind of insistence on one's own language, of which the French have often been accused, may not only impair understanding of the form of what has been said, it can also arouse defensive attitudes which may extend into the content of the message. The provision by the French Ministry of Foreign Affairs for all EU individuals subject to its directives: "*les Français parlent leur langue*" (Van Parijs 2011: 214, note 17) may sometimes be associated with this unfavourable effect, which is detrimental to core objectives. However, similar directives about the use of German can be found in German Government offices. For example, one "code of behaviour" from the Federal Ministry of Finance for individuals subject to its directives in EU institutions is worded as follows:

1. Participation at meetings/conferences (regardless of whether Commission or Council) shall take place only if:

    •   A German version of any preparatory documents is presented promptly together with the invitations; and
    •   Interpreting into German and from German is ensured.
    [. . .]

3. In the meetings, only German shall be spoken by German representatives.

    (Federal Ministry for Finances, Department for European Policy (June 2000) *EU-Handbuch. EU-Verfahren und -Unterrichtsaufgaben der Bundesregierung, insbesondere im parlamentarischen Raum.* Dept. EA1: 85).

So far as I know, this provision still applies today but has presumably never been consistently followed. It was no doubt related to a similar ruling adopted shortly before, about which the Foreign Office in Berlin gave me the following statement: "The Secretaries of State for Europe of the Federal Ministries adopted the following resolution in February 2000: 'In the event of meetings at EU ministerial level, Federal Ministries shall not take part in such meetings either at political or operational level unless full, active and passive interpreting is provided for the German language'" (Frank Werner, Dept. E01, email 5 July 2012). Point 3 of the ruling cited above is implied here in principle; but limited to "meetings at EU ministerial level". Criticism of such rulings on principle seems inappropriate, if they aim only to increase the parity of German as an EU working language compared with English and French, as suggested by the statutory parity of the three languages since 1993 (Ch. H.4.2). At the time of the resolution, it was certainly also an urgent goal to reduce the competitive, linguistic disadvantage of German companies in gaining access to EU orders – because at that time, Germany was still an economic concern to Europe. Having said this, it is difficult to estimate the extent to which greater parity of German with English and French is achieved by such rulings, rather than potentially counter-productive, defensive reactions. This certainly depends to a high degree upon diplomatic sensitivity and skillful handling.

But how can politicians be expected to respond to the complicated conditions of language choice which academics/scientists are only beginning to comprehend (Ch. A.6; F.2)? There are in fact pointers indicating that many politicians are aware of the potential impact of language choice on the position of languages. For example, in one questionnaire of MEPs from Germany and Austria in 2004 (total response n= 25, 21% of those approached) 52% declared that they tried to strengthen the position of German in the EU by using German, and a further 18% that they made an active effort towards the strengthening of German, e.g. by trying to motivate colleagues correspondingly. Only 28% denied making any such effort – mostly with reference to more important European interests – (one respondent gave no answer).

Nevertheless, the investigators still came to the same negative conclusion, "that the questioned German members of parliament [EU Parliament! U.A.] are not making any special effort to promote their language" (Ollila/ Partanen 2004 – no page numbers). Politicians' awareness of the effects of language choice on the international position of German is sharpened by media reports about associated conflicts. Once again, the German-Finnish conflict about German as a working language in informal meetings of the Council of Europe (Kelletat 2001a; Ch. H.4.4) and the refusal by German Foreign Minister Guido Westerwelle to answer in English a question asked by a BBC reporter in English (ramonschack.word press.com/2009/09/29/7334/; Ch. A.5) provide relevant examples. The media hype around such events does sensitise diplomats and others to the problems of language choice in international contacts, but this in itself does not provide an appropriate basis for practical action, at least not with any sense of certainty. Even with a full awareness of their own language interests, especially strengthening the position of German, German diplomats must keep their core objectives in view and focus on linguistic comprehensibility, circumspection about national interests (because of German history) and politeness. Sometimes, they must also demonstrate a knowledge of foreign languages and cosmopolitanism. Critics of missed opportunities to speak German often highlight such efforts, attributing them to the pitiful motivation of showing off. But, conversely, Westerwelle's refusal to speak English has also been denounced from the other side as a lack of cosmopolitan openness – and long afterwards he [himself! U.A.] conceded that it was an error, which he attributed to "residual alcohol from a victory party", and confessed, that his refusal to speak English:"worried me for a whole year" ("Westerwelle regrets statement about decadence", *WAZ* 23 March 2013). By contrast, I evaluate his refusal to speak English at the press conference, which was, after all, directed primarily to a German public, as entirely appropriate, and as a signal to foreign journalists that they require a knowledge of German if they are to work efficiently in Germany.

A comment by the Bundestag Vice-President at that time, Johannes Singhammer (CSU), provides an example acting in the opposite direction by critiquing the fact:

> that German Minister of Defence Ursula von der Leyen (CDU) delivered her speech on German defence policy at the security conference in English. Singhammer told the newspaper '*Münchner Merkur*':'I would urgently advise that something of this nature should be done in German. The most important international conference which we have in Germany should also be a showcase for the German language.' He said it was difficult, for example, in the EU Commission in Brussels to fight for the German language, 'if we don't speak it ourselves. It is a problem for the German elite that they're so willing to show off their knowledge of English.' [...] According to information from the conference organisers, speakers were free to choose which language they spoke, simultaneous interpreters were said to have been available.
>
> *(www.merkur-online.de/aktuelles/politik/viel-englisch-singhammer-ruegt-leyen-3349115.html)*

In fact, this event took place in Munich, i.e. in Germany (on 31 January 2014). But the public was decidedly international, including largely members of NATO, in which German is not an official language (Ch. H.3). In this sense, von der Leyen's language choice was not wrong – although it is difficult to assess whether a presentation in German (with simultaneous interpretation) would have been detrimental to the effect intended by the speaker.

In concluding the present chapter, two points deserve special emphasis. Firstly, I would like to reiterate a point I made about international business contacts (Ch. F.2). *It is important to consider whether audiences are speakers, learners or teachers of German.* If they are, it is generally advisable to use German. Harald Weydt (2004: 127) perspicaciously warned against the misinterpretation, "that it is a priori polite to use English every time we speak to a non-German. This can be a considerable insult". Regarding learners and teachers of German, this effect can be explained based on politeness theory as conceived by Penelope Brown and Stephen Levinson (1987) in continuation of Erving Goffman's (2003) terminology, according to which rudeness is "face-threatening". Accordingly, learners or teachers of German may interpret a refusal to speak German as meaning that they are perceived as not having an adequate knowledge of German. Of course, this does not mean that one should insist on German if the people addressed cannot speak German well or do not like to hear it or speak it. With a larger public, it is difficult to assess preferences. But preliminary enquiries and partial consideration if wishes are expressed spontaneously may be helpful: short-term code switching into German, supported by simultaneous interpreting if available or spontaneous self-interpreting into English (if possible).

One tip for appropriate language choice worth taking to heart is a *change of perspective.* What would be the impact of a person with a different native language or official language of similar international ranking (Ch. A.7) in a similar situation? In other words, taking up the examples of Westerwelle and von der Leyen – what if a French or Italian Foreign Minister at a press conference addressed to their own population in Paris or Rome were not to answer in English a question asked in English by a British journalist? Or what if a French or Italian defence Minister were to give a (short) presentation in their native language (with simultaneous interpreting into English) at a specialist conference? In fact, a reliable evaluation of the effect would require empirical investigation. But even without this safety measure, it seems probable that the damage to their country would not be great in either case, and that certain benefits could not be precluded. Among other factors, these benefits would emerge from the message to learners and teachers of the foreign language that the native-language community and official-language community are aware of maintaining or strengthening the global position of their own language and that the language is also acceptable on the international stage – if appropriate interpreting is available.

At least a short greeting in German is almost always appropriate. In other circumstances, giving priority of use to German would be advisable e.g. for Guttenberg's press conference at the EU Commission, because German is a declared working language of the Commission. In the example of the Goethe-Institut in Paris mentioned above, the use of German would also have been appropriate. In such cases, with relatively few participants, whispered interpreting can often be arranged for individual participants who know no German. In personal contacts, one should never refuse to speak German if it is desired or accepted. With groups or public speeches, the presence of attendees with a knowledge of German can easily be determined by asking the audience. If everyone present speaks German, the choice of German need hardly be a problem. However, everybody should be asked openly whether they agree and only then should German be spoken. With a larger audience, the emergency measure of whispered interpreting is generally difficult or intrusive. In special situations, it may be appropriate to speak one's own language even if listeners do not understand it, for example, to demonstrate political autonomy. But simultaneous interpreting must then be provided for the entire audience. Furthermore, to avoid the impression of rudeness or domineering conduct, symbolic inclusion of the language predominant among the audience or at least of a lingua franca, generally English may be advisable (cf. Ch. A.6). At celebrations of German–French friendship on 8 July 2012 in Reims (France), Federal Chancellor Angela Merkel provided one successful example by weaving into her speech, which was otherwise held entirely in German, the words "*Vive l'amitié franco-allemande!*" – Thereby repeating verbatim the offer of friendship made by President de Gaulle 50 years previously during his visit to Germany ("*Merkel: Vive l'amitié franco-allemande!*", *FAZ* 9 July 2012: 2). On the fiftieth anniversary of de Gaulle's invocation of international friendship, French President François Hollande also took up this idea in the opening speech he made at celebrations in Ludwigsburg on 21/22 September 2012, by shouting out "*Es lebe die deutsch-französische Freundschaft!*" [Long live German-French friendship!] (www.tagesschau.de/inland/deutsch-franzoesische-freundschaft102.html).

I

GERMAN IN MEDIA AND LANGUAGE ARTS OUTSIDE THE GERMAN-LANGUAGE TERRITORY

1. Media

1.1 Media and medial forms of communication: typology and methodology

In this chapter, "media" are understood not in the broadest sense, as all components necessary for the transmission of information between senders and receivers (light rays, paper, soundwaves etc.), but in the narrower sense of "medial forms of communication" defined by Ulrich Schmitz (2004: 58). Indeed, subdividing the chapter into two sections "media" and "language arts" only makes sense with this narrower definition. The section on media is the more dynamic of the two. Electronic media and the opportunities for communication opened by them have developed rapidly in recent history, and a slackening of pace is unlikely. According to one assessment, the most important electronic media include telegraphy, telephony, broadcasting, with *radio* and *TV*, *Internet*, intranet, CD-ROM, e-book, electronic newspaper and *mobile phone* (de.wikipedia.org/wiki/Elektronisch_Medien). In the list, I have italicised the media to be discussed in the present chapter. The computer is an obvious prerequisite for many of these examples. Internet-based media (Ch. I.1.4), and among them the rapidly developing social media (Ch. I.1.4.2), are of special significance. These Internet-based media are often grouped together under the heading of "new media". But more traditional media continue to exist alongside them, especially the print media, such as newspapers, magazines and books, as well as photography, especially film. Schmitz (2004: 58) names the following medial forms of communication: books, the press, radio, TV, video/DVD, cinema – telephone, fax, SMS, computer (with hypermedia, chat, email). He also mentions "incidental media", such as billboards and product labelling (ibid: 60) to which recipients or consumers are exposed randomly, without actively selecting them. Based on more recent developments, smart phones and tablets must be added to this list, creating overlaps with other forms of communication, such as the telephone. I shall not attempt a systematic classification here, especially in view of the pace of current developments. However, one important distinction must be made between unilateral and bilateral directions of communication, which I have separated with a hyphen in the list of medial forms of communication above. Most of the "new media", or more explicitly, *new medial forms of communication*, belong in the latter group. The group comprising different options for bilateral communication includes the various forms of *social media.* The rapid development of these social media is evident, e.g. from the fact that successful platforms such as *Facebook* and *Twitter* were founded only in 2004 and 2006 respectively (Ch. I.1.4.2).

Questions relevant to the position of German among these media overlap with many other topics in the present book, especially regarding language choice within specific social groups and action fields, although the perspective is sometimes different. The overlap is evident, for example, in the "target audience" of the *Deutsche Welle* radio broadcaster (1986: 5). The subdivision indicated below still applies today (see Ch. I.1.3), and the relevant groups have already been discussed in preceding chapters (refs. in square brackets). Target audiences for *Deutsche Welle* have been defined as follows: "On one hand, listeners of German origin all over the world [Ch. E. Minorities], on the other hand, German-speaking citizens living temporarily abroad [Ch. F. Business economy; Ch. H Politics and Diplomacy] and the many foreigners who are interested either in Germany or in learning German, or who want to perfect their German-language skills [Ch. J. German as a Foreign Language]. The target group also includes the now considerable number of holidaymakers abroad [mentioned in Ch. E.5] for whom *Deutsche Welle* guarantees contact with their home country through its range of programmes. Although these groups have been mentioned in previous chapters, medial forms of communication were not discussed and thus constitute an independent topic for the present chapter.

Research on the medial forms of communication relevant to the questions raised here is less developed than for any other chapter. This is surprising because the overall scope of research on the media is extremely broad (cf. the extensive bibliography even in the somewhat dated book by Schmitz 2004: 133–206). Above all, there is a lack of investigations and data on the new media relating to languages and language choices by "senders" and "receivers", as they are designated in traditional communications science, especially a lack of quantified results and developmental trends.

Even for the traditional media, there are often only isolated references rather than precise data, but having said this, the available data do reveal overarching trends. One example is cinema, where there are clear indications that the international position of German has deteriorated. A news item such as the following from the early 1930s would be inconceivable today: "Paraguay: German film industry competing with America (20 German films in Asuncion)" (*Mitteilung der Akademie* [. . .]/ *Deutsche Akademie* 11 (1) 1933: 109). By contrast with its once competitive position, the German film industry today compares with the international prestige of the American film industry rather on the scale of a daisy to a giant redwood tree. The global presence of the German and English languages in cinema films has diverged correspondingly. Even in German-speaking countries and regions, films from the English-speaking world predominate. This is evident from the fact that the titles of English-language films are often no longer translated into German even for the German-language territory. In Germany, Suzanne Hilgendorf (2013) investigated every conceivable transitional form from purely English-language titles through diverse language mixtures to purely German language titles, including specially formulated titles in English for films from the English-speaking countries. However, she was surprised that all films were still dubbed – by contrast with the subtitling found in relatively smaller language territories. Her explanation for the openness towards English in film titles, with resistance to English in the action of the film, boils down, on one hand, to a capitulation before the higher prestige of English, which also makes English suitable for advertising in Germany, and on the other hand, to a desire among German-speakers to maintain their own language (ibid: 182). By contrast, even German-language film titles would cause a stir in the English-language territory. Investigations of such shifts and discrepancies could also reveal the extent to which the international dominance of English favours global distribution of films and other medial forms of communication from English-speaking countries, especially the USA. For example, the film industry promotes the spread of English, and presumably, what is involved here is a self-perpetuating feedback process – but conversely, in the case of German film and German-language films, a self-harming feedback process.

In general, the medial forms of communication are only relevant to the present book in so far as they mediate international communication, especially international communication in the narrower sense (international and at the same time interlingual; Ch. A.3). As with other chapters in the book, there is a shortage of direct data, and I must rely largely on indicators for this kind of communication (Ch. A.3, towards the end). If, for example, the frequency of occurrence of German-language radio broadcasts outside the German-language territory is taken as an indicator, this presupposes at least that the broadcasts are listened to in the first place. If reception is limited to native speakers of German, then only international communication in the broad sense is involved. International communication in the narrower sense requires FL speakers (non-native speakers) of German. Regarding the groups of listeners cited above for the German-language programme *Deutsche Welle*, these would comprise only "foreigners who are interested in Germany and learning German". The other named groups of listeners are native speakers. It can be assumed that English-language broadcasts attract a considerably higher proportion of non-native speakers because, not only is interest in the native-language countries – USA, UK and so on – broader, but English is also learnt overwhelmingly more frequently as a foreign language (Ch. J.7). Such differences must be borne in mind when drawing inferences from broadcast frequencies to the scope of international communication and making comparisons between languages based on these, where the orders of magnitude cannot be estimated with any degree of certainty. Even if English is broadcast less than another language, it cannot be reliably inferred from this that less international communication in the narrower sense takes place. Conversely, with a greater broadcasting frequency in English, greater frequency of international communication in English is extremely probable. At least, such cautions can mitigate the associated possibility of false inferences and provide motivation to look elsewhere for empirical background. By contrast with a complete absence of quantification which leaves the door open for all kinds of speculation, even this level of quantification does provide pointers. The same considerations apply for newspapers and magazines, which will be addressed in the next section.

1.2 The press

1.2.1 Press exports from German-speaking countries

Anyone who has seen shops and kiosks selling newspapers and magazines in tourist areas and in the main streets of world cities will no doubt have noticed German-language newspapers and magazines, such as *Die Zeit, Der Spiegel, Focus, Bild, Bunte, Neue Post* or *Freizeit Revue*, although only a few copies may be available. Now, it is obvious that no one has a complete overview of the German-language press on sale outside the German-language territory, as shown by research I carried out around 1990 (Ammon 1991a: 378f.). Nevertheless, one of the largest distribution organisations, *der Deutsche Pressevertrieb GmbH* (DPV, website: www.dpv.de/kontakt/) kindly offered me some relevant export figures. Table I.1.2–1 provides evidence for the export of newspapers and magazines from Germany to the 25 highest ranking press export countries (among a total of 124 such countries) – German-speaking countries such as Austria, Switzerland and Luxembourg are less relevant for the present book. These statistics do not consider languages of publication, so that printed matter not in German may also be included; furthermore, the figures do not include the number but only the value (in €), which presumably shows a positive

Table I.1.2–1 Development of the export value of newspapers and magazines from Germany in 2008–2012 in €

Countries Year	2008	2009	2010	2011	2012
1. Austria	237,599	214,572	217,871	197,664	218,815
2. Switzerland	157,666	158,311	156,935	175,804	159,686
3. France	89,278	72,240	69,437	67,379	71,270
4. Netherlands	46,976	44,224	56,941	52,491	43,892
5. Italy	50,734	46,454	48,294	50,258	48,492
6. Spain	40,121	32,536	36,420	39,830	38,862
7. UK	42,334	33,973	30,877	25,123	12,758
8. Belgium	25,604	23,070	26,423	25,818	20,287
9. Denmark	23,589	23,474	19,091	22,730	25,056
10. Luxembourg	19,935	20,158	21,909	21,396	22,052
11. Russian Federation	44,669	16,333	12,112	7,981	7,434
12. Czech Republic	13,316	11,131	13,983	8,436	7,180
13. Sweden	9,873	7,352	7,943	8,052	7,653
14. Greece	8,300	6,827	7,178	6,339	5,381
15. Hungary	4,978	4,803	4,671	5,265	4,587
16. Portugal	4,899	5,336	4,291	4,585	4,143
17. Norway	6,784	4,888	3,923	4,266	3,163
18. Slovenia	3,749	4,190	4,592	4,898	4,506
19. Poland	4,323	4,019	4,405	3,578	5,072
20. Finland	3,180	2,983	5,060	5,413	3,980
21. People's Republic of China	3,018	2,788	3,443	3,979	4,322
22. USA	3,885	2,932	2,712	2,543	2,415
23. Turkey	2,760	2,204	2,110	2,175	1,989
24. Slovakia	1,803	1,613	1,506	1,475	1,271
25. Ukraine	1,246	1,358	1,363	1,626	1,400
Total exports to countries worldwide	863,886	758,887	773,779	759,192	734,424

(*Source*: based on information from Angela Kohl, Project Director of *DPV Deutscher Pressevertrieb GmbH*, 9 December 2013)

correlation with the number of items. In fact, economic performance shows an overall decline during the five years 2008–2012, but not by any means for all countries. On the contrary, the data show an increase for Switzerland, Denmark, Luxembourg, Slovenia, Poland, Finland, China and Ukraine, contrasting with the marked decline in the UK, Russia, Czech Republic, a moderate decline in Greece, USA, Turkey, Slovakia, with a less pronounced decline for other countries.

Since the explanation for these changes in performance remains very hypothetical, I shall limit myself to suggestions, also assuming that the decline in monetary value corresponds to a decline in the number of items. For many developments, changes in tourist figures from the German-speaking countries may be a factor, e.g. for the sharp rise in Poland from 2011 to 2012, or less spectacularly in Denmark, Slovenia and Finland. Intensified business relations with the German-speaking countries, with more travellers and expatriates, are another potential factor, possibly for China, and also for Ukraine. Conversely, the turn towards English or other foreign languages by expatriates and visitors from the German-speaking countries may have reduced the demand for German-language printed matter, e.g. in the UK, USA and Hong Kong. But these questionable factors require more focussed investigation.

I could not obtain corresponding data for exports from the other German-speaking countries (Ch. D.). Comparison with other international languages would also be interesting, but it can be assumed that English-language printed matter, especially from the USA and the UK predominates worldwide. French-language printed matter is also more widely distributed outside its language territory than German-language equivalents. However, such assumptions about languages other than English also require checking.

1.2.2 German-language press abroad

Despite the overall decline in exports of German-language newspapers and magazines to other language territories suggested by data from Germany, there should still be a demand for such media. Many people living abroad wish to keep up to date with news and entertainment from their home country and in their own language. It would therefore be interesting to know the extent to which exported print media in different languages are also read by non-native speakers. Having said this, print media may also be under increasing pressure from electronic media, especially the new media (Ch. I.1.4), via laptops, tablets, smartphones and similar which are used during travel. A distinction must be made between newspapers and magazines published inside a language territory (editorially processed but not necessarily printed there) and those published outside, even if some are distributed inside the same territory. For example, the German-language newspaper *Die Zeit* is published in Germany, but when it is distributed in Australia, it belongs to the first category (published internally in the German-language territory and distributed externally); by contrast, *Die Woche in Australien*, which is published in Australia and also distributed there, belongs to the second category (externally published and externally distributed, by German Language Press Pty. Ltd., P.O. Box 279, Five Dock NSW 2046, Sydney). It seems that externally published print media are also often distributed externally, but in some cases, also outside the country in which they are published, e.g. *Die Woche in Australien* also in New Zealand, and the Namibian *Allgemeine Zeitung* also in South Africa. In isolated cases, they are even sold in the German-speaking countries. An up-to-date overview of externally published, German-language periodicals is provided by the *Handbuch der deutschsprachigen Presse im Ausland* (Akstinat 2012/ 13). Admittedly, apart from newspapers and magazines, it contains other periodicals, as the subtitle shows: "*Verzeichnis deutschsprachiger Zeitungen, Zeitschriften, Mitteilungsblätter und Jahrbücher außerhalb Deutschlands, Österreichs, Luxemburgs, Liechtensteins und der Schweiz*": church bulletins, newsletters, society bulletins, magazines and similar. In the absence of any clear demarcation of genre, I have decided on an overall count per country (Table I.1.2–2). In this Table, I added findings from earlier accounts to Akstinat's figures (details in Ammon 1991a: 380–383). Table I.1.2–2 shows the countries according to the number of the title in Akstinat (2012/13) in a rank ordering and arranged alphabetically when the figures are the same. The current figures are printed in bold and appear only once at each rank level; other, earlier figures, from 1984, are added in brackets.

For the number in brackets, I selected the larger of the numbers in the two sources. In the case of the higher-ranking countries, explanatory notes have been added in some cases (in italics in the third column). In Italy and Belgium, German is a regional official language, in South Tyrol and Eastern Belgium respectively (Ch. D.3.2; D.3.1), where most of the German-language periodicals therefore appear. The USA and Canada are migration destinations, with immigrants from German-speaking countries who are in some cases not yet assimilated. These also include religious minorities who adhere to their German language of origin more firmly than other immigrants (Ch. E.4.11). Other migration destinations with religious and sometimes other German-language minorities include Brazil, Paraguay, Chile, Uruguay and Bolivia in the rank

Table I.1.2–2 German-language periodicals outside the German-speaking countries – rank ordering by frequency

Rank Countries		Number of periodicals		Explanatory note
1.	Italy	**301**	(59)	*German regional official language*
2.	Spain	**69**	(16)	Holiday destination
3.	USA	**66**	(48)	Immigration destination
4.	Belgium	**56**	(35)	*German regional official language*
5.	Poland	**52**	(7)	*Neighbour and minority*
6.	France	**51**	(33)	*Neighbour and minority*
7.	Romania	**49**	(19)	*Minority*
8.	Hungary	**42**	(14)	*Neighbour and minority*
9.	Canada	**40**	(32)	Immigration destination
10.	Russia	**36**	(14 USSR)	*Minority*
11.	Denmark	**33**	(11)	*Neighbour and minority*
12.	UK	**30**	(13), South Africa (23)	
13.	Brazil	**26**	(17)	*Minority*
14.	Australia	**25**	(20), Czech R. 25 (21 Czechoslovakia)	
15.	Namibia	**18**	(17)	*Minority*
16.	South Korea	**17**	(n.d.), Netherlands (12)	
17.	Turkey	**16**	(6), Japan (5)	
18.	Croatia	**14**	(3 Yugoslavia), Finland (10)	
19.	Paraguay	**13**	(6)	*Minority*
20.	Sweden	**11**	(13)	*Lutheran religion*
21.	Egypt	**10**	(n.d.), Israel (14)	
22.	Greece	**9**	(5), Mexico (4), Portugal (7), Thailand (1)	
23.	China	**8**	(4), Slovakia 25 (21 Czechoslovakia) Slovenia (3 Yugoslavia)	
24.	Chile	**7**	(6)	*Minority*
25.	Argentina	**6**	(17), Estonia (14 USSR), Norway (1), Peru (2)	
26.	Bulgaria	**5**	(3), India (6), Ukraine (14 USSR), Uruguay (3)	
27.	Azerbaijan	**4**	(14 USSR), Bolivia (3), Indonesia (1), Kenya (2), Latvia (14 USSR), Mongolia (14 USSR), Singapore (1), United Arab Emirates 4 (1)	
28.	Ireland	**3**	(1), Columbia (3), New Zealand (n.d.), Taiwan (n.d.), Venezuela (3)	
29.	Ethiopia	**2**	(n.d.), Costa Rica (n.d.), Ecuador (2), Iran (1), Kazakhstan (14 USSR), Lithuania (14 USSR), Malaysia, (n.d.), Malta (1), Morocco (n.d.), Tunisia (n.d.)	
30.	Albania	**1**	(n.d.), Belize (n.d.), Bosnia and Herzegovina (3 Yugoslavia), Dominican Republic (n.d.), El Salvador (n.d.), Georgia (14 USSR), Guatemala (n.d.), Honduras (n.d.), Iceland (n.d.), Jordan (1), Cameroon (n.d.), Cuba (n.d.), Lebanon (1), Nigeria (n.d.), Zimbabwe (1), Surinam (n.d.), Tanzania (n.d.), Vatican City (1), White Russia (14 USSR), Cyprus (1)	

(*Sources*: current figures, bold, Akstinat 2012/13; figures from 1984, bracketed, Presse- und Informationsamt der Stadt Wuppertal 1984; Verein für das Deutschtum im Ausland 1984; n.d. = no data)

ordering shown in Table I.1.2–2. They are also discussed in Ch. E.4.11 – and in Ch. C.1 in the context of the total number of German native speakers. Table C.1–2 lists other countries from Table I.1.2–2 with German-language minorities. One special minority of this kind originating from the Nazi period still lives in Israel (Pazi 1979; Betten/ Dunour 2000; Betten 2011; Zimmermann/ Hotam 2005; Zabel 2006). The diverse conditions for language maintenance among German-speaking minorities are explained in Ch. E.1; E.2. Key factors include geographical proximity to German-speaking countries, as in the case of Poland (Ch. E.4.4), France (Ch. E.4.3), Romania (Ch. E.4.7), Hungary (Ch. E.4.6), Denmark (Ch. E.4.2), Croatia and Finland (ranked in Table I.1.2–1), or less frequently, special historical connections, such as the special case of Namibia with a German-speaking minority dating back to the German colonial period (Ch. E.4.9). Such minorities also often support German-language periodicals. In many places, comparable support is provided by tourism or retirement colonies from German-speaking countries (Ch. E.5), as in Spain, Turkey and Greece. German-language periodicals for German Philology and Linguistics and the teaching of German as a foreign language, which carry weight in the UK (Ch. K.9.3), South Korea and Japan (Ch. K.9.14), are a special case.

For the present book, more accurate insights into the reception of the periodicals would be of interest, especially to assess their effect on the maintenance of German at local level. Fluctuation of these periodicals suggests a limited language-maintaining effect. Some time ago, the Verein für das Deutschtum im Ausland (1984: 7) drew attention to this fluctuation, "because titles are steadily being lost (as a result of the weak financial basis in many locations), and new publications are being founded". Problems identified by Akstinat (2012/13: 14) reveal similar characteristics: the "Assimilation Problem: declining reader numbers, e.g. because Germans living abroad unlearn the German language" or the "Next-Generation Problem: many media providers have difficulty finding employees with adequate German-language skills + adequate specialist knowledge locally". Titles with high frequency or circulation and daily newspapers are a rarity. Table I.1.2–3 contains all titles which appeared weekly at least five times in the early 1980s (City of Wuppertal 1984) together with updated figures for the present, around 30 years later (after Akstinat 2012/13).

Table I.1.2–3 German-language dailies outside the German-speaking countries with circulation in the early 1980s and around 2012

	Early 1980s		Around 2012
Italy	*Dolomiten*	30,000	50,000–80,000
Belgium	*Grenz-Echo*	13,000	13,000
France	*Dernieres Nouvelles D'Alsace*	250,000	Only in French since 2012
	L'Alsace	134,000	Only German insert: 4,000
Denmark	*Nordschleswiger*	3,000	3,000
Romania	*Neue Banater Zeitung*	18,000	n.d.
	Neuer Weg	40,000	*Allgemeine Deutsche Zeitung* 3,000
Hungary	*Neueste Nachrichten*	15,000	n.d.
Soviet Union/ (Russia)	*Freundschaft* (since 1 January 1990 *Deutsche Allgemeine*)	?	n.d.
Namibia	*Allgemeine Zeitung*	5,000	5,000–6,000
Israel	*Israel-Nachrichten*	?	n.d.

(*Sources*: Presse- und Informationsamt der Stadt Wuppertal 1984; Akstinat 2012/13; n.d. = no data)

Dernieres Nouvelles D'Alscace was previously bilingual German and French, but today it only contains a German-language insert for subscribers by special request. *L'Alscace* was also once bilingual and today has only a German insert with a circulation of 4,000. For Romania, the *Allgemeine Deutsche Zeitung für Rumänien*, according to the complete title, the "only German-language newspaper in Eastern Europe" (Akstinat 2012/13: 214) is the successor of *Neuer Weg* (until 1992). No data are provided in Akstinat (ibid) for the *Neue Banater Zeitung*. Akstinat (ibid) also contains no data for the *Neueste Nachrichten* in Hungary; there is no daily newspaper there but only the weekly *Neue Zeitung*. For Russia also, there are no data in Akstinat (ibid) on *Freundschaft* or *Deutsche Allgemeine*; there is no daily newspaper in Russia but only the bilingual German/Russian weekly *Ihre Zeitung*. Akstinat (ibid) also has no data for the *Israel-Nachrichten* in Israel; there is no longer even a weekly newspaper there. Stability or expansion are to be found only in Italy (South Tyrol; Ch. D.3.2), Belgium (bilingual community; Ch. D.3.1), Denmark and Namibia (Ch. E.4.2; E.4.9). A simplified explanation is that, in the first two cases, status as a regional official language; in the latter two cases, generous minority laws, proximity to Germany and/or pride in their own language and ethnicity, and a commitment to language maintenance, offer the required protection. In all other cases, a sometimes dramatic decline is identifiable, also determined by language shift from the minority language German to the surrounding majority language. Having said this, the move towards the new media (I.1.4) may also play a role, not least because of access to online versions of newspapers and magazines from the German-speaking countries.

The dwindling of German-language periodicals has been evident for a considerable time. For example, the *Handbuch der deutschsprachigen Zeitungen im Ausland* still shows 995 German-language "newspapers" for the 1930s (Heide 1935) outside the circumscribed German-language territory. For comparison with more recent figures, 705 must be subtracted from the total number of 1,700, namely 236 in Austria, 444 in Switzerland, 3 in Liechtenstein and 22 in Luxembourg. These countries are missing in the catalogue of the Presse- und Informationsamt der Stadt Wuppertal (1984), which provides a suitable comparison. Despite all the defects in terms of comparability, the total number of newspapers in the Wuppertal catalogue is only about half the figure shown in Heide: 508 compared with 995. A similar picture reaching further back in history is obtained for the USA, which, in the early 1980s, "as the most important migration destination" still had the "largest number of German-language newspapers and magazines" (Presse- und Informationsamt der Stadt Wuppertal 1984: 16), but at the same time, showed a clearly marked decline (Table I.1.2–4)

Table I.1.2–4 Number of German-language newspapers in the USA between 1732–1983

Year	Number of newspapers	
1732	1	(Benjamin Franklin)
1840	40	
1860	approx. 80	
1890	727	
1914	537	
1930s	174	
1960	69	
1983	16	(No more daily newspapers)

(*Sources: Forschungsstandbericht Deutsch als Muttersprache im nichtdeutschsprachigen Ausland* 1988: 174; Heide 1935)

Table I.1.2–5 Circulation of German-language newspapers and magazines remaining in the USA until 1980

	Around 1930	*Around 1980*
Newspapers Magazines	28,000 weekly (*Sonntagspost*, Chicago)	10,000 weekly (*Sonntagspost und Milwaukee Deutsche Zeitung*, Chicago)
	? daily (*Milwaukee Deutsche Zeitung*, Milwaukee)	
	? 16,800 daily (*Detroiter Abendpost*, Detroit)	11,800 weekly (*Nordamerikanische Wochen-Post und (Detroiter Abendpost*, Detroit)
	17,800 weekly (*Eintracht*, Chicago)	6,000 weekly (*Eintracht*, Shokie, Ill.)
	15,000 weekdays (*Wächter und Anzeiger*, Cleveland, Ohio)	3,500 weekly (*Wächter und Anzeiger*, (Cleveland, Ohio)
	2,000 to 3,000). weekly (*California Staats-Zeitung*, Los Angeles)	16,500 weekly (*California Staats-Zeitung*, *und Neue Zeitung*, Los Angeles)
	?	38,500 monthly (*Die Hausfrau*, Chicago)
	56,000 monthly (*Die Hausfrau*, Milwaukee)	

(*Sources*: Heide 1935; Presse- und Informationsamt der Stadt Wuppertal 1984; ? = title or circulation missing in Heide 1935)

The addition in brackets in the last line of Table I.1.2–4 suggests that this is not a matter of concentration, where circulation numbers grow against a decline in the number of titles. On the contrary, Table I.1.2–5 shows the following mutually reinforcing trends: 1) decline in the level of circulation; 2) slowing down of frequency of publication (from daily to weekly); and 3) amalgamation of publications. A similar decline would presumably also be demonstrable for most German-language periodicals outside the German-speaking countries (Ch. E).

In Australia, the German-language press is the oldest foreign-language press there; it began with the *Deutsche Post fuer die Australischen Kolonien*, founded by Carl Kornhardt (Adelaide, 6

January 1848) and developed great diversity before WWI until a general ban on German-language printed matter was introduced by the Australian Government in 1917. After WWI, the German-language press was redeveloped but succumbed again in WWII. It was resurrected a third time until, finally, by the end of the 1950s/beginning of the 1960s, it stagnated and died out (Gilson/ Zubrzycki 1967: 4–13, 132–136). A change in this trend seems unlikely. Kurt Schnöring has pointed out that the German-language print media are fighting for survival in many places, especially in South America and North America (Presse- und Informationsamt der Stadt Wuppertal 1984: 15–18). The "problems of German-language foreign publications" already mentioned and listed by Akstinat (2012/13:14) also fit with this picture. The decline in externally published German-language print media has been caused substantially by the linguistic assimilation of German-speaking immigrants and minorities (Ch. E). This development has not been compensated by expansion of international commercial ties and tourism. The fact that the periodicals of the German Chambers of Commerce Abroad are increasingly being replaced by websites is also symptomatic of this (Ch. F.4).

Comparison with the print media of other international languages (Ch. A.7) would be worthwhile, but unfortunately, I have not had access to usable figures. Global news agencies available for these languages, which, admittedly, do not serve only the press, provide a rough indication of the stronger position of English, but also of French and Chinese. Thomas L. McPhail (2007: 175–191) designates the following organisations as by far the most comprehensive "Global News Agencies": *Reuters* (UK), *The Associated Press, United Press International, Bloomberg, Dow Jones & Company* (all four in the USA), *Agence France-Presse* (France) and *Xinhua* (China). However, he does not mention the *Deutsche Presseagentur* (dpa) although it is presented on the Internet as "one of the world's leading news agencies" (www.dpa.de/englisch.82.0.html). Presumably, its orientation is less global than the other agencies named by McPhail. But McPhail does not offer any explicit correlation between the international position of press agencies or even between press and language.

1.3 Broadcasting

1.3.1 Overseas broadcasting from German-speaking countries

The term broadcasting includes audio broadcasting or radio, which I will discuss first, and television, which will be addressed in the next subsection. International communication in German takes place primarily via transmitters located in the German-speaking countries which broadcast abroad (foreign services), but also via transmitters in other countries which broadcast in German (German-language foreign broadcasters; Ch. I.1.3.2). The foreign services of the German-speaking countries have become more restricted in recent decades. In March 2003, *Radio Österreich International* (*RÖI*), which had provided German-language overseas broadcasts on shortwave since 1955, ceased broadcasting. Private follow-on operations have now fallen silent, and no alternative has been launched via the Internet. The *Schweizer Radio International* (*SRI*), which had broadcast on shortwave since the 1930s in the three official languages, i.e. including German (Ch. D.2.4), ceased operating on 30 October 2004. It now provides news bulletins on the Internet at <swissinfo> in the national official languages German, French, Italian, but not Romansh, and in seven other international languages (in 2013). Germany's overseas broadcasting has also declined. After reunification, the GDR broadcaster *Radio Berlin International* (*RBI*) closed on 3 October 1990, and 21 of the 130 employees were taken on by *Deutsche Welle* in the FRG and then in unified Germany ("*Kleine Meldungen*", *FAZ* 15 October 1990), which is now the only overseas broadcaster among the German-speaking countries. The once thriving shortwave-radio service in German has been abandoned and now broadcasts only in 14 other languages (www.dw.de/frequenz%C3%BCbersichten-radio/a-435653).

However, radio services from foreign broadcasters in other countries, especially on shortwave, have also been reduced, even for large international languages, e.g. *Radio China International, Voice of America, Stimme Russlands* (Голос России/Golos Rossii), *BBC World Service, Radio France Internationale, Radio Japan* (NHK) and *Radio Exterior de España* (a comprehensive list of "International overseas broadcasters" with shortwave broadcasts is available at de.wikipedia.org.wiki/ Kurzwellenrundfunk#Auswahl_einiger_Kurzwellensender).

The forerunners of the *Deutsche Welle* were founded in the 1920s (for historical accounts, see Pieper 2000; Deutsche Welle 2003; Ammon 1991a: 365–367). A broadcaster of the same name was founded in 1926 in combination with the *Weltrundfunksender* [transmitter for international radio broadcasting] at Königs Wusterhausen in 1928, which broadcast from 1929 onwards to North, Central and South America, Africa and Eastern Asia. The Nazi government took over the broadcaster as the *Deutscher Kurzwellensender*, exploiting it for propaganda. In 1953, in the FRG, this was followed by the *Deutsche Welle* based in Cologne as the public-service broadcaster commissioned to provide balanced news reporting and as "Germany's visiting card" (Krasteva 2007). This necessitated a language choice which would reach the maximum number of opinion makers in the world; it was therefore impossible not to use English and other international languages ("*Alles auf Englisch*", *FAZ* 21 January 2014: 31). A second goal, not voiced so frequently in public, is the promotion or distribution of German language and culture in the world (see Ch. K). Many people, especially Germanists, may see this as the primary goal and criticise the restriction of German as a broadcasting language in favour of other languages, especially English. In fact, the second part of the broadcaster's commission reads as follows: "The *Deutsche Welle* shall therefore especially promote the German language" (*DW-Gesetz* 2005, para 4, last sentence) – it might therefore be hoped that as many German-speakers or people interested in the German language and culture overseas should be reached as possible. With both tasks in mind, the choice between German and English or other languages sometimes becomes a difficult balancing act (see Ch. A.2). As already mentioned, the remaining German-language broadcasts – no longer available on shortwave – are directed primarily towards three target groups: 1) emigrants from the German-speaking countries and regions including German-speaking minorities; 2) expatriates, in the sense of all citizens and residents of German-speaking countries and regions living temporarily abroad (business people, diplomats, academics, teachers, development workers, tourists) and 3) learners or speakers of German as a foreign language (Krasteva 2007: 18). Over the years, the target regions for German-language broadcasts have shifted less than for foreign language broadcasts which are motivated more by political and economic concerns, e.g. orientation towards the Islamic world (ibid: 17). While the traditional target groups of emigrants and minorities of German origin are losing importance, expatriates and learners of German as a foreign language are becoming more significant. The home page (www.dw.de) and special webpages in 30 languages are extremely informative about the *Deutsche Welle*.

Deutsche Welle television plays a prominent role among present-day broadcasts. There are six channels, each for specific regions of the world and with specific broadcasting languages; the reception regions overlap at the margins:

- Europe (from Greenland to beyond the Urals and from Spitsbergen to the northern edge of Africa, including the Middle East): 18 hours in English and six hours in German;
- America (the whole of North America and South America): 20 hours in German, four hours in English;

- Latin America (the whole of South America and parts of North America into the USA): 24 hours Spanish;
- Arabic world (all Arabic countries, Middle East and North Africa): ten hours in Arabic and 14 hours in English;
- Asia (the whole of Asia and Oceania including Australia and New Zealand, also Eastern Europe and the Middle East): 24 hours in German (www.dw.de/programm/tv-programm/s-4765-9798).

A sixth channel, the basic *Deutsche Welle* channel is additionally available to viewers in Asia, round-the-clock in English, its broadcasts are also available in North America, Africa and Australia. On television, German is therefore restricted to Europe, North and South America, and Asia, but is absent throughout Africa. This absence has been severely criticised for a considerable time (e.g. Franz Stark 2000c), and there are still grounds for this criticism. The webpage of the *Deutsche Welle* provides a map with 27 localities – distributed across all broadcast territories around the world – each of which can be clicked individually to inspect broadcasting terms. However, access to broadcasts in many countries still leaves something to be desired.

1.3.2 German-language foreign broadcasting

In addition to the foreign services of German-speaking countries – and by analogy with the press – there are also German-language foreign broadcasts produced in non-German-speaking countries and broadcast from there. They are largely restricted to audio broadcasting and webpages on the Internet; TV programmes are isolated, often short-lived exceptions. Accordingly, the broadcasters or broadcasts are often designated as "German Radio Abroad". But their existence is often endangered in a similar way to the German-language press abroad (Ch. I.1.2.2), and there is a trend towards technical conversion to satellite and/or Internet. Table I.1.3–1 gives an impression of this conversion. The table shows countries with German-language broadcasts from large, usually public sector broadcasters from a relatively old webpage (www.press-guide.com/radio.htm), presumably around 1989. However, Portugal is missing, because its German service was closed in September 1988, by contrast with South Africa, where Radio RSA did not close its German-language broadcasts until 30 April 1990 (www.jans-radioseiten.de/im.html). Accordingly, at that time there were 45 non-German-speaking countries with German-speaking

Table I.1.3–1 Countries with German-language radio programmes from large, generally state-run broadcasters (as at November 2013; ? = converted transmission technology; ?? = no more German-language broadcast)

Egypt	Ecuador	?? Canada	Russia	? Czech Republic
Albania	?? France	Kazakhstan	?? Sweden	Turkey
Argentina	Georgia	Korea (South)	*Serbia	Tunisia
Armenia	Greece	Korea (North)	? Slovakia	Ukraine
Azerbaijan	Indonesia	?? Malta	Slovenia	?? Hungary
Australia	Iran	Namibia	Spain	?? USA
?? Brazil	Iraq	Paraguay	Syria	?? Uzbekistan
? Bulgaria	Israel	? Poland	Taiwan	? Vatican City
China	?? Japan	Romania	Thailand	White Russia

(*Sources*: www.press-guide.com/radio.htm; www.jans-radioseiten.de/im.html)

broadcasts in their public sector broadcasting – Switzerland, Belgium and Italy are not included. Instead of "Serbia" (marked with an asterisk), this is still called "Yugoslavia"; however, "Radio Yugoslavia, International Radio of Serbia and Montenegro", as it was known, was stationed in Belgrade. I compared this list with a more up-to-date webpage which reports on the reduction of broadcasters from September 1988 to September 2013 and is entitled: "In memoriam – German on shortwave and medium wave"; it begins with the words: "For several years there has been a trend for stations to abandon their [German-language! U.A.] broadcasts on short-wave and medium wave completely or for individual language services to be closed" (www. jans-radioseiten.de/im.html). Table I.1.3–1 provides evidence that the large, generally state-run broadcasters in nine countries have completely closed their German-language broadcasts in recent years; at least six further broadcasts should be added to this, which are not named in the comparison table, namely, Afghanistan, Finland, UK, Italy, Portugal and South Africa. This amounts to a loss of German-language radio broadcasts by major broadcasters in at least 15 countries (for details of the earlier reductions, see Ammon 1991a: 369).

In parallel with these developments, so many new, private broadcasters and broadcasts have arisen that a full overview is no longer possible. However, the webpage www.medienindex. de/Radio_Deutsch_Ausland.htm/ provides relevant pointers. This also shows the considerable fluctuation of often underfinanced broadcasters. Of the 53 named foreign broadcasters, 21 are already out of operation ("*EINGESTELLT* [closed] "*ZZT OFF AIR*" [currently off air] etc.). Having said this, the list does include the webpage of the *German-American Radio Program*, which refers to 51 US states with German-language programmes (www.cazoo.org/GARadio.htm).

I was not able to carry out a serious quantitative comparison of German with other languages regarding the scope of broadcasts outside each of the home-language territories because of lack of appropriate sources. In an earlier attempt for radio broadcasts (Ammon 1991a: 374–377), I relied substantially on the *World Radio TV Handbook* (1989). However, under the heading "International Radio", the more recent additions list only a small fraction of the countries in the world, which are of diverse size and economic importance (*World Radio TV Handbook. Volume 66*–2012 (2011): 431–510; *Volume 68*–2014 (2013): 443–514). This restriction of countries presumably reflects the decline in international radio channels in recent history. Table I.1.3–2 gives an overview of the broadcast languages for international radio broadcasters in major countries and international languages, wherever data was available. The English language has not been included, because it is present in every case. Where several broadcasters were listed, e.g. in the USA, or multiple occurrences of one language in the same country, this was only counted once; broadcasting times of different lengths were not considered.

The position of German as an international radio-broadcasting language seems rather weak. The relatively small number of countries with German as an official language of state and their regional limitation to central Europe (Ch. D) as well as the limited function of German in diplomacy (Ch. H.1; H.3) presumably also have an effect here. However, in the contemporary world, international radio broadcasts are no longer important components of the international position of languages because of the other medial forms of communication.

1.4 New media

1.4.1 Internet

Like everything new, the "new media" will only be new for a limited time. A glance at older titles on the subject makes this immediately apparent. For example, searching through a volume by Hilmar Hoffmann (2000) subtitled "New Media" for references to "social media" such

Table I.1.3–2 Broadcast languages in international radio channels of large countries (- = own official language of state)

Languages Countries	Arabic	Chinese	French	German	Hindi
Australia		x			x
China	x	-	x	x	x
France		x	-		
UK	x		x		x
Italy	x		x		
India	x	x	x		
Indonesia	x	x	x	x	
Japan	x	x	x		x
Canada	x	x	-		x
Nigeria	x		x		
Poland				x	
Russia	x	x	x	x	
South Africa			x	x	
USA	x	x	x	x	x
Total	10	8	10	6	6

Languages Countries	Japanese	Malaysian	Portuguese	Russian	Spanish	Swahili
Australia	x	x				
China	x	x	x	x	x	x
France			x	x	x	x
UK				x		
Italy						
India	x	x			x	
Indonesia	x	-			x	
Japan	-	x	x	x	x	x
Canada	x		x	x	x	x
Nigeria						x
Poland				x		
Russia	x		x	-	x	
South Africa			x			x
USA		x	x	x	x	x
Total	6	5	7	7	8	7

(*Source: World Radio TV Handbook. Volume 66–2012* (2011): 431–510)

as Facebook or Twitter, which have gained worldwide popularity since this book was written, would be utterly frustrating. The scope of the term "new media" therefore changes with time. But it is acceptable to see in it an approximate correspondence with the Internet; the same applies to the subset of "social media" (Ch. I.1.4.2). The following discussion is based partly on my own previous research (Ammon 2000e, 2006c), supplemented with more recent information.

No technological advance has been more strongly associated with the English-speaking world than the computer and the Internet. One indication for this is that most languages in the world borrow English-language terms, sometimes with structural adaptation (*Computer, Internet,*

Hardware; Webseite, Netzwerk and so on). Although the *European Centre for Particle Physics* (CERN) played a part in developing the *World Wide Web* (WWW), it was still the USA which provided the incentive and most of the development, e.g. via the *Advanced Research Projects Network (Arpanet)*. So, it is no coincidence that the English-language has assumed a priority position on the Internet from the very outset. David Crystal (1997: 11) has argued the need for a global language partly with reference to the Internet. "Why do we need a global language? [. . .] A conversation over the Internet between academic physicists in Sweden, Italy, and India is at present practicable only if a common language is available". Initially, he saw no need whatsoever for other languages on the Internet: "[I]f you want to take full advantage of the Internet there is only one way to do it: learn English [. . .]". Having said this, a short time later, in a book devoted specially to the Internet, Crystal (2001) made a U-turn and stressed the emergence of other Internet languages. He then presented the Internet as a promising medium for the use and continuation of smaller languages, because it is considerably more cost favourable to publish on the Internet than through traditional media. David Graddol (1997) had highlighted this opportunity somewhat earlier in a book published for the British Council on the spread of the English language. Before turning to the Internet, he inserts a chapter on "The growth of local communities" considering non-public intranets of groups, especially companies abroad. "This may [. . .] permit, say, a Swiss-based company to maintain a German speaking culture amongst its employees". But he also sees room for languages other than English in the actual Internet, especially on webpages and emails. The present book is concerned primarily with Internet communication in German, especially international communication in the narrower sense (Ch. A.3), that is, with the participation of non-native speakers of German of different nationality. However, as with other topics, there is a lack of relevant data which could take us beyond the anecdotal. The numerical data available are largely restricted to the frequency of use of languages without specification of interlingual or intra-lingual use, but if distortions are carefully considered, this is still a more informative indicator for the scope of international communication than nothing at all.

The frequency of use of languages on the Internet is generally measured by the number of homepages, websites, Internet users or Internet views/hits (a critical methodological overview is given in Gerrand 2008: 2–7); there are no comparative figures on the more specialised use of the Internet for emails, chats, Internet telephony or social networks. It is often necessary to infer figures for languages from the figures for countries. Relatively informative figures, including some older figures, have been summarised in Table I.1.4–1 (with generous assistance of Enrique de Argaez, *CEO of Miniwatts Marketing Group* (email 5 December 2013); see also Ammon 2006c: 45f).

German does worse for the parameter number of Internet users than for websites and home-pages because of its speaker numbers. In terms of number of native speakers, German is only in approximately tenth position of all languages (Ch. C.2: Table C.2–1). However, proportionally, the rank position of German by number of Internet users is still relatively high. An overview of various estimation attempts is given in Table I.1.4–2. Column 2 here is not very informative because, apart from English and German, only romance languages have been included. On the one hand, the total number of native speakers for the individual languages has been used for col-umn 3 and, on the other hand, the percentages of Internet users in the most important countries with such native speakers. Because of different sources for Germany, Austria, Switzerland, Italy and the USA, this gave, e.g. for German, a total number of 55.3 million native-speaker Internet users. As this example shows, the figures included are in fact largely incomplete, but they do still include most native speakers. Presumably, a similar approach was used for column 4, but the relevant details are not available.

The course of development reflected in these various figures can be summarised as follows: German language plays a considerable role on the Internet although it is in the second division,

Table I.1.4–1 Worldwide language shares on the Internet between 1995–2010, based on homepages and webpages (percentage)

	1995	1997	1999		2002		2010
English	84.3	82.3	62	English	56.4	English	55.4
German	4.5	4.0	13	German	7.7	Russian	6.1
Japanese	3.1	1.6	5	French	5.6	German	5.9
French	1.8	1.5	4	Japanese	4.9	Japanese	4.9
Spanish	1.2	1.1	2	Spanish	3.0	Spanish	4.5
Swedish	1.1	0.6	2	Chinese	2.4	French	3.9
Italian	1.0	0.8	2	Italian	2.0	Chinese	3.7
Portuguese	0.7	0.7	2	Dutch	1.9	Portuguese	2.3
Dutch	0.6	0.4	1	Russian	1.7	Polish	1.8
Norwegian	0.6	0.3	0.5	Korean	1.5	Italian	1.7
	(Graddol 1997: 51)	(Crystal 2001: 217)	(Ammon 2000: 251.)	(*Netz-Tipp-Studie* 19 September 2005) (www.netz-tipp. de/sprachen. html)		*Content Languages for Websites 2010*	

Table I.1.4–2 Worldwide language shares based on Internet users between 1998–2011 (percentage)

English	56	English	47.6	English	35.2	English	26.8
Spanish	24	German	6.1	Chinese	13.7	Chinese	24.2
Japanese	22	Spanish	4.5	Spanish	9.0	Spanish	7.8
German	13	Portuguese	3.7	Japanese	8.4	Japanese	4.7
French	10	French	3.1	German	6.9	Portuguese	3.9
Chinese	6	Italian	2.5	French	4.2	German	3.6
Swedish	4	Romanian	0.13	Korean	3.9	Arabic	3.3
Dutch	4			Italian	3.8	French	3.0
Italian	4			Portuguese	3.1	Russian	3.0
				Dutch	1.7	Korean	2.0
USA Today, Oct. 1998 – Information from Franz Stark		*Global Reach*, March 2001 (www.glreach. com)		*Global Reach*, Sept. 2004 (www. global-reach.biz/ globstats/index. php3)		*Internet World Stats*, May 2011 (www. internetworldstats. com/stats7.htm)	

alongside Spanish, Japanese, Portuguese, Arabic and French. By contrast, English and Chinese are in the first division, Chinese especially with reference to user numbers. As always, English is in a class of its own, especially for international communication in the narrower sense (international and interlingual, Ch. A.3) – although based only on user numbers, it has already been surpassed by Chinese, as predicted a considerable time ago (e.g. "Chinese to become most-used language on web", *Financial Times* 7 December 2001: 12).

Internet World Stats (www.internetworldstats.com/stats7.htm) provides two further interesting sets of figures, namely "Internet Penetration by Language" and "Growth [of Languages] on the Internet 2000–2011". The first is defined as a quotient of the number of Internet users of the respective language divided by its total speaker number (native speakers); the "Growth [of Languages] on the Internet" is defined as the increase in users over the respective time interval.

Table I.1.4–3 Internet Penetration by Language 2011 and Growth of Languages in Internet 2000–2011 for languages with most users (percentage of speakers or Internet users)

Internet-penetration		Internet-growth	
German	79.5	Arabic	2,501.2
Japanese	78.4	Russian	1,825.8
Korean	55.2	Chinese	1,478.7
English	43.4	Portuguese	990.1
Russian	42.8	Spanish	807.4
Spanish	39.0	French	398.2
Chinese	37.2	English	301.4
Portuguese	32.5	German	174.1
Arabic	18.8	Japanese	110.7
French	17.2	Korean	107.1

(*Source*: *Internet World Stats*, May 2011 www.internetworldstats.com/stats7.htm)

Perhaps the greatest uncertainty is in the estimated total speaker numbers, which are not disclosed. In Table I.1.4–3, I have ranked these figures. Since the source is restricted to the ten languages with largest user numbers, which are also languages with large speaker numbers, the possibility cannot be precluded that many languages with relatively smaller speaker numbers might have had relatively higher penetration and higher growth.

There is an explanation – although it is a blanket explanation – for the immense differences in Internet growth. Language communities which engaged early with the Internet show a relatively smaller growth than latecomers, because their capacity had already been largely exhausted by the start of the measurement period. These are generally language communities which were already technologically highly developed when the Internet was introduced. Compared with these, the languages of technologically later-developing countries had greater opportunities for growth.

It is surprising that German is at the top for Internet penetration (among the ten languages with highest Internet use). Could this finding derive from the fact that the total speaker number for German, the denominator of the quotient, has been set too low? Other data contradict this suspicion. Then again, contrary to the occasional prophesies of doom, is it true that the Germans are especially keen Internet users? According to analysis of the figures from *Internet World Stats* based on the 20 individual states with the largest number of inhabitants worldwide by the Instituto Cervantes (2013: 45), this does seem to be the case. Because, according to this analysis, the UK (83.6%) is the only state placed slightly above Germany (83.0% for Internet penetration (*Penetración*), which may, however, be compensated for English as a whole by English-speaking countries with low penetration. Checking this finding for German would be a manageable research project.

Another indicator for the keen Internet use by German-speakers is the strong position of the German language in the Internet encyclopaedia *Wikipedia*. Compared with previous years, German had fallen by one rank position from position 2 to position 3 (for previous position, see Ammon 2006c: 49), which is also noteworthy. At the end of 2013, the ten most strongly participating languages showed the figures for articles and users listed in Table I.1.4-4 below – the length of articles and duration of use were not considered. The large number of articles for Dutch was surprising in view of the low number of "active users" (defined based on at least five contributions per month; Komus/ Wauch 2008: 56). By 2018, German was back in position 2, behind English but ahead of French, Russian, Italian, Spanish and Polish (https://en.wikipedia.org).

Table I.1.4–4 Languages with the largest number of articles in *Wikipedia* at the end of 2013: Number of articles and active users

Languages	Articles	Active users	Languages	Articles	Active users
1. English	4,354,737	127,156	6. Italian	1,071,258	8,224
2. Dutch	1,701,059	4,070	7. Russian	1,054,089	10,874
3. German	1,642,592	20,298	8. Spanish	1,052,656	17,089
4. Swedish	1,594,933	2,741	9. Polish	1,005,071	4,177
5. French	1,436,906	16,329	10. Wáray-Wáray	919,683	90

By contrast, the German-language community does not take the lead in its efforts to use the Internet for "Internet activity relating to political development and human rights". Here, Germany was only in position 16 in 2013, behind Austria in position 14 and Switzerland in position 17 (thewebindex.org/data/index or wikipedia.org/wiki/Web_index). The *Web Index* used as a measure here comprises four components with equal weighting: "*universal access* to the web", "*relevant content*", "*freedom and openness* [of access]" and "*impact and empowerment*". This represents an attempt to measure the political commitment of Internet users and their effect on global development. The fact that Germany only reached 16th position has been taken as a sign of political disaffection by Germans (www.dw.de/web-index-warns-against-online-ignorance/a-17249548); however, the validity of the measure applied – but not the political relevance of the question – seems doubtful to me.

Countless research perspectives have been opened by the Internet. One example is an investigation by Jannis Androutsopoulos (2006), into how "diaspora minorities" in Germany – one could also speak of migrants or immigrants – foster their ethnic identity via websites: Turkish, Russian, Indian and other groups. In this context, the language choice of their websites varies from dominance of the majority language (that is German) through parity of both languages to dominance of the native language (e.g. Turkish; see also Ch. J.9.7). Such investigations would also be interesting for German minorities (outside the German-language territory) (Ch. E). Perhaps websites play a role not only for internal cohesion and language maintenance, but also for language archipelagos (Ch. E.4.11).

1.4.2 Social media

Social media includes digital media and medial forms of communication which allow interactive feedback and, accordingly, an exchange of information and collective production of Internet texts. The most familiar form is *email*, which is often overlooked in this category, possibly because of its relatively long history and wide distribution, in favour of the more recent forms of social media such as *Blogs, Facebook, Twitter, LinkedIn* and more specialised forms such as *Researchgate* etc. The history of the various social media, their purposes and functions are described in detail with practical guidelines in Wikipedia articles and on specialist websites. In view of the pace of change and for personal reasons (including my age which reduces my motivation to keep up with the latest developments), I can offer little more on social media than to encourage future research. I have limited myself largely to Facebook and Twitter because of their greater popularity and because for them at least, there is some relevant information available. Even regarding the medium of email, there is a lack of comprehensive investigations. This applies especially for the specific research question posed in this context about the extent to which international communication, primarily international communication in the narrower sense, takes place in German (Ch. A.3). The question invites further sub-questions about the extent to which social media can promote or impair the international use of languages such as German and give additional impetus to English as the global lingua franca. There seems so far to be hardly any relevant research on these more specialised questions. I considered gathering information through the *Association of Internet Researchers (AoIR)* (aoir.org/) or its German counterpart the *Deutsche Gesellschaft für Online Forschung* (DGOF) (www.dgof.de/); however, the effort required seemed excessive. An email (25 November 2013) from Thorsten Strufe, Head of the Peer-to-Peer Networking Group at the Technical University of Darmstadt, which referred specifically to Facebook precisely captures the tone of many replies to my requests for advice: "I have now found time to look through our data records. Of course, we don't have a complete overview or detailed statistics. But it looks as if the German language is not widely distributed in the data we have. The only exception seems to be university communities, in which various foreign students converse with German students (student clubs/societies). Apart from these, most social groups consisting exclusively of Germans also tend to converse in English (possibly assuming international visibility)".

Based on direct questioning, especially of participants in my own seminars, I can confirm – of course, without statistical representativeness – that a great deal is "posted" in German in Facebook "friend groups" in which German native speakers and also FL speakers of German take part. However, the picture is very varied. My questionnaire to approximately 25 students, which was distributed further by the students in a snowball process, was worded as follows:

> If you are active in a "friend group" on Facebook or another form of social-media communication [...], I would be grateful for information about the language choices made in the group. Please try to estimate:
>
> 1) The (approximate) make-up of your group based on nationality and native languages (rough figures),
> 2) Which languages are used in the group in total (if possible, rough estimate of figures) and
> 3) Which nationalities and native speakers post their messages mainly in which language (possibly indicate individual preferences or variable types of behaviour).

The following responses were received; it is not meaningful to quantify the results because the numbers were too small:

Friend group of German male with 128 friends: all with German nationality apart from 3 Persians, 2 Argentinians, 2 French, 2 Spanish, 1 Croatian, 1 Malaysian, 1 Serbian (all with native language only German), 3 Swedish friends (2 native language also German) (all posted almost exclusively in German), 2 Turkish friends (1 native language also German, 1 native language also German + English: almost exclusively in Turkish), 1 friend from Thailand (native language also German: almost exclusively in English), 1 USA, 1 England, 1 (all native language also German: exclusively in English), 1 Scotland, 1 Canada, 1 Italy (native languages unknown).

Overarching rules for language choice:

- If native language German is not recognisable, then exclusively in the language of the country
- If native language German is recognisable, then in German and language of the country
- 1 German male, who lives in Sweden: exclusively in Swedish

- 1 German female in Australia, 1 German female in New Zealand, both exclusively in English
- 10–15% of the Germans also communicate in English, because of many international friends (JE, email 6 January 2014).

Friend group of a German female with 123 mostly university friends: 101 German friends, 12 Swiss, 4 Russian and 1 American, 1 Chilean, 1 French, 1 Spanish, 1 Czech and 1 Venezuelan: 80% in German, 10% English and in each case 2% French, Russian, Spanish and Czech. German academics, often in English, also among themselves. Native speakers of other languages generally in their own language among themselves, but also with comments in German (Karin Schneider-Wiejowski, email 11 December 2013).

Friend group of a German male, some university friends, some non-university, undefined group size: approximately 70% German, 11% Russian and in each case 1–2% Austrian, Polish, Turkish and 1 or 2 Brazilian, Canadian, Chilean, Croatian, Dutch, English, French, Greek, Indian, Indonesian, Italian, Japanese, Mexican, Persian, Portuguese, Serbian, Swedish, Swiss, Tunisian, Ukrainian, US American and Hungarian friends: approximately 72% in German, 13% in Russian, 10% in English, 1% in Portuguese and Spanish and <1% in Croatian, Dutch, French, Greek, Indian, Indonesia, Italian, Japanese, Polish, Serbian and Turkish. Published Facebook comments exclusively in German (65%), English (20%), Russian (12%), Spanish, Portuguese, French (1% each) and Indonesian (<1%). "I personally communicate with the corresponding Facebook friends and on the Facebook platform approximately 70% in German, 20% in English and 10% in Russian (Tim Brüning, email 11 December 2013).

Friend group of a Chinese female, mostly students, with approximately 90 friends: approximately 80 German friends, 4 Chinese, 3 Russian and 3 Moroccan: exclusively in German (Yanjun Wang, oral communication).

Friend group of a Chinese female with 270 friends: approximately 100 German friends, 60 American, 50 Chinese, otherwise from various countries: approximately 60% in own native language, but also in English and German as lingua franca ("if communicating with friends who do not come from the same country"). This informant additionally reported a "group of friends" in Düsseldorf, outside Facebook, many of them "expats", who mostly spoke English, even among themselves, including Germans who only spoke English to one another (Wenting Sheng, email 12 December 2013).

Friend group of a Chinese female, undefined group size, proportion of Germans approximately 85%, otherwise predominantly Chinese: all in their own native language among themselves, but Chinese friends predominantly in English with speakers of other languages. It was said to be the same for other Chinese people and people of other nationalities abroad who generally use their native language among themselves but English with speakers of other languages. "But with me, people speak German (because they are also German teachers)" (Han Guo, email 15 December 2013).

There is no evidence of a noticeable increase in the use of English as a lingua franca. But where members of a university are involved, they are mostly in the humanities and social sciences. Would a different picture appear in groups of natural scientists and structural scientists made up of similar proportions of nationalities and languages (cf. Ch. G.8)? Friend groups distributed more broadly including non-German-speaking countries would also be interesting. And do teachers and learners of German as a foreign language from different countries post to each other in German? And who else may do this? Under which conditions does this occur or not – in the spirit of Joshua Fishman's "Who speaks what language to whom and when?" (1965)?

Examples of language use and language choice on Facebook outside the academic world are given by Jordan Kraemer (2014) based on observations in Berlin. He sees parallels between the social relationships established and language choice. In highly international groups, a broadly conceived American concept of friendship predominated. There were only "friends", no "acquaintances", or in German only "*Freunde*" and no "*Bekannte*" (ibid: 54–56, 71). At the same time, the use of English was very dominant (ibid: 62, 66). Kraemer sees a possible explanation for the generalisation of US social relationships in the prestige and power relations between nations: "especially given its [Facebook's! U.A.] origin as an elite site for Harvard students [. . .]" (ibid: 59). Having said this, the function of English as a global lingua franca seems to me the more important factor in this language choice. By contrast, groups comprising predominantly Germans distinguish relatively consistently between "*Freunde*" and "*Bekannte*", which was translated into English as "close friends" and "acquaintances". Nowadays, these "options" are generally available, "to improve privacy management" (ibid: 72). The investigated groups of less international composition often posted "primarily in German". Groups of international composition preferred English. However, there were also Germans among them, even in the USA and Canada, who "posted both English and German, depending on the context" (ibid: 69).

Jennifer Dailey-O'Cains (2013) shows interesting differences between language communities by comparing bloggers in Germany and the Netherlands, in fact in "lifejournal blogs", in which "interconnectivity" between communicants "makes them more similar to social networking sites like Facebook"; ibid: 149). In 1,000 online conversations with women aged between 20 and 30, she found that the Dutch women not only used considerably more English than the Germans, but also took this for granted to a greater extent. Germans tend to "flag" the use of English or the switch to English, that is, they make a conscious language choice, while the Dutch use English almost as unconsciously as their own Dutch (ibid: 162). Dailey-O'Cains (2013: 163) explains the divergence with reference to the difference in size between the two language communities and therefore the different position of German and Dutch in the global language constellation (cf. Ch. A.7). Different attitudes towards English follow from this; the Dutch tend to see English as a global lingua franca, while the Germans consider it rather a foreign language and the language of the English-speaking countries. These findings prompt further comparisons between languages, including the international languages.

The Annual Report of the Instituto Cervantes (2013) also guided me in this direction for Facebook and Twitter (information from Alf Monjour; email 9 December 2013). Its findings still require further checking. The figures for Facebook originate from *Socialbakers*, a "Czech-based company that provides social media network statistics and analysis from Facebook, Twitter, Google +, LinkedIn and YouTube, helping companies monitor the effectiveness of their social media campaigns" (en.wikipedia.org/wiki/Socialbakers). Table I.1.4–5 provides an overview of the languages growing most rapidly in Facebook according to this source – the origin of the figures remains uncertain.

According to this data, German is relatively low down the chart but has risen during the investigated period by one rank position and, *proportionally* (note this narrowing of the specification!), German shows the third strongest growth of the languages included. Only Portuguese and Arabic show stronger growth. The source comments on the proportional boost in growth of German as follows: "And why is the German language so popular? Because it's the second fastest growing Facebook country in Europe!".

For Twitter, the available information relating to the topic of this book is even more fragmentary. Mocanu et al. (2012: arxiv.org/pdf/1212.5238v1.pdf) discuss possibilities for quantification of diverse aspects of social media; but the fragmentary findings still require completion and checking. For example, under *Figure 2*, a rank ordering of countries is provided based on Twitter

Table 1.1.4–5 The ten languages most strongly represented and growing fastest in Facebook

Languages	Users in millions		Increase in users in millions	
	November 2012	May 2010	Languages	May 2010 – November 2012
English	359.8	213.2	English	146.6
Spanish	142.9	61.2	Spanish	81.6
Portuguese	58.5	6.1	Portuguese	52.4
French	44.4	23.5	French	20.9
Indonesian	43.8	20.5	Indonesian	20.4
Turkish	31.7	21.9	German	19.5
German	30.8	11.3	Arabic	16.7
Italian	23.9	16.2	Chinese	10.5
Arabic	20.2	3.5	Turkish	9.8
Chinese	20.1	9.6	Italian	7.7

(*Source*: www.socialbakers.com/blog/1064-top-10-fastest-growing-facebook-languages)

users per head of the population, where Germany is ranked in 7th position (behind Kuwait, Spain, South Korea, Brazil, Indonesia and France, but ahead of Ukraine and Poland – this is the sequence of the ten highest ranked countries). In another part of the same figure, a rank ordering of countries is shown based on "Twitter users over a population of 1000 individuals". According to this, Germany is in third position, behind the USA and Canada and ahead of France, UK, Indonesia, Italy and the Netherlands. Having said this, another rank ordering in *Figure 4* in this source is not completely compatible with these figures. This relates to languages, not countries, and in fact to the probability of the "number of daily tweets grouped by language". Languages in which there is probably more tweeting per day are ranked higher than those in which this probably occurs less. Here, German is no longer even represented, this time among the eight highest-ranking languages, which include only English, Spanish, Portuguese, Indonesian, Japanese, Dutch, Italian and French – in this order. Figures from *Statista*, "the world's largest statistical portal" point in the same direction. Here also, German was not present in an analysis carried out in September 2013 of the ten most frequently tweeted languages worldwide, for which the following proportions were shown: English 34%, Japanese 16%, Spanish 12%, Malay 8%, Portuguese 6%, Arabic 6%, French 2%, Turkish 2%, Thai 1% and Korean 1%. German was only among the "other languages" with proportions <1%, which were not listed individually (www.social-secrets.com/2013/12/twitter-nutzer-sprechen-nur-selten-deutsch/ → Button "News"). One obvious explanation for this weak position of German would be that German-speakers simply tweet less compared with speakers of many other languages. Another possibly supplementary explanation would be that, when tweeting, German-speakers tend to use a foreign language rather than their own.

A technically sophisticated analysis carried out specially for me by Chris Biemann (Head of Language Technology in the Computer Science Department, Technical University Darmstadt) and his colleague Uli Fahrer provides important pointers for both the above hypotheses. They subdivided the world into the German official-language territory on the one hand (Germany, Austria, German-speaking Switzerland, Liechtenstein, Luxembourg, Eastern Belgium and South Tyrol; cf. Ch. D), and the rest of the world on the other hand. From the totality of tweets sent worldwide in 2012 and 2013, they selected a random sample of 1%. Using the program *Geotag*, all tweets for which the geographical origin could be determined, were filtered out, approximately

Table I.1.4–6 Percentage of tweets in worldwide circulation inside and outside the German official-language territory in 2012 and 2013, subdivided into four quarters

Quarter years	2012–1	2012–2	2012–3	2012–4
German outside	0.03	0.04	0.03	0.03
Non-German outside	99.24	99.25	99.36	99.46
German inside	0.29	0.28	0.21	0.16
Non-German inside	0.44	0.44	0.40	0.35
Quarter years	2013–1	2013–2	2013–3	2013–4
German outside	0.04	0.04	0.04	0.03
Non-German outside	99.51	99.51	99.58	99.64
German inside	0.15	0.15	0.12	0.11
Non-German inside	0.31	0.31	0.26	0.22

(*Source*: analysis Chris Biemann and Uli Fahrer, *Technische Universität Darmstadt*)

19.4 million. By means of two mutually controlling language recognition programs (*chromium-language-detector* and *github.com/shuyo/Idig*), these were then subdivided into German-speaking and non-German-speaking. Distribution between the German official language territory and the rest of the world was then determined. Two of the findings were particularly informative for our research question (Table I.1.4–6). First, that the total proportion of tweets sent in the German-language territory over this period declined from 0.73% (0.29 + 0.44) to 0.33% (0.11 + 0.22 to), i.e. to less than half.

"This comes about as a result of the larger growth of Twitter worldwide [compared with the German official-language territory]; the absolute figures are more or less stable" (email from Biemann 22 February 2014). So, based on tweeting, the German official-language territory falls short compared with the rest of the world. The second most important finding was that non-German language tweets inside the German official-language territory were more numerous than the German-language tweets and declined less markedly than the German-language tweets. The number of non-German-language tweets only halved (from 0.44% to 0.22%), while the German-language tweets fell by almost a third (from 0.29% to 0.11%). The proportion of German-language tweets therefore declined relative to the non-German-language tweets, which is equivalent to saying that the proportion of non-German-language tweets grew. These findings confirm both the preceding assumptions, namely that German-speakers tweet relatively less frequently than the speakers of many other languages, and that German-speakers tend to use a language other than their own when tweeting. Both hypotheses suggest that at least Twitter – if not the other social media – are more damaging, on average or in total, than supportive of the global position of German. Having said this, the hypothesis requires further research in view of the dynamic growth of the social media.

2. Language arts

2.1 Explanation of terms

The heading "language arts" is not intended as a normative claim about high artistic quality, such as might be suggested by the once popular textbook on German literature *Das sprachliche Kunstwerk* [The Work of Art in Language] by Wolfgang Kayser (1948). On the contrary, the title is to be taken only as a common denominator for the next two sub-sections. However, these are distinct from the preceding sub-sections of Ch. I in that they narrow the focus to aesthetic texts or texts with an aesthetic claim. This specification is particularly important in the case of Ch. I.2.2, because external forms such as the book, have been discussed in earlier chapters, for instance, in Ch. G *Science and scholarship*, but with a different focus. In that context, the focus was factual, whereas, for Ch. I.2.2, *Poetry and fiction [Belletristik]*, the central focus can be characterised as aesthetic entertainment, edification or something along those lines. This also applies to some extent for Ch. I.2.3 *Vocal music* – where narrowing the focus with the modifier *Vocal* seems almost redundant given the topic of the book. The sub-heading in this case is merely intended to avert potential irritation or confusion if readers consider only the title and immediately think of instrumental music when they see the word *music*. Having said this, as with almost all the topics in the present book, precise definitions are problematic. For example, there are also scholarly and scientific publications (the topic of Ch. G) which simultaneously make a claim to entertain. Similarly, music with a language component, such as a choral movement in a symphony, is often allocated to instrumental music because the instrumental component predominates. I include this kind of music in Ch. I.2.3 under the heading of vocal music, e.g. the 4th movement of Beethoven's Ninth Symphony, which is mentioned in that section.

2.2 *Poetry and fiction* [Belletristik]

This section concentrates largely on the fictional book – and therefore on a specific form of medial communication, contrasting with newspapers or magazines (Ch. I.1.2). Many Germanists may be frustrated by this limitation and indeed by the restriction of poetry and fiction to a subsection of this book on the global position of German. Poetry and fiction are the centre of interest for Germanists and carry considerable weight in German Philology and Linguistics abroad, in intercultural German Studies and even in German as a foreign language (GFL). This is immediately evident from the respect they receive in relevant institutional periodicals, such as the *Jahrbuch für Internationale Germanistik, Jahrbuch Deutsch als Fremdsprache/Intercultural German Studies* and the periodicals of the national societies for German Philology and Linguistics and GFL and applies especially to the literary book [*das belletristische Buch*]. It is possible that the significance of the literary book, or of poetry and fiction in their entirety, for the global position of German may be over-represented as a result. Heinz Kloss (1952: 29) warned of this long ago, pointing out that linguistic functions other than the aesthetic predominate "because the broad masses of people of all classes do not in fact write epics and poems and, alas, only a small minority reads epics and poems. Most people only read newspaper articles, church notices, letters, invoices and academic articles [. . .]".

Printed media are now challenged by the increasing significance of electronic media; the printed book must face the e-book. And yet, precisely in fictional writing, the bound, codex book presumably also retains a permanently secure position for communication among broad social groups. One relevant indicator is the growth of the book market in Germany: "Which group of goods is most important for the book market [in Germany! U.A.]? [. . .] [U]nquestionably fiction [*Belletristik*]. With a share of 35.0%, it is the main component in the total turnover of the industry and has therefore continued to strengthen its ascendancy [. . .]. In 2003, the first year of data collection, the proportion was 29.5% [. . .] (Börsenverein des Deutschen Buchhandels 2013: 13; information from Tobias Voss, CEO of International Markets of the Frankfurt Book Fair). However, these figures relate to market shares in monetary value, not the number of books. For a considerable time, this proportion has remained relatively constant: 1994 approximately 18.4% and 2011 approximately 18.5% of all books published in Germany, of which the total grew from 1994: 70,643 to 2011: 82,048. For titles in poetry and fiction, the figures were: 1994: 12,998 and 2011: 15,141 (calculated from percentages based on Volpers 2002: 2652 and Frankfurt Book Fair 2013: [4]).

It would also be relevant to our research question that these figures include not only authors from Germany or German-speaking countries or regions and not only German-language texts, although most are German-language texts. I was not able to determine this proportion, because the companies operating in the book trade do not generally have the statistics required. In the German-language territory, companies are organised within the *Börsenverein des Deutschen Buchhandels* (Germany), the *Schweizer Buchhändler- und Verleger-Verband* (SBVV) and the *Hauptverband des österreichischen Buchhandels* (de.wikipedia.org/wiki/Buchhandel). Based on the total number of books produced, Germany ranked third among all countries in the world in 1994, behind China and the UK and ahead of USA and France (Volpers 2002: 2652). By contrast, in 2011, it was only in position 6, behind the USA, China, UK, Russia and India, but ahead of Japan and Iran (en.wikipedia.org/wiki/Books_published_per_country_per_year). In this context, the proportion of e-books is increasing. Several years ago, it was announced: "Some 1300 German-language publishers have already made their in-copyright titles available in the *Libreka!* database, with 400 of them offering their e-books for sale on the platform" (publishing perspectives. com/2010/11/germanys-libreka-e-book store-opens-doors-to-us-and-foreign-publishers/ – announcement 12 November 2010). The *Online-Adressbuch des Deutschen Buchhandels* stated: "Currently there are 270,000 e-books for sale and more than 1.2 million books fully digitalised and searchable on Libreka! Amounting to more than 15 million book pages". But this certainly also included books published outside the German-speaking countries (www.mvb-online. de/international-clients/international-clients.html). *Libreka!* is a project of the *Börsenverein des Deutschen Buchhandels* for storage, searching, display and sale of digital versions of printed books. In fact, coming from nowhere, the e-book has experienced an explosive growth; but its share in the German book market in 2012 reached only 2.4% (*Börsenverein des Deutschen Buchhandels* 2013: 23). In future, it is likely to characterise the type and frequency of international communication occurring through books.

Although it may not be possible to draw precise conclusions about the scope of international communication, book exports do give a rough indication of international communication (between German native speakers and German FL speakers; Ch. A.3). In any case, communication occurs in multiple stages between authorship and reception of books, involving publishers' readers, editors, translators, reviewers, sales and purchasing personnel in addition to authors and readers. But above all, the statistics available for our research question are approximate. Book exports from Germany are classified according to "continents" and fiction is not considered separately. In 2011, a total of 1,182,889 books were exported from Germany, of which 1,028,752 (86% of all exported books) were exported to foreign countries in Europe, including German-speaking countries and regions, 34,318 (2%) to Africa, 62,872 (5%) to America, 54,182 (4%) to Asia and 2,703 (0.2%) to Australia (Börsenverein des Deutschen Buchhandels 2013: 144). Bearing in mind that this by no means only relates to fiction and that books in languages other than German may be included, these figures seem modest. It was not possible to determine the exact export destinations for the more recent period. The extent to which my findings from research carried out more than 20 years ago (from *Adressbuch für den deutschsprachigen Buchhandel* 1990/91: 733ff.; Ammon 1991a: 392–394) might still be valid remains doubtful. Around 1990, the book trade in the Federal Republic of Germany, Austria and Switzerland was engaged in business associations with 3,530 foreign book trading companies distributed in 79 countries: 25 in Europe, 17 in North and South America, 12 in Africa, 21 in Asia and four in the Pacific region (ibid: 735–830). The large number of German names, including company names, among the addresses was remarkable, e.g. *Gutenberg-Buchhandlung* (Brussels), *Bauzentrum Buchhandel* (Oslo), *Aufrechter Gang, Buchimport* (Lund, Sweden), *Deutsche Buchhandlung* (Teheran), *Buch-Bruecke* (Ballston Lake, NY, USA), *Lehmann, Ludwig, Buchhhandlung* (Montevideo, Uruguay), *Luederitzbuchter Buchhandlung* (Luederitz, Namibia) etc. A name in the national language also often appeared on German books, e.g. *Calligrammes, Librairie Allemande* (Paris), *Türk-Alman Kitap Evi* (Istambul), *German Book Post Language Center* (Breiningsville, PA, USA), *German Book Boutiques Ltd.* (Ottawa, Canada), *Livraria Alemao Ltda* (Blumenau, Brazil), *Libreria Alemana S.R.L.* (Asunción, Paraguay), *German Book Centre* (Madras, India) etc. These are often university or international bookshops. Neither the proportion of German-language titles nor the proportion of fiction among the inventory was disclosed. Performance differed in different countries, but with the overarching trend of a gradual decline in demand for German-language books, including fiction.

This was especially obvious in the USA. When Suhrkamp-Verlag abandoned direct distribution of German titles in the USA towards the end of 1989, the publisher's representative explained, "[o]f course that was a reaction to the fact that an already small market is continuing to shrink [. . .]". This reference should be understood in the sense that the focus of German Philology and Linguistics has shifted towards language acquisition, i.e. it is turning away from the reading of German-language poetry and fiction ("Goethe, Foucault and the others", *FAZ* 5 December 1989). At the same time, German textbooks from Germany showed increased sales, also in the USA, based on an initially significant increase in learning German as a foreign language after the opening of the Berlin wall ("*Das Interesse für die deutsche Sprache wächst schon*", *FAZ* 15 October 1990; also, Ch. J.2). That political change presumably also aroused increased interest in German-language fiction in many places. At least, two bookshops in Paris (*Calligrammes. Librairie Allemande* and *Le Roi des Aulnes. Librairie-Galerie des Pays de Langue Allemande*) which both saw a rise in demand for German-language fiction in France, confirmed this in response to my letters (April 1990). However, even at that time, approximately 80% of all books imported into France were in English, with continuing growth ("*Channel crossing. Englische Bücher sind in Frankreich mehr gefragt*" [English books are more in demand in France], *Spotlight* 1991 (1): 22). According to more recent indicators, demand for German-language fiction in the non-German speaking foreign countries has faded.

Access to German-language fiction for non-German-speakers is also available via many German (speaking) minorities which publish German-language poetry and fiction without official status of the German language (Ch. E). This still applies today for Romania (Ch. E.4.7) and Namibia (E.4.9) and – in residual form – for Alsace in France (E.4.3). Detailed investigation of current circumstances, especially the extent to which speakers of the respective majority language or neighbouring minority languages consider this literature or are motivated to learn German as a result would be a desirable topic for future research.

Some of the most important German-language authors in modern history, such as Franz Kafka, Max Brod and Franz Werfel (Czech majority region), Paul Celan (Ukrainian majority region), Elias Canetti (Bulgarian and neighbouring Romanian majority region; Nobel prize 1981) and Herta Müller (Romanian majority region; Nobel Prize 2009), come from minority territories. Emigrants in the 1930s and 1940s fleeing National Socialism found themselves in a similar communication situation; most, and the most famous of them, lived in the USA at least for a time, such as Heinrich and Thomas Mann (Nobel prize 1929), Bertolt Brecht, Alfred Döblin, Carl Zuckmayer and Lion Feuchtwanger. In addition to such celebrities, there were numerous other authors writing in German in German-(speaking) minority regions, who were, and still are, valued by connoisseurs. Details are given in the series *Auslandsdeutsche Literatur der Gegenwart* published by Alexander Ritter (1974ff., 25 volumes; Hildesheim: Olms). It provides an overview of German-language literature in individual regions, such as Kazakhstan and the former Volga Republic with the Ukraine (USSR, two volumes), Romania, Alsace (six volumes), South Tyrol, USA, Canada (Ontario), South-Eastern Europe, Hungary and Israel – also Eastern Belgium and Luxembourg, where German is an official language of state. Many volumes are dedicated to individual authors, such as Nikolaus Berwanger, who migrated from Romania to the FRG (two volumes) and Benno Fruchtmann, Israel, and Adrien Fink, Alsace. Volume 15 contains a bibliography by Hartmut Fröschle on "German Language and German-language Literature Abroad". There are also special bibliographies or histories of literature on individual minority regions, e.g. the *Schriftsteller-Lexikon der Siebenbürger Deutschen* ([1868], Vol. 10, Harald Roth (ed.) 2012).

German-language books by authors of foreign-language origin who have migrated into the German-language territory constitute a separate topic, which is relevant to German as a second language (Ch. A.3) and to the position of German in the world. These authors also include respected names, such as Lev Kopelew, Wladimir Kaminer and Olga Martynova (caution: ≠ there is an author with the same name in the bibliography of the present book!) (native language Russian), Libuse Moniková (native language Czech), Guilermo Aparicio (native language Spanish), Irena Habalik (native language Polish), Joao Costa (native language Portuguese), Ertunç Barin, Zafer Senocak, Rumjana Zacharieva and Feridun Zaimoglu (native language Turkish), Nino Haratschiwili (native language Georgian) and Yoko Tawada (native language Japanese).

As early as 1985, there were 330 participants in a competition for authors of non-German native language writing in German, of whom around three quarters lived in the FRG. Almost onethird were Turkish (*Informationen Deutsch als Fremdsprache* 13 (3) 1986: 284). An overview of this topic is provided in Corino (1981), Ackermann (1985), Ackermann/ Weinrich (1986) and Serke (1984, 1987). Since 1985, the Robert Bosch Foundation has awarded the Adelbert-von-Chamisso Prize to authors of non-German native language writing in German. By 2013, a total of 65 prizes had been awarded to authors from more than 20 countries of origin. Beyond this, "an 'honorary award of the Adelbert-von-Chamisso Prize of the Robert Bosch Foundation' [. . .] has been granted to 3 people, whose life's work has been especially influential in the sense of the prize: Jiři Gruša, Imre Kertész and Harald Weinrich". The prize honours "authors whose work is characterised by cultural exchange. The prize winners also share an exceptional relationship with language which enriches German literature" (www.bosch stiftung.de/content/ language1/html/14169.asp). Weinrich is considered the discoverer of this "migration literature", which began life as "*Gastarbeiterliteratur*". It has become a flagship for German external cultural policy. For example, the *Deutsches Haus* in New York organised a conference "German Literature Transnational: featuring 'the celebrated Turkish-German author' Emine Sevgi Özdamar", in New York on 26 February 2014, who was, at the same time, appointed to the "DAAD Distinguished Chair in Contemporary Poetics" (co-funded by Germany) at New York University. This author is also a holder of the Adelbert-von-Chamisso Prize (1999). What remains to be carried out here is a – methodologically challenging – investigation of the extent to which this kind of literature arouses additional international interest in German language and culture.

Translations from German into other languages presumably contribute to this process, and this represents another potentially interesting research project (once again, the relevant data are from Tobias Voss and Enrico Turrin, Deputy Director of the Federation of European Publishers). Heinz Kloss construed translations from a language as an indicator for its international rank or position in the world: "A further measure for the international ranking of languages is whether a large number of books have been translated from it [sic!] into other languages". However, he rightly imposes two limits on the validity of this indicator: 1) "In many cases, the large number of translations is explained primarily not with reference to international position but rather with reference to the internal ranking of a language within a country". He refers here to multilingual countries which promote translations into their other official languages. 2) "Furthermore, it must be borne in mind that the increasing spread of a language abroad can mean precisely that translations into this language become, to a certain extent, superfluous or at least less urgent". Here, he is touching on an effect of translations into other languages which possibly inhibits the international spread of the source language – to the extent that the learning of the source language seems superfluous, because the interesting texts have, apparently, already been translated. Conversely, translations also can arouse interest in the source language: its literature may appear so rich through translation, that it becomes worthwhile to learn, because there is certainly a great deal which has not been translated. Translators, language teachers and media experts are keen to grasp professional opportunities arising from their skills in this context.

From this perspective, translations into German (German as target language) are less relevant than translations from German (German as source language). But I would still like to touch briefly on translations from German. Table I.2–1 shows the eight most frequent source languages for translations into German and the eight most frequently learned foreign languages in Germany. The rankings for the annual figures named correspond broadly to a long-term trend. The data for 2008 to 2012 (Börsenverein des Deutschen Buchhandels 2013: 97) provide evidence for this. The figures for 2009 in Table I.2–1 were selected because of their proximity in time to the available figures for foreign language learning. They cover all types of publication. Figures relating specifically to fiction translations were available only for 2012, and only for the source languages, not in the other direction. The figures in Table I.2–1 show an approximately parallel ranking based on frequency between translations into German and foreign languages learnt in Germany, however, more so in the higher rankings than in the lower. This parallelism could be determined by bilateral effects which cannot be precluded: on one hand, it could be that foreign-language skills already available in Germany motivate translations from the respective languages; on the other hand, the translations from other languages may motivate people to learn. Presumably, the former carries more weight – but the opposite, particularly interesting effect cannot be precluded in the present context either. Comparing texts of all types and genres (row 2) with exclusively fictional texts (row 3), it is remarkable that the larger, international

Table I.2–1 The eight most frequently learnt foreign languages in secondary schools in Germany in the school year 2006/7, and the most frequent source languages for translations into German (German as target language) for texts of every kind in 2009 and for fiction and poetry 2012

FL learners	English	French	Latin	Spanish
2006/7	7,372,865	1,696,411	825,275	285,480
Translation all	English	French	Japanese	Italian
2009	6,874	1,078	547	333
Translations of fiction/poetry	English	French	Italian	Swedish
2012	3,196	278	115	112
FL learners	Russian	Italian	Greek	Turkish
2006/7	99,991	52,111	15,909	10,977
Translation all	Dutch	Swedish	Russian	Spanish
2009	219	205	194	182
Translations of fiction/poetry	Russian	Dutch	Norwegian	Danish
2012	70	50	41	30

(*Sources*: Quetz 2010: 174; Börsenverein des Deutschen Buchhandels 2013: 97; de.statista.com/statistik/daten/studie/194342/umfrage/buchmarkt-hoerbuch-umsatz-nach-warengruppen/)

languages predominate more strongly in the former case (row 2) than in the latter (row 3). Presumably, more scientific texts are present in the former case, which, in the latter case, in the smaller language communities (Scandinavia, the Netherlands, Flemish Belgium), are already published predominantly in English. However, the small language communities still have a rich fictional literature in their own languages.

Table I.2–2 shows the eight most frequent target languages for translations from German; separate figures for poetry and fiction were not available.

The target languages for translations from German are evidently very different from the source languages. They correlate more closely with the language territories or countries in which German is learnt as a foreign language. Compare with maps J.7–1 and J.7.2 towards the end of Ch. J.7 and Ch. J.9.2–J.9.15. Furthermore, the target languages for translations from German reveal shifts of interest in recent history, both for the learning of German as a foreign language (GFL) and in commercial terms. This applies especially for the decline in Eastern European languages and countries, and the growth of Chinese and China.

For Tables I.2–1 and I.2–2, I selected the absolute figures, because this shows the orders of magnitude. These reveal the asymmetry of the generally smaller number of translations from German (German as source language) than into German (German as target language), but also that this asymmetry is based only on some of the languages: the extreme is with English, also French, less so for Japanese and Swedish (see also Table I.2–3). Evidently, the German-speaking countries find the texts produced in these languages, especially in English, more interesting than vice versa. In the case of English, the eagerness to translate is more surprising, because knowledge of this language, at least a reading knowledge, is more widely distributed in the German-language community than for any other foreign language – as shown in Table I.2–1 (also Quetz 2010; Ammon 2006f.; Hüllen 2007; Gerhards 2010; H. Wagener 2012). By contrast, for speakers

Table I.2–2 The eight most frequent target languages for translations from German

2008	Polish	Russian	Czech	Chinese	English	Korean	Italian	Spanish
	765	572	555	518	472	460	455	427
2010	Chinese	Spanish	Polish	Czech	French	Dutch	Russian	English
	876	638	588	526	516	451	396	390
2012	Chinese	English	Spanish	Czech	Italian	Polish	Russian	French
	1,055	529	434	405	392	367	331	330

(*Source*: Börsenverein des Deutschen Buchhandels 2013: 112)

Table I.2–3 Comparison of source and target languages for translations from/into German

Source languages	Engl.	French	Japanese	Italian
Rankings 2009	6,874	1,078	547	333
Target languages 2009	472	347	150	455
Target languages	Polish	Russian	Czech	Chinese
Rankings 2008	765	572	555	518
Source languages	Dutch	Swedish	Russian	Spanish
Rankings 2009	219	205	194	182
Target languages 2009	306	83	572	427
Target languages	English	Korean	Italian	Spanish
Rankings 2008	472	460	455	427

(Source for Tables I.2–1, I.2–2; Börsenverein des Deutschen Buchhandels 2013: 112)

of the languages shown in Table I.2–3, Italian, Dutch, Russian and Spanish, texts from German are evidently more interesting than vice versa.

Caution is required in explaining and especially evaluating these figures. It is in no sense possible to infer the "objective" quality or significance of texts in the different languages – however this is defined – directly from such asymmetries. Many language communities may translate less from other languages than would be good for them, simply because of a lack of corresponding foreign-language skills. This suspicion is suggested in the English-speaking countries – because "only about 3% of all books in the United States [from the context, this must mean 'United Kingdom'! U.A.] are works in translation. [. . .] And that 3% figure includes all books in translation – in terms of poetry and fiction, the number is actually closer to 0.7%" (Donahay 2012: 5; also 26). By contrast, titles translated from English alone represent around 7% of book production in Germany (93,124 in 2009, according to the Börsenverein des Deutschen Buchhandels 2013: 80). In this context, the proportion of people with a reading knowledge of German in the English-speaking countries is much smaller than that of people with a reading knowledge of English in the German-speaking countries. The greater readiness to translate in the German-language community compared with the English-language community may have diverse reasons. One possible reason is that, on average, the English-language texts contain more innovative, interesting information. Poetry and fiction in fact represent only a fraction. Because of possible discrepancies in information, reference could be made here to the different number of Nobel prizes among German-speaking and English-speaking academics (cf. Ch. G.1; G.9).

Werner Bormann (1973: 30f.) offers evidence for the fact that the asymmetries in translation identified between these languages, especially English and French, have a long tradition. He refers to a "cultural balance sheet"; but I find *translation balance sheet* more appropriate here. From around 1969 until the 1980s, the balance sheet for German is only negative compared with English and French; but positive compared with all other nine comparable languages: Dutch, Spanish, Italian, Hungarian, Danish, Czech, Polish, Swedish and Russian (Bormann's sequence). In addition to Bormann's figures for 1969 (1973: 31), I have included the figures for subsequent years for other languages where data were available, and in fact from the UNESCO *Statistical Yearbook* (1981, 1985, 1987). For reasons of visual clarity and to achieve broader representativeness, I have formed averages from several years (1975–1978 and 1979–1982) (Table I.2–4). The positive balance sheet compared with Russian in the 1970s subsequently veered into the negative, presumably partly because of the dependence of the then GDR upon the Soviet Union. For French, it should be borne in mind that for a considerable time, the French government has generously sponsored translations from French into other languages.

Since primarily poetry and fiction are involved here, Table I.2–5 now provides a rank ordering of the previously included ten languages according to the number of poetry and fictional books translated from these languages ("Literature" in UNESCO *Statistical Yearbook* 1971, 1980s, 1988). It was prepared based on the average number of translations in the years 1967–1969, 1973–1975 and 1980–1982 (extreme values in brackets). Unfortunately, the more recent UNESCO yearbooks no longer contain the corresponding statistics – possibly because of the questionable reliability of some of the data. The fourth place for German in this balance sheet comes close to the prestige enjoyed by German as a language of literature elsewhere, which presumably relies especially on "connoisseur literature".

A serious comparative evaluation of the poetry and fiction of different languages would presumably overstretch many experts in comparative literature. Comparative listings of literature by language are seldom found (example: Amiet 1932). I have therefore had to make do with rough pointers, such as how the ranking of German-language fiction may be perceived by the wider global public compared with the literatures of other languages. Presumably the allocation of

Table I.2–4 Translation balance sheet between German and other languages

	1969	1975–1978	1979–1982
German – > English	674	713	865
	− 1404	− 3627	− 3932
English – > German	2078	4340	4797
German – > French	422	505	505
	− 170	− 556	− 662
French – > German	592	1061	1167
German – > Russian	111	97	169
	+ 20	− 638	− 465
Russian – > German	91	735	634
German – > Spanish	372	731	715
	+314	+615	+201
Spanish – > German	58	116	514
German – > Italian	331	276	297
	+234	+ 27	+ 36
Italian – > German	97	249	261
German – > Japanese		256	205
		+236	+178
Japanese – > German		20	27
German – > Arabic		17	18
		− 3	− 6
Arabic – > German		20	12

(*Sources*: Bormann 1973: 31; UNESCO *Statistical Yearbook* 1981, 1985, 1987)

Table I.2–5 Average number of translations of poetry and fictional books from ten languages 1967–1982

1. English	10,112	(7,368/ 12,841)
2. French	2,562	(2,322/ 3,031)
3. Russian	1,750	(1,448/ 2,098)
4. German	1,416	(1,272/ 1,688)
5. Spanish	527	(313/ 1,080)
6. Italian	482	(405/ 561)
7. Japanese	92	(52/ 148)
8. Arabic	72	(38/ 120)
9. Chinese	66	(48/ 101)
10. Portuguese	64	(41/ 120)

(*Source*: UNESCO *Statistical Yearbook* 1971, 1980, 1988)

Nobel prizes, the most prestigious literary award in the world, has some influence on this. The stimulus to read fiction in the original language might depend somewhat on the ranking of the literature of a language perceived in this way, and may therefore lead people to learn the language. A total of 13 Nobel prizes for literature had been awarded to German-speaking authors, i.e. to the German language by 2013. The prize winners were Theodor Mommsen 1902, Rudolf Eucken 1908, Paul Heyse 1910, Gerhard Hauptmann 1912, Carl Spitteler 1919, Thomas Mann 1929, Herman Hesse 1946, Nelly Sachs 1966, Heinrich Böll 1972, Elias Canetti 1981, Günter

Table I.2–6 Distribution of Nobel prizes for literature between languages up to 2013

	English	*French*	*German*	*Spanish*	*Swedish*	*Italian*	*Russian*
1901–1910	1	1.5	3	1	1	1	–
1911–1920 (not 1914)	0.5	2	2	–	1	–	–
1921–1930	3	2	1	1	–	1	–
1931–1940 (not 1940)	3	1	–	–	1	1	1
1941–1950 (not 1941–1943)	3	1	1	1	–	–	
1951–1960	2	3	–	1	1	1	1
1961–1970	1	2	1	1	–	–	2
1971–1980	3	–	1	2	2	1	
1981–1990	2	1	1	3	–	–	1
1991–2000	4	–	1	–	–	1	
2001–2010	4	1	2	1	–	–	
2010–2013	1	–	–	–	1	–	
Total	27.5	14.5	13	11	7	6	5

Grass 1999, Elfriede Jellinek 2004 and Herta Müller 2009. Table I.2–6 provides an overview of the distribution of Nobel prizes between languages. The language of each prize winner has been allocated the value 1, even if two authors shared the prize. However, if an author wrote in two languages (e.g. Czeslaw Milosz: English and Polish), each of the two languages was only allocated the value 1/2. Only languages with a total of at least five Nobel prizes have been included and ranked from left to right.

The other Nobel prizes were distributed as follows: Danish 3, Norwegian 3, Polish 3, Chinese 2, Japanese 2, Modern Greek 2, Arabic 1, Finnish 1, Yiddish 1 (2 x ½), Portuguese 1, Serbo-Croat 1, Czech 1, Turkish 1, Hungarian 1, Bengali ½, Icelandic ½, Hebrew ½ and Occitan ½. Accordingly, many languages, including EU official languages, are still without a Nobel prize.

German ranks third, behind English and French, but ahead of Spanish. English is clearly in the lead, but by a smaller margin than for many parameters in book production. It is therefore entirely justifiable to suppose a significant position for German in the perceived "connoisseur literature". Having said this, the performance characteristic is less favourable than for many other languages. For example, the considerable growth of Spanish and Russian compared with the other larger European languages is remarkable. It becomes clearer when the ten-year steps are combined into just three time segments, and even clearer with just two time segments, which leads to the following proportions for the period up to 1950 compared with the period following this: English 10 ½: 17, French 7 ½: 7, German 7:6, Spanish 3:8, Swedish 3:3, Italian 3:3 and Russian 1:4. Looked at in this way, German and French, show the most marked stagnation, creating the impression that both languages have lost prestige in literature, especially compared with Spanish and Russian. Having said this, one must keep in mind the statistically small totals, which certainly cannot serve as a basis for predicting the future.

2.3 Vocal music

I have limited my discussion here to music *in conjunction with* language to avoid confusion with the distribution of music of all kinds, which might be suggested, e.g. by the metaphor of music as a "world language". *Vocal music* as I designate it, includes all musical works with a language component, even if they are generally thought of as instrumental music when the total language component is less important than the instrumental components. But such vocal music can also be received without understanding the text, e.g. operas with Italian *libretti* without knowing Italian, French-language *chansons* without knowing French etc. Even vocal production, the singing of foreign-language texts, may involve only an imitation of sounds without real knowledge of the respective language. The distribution of vocal music in a given language should therefore not be equated with the distribution of that language itself; although, having said this, there is presumably a loose correlation. At least, this assumption probably underlies claims I have sometimes heard that internationally successful German bands have boosted listeners' motivation to learn German. For example, the president of the Goethe-Institut, Klaus-Dieter Lehmann, has been quoted as follows: "We are currently overbooked for German language in the Goethe Institutes in France and Israel, just because of the appearance of 'Tokio Hotel'", a band which sings in German (www.dradio.de/dkultur/sendungen/fazit/904337/). In fact, regular reception or even production of vocal music in a foreign language could prompt the need for at least an elementary knowledge of the language required to understand the text approximately, and this could contribute to the positive evaluation of the language and promote listeners' readiness to learn. In this sense, rock music and pop music therefore presumably contribute to the worldwide distribution of English. Conversely, existing knowledge of a language facilitates access to the respective vocal music via a feedback mechanism between the distribution of a language and the associated vocal music.

Let us first consider reception, starting with classical German vocal music. This music, including cantatas, oratorios, masses, operas, operettas and art songs, is received worldwide, but its share in the totality of vocal music received outside the German-language territory is relatively small. The classification applies specially to live performances but also to sound media (CDs, videos, films and the Internet) and mass media (radio, TV). However, in this context, relevant figures were not available to me, not even for the frequency of translations or subtitling, e.g. for opera performances. A comprehensive investigation, in which individual genres would have to be considered separately, would therefore be extremely relevant. Especially in opera, the predominance of Italian is beyond doubt. Reports, such as the following on the 200th anniversary of the birth of Richard Wagner, are typical: "Admittedly, the number of Verdi performances this year significantly exceeds Wagner events. In terms of global popularity, the Italian composer has always been a little ahead of his German rival" (*Saarbrücker Zeitung* 19 July 2013). Investigations of individual genres reveal connections with the history of German as a foreign language in many countries, e.g. in Japan. Many Japanese towns celebrate New Year's Eve with performances of the 4th movement of Beethoven's Ninth Symphony sung by large amateur choruses, always with the original German text (Ziegler 1994). A general love of German classical music is clearly involved, as suggested by a report that "For 120 years, the three 'Bs' Bach, Beethoven and Brahms, have dominated Japanese musical life – so much so that even today, the most popular song at Christmastime is still '*Freude, schöner Götterfunke*'" ("Mozart – *fernöstlich*", *FAZ* 17 October 1990). Such musical preferences are probably connected with the traditional but declining importance of German as a foreign language in Japan (Ammon 1994d: contributions by Hirataka 1994; Naka 1994; Haarmann 1994; Ch. J.9.14).

Historically, the German "*Volkslied*" [folksong] used to be a very popular genre in the German-language territory and was respected by the outside world. Friedrich Engels himself ([1839] 1970: 417) recommended these "*Volkslieder*, which are known throughout Germany and of which we can indeed be proud" to the workers of his town, Elberfeld, in preference to the often "extremely vulgar *Zotenlieder* [bawdy songs]". The quotation shows that the *Volkslieder* were not only appreciated by conservative groups. However, they have only been maintained – to a certain extent – among these groups. One reason for the broad turn away from *Volkslieder* was no doubt the fact that they were preferred by the Nazis and other German nationalist groups because they were felt to signify a high level of German "*Volksgeist*". The German *Volkslieder* exemplify how linguistic forms and symbols can be permanently discredited through political misuse. Other reasons for the low esteem felt by the *Volkslieder* in recent history, e.g. that they express an outdated worldview or attitude towards life, seem less important because they are equally applicable to other, less disparaged genres of vocal music.

I will return to the ongoing, special fostering of German folk music later in this chapter, but first I must outline the adaptation of German popular song towards the genres developed in the English-speaking world. The outline should be prefaced with the comment that the German language plays only a subordinate role in these genres and is therefore seldom heard outside the German-language territory. Groups such as *Tokio Hotel*, which caused a temporary sensation because of their international success, have often shifted to English-language texts for international performances. I can only give a simplified sketch of such developments (for further details, see Mahlmann/ Zombik 2002: especially 2683). This trend should probably be understood less as a continuation of the actual *Volkslied* tradition than as a continuation of the tradition of "*volkstümliche Lieder*" [popular, folk-like songs], a specific kind of "*Schlager*" ["hit" songs]. Since the advent of mass media communication, these have played an important role for the broad population in the German-language territory. It must be conceded that they did not reach far beyond this, and, until well into the 1960s, songs in this tradition were sung almost exclusively in German: to such an extent that American singers of related genres who performed in Germany sometimes also sang in German. Examples include Bill Ramsey, who then became a German, Johnny Cash and even Elvis Presley, but with German *Volkslieder* and not in the individualist genre of rock 'n' roll. The extent to which folk-like music in Germany continued in the German language into the 1960s can be gathered from the fact that even the Beatles tried to access the German market in German, with German-language versions of "*Sie liebt dich*" (*She Loves You*) and "*Komm gib mir deine Hand*" (*I Want to Hold Your Hand*). The translator was the Luxembourg singer and radio presenter Camillo Felgen writing under the pen name of Jean Nicolas (en.wikipedia.org/wiki/Komm,_gib_mir_deine_Hand/Sie_liebt_dich). But the success of these German-language versions by the Beatles was strongly eclipsed by the English-language titles which were much more popular in Germany, and the Beatles quickly abandoned singing in German. In fact, the turn by the German public in the 1960s towards English-language songs, not only by the Beatles, was overwhelming; and it has been maintained ever since. One retrospective judgement of the Beatles' attempts at singing in German sums it up: "Today such an idea seems laughable [. . .]" (german.about.com/library/blmus_beatles.htm). The awakening which followed the post-war repression of Nazi crimes may furnish a provisional explanation for German citizens' openness towards the English language – which has often been criticised by "friends of the German language". Openness towards English coincided with the rise of the student movements which attempted to come to terms with their own German past. In this context, a broad but mostly academic social group became aware and acknowledged that the Nazi crimes and the preceding chauvinism of the German nationalist movement and the German Empire had all been organised and propagated in German. One consequence of this growing awareness was to associate the German language with that now hated way of thinking. Added to this was the – by no means far-fetched – idea that the German language was also thought of in this way worldwide. However, the complex topic of politically motivated negative attitudes towards the German language can only be touched upon here. To mention just a few examples, publications such as the following give an impression of the complexity: *Aus dem Wörterbuch des*

Unmenschen [From the dictionary of the monster] (Sternberger/ Storz/ Süskind 1957, several editions), "*Lingua Tertiae Imperii/LIT*" (in Klemperer 1966), retrospectively also conferences such as the 2002 annual conference "*Deutsch von außen*" of the Institute for German Language (see also "*Hässlich und schwierig*"? [Ugly and difficult?] *FR* 26 March 2002: 20) and references to German as a "barked language" (Trabant 2007). Counter arguments to the effect that it was not the language but certain groups among the German people, but by no means all of them, who caused the evil, and references to the humanist and classical tradition of German philosophy which was also articulated through the German language, have not succeeded in compensating this loss of prestige. However, damaged linguistic prestige was presumably less important for the turn away from popular German-language vocal music than other factors, such as the medial and economic superiority of the English-speaking world.

Especially the genres of popular music, such as rock, pop and later hip-hop, rap and others (for details of "fashion cycles" see Mahlmann/ Zombik 2002: 2682f.), which were characterised by English-language culture anyway, were now also given mostly English-language texts even by German-speaking composers and performers. How else could German-language popular vocal music be distributed and received outside the German-language territory? Almost all language communities must have been in a similar position relative to English. The English-language community – rather than the language – dominated the relevant musical genres worldwide. The same applies to jazz, the associated songs and musicals – which now often took precedence over operetta even in the German-language territory – although the texts of musicals were often translated into the local language. To understand the swing from German to English, just think back to the times when Italian and French operas were still performed in Germany with *libretti* translated into German, up to the 1970s ("*Als Alfredo noch Alfred hieß*", *WAZ* 23 August 2013; *Flieg, Gedanke. Verdi auf Deutsch.* EMI Elektrola, 10 CDs with premieres). Then again, Udo Lindenberg recently declared it "*superwichtig*" that his German-language musical *Hinterm Horizont* was provided with English subtitles for the performance on the Potsdamer Platz in Berlin (*WAZ* 14 January 2014).

By contrast with the isolated German-language song outside the German-language territory, this mass of English-language music presumably provides a strong motivation to learn English. The effect on the young generation has been emphasised from various perspectives (e.g. Crystal 2003: 100–104; for Czechoslovakia, see Prucha 1983: 178). Primary schoolchildren have often confessed to me that they wanted to learn English so that they could understand their favourite songs. In 1990, I gave a questionnaire to school pupils in years 3 and 4 in Duisburg-Homberg with the following questions: 1a) "What is your favourite song?", 1b) "Which language is it in?", 1c) "What does the text mean?", 2a) "Which other song do you like a lot?", with 2b) and 2c) corresponding to 1b) and 1c). 36 of the respondents (57%, n = 63) named an English-language song as their favourite, 27 of them David Hasselhoff's "I've been looking for freedom". Only 19 (30%) named a German-language song as their favourite; one named a Portuguese-language song. Surprisingly, 5 of the 19 informants with a German-language favourite song indicated English as the language of the text. Had the greater prestige of English tricked them into this incorrect answer, because, among school pupils, it counted for more than a song in German, or had they just misheard the text? The level of ignorance of the English-language texts was astonishing. None wrote the title without mistakes; the answers were garbled, such as *Apiluki fon Fiden, Apip luken vor Fridom, Lukin vor enfredom, Abel loking wor frieden, Ape lukin vor fredom, Abkink Forfriedom* and so forth. The meaning was also misunderstood, in every case hovering around the two keywords *Süden* and *Frieden* (peace instead of freedom), e.g. "*auf der Strasse nach Süden*: on the road to the south" or "*Ich suche Frieden*: I'm looking for peace". At the same time, this small-scale survey shows that songs can be appreciated even without understanding the text, especially if the content has pleasant associations. But the higher prestige of English compared with German certainly contributed to the children's acceptance of the songs.

Statements by some German performers of popular music who prefer English-language texts for reasons of personal identity point in a somewhat different direction. When asked why she did not even sing one German-language text, Sabine Sabine [sic!] replied: "It doesn't sound right; it's just not me" (WDR 1, Landesstudio Dortmund 9 February 1990). Many German-speaking singers of popular songs therefore find their own identity more in English than in German-language texts. This question also faces people who listen to such songs in German-speaking countries and regions. On the question of identity, it is worth remembering that in the celebrations for the unification of Germany in Berlin during the night from 2 to 3 October 1990, British-Irish singer, Chris de Burgh, was a key performer, singing exclusively English-language songs. So, German unification took place against a soundtrack of English-language songs. However, this does suggest that most present-day Germans are not language chauvinists (on this question, see Hoberg/ Eichhoff–Cyrus/ Schulz 2008: 36–40). But, nowadays, the size of the global market also plays a significant part in the choice of the English language by German singers.

A form of counter movement against the complete anglicisation of popular music in the German-speaking world was started by the *Neue Deutsche Welle* [New German Wave] which came into being towards the end of the 1970s. It emerged from English-speaking role models but then broke away linguistically and even found fans outside the German-language territory, which makes it especially interesting for the topic of this book: "[I]t quickly developed into an original and distinct style, influenced in no small part by the different sound and rhythm of the German language which many of the bands had adapted from early on" (en.wikipedia.org/wiki/Neue_Deutsche_Welle). Famous interpreters and "Bands", which they were still called despite their Germanness, included Nena, Ideal, Spliff, Joachim Witt Trio and – to stretch the term somewhat – also including BAP and Udo Lindenberg. The only German-speaking singer included in the RTL list of "most successful hits in the world", the Austrian singer-songwriter Falco, was also among them. Perhaps it is an indication of the limits on global success that Falco's song "*Rock me Amadeus*" was only partly in German and had an English-language title. The international success of the *Neue Deutsche Welle* as a movement also remained limited. Having said that, there were successes in several countries which resonated for a considerable time afterwards. For instance, I recall Nena's "*99 Luftballons*" from my visits to Russia long after the start of the new millennium. In fact, it was only the English-language translation "*99 Red Balloons*" which succeeded in "topping the charts in the UK, Canada and Ireland". But the German-language version remained popular even in many English-speaking countries: "American and Australian audiences preferred the original German version, which became the highest Billboard charting German song in US history when it peaked at number 2 in the US" (en.wikipedia.org/wiki/99_Luftballons). This claim is not confirmed by the "list of German number one hits abroad", which shows a number one for the German-language version in New Zealand, but only for the English-language version in Australia, and in the USA, the list does not mention Nena at all (de.wikipedia.orf/wiki/List_er_deutschen-Nummer-ein-Hits_im_Ausland). This list "contains German and German-speaking artists, songs and albums which made it outside Germany, Austria and Switzerland to number one in the official singles or album charts there" (ibid: 3; entire list 3–18). It included German-language titles in the following countries: Belgium (only Flanders), Czech Republic, Denmark, Finland, Ireland, Italy, New Zealand, the Netherlands, Norway and Sweden. Countries in which "Germans, German-speaking artists, songs and albums" reached number one with English-speaking titles were: Australia, Belgium (Wallonia), France, Greece, Georgia, Hungary, Poland, Portugal, Romania, USA and UK – i.e. a total of 20.

Apart from a few lone pioneers such as Freddie Quinn in Flanders (1956) or Heintje in the Netherlands (1968), German-language successes are clustered at the beginning of the 1980s. After that time, there are only isolated hits: Matthias Reim (*"Verdammt, ich lieb' Dich"*) 1990, Mo-Do (*"Eins, zwei Polizei"*) 1994, Schnappi (*"Schnappi, das kleine Krokodil"*) 2005 and Hansi Hinterseer (*"Ich hab dich einfach lieb"*) 2010, along with several from Rammstein between 2004 and 2009 (*"Reise, Reise"*; *"Rosenrot"*; *"Völkerball"*; *"Liebe ist für alle da"*; details of hits in America, see: www.testspiel.de/doku-rammstein-in-amerika/320692/). All in all, the international success of the *Neue Deutsche Welle*, which I have defined broadly here, was limited. It "quickly ebbed away without substantial international resonance, but more could not have been expected because of the German-language performances" (Mahlmann/ Zombig 2002: 2686). Ultimately, the German language may have stood in the way of international distribution. But the recognisable German origin of the music may have had the same effect. Based on the explanations already given, "it is easier for German artists to succeed if the origin and identity of the music cannot be too easily recognised" (ibid). Accordingly, attempts to strengthen the global position of German based on German-language vocal music should be discouraged, and instead, the German language should give way to avoid harming the distribution of music from Germany. This fits with the fact that *Tokio Hotel* does not appear as number one anywhere in the named charts, and neither do any other German-speaking performers who have been successful inside the German-language territory and who have appeared after unification under the influence of the new federal states.

On balance, the *Neue Deutsche Welle* and subsequent German-language performers have hardly encroached on the dominance of English-language titles in the mass media in German-speaking countries and regions. Complaints by German singers that German listeners are rejecting German-language texts are also ineffectual, e.g. the comments by Jürgen Drews who sees himself as a victim of this attitude: "English texts are not more intelligent than ours, they just have the advantage that no one can understand them" (*Hörzu* 29, 13 July 1990: 13). The same report, acrimoniously entitled *"Wir singen deutsch – leider"*, quotes rock singer Veronika Fischer, who migrated from the GDR to the FRG in 1980, as saying: "Over there in the GDR, there were 2500 people in my audiences, there are only 400 here. I'm a German and I want to express myself in my own language, but there's no money in it. I can't help thinking about the idea of singing in English".

A study of 94 German public-sector and private radio channels between May 2001 and April 2002 commissioned by the then German Minister of State for Culture Julian Nida-Rümelin found that German-language titles predominated only in broadcast profiles for "German '*Schlager*', oldies, '*Volksmusik*'". By contrast, in the broadcast profiles for "Rock and pop mainstream formats", German productions amounted to only around 10 to 20%. "The proportion of German-language titles is generally significantly below 10%. Among the 94 channels investigated, 51 showed less than 5% German-language titles. Even so, with 39 million listeners, these broadcasters still reach every second listener" (Hoeren 2003: 4). These findings contributed to the German Bundestag addressing the topic (information from Bundestag Vice-President Antje Vollmer; also *"Pop im Parlament"*, *RP* 30 September 2004: A7). In 2004, the governing groups of the SPD, *Bündnis* 90 and *Die Grünen* as well as MPs from the opposition CDU and CSU parties submitted requests "For a commitment by public sector and private radio broadcasters to promote diversity in the field of pop and rock music from Germany" and respectively "For a voluntary commitment by radio broadcasters to promote German-language music" (Bundestag document 15/4521 and 15/4495, 149th session of the Bundestag 17 December 2004, stenographic report: 14022). Among the reasons given, it was complained that radio broadcasters often ignored "excellent" German-language music. The bands *"Juli"*, *"Silbermond"*,

"*2raumwohnung*" and the performers Patrick Nuo and Yvonne Catterfeld were named (ibid: 14024). While initially, the SPD inclined towards future introduction of a radio quota – referencing the efficacy of a corresponding ruling in France – with "approximately 35% German-language music or music produced in Germany" (ibid); but ultimately, all the petitioners agreed that only a "voluntary commitment to music sung in German or produced in Germany" could be considered (ibid: 14024). The comment by Gitta Connemann (CDU/CSU), who delivered the closing speech to general applause, is worth mentioning: "[. . .] The *quota* is passé, even if the request from the Red-Green coalition sounds different and if there is reference in it to a proportion of 'approximately 35%'. Ultimately, broadcasters should undertake their own commitment" (ibid: 14029). The reference to France introduced into the discussion previously had obviously been dropped by the end of the debate: "after the proportion of French music on the radio grew to 40% as a result of the quota introduced there in 1994, sales of national CDs also rose steeply" (ibid: 14023).

Whether this Bundestag involvement with the topic contributed to increasing the proportion of German or German-language music in the media has not been investigated. By contrast with the German policy, other countries had taken up the issue a decade earlier and introduced binding rules (Wedell/ Henley 2002: 2692). Even in the Bundestag discussion at the time, it was stated: "A total of 29 countries have a quota" (stenographic report: 14022, 14026). The Bundestag may have been held back from issuing a legally binding ruling by the possibility of legal difficulties (for details, see Hoeren 2003), but these were hardly mentioned in the handling of this topic which lasted only half an hour (report: 14025).

Other attempts to resist the dominance of English-language popular vocal music have not been particularly successful. One example was the broadcasts by WDR 4 (since 1 January 1984) focussing on German-language light music, which were followed by Radio Bremen 3 and Hessischer Rundfunk 4. "SPIDEM", an umbrella organisation for German music, supported these efforts (details from General Secretary Gabriel Steinschulte), e.g. by awarding the SPIDEM-Kristall to the artistic director of WDR, Friedrich Nowottny, for his services to WDR 4 (*Musikspiegel* 23 September 1987: 1–3). Poor quality and lack of reference to the *Zeitgeist* were diagnosed as causes for the slow distribution, especially in the case of German *hit songs*.

The "Eurovision Song Contest" also shows that support for German texts outside the German-language territory is dwindling (conception and history in John K O'Connor *The Eurovision Song Contest* 2010; Feddersen 2002; en.wikipedia.org/wiki/Eurovision_Song_Context). The question of language choice has been investigated by Eva Maria Klapheck (2004) whose findings form the basis for part of the following discussion. The first contest in Lugano was advertised on German TV under the title "*Grand Prix Eurovision de la Chanson*" (ibid: 13), which serves as a reminder of German acceptance of the priority of French over German as the language of Europe (Ch. H.4.2), but also acted as a kind of homage to French throughout the contest. The English-language title became established only in the 1990s. All styles of popular music are offered, but no "'serious music' (opera, symphony)" or "progressive or radical styles", such as heavy metal, hard rock and techno – although there were no clear boundaries (ibid: 15). The performers each represent their own country. Like the conception of Europe held by the Council of Europe (Ch. H.3), the orientation towards Europe was geographically broad from the start, and today even includes non-European countries, especially Arabic countries and Israel. To this extent, the contest provides hints at the international position of languages in popular vocal music. The realisation that it can contribute to strengthening or weakening the position of languages was presumably one of the reasons why the language question proved awkward and was disputed. "Until 1964, songs were always performed in the national language [of the country represented by the performers! U.A.]. In this respect, there was only one exception: in 1961, Lale Andersen, the contestant for Germany, sang the refrain of her song in French". In 1965, the rule relating to the language of the performers' own country was lifted but reintroduced again in the following year and then dropped again in 1973 (Klapheck 2004: 19f). The German delegation was unable to find a clear line for a considerable time. For example, in 1977, it agreed to the specification of national languages but at the same time, for the same year, requested an exception for Germany for the song "Telegram" for the first time written entirely in English (performed by Silver Convention). Apart from this exception, the specification of national languages remained intact for the following 22 years (Klapheck 2004: 20). Finally, it was again the German delegation, under the leadership of NDR editor Jürgen Meier-Beer, which urged for a free choice of languages for all participating countries from 1999: the wording of the official ruling is, "Participating Broadcasters may decide what language their artists may sing in" (ibid: 21). This was followed by a "stampede" towards English, as Abram de Swaan (2001a: 171) characterised the worldwide rush for this language. In the period from 1999 to 2004 alone, the proportion of English-language contributions from non-English-speaking countries increased from 35% (nine of the total of 23) to 58% (21 of the total of 36 participants; Klapheck 2004: 95) against a baseline of 0% resulting from the language ruling. Furthermore, between 1999 and 2004, all the prizes went to English-language titles, of which, by the way, none was from an English-speaking country: 1999 Sweden, 2000 Denmark, 2001 Estonia, 2002 Latvia, 2003 Turkey, 2004 Ukraine. Only in the last case, the text was partly in Ukrainian in addition to English (ibid: 98). It can be well imagined that these prizes motivated contestants increasingly to choose English. While performers from Germany sang almost exclusively in German until 2001, from 2002 onwards they shifted consistently to English. The only exception was Roger Cicero with "*Frauen regier'n die Welt*", but, the fact that he only reached 19th place did not encourage further use of German (list and rankings of German participants at de.wikipedia. org/wiki/Deutschland_beim_Eurovision_Song_Context).

Overall, German has played a very modest role in this international song contest. The language achieved victory only twice, in 1966 and 1982, out of a total of 58 contests (1956–2013). Added to this, French also played a part on both occasions. In 1966, with Udo Jürgens performing a song with the French title "*Merci Chérie*", and in 1982, in the performer's name "Nicole" ("*Ein bisschen Frieden*") – where this French-sounding name stretches the point a little. The latter song was the only victory for Germany with a completely German-language song (Udo Jürgens is Austrian); the second win for Germany, by Lena in 2010, was for the completely English-language song "*Satellite*". Austria's second win with "*Rise Like a Phoenix*" in 2014 by transgressive and demonstratively intersexual performer Conchita Wurst, was entirely in English. It is tempting to think that, with their push for free language choice, the German delegation wanted to release the German-speaking countries from their linguistic disadvantage in the competition (resulting from continuing associations of the German language with racism and chauvinism and recent accusations of economic high-handedness by Germany, the largest of the German-speaking countries). At least, the low number of only two winning titles in German is compatible with this assumption, if it is compared with the number of speakers of German in Europe (Ch. H.4.4: Table H.4.4–2). By contrast, 29 winning titles were in English, 14 in French and three each in Dutch and Hebrew. Only two winning songs were in Italian and Spanish – and perhaps less surprisingly – in Norwegian and Swedish. All other languages achieved even fewer winning titles (one or none). It is also remarkable and revealing of the value attributed to French and German that both winning performers from Switzerland and all five winners from Luxembourg sang in French, thereby gaining half the winning titles for the French language (en. wikipedia.org/wiki/List_of_Eurovision_Song_Contest_winners: 13). However, the moderate achievement of Italian and Spanish titles urges caution towards explanations based on prejudices against languages or speakers. What is certain is that the Eurovision Song Contest does not testify to a significant international position of the German language in popular vocal music.

Other styles of German vocal music differ from the music in the Eurovision Song Contest through their broadly defined folk-like style, as cultivated e.g. by Hannes Wader or Reinhard Mey, who also sings in French (information from Ulrike Schulz) and achieved success in France as "Frédérik Mey". In 1968, Mey was the first non-French singer to win the *Prix International de la Chanson Française* (en.wikipedia.org/wiki/Reinhard_Mey). Hannes Wader failed to achieve international success on this scale, no doubt because of his adherence to German, although he was internationally popular in left-wing circles (en.wikipedia.org/wiki/Hannes_Wader). Heino represents a more conservative tradition of German "*Volkslied*", including his recent composi- tions orientated towards this genre (en.wikipedia.org/wiki/Heino). He also has a limited inter- national fan base, where he enjoys cult status, especially among emigrants, expatriates from German-speaking countries and German-speaking minorities. The ARTE TV show "Heino – Made in Germany" (14 December 2013: 213: 5–22:35) about his performances abroad clearly suggests an impact on the maintenance of German abroad, which includes other singers in the "*volkstümlich*" tradition.

A similar effect in a different guise can be identified in the German-language choirs which exist in many non-German-speaking countries. I should first reiterate that it is possible to enjoy and even sing vocal music without accurately understanding the texts or knowing the language very well. However, if language is expressly highlighted as a programmatic element of the music, as in the case of the German-language choirs, this generally requires at least a limited knowledge of the language. The "*Zentralstelle für den deutschsprachigen Chorgesang in der Welt*" in Solingen, which was founded in 1976, gathers data on German-language choirs outside the German-language territory and supports them with materials and educational events (www. chorfestival-solingen.de). The "*Stiftung Volkslied*" has been operating along the same lines in Kas- sel since 1973. Its objectives are the "distribution and promotion of the *Volkslied* and religious song in Germany and abroad. Distribution of songbooks, choir literature, musical comedies and plays for amateur performers to every continent. Suppliers of songbooks to German choirs, pri- vate schools, kindergartens and old people's homes" (www.kulturfoerderung.org/dizk/details. htm?idKey=showOrgadetails&idValue=946&selectedLocale=de).

The former director of the *Zentralstelle*, Ulrich Renner, sent me a list of choirs for the period around 1986. Figures for 2013 were provided by my present contact, Dieter Lein. I have listed these figures in Table I.2–7, admittedly without Austria (with seven choirs in 2013), Switzerland (four), Belgium, Italy and Liechtenstein (two each). These figures are evidently incomplete, with gaps especially in the 1986 allocation to countries. I have attempted to fill these gaps based on data in the *Jahrbuch des Deutschen Sängerbundes* 42 (1986. Cologne: *Verlags- und Vertriebsgesellschaft für Chordbedarf*, 176–187). Accordingly, the figure for Brazil at that time comprises 69 choirs listed there + 120 other Brazilian choirs known to the *Zentralstelle*. By contrast, the choirs in the recent list were allocated consistently to the countries. The differences between the two lists are therefore determined primarily by gaps in the data for 1986, in some cases also through *de facto* changes. For example, on one hand, 17 choirs have been deleted from the list since 2008 alone, because they have been dissolved, six of them in Brazil; on the other hand, however, new choirs have been adopted in Brazil, China, Japan, Mexico, Russia and South Africa (email Dieter Lein 17 December 2013). A considerable number of new entries after 1990 originate from the terri- tory of the former Soviet Union, where contacts could not be established previously. These cer- tainly also include newly founded choirs. Whether the number of choirs in total has increased, as this summary suggests, would require further checking.

Table I.2–7 Number of German-language choirs outside the German-language territory

	2013	1986
USA	170	164
Hungary	158	n.d.
Brazil	56	189
Canada	43	38
South Africa	22	8
Australia	18	14
Argentina	13	17
Paraguay	10	n.d.
Chile	9	8
Poland	8	n.d.
Mexico	7	n.d.
Netherlands	5	n.d.
Namibia	3	11
Finland, Kazakhstan, Japan, Zaire	2	n.d.
Armenia, Bulgaria, Cameroon, China, Colombia, France, New Zealand, Sweden, Togo, Ukraine, Venezuela	1	n.d.
Total	**541**	**449**

The distribution between countries suggests that the choirs were founded mostly by people of German origin and serve to promote the culture and traditions of German-speaking immigrants and minorities (Ch. E.3). In many cases, the regional origins of these immigrants are evident from the names for the choirs: *Banater Männerchor* (Cleveland), *Rheinischer Gesang-verein* (Chicago), *Schwäbischer Männerchor* (Detroit), *Schweizer Männerchor* (Edmonton, Canada), *Donauschwaben-Verein* (Buenos Aires). However, almost all choirs are open to people who are not of German origin. Not only these choir members, but also members of German origin often have only a limited knowledge of German. Membership of the choir sometimes leads them to learn German or improve their knowledge, especially if they have a leadership role. Choral conductors are specially encouraged by the *Zentralstelle* to learn German. Training in "*deutscher Hochsprache*" is a component of the choral-conductor seminars provided in Solingen, not only for GFL speakers but also for native speakers if they only speak dialect. Having said this, accepting non-German-speaking members in the choirs not only brings new speakers to the German language, it often makes routine use of German more difficult. Even if only a few members understand no German, important matters must be discussed in the local majority language – English, Portuguese, Russian etc. At present, no one seems to have an overview of the extent to which German is still spoken between members of the German-language choirs. Around 1990, Ulrich Renner estimated that this was the case in approximately 30% of the choirs served by the *Zentralstelle*. In commemorative publications or *Festschriften* produced by the societies, which are generally bilingual, especially in the USA, but also often only monolingual English, complaints are often raised about the rampant indifference to the German language. An interest in the maintenance of German is found only rarely, as in the following rather dated example: "There are many signs which satisfy the desire to maintain German language and culture. Some societies have already set up collaborative arrangements with other German schools and societies; some organisations are working to establish contacts between people living in the German-language territory in Europe and their relations and friends abroad [. . .]" (*A Commemoration of 60 years' service to the German-language community. La Sociedad Coral Alemana Villa Ballester en su 60° aniversario.* [1983]. Villa Ballester, Argentina: 5). Alongside choirs of German-speaking emigrants and minorities, the *Zentralstelle* in Solingen also supports choirs of local German-speaking personnel in embassies and companies, i.e. expatriates (Ch. E.5). In isolated cases, the choirs supported also consciously cultivate vocal music in other languages, especially in countries without significant immigration from the German-language territory, e.g. Japan or Zaire. Presumably, the knowledge of German cultivated there is hardly more than required to pronounce the song texts. Having said this, letters to these choirs from Solingen are generally written in German, but not the replies.

J

GERMAN AS A FOREIGN LANGUAGE (GFL) OUTSIDE THE GERMAN OFFICIAL-LANGUAGE TERRITORY

1. Explanation of themes and terms

The *German official-language territory* includes Germany, Austria, Switzerland (German-speaking region), Liechtenstein, Luxembourg, Eastern Belgium and South Tyrol in Italy (Ch. D.1: Map D.1–1). This chapter relates to the rest of the world outside this territory. But the chapter is not strictly limited to German as a foreign language (GFL); it also touches on German as a native language (especially Ch. J.3) and *Germanistik* [German Language and Literature and German Studies] (especially Ch. J.4). By contrast with my earlier book, *Die internationale Stellung der deutschen Sprache* (1991a: 511–523), the section on "Church activities overseas", which was orientated primarily towards German-(speaking) minorities and expatriates and therefore related more to native speakers than FL speakers, has been not been included here (cf. Ch. E and especially E.5). For the same reason, the topic of "German Schools Abroad" (Ch. J.3) has been dealt with more concisely (Ammon 1991a: 442–455) but refers more consistently to schools of German-speaking countries other than Germany. In fact, the schools abroad of the German-speaking countries do largely serve German-(speaking) minorities and expatriates, i.e. German native speakers, but, as suggested by the frequently used designation "encounter schools" [*Begegnungsschulen*], they are open towards GFL learners. These schools are also considered in Ch. K "Policies for promoting the German language in the world", especially Ch. K.3.

Even the concepts of "foreign language" and "native language" (Ch. A.3; Dietrich 2004a, b; Davies 2003) imply that a strict limitation of Ch. J to German as a *foreign language* will not be possible. It will therefore also be important to distinguish the relationship between individuals and their language from the curricular position of the language in schools and universities. For example, *within the curriculum*, German can be considered a "foreign language", as it generally is outside the official German-language territory, but, at the same time, for some students and/or teachers, German may be their own *individual* native language. This is typical for German-speaking emigrants living in a non-German-speaking country who are not yet linguistically assimilated but also for German-speaking minorities (Ch. E) who adhere to German as their family language and native language. Many of these people still consider themselves native speakers even if their command of German is incomplete. As a result, the term *native language of a person* can be defined differently, namely: 1) based on tradition in the family (language of origin); so that the person considers German as their "native language" or "identifies" with German; 2) as the first language learnt during their life history (first language); 3) as the language in which they were socialised; 4) as the language of which they have a secure knowledge. The various possibilities can diverge or converge. In general, the figures cited in the following sections relate to GFL in the curricular sense, i.e. to learners or teachers of German as a foreign language, including individual native speakers of German.

In most cases, German is only a school subject, not the language of instruction. This is a significant difference because the language of instruction presupposes a considerably higher skill level than a mere school subject. It is used not only within specific language lessons, but also in other subjects as a means of communication. Even with German-speaking minorities, German is often only a school subject, or it may be a language of instruction only in afternoon classes or weekend classes. By contrast, in "Schools Abroad" [*Auslandsschulen*] of the German-speaking countries, German is a language of instruction – although not the sole language of instruction. For all these reasons, the distinction between the curricular position of German as a native language or as a foreign language is important. Position as a foreign-language school subject can be further subdivided as follows.

1) *Based on selectability*:

   - As a *compulsory subject*; outside the official German-language territory, German is a compulsory subject only in some non-German-speaking parts of Switzerland;
   - As an *elective subject*, among several languages, one of which must be chosen, which has consequences for German depending on the composition of the group;
   - As a *merely optional subject*, generally also among several languages, one of which may, but need not, be selected;
   - *Not selectable*, i.e. not provided at all.

2) *Within the ascending sequence of school classes or semesters*:

   - As the *first foreign language*, in the lowest class in which foreign languages are provided; almost everywhere, this applies only to English, but German is possible in Russia (Ch. J.9.6);
   - As a *second foreign language*;
   - As a *third foreign language*; very rare indeed.

Unfortunately, there is no worldwide overview of GFL relating to these distinctions, not even for the countries selected here (Ch. J.9.2–J.9.15).

2. German as a foreign language (GFL) in schools

Numerous investigations have confirmed that schools with German as a school subject, or especially as a language of instruction, are highly significant for the ongoing transmission of German-language skills into the future. German in schools guarantees more stable learning than extracurricular provisions. But it also ensures a more thorough learning, because most countries which teach German in schools also allow further study at university. For example, at the start of 2010, German teaching was provided in schools but not in universities only in Bosnia and Herzegovina, Costa Rica, Kenya, Kuwait, Mozambique, Uruguay and Trinidad and Tobago – that is, in just eight among a total of 136 countries offering German instruction (Netzwerk Deutsch 2010). This creates the false impression of a lack of learning opportunities in universities, but the source gives no information about opportunities for *Germanistik* [German Language and

Literature or German Studies] which existed to a varying degree. Learning German in school often motivates students to continue at university, even if this is sometimes just to avoid wasting an educational investment. Different sources have confirmed this, e.g. for Australia: "A relatively large number of responses [...] relate to the desire to continue with German after having started it at school or abroad" (G. Schmidt 2011: 127; also, Ammon 1991b: 57–64). An early start in primary school or even kindergarten, which would be extremely beneficial for basic learning, is rare, although worldwide investigations offer no relevant data here (StADaF 2005; Netzwerk Deutsch 2010; Auswärtiges Amt [German Foreign Office] 2015).

Before considering the present situation in schools, it will be advisable to look back at the history, amongst other reasons in view of the developing relationships with other foreign languages. In normal schools, GFL instruction was only introduced in the nineteenth century (before this it was generally only available outside the school curriculum; details, see Glück 2002, 2013, details of an early textbook in van der Lubbe 2007). More detailed retrospective accounts are also provided in investigations of individual countries (e.g. Lévy 1950/52 for France; Ortmanns 1993 for the UK). But the present account does not begin until the twentieth century and it concentrates on the following parameters: (1) number of countries with school GFL instruction, (2) number of GFL students and (3) duration of learning (as a rough indicator for language skills attained). In fact, most of the available data show gaps for all three parameters; they do allow a comparison between German and other foreign languages often learnt during the period under investigation, but not seamlessly up to the present. Worldwide developments in school FL instruction from the beginning of the twentieth century (1908) until shortly before WWII (1938) have been analysed statistically by Walter Fränzel (1938, 1939). He relies on analyses by Viktor Franke (1937a, b) of reports from education ministers in 48 countries of the *Bureau International d'Education* (at that time in Geneva). Further information on the period before WWII is provided by Franz Thierfelder (1928, 1929, 1930, 1931a, 1933, 1936), but I have relied here primarily on Fränzel's statistics. The 48 countries in the *Bureau International d'Education* represented the bulk of the countries in the world at that time, although some important countries were absent: The Soviet Union, Austria, Czechoslovakia, South Africa and most of the colonies and mandated territories (list of countries included in Fränzel 1939: 105, note 1). For countries which did not exist continuously during the investigated period from 1908 to 1938, foreign language instruction in the relevant regions was taken as the basis for analysis. The totals on which Figure J.2–1 is based are the arithmetic mean calculated for all points in time based on the population of each country (see Fränzel 1939: 105–108, 110–116). Accordingly, at that time, German was in third position of all foreign languages in the world, with the peak (admittedly only weakly marked) before WWI. During this war, there was a marked decline, which was followed, in the 1920s, by a period of recovery, but the pre-war level was never reached again, and the proportion declined again in the 1930s. The general trend for French also shows a decline. One remarkable feature is the intermediate phase during WWI, running contrary to German and suggesting a shift from German to French. The steadily rising overall trend for English, which was already the globally dominant foreign language at that time, contrasts with both these languages and, at a much lower level, with Spanish and even Italian.

The downturn for German in WWI originated from a decline in the English-speaking countries, the most important of which, even at that time, was the USA, based on population and economy. Before WWI, German was the most-learnt foreign language in the USA. For 1910, Fränzel (1939: 111) recorded proportions of foreign-language instruction in the USA at 65.6% for German, compared with 32.6% for French and 8% for Spanish. According to Gilbert (1981: 263), there were 216,869 learners of German at US High Schools in 1910 and only 90,591 learners of French. But after the entry of the USA into the war, German teaching was almost

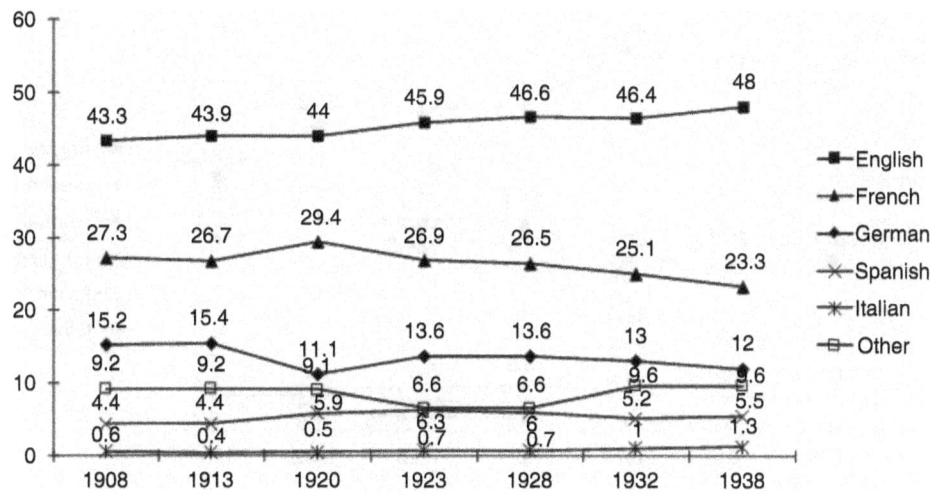

Figure J.2–1 Proportions of five languages in FL teaching in schools worldwide between 1908–1938
(*Source*: after Fränzel 1939: 110–115)

completely abandoned, especially in favour of French, but also Spanish. For 1922, Gilbert (1981: 263) recorded only 13,385 learners of German at US High Schools compared with 345,650 learners of French. German was never to regain its former position and remained significantly behind French and Spanish, which switched positions after WWII (Gilbert 1981; Pentlin 1977). Other English-speaking countries such as Australia, Canada and the UK also experienced a collapse of GFL after WWI from which they never recovered.

Moreover, there were isolated, minor setbacks for German even before WWI. One example is Argentina, where, like Italian, German was dropped from the curriculum because of lack of demand in 1912, while English and French were retained (Fränzel 1939: 11). For France also, Lévy (1952: 174) records minor losses for German even before WWI. At the time, German was positioned above all other foreign languages: "*Paris montre cependant dès avant le guerre un léger, mais constant fléchissement de l'allemand*". Schwarzkopff (1987) relativizes WWI as a factor for the decline of German (as a native language) in the USA but does not trivialise its importance. This effect is reminiscent of the initially hardly discernible proportional losses for German as an academic language (Ch. G.1). The trends may have been linked as consequences of the rise of the USA, which, even before WWI, had surpassed the German Empire economically and was approaching the global hegemony it has enjoyed ever since. Even without wars and Nazism, the German language would presumably have fallen behind in its international position relative to English, although less dramatically than it did in the wake of those catastrophes (cf. Ch. G.9).

Losses in overseas countries, especially the USA, intensified the restriction of GFL to Europe, where, before WWI, German was concentrated more strongly than English (EFL). For example, with reference to 1908, Fränzel (1939: 109) claims, "In Europe, German is still ahead of English [and behind French! U.A.] but declining strongly overseas [. . .]". This geographical distribution was intensified after WWI. Concentration in Europe was additionally promoted by the new countries in Eastern Europe, which had been formed from former components of Russia and in which GFL also gained a strong position. The situation is reminiscent of parallels in the strengthening of GFL after 1989 following the dissolution of the Soviet Union. The centring of GFL in

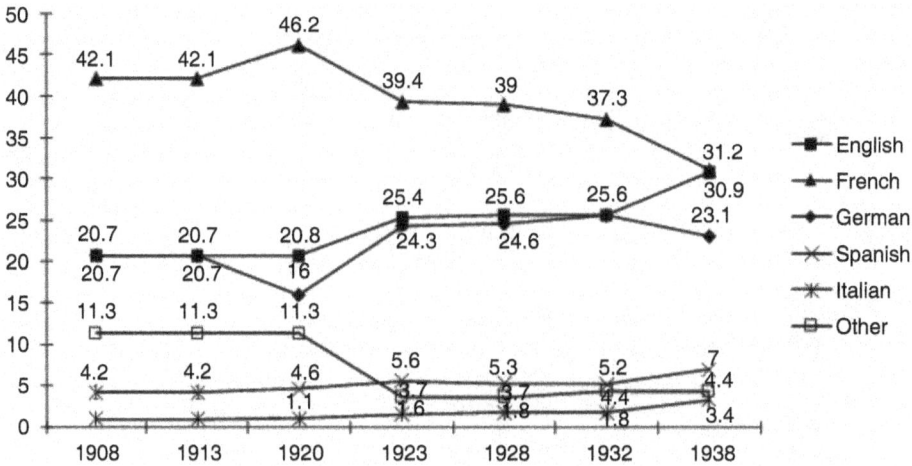

Figure J.2–2 Proportions of five languages in FL teaching in schools in Europe between 1908–1938
(*Source*: after Fränzel 1939: 110–115)

Europe is illustrated by the higher proportion of GFL in Figure J.2–2 (Europe) compared with Figure J.2–1 (global).

It is remarkable that, between the two world wars, the proportion of German within FL instruction did not rise continuously in Europe but fell again from 1932–1938 (from 25.6% to 23.1%). Incidentally, this was similar for French but contrasts with the steady rise of English. In some countries, having been introduced and promoted to the position of a compulsory school subject, GFL was demoted again, especially e.g. in Latvia and Estonia, to a lesser extent in Lithuania, Yugoslavia (at that time "Southern Slavia") and Portugal – and in individual overseas countries, such as Uruguay (Fränzel 1939: 114). The demotion occurred in each case after Nazism had seized power in Germany, often as a defensive move against this. This motive for demoting German has been reported by Thierfelder (1938: 129–136; also 1936) with reference to Latvia, Estonia and Lithuania. In other cases, demand was the decisive factor for the decline, e.g. in Portugal and Spain (suggested in Thierfelder 1938: 180f.). The governments in these countries, which sympathised with the Nazis, initially strengthened the position of GFL but were not able to maintain this because of lack of demand, so that English, and for a time also French, became more important. Other individual countries in which GFL was initially dominant also tended towards English before WWII. Thierfelder (1938: 137) explains that "[I]n Finland also, there are growing signs that English is advancing". Nevertheless, to German experts before WWII, the situation still seemed to resemble the situation before WWI, in that "in general, there are only the three modern languages [modern foreign languages! U.A.] [...], German, French and English in the entire world. Alongside these, Italian and Spanish play only a subordinate role, as do the other languages" (Franke 1937a: 138).

The status of GFL as a compulsory subject in senior schools shows that the setbacks for GFL had, so far, not been dramatic, even bearing in mind that English and French were also often compulsory subjects alongside German. Table J.2–1 includes countries with GFL as a compulsory subject in senior schools in 1908 and 1938. It is possible that quantitative considerations also influenced Fränzel's (1939) data, and it may therefore be more appropriate to speak of a "widespread compulsory subject". The gaps mark changes after which the number of countries

Table J.2–1 Countries and regions with GFL as a compulsory subject in senior schools 1908 and 1938

1908	1938
Belgium	Belgium
Denmark	Denmark
–	Finland
France	France
Iceland	Iceland
–	Lithuania
Luxembourg	Luxembourg
–	Netherlands
Norway	Norway
Romania	Romania
Sweden	Sweden
Switzerland	Switzerland (non-German-speaking regions in both cases)
Czechoslovakia	Czechoslovakia
Hungary	Hungary
Argentina	–
Japan	Japan

(*Source*: after Fränzel 1938: 191–193; 1939: 110–115)

with GFL as a compulsory subject in 1938 was even greater than in 1908 (n=15 compared with 13) – but this was because of countries newly formed in 1918. With reference to Table J.2–1, it should be borne in mind that position as a compulsory subject in (senior) schools cannot provide reliable information about the proportion of GFL within foreign language instruction. For example, after the formation of Poland, "the focus [of FL instruction! U.A.] shifted to German", which even in the 1930s had been the most frequently learnt foreign language, but only as an elective subject, together with French (Thierfelder 1938: 128). What is more, German was also a native-language subject in Poland because of the considerable German-speaking population there following the Treaty of Versailles.

After WWII, GFL lost its position as a compulsory school subject in most countries, especially its leading position in the ascending sequence of school classes. The only exceptions are the non-German-speaking parts of Switzerland, where its status as a national official language has also strengthened the position of German as a foreign language up to the present (Ch. D.2.4). Otherwise, German did not remain the predominant foreign language in schools in any country, not even on an equal footing with another foreign language. After 1945, English was the most-learnt foreign language almost worldwide, apart from most of the Warsaw Pact countries, other than isolated cases there, such as Hungary (Bassola 1995: 233; Földes 2004b: 112). But in Hungary also, Russian was initially the most frequently learnt foreign language, followed by English in the 1990s (Földes 2004b: 115; 2004a: 17). By contrast, in the English-speaking world, French, or Spanish, rose to first position – from which they will presumably not be relegated in the foreseeable future, not even by Chinese.

There is insufficient data for a representative worldwide comparison of foreign languages. Total learner numbers for various languages will be discussed in Ch. J.7. But there are relatively secure figures, especially for GFL between 1979 and 2015: for the early years in the *Bericht der Bundesregierung über die deutsche Sprache in der Welt* [German Government Report on German in the World] (1985) and the *ADaF-Auswertung* (1990) *Deutsch als Fremdsprache in den Gastländern*

Table J.2–2 Numbers of GFL learners in schools from 1979–2015; ★ = accurate figure not available

1979	1985	1995	2000	2005	2010	2015
16,363,000	15,079,640	16,686,782	17,163,871	14,498,374	★12,800,000	13,456,790

(*Sources: Sprachatlas* 1979; *Bericht der Bundesregierung über die deutsche Sprache in der Welt* 1985; Goethe-Institut 2000: 10; StaDaF 2005: 15; Netzwerk Deutsch 2010: 12; Auswärtiges Amt 2015: 16)

des Goethe-Instituts [GFL in the host countries of the Goethe-Institut], both evaluated in my book *Die internationale Stellung der deutschen Sprache* (1991a: 432–437). In 1982/83, GFL was learnt in schools in 88 countries, and in 1988, in 83 countries, with a rising trend in 41 countries and a falling trend in 28 countries. But this does not lead to an overall growth in the total number of GFL learners, because even a comparison with an earlier estimate reveals a decline. The figures for 1979 (*Sprachatlas* 1979) were higher than for 1985 (*Bericht der Bundesregierung über die deutsche Sprache in der Welt* 1985), with 16.4m (16,353,000) compared with 15.1m (15,079,640); but this decline may have been influenced by previously exaggerated figures for the Soviet Union (Sturm 1987b: 11). In general, caution is required with such figures.

For example, alongside various minor discrepancies in Netzwerk Deutsch 2010 (p. 12), the figure of 12,303,657 for "GFL learners in schools in 2010" was initially recognisably too low, as was the total number of learners ("total learners of German") (14,042,789; ibid). In response to my inquiry, the director in charge of the evaluation, Rolf C. Peter (Goethe-Institut) commissioned a follow-up investigation, which led to an increase in the total learner numbers to 14,500,940 (email Nadja Kranz 01. April 2011). Evaluation of the detail then showed a rise primarily in learners in schools, in fact, up to the number I have estimated and marked with an asterisk in Table J.2–2, which was then raised again in Auswärtiges Amt 2015 (p. 16) (to 12,825,297 – for 2010! – not to be confused with the even higher figure for 2015).

In general, these figures should be realistic, also for the current growth in learners (Table J.2–2: last column). Whether and for how long this increase will last is difficult to predict. The following factors play a part in the interplay of forces:

1) The spread of English as global lingua franca (Crystal 2003; Graddol 2000, 2006), so that a knowledge of other foreign languages, including German, appears less urgent (Ch. A.4; A.6). This impression, which is not entirely misguided, has presumably contributed to the relegation of GFL to a secondary, no longer even compulsory position as a foreign language in schools, but also to a general decline in foreign-language learning in English-speaking countries (Ch. J.9.3; J.9.10);

2) Energetic promotion of English learning in German-speaking countries (and most other countries), which can reinforce the impression among foreigners that a knowledge of German and other foreign languages is gradually becoming less important for contact with native speakers (H. Wagener 2012; Quetz 2010);

3) The rise of competing international languages, especially Japanese and Chinese, alongside the traditional international languages which include German. These augment the number of foreign languages offered in schools and reduce the numbers of learners of the traditional foreign languages;

4) The increase in content of teaching and learning at school in line with scientific/technological progress: in natural sciences, social and political sciences, IT and media studies. With reference to these additional demands, Vitek Dovalil (2010) raised the following question

about GFL and other foreign languages in his country: "Are two foreign languages in the Czech Republic realistic?".

These trends, which weaken GFL learning, have been compensated or overcome by strengthening factors, especially the following:

5) Reunification of Germany, the perception of the growing economic and political importance of this now larger country has prompted and motivated the learning of German, which was, to some extent, supported by the German government, not least in Eastern Europe. This presumably accounts for the increase in learner numbers shown in Table J.2–2 for 1995 and 2000;

6) After this, factors 1) to 4) reasserted themselves; but the decline in learning German which they caused has recently been weakened again if not reversed by a now modified factor 5), based on the economic strength and influence of Germany and the other German-speaking countries. This new image of the German speaking-countries, also as preferred destinations for migrants and refugees, has certainly contributed to the fact that GFL learner numbers have recently started to grow again (cf. e.g. Ch. J.9.4; J.9.8; J.9.12; J.9.13). At least, this is how the German Foreign Office (Auswärtiges Amt 2015: 5–8) interprets the trend, for which various investigations, including suggestions for further support, are planned or already in progress (see also Ch. K.3; K.4; Ammon/ G. Schmidt 2019).

3. German Schools Abroad from the German-speaking countries

The German Schools Abroad form an important component of Germany's soft-power policy (for the term and theoretical background, see Nye 1990a, b; 2004; Maaß 2009a, b). A speech by former German Foreign Minister Frank-Walter Steinmeier at the "World Congress of German Schools Abroad" (4 June 2014 in Berlin – email German Foreign Office 5 June 2014) contains a relevant analysis. The following passage is taken from it:

> New powers are emerging in Asia and Latin America. [. . .] This is not a cause for complacency – quite the contrary. Let us accept the competition with open arms and share with the world the very best we have to offer: the legacy of the European Enlightenment. [. . .] In fact, this is precisely what the policy for foreign culture and education is attempting to do: the Goethe-Institut, the German Academic Exchange Service [DAAD] and the broad network for disseminating German art, literature, music and language to the world. And above all, it is you [all the active attendees! U.A.] in the German Schools Abroad operation – every day, on 5 continents, in 141 schools abroad and more than 1800 partner schools [all the former and most of the latter are *Sprachdiplomschulen* (DSD) . . .]. And we have therefore, for the first time, enshrined the funding for the DSD schools in the new law on Schools Abroad, based on the Public Funding Law [*Zuwendungsrecht*]. [. . .] We cannot expect masses of young people in their early 20s to come flooding into Germany from overseas to study, if they have never previously had contact with the German language. We must therefore keep these potential students' entire educational trajectory in view, and with this in mind, our national educational provision and the instruments of our external education policy must be harnessed together in an integrated manner [. . .].

In the speech, the Foreign Minister draws a wide arc from schools to universities and research. Alongside specific course contents, the global position of German must also be strengthened, although this may be a secondary objective rather than a primary goal. The German Schools

Abroad contribute to this by supporting the native-language skills of the children of emigrants (minorities or "German diaspora") and expatriates (Ch. E.). They can also strengthen the position of German by giving children of local populations who attend these schools a solid grounding in German as a foreign language (GFL). In the German Schools Abroad, the language provision is more thorough than in normal GFL lessons because German is not only a school subject; it is also the language of instruction. Sound knowledge of German acquired in this way can motivate learners to establish contacts with the German-speaking countries, thereby maintaining and deepening their language skills. German Schools Abroad have therefore long been regarded as an extremely important instrument for disseminating German language and culture in the world (Ch. K.2; K.3.2; K.4; Schönrock/ Krath 2014; *ABC des Auslandsschulwesens* 2013). The new legal basis to which Steinmeier referred in the speech is the *Law on the Promotion of German Schools Abroad* resolved on 1 January 2014 (*Auslandsschulgesetz/ ASchulG*: npl. ly.gov.tw/pdf/8415.pdf). According to culture politician Peter Gauweiler, the law is supposed to strengthen German cultural policy, because "[f]or the first time in their 100-year history, the German Schools Abroad have a legal claim for support from the Federal German Government" (*Begegnung* 35 (1) 2014: 9).

The German Schools Abroad are administered by the Central Office for Schools Abroad (ZfA) under specialist supervision of the Foreign Office. The ZfA also publishes the periodical *Begegnung. Deutsche schulische Arbeit im Ausland* [Encounter. German Schools at Work Abroad], which is published annually and provides relevant information on individual schools and more general matters. For example, there is an overview of "German schools working abroad" (Schönrock/ Krath 2014) which describes the 141 German Schools Abroad and related types of schools, which are also supported by the ZfA, sometimes in collaboration with the Goethe-Institut: the 1,100 DSD schools, which offer a diploma qualification allowing access to universities in Germany; and, at the time, 1,700 (but now more than 2,000) PASCH schools, which have been established since 2008 through the partner schools initiative (Ch. K.3.2). These schools also actively promote the subject of German as a foreign language (GFL).

The designation "*Auslandschule*" [school abroad] is not restricted to Germany; three of the four other German-speaking countries also provide this type of school (Ch. B.4):

- Germany; 141 *Deutsche Auslandsschulen* [German Schools Abroad] (global overview Ch. K.3.3: Map K.3.3–1);
- Austria: 8 *Österreichische Auslandsschulen* (www.bmukk.gv.at/schulen/schulen/ausland/oes-terr_auslandsschulen.xml; Ch. K.4);
- Switzerland: 17 *Schweizer Schulen im Ausland* (unterricht.educa.ch/de/schweizerschulen-ausland; Ch. K.4).

Most of these schools are located outside the German-speaking countries, except Austria's "*formatio – Bilinguale Privatschule*" in Liechtenstein (with German and English as the languages of instruction), the German "*Deutsche Schule in Genf (DAS)*", which is, in fact, in a German-speaking country but located outside the German official-language territory (Map D.1–1). Furthermore, there are three German Schools Abroad inside the German official-language territory but outside the German-speaking countries, namely, in Eupen (Eastern Belgium): the "*Robert Schumann Institut*", the "*Königliches Athenäum*" and the "*Pater-Damian-Sekundarschule*".

In most schools abroad from a German-speaking country, German is both a language of instruction and a school subject, as a native language (GNL) or as a foreign language (GFL). However, not all schools (outside the German-speaking countries or outside the German official-language territory) with German as a language of instruction are necessarily also schools abroad of a German-speaking country. They only have this status if, at the same time, they offer school-leaving qualifications from a German-speaking country, rather than just local school-leaving qualifications. It would require a separate investigation to determine which schools precisely offer German as a language of instruction but are not at the same time schools abroad. All schools abroad of a German-speaking country are orientated towards the curricula and educational laws of the German-speaking country which funds them and of the country in which they are located.

The "European schools" funded by the EU are a separate category. They are, in principle, for the children of EU officials but are also often open to local students (de.wikipedia.org/wiki/Europäische_Schulen). These European Schools in various EU Member States provide school curricula in several languages, always including German. Schools currently being opened which are not funded by the EU follow the same model as the existing 14 schools of this type. Their primary aim is to prepare children for their homeland school system when they return. However, the European Schools are less open to local students than the schools abroad of the German-speaking countries. The proportion of local students in schools abroad has increased over time. In German Schools Abroad, it was around 75% in spring 2014 (email Judith Weyer, ZfA, 28 February 2014), but no upper limit has been fixed. By contrast, for the *Schweizer Schulen im Ausland*, a "minimum percentage of Swiss students" is stipulated, but the level varies to some extent (email Irène Spicher, Director of *educationsuisse*, 13 January 2014). German is not consistently prioritised in the schools abroad of Switzerland, which, it should be remembered, is a multilingual country (Ch. D.2.4). But 15 of the 17 schools have German-speaking "patron Cantons", and German is therefore their sole "*Basissprache*" and therefore language of instruction. There are exceptions, such as the school in Bogotá (Colombia), which provides a French-language division alongside the German-language division, from kindergarten through to the Swiss "*Maturität*" certificate; and the "*Deutsch-Schweizerische Internationale Schule* Hong Kong", with English alongside German as a language of instruction, which is, in fact, one of the German Schools Abroad but is supported by Switzerland which supplies teaching staff. "The Austrian Schools Abroad are attended primarily by students from the host country, i.e. the Austrian teaching staff teach their subjects in German, to students whose native language is not German. [. . .] The majority of students attending the *Österreichische Schule Liechtenstein* [. . .] are German speakers; teaching is provided bilingually in German and English" (www.weltweitunterrichten.at/site/auslandsschulen/taetigkeit?SWS=36de043bc08434232591b083a0f3c568).

4. GFL, German Language and Literature and German Studies in universities

In universities, a distinction must be made between the study of German Language and Literature or *Germanistik*, and the more practical orientation of language learning (subsidiary, academic language courses), which are often associated with the study of other subjects. Especially in English-speaking countries, *German Studies*, in which knowledge of the German language often plays a subordinate role by comparison with *German Language and Literature*, represent an additional field of study (for the USA: Lohner/ Nollendorfs 1976; Nollendorfs/ Markgraf 1986; Lützeler 1990; Australia: Veit 1984; India: Ganeshan 1990). This certainly applies for fields of study which cover more than one country or multilingual cultural domains, such as *European Studies*, where German may, but need not, be subsumed under the *Language Studies* component (introductory: en.wikipedia.org/wiki/European_studies). It remains an open question here whether these fields of study support or are detrimental to the learning of German overall, either providing new motives for learning German or opportunities for avoiding learning

German. For reasons of scope, I shall restrict the discussion in this chapter to *Germanistik* [German Language and Literature] and German as a foreign language (GFL) in universities.

An initial impression of the global distribution of German Language and Literature is provided by the *Online-Verzeichnis der Hochschulgermanistik – Germanistenverzeichnis* of the German Association of Germanists (DGV) and the German Academic Exchange Service (DAAD), which contains data about Germanists up to the date referenced here in 74 countries: from Albania to Zimbabwe (www.germanistenverzeichnis.phil.uni-erlangen.de/cgi-bin/gvz_ausgabe_int.pl). Recent global statistics on the German language (Netzwerk 2010; Auswärtiges Amt 2015) do not contain figures on German Language and Literature, and it is therefore not possible to infer in which countries and in how many countries German is represented in universities. In the 2005 investigation, there are figures for "*Germanistik-Studierende*" in 89 countries, but, in some cases, these are very low (e.g. in Malta 5; StADaF 2005: 12). Accurate figures cannot easily be derived from the overview of courses in German Language and Literature and German by Björn Akstinat ([1997] 2009: 50–89; also Ch. J.6). It is common to all sources that the total number of Germanists in universities outside the German official-language territory, who will often subsequently become German teachers, is significantly smaller than the figures for mere learners of German (Table J.4–1). The latter group, with German as a subsidiary subject or "academic German", has also received increasing attention for some time now (e.g. in Japan: Yamaji 1994; Korea: Yang 2003; China: J. Zhu 2007; Russia: Titkova 2011). The figures for this group have been rising for decades, while those for Germanists have been falling.

Comparing the university setting with the school setting creates the impression that there are long-term, approximately parallel upward or downward trends, e.g. with reference to the decline, on the one hand, of German Language and Literature and GFL in universities and, on the other hand, of the learning of German in schools after WWI in the English-speaking countries and in France (Ch. J.2). According to Kloss (1971: 118f.), German was the preferred foreign language in the USA, not only in schools but also in colleges and universities, when the USA joined the war in 1917, which was then followed by a serious collapse at both educational levels after the war. In France also, Lévy (1952: 224–228) reports a decline after the war in schools and universities, *Grandes Écoles*, military colleges (*Écoles Militaires*) and especially polytechnic colleges (*Écoles Polytechniques*). "*Encore en 1917, il y a 77% de germanisants contre 23% d'anglicisants. En 1929 [. . .] il est tombé à 37% pour l'allemand contre 63% pour l'anglais*" (ibid: 226). It is obvious that the dwindling of German teaching in schools restricts employment opportunities for Germanists, and also German teaching in school guarantees a trained and qualified successor generation for German Language and Literature in universities. To this extent, the claim made in the German government report [*Bericht der Bundesregierung*] (1985: 7) still applies today: "research in German Language and Literature and research related to Germany can only flourish in countries in which there are sufficient employment opportunities for German teachers in schools [. . .]". By contrast, the mere learning of German

Table J.4–1 Numbers of Germanists and GFL learners at universities in the period 1985–2015

	1985	*1995*	*2000*	*2005*	*2010*	*2015*
German Lang. and Lit.	88,007	728,160	427,689	146,779	[117,890]	[109,098]
GFL learners in universities	1,310,511	2,096,945	2,046,632	1,649,564	[1,355,733]	[1,226,245]
Total numbers	1,398,518	2,825,105	2,474,321	1,796,343	1,473,623	1,335,343

(*Sources for 1985 and 1995*: Goethe-Institut 2000: 175; for 2000 and 2005: StADaF 2005: 15 and 8; for 2010: Netzwerk 2010: 12; for 2015: Auswärtiges Amt 2015: 16)

in universities – generally alongside other studies – is less dependent upon schools. Stuck-enschmidt (1989: 17) has shown corresponding developments in Japan (Ch. J.9.14). But in Japan, German did not suffer a dramatic loss of position until after WWII (Hirataka 1994). Before that, German enjoyed high prestige both as a school subject and as an academic for-eign language (contributions in Ammon 1994d) – but, contrary to some exaggerated claims, it was never really higher than English. A serious decline occurred after the war. "Since then, the existence of German in Japan has cowered under the overwhelming shadow of English" (Ueda 1989: 33). At school level, German was limited to a few schools in the private sector (Itoi 1994), after which German Language and Literature also dwindled (Nakajima 1994). Only GFL in universities as a subsidiary to other subjects has remained widespread, but in recent decades, this has also been on the decline (Yamaji 1994) – based on competition with Asian foreign languages (Chinese, Korean) which have greater practical relevance (see Ch. F.6; J.9.14).

Various worldwide investigations including figures for learning German in schools (Ch. J.2) provide a quantitative overview of the study of German Language and Literature and GFL teaching in universities in non-German-speaking countries. However, comparison of the figures for different years requires interpretation and supplementary calculations. For 1985 and 1995, the respective "number of students of German Language and Literature" and the "number of participants in university language courses" can be derived without difficulty from Goethe-Institut 2000 (page 175). For 2000 and 2005, StDaF 2005 (page 15) names "Total students of German" and separately "Students of German Language and Literature". The following expla-nation relates to the former group (ibid: 8, note 7):

> These figures include students on 'university courses relevant to German' and stu-dents of German Language and Literature: German within the framework of language courses = German as language-course instruction; as a subsidiary subject, optional or elective course; in combined courses with another degree program; or as a course option accompanying vocational-technical degree programmes; as well as studying (as major or subsidiary subject) German Language and Literature, a training course for German teachers or interpreters, and, of course, studying German in combination with another subject.

I have therefore subtracted the number of "students of German Language and Literature" from the number of "Students of German in total" to obtain the number of GFL learners (third row, Table J.4–1). For 2010 and 2015, Netzwerk 2010 (page 12) and Auswärtiges Amt 2015 (page 16) refer only to "Total students learning German in 2010" and respectively Students learning German in 2015", without giving details of German Language and Literature. Accord-ingly, these figures presumably include both GFL learners and Germanists, no doubt with a smaller proportion of Germanists. With the same proportions as in 2005, this would give the hypothetical figures indicated in each case in square brackets. (In Auswärtiges Amt 2015 (page 16), the number for 2010 is indicated as somewhat higher than in Netzwerk 2010; but the scal-ing is still based on the latter.)

Despite gaps in the data, the following trends are still quite clear. GFL learners in universities are considerably more numerous than students of German Language and Literature, and the numerical difference is growing (1985–2015). In this context, there may be some doubt about the figures for 1985 (Table J.4–1) because the eightfold increase in Germanists from 1985 to 1995 seems exaggerated, despite the influence of reunification, among other reasons, because the number of GFL learners did not even double during the same period. Presumably, in the count in 1985, Germanists and GFL learners were not adequately differentiated. By contrast, the proportions in subsequent years are comprehensible and show a continuous drift towards GFL learners. "Number of Germanists : Number of academic GFL learners", in 1995–1 : 2.88; in 2000–1 : 4.79; in 2005–1 : 11.2. The figures in square brackets in Table J.4–1 have been numerically simulated – extremely hypothetically – from the figures for 2005. After 1995, following the rise between 1985 and 1995, which was presumably initiated by reunification, the total figure declined steadily. Based on this trend, it can be assumed that the more recent, slight rise in the total number of German learners is attributable less to the universities than to other educational institutions, no doubt primarily the schools: for 2015: 15.4m, compared with 2010: 14.7m, rising to 14.9m if Goethe Institutes are included (Auswärtiges Amt 2015: 6; also Ch. J.2).

In my view, the consequences of this curricular shift have so far not been adequately researched, especially not the effects of the dramatic decline in the number of Germanists (Table J.4–1: second row). Over the ten years with relatively secure figures, 1995 to 2005, they decline from 728,160 via 427,689 to 146,779, i.e. to approximately just a fifth. The associated, inevitable fate of Germanists must be a cause of concern for everyone sensitive to social change. Two consequences can be assumed: on one hand, losses of entire academic posts and, on the other hand, a downgrading of academic teaching to mere language instruction. Numerous colleagues have reported such developments to me orally and in written reports, expressing a mixture of sheer anxiety about survival and humiliation at being forced to switch to more superficial teaching, in some cases even to teaching English. This relates especially to countries with a long tradition of learning German and German Language and Literature (such as Japan, Korea, Russia, Europe in the narrower sense and countries associated with European emigration; Ch. J.9.2–J.9.15). However, it would be worthwhile to investigate not only such negative developments but also the opening of new opportunities, especially associated with the growing subject of GFL (see e.g. Ch. J.5; J.9.2; J.9.15). With sustained economic development in German-speaking countries, such new openings do indeed have a long-term perspective and, to some extent, may even revitalise the study of German Language and Literature.

5. GFL in extracurricular and extramural education

This rather diffuse domain includes mass media language courses (radio, TV), including self-instruction by means of various media (textbooks, online, Internet), and personal instruction with teachers. It covers foreign-language teaching in cultural institutes (e.g. Goethe-Institut) and educational facilities supplementing schooling: vocational (e.g. Carl-Duisburg language centres) and general educational (e.g. evening classes), as well as language courses in companies, abroad and at home, private language schools (e.g. Berlitz) and finally individual learning, e.g. through foreign-language tourism. It will only be possible to provide a rough sketch of this diversity, focussing on the following types of GFL courses:

1) In German companies abroad;
2) Via mass media: radio, television and Internet;
3) In state-run cultural institutes, especially the Goethe-Institut; and
4) In private schools (e.g. Berlitz schools).

I have reasonably representative worldwide figures only for 2) to 4), and comparative figures with other languages only for 4).

For type 1), GFL courses in foreign companies would also be interesting, but relevant data were not available. Information on GFL courses in German companies is also fragmentary.

Relevant courses, especially abroad for local employees, must not be confused with "German company schools" for the children of expatriates, employees from German-speaking countries living temporarily abroad (see Werner 1986b) and must certainly not be confused with German Schools Abroad (Ch. J.3). Information about GFL courses in German companies abroad which go beyond isolated examples is in short supply. But there is one report by Natalia Troshina (2011) on Russia. Cross-national data evidently exist only for earlier periods. For example, for 1988, the following figures are certainly only estimates relating to GFL courses in Federal German companies in 19 non-German-speaking countries (participant numbers in brackets. Source: *ADaF-Auswertung* 1990):

Europe:	Belgium (100), Denmark (55), Netherlands (?), Sweden (200);
North America:	USA (300);
Latin America:	Argentina (1000), Brazil (1000), Mexico (560), Peru (33), Venezuelan (40);
Africa:	Ivory Coast (22), Ghana (10), Nigeria (55);
Asia and Oceania:	Hong Kong (30), India (1800), Malaysia (91), New Zealand (150), Sri Lanka (30), South Korea (30).

For type 2) (GFL courses via radio, TV and Internet), the availability of data is more favourable – among other reasons, because governments often support these courses, making them more easily identifiable. However, because of limited working capacity, I was not able to carry out a comparative investigation of different languages. Regarding the promotion of such courses by governments, there are thematic overlaps here with chapter K "Policies for promoting the German language in the world", especially K.3.1 and K.3.3. Relevant GFL courses often reach large numbers of participants; but the level of learning achievement generally remains obscure. In particular, "the German Foreign Office has encouraged the development of various radio and television language courses which can reach a considerably larger number of learners than other means of language promotion" (*Bericht* 1985: 11). Radio and television GFL courses have also been developed and broadcast in non-German-speaking countries. In some, they have a long tradition and have reached large numbers of participants, e.g. in Japan in the 1980s, with around 400,000 annually (Stuckenschmidt 1989: 19; also, Sekiguchi 1994; for Korea, see Kang 2003).

A cross-national overview for 1988, covering the 72 countries with Goethe Institutes at that time is provided in the *ADaF-Auswertung* 1990. For each country, the overview contains the number of GFL radio or TV courses "with several episodes in a series" (note in the investigation questionnaire); however, participant numbers are not available. Only 26 of the 72 countries recorded GFL media courses of one kind or another; Japan stands out with four courses per year (two on radio and two on TV). In this context, all 72 countries hosted Goethe Institutes and were therefore certainly more closely associated with the German language than other countries. The courses were distributed as follows (number of radio courses/number of TV courses; – = no data):

Europe:	Belgium (0/2), Finland (1/1), Greece (1/1), UK (0/1), Ireland (2/1); Iceland (1/1), Italy (0/1), Norway (1/1), Sweden (1/1), Hungary (1/0), Cyprus (1/-);
North America:	Canada (0/1), USA (1/1);
Latin America:	Argentina (0/1), Brazil (1/0), Chile (-/1), Costa Rica (2/1), Mexico (2/1), Uruguay (1/0);
Middle East:	Egypt (1/0);
Asia and Oceania:	Australia (1/1), Japan (2/2), Philippines (1/0), Sri Lanka (0/1), South Korea (1/1), Thailand (2/0).

The concentration in Europe is evident, and neighbouring countries such as Denmark and the Netherlands were also able to draw on the German-language territory.

There is an impressive array of courses from *Deutsche Welle* (DW), by far the most important broadcaster of GFL courses (data from Werner Neven, DW, email 17 February 2014). Starting in 1957 with the course "*Lernt Deutsch bei der Deutschen Welle*", a total of 25 courses had been created by 2013. At the beginning of 2014, 12 online courses for GFL learners were broadcast and one for GFL teachers: "*Deutsch unterrichten. Praktische Angebote für Lehrer*" (overview: www.dw.de/popups/pdf/29149215/deutsch-zum-mitnehmen-deutsch-pdf.pdf). Accesses (*Page Impressions*) to the online courses were stable at around 6 million per month. Admittedly, teaching/learning performance remains uncertain, because there are no performance checks, and no certificates are issued; but self-monitoring and corrections are available for users. A flood of almost exclusively positive feedback emails confirms the positive reception worldwide. DW sent me convincing examples of emails from France, Spain, Czech Republic, Poland, Ukraine, South Korea, Senegal and Ecuador. The growth in popularity is certainly associated with the general proliferation of different types of media and broader ownership of media. In many cases, limited provision of German in schools provides motivation (Ch. I.2, end) to learn via the media – as do extracurricular and extramural adult education.

For type 3), German courses in state-run cultural institutes, the Goethe-Institut has always played a prominent role for GFL because of its long tradition (dating back to 1932, re-founded in 1951; Ch. K.2; K.3.1) and its worldwide representation with 158 institutes (in 2013), of which 145 are abroad in 92 countries (*Jahrbuch* [*Goethe-Institut*] 2012/13:105; Map K.3.3–1; further details on participant numbers in GFL courses are given below). The Austrian Institutes (*Österreich Institut*; Ch. K.4) also offer GFL courses. Founded in 1997, there were ten institutes in 2013, nine of which are abroad in Eastern and Southern Europe, with approximately 10,000 GFL course participants over the year (de.wikipedia.org/wiki/%C3%96sterreich_Institut). In its total of 12 *Kultur- und Informationszentren*, the GDR also offered GFL courses, the quality of which was celebrated, although participant numbers remained modest. These centres were mostly in the Warsaw-Pact countries, and in Paris, Helsinki, Stockholm, Cairo, Damascus and Beirut. Unlike the Goethe-Institut, the *Herder-Institut* of the Karl-Marx University in Leipzig (Ch. K.3.1), which supervised the centres, did not itself offer GFL courses for adult education but only to prepare foreigners for university degree courses. It is evident from the Goethe-Institut yearbooks that, after courses were resumed in 1951, the figures for course participants grew rapidly, although not consistently. For the early years, participant numbers cannot be obtained without considerable difficulty, and even for more recent decades, it is necessary to inspect the yearbooks closely. I am grateful to members of the Goethe-Institut for providing me with the figures: Gabriele Siemers for 1982/83 to 1990 and Ursula Obers-Kraft for 1995 to 2012 (email 16 January 2014). The two sets of figures are not directly comparable, because the older figures relate to teaching units (courses) at given times (course participants); while the more recent figures relate to the whole year (participants per year). For this reason, the sets of figures are shown separately in Table J.5–1. For the more recent period, examination participants were available in addition to the participants per year.

While the home institutes occasionally showed a decline in the 1980s, there was steady, but sometimes modest growth for institutes located abroad. Between 1989 and 1995, there was an abrupt change, which was certainly associated with the reunification of Germany and the associated hopes for a revival of the country – but possibly even more so with the relocation of institutes from low-population countries to high-population countries, e.g. from Scandinavia to China and Russia. Added to this, in recent history, was the attraction of the labour market in the German-speaking countries for Mediterranean countries suffering from low employment.

Table J.5–1 GFL learners in Goethe Institutes abroad: participants by course around 1967 to 1990 and participants by year and examinees from 1995 to 2013

Participants / course	Participants / year		Examinees
1967 approx.	65,000	1995	157,695	47,760
1982/83	69,028	1997	147,504	51,542
1984	69,065	1999	149,765	50,868
1985	70,608	2001	152,565	63,104
1986	72,291	2003	155,031	78,350
1987	75,538	2005	159,820	91,366
1988	76,139	2007	175,990	109,129
1989	80,100	2009	184,219	161,692
1990	97,085	2011	197,951	184,027
		2012	207,113	201,345
		2013	220,486	245,955

(*Sources: Bericht 1967*: 14; figures for 1982/83 to 1990 from Gabriele Siemers, 1995 to 2013 from Ursula Obers-Kraft, Ingrid Köster and Herbert Moosbauer, all from the Goethe-Institut)

Reports such as the following allude to this situation (the figures do not always agree accurately, because final calculations have not been completed; cf. Table J.5–1): "After years of relatively constant demand, two-digit growth rates were achieved in 2011. In the worldwide network of the Goethe-Institut, there was a total of 234,587 course participants, 16,400 more than in 2010. Particularly strong growth was recorded in Spain (35% increase), Portugal (20%) and Italy (14%) from 2010 to 2011. Greece also recorded a growth of just under 10%" (*Reportagen, Bilder, Gespräche. Das Magazin des Goethe-Instituts* 2 December 2012: 5). The strong growth in examinees compared with mere participants supports this explanation. In fact, it is difficult to explain this other than by reference to the increase in practical, especially vocational motives for learning German (see Ch. J.8). The numerical proportions of examinations to participants in 1995 were around 1 : 3.3; in 2001, around 1 : 2.4; in 2007, around 1 : 1.6; in 2003, around 1 : 0.9 (47,760 : 157,695; 63,104 : 152,565; 109,129 : 175,990; 220,486 : 245,955). The number of examinations therefore finally exceeded the number of course participants.

For type 4), the private language schools, absolute numbers of learners are difficult to obtain because it is obviously desirable to guard them from competitors. These schools are more willing to publish just the proportions of different languages. The following data from different countries show that German is entirely within the group of languages frequently offered and learnt, together with French, Spanish and other international languages (Ch. A.7). However, as with most other international languages, the average proportion of learners and teaching hours for German is below 10%, – by contrast with English, where this figure ranges around 70 to 80%. Detailed investigations for German, although not always with very recent figures, are available for Japan (Noro 1994), Korea (Lee 2003) and Russia (Kostrova 2011). For a worldwide overview, the Berlitz language schools provided me with data for various languages which also show developmental trends – but for commercial reasons, these are only in the form of percentages rather than absolute figures. The figures do not relate to learners, but to teaching hours per language and are therefore dependent both on the number of learners and on the duration of the courses. Figures for the early 1970s, without precise details of years, were provided by Peter Nelde (1975: 37); for 1989, they were provided by Wolfgang Wiedeler (head office of the Berlitz language school in Frankfurt), for 2012, by Heino Sieberath (Marketing Director, Berlitz

Table J.5–2 Proportions of languages among teaching hours in the Berlitz schools (percentages)

	Total		Regional Distribution		
	Start of 1970s	1989/2012	Europe 1989/2012	North+Latin/ all America 1989/2012	Asia 1989/2012
English	42	63/71.8	37/62.8	12+21/74.2	30/81.4
German	12	8/ 6.9	64/15.5	23+ 6/ 1.5	7/ 1.0
French	25	11/ 5.9	54/ 8.0	34+ 5/ 7.4	7/ 1.3
Spanish	12	9/ 3.8	24/ 3.0	62 +12/ 7.9	2/ 0.6
Chinese	-	-/ 2.3	-/ 0.3	-/ 1.2	-/ 6.1
Dutch	-	1/ 1.3	96/ 3.2	4+ -/ 0.1	-/ 0.0
Portuguese	-	1/ 1.2	28/ 0.5	36 +30/ 2.8	6/ 0.3
Italian	-	3/ 0.9	58/ 1.4	36+ 3/ 0.8	3/ 0.3
Japanese	-	2/ 0.6	9/ 0.2	53+ -/ 0.7	38/ 1.2
Russian	-	-/ 0.1	-/ 0.9	-/ 0.8	-/ 0.1
Other	9	2/ 4.7	25/ 4.1	36 +25/ 2.7	14/ 7.7

Note: rank ordering based on proportions in 2012. – = no data. The last three columns show the distributions of each language (=100%) between the continents

Deutschland, email 10 January 2014). In the two left-hand columns, Table J.5–2 shows the worldwide proportions of languages at the start of the 1970s, in 1989 and in 2012 (1989/2012); the regional distribution of proportions in 1989 and 2012 is shown in the three columns on the right (1989/2012) (always in the categories given in the Berlitz statistics).

The most noticeable change during the investigated period of approximately 15 years is the growth of English and the decline of French, and to a lesser extent German and Spanish. German, French and somewhat further behind Spanish (based on 2012 ranking) are relatively close together. Changes in less frequently demanded languages cannot be determined precisely because of lack of comparative figures (older figures not itemized). The regional distributions are remarkable. For example, German, French and Italian have their primary focus in Europe with a secondary focus in North America, while the reverse is the case for Spanish. English is distributed most uniformly of all languages worldwide, with obvious lower significance (as a foreign language!) in the principal native-language region of North America. Among previously less frequently learnt languages, Chinese has grown significantly. German lost position less than French or Spanish and, in 2012, was ahead of both languages, although only slightly. On one hand, this could be attributable to the now well-known strong economic position of the German-speaking countries and the associated aspirations, as already mentioned for the Goethe-Institut; in individual cases, it may also be attributable to the limited regular provision of German in schools, which drives a stronger demand for extracurricular learning opportunities.

6. German-language degree programmes and educational events in universities

In many countries, universities try to attract foreign students with foreign-language degree programmes. Among these foreign-language degree programmes and educational events, the English language is generally so prominent that the relatively scarce offerings in other foreign languages can go unnoticed. This general picture matches the German-speaking countries (cf. Ch. G.8) but also countries with other languages throughout the world. However, even outside the German official-language territory, there are degree programmes and educational events in German which, it can safely be assumed, are intended to attract students from the German-speaking countries. In some cases, other motives play a part, such as efforts to serve German-(speaking) minorities already existing in the country, to improve cooperation with universities in German-speaking countries and to secure financial support from those countries. But such German-language provision does not target only the German-speaking countries; the courses are also relevant for students from the host countries themselves and therefore for German as a foreign language (GFL).

It is difficult to acquire representative data about students and whether German is their native language or a foreign language. Even obtaining an overview of "German-language courses in universities worldwide" is not easy – although a book with precisely this title exists; indeed, at the time of writing the present chapter, it is already in its sixth edition (Akstinat [1997] 2009). The book in question is intended as a guide for students interested in German-language study opportunities outside the German-speaking countries and is subdivided into a total of 73 subjects. However, the details about degree programmes and lectures remain very broad. "Specific questions relating to admission requirements, student fees, entry requirements etc. should be addressed directly to the relevant universities" (ibid: 5). The function of the German language in each degree programme is seldom explained, and most of the details given are sobering. For example, with reference to the ten degree programmes named at the German University in Cairo: "The principal teaching language is English, but lecturers can generally also speak German" (ibid: 26). This comment suggests that there is no teaching in German at all – which is, in fact, the case (Ch. J.9.8). The many examples in which no language is specified might give the impression that the entire degree programme could be completed in German, which is certainly not generally the case. Checking individual courses quickly shows that German is not the teaching language even in degree programmes with headings such as "German Language and Literature/ German (a selection)", where it would seem most likely and where most entries occur (40 of 147 pages; ibid: 50–89 of 11–157). Presumably, there are teaching events in German in some of these, especially in German Language and Literature, but there are certainly more in the respective official language of state or in English. Precise details would be desirable here – but obtaining them is easier said than done. At the very least, appropriate warnings in the preface of the book would be appropriate.

Instead of a quantitative evaluation of the book for all 73 subjects, leading to a rather dry, merely numerical outcome compared with the effort involved, it would seem more illuminating to offer brief descriptions of prominent cases of individual universities with German-language degree programmes or components. One such example is the *Andrássy Gyula German-Language University, Budapest*, founded in 2002 (Hungary; also Ch. E.4.6); the university offers six degree programmes which can be studied entirely in German, namely: business economics, European studies, engineering, politics, law (jurisprudence) and transport studies (automobile technology) (ibid: 23, 48, 105, 132, 137, 150). The *German University Cairo* in Egypt mentioned previously, where teaching is, in fact, entirely in English, but where all students must learn German alongside their studies (unless they already know it), admittedly only up to competence level A2 of the Common European Reference Framework, and where most lecturers have a knowledge of German, provides another interesting example. This university offers degree programmes in the following subjects or subject combinations: business studies, biotechnology, design, German Language and Literature/German, information technology, engineering, materials science, media technology, pharmacy, business administration and engineering (ibid: 14, 26, 29, 50, 93, 98, 118, 121, 128, 155). The *Marmara University* in Istanbul (Turkey; also Ch. J.9.7), the *German-Jordanian University* near Amman (Jordan) and the *Vietnamese-German University* in Thu Dan Mot

City (Vietnam), each with German as one of several teaching languages, should also be included in the list (see the relevant Wikipedia articles). Akstinat's book (2009: 20) advertises one of the universities as follows: "Did you know that among all universities outside the German-language territory, the University of Klausenburg in Romania offers most German-language degree programmes?" (also Ch. E.4.7), and Akstinat names no less than 21 degree programmes for this university "*Babeş-Bolyai*" in Cluj-Napoca/ Klausenburg, including five "Masters' programmes", the others being "BA programmes" (ibid: [161]). In fact, once again, the proportions of German-language are not given; but there is one impressive historical reference: "The university was founded in 1776 as a German-language university" (ibid: 19), and a detailed listing of relevant degree programmes, which I will not name in detail here (ibid: 19, 20, 25, 28, 33, 42, 49, 91, 100, 104, 106, 108, 118, 120, 127, 129, 131, 140, 147, 151, 152).

Apart from entirely "German" universities, founded with German assistance, or largely "German-language" universities, there are also smaller German-language departments, e.g. the *Chinese-German University College* (CDHK) at the Tongji University in Shanghai (China) founded in 1998. It is supported by the Volkswagen car company, and German professors teach within self-contained teaching modules. The reference in Akstinat (2009: 10) is: "Our strengths: 30 founders' professorial chairs – extensive industrial contacts – 20 German partner universities – international research projects – blocks of lectures with German professors – introduction to Chinese language and culture". In detail, the following subjects are offered: business economics, electro-technology, engineering, mechanical engineering, law (jurisprudence), transport studies (automobile technology) (ibid: 15, 18, 39, 98, 114, 133, 150). The *Europainstitut Klaus Mehnert* at the Kaliningrad State Technical University in Kaliningrad (formerly *Königsberg*, now in Russia; ibid: 47, [162]) also deserves mention. Initiated by the political scientist Winfried Böttcher, from Aachen, and founded in 2005, it offers a one-year "European studies" course, entirely in German, which regularly has around 20 participants – despite the high student fees. Approximately 90% are non-native speakers of German, most of whom are from the CIS states, and approximately 10% are native speakers from various German-speaking countries. The teaching programme is delivered entirely in German, but participants already know English and additionally learn French within the programme. The curriculum comprises one-week modules on many aspects of European politics. Lecturers, who teach in a cycle, are specialists on the theme of the module and mostly come from Germany, but some are also FL speakers of German from non-German-speaking countries. I taught there myself for several years and wish that the strong motivation and qualifications achieved by students on these German-language degree programmes could be emulated worldwide.

7. Total learner numbers and worldwide distribution of GFL

As with other chapters in this book, it will not be possible to give precise figures in this chapter, although orders of magnitude can be indicated, and these do provide important insights – in the sense of a comment made by mathematician Rudolf Taschner (2013: 53–55): "What people want to know is not calculation but estimation". In fact, accurate worldwide figures on the learning of a language as a foreign language are unavailable, or at least accessible only for the larger international languages (Ch. A.7). A comparison between languages is made additionally difficult by the fact that the available figures diverge in timescale and levels of skill (competences), if the latter are specified at all. In this context, the figures for German as a foreign language (GFL) tend to be more reliable than for many other languages. The following total figures include all learners and students at regular schools, universities (including Germanists) and outside schools, including adult education (for GFL pupil numbers see Ch. J.2).

Table J.7–1 Total learner figures for German as a foreign language 1995–2015

1995	19,511,887
2000	20,167,616
2005	16,780,701
2010	14,883,608
2015	15,455,452

(*Sources*: for 1995: Goethe-Institut 2000: 10; for 2000 and 2005: StADaF 2005: 15; for 2010 and 2015: Auswärtiges Amt 2015: 16)

Table J.7–2 Number of countries with GFL teaching in school from 1982/83–2015 (Named countries with learner number 0 have not been counted, although they may have offered GFL teaching)

1982/83	1985	1995	2005	2010	2015
Bericht	Goethe-Institut	Goethe-Institut	StADaF	Netzwerk Deutsch	Auswärtiges Amt
1985	2000	2000	2005	2010	2015
88	74	100	115	90	109

The "zigzag" development (growth 1995–2000, decline 2000–2010, renewed growth 2010–2015) can be explained by analogy with the development of student numbers, including the trend towards an overarching decline. The decline here is determined mainly by the spread of English as the world lingua franca (Crystal 2003; Graddol 2000, 2006), in consequence of which knowledge of other foreign languages, including German, seems less urgent – and may indeed be less urgent for practical communication (see Ch. A.4; A.7.2). Another reason for the decline is the rise of new international languages, e.g. Japanese and Chinese, which draw learners away from the traditional foreign languages, including German. The upturns before 2000 were driven by the reunification of Germany together with ideas about its future economic and political importance; and leading up to 2015 by the actual economic and political stability of the German-speaking countries, including the effect of attracting migrants and refugees. However, at least so far, the upward trends appear to have been too weak to counteract the downward pull.

Alongside the number of GFL learners, the number of countries in which GFL is learnt is also relevant, especially regarding language policy measures. But, as indicators for the global position of German or other languages, these two parameters should be kept apart. Having said this, there is a rough parallelism in the peak-and-trough development when comparing Table J.7–2 with Table J.2–2. In each case, a rising trend leads up to 2000 and then again up to 2015. Between these peaks, there are divergences with numerical gaps, but these cannot be attributed to increased inertia from the number of countries, because, in recent times, this factor is even more mobile than the number of learners.

Maps J.7–1 and J.7–2 provide a clearer overview of the global geography of GFL. The maps show the global distribution of learners in schools and universities (including Germanists) around 1995 (year of investigation – year of publication 2000) and 2010. The darker the colour, the greater the density of learning.

Learner density was calculated by dividing the learner number (GFL learners including Germanists) for each country by the population and then arranging the countries in quartiles (25% each) (higher quartiles in darker colour). The basic course of distribution over this time interval remained relatively uniform – apart from geographically relatively small shifts, especially in Africa, where Central African States were added, and states such as Libya, experiencing

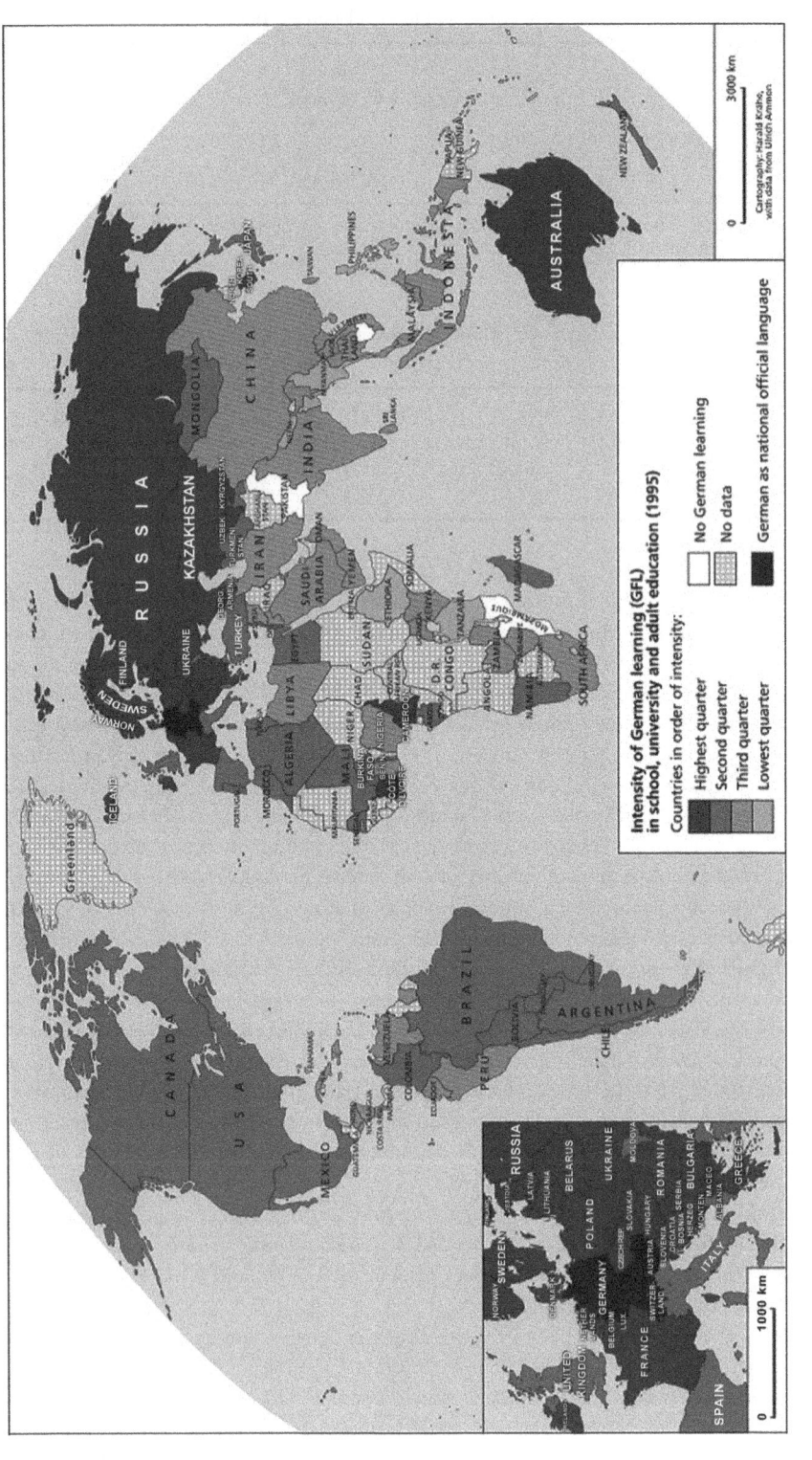

Map J.7–1 German as a foreign language worldwide around 1995, intensity of learning based on total number of all types of learners (Goethe-Institut 2000: "Students of German Language and Literature" + "Participants in academic language courses")

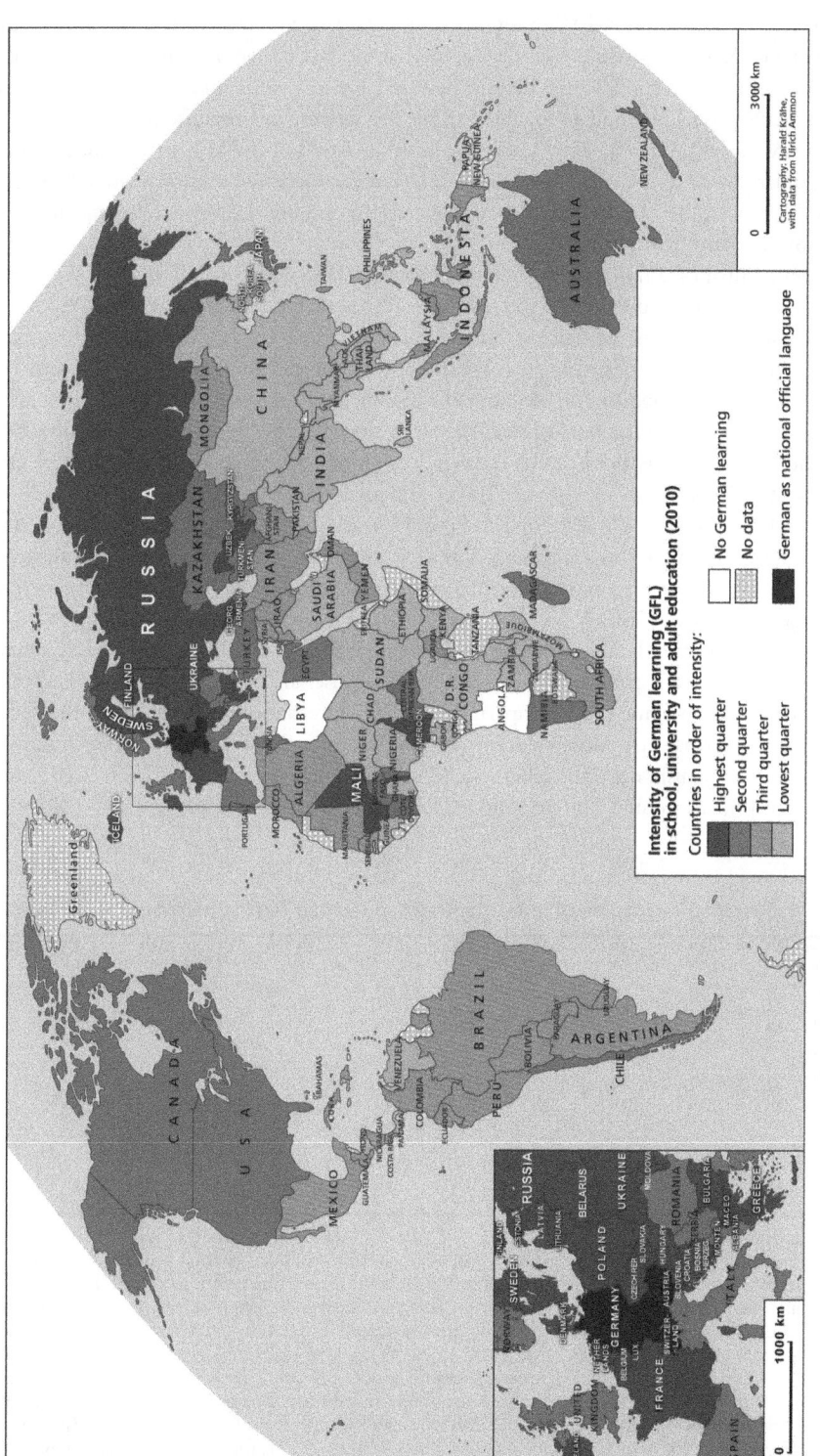

Map J.7-2 German as a foreign language worldwide around 2010, intensity of learning based on total number of all types of learners

(*Source*: Netzwerk Deutsch 2010: "Total German learners")

political revolutions, disappeared. With reference to Abram de Swaan's (2001a) "communication potential of a language" ("Q-value"), I have criticised the fact (Ch. A.7) that it relates languages to complete countries, regardless of whether they are large in area or small in area, e.g. to Russia and Japan. Both maps J.7–1 and J.7–2 also exhibit this defect. To minimise it, in my contribution to the *Nationalatlas der Bundesrepublik Deutschland* (Ammon 2005f.), settlement regions in countries of large area were also marked (ibid: 111); but the increased accuracy blurs the broader overview. Moreover, the question of how the learner figures are distributed among the settlement regions remains open.

Based on comparative figures with other languages, strong claims to validity and representativeness cannot be justified with the current state of research. Serious comparative figures for languages based on learners of German as a foreign language are in short supply, because, in many cases, the data collection remains obscure. For example, figures from the Instituto Cervantes (2013: 11 – provided by Alf Monjour) on the "*Idiomas más estudiados como lengua extranjera*" create a more serious impression than they may deserve. The figures are presumably based only on the Berlitz schools, because the only indication of a source reads: "*Primer Informe Berliz* [sic!] *sobre el estudio del español en el mondo*, 2005", and gives only percentages, which is typical for the Berlitz schools (see Ch. J.5). But, on this basis, FL learners worldwide were measured as follows: English 69%, French 7%, Spanish 6%, German 5%, Italian 2%, Chinese 2% [in this order!] and "*Resto*" 9%. My own attempt to determine absolute figures based on multiple sources led to the results listed in Table J.7–3.

Despite all the imponderables, the orders of magnitude should be approximately correct. Figures for English seem particularly questionable because the sources relate to FL speakers rather than FL learners; however, comparison of other international languages in the second rank relative to German are more relevant anyway. In isolated cases, much higher figures are in circulation for Spanish, e.g. "50 million to 70 million non-native learners" for 2010 (Montgomery 2013: 46), but I could find no solid evidence for this (I was unable to access the website

Table J.7–3 FL learners of international languages worldwide around 2005 in millions

1. English	750 ≤ 1,000, possibly > 2,000
2. French	82.5
3. Chinese	30 (with estimates from 3 ≤ 30)
4. German	16.7
5. Spanish	14
6. Italian	3 ≤ 14
7. Japanese	3
Portuguese	?
Russian	?

(Sources: for English: Crystal, 1997a: 61; 2003: 68f., 1997b: 360, who estimates "non-native speakers", who are not exactly identical with learners, at 530–830m (1,200–1,500m in total minus 670m "native or near-native speakers") and respectively at possibly > 1,000, with reservations in 2003: 68). But the figures have continued to rise and are certainly higher for the actual learners (Graddol 2006); for French: www.diplomatie.gouv.fr/en/france-priorities_1/francophony-french-language_1113/french-language_1934/promoting-french_4450/global-initiatives_4451/promoting-and-teaching-french-abroad_6881.html?var_recherche= french+learners); for Chinese: Graddol (2006: 63) 30m, with the note that the Chinese government is expecting 100m "in the next few years", but based on estimates by Markus Taube, East Asian Studies, University of Duisburg-Essen, and the Professional Association for Chinese, barely > 3m; for German: StADaF 2005: 15; for Spanish: *Enciclopedia del Español* 2006: 25, 27; for Italian: estimate by Andrea E. Samà, Director of the Cultural Division of the Italian Embassy in Berlin; for Japanese: Japan Foundation 2008: 1; for Portuguese and Russian, no figures supported by sources. Details in Ammon 2010c: 105)

named by Montgomery). The figures for French are possibly overinflated because FL speakers were counted for the West-African countries instead of SL speakers (Ch. A.3), which may have been more appropriate, as French is an official language there. In general, given the geographical limitation of the German-speaking countries and official-language territories to Central Europe (Ch. D) and the weak position of German in international organisations (Ch. H), German is maintaining its position well in this highly competitive field. In this context, reference should also be made to the – admittedly modest – rise in learner numbers for 2015 to 15,455,452 (Table J.7–1).

For the global position of languages, it would be particularly interesting to consider figures for people using the languages (listening, speaking, reading and writing; Ch. A.3). But this ultimately leads to a blind alley. For example, Montgomery (2013: 45) names the following "Number[s] of non-native speakers" for the ten languages with most native speakers, "who employ each language for actual communication" (in millions): English 1,500–1,600, Hindi 120–150, Arabic 100–150, Russian 75–100, Spanish 50–70, Bengali 30–50, Chinese and Portuguese 15–20, German 10–20, Japanese <10. French is not included, because Montgomery does not list it among the ten languages with most native speakers, a limitation he has adopted here. In fact, there is a lack of sound evidence for these figures, but low user numbers for GFL do serve as a reminder of the limitations on use addressed in the present book. Possible causes might include the hyper-radical shift from German to English as a language of science and scholarship, especially in the natural sciences (Ch. G.1; G.3), which also minimises the option of using German for non-German-speaking scientists and scholars (Ammon 1998: 99f., 120f.); but would also include exaggerated ideas about politeness among German native speakers who speak English with all foreigners, even foreigners with a good knowledge of German and the readiness to use this knowledge (examples in Ch. A.6; F.2; F.5; H.3; I.5; Weydt 2004).

8. Motives (subjective reasons) for GFL learning

Why do people learn German as a foreign language (GFL) in schools and universities, and why do they study German or German Language and Literature? What are the motives or subjective reasons for this choice? This question, which will be raised several times for different circumstances in different countries (Ch. J.9.2–J.9.15), is complex and can be addressed here only with reference to a few aspects which deserve special attention. Initially, it will be helpful to distinguish between choosing a language as a subject for learning or study and choosing it for communication (in specific situations): for which purpose do I learn or study German – why do I speak German (in such situations) (see also Ch. A.6)? This chapter is concerned primarily with the former choice; the choice of German for communication has been discussed in many other chapters of the book (e.g. language choice in international business contacts, Ch. F.2, and in diplomacy, Ch. H.5.3).

The relationship between the terms *motive* (synonymous with *subjective reason*) and *motivation* also requires clarification. In addition to its use as a mere synonym, *motivation* is sometimes used to specify the learners' eagerness to learn or to study and their endurance or stamina. The question thus points towards pedagogy and the teaching methods which can encourage the maximum, most enduring eagerness to learn (precisely the "motivation" required). But I cannot engage with this broad and complex set of questions in the present book. As far as possible, I shall speak only of *motives* or *subjective reasons* but not of *motivation*. In the specialist literature, the term *motivation* tends to predominate, e.g. without reference to GFL, in Gardner/ Lambert 1959, 1972; Gardner/ McIntyre 1991; Gardner 2001; and with reference to GFL, in Riemer/ Schlak 2004; Riemer 2010, 2011; Mackiewicz 2013, 2014. Others have restricted themselves to *motives*, e.g. with reference to GFL: Ammon 1991b; Honda 1994; Kwon 2003; Voronina 2011; by contrast, G. Schmidt 2011 additionally speaks of "motivation" and "reason". However, all the articles listed here are relevant to the *motives* or *subjective reasons* for choosing GFL as a subject of learning.

Asking school pupils and university students why they learn or study German evokes diverse responses. The following list is a selection from different places, under different circumstances; only the gist of the responses has been reproduced rather than quoting them literally. An overarching category, to which the relevant response/s can be allocated, has been added in brackets. I will return to this point later. Where several responses are allocated to the same category, they are separated by a stroke.

I learn German:

1) Because, in my school, I had to learn two foreign languages, and, apart from English, there was only German (this is a cause, not a motive);
2) Because I would like to study in Austria/ because I would like to work in Germany (instrumental motive);
3) Because I would like to emigrate to German-speaking Switzerland/ Germany (integrative motive)
4) Because my family originates from Austria/ because we are Lutherans/ because my father learned German (identificatory motive);
5) Because I value German culture/ because I like German music (cultural motive);
6) Because the German language is a challenge (performance-driven motive).

Further examples can be found e.g. in the work of Claudia Riemer (references in Riemer 2011) and corroborating responses previously given in Ammon 1991b (30–37) and G. Schmidt 2011 (108–111); other conceivable responses can be derived from vocational objectives attainable with a knowledge of German (e.g. Ammon 1991b: 184–188). The appended overarching categories are suggestions which may also turn out differently depending on the typology of motives for language choice. The concept of "motive/subjective reason" is considered important in explanations of human agency/action and can be distinguished from the concept of "'cause" – where many experts consider motives/subjective reasons to be special cases of causes or subsume both under the term *grounds/reasons*. I tend towards the view presented e.g. by Georg H. von Wright in his book *Explanation and Understanding* (1971) that "grounds" and "causes" should be kept distinct. Causes are objective and exist before and independently of the action, whereas *motives* are subjective and are inseparably associated with the action. They are directed towards the future, towards goals of the acting subject/actor. Accordingly, e.g. in response 1) above, school curricula, are (objective) causes for specific languages being learnt rather than others, while responses 2) to 6) name (subjective) motives explaining why the respondents specifically want to learn German. In this context, *subjective reasons* are associated more with the terminology of action theories, and *motives* with psychology, but, for our purposes, they can be taken as synonyms. *Motives* in the sense of social psychology can be allocated to the overarching category of attitudes and can therefore be analysed based on cognitive, affective and pragmatic aspects. *Subjective reasons* in the sense of action theory are associated instead with intentions and decisions (see Janich 2004 on conscious decisions, especially with reference to language culture). Such considerations can lead to traditional philosophical questions about human free will, which I shall not pursue here. In the following discussion, I shall not always distinguish strictly between the terminologies of causes and motives, especially if the distinction seems artificial in view of less rigorous terminology used in the specialist literature. Maciej Mackiewicz (2014: Ch. 2.4) attempts to attribute motives for foreign language learning, possibly also for language choice, to deeper, underlying causes and, in this context, relies on Abraham Maslow's "hierarchy of needs" (Maslow 1967). The discussion shows that the connection between ontogenetically developing needs and the reasons for learning foreign languages and the choice of specific foreign languages can be complicated by many different factors (causes and motives).

One important question for the empirical investigation of motives is the degree to which actors are conscious of their motives. Actors can only be questioned (in questionnaires or interviews) if they are conscious of their motives. In this context, lack of consciousness at the time of the action cannot be precluded. We must often admit that we do not know why we did something and may subsequently speculate about it or may receive prompts from others. Motives claimed in responses to questions should therefore not be accepted without reservation as actual motives – although there is often no other access to the actual motives than via a statement by the actors. Nevertheless, even with the best intentions of the respondents, their statements may be incorrect – especially if the action, such as the choice of GFL or another foreign language, lies a long way back in time or if conceivable motives are suggested by outside parties. Just consider the miracles on which religions are based, which David Hume ([1748] 2008: 79–95) attributed to faulty perception, or faulty memory or reporting. For our topic, a positive correlation between statements and facts (actual motives) often seems possible. This is in contrast with miracles, which, at least according to Hume, are incompatible, by definition, with natural laws (and therefore not true). It should also be remembered that motives can change during the learning process and subsequent characteristics can be superimposed on earlier characteristics, so that motives, as well as the statements about them should strictly be marked with time indices. This applies equally to the degree of eagerness to learn, in the sense of motivation as defined at the beginning of the chapter. Learning endurance and the sustainability of teaching depend upon developments over time – including breaking off the learning process or even switching to another language (see Jansen/ Schmidt 2011). A variety of causes and motives also comes into question in this context. Regarding breaches and continuities, what is of special interest here is why which respondents *give up* or *continue* learning German.

There remains the task of providing an appropriate typology of motives for language choices for learning in the following descriptions of GFL in individual countries (Ch. J.9.2–J.9.15). By contrast with a random classification, this typology should furnish an approach to explaining the circumstances to be described. The question may deserve a more thorough discussion of the extensive specialist literature than was possible for me here. A broadly accepted, rough classification originates from Gardner/ Lambert (1959; refined in Gardner/ Lambert 1972; Gardner/ McIntyre 1991; Gardner 2001), namely, the distinction between *instrumental* and *integrative motives* (generally referred to as *motivation* by these authors). According to one current specification, instrumental motives are orientated towards economic or vocational goals and integrative motives are orientated towards integration within social groups. Responses 2) and 3) at the beginning of this chapter represent examples of this. The Canadian researchers Gardner and Lambert were referring especially to non-English-speaking people, many of whom learn English with the goal of vocational or career-related promotion and others to integrate themselves into English-speaking society – where, of course, both motives may also be active at the same time. Correspondingly, the learning of German can also relate to career and/or integration, e.g. for migrants. Gardner's dichotomy has sometimes been criticised as oversimplified (see e.g. G. Schmidt 2011: 143–148).

In fact, it is easy to find motives which cannot be seamlessly classified into this system, e.g. response 4) at the beginning of the chapter. Instead of a questionable allocation to either integrative or instrumental motives, a reference to group identity seems more appropriate here.

Knowledge of German belongs precisely to the identity of a person of Austrian origin or a Lutheran. The same applies for the family identity based on a father's learning of German as a foreign language. In fact, a person is already a group member and, to that extent, already integrated; but the linguistic symbol for group membership, the personal group identity, is missing. Correspondingly, there are motives of role identity, a more specific type of social identity for individuals (Ch. B.3), for example, if a foreign ambassador in Germany learns German in line with their professional role. The instrumentality of this motive is not necessarily exhausted as soon as the targeted vocational goal has been attained. One can also speak of *identity-related* or *identificatory* motives. The motives in Gardner's dichotomy do not fit neatly with response 5) above: "Because I value German culture/ because I like German music". Gabriele Schmidt (2011: 148–150) found considerable evidence for this group of motives "interest in German culture and therefore also in the German language" in Australia (Ch. J.9.15). This suggests a *cultural motive* for choosing a language as a foreign language to learn. Finally, responses like 6) above do not fit into any of the previous categories. Taking the difficulty, and perhaps additionally, the beauty of the German language as a motive for learning German often used to be given in responses from France. German was said to be something "for clever people", as Harald Weinrich claimed; and even today, the Goethe-Institut bases its language competitions on this motto ("*Deutsch für helle Köpfe*" [German for bright people], e.g. www.goethe.de/ins/cz/prj/hel/deindex.htm). I have called this the performance-related motive [*leistungssuchendes Motiv*]. Rather like a mountaineer, learners take on the challenge of learning a language which is considered difficult just to prove that they can. This is still an autonomous motive, although other motives, e.g. instrumental motives, may resonate with it, for example, the fact that the effort of learning can also be beneficial for one's career. The above typology, which is doubtless in need of further improvement, nevertheless seemed appropriate to characterise the GFL situation in individual countries. It has not been developed sufficiently for consistent application in the short descriptions offered in Chapters J.9.2–J.9.15, and I therefore refer to it only occasionally in that context.

9. GFL and *Germanistik* (German Language and Literature) in selected countries

9.1 Choice of countries and plan for the following descriptions

Subsections J.9.2–J.9.15 describe the position of German as a foreign language (GFL) and *Germanistik* (German Language and Literature) in 14 countries. I have chosen the countries to achieve the most even distribution possible both between the continents and based on their size. Giving precedence to large countries is problematic because the circumstances in small countries may be more interesting in several respects. However, global representativeness seemed important as an overarching perspective, especially since I would not have been able to include enough countries for a systematic comparison of large and small countries. The level of existing research on the countries selected varies widely. Relevant accounts can be found by searching Google for "*Deutsche Sprache* in X" – "German language in X" (X = name of the country), although the reliability of such accounts must always be monitored. But even here, it is evident that conditions in relatively large countries can diverge widely – depending on relations with the German-speaking countries, on political and social structure, education system, as well as traditions of foreign-language learning, especially learning and studying German in schools and universities. Despite all the variations, it is still possible to identify aspects which allow a comparison of the countries based on the position of GFL and German Language and Literature. If they can be related to theories for maintaining the position of foreign languages (GFL) and of philology and linguistics (German Language and Literature) in a society or a country, these aspects give pointers for the position of GFL and German Language and Literature, indicating the chances for maintaining this position.

I have intentionally referred to theories in the plural here, because there is evidently no single, coherent theory about this complex question but only a range of different approaches. Some of the general approaches have been addressed in Ch. A while more specific approaches are outlined in the subsequent chapters B to I and J.2 to J.8. At least implicitly, the many available descriptions of "German (GFL) or German Language and Literature in individual countries", e.g. for 40 countries in the handbook *Deutsch als Fremdsprache* (Helbig/ Götze/ Henrici/ Krumm 2001, Vol. 2: 1424–1690) or for 55 countries in the handbook *Deutsch als Fremd- und Zweitsprache* (Krumm/ Fandrych/ Hufeisen/ Riemer 2010, Vol. 2: 1602–1842) all relate to such theoretical approaches. Unfortunately, these collections are not prefaced by any explicit criteria for the descriptions they contain. But, in some cases, such criteria can be abstracted from them. This is possible with the descriptions of GFL and German Language and Literature for individual countries in *Info DaF* – to name just two examples – for Australia, by Jäger/ Jasny (2007) or Indonesia, by Kohlauf/ Maintz (2001), or with the descriptions in the *Jahrbuch für Internationale Germanistik* and the *Berichte aus dem Internationalen Wissenschaflichen Rat* of the Institute for German Language. I mention just a few of them here which refer to the countries described in chapters J.9.2–J.9.15: France (Schneider-Mizony 2002, 2008; Dalmas/ Metrich 2004, 2008), Turkey (Tapan 2002; Ülkü 2004; Akdoğan 2008), Japan (Takahashi 2002), Italy (Moraldo 2003; Di Meola/ Tonelli 2008), UK (Durrell 2004a, b; 2007, 2008), USA (Lovik 2004a, b; Louden/ Lovik 2008), Brazil (Kaufmann 2003), Russia (Dobrovols'kij 2004, 2008; Troshina 2004), China (Hernig/ Zhu 2004), Australia (Kretzenbacher 2006; Clyne 2008). The books *Deutsch in Japan/ Korea/ China/ Russland* (Ammon 1994d; Ammon/ Chong 2003; Ammon/ Reinbothe/ Zhu 2007; Ammon/ Kemper 2011) also discuss aspects relevant to the descriptions. Finally, commentaries on the maintenance of German and German Language and Literature can also be found in cross-national descriptions, e.g. by Duesberg (2006) and in introductions to the subject of German as a Foreign Language, e.g. by Huneke/ Steinig (2003) or Hernig (2005).

The brevity of the individual descriptions, which was necessary to keep down the length of chapters J.9.2–J.9.15, required my concentration on a small number of informative aspects. These are not restricted to topics for which most information was available or accessible but also deliberately include aspects which open new areas of research. Having said this, I avoided a rigidly schematic approach to the description. Many gaps in the data could not be closed despite extensive assistance from local experts, who are named in each case. With these limitations, the following aspects therefore provide a descriptive plan applied to all 14 countries:

1) Level of economic development of the country and business relationships with the German-speaking countries, primarily with Germany;
2) Linguistic diversity of the country, international position of its own national official languages, German-(speaking) minorities, tradition of learning German;
3) Legal and curricular basis for GFL at school level;
4) Learners of GFL at school level;
5) Legal and curricular basis for GFL and German Language and Literature at university level;
6) Learners of GFL and students of German Language and Literature at university level;
7) Learners of GFL outside school and in adult education;
8) Causes and motives for the choice of GFL or German Language and Literature in school and university;

9) Vocational prospects for GFL learners and Germanists;
10) Promotion of GFL and German Language and Literature by the German-speaking countries and by local organisations.

9.2 France

This chapter has been checked and amplified primarily by Martine Dalmas (Université Paris-Sorbonne) and Odile Schneider-Mizony (Université de Strasbourg). The principal sources included Dalmas 2010; Dalmas/ Metrich 2004, 2008; Schneider-Mizony 2002, 2007, 2010; Schmale 2007a, b. Concise historical background was provided by Artur Rosenberg (1953). France's economic relations are closer with Germany than with any other country (17% of French imports, 16% of exports in 2011; *Fischer Weltalmanach* 2013: 157f.). For many years, both countries have declared an especially close friendship – after enmity lasting hundreds of years, up to the end of WWII. However, GFL in France has fallen far behind English and behind Spanish – incidentally, almost in mirror image to the position of French in Germany. Repeated public warnings from both French and German business and government (for which there is considerable evidence on the Internet) have failed to reverse this trend. Commercial promises from the German-speaking countries evidently motivate French people to learn the language less than the allure of the Spanish-speaking world (work here – holidays there); added to this is the fact that the romance "sister language" is easier to learn. This agrees with findings by Claudia Riemer (2011: 335), that, in the German-learning biographies of French people, "instrumental motives feature very rarely, significantly less than in other countries" (but admittedly, for a very small sample size: 28 learners at the Goethe-Institut in Nancy; page 332). In France, GFL is faced with competition not only from the over-powerful English and the popular Spanish, but with around ten others, including almost all international languages (Ch. A.7) and a further six regional languages in specific regions. Bilingual schools have been established for these, from which German benefits in Alsace and Lorraine – although not necessarily as a foreign language (Ch. E.4.3). However, German can be learnt as a foreign language throughout the country, although by no means in all schools.

At primary level, English almost has a monopoly. At secondary school level, bilingual classes (*classes bilangues*) have existed in the *collèges* since 2000, in Alsace, with a focus on German. On one hand, the combination with English in these classes has strengthened German, but on the other hand, German has also been weakened as a second foreign language, because it has been pushed out of many other *collèges* as a result. In the *lycées*, which correspond to the higher types of school including the *Gymnasium* in Germany, there is intense language competition, with the now stable rank ordering: English (absolutely dominant) > Spanish > German. Since 1992, many *collèges* and *lycées* have had European Sections (*sections européennes*) with intensified foreign languages, two of which act as languages of instruction. But here also, English is dominant. The *Abibac*, a combination of the German *Abitur* and the French *baccalauréat*, does support German. But the lack of German teachers, leading to frequent cancellation of lessons, is an overarching problem. Table J.9.2–1 shows the development of learner numbers at secondary level (*second degré*), i.e. *collèges* and *lycées*, in the three foreign languages predominant throughout the country.

The figures show a dramatic decline until around 2007, followed by stabilisation. It is uncertain whether this stabilisation will be maintained. For the most recent period (when the report was produced), I have no absolute figures for comparison but only percentages (relative to the total number of secondary school pupils). For 2013: German 15.3%, Spanish 46.1%, English 98.2%. From 2006, there have been fluctuations, with the high points repeatedly celebrated in the press (e.g. "Revival of German language in France but . . .", *Journal Interparlementaire*

Table J.9.2–1 Learners of GFL at secondary level compared with Spanish and English as foreign languages from 1995–2011

	1995	*2000*	*2005*	*2007*	*2009*	*2011*
German	1,312,119	1,031,144	843,963	821,082	820,946	828,377
	22.9%	18.5%	15.5%	15.4%	15.5%	15.3%
Spanish	1,657,201	1,911,789	2,161,726	2,111,391	2,180,769	2,394,277
	28.9%	34.2%	39.6%	39.4%	41.1%	44.2%
English	5,334,128	5,324,662	5,303,854	5,210,348	5,198,267	5,331,088
	93%	95.3%	97.2%	97.6%	98%	98.4%

(*Source*: Hannequart 2013: [1] – information from Martine Dalmas)

franco-allemand 1 April 2007; dfizeitungjournalinterparlementaire.wordpress.com/2007/04/01/aufschwung-der-deutschen-sprache-in-frankreich-aber-%E2%80%A6/). For the period from 2010 to 2015), a further decline in GFL learners at schools of 1.9% was recorded (by 19,136, to 998,749; Auswärtiges Amt 2015: 10). However, signs of consolidation prevail. The Football World Cup 2006 in Germany, to which a growth in friendliness towards the German language is sometimes ascribed, presumably contributed less to this than Germany's economic recovery after the burden of reunification, which promises increased vocational benefits from a knowledge of German. As in most other countries, German Language and Literature at university, operating at a high level of scholarship, has lost ground seriously, while German in degree programmes of applied foreign languages (*langues étrangères appliquées*) and especially learning German as a subsidiary, alongside other subjects (*langue pour spécialistes d'autres disciplines/LAND-SAD*) has gained in popularity: in the natural sciences and technology, but also in law and humanities. German Language and Literature now also participates in these arrangements – which strengthens the subject. The fact that German Language and Literature benefits from this, is shown by the development of student numbers in 1985: 12,000, 1995: 18,000 and 2005: 20,000. However, these remain far behind the brilliant rise in learning German as a subsidiary, alongside other subjects – from 1995: 49,772 to 2005: 150,000 (same sources as for Table J.9.2–1, with gaps for the other years). Moreover, there has been a recent expansion of *bidisiplinarité*, with subject combinations, such as German Language and Literature + history, German Language and Literature + mathematics, also with other languages and natural sciences, after which students are awarded two bachelor degrees. It is presumably also instrumental, vocational motives which have increased the numbers of GFL learners in extracurricular/extramural institutions (excluding Goethe Institutes) – from 1985: 15,000 and 1995: 12,000 to 2005: 34,000 (Goethe-Institut 2000: [168]; StDaF 2005: 9). These developments have recently been detected by the Goethe Institutes, as combined figures from the institutes show (Bordeaux, Lille, Lyon, Marseille, Nancy, Paris, Strasbourg, Toulouse): 1990: P – 11,312, E – 1,308; 2012: P – 4,660, E – 1,383; 2013: P – 4,774, E – 1,440 (P = course participants, E = examinations; information from Ingrid Köster and Herbert Moosbauer, Goethe-Institut, Munich) – but with a slight decline in 2015 to P – 4,527 (Auswärtiges Amt 2015: 10). Accordingly, after a relatively dramatic decline, the situation has stabilised with reference to course participants and examinations. The earlier decline may have been intensified by restrictions on the provision of courses which now exist only in Lyon, Nancy, Toulouse and, with the bulk of participants, Paris. High instruction fees (e.g. in Nancy €930 for a one-year course of three hours per week, several times the cost for a year of study at university; email from Odile Schneider-Mizoni, 7 March 2014) also have a retarding effect. Such course fees drive the search for more cost-favourable learning opportunities, e.g. media-supported self-instruction. In the case of the Goethe Institutes, this leads to lower numbers of course participants and higher numbers of exam participants. In France, the figures do not show this effect, but they certainly do in other countries (e.g. Italy, Ch. J.9.4, and Japan, Ch. J.9.14).

The learning of German in France receives French, German and Austrian support, with the roles reversed for the learning of French in Germany. The legal basis is formed by the *Élysée*-Treaty of 1963, by means of which the *Deutsch-französisches Jugendwerk (DFJW)/Office franco-allemand pour la jeunesse (OFAJ)* was founded, and which has since supported more than 300,000 meetings and exchanges. The *Deutsch-französische Hochschule/Université franco-allemande*, which was founded in 1997, with its administrative base in Saarbrücken is also worth noting, with its approximately 135 bilingual and sometimes trilingual degree programmes in numerous partner French and German universities. Alongside the Goethe Institutes, two German Schools Abroad (Paris, Toulouse) and 25 DSD schools (offering the German *Sprachdiplom*) must also be mentioned. Furthermore, the German Academic Exchange Service (DAAD) participates in the promotion of German with 50 lectorships in French universities, together with – on a smaller scale – the Austrian Exchange Service. These facilities are further supported by campaigns, such as *DeutschMobil*, which have promoted the learning of German in France and in other countries. The promotion of German by associations of German teachers, especially the *French Association of German Teachers/Association pour le Développement de l'Enseignement de l'Allemand en France* (ADEAF – President Jean-Michel Hannequart), and the *Internationale Vereinigung für Germanistik* (IVG; President Jean-Marie Valentin 2000–2005 and World Congress in Paris 2005).

9.3 United Kingdom

This chapter has been checked and amplified by Martin Durrell (University of Manchester) and Gertrud Reershemius (Aston University, Birmingham). The principal sources included Rösler 2001; Durrell 2004a, b; 2007, 2008; Reershemius 2010; Gould/ Riordan 2010; Mulkerne/ Graham 2011; historical perspective was provided by Ortmann 1993. British economic ties with Germany are closer than with any other country, with a predominance of imports from Germany to the UK (13% of British imports, 11% of exports in 2011; *Fischer Weltalmanach* 2013: 177). The UK is striving to expand its economic relations with Asia, especially China, which also strengthens interest in the Chinese language ("Mandarin & Money", *SZ* 6 December 2013) and therefore intensifies competition with the traditional foreign languages. The UK has two acknowledged, indigenous (autochthonous) minority languages from the Celtic language family: Welsh and Gaelic; in their respective regions, they are also school subjects and even languages of instruction. Added to these in more recent history are various allochthonous, immigrant languages from other countries, resulting from Britain's colonial history (V. Edwards 2008). Further competition for the traditional foreign languages can derive from both sides. However, another consequence of British colonialism has had a considerably more powerful effect on foreign-language learning: the current position of the English language as the global lingua franca (Gould/ Riordan 2010: 205f.; Ch. A.7; A.11; Graddol 1997, 2000, 2006). As a result, many UK citizens evidently consider it superfluous to learn foreign languages at all. The extent to which these people are deluding themselves and overestimating the global spread of English forms a backdrop to the learning of foreign languages, including German, in this island realm.

A look back at the history shows that, in the UK, as in other (English-speaking) countries, learning German has been declining since WWI, albeit with occasional periods of recovery (Ch. J.2). In recent years in the UK, these developments have been perceived as life-threatening for institutions concerned with the teaching and learning of German and for those employed in them. Alarm calls from business, in some cases scientifically supported (Hagen 1986, 1988; Ch. F.6), finally stirred the British Government, motivating government funding measures for foreign-language learning, including the learning of German (Durrell 2007: 38–44). However, any sustainable effect seems doubtful, possibly because the British Government is also ultimately relying on the global position of English. Attempts to strengthen foreign-language learning have been counterbalanced by the fact that "the teaching of modern foreign languages in state-run comprehensive schools [became! U.A.] optional from September 2004". "[I]n fact, state-run comprehensive schools have dramatically reduced their teaching provision in modern foreign languages, while they remain part of the compulsory educational canon in private schools and *grammar schools* in the UK" (Reershemius 2010: 1674f.). As a result, foreign-language learning has become entirely an elite privilege, so that the social strata more remote from education do not benefit from it. Added to this, German enjoys the "bonus" of being considered particularly difficult.

With reference to learner numbers, there is no doubt that these have fallen dramatically since the 1990s, and German has lost its position as the second most frequently learnt foreign-language to Spanish. Since WWI, French has been and continues to be the most learnt foreign-language with a considerable margin. In view of the fragmentation of the UK school system, school-leaving examinations illustrate the course of these figures – in a potentially informative manner – for the three most important foreign languages included in Table J.9.3–1. A distinction is made between *General Certificate of Secondary Education* (GCSE), a kind of post-16 leaving certificate and *General Certificate of Education, Advanced Level*: (GCE A-level), at university entrance level.

As can be seen, the figures for German and French have fallen continuously, especially at the less demanding GCSE-level. However, in recent history, the figures for the more demanding (GCE) A-level have stabilised (in Table J.9.3–1, in 2007), a point to which I shall return. More recent figures for the (GCE) A-level were not available. However, at this level, Spanish was already catching up with German in 2005. At the simpler GCSE-level, Spanish does not catch up with German until later (according to Table J.9.3–1, in 2011). Spanish now seems to have overtaken German at all levels, including universities (see Reershemius 2010: passim).

Table J.9.3–1 Examination passes at the level of the *General Certificate of Secondary Education: GCSE* in England and Wales and the *General Certificate of Education, Advanced Level: GCE A-level* in England, Wales and Northern Ireland

	2001		2003		2005	
	GCSE	*A-level*	*GCSE*	*A-level*	*GCSE*	*A-level*
French	321,207	18,407	304,472	15,335	244,800	14,248
German	130,627	8,575	120,659	6,876	99,200	5,834
Spanish	45,629	5,743	51,299	5,748	52,200	6,173

	2007		2011
	GCSE	*A-level*	*GCSE*
French	189,400	14,615	141,700
German	75,800	6,406	58,300
Spanish	53,800	7,152	58,700

(*Source 2001–2007*: Durrell 2008: 83f., 2011: www.cilt.org.uk/home/research_and_statistics/language_trends_surveys/secondary/2011.aspx, information from Durrell)

Table J.9.3–2 Learners of German, including Germanists, at universities from 1995–2015

	1995	2000	2005	2010	2015
Universities: Learners of German and Germanists	5,884	[8,800]	5,325	4,920	11,000

(*Sources for 1995*: Goethe-Institut 2000: [168]; for 2000 and 2005: StADaF 2005: 9; for 2010: Netzwerk Deutsch 2010: 6; Auswärtiges Amt 2015: 11. The figure in square brackets is derived from the fact that the source for 2005 indicates the difference from the unnamed figures for "Total learners of German" in 2000 as "3,565")

The decline in German is incisive. For example, in 1994, 21% of a yearly cohort still learnt German in state-run schools in England; by 2009, the figure was only 11%. A similar picture is found in the other parts of the UK. These developments have also impacted on universities, especially on German Language and Literature. In 2000, 126 still offered German Language and Literature/German Studies, but by 2006, this had declined to 65 (Reershemius 2010: 1667f.; Durrell 2007: 47–50; 2008: 86). In this context, German Language and Literature/ German Studies degree programmes work at an academically high level, although often with minimal staffing (Durrell 2008: 87–89). German Language and Literature/German Studies is evidently affected by a decline in student numbers parallel to the decline in learners of German at school (Durrell 2007: 50). By contrast, learning German alongside other university courses appears to be enjoying increasing demand, as in other countries. One indicator for this may be the increase in A-levels in Table J.9.3–1 in 2007. Figures determined on behalf of the Goethe-Institut certainly point in this direction (Table J.9.3–2). For James Coleman (2004, 2012) and Michael Worton (2009), these figures illustrate a shift of language learning into university language centres and a separation between research and teaching within the discipline.

Data in corresponding tables in the following chapters J.9.4–J.9.15 labelled "Learners of German and Germanists" are designated differently in different sources. However, the extensive agreement in content can be inferred from the context of the other categories. An explicit definition is found only in StADaF 2005 (p. 8, note 7), in fact, for the designation "Total students of German": "This includes students on 'degree programmes relevant to German' and students of German Language and Literature: German within the framework of language courses = German as language-course instruction; as a subsidiary subject; optional or compulsory course; in subject combinations with another degree programme; or as a course option in specialist vocational degree programmes; and the study (as principal or subsidiary subject) of German Language and Literature; German teacher or interpreter training; and studies of Germany combined with another subject". For further definition see Ch. J.9.4, below Table J.9.4–2.

It is surprising that Spanish has taken the lead over German because German seems economically more promising. This assessment is suggested on one hand by ongoing comparisons in the media in EU countries; on the other hand, it has been underlined by British experts based on relevant investigations in the UK: "German was the most requested language across all positions in the past 12 months; 1,581 jobs required German, about 25% of the total" (Mulkerne/ Graham 2011: 38). Furthermore, German is still the more important international academic language, at least with reference to number of publications (Ch. G.3–G.7). Other motives for learning foreign languages clearly carry more weight and not only here. Spanish is associated with "holidays abroad and Latin America which is perceived as exotic"; by contrast, German is associated "at worst with the Second World War" or with "humourless, but effective contemporaries" (Reershemius 2010: 1675). However, the increase in German learning mentioned above may indicate a change in the trend. Apart from rising numbers in universities, the figures for extracurricular language learning

Table J.9.3–3 Figures for course and exam participants of the Goethe-Institut in the UK from 1990–2015

	1990	2000	2005	2010	2011	2012	2013	2015
Course participants	6,300	3,121	2,938	2,689	2,405	3,004	3,086	3,154
Examinees	369	214	229	164	153	220	347	

Source: (Data from Ingrid Köster and Herbert Moosbauer, Goethe-Institut, Munich; Auswärtiges Amt 2015: 11)

are also growing. For example, especially in Goethe Institutes (Table J.9.3–3) – although Goethe Institutes now only exist in London and Glasgow, since Manchester and York were closed after the collapse of the Soviet Union to release financial support for the institutes in Eastern Europe and Asia. But the fact that learner numbers in the UK are growing, could also be driven by instrumental motives, by the improved economic situation in Germany, which is also perceived in the UK. Moreover, Germany's image there has also brightened ("*London entdeckt die Liebe zu den Deutschen*" [London finds love for Germans], *FAZ* 27 February 2014: 3). Perhaps the Football World Cup in 2006 also contributed to breaking down timeworn stereotypes.

Renewed interest in the German language has presumably also been supported by the promotion of German by Germany and Austria. Among others, the two Goethe Institutes, the German School Abroad and the DSD school in London (offering the German *Sprachdiplom*), the German Academic Exchange Service (DAAD), the Austrian Exchange Service (OeAD) and the Alexander von Humboldt Foundation, which funds visits to Germany for UK lecturers, have contributed to this effect. The country's own organisations, with their marketing and lobbying work, must not be forgotten, especially the *Association for German Studies in Great Britain and Ireland* (ASG). But a return to the former level of foreign-language learning for the UK or the other English-speaking countries can no longer be expected. This is also shown by a consideration of the academic scene. Even for British academics, knowledge, at least a reading knowledge, of several foreign languages used to be taken for granted (Ch. G.1). One somewhat dated example is Charles Darwin, who, in his book *The Descent of Man* [. . .] 1871 (2011: 7–10 and passim), which is relevant far beyond its disciplinary boundaries, quotes from the following languages without translating the quotations: German, French, Italian and Latin. He therefore not only had a knowledge of these languages himself but expected it of his readers. By contrast, UK natural scientists nowadays cause a stir even if they quote in one language other than their own (Ch. G.3).

9.4 Italy

This chapter has been checked and amplified by Claudio Di Meola (Universita di Roma "La Sapienza"), Sandro M. Moraldo (Universita di Bologna, Campus di Forli) and Goranka Rocco (Università degli Studi di Trieste). The main sources included Ponti 2001; Moraldo 2003, 2009, 2010, 2013; Foschi Albert 2005; Foschi Albert/ Hepp 2010; Di Meola/ Tonelli 2008; Rocco 2010, 2014; Langé/ Scifo 2012. Italy's economic relations with Germany are closer than with any other country (16% of Italian imports, 13% of exports in 2011; *Fischer Weltalmanach* 2013: 232). It is therefore not surprising that, in a 2011 survey of Italian businesses which asked about the most important foreign languages, German was the second most frequently named language (18.8%), a long way behind English (59%), but ahead of French (16.2%) and especially Spanish (4.3%) (Moraldo 2013: 402). Motives for learning German therefore reflect economic considerations, including employment or further education in a German-speaking country (cf. Ch. F.6), amongst other reasons, because of youth unemployment.

Italian is an international language (Ch. A.3; A.7) in many respects of similar ranking to German. It competes with German as a foreign language in many parts of the world, inside the EU and outside, e.g. in Australia (Ch. J.9.15), but this does not impact on German as a foreign language (GFL) in Italy. The other official languages or minority languages in Italy also hardly influence GFL, apart from French in the Aosta Valley, which limits other foreign languages there, but with reference to the whole country, has little influence. German as a native language, official language and language of school instruction in Southern Tyrol (Ch. D.3.2) is not addressed in this chapter which is concerned exclusively with GFL.

Italy has taken the EU language-education goals seriously and, in 2005, moved foreign-language teaching forward to the start of primary education. Initially, it also made the acquisition of two foreign languages (two FL) alongside the native language (NL) compulsory (NL + 2 FS; Kruse 2012); but, one year later, this was withdrawn, and schools were allowed to use the number of hours for the second foreign language for "intensified English" (*inglese potenziato*), "to achieve a near-native-language competence in English" (Moraldo 2013: 397; Foschi Albert/ Hepp 2010: 1695). Many schools exploited this opportunity, in the period 2009–2012 for almost 3,000 classes, especially private schools 27% (Moraldo ibid). Furthermore, English became the compulsory first foreign language for all schools and, in fact, throughout the entire schooling period through to school leaving (*Maturità*). As a result, conditions in Italy largely resemble the "foreign-language monoculture" diagnosed in other EU Member States (Quetz 2010). However, the second foreign languages, including German, do still play a role: in the rank ordering of learner numbers in schools: English, French, Spanish and German. German is therefore in fourth position, stronger in the north than in the south of the country. Table J.9.4–1 gives an overview of the figures.

Despite the gaps, especially in the comparative figures for 2015 (also in the sources), it is possible to identify trends. The learner numbers increase over the documented period for all foreign languages, but less markedly for German than for Spanish, and even less so for French, which however remains the second most frequent foreign language with a considerable margin. English is clearly alone at the top and will be learnt by all school pupils in future. One relevant aspect for German cannot be derived from Table J.9.4–1: at Secondary Level II, German has fared better than in the lower schooling levels. This is evident from a comparison of German (2004/5: 196,631, 2008/9: 198,365) with Spanish (2004/5: 79,911, 2008/9: 124,525) (Foschi Albert/ Hepp 2010: 1695), which is, however, also catching up here. Presumably, the strength of German at the highest schooling level originates from the fact that the motives for language choice which favoured German, such as vocational benefits, come into play. Table J.9.4–2 gives an overview of German in schools and universities.

Table J.9.4–1 Figures for foreign-language learners in schools in Italy

Schooling level	Secondary level I			All levels	
School year	2004/5	2007/8	2011/12	2008/9	2015
English	1,599,428	1,723,615	n.d.	7,209,773	n.d.
French	830,700	1,294,015	1,234,715	2,086,085	n.d.
Spanish	64,538	276,298	363,696	409,426	n.d.
German	87,316	148,470	152,799	402,794	398,483

(*Sources*: Moraldo 2013: 400; Foschi Albert/ Hepp 2010: 1695; Auswärtiges Amt 2015: 13)

Table J.9.4–2 Learners of German and Germanists in Italian schools and universities

Schools	1985	1995	2000	2005	2010	2015
	270,513	195,957	[210,598]	228,314	401,577	398,483
Universities: Learners of German and Germanists	4,500	10,000	[37,800]	30,000	30,000	30,000
Of which Germanists	4,500	10,000	n.d.	13,000	n.d.	n.d.

(*Sources for 1985 and 1995*: Goethe-Institut 2000: [169]; for 2000 and 2005: StADaF 2005: 10; for 2010: Netzwerk Deutsch 2010: 7; 2015: Auswärtiges Amt 2015: 13)

The figures are estimates. Comparability over the years is additionally impaired by the variability of terms. For example, in Table J.9.4–2, I have subsumed under the heading "Schools": "School pupils learning German in secondary schools" (Goethe-Institut 2000) and "GFL learners in schools" (StDaF 2005; Auswärtiges Amt 2015). The heading "Universities: Learners of German and Germanists" (definition Ch. J.9.2, below Table J.9.3–2) subsumes the sum of "Number of students of German Language and Literature"; "Number of participants in academic language courses" – the latter are missing for Italy for 1985 and 1990, so that the total is identical with the number of Germanists (both data Goethe-Institut 2000); "Total students of German" (Netzwerk Deutsch 2010); "Students learning German" (Auswärtiges Amt 2015). Furthermore, Germanists are not always listed separately in the sources. The figures in square brackets reflect the fact that the source for 2005 indicates the difference from the unnamed figure for "GFL learners in schools" in 2000 as "17,716" and for "Total students of German" as "7,800".

After the decline at the end of the last century, the revival in schools and the continuity in the universities are noteworthy. The reason is presumably the university reform introduced in 2001 (Di Meola/ Tonelli 2008; Moraldo: 14), which "introduced numerous established posts" for linguistics through separation from literary studies and strengthened its academic standard (Di Meola/ Tonelli 2008: 41f.). However, relegation of GFL in schools only to a second foreign language and, in some cases, replacement with English led to a "rising number of complete beginners" in universities (ibid: 43).

While French may benefit from its priority in EU institutions, German has a more diverse, vocation-related basis (Moraldo 2013: 402f.). This might also explain the high number of examinees in the Goethe Institutes (Genoa, Milan, Naples, Palermo, Rome, Trieste and Turin taken together), which exceeds the number of course participants: 1990: P – 8,052, E – 2,029; 2012: P – 5,065, E – 15,774; 2013: P – 6,145, E – 15,708 (P = course participants, E = examinations; information from Ingrid Köster, Herbert Moosbauer, Goethe-Institut, Munich). In surveys, "employment opportunities" was given as the main reason for choice of GFL: in 2007/8 for 71% (n = 500) and 2013 for 81% (n= 300) of students; but academic-scientific practical benefits also showed a growth from 9% to 19% (Rocco 2010, 2014). By contrast, both investigations show a decline of the traditionally dominant interest in German culture and way of life: 2007/8–46%, 2013–38% nominations (Rocco 2010: 79–83, 121–126; 2014). Among students of German Language and Literature, around half are hoping for jobs in education, as teachers at schools or universities, which seems realistic, but only for approximately 20%. Other employment opportunities include tourism, Italian industry, also in Joint Ventures (business correspondence), or as different types of translator (Foschi Albert/ Hepp 2010: 1696).

GFL and German Language and Literature in Italy are also promoted by the German-speaking countries. The funding institutions include the Austria Institute in Rome and the seven Goethe Institutes and four Goethe Centres (as at 2012). Various German cultural centres with "activities for the promotion of the German language and culture" also exist (cms.ifa.de/popup/italien/kulturgesellschaft-acit-und-icit/). Furthermore, the following institutions offer German as a language of instruction: four Swiss Schools Abroad (in Bergamo, Catania, Milan, Rome – another in Como teaches in Italian) and three German Schools Abroad (in Genoa, Milan, Rome) and, with intensified GFL teaching, 27 DSD schools (providing the German *Sprachdiplom*). The German Academic Exchange Service (DAAD) contributes to the promotion of GFL with lectorships (12 in 2014), intensive German courses and grants for Italian and German students and guest lecturers. The German Ministry for Family Affairs provides financial assistance for vocational German courses relating to the introduction of the dual vocational training system in Italy, and the Alexander von Humboldt Foundation supports research visits by Italian academics to Germany. There is financial support from Austria and Switzerland for conferences and events promoting GFL. Finally, professional associations also play a role, the Italian German Teachers' Association (*Associazione Nazionale Insegnanti Lingue Straniere*), which is a member of the International German Teachers' Association (IDV), whose president has been Marianne Hepp (Università degli Studi di Pisa) (since 2009), the Italian Association of Germanists (*Associazione Italiana di Germanistica*) and the *International Association for Germanic Studies* (IVG), whose president since 2015 has been Laura Auteri (Università degli Studi di Palermo), where the next IVG World Congress is to take place in 2020.

9.5 Poland

This chapter has been checked and amplified by Sambor Grucza (Uniwersytet Warszawski) and Maciej Mackiewicz (Uniwersytet im. Adama Mickiewicza w Poznaniu). Other sources included Oschlies 1982; Orlowski 1988; F. Grucza 2001, 2010, 2014; F. Grucza et al. 1999; Czarnecki 2004; Mackiewicz 2013, 2014. Poland's economic relations with the German-speaking countries are close, closer with Germany than with any other country in the world. In 2011, 26% of Polish exports went to Germany (France, UK and Czech Republic are in second place with 6% each), and 22% of Polish imports come from Germany (Russia is in second place with 12%) (*Fischer Weltalmanach* 2013: 368). There has also been intensive economic migration and commuting, more from Poland to Germany than vice versa, since the lifting of employment restrictions for countries recently joining the EU on 1 May 2004. In addition to a long tradition, there are therefore instrumental motives for learning German in Poland. "No doubt many people learn German primarily for economic reasons, in other words because they anticipate better job prospects or a better position at work" (F. Grucza 1995: 720, similar comment in Mackiewicz 2014: 103–105). For the present period, however, Sambor Grucza (email 31 March 2014) has claimed: "Most learners of German in Poland are aiming for a job in Poland", rather than in a German-speaking country. For school pupils, there is also an external compulsion to learn German, in the sense of a cause rather than a motive (J.8). Accordingly, when sixth formers (n= 675) were asked why they "started learning German", 58% replied: "I had to choose the language at school" – contrasted with only 27% who said, "I would like to communicate with German-speakers". Only in this case can instrumental, vocational or education-related motives be assumed, possibly together with an integrative motive, e.g. the desire for social integration during a stay in a German-speaking country (Mackiewicz 2013: 29f). More strongly marked motivation towards GFL learning in the west of Poland than in the east (ibid: 32) may be attributable to instrumental rather than integrative motives (cf. Ch. J.8). For the German-(speaking) minority in the west of Poland, in the region of Silesia, which belonged to Germany until 1945, identity-related motives are also conceivable (Ch. J.8). There are still traces of German as a native language (GNL) there, but among the younger generation, only as a second native language (Ch. E.4.4). But the present chapter is concerned only with GFL. In this context, the motivational impact of attitudes towards Germans and Germany is less easy to explain. It is still characterised by the history of oppression associated with Prussia, Austria and subsequently with Germany: from the partition of Poland at the end of the eighteenth century to the end of WWII, interrupted only by the inter-war years (F. Grucza 1995: 717–719; 2001: 1529f., 2014: 14–17; Ch. E.4.4, beginning). After 1945, this was followed by a much shorter period of suppression of everything German. But the Polish image of Germany also has positive aspects, including much which is considered stereotypical of Prussian "principles", e.g. "order" (F. Grucza 2014: 27). In general, relations between Poland and Germany have improved in recent history, although not to the same extent as those between France and Germany (Ch. E.4.3; J.9.2).

For historical, political and economic reasons, linguistic relations are also less symmetrical than those between France and Germany, to the extent that Polish is learnt significantly less in the German-speaking countries than German in Poland. Efforts on both sides have only managed to mitigate this asymmetry but not to remove it. One example of successful mutuality is the *Europa-Universität Viadrina* in Frankfurt an der Oder, which offers German-language and Polish-language degree programmes. However, it is noteworthy that English-language degree programmes are also offered there (as throughout Europe; Ammon/ McConnell 2002), which shows that English is still the most-learnt foreign language in Poland (as in Germany and worldwide). Nevertheless, German is the second most frequently learnt foreign language in Poland.

One important support for GFL was the introduction of a second compulsory foreign language in grammar schools starting in the school year 2009/10 – corresponding to the EU education target for all citizens: "native language +2 [foreign languages]" (see Kruse 2012). "Even in the first school year after the expansion of compulsory foreign-language learning, the number of learners of German in grammar schools increased by more than 48% [. . .]" (Mackiewicz 2013: 24). However, it has not been possible to resist the trend for German to lose ground to English (ibid: 25f.; F. Grucza 2014: 23f.). Nevertheless, Poland recently became the country with most GFL learners: 2,288,125 ("Total learners of German" in Auswärtiges Amt 2015: 16, 21), ahead of the UK (1,547,994; ibid: 13) and the Russian Federation with 1,546,062 (ibid: 16, 25), which previously occupied first position. Despite the Nazi atrocities, German began to be learnt again soon after 1945. In the 1980s, there were reports such as "German language is in demand again in Poland. 200,000 school pupils are learning German as an optional language of the West" (Oschlies 1982), and again an "Olympics for German in Poland" (Orlowski 1988). The sovereignty of Poland after the dissolution of the Soviet Union and after joining the EU have accelerated these developments. At the beginning of the period, English, German and Russian 1995: 723f., 2001: 1534f.). For the period 1993–1996, Table J.9.5–1 shows an increase of German, English and French, and the decline of Russian in all types of school at secondary level.

Table J.9.5–1 Foreign-language learners in schools in Poland in thousands, 1993 and 1996

	General grammar schools				Specialist grammar schools				Vocational schools			
	G	E	R	F	G	E	R	F	G	E	R	F
1993	334	421	274	118	332	280	178	47	115	56	512	11
1996	420	579	223	127	386	405	130	56	134	67	408	12

Note: G = German, E = English, R = Russian, F = French

(*Source*: F. Grucza et al. 1999: 125)

Table J.9.5–2 Learners of German and Germanists in Polish schools and universities from 1985–2015

	1985	1995	2000	2005	2010	2015
Schools	453,000	780,500	[2,131,781]	2,194,000	2,328,940	2,139,070
Universities: Learners of German and Germanists	22,267	85,751	n.d.	n.d.	16,540	96,555
Of which Germanists	2,267	9,266	n.d.	14,300	n.d.	n.d.

(*Sources for 1985 and 1995*: Goethe-Institut 2000: [173]; for 2000 and 2005: StADaF 2005: 13; for 2010: Netzwerk Deutsch 2010: 10; Auswärtiges Amt 2015: 16)

However, in vocational schools, German and especially Russian rank ahead of English, because of language requirements in non-academic sectors and possibly also because teachers of Russian must still be employed (email Mackiewicz 6 April 2014). The fact that German is still behind English but ahead of French shows that economic benefits can motivate more strongly to learn a foreign language than political friendship, since Poland's relationship with France has a longer tradition than its friendship with Germany. The development of the figures for GFL learners and students of German Language and Literature over the years is shown in Table J.9.5–2.

The figures are estimates. Comparability against time is impaired by the variability of the terms. In Table J.9.5–2, I have subsumed under the heading "Schools": "School pupils learning German in secondary schools" (Goethe-Institut 2000) and "GFL learners in schools" (StADaF 2005; Auswärtiges Amt 2015). The heading "Universities: Learners of German and Germanists (definition Ch. J.9.3, below Table J.9.3–2) subsumes the sum of "Number of students of German Language and Literature" + "Number of participants in academic language courses (both data Goethe-Institut 2000); "Total students of German" (StADaF 2005); "Students learning German" (Auswärtiges Amt 2015). The Germanists are not always listed separately in the sources. The figure in square brackets reflects the fact that the source for 2005 indicates the difference from the unnamed figure for "GFL learners in schools" in 2000 as "62,219".

Despite questionable accuracy, it is evident that the figures in schools have risen markedly, with a slight decline in recent years – whereas, in universities, a recent sharp increase is particularly noticeable. The high figures in schools are co-determined by the fact that learning German is compulsory. For example, in the school year 2011/2012, approximately 1,869,000 school pupils learning German (38.9%) were registered within the compulsory GFL instruction (ORE 2013: 4). Beyond this, the motive for choosing GFL was certainly more practical, vocational rather than academic. This fits with the "territorial distribution of learners of German; German is naturally chosen most frequently in the western regions of Poland, especially at the Polish-German border" (F. Grucza 2010: 1761), where, in the region around Opole/*Oppeln* in Upper Silesia, it is sometimes difficult to distinguish between GFL and GNL (second native language).

Vocational motives contribute to the fact that GFL "is also offered in many extracurricular facilities", but that this "is difficult to register statistically" (F. Grucza 2010: 1761, 2014: 24). A long-term overview of participation in the Goethe Institutes shows the following development, taking Krakau and Warsaw together (P = course participants, E = examinations). 1990: P – 0, E – 0; 2000: P – 2,529, E – 1,145; 2005: P – 2,834, E – 628; 2010: P – 2,600, E – 534; 2012: P – 2,857, E – 66; 2013: P – 2,930, E – 864 (information from Ingrid Köster and Herbert Moosbauer, *Goethe-Institut*, Munich). In 1990, there were, so far, no courses available. After that, the overarching trend is stable, with a rise in recent years. The development of German Language and Literature deserves separate consideration (details in F. Grucza 2001: 1535–1542). During the Prussian period (from the 18th century), Polish people hardly ever occupied professorial chairs in German Language and Literature, but after 1918, they gained access to additionally established professorships. Links with this tradition, which had been interrupted by the Nazis, were re-established after 1945; but further development was not possible until the post-Stalin era, after 1956. Developments beyond literature studies included the establishment of linguistics and then translation studies, regional studies and pedagogy, orientated towards GFL and even GNL teaching ("a five-part concept of German Language and Literature"). But even today, the subject, especially teacher training and the appointment of teachers, suffers from financial difficulties (ibid: 1540–1542; for more recent developments in German Language and Literature see F. Grucza 2010: 1763–1765).

GFL and German Language and Literature are supported by the German-speaking countries, primarily Germany. After the dissolution of the Soviet Union, extensive further training measures for German teachers were "often supported by German funding" (Mackiewicz 2013: 25). In the Goethe-Institut project "*Deutsch-Wagen-Tour*" [German Roadshow], special vehicles full of interesting language-teaching resources visited schools around Poland (and similarly in France) to promote the learning of German (Mackiewicz 2013). The project seems to have been successful, because 58% of school pupils questioned after the first cycle indicated that they now "enjoyed learning German more" (ibid: 34). Two Goethe Institutes (in Warsaw and Kraków) and the Goethe Centre in Lublin took part in the GFL promotion, as did three Austria Institutes (Warsaw, Kraków and *Breslau*/Wrocław), the German School Abroad in Warsaw and 94 DSD schools (offering the German *Sprachdiplom*). Added to this, German lectors in Poland have been financed by the German Academic Exchange Service (DAAD), and there are grants for Polish and German students and guest lecturers, grants from the Alexander von Humboldt Foundation for visits by Polish lecturers to Germany and financial support for events, including conferences, promoting German. These include contributions from Austria and Switzerland. The *Polish German Teachers' Association* (PSNJN), which is a member of the *International German Teachers' Association* (IDV), the *Association of Polish Germanists* (VPG) (Czarnecki 2004: 47) and the large membership numbers of Polish Germanists in the *International Association for Germanic Studies* (IVG) all deserve mention here. Warsaw Germanist Franciszek Grucza was president of the IVG from 2005 to 2010 and organised its World Congress in 2010 in Warsaw.

9.6 Russia (Russian Federation)

This chapter has been checked and amplified by Dirk Kemper (Russian State University for Humanities Moscow/RGGU) and Natalia Troshina (Institute for Humanities at the Academy of Sciences of Russia, Moscow). Other sources included Domaschnew 2001; Dobrovolśkij 2004, 2008; Dubinin 2005; Troshina 2004, 2010, 2011, 2013; Kemper 2011; Voronina 2011; Perfilowa 2011; Titkova 2011; Kostrova 2011; Alexkseeva 2011; Guseynova 2011; Martynova 2011, 2012; Radtschenko 2011a, b; Baur/ Chlosta/ Wenderoff 2000; Baur/ Bampoija/ Schymicik 2011a, b. In summary, the Russian Federation's economic relations with Germany are closer than with any country other than China and the Netherlands (12% of Russian imports (China 16%), 7% of exports (the Netherlands 12%, China 7%) in 2011; *Fischer Weltalmanach* 2013: 377); Germany imports valuable raw materials from Russia, especially natural gas. The official name of the state "Russian Federation" gives consideration to the approximately 100 ethnic minorities (de. wikipedia.org/wiki/Russland#V.C3.B6lker_und_Sprachen), which include a German minority, for whom German was traditionally their native language (Ch. E.4.8), but this minority has dwindled through emigration.

Learning German as a foreign language (GFL) has a long tradition in Russia (Perfilowa 2011; Dubinin 2005); in recent history, Russia had the largest number of GFL learners worldwide, until

Poland took over this position (Netzwerk Deutsch 2010; Ch. J.9.5). German was promoted by the Soviet Union as the language of the GDR, which was faithful to party principles and economically and technically comparatively flourishing; German was also in competition with English which was taken as a symbol of capitalism. Based on one quotation from the 1950s, 60% of university foreign-language teaching was said to have been devoted to English, 20% to German and a further 20% to other languages, including French (as today, in Belorussia). Around the turn-of-the-century, Anatoli Domaschnew (2001: 1557) contrasted complaints about the decline of GFL, which were widespread elsewhere, with the "stability of the position of German as a school subject" and the "general interest in the German language" in Russia. However, as is the case worldwide, English then became the dominant foreign language (Dobrovolśkij 2004: 67).

Nevertheless, German continues to hold second place – although there is a wide margin. Maintaining this position relies on the fact that schools offer a second foreign language, and, for a time, this seemed to be compulsory at least in state schools (Perfilowa 2011: 153; Ammon/ Kemper 2011: 12). However, recent Russian legislation on schooling (applicable since 2013) contains only a corresponding recommendation, without any obligation. Furthermore, the choice of foreign languages is left to school management (Tatjuana Egorowa, Goethe-Institut Moscow, email 4 April 2014). In fact, German can still be chosen as the first foreign language in many schools, although school pupils overwhelmingly prefer English. German still has a respectable position as a second foreign language, which is supported by the economic conditions in the German-speaking countries; but the considerable decline is unmistakable. Table J.9.6–1 provides an overview.

The figures are estimates. Comparability over the years is impaired by the variability of the terms. In Table J.9.6–1, I have subsumed under the heading "Schools": "School pupils learning German in secondary schools" (Goethe-Institut 2000) and "GFL learners in schools" (StADaF 2005; Auswärtiges Amt 2015). The heading "Universities: Learners of German and Germanists (definition Ch. J.9.3, below Table J.9.3–2) subsumes the sum of "Number of students of German Language and Literature" + "Number of participants in academic language courses (both data Goethe-Institut 2000), "Total students of German" (StADaF 2005), "Total students learning German" (Netzwerk Deutsch 2010), "Students learning German" (Auswärtiges Amt 2015). The Germanists are not always listed separately in the sources. The figures for students of German Language and Literature are presumably contained within the figures for "Universities: Learners of German and Germanists" (definition Ch. J.9.3, below Table J.9.3–2). The figures in the square brackets reflect the fact that the source for 2005 indicates the difference from the figure for "GFL learners in schools" in 2000 as "1,427,828" and "Total learners of German in universities" as "132,500".

Despite the inaccuracy, there is no doubt about the consistent, strong decline in these figures. For schools, the figures for shorter, more recent periods also confirm this, e.g. the GFL school

Table J.9.6–1 Learners of German and Germanists in Russian schools and universities from 1985–2015

	1985	*1995*	*2000*	*2005*	*2010*	*2015*
Schools	9,200,000	3,868,969	[4,000,000]	2,572,172	1,612,512	1,129,018
Universities: Learners of German and Germanists	185,000	1,371,882	[617,500]	750,000	700,000	400,000
Of which Germanists	n.d.	n.d.	n.d.	14,300	n.d.	n.d.

(*Sources for 1985 and 1995*: Goethe-Institut 2000: [173]; for 2000 and 2005: StADaF 2005: 13; for 2010: Netzwerk Deutsch 2010: 10; Auswärtiges Amt 2015: 16)

Table J.9.6–2 GFL school leavers from different types of school (based on Troshina 2010: 1777)

	General schools	Schools with extended GFL teaching	Grammar schools	Lycées	Σ
School year 2006/7	382,133	4,993	4,058	1,069	392,253
School year 2007/8	309,280	5,461	3,493	711	318,945

Table J.9.6–3 Participants in courses and in examinations in Goethe Institutes in Russia from 1990–2013 (information from Ingrid Köster and Herbert Moosbauer, Goethe-Institut, Munich)

	1990	1995	2000	2005	2010	2011	2012	2013
Course participants	0	1,279	2,733	5,221	7,089	7,364	7,673	8007
Examinees	0	140	227	323	2,343	2,981	3,398	4,093

leavers from different types of school (e.g. from 2006/7 to 2007/8; Table J.9.6–2). However, a quantitative decline does not always correspond to a qualitative decline, because it has often reduced several years of ineffective instruction. Where German has a vocational function or provides qualifications for further study, demand and level of education remain high. For universities, a considerable proportion relates to German teaching alongside other studies. Presumably, the institutions were grouped differently for the counts in 1985 and 1995, so that the decline in the schools seems exaggerated.

Nevertheless, complaints are still heard from the universities about a deterioration of German-language skills among school leavers, who must attend extension courses in German, often outside university. While German has almost completely lost its position as an international academic language, it has recently become more "in-demand" for study visits to German universities. The shift from the severely depleted German Language and Literature to learning German as a subsidiary alongside other studies is evident here (cf. Ch. J.4). Regarding extracurricular/extra mural learning of German (without Goethe Institutes), only the figure for 1995 is available: 530 participants (Goethe-Institut 2000: [173]). Olga Kostrova (2011) describes a wide range of private language schools. These resemble the "European adult-education colleges" (*Volkshochschule* VHS) and are used in "preparation for study abroad or for the unified state examination, preschool development, professional career, tourism and the quest for identity" (ibid: 241); however, Kostrova does not give learner numbers. Presumably, the extracurricular/extramural learning of German (without Goethe Institutes) has developed approximately parallel to the learning of German in Goethe Institutes. Table J.9.6–3 shows the combined figures for all Goethe Institutes in Russia. However, during the entire period, only the two institutes in Moscow and St Petersburg offered courses and examinations, but not the third Institute in Novosibirsk. The figures show a steady rise over the whole period from 1995 to 2013. Although the figures are modest, they do show a continuing interest in German – by contrast with the over-pessimistic statements about the future of GFL in Russia which are sometimes heard.

There are evidently still instrumental motives for choosing GFL orientated towards professional careers and corresponding to the Goethe-Institut slogan created by Jutta Limbach: "English is a must, German is a plus!". In many professions, a knowledge of German represents an additional qualification (Titkova 2011; Martynova 2011, 2012); further evidence is provided by various in-company German-teaching facilities in Russia (Troshina 2011). With German as a second foreign language, school pupils and students can hope for improved career opportunities (Vornonina 2011; Radschenko 2011a; Ch. F.6), also based on special training, e.g. for translators (Alekseeva 2011).

In view of such demand, German teaching has also been modernised in pedagogical and methodological terms (Perfilowa 2011) – although many promising approaches, e.g. bilingual learning in schools or specialist German-language instruction in universities (Baur/ Chlosta/ Wenderoff 2000 and respectively Baur/ Mamporija/ Schymicik 2011a, b) have often not been adopted in practice. Linguistics and GFL form the core of German Studies understood in this way (Troshina 2010: 1780; Dobrovolśkij 2008: 48), often under the label "Intercultural Communication". Literary studies are often located in different institutes or under different professorships (e.g. professorships for world literature) and often have an explicit or implicit comparative orientation (Kemper 2011). As a reaction to the separation of research (Academy) and teaching (University) which has been lifted since the 1990s, dissertations in linguistics and in literary studies have a tendency towards scientification and internationalisation. Empirical investigations would be desirable in this context.

In Russia also, GFL and German Language and Literature are supported by the German-speaking countries, primarily Germany (Ammon 2011d). In addition to the three Goethe Institutes in the country (Ebert 2011), there are: the Austrian Cultural Forum (Gerschner 2011); the German-Russian Centres, especially the German-Russian Centre in Moscow, which also serves the German minority (Troshina 2010: 1775f.); 2 German Schools Abroad (Moscow, St Petersburg) and 90 DSD schools (offering the German *Sprachdiplom*); the German Academic Exchange Service (DAAD) (Berghorn 2011) with a relatively large number of lectorships and grants for Russian and German students and guest lecturers; the Alexander von Humboldt Foundation (Radschenko 2011b), which allows contacts between German and Russian academics and visits to Germany and provides financial support for German-promoting events, including conferences, to which Austria and Switzerland also contribute. Added to these are the organisational and marketing activities of the Russian Association of Germanists and German Teachers (Guseynova 2011), which, together with its ten federal associations, is a member of the International German Teachers Association (IDV; www.idvnetz.org/verbaende_weltweit/ verbaende_weltweit.htm), and of the Russian Association of Germanists (Belobratow 2011).

9.7 Turkey

This chapter has been checked and amplified by Feruzan Gündoğar (Akdoğan) (Marmara-University) and Nilüfer Tapan (University of Istanbul). Other sources included Knöß 1986; Emmert 1987; Tapan 1996, 2001, 2002, 2004, 2010; Torgay 1997; Balci 1997; Polat/ Tapan 2003; Polat 2004; Kuruyazıcı 2004; Ozil 2004; Ülkü 2004; Akdoğan 2003, 2004, 2008. Turkey's economic relations with the German-speaking countries are close, closer with Germany than with any other country. In 2011, 10% of Turkish exports went to Germany, more than to any other country, and 10% of Turkish imports came from Germany (a similar volume of 10% was imported only from Russia; *Fischer Weltalmanach* 2013: 469). Added to these aspects are close personal connections based on the extensive migration from Turkey to Germany: "most of the 15.96 million people with a migration background originate from Turkey (18.5%), followed by Poland (9.2%) and Russia (7.7%)" (www.bpb.de/nachschlagen/zahlen-und-fakten/soziale-situation-in-deutschlan d/61646/migrationshintergrund-i). Many of these immigrants are second-language speakers of German (Ch. A.3), or their children have become SL-German speakers (Ch. C.1). Approximately 3 million people of Turkish origin live in Germany, and approximately 2 million, with descendants up to 5 million (Ch. E.5), have returned to Turkey.

These migrations and continuing connections also have an impact on the teaching of GFL in Turkey (Tapan 2001: 1567–1570, 2010: 1818). One consequence is that, in many Turkish universities, students with very poor knowledge of German sit side-by-side with students with almost native-language German skills (Ozil 2004: 271). For a short time, there were reintegration schools with German as a language of instruction in some subjects (Emmert 1987: 67). These were then transformed into the so-called "Andolus foreign-language specialist schools". This development has contributed to making German the second most important foreign language in Turkey behind English but ahead of French, which was more prominent until the 1980s (Knöß 1986: 241; Emmert 1987: 64). German serves the numerous business connections between Turkey and the German-speaking countries as well as tourism, especially from Germany (Balci 1997: 621; Torgay 1997). For a time, remigration covered the demand for German-language skills, which, on occasion, brought the subject GFL into crisis and caused difficulties for German teachers, but this situation has since been moderated (Balci 1997; Tapan 2010: 1821f.). Nowadays, instrumental motives related to study and vocation are key for the choice of GFL. However, integrative motives also play a role for the descendants of family members in the German-speaking countries. For returners from Germany who are sometimes referred to as "*Deutschländer*" identity-related motives may also be involved (cf. Ch. J.8). By contrast, the continuation of an academic tradition, which had been strengthened by German university teachers fleeing from Nazism to Turkey in 1933, is rather modest. These academics made an important contribution to the foundation of new universities in Istanbul and Ankara and to the development of German Language and Literature in Turkey (Kuruyazici 2004; Emmert 1987: 61f.). At that time, lectures were often delivered in German. By contrast, present-day universities with German-language degree programmes are innovative institutions which do not draw on this tradition: the *Marmara University* with teaching provision in four languages (Turkish, English, German, French), 14 sites and 103 degree programmes, and the *Turkish-German University in Istanbul*, which is presently being set up with five faculties (de.wikipedia.org/wiki/Marmara-Universit%C3%A4t;de.wikipe dia.org/wiki/T%C3%BCrkisch-Deutsche_Universit%C3%A4t).

However, it is the schools which form the broad basis for GFL in Turkey. At least, the old tradition of the *Deutsche Schule* and the Austrian *St.-Georgs-Gymnasium*, founded in 1886 and respectively 1889 in Istanbul, was orientated primarily towards German as a native language. GFL only came into being later. The school reform of 1997 was decisive for the present-day situation (Tapan 2010: 1817–1821; for historical conditions, see Emmert 1987). This reform was modified in 2011. The reform made foreign-language teaching in state-run schools generally compulsory from the fourth year of schooling at primary level. At secondary level, a second foreign language is added as an option in state-run grammar schools; it is compulsory in the "Anadolu-grammar schools (*Anadolu Liseleri*) with a focus on foreign languages". In both cases, English, German and French are elective subjects, which means that, especially at primary level, almost all school pupils choose English – apart from a few private schools which offer German as the first foreign language from the first year of schooling. These are, in fact, limited to major cities, and there are very few of them, but they are very much in demand because of the quality of instruction and the strong focus on German teaching. The German Schools Abroad (one in Ankara, three in Istanbul), which design their curriculum more freely, are a special case. The Anadolu grammar schools with German as the first foreign language, of which there are 30 nationwide, therefore play an important part. For most, German is indeed the main foreign language with a large number of teaching hours, but German is a language of instruction only in 12 of these schools (of course, with a Turkish curriculum and compulsory knowledge of Turkish). Support from Germany includes the provision of teachers. Turkey's efforts to join the EU played a role in expanding foreign-language instruction to include a

Table J.9.7–1 Learners of German and Germanists in Turkish schools and universities from 1985–2015

	1985	1995	2000	2005	2010	2015
Schools	280,000	80,000	[225,000]	260,000	309,069	450,000
Universities: Learners of German and Germanists	2,500	7,412	[34,450]	20,000	7,691	8,705
Of which Germanists	1,000	6,142	n.d.	3,000	n.d.	n.d.

(*Sources for 1985 and 1995*: Goethe-Institut 2000: [175]; for 2000 and 2005: StADaF 2005: 15; for 2010: Netzwerk Deutsch 2010: 12; Auswärtiges Amt 2015: 17)

second foreign language, in line with the educational goal recommended for all EU citizens of: "native language +2 [foreign languages]" (Kruse 2012). Pupil numbers indicate the position of the three most important foreign languages in Turkey. In the school year 2007/8, they were distributed as follows in primary//secondary level: English 6,392,318// 2,530,286 – German 33,060//258,089 – French 9,382//22,580 (Tapan 2010: 1819). Table J.9.7–1 shows the long-term development for GFL and German Language and Literature (somewhat older figures with gaps can be found in Knöß 1986.

The figures are estimates. Comparability over the years is impaired by the variability of the terms. In Table J.9.7–1, I have subsumed under the heading "Schools": "School pupils learning German in secondary schools" (Goethe-Institut 2000) and "GFL learners in schools" (StADaF 2005; Auswärtiges Amt 2015). The heading "Universities: Learners of German and Germanists (definition Ch. J.9.3, below Table J.9.3–2) subsumes the sum of "Number of students of German Language and Literature" + "Number of participants in academic language courses (both data Goethe-Institut 2000); "Total students of German" (StADaF 2005); "Total students learning German" (Netzwerk Deutsch 2010); "Students learning German" (Auswärtiges Amt 2015). The Germanists are only occasionally listed separately in the sources. The figures in the square brackets reflect the fact that the source for 2005 indicates the difference from the figure for "GFL learners in schools" in 2000 as "35,000" and "Total learners of German in universities" as "14,450".

Despite questionable accuracy, an overarching upward trend for schools and universities is evident. The downturn in schools from 1985 to 1995 may have been determined by remigration, because returners with good German-language skills saw no need for additional German instruction. The large numbers in schools compared with universities and the growth – although the evidence for this is weak – of mere learners of academic German by contrast with Germanists suggest practical interests rather than scholarly or scientific interests, which would correspond with the intensive business relations between Turkey and Germany. Instrumental, vocational motives have also presumably enlivened GFL learning in extracurricular/extramural facilities. Figures without the Goethe Institutes are available for 1985: 4,100, 1995: 2,000 (Goethe-Institut 2000: [175]) and 2005: 8,000 (StADaF 2005: 15). Participation in the Goethe Institutes developed as follows, in a long-term overview: Ankara, Istanbul and Izmir taken together (P = course participants, E = examinations): 1990: P – 13,084, E – 668; 2000: P – 9,729, E – 133; 2012: P – 8,261, E – 12,847; 2013: P – 9,420, E – 11,811 (information from Ingrid Köster and Herbert Moosbauer, Goethe-Institut, Munich). The overarching trend is a slight decline in participants, but recently a significant increase in examinations. Certification of German-language skills is therefore valued, which may be linked with intentions to study in German-speaking countries or vocational plans. One important step forward for GFL in Turkey is the modernisation of teacher training, not least for German as a second foreign language (behind English), which may be orientated towards the country's attempt to obtain membership of the EU. Accordingly, the training of GFL teachers in Turkey has presently attained an international level. There are several thorough accounts of this (Akdoğan 2003, 2004, 2007; Polat 2004; Tapan 2004; Polat/ Tapan 2003). In conjunction with the improvement of training, the teaching profession has also become more attractive (Ülkü 2004: 83f.). In universities, there are different professorial chairs for German Language and Literature and the training of German teachers.

In Turkey also, GFL and German Language and Literature are supported by the German-speaking countries, primarily Germany. One tradition-rich institution is the Austrian grammar school *St. Georgs-Kolleg* in Istanbul (de.wikipedia.org/wiki/St._Georgs-Kolleg; Emmert 1987: 61). From the German side, the three Goethe Institutes are important, as are the four German Schools Abroad (one in Ankara, three in Istanbul) and 17 DSD schools (offering the German *Sprachdiplom*). The German Academic Exchange Service (DAAD) funds lectors from Germany and grants for Turkish and German students and guest lecturers. The Alexander von Humboldt Foundation supports visits to Germany by Turkish lecturers. Added to these measures, there is funding for events promoting German, including conferences, to which Austria and Switzerland also contribute. Local organisations play an important role in promoting GFL and German Language and Literature: the *Turkish Association of German Teachers* (TAÖD), which is a member of the International German Teachers Association (IDV), and the Turkish Germanists' Association (GERDER), with numerous members in the *International Association for Germanic Studies* (IVG). Both associations issue regular publications and organise conferences.

9.8 Egypt

This chapter has been checked and amplified by Imam Shalabi (Ain-Shams-University, Cairo) and Julia Wolbergs (DAAD, Cairo). Other sources included Aref 1983/ 84; Gottzmann 1984; Rau 1986; Arras 2001; Böhm 2003: 182–197; M. Maher 2008 and Khattab 2010. Egypt fosters close economic relations with the German-speaking countries. In 2011, 8% of Egyptian imports came from Germany (more goods were imported only from the USA and China, 9% each); however, regarding exports, some six countries are ahead of Germany (*Fischer Weltalmanach* 2013: 26). Political uncertainty has inhibited tourism from the German-speaking countries which used to be intensive; significant instrumental motives for learning GFL were associated with this (Arras 2001: 1607).

The sole official language of Egypt is Arabic. The variety of Egyptian Arabic spoken in Egypt is understood in all Arabic countries; alongside this, High (*Qur'anic*) Arabic functions as a written language. Among the educated social strata, French and increasingly English are widespread as foreign languages (Böhm 2003: 185). GFL is subordinate to these two foreign languages and restricted to a few institutions. One of these is the *Deutsche Universität in Kairo*, opened in 2003, which is generally advertised as the *German University Cairo (GUC)*: "The language of instruction is English, but courses in the German-Learning Centre of the GUC are compulsory for all students" (www.daad.de /hochschulen/hochschul projekte-ausland/hochschulen-ausland/18489.de.htm). Accordingly, all 7,500 students acquire German-language skills. This is compulsory up to competence level A2 of the Common European Reference Framework (Quetz 2002) and voluntary beyond this level. In schools, GFL has a long history, although it is institutionally limited. The oldest evidence of this history is interesting because of the designation as "*österreichische Sprache*" (*al-Lugha en-nimsayewa*, instead of *deutsche Sprache* (Khattab 2010: 1603). At the time, in 1863, Austria was still the leading power in the movement for German unification, before it was pushed out in 1866 in the battle at *Königgrätz* (Czech: *Hradec Králové*) (for the linguistic consequences, see Ammon 1995a: 120f.). There has been a continuous tradition of German teaching since the late nineteenth century and early twentieth century, and in fact in the *Deutsche Schulen der Borromäerinnen (DSB)*, in Alexandria (since 1884), in Cairo (since 1904), and in the *Deutsche Evangelische Oberschule (DEO)* in Cairo, which are among the eight German Schools Abroad. They are simultaneously partner schools (PASCH-schools), supervised by the Central Office for Schools Abroad (ZfA). Added to these are the three German-Language-Diploma-Schools (DSD schools) and 18 FIT schools (subject specific, for individualised, specialist training), both groups are supervised by the Goethe-Institut (Ch. J.3). Furthermore, since 1957 (Aref 1983/ 84:44), German has been introduced gradually in many schools as a second foreign language, ranking behind English and as an alternative to French. In the school year 1997/98, these included 211 public sector and 40 private sector schools (Arras 2001: 1604). I was not able to verify these figures in 2014. The DAAD office in Cairo sent me the following information (email 7 April 2014, content abbreviated):

> In normal state-run schools, English is a compulsory subject from Class 6. A second foreign language is also compulsory from Class 10; generally, as an elective between French or German. In other schools offering general education (including experimental schools, low-cost public-sector elite schools and so on), foreign-language teaching often begins in Class 1 with English or French, and the second foreign language is introduced in Class 4, and also includes German. In private schools offering general education, all variants are possible from kindergarten upwards. In the private sector, there is currently a growing demand for German, and in many, German is also offered as the first foreign language.

Six state-run universities also offer degree programmes in German Language and Literature and GFL (Ain Shams, Al-Azhar, Cairo, Minia, Minofeia, Helwan); Ain Shams and Azhar universities are prominent among these. Alongside literature and linguistics, translation and translation studies are important components of research and teaching. At the Azhar University, GFL is integrated into Islamic Studies. During a visit there several years ago, students explained to me the special relevance of a knowledge of German. For them, it is apparently important to explain Islam to German-speakers e.g. by correcting the meaning of *Jihad*. This is not, as often assumed, a "holy war" but rather a "serious effort – along the road towards God". This clearly Islamic motive for learning German has remained obscure to me. Table J.9.8–1 shows the development of the figures over the period 1985–2015.

The figures are estimates. Comparability over the years is impaired by the variability of the terms. In Table J.9.8–1, I have subsumed under the heading "Schools": "School pupils learning

Table J.9.8–1 Learners of German and Germanists in Egyptian schools and universities from 1985–2015

	1985	1995	2000	2005	2010	2015
Schools	9,200	83,600	[100,000]	72,279	100,000	229,420
Universities: Learners of German and Germanists	1,720	7,770	[6,000]	14,369	12,695	12,078
Of which Germanists	1,170	2,400	n.d.	4,937	4,715	n.d.

(*Sources for 1985 and 1995*: Goethe-Institut 2000: [166]; for 2000 and 2005: StADaF 2005: 8; for 2010: Netzwerk Deutsch 2010: 4; for "Germanists" see 2010 Julia Wolbergs (email 31 March 2014); Auswärtiges Amt 2015: 11)

German in secondary schools" (Goethe-Institut 2000) and "GFL learners in schools" (StADaF 2005; Auswärtiges Amt 2015). The heading "Universities: Learners of German and Germanists (definition Ch. J.9.3, below Table J.9.3–2) subsumes the sum of "Number of students of German Language and Literature" + "Number of participants in academic language courses (both data Goethe-Institut 2000); "Total students of German" (StADaF 2005); "Total students learning German" (Netzwerk Deutsch 2010); "Students learning German" (Auswärtiges Amt 2015). The Germanists are not always listed separately in the sources. The figures in the square brackets reflect the fact that the source for 2005 indicates the difference from the figure for "GFL learners in schools" in 2000 as "-27,721" and "Total learners of German in universities" as "8,369".

Despite the questionable accuracy, the figures for schools and universities have evidently risen strongly. Similar figures in Böhm (2003: 186) provide further evidence especially for schools. The development of German Language and Literature could be subject to the following problems: the "course content is no longer appropriate for the present situation in the country [. . .]. With the discontinuation of guaranteed employment in the civil service in 1998, it has become more difficult for graduates of German Language and Literature to find work". In this context, tried and tested approaches are being continued (Gottzmann 1984; Rau 1986): on one hand, towards "methodological/pedagogical questions about the teaching of German as a foreign language" for future teachers and, on the other hand, towards German-language skills, including specialist skills useful in the economy, including tourism, and in academia (Arras 2001: 1606f.). Contradicting this position, there have been warnings against too close a reference to actual life, because, although there are numerous vocational goals: "translator, interpreter, German teacher [. . .], in tourism [. . .], in the press, radio and television [. . .], in the Foreign Ministry [. . .]; one could even become an ambassador", in general, opportunities remain limited (M. Maher 2008: 8). In this context, Maher has called for continuing education towards "intellectual goals" and an appreciation of German literature (ibid: 12–15). Since the winter semester of 2008, a bi-national GFL master degree programme in cooperation with Ain Shams University and the University of Leipzig has been run within the framework of the Bologna process. Other masters degree programmes are being developed at Ain Shams and Azhar Universities in partnership with other German universities.

However, these developments, including the figures for language learners, tend towards the practical direction, driven by instrumental motives. The figures show a sharply rising trend (Table J.9.8–1: fields 1 and 2). This applies less in the case of GFL learners in extracurricular/extramural teaching facilities. For facilities excluding the Goethe Institutes, the figures are as follows, for 1985: 4,150, 1995: 150 (Goethe-Institut 2000: [166]) and 2005: 800 (StADaF 2005: 8). Within the Goethe Institutes, participation has developed as follows, in a long-term overview with Cairo and Alexandria combined (P = course participants, E = examinations): 1990: P – 5,118, E – 253; 2000: P – 5,292, E – 112; 2010: P – 7,455, E – 1,168; 2013: P – 7,105, E – 3,624 (data from Ingrid Köster and Herbert Moosbauer, Goethe-Institut, Munich). In this context, especially the number of examinees shows a rise in interest. At the Goethe Institutes, students' readiness to learn GFL has certainly been slowed down by financial concerns, because the courses are expensive – as in many other places – relative to average earnings in Egypt. Furthermore, government cutbacks have restricted school resources, also with reference to the number and salaries of teachers (Böhm 2003: 184), more recently, this has been intensified by the uncertain political situation.

GFL and German Language and Literature in Egypt are also funded by the German-speaking countries, primarily Germany. In addition to the two Goethe Institutes, there are eight German Schools Abroad, which are also PASCH-schools (two in Alexandria, five in Cairo, one in Hurghada) and another 21 PASCH schools (three DSD schools and 18 FIT schools). Added to these, there are seven DAAD lectorships (including two locally recruited lectorships) and two language assistants, together with extensive individual funding by the DAAD; no less than 2,016 people received awards in 2012, including Egyptian and German students and guest lecturers. Grants from the Alexander von Humboldt Foundation for visits by Egyptian lecturers to Germany and regular financial support for events promoting German, including conferences, also deserve mention. Austria and Switzerland contribute to these funding measures. One recent, successful example was the German teachers' conference at the Goethe-Institut in Cairo on 02.11.2013. The *Egyptian Association of German Teachers*, which is a member of the International Association of German Teachers (IDV) and its numerous activities must also be mentioned. However, Egypt does not have its own association for Germanists.

9.9 South Africa

This chapter has been checked and amplified by Carlotta von Maltzan (University of Stellenbosch) and Kathleen Thorpe (University of the Witwatersrand, Johannesburg). Other sources included Welz 1986; Blumer 1987; Bodenstein 1995; Schmitt 1995; Kußler 2001; Böhm 2003: 589–633; Annas 2004; Laurien 2006; Rode 2008; von Maltzan 2009, 2010; Augart 2012. The Republic of South Africa fosters close economic relations with the German-speaking countries, closer with Germany than with any other European country: 11% of South African imports in 2011 (more came only from China, 14%), 7% of South African exports (more goods are exported to China 14%, USA 10%, Japan 9%) (*Fischer Weltalmanach* 2013: 439). Added to this is the local economic presence: "Some 600 German companies have subsidiaries in South Africa and employ in total more than 90,000 people. Some of these companies are among the most important and advanced production operations in the country" (www.southafrica.diplo.de/ Vertretung/suedafrika/de/06__Wirtschaft/1__Deutschl__Suedafrika/DEU__Firmen.htm). There is therefore a basis for instrumental, vocational motives for learning German as a foreign language (GFL), to which the extensive tourism from the German-speaking countries also contributes (Kußler 2001: 372).

Since the overthrow of racial apartheid in the political revolution of 1994, 11 official languages of state are acknowledged in the constitution, two of European provenance (English, Afrikaans) and nine African languages (von Maltzan 2009: 205; Böhm 2003: 599, 603–606). English is now the most widely distributed language and is learnt in school by almost all inhabitants. In the case of native speakers of other languages X, GFL in school can be ranked only in third place (after X + English). Furthermore, German is less present as a foreign language in the rest of Africa than French and Portuguese; it also competes with languages like Arabic, Spanish, Italian and others (Böhm 2003: 609; von Maltzan 2009; literature references in Augart 2012: 8). Nevertheless, in the constitution, German is expressly claimed as a "language of South Africa"; in addition to the official languages, "a number of other languages are named in the constitution, which are not counted among the national languages, but [. . .] are [e]xplicitly named as worthy of promotion [. . .] (Ch. 1, §6), [namely] German, Greek, Gujarati, Hindi, Portuguese, Tamil, Telugu and Urdu" (von Maltzan 2009: 206). However, the following also applies: "The named languages, including German, are listed only by way of example and represent an open continuum in which, according to the constitution, in principle, every language which is spoken in South Africa can enjoy the status of a South African language worthy of protection" (Laurien 2006: 440). It is questionable whether this nomination of German and its position as a native language have a positive effect on GFL, which could therefore appear less in need of promotion (Kußler 2001: 1615f.; Augart 2012: 11. See also the neighbouring country Namibia, Ch. E.4.9).

There is evidence of German teaching in South Africa only since the first half of the nineteenth century (Kußler 1999: 365). Later, in the wake of apartheid, it was largely limited to schools for "whites" (von Maltzan 2010: 1806), mainly for Afrikaans speakers. Its problematic association with apartheid is evident from the accounts by Welz (1986) and Blumer (1987). Alterations in admission requirements for universities also had a detrimental effect: "The steady decline of GFL began at the end of the 1970s with the abandonment of the so-called third language (after English and Afrikaans) as a condition for university admission" (von Maltzan 2010: 1806). Eckhard Bodenstein (1995: 47) provides evidence for the decline in schools in the period 1989–1992, including the anticipated redistribution of educational resources to schools when the end of apartheid was in sight. This has had a detrimental after-effect on GFL teaching even up to the present. Referencing Bodenstein, Marco Schmidt (1995: 56) of the German General Consulate in Cape Town gave South Africans the following contrasting but slightly exaggerated warning: "[A] language such as German is an asset comparable to computer skills for finding meaningful employment in an economy which will attract ever-increasing German investment". Despite this caution, recent developments have been characterised by a considerable decline in schools and universities, as an after-effect of apartheid (Kußler 1999: 367f., 370) and based on the growing function of English compared with all other languages, including German. Table J.9.9–1 gives an overview of these developments.

The figures are estimates. Comparability over the years is impaired by the variability of the terms. In Table J.9.9–1, I have subsumed under the heading "Schools": "School pupils learning German in secondary schools" (Goethe-Institut 2000) and "GFL learners in schools" (StADaF 2005; Auswärtiges Amt 2015). The heading "Universities: Learners of German and Germanists (definition Ch. J.9.3, below Table J.9.3–2) subsumes the sum of "Number of students of German Language and Literature" + "Number of participants in academic language courses (both data Goethe-Institut 2000); "Total students of German" (StADaF 2005); "Total students learning German" (Netzwerk Deutsch 2010); "Students learning German" (Auswärtiges Amt 2015). The Germanists are not always listed separately in the sources. The figures in square brackets reflect the fact that the source for 2005 indicates the difference from the figure for "GFL learners in schools" in 2000 as "3,400" and "Total learners of German in universities" as "390".

Despite the questionable accuracy, a strong overarching decline is evident. Today, one problem typical for emerging countries and especially for developing countries is the lack of teachers, resulting from the relatively poor pay conditions (Rode 2008). In fact, German-language skills not acquired in school can, in some cases, be supplemented through extracurricular means. In a long-term overview, participation at the Goethe-Institut in Johannesburg and the Goethe Centre in Cape Town, which was opened in 1999, developed as follows (P = course participants, E = examinations): 2000: P – 337, E – 31; 2005: P – 273, E – 18; 2010: P – 0, E – 129; 2011: P – 340, E – 202; 2012: P – 0, E – 182; 2013: P – 422, E – 221 (information from Ingrid Köster and Herbert Moosbauer, Goethe-Institut, Munich). In recent years, so far as can be identified,

Table J.9.9–1 Learners of German and Germanists in South African schools and universities from 1985–2015

	1985	1995	2000	2005	2010	2015
Schools	32,000	11,120	[8,500]	11,900	7,523	7,908
Universities: Learners of German and Germanists	3,009	628	[967]	1,357	1,000	871
Of which Germanists	3,009	628	1999:861	266	n.d.	n.d.

(*Sources for 1985 and 1995*: Goethe-Institut 2000: [174]; for 2000 and 2005: StADaF 2005: 14; for 2010: Netzwerk Deutsch 2010: 11; for Germanists 1883–1999: Böhm 2003: 611; Auswärtiges Amt 2015: 17)

Table J.9.9–2 Student and learner numbers for all degree programmes in three languages at University of Stellenbosch from 1997–2014 (Information from Carlotta von Maltzan)

	1997	2000	2004	2008	2012	2013	2014
German	218	261	258	329	306	316	319
French	155	228	289	337	310	348	366
Chinese	0	19	35	95	110	93	83

the overarching trend for GFL in all institutions taken together is stability or even growth. It is presumably the image of the economic stability of the German-speaking countries, which is nowadays distributed worldwide, which exerts this influence here as elsewhere (e.g. in France and Italy, Ch. J.9.2; J.9.4). Table J.9.9–2 below provides evidence for the stability of demand at the University of Stellenbosch; admittedly, this applies more for French. But the comparison of languages should not be generalised, because Stellenbosch has the largest German department in South Africa and the only remaining professorship for German Language and Literature.

Preliminary losses and redundancies were severe. Especially in German Language and Literature, there was a sharp decline in German learners and students (see Table J.9.9–1) accompanied by cutting back of posts and entire departments (Kußler 2001: 1616; von Maltzan 2009: 211). The adherence of German Language and Literature to traditional literary content may have contributed to this, as suggested by the list of contents in specialist periodicals: *Acta Germanica / German Studies in Africa: Yearbook of the Association of Germanists in South Africa* (from 1966) and also *Deutschunterricht in Südlichen Afrika* (DUSA) (until 1998), which was orientated more closely to school level and is now entitled *Deutschunterricht in Südafrika* (DUSA) and eDUSA in electronic form (www.sagv.org.za/publ_dusa.htm). But the gradual transition to the broader thematic content of German Studies, which is also evident in more recent teaching programmes, is already evident here (Augart 2012: 11–15, 17–19; regarding cutbacks and compensating regional cooperation, see Annas 2004: 186). There appear to be no valid investigations on the motives for the choice of GFL in schools or universities – including German Language and Literature – or on subsequent employment prospects for South Africa. The following motives seem likely: the prospect of employment in subsidiaries of German companies in South Africa; or in South African companies with corresponding business relations; or the desire to study or work for a period in a German-speaking country; no doubt after working in schools and universities and despite limited opportunities.

GFL and German Language and Literature in South Africa are also supported by the German-speaking countries, primarily Germany (Kußler 2001: 369; von Maltzan 2010: 1806). The Goethe-Institut in Johannesburg and the Goethe Centre in Cape Town also play an important part, especially because of their conferences for GFL teachers (www.goethe.de/ins/za/de/joh/acv. cfm?fure action=events.details&event_id=8048937), as do the four German Schools Abroad (Hermannsburg, Johannesburg, Cape Town, Pretoria) and 11 DSD schools (offering the German *Sprachdiplom*). The German diplomatic service also emphasises the following key German funding measures:

German Academic Exchange Service (DAAD), Alexander von Humboldt Foundation (AvH) and German Research Community (DFG) [. . .]. There are more than 90 formalised university-cooperation agreements. Since 1997, the DAAD has operated an information office (consultation about grants) at the Witwatersrand University of

Johannesburg [. . .]. In 2009, the DAAD also issued around 150 grants, including 'Sur-
place' and for study in Germany.

(www.southafrica.diplo.de/Vertretung/suedafrika/de/07_Kultur/Kultur/
Kulturbeziehung_DE_SA.html)

Added to these are the DAAD language assistants in Johannesburg, Cape Town and Stellenbosch. There is support for events promoting the German language, including conferences;
this is also provided by Austria and Switzerland. Finally, the organisational and promotional
activities of the following South African associations: *Germanistenverband im Südlichen Afrika/
Association for German Studies in Southern Africa*, with members in the *International Association for
Germanic Studies* (IVG), and the *Deutsche Pädagogische Vereinigung im Südlichen Afrika*, a member
of the *International Association of German Teachers* (IDV), also make an important contribution
to the promotion of GFL.

9.10 USA

This chapter has been checked and amplified by Monika Chavez (University of Wisconsin,
Madison) and Thomas Lovik (Michigan State University, East Lansing). Other sources included
Gilbert 1971; Arnold 1983; Huffines 1986; Trommler 1986, 1989; Lützeler 1990; Byrnes 1996;
Bister-Broosen/ Good 1997; Hermand 1999; James/ Tschirner 2001; Andress et al. 2002; Lovik
2003, 2004; Louden/ Lovik 2008; Davidheiser/ Wolf 2009; ACTFL 2010; Furman/ Goldberg/
Lusin 2010; Tatlock 2010 and Ecke 2010, 2011. The USA fosters more intensive economic rela-
tions with Germany than with any other European country apart from the UK, but even more
intensive economic relations are maintained with a series of non-European countries: Germany
supplied 5% of US imports in 2011 (18% from China, 14% from Canada, 12% Mexico, 6%
Japan), and received 3% of US exports (Canada 19%, Mexico 13%, China 7%, Japan 5%, UK 4%)
(*Fischer Weltalmanach* 2013: 492). However, motives relating to the economy and corresponding
vocational motives for the choice of German as a foreign language (GFL) seem to play only
a limited role (Hermand 1999: 335). Nevertheless, with reference to her university, Monika
Chavez (email 18 March 2014) explained that "a larger percentage of our students (not majors,
but language learners – although there are some majors among them) come from engineering
or various biosciences. [. . .] Placements [in Germany! U.A.] are certainly a big attraction [. . .];
many advisers insist on their students learning German (so they can also study or work in Germany". Condray (2007) gives an inspiring account of the DAAD programme *Research Internships
in Science and Engineering* (RISE). As an indicator of instrumental motivation, Chavez underlines
the fact that the proportion of men learning German is significantly higher than e.g. for French.
Asian people also seem to prefer German, presumably with a view to employment, but possibly
also because they have become familiar with German in their countries of origin.

Another basis for foreign language choice derives from the long tradition of immigration
from German-speaking countries, although the religious "language islands" (Ch. E.4.11) are
of subordinate significance for GFL. For a considerable time now, "German has been the most
frequently reported category of ancestry in the US", also in the 2005 census, the most recent
census at my disposal (Ecke 2011: 57). The category is based, here, on an ethnic understanding
of "German" associated with the language of origin, which also includes all German-speaking
countries (Ch. B.3; B.4). The number of publications about "Germans" in the USA and their
immigration history is incalculably large, but Gilbert (1971), Huffines (1986) and especially
Trommler (1986) deserve special mention. The large number of immigrants – alongside the
political, economic and academic significance of the German-speaking countries – contributed

to the fact that German was the most learnt foreign language in the USA before WWI (Ch. J.2). In consequence of this war, and ever since, German is now only in third position with a large interval behind Spanish and French. Various findings support the view that ethnic origin continues to have an after-effect on foreign language choice. For example, 59% of GFL school students at high schools (n= 4,711) named "family background" as a reason for their choice of GFL (Andress et al. 2002: 3; Ecke 2011: 56; see Ch. J.8 on the difference between "named reason" and "actual motive"). The *Census Bureau American Community Survey* of 2014 confirms that German is still used relatively frequently as a home language; www.census.gov/acs/www/). In 16 Federal States, German was the third most frequent home language – admittedly considerably behind English and Spanish. Based on speaker numbers throughout the USA, German is also behind Chinese ("*Let's talk Deutsch*", *SZ* 14 May 2014).

In the USA, the language of instruction in all schools and universities is specified by law. It is generally English, apart from exceptions, such as religious minorities. But the choice of languages offered as school subjects is largely at the discretion of individual institutions. This depends mainly on demand, e.g. from parents, pupils and students. Table J.9.10–1 summarises the development of these figures. It can be assumed that the figures for "Universities: Learners of German and Germanists" and "Of which Germanists" have become muddled in the sources for 1985 and 1995. However, if this and other gaps are disregarded, the figures do agree with the other data. This applies especially for the growth of GFL in schools in the early 1990s.

The figures are estimates. Comparability over the years is impaired by the variability of the terms. In Table J.9.10–1, I have subsumed under the heading "Schools": "School pupils learning German in secondary schools" (Goethe-Institut 2000) and "GFL learners in schools" (StADaF 2005; Auswärtiges Amt 2015). The heading "Universities: Learners of German and Germanists (definition Ch. J.9.3, below Table J.9.3–2) subsumes the sum of "Number of students of German Language and Literature" + "Number of participants in academic language courses (both data Goethe-Institut 2000); "Total students of German" (StADaF 2005); "Total students learning German" (Netzwerk Deutsch 2010); "Students learning German" (Auswärtiges Amt 2015). Since the data for "Number of participants in academic language courses" are missing for 1995, I have used the "Number of students of German Language and Literature" for "Universities: Total learners of German". Germanists are not always listed separately in the sources. The figures in square brackets reflect the fact that the source for 2005 indicates the difference from the figure for "GFL learners in schools" in 2000 as "-40,239" and "Total learners of German in universities" as "2,080".

The increase after the reunification of Germany was followed by a decline (see Lovik 2003: 26f., 2004: 97f.; James/ Tschirner 2001: 1425) and, more recently, another – modest – "upward trend" (Ecke 2011: 62; Louden/ Lovik 2008: 75f.). This is confirmed by the *American Council on the Teaching of Foreign Languages* (ACTFL 2010: 8). Furman/ Goldberg/ Lusin (2010: 3, 11)

Table J.9.10–1 Learners of German and Germanists in US schools and universities from 1985–2015

	1985	*1995*	*2000*	*2005*	*2010*	*2015*
Schools	319,913	415,000	[373,234]	332,995	400,000	400,000
Universities: Learners of German and Germanists	151,000	108,263	[89,020]	91,100	94,265	96,349
Of which Germanists	1,000	108,263	n.d.	7,000	n.d.	n.d.

(*Sources for 1985 and 1995*: Goethe-Institut 2000: [175]; for 2000 and 2005: StADaF 2005: 15; for 2010: Netzwerk Deutsch 2010: 12; Auswärtiges Amt 2015: 18)

also found a "modest gain" for GFL of 2.2% in universities in 2009 (compared with the year before). This may be an indication of the importance of guarding the "flame" kindled in the high schools and carrying it to the universities (Davidheiser/ Wolf 2009). Apart from the three leading foreign languages, Spanish, French and German, isolated other languages have also made gains recently, especially Chinese, but overall, based on learner numbers, these languages are still in the background.

Ultimately, despite various attempts (Condray 2007; Chavez, start of this chapter), what GFL lacks here is the spark of instrumental motivation. One survey of learners of German in universities in North Carolina showed a diversity of reasons for their language choice (Bister-Broosen/ Good: 55), the most frequent were "travel", with "German origins" at 12.5%. Regarding the weakness of instrumental motives, the USA resembles other countries which are geographically remote from the German-speaking countries and economically and technologically highly developed (e.g. Japan, Ch. J.9.14). The motive of wanting to study or work in a German-speaking country plays a less important role. In this context, Germany is only seventh in priority, behind the UK, Italy, Spain, France, China and Australia (Ecke 2011: 65). However, "study abroad" itself has multiple motives. Presumably, the image of English as a world lingua franca, with which people believe they can communicate successfully everywhere (see Ch. A.7), and which is also distributed in other English-speaking countries, such as the UK and Australia (Ch. J.9.3; J.9.15), is even more damaging to the instrumental motives for learning foreign languages, especially GFL. Here as elsewhere, this assessment may be exaggerated, but is not entirely false – as shown e.g. by the language choice of subsidiaries of German companies in the USA.

Tradition, the quest for ethnic origins or identity, the culture associated with the German language (as in Japan and Australia) and, not least, trends in fashion, play a role in the choice of GFL alongside or instead of instrumental motives. The recent moderate upturn may have been favoured by the fact that the image of Germany and the German people has improved in recent years. In a survey carried out in 2009, approximately half of the Americans questioned, especially young university graduates, had a positive image of Germany: as an important economic partner, especially in high-end technology – but Germany only reached fifth place in political cooperation ("*Die Deutschen sind wieder wer in den USA*", www.spiegel.de/politik/ausland/0,1518,681124,00. html, 2010). Some of the senseless reasons given for learning German (e.g. "*Have you hier Schillers Jungfrau von New Orleans'?*, FAZ 8 March 2014: 9) suggest that the trend towards GFL is partly driven by fashion. But, in general – despite the occasional diagnosis of "galloping consumption" (Arnold 1983: 73), the survival of GFL in the USA is not under serious threat.

Tatlock (2010) presents an encouraging and realistic outlook with detailed figures for individual states, universities, students and PhD students. Many US job lists are similarly encouraging, e.g. "that there is a continuous strong interest in and need for teachers of German" (Ecke 2011: 69, also 70–73; counterbalanced in Lovik 2003: 27). Heide Byrnes (1996: 259–261) has proposed a bold "Action Plan for the Profession" based on reports from specialist meetings. By contrast, once again, the small number of examinations in Goethe Institutes compared with course participants points towards weak instrumental motivation: certification for German-language skills is not required; the relative scarcity of institutes given the size of the country may also betray a weak instrumental motivation. There are Goethe Institutes in Boston, Chicago, Los Angeles, New York, San Francisco, Washington DC; Goethe Centres in Atlanta, Cincinnati, Houston, Seattle, Saint Louis. The figures for all institutes combined (Goethe-Institut P = course participants, E = examinations: 1990: P – 3,432, E – 287; 2012: P – 2,936, E – 448; 2013: P – 2,878, E – 591. (Information from Ingrid Köster and Herbert Moosbauer, Goethe-Institut, Munich.)

The USA has itself contributed to the erosion of instrumental motives for all foreign-language learning, not least by dropping the "foreign-language requirement" for universities since the 1960s (Ch. G.1; also, Ammon 1998: 13f.). As a result, globally dominant academic centres have lost the ability to communicate with the outside world in other languages, such as German, so that other countries are now forced to switch to English. Having said this, faced with such challenges to its survival, German Language and Literature in the US has developed an impressive diversity of teaching content and research interests (Classen 1988: 371; Trommler 1989; Lützeler 1990; James/ Tschirner 2001: 1426; Lovik 2004: 98–100; Louden/ Lovik 2008: 77–79; Ecke 2010: 1836f.).

Despite criticism (*"Die Bildungspolitik schläft mal wieder"*, *FAZ* 12 September 2012: N5), the promotion of GFL and German Language and Literature in the USA by the German-speaking countries is still respectable. In addition to the six Goethe Institutes and five Goethe-Centres, there are five German Schools Abroad (Boston, New York, Portland OR, Silicon Valley CA, Washington DC) and 92 DSD schools (offering the German *Sprachdiplom*). Furthermore, the German Academic Exchange Service (DAAD) finances German lectorships and grants for American and German students and guest lecturers; the Alexander von Humboldt Foundation supports visits to Germany by American lecturers and regularly alerts the *Deutsches Haus* in New York about contemporary culture in the German-speaking countries. Added to this, support for conferences and mutual visits is available from different sources, including Austria and Switzerland. Support by the USA's own organisations for GFL and teachers of German Language and Literature also deserves mention, especially the *American Association of Teachers of German* (AATG), *German Studies Association* (GSU), *Society of German-American Studies* (SGAS) and the *Society of Germanic Linguistics* (SGL) (James/ Tschirner 2001: 1424, 1429).

9.11 Brazil

This chapter has been checked and amplified by Katja Reinecke (DAAD São Paulo) Paolo Soethe (*Universidade Federal do Paraná* (UFPR) in Curitiba) and José Simões (*Universidade de São Paulo*)). Other sources included: Jacobi 1979; Rosenthal 1980; Leutner 1989; Altenhofen 1996; Xavier de Oliveira 1997; Sartingen 2001; Oliveira 2002; Galle 2002; Heise/ Aron 2002; Nitschak 2002; Altenhofen/ Gonzaga de Souza 2003; G. Kaufmann 2003; Soethe 2002, 2010. Brazil fosters close economic relations with the German-speaking countries, closer with Germany than with any other European country apart from exports to the Netherlands: 7% of Brazilian imports (from the USA 15%, China 15%, Argentina 8%), 4% of Brazilian exports (China 17%, USA 10%, Argentina 9%, the Netherlands 5%, Japan 4%) (*Fischer Weltalmanach* 2013: 69). São Paulo "is [or is taken to be! U.A.] the largest 'German' industrial city worldwide with more than 1,000 subsidiaries of German companies" (Soethe 2010: 1624). At the opening of the Brazilian German-Teachers' Congress in São Leopoldo in 2002, the German ambassador in Brazil referred to a "strategic partnership", especially regarding economic cooperation (Kaestner 2003). The two countries also share common political interests, e.g. in each having a permanent seat on the UN Security Council. Paolo Soethe (email 29 April 2014) anticipates a considerable influence on GFL and German Language and Literature in Brazil from the German programme *Wissenschaft ohne Grenzen* [Science without frontiers] (see: www.csf-alemanha.de/de/index.html).

The cities of São Paulo and São Leopoldo represent two regions which, although they merge into one another, differ with reference to the German language. São Leopoldo, in the conurbation of the city of Porto Allegre, is characteristic for the regions of the three southern Federal States, Rio Grande do Sul, Santa Catarina and Paraná, where descendants from the German-speaking countries are concentrated, many of whom still adhere to German as their home language, i.e. a second native language (GNL) alongside Portuguese (Ch. E.4.10; Altenhofen 1996; Damke 1997). An expert on local conditions here once wrote: "Apart from Europe, there is nowhere with so many German-speakers as in the south of Brazil" (Kaufmann 2003: 29). But what was meant was primarily German as a native language (which is dealt with in Ch. E.4.10 and not in the present chapter); nevertheless, because of rampant linguistic shifting, German as a foreign language (GFL) is also becoming increasingly important. At least, during school visits I made there in 2008, I had the impression that native-language school pupils were disaffected about learning German, especially in the form of GFL, as also noted by Jacobi (1979). This is still the case in the adjoining Federal State of São Paulo to the north, but decreasingly so to the south (Soethe 2010: 1624). A recently established home-study course has managed to generate brisk demand (email Simões 28April 2014).

Brazilian schooling regulations stipulate Portuguese as the language of instruction, introducing a foreign language only from Class 5. Although there is a free choice, it is generally for English or Spanish. At secondary level, a second foreign language is added, for which the central Brazilian government favours Spanish, amongst other reasons to integrate the country within the Latin American economic zone Mercosul (Portuguese)/Mercosur (Spanish). Since 2010, Spanish has been a compulsory subject, only in Classes 9 to 11 and only as a curricular provision; it is not compulsory for school pupils. As a result, the negative impact on German, which is offered from Class 5 onwards, is limited (email Soethe 29April 2014; Soethe/ Weininger 2009). For the first foreign language, in the three southern states, the procedure is "often that German is taught from Class 5 (sometimes even earlier) up to Class 8, but pupils switch to English in the last three years of schooling" (Kaufmann 2003: 32). The position of Italian is similar because of the similar numbers of immigrants from the native country. As in other emerging countries, there is also a lack of well-trained foreign-language teachers in Brazil (Xavier de Oliveira 1997: 24; Soethe 2010: 1625). The language centres (*Centros de Estudo de Linguas*) established in various cities in the Federal State of São Paulo with GFL as an optional subject for school pupils in public sector schools do provide a balance (email Simões 28 April 2014). English is almost exclusively relevant for the foreign-language components of university admission examinations, which has an unfavourable impact on GFL and on the maintenance of native-language German. Because of limited interest in the schools, even Germanists often begin their studies with weak German-language skills (Heise/ Aron 2002: 53). German Language and Literature is offered in 16 universities, with the largest department in the country in the University of São Paulo (ibid: 54f.). Alongside this, GFL is available at different levels as a subsidiary subject. Since 2009, in collaboration with the University of Leipzig; the Federal University of Paraná in Curitiba has provided a bilateral master's degree programme in German as a foreign language. In many places, German Language and Literature is seen to be facing a crisis (Rosenthal 1980; Heise/ Aron 2002) and efforts are being made to expand into cultural studies (Sartingen 2001: 1447; Galle 2002; Nitschak 2002), translation studies, linguistics, GFL and the local context (Oliveira 2002; Soethe 2002) or cooperation with other subjects, e.g. philosophy (Altenhofen/ Gonzaga de Souza 2003). The vocational goals of Germanists range from teaching, university lecturing and translating (Leutner 1989) to working in the subsidiaries of German companies or in Brazilian firms associated with the German-speaking countries (Sartingen 2001: 1447). Possibly because of the large distance involved, tourism hardly plays a role. However, figures for learners and students show an overarching favourable development (Table J.9.11–1).

The figures are estimates. Comparability over the years is impaired by the variability of the terms. In Table J.9.11–1, I have subsumed under the heading "Schools": "School pupils learning German in secondary schools" (Goethe-Institut 2000) and "GFL learners in schools" (StADaF 2005; Auswärtiges Amt 2015). The heading "Universities: Learners of German and Germanists (definition Ch. J.9.3, below Table J.9.3–2) subsumes the sum of "Number of students of German Language and Literature" + "Number of participants in academic language courses (both

Table J.9.11–1 Learners of German and Germanists in Brazilian schools and universities from 1985–2015

	1985	1995	2000	2005	2010	2015
Schools	17,900	7,915	[51,000]	52,000	65,430	79,541
Universities: Learners of German and Germanists	2,726	5,476	[4,925]	6,500	9,750	12,910
Of which Germanists	1,236	2,176	n.d.	2.000	n.d.	n.d.

(*Sources for 1985 and 1995*: Goethe-Institut 2000: [167]; for 2000 and 2005: StADaF 2005: 08; for 2010: Netzwerk Deutsch 2010: 5; Auswärtiges Amt 2015: 11)

data Goethe-Institut 2000); "Total students of German" (StADaF 2005); "Total students learning German" (Netzwerk Deutsch 2010); "Students learning German" (Auswärtiges Amt 2015). The Germanists are not always listed separately in the sources. The figures in square brackets reflect the fact that the source for 2005 indicates the difference from the figure for "GFL learners in schools" in 2000 as "1,000" and "Total learners of German in universities" as "1,585".

Despite questionable accuracy, it is evident that the figures for GFL learners in schools and universities have risen significantly (confirmed by Soethe 2010: 1626), remaining stable for Germanists, as far as this can be judged. The latter point is also supported by the number of approximately 100 students of German Language and Literature starting their course every year at the University of São Paulo (email Simões 28 April 2014). The increase in learners of German in universities suggests that German-language skills are considered vocationally useful (ibid: 1627) or relevant for study or placement in the German-speaking countries – and this corresponds with positive media reports about the German-speaking countries. It would be a worthwhile research project to investigate the extent to which identity-related motives based on German origins might play a role beyond instrumental motives (Ch. J.8; E.4.10). GFL learning in extra-curricular/extramural facilities also suggests instrumental motivation, and figures (excluding the Goethe Institutes) are available for 1985: 11,600, 1995: 5,700 (Goethe-Institut 2000: [167]), 2005: 12,000 (StADaF 2005: 8) and 2010: 16,788 (Netzwerk Deutsch 2010: 5), which show a clear upward trend. By contrast, in the Goethe Institutes themselves, long-term participation has developed as follows, with Belo Horizonte, Brasilia, Curitiba, Porto Alegre, Rio de Janeiro, Salvador Bahia and São Paulo combined (P = course participants, E = examinations): 1990: P – 14,030, E – 1,338; 2012: P – 8,938, E – 802; 2013 P – 8,616, E – 1,465. The overarching trend is downwards, i.e. a decline in course participants, but – especially recently – an increase in examinations. The decline could be influenced by the high fees which motivate the more cost-favourable attendance at language courses in universities, followed by subsequent certification in the Goethe Institutes (Kaufman 2003: 38).

Since 2013, the Brazilian Federal Government has supported the training of German teachers for public sector schools; after English, German is the second foreign language to receive such support from the Federal Ministerial Agency CAPES. There is also considerable support for GFL and German Language and Literature from the German-speaking countries, primarily from Germany. In addition to the seven Goethe Institutes and the Goethe Centre in the capital Brasília, there are two Swiss Schools Abroad (in Curitiba and São Paulo), four German Schools Abroad (two in São Paulo, one each in Valinhos by Campinas and Rio de Janeiro) and 18 DSD schools (offering the German *Sprachdiplom*), as well as a relatively large number of additional PASCH schools (partners with schools in Germany). The German Schools Abroad worldwide are also PASCH schools (information from Judith Weyer, ZfA, email 28 February 2014). Added to this, there are German lectorships in Brazil, guest visits by German and Brazilian university teachers in each other's country funded by the German Academic Exchange Service (DAAD). The Alexander von Humboldt Foundation has financed grants for outstanding Brazilian lecturers, since 2010 in a joint programme with the Brazilian funding agency CAPES. Finally, financial support for German-promoting events including conferences is available, with the participation of Austria and Switzerland (see e.g. the publishing information in Kaufmann/ Lenhard Brede-meier/ Volkmann 2003). Scientific-technical cooperation, including mutual visits by academics, is supported from both sides (even around the year 2000, approximately 50 academics participated each year; Sartingen 2001: 1446). This support through various forms of cooperation also benefits GFL, e.g. in the *Centre for Brazilian-German Cooperation/Centro de Cooperacao Internacional Brasil-Alemanha* in Curitiba (www.cciba.ufpr.br/site_german/institucional/objetivos.html).

Finally, the *Brazilian Association of German Teachers/Associação Brasiliera de Associações de Profes-sores de Alemão (ABraPA)* (with some 900 members), which is a member of the *International Association of German Teachers (IDV)*, and the *Lateinamerikanische Germanistenverband*, with members in the *International Association for Germanic Studies (IVG)* play a significant role in promoting GFL and German Language and Literature. The *Brazilian Association of Germanists/Brasilianischer Germanistenverband* was founded in 2013.

9.12 India

This chapter has been checked and amplified by Anja Hallacker (DAAD Pune) and Reckha Kamath Rajan (Jawaharlal Nehru University, New Delhi). Other sources included Dasgupta 1978; Sasalatti 1978, 1990; Ganeshan 1990; Mohr-Sobkowiak 2005; Bhatti 2001, 2007; *Deutscher Akademischer Austauschdienst* (DAAD) 2006; Rajan 2001, 2010. India imports more from Germany and Switzerland than from any other European country and, in Europe, only exports more to the UK and the Netherlands than to Germany; 4% of Indian imports came respectively from Germany and Switzerland in 2011 (12% from China, UAE 7%, Saudi Arabia 5%, USA 6%, Saudi Arabia 5%, Australia 5%, Iran 4%); and 3% of Indian exports went to Germany (UAE 14%, USA 11%, China 10%, Singapore, UK, the Netherlands 4% each) (*Fischer Weltalmanach* 2013: 196). Subsidiaries of German companies are concentrated in many regions of India, e.g. around Bangalore, New Delhi and Pune. India is gradually becoming the most populous country in the world (approximately 1.21 billion inhabitants according to 2011 census. *Fischer Weltalmanach* 2013: 196) and has many languages. India has 23 official languages of state: two national (Hindi, English) and 21 regional languages, including the inter-regional federal-state language Sanskrit. In fact, English is not in the constitution but functions as a dominant, national official language. Added to these languages, there are around 100 minority languages (de.wikipedia.org/wiki/ Sprachen_Indiens). However, there is no evidence correlating the membership of language groups with the learning of German; in the case of native speakers of non-official minority languages, the language burden may have a detrimental effect, despite individual multilingualism.

For many years, German has been a respected although not dominant foreign language in India. Even relatively recent situation reports still record a modest position (e.g. Rajan 2001, 2010), and this is especially true of older accounts (e.g. Dasgupta 1978; Sasalatti 1978, 1990; Ganeshan 1990). French has a longer and more robust tradition. Based on learner numbers, Japanese has also ranked ahead of German for a considerable time, and the same applies, certainly more recently, for Chinese, possibly also Portuguese and Spanish. English is not considered a foreign language. I was not able to determine the current ranking for foreign languages. Rekha Rajan (email 19 March 2014) presumes a recently strengthened position for German, possibly ahead of some of the languages named here, even perhaps of Japanese and Chinese. Position in schools is variable: elective or only optional subject, beginning at primary level or not until secondary level, in conjunction with one or more other foreign languages; the culturally auton-omous Federal States allow schools a wide margin for decision-making, especially the numerous private schools.

Among Indians, instrumental, vocational motives for the choice of German as a foreign lan-guage (GFL) predominate; this also applies for German Language and Literature. The motives are based on the perception of political and economic stability in the German-speaking coun-tries (Survey of pupils in Mumbai, Mohr-Sobkowiak 2005: 154–190, see 179) and the demand for skilled personnel. These motives also relate learning German as a subsidiary subject. Hitherto inadequate German-language skills were exposed through the "Blue card" campaign by Ger-many (analogous to the US "Green card" scheme), which was intended to attract IT specialists, but was not fully successful. Among the barriers diagnosed for Indians were "the language, eat-ing habits and cultural differences" ("*Deutschland? Muss nicht sein*", *Der Spiegel* 11 May 2012). At the very least, the language barrier had to be overcome. In fact, there were many accounts of rising learner numbers, e.g. during the visit by a former German Foreign Minister in 2011 in New Delhi: "Westerwelle was impressed by school pupils' interest in Germany and the Ger-man language [. . .]: 'We would like a total of 1000 schools in India to offer German as a foreign language in the next few years'" ("'*Deutsch an 1000 Schulen' in Indien*", *Magazin für Europa und Internationales* 1 (2012). Table J.9.12–1 provides an overview of developments in India.

The figures are estimates. Comparability over the years is impaired by the variability of the terms. In Table J.9.12–1, I have subsumed under the heading "Schools":"School pupils learning German in secondary schools" (Goethe-Institut 2000) and "GFL learners in schools" (StADaF 2005; Auswärtiges Amt 2015). The heading "Universities: Learners of German and Germanists (definition Ch. J.9.3, below Table J.9.3–2) subsumes the sum of "Number of students of Ger-man Language and Literature" + "Number of participants in academic language courses (both data Goethe-Institut 2000);"Total students of German" (StADaF 2005);"Total students learning German" (Netzwerk Deutsch 2010);"Students learning German" (Auswärtiges Amt 2015). The Germanists are not always listed separately in the sources. The figures in square brackets reflect the fact that the source for 2005 indicates the difference from the figure for "GFL learners in schools" in 2000 as "2,100" and "Total learners of German in universities" as "300".

Despite questionable accuracy, it is evident that the GFL learners have shown a steady and recently strong increase, especially in schools. The figures for universities in Table 9.12–1 may relate, here as in many other cases, to the declining number of Germanists without other learners of German. This would also explain why the figure for "Total learners of German" at 154,300 (Auswärtiges Amt 2015: 13) is considerably higher than the sum of the figures for schools + universities in Table J.9.12–1 (last column). However, these still modest figures (similar in Rajan 2010: 1680) should be compared with German media reports, such as the following: "German has been taught for decades at the RA Podar College [in Mumbai! U.A.]. Other schools are now

Table J.9.12–1 Learners of German and Germanists in Indian schools and universities from 1985–2015

	1985	*1995*	*2000*	*2005*	*2010*	*2015*
Schools	1,943	870	[12,800]	14,900	18,550	107,000
Universities: Learners of German and Germanists	4,800	4,498	[4,200]	4,500	11,000	2,300
Of which Germanists	4,800	2,224	n.d.	230	n.d.	n.d.

(*Sources for 1985 and 1995*: Goethe-Institut 2000: [169]; for 2000 and 2005: StADaF 2005: 10; for 2010: Netzwerk Deutsch 2010: 6; Auswärtiges Amt 2015: 13)

following suit, for example the Kendriya Vidyalaya schools. This chain of schools for the children of government employees would like to offer German to at least 1,000 of their schools by 2017. Approximately 1 million school pupils would then be able to learn German as their first foreign language" ("'*Namaste und Guten Tag!*' – *Deutschlernen in Indien*", *Deutsche Welle* 1 October 2013: www.dw.de/namaste-und-guten-tag-deutschlernen-in-indien/a-17114871). Rekha Rajan (2010: 1685) is right to suggest the concern that this development "depends significantly on conditions in the employment market", which "have been registered [. . .] seismographically" – and could also be reversed.

The Goethe Institutes also confirm a rise in demand so far. In long-term overview, participation has developed as follows, taking Bangalore, Madras, Hyderabad, Calcutta, Mumbai, New Delhi and Pune together (P = course participants, E = examinations): 1990: P – 6,118, E – 919; 2012: P – 13,116, E – 16,897; 2013: P – 14,511, E – 23,071 (information from Ingrid Köster and Herbert Moosbauer, Goethe-Institut, Munich). In this context, the stronger increase in examinations than in course participants is remarkable and suggests an acquisition of German-language skills elsewhere; in fact, the Goethe Institutes have reached the limits of their capacity, for which reason private schools prepare students for the Goethe examinations, possibly at more favourable costs. Alongside the provision of German teaching, the subject of German Language and Literature also has a broad interest base (see e.g. Bhatti 2001, 2007; Rajan 2010: 1681–1683; Mohr-Sobkowiak 2005; schon 1990 Ganeshan). This breadth is also shown by the periodical *German Studies in India. Aktuelle Beiträge aus der indischen Germanistik/Germanistik in Indien* (Munich: Iudicium, since 2006), which covers colonial history and cultural studies alongside literature and linguistics.

GFL and German Language and Literature in India are also supported by the German-speaking countries, primarily Germany. The Goethe-Institut/*Max Müller Bhavan* (named after the famous Indologist) is particularly important; in addition to five regular institutes in Chennai, Calcutta, Mumbai, New Delhi and Pune, it includes a further seven Goethe Centres in Ahmedabad, Chandigarh, Coimbatore, Hyderabad, Jaipur, Rourkela and Trivandrum. Two German Schools Abroad (Mumbai, New Delhi) and 11 DSD schools (offering the German *Sprachdiplom*) are also significant, as is the German Academic Exchange Service (DAAD), offering lectorships in various universities and financing grants for Indian and German students and guest lecturers. The Alexander von Humboldt Foundation also funds visits to Germany by Indian lecturers. Funding for German-promoting events, to which Austria and Switzerland contribute, is also available. The *Goethe-Society India* (goetheindia.wordpress.com/), which organises specialist conferences for Germanists also supported by the DAAD, and the work of institutional partnerships for German Language and Literature (e.g. with the universities of Göttingen, Pune and Mumbai) also play a significant role. Associations representing the interests of schoolteachers (Rajan 2010: 1684), such as the *IndoGerman Teachers Association*, which is a member of the *International Association of German Teachers* (IDV), and the membership of university teachers in the *International Association for Germanic Studies* (IVG) also deserve mention.

9.13 China

This chapter has been checked and amplified by Yu Chen (Tongji University Shanghai) and Jun He (Southwest Jiaotong University, Chengdu); I also received significant information from Jianhua Zhu. Other sources included Ciu 2007 [correct name: Xiaohu Feng]; Fan/ Li 2007; Fluck 1985, 2007; H.-W. Hess 1992, 2001, 2007; Zhao 1999; Gauler/ Treter 2007; Hernig 2007, 2010; Kong 2007; Reinbothe 1992, 2007a, b; Hansgünther Schmidt 2007a, b; Song 2007; Wang 2007; J. Zhu 2007; X. Zhu 2007; Huang 2011; Chen 2012; He 2013. China has thriving economic relations with the German-speaking countries, more thriving with Germany than with any other European country; however, some non-European countries rank ahead of Germany: 5% of Chinese imports in 2011 came from Germany (11% from Japan, South Korea 9%, Republic of China [Taiwan] 7%, USA 7%, Australia 5%), 4% of Chinese exports went to Germany (USA 17%, Hong Kong 14%, Japan 8%, South Korea 4%) (*Fischer Weltalmanach* 2013: 84 – separate data for Republic of China [Taiwan] and Hong Kong). Throughout China, Chinese (Mandarin-Chinese/Putonghua) is the official language and the language of schooling, to which officially, "dialects" (*Pinyin fangyan*) are allocated very generously, which, in fact, have the same written form but can also be taken as independent languages because of their linguistic distance from Mandarin-Chinese (Ch. B.1; B.2). Furthermore, alongside the majority Han-Chinese, there are 55 national minorities: 53 of which with recognised independent languages (german.china. org.cn/pressconference/ 2011–02/14/content_ 21916648.htm). Overall, more than 80 indige-nous languages are recognised in China (www.moe.edu.cn/publicfiles/business/htmlfiles/moe/ s5990/ 201111/ 126551. html).

GFL was introduced into China in 1871, the year in which the German Empire was founded, to train interpreters for the diplomatic service. During the subsequent German colonial period, German schools and universities were set up in the province of Kiautschou (Jiaozhou, capital city Tsingtau, now Qingdao), and in Shanghai and Hangkou (Reinbothe 1992, 2000, 2007a, b). After Germany lost the province of Kiautschou to Japan in WWI – it had been conceded under German pressure in a lease in 1898 – these educational facilities continued to operate, but only to a limited extent. In 1922, German Language and Literature was even established at the University of Peking. But in the 1930s, under the regime of Chiang Kai-shek (Hernig 2010: 1637f.; Reinbothe 2000, 2007c), almost all facilities disappeared. After fresh starts around 1950 in cooperation with the GDR and setbacks during the Cultural Revolution (1966–1976), GFL and German Language and Literature achieved a secure, although initially uncertain position in terms of practical application, within the Chinese educational and academic landscape in the 1980s (Hess 1992).

The figures for learners in schools and universities provide an indicator of developments as shown in Table J.9.13–1.

The figures are estimates. Comparability over the years is impaired by the variability of the terms. In Table J.9.13–1, I have subsumed under the heading "Schools": "School pupils learning German in secondary schools" (Goethe-Institut 2000) and "GFL learners in schools" (StADaF 2005; Auswärtiges Amt 2015). The heading "Universities: Learners of German and Germanists (definition Ch. J.9.3, below Table J.9.3–2) subsumes the sum of "Number of students of Ger-man Language and Literature" + "Number of participants in academic language courses (both data Goethe-Institut 2000); "Total students of German" (StADaF 2005); "Total students learning German" (Netzwerk Deutsch 2010); "Students learning German" (Auswärtiges Amt 2015). The

Table J.9.13–1 Learners of German and Germanists in Chinese schools and universities from 1985–2015

	1985	1995	2000	2005	2010	2015
Schools	400	750	[600]	1,760	5,900	12,200
Universities: Learners of German and Germanists	1,300	18,460	[12,790]	30,010	35,000	44,945
Of which Germanists	1,300	2,000	n.d.	6,200	n.d.	n.d.

(*Sources for 1985 and 1995*: Goethe-Institut 2000: [167]; for 2000 and 2005: StADaF 2005: 09; for 2010: Netzwerk Deutsch 2010: 5; Auswärtiges Amt 2015: 12)

figures in square brackets reflect the fact that the source for 2005 indicates the difference from the figure for "GFL learners in schools" in 2000 as "1,160" and "Total learners of German in universities" as "17,210".

Despite limited accuracy, the figures do provide evidence for a strong increase both in schools and universities, which is further confirmed by various investigations of specific details (e.g. Hernig 2010; Song 2007; Kong 2007). "Not only the numbers of school pupils in the subject 'German as the first foreign language', but also the figures for 'German as the second foreign language' show a clear upward trend", was one comment on the 6,000 GFL school pupils in 60 primary and middle schools in Shanghai alone in 2005 (2007: 122); the same direction is evident in the development of student and learner numbers (e.g. Kong 2007: 124). For 2010, the total figure for all educational levels was still recorded as 40,900 (Netzwerk 2010: 5), but for 2015, it had already risen to 117,487 ("Total learners of German" in Auswärtiges Amt 2015: 12). Compared with other demographic figures for China, these are admittedly extremely small. For example, in 2005, the proportion of students of German among 523,211 foreign-language students working towards a bachelor's degree in "regular Higher Education Institutions" was only 1.2% (www.moe.edu.cn /publicfiles/business/htmlfiles/moe/s6200/201201/129 594.html). In 2009, Premier Wen Jiabao claimed that the number of learners of English in China was more than 300 million (Montgomery 2013: 6). According to these figures, there would be more than 7,000 learners of English (more precisely 7,160) for every one learner of German. In fact, German is admitted as the first foreign language in Chinese schools but is generally learnt only as the second foreign language. Based on frequency of choice, it ranks not only far behind English but also behind Japanese and recently also behind French. However, in this context, I did not have accurate figures at my disposal. The rise of French is partly supported by its position as a working language of the EU and of international organisations (Ch. H.3, H.4.2), but also as the official language of West African States with economic relations with China.

In universities, "German as a subsidiary subject" (J. Zhu 2007) must be distinguished from German Language and Literature (Kong 2007). In the former subject, which has developed very rapidly in recent decades, German is learnt alongside other subjects, such as economics, engineering or natural sciences. For example, from 1995 to 2005, the number of universities with a unified examination "Academic German Level 4" rose from 17 to 112, and the number of examinees from 1,012 to 5,515 (J. Zhu 2007: 150). German Language and Literature is also often studied in conjunction with other subjects, where language and linguistics then form focal points. However, German literature is also studied, but often expanded interculturally (Kong 2007: 126–132). Complaints about a lack of learners or students are seldom heard; on the contrary – as is almost typical for "German studies abroad" – complaints are more likely about the academic shortfall relative to the study of German Language and Literature in the German-speaking countries (ibid: 138). The figures for German and German Language and Literature departments provide evidence for the expansion of degree programmes, e.g. from 2006 to 2012/13: bachelor degrees at 106 universities (2006 at 50), master degrees at 35 (19 in 2006) and PhD/Dr at 12 (six in 2006) (emails Chen 1 March 2014 and He 13 March 2014; He 2013: 87; Kong 2007: 139f.). These figures include only the state-run universities, generally with four-year bachelor's degree programmes in German Language and Literature, but not the vocational or junior colleges.

Interest in German as a subsidiary subject and a "foreign-language subject" (Fluck 1985, 2007) reveals predominantly instrumental motives for learning German (Zhao 1999), by contrast with the "Art of killing dragons" (Hess 1992), which was once perceived as relatively useless. A comparison of motives for subject choice in 1989 with those from 2003 demonstrates this shift. In the degree programme German Language and Literature in 1989, the motive "good employment opportunities" ranked in third place (first place: "no other choice was recommended"); by contrast, in 2003, it was in first place. For the subsidiary German courses, in 1989, the motive "To study/live in Germany" did not appear at all, whereas in 2003, it occupied first place (Fan/ Li 2007: 199–203). In an investigation carried out in 2009 (n = 215 students of German Language and Literature at six universities), "Interest in studying and living in German-speaking countries" was in first place with a wide margin – because, as the investigators explain, "studying in the English-speaking countries is considerably more expensive" and the "[German! U.A.] universities have quite a good reputation worldwide". "Many students even want to find employment in Germany after their studies and then to be able to live in Germany in the long term. And a knowledge of the language is the most important prerequisite" (Huang 2011: 8). The integrative motive of wanting to become integrated in a German environment possibly comes into play here (Ch. J.8). The shifts in motive match changing framework conditions, especially the increasingly intensive economic relations between China and the German-speaking countries (with approximately 1,200 German companies around 2010 in the conurbation around Shanghai alone; Hernig 2010: 1641). The more expensive student fees in China and switching from state allocation of employment to searching independently for employment after university also contribute to this (Fan/ Li 2007: 198). This intensifies the pressure to choose a subject which will be useful for further training and vocational success and still applies despite dampened appraisals of employment prospects: only half of the students of German and German Language and Literature (n= 531) questioned in 2003 judged their employment prospects to be "fairly good", the other half estimated their chances as "fairly poor" (X. Zhu 2007: 218 – based on Yuqing Wei 2003: manuscript). However, the positive responses clearly relate to careers – by contrast with the former "Art of killing dragons". One difficulty is still the limited use of German in German firms in China (see Wang 2007; Ch. F.6). Nevertheless, a knowledge of German is rightly considered the "'Plus" promised by the *Goethe-Institut* for appointments in German and even Chinese companies. Furthermore, for German Language and Literature, the traditional activities as schoolteacher, university lecturer or private German instruction are still possible.

The figures for GFL learners in extracurricular/extramural facilities also show an upward trend. In the Goethe Institutes, in long-term overview, participation has developed as follows, with Beijing, Hong Kong and the Goethe-Institut liaison office in Shanghai taken together (P = course participants, E = examinations): 1990: P – 4,406, E – 102; 2012: P – 6,476, E – 2,248; 2013: P – 6,919, E – 5,219 (information from Ingrid Köster and Herbert Moosbauer, Goethe-Institut, Munich). The growth in examinations is noteworthy and certainly includes spouses, who must be able to demonstrate the admittedly low competence level A1 of the Common European Reference Framework (Quetz 2002) required for a family move to a German-speaking country. The predominant motive for learning German today is studying in a German-speaking country, especially Germany, where Chinese students (as in many other countries) now represent the largest group of foreign students; or more precisely, the largest group of students among *Bildungsausländer* (foreigners educated abroad). If those educated in German-speaking countries are included (*Bildungsinländer*), Turkish students form a group of similar size. Chinese university students in Germany have a long history which dates to 1860 (Harnisch 1999; more generally on history Kaderas/ Meng 2000; Meng 2005). To some extent, this continues to nourish the good reputation of German universities, which, it must be admitted, has nowadays been surpassed by the more expensive, English-speaking institutions. However, in the long term, German universities may lose power as engines driving the learning of German because of the English-language degree programmes they now offer (Ch. G.8). They could create the impression that a knowledge of German is no longer required at all to study in a German-speaking country (see also H. Wagener 2012). However, it has so far not been possible to demonstrate this effect (He 2013). The stagnation of German-language skills (instead of improvement) among many Chinese students during their study visits in Germany (Chen 2012) is attributable less to the English-language degree programmes than to lack of contact with German people.

GFL and German Language and Literature in China are also promoted by the German-speaking countries, primarily Germany. On 26 May 2013, German Chancellor Angela Merkel and Chinese Premier Li Keqiang opened the German-Chinese Year of Language 2013/14 in Berlin, with many cultural events and a "German Roadshow" campaign (cf. Poland, Ch. J.9.5). The – politically motivated – Chinese-government restriction of Goethe Institutes to just two (Peking, Hong Kong; Gauler/ Treter 2007) has been obstructive, but, by spring 2014, six Goethe-Language Centres, all offering German courses, had been added (Shanghai, Tianjin, Qingdao, Nanjing, Chongqing and Shenyang). There are also four German Schools Abroad (Changchun, Hong Kong, Beijing, Shanghai) and 47 DSD schools (offering the German *Sprachdiplom*). In total, 103 schools with German as a foreign language (always alongside English) are supported by Germany, 62 by the Goethe Institutes and Centres and 41 by the Central Office for Schools Abroad (ZfA) (www.china.diplo.de/contentblob/ 3433562/ Daten/ 3134474/ PASCH_Schulliste_dd.pdf; for the ZfA, see Hansgünther Schmidt 2007a: 302f.). Support from the DAAD (ibid), the provision of lectors from Austria (Hernig 2007: 266f.), grants from the Alexander von Humboldt Foundation for visits to Germany by Chinese lecturers (Ciu 2007: 282–290) and various forms of support from German Federal States, political and private bodies (Hansgünther Schmidt 2007a: 303) are also important. Moreover, professional associations such as the *Chinese Association of German Teachers*, which is a member of the *International Association of German Teachers* (IDV), and the *Chinese Association of Germanists*, with many members in the *International Association for Germanic Studies* (IVG) have provided a considerable promotional impact for GFL and German Language and Literature. In 2010/2015, the president of the IVG was Chinese Germanist Jianhua Zhu from Tongji-University in Shanghai, who also organised the 2015 World Congress at his university.

9.14 Japan

This chapter has been checked and amplified by Shinichi Sambe (Keio-University, Tokyo) and Hideaki Takahashi (Kansai-University, Osaka). Other sources included Hirataka 1994, 2007; Takahashi 2002; Hayakawa 1994; Honda 1994; Itoi 1994; S. Kaufmann 1994; Naka 1994; Nakajima 1994; Shimokawa 1994; Yamaji 1994; Sekiguchi 1994; U. Ueda/ Takei 1994; Y. Ueda 1997; Sugitani 2001, 2010; Sambe 2013. Japan has closer economic relations with Germany than with any other European country. However, in 2011, Japan's imports from Germany were behind those from eight non-European countries, headed by China at 22%. Regarding exports from Japan, Germany was in seventh place of all countries with 3%, behind China 15%, USA 15%, South Korea 8%, Republic of China [Taiwan] 6%, Thailand 5% and Singapore 3% (*Fischer Weltalmanach* 2013: 236). Economic factors therefore hardly form a basis for a broad learning of German as a foreign language (GFL) (Takahashi 2002: 34). To some extent, GFL in Japan still feeds on the tradition reaching back to the modernisation and orientation of Japan towards the west following the removal of the Shogunate (1868). At that time, Wilhelmine Germany seemed an appropriate model for the new Meiji Empire (1868–1912), more so, in fact, than the more democratic French and English-speaking forms of state, and because of German victory over France (1871) and the academic prowess of German universities (Naka 1994: 242–244; Ch. G.1). Until the end of WWII, German, French and English were approximately equally ranked foreign languages in Japan. Only afterwards did English achieve the overarching, dominant position (Hirataka 1994) which has since been consolidated. Above all, English has achieved almost

Table J.9.14–1 Learners of German and Germanists in Japanese schools and universities from 1985–2015

	1985	1995	2000	2005	2010	2015
Schools	4,000	5,000	[23,000]	4,548	4,000	3,348
Universities: Learners of German and Germanists	753,000	400,000	[246,465]	345,196	285,000	224,000
Of which Germanists	3,000	380,000	n.d.	1,650	n.d.	n.d.

(*Sources for 1985 and 1995*: Goethe-Institut 2000: [169]; for 2000 and 2005: StADaF 2005: 10; for 2010: Netzwerk Deutsch 2010: 7; Auswärtiges Amt 2015: 13)

a monopoly position in schools. Based on learner numbers, GFL has now also fallen behind the foreign languages Chinese, Korean and possibly also French. The dominance of English is evident from the following report about university admissions (email Hideaki Takahashi 21 March 2014): "In January, admission examinations for universities are held [. . .]. All state-run, prefectural and municipal universities and many private universities take part. In 2014, there were 560,672 examinees. The heading "foreign language" allows a choice of five foreign languages: English, German, French, Chinese and Korean. This year, almost all examinees (approximately 99.8%) chose English". However, German recently gained an advantage compared with many other foreign languages. German overtook French in the university examinations in 2014 (n = 147 compared with n = 134 examinations), having lagged behind French for the previous ten years. Presumably, the economic strength of the German-speaking countries widely published in the media has provided momentum; but the effect was insufficient to overtake Chinese (n = 449) or Korean (n = 161) (figures from Takahashi, ibid). The overview of developments in Table J.9.14–1 shows a further decline rather than an upward trend.

The figures are estimates. Comparability over the years is impaired by the variability of the terms. In Table J.9.14–1, I have subsumed under the heading "Schools": "School pupils learning German in secondary schools" (Goethe-Institut 2000) and "GFL learners in schools" (StADaF 2005; Auswärtiges Amt 2015). The heading "Universities: Learners of German and Germanists (definition Ch. J.9.3, below Table J.9.3–2) subsumes the sum of "Number of students of German Language and Literature" + "Number of participants in academic language courses (both data Goethe-Institut 2000); "Total students of German" (StADaF 2005); "Total students learning German" (Netzwerk Deutsch 2010); "Students learning German" (Auswärtiges Amt 2015). In the sources, the Germanists are not always listed separately. The figures in square brackets reflect the fact that the source for 2005 indicates the difference from the figure for "GFL learners in schools" in 2000 as "-18,452" and "Total learners of German in universities" as "98,731".

Despite inaccuracy, the figures in Table J.9.14–1 unmistakably show an overall strong decline. In the sources for 1985 and 1995, the figures have certainly become transposed ("Number of students of German Language and literature" 1985: 3000, 1995: 380,000; "Number of participants in academic language courses" 1985: 750,000; 1995: 20,000), presumably because of uncertainties in allocating the two groups of GFL-learners and Germanists. The much larger figures in the universities than in the schools could contribute to confusion, but possibly also the teaching objectives, which were largely restricted to linguistic skills even in the universities, without German Language and Literature. Incidentally, these also offer teachers "little opportunity [. . .] to savour their expertise as specialist academics", where they are in fact "not qualified as language teachers, but as Germanists [. . .]" (Nakjima 1994: 250f.). For learners, a practically useful level of knowledge in German is difficult to achieve because of the late start of learning, the short learning time and the linguistic distance from the starting language (for a critical view, see Hirataka 2007: 111–113). Only a few schools, often private schools, generally in conjunction with universities with a long tradition of German and German Language and Literature, allow an early start of learning with German as the first foreign language, e.g. the Dokkyo Upper School (Itoi 1994: 213f.). Furthermore, in 2013, 72 public sector schools and 58 private upper schools offered GFL as a second foreign language alongside other languages (information from Shinichi Sambe; older figures in Sugitani 2001: 1587f.). Moreover, GFL can be chosen in some 40 private universities as an entrance examination subject (*Deutschunterricht in Japan* (2012) 17; older figures in Itoi 1994: 215–219). However, the bulk of GFL learners are in universities (Jamaji 1994; Nakajima 1994). The decline in GFL learners is not only determined by competition with other, especially Asian, foreign languages, such as Chinese and Korean, but also by the university reform of 1991 (Shimokawa 1994). Until then, universities had to oblige all students to learn a second foreign language, even if this was only for two years, with a few hours a week. The reform allowed universities to abandon the compulsory second foreign language, so that many have limited themselves to English as the sole, compulsory subsidiary foreign language. The schools which still offered GFL now design their curriculum independently from university requirements.

A basic lack of instrumental motives for choosing GFL (see Ch. J.8) causes special difficulties, especially the extensive loss of the previous practical usefulness of German as an academic language (Ch. G.1). Where individual sub-disciplines continue learning German as a subsidiary, this hardly has further practical significance. This is especially true of medicine, for which a knowledge of German was once taken for granted, because Japanese doctors even used to write their medical records and case histories in German (Kakinuma 1994). Knowledge of German is still relevant only for some of the humanities and some sub-disciplines of law, because of Japanese legal traditions in civil law and criminal law (Mori 1994: 56). Even for international business contacts, GFL hardly offers advantages, because it is generally possible to communicate with the German-speaking countries and companies without great difficulty in English. Within subsidiaries in Japan, German companies now rarely communicate in German (Coulmas 1994; Ch. F.6; also F.8). As a result, learners "have no clear motives [any longer! U.A.] for choosing German" (Honda 1994: 275). This also strengthens the tendency to broaden the subject and possibly to dilute it: "within German Studies, 'Area Studies' are gradually becoming established alongside the traditional topics of linguistics and literature. Germanists, who are suffering from the decline of German, are looking for new approaches [. . .]" (Takahashi 2002: 37; also, Sugitani 2001: 1592). In conjunction with this, a "motivation syndrome" has begun to take shape for GFL and German Language and Literature, which can be summed up by the label "culture". GFL is learnt and German Language and Literature are studied because German is a language associated with a rich culture. The motive "interest in the associated culture" is affirmed more frequently for German Language and Literature than for other comparable subjects (Honda 1994: 277). This motive is also based on the long tradition of GFL and German Language and Literature, which is already almost part of Japanese culture and handed down from parents to children as a motive for studying. In fact, this does not preclude certain instrumental motives. For example, the question "Do you want to choose an occupation in future in which you will be able to use your knowledge of German?" was answered in the affirmative by 71% of Germanists (Ueda/ Takei 1994). But such motives remain vague, because it is unclear whether such occupations even exist. One indicator for the low practical usefulness is the meagre provision of German courses in private Japanese language schools (Noro 1994: 315). Free television and radio courses have achieved a greater popularity (Sekiguchi 1994; Takahashi 2002: 36). Limited participation in Goethe-Institut language courses is another sign of lack of instrumental motives. In long-term overview, this has developed as follows in the institutes in Tokyo, Kyoto and Osaka taken together (P = course participants, E = examinations): 1990: P – 7,118, E – 617; 2012: P – 4,670, E – 223; 2013: P – 1,216, E – 2,086 (information from Ingrid Köster and Herbert Moosbauer, Goethe-Institut, Munich). However, despite the decline in course participants, the strong increase in examinees does still suggest instrumental motives. But the increase may also be co-determined by a need for certification which is independent of practical usefulness, but which avoids course fees at the Goethe-Institut, possibly through media-supported instruction. This overall assessment of the situation is shared by Japanese professors of German Language and Literature, e.g. Shinichi Sambe (email 2 October 2013): "[T]he question of which foreign languages are important for the Japanese economy is not really taken seriously in Japan. That is, people do not [. . .] even ask; they just assume that, other than English, there are no useful languages where business and trade are concerned".

> Hardly anyone in Japan learns German for commercial reasons. German is learnt as a language of culture. That is, in fact, both the weakness and the strength of German instruction in Japan. Because learning has nothing to do [. . .] with external commercial motives or social climbing, i.e., it has no influence on the teaching of German. But there are always internally motivated learners; there are not many of them, but they tend to be very dedicated.
>
> *(details in Sambe 2013)*

This picture of GFL resembles other highly developed countries, including English-speaking countries (cf. Australia, Ch. J.9.15) which are geographically remote from the German-language territory. Nevertheless – and this is important for the topic of the present book – it is associated with the prospect of an admittedly modest stability for GFL and German Language and Literature.

In Japan, this situation is also supported by the German-speaking countries, primarily Germany. In addition to the three Goethe Institutes (S. Kaufmann 1994), the following deserve mention: the two German Schools Abroad in Kobe and "Tokyo Yokohama" (www.dsty.ac.jp/ja); the German Academic Exchange Service (DAAD), with its grants for Japanese and German students and guest lecturers (but there have been no more lectors from Germany for around 20 years); the Alexander von Humboldt Foundation supporting visits to Germany by Japanese lecturers; and the Japanese professional associations: *Association of Teachers of German in Japan* (VDJ) (until May 2013: *Japanese German Teachers' Association* (JDV)) with the umbrella organisation, the *Japanese Society for German Language and Literature* (JGG) (Sugitani 2010: 1699f.). The membership of many Japanese Germanists in the *International Association for Germanic Studies* (IVG) is also of great importance. The president from 1985–1990 was Eijiro Iwasaki, who organised the World Congress of the IVG in 1990 in Tokyo.

9.15 Australia

This chapter has been checked and amplified by Gabriele Schmidt (Australian National University, Canberra) and Brian Taylor (University of Sydney). Other sources included Ammon 1991b; G. Schmidt 1998, 2011; Truckbrodt/ Kretzenbacher 2001; Kretzenbacher 2006, 2010, 2011; Jäger/ Jasny 2007; Clyne 2008; C. Nettelbeck et al. 2008; Taylor 2013. On one hand, Jäger/ Jasny 2007 and, on the other, Clyne 2008 provide examples of decidedly optimistic and respectively pessimistic evaluations of the same factual situation regarding German as a foreign language (GFL) and German Language and Literature in Australia. Australia has a highly developed economy which produces more raw materials than finished products and exports primarily to the neighbouring Asian countries. By comparison, economic relations with Europe are modest but more intensive with Germany than with any other European countries apart from the UK. In this context, imports from Germany outweigh exports to Germany (5% of all Australian imports 2010; *Fischer Weltalmanach* 2013: 48) – which motivates the learning of German less than vice versa (Ch. F.1; F.2). Economics and geographical proximity favour the turn towards the Asian languages, primarily Japanese since the 1980s, but more recently Chinese. However, the traditional European foreign languages have been maintained in schools and universities, including GFL and German Language and Literature. In this context, as another English-language immigration destination, Australia resembles the USA, which is also officially monolingual (national official language exclusively English; Ch. J.9.10), and Canada (in spite of its two official languages English and French), because all three countries show a similar trend towards multiculturalism (see Clyne 1982b; Lo Bianco 1987; Petersen 1993; Kretzenbacher 2006: 15).

In the 1970s, these developments raised awareness of *LOTEs* (*languages other than English*) and led to the programme of community languages (*Stadtteilsprachen*) in schools. This programme focuses primary school pupils' attention on immigration languages predominant within each part of the town, including German, although this tends to be an exception (Clyne 1982b, 1991). But linguistic diversity in Australia also includes vestiges of languages spoken by the original inhabitants (*aborigines*), which are fostered in a similar way. As in the rest of the English-speaking world, since WWI, German has fallen behind the other European foreign languages, French and, in this case, sometimes Italian. However, economic reasons and German-speaking immigrants (with local consolidation, forming language minorities) have assisted the maintenance of GFL and German Language and Literature (Clyne 1981, 1982a; Harmstorf/ Cigler 1985; Jurgensen/ Corkhill 1988); although in some cases, they also quickly shifted to English (Clyne 2008: 10, 12). Between 2006 and 2011, German fell back from ninth most frequent to eleventh most frequent home language (in each case 0.4% of the Australian population; Australian Bureau of Statistics 2012: Languages Spoken at Home).

GFL is taught in public sector schools in all six Federal States and in the Australian Capital Territory, with focal points in Victoria, New South Wales, Queensland and South Australia. GFL profits from the fact that the new national curriculum in all Federal States has made foreign-language instruction in public sector schools compulsory (www.smh.com.au/national/education/ chinese-italian-lead-new-curriculum-20110131-1ab54.html). However, GFL suffers from the short duration of this obligation (often only two years; details in Jäger/ Jasny 2007: 477; Kretzenbacher 2006: 17 on Victoria), for which reason students of German at universities often require introductory language courses. Over the last few decades, the number of universities with GFL and German Language and Literature has remained stable, but not without institutional downgrading. In 2007, there were "14 state-funded universities with German Language and Literature +3 universities with German courses" – but now only two professorships in German, in Brisbane and Melbourne, which used to exist in almost all universities (email Brian Taylor March 2014 – contrast with the incorrect information in Jäger/ Jasny 2007: 473, after Corkhill 2003: 123, to the effect that there are no longer any professorships in German). Table J.9.15–1 gives an overview against time.

The figures are estimates. Comparability over the years is impaired by the variability of the terms. In Table J.9.15–1, I have subsumed under the heading "Schools": "School pupils learning German in secondary schools" (Goethe-Institut 2000) and "GFL learners in schools" (StADaF 2005; Auswärtiges Amt 2015). The heading "Universities: Learners of German and Germanists (definition Ch. J.9.3, below Table J.9.3–2) subsumes the sum of "Number of students of German Language and Literature" + "Number of participants in academic language courses (both data Goethe-Institut 2000); "Total students of German" (StADaF 2005); "Total students learning

Table J.9.15–1 Learners of German and Germanists in Australian schools, extracurricular facilities and universities from 1985–2015

	1985	1995	2000	2005	2010	2015
Schools	107,985	61,000	[142,300]	142,300	98,000	100,800
Universities: Learners of German and Germanists	2,007	4,080	[3,655]	3,000	3,000	2,940
Of which Germanists	2,007	2,280	n.d.	1,500	n.d.	n.d.
GFL learners extracurricular/extramural (without Goethe-Institut)	n.d.	2,300	n.d.	5,000	6,000	231

(*Sources for 1985 and 1995:* Goethe-Institut 2000: [166]; for 2000 and 2005: StADaF 2005: 8; for 2010: Netzwerk Deutsch 2010: 4, Auswärtiges Amt 2015: 11)

German" (Netzwerk Deutsch 2010); "Students learning German" (Auswärtiges Amt 2015). In the sources, the Germanists are not always listed separately. The figures in square brackets reflect the fact that the source for 2005 indicates the difference from the figure for "GFL learners in schools" in 2000 as "0" and "Total learners of German in universities" as "655". A more detailed breakdown and comparisons with other industrial countries is given in Kretzenbacher (2011: 44 and 45–52).

Despite some doubts about accuracy, the figures in universities seem to have remained more stable than in the schools. Slightly rising student numbers are reported for individual Federal States, such as Victoria, Queensland and South Australia (Jäger/ Jasny 2007: 474). As already mentioned, the growing numbers of students starting university courses with weak German-language skills match the weaker development in schools in recent years (Jansen/ G. Schmidt 2011: 166; G. Schmidt 2011: 87, 122f.). They tend to break off their studies: around 70% of inadequately linguistically prepared students after two years at the latest (Jansen/ G. Schmidt 2011: 166). In view of their skittishness in recent years, the figures for GFL learners in extracurricular/ extramural facilities (without the Goethe Institutes) are questionable. In the Goethe Institutes, participation has developed as follows, combining Sydney and Melbourne – because of the closure of the Goethe-Institut (in 1998), there was no provision in Canberra over the whole period – (P = course participants, E = examinations): 1990: P – 2,227, E – 106; 2012: P – 2,189, E – 194; 2013: P – 1,926, E – 198 (information from Ingrid Köster and Herbert Moosbauer, Goethe-Institut, Munich). The overarching trend is stable with a rise in examinations, which suggests that instrumental, vocational motives still play a part here.

Nevertheless, the large geographical distance and rather weak economic contacts with the German-speaking countries invite the question of why German is still learnt, and German Language and Literature still studied at all. Surveys of students of German revealed a plurality of reasons for choosing the language and the subject (Ammon 1991b; Petersen 1993; G. Schmidt 2011: 152) – where the possible discrepancy between named reasons and actual motives should be remembered (Ch. J.8). A similar diversity is to be found in students' vocational aspirations and presumably also in the occupations taken up by learners of German in Australia – although this has not been investigated in greater detail (Ammon 1991b: 184–188; Kretzenbacher/ Truckenbrodt 2001: 1656; G. Schmidt 2011: 127).

However, there was frequent clustering among the reasons and motives, e.g. in my own investigation around the following three responses, which are at least not unconnected: "to communicate with German-speakers abroad", "to travel to a German-speaking country as a tourist" and "because German improves my professional qualifications" (Ammon 1991b: 43–53). Moreover, among students of German, the proportion with origins in a German-speaking country was several times higher than in the total Australian population (ibid: 71–89) – which matches the fact that communities of German origin often run native-language Saturday schools (older figures, see Clyne 1981: 41; on the Internet, e.g. www.australien.diplo.de/Vertretung/australien/de/GK-Sydney/ Sonnabendschule_Sydney_Weihnachtsfeier2013.html).

Gabriele Schmidt's (2011: 148) comprehensive investigation exposed the following composite motive: "A general interest in the German language and culture". A diversity of interests among Australian Germanists therefore possibly converges in this manner (see Kretzenbacher 2006: 23–25), to some extent, also explaining the correlation between language and culture mentioned (G. Schmidt 2001: 148–161). This could almost be conceptualised as a *myth* (in the English sense of the word) about the cultural achievements of the German-speaking countries, on which the continuing demand for a reading knowledge of German among doctoral candidates in the humanities seems to feed. One course organiser at the University of Sydney explained, "the flow of students interested in my reading courses has increased so much this year that, just 'in terms of space', I don't know if I can fit them all in" (email Brian Taylor 4 March 2014; Taylor 2013).

The promotion of GFL and German Language and Literature in Australia by the German-speaking countries is rather modest (Kretzenbacher 2006: 21–23). Closure of the Goethe-Institut in Canberra (1998), as mentioned above, is symptomatic. However, mention must be made of the two German Schools Abroad in Sydney and Melbourne, the DSD schools (offering the German *Sprachdiplom*) and lectorships and grants from the DAAD. Furthermore, the conferences organised by the *Network of Australian Teachers of German* (NATG) and its active branches in almost all Federal States (network magazine: *Szene* – www.ausdaf.edu.au/) are also effective promotional means. The Network is a member of the *International Association of German Teachers* (IDV).

10. Factors strengthening and weakening the position of GFL within a country

It would be desirable to provide a typology of countries based on the chances of maintaining the position of German as a foreign language (GFL), so that all countries in the world could be arranged, at least in the form of a rank ordering, but even better along a (numerical) ratio scale. One prerequisite would be an appropriate approach for assessing countries. A suitable starting point might be the proportions of GFL learners and GFL speakers in the total population, including the level of GFL competence. However, corresponding data are not available. Indeed, there is a lack of knowledge about other factors strengthening or weakening GFL in individual countries and about their relative weighting and interaction. In the following list of possible factors, I have generally avoided citing evidence, either because it seemed plausible that the factors are effective in the sense named (admittedly without my being able to indicate their corresponding weighting) or because it would be too effort-intensive to provide convincing evidence of their efficacy. The numbering is not meant to suggest weighting but is intended only for reference purposes.

1) *English speaking within the country (Anglophonie)*: In an English-speaking country (e.g. the UK), foreign-language learning is often limited. This can be detrimental to the learning of German. The belief that English is increasingly enough for worldwide communication in the present period of globalisation may be widespread (cf. Ch. A.7). The UK is one example, with short, compulsory foreign-language learning in schools for general education (Eurydice 2008: 29 – eacea.ec.europa.eu/education/eurydice/ documents/key_data_series/095EN.pd);

2) *English speaking within the country (Anglophonie)* + *other official or national language/ s*: If an English-speaking country has a second official or national language, this can further inhibit foreign-language learning. With such a language constellation, real "foreign" languages are relegated to third place in school (for a long time now, Ireland has had no compulsory foreign-language learning in schools for general education (ibid: 28);

3) *Friendliness of the country towards English (Anglophilie)*: If the country is not an English-speaking country but is friendly towards English and largely committed to English as the world lingua franca, this tends to inhibit any other foreign-language learning. The Scandinavian countries and the Netherlands are examples of countries which have restricted their former foreign-language multilingualism in favour of a predominance of English. The belief that other international languages are more of a burden than an enrichment contributes to this. Added to this is the – not entirely false – belief, which is additionally detrimental to GFL learning, that it is possible to communicate reasonably effectively with German-speakers and in German-speaking countries in English;

4) *Educational legislation on foreign-language learning*: This is a complex factor which can be differentiated at multiple levels, in fact, at least in the following respects: position of the foreign languages in the curriculum i) compulsory; ii) elective from a bundle of languages (one of which is compulsory); or iii) optional from a bundle of languages (one of which is optional); iv) number of languages in each bundle; v) levels of schooling for language learning; vi) duration of learning (total number of hours); vii) function of the knowledge of language within the educational programme (e.g. compulsory or optional part of university admission examinations). The following examples are based on the many possible combinations.

   a) *English as the sole compulsory foreign language*: Other foreign languages are only optional subjects (e.g. South Korea). The detriment to GFL is obvious, especially with a relatively large number of optional languages;

   b) *Only one compulsory foreign language as an elective subject from several languages*: If English is among these languages, which is nowadays always the case (e.g. Brazil), the choice is predominantly for English. However, if German is also among the elective languages, GFL has more of a chance than in the case of 4a);

   c) *Two compulsory foreign languages* (e.g. Italy, France). GFL is then often a component of the second, subordinate elective bundle. Of course, it promotes GFL if two foreign languages are compulsory and GFL is one of them. The European Union also recommends two compulsory foreign languages for all Member States (Kruse 2012). The Goethe-Institut and all GFL professors, e.g. – to mention just one beacon – Hans-Jürgen Krumm (Netzwerk Deutsch 2010: 2; Krumm 2000a, b; 2002, 2003, 2004), have been canvassing for this for years, of course, including GFL.

With the following factors, it can be assumed that many are causally connected and correlate statistically, but I shall not always reference this explicitly.

5) *Geographical distance from the German-speaking countries*: Geographical proximity is more beneficial to GFL learning, especially for the motivation to learn German (language choice and eagerness to learn), than geographical distance. Compare, for example, Poland with South Korea (Ch. J.9.5; Ammon/ Chong 2003);

6) *Intensity of economic contacts with the German-speaking countries*: Greater intensity of such contacts is beneficial to GFL learning. Even if the comparison of individual countries is not

absolutely convincing because of other simultaneously acting factors, it is still relevant to compare e.g. Brazil and Venezuela. In this context, it must be considered that the figures named are only a weak reflection of the economic involvement with the German-speaking countries which diverge even more strongly between the two countries.

Exports to Germany 2011: Brazil 4%, Germany is sixth largest export market; – for Venezuela, Germany is not even among the seven largest export markets. *Imports from Germany 2011*: Brazil 7%, Germany is fourth largest import market; – Venezuela 4%, Germany is only sixth largest import market (*Fischer Weltalmanach* 2013: 69, 488).

GFL learners 2010: Brazil 91,788 (inhabitants 190,755,799) – Venezuela 2,391 (inhabitants 27,150,094) (Netzwerk Deutsch 2010: 5, 12; *Fischer Weltalmanach 2013*: 69, 488). The proportion of GFL learners in the population of Brazil is more than five times as large as the population of Venezuela (n population : n GFL learners – Brazil 11,355; Venezuela 2,079);

7) *Level of technological development compared with the German-speaking countries*: An ambivalent factor. On one hand, it can influence GFL learning based on school provision dependent upon this factor (I will return to this later: factors 12 to 14), but, on the other hand, it can also influence motivation to learn GFL. For economically and technologically developing or emerging countries, further education/study and vocational opportunities in the German-speaking countries are attractive. But GFL skills seem to be appropriate only if there is a genuine requirement. To promote GFL learning, the abandonment of German in favour of English in universities and companies in German-speaking countries must, therefore, not be exaggerated (cf. in this respect, Ch. F.1; F.5; G.1; G.8; H. Wagener 2012; He 2013);

8) *Educational prospects in the home country resulting from GFL skills*: It is detrimental to GFL if GFL skills offer no advantages for further education in the home country. This applies for access to higher levels of schooling and for university admissions, as already mentioned under 4 (point vii). In many countries, knowledge of GFL is irrelevant in this respect. In South Africa, for example, because of the "abandonment of the so-called third language (after English and Afrikaans) as a condition for admission to university" (von Maltzan 2010: 1806; Ch. J.9.9);

9) *Vocational prospects in the home country resulting from GFL skills*: The parallels with factor 8 are obvious. The relevance of GFL skills to vocational activities diminishes if local companies treat them as superfluous. This attitude has been reported from many countries and their companies, e.g. Japan (Ch. J.9.14). It may be reinforced, especially if companies from German-speaking countries do not value communicating in German, either at home or abroad (cf. Ch. F.1; F.5; F.7);

10) *The tradition of GFL in the respective country*: A long tradition of GFL in the country stabilises the position of GFL. By contrast, if there is no such tradition, it is difficult to establish and develop GFL. There is a lack of trained teachers in schools and universities who – possibly for personal motives – are committed to the subject and qualified to teach or instruct. Once again, it is difficult to compare countries because of additional factors. But it is obvious that dramatic differences between many countries are partly determined by this factor. The following examples give population : GFL learner numbers, and then, after a stroke, the proportions.

China 1,333,724,852 : 40,900 / 32,609 : 1, Mexico 112,336,538 : 41,000 / 2,740 : 1, USA 308,745,538 : 494,264 / 625 : 1 (In each case, sources Netzwerk Deutsch 2010, figures for 2010; *Fischer Weltalmanach* 2013, figures for 2011.)

Accordingly, in the USA, proportionally to the population, 4.4 times more GFL is learnt than in Mexico and 52.2 times more than in China – and this is despite the detriment to GFL learning in the USA caused by factor 1 "English-speaking country"! This striking discrepancy points directly towards the next factor;

11) *Current or enduring immigration from the German-speaking countries and existing German (speaking) minority*: Both parts of this factor, which I have combined for the sake of brevity, promote GFL learning, or their absence is detrimental to GFL. At least some of the immigrants will switch in the third generation to the language of the destination country. In language islands, a language shift also sometimes occurs at the margins. However, even linguistically assimilated groups often motivate their children to learn GFL and try to set up this possibility. This strengthens the position of GFL in the relevant country (cf. Ch. J.9.5; J.9.10; J.9.11; J.9.15; for German-(speaking) minorities, e.g. in France, Brazil and USA, see Ch. E.4.3; E.4.10; E.4.11).

The following factors are more trivial in the sense that they are often addressed within the subject of GFL because they are experienced more directly there than the previous factors. Factor 14 is one of the acknowledged objectives of GFL;

12) *Provision of schooling in the country*: Apart from foreign-language educational legislation (factor 4), the observance of existing laws is also an important factor. Amongst others, it depends on the provision of schooling. Especially in developing countries, this is a rapidly growing problem. One indicator is the extent of illiteracy, which is high in many African countries and in India. In 2007/8, it was still around 60–70% of the population in places (www.laenderdaten.de/bildung/ alphabetisierung.aspx). Even the finest foreign-language educational legislation and the best motivation are of no use to people who cannot attend school at all;

13) *Availability of teachers*: A serious lack of GFL teachers is reported from many countries including rich countries e.g. France (Ch. J.9.2). The reasons are often complex. But the relatively poor pay for teachers frequently induces graduates in German Language and Literature to seek other employment opportunities. It is obvious that inadequate provision for GFL learning and the cancellation of lessons are detrimental to GFL. Poor teacher remuneration also has a demotivating effect on students learning GFL with a view to a career in teaching, because it undermines the prestige of this career;

14) *Qualification of teachers*: Pedagogical deficiencies in GFL teaching are among the common reasons for students' dislike of learning German, often associated with a reference to the grammar-translation method, which is thought to originate from Germany. It seems that the reality content of such *clichés* has not yet been convincingly overcome, especially by comparison with other foreign language subjects – but this is urgently required. The subject of GFL must energetically apply itself to improving pedagogy and teaching methods!

15) *Promotion of GFL by the German-speaking countries* and by each country in which GFL is taught and learnt in schools and universities. The next chapter, Ch. K, which is the last chapter of the book, deals specifically with the promotion of GFL by the German-speaking countries. But examples have already been given in each case at the end of Chapters J.9.2 to J.9.15. There can be little doubt that such promotional effort generally strengthens the position of GFL. Nevertheless, like all the factors named here, the outcome is difficult to assess, especially the impact of individual funding components. This seems to me to be a substantive explanation for the scant appreciation of funding policies and the associated

measures. Isolated investigations have provided evidence, e.g. for the impact of the German Roadshow campaign in Poland (Mackiewicz 2013), but many reports of successful measures are based primarily on intuition and one-off observations, although they are often delivered with great conviction, as with the following example: "Language initiatives, such as the large-scale PASCH partner-school initiatives or major thematic projects such as 'Languages without Frontiers' are proving to be an appropriate and successful instrument for combating a downward trend [in GFL! U.A.]" (Netzwerk Deutsch 2010: 2). I must stress that while the positive assessment in this example seems plausible, and I consider it defensible with reference to the topic under discussion, experts should still be mindful of the frequent lack of compelling evidence.

K
POLICIES FOR PROMOTING THE GERMAN LANGUAGE IN THE WORLD

1. Concepts, terminology and framework conditions

1.1 "Language promotion", "Language-spread policy", "External language policy"

This chapter is primarily concerned with government policies on language/s, which are orientated – as a component of a country's foreign policy – towards foreign states and territories. Terminology in German for policies of this kind is not unified. The following terms are largely synonymous but with a different emphasis:

1) *External language policy (ELP)* [*Auswärtige Sprachpolitik/ ASP*] (Andrei/ Rittberger 2009; A. Schneider 2000), as a component of *External cultural policy (ECP)* [*Auswärtige Kulturpolitik/ AKP*], which, in turn, is part of *Foreign Policy (FP)* [*Außenpolitik/ AP*] (ELP ⊂ ECP ⊂ FP). The opposite term is *Internal/ Domestic* [*Innere*] *Language Policy* etc. Since 2000 (Ch. K.3.2), the designation for ECP in Germany has been expanded to *External Cultural and Educational Policy (ECEP)* [*Auswärtige Kultur- und Bildungspolitik/ AKBP*], although *External cultural policy (ECP)* is still used.

2) More technical terms are: *External Language Promotion* [*Förderungs-*] *Policy (ELPP)* (also *External Language Promotion*) – with variations such as *External Language-Spread* [*Verbreitungs-*] *Policy (ELSP)* and *External Language Maintenance* [*Erhalt/ ungs-*] *Policy (ELMP)* (ELPP = ELSP ∪ ELMP; Ammon 1991a: 524–528), although these abbreviations are seldom used.

3) Within sociolinguistics, designations would be plausible, but hardly occur, such as *External Language Status Policy* or *External Language Corpus Policy*, corresponding to the distinction between *Language Status Planning* and *Language Corpus Planning* (Haugen 1966, 1987), or *External Language Position Policy*, which not only relates to status in the legal sense but also to the function or use of the language (Ch. D.1).

By contrast, the term *Language Export* is impractical because of the possibility of misunderstanding, since – by way of distinction from other exports – no change of ownership takes place.

In earlier accounts, I have used the term *Language Spread Policy (LSP)* for the generic concept (Ammon 1989c: 229f., 1990d, 1991a: 524–528), because this seemed to express most clearly the primary intention of such policies and because of the sociolinguistic term *language spread* (Cooper 1982; Lowenberg 1988). The same applies for the term *language spread policy*, which I coined for the volumes of the *International Journal of the Sociology of Language* 95 (1992); 107 (1994) I edited. However, politicians avoid this term, presumably because of possible associations with *linguistic imperialism* (Phillipson 1992). In Germany, the political discourse tends more towards the term *language promotion* (Auswärtiges Amt 1973: 18; *Bericht* 1985: 4, 6, 11, 17; Witte 1985c; H. Hoffmann 2000). It seems more suitable as the generic term for a policy on language spread and on language maintenance – the latter objective being more obvious here in view of the current global position of German. The term *language promotion policy* or the shorter version *language promotion* therefore seems more appropriate to me nowadays than *language spread policy*. However, in unambiguous cases, it is advisable to speak directly of *language spread policy* (Ch. K.2), and *language maintenance policy* in the contrary case.

What is involved in this context are external policies rather than internal policies. This already almost suggests a primary reference to the position of the language rather than to its structure, which is not the case when language policy is discussed as a component of internal policy. In the latter case, policies are orientated not only towards the position of a language within a national territory or society, but also towards its structure, that is, grammar and vocabulary (legal or academic terminology, possibly entrusted to a language academy) or, notoriously in the case of German, towards spelling. But a terminological distinction between *language position policy* and *language structure policy* would still be possible in this context. However, language structure policy (language corpus policy) is only touched upon briefly in this book (e.g. in Ch. G.11) – and I shall not dwell on this terminological distinction.

According to definition, *external language policy* (or *language promotion policy*) in the sense used does not include a policy which has a language-maintaining or language-spreading effect without the corresponding intention (as an unintended consequence of the policy; an effect of the "invisible hand", Ch. A.2). However, a successful economic policy or academic policy may promote a language more effectively than a (deliberate) language promotion policy. This assumption is suggested e.g. by the GFL learner numbers in Mediterranean countries, which have been rising in recent years (Ch. J.4, towards the end; J.9.4). Such examples can also be instructive for external language policy by showing the limits of an excessively narrow reference to language.

Another case is the type of external language policy which is not declared as such or which is even deliberately concealed. Embarrassing German examples are provided in the *Geheime Denkschrift des Auswärtigen Amtes über das deutsche Auslandsschulwesen* [Secret Memorandum of the Foreign Office on German Schools Abroad] April 1914 (facsimile in Düwell 1976: 268–370) or in Georg Schmidt-Rohr's 1940 plan for a *Geheimes politisches Sprachamt*, [Secret Political Language Office] with the goal of making German into the "world language" (Simon 1979b: 164–170, p. 167; Ch. K.2). As with many other policies, a temptation "not to advertise too loudly" the policy-makers' genuine intention is also sometimes found in the context of external language policy. As a result, such policies often go unnoticed, even by supposed experts. For example, quite a few sociolinguists initially denied the existence of any such policies when I asked them for reports about their countries' external language policy – until they discovered these policies (in preparing their contributions to the volumes of the *International Journal of the Sociology of Language* mentioned above). Malicious observers interpreted the "great Europe speech" by German Federal President Joachim Gauck (in Berlin 22 February 2013) as an example of concealing his country's language promotion plans. For all his declared appreciation of multilingualism, Gauck only mentions English as a possible "common language of communication" in Europe, which the younger generation is already "growing up with as a lingua franca". By claiming, "that both can live side-by-side in Europe: culturalization in the native language with its poetry alongside practicable English for all stations and ages of life", he implicitly denied his own language any function as a lingua franca and position as an international language (with the same applying to French, Spanish and Italian) (www.bundespraesident.de/SharedDocs/Reden/DE/Joachim-Gauck/Reden/2013/02/130222 *External Language Status Policy External Language Status Policy* – Europa.html). This insinuation would be difficult to reconcile with the German Government's external language policy – and, it must be said, also with other language policies of EU countries (Ch. H.4.6). To designate different degrees of publicness, a distinction can be made between *declared* and *non-declared* external language policy, and the latter can be further differentiated into *tacit* and (intentionally) *secret* policies.

Basically, any organisation which has enough autonomy and resources at its disposal can operate a language policy. Examples include international organisations, religious communities (churches), companies, scientific and educational institutions and private associations. Such policies have been touched upon in previous chapters of the book, e.g. in references to the codification of "rules" or "statutes" (of the UN, universities etc.). However, through their governments, states have the most comprehensive opportunities, and the present chapter is largely limited to this context (apart from Ch. K.3.4; K.3.5). On closer inspection, it becomes evident that most states do operate external language policies – although often (necessarily) only at a rudimentary level – and, try to promote and ideally spread "their" own language/s (Ch. K.5).

1.2 Own language as a cross-cutting task [Querschnittsaufgabe] in external cultural policy

A task which is relevant beyond its specific domain, in the case of politics beyond its specific political domain, can be described as *cross-cutting* or *cross-sectional*. In this sense, for example, the German language is relevant beyond the external language policy (ELP) of Germany or of the German-speaking countries to other domains of external cultural policy and even beyond that to other domains of foreign policy. Therefore, even language-independent aspects of external cultural policy, such as instrumental music, painting or sports, could be carried out with an eye to external language policy. Almost all activities within external cultural policy offer opportunities for using participants' own language, i.e. they can cohere with it. The "actors" are almost always faced with the choice of using their own language or a foreign language, or of promoting that use or not. This relates, for example, to the communication necessary for art exhibitions or music performances abroad, including written explanations. Should this communication take place e.g. exclusively in English or (partially) also in German?

Such connections between own language and own cultural activities and the potential use of the participants' own language are hardly ever put clearly or discussed openly in official statements on external language policy or external cultural policy (ECP), not even when commissioned by the German Bundestag or the German Government (cf., e.g. resolutions dated 15 June 1994; *Bundestagsdrucksache* 12/ 790; *Bundesregierung* 2014: 17. *Bericht der Bundesregierung Auswärtige Kultur- und Bildungspolitik*). In these reports, attention even tends to be focussed merely on learning the language, without addressing language use. For example, with reference to the overseas broadcaster *Deutsche Welle*, German language courses are more likely to be discussed than the question of German as a broadcasting language or the suppression of German by other broadcasting languages (see Ch. J.1.3.2). It seems to me that such deficiencies are determined by the lack of a clear distinction between teaching German (as a foreign language/GFL) and the use of German, where the use of German and the significance of its use tend to be obscured from view. By contrast, one of the aims of this book has been to describe and to justify connections between the choice of German for use (for communication) and for learning – and the position of German not only locally, but also internationally or globally (Ch. A.2; A.6; F.2; H.4.2; H.4.6). The adequate language choice for communication (use of the language) in all situations relevant for the global position of German ought, more clearly than it has been hitherto, to be an objective within the external language policy of German-speaking countries: with the goal of motivating a choice which could strengthen the position of German locally and globally. In the chapters mentioned, I have attempted to show the difficulties of such language choices, which are also associated with the difficulty of providing an appropriate policy. The difficulty arises from the fact that, on one hand, the position of other relevant languages must also be taken into consideration, not least in view of the global language constellation (circumspect policy; Ch. A.7), and, on the other hand, doing justice to the linguistic interests of the other actors (respectful policy). But, in every case, external cultural policy is faced with the question of choosing a language for use which serves its goals. Beyond any other goals of the external cultural policy, these goals should relate to the interest of all German-speakers or to the entire German-language community in a strong global position for German (Ch. A.1) – at the same time as respecting the interests of other countries and language communities (see Ch. K.5).

Among its other goals, an external language policy which is guided by a (respectful) interest in a stronger position for the home language, should not lose sight of the following goals: maintaining or gaining as many speakers as possible (Ch. C; E), anchoring the German language, both legally/by statute and also regarding its use in as many states as possible, e.g. as an official language (Ch. D) or as a protected minority language (Ch. E), in the business economy, e.g. within companies (Ch. F), in science and scholarship, e.g. in universities (Ch. G), in diplomacy, e.g. in international organisations (Ch. H) and in other action fields (Ch. I); moreover – and this, at least, is already within the focus of current external cultural policy – maintaining or gaining the maximum possible number of learners of GFL (Ch. J).

2. Germany's language-spread policy up to the fall of the Nazi state

The largest German-speaking country has also pursued the most comprehensive external language policy and for that reason alone occupies the central position in this chapter. But it was Kaiser Josef II (reign as Kaiser 1765–1790) who undertook a spectacular early attempt at *internal* language policy in 1784 with a decree which declared German the national official language of the entire, multilingual Habsburg Monarchy (also known as the *Danube Monarchy* or the *Habsburg Empire*). However, on his deathbed (1790) Josef II had to withdraw the decree under pressure from Hungary (Stark 2002: 92). His attempt to assert an official language of state was intended primarily to simplify administration. But – in the spirit of enlightened absolutism – the idea that linguistic unification would allow all citizens to perceive their political rights more effectively was presumably already in play, corresponding to the assertion of the French language only a little later in revolutionary France. A later example of the internal spread of German was the Prussian schooling policy for the Polish-speaking population before WWI (Glück 1979). This limited the use of the Polish native language in school teaching to residual elements, such as the teaching of religion. The ruling was in no sense democratically motivated; it was designed to secure linguistic and therefore also ethnic assimilation to the German majority population. However, the present book is concerned less with internal than with external language policy.

Germany's external language policy (ELP) also began at the time of the last example, and indeed, as in other states, as a part of an external cultural policy (ECP) and therefore a foreign policy. It should be mentioned incidentally that Austria-Hungary had already initiated an external language policy in favour of German before WWI. Indicators can be seen in the foundation of Austrian schools abroad, e.g. the *St Georgs-Gymnasium* and the *Deutsches Gymnasium* in

Constantinople/Istanbul, both in 1868 (Emmert 1987: 61; Ch. K.9.7). However, Germany's policy was more comprehensive and more sustained. As Chancellor of the German Empire, founded in 1871, Bismarck launched the first stages. He introduced German instead of French for internal reports from external diplomatic agencies of the Empire. Later, he insisted on German as the language of correspondence for the Empire, even in correspondence with France, which, however, adhered to French. Bismarck attempted to replace French with German for correspondence with all foreign agencies in Berlin; though France refused to reply in German (Ch. H.5.2). Bismarck also strove to establish German as an international treaty language (Ch. H.1; H.2).

Imperial promotion of German schools abroad from 1878 (establishment of the *Reichsschulfonds*; Düwell 1976: 59) was also intended, alongside more comprehensive designs, to assist the spread of the German language. The policy was encouraged by Heinrich von Treitschke, a member of the Reichstag from 1871 to 1884 and a politically influential historian in the period before WWI, whose wise saying, "Germany's prospects will depend substantially upon how many people speak German in future" has been quoted in public speeches (Reinbothe 1992: 103f.). In 1906, a special Schools Division was founded for the schools abroad which were developed further to form a new type of school: "propaganda schools" [*Propagandaschulen*] (Düwell 1976: 60f) – although, at that time, the word *propaganda* meant simply "canvassing (generally for political ideas)", without the subsequent aggressiveness associated with the Nazi period. The spread of the German language as one of the goals of the external cultural policy (ECP) began to take on clear contours with the official School Division and the German Schools Abroad. This is clearly articulated in the secret *Geheime Denkschrift des Auswärtigen Amtes über das deutsche Auslandsschulwesen* of April 1914, where it is claimed: "In recent years, approximately since 1906, a movement has begun which sets important new tasks for the German Schools Abroad. It is based on the view that, to a greater extent than hitherto, these schools could spread knowledge of the German language and disseminate correct ideas about Germany among foreign people, acquainting as many indigenous groups as possible with German customs and education in order to win them as friends for Germany". This document also claims with satisfaction that, although they did not teach exclusively in German, "[. . .] the use of German as a language of teaching in the German Schools Abroad has generally increased since the turn-of-the-century [. . .]" (quoted after Düwell 1976: 271, 295).

Government policy was supplemented by private associations, which were generally funded by the government. Prominent among these was the *Allgemeiner deutscher Schulverein* founded in 1881, whose activities soon went beyond the promotion of the German Schools Abroad. In 1901, it changed its name to the *Verein für das Deutschtum im Ausland* (*VDA* – Society for German Culture Abroad) and continued under this name until 1970, in the FRG, with the support of the German Foreign Office (after that, with a new programme, under the name of *Gesellschaft für Deutsche Kulturbeziehungen im Ausland*, and from 1998: *Verein für Deutsche Kulturbeziehungen im Ausland e. V.* (*VDA*); see Ch. K.3.4). As a curiosity which sheds light on imperial ambitions around the time of WWI, mention should also be made of proposals for a simplified German, primarily with simplified grammar, which was to be spread in the sphere of German influence, especially the colonies. Such projects had a certain similarity with Ogden's (1934) and Richards' (1943) subsequent "Basic English". However, the proposals by Salzmann (1913), Baumann (1915) and Schwörer (1916) did not attract government support.

During the Weimar Republic, the ECP became an important part of German foreign policy. This applies especially to the German Schools Abroad, most of which had been closed or confiscated in the war, and efforts were now being made to restore them. "In the period 1919–1935, 51 schools were reopened or newly founded in Europe, 22 in Asia, 23 in Africa and 64 in South America. The number of pupils rose to a total well above 80,000. Even by the mid-1920s, they had returned to the pre-war level. By way of further support, the Schools Division of the Foreign Office [a legacy from the Kaiser's time! U.A.] sent teaching materials to the Schools Abroad and continued to provide German teaching staff to the schools" (Waibel 2010: 13f.). In the German Schools Abroad, German was the language of teaching at least for some subjects, especially in the subject German itself but also in history and geography. The ECP of the Weimar Republic can be explained, on one hand, with reference to the effort to keep together the German "nation" (in the ethnic sense of cultural and linguistic nation; Ch. B.3), as far as possible worldwide, but on the other hand, as a form of compensation for other possibilities for political action which had been reduced in consequence of the loss of the war. France had reacted in a similar manner after the defeat in 1871. The founding of the *Alliance Française* in 1883 can be regarded as an indicator for France's expanded ECP at that time. In both cases, the latent hope of occasionally winning back territories lost in the war through language maintenance presumably played a part here (Ammon 2000a). This was highly conflict-laden because of flagrant incongruities between ethnic and political boundaries and affiliations, especially in Europe (see Rundle 1944). (It has become so again recently, but with different ethnic groups and nations.)

In 1919, a dedicated Culture Department was established within the German Foreign Office (Auswärtiges Amt/AA). After a turbulent intervening history, its successor has become *Abteilung 6: Kultur und Kommunikation* of the present-day AA (Ch. K.3.2, beginning). In subsequent years, but also even before, several institutions were founded whose objectives included spreading the German language (Abelein 1968: 116f.). These still exist in Germany today but, of course, with different objectives and, in some cases, modified names (Ch. K.3.3). Arranged according to significance for the promotion of German, the most important are:

- *Goethe-Institut (G-I)*, which was formed from the "Practical Department" of the *Deutsche Akademie* set up in 1925 and founded in 1932 to celebrate the centenary of the death of Goethe ("Foundation of a Goethe-Institut of the German Academy for the further training of foreign German teachers in Munich" in *Mitteilungen der Akademie* [...] 1, April 1932: 1–3; Düwell 1976: 124; E. Michels 2005: 80–83; 222–227). Because of the Nazi past, but also the widening of its aims, the present-day Goethe-Institut prefers to begin its own accounts of its history with the refoundation in 1951.

- *Deutscher Akademischer Austausch Dienst (DAAD)*, also originated in 1925 (founded in Heidelberg; Alter 2000b: 21), its main purpose, corresponding to the name, is to intensify exchange between German and foreign academics, students, teachers and researchers, which also benefits German Language and Literature and therefore the global position of German (Laitenberger 1976, 2000; Schulz 1975; Scheibe 1975; Alter 2000a, b).

- *Deutsches Ausland-Institut (DAI)*, founded in 1917 in Stuttgart to foster relations with "German culture abroad", minorities and emigrants from the German-speaking countries and therefore also maintenance of the German language abroad. Now known as the *Institut für Auslandsbeziehungen* (ifa) (E. Ritter 1976; "75 years Institut für Auslandsbeziehungen Stuttgart 1917 to 1992" in *Zeitschrift für Kulturaustausch* 42 (1) 1992: 143–155).

- *Alexander von Humboldt-Stiftung (AvH)*, re-founded in 1925 – after the bankruptcy in 1923 of the foundation formed in 1860, one year after the death of Alexander von Humboldt. It aims to attract high-ranking foreign academics to make visits to Germany and to support them during their stay – a knowledge of German could play a part in selection, support and maintaining contact (for history, see C. Jansen/ Nensa 2004).

All these organisations were and still are constituted as associations under private law with the AvH constituted as a foundation. They operate "less bureaucratically than government authorities" and do not arouse "suspicion abroad that Germany is seeking to pursue political goals through cultural activities" (Niere 1977: 10f.) – which, admittedly, was and still is the case. Not only do they pursue in basic outline goals specified by the government; they are also largely financed by the government. The German Foreign Office is responsible for them, more specifically its Culture Department. Even today, the external cultural policy, specifically the external language policy (ELP), is still structured based on government-supervised "mediating organisations" [*Mittlerorganisationen*] *constituted* under private law (Witte/ Akalin 1985: 7; Maaß 2009c; Ch. K.3.3).

Alongside these organisations, there were and still are purely government organisations for the ELP. These included the Schools Division of the Foreign Office already mentioned, which was taken over from the Wilhelmine period and supervised the Schools Abroad. During Nazi times, its responsibilities merged with those of the "Division (EIIIb) of the *Reichserziehungsministerium*, founded in 1934", which was concerned "with questions regarding the Schools Abroad (e.g. provision of teachers, school curricula, recognition of certificates etc.). This Division was formed from a Division of the 11th Prussian Ministry for Culture" (Waibel 2010: 10f.). To some extent, it continues in present-day Germany in the *Zentralstelle für das Auslandschulwesen/ZFA* [Central Office for Schools Abroad].

The *Weltrundfunksender*, which was founded and began radio broadcasting in 1929, was also significant. It broadcast around the world in German and therefore also supported language maintenance among emigrants and German-speaking minorities. At the same time, purely private institutions were also formed, which contributed to the external spread of German in a similar way, e.g., in 1926, the *Amerika-Werkstudentendienst*, which organised mutual internship exchanges between Germany and the USA. The *Carl Duisberg Gesellschaft* was re-founded as a successor by the Federal Government and the Federal States in 1949. It was named after the initiator, Director General of the Bayer paint factories (M. Schneider 1989) but was absorbed, in 2002, into *Internationale Weiterbildung und Entwicklung GmbH (InWent)* (www.cdg.de/verein_geschichte.htm).

Under Nazism, all organisations constituted under private law lost their autonomy, sometimes with and sometimes without internal resistance (for Goethe-Institut: E. Michels 2005; for DAAD: G. Schulz 1975; Laitenberger 1976, 2000; for *Deutsches Auslandsinstitut/ Institut für Auslandsbeziehungen*: Gesche 2006). The Culture Department of the Foreign Office was renamed as the "*Kulturpolitische Abteilung*" and placed as far as possible at the disposal of National Socialist propaganda. In consequence, in the mid-1930s, especially in the Baltic states, Sweden and the USA, German teaching "sensitively" receded (Thierfelder 1936: 44; Ch. J.2). Government organisations were taken over by the Nazis without ceremony. The same applies for the *Weltrundfunksender*, which the National Socialist government renamed as the *Deutscher Kurzwellensender* and utilised for propaganda abroad. It also served the spread of German abroad through German-language broadcasts and subsequently additional German-language courses. In the subsequent FRG, the redesigned *Deutsche Welle (DW)* was founded in 1953 as an overseas broadcaster. In the GDR, *Radio Berlin International* (RBI) was formed in 1959. Deutsche Welle took over the RBI's broadcasting capacities in 1990 (Ch. I.1.3.1).

According to Nazi beliefs, on the one hand, German was to become, as far as possible, a "world language" as conceived e.g. by Thierfelder (1938). On the other hand, during the war, there were also efforts to restrict knowledge of German according to racist perspectives, e.g. for Ukrainians and Russians, by contrast with the Baltic population; German was portrayed as the language of the "master race" (G. Klein 1984: 109). Dirk Scholten (2000a, b) investigated the wartime ELP of the Nazi state for Luxembourg, Eastern Central and Eastern Europe. In fact, substantial points of the policy were kept secret, and it is possible to distinguish between "declared", "non-declared" and, as a special case of the latter category, "secret" language-spread policies. In general, German was provided as the sole official language for annexed states and national territories; it was supposed to become the native language later, following compulsory language shifting and expulsion of parts of the population. The procedure in occupied territories was different.

In Alsace and Lorraine (cf. Ch. E.4.3), French was to be completely replaced by German through expulsion of the French-speaking population, and French was to be entirely replaced by German as the official language and language of schooling. The policy included rulings such as the following: "Inscriptions on gravestones and grave monuments may, in future, be written only in German; this provision applies both for the initial inscription and also for any renewal of existing inscriptions" (Secretariat of the Court of Justice 1948; Volume 6:470–483, p. 483).

In Luxembourg (cf. Ch. D.2.5), French was banned as the language of teaching and Luxemburgish was discredited as a mere (admittedly "German") dialect, "the fostering of which in no sense corresponds with the *Führer's* wishes" (Scholten 2000a: 130, 132). In October 1941, a referendum was supposed to legitimise the annexation of the country through a popular declaration in favour of German as the "native language" and "membership of the German *Volk*". However, this plan was aborted when initial results showed that more than 90% of the population had declared Luxemburgish as their native language and ethnicity (ibid: 127f.). But the country was annexed anyway and, in August 1942, declared a part of the "*Großdeutsches Reich*".

For the Netherlands and Flemish-speaking Belgium (Flanders), there were proposals to persuade the population that Flemish was only a dialect of German (cf. Ch. B.1; B.2). The idea was ultimately to achieve a voluntary linguistic – and subsequently also political – annexation in this manner. Georg Schmidt-Rohr's suggestion that "it has been shown time and again and very skillfully using the resources of mass manipulation, that, in so far as they speak a dialect, Dutch and Flemish people are speaking a German dialect" evidently also has this approach in mind. With these resources, therefore, positive evaluation of their own language – or their "language loyalty" (Greule 1999) – was to be undermined. "Faced with this written language [German! U.A.], the Dutch people themselves have the feeling that [Dutch] is actually not a proper, cultural language [. . .], but really probably just a written dialect [. . .]. Undermining the self-confidence of the Dutch people with all the resulting political feedback, with the need for closer reliance on the German *Muttervolk* [mother-tongue ethnic group] should not be so difficult [. . .]" (Quotation from Simon 1979b: 169). But this proposal was not supported officially, among other reasons because it was considered unrealistic (Simon 1979b: 172f.). However, during the period of German occupation, the provision of German-language newspapers (C. Sauer 1989) and radio broadcasts was considerably expanded. This may have been co-determined primarily by practical considerations but was possibly also guided by the intention of familiarising the Dutch people with the German language and with the prospect of shifting to German in the long term.

In every case, this was what was planned for Czechia, if not for all of Czechoslovakia – where the racist distinction between "Germanisable" and "non-Germanisable" people was imposed for large parts of Eastern Central and Eastern Europe; the former group were to be linguistically and ethnically assimilated and the latter suppressed, expelled or even annihilated. After the territory of Czechoslovakia, which had so far been *Sudeten* German, had been annexed to Nazi-Germany in September 1938, the remaining Czech population was denied any minority rights, which had previously been demanded by Germany – not entirely without justification – for the Sudeten Germans. Because of the repressive measures, approximately 500,000 ethnic Czechs had already left this region, which was to be radically Germanised, by May 1939 (Scholten 2000a: 134–148). For the remainder of Czechia, which was declared the Nazi-German "Protectorate of

Bohemia and Moravia" in March 1939, the same language-policy goals were set, but they could not be fully implemented because of the Russian campaign (ibid: 148–153, 158–162, 177–179, 186–200). This involved the introduction of German as the official language of state, expansion of German as the language of teaching in schools (which was only possible to a limited extent in the short time available; ibid: 179) and of German as the language of teaching at the Karls-University in Prague, where teaching had to be abandoned for years as a result. German kindergarten teachers were appointed everywhere; Czech schools were either closed or attendance was prohibited. The Czech government had to accept a German in the Cabinet, so that German became the sole working language, as was also stipulated for the entire government administration (Secretariat of the Court of Justice 1948, Vol. 26:469–473). This policy was implemented with the goal of depriving the Czech language of all higher cultural functions.

In Slovakia, which became independent in 1938, German-language schooling with German as the language of teaching was expanded under pressure from Germany, and German was established in all schools as the first foreign language (Scholten 2000a: 180–185). At the University of Bratislava, a *Deutsches Wisssenschaftliches Institut* (*DWI*) was designed to secure the priority position of German as an academic language (ibid: 162–165).

In the occupied parts of Poland, on 26 October 1939, by order of the German Governor General, Hans Frank, German became the sole official language (§9 of the Order). The Governor General's orders were also issued in Polish, but the German text was binding (§10 of the Order. Secretariat of the Court of Justice 1948, Vol. 32:304). "Racially valuable" parts of the population could declare their Germanness (cf. Ch. E.4.4); but they were offered "favourable living conditions" only "subject to the condition that they would ensure that their children learn the German language and familiarise themselves with German thought" (Secretariat of the Court of Justice 1948, Vol. 26:41). By contrast, the "non-Germanisable" parts of the population were not to attend German schools and not to be provided with a knowledge of German (ibid: 223f.).

Hungary was allied with Nazi-Germany but remained independent – until occupation by German troops in March 1944. In fact, Nazi-Germany had previously tried to protect the German-(speaking) minority (Ch. E.4.6) from Hungarian pressure towards assimilation but achieved relatively little (Scholten 2000a: 201–246). By contrast, the establishment of a nationwide network of lectors from the *Deutsche Akademie* during the war was successful (ibid: 229–242). Broadcasting German-language courses on the radio became possible only after the occupation of the country (ibid: 242).

The details of Nazi external language policy have been described explicitly by Scholten (2000a), especially for the Baltics (Estonia, Latvia, Lithuania), Belarus, Russia and the Ukraine. The overarching objective was "assimilation of the racially suitable" and expulsion or subjection and rendering servile of "larger racially inferior groups of the population" (ibid: 248). The German language was not to be forced upon the latter group but, instead, withheld from them (2000b). Securing mastery over the "racially inferior populations", the proportion of whom was estimated to be larger towards the east, was to be achieved by destroying their education system and their culture, and by withholding comprehensive knowledge of German, apart from a minimum level required for the communication of orders. This policy is reminiscent of the simplified "colonial German" of E. Schwörer (1916: 20), which has already been mentioned, because this was also supposed to be "nothing more than a paltry but very useful maid servant alongside its superior, High-German sister". However, unrestricted Standard-German was to become the official language, the language of education and culture – expressions which perhaps merit inverted commas here – of the unified "*Großdeutsches Reich*".

The National Socialist policy of expansion and restriction of German has been outlined here to give an idea of the political legacy inherited by the German-speaking countries after WWII in their renewed efforts "to promote German abroad". Forcing the German language on other peoples was a relatively harmless part of Nazi policy compared with the violation of ethnic and human rights, military conquest and devastation, and genocide based on Nazi racist ideology. After these events, German was considered less the language of Goethe than the language of Hitler and Auschwitz and was presumably judged by many people much as it was by Anne Frank's family in conversations in their hideaway in Amsterdam which permitted only "all languages of culture, and so *not German*" ("*toegestaan zijn alle cultuurtaalen, dus geen Duits*". Anne Frank 1947: 46 – emphasis U.A.).

However, despite the understandable aversion to German, many people retained a memory of more humane and worthy traditions in German language and culture. Even people who had been affected particularly brutally by National Socialist crimes. I mention the respected literary critic Marcel Reich-Ranicki as just one example. And some groups of "*Jeckes*", the Jews who fled the German-speaking countries, often making a narrow escape to Israel, and who nurtured amongst themselves a cultivated German language and German culture, have also preserved this attitude (Betten 2011; Betten/ Dunour 2000; contributions in Zabel 2006).

3. Germany's external language policy after WWII

3.1 Overview of external language policy in the FRG, GDR and unified Germany

Despite the burden of its history, the *Bundesrepublik Deutschland/Federal Republic of Germany* (FRG), formed in the West through the division of Germany, succeeded in developing a new external cultural policy (ECP) with an external language policy (ELP). Its organisational centre was the German Foreign Office re-founded in 1951 (in Bonn until 1999, then in Berlin). Once again, special responsibilities were given to Department 6: *Culture Department*, which played a key role in the re-founding and new foundation of "mediating organisations" [*Mittlerorganisationen*] (for this term, see Ch. K.3.3), in some cases with revised and expanded objectives. The organisations named first here (*Goethe-Institut* to *Deutsche Welle* and *Alexander von Humboldt Foundation*) are the most important for the ECP (references in brackets). In view of the description already given in Ch. K.2, a few keywords will suffice here, also with reference to the history. The same applies for newly founded organisations (*Deutsche UNESCO-Kommission* to *Deutsche Gesellschaft für Internationale Zusammenarbeit*), which are less relevant to the ELP.

- *Goethe-Institut* (*G-I*; Munich), re-founded in 1951, entered in the register of associations 1952, with amended title "for the cultivation of the German language abroad" instead of "for the further training of foreign German teachers" from the original foundation in 1932 (E. Michels);
- *Deutscher Akademischer Austauschdienst* (*DAAD*; Bonn), re-founded in 1950, initially founded in 1925 (Alter 2000b);
- *Institut für Auslandsbeziehungen* (*ifa*; Stuttgart), re-founded in 1949, initially founded 1917 as *Deutsches Ausland-Institut* (*DAI*) ("75 years Institute for Foreign Relations Stuttgart 1917 to 1992" (1992) in the *Zeitschrift für Kulturaustausch* 42 (1): 143–155);
- *Zentralstelle für das Auslandwesen* (*ZfA*), government authority for the Schools Abroad, newly founded in 1960 within the Federal Office for Administration (Cologne) – a kind of

continuation of the Schools Division of the Foreign Office founded in 1906 (Waibel 2010: 10f.; Ch. K.2);

- *Deutsche Welle* (*DW*; Cologne), government broadcaster, re-founded in 1953, initially founded in 1929 as *Weltrundfunksender* (Dorr/ Schiedermair 2003; Krasteva 2007);
- *Alexander von Humboldt-Stiftung* (*AvH*; Bonn), re-founded in 1953, initially founded in 1925 (C. Jansen/ Nensa 2004).

Other new foundations:

- *Deutsche UNESCO-Kommission* (Bonn), initially founded in 1950;
- *Haus der Kulturen der Welt* (*HKW*; Berlin), initially founded 1989;
- *(Deutsche) Gesellschaft für Internationale Zusammenarbeit* (*GIZ*; Bonn/Eschborn), initially founded in 2011 through the merger of the *Deutsche Entwicklungsdienst* (*DED*; initially founded in 1963), *Deutsche Gesellschaft für Technische Zusammenarbeit* (*GTZ*; initially founded in 1975) and *Internationale Weiterbildung und Entwicklung* (*InWent*; initially founded in 2002, with the inclusion of the *Carl Duisberg Gesellschaft* re-founded in 1949 as the successor of the *Amerika-Werkstudentendienst*, initially founded in 1926); (all, apart from GIZ, in Maaß 2009c: 269, 276–280).

The work of these organisations was backed by Willy Brandt, Foreign Minister (1966–1969), whose appreciation of the relevant policies led to the saying that the "external cultural policy was the *third column* of German foreign policy", alongside security and external economic policy. However, as early as 1912, cultural historian Karl Lamprecht had already mooted the idea that external cultural policy is a continuation of *Machtpolitik* (power policy; E. Michels 2005: 17), and American political scientist Joseph Nye (1999, 2004) has taken the idea further with the now sloganized term "soft power": the attempt to influence other countries via cultural activities in addition to or instead of economic or military pressure. However, Brandt's emphasis was more strongly on mutuality between countries.

An overview of the state of the FRG's external cultural policy in the 1980s is provided in the *Federal Government Report on the German Language in the World* (1985: 22–27). I have described the history of the discussion of these policies in the Bundestag in Ammon 1989c (see also Bohrer 1988). The descriptions cover the most important official documents up to this time, such as the Federal Government reports of 1967 (*Situation of the German Language in the World*) and 1985 (*Federal Government Report on the German Language in the World*), including the goals, methods and instruments of the FRG's external language policy. The political situation in the divided country necessitated a policy which is more appropriately described as "language promotion" rather than "language spread" (Ch. K.1), which also corresponds more closely to the altered global position of German, relating more to maintenance than spread (Ch. A.11). But it is evident that, throughout the history of the FRG, the ELP has grown, and the range of people involved and resources applied has multiplied since the 1950s. Furthermore, the ELP has become established as an independent part of the ECP, although it has always been integrated with the other parts. One indicator for this is the establishment, in February 1988, of a dedicated divisional office "German Language" (Division 605) within Department 6, the Culture Department of the German Foreign Office. However, this was followed by a restructuring and change of responsibilities, as the name of a division with the same number in 2014 suggests: "Division 605 (German Schools Abroad, PASCH and Sport)", so that there is now no longer a dedicated Division for "German Language" (Ch. K.3.2, beginning). The high status accorded to the ELP is revealed through public statements, through the commitment of the director of the Culture Department (1983–1991), Barthold C. Witte (e.g. 1983, 1984, 1985c, 1987; Witte/ Akalin 1985; Wehrmann 1988), and through the financial benefits granted to the "promotional division for German language" which, at times exceeded 50% of the total expenditure of the Culture Department, e.g. 1984: DM 424.4 of 761.2 m; 1986: DM 445.6 of 808.3 m (Department for External cultural policy of the German Foreign Office 1988: 15, 95). At times, the ELP was considered crucial for the ECP and may even have been significant for the entire foreign policy. In the 1980s – responding to the idea that German was experiencing a global decline – ELP was intensified, which is evident from the increased financing and government declarations by Chancellor Helmut Kohl on 4 March 1983 and 18 March 1987, in which he announced that he wanted "once more to spread the German language abroad" and "to promote the spread of the German language, our mother tongue, robustly throughout the world in future" (*Bundestagsprotokolle* 67C and respectively 64D). This position was echoed by demands from other politicians regarding German as a foreign language (GFL), to "shift the existing policy of meeting demand to a policy of demand creation" (Minister of State, Jürgen Möllemann in discussion of the Report. German Bundestag, Public Relations Division 1986: 12). The Goethe-Institut launched an advertising campaign abroad for the learning of German (*auf deutsch. Zur Werbung für Deutsch als Fremdsprache*, no date given; Department for External cultural Policy of the German Foreign Office 1988: 16f.), supported by posters with texts such as "*Kan Du tyska?*" "*Aprenda Alemão*", "*Aprender Alemão Compensa!*", "*L'Anglais tout seul ne suffit plus. Apprenez l'Allemand*", "What About Learning German?". Intensification of the ELP presumably grew not only from the recognisably dwindling global position of German, especially compared with English, but also in response to increasing German economic power with the exaggerated self-image of an "economic giant and political dwarf".

The *Deutsche Demokratische Republik (DDR)* German Democratic Republic/ GDR), which was formed in the former central and eastern region of Germany, also developed an ELP, which has been described and analysed by Martin Praxenthaler (2000, 2002). His choice of the term "language spread policy" was possibly influenced by my own earlier choice of terms (Ammon 1989c, 1990d, 1991a: 524–566). But observers may be surprised by Praxenthaler's choice of terms here and even by the discovery that the GDR did indeed have an external language policy – because of the criticisms in the GDR about the "language-policy imperialism" of capitalist countries expressed by GDR politicians, such as Klaus Zorn (1980: 1982; cf. contributions in *Imperialistische Sprachpolitik in den 70er und zu Beginn der 80er Jahre* 1983). In this context, the GDR's ECP served to distribute citizens' own political ideas more openly than that of the FRG. Its breadth is shown by Praxenthaler's (2002) chapter headings, such as "Studying in the GDR for Foreign Students" (ibid: 208–216), "German Teaching in Schools", "German Language and Literature in Universities", "German in the Media", "German Speaking Minorities", and "Lectors in Universities in the Host Countries" (ibid: 245–259). However, the GDR's external language policy was necessarily limited largely to the socialist countries, except for Scandinavia – and conversely, the socialist countries were correspondingly inaccessible to the FRG for its external language policy. The GFL pedagogy developed in the GDR was built on a solid theoretical-grammatical base and was also respected in the FRG. It was supervised by the *Herder-Institut* in Leipzig, which had begun with GFL teaching as early as 1951, although the institute was not officially founded until 1961, and its title was supplemented with the following: *Vorstudienanstalt für ausländische Studierende in der DDR und Stätte zur Förderung deutscher Sprachkenntnisse im Ausland* [Preparatory Studies Centre for Foreign Students in the GDR and Centre for Promotion of the German Language Abroad] (www.uni-leipzig.de/herder/hi.site,postext,chronologie.html? PHPSESSID=1dpvgmfgbhck7 nk257q3a8ai9l0uqeio). This supplement to the title reveals the institute's primary objective of linguistic preparation of foreign students. The director for many years was Gerhard Helbig, a world-renowned grammar researcher. The Herder-Institut (www. uni-leipzig.de/herder/) was subsequently absorbed into the unified Germany and, since 2007, has been directed by Christian Fandrych. But to the regret of many experts, large parts of the GDR external language policy have not been continued.

However, the *Bundesrepublik Deutschland/ BRD* (Federal Republic of Germany) – abbreviated here as *Germany* – which became politically more important after reunification, has intensified its ELP. To some extent, the policy was orientated towards the position of German in the European Union (Ch. H.4.2; Ammon 2009a: 124–126). For example, German EU officials (who were not legally bound by instructions from the German Government) were nevertheless instructed to insist on German-language consultation documents (Andrei/ Rittberger 2009: 44); and Chancellor Helmut Kohl had demanded that German should receive the status of a working language of the Commission, which Commission President Jacques Delors finally allowed with the decree that "Documents for internal use by the Commission [. . .] should be prepared in the working languages German, English and French" (*EG-Nachrichten* 34, 6 September 1993: 4). However, like other attempts to strengthen the position of German in the EU institutions, the effect lagged far behind Germany's wishes. It would thus not be an exaggeration to evaluate Germany's ELP relative to the EU as having substantially failed (Ch. H.4.2; H.4.4; H.4.6). This is symbolically evident from the fact that, even today, in public appearances of the Commission, the "working language" German does not appear on text banners, which still show only English and French. This failure is in line with the failure to achieve the position of an official language in the United Nations, which was not even applied for when the Federal Republic joined in 1973 (Ch. H.3).

Efforts to strengthen the position of German in Eastern Europe after the dissolution of the Soviet Union, where many hoped for a "renaissance of German language and culture", as former Premier of Baden-Württemberg, Lothar Späth (1990: 322) once put it, also failed. In this context, "the German language was promoted in Central and Eastern Europe with a comprehensive special programme" (Maaß 2009b: 27; in detail, Axel Schneider 2000: 83–299). It included – with the participation of all "mediating organisations" (Ch. K.3.3) – school teaching, universities, adult language courses and development and use of media – but was also largely unsuccessful (Stevenson/ Carl 2010: 45–50; Born/ Stickel 1993). But it would be incorrect to deny Germany's ELP at that time any impact, because, without it, German may not have achieved second place among school foreign languages in large parts of Eastern Central and Eastern Europe, where it is surpassed only – with wide margin – by English (Ch. J.7; Maps J.7–1 and J.7–2; J.9.5; J.9.6).

Failure of key ELP objectives may have been the underlying reason for dwindling commitment to ELP by the Red-Green coalition (1998–2005) under Foreign Minister Joschka Fischer (1998–2005), as revealed in his programmatic paper "*Auswärtige Kulturpolitik – Konzeption 2000*" (www.ifa.de/ fileadmin/pdf/aa/akbp_konzeption2000.pdf). In fact, the document contains objectives and principles which seem important, such as "the maintenance and strengthening of the German language as a key to the German culture and the provision of Schools Abroad" – but they occur low down the list (point 6 of 9). In the immediately following List II of "current challenges" for German external cultural policy "in a changing world", the promotion of German is not even mentioned, only the "preservation and promotion of the diversity of European languages" (point 5). In "List III. Strategy for the immediate future", the promotion of German does occur again but only under point 8 (of 12). Here, it is stated that: "[P]romoting the demand for the German language, and exchange and encounter programmes for multipliers will therefore be of increasing importance". After touching on the topic occasionally, the overview of institutions and improvements in the efficiency of ECP ends with the warning (point 4) that the "promotion of the German language" in the world will only be credible, "if the goal of multilingualism in Germany is also taken seriously" by "expanding foreign-language teaching in schools [. . .]". It might therefore be suspected that Germany has not fulfilled this condition (cf. Quetz 2010) – and the promotion of German will remain a vain effort. Admittedly, the limits on ECP which are discernible at this time were also determined by financial constraints. But the financial cutbacks and commitments to intensify self-financing by the organisations involved impacted most strongly on ELP. According to "IV. Strategy papers", the Goethe-Institut is "affected in a particularly visible manner by structural cutbacks", and the reduction of structural costs takes place "primarily to the detriment [. . .] of the Schools Abroad" ("Budget and structural questions": points 3 and respectively 2, similarly in "Schools Abroad": point 4). Not until subsequent governments were in power could these cutbacks be reversed; the Goethe-Institut was then more generously funded, and the German Schools Abroad were placed on a secure legal footing (Ch. K.3.2).

However, it is remarkable that the ELP of the FRG and then of the unified Germany was supported by all political parties represented in the Bundestag, although to a different extent (see also 1989c, 1991a: 540–544). This applies especially to the following aspects, which were developed by way of distinction from German policy before 1945:

(1) Publicness of the ELP, as for the entire ECP (*Bericht* 1985: 5). Secrecy shrouding previous policies (cf. Ch. K.2) is considered incompatible with democratic principles;
(2) Declared readiness for mutual language learning; the will to learn other languages ourselves alongside the desire that others should learn German (*Bericht* 1985: 7. But for limits on *de facto* readiness to learn, see Quetz 2010);
(3) Goal of improving the image of Germany abroad, which was destroyed by Nazism, and making serious efforts to achieve this.

In proportion to the consensus between parties, dissent is minimal. It is co-determined by fluctuations between the roles of government and opposition: the opposition tends to demand from the government a greater commitment to German in the ELP, and this includes the otherwise rather reticent SPD (details in Ammon 1989c: 235, 237, 254, 258). Their reticence is evident e.g. in the fact that Willy Brandt was the only SPD Chancellor who even touched on the topic in his government policy statement, by expressing the "wish that our language might have a life outside". By contrast with subsequent statements by Helmut Kohl, Brandt's intention is less with the spread of German than with issuing a warning not "to allow" our own language "to atrophy from the inside" (18 January 1973; *Bundestagprotokolle* 130C). This position corresponded with the wording in the *Leitsätze für die auswärtige Kulturpolitik* [guidelines for external cultural policy (Auswärtiges Amt, December 1970) issued approximately one year after the start of the social-liberal coalition, which was characteristic of the SPD. The document states that "The German language is the bearer, not the goal of our activities abroad". It continues, "[T]here are traditional German language territories in which the promotion of German can be intensified; in other parts of the world, it may be more expedient for the goals of exchange and collaboration to use the most customary language in each context as a means of communication" (ibid: 10). By contrast, documents characteristic of the CDU/CSU typically discuss the "responsibility and duty of the government of the largest German-speaking country to commit itself to the most comprehensive possible spread and assertion of its language abroad" (*Bericht* 1985: 6). Having said this, the two major parties ultimately differ only in nuance.

The FDP occasionally tended towards a more active policy, e.g. Minister of State Jürgen Möllemann, but it sometimes showed even greater reticence, e.g. German MP Hildegard

Hamm-Brücher (Deutscher Bundestag, Public Relations Division 1986: 11–13, 23–28). *Die Grünen*, subsequently *Bündnis 90/Die Grünen* and die *Linkspartei PDS*, subsequently *Die Linke*, generally tended towards reticence but, in principle, did not question the ELP or attempts at strengthening the global position of German. As one among various possible indicators for an affirmative attitude, the commitment and support shown by the culture-policy spokesperson of the Green Bundestag faction, Antje Vollmer (*RP Online* 1 April 2004; Ch. I.2.3) for a "German music quota", favouring an increased proportion of German language, should also be remembered. This also seems compatible with approval, if not explicit support, for external policies for maintaining the position of German. However, the German Government is not always tentative in its choice of wording for the ELP. Occasionally, for example, it grasps the nettle in describing its overarching goal as "the *spread* of the German language in Europe and in the world" (www. auswaertiges-amt.de/DE/Aussenpolitik/ KulturDialog/ ZieleUndPartner/ZielePartner_node. html; emphasis U.A.).

3.2 Recent developments

A comprehensive account would need to include all ministries in the governments of the German-speaking countries concerned with external language policy (ELP), which will not be possible within the present context. The diversity of responsibilities can perhaps be suggested based on the example of the German government, to which I restrict myself here. In Germany, superordinate responsibility lies with the German Foreign Office (Auswärtiges Amt/AA), but other ministries are involved, especially the Federal Ministries for Education and Research and for Economic Cooperation and Development. Among the nine or ten departments of the Foreign Office – depending on the method of counting – Department 6: *Culture and Communication* is of primary importance. Its "task [. . .] is the planning, coordination and control of German external cultural and educational policy, communications and media policy and political public-relations work" (www.auswaertiges-amt.de/DE/AAmt/Abteilungen/ KulturUndKommunika-tion _node.html).

However, the following departments also play a part in ELP (indicated here with their official reference number): 1 *Central Department* and 7 *Diplomatic Protocol*. And within the Department for *Culture and Communication*, it is primarily the following operational units which are concerned with ELP (information gratefully received from Gunnar Hille and Jakob Haselhuber): 606–9 "German as a foreign language"; Division 600 "Strategy and Planning External Cultural and Educational Policy, Communication and Image of Germany Abroad (*DiA*), European Cultural and Media Policy"; 601 (Europe, USA, Canada, Russia, Turkey, Central Asia and Caucasus), 602 (Africa, Asia, Australia, Pacific, Latin America and Caribbean), 603 ("Multilateral Culture and Media Policy; Transregional cultural projects; Promotion of the Arts, Literature and Film"), 605 (German Schools Abroad, PASCH and Sport), 606 (Overseas Operations of German Cultural Institutes such as the Goethe-Institut and the Institute for Foreign Relations), 604 (Science and Scholarship, Universities, German Archaeological Institute), 608 (Communications Abroad, Internet Editing, Internet Pages of Diplomatic Missions, Deutschland Centres, Web 2.0, Intranet Editing; Audiovisual Products, *Deutsche Welle*, Federal Government Visitor Programmes); and 609 ("Cultural, Educational and Media Relations" with the Maghreb, Near East and Middle East, and "Dialogue with the Islamic World"). Beyond these, divisions within other departments have responsibilities relating to the German language, such as division E01 in the Europe Department for "the language question in the EU", division 405 for the "external scientific policy (*Deutsche Wissenschafts- und Innovationshäuser*)" and for international research policy; and division 105 "Language Services" (with the operational unit "Language Centre". For anyone on the outside, this complicated structure is reminiscent of Kafka's *The Castle.* An organisational diagram can be found on the Foreign Office homepage: www.auswaertiges-amt.de/cae/servlet/contentblob/382698/publicationFile/ 195722/Organisationsplan-Druckversion.pdf.

In recent years, at least the mediating organisations (Ch. K.3.3) controlled by the Foreign Office have acknowledged the need to rationalise the ELP, forming the following mergers and cooperative projects:

- Goethe-Institut and Inter-Nationes (in 2000): with the provisional title *Goethe-Institut Inter-Nationes* (2001–2003), which was then shortened to *Goethe-Institut*, again revealing the asymmetry of the connection;
- *Deutscher Sprachrat* [German Language Council] (2003): a working group of the German Academic Exchange Service (*DAAD*), the Society for German Language (*GfdS*), the Goethe-Institut (*G-I*), and the Institute for German Language (*IDS*), which is primarily concerned with the "domestic language culture" but also with "promoting the position of German abroad" (www.deutscher-sprachrat.de/ziele-und-aufgaben/);
- *Netzwerk Deutsch* (even before 2010): an "Initiative of the Foreign Office, the German Academic Exchange Service, the Goethe-Institut and the Central Office for German Schools Abroad (*ZfA*) for the promotion of German as a foreign language" (www.goethe.de/uun/pub/ de5759780.htm). Amongst other work, it has collaborated in registering learner numbers for GFL worldwide (Netzwerk Deutsch 2010; Auswärtiges Amt 2015), but, in many countries, it also coordinates promotion of the German language, generally in collaboration with the local German embassies.

The following external cultural and education policy (ECEP) initiatives and innovations are particularly relevant to Germany's ELP on the global position of German:

1) School level

   a) The partner-school initiative/*PASCH* (www.pasch-net.de/udi/web/ deindex. Htm. Ch. J.3; K.3.3); and
   b) The Law on Schools Abroad (Ch. J.3).

2) University level

   a) International degree programmes (Ch. G.8);
   b) *Initiative Außenwissenschaftspolitik*, initiative on external academic policy (Ch. K.3.3).

Point 1a): The "PASCH-Initiative (Schools: Partners for the Future)" originated in 2008 at the instigation of the Foreign Minister, Frank-Walter Steinmeier, and has developed brilliantly. By spring 2014, around 1,800 schools in 115 non-German-speaking countries worldwide had joined. They delivered GFL teaching in partnership with schools in Germany, in situations in which German is generally the second foreign language. The approximately 550 "*Fit-Schulen*" (also *FIT-Schulen*), which establish and extend GFL teaching under the supervision of the Goethe-Institut, enjoy a special status (email Judith Weyer, ZfA, 28 February 2014; Bundesregierung 2014: 22, 26). Thanks to the *PASCH* initiative, the group of *DSD*-schools (*Deutsches-Sprachdiplom-Schulen*) has also been expanded, although by no means all PASCH schools are also DSD schools (see Ch. K.3.3; Map K.3.3–1 for the DSD schools).

   Point 1b): The *Law on the Promotion of German Schools Abroad (Auslandsschulgesetz/ASchulG)*, which came into force on 1 January 2014, applies to the 141 relevant schools, all of which are located outside the German-language territory (npl.ly.gov.tw/pdf/8415.pdf; Ch. K.3.3: Map

K.3.3–1). It regulates the legal claim of the German Schools Abroad for funding by the Federal Republic of Germany. However, this status can be withdrawn from any school "on serious grounds at any time and with immediate effect or with an appropriate period of notice [. . .] by the Federal Government or by the sponsor of the school (§ 3 (2)). "A German School Abroad is fundable if" as one of six conditions, "it offers German-language teaching and leaving certificates characterised by the German language [. . .]" (§ 8 (1)). These include, annually, at least twelve "mixed-language International Baccalaureates [. . .] subject to recognition by the Standing Conference of Ministers of Education and Cultural Affairs" (§ 2 (2)), to which "German *Sprachdiplom der Kultusministerkonferenz* levels I and II" can be added (§ 2 (3)). In every case, due attention is paid to sound knowledge of German, and (with reasonable local participation) the promotion of the schools is secured. Promotional measures include the provision of teaching staff and financial support. The German Schools Abroad therefore have planning security, because a loss of their status and their claim to support remains an exceptional case under the control of the school itself.

Point 2a): The introduction of international degree programmes in German universities towards the end of the last century presumably has a lasting effect on German as an academic language (Ch. G.6). It has certainly contributed to the opening of German universities for foreign students and academics, so that "Germany has become one of the most attractive sites worldwide" as the Federal Minister for Education and Research, Johanna Wanka, has often stressed (www.bmbf.de/press/3611.php). The number of foreign students provides an indicator – based on student numbers, Germany is now in third or fourth position worldwide, behind the USA and the UK and approximately level with France. However, this development brings German as an academic language and GFL into the dilemma, on the one hand, of admitting English for university teaching and, on the other hand, maintaining German in this function (see the memorandum on German as an Academic Language by the DAAD, 2010: "Open to English, committed to German"; www.daad.de/portrait/presse/pressemitteilungen/2010/13058. de.html; "Joint declaration by the President of the Alexander von Humboldt Foundation, DAAD and German Rectors' Conference [HRK]" in 2009; www.goethe.de/Ihr/prj/diw/dos/ de7753902.htm). However, the balance is difficult, as suggested by relevant investigations (e.g. Fandrych/ Sedlaczek 2012). A trend could develop to the effect that German in German universities becomes increasingly limited to social functions, for establishing contacts, while English becomes the predominant academic language, especially in the natural sciences and social sciences (Ch. G.3; G.5).

Point 2b): The *Initiative Außenwissenschaftspolitik* opened with a "Start-up Conference of the German Foreign Office" on 19/20 January 2009 on the topic of "External policy for science and scholarship: – education, science and research as key elements of German foreign policy". Among the many resulting incentives, the "Projects for German universities abroad", as they are referenced by the DAAD, are the most visible outcome (Ch. J.6). The most promising projects are supervised primarily by the DAAD on behalf of the Foreign Office. In summer 2014, 55 study places were offered outside the German-language territory, in cooperation with German universities (information from Roman Luckscheiter, DAAD). They included a series of sometimes admittedly quite small universities, such as the Vietnamese German University/VGU, *Türkisch-Deutsche Universität/TDU*, German University Kairo/GUC, German-Jordanian University/GJU, *Deutsch-Kasachische Universität/DKU* and *Andrássy Gyula Deutschsprachige Universität Budapest/AUB*. Added to these are individual institutes or degree programmes in different faculties, e.g. the *Chinesisch-Deutsches Hochschulkolleg* at the Tongji University in Shanghai, Civic Engineering at the Zhejang University of Science and Technology in Hangzhou, both in China. The predominant language of teaching is generally English, with German as something of an exception, especially in individual degree programmes, but not in entire universities. However, subsidiary GFL courses are almost always compulsory, but generally only up to level A1 or A2 of the Common European Reference Framework (Quetz 2002). This allows the link with German-speaking countries, which can then be further consolidated.

The new initiatives have been bolstered by intensive advertising including campaigns abroad. Examples included the bilateral Language Years, such as the German-Indian (2011/12), German-Brazilian (2012/ 13) and German-Chinese Language Year (2013/ 14), and the German-Russian Year of Language and Literature (2014/15). These joint events are intended to show that Germany "takes seriously" not only the promotion of its own language, but also "the goal of multilingualism" in the form of an "expansion of foreign-language teaching in schools" (point 4 of *Konzeption 2000*; Ch. K.3, towards the end). In September 2011, the German Foreign Office presented a new plan for the ECEP which was discussed and resolved in the Bundestag on 21 of March 2013 (bundestag.de/dokumente/textarchiv/2013/43457906_kw12_sp_auswaertige_kulturpolitik/index.html).

In a major parliamentary interpellation by the SPD faction ahead of the Bundestag debate, this concept was criticised for introducing a paradigm shift into the ECEP in the direction towards Joseph Nye's "Cultural Diplomacy" (Nye 1999a, 2004; Ch. K.3.1), because the previous mutuality with partner countries had allegedly been neglected in favour of unilateral influence by Germany (Bundestag document 17/ 9839). The Federal Government replied that, as always, what was involved was a "strengthening of Europe, securing peace and shaping globalisation in a responsible manner with old friends and new partners – these are still the predominant goals of the ECEP. Concerns about a paradigm shift in the ECEP are unfounded" (dip21.bundestag.de/ dip21/btd/17/119/ 1711981.pdf). The disagreement widens into the difference between a neoliberal ECP or ECEP guided primarily by self-interest, and a constructivist policy orientated towards superordinate values (Ch. K.3.6).

3.3 Mediating organisations

The "mediating organisations" (*Mittlerorganisationen*) – as they are aptly known – are characteristic for the "German model" for external cultural policy (ECP) (Maaß 2009c; Ch. K.2). The six organisations most strongly involved with the ECP are: Goethe-Institut (G-I), German Academic Exchange Service (DAAD), Institute for International Relations (ifa), Alexander von Humboldt Foundation (AvH, less concerned with ELP), Central Office for German Schools Abroad (ZfA) and *Deutsche Welle* (DW) (the last two are not mediating organisations in the narrow sense; for G-I, DAAD and ZfA see Ortner/ Ruckteschell-Katte 2010: 133–137). Political foundations (Pogorelskaja 2009b) and research institutions, e.g. the Institute for German Language (*IDS*), which touch on ELP, also deserve mention, but I shall not describe them in greater detail here. However, the term *mediating organisation* requires some explanation.

These organisations are in fact subject to government framework conditions and largely rely on government finance, but they have the legal form of a private organisation, such as an association [*Verein*] or foundation [*Stiftung*]. In this way, they combine government supervision with the broad manoeuvrability typical of private organisations. One feature essential for our topic is the object of mediating or disseminating the culture and language of their own country to the outside world. Having said this, especially in Germany, there are other, purely government and purely private organisations (Ch. K.3.4), which also act as mediators for culture or language abroad. These include organisations which receive government financial aid, but do not furnish any special rights to the state (since they are part of the state) and are therefore not actually mediating organisations. By contrast, in mediating organisations, government influence on structure and objectives is contractually codified. However, with a broad understanding, many organisations without any private-law status are counted among them (Maaß 2009c: 278), especially the Central Office for German Schools Abroad (ZfA), which is a department of the Federal Administration Office and is entirely subject to the administrative supervision of the Federal Ministry for the Interior. The advantage of mediating organisations – and this is the concept behind their formation – is that they operate more efficiently and arouse less suspicion abroad that Germany might be pursuing political ends under the guise of cultural activities. Their relatively broad room for manoeuvre has only once been restricted so drastically that it was incompatible with their objective of cultural mediation and promotion of the German language abroad, namely during the Nazi period. Apart from gains in Germany's image obtained through the mediation of culture and language apparently independently of vested interests and political influence, their advantages to the state include increased continuity of activities and impact compared with more direct government control, which could be destroyed in the case of a change of government. The German model has accordingly found imitators, at least in initial approach, in Japan, Spain and more recently China (Ch. K.5).

The most important government actors, which specify and financially support the aims of the German mediating organisations at least in their basic outlines, are the German Foreign Office (*AA*), especially the Department for "Culture and Communication", the Federal Ministry for Education and Research (*BMBF*), the Commissioner of the Federal Government for Culture and Media (*BKM*) and – corresponding to the German federal constitution – the Standing Conference of Ministers of Education and Cultural Affairs of the Federal States (*KMK*) (www. ifa.de/kultur-und-aussenpolitik/themen/grundla gen -der-akbp/akteure/html). In the following individual descriptions, I have outlined relationships with the government, based on framework agreements or articles of association as well as objectives and activities, where these are relevant for ELP, although these are admittedly sometimes difficult to differentiate.

Turning first to the *Goethe-Institut e. V.* (*G-I*) (Head office: Munich; for recent history see Niere 1977; Kathe 2005; E. Michels 2005). This is the only mediating organisation in the narrower sense of which the articles of association explicitly name the ELP as an objective, in fact, the primary objective. It remains unclear whether this means that it is also the first priority, and this has been disputed in various ways during the history of the Goethe-Institut. The wording of the objectives is as follows: "The purpose of the Association shall be to promote knowledge of the German language abroad, to foster international cultural cooperation and communicate a comprehensive image of Germany by providing information on cultural, social and political life" (§ 2 paragraph 1 of the Articles of Association of 21.09.2000 in the version of 20 November 2009; www.goethe.de/mmo/priv/1223959-STANDARD. pdf). However, for the Goethe-Institut, the ELP is of special importance in that it represents a substantial source of income. With reference to its ELP, especially the teaching of German, the Goethe-Institut differs from the other mediating organisations which do not have a source of income on this scale. For example, the independently earned component in the Goethe-Institut budget 2012/13 amounted to €135m, that is, a good third (34%) of the total income of €336m. But it is questionable whether this independent component in fact guarantees greater independence from the state; this factor varies from organisation to organisation. In the case of the Goethe-Institut, it is based on the framework agreement with the Foreign Office of 1969, which was renewed in 2001 (Ammon 1991a: 549; Maaß 2009c: 272). According to this agreement, the establishment or closure of a Goethe-Institut requires the approval of the Foreign Office. The Foreign Office can also demand immediate suspension of employees working abroad if, in the opinion of the Foreign Office, they are damaging Germany's image or could lead to a burden on the relations with the host country or third countries.

Finally, on serious political grounds, the Foreign Office can request measures under the contractual obligations of a Goethe-Institut.

The breadth of distribution and global position of the Goethe-Institut is impressive. In 2012, the organisation had at its disposal 158 regular "Goethe Institutes" (including liaison offices) in 93 countries and more than 3,040 employees (*Jahrbuch* 2012/13: 177). Map K.3.3–1 gives an overview of the global distribution. The full, regular Goethe Institutes were supplemented with 39 more restricted Goethe-Centres in 23 countries, most of which were simultaneously "foreign-German cultural societies". Beyond this, the organisation is integrated with other facilities abroad:

> The Goethe-Institut promotes public libraries and similar resources in the host countries. Worldwide, there are cooperative projects with 77 German reading rooms, dialogue points, Germany meeting points, and respectively information and learning centres. They are supplied with media by the Goethe-Institut [. . .]" (www.goethe.de/ uun/adr/wwt/kop/deindex.htm).
>
> 'The partner libraries [provide! U.A.] appropriate rooming facilities, German-speaking specialist staff and library infrastructure. The Goethe-Institut ensures a basic annual provision of media, technical equipment and further training for local staff.' 'At present, alongside 95 libraries in Goethe Institutes, there are 89 joint ventures: 11 'dialogue points', 10 of which in North Africa and the Middle East, 1 in Southern Asia. 5 information and learning centres: 4 in China, 1 in Mongolia. 41 reading rooms, 30 of which in Eastern Europe and Central Asia, 2 in China and 9 in South Eastern Europe. 32 partner libraries are in Central and Eastern Europe.'
>
> *(www.goethe.de/ins/prj/les/deindex.htm – order modified)*

The language courses strengthen the global position of German most directly. In 2012, the Goethe-Institut provided 17,161 such courses with 207,113 participants abroad, together with 5,999 courses with 39,453 participants in Germany (*Jahrbuch* 2012/13: 177). The "Pedagogical Liaison Work" of the Goethe-Institut with schools abroad which teach GFL is also especially significant. Schools receive advice, access to German-language literature, information and even teaching materials. The work of the *PASCH* schools ("Schools: Partners for the Future", since 2008) is also important: "The Goethe-Institut supervises around 500 of these PASCH schools in more than 110 countries" (www.goethe.de/ins/ in/ned/lhr/spz/deindex.htm; for PASCH-schools see below: *Zentralstelle für das Auslandsschulwesen* (*ZfA*); also Ch. J.3; K.2, towards the end; K.3.2). Finally, the promotional campaigns for GFL launched by the Goethe-Institut deserve special mention, e.g. the *German-Roadshow* in France and Poland (Ch. J.9.2; J.9.5).

Promoting the German language is not specified as an objective for the *Deutscher Akademischer Austauschdienst e. V./German Academic Exchange Service* (*DAAD*) (Head office: Bonn; for recent history, see Alter 2000b), either in its articles of association or in the framework agreement with the government. Nevertheless, the DAAD is committed to this objective. The organisation's budget gives an impression of the scale of its activities. In 2012, the total budget ran to €411m (German Foreign Office €178.0m; Federal Ministry for Education and Research: €99.0m; Federal Ministry for Economic Collaboration and Development: €38.0m; European Union €58.0m, other: €38.0m; de.wikipedia.org/wiki/Deutscher_Akademischer_Austauschdienst). The ministries providing this finance are represented in the advisory board of the DAAD (§ 14, Articles of Association entering into force on 01.01.2013: www.daad.de/portrait/structure/satzung/08952.de.html). The purpose of the association is specified in the Articles as follows: "(1) [. . .] promotion of science, scholarship and research, education and training, art, culture and international understanding. (2) [This] is to be realised especially by cultivating academic relations abroad. Through ideas and finance, the Association shall mediate and promote international mobility and collaboration, as well as academic and student exchange. (3) It shall support activities serving the same objectives in universities and other academic and educational institutions". It is evident that these objectives may require language-policy decisions, even if they are not named in the articles of association. One example is the English-language degree programmes in German universities. Their introduction from the winter semester 1997/98 was supported by the DAAD – in conformity with the Articles of Association: §2(2) "Cultivating academic relations abroad" and received funding from the Federal Ministry for Education, Science, Research and Technology (bmb+f) (Ammon 1998: 230, 227–252; Motz 2005a). However, the DAAD has been criticised because these degree programmes may allegedly damage German as an international or academic language. In response, the DAAD and the bmb+f (Wahl 2005) raised the hope that, through the influx of foreigners into German universities, they would also be able to secure the global position of German (Ch. G.8). This argument and similar criticisms (e.g. Weydt 2004) have sharpened the language-policy awareness of the DAAD. "In this context, it is also evident that the DAAD has declared the promotion of German Language and Literature and the promotion of German language in universities abroad as among its core strategic objectives" (G. Schneider 2012: 245). The DAAD now explains that one of four reasons why it would like to "create globally open structures" is "[. . .] that German remains an important cultural and academic language". With this in mind, one item in the DAAD budget was worded as follows for 2013: "Promotion of German Language and Literature and German language: €48m" (www.daad.de/medien/ausland/dokumente/11_2013_das_lektorenprogrammdes_daad_im_ueberblick_neues_layout.pdf).

Of course, all the DAAD programmes offer opportunities for promoting GFL, German language and literature. But the lector programme, "as the core element in the DAAD promotion of German language and literature" is specifically orientated towards German language and literature and GFL, with the description: "German language, German language and literature and German studies are promoted in such a manner that the German culture is present in the partner countries; that academic disciplines relating to Germany are strengthened in universities; that elites and successive generations are trained for collaboration with Germany; and that German is strengthened as an academic language" (www.daad.de/medien/ausland/dokumente/11_2013). Of the €48m provided for the promotion of German language and literature and German language in the budget for 2013, €21.7m (47%) were used for the lector programme, the remainder for university summer courses, "special measures for German language in Central and Eastern Europe", conferences and so on. The lectors offer support in many departments of German language and literature and GFL abroad. University lectors – approximately 75% of all lectorships are "regular lectors *Regellektoren*" – have a teaching commitment from 12 to 15 hours per week "in the fields of German language and literature/German studies, teacher training, interpreter and translator training and/or German for students in all faculties"; two to four hours consultation work are generally added to this (ibid). The total numbers and worldwide presence are impressive: distributed among 39 countries in "Europe" (in the broader sense of the Council of Europe, including Turkey, Russia and Kazakhstan) and 19 countries "overseas" in 2012 (ibid). The DAAD provides additional GFL funding via the *Pädagogischer Austauschdienst (PAD)*, founded in 1952 and affiliated to the Standing Conference of Ministers of Education and Cultural Affairs (KMK). The *PAD* supervises thousands of German school pupils on exchanges abroad (Federal Government [Germany] 2014: 113f.). In 2013, Australia, Belgium, Canada, China, France, Ireland, Italy, Mexico, New Zealand, Switzerland, Spain, UK, and the USA participated in such exchange programmes. Finally, DAAD support for the PASCH-programme (Ch. K.3.2), which every year finances a complete university degree programme in Germany for 120 foreign PASCH school leavers (www.pasch-net.de/mag/akt/a12/de3344312.htm), deserves special mention.

The *Institut für Auslandsbeziehungen e. V./Institute for International Relations* (*ifa*) is among the smaller mediating organisations with an annual budget of approximately €20m (2012: €20.214m, of which Foreign Office €19.164m; Federal State of *Baden-Württemberg* €0.7 to €2m; State capital, Stuttgart, €0.328m; information from Gudrun Czekalla, ifa, email 28.05.2014). The relationship with the government is specified in the Articles of Association (version 4 December 2003, paragraph 2.3) as follows:

> 'Ordinary members' are "[t]he Federal Republic of Germany, represented by two voting representatives from the Foreign Office and one voting representative of the Office for Culture and Media (formerly BMI), the State of Baden-Württemberg, represented respectively by one voting representative of the Ministry for Science, Research and the Arts and of the Ministry of Finance; the State capital, Stuttgart, represented by one voting representative of the Culture Division, as awarding authorities [...]". The purpose of the Association is defined in Paragraph 2.1: 'Within the cultural field, the Association shall operate on the basis of the conception of the External cultural Policy of the Foreign Office, especially in the fields of art and culture, education, training, science, information and documentation. Additionally, the ifa shall run German courses with regional studies.'
>
> *(www.ifa.de/fileadmin/pdf/ifa/satzung.pdf/ifa/satzung.pdf)*

The last sentence should not be understood only in the sense of *external language policy* (ELP); recently, it has been more concerned with integrational German courses and courses providing vocational qualifications, which are implemented at the ifa German College in Stuttgart (cms.ifa.de/deutschkurse/kurse-und-pruefungen-im-ueberblick/). However, ifa also participates in German teaching abroad. For example, the following statement appears on one DAAD website: "3,000 language learners from 100 countries learn GFL with the support of the ifa. A special ifa programme supports the German minority in Central and Eastern Europe. ifa is represented in many countries with an assistant programme, consultants for cultural and language exchange and promotion programmes" (www.daad.org.ua/de/2.5.2.6 html). Above all, promotion of German-(speaking) minorities in Eastern Europe (Ch. E.4.4–E.4.8) has also included German teaching. Finally, the ifa-research programme "Culture and External Policy", which also promotes investigations of ELP (e.g. funding the study *Deutsch sprechen in Frankreich* by Matthias Lahr-Kurten (2012)) and the RAVE Research prize for dissertations on ELP, e.g. by Dirk Scholten (2000a), Verena Andrei (2008) and Jan Kruse (2012).

The *Alexander von Humboldt Stiftung/Alexander von Humboldt Foundation* (*AvH*) is a relatively large mediating organisation with a budget of €112.5m in 2012, with the following shares from different Federal Ministries (Foreign Office 34.8%; Federal Ministry for Education and Research 55.8%; Federal Ministry for Economic Cooperation 4.9% and others; causaschavan.files.wordpress.com.2013/02/ forschungsorganisationen.pdf). However, the ELP is not among its objectives in any agreement; only the following description appears in the Articles of Association:

> 'The purpose of the Foundation is to promote science, scholarship and research together with intercultural understanding.' "The purpose of the Articles of Association shall be realised especially in that the Foundation shall grant the possibility to carry out a research project in the Federal Republic of Germany to academically

highly qualified academics of foreign nationality, regardless of their gender, ethnic origin and nationality, religion or philosophy, through the provision of research grants and research prizes; shall undertake other measures for promoting international academic cooperation; and shall maintain and promote the resulting connections.'

(www.humboldt-foundation.de/web/docs/F21852/satzung.pdf)

Approximately two thirds of the grants go to the natural sciences, one third to the humanities. Among the humanities grants from 2008 to 2012, only 6.75 went to Germanists (45 of 666); the average rate was therefore hardly higher than all humanities: 39.1% (45 of 115 applications) compared with 33.3% (666 of 2002 applications (Alexander von Humboldt-Stiftung 2013: 60). However, many academics from other disciplines are certainly led towards the German language as a result of the grants, amongst other reasons because of the lifelong after-care for alumni (www.humboldt-foundation.de/web/alumnifoerderung-ausland.html). Beyond this, the AvH also sometimes spontaneously engages with the ELP, especially through conferences, e.g. together with the broadcaster *Deutsche Welle* in 2006 in Bonn, entitled: "Does Germany need a more aware, cohesive language policy?" (www.humboldt-foundation.de/ web/2401. html; discussion in: www.humboldt-foundation.de/pls/web/docs/F1542/sprachenpolitik.pdf).

The organisations discussed so far are mediating organisations in the narrower sense, with a combination of private-law constitution and government control. However, the two following, purely government organisations also play an important role in the German Government's ELP.

Regarding its importance for the ELP, the *Zentralstelle für das Auslandschulwesen/Central Office for German Schools Abroad (ZfA)* ranks very high (Head office: since February 2014 in Bonn, previously in Cologne; see also Ch. J.3; K.3.2)."The ZfA is a department of the *BVA [Bundesverwaltungsamt!* U.A.; Federal Office for Administration], but regarding its responsibilities for German school activities abroad, it is under the specialist supervision of the Foreign Office"."The ZfA is [. . .] a department within an authority" ("Interview with the President of the BVA, Christoph Verenkotte", *Begegnung* Vol. 31(3), 2010: 8f.). In the same interview, the President of the BVA emphasises the structurally determined, straightforward process of decision-making with the Foreign Office and the excellent cooperation with Goethe-Institut and DAAD. In 2013, the ZfA had €208m at its disposal for school work abroad (Federal Government [Germany] 2014: 113). "[W]ith approximately 90 employees and around 50 specialist consultants, it organises schooling abroad" (www.bva.bund.de/DE/Organisation/Abteilungen/ Abteilung_ZfA/zfa_ node.html). The organisation's main objective is to supervise the 141 German Schools Abroad, 1,050 *DSD* schools (Map K.3.3–1) and 1,200 (now 1,300? U.A.] *PASCH*-schools ("Schools: Partners for the Future", since 2008) (figures from February 2014; Judith Weyer, ZfA, email 28 February 2014). In total, there are more than 1,800 PASCH schools, but 500 of these are co-supervised by the Goethe-Institut (see above). Provision by the ZfA "includes the supply of German-teaching staff abroad and the qualitative development of the schools. Because the actual promotional work is the education of school-age pupils [. . .]. With more than 390,000 children and young people, the schools are far from a niche project" (Joachim Lauer, Director of the ZfA in www.bva.bund.de/SharedDocs/Downloads/ DE/ZfA/ Jahrbuch/Jahrbuch2011_2012. pdf?__blob=publicationFile&v=2). In this context, some 2,000 teachers from Germany are in active service abroad at any time.

The DSD schools (*Sprachdiplomschulen*) offer the German *Sprachdiplom* (DSD) of the Standing Conference of Ministers of Education and Cultural Affairs. With DSD I (competence level A2/ B1 of the Common European Reference Framework; Quetz 2002), foreigners can gain access to a preparatory college in Germany (http://de.wikipedia.org/wiki/Studienkolleg). The second level, DSD II, corresponds to linguistic competence level B2/ C1 and represents the

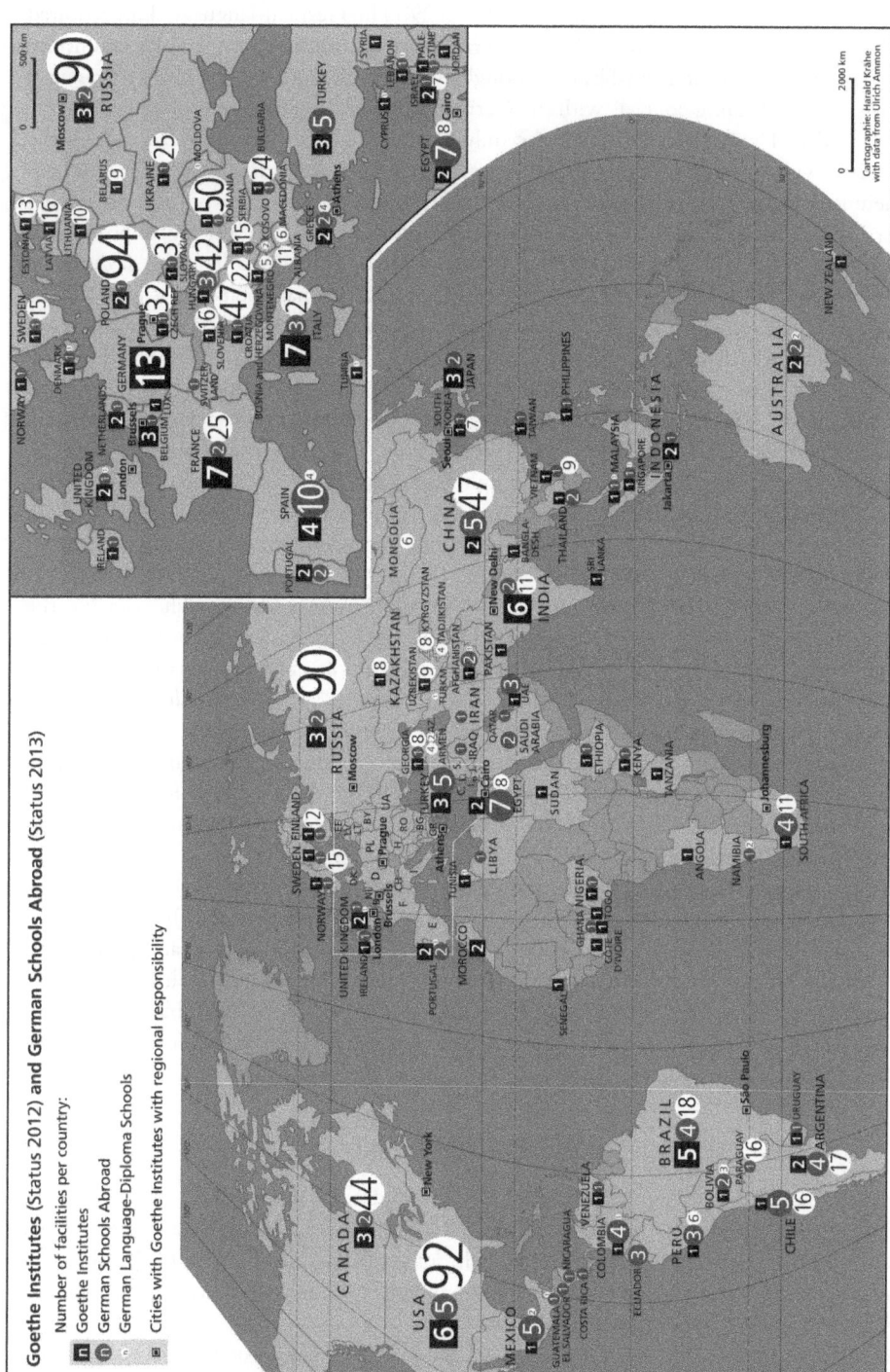

Map K.3.3–1 Goethe Institutes and German Schools Abroad worldwide and in Europe

"language qualification, required formally and in terms of content, for study [at a German university! U.A.] [. . .]" (Georg Krawitz, *BVA* 2013a: 29). The German-language skills acquired through schools supervised by the ZfA are generally very sound. Moreover, good relationships with Germany are also often established through the schools. Both these factors represent a sound basis for continuing contacts with the German-speaking countries.

Like the ZfA, Deutsche Welle (DW), the only German overseas broadcaster, is among the organisations with a potentially considerable impact on the global position of German. But here also, there is no private-law constitution. Deutsche Welle is a public-sector broadcaster subject to federal law, financed from radio fees (for information on its impact on the global position of German, see Ch. I.1.3.1). In 2012, DW had a total budget of €271m and has been at this level for several years (Berthold Stevens, DW, email 13 May 2014). Its main objective is to provide a balanced view of Germany and the German perspective on the world, for which reason it has also sometimes been characterised as "Germany's visiting card" (Krasteva 2007). However, the legal description of its objectives reads as follows: "Deutsche Welle thus especially promotes the German language" (DW-Gesetz 2005, § 4, last sentence). This involves broadcasting in German alongside numerous other languages to reach large numbers of listeners and viewers. Through German-language broadcasts, Deutsche Welle upholds at least the receptive use of the language within its broadcast territory. In this context, it is directed primarily towards 1) emigrants from the German-speaking countries and German-speaking minorities; 2) expatriates, i.e. citizens and inhabitants of German-speaking countries resident overseas: businesspeople, diplomats, academics, teachers, tourists etc. (Ch. E.5); and 3) GFL teachers and learners who can use the broadcasts to improve their knowledge of German. A regular provision of German-language courses contributes to the global promotion of German. One current example is a Telenovela (a broadcast in the form of a serialised novel), which runs online ("*Jojo sucht das Glück*" [Jojo looks for happiness]). Websites such as www.google.com/#q=Deutsche+Welle provide further information. An impression of the large numbers of people interested in German courses of this kind can be gained from reports such as "241,091 people like DW – Learn German" (*DEUTSCH LERNEN* | DW.DE – 03.12.2013). Deutsche Welle has a tradition as a "global classroom" for German teaching (Weirich 2000).

It would be interesting to compare the regional distribution of Germany's mediating organisations and their activities with Germany's diplomatic missions abroad, with which they are in frequent contact: at the time of writing, there were 148 embassies, 60 general and professional consulates, 12 permanent representations and eight other agencies abroad, as well as 354 honorary consuls. A complete list, without honorary consuls, but including cartographic overviews of countries worldwide, apart from small white spots in Central Africa, South America and Oceania), can be found at: de.wikipedia.org/wiki/Liste_deutscher_Auslandsvertretungen.

3.4 Private associations

Alongside the mediating organisations which operate under the framework conditions of the government, many private societies, associations and foundations also contribute to the external promotion of the German language. The difficulty of providing an overview of this situation is illustrated below in the Federal Government's incomplete response to a major parliamentary interpellation from the opposition in September 2011.

"121. Which private foundations invest on a large scale in the field of external cultural and educational policy?

According to information from the Federal Association of German Foundations e.V., there are currently approximately 19,000 nonprofit foundations in Germany. The 3,700 members registered with the Federal Association of German Foundations e.V. all have specific thematic or regional focuses. This also applies for their respective commitments at home and abroad. Detailed, complete and reliable data on planned and actual spending in the field of external cultural and educational policy can be obtained from the articles of association and annual reports of the individual foundations. The Federal Government does not have at its disposal a corresponding listing or statistical evaluation. Some partnerships in the field of ECEP have existed for many years, e.g. with the Robert Bosch Foundation GmbH, the Allianz Cultural Foundation and the Haniel Foundation" (Response from the Federal Government to the major interpellation by the [. . .] SPD [. . .], dated September 2011; dip21.bundestag.de/dip21/btd/17/119/1711981.pdf).

My discussion of the involvement of private associations with the subdomain of external language policy (ELP) within the external cultural and educational policy (ECEP) must therefore remain correspondingly incomplete. The list of foundations would have to be supplemented with private associations and other NGOs (Pogorelskaja 2009a). Pointers in this direction are provided by a – now somewhat dated – inventory entitled *Förderung der Sprachkultur in Deutschland* [Promotion of language culture in Germany] (*Gesellschaft für deutsche Sprache/Institut für Deutsche Sprache* 1999). For this project, letters were addressed to "380 facilities, of which 135 have been registered in the handbook" (ibid: XI). Most of the mediating organisations discussed in Ch. K.3.3 are included in this list. In the case of the purely private organisations, the ELP is not explicitly named anywhere as an action field, although they are entirely capable of conducting a language policy (Ch. K.1.1, towards the end). However, many foundations which are important in this context are missing, such as the *Robert Bosch Foundation* (Stuttgart; Theiner 2009: 310) and the *Marga und Kurt Möllgaard-Stiftung* (Essen). In fact, promoting the German language is not a declared goal of these organisations, although, to some extent, possibly unintentionally, it is certainly a side-effect, e.g. for the Möllgaard Foundation with its focus on "promotion of international scientific cooperation (stiftungen.stifterverband.info/t130_moellgaard/). This also applies to the Robert Bosch Foundation, one of the largest German industrial foundations, which cultivates primarily German-French, German-American, German-Polish/Eastern Central European and German-Chinese relations within its broad range of activities. For more than 20 years, it has supplied and financed German-speaking lectors abroad, thereby contributing to the external promotion of German (www.bosch-stiftung.de/content/language1/html/13919. asp). Another example of indirect promotion is the Fritz Thyssen Foundation, which [supports] "international grants and exchange programmes [. . .]" as well as "projects, in which German and foreign scientists work together" (for examples see: www. www.fritz-thyssen-stiftung.de/ foerderung/ sonderprogramme /internationale-stipendien-und-aus tauschprogramme/).

At the level of research, the Volkswagen Foundation also strengthens the global position of German by raising awareness about problems, e.g. the programme "German plus – Science is Multilingual", which promotes multilingual student courses and translations of German-language scientific works, as well as research and conferences on multilingualism in the sciences, and German as an international academic language (Oberreuter/ Krull/ Meyer/ Ehlich 2012).

This applies especially where the promotion of the German language abroad is an explicit goal; strictly speaking, real ELP is involved only in such cases (Ch. K.1). Examples include various organisations which are supported financially by the German Government but not subject to its supervision and are therefore not mediating organisations in the narrower sense (Ch. K.3.3, beginning). The following are particularly important:

- *Verein für Deutsche Kulturbeziehungen im Ausland e.V.* (VDA – *Association for German Cultural Relations Abroad*); this has been the name since 1998, but the association looks back on a long tradition with many changes of name and political orientation. In the FRG, the long-standing name since 1881, *Allgemeiner Deutscher Schulverein*, was changed into the *Verein für das Deutschtum im Ausland (VDA)* (1955–1970) and after that into *Verein für Deutsche Kulturbeziehungen im Ausland (VDA)* (de.wikipedia.org/wiki/Veein_f%C3%BCr_ Deutsche_Kulturbeziehungen_im_Ausland). According to the Articles of Association (of 6 November 1998, § 3 (1)), it is concerned with "the promotion and maintenance of German culture abroad, unhindered use and cultivation of the mother tongue, the realisation of human rights and ethnic rights, and minority rights protection for Germans abroad" (www. vda-kultur.de/ media/ external-downloads/_administrative-pdfs/vda-satzung); it also promotes school exchanges to Germany.

* *Internationale Medienhilfe (IMH)*, founded in the early 1990s by Björn Akstinat (Akstinat 2012/13). It largely took over the objectives of the former *Internationale Assoziation Deutschsprachiger Medien* (iadm) and promotes German-language media outside the German-language territory. It describes itself as "acting in an honorary capacity as an independent self-help organisation and workgroup of intercultural and respectively international media from all parts of the globe" (www.imh-deutschland.de/page/index.php).

Associations with a closer focus on language are of particular interest here; among these, three are prominent with reference to ELP: *Gesellschaft für deutsche Sprache, Verein Deutsche Sprache* and *Verein für Sprachpflege*.

The *Gesellschaft für deutsche Sprache e.V.* (*GfdS*) (Wiesbaden) has a long history which began as the *Allgemeiner Deutscher Sprachverein (ADSV)* founded in 1885; after re-foundation in 1947, it distanced itself from previous chauvinistic and linguistically purist tendencies. In 2014, the society had "around 3,000 members at home and abroad" (www.gfds.de/wir-ueber-uns/mit glied-werden/). In addition to internal resources, it is financially supported "by the Federal Government (Commissioner for Culture and Media) based on a resolution by the German Bundestag and the governments of the Federal States (Standing Conference of Ministers of Education and Cultural Affairs, KMK)" (www. gfds.de/ wir-ueber-uns/). However, according to the Articles of Association (§1), it is "a politically independent society for cultivating and researching contemporary German language" and according to (§2), it seeks "a) to help all who require advice in linguistic matters; b) to awaken and promote understanding of the nature, significance and performance of the language; c) to prompt the German-language community to pay attention to language and to deepen its sense of language; d) to carry out application-related research in the field of contemporary German language" (www.gfds.de/wir-ueber-uns/satzung/). Furthermore, it aims to deepen awareness of the German language, making its function visible at a global level. Its two periodicals, *Muttersprache* and *Der Sprachdienst*, together with worldwide networking, serve this end. It has "branches" in 57 cities and 38 countries outside Germany (www.gfds.de/ zweige-in-ausland/zweige-im-ausland/). By contrast with the societies named below, the GfdS distances itself from linguistic purism and the battle against anglicisms. However, in many lectures and publications, its former president (1999–2011), Rudolf Hoberg (e.g. 2002a, b, c, 2004, 2012), has drawn attention to the global loss of position of German, but without presenting concrete proposals for ELP. This corresponds with the primarily academic rather than political self-image of the association. Again, by contrast with the following societies, members are largely qualified linguists and include many university teachers. Through the GfdS, some have developed an interest in ELP and contributed to deeper understanding through their own academic work.

The *Verein Deutsche Sprache e.V.* (*VDS*) (Dortmund) was founded as recently as 1997 by statistics professor Walter Kramer, who is still the society president. Until 2000, the name was *Verein zur Wahrung der deutschen Sprache* (*VWDS* – Association for the preservation of the German language). An account of the history of the VDS, including goals and activities, has been provided by Karoline Wirth (2010). The VDS does not receive government financial support, which it does not need because of its large contribution-paying membership: in spring 2014 "36,000 people from almost all countries, cultures, parties, age groups and occupations. One third of these are friends of the German language from Asia and Africa alone (www.vds-ev.de/verein). In the early years, the VDS focussed almost exclusively on opposing the (widespread preference for) borrowings from English, against which members targeted books such as the *Wörterbuch überflüssiger Anglizismen* [Dictionary of superfluous anglicisms] (Barzsch/ Pogarell/ Schröder [1999] 2003), attacking them with deprecating designations, e.g. in the book *Denglisch, nein danke!* (Zabel [2001] 2003). However, the VDS has widened its view, campaigning, amongst other goals, for greater parity of German with English and French as an EU working language (e.g. Voslamber 2006). The VDS is also opposed to excessive English in German universities, in the advisory boards of German business, in popular music in the mass media, in appearances by German personalities abroad; it also argues for increased rights for German-(speaking) minorities outside the German-language territory. Its quarterly periodical *Sprachnachrichten* regularly publishes contributions on these and similar topics.

From the point of view of the GfdS, the VDS may seem academically questionable or even populist, but, from the point of view of the VDS (and especially from that of the GfdS), similar criticisms might apply to the position of the *Verein für Sprachpflege e. V.* (*VfS* – Association for language preservation) (Erlangen). This society dates back to 1971, when it was known as the "*Hamburger Verein für Sprachpflege*"; it was then re-formed from its regional branch at the initiative of Hans-Manfred Niedetzky, the president of the VfS from 2001 to 2005, who was succeeded by Thomas Paulwitz (www.nuernbergwiki.de/index.php/Verein_f%C3%BCr _Sprachpflege). In addition to its opposition to anglicisms, the VfS still campaigns against the German spelling reform but also works to strengthen the position of German outside the German-speaking countries. Its quarterly periodical *Deutsche Sprachwelt* (*DSW*) is directed more towards politicians committed to language policy than to academic linguists, but it possibly reaches out to a quite a broad readership.

3.5 Associations of German teachers and Germanists

Like many of the private associations described in Ch. K.3.4, associations of German teachers and Germanists also often receive government support, especially for conferences and publications. In an earlier account, I characterised these associations as "lobbies for the German language" (Ammon 1991a: 507–511). Their members often have a professional interest in ensuring that as many people as possible in the world learn German or study German language and literature. They are therefore motivated "instrumentally" (Ch. J.8), although sometimes not exclusively instrumentally, towards a strong global position for German. Accordingly, they are sensitive to global changes in the position of German as a foreign language (GFL), especially the turn towards English and the demotion of other foreign languages, including German; and they are sensitive to the trend among educational policymakers and defenders of globalisation, also discernible in the English-speaking countries, towards English as potentially the sole foreign language, with other foreign languages required only for specialists and enthusiasts (Ch. J.9.3; J.9.10; J.9.15). Worldwide, German is, in fact, still mostly a second foreign language, always behind English (Ch. J.2, towards the end), and even with this subordinate position, feels the pressure from other foreign languages: traditional languages such as Spanish, or rising languages such as Chinese (Ch. J.7). One typical expression of current interests among professional associations, which is especially relevant here, is the conference publication from the "12th International

Conference of German Teachers" (30 July – 4 August 2001 in Lucerne/Switzerland) entitled: "*Mehr* Sprache – mehr*sprachig* mit *Deutsch*. Didaktische und politische Perspektiven". [*More* language – multi-*lingual* with *German*] (G. Schneider/ Clalüna 2003) According to this title, foreign-language teaching should indeed be multilingual (but not orientated exclusively towards English), and German should be included within the package; anything less would hardly be acceptable.

Of course, associations of German teachers and Germanists also serve professional exchange within the discipline. But even this is not disinterested, because the improvement of instruction, teaching and research is considered strengthening for the discipline and as a defence against cutbacks in posts, especially as the German language is still associated with difficulty for learners, and German teaching is associated with monotonous teaching methods in the alleged tradition of the "grammar-translation method". Defending oneself against this kind of vilification is more successful in associations than by individuals, especially if the associations are led by advocates experienced in arguing the case. Associations often have at their disposal externally effective organs of publication, which promote cohesion, assist the activities and further development of members, and can integrate other groups with similar disciplinary interests (language disciplines, literature disciplines, philology). Examples of such publications include *Germanistische Mitteilungen des Belgischen Germanisten- und Deutschlehrer-Verbands* (www.bgdv.be/gm.html), *Deutschunterricht in Japan* (since 1996, previously *Bericht des Japanischen Deutschlehrerverbandes*) of the *Association of German Teachers in Japan* (VDJ) (since 2013, previously *Japanischer Deutschlehrerverband* (JDV) (www.vdjapan.org/bericht/bericht-top.html) or *The German Quarterly/Die Unterrichtspraxis des Verbandes der amerikanischen Deutschlehrer* (*American Association of Teachers of German* (AATG)) (www. aatg.org/). It is evident from their webpages how the associations of German teachers and/or Germanists promote their discipline and therefore also the position of German in their own country. For example, the webpage of the AATG also links to the regularly appearing *Newsletter*. The Association was founded in 1926, during the period of crisis for the German language in the USA after WWI (Ch. J.2) and had approximately 4,000 members in 2013 (but it still had around 6,500 in 1990; Ammon 1991a: 509). The webpage leaves no doubt about the professional interests of members: "The American Association of Teachers of German supports the teaching of the German language and German-speaking cultures in elementary, secondary and post-secondary education in the United States. The AATG promotes the study of the German-speaking world in all its linguistic, cultural and ethnic diversity, and endeavours to prepare students as transnational, transcultural learners and active, multilingual participants in a globalized world".

The National German teachers' associations are generally members of the *Internationaler Deutschlehrerverband* (IDV), founded in 1968 (references from IDV president Marianne Hepp, email 28 May 2014; Sorger 2012; Hufeisen/ Sorger 2010: 167f.). In 2012, 104 associations from 86 countries belonged to the umbrella organisation – these included several associations in the following countries: Algeria two, Denmark five, Germany two, Hungary two, Italy two, Russian Federation ten, Switzerland two (www.idvnetz.org/verbaende_weltweit/ verbaende_weltweit. htm). In 2012, the IDV had approximately 25,000 paying members (and as many non-paying members) and "represented" the interests of around 250,000 German teachers (www.dadkhah. de/idv/). The "International Conferences of German Teachers", which takes place every four years, most recently in Jena 2009, Bolzano 2013 and Freiburg/Fribourg (Switzerland) 2017), have demonstrated the importance and articulated the claims of the Association, which can also influence educational policy and capture media attention. Since 2009, the president of the IDV has been Marianne Hepp (*Universitate degli Studi de Pisa*). Table K.3.5–1 gives an overview of countries with national German teachers' associations recognised by the IDV and acknowledged

Table K.3.5–1 National German-teachers' associations in the International German Teachers' Association (IDV) in 86 countries in the world in 2012

Albania	Denmark (5)	Latvia	Senegal
Algeria (2)	Ecuador	Lithuania	Serbia
Argentina	Egypt	Luxembourg	Slovakia
Armenia	Estonia	Macedonia	Slovenia
Australia	Finland	Madagascar	South Africa
Austria	France	Malaysia	South Korea
Belgium	Georgia	Mali	Spain
Belarus	Germany (2)	Mexico	Sweden
Benin	Ghana	Moldovia	Switzerland (2)
Bolivia	Greece	Mongolia	Taiwan
Bosnia and Herzegovina	Guatemala	Morocco	Thailand
Brazil	Hungary	Netherlands	Togo
Bulgaria	Iceland	New Zealand	Tunisia
Burkina Faso	India	Nigeria	Turkey
Cameroon	Indonesia	Norway	UK
Canada	Ireland	Paraguay	Ukraine (2)
Chechnya	Israel	Peru	Uruguay
Chile	Italy (2)	Poland	USA
Colombia	Japan	Portugal	Uzbekistan
Côte D'Ivoire	Kazakhstan	Romania	Venezuela
Croatia	Kirgizstan	Russian Fed. (10)	Vietnam
Cuba	Kosovo		

(*Source*: www.idvnetz.org/verbaende_weltweit/verbaende_weltweit.htm)

as members in 2012 (in the case of several associations, the number is given in brackets). The People's Republic of China is missing because the Association ceased cooperation years ago; but there is now a prospect of its returning. The distribution shows a certain concentration in Europe (in the extended sense of the Council of Europe; Ch. H.3). However, a closer analysis, including membership numbers of the individual associations, would presumably show an approximate agreement (positive correlation) with the distribution of GFL learning in the world (see Ch. J.7: Maps J.7–1; J.7–2) – this could make a possible future research project.

In fact, there are members of the IDV who are interested in the linguistics of the German language, especially language pedagogy; but at university level, the bulk of Germanists are members of different organisations, especially for literary studies and for linguistics. On one hand, there is a series of national Germanists' associations (www.germanistik.net/fachverbande.htm). On the other hand, there are transnational Germanists' associations, e.g. the *Mitteleuropäische Germanistenverband* (*MGV*), which, according to §2 of its Articles of Association, regards itself "as a union of Germanists from the countries of Eastern Central, South Eastern and North Eastern Europe, Germany, Austria and Switzerland" and in which, according to §6 "representatives of the discipline from the countries listed in §2" "can become ordinary members [. . .]" (mgv-portal.eu/uploads/Satzung.pdf). Finally, Germanists are organised independently of national or transnational associations worldwide as individual members of the *Internationale Vereinigung für Germanistik* (IVG) (Hufeisen/ Sorger 2010: 168f.). This was founded in 1951 in Florence and has no national associations. Until quite recently, the Association was still called the *Internationale Vereinigung für Germanische Sprach- und Literaturwissenschaft* (*IVG*), where this title expresses its comprehensive understanding of the discipline. It includes the study of "Afrikaans, Old-German,

German, Friesian, Yiddish, Dutch and Nordic languages and literatures" (IVG Articles of Association, §1). However, at least qualitatively, German language and literature predominate, and German is the sole working language in practice. The goal of the IVG is "to promote German Language and Literature through international cooperation" (IVG Articles of Association, §1). The IVG works towards this goal, amongst other activities, through its publications, including primarily the *Jahrbuch für Internationale Germanistik*, and through public relations work, especially at its international congresses held at five-yearly intervals, in recent years, accompanied by extensive congress publications. The most recent of these congresses were held in Vienna (11–16 September 2000), Paris (26 August – 3 September 2005), Warsaw (30 July – 7 August 2010) and Shanghai (24 – 30 August 2015) (Full overview in de.wikipedia.org/ wiki/Internationale_Vereinigung_ f%C3%BCr_ Germanische_ Sprach-_und_ Literaturwissenschaft). In each case, press releases show the extent to which local Germanists hope to boost their discipline and strengthen the position of German, especially GFL, in their own country and worldwide. The president of the IVG from 2010–2015 was Jianhua Zhu (Zhu is the family name), Tongji University, Shanghai (China), and, since that time has been Laura Auteri, Università degli Studi de Palermo (Italy). Because of the lack of national associations and the time interval between congresses, membership of the IVG sometimes fluctuates considerably – with a roughly estimated average over recent years of around 2,000. Apart from subject-specific associations, which relate to individual languages or groups of closely related languages, there are associations orientated towards several languages, national associations such as the French *Fédération Internationale des professeurs de langues vivantes (FIPLV)* (Hufeisen/ Sorger 2010: 169f.), the German *Gesellschaft für Angewandte Linguistik* (GAL) and the American *Modern Language Association (MLA)*, and its international affiliations, e.g. for the sister associations of the GAL, the *International Association of Applied Linguistics (AILA)*. These organisations also resist limitations on the training and teaching of individual languages as foreign languages. But presumably, for GFL and German language and literature, "transnational networks between Germany, Austria and Switzerland, are more effective" (Hufeisen/ Sorger 2010: 170f.).

3.6 Evaluation and explanation of Germany's external language policy

This chapter is not concerned with assessing Germany's external language policy (ELP) based on the extent to which postulated goals for strengthening the position of German have been actualised by the methods applied. Individual findings available to me do not give an adequately representative picture for that purpose. However, one example of such an individual evaluation is Maciej Mackiewicz's (2013: 34; Ch. J.9.5) questioning of school pupils after the *Deutsch-Wagen-Tour/Roadshow* in Poland. It showed that even after the first phase of the roadshow, 58% of participants claimed they had "an increased desire to learn German" – which prompts comparative investigations of other countries visited by the *Deutsch-Wagen-Tour* (J.9.2; J.9.13). But evaluation of such promotional measures could be orientated in several directions. More inclusive indicators for success can be found in questions relating to the external cultural policy (ECP), e.g. in the "Response by the Federal Government to a major parliamentary interpellation [. . .] from the SPD parliamentary faction – document 17/ 9839 – Paradigm shift in the conception of external cultural and educational policy of the German Foreign Office in September 2011":

Question 27: "Have the '*Deutschlandjahre*' ('Year of Germany' campaigns, e.g. in China) been evaluated with reference to their efficiency in the use of material resources, sustainability or reaching the target public, and if yes, what are the results?"

Response: "In China, the campaign locations in Shenyang and Wuhan (spring and respectively autumn 2009) were evaluated or an opinion poll was carried out. The evaluation in Shenyang came to the result that the goals of the event series 'Germany and China – On the Move Together' (1. Promotion of German-Chinese cooperation, 2. Opening of new regions: 3. Strengthening the image of Germany) were achieved. With the Year of Germany, the Goethe-Institut successfully gained footholds and consolidated its presence throughout the country. In Chongqing, within the context of this event series, for example after the '*Deutschland-promenade*' in spring 2008, the Goethe-Institut reported a discernible increase in demand for German courses and has also been offering them there since that time. The opinion poll in Wuhan showed a clear increase in knowledge about Germany and interest in Germany".

Question 42: "According to which criteria does the Federal Government assess the success of the external cultural and educational policy, and, in this context, how does it evaluate the number of foreign agencies?"

Response: "Apart from the use of targeted evaluations explained in the response to question 27, the success of ECEP measures abroad is assessed based on a continuous comparison between target specifications (target agreements) and de-facto results. In this context, our agencies abroad have an important task. They report regularly on the status of the ECEP in their host countries. In future, an important prerequisite for the achievement of these goals will still be a commensurate number of foreign agencies" (dip21.bundestag.de/dip21/btd/17/119/1711981.pdf).

This gives an impression of an evaluation comprising a plurality of dimensions. For example, measures (within the Year of Germany) which are not directed specifically towards the promotion of language, can also favour this goal (demand for German courses at the Goethe-Institut). But are there other effects which go beyond the Goethe-Institut and are possibly more sustainable? Investigations which probe more deeply than mere claims and include changes in action are more difficult. And assessing long-term, sustainable effects generally requires a considerable time commitment. Furthermore, the findings can expose cost-benefit questions and therefore possibly fundamental questions about external language promotion. These may even relate to the choice between external promotion of German and (even) stronger openness towards English as the principal language for international communication by Germany or German-speaking countries (for German as an academic language, see Ammon 1998: 252–286).

Rather than entering a laborious discussion of these questions, the present chapter is limited to the causes and evaluation of Germany's ELP from the perspective of different foreign-policy theories (external policy). In this context, I rely on analyses by Verena Andrei and Volker Rittberger (2009), which are based on preliminary work by Rittberger and a comprehensive investigation by Andrei (2008). The analyses put forward by Andrei/ Rittberger integrate the ELP and external cultural policy (ECP) as the "third column of (German) foreign-policy", i.e. within a foreign policy characterised by the two traditional columns of security policy and external economic policy, thereby alluding to a statement ascribed to Willy Brandt during his period as Foreign Minister (1966–1969) and subsequently sloganized. Joseph Nye's (1990a, b; 2004) characterisation of the ECP, which also includes the ELP, as a form of "soft power", points in the same direction. The foreign policy theories applied by Andrei and Rittberger (2009) are not merely descriptive; they are attempts to explain why certain external policies are as they are, and what motivates the actors involved. These are aligned with the three major political orientations of *neorealism* (ibid: 34–37), *utilitarian liberalism* (ibid: 37–40) and *constructivism* (ibid: 40–42) and are assessed with reference to two key objectives of Germany's ELP after the reunification of the country and the dissolution of the Soviet Union, namely strengthening of the position of the German language: 1) "in the states of Central and South Eastern Europe" and 2) "as a working language in the European Union" (ibid: 42–60).

The neorealist theory of external policy assumes an anarchic and variable structure in the international relations between states. In this context, individual states are intent upon preserving a high degree of autonomy, which is based on economic strength, size of territory and influence over other states. Strengthening this influence was and presumably still is a substantial motive for Germany's ELP of promoting the German language in Central and South Eastern Europe and as a working language in the EU institutions. However, both attempts enjoyed only limited success, because – contrary to the policy objective – as a foreign language in Central and South Eastern Europe, German remained far behind English, and similarly, as a working language, even behind French (ibid: 44–48; see also Ch. K.3.1; K.3.2, beginning).

The foreign policy theory of utilitarian liberalism does not relate directly to entire states as actors, but rather to the predominant interest groups regarded in terms of power policy. These have two basic interests: preservation or enlargement of 1) power and 2) wealth. In this context, the actors can be subdivided into two major groups: on one hand, the representatives of politics and administration and, on the other hand, private organisations and citizen groups. The first group is primarily interested in positions, and the second in the preservation of ownership and income, in addition to more specialised goals, including non-material goals. In the event of a loss of autonomy of their state, both groups are threatened with losses regarding their decision-making competencies. Network analyses are particularly appropriate for more detailed investigation of such interests and actions. Actors associated with politics and administration had contrary preferences regarding the promotion of German: because of the costs, the Finance Minister tended to be disinclined, while the Foreign Minister and other ministries involved in the promotional activities were more in favour, if only because of the increased allocation of resources. This last point also applies for implementing organisations, such as the Central Office for German Schools Abroad (ZfA), the Goethe-Institut (G-I), the German Academic Exchange Service (DAAD) and the Institute for International Relations (ifa), which all welcomed gains in competencies and resources. Private actors, such as the Association of Chambers of Industry and Commerce, also favoured the promotion of German, because they "hoped for commercial advantages [. . .] from an improved knowledge of German among their business partners (in the countries of Central and South Eastern Europe! U.A.]". By contrast with the neorealist view, however, agreement was divided: "overall, there is [even! U.A.] a stalemate situation between Federal Minister of Finance and Foreign Minister [. . .]" (ibid: 50f.). By contrast, all actors supported the policy for strengthening the position of German in the EU committees. Representatives of politics and administration saw advantages for influencing EU legislation if the government bills were available in German and not only in English and French (which was in fact achieved through German demands, especially by Helmut Kohl; Ch. H.4.2). And, for private sector actors, especially German companies, it is obviously advantageous if, for example, Europe-wide bids from the Commission also appear in German, which was also largely achieved (ibid: 51–54).

The constructivist theory of foreign policy is based on an understanding of political actors as the bearers of roles who act primarily through norms and values internalised by socialisation, the broad acknowledgement of which also finds expression in the prevailing law (ibid: 40–42). For the German ELP, this leads to the support of minority rights, also for "the culture and language of German minorities in Eastern Europe", among other factors. In this respect, "even before 1990, it is possible to speak of a consensus on the ECP which includes all parties represented in the Bundestag [...]" (ibid: 56f.). However, "the minimal consideration of languages from CSOE (Central and South Eastern Europe! U.A.] in German schooling" (ibid: 58) contradicts the constructivist explanation of the German ELP after reunification. Moreover, strengthening the position of German in the EU institutions is hardly compatible with the values otherwise pro-claimed by Germany, especially regarding linguistic diversity. Diversity requires equality between all EU official languages (but this would not achieve efficient operating of the EU institutions). In view of such discrepancies between claims and reality for the policy of strengthening the position of German, "the explanatory value of the constructivist theory is drawn into doubt". This policy does not follow the values otherwise represented by the associated actors and was not successful in this sense (ibid: 58–60).

Regarding the explanatory value of the three foreign policy theories with reference to the two components investigated, the conclusion reached by Andrei/ Rittberger (2009: 60) is there-fore coherent: "Accordingly, the German ELP after 1990 as a whole could be best explained based on the (modified) neorealist theory as a form of an intensified power policy in the sense of a policy of cultural influence and defence" (ibid: 60). It followed the principles and regulari-ties assumed by the utilitarian and constructivist theories only to a very limited degree. Apart from obvious criticisms of political incompetence, because substantial goals were missed, the findings also prompt moral criticism of the deviation from the constructivist line because of the incompatibility between declared norms and actual policy. Was the German ELP after 1990 guided more by self-interest than by superordinate values? But, then, could a fundamentally different language policy have been expected from a German government? Anyway, what was involved was only "soft power"; it was not a brutal military or economic policy, and not a case of indubitable oppression. At least, with such "soft" policies, could a government afford to neglect the direct interests of its own country, its own population and its own language community and to subordinate them to higher, more universal human interests (see e.g. Stickel 2007a; Ammon 2007b)? And would this apply in the light of the barely disputable fact that, ultimately, not even a single country does pursue such selfless policies (Ch. K.5)? I leave the answer to this question, which leads into deep philosophical waters, to the reader.

4. External-language policies of the other German-speaking countries

The external-language policies (ELP) of the other German-speaking countries (Ch. B.4; Ch. D) are more modest than the German ELP, not least because of their smaller size. Nevertheless, Austria's ELP is quite considerable (de Cillia 2012a: 242–245; Ortner/ von Ruckteschell-Katte 2010: 138–142; Muhr 1997). There was a long tradition of teaching GFL dating to the time of Maria Theresia (Queen of Austria and Hungary 1740, Empress of the Holy Roman Empire 1745, both until 1780) and extending throughout Austria's subsequent history (Goebl 1997, 1999) until the end of WWI. Austria's ELP saw a new start after WWII in the 1960s, with the establishment of GFL in the 1980s and consolidation of the subject after 1990 (Boeckmann 2010: 72–78). Austria created a "Cultural Policy Section", currently in the "Federal Ministry for Europe, Integration and Foreign Affairs", with responsibility for government planning of the ELP, to which the Ministry for Science and Education also contribute, especially through the Division for "Culture and Language" (Ortner/ Ruckteschell-Katte 2010: 142). Former direc-tor of the Cultural Policy Section, Wolfgang Schallenberg (1987: 193), described the Austrian position, which still applies today, as follows: even if "the spread of the German language as such cannot be the primary aim of Austria's cultural activities, the Austrian government's external cultural policy still [makes] its own, no doubt modest, contribution to the spread of German".

By way of further limitation, he added "it is even more important – and this also applies to other small and medium-sized countries – for us Austrians to learn foreign languages than it is for large numbers of foreigners to acquire the language we speak". This quotation sheds light on the circumstance that, like other Eastern Central European countries following the dissolution of the Soviet Union, Austria adopted observer status within Francophonie, complying with the wishes of France to promote the use of French (Ch. K.5: paragraph on "France").

One important organisation for Austria's external promotion of German is the *Österreich Institut*, which was founded in 1997, to some extent based on the model of the Goethe-Institut. By 2013, it had already set up ten institutes abroad: in Belgrade, Brno, Bratislava, Budapest, Kraków, Ljubljana, Rome, Warsaw, Wrocław (Breslau) and Istanbul (www.bmeia.gv.at/ aussen-ministerium/aussenpolitik/auslandskultur/oestereich-institut-gmbh.html). All these institutes offer GFL courses. In recent years, the number of participants has been around 10,000 per year. As with the Goethe-Institut, there has been a clearly increasing trend more recently (Ch. J.5; Table J.5–1) (www.oesterreichinstitut.at). As a mediating organisation, the Österreich Institut is largely self-financing, especially from course fees. To provide an academic basis for GFL teaching and for the training of teaching staff, GFL professorships have been established in Vienna and Graz (Boeckmann 2010: 76; for details of Austrian GFL associations, see Sorger 2010; Ch. K.3.5).

The eight Austrian Schools Abroad – one of them the bilingual *formatio – Bilinguale Privats-chule*, in Liechtenstein, that is, inside the German-language territory – also serve the promotion of German. Of the other schools, mostly grammar schools, two are in Budapest, with one each in Istanbul, Prague, Shkodra (Albania), Guatemala Ciudad (Guatemala) and Querétaro (Mexico) (www.bmukk.gv.at/schulen/schulen/ausland/oesterr_auslandsschulen.xml). The pupils attending these schools originate primarily from the host country; but most of the teachers are sent from Austria and teach in German (www.weltweitunterrichten.at/site/auslandsschu len/taetig keit?SWS=36de043bc08434232591b083a0f3c568). Furthermore, Austria is committed to the education and further training of foreign German teachers. Added to these factors which contribute to the promotion of German abroad, numerous lectors and language assistants are sent to foreign language universities in countries abroad, in approximately 130 sites in 2012 (de Cillia 2012a: 242). Austrian efforts to promote German abroad also include the development of an Austrian GFL language diploma and, in conjunction with other German-speaking countries, a common examination format "*Zertifikat Deutsch*".

Compared with Austria, Switzerland is reticent in its external promotional policy for German. "Cultural policy in Switzerland is positioned differently because, by contrast with Germany and Austria, we have four national languages. There are no institutions which promote the German language or German teaching abroad" (Information in a letter from Swiss cultural foundation *Pro Helvetia*, which finances cultural exchange with foreign countries, 28 November 1990). Although the title of one book by Carmela Ahokas (2003), "The Promotion of the German Language in Switzerland", seems promising, the book also creates a similar impression. It is limited almost exclusively to circumstances inside Switzerland. Only the short chapter "Swiss Schools Abroad" (ibid: 75–78) reaches outwards. Nevertheless, the promotion of German described in this chapter is considerable, because Switzerland does indeed have 17 "Swiss Schools Abroad" " (unterricht.educa.ch/ de/schweizerschulen-ausland; Ch. J.3). But in these schools, there must be "a minimum percentage of Swiss school pupils", the magnitude of which is variable (information from Irene Spicher, Co-Managing Director of the responsible committee *educationsuisse*, email 13 January 2014). 15 schools have German-speaking "patron Cantons" and German as "*Basissprache*" and therefore also the language of teaching. The school in Bogotà (Colombia) also has a branch with French in addition to the German branch. The "German-Swiss International School Hong Kong" which also has English alongside German as a language of teaching, is a German School Abroad (Ch. J.3) with three members of the teaching staff funded by Switzerland. The 15 Swiss Schools Abroad with German as language of teaching are (alphabetically by country) in São Paulo, Curitiba (both in Brazil), Santiago (Chile), Bergamo, Catania, Milan, Rome (all four in Italy – another school in Como teaches in Italian), Mexico City, Cuernavaca, Querétaro (all three in Mexico), Lima (Peru), Singapore (Singapore), Barcelona, Madrid (both in Spain) and Bangkok (Thailand) (unterricht.educa.ch/de/schweizerschulen-ausland). In cultural contacts with foreign countries, balanced consideration is given to all four national languages. And this also promotes German, for example, through gifts of books to universities and libraries abroad, poetry readings, often in cooperation with Goethe Institutes, and foreign visits by guest lecturers. Furthermore, Switzerland provides preparatory German-language courses for foreign students at the German-speaking Swiss universities.

The fact that four languages are spoken, and the promotion of German is directed more inwards than outwards means that German as a second language (GSL) is a more important school subject than German as a foreign language (GFL). This is evident from the article by Michael Langner (2010) on "Developments of German as a Foreign and Second Language in Switzerland", which addresses almost exclusively GSL. The only GFL professorship in Freiburg/Fribourg is "associated with the bilingualism of this university and the associated need to offer subsidiary and study-specific language teaching for German (and French) as academic languages" (ibid: 83). The presentation of "Institutions and Associations for German as a Foreign and Second Language in Switzerland" by Monika Clalüna (2010) shows a similar weighting. Apart from the Swiss Schools Abroad and Pro Helvetia, Clalüna does not mention any institutions abroad of significant scale. There are also no associations with this orientation, apart from the *Arbeitskreis Deutsch als Fremdsprache* (*AkDaF*; ibid: 162–164). Moreover, external observers might take away the impression that Switzerland prefers French to German. This does apply especially for international communication between diplomats, who use German almost exclusively with German-speaking partners, but otherwise tend to use French more often, alongside English. Furthermore, the preference among German-Swiss people for their dialect reveals a certain antipathy towards High German and indirectly towards the German language overall; there is no corresponding effect in French-speaking or Italian-speaking Switzerland. Switzerland's full membership of Francophonie is sometimes celebrated in a way which would hardly be imaginable for membership of the German-language community, e.g. at the Francophonie Summit in Montreux (Canton Waadt) in 2010 (www.swissinfo.ch/ger/specials/frankophonie-gipfel/Auch_die_Schweiz_profitiert_vom_Frankophonie-Gipfel.html?cid=28570518).

Presumably, very few observers would expect a policy for external promotion of German from Liechtenstein, the smallest German-speaking country. But in various ways, Liechtenstein has shown astonishing commitment, e.g. in the – ultimately unsuccessful – attempt to achieve the position of German as an official language of the Council of Europe (Ch. H.4.6).

5. External-language policies of countries with languages other than German

A glance at the "*Liste nationaler Kulturinstitute*" [List of national cultural institutes] in Wikipedia (de.wikipedia.org/wiki/Liste_nationaler_Kulturinstitute) might give the impression that many countries pursue at least an external cultural policy (ECP), but probably also external-language policies (ELP). Most of the 30 institutes named are less responsible for national culture as such than for the ECP of their countries (e.g. China: Confucius Institute; Germany: *Goethe-Institut, Institut für Auslandsbeziehungen*; France: *Alliance française, Institut française*; Italy: *Società Dante Alighieri; Istituto Italiano di Cultura*; Japan: Japan Foundation; Austria: *Österreichisches Kulturforum,*

Österreich Institut; Spain: Institut Cervantes; South Korea: Korean Cultural Centre; Turkey Yunnus Emre Cultural Institute; United Kingdom: British Council etc.). As different types of mediating organisation, most of these also pursue an ELP. More detailed but now relatively dated summaries of the ELP of various countries can be found in Ammon/ Kleineidam (1992) and Ammon (1994). In general, countries with the same language (national official language and majority native language) cooperate in the external promotion of their shared language. However, there are also often minor contests between them for zones of influence and viability of the respective national language varieties. For example, the UK would prefer to promote British English rather than US English; Portugal prefers Lusitanian Portuguese, whereas Brazil prefers Latin American Portuguese; Spain prefers Iberian Spanish; Argentina prefers Latin American Spanish; Germany prefers "Teutonic German" while Austria prefers "Austrian German" and so on (for pluricentric languages, see e.g. Clyne 1992; Ammon 2005d). In general, however, the common language unites more strongly than differences in national varieties divide, so that the different centres for the same pluricentric language cooperate more than they compete.

Cooperation on language policy between countries with different languages is more difficult. It presents a task of the form *"do ut des"* (I give, so that you give), which is potentially advantageous to all participants. But such cooperation is generally restricted to situations faced with a clear threat, where both (or several) sides involved are otherwise afraid of serious losses or failure. Japanese author, Seiei Shinohara (2000: 47) has described one historical curiosity; he was a funded student in Germany during WWII and, in 1944, was invited by the Japanese Embassy in Berlin and the German Foreign Office to be the first person to teach Japanese in a German school: "As I was told by the gentlemen representing the two authorities, after the victorious end of the war [. . .], teaching in the Japanese language was to be provided in all grammar schools in Germany instead of English, and teaching in German was to be given in all middle schools in Japan instead of English". This was obviously a project as lacking in realism as the German-Japanese "final victory"! However, there have also been more realistic attempts at ELP cooperation between countries with international languages in the second rank (Ch. A.7), especially when they are driven by concern over the further (or ultimately total) loss of the international position of their language to the "over-powerful" English. I have myself suggested that possibilities for this kind of cooperation on language policy should be investigated (Ammon 2007a). But so far, only initial steps have been made, e.g. between Germany and France: in the "Common German-French language instruction" for EU institutions (Ammon 2009a: 125f.; Ch. H.4.2) or in the case of advertising in one's own country for the language of the other country as a foreign language (Ch. J.9.2). Matthias Lahr-Kurten (2012) describes opportunities for "speaking German in France" and "practices for promoting the German language within the French education system", which presuppose a basic cooperative attitude towards the language community of the other. Having said this, the readiness required for this is generally limited to foreign language teachers and other commercially interested groups. The predominant attitude, also among planners and principal actors of the ELP, tends to be characterised by competitive thinking. It is therefore more accurate to speak, like Kurt-Jürgen Maaß (2013: 13f.) of the "competition" between countries with international languages of the second rank, especially over position as a second foreign language in the school and university curricula of other countries. Since the first foreign language is almost always English, the English-speaking countries seem to rise above this competition.

But competitive thinking hinders cooperation. This is evident from the way in which competitors tend to be more aware of reluctance to cooperate in others than in themselves. I must admit to this in my own perception of an apparent lack of linguistic solidarity, e.g. by France more than Germany regarding the lack of French support in improving the position of German in EU institutions (Ammon 2007b) and the absence of German-language text panels in museums and exhibitions in France, e.g. at the Paris Exhibition 2014 on the German von Humboldt brothers ("*Unsere Brüder Humboldt*", *FAZ* 19 May 2014: 9). By contrast, the absence of French text panels in Germany is less noticeable to me. I am aware of a correspondingly asymmetric perception and attitude among many Germans and, vice versa, among French people. It grows from a subconscious linguistic suspicion, which stands in the way of cooperation. The actors involved easily slip into a kind of prisoner dilemma in which neither party reaches an optimal solution (see Ch. A.2).

Indeed, these difficulties run even deeper, prompting the question: what might an optimal, fair solution look like? The complexity required in any satisfactory answer to this question has been suggested by one of the pioneers in the field of linguistic justice, at least on my understanding of his thinking: external promotion of languages other than English would ultimately be unfair in general and, in fact, relative to all language communities which do not have an international language at their disposal (Ch. A.7). Because for them, every additional international language – in addition to the world language English – would represent more of a burden than an enrichment (van Parijs 2001a, 2004a, b; 2007b, 2011). Nevertheless, in my estimation, this inference requires further investigation and presumably greater differentiation. But I turn now to the ELP of individual countries, pruned down to a manageable selection.

United Kingdom and USA, with one language, English, which essentially requires no promotion (Grin 1999a, b, 2000). In fact, its spread is self-propelling, because almost everyone would like to learn this most widely distributed language to avoid depriving themselves of important opportunities for communication and thereby harming themselves. Despite this fact, the British Council is, without competition, the largest language-promoting organisation worldwide, and this includes reference to client numbers (Lutzmann/ Schneider 2009). It is also the most profitable, possibly even the only organisation with – saturated – pure profit, which contributes to the enormous profit of the British language industry (Grin 2001, 2004b), which relies, in turn, on the global position of English (Crystal 1985, 2003; Graddol 2000, 2006). The policy which has led to this position has been extensively criticised as "language imperialism", especially in the work of Robert Phillipson (1992, 2000, 2006b, c) and his wife Tove Skutnabb-Kangas (Phillipson/ Skutnabb-Kangas 1994, 1999). However, the further spread of English nowadays no longer requires any imperialistic policies, because the non-English-speaking world is now reliant on this language. It would experience serious communication crises if the English-speaking countries were to prohibit the use of English, which, admittedly, they cannot do. The USA has no government language-promoting organisations, but does promote English and English teaching whenever required, contributing to the further spread of English through worldwide media presence and through its schools and universities, which exist in many countries (with English as the language of teaching and a subject for study (R. Hoffmann 2009: 362f., 366).

France has a reputation as the country with the most elaborate and sophisticated language-promotion policy worldwide; and this is presumably well-founded. It promotes the French language not only externally (Kleineidam 1992; Christ 2000; Lutzmann/ Schneider 2009), but also internally within its own country (Braselmann 1999; Braselmann/ Ohnheiser 2008; Ch. E.4.3). The *Organisation Internationale de la Francophonie*, abbreviated as *Francophonie*, of which all countries with official language French are full members and at the head of which sits no less an authority than the President of France, plays an important role for the worldwide promotion of French. The extended circle of Francophonie includes countries which acknowledge and promote French especially as a language of culture. Together with these countries, Francophonie comprised 77 countries in 2014. They include all Eastern Central European countries apart from Belarus and Russia, which France was able to win over to an observer status within

Francophonie after the dissolution of the Soviet Union (en.wikipedia.org/wiki/File:Map-Fran cophonie_organisation_fr.svg). As a result, Francophonie occupies an impressive area on world maps. Switzerland and Luxembourg are full members; and even Austria has been a member with observer status since 2004 (www.bmeia.gv.at/ aussenministerium/ pressenews/ presseaussendun gen/ 2004/oesterreich-erlangt-beobachterstatus-bei-der-organisation-der-franko phonie.html). This impressive organisation supports the official status of French in international organisations (Ch. H.3) and its continuing position within diplomacy and the EU institutions (Ch. H.4.2). The government-run *Institut français* is responsible for external promotion of French; it is supported by the *Centres culturels* with responsibility for other aspects of culture and by the *Alliance française*, which acts in a mediating function to promote the language. Since its foundation in 1983, this organisation looks back over a long tradition and today comprises approximately 800 branches in 133 countries (de.wikipedia.org/wiki/ Alliance_fran%C3%A7aise).

Italy also has a considerable tradition in external language policy, which has been described by Mariella Totaro-Genevois (2005; also Lutzmann/ Schneider 2009: 374 f.; De Mauro/Vedovidelli 1994). The *Società Dante Alighieri*, which is primarily responsible for Italy's practical ELP, was founded in 1889 and could have been the model for the naming of the Goethe-Institut, setting a precedent by foregrounding the country's most famous poet. Italy's ELP is orientated not only towards Italian as a foreign language, but also towards its maintenance as a native language among the numerous emigrants and many Italian(-speaking) minorities. More than 500 Italian schools abroad are included within the network of Italy's ELP. As in Germany, the government Foreign Ministry is responsible for the ELP. It has connections with the approximately 450 committees of the *Società Dante Alighieri*, which provide teaching in Italian as a foreign language in 60 countries distributed in all continents. The Società receives government subsidies and functions as a kind of mediating organisation (Totaro-Genevois 2005: 88–90; de.wiki pedia.org/ wiki/Societ%C3%A0_Dante_Alighieri).

Spain developed a new ELP after the Franco dictatorship (Lutzmann/ Schneider 2009: 377f.; de Cock 2008). Accordingly, its *Instituto Cervantes*, which is primarily entrusted with the ELP is still relatively young having been founded only in 1991 (de.wikipedia. org/wiki/Instituto_Cervantes) as successor to the *Institutos de España*. Its naming also takes up the Italian-German model by referencing the most famous national poet, and it expressly undertook to operate "*como el Goethe-Institut en Alemania*" and other similar institutions (Sanchez 1992: 58–60). The Instituto Cervantes is a mediating organisation, financed and supervised by the Foreign Ministry; it comprises more than 70 centres distributed among all continents. It has attracted attention in many countries, including within Europe, through intensive advertising and has generated a lively demand for its courses in Spanish as a foreign language. In the German-language territory alone, there are examination centres in six Cervantes Institutes, and worldwide, in some 800 institutes in more than 100 countries (www.studyinspain.info/ reportajes/propuestas/El-Instituto-Cervantes-el-espaol-en-el-mundo/?l=en). The Institute's ambitions are evident from announcements by the new director of the Instituto Cervantes since 2012, who was previously president of the national language institute *Real Academia Española*: "*Nuestro gran proyecto es implantar el Cervantes en las mejores universidades de Estado Unidos*" (*Mercurio/Fundación José Manuel Lara* 143, September 2012: title page).

Portugal pursues its ELP together with and to some extent in the shadow of the incomparably larger Brazil (da Silva/ Klein Gunnewick 1992). In 1992, it founded the *Instituto Camões* (successor to the *Instituto da Cultura e Lingua Portuguesa*) as a "mediating organisation" which – as with other countries – is financially supported and co-controlled by the Portuguese Foreign Office (Lutzmann/ Schneider 2009: 376f.). Once again, the reference to the national poet, Luis de Camões, follows the same model as the Goethe-Institut. The Instituto Camões has language institutes in 38 cities and 27 countries (de.wikipedia.org/wiki/Instituto_Cam%C3%B5es); Schneider/ Lutzmann (2009: 376) noted as many as "48 language centres worldwide" and "23 cultural centres". The regional foci are in Africa and Europe; Brazil has responsibility for America. Current news about individual institutes can be found at: www.instituto-camoes.pt.

Russia has a long tradition of promoting its own language. During the Soviet period, especially since the leadership of Stalin, this also extended towards non-Russian peoples within the Soviet Union and foreign countries (Haarmann 1992). One component of the Soviet ELP was the assertion of Russian as the first, compulsory foreign language in schools in all member states of Comecon and the Warsaw Pact, and as the sole, or at least a first-ranking, working language in all joint institutions. The ELP was redesigned after the collapse of the Soviet Union, but despite setbacks with the learning of Russian outside the new Russian Federation, it was able to build upon the knowledge of Russian distributed during the Soviet period. More recent ELP is directed towards language maintenance for the Russian(-speaking) minorities, which are regarded as a "diaspora", especially in the countries of the CIS (Community of Independent States), but also towards the promotion of learning Russian as a foreign language (Bälz 2009: 411–417). This includes supporting "Centres for the Russian Language" abroad (e.g. in *Frankfurt am Main* and Vienna), the "International Association for Teachers of the Russian Language" (*Meždunarodnaja associacija propodavatelej russkogo jazyka i literatury*) and promotional campaigns such as the "Year of the Russian Language 2007" and the programme "The Russian Language (2011–2015)", especially also for Germany (deu.rs.gov.ru/de/node/752). To all appearances, external language promotion takes priority over cultural promotion in the narrower sense (Bälz 2009: 422).

In previous, imperial periods of its history, *Japan* pursued an energetic colonial ELP in Korea, parts of China, and especially in Manchuria (Hirataka 1992: 93–95). Modern promotion of Japanese began only in the 1980s in conjunction with the economic upturn (ibid: 95–107) and rising demand for knowledge of Japanese abroad (Coulmas 1989). The policy was developed primarily by the *Japan Foundation* (Kawamura 2009: 391), which is subordinate to the Japanese Foreign Ministry and today comprises 21 branches in 19 countries (de.wikipedia.org/wiki/Japan_Foundation). In the early years of the new ELP, providing the start-up finance for professorships in Japanese played a considerable role (Hirataka 1992: 96); additional financing was then gradually transferred to the recipient universities. In the most recent period, a key term in Japanese external cultural and language policy has become "international exchange" (*kokusaika*). In conjunction with this concept, Japan has tried, possibly more than other countries, to improve knowledge of English within its own country, which seems to be more important to Japan than promoting its own language abroad (Kawamura 2009: 392). After many years of successful spread of Japanese as a foreign language, especially in the neighbouring countries of Asia and Oceania, Japanese has recently been overtaken in many places by Chinese as a foreign language.

China has become "a competitor [. . .] which must be taken seriously" (Maaß 2013: 14) by all countries worldwide regarding external cultural policy and language policy (Sheng 2015; Gil 2017 – the latter title has not been evaluated). This is hardly surprising as China is currently the USA's only serious competitor for position as the world's leading power. The most important institution for China's ELP is the *Confucius Institute* which is largely under state control, so that, in the absence of a private-law constitution, it can hardly be described as a mediating organisation. "In general, they [the Confucius Institutes! U.A.] are tasked with spreading the Chinese language and improving understanding within and about China" (Hartig 2009: 405). Development of the Institutes took place at a similar speed to China's economic upturn, the initial impetus having apparently come from the former Chinese ambassador in Berlin, possibly because of his acquaintance with the Goethe-Institut. The first Confucius Institute was opened in Seoul in 2004, and by "December 2008, there were 249 Confucius Institutes and 56 Confucius classrooms in 78 countries" (Hartig 2009: 405). "In founding the Institutes, recourse was taken to the existing infrastructure in the host countries, such as universities, associations or chambers of commerce" (de.wikipedia.org/wiki/Konfuzius-Institut). This procedure has considerably accelerated their expansion. "Within only 10 years, 440 of these cultural institutions and 640 so-called Confucius classrooms have been established in 120 countries", almost always in cooperation with local partners (universities or local authorities), which have provided "rooming facilities, local employees and 50% of the project funds", while the Chinese side paid a start-up contribution and supplied the other half of the running costs as well as teaching staff and materials. The *Hanban* national management committee of the Confucius Institutes has also recently been trying to achieve sustainable qualitative improvements, especially in teaching methods. As part of this effort, model institutes are to be set up, but the total number of institutes may in fact be reduced (Hartig 2014: 61). As with Japanese, the spread of Chinese is also hindered to some extent because of the effort required to learn the written form. But, in view of the economic potential of the parent country, it must be anticipated that Chinese will eventually become established as one of the most learnt foreign languages in the world – however, without endangering the global position of English, at least, not in the foreseeable future (see also Ch. J.7; J.9.13).

BIBLIOGRAPHY

Most of the titles listed here are cited in the text. However, additional titles which are relevant to the topic of the book have also been included. Web pages mentioned only once in the book have been referenced at the appropriate place in the text.

ABC des Auslandsschulwesens ([2013] n.d.) Zentralstelle für das Auslandsschulwesen (ed.) Köln.

Abel, Andrea/ Stuflesser, Mathias/ Voltmer, Leonhard (eds.) (2007) *Aspects of Multilingualism in European Border Regions: Insights from Alsace, Eastern Macedonia and Thrace, the Lublin Voivodeship and South Tyrol.* Bozen: EURAC Research.

Abelein, Manfred (1968) *Die Kulturpolitik des deutschen Reiches und der Bundesrepublik Deutschland und ihre verfassungsrechtlichen Probleme.* Köln/ Opladen: Westdeutscher Verlag.

Abfalterer, Heidemaria (2007) *Der Südtiroler Sonderwortschatz aus plurizentrischer Sicht. Lexikalisch-semantische Besonderheiten im Standarddeutsch Südtirols.* Innsbruck: Innsbruck University Press.

Abteilung für Auswärtige Kulturpolitik des Auswärtigen Amtes (ed.) (1988) *Auswärtige Kulturpolitik 1984– 1986.* Bonn.

Ackermann, Irmgard/ Weinrich, Harald (eds.) (1986) *Eine nicht nur deutsche Literatur. Zur Standortbestimmung der Ausländerliteratur.* München/ Zürich: Piper.

[ACTFL] American Council on the Teaching of Foreign Languages (2010) *Foreign Language Enrollments in K-12 Public Schools: Are Students Prepared for a Global Society?* Alexandria, VA: American Council on the Teaching of Foreign Languages. (www.actfl.org/sites/default/files/pdfs/ReportSummary2011.pdf)

ADaF-Auswertung (1990) *Deutsch als Fremdsprache in den Gastländern des Goethe-Instituts.* Zusammengest. vom Referat 02. München: Goethe-Institut.

Adams, Willi P. (1990) *The German Americans: An Ethnic Experience.* Indianapolis: Max Kade German Center.

ADAWiS (2013) *Die Sprache von Forschung und Lehre: Welche – Wo, für Wen? Dokumentation einer Podiumsdiskussion des Arbeitskreises Deutsch als Fremdsprache (ADAWiS) e. V. und der Freien Universität Berlin am 29. Januar 2013 in Berlin.* Berlin: Arbeitskreis Deutsch als Fremdsprache.

Adler, Robert/ Ewing, John/ Taylor, Peter (2008) *Citation Statistics. A Report from the International Mathematics Union (IMU) in cooperation with the International Council of Industrial and Applied Mathematics (ICIAM) and the Institute of Mathematical Statistics (IMS).* (www.mathunion.org/fileadmin/IMU/Report/ CitationStatistics.pdf)

Adressbuch 1990/91 für den deutschsprachigen Buchhandel (1990) Frankfurt a.M.: Buchhändler- Vereinigung GmbH.

Ahlzweig, Claus (1989) Die deutsche Nation und ihre Muttersprache. In Ehlich, K. (ed.) *Sprache im Faschismus.* Frankfurt a.M.: Suhrkamp, 35–57.

Ahokas, Carmela (2003) *Die Förderung der deutschen Sprache durch die Schweiz. Möglichkeiten und Einschränkungen.* Frankfurt a.M.: Lang. Ahrens, Rüdiger (ed.) (2003) *Europäische Sprachenpolitik. European Language Policy.* Heidelberg: Winter.

Airey, John/ Linder, Cedric (2006) Language and the experience of learning university physics in Sweden. *European Journal of Physics* 27: 553–560.

Aiyepeku, Wilson O. (1973) The languages and format of geographical literature: A comparative study. *International Library Review* 5: 53–62.

Akdoğan, Feruzan (2003) Deutsch als Fremdsprache in der Türkei. Bestandaufnahme und Prognosen. *Info DaF* 30 (1): 46–55.

—— (2004) Das neue Ausbildungsprogramm für Deutschlehrer an türkischen Universitäten. Kompatibel – zukunftsträchtig? *Info DaF* 31 (4): 475–482.

—— (2008) Die Deutschlehrerausbildung an türkischen Universitäten. *Jahrbuch für internationale Germanistik* 39 (2): 17–26.

Akstinat, Björn [1997] (2009) *Deutschsprachige Studienangebote weltweit. Verzeichnis der Kontaktadressen zu deutschsprachigen Vorlesungen und Studiengängen an Universitäten und Hochschulen außerhalb Deutschlands, Österreichs, Luxemburgs, Liechtensteins und der Schweiz* [German-language part! et al.]. 6th expanded edition Köln: Internationale Medienhilfe (IHM).

—— (2012/13) *Handbuch der deutschsprachigen Presse im Ausland. Verzeichnis deutschsprachiger Zeitungen, Zeitschriften, Mitteilungsblätter und Jahrbücher außerhalb Deutschlands, Österreichs, Luxemburgs, Liechtensteins und der Schweiz.* Berlin: Internationale Medienhilfe (IHM).

Alber, Siegbert (2004) Die Rolle der deutschen Sprache im Gerichtshof der Europäischen Gemeinschaften. In Lohse, 51–72.

Alekseeva, Irina (2011) Dolmetscher- und Übersetzer-Ausbildung in Russland. In Ammon/ Kemper, 128–137.

Alexander von Humboldt-Stiftung (2013) *Jahresbericht 2012.* Bonn-Bad Godesberg: Alexander von Humboldt-Stiftung. (www.humboldt-foundation.de/pls/web/docs/F2691/jahresbericht_2012.pdf.)

Allard, R[eál]/ Landry, R[odrigue] (1992) Ethnolinguistic vitality beliefs and language maintenance and loss. In Fase/ Jaspaert/ Kroon, 171–195.

—— / —— (1994) Subjective ethnolinguistic vitality: a comparison of two measures. *International Journal of the Sociology of Language* 108: 117–144.

Allert, William A. (2006) Die Hutterer – Teile alles, vertraue auf Gott. Die Gemeinde von Surprise Creek lebt noch streng nach den Regeln ihrer Vorväter. *National Geographic Deutschland* (September): 64–91.

Altenhofen, Cléo V. (1996) *Hunsrückisch in Rio Grande do Sul. Ein Beitrag zur Beschreibung einer deutschbrasilianischen Dialektvarietät im Kontakt mit dem Portugiesischen.* Stuttgart: Steiner.

—— (2013) Dachsprachenwechsel und Varietätenabgrenzung im Kontakt zwischen Hunsrückisch und Portugiesisch in Brasilien. In *Festschrift für Harald Thun zum 60. Geburtstag.* Kiel: Westensee-Verlag.

—— / Gonzaga de Souza, Draiton (2003) Ensino de Leitura de Textos de Filosofia e Letras em Alemão: Uma Experiência Interdisciplinar. In Kaufmann/ Lenhard Bredemeier/ Volkmann, 179–193.

Alter, Peter (1981) Internationale Wissenschaft und nationale Politik. Zur Zusammenarbeit der wissenschaftlichen Akademien im frühen 20. Jahrhundert. In Kettenacker, L./ Schlenke, M./ Seier, H. (eds.) *Studien zur Geschichte Englands und der deutsch-britischen Beziehungen. Festschrift für Paul Kluke.* München: Fink, 201–221.

—— (1985) *Nationalismus.* Frankfurt a.M.: Suhrkamp.

—— (1987) *The Reluctant Patron. Science and the State in Britain 1850–1920* [Tr. (1982) *Wissenschaft, Staat, Mäzene. Anfänge moderner Wissenschaftspolitik in Großbritannien 1850–1920*]. Stuttgart: Klett-Cotta. Oxford/ Hamburg/ New York: Berg.

—— (ed.) (2000a) *Der DAAD in der Zeit. Geschichte, Gegenwart und zukünftige Aufgaben – vierzehn Essays.* Bonn: Deutscher Akademischer Austauschdienst (DAAD).

—— (2000b) Der DAAD seit seiner Wiedergründung 1950. In Alter 2000a, 50–105.

Altermatt, Urs (1995) Die mehrsprachige Schweiz – Modell für Europa? In Altermatt, U./ Brix, E. (eds.) *Schweiz und Österreich. Eine Nachbarschaft in Mitteleuropa.* Wien/ Köln/ Weimar: Böhlau, 39–49.

Althof, Hans-Joachim (ed.) (1990) *Deutschlandstudien international. Dokumentation des Wolfenbütteler DAAD-Symposiums 1988.* Bonn-Bad-Godesberg: DAAD.

AMGO e.V. (2012) *Wie ringen Volksgruppen in der EU für die Umsetzung von Minderheitengesetzen? Eine Analyse am Beispiel der Republik Polen und dem Fall der verhinderten Schließung der "Zweisprachigen Grundschule Nr. 5 – Ratibor-Studen" – einer Schule für die deutsche Volksgruppe.* Bonn: Gesellschaft zur Unterstützung der Deutschen in Schlesien, Ostbrandenburg, Pommern, Ost- und Westpreußen e.V.

Amiet, William A. (1932) *Literature by Languages. A Roll Call.* Sydney: Angus & Robertson.

Ammon, Carola (1995) *Deutsch als Fremdsprache an israelischen Gymnasien.* Tel Aviv: Goethe Institute.

Ammon, Ulrich [1972] (1973) *Dialekt, soziale Ungleichheit und Schule.* 2nd revised edition. Weinheim/ Basel: Beltz.

―――― (1975) Zur Soziologie der Fremdsprachenkenntnisse – mit besonderer Berücksichtigung des deutschsprachigen Gebiets. In Ammon, U./ Simon, G. *Neue Aspekte der Soziolinguistik.* Weinheim/ Basel: Beltz, 121–155.

―――― (1987) "Language – variety/ standard variety – dialect." In Ammon/ Dittmar/ Mattheier, 316335.

―――― (1989a) Die Schwierigkeiten der deutschen Sprachgemeinschaft aufgrund der Dominanz der englischen Sprache. *Zeitschrift für Sprachwissenschaft* 8 (2): 257–272.

―――― (1989b) Towards a descriptive framework for the status/ function (social position) of a language within a country. In Ammon 1989d, 21–106.

―――― (1989c) Zur Geschichte der Sprachverbreitungspolitik der Bundesrepublik Deutschland von den Anfängen bis 1985: Kommentierte Dokumentation der Diskussion im Bundestag mit anschließendem Ausblick. *Deutsche Sprache* 3: 229–263.

―――― (ed.) (1989d) *Status and Function of Languages and Language Varieties.* Berlin/ New York: de Gruyter.

―――― (1990a) German as an international language. *International Journal of the Sociology of Language* 83: 135–170.

―――― (1990b) Deutsch, Englisch, Russisch und Französisch als Linguae francae in Osteuropa: eine Expertenbefragung. *Germanistische Mitteilungen* 32: 67–81.

―――― (1990c) German or English? The problems of language choice experienced by German-speaking scientists. In Nelde, P. H. (ed.) *Language Conflict and Minorities/ Sprachkonflikte und Minderheiten.* Bonn: Dümmler, 33–51.

―――― (1990d) Vorüberlegungen zur Analyse von Sprachverbreitungspolitik (SVP) am Beispiel der Bundesrepublik Deutschland (BRD). In Spillner, B. (ed.) *Sprache und Politik.* Frankfurt a.M.: Lang, 48–51.

―――― (1990e) Deutsch unter Druck der englischen Sprache. *Sprachreport* (2): 6–8.

―――― (1990f) Schwierigkeiten der deutschen Sprachgemeinschaft aufgrund der Dominanz der englischen Sprache. In Spillner, B. (ed.) *Interkulturelle Kommunikation.* Frankfurt a.M.: Lang, 68–70.

―――― (1991a) *Die internationale Stellung der deutschen Sprache.* Berlin/ New York: de Gruyter.

―――― (1991b) *Studienmotive und Deutschenbild australischer Deutschstudenten und -studentinnen.* Wiesbaden/ Stuttgart: Steiner.

―――― (1991c) Die Stellung der deutschen Sprache in Europa und in der Welt im Verhältnis zu ihrer Stellung in den EG-Gremien. *Sociolinguistica* 5: 70–84.

―――― (1991d) On the status and changes in the status of German as a language of diplomacy. In Ammon/ Hellinger, 421–438.

―――― (1991e) The status of German and other languages in the European Community (EC). In Coulmas, 241–254.

―――― (1991f) "Standard linguistic form", "standard variety" and "standard language" on the basis of H. von Wright's norm theory. *Indian Journal of Applied Linguistics* 17 (1): 21–43. Reprinted in S. I. Hasnain (ed.) (1995) *Standardization and Modernization: Dynamics of Language Planning.* New Delhi: Bahri Publications, 21–43.

―――― (1992a) Zur Stellung der deutschen Sprache in Japan. *Muttersprache* 102: 204–217.

―――― (1992b) The Federal Republic of Germany's policy of spreading German. *International Journal of the Sociology of Language* 95: 33–50.

―――― (1993) Über die Geschichte und derzeitige Situation von Deutsch als Fremdsprache in der Welt. *Deutsch als Fremdsprache* 30 (1):10–17.

―――― (1994a) The present dominance of English in Europe. With an outlook on possible solutions to the European language problems. *Sociolinguistica* 8: 1–14.

―――― (1994b) International languages. In Bolinger, D./ Simpson, J. M.Y. (eds.) *Encyclopedia of Language & Linguistics,* Vol. 4. Oxford: Pergamon, 1725–1730.

―――― (1994c) unter Mitwirkung von Naoki Kato. Stellenanzeigen mit gewünschten Deutschkenntnissen – im Verhältnis zu anderen Fremdsprachen. In Ammon 1994d, 103–114.

―――― (ed.) (1994d) *Die deutsche Sprache in Japan: Verwendung und Studium.* München: Iudicium.

―――― (ed.) (1994e) *Language Spread Policy.* Vol. 2: *Languages of Former Colonies and of Former Colonial Powers* (International Journal of the Sociology of Language 107).

―――― (1995a) *Die deutsche Sprache in Deutschland, Österreich und der Schweiz. Das Problem der nationalen Varietäten.* Berlin/ New York: de Gruyter.

―――― (1995b) To what extent is German an international language? In Stevenson, P. (ed.) *The German Language and the Real World.* Oxford: Clarendon, 15–53.

―――― (1996) "Gibt es eine österreichische Sprache?" *Die Unterrichtspraxis/ Teaching German* 29 (2): 131–136.

———— (1998) *Ist Deutsch noch internationale Wissenschaftssprache? Englisch auch für die Lehre an den deutschsprachigen Hochschulen.* Berlin/ New York: de Gruyter.

———— (1999) Deutsch als Wissenschaftssprache: die Entwicklung im 20. Jahrhundert und die Zukunftsperspektive. In Wiegand, 668–685.

———— (2000a) Auf welchen Interessen beruht Sprachförderungspolitik? Ansätze einer erklärenden Theorie. In Ammon 2000c, 135–150.

———— (2000b) Entwicklung der deutschen Wissenschaftssprache im 20. Jahrhundert. In Debus/ Kollmann/ Pörksen, 59–81.

———— (ed.) (2000c) *Sprachförderung. Schlüssel auswärtiger Kulturpolitik.* Frankfurt a.M.: Lang.

———— (2000d) Weltmacht Englisch? *Merkur* 54: 867–877.

———— (2000e) Das Internet und die internationale Stellung der deutschen Sprache. In Hoffmann, 241–260.

———— (ed.) (2001a) *The Dominance of English as a Language of Science. Effects on Other Languages and Language Communities.* Berlin/ New York: Mouton de Gruyter.

———— (2001b) English as a future language of teaching at German universities? A question of difficult consequences, posed by the decline of German as a language of science. In Ammon 2001a, 343–361.

———— (2002) Die Stellung der deutschen Sprache in Europa und Modelle der Mehrsprachigkeit. In Kelz, 19–35.

———— (2003a) The international standing of the German language. In Maurais/ Morris, 231–249.

———— (2003b) Language and identity. With an outlook on scientific communication and on the language situation in the European Union. In Vielberth, J./ Drexel, G. (ed.) *Linguistic Cultural Identity and International Communication. Maintaining Language Diversity in the Face of Globalization.* Saarbrücken: AQ-Verlag, 125–136.

———— (2003c) Global English and the non-native speaker: overcoming disadvantages. In Tonkin, H./ Reagan, T. (eds.) (2003) *Language in the Twenty-First Century.* Amsterdam/ Philadelphia: John Benjamins Publishing Company, 23–34.

———— (2004a) Funktionale Typen und Statustypen von Sprachsystemen. In Ammon/ Mattheier/ Dittmar/ Trudgill, 179–187.

———— (2004b) Standard variety. In Ammon/ Dittmar/ Mattheier/ Trudgill, 273–283.

———— (2004c) Der Status des Deutschen in Remigrationsländern: Weder Nationalsprache noch Lingua Franca. In F. Januschek (ed.) *Multisprech vor den Toren der EU.* Oldenburg: Bibliotheks- und Informationssystem der Carl von Ossietzky Universität, 38–48.

———— (2005a) Some problems of EU language policy and discussion of possible solutions. In Banti, G./ Marra, A./ Vineis, E. (eds.) *Atti del 4° congresso di studi dell' Associazione Italiana di Linguistica Applicata.* Perugia: Guerra, 193–207.

———— (2005b) Standard und variation: norm, autorität, legitimation. In Eichinger, L. M./ Kallmeyer, W. (eds.) *Standardvariation. Wie viel Variation verträgt die deutsche Sprache?* Berlin/ New York: de Gruyter, 28–40.

———— (2005c) Umkämpftes Privileg – Die deutsche Sprache. In Maaß 2005, 85–94.

———— (2005d) Pluricentric and divided languages. In Ammon/ Dittmar/ Mattheier/ Trudgill, 15361542.

———— (2005e) Demokratisches Deutsch im demokratischen Europa. Die deutsche Sprache als Arbeits- und Verkehrssprache. In Kilian, J. (ed.) *Sprache und Politik. Deutsch im demokratischen Staat.* Mannheim: Dudenverlag, 314–328.

———— (2005f) Die Stellung der deutschen Sprache in der Welt von heute. In Leibniz-Institut für Länderkunde (ed.) *Nationalatlas der Bundesrepublik Deutschland,* Vol. 11: *Deutschland in der Welt.* München: Elsevier, 110f.

———— (2006a) Ist die auswärtige Förderung von Sprachen wie Deutsch oder Japanisch heute noch zeitgemäß? *Deutsch als Fremdsprache* 43 (2): 79–87.

———— (2006b) Die deutschsprachigen Länder. In Ammon/ Mattheier/ Dittmar/ Trudgill, 1765–1772.

———— (2006c) Die Stellung der deutschen Sprache im Internet. In Schlobinski, 38–51.

———— (2006d) Language planning for international scientific communication: an overview of questions and political polutions. *Current Issues in Language Planning* 7 (1): 1–30.

———— (2006e) The dominance of languages and language communities in the European Union (EU) and the consequences. In Pütz, Martin et al. (eds.) *"Along the Routes to Power". Explorations of Empowerment through Language.* Berlin/ New York: de Gruyter, 217–241.

———— (2006f) The status and function of English in Germany. *Revista Canaria de Estudios Ingleses* 53: 27–35.

———— (2006g) Language conflicts in the European Union. On finding a politically acceptable and practicable solution for EU institutions that satisfies diverging interests. *International Journal of Applied Linguistics* 16 (39): 319–338.

———— (2007a) Is the promotion of languages such as German and Japanese abroad still appropriate today? In Coulmas, F. (ed.) *Language Regimes in Transformation. Future Prospects for German and Japanese in Science, Economy, and Politics.* Berlin: de Gruyter, 53–70.

———— (2007b) Die Wichtigkeit und Schwierigkeit von Deutsch als Arbeitssprache in den EU Institutionen. *Muttersprache* 117 (2): 98–110.

———— (2007c) Deutschsprachige Minderheiten in Europa im Vergleich zum Elsass. In Darquennes, J. (ed.) *Kontaktlinguistik und Sprachminderheiten.* St. Augustin: Asgard, 103–116.

———— (2007d) Global scientific communication: open questions and policy suggestions. *AILA Review* 20: 123–134.

———— (2009a) Umkämpftes Privileg – Die deutsche Sprache. In Maaß (2009a), 113–126.

———— (2009b) Über die Dilemmata jeglicher EU-Sprachenpolitik. In Stickel (2009a), 19–34.

———— (2009c) Thesen zur Abträglichkeit der EU-Sprachenpolitik für Deutsch als Fremdsprache. *Der Sprachspiegel* 53 (1): 16–19.

———— (2009d) Sprachwahl und Macht. In Enell-Nilsson, M./ Nissilä, N. (eds.) *Käännösteoria, Ammattikielet ja Monikielisyys Vakki-symposiumi XXIX. Vaasa 13. – 14.2.2009* (Publications of the Research Group for the Theory of Translation, LSP and Multilingualism at the University of Vaasa 36). Vaasa: Universität Vaasa, 10–29.

———— (2010a) Western Europe. In Fishman, J./ García, O. (eds.) *Handbook of Language and Ethnic Identity. Disciplinary and Regional Perspectives.* Vol. 1. 2nd edition, Oxford/ New York: Oxford University Press, 207–220.

———— (2010b) The hegemony of English. In International Social Science Council (ed.) *World Social Science Report: Knowledge Divides.* Paris: UNESCO, 154f.

———— (2010c) The concept of "world language": ranks and degrees. In Coupland, 101–122.

———— (2010d) English and other international languages under the impact of globalization. *Neuphilologische Mitteilungen* 61 (1): 9–28.

———— (2010e) Why accepting one common language plus preserving all the other languages as national or minority languages would not solve the European language conflicts. In de Cillia, R. et al. (eds.) *Diskurs – Politik – Identität. Festschrift für Ruth Wodak.* Tübingen: Stauffenburg, 1–6.

———— (2010f) Die Verbreitung des Deutschen in der Welt. In Krumm/ Fandrych/ Hufeisen/ Riemer, Vol. 1, 89–107.

———— (2011a) A checklist of sociolinguistic language maintenance indicators for diaspora minorities (with a focus on German examples). In Moretti/ Pandolfi/ Casoni, 43–63.

———— (2011b) Deutsch als plurizentrische Sprache – mit Hinweisen auf die Nachfolgestaaten des früheren Jugoslawien. In Gavrić, S. (ed.) *Sprach(en)politik in Bosnien und Herzegowina und im deutschsprachigen Raum. Sammelband zur gleichnamigen Konferenz vom 22. März 2011 in Sarajevo.* Sarajevo: Goethe-Institut/ Österreichische Botschaft/ Schweizer Botschaft, 38–46.

———— (2011c) Deutsch im Verhältnis zu anderen internationalen Sprachen – mit Ausblicken auf die Relevanz für die Germanistik in Israel. In Kohlross/ Mittelmann, 247–268.

———— (2011d) Die Politik der deutschsprachigen Länder zur Förderung der deutschen Sprache in Russland. In Ammon/ Kemper, 327–343.

———— (2012a) Die Bedeutung der deutschen Sprache in Namibia für die deutschsprachigen Länder und aus europäischer Sicht. In *Sprachenvielfalt in Namibia*, 62–67.

———— (2012b) Prestige planning. In *The Encyclopedia of Applied Linguistics.* Wiley Online Library. (www.onlinelibrary.wiley.com/doi/10.1002/9781405198431.wbeal0952/full)

———— (2012c) Linguistic inequality and its effects on participation in scientific discourse and on global knowledge accumulation – With a closer look at the problems of the second-rank language communities. *Applied Linguistics Review* 3 (2): 333–355.

———— (2012d) Die Nischenfächer für Deutsch als internationale Wissenschaftssprache und die Zukunftsperspektiven. *Quo Vadis Romania?* 40: 39–61.

———— (2012e) Language policy in the European Union (EU). In Spolsky, B. (ed.) *The Cambridge Handbook of Language Policy.* Cambridge, UK: Cambridge University Press, 570–591.

———— (2013) Wissenschaftssprachen im Wandel der Zeiten. In Neck, R./ Schmidinger, H./ Weigelin-Schwiedrzik (eds.) *Kommunikation – Objekt und Agens von Wissenschaft.* Wien/ Köln/ Weimar: Böhlau, 45–70.

————— (2015) *Die Stellung der deutschen Sprache in der Welt*. Berlin/ München/ Boston: de Gruyter.

————— (2017) On the social forces that determine what is standard in a language – with a look at the norms of non-standard language varieties. In Pandolfi, E. M./ Miecznikowski, J./ Christopher, S./ Kambers, A. (eds.) *Studies on Language Norms in Context*. Frankfurt a. M. etc.: Lang, 17–35.

————— / Bickel, Hans/ Ebner, Jakob et al. (2004) *Variantenwörterbuch des Deutschen. Die Standardsprache in Österreich, der Schweiz und Deutschland sowie in Liechtenstein, Luxemburg, Ostbelgien und Südtirol*. Berlin/ New York: de Gruyter.

—————/ Bickel, Hans/ Lenz, Alexandra N. (2013/16) *Variantenwörterbuch des Deutschen. Die Standardsprache in Österreich, der Schweiz, Deutschland, Liechtenstein, Luxemburg, Ostbelgien und Südtirol sowie Rumänien, Namibia und Mennonitensiedlungen*. 2., completely revised and expanded ed. Berlin/ Boston: de Gruyter.

————— / Chong, Si-Ho (eds.) (2003) *Die Deutsche Sprache in Korea. Geschichte und Gegenwart*. München: Iudicium.

————— / Dittmar, Norbert/ Mattheier, Klaus J. (eds.) (1987/ 88) *Sociolinguistics. An International Handbook of the Science of Language and Society*, 2 vols. Berlin/ New York: de Gruyter.

————— / Dittmar, Norbert/ Mattheier, Klaus J./ Trudgill, Peter (eds.) (2004/ 2005/ 2006) *Sociolinguistics. An International Handbook of the Science of Language and Society*, 3 vols., 2nd completely revised edition, Berlin/ New York: de Gruyter.

————— / Haarmann, Harald (eds.) (1991) *Status und Funktion der Sprachen in den Institutionen der Europäischen Gemeinschaft/ Focus: Status and Function of the Languages in the Political Bodies of the European Community/ Thème principal: Status et fonction des langues dans les organes de la Communauté Europénne* (Sociolinguistica 5).

————— / Haarmann, Harald (eds.) (2008) *Wieser Enzyklopädie Sprachen des europäischen Westens/ Wieser Encyclopaedia Western European Languages*. 2 vols. Klagenfurt: Wieser.

————— / Hellinger, Marlis (eds.) (1991) *Status Change of Languages*. Berlin/ New York: de Gruyter.

————— / Kemper, Dirk (eds.) (2011) *Die deutsche Sprache in Russland. Geschichte, Gegenwart, Zukunftsperspektiven*. München: Iudicium.

————— / Kleineidam, Hartmut (eds.) (1992) *Language Spread Policy*. Vol. I: *Languages of Former Colonial Powers* (International Journal of the Sociology of Language 95).

————— / Kruse, Jan (2013) Does translation support multilingualism in the EU? Promises and reality – the example of German. *International Journal of Applied Linguistics* 23 (1): 15–30.

————— / McConnell, Grant (2002) *English as an Academic Language in Europe. A Survey of its Use in Teaching*. Frankfurt a. M.: Lang.

————— / Michels, Stefan (1994) Die derzeitige Rolle der deutschen Sprache im Verhältnis zu anderen Fremdsprachen in der internationalen Kommunikation japanischer Natur- und Geisteswissenschaften. In Ammon 1994d, 15–33.

————— / Reinbothe, Roswitha/ Zhu, Jianhua (eds.) (2007) *Die deutsche Sprache in China. Geschichte, Gegenwart, Zukunftsperspektiven*. München: Iudicium.

Andersen, H./ Rasmussen, E. (2004) The role of language skills in corporate communication. *Corporate Communications: An International Journal* 9 (3): 231–242.

Andersen, Uwe/ Woyke, Wieland (eds.) (1985) *Handwörterbuch Internationale Organisationen* (UTB 1299). Opladen: Leske und Budrich.

Anderson, Benedict (1983) *Imagined Communities*. London: Verso.

Andmussen, R. L. (1967) Trends in the Ph. D. requirement. *Modern Language Journal* (October): 346–349.

Andrei, Verena (2008) *Die auswärtige Sprachpolitik der Bundesrepublik Deutschland gegenüber den Staaten Mittel- und Südosteuropas und in der Europäischen Union. Eine theoriegeleitete Außenpolitikanalyse*. Diss. Universität Tübingen. (www.tobias-lib.ub.uni-tuebingen.de/volltexte/2008/3275)

————— / Rittberger, Volker (2009) Macht, Interessen und Normen: Auswärtige Kulturpolitik und Außenpolitiktheorien illustriert am Beispiel der deutschen auswärtigen Sprachpolitik. In Maaß 2009a, 33–60.

Andress, Reinhard et al. (2002) Maintaining the momentum from high school to college: report and recommendations. *Die Unterrichtspraxis/ Teaching German* 35: 1–14.

Androutsopoulos, Jannis K. (2006) Multilingualism, diaspora, and the Internet: codes and identities on German-based diaspora websites. *Journal of Sociolinguistics* 10: 520–547.

————— / Ziegler, Evelyn (eds.) (2003) *"Standardfragen". Soziolinguistische Perspektiven auf Sprachgeschichte, Sprachkontakt und Sprachvariation*. Frankfurt a. M.: Lang.

Angelo, Miatello (1988) *United Nations Organization: Multilingual Glossary [English-French German-Italian-Arab]*. Bern: Lang.

Annas, Rolf (2004) Zur Situation des Faches Deutsch an südafrikanischen Universitäten. *Acta Germanica* 30/31: 181–191.

Aoki, Toshio (1989) Wozu lernt man Deutsch? Weder praxisorientiert noch bildungsorientiert. In Bauer 1989b, 68–74.

Archan, Sabine/ Dornmayr, Helmut (2006) *Fremdsprachenbedarf und -kompetenzen. Unternehmensbefragung zu Ausbildungsqualität und Weiterbildungsbedarf.* Wien: Institut für Bildungsforschung der Wirtschaft.

Aref, Anke (1983/ 84) Deutsch als Fremdsprache in Ägypten. *Info DaF* 2: 44–47.

Arnold, Hans (1980) *Auswärtige Kulturpolitik. Ein Überblick aus deutscher Sicht.* München: Hanser.

Arnold, Herbert (1983) Fremdsprache Deutsch und Deutschlandkunde in den USA. *Linguistische Berichte* 84: 73–84.

Arras, Ulrike (2001) Deutschunterricht und Germanistikstudium in Ägypten. In Helbig/ Götze/ Henrici/ Krumm, Vol. 2: 1601–1609.

Arts & Humanities Citation Index (A&HCI) (1975ff.). Institute for Scientific Information/ Thomson Reuters.

Ash, Mitchell G. (1983) Die deutschsprachige Psychologie im Exil: Forschungsansätze und ergebnisse zum Problem des Wissenstransfers. In Lüer, G. (ed.) *Bericht über den 33. Kongreß der Deutschen Gesellschaft für Psychologie in Mainz 1982,* Vol. 1. Göttingen: Hogrefe, 106–113.

Askedal, John Ole (2000) Hochdeutsch und Philosophie auf Norwegisch. In Naumann/ Müller, 183–209.

Assemblée nationale (France) (2003) *Rapport d'information déposé par la délégation de l'Assemblée nationale pour l'union européenne sur la diversité linguistique dans l'Union européenne* (Rapport Herbillon). (www.elections-legislatives.fr/ 12/ europe/ rap-info/ i0902.asp)

Asserate, Asfa-Wossen (2013) *Deutsche Tugenden. Von "Anmut" bis "Weltschmerz".* München: Beck.

Auburger, Leopold/ Kloss, Heinz (eds.) (1977) *Deutsch als Muttersprache in Kanada.* Mannheim: Institut für deutsche Sprache.

———— / Kloss, Heinz (eds.) (1979) *Deutsche Sprachkontakte in Übersee, nebst einem Beitrag zur Theorie der Sprachkontaktforschung.* Tübingen: Narr.

———— / Kloss, Heinz/ Rupp, Heinz (eds.) (1979) *Deutsch als Muttersprache in den Vereinigten Staaten, Teil I: Der Mittelwesten.* Wiesbaden: Steiner.

"Aufruf an die Kulturwelt!" from 4th October 1914. reprinted in Kellermann, Hermann. (1915) (ed.) *Der Krieg der Geister. Eine Auslese deutscher und ausländischer Stimmen zum Weltkriege 1914.* Dresden: Duncker, 64–68.

Augart, Julia (2012) (Süd-)Afrikanische Germanistik. (electronic version) *Deutschunterricht in Südafrika (eDuSa)* 7 (1): 7–22. (www.sagv.org.za/ publ_dusa.htm)

Augustin, Matthias (2003a) Offizielle Sprache und Sprachwahl der in Korea ansässigen Betriebe deutschsprachiger Länder. In Ammon/ Chong, 95–108.

———— (2003b) Stellenangebote mit gewünschten Kenntnissen in Deutsch und anderen Fremdsprachen. In Ammon/ Chong, 141–158.

Australian Bureau of Statistics (2012) *For a brighter future.* Canberra. (www.abs.gov.au/ census)

Auswärtiges Amt (2.7.1973) *Auswärtige Kulturpolitik der Bundesrepublik Deutschland. Gesamtplan 1973–1976.* Bonn.

Auswärtiges Amt (16.03.2006) *Bericht der Bundesregierung zur Auswärtigen Kulturpolitik 2004.* Berlin.

Auswärtiges Amt (2015) *Deutsch als Fremdsprache weltweit. Datenerhebung 2015.* Berlin.

Auswärtiges Amt, Referat für Öffentlichkeitsarbeit (ed.) (1978) *Auswärtige Kulturpolitik im Schulwesen. Rahmenplan für Auslandsschulen, Sprachförderung und internationale Zusammenarbeit* (Bundestagsdrucksache 8/ 2103). Bonn.Baasner, Frank (2007) Mehrsprachigkeit in Europa: Überlegungen unter besonderer Berücksichtigung von Deutsch und Französisch. In Bergsdorf, Wolfgang (ed.) *Erbfreunde.* Erfurt: Universität: 37–52.

Bach, Adolf (1950) *Deutsche Mundartforschung. Ihre Wege, Ergebnisse und Aufgaben.* Heidelberg: Winter.

Backhaus, Peter (2007) *Linguistic Landscape. A Comparative Study of Urban Multilingualism in Tokyo.* Clevedon/ Buffalo/ Toronto: Multilingual Matters.

Baer, Emil (1936) *Alemannisch. Die Rettung der Eidgenössischen Seele.* Zürich/ Leipzig/ Stuttgart: Rascher.

Baethge, Christopher (2008) Die Sprachen der Medizin. *Deutsches Ärzteblatt* 105 (3): 37–40.

———— (2009) Wissenschaftliches Publizieren auf Deutsch ist ein Anachronismus – Kontra. *Psychiatrische Praxis* 36: 157–159.

———— (2011) Die Lage der Wissenschaftssprache Deutsch in der Medizin. In Wieland, E./ Glück, H./ Pretscher, S. (eds.) *Wissen schaffen – Wissen kommunizieren. Wissenschaftssprachen in Geschichte und Gegenwart.* Wiesbaden: Harrasowitz: 109–117.

Baier, Hannelore/ Bottesch, Martin/ Nowak, Dieter/ Wiecken, Alfred/ Ziegler, Winfried (2011) *Geschichte und Traditionen der deutschen Minderheit in Rumänien. Lehrbuch für die 6. und 7. Klasse der Schulen mit deutscher Unterrichtssprache.* 4th edition Mediaş: Central.

Baker, Steven J. (ed.) (2002) *Language Policy: Lessons from Global Models.* Monterey: Monterey Institute of International Studies.

Balay, Robert/ Carrington, Vee F. (Anoc.)/ Martin, Murray S. (Assist.) (1996) *Guide to Reference Books.* 11th ed. Chicago/ London: American Library Association.

Baldauf, Richard, B. (1986) Linguistic constraints on participation in psychology. *American Psychologist* 41: 220–224.

————— / Jernudd, Björn H. (1983) Language use patterns in the fisheries periodical literature. *Scientometrics* 5 (4): 245–255.

Balci, Tahir (1997) Das Germanistik- bzw. DaF-Studium in der Türkei. *Info DaF* 24 (5): 621–624. Ball, Rafael/ Tunger, Dirk (2005) *Bibliometrische Analysen – Daten, Fakten und Methoden. Grundwissen Bibliometrie für Wissenschaftler, Wissenschaftsmanager, Forschungseinrichtungen und Hochschulen.* Jülich: Forschungszentrum Zentralbibliothek.

Bälz, Ottilie (2009) Ein weltweites Bild verändern – die Auswärtige Kulturpolitik der Russischen Föderation. In Maaß 2009a: 411–427.

Banks, Arthur S./ Muller, T. C. (eds.) [1928] (1987) *Political Handbook of the World: 1987. Governmental and Intergovernmental Organizations as of March 15, 1987.* Binghamton, NY: CSA Publications.

————— / ————— / Overstreet, William R. (eds.) [1928] (2007) *Political Handbook of the World: 2007.* Washington, DC: CQ Press.

Bär, Günter (1974) Deutsch als außenpolitischer Faktor. *Sprache im technischen Zeitalter* 50: 113–120, 51: 294–296.

Barbasina, Elvira (1999) Die Assimilation der Deutschen in Sibirien nach 1945. In Barbasira, E./ Brandes, D./ Neutatz, D. (eds.) *Die Russlanddeutschen in Russland und Deutschland. Selbstbilder/ Fremdbilder/ Aspekte der Wirklichkeit.* Essen: Klartext, 155–175.

Barbour, Stephan (2001) Accents, dialects and languages. National differences in the evaluation of language varieties. *Sociolinguistica* 14: 5–10.

————— (2004) National language and official language. In Ammon/ Dittmar/ Mattheier/ Trudgill, 288295. Barcan, Monica/ Millitz, Adalbert (1977) *Die deutsche Nationalität in Rumänien.* Bukarest: Kriterion.

Barinaga, Marcia (1995) Brain Researchers Speak a Common Language. *Science* 270: 1437f. Barker, B. (1966) *Characteristics of the Scientific Literature Cited by Chemists of the Soviet Union.* University of Illinois: PhD in Library Science.

Barkowski, Hans/ Demmig, Silvia/ Funk, Hermann/ Würz, Ulrike (eds.) (2009) *Deutsch bewegt. Entwicklungen in der Auslandsgermanistik und Deutsch als Fremd- und Zweitsprache. Dokumentation der Plenarvorträge der XIV. Internationalen Tagung der Deutschlehrerinnen und Deutschlehrer IDT Jena-Weimar.* Baltmannsweiler: Schneider.

————— / Faistauer, Renate (eds.) (2002) . . . *in Sachen Deutsch als Fremdsprache. Sprachpolitik – Unterricht – Interkulturelle Begegnung. Festschrift für Hans-Jürgen Krumm zum 60. Geburtstag.* Hohengehren: Schneider.

Bärnert-Fürst, Ute (1994) Conservation and Displacement Processes of the German Language Speech Community on Panambi, Rio Grande do Sul, Brazil. In Berend/ Mattheier, 273–287.

Bartsch, Renate (1985) *Sprachnormen: Theorie und Praxis.* Tübingen: Niemeyer.

Bartzsch, Rudolf/ Pogarell, Reiner/ Schröder, Markus [1999] (2003) *Wörterbuch überflüssiger Anglizismen.* 5th Paderborn: IFB Verlag.

Baschera, Marco (2008) Welche Fremdsprachen in den Deutschschweizer Schulen? In Moraldo, 215–224.

Bassola, Péter (1995) *Deutsch in Ungarn – in Geschichte und Gegenwart.* Heidelberg: Julius Groos.

————— / Földes, Csaba/ Hessky, Regina (2004) Ungarn. In Institut für Deutsche Sprache, 87–94.

————— / ————— / ————— / (2008) Ungarn. In Institut für Deutsche Sprache, 63–72.

Bauer, Hans L. (1989a) Eine Marktforschungsstudie zu Deutsch als Fremdsprache in Japan. In Bauer 1989b, 201–219.

————— (ed.) (1989b) *deutsch als zweite fremdsprache in der gegenwärtigen japanischen gesellschaft.* München: Iudicium.

Baumann, Adalbert (1915) *Wede, die Verständigungssprache der Zentralmächte und ihrer Freunde, die neue Welt-Hilfs-Sprache.* Diessen vor München: Huber.

Baur, Arthur (1983) *Was ist eigentlich Schweizerdeutsch?* Winterthur: Gemsberg.

Baur, Rupprecht/ Chlosta, Christoph/ Wenderoff, Claus (2000) Bilingualer Unterricht in Russland – ein konkretes Beispiel zur Förderung des Deutschen. In Ammon 2000c, 83–91.

————— / ————— / Schroeder, Christoph (2004) Was sprecht ihr vornehmlich zu Hause? *Essener Unikate* 24 (1): 96–105. (www.uni-due.de/unikate/ressourcen/grafiken/PDF%27s/EU_24/24_baur.pdf)

————— / Mamporija, Irina/ Schymiczek, Nelly (2011a) Bilinguales Lernen an russischen Schulen. In Ammon/ Kemper, 159–186.

————— / ————— / ————— (2011b) Fachunterricht in deutscher Sprache an russischen Hochschulen. In Ammon/ Kemper, 174–186.

Baur, Siegfried (2009) Ausblicke und neue Aspekte im 21. Jahrhundert. In Baur/ Mezzalira/ Pichler, 389–428.

——— / Mezzalira, Giorgio/ Pichler, Walter (2009) *Die Sprache der Anderen. Aspekte der Sprachen- und Schulpolitik in Südtirol von 1945 bis heute.* Meran: Alpha & Beta Verlag.

Bausch, Karl-Richard (2003) Deutsch *nach* Englisch? Besser: Deutsch *mit* Englisch! – Zu den Spezifika des Lehrens und Lernens von Deutsch als zweiter bzw. weiterer Fremdsprache. In Schneider/ Clalüna, 28–38.

Bausinger, Hermann (ed.) (1990) *Gesprochene Sprache. Festschrift für Arno Ruoff zum 60. Geburtstag.* Tübingen: Ludwig-Uhland-Institut für empirische Kulturwissenschaft.

——— (2000) *Typisch deutsch. Wie deutsch sind die Deutschen?* München: Beck.

Beacco, Jean-Claude/ Byram, Michael (2003) *Guide pour l'élaboration des politiques linguistiques éducatives en Europe. De la diversité linguistique à l'éducation plurilingue.* Straßburg: Conseil de l'Europe (Division des politiques linguistiques).

Bechdolf, Ute/ Johler, Reinhard/ Tonn, Horst (2007) *Amerikanisierung – Globalisierung. Transnationale Prozesse im europäischen Alltag.* Trier: WVT.

Beck, Ulrich (1997) *Was ist Globalisierung?* Frankfurt a.M.: Suhrkamp.

Becker, Joachim H. (1980) Englischsprachige Publikationen deutscher Psychologen. Trends, Inhalte, Herkunft, internationale Aufnahme. *Psychologische Beiträge* 22: 356–371.

——— (1981) Wen interessiert die deutsche Sozialpsychologie? Rezipienten und Rezipiertes der 'Zeitschrift für Sozialpsychologie 3'. *Zeitschrift für Sozialpsychologie* 12: 325–335.

——— (1983) Englischsprachig publizieren – ein Vergleich deutscher Psychologen mit deutschen Forschern aus anderen Disziplinen und eine Analyse von Autoren und Rezipienten der Zeitschrift ‚Psychologische Forschung/ Psychological Research' vor und nach der Titeländerung. In Lüer, 116–119.

——— (1984) German-language psychological journals: an overview. *The German Journal of Psychology* 8: 323–344.

——— (1994a) Produzieren produktive deutsche Psychologen zunehmend in englischer Sprache? *Psychologische Rundschau* 45: 234–238.

——— (1994b) Provinzbühne oder Metropolitan Opera – das Forum entscheidet über das Publikum . . . auch beim Publizieren. In *Tätigkeitsbericht der Zentralstelle für Psychologische Information und Dokumentation.* Trier: Universität, Sonderanhang, 1.12.

Bedi, Lasme E. (2006) *Deutsch in Afrika: Vergangenheit, Gegenwart, Zukunft.* Hamburg: Dr. Kovač.

Beer, Alexander (1998) The concept of corporate language and its impact on business performance. In Rainer, F./ Stegu, M. (eds.) *Wirtschaftssprache. Anglistische, germanistische, romanistischen und slavistische Beiträge. Gewidmet Peter Schifko zum 60. Geburtstag.* Frankfurt a.M.: Lang, 95–107.

Beersmans, Frans (1987) Deutsch als Fremdsprache in den Niederlanden. In Sturm (1987a), 3546.

Behbud, Gholam Dastgir (2006) Deutsch in Afghanistan. *Jahrbuch für Internationale Germanistik* 38 (2): 35–47.

von Behr, Marhild (2001) Internationalisierungsstrategien kleiner und mittlerer Unternehmen. *Dortmund: Arbeitsgruppe des Lehrstuhls Technik und Gesellschaft,* Nr. 9/2001. (www.isf-muenchen.de/pdf/uniDo_AP%209%202001.pdf)

Behrens, Julia/ Fischer, Lars/ Minks, Karl-Heinz/ Rösler, Lena (2010) *Die internationale Positionierung der Geisteswissenschaften in Deutschland. Eine empirische Untersuchung.* Hannover: HIS Hochschulinformationssystem. (www.his.de/publikation/bericht)

Beidelmann, T. O. (1986) On J. Zwernemann's Culture History and African Anthropology. *Anthropos* 81 (4/ 6): 661–671.

Beierwaltes, Andreas (2000) *Demokratie und Medien. Der Begriff der Öffentlichkeit und seine Bedeutung für die Demokratie in Europa.* Baden-Baden: Nomos.

——— (2001) Sprachenvielfalt in der EU – Grenze einer Demokratisierung Europas? Bonn: Zentrum für Europäische Integrationsforschung.

Beilsteins Handbuch der Organischen Chemie [1918ff.] (1919ff.) Published by the Deutsche Chemische Gesellschaft. 4th edition, Berlin: Springer.

Beilstein Handbook of Organic Chemistry (1984) 4th edition, Berlin/ Heidelberg/ New York/ Tokyo: Springer.

Belcher, Diane (2007) Seeking acceptance in an English-only research world. *Journal of Second Language Writing* 16 (1): 1–22.

Belke, Gerlind (2011) *Zweisprachige Erziehung in Schweden.* Universität Duisburg-Essen/ Stiftung Mercator: proDaZ. (www.uni-due.de/imperia/md/content/prodaz/zweisprachige_erziehung_in_schweden.pdf)

Belobratow, Aleksandr (2011) Der Russische Germanistenverband: Gründe, Motivation und Realisationen. In Ammon/ Kemper, 389–393.

Ben-David, Joseph (1977) *Centers of Learning. Britain, France, Germany, United States.* New York: McGraw-Hill.

Beneke, Jürgen (1981) Foreign language on the top floor: European executive managers evaluate their foreign-language needs. In Freudenstein/ Reneke/ Pönisch, 23–41.

—— / Freudenstein, Reinhold (1994) *Die Sprache des Kunden: Fremdsprachenlernen für Wirtschaft und Beruf.* Bonn: Dümmler.

Benfield, John R./ Howard Kathryn M. (2000) The language of science. *European Journal of Cardio-Thoracic Surgery* 18: 642–648.

—— / Feak, Christine B. (2006) How authors can cope with the burden of English as an international language. *Chest* 129: 1728–1730.

Berberis, Paola/ Ekna, Bruno (1987) *Deutsch im Hotel 1,2. Kommunikatives Lehrwerk für Deutschlerner im Fach Hotelgewerbe/ Gastronomie.* Ismaning: Hueber.

Berchem, Theodor (2003) "If only we had the words, we would not need weapons": Deliberation on a European language policy. In Ahrens, 23–33.

Berend, Nina (1994) Sprachinseldialekte in Auflösung. In Berend/ Mattheier, 319–331.

—— (2006) Zur Geschichte und Gegenwart der deutschen Sprachinseln in Russland und der ehemaligen Sowjetunion. In Berend/ Knipf-Komlósi, 77–88.

—— (2011) Die Aufnahme deutscher Siedler und die Bildung von Sprachinseln in Russland seit Katharina II. In Ammon/ Kemper, 60–72.

—— / Knipf-Komlósi, Elisabeth (eds.) (2006) *Sprachinselwelten – The World of Language Islands.* Frankfurt a.M.: Lang.

—— / Mattheier, Klaus J. (eds.) (1994) *Sprachinselforschung. Eine Gedenkschrift für Hugo Jedig.* Frankfurt a. M.: Lang.– / Riehl, Claudia M. (2008) Russland. In Eichinger/ Plewnia/ Riehl, 17–58.

Berg, Guy (1993) *"Mir wëlle bleiwe, wat mir sin". Soziolinguistische und sprachtypologische Betrachtungen zur luxemburgischen Mehrsprachigkeit.* Tübingen: Niemeyer.

Berge, Frank/ Grasse, Alexander (2003) *Zerfall – oder föderales Zukunftsmodell? Der flämischwallonische Konflik und die Deutschsprachige Gemeinschaft.* Opladen: Leske + Budrich.

Bergem, Wolfgang (2000) Culture, identity, and distinction: ethnic minorities between Scylla and Charybdis. In Wolff, 1–12.

Berghorn, Gregor (2011) Der Deutsche Akademische Austauschdienst (DAAD) in Russland. In Ammon/ Kemper, 361–374.

Van Bergijk, D. (1983) The World Transindex, a data base on existing scientific translations: an aid to overcome the language barrier. *Multilingua* 2 (1): 27–31.

Bergmann, Klaus/ Siebel, Wolf (1987) *Sender & Frequenzen 1988.* Meckenheim: Siebel Verlag. *Bericht der Bundesregierung* (1967) *Die Situation der deutschen Sprache in der Welt* (Bundestagsdrucksache V/ 2344). Bonn.

Bericht der Bundesregierung (1985) *Die Stellung der deutschen Sprache in der Welt* (Bundestagsdrucksache 10/ 3784). Bonn.

Bericht der Bundesregierung über Stand und Entwicklung der deutschen Schulen im Ausland (1988) (Bundestagsdrucksache 11/ 1642). Bonn.

Bericht der Bundesregierung über die Integration der Bundesrepublik Deutschland in die Europäische Union (22.03.1994) Reporting period 1st July to 31st December 1993. (Bundesrat Drucksache 245/ 94). Bonn.

Bericht der Bundesregierung zur Auswärtigen Kulturpolitik 2000 (15.08.2001) (Deutscher Bundestag Drucksache 14/ 6825, 14th election period). (dip21.bundestag.de/ dip21/ btd/ 14/ 068/ 1406825.pdf)

Berlin-Brandenburgische Akademie der Wissenschaften (ed.) (2011) *Welche Sprache(n) spricht die Wissenschaft? Streitgespräche in den Wissenschaftlichen Sitzungen der Versammlung der Akademiemitglieder am 2. Juli und am 26. November 2010* (Debatte, Heft 10). Berlin: Berlin-Brandenburgische Akademie der Wissenschaften.

Bernath, Arpad (2004) Gefahren und Chancen für die Behauptung des Deutschen als Fremdsprache im 21. Jahrhundert. In Goltschnigg/ Schwob, 129–133.

—— / Csuri, Karoly (2004) Die deutsche Sprache im ungarischen Hochschulwesen. In Goltschnigg/ Schwob, 137–139.

Bernhard, Gerald (2008) Immigrantensprachen in Italien. In Ammon/ Haarmann, 533–553.

Bernheim, Ernst [1914] (1960) *Lehrbuch der historischen Methode und der Geschichtsphilosophie. Mit Nachweis der wichtigsten Quellen und Hilfsmittel zum Studium der Geschichte.* 5th revised edition, New York: Franklin [reprint of 1914 edition].

Berns, Margie (1992) Bilingualism with English as the other tongue. English in the German legal domain. *World Englishes* 11 (2–3): 155–161.

———— (1995a) English in Europe: Whose language, which culture? *International Journal of Applied Linguistics* 5 (1): 21–32.

———— (1995b) English in the European Union. *English Today* 11 (3): 3–11.

———— / de Bot, Kees/ Hasebrink, Uwe (2007) *In the Presence of English. Media and European Youth*. New York: Springer.

Bertelsmann, Werner (1970) *Die Minderheitenrechte der deutschsprachigen Bevölkerung in Südwestafrika*. Diss. Universität Göttingen.

———— [1978] (1982) *Gutachten über die rechtliche Stellung der deutschen Sprache in Südwestafrika/ Namibia*. Ergänzt durch Auslassungen von D. H. Van Wyk. Windhoek: Interessengemeinschaft deutscher Südwester.

———— (1979) *Die deutsche Sprachgruppe Südwestafrikas in Politik und Recht seit 1915*. Windhoek: Meinert.

———— (1980) *Die deutsche Sprachgruppe Südwestafrikas in Politik und Recht seit 1915*. Stuttgart: Steiner.

Betten, Anne (2011) Sprachheimat vs Familiensprache. Die Transformation der deutschen Sprache von der 1. zur 2. Generation der Jeckes. In Kohlross/ Mittelmann, 205–229.

———— / Dunour, Miryam (eds.) (2000) *Sprachbewahrung nach der Emigration. Das Deutsch der 20er Jahre in Israel*. Tübingen: Niemeyer.

Beyerchen, Alan D. (1982) *Wissenschaftler unter Hitler. Physiker im Dritten Reich*. Frankfurt a. M./ Berlin/ Wien: Ullstein.

Beyermann, Klaus (1985) Bedeutung und Organisation des Ausländerstudiums in der Bundesrepublik Deutschland und Berlin (West). *Info DaF* 12 (4): 380–384.

Bhatti, Anil (2001) Nationales und Internationales. Eine literaturwissenschaftliche Anmerkung aus Indien. In Deutscher Akademischer Austauschdienst (ed.) *Jacob- und Wilhelm-Grimm Preis des Deutschen Akademischen Austauschdienstes*. Bonn: DAAD, 13–29.

———— (2007) Germanistik in Indien. Eine Miszelle vom Umgang mit dem Sprachrepertoire. In Bode/ Jecht, 236–242.

Bianco, Joseph L. (1987) *National Policy on Languages*. Canberra: Australian Government Publishing Service.

Biehl, Jürgen (2008) Jiddisch (Yiddish). In Ammon/ Haarmann, Vol. 2, 7–20.

Biere, Bernd U./ Liebert, Wolf-Adreas (eds.) (1997) *Metaphern, Medien, Wissenschaft: Zur Vermittlung der AIDS-Forschung in Presse und Rundfunk*. Opladen: Westdeutscher Verlag. *Biological Abstracts* (1927ff.). Philadelphia: BIOSIS.

Bister-Broosen, Helga (1998) *Sprachkontakte und Sprachattitüden Jugendlicher im Elsass und in Baden. Vergleichende soziolinguistische Untersuchungen in Colmar (Frankreich) und in Freiburg und Müllheim (Deutschland)*. Frankfurt a.M.: Lang.

———— / Good, Kathryn (1997) Fremdsprachenwahl an amerikanischen Universitäten: Eine Umfrage in North Carolina. In Moelleken, W. W./ Weber, P. J. (eds.) *Neue Forschungsarbeiten zur Kontaktlinguistik*. Bonn: Dümmler, 52–58.

Blanke, Detlev/ Scharnhorst, Jürgen (eds.) (2007) *Sprachenpolitik und Sprachkultur*. Frankfurt a.M.: Lang.

Blankenhorn, Renate (2008) Die russlanddeutsche Minderheit in Sibirien. In Eichinger/ Plewnia/ Riehl, 59–70.

Bleich, Carola (2005) Eine Umfrage zum Stellenwert der deutschen Sprache im schwedischdeutschen Wirtschaftsleben. In Van Leewen, 275–287.

Blick auf den Bundesstaat Belgien. Ich informiere mich über die Reform (1989) Brüssel: Belgisches Institut für Information und Dokumentation.

Bliesener, Ulrich (2003) European language policy – frustration and hope. In Ahrenz, 75–98.

———— (2005) Sprachen in Europa – einige Beobachtungen und Anmerkungen. In Van Leewen, 203–217.

Blommaert, Jan (2010) *The Sociolinguistics of Globalization*. Cambridge, UK: Cambridge University Press.

———— (2013) *Ethnography, Superdiversity and Linguistic Landscapes: Chronicles of Complexity*. Bristol: Multilingual Matters.

Blumenwitz, Dieter/ Gornig, Gilbert H./ Murswiek, Dietrich (eds.) (1999) Fortschritte im Beitrittsprozess der Staaten Ostmittel-, Ost- und Südeuropas zur Europäischen Union. Regelungen und Konsequenzen für die deutschen Volksgruppen und Minderheiten. Köln: Verlag Wissenschaft und Politik.

Blumer, Arnold (1987) Wider die ‚Kofferträger‘ oder Bemerkungen zu Entwicklungsbedingungen einer südafrikanischen Germanistik. *Jahrbuch Deutsch als Fremdsprache* 13: 312–321.

Blümle, A./ Antes, G. (2006) Handsuche nach randomisierten kontrollierten Studien in deutschen medizinischen Zeitschriften. *Deutsche Medizinische Wochenschrift* 133: 230–234.

Böckenförde, Ernst-Wolfgang (1999) Die Schweiz – Vorbild für Europa? In ders. *Staat, Nation, Europa: Studien zur Staatslehre, Verfassungstheorie und Rechtsphilosophie*. Frankfurt a.M.: Suhrkamp.

Bode, Christian/ Jecht, Dorothea (eds.) (2007) *20 Jahre "Wandel durch Austausch". Festschrift für Prof. Dr. Dr. h.c. mult. Theodor Berchem.* Bonn: Deutscher Akademischer Austauschdienst.

Bodenstein, Eckhard W. (1995) Die Rolle der deutschen Sprache in Südafrika. *Deutschunterricht im Südlichen Afrika (DUSA)* 26: 34–53.

Boeckmann, Klaus-Börge (2010) Entwicklungen von Deutsch als Fremd- und Zweitsprache in Österreich. In Krumm/ Fandrych/ Hufeisen/ Riemer, Vol. 1, 72–80.

Boehnke, Klaus/ Boehnke, Mandy (2007) Die Jacobs University Bremen als Fallbeispiel für Sprachpolitik im tertiären Bildungssektor. *Fremdsprachen Lehren und Lernen* 36: 171–184.

Boemeke, Manfred F./ Feldman, Gerald D./ Glaser, Elisabeth (eds.) (1998) *The Treaty of Versailles. A Reassessment After 75 Years.* Cambridge: Cambridge University Press.

Bogen, James/ Woodward, James (1988) Saving the phenomena. *The Philosophical Review* 57 (3): 303–352.

Böhm, Michael A. (2003) *Deutsch in Afrika. Die Stellung der deutschen Sprache in Afrika vor dem Hintergrund der bildung- und sprachpolitischen Gegebenheiten sowie der deutschen Auswärtigen Kulturpolitik.* Frankfurt a.M.: Lang.

Böhmer, Maria/ Zoepffel-Tassenari [1984] (1997) *Il tedesco scientifico: Wissenschaftsdeutsch*, 2nd revised edition. Rome: Bulzoni.

Bohrer, Kurt-Friedrich (1988) Auswärtige Kulturpolitik der Bundesrepublik Deutschland 1976–1986. *Jahrbuch Deutsch als Fremdsprache 1987* 13: 362–401.

Boia, Lucian et al. (eds.) (1991) *Great Historians of the Modern Age. An International Dictionary.* New York/ Westport, Conn./ London: Greenwood. Bormann, Werner (1973) Die Position der deutschen Sprache. *La mondo linguo problemo* 5 (13): 18–34.

Born, Joachim (1995) Minderheiten, Sprachkontakt und Spracherhalt in Brasilien. In Kattenbusch, D. (ed.) *Minderheiten in der Romania.* Wilhelmsfeld: gottfried egert verlag, 129158.

——— (2003) Regression, convergence, internal development. The loss of the dative case in German-American dialects. In Keel/ Mattheier, 151–164.

——— / Dickgiesser, Sylvia (1989) *Deutschsprachige Minderheiten. Ein Überblick über den Stand der Forschung für 27 Länder.* Mannheim: Institut für deutsche Sprache.

——— / Jakob, Gerhard (1990) *Deutschsprachige Gruppen am Rande und außerhalb des geschlossenen deutschen Sprachgebiets. Eine bibliographische Dokumentation von Literatur zum Thema "Sprache" aus der Zeit nach 1945.* 2nd edition, Mannheim: Institut für deutsche Sprache.

——— / Stickel, Gerhard (eds.) (1993) *Deutsch als Verkehrssprache in Europa.* Berlin: de Gruyter.

Börsenverein des deutschen Buchhandels (ed.) (1985/ 2013) *Buch und Buchhandel in Zahlen/ 2013.* Frankfurt: Marketing und Verlagsservice des Buchhandels.

Bosch, Gloria/ Schlak, Torsten (2013) Konzepte und Methoden bedarfsanalytischer Untersuchungen am Beispiel von Deutsch als Fremdsprache im Tourismus (DaFT) auf Mallorca. In G. Bosch/ T. Schlak (eds.) *Foreign Languages for Tourism. Research and Practice.* Bern: Lang, 165–184.

de Bot, Kees (1996) Language loss. In Goebl/ Nelde/ Zdeněk/ Wölck, 579–585.

——— et al. (2001) Institutional status and use of national languages in Europe. Contributions to the development of a European languague policy. In de Bot et al. (eds.) *Institutional Status and Use of National Languages in Europe.* St. Augustin: Asgard, 3–17.

Botanisches Zentralblatt. Referierendes Zentralblatt für das Gesamtgebiet der Botanik (18801945). Jena: Fischer.

Bothorel-Witz, Arlette (2001) L'allemand en Alsace: mythes et réalités. I. – Les aspects contradictoires de la place de l'allemand dans l'imaginaire de locuteurs et dans leurs productions dialectales. In Hartweg, F./ Staiber, M. (eds.) *Mémoire et frontieres. Hommage à Adrien Finck.* Strassbourg: Presses universitaires, 117–140.

——— / Choremi, Thiresia (2009) Le plurilinguisme dans les entreprises à vocation internationale. Comment saisir ce phénomène pluridimensionnel à travers le discours des acteurs? *Sociolinguistica* 23: 104–130.

Bottesch, Johanna (2008) Rumänien. In Eichinger/ Plewnia/ Riehl, 329–392.

Bottesch, Martin (1997) *Deutsch sprechen in siebenbürgischen Schulen.* Sibiu/ Hermannstadt: Honterus.

——— / Grieshofer, Franz/ Schabus, Wilfried (2002) *Die Siebenbürgischen Landler. Eine Spurensicherung.* 2 Bände. Wien: Böhlau.

Böttger, Claudia (2007) *Lost in Translation? An Analysis of the Role of English as the Lingua Franca of Multilingual Business Communication.* Hamburg: Dr. Kovač.

Bourdieu, Pierre (1980) *La distinction.* Paris: Éditions de Minuit.

——— (1982) *Ce que parler veut dire: L'économie des échanges linguistiques.* Paris: Éditions Fayard.

—— / de Swaan, Abram/ Hagège, Claude/ Fumaroli, Marc/ Wallerstein, Immanuel (2001) Quelles langues pour une Europe démocratique? *Raisons politiques* 2: 41–64.

Bourhis, R[ichard] Y. (2001) Reversing language shift in Quebec. In Fishman 2001a, 101–141.

—— / Giles, Howard/ Rosenthal, Doreen (1981) Notes on the construction of a ‚subjective vitality questionnaire' for ethnolinguistic groups. *Journal of Multilingual and Multicultural Development* 2 (2). 145–155.

—— / Lepicq, Dominique (2004) *La vitalité de communautés francophones et anglophones du Quebéc: bilan et perspectives depuis la lois 101.* (Concordia-UQUAM Chair in Ethnic Studies Research Paper 11). Montréal: Concordia-UQUAM.

—— / Maass, Anne (2005) Linguistic prejudice and stereotypes. In Ammon, 1587–1601.

Bouthier, Rita (2005) Deutschlernen in Albanien. *Jahrbuch für Internationale Germanistik* 37 (1): 87–97.

Bowen, David (1980) Death of a monoglot salesman. *Marketing* July 16: 28f.

Bradean-Ebinger, Nelu (1999) Kann eine Volksgruppe ohne Muttersprache bestehen? *Suevia Pannonica. Archiv der Deutschen aus Ungarn* 17 (27): 23–36.

Braga, Giorgio (1979) International languages: concept and problems. *International Journal of the Sociology of Language* 22: 27–49.

Brandt, Carsten (1992) *Sprache und Sprachgebrauch der Mennoniten in Mexiko.* Marburg: Elwert.

Braselmann, Petra (1999) *Sprachpolitik und Sprachbewusstsein in Frankreich heute.* Tübingen: Niemeyer.

—— / Ohnheiser, Ingeborg (eds.) *Frankreich als Vorbild? Sprachpolitik und Sprachgesetzgebung in europäischen Ländern.* Innsbruck: innsburg university press.

Bratt Paulston, Christina (1993) *Language Maintenance and Language Shift.* Amsterdam: Benjamins.

—— / Peckham, Donald (eds.) (1998) *Linguistic Minorities in Central and Eastern Europe.* Clevedon, UK: Multilingual Matters.

Braun, Frank X. (1954) German for Research. *German Quarterly* 27: 116–121.

Braun, Michael (1984) Nochmals: Germanistik und Deutschunterricht in Südafrika. *Deutschunterricht in Südafrika* 15 (1): 23–28.

Braun, Peter (1986) Die deutsche Sprache im europäischen Vergleich. *Muttersprache* 96: 330344.

—— / Schaeder, Burkhard/ Volmert, Johannes (eds.) (1990) *Internationalismen. Studien zur interlingualen Lexikologie und Lexikographie.* Tübingen: Niemeyer.

Braun, Sabine/ Kohn, Kurt (eds.) (2005) Sprache[n] in der Wissensgesellschaft. Proceedings der 34. Jahrestagung der Gesellschaft für Angewandte Linguistik. Frankfurt a.M.: Lang.

Braun, T./ Glänzel, W./ Schubert, A. (1987) One more version of the facts and figures on publication output and relative citation impact in the life sciences and chemistry. *Scientometrics* 11 (3/4): 127–140.

Braun, T. et al. (1994) World science in the eighties. National performance in publication output and citation impact, 1985–1989 versus 1980–1984. Part I: all science fields combined, physics and chemistry; Part II: lfe science, engineering, and mathematics. *Scientometrics* 29 (3): 299–334; 31 (1): 3–30.

Bräuninger, Michael/ Haucap, Justus/ Muck, Johannes (2011) Was lesen und schätzen Ökonomen im Jahr 2011? *DICE Ordnungspolitische Perspektiven* 18. Heinrich-Heine-Universität Düsseldorf, Wirtschaftswissenschaftliche Fakultät, Düsseldorf Institute for Competition Economics (DICE). (www.d-nb. info/1014893607/34)

Brednich, Rolf W. (1998) *Die Hutterer. Eine alternative Kultur in der modernen Welt.* Freiburg i. Br./ Basel/ Wien: Herder.

Brenn, Wolfgang (1989) Deutschspracherwerb außerhalb der Universität. In Brenn/ Dillmann, 187–210.

—— / Dillmann, Gerhard (eds.) (1989) *Deutsch als Fremdsprache und Germanistik in Japan.* Bonn: Deutscher Akademischer Austauschdienst.

Brenzinger, Matthias (1992) *Language Death. Factual and Theoretical Explorations with Special Reference to East Africa.* Berlin/ New York: Mouton de Gruyter.

Bretzler, Gerrit (1976) Die deutsche Sprache als Bestandteil der auswärtigen Kulturpolitik in Entwicklungsländern. *Zeitschrift für Kulturaustausch* 26: 52–62.

Breuker, Pieter (2001) The development of Standard West Friesian. In Munske, 711–721.

Bright, William (ed.) (1966) *Sociolinguistics. Proceedings of the UCLA Sociolinguistics Conference, 1964.* The Hague/ Paris: Mouton & Co.

Brizic, Katharina (2009) Familiensprache als Kapital. In *Puhalo, N./ Kerschhofer-Puhalo, N./ Plutzar, V.* (eds.) Nachhaltige Sprachförderung. Innsbruck/ Wien: StudienVerlag, 136–151.

Broadbridge, Judith (2000) The ethnolinguistic vitality of Alsatian-speakers in Southern Alsace. In Wolff, 47–62.

vom Brocke, Bernhard (ed.) (1985) Wissenschaft und Militarismus'. Der Aufruf der 93 'An die Kulturwelt!' und der Zusammenbruch der internationalen Gelehrtenrepublik im Ersten Weltkrieg. In Calder, W.

M./ Flashar, H./ Lindken, T. (eds.) *Wilamowitz nach 50 Jahren.* Darmstadt: Wissenschaftliche Buchgesellschaft, 649–719.

———— (1990) Die Kaiser-Wilhelm-Gesellschaft in der Weimarer Republik. Ausbau zu einer gesamtdeutschen Forschungsorganisation (1918–1933). In Vierhaus/ vom Brocke, 197–355.

———— (1996) Die Kaiser-Wilhelm-/ Max-Planck-Gesellschaft und ihre Institute zwischen Universität und Akademie. Strukturprobleme und Historiographie. In vom Brocke/ Laitko, 1–32.

———— (2005) Universitäts- und Wissenschaftsfinanzierung im 19./20. Jahrhundert. Zugleich ein Kommentar zu Teil II. In Schwinges, R. Ch. (ed.) *Finanzierung von Universität und Wissenschaft in Vergangenheit und Gegenwart.* Basel: Schwabe, 343–462.

———— / Laitko, Hubert (eds.) (1996) *Die Kaiser-Wilhelm-/ Max-Planck-Gesellschaft und ihre Institute. Studien zu ihrer Geschichte: Das Harnack-Prinzip.* Berlin/ New York: de Gruyter.

Brod, Richard J. (1987) *Foreign Language Enrollments in US Institutions of Higher Education – Fall 1986.* [New York, NY]: Modern Language Association.

———— (2001) A forecast for tertiary foreign-language education in the United States. *Forum for Modern Language Studies* 37 (4): 368–381.

———— / Huber, Bettina J. (1996) The MLA-Survey of foreign language entrance and degree requirements, 1994–1995. *ADFL Bulletin* 28 (1, Fall): 35–43.

Brown, Eric et al. (eds.) (1986) *German in the United Kingdom. Issues and Opportunities.* London: Centre for Information on Language Teaching and Research.

Brown, Penelope (2005) Linguistic politeness. In Ammon/ Dittmar/ Mattheir/ Trudgill, 14101415.

———— / Levinson, Stephen C. [1978] (1987) *Politeness. Some Universals in Language Use.* Cambridge, UK: Cambridge University Press.

Brown, Roger/ Gilman, Albert (1960) The pronouns of power and solidarity. In Sebeok, T. A. (ed.) *Style in Language.* New York: MIT Press, 253–276.

Bruha, Thomas/ Seeler, Hans-Joachim (eds.) (1998) *Die Europäische Union und ihre Sprachen. Interdisziplinäres Symposium zur Vielsprachigkeit als Herausforderung und Problematik des europäischen Einigungsprozesses. Gespräch zwischen Wissenschaft und Praxis.* Baden-Baden: Nomos.

Bruhl, Viktor (2003) *Die Deutschen in Sibirien. Eine hundertjährige Geschichte von der Ansiedlung bis zur Auswanderung.* 2 Vols. Nürnberg: Historischer Forschungsverein der Deutschen aus Russland.

Brüll, Christoph (2005) Un passé mouvementé: l'histoire de la Communauté germanophone de Belgique. In Stangherlin, 17–48.

Brumback, Roger A. (2008) Worshiping false idols: the impact factor dilemma. *Journal of Child Neurology* 23 (4): 365–367.

Brunotte, Thomas (2012) Deutsch als Wissenschaftssprache fördern – was Stiftungen tun können. In Oberreuter/ Krull/ Meyer/ Ehlich, 251–262.

Brutt-Griffler, Janina (2002) *World English: A Study of Its Development.* Clevedon: Multilingual Matters.

———— (2008) Intellectual culture and cultural imperialism: implications of the growing dominance of English in academia. In Gnutzmann (2008a), 59–72.

Bühler, Karl [1934] (1965) *Sprachtheorie. Die Darstellungsfunktion von Sprache.* 2nd unamended edition Stuttgart: Gustav Fischer.

Bullivant, Keith (1985) Kontroversen, alte und neue. VII. Weltkongreß der Germanisten in Göttingen. *Kulturchronik* 3 (6): 44–46.

Bundesamt für Migration und Flüchtlinge (ed.) (2010) *Bundesweites Integrationsprogramm. Angebote der Integrationsförderung in Deutschland – Empfehlungen zu ihrer Weiterentwicklung.* Nürnberg. (www.bmi.bund.de/ SharedDocs/Downloads/DE/Broschueren/2010/integrationsprogram m.pdf?__blob=publicationFile)

Bundesrat (2002) *Entschließung des Bundesrates zur Gleichberechtigung der deutschen Sprache auf europäischer Ebene.* Drucksache 175/04 (Beschluss) 12.03.2004.

Bundesregierung [Deutschland] (12.02.2014) *17. Bericht der Bundesregierung Auswärtige Kultur- und Bildungspolitik.* (www.auswaertigesamt.de/cae/servlet/contentblob/670488/publicationFile/189745/AKBP-Bericht_20122013.pdf)

Bundesverwaltungsamt – Zentralstelle für das Auslandsschulwesen (ed.) (2013a) *Deutsches Sprachdiplom der Kultusministerkonferenz. 40 Jahre DSD.* Paderborn: Bonifatius-Verlag. (2013b – Stand 3/ 2013) *Auslandsschulverzeichnis.* (www.auslandsschulwesen.de/nn_2167846/Auslandsschulwesen/Auslandsschulverzeic hnis/Schulverzeichnis/schulverzeichnis-inhalt.html)

———— (2014) *ABC des Auslandsschulwesens.* (www.bva.bund.de/DE/Organisation/Abteilungen/ Abteilung_ZfA/DieZfA/ABC/ABC.pdf?__blob=publicationFile&v=2)

Bungarten, Theo (1996) Mehrsprachigkeit in der Wirtschaft. In Goebl/ Nelde/ Starý/ Wölck, Vol. 1, 414–421.

———— (ed.) (1999a) *Wirtschaftshandeln. Kommunikation in Management, Marketing und Ausbildung.* Tostedt: Attikon.

———— (ed.) (1999b) *Sprache und Kultur in der interkulturellen Marketing-Kommunikation. Mit 1000 aktuellen Literaturhinweisen zur Theorie und Praxis der Marketingkommunikation.* 2nd revised and expanded edition, Tostedt: Attikon.

———— (1999c) Fremdsprachen und Mehrsprachigkeit in der Wirtschaft. In Bungarten (1999a), 113122.

———— (1999d) Fremdsprachenbedarf, Fremdsprachengebrauch, Fremdsprachenausbildung und Mehrsprachigkeit in der Wirtschaft. Eine Auswahl aktueller Literatur. In Bungarten (1999a), 269–329.

———— (2001) Motive der Sprachenwahl und des Sprachgebrauchs in der europäischen Wirtschaft. In de Bot, C./ Kroon, S./ Nelde, P. H./ Van de Velde, H. (eds.) *Institutional status and use of national languages in Europe.* Sankt Augustin: Dümmler, 19–40.

Burgess, Sally/ Fumero Pérez, Maria del Carmen/ Díaz Galán, Ana (2006) Mismatches and missed opportunities? A case study of a Non-English-speaking background research writer. In Carretero, M. et al. (eds.) *Volumen homenaje a Angela Downing.* Madrid: Editorial Complutense, 68–74.

Burgoon, J./ Stern, L./ Dillman, L. (1995) *Interpersonal Adaption: Dyadic Interaction Patterns.* New York: Cambridge University Press.

Burney, Pierre (1966) Les *langues internationales.* 2nd edition, Paris: Presses Universitaires de France.

Burrough-Boenisch, Joy (2006) Negotiable acceptability: reflections on the interactions between language professionals in Europe and NNS scientists wishing to publish in English. *Current Issues in Language Planning* 7 (1): 31–43.

Bußmann, Hadumod (1983) (1990) *Lexikon der Sprachwissenschaft.* 2nd completely revised edition, Stuttgart: Kröner.

Byram, Michael (1986) *Minority Education and Ethnic Survival. Case Study of a German School in Denmark.* Clevedon: Multilingual Matters.

———— (1988) Bilingualism and education in two German minorities. *Journal of Multilingual and Multicultural Development* 9: 387–397.

Byrnes, Heidi (1996) The future of German in American education: a summary report. *Die Unterrichtspraxis/ Teaching German* 29: 253–261.

Cadiot, Pierre (1980) Situation linguistique de la Moselle germanophone: un triangle glossique. In Nelde, P. (ed.) *Sprachkontakt und Sprachkonflikt.* Wiesbaden: Steiner, 325–334.

———— / Lepicq, Dominique (1987) Roofless dialects (roofless speech). In Ammon/ Mattheier/ Dittmar, 755–767.

Calvet, Louis-Jean (1999) *Pour une écologie des langues du monde.* [Paris]: Plon.

———— (2002) *Le marché aux langues. Les effets linguistiques de la mondialisation.* Paris: Plon.

Campbell, George L. (1991) *Compendium of the World's Languages.* London: Routledge.

———— (1995) *Concise Compendium of the World's Languages.* London: Routledge.

Canagarajah, A. Suresh (1999) *Resisting Linguistic Imperialism in English Teaching.* Oxford: Oxford University Press.

———— (2002) *A Geopolitics of Academic Writing.* Pittsburgh: University of Pittsburgh Press.

Cannon, John et al. (eds.) (1988) *The Blackwell Dictionary of Historians.* Oxford: Blackwell.

Capella, J. (1997) The development of theory about automated patterns of face-to-face human interaction. In Philipsen, G./ Albrecht, T. (eds.) *Developing Commuication Theories.* Albany: SUNY Press, 57–83.

Carl, Jenny/ Stevenson, Patrick (2009) *Language, Discourse and Identity in Central Europe: The German Language in a Multilingual Space.* Basingstoke: Palgrave Macmillan.

Carli, Augusto (2009) Le concept de 'vitalité linguistique' à l'exemple des 'langues minoritaires', des 'langues moins utilisées' es des 'langues majoritaires'. In Stickel (2009a), 103–113.

———— / Ammon, Ulrich (eds.) (2007) *Linguistic Inequality in Scientific Communication Today.* Amsterdam/ Philadelphia: John Benjamins (AILA Review 20).

———— / Calaresu, Emilia (2003) Le lingue della comunicazione scientifica. La produzione e la diffusione del sapere specialistico in Italia. In Valentini, A./ Molinelli, P./ Cuzzolin, P./ Bernini, G. (eds.) *Ecologia linguistica.* Roma: Bulzoni, 27–74. Carmel, Alex (1973) *Die Siedlungen der Württembergischen Templer in Palästina 1868–1918.* Stuttgart: W. Kohlhammer.

Carton Fernand/ Delefosse, J. M. Odéric (eds.) (1994) *Les langues dans l'Europe de demain.* Paris: Presses de la Sorbonne Nouvelle.

CAS Statistical Summary 1907–1996 (1997) Columbus, OH: Chemical Abstracts; A Division of the American Chemical Society.

Casad, Eugene (2005) Analyses of intelligibility. In Ammon/ Dittmar/ Mattheier/ Trudgill, 12611272.

Castles, S. (1999) Globalization, multicultural citizenship and transnational democracy. In Hage, G./ Couch, R. (eds.) *The Future of Multiculturalism*. Sydney: Sydney Research Institute for the Humanities and the Social Science.

Castonguay, Charles (2005) *Les indicateurs généraux de vitalité de langues au Québec: comparabilité et tendances 1971–2001.* Gouvernement du Québec: Bibliothèque nationale du Québec.

Centre d'Information et de Recherche pour l'Enseignement et l'Emploi des Langues (ed.) (1979) *L'Enseignement de l'Allemand en France*, 2 vols. Paris.

Cerquiglini, Bernard (2004) La place du français dans la vie économique. *Le Français dans le monde* (janvier): 40–44.

Chamber of Commerce Hamburg (1989/ 2005) (see: https://en.wikipedia.org/wiki/Hamburg_Chamber_of_Commerce).

Chambers, J. K./ Trudgill, Peter (1980) *Dialectology.* Cambridge: Cambridge University Press.

de Chambrun, N./ Reinhardt, A. M. (1981) Publish (in English) or perish. In de Chambrun, *Le français chassé des sciences*. Paris: CIREEL, 15–20.

Chartier, Roger/ Corsi, Pietro (eds.) (1996) *Sciences et langues en Europe*. [Paris:] École des Hautes Études en Sciences Sociales.

Chaudenson, Robert (ed.) (2001) *L'Europe parlera-t-elle anglais demain?* [Paris:] Institut de la Francophonie/ L'Harmattan.

——— (2003) Geolinguistics, geopolitics, geostrategy: the case of French. In Maurais/ Morris, 291297.

Chemical Abstracts (1907ff.) Columbus, OH: Chemical Abstracts; A Division of the American Chemical.

Chemisches Zentralblatt (1830–1969). Berlin: Deutsche Akadamie der Wissenschaften [1830–1848 *Pharmaceutisches Centralblatt*; 1849–1855 *Chemisch-Pharmaceutisches Centralblatt*; 1856–1896 *Chemisches Centralblatt*; 1897–1969 *Chemisches Zentralblatt*].

Chen, Yu (2012) *Verbessern chinesische Studierende ihre Sprechfähigkeit im Deutschen während des Fachstudiums in Deutschland? Eine empirische Untersuchung unter Berücksichtigung sozialer Aspekte.* Frankfurt a. M.: Lang.

Cho, Chang-Sub/ Cheon, Mi-Ae (2003) Die Anfänge der Germanistik in Korea. In Ammon/ Chong, 203–212.

Chong, Si Ho (2001) *Offener Brief an die Bundesregierung in Berlin und Wien . . . Pressemitteilung des Vereins Deutsche Sprache 16.5.2001.* (www.vds-ev.de/ presse/ pressemitteilungen/ archiv/ 2001_16_05.php)

——— (2002) Zum Rückgang des Deutschen und zum Umbruch der Germanistik in Korea. *Jahrbuch für Internationale Germanistik* 34 (1): 43–47.

——— (2003a) Zum Übergang von Deutsch auf Englisch in der medizinischen Ausbildung in Korea. In Ammon/ Chong, 27–42.

——— (2003b) Die Hintergründe der Zurückdrängung von Deutsch an den koreanischen Schulen und Hochschulen nach 1945. Ammon/ Chong, 229–244.

——— (2003c) Gründe für die größere Attraktivität von Englisch, Japanisch und Chinesisch als Deutsch in Korea. In Ammon/ Chong, 297–316.

——— (2006) Dolchstoß aus Deutschland. *Sprachnachrichten* 01/ 2006: 29.

Christ, Herbert (1980) *Fremdsprachenunterricht und Sprachenkonflikt.* Stuttgart: Klett.

——— (1987) Deutsch als Fremdsprache: Bedarf und Nachfrage in sprachenpolitischer Betrachtungsweise. In Sturm (1987a), 207–215.

——— (2000) Zur französischen Sprachpolitik. Der Blick nach innen und außen. In Ammon 2000c, 103–119.

——— / Schwarze, Angela (eds.) (1985) *Fremdsprachenunterricht in der Wirtschaft. Bestandsaufnahmen und Perspektiven.* Tübingen: Narr.

——— et al. (eds.) (1980) *Fremdsprachenpolitik in Europa. Homburger Empfehlungen für eine sprachenteilige Gesellschaft.* Augsburg: Universität Augsburg. Christen, Bernd (2005) La traduction en langue allemande des textes normatifs. In Stangherlin, 93–116.

Christiansen, Pia Vanting (2006) Language policy in the European Union. European/ English/ Elite/ Equal/ Esperanto Union? *Language Problems & Language Planning* 30 (1): 2144 (24).

Chung, Wan-Shik (2003) Lehnwörter aus dem Deutschen im Koreanischen. In Ammon/ Chong, 187–200.

Church, Jeffrey/ King, Ian (2003) Bilingualism and network externalities. *Canadian Journal of Economics/ Revue canadienne d'économique* 26: 337–345.

de Cillia, Rudolf (1997) "Alles bleibt, wie es ißt". Österreichs EU-Beitritt und die Frage des österreichischen Deutsch. *Jahrbuch Deutsch als Fremdsprache* 23: 239–258.

—— (1998) *"Burenwurscht bleibt Burenwurscht"*. *Sprachenpolitik und gesellschaftliche Mehrsprachigkeit in Österreich.* Klagenfurt/ Celovec: Drava.

—— (2012a) Zur sprachlichen und sprachenrechtlichen Situation in Österreich. In Grucza, F. (ed.) *Vielheit und Einheit der Germanistik weltweit.*Vol. 2 *Eröffnungsvorträge – Diskussionsforen.* Frankfurt a.M.: Lang, 241–245.

—— (2012b) Migration und Sprache/n. In Fassmann, H./ Dahlvik, J. (eds.) *Migrations- und Integrationsforschung – multidisziplinäre Perspektiven. Ein Reader.* 2nd revised edition Göttingen: V & R Unipress, 185–212.

—— / Krumm, Hans-Jürgen (2010) Fremdsprachenunterricht in Österreich. *Sociolinguistica* 24: 153–169.

—— / Schweiger, Teresa (2001) English as a language of instruction at Austrian universities. In Ammon, 363–387.

—— / Wodak, Ruth (2006) *Ist Österreich ein "deutsches" Land? Sprachenpolitik und Identität in der Zweiten Republik.* Innsbruck et al.: StudienVerlag.Cink, Pavel (1999) Jazyková politika v nové Evropě [Sprachenpolitik im neuen Europa]. In Krumm, 30–39.

Cioffi-Revilla, Claudio/ Merrit, Richard L./ Zinnes, Dina A. (eds.) (1987) *Communication and Interaction in Global Politics.* Beverly Hills/ London/ New Delhi: Sage Publications.

Ciu, Shaina [correct name: Feng, Xiaohu] (2007) Die Alexander von Humboldt-Stiftung in China. In Ammon/ Reinbothe/ Zhu, 277–290.

Claessen, J. F. M./Van Galen, A. M./ Oud-de Glas, M. (1978) *De behoeften aan moderne vreemde talen. Een oderzock onder bedrijven en overheidsdiensten.* Nijmegen: Instituut voor toegepaste Sociologie.

—— / —— / —— (1979) *Bedrijven en overheidsdiensten en behoeften aan moderne vreemde talen.* 's-Gravenshage: Staatsuitgeverij.

Clalüna, Monika (2010) Institutionen und Verbände für Deutsch als Zweit- und Fremdsprache in der Schweiz. In Krumm/ Fandrych/ Hufeisen/ Riemer,Vol. 1, 160–166.

Clark, Cal/ Merrit, Richard L. (1987) European community and Intra-European communications: the evidence of mail flows. In Cioffi-Revilla/ Merrit/ Zinnes, 209–235.

Clarke, W. M. (2000) The use of foreign languages by Irish exporters. *European Journal of Marketing* 34.1/ 2: 80–90.

Clyne, Michael G. (1974) Gegenwärtiger Stand der deutschen Sprache in Australien. In Kloss, 119–138.

—— (1975) *Forschungsbericht Sprachkontakt. Untersuchungsergebnisse und praktische Probleme.* Kronberg/ Ts.: Scriptor.

—— (1976) The languages of German-Australian industry. In Clyne, M. G. (ed.) *Australia Talks.* Canberra: Research School of Pacific Linguistics, 117–129.

—— (1977) European multinational companies in Australia and the exportation of languages. *Institut voor Toegepaste Linguistiek* 37: 83–91.

—— (1981) *Deutsch als Muttersprache in Australien. Zur Ökologie einer Einwanderersprache.* Wiesbaden: Steiner.

—— (1982a) Die deutsche Sprache in Australien. *Germanistische Mitteilungen* 15: 59–67.

—— (1982b) *Multilingual Australia.* Melbourne: River Seine Publications.

—— (1984a) Wissenschaftliche Texte Englisch- und Deutschsprachiger: Textstrukturelle Vergleiche. *Studium Linguistik* 15: 92–97.

—— (1984b) *Language and Society in the German-Speaking Countries.* Cambridge: Cambridge University Press.

—— (1987a) Zur Lage der Einwanderersprachen in Australien. In Weber, W. (ed.) *Einwanderungsland Australien.* Frankfurt a.M.: Athenäum, 133–152.

—— (1987b) Cultural differences in the organization of academic texts. *Journal of Pragmatics* 11 (1): 211–247.

—— (1991) The sociocultural dimension: the dilemma of the German-speaking scholar. In Schröder, Hartmut (ed.) *Subject-oriented Texts. Languages for Special Purposes and Text Theory.* Berlin/ New York: de Gruyter, 49–67.

—— (ed.) (1992) *Pluricentric Languages. Differing Norms in Different Nations.* Berlin/ New York: Mouton de Gruyter.

—— (1994) What can we learn from Sprachinseln? Some observations on "Australian German". In Berend/ Mattheier, 105–122.

—— (1995) *The German Language in a Changing Europe.* Cambridge: Cambridge University Press.

—— (2001) Can the shift from immigrant languages be reversed in Australia? In Fishman 2001a, 364–390.

———— (2003) *Dynamics of Language Contact: English and Immigrant Languages.* Cambridge: Cambridge University Press.

———— (2004) Pluricentric language. In Ammon/ Dittmar/ Mattheier/ Trudgill, 296–299.

———— (2006) Braucht Deutschland eine bewusste kohäsive Sprachenpolitik – Deutsch, Englisch als Lingua franca und Mehrsprachigkeit? (Hauptvortrag). (www.humboldt-foundation.de/ de/ netzwerk/ veranstalt/ hoersaal/ ebook_expert_09_2006/ clyne.pdf).

———— (2008) Australien. In Institut für Deutsche Sprache, 9–14.

———— /Hoeks, Jimmy/ Kreutz, Heinz-Josef (1988) Cross-cultural responses to academic discourse patterns. *Folia Linguistica* 22 (3–4): 457–473.

Coates, R. (2002) Language and publication in Cardiovascular Research articles. *Cardiovascular Research* 53: 279–285.

de Cock, Barbara (2008) Instituciones españolas de cara a la difusión de la lengua. Con atención particular a la situación en Bélgica, Estados Unidos y Canadá. *Bulletin hispanique* 110 (2): 681–724.

Cohen, Israel (1918) *The German Attack on the Hebrew Schools in Palestine.* London: Jewish Chronicle and Jewish World.

Cohen, Marcel (1956) *Pour une sociologie du langage.* Paris: Albin Michel.

Cohen, Ulrike/ Osterloh, Karl-Heinz (1981) *Zimmer frei. Deutsch in Hotel und Restaurant. Ein Sprachkurs für Hotelmitarbeiter.* Berlin: Langenscheidt.

———— / ———— (1986) *Herzlich willkommen. Deutsch für Fortgeschrittene in Hotel, Restaurant und Tourismus.* Berlin: Langenscheidt.

Coleman, James A. (2004) Modern languages in British Universities: past and present. *Arts & Humanities in Higher Education* 3 (2): 147–162.

———— (2012) Non-specialist linguists in the United Kingdom in the context of the Englishisation of European Higher Education. *Fremdsprachen Lehren und Lernen* 41: 9–24.

Coles, Peter (1989) Protest as Pasteur speaks English. *Nature* 338: 448.

Colliander, Peter (2009) Die Zukunftsperspektiven des Deutschen als Fremdsprache im Ausland (DaFiA) am Beispiel Dänemark – ein persönlicher Blick. In Barkowski/ Demmig/ Funk/ Würz, 107–117.

Collins, Joseph W./ Rutledge, John B. (1996) *Köttelwesch* on the cutting board: analyzing the literature of Germanistik. *Collection Management* 20 (3/ 4): 73–84.

Commission Européenne (ed.) (2001) *L'enseignement des langues étrangères en milieu scolaire en Europe.* Bruxelles: Commission Européenne, DG Éducation et culture.

———— (2004) *Promouvoir l'apprentissage des langues et la diversité linguistique. Plan d'action 2004–2006.* Bruxelles: Commission Européenne, DG Éducation et culture.

CompactMATH (O.J.) *Zentralblatt für Mathematik und ihre Grenzgebiete/ Mathematics Abstracts.* Vol. 1–99: MATH Database 1931–1969; vol. 201–549: MATH Database 1970–1984. Berlin/ Heidelberg: Springer.

Comrie, Bernard (ed.) [1987] (1990) *The World's Major Languages.* London/ Sydney: Croom Helm.

Condray, Kathleen (2007) Using RISE to promote German: making the case for practical work experience abroad to engineering students and faculty. *Die Unterrichtspraxis/ Teaching German* 40 (1): 61–66.

Connell, R. W./ Wood, Julian (2002) Globalisation and sScientific labour: patterns in a lifehistory study of intellectual workers in the periphery. *Journal of Sociology* 38 (2): 167190.

Conrad, Andrew W./ Fishman, Joshua A. (1977) English as a world language: the evidence. In Fishman/ Cooper/ Conrad, 3–76.

A Contemporary German Science Reader: Biology, Chemistry, Physics, Engineering, Manufacturing, Medicine, Psychology, General Science [1948, 1955, 1957, 1963] (1966) New York: Holt, Rinehart and Winston.

Conzen, Kathleen N. (1986) Deutschamerikaner und die Erfindung der Ethnizität. In Trommler, 148–164.

———— (2003) *Germans in Minnesota.* St. Paul: Minnesota Historical Society Press.

Cooper, Robert L. (ed.) (1982) *Language Spread. Studies in Diffusion and Social Change.* Bloomington: Indiana University Press.

———— (1989) *Language Planning and Social Change.* Cambridge/ New York: Cambridge University Press.

Cordell, Karl (2000) Poland's German minority. In Wolff, 75–96.

Corino, Karl (ed.) (1981) *Autoren im Exil.* Frankfurt a.M.: Fischer.

Corkhill, Alan (2003) Whither goeth Australasian German Studies? Some personal observations. *AUMLA* 100: 122–133.

Coulmas, Florian (1985) *Sprache und Staat.* Studien zur Sprachplanung (Sammlung Göschen, 2501). Berlin/ New York: de Gruyter.

———— (1987) Why Speak English? In Knapp, K./ Enninger, W./ Knapp-Potthoff, A. (eds.) *Analyzing Intercultural Communication.* Berlin: de Gruyter, 93–107.

—— (1989) The surge of Japanese. *International Journal of the Sociology of Language* 80: 115–131.

—— (1990) The status of German: some suggestions for future research. *International Journal of the Sociology of Language* 83: 171–185.

—— (1991a) Die Sprachenregelung in den Organen der EG als Teil einer europäischen Sprachenpolitik. *Sociolinguistica* 5: 24–36.

—— (1991b) European integration and the idea of the national language: ideological roots and economic consequences. In Coulmas 1991c, 1–43.

—— (ed.) (1991c) *A Language Policy for the European Community. Prospects and Quanderies.* Berlin/ New York: de Gruyter.

—— (1992a) *Die Wirtschaft mit der Sprache. Eine sprachsoziologische Studie.* Frankfurt a.M.: Suhrkamp.

—— (1992b) *Language and Economy.* Oxford, UK/ Cambridge, USA: Blackwell.

—— (1994) Deutsch in japanischen Niederlassungen deutscher Firmen. In Ammon 1994d, 71–82.

—— (2005a) *Sociolinguistics. The Study of Speakers' Choices.* Cambridge: Cambridge University Press.

—— (2005b) Economic aspects of languages. In Ammon/ Dittmar/ Mattheier/ Trudgill, 1667–1673.

—— (2007) English monolingualism in scientific communication and progress in science, good or bad? *AILA Review* 20: 5–14.

—— (2010) Eine Lingua Franca für die Wissenschaft ist eine Bereicherung. *NZZ* 19.01.: 13.

Coupland, Nikolas (ed.) (2010) *The Handbook of Language and Globalization.* Malden, MA/ Oxford: Blackwell.

Crawford, Elisabeth/ Shinn, Terry/ Sörlin, Sverker (eds.) (1993a) *Denationalizing Science. The Context of International Scientific Practice.* Dordrecht/ Boston/ London: Kluwer Acad. Publ.

—— / —— / —— (1993b) The nationalization and denationalization of the Science: An introductory essay. In Crawford/ Shinn/ Sörlin (1993a), 1–42.

Cremer, Rolf/ Willes, Mary (1994) Overcoming language barriers to international trade: a text based study of the language of Deals. *Journal of Asian Pacific Communications* 5: 147161.

Cresswell, John (1994) *Research Design: Qualitative and Quantitative Approaches.* Thousand Oaks, CA: Sage.

Crystal, David (1985) How Many Millions? The Statistics of English Today. *English Today* 1: 7–9.

—— [1987] (2010) *The Cambridge Encyclopedia of Language,* 3rd edition. Cambridge: Cambridge: University Press.

—— [1997] (2003) *English as a Global Language,* 2nd edition. Cambridge: Cambridge University Press.

—— (2001) *Language and the Internet.* Cambridge, UK: Cambridge University Press.

Culbert, S. (1977) The principal languages in the world. In *The World Almanach.* New York: Newspapers Enterprises, 226.

Cullars, John (1992) Citation characteristics of monographs in the fine arts. *Library Quarterly* 62: 325–342.

—— (1996) Citation characteristics of French and German fine arts monographs. *Library Quarterly* 66: 138–160.

Cummins, Jim (1995) Forging identities in the preschool: competing discourses and their relationship to research. In Fase/ Jaspaert/ Kroon, 7–23.

Curry, Mary Jane/ Lillis, Theresa (2004) Multilingual scholars and the imperative to publish in English: negotiating interests, demands and rewards. *TESOL Quarterly* 38.4: 663–688.

Czarnecki, Thomas (2004) Polen. In Institut für Deutsche Sprache, 9–14.

Czerwon, H.-J./ Havemann, F. (1993) Influence of publication languages on the citation rate of scientific articles: a case study of East German journals. *Scientometrics* 26 (1): 51–63.

Dahinden, Janine (2005) *Prishtina – Schlieren. Albanische Migrationsnetzwerke im transnationalen Raum.* Zürich: Seismo.

Dahme-Zachos, Andrea (2001) *Zum Zusammenhang von Lebensgeschichte mit kollektiver Geschichte und kollektiven Identitäten bei der deutschsprachigen Minderheit und ihren Nachkommen in Brasilien – eine biographieanalytische Arbeit.* Sankt Augustin: Michael Itschert, Gardez.

Dahrendorf, Ralf (1965) *Homo Sociologicus: ein Versuch zur Geschichte, Bedeutung und Kritik der Kategorie der sozialen Rolle.* Köln/ Opladen: Westdeutscher Verlag.

Dailey-O'Cain, Jennifer (2013) The use and the discursive functions of English in native language online conversations among Dutch and German youth. *Sociolinguistica* 23: 146166.

Dalby, David (1998) *The Linguasphere: From Person to Planet.* Hebron, Wales: Linguasphere Press.

—— (1999/2000) *The Linguasphere Register of the World's Languages and Speech Communities.* 2 Vols. Hebron, Wales: Linguasphere Press/ Gwasg y Byd Iaith.

—— (2000) The Linguasphere: a new nindow on the World's languages. *The Linguist* (August).

—— (2003) *Language in Danger.* London: Allen Lane/ The Penguin Press.

Dalmas, Martine (2010) Deutsch in Frankreich. In Krumm/ Fandrych/ Hufeisen/ Riemer, Vol. 2, 1658–1664.

———— / Metrich, René (2004) Frankreich. In Institut für Deutsche Sprache, 21–26.

———— / ———— (2008) Frankreich. In Institut für Deutsche Sprache, 23–30.

Dalmazzone, Silvana (1999) Economics of language: a network externalities approach. In Breton, A. (ed.) *Exploring the Economics of Language.* Ottawa: Department of Canadian Heritage, 63–87.

Damke, Ciro (1997) *Sprachgebrauch und Sprachkontakt in der deutschen Sprachinsel in Südbrasilien.* Frankfurt a. M.: Lang.

Damus, Sahra (2011) Irreguläre Morphologie in deutschen Sprachinseln im Altai. Erste Ergebnisse aus einem Projekt an der Schnittstelle von Sprachwandelforschung und Soziolinguistik. In Djatlowa, W. (ed.) *Forschungen deutscher Dialekte in Russland: Geschichte, Gegenwart und Zukunft russlanddeutscher Sprachinseldialektologie: Vorträge der internationalen wissenschaftlich-praktischen Sprachkonferenz, Moskau 2529 Juni 2011.* Moskau: IVDK-Press, 32–36.

Darquennes, Jeroen (2004) *The German Language in Education in Belgium.* Leeuwarden/ Ljouwert: Mercator Education.

———— (2005) *Sprachrevitalisierung aus kontaktlinguistischer Sicht. Theorie und Praxis am Beispiel Altbelgien-Süd.* St. Augustin: Asgard.

———— (2011a) Sprachwechsel, Spracherhalt und Sprachrevitalisierung im Areler Land von 1839 bis zur Gegenwart. In Gilles, P./ Wagner, M. (eds.): *Linguistische und soziolinguistische Bausteine der Luxemburgistik.* Frankfurt a. M.: Lang, 235–256.

———— (2011b) A historical sociolinguistic account of language shift and language maintenance in the Areler Land (1839–2010). In Moretti/ Pandolfi/ Casoni, 93–110.

———— (2013) Deutsch als Muttersprache in Belgien: Forschungsstand und Forschungsperspektiven. In Schneider-Wiejowski/ Kellermeier-Rehbein/ Haselhuber, 349–368.

Darwin, Charles [1859] (O.J.) *The Origin of Species* (Anchor Books). Gardin City, NY: Dolphin & Company.

———— [1871] (2011) *The Descent of Man, and Selection in Relation to Sex,* 2 Vols. Madison Park: Pacific Publishing Studio.

Dasgupta, Shyamal (1978) Deutsch als Fremdsprache in Indien. *Jahrbuch Deutsch als Fremdsprache* 4: 296–308.

Dauzat, Albert (1953) *L'Europe linguistique,* 2nd edition. Paris: Payot.

Davidheiser, James C. (1993) Soll Deutsch die dritte Arbeitssprache der Europäischen Gemeinschaft werden? *Die Unterrichtspraxis/ Teaching German* 26: 176–184.

———— / Wolf, Gregory (2009) Fanning the flames: best practises for ensuring the survival of small German programs. *Die Unterrichtspraxis/ Teaching German* 42: 60–67.

Davies, Alan (2003) *The Native Speaker: Myth and Reality.* Clevedon: Multilingual Matters.

Davis, Elisabeth B. (1987) *Guide to Information Sources in the Botanical Sciences.* Littleton, Colorado: Libraries Unlimited.

———— / Schmidt, Diane (1995) *Using the Biological Literature. A Practical Guide.* 2nd., rev. ed. New York/ Basel/ Hong Kong: Marcel Dekker.

Davis, Kathryn A. (1989) *Social Organization of Language Behavior in Luxembourg. Implications for Language Planning.* Phil. Diss. Stanford University.

Davis, M. (2004) GDP by Language. Unicode Technical Note # 13. (www.unicode.org/ notes/ tn13/ tn13-1.html)

Dawkins, Richard (2011) *The Magic of Reality. How we Know What's Really Ttrue.* London: Bantam Press.

Debus, Friedhelm/ Kollmann, Franz Gustav/ Pörksen, Uwe (eds.) (2000) *Deutsch als Wissenschaftssprache im 20. Jahrhundert. Vorträge des Internationalen Symposions vom 18./ 19. Januar 2000.* Stuttgart: Steiner.

Décsy, Gyula (1973) *Die linguistische Struktur Europas.* Wiesbaden: Harrassowitz.

Deminger, Szilvia (2004) *Spracherhalt und Sprachverlust in einer Sprachinselsituation.* Frankfurt a.M.: Lang.

Demokratischer Verband der Ungarndeutschen (ed.) (1988) *7. Kongreß der Ungarndeutschen/ Magyarorsz gi Németek 7. Kongresszusa.* Budapest: Selbstverlag des Demokratischen Verbandes der Ungarndeutschen.

Dermaut, Nadine/ Van Baelen, Greta/ Kern, Rudolf (1983) Untersuchung über die Situation des Deutschen als Fremdsprache in Belgien. *Deutsch als Fremdsprache in Belgien*: 52–212.

Desselmann, Günther/ Wazel, Gerhard (1979) Deutsch als Fremdsprache in der Deutschen Demokratischen Republik. *Moderna språk* 72 (3): 233–238.

Detering, Heinrich (2000) Deutsch als Sprache germanistischer Literaturwissenschaften. Erfahrungen und Thesen. In Debus/ Kollmann/ Pörksen, 159–177.

Deutsch-Italienische Handelskammer (2008) *Deutsche Unternehmen auf dem italienischen Markt: Erfahrungen und Erfolgsfaktoren. Umfrage zum deutschen Export nach Italien 2007/2008.* (www.ahkitalien.it/fileadmin/

ahk_italien/Dokumente/Publikationen/Umfragen/Deutsche_Exportunternehmen/1-Exportum-frage_2007-2008-_Deutsch_01.pdf)

———— (2010) *Italienische Unternehmen auf dem deutschen Markt Erfahrungen und Erfolgsfaktoren Umfrage zum italienischen Export nach Deutschland 2009.* (www.ahkitalien.it/fileadmin/ahk_italien/Dokumente/Pub-likationen/Umfragen/Italienisc   he_Exportunternehmen/DE-Umfrage_screen_30_03-sito_01.pdf)

Deutsch wieder Amtssprache in Namibia (1984). *Europa Ethnica* 41: 173.

Deutsche Akademie für Sprache und Dichtung/ Union der deutschen Akademien der Wissenschaften (eds.) (2013) *Reichtum und Armut der deutschen Sprache. Erster Bericht zur Lage der deutschen Sprache.* Mit Beiträgen von Ludwig Eichinger, Peter Eisenberg, Wolfgang Klein, Angelika Storrer. Berlin/ New York: de Gruyter.

Deutsche Forschungsgemeinschaft (2009) Alternativen zum European Reference Index for the Humanities (ERIC): DFG sucht nach bibliometrischen Ansätzen für die Geistes- und Sozialwissenschaften. *DFG Aktuell* (4).

Deutsche Speisekarte (1911) *Verdeutschung der in der Küche und im Gasthofswesen gebräuchlichen entbehrlichen Fremdwörter* (Verdeutschungsbücher des Allgemeinen Deutschen Sprachvereins 1). Berlin: Verlag des Allgemeinen Deutschen Sprachvereins.

Deutsche Sprache und Literatur an der Universität Sao Paulo (1980) *Lingua e literatura aleman, Suppl*: 3–24.

Deutsche Welle (ed.) (n.d.) *Deutsche Welle Technik.* 5th edition Köln.

———— (ed.) (1986) *Deutsche Welle. Auslandsrundfunk der Bundesrepublik Deutschland.* Köln: DW Hausdruckerei.

———— (ed.) (September 1988) *Umfrage im Ausland zur Nutzung internationaler Medien unter Berücksichtigung der DEUTSCHEN WELLE, April 1988.* Köln (hektographiert).

———— (ed.) (2000/ 2002) *Passé und mega-out? Zur Zukunft der deutschen Sprache im Zeitalter von Globalisierung und Multimedia.* Köln: Deutsche Welle/ Berlin: Vista.

———— (2003) *50 Jahre aus der Mitte Europas/ 50 Years at the Heart of Europe. Festschrift.* Bonn: Deutsche Welle.

Deutscher Akademischer Austauschdienst (DAAD) (1997a) *Undergraduate Degree Programms in English.* Bonn: DAAD.

———— (1997b) *Postgraduate Degree Programms in English and German.* Bonn: DAAD.

———— (ed.) (2002) *Germanistentreffen: Deutschland – Argentinien, Brasilien, Chile, Kolumbien, Kuba, Mexiko, Venezuela 8. – 12.10.2001.* Bonn: [DAAD].

———— (2004a) *Betreuung, Zulassung, Ausländerrecht* (Die internationale Hochschule: Ein Handbuch für Politik und Praxis, 7). Bielefeld: Bertelsmann.

———— (ed.) (2004b) *Deutsch und Fremdsprachen* (Die internationale Hochschule: Ein Handbuch für Politik und Praxis, 8). Bielefeld: Bertelsmann.

———— (ed.) (2004c) *Deutsche Studienangebote im Ausland* (Die internationale Hochschule: Ein Handbuch für Politik und Praxis, 10). Bielefeld: Bertelsmann.

———— (ed.) (2006) Jecht, Dorothea/ Mazumdar, Shaswati (red.) *German Studies in India. Aktuelle Beiträge aus der indischen Germanistik/ Germanistik in Indien.* München: Iudicium.

———— (2010) *Memorandum zur Förderung des Deutschen als Wissenschaftssprache.* Bonn: DAAD.

Deutscher Bundesrat (2004) *Entschließung des Bundesrates zur Gleichberechtigung der deutschen Sprache auf europäischer Ebene* (Bundesratsdrucksache 175/ 04).

Deutscher Bundestag (1981) *Antwort der Bundesregierung auf die Anfrage des Abgeordneten Schäfer (FDP) betr. ausländischer Studienbewerber* (Bundestagsdrucksache 9/ 523). Bonn.

———— (2003) *Deutsch als Arbeitssprache auf europäischer Ebene festigen – Verstärkte Förderung von Deutsch als erlernbare Sprache im Ausland. Antrag der Fraktionen SPD, CDU/ CSU, BÜNDNIS 90/ DIE GRÜNEN und FDP* (Bundestagsdrucksache 15/ 1574). Berlin.

———— Referat Öffentlichkeitsarbeit (ed.) (1986) *Die deutsche Sprache in der Welt. Anhörung des Auswärtigen Ausschusses am 18. Juni 1986 und Aussprache im Plenum des Deutschen Bundestages* (Zur Sache, 5). Bonn.

Deutscher Sprachatlas (1927–1956) 23 Lieferungen. Wenker, Georg (founder), Wrede, Ferdinand (beginn.), Mitzka, Walter/ Martin, Bernhard (successor). Marburg: Elwert.

Deutsches Minderheitensprachen-Gesetz. Gesetz zu der Europäischen Charta der Regional- oder Minderheitensprachen des Europarats vom 5. November 1992/ vom 9. Juli 1998 (BGB1.II 1314).

Dickson, David (1989) "L'Affaire Pasteur" Prompts Canadian Outcry. *Science* 244: 280f.

Die deutsche Sprache in der Welt. Deutschunterricht in 60 Ländern (1979) *Auslandskurier* 20 (8): 22.

Diel, Paulo F. (2001) *"Ein katholisches Volk, aber eine Herde ohne Hirte". Der Anteil deutscher Orden und Kongregationen an der Bewahrung deutscher Kultur und an der Erneuerung der katholischen Kirche in Süd-Brasilien.* Sankt Augustin: Gardez.

Dietrich, Rainer (2004a) Erstsprache – Muttersprache/ First language – Mother tongue. In Ammon/ Dittmar/ Mattheier/ Trudgill, 305–311.

――――― (2004b) Zweitsprache – Fremdsprache/ Second language – Foreign language. In Ammon/ Dittmar/ Mattheier/ Trudgill, 311–314.

Dietz, Barbara/ Hilkes, Peter (1988) Deutsch in der Sowjetunion. Zahlen, Fakten und neue Forschungsperspektiven. *Aus Politik und Zeitgeschichte* 50: 3–13.

Dimova, Ana (2010) Deutsch in Bulgarien. In Krumm/ Fandrych/ Hufeisen/ Riemer, Vol. 2, 16281632.

Dingeldein, Heinrich (2004) Die deutsche Sprache und das deutschsprachige Schulwesen in Rumänien. (www.alsace.iufm.fr/web/connaitr.cfeb/regards_extererieurws.pdf) – (2006) Die deutsche Sprache und ihre Erscheinungsformen in Rumänien. Historische Grundlegung und aktuelle Entwicklungstendenzen. In Berend/ Knipf-Komlósi, 57–75.

Diodato, Virgil (1990) The use of English language in non-U.S. Science journals: a case study of Mathematics publications, 1970–1985. *Library & Information Science Research* 12: 355371.

Djatlova, Valentina (2011) Deutsch und Russisch als Sprachen der Russlanddeutschen heute. In Ammon/ Kemper, 397–408.

Dobelli, Rolf (2011) *Die Kunst des klaren Denkens. 52 Denkfehler, die sie besser anderen überlassen.* München: Hanser.

――――― (2012) *Die Kunst des klugen Handelns. 52 Irrwege, die Sie besser anderen überlassen.* München: Hanser.

Dobrovolśkij, Dmitrij (2004) Russland. In Institut für Deutsche Sprache, 63–68.

――――― (2008) Russland. In Institut für Deutsche Sprache, 47f.

Doi, Takeo [engl. 1973] (1982) *Amae. Freiheit in Geborgenheit. Zur Struktur japanischer Psyche.* Frankfurt a.M.: Suhrkamp.

Dolde, Kerstin/ Lüsebrink, Claire/ Rowley, Anthony/ Schnabel, Michael/ Warter, Monika (1988) *Gebietsartikel Südtirol.* Universität Bayreuth: Universitätsdruck.

Domaschnew, Anatoli I. (1994) Englisch als die einzige Verkehrssprache des zukünftigen Europa? Eine Stellungnahme aus osteuropäischer Sicht. *Sociolinguistica* 8: 26–43.

――――― (2001) Deutschunterricht und Gemanistikstudium in Russland. In Helbig/ Götze/ Henrici/ Krumm, Vol. 2: 1556–1560.

Dominian, Leon (1917) *The Frontiers of Language and Nationality in Europe.* New York: Henry Holt and Company.

Donahay, Jasmine (2012) *Publishing Data and Statistics on Translated Literature in the United Kingdom and Ireland.* Aberystwyth University, Wales, UK: Mercator Institute for Media, Languages and Culture.

von Donat, Marcell (1999) Amts- und Arbeitssprachen der EU: Vielsprachigkeit und Demokratieverständnis. *EUmagazin* 12: 18f., 22.

Dörr, Dieter/ Schiedermair, Stephanie (2003) *Die Deutsche Welle. Die Funktion, der Auftrag, die Aufgaben und die Finanzierung heute.* Frankfurt a. M.: Lang.

Dovalil, Vítek (2006) Sprachenpolitik in der Tschechischen Republik (unter besonderer Berücksichtigung der Beziehungen zur EU und zum Europarat). *Interlinguistische Informationen. Mitteilungsblatt der Gesellschaft für Interlinguistik e. V.* Beiheft 13: 105–119.

――――― (2010) Sind zwei Fremdsprachen in der Tschechischen Repulik realistisch? Zu den aktuellen Problemen der tschechischen Spracherwerbsplanung. *Sociolinguistica* 24: 43–60.

Drahota-Szabó, Erzsébet (2010) Deutsch in Ungarn. In Krumm/ Fandrych/ Hufeisen/ Riemer, Vol. 2, 1727–1833.

30 Jahre Ausländerstudium in der DDR – 25 Jahre Herder-Institut der Karl-Marx-Universität Leipzig (1981) *Reden anläßlich der Festveranstaltungen am 12. Juni 1981.* Leipzig: KarlMarx-Universität.

300 Jahre Zusammenleben (1988) *Aus der Geschichte der Ungarndeutschen/ 300 éves együttélés – A magyarországi németek történetéböl.* Budapest: Tankönyvkiadó.

Drewer, Petra (2003) *Die kognitive Metapher als Werkzeug des Denkens. Zur Rolle der Analogie bei der Gewinnung und Vermittlung wissenschaftlicher Erkenntnisse.* Tübingen: Narr.

Drews, Albert (ed.) (2012) *Außenkulturpolitik. Aktuelle Herausforderungen in einer Welt im Umbruch. 57. Loccumer Kulturpolitisches Kolloquium* (Loccumer Protokolle 10/11). Rehburg-Loccum: Evangelische Akademie Loccum.

Drömert, Irene (1999) Die Sprache des Unternehmens – Bedeutung, Ausprägungsformen und Gestaltungsmöglichkeiten. In Bungarten 1999a, 141–152.

Dubinin, Sergej I. (2005) Zur Rezeption und Akzeptanz der deutschen Sprache in Russland. *Das Wort* (Moskau/ Bonn): 27–44.

———— (2011) Die Wolgadeutschen und ihre Autonome Republik (1924–1941). In Ammon/ Kemper, 8294.

Dück, Elvine S. (2011) *Vitalidade linguística do Plautdietsch em contato variedades Standard faladas em comunidades menonitas no Brasil.* Unpublished dissertation Universidade Federal do Rio Grande do Sul, Porto Alegre.

Duesberg, Peter (2006) DaF International. Aktuelle Tendenzen weltweit und Herausforderungen für die deutschsprachigen Länder. *Jahrbuch für Internationale Germanistik* 38 (2): 47–77.

Duke, Janet/ Hufeisen, Britta/ Lutjeharms, Madeline (2004) Die sieben Siebe des EuroCom für den multilingualen Einstieg in die Welt der germanischen Sprachen. In Klien, H./ Rutke, D. (eds.) *Neuere Forschungen zur europäischen Interkomprehension.* Aachen: Shaker, 109134.

Dundler, Franz (1988) *Urlaubsreisen 1954–1987. 34 Jahre Erfassung des touristischen Verhaltens der deutschen durch soziologische Stichprobenuntersuchungen.* Starnberg: Studienkreis für Tourismus.

Dunja-Blajberg, Jennifer (1980) *Sprache und Politik in Südwestafrika. Stellung und Funktion der Sprachen unter dem Apartheid-System.* Bonn: Informationsstelle Südliches Afrika e.V.

Durand, Charles X. (2001) *La mise en place des monopoles du savoir.* Paris: L'Harmattan.

———— (2006) If it's not in English, it's not worth reading!. *Current Issues in Language Planning* 7 (1): 44–60.

During, Florence (1995) Status et usage des langues au Conseil de l'Europe. *Terminologie et traduction* 3: 39–120.

Dürmüller, Urs (1986) The status of English in multilingual Switzerland. *Bulletin CILA* 44: 7–38.

———— (1991) Swiss multilingualism and intranational communication. *Sociolinguistica* 5: 111–159.

———— (1994) Multilingual talk or English only? The Swiss experience. *Sociolinguistica* 8: 44–64.

———— (2001) The presence of English at Swiss universities. In Ammon, 389–403.

———— (2002) English in Switzerland: from foreign language to lingua franca. In Allerton, D. J. (eds.) *Perspectives on English as a World Language.* Basel: Schwabe, 115–123.

Durrell, Martin (2002) Die Sprachenpolitik der Europäischen Union aus britischer Sicht. In Hoberg (2002a), 286–297.

———— (2003) Register, Variation und Fremdsprachenvermittlung. Zum Problem des Deutschunterrichts in Großbritannien. In Stickel, 239–258.

———— (2004a) Status der deutschen Sprache im Vereinigten Königreich und in Nordirland. In Institut für Deutsche Sprache, 29–33.

———— (2004b) Perspektiven für den Deutschunterricht und die Germanistik im Vereinigten Königreich Großbritannien und Nordirland. *Jahrbuch für Internationale Germanistik* 34 (1): 19–24.

———— (2007) Zum gegenwärtigen Stand des Deutschunterrichts und der Germanistik in Großbritannien. *Jahrbuch für Internationale Germanistik* 39 (2): 37–50.

———— (2008) Vereinigtes Königreich von Großbritannien und Nordirland. In Institut für Deutsche Sprache, 81–91.

———— (2013) [Review of] Christian Fandrych und Betina Sedlaczek, unter Mitarbeit von Erwin Tschirner und Beate Reinhold, "I need German for my life". Eine empirische Studie zur Sprachsituation in englischsprachigen Studiengängen in Deutschland [. . .]. *Zeitschrift für Dialektologie und Linguistik* 40 (2): 64–68.

Dürscheid, Christa/ Businger, Martin (2006) *Schweizer Standarddeutsch. Beiträge zur Varietätenlinguistik.* Tübingen: Narr.

Durzak, Manfred/ Kuruyazızı, Nilüfer (eds.) *Interkulturelle Begegnungen. Festschrift für Şara Sayın.* Würzburg: Königshausen & Neumann.

Duschanek, Michael (1997a) Sprachenkarte Tschechiens und der Slowakei. In Goebl/ Nelde/ Starý/ Wölck, 2041–2043.

———— (1997b) Sprachenkarte von Ungarn. In Goebl/ Nelde/ Starý/ Wölck, 2045–2047.

Düwell, Kurt (1976) *Deutschlands auswärtige Kulturpolitik 1918–1932. Grundlinien und Dokumente.* Köln/ Wien: Böhlau.

———— (2000) Der DAAD im Spannungsfeld zwischen Hochschulen und Regierungen seit 1950. In Alter, 106–129.

———— (2009) Zwischen Propaganda und Friedensarbeit – 100 Jahre Geschichte der deutschen Auswärtige Kulturpolitik. In Maaß (2009a), 61–111.

———— / Link, Werner (eds.) (1981) *Deutsche auswärtige Kulturpolitik seit 1871. Geschichte und Struktur: Referate eines interdisziplinären Symposions.* Köln/ Wien: Böhlau.

Dyck, Cornelius J. [1967] (1993) *An Introduction to Mennonite History. A Popular History of the Anabaptists and the Mennonites.* 3rd edition, Scottdale, Penn./ Waterloo, Ontario: Harold Press.

Earls, Clive W. (2013a) Setting the Catherine Wheel in motion: an exploration of "Englishization" in the German higher education system. *Language Problems and Language Planning* 37 (2): 125–150.

——— (2013b) *An Exploration of Language-in-Education Policy and Practice: The Experience of English-Medium Degree Programmes in Germany.* Unpublished Ph.D thesis University of Limerick (Ireland).

——— (2014) Striking the balance: the role of English and German in a multilingual English-medium degree programme in German higher education. *Current Issues in Language Planning* 15: 153–173.

Ebert, Johannes (2011) Die Goethe-Institute in Russland. In Ammon/ Kemper, 347–360.

Ebner, Jakob [1969] (2009) *Wie sagt man in Österreich? Wörterbuch des österreichischen Deutsch.* 4th edition, Mannheim: Dudenverlag.

Ecke, Peter (2010) Deutsch in USA. In Krumm/ Fandrych/ Hufeisen/ Riemer, Vol. 2, 1833–1839.

——— (2011) The state of German in the United States: a statistical portrait and a call for teachers. *German as a Foreign Language (GEL)* (2): 55–83.

Eder, Klaus (2000) Zur Transformation nationalstaatlicher Öffentlichkeit in Europa. Von der Sprachgemeinschaft zur issuespezifischen Kommunikationsgemeinschaft. *Berliner Journal für Soziologie* 10: 167–184.

Eder, Ulrike (2010) Entwicklungen von Deutsch als Fremdsprache in Deutschland nach 1945. In Krumm/ Fandrych/ Hufeisen/ Riemer, Vol. 1, 44–62.

Edwards, J. A./ Kingscott, A. G. (eds.) [1994] (1997) *Language Industries Atlas.* 2nd edition, Amsterdam: IOS Press.

Edwards, John (1984) *Linguistic Minorities, Policies and Pluralism.* London: Academic Press.

——— (1992) Sociopolitical aspects of language maintenance and loss: towards a typology of minority language situations. In Fase/ Jaspaert/ Kroon, 37–54.

——— (2009) *Language and Identity. An Introduction.* Cambridge, UK: Cambridge University Press.

——— (2010) *Minority Languages and Group Identity. Cases and Categories.* Amsterdam/ Philadephia: John Benjamins.

Edwards, Viv (1981) Sprachgebrauch und Sprachkompetenz bei mehrsprachigen Kindern im Südtiroler Unterland. In Meid, W./ Heller, K. (eds.) *Sprachkontakt als Ursache von Veränderungen der Sprach- und Bewußtseinsstruktur.* Innsbruck: Institut für Sprachwissenschaft der Universität, 67–82.– (1982) Die deutsche Sprache in Italien. *Germanistische Mitteilungen* 15: 69–80.

——— (1990) Zur Sprachsituation in Südtirol: Auf der Suche nach Konsens. *Deutsche Sprache* 4: 7688.

——— (2008) Immigrant Languages in the UK. In Ammon/ Haarmann, Vol. 1, 471–487.

Egger, Kurt (1977) *Zweisprachigkeit in Südtirol. Probleme zweier Volksgruppen an der Sprachgrenze.* Bozen: Athesia.

——— (1990) Zur Sprachsituation in Südtirol: Auf der Suche nach Konsens. *Deutsche Sprache* 4: 7688.

——— / Heller, Karin (1997) Italienisch – Deutsch. In Goebl, H./ Nelde, P. H./ Zdeněk, S./ Wölck, W. (eds.) *Kontaktlinguistik/ Contact Linguistics/ Linguistique de contact.* Vol. 2. Berlin/ New York: de Gruyter, 1350–1357.

——— / Lanthaler, Franz (eds.) (2001) *Die deutsche Sprache in Südtirol. Einheitssprache und regionale Vielfalt.* Wien: Folio.

Ehala, Martin (2009) An evaluation matrix for ethnolinguistic vitality. In Pertot, S./ Priestly, T. M. S./ Williams C. H. (eds.) *Rights, Promotion and Integration Issues for Minority Languages in Europe.* Basingstoke, UK: Palgrave Macmillan, 123–137.

Ehlich, Konrad (1993) Deutsch als fremde Wissenschaftssprache. *Jahrbuch Deutsch als Fremdsprache* 19: 13–42.

——— (2002) Die Zukunft des Deutschen und anderer Sprachen – außer der englischen – in der wissenschaftlichen Kommunikation. In Hoberg (2002a), 44–53.

——— (2004) The future of German and other non-English languages for academic communication. In Gardt/ Hüppauf, 173–184.

——— (2005) Deutsch als Medium wissenschaftlichen Arbeitens. In Motz (2005a), 41–51.

——— (2006) Die internationale Valenz des Deutschen und die europäische Sprachenpolitik. *Cadernos do cieg* 24 (Coimbra): 9–35.

——— (2010) Die deutsche Sprache in der Sprachenpolitik europäischer Institutionen. In Krumm/ Fandrych/ Hufeisen/ Riemer, Vol. 1, 124–132.

——— / Heller, Dorothee (eds.) (2006) *Die Wissenschaft und ihre Sprachen.* Bern: Lang.

——— / Issel, Burkhard/ Zickfeld, August Wilhelm (ed.) (2001) *Deutsch in Norwegen. Neue Beiträge zum Gespräch zwischen Germanistik, Lehrerausbildung und Schule.* Regensburg: Fachverband Deutsch als Fremdsprache, 89–106.

Eichhoff, Jürgen (1976) Bibliography of German Dialects spoken in the United States and Canada, and Problems of German-English Language Contact, especially in North-America 1968–1976 with pre-1968 Supplements. *Monatshefte* 68: 196–208.

——— (1986) Die deutsche Sprache in Amerika. In Trommler, 235–252.

——— (1993) 'Ich bin ein Berliner': a history and a linguistic clarification. *Monatshefte* 85: 71–80.

Eichinger, Ludwig M. (1994) Sprachliche Kosten-Nutzen-Rechnungen und die Stabilität mehrsprachiger Gemeinschaften. In Helfrich, U./ Riehl, C. *Mehrsprachigkeit in Europa.* Wilhelmsfeld: 31–54.

——— (1995) Regionaler Sprachkontakt und fremdsprachliche Norm. Form und Verwendung der deutschen Standardsprache in Ungarn. In Wodak/ de Cillia, 53–62.

——— (1996) Südtirol. In Hinderling/ Eichinger, 199–262.

——— (2003) Island Hopping: Vom Nutzen und Vergnügen des Vergleichs von Sprachinseln. In Androutsopoulos/ Ziegler, 83–107.

——— (2006) Soziolinguistik und Sprachminderheiten. In Ammon/ Dittmar/ Mattheier/ Trudgill, 2473–2484.

——— / Plewnia, Albrecht/ Riehl, Claudia Maria (eds.) (2008) *Handbuch der deutschen Sprachminderheiten in Mittel- und Osteuropa.* Tübingen: Narr.

——— / Schoel, Christiane/ Stahlberg, Dagmar (eds.) (2012) *Sprache und Einstellungen. Spracheinstellungen aus sprachwissenschaftlicher und sozialpsychologischer Perspektive. Mit einer Sprachstandserhebung zum Deutschen von Gerhard Stickel.* Tübingen: Narr.

Eins, Wieland/ Glück, Helmut/ Pretscher, Sabine (eds.) (2011) *Wissen schaffen – Wissen kommunizieren. Wissenschaftssprachen in Geschichte und Gegenwart.* Wiesbaden: Harrassowitz.

Eisenberg, Peter [1986] (1999/2001) *Grundriß der deutschen Grammatik.* Vol. 2. *Der Satz.* Stuttgart/ Weimar: Metzler.

——— (1987) Wie lassen sich Ansehen und Wirkung der deutschen Sprachwissenschaft ermitteln? *Zeitschrift für germanistische Linguistik* 15: 228–230.

——— (1998) *Grundriß der deutschen Grammatik.* Vol. 1. *Das Wort.* Stuttgart/ Weimar: Metzler.

——— (2011) *Das Fremdwort im Deutschen.* Berlin/ New York: de Gruyter.

——— (2012) Das Ende vor Augen? Über das Erhalten des Deutschen als Wissenschaftssprache. *Gegenworte* (Zwischen den Wissenschaften) 28: 52–55. (www.edoc.bbaw.de/volltexte/2013/2341/pdf/16_GW28_Eisenberg.pdf) Auch in ADAWiS 2013.

Eisfeld, Alfred (1999) *Die Russlanddeutschen.* Mit Beiträgen von Detlev Brandes und Wilhelm Kahle. 2nd revised edition, München: Langen Müller.

ELAN (2006) *Auswirkungen mangelnder Fremdspachenkenntnisse in den Unternehmen auf die europäische Wirtschaft.* London/ Newcastle upon Tyne: CILT/ Interact International. de Elera, Alvaro (2004) Unión Europea y Multilingüismo [European Union and multilingualism]. *Revista española de derecho europeo* 9 (1): 85–138.

Eleta, Irene (2012) *Multilingual Use of Twitter: Social Networks and Language Choice.* Seattle, WA, February 11–15. (www.dl.acm.org/citation.cfm?id=2141512.2141621&coll=DL&dl=GUIDE&CFID=26766136 3&CFTOKEN=33283622)

Elmentaler, Michael (ed.) (2009a) *Deutsch und seine Nachbarn.* Frankfurt a.M.: Lang.

——— (2009b) Hochdeutsch und Platt – zwei ungleiche Nachbarn. In Elmentaler, 31–45.

Van Els, Theo (2001) The European Union, its institutions and its languages: some language political observations. *Current Issues in Language Planning* 2 (4): 311–360.

——— (2003) Language policy of and for the European Union. In Ahrenz, 45–56.

——— (2005a) Multilingualism in the European Union. *International Journal of Applied Linguistics* 15 (3): 263–281.

——— (2005b) An update on the European Union, its institutions and its languages: some language political observations. In Baldauf, R./ Kaplan, R. B. (eds.) *Language Planning and Policy in Europe. Vol. 2. The Czech Republic, The European Union and Nothern Ireland.* Clevedon: Multilingual Matters: 252–256.

——— (2007) Sprachenpolitik der Europäischen Union. Wie wird es der deutschen Sprache ergehen? *Muttersprache* 117 (2): 124–134.

——— / Oud-de Glas, Maria (eds.) (1983) *Research into Foreign Language Needs.* Augsburg: Universität Augsburg.

Emmert, Hans D. (1987) Deutsch als Fremdsprache und Germanistik in der Türkei. In Sturm (1987), 61–73.

Empfehlungen des Vorstandes der Deutschen Gesellschaft für Pychologie zur Fortentwicklung deutschsprachiger Fachzeitschriften der Psychologie (1985) *Pychologische Rundschau* 36: 62–66.

Enciclopedia del Español en el Mundo (2006) (Annuario del Instituto Cervantes, 2006–7). Madrid: Instituto Cervantes.

Engels, Dietrich/ Köller, Regine/ Koopmans, Ruud/ Höhne, Jutta (2011) *Zweiter Integrationsbericht erstellt für die Beauftragte der Bundesregierung für Migration, Flüchtlinge und Integration.* Köln: ISG Institut für Sozialforschung und Gesellschaftspolitik/ Berlin: Wissenschaftszentrum Berlin für Sozialforschung.

Engels, Friedrich [1839] (1970) Briefe aus dem Wuppertal. In *Karl Marx / Friedrich Engels Werke*, Vol. 1. Berlin: Dietz, 415–432.

English only? In Europe (1994) Sociolinguistica 8. Tübingen: Niemeyer.

Engombe, Lucia (2004) *Kind Nr. 95. Meine deutsch-afrikanische Odyssee*. Berlin: Ullstein.

Enninger, Werner (ed.) (1983) *Word List of Pennsylvania German – as Spoken by the Old Order Amish of Kent County, Delaware*. Essen: University of Essen Printing Office.

———— / Raith, Joachim/ Wandt, Karl-Heinz (eds.) (1989) *Studies on the Languages and the Verbal Behavior of the Pennsylvania Germans II*. Stuttgart: Steiner.

Erb, Maria (1994) Zur interdisziplinären Untersuchung der natürlichen Zweisprachigkeit am Beispiel des Ungarndeutschen. In Berend/ Mattheier, 263–271.

———— (1995) Die Rolle der deutschsprachigen Medien bei den Ungarndeutschen. Beiträge zur Volkskunde der Ungarndeutschen 12: 28–37.

———— (2010) Sprachgebrauch der Ungarndeutschen: Geschichte – Tendenzen – Perspektiven. In Kostrzewa/ Rada/ Knipf-Komlósi, 118–146.

———— / Knipf-Komlósi, Elisabeth (eds.) (2006) *Tradition und Innovation. Neuere Forschungen zur Sprache der Ungarndeutschen* (Reihe Ungarndeutscher Studien 7). Budapest: Elte.

Eriksen, Lars H. (1986) Fall und Gegenfall. Ein Vergleich der Stellung und Sprache der deutschen Minderheit in Dänemark und der dänischen in Deutschland aus sprach-rechtlicher Sicht. In Hinderling, 149–187.

Erling, Elizabeth J. (2004) *Globalization, English and the German University Classroom: A Sociolinguistic Profile of Students of English at the Freie Universität Berlin*. University of Edinburgh: PhD Thesis.

———— / Hilgendorf, Suzanne K. (2006a). English in the German university: a means of disadvantage or empowerment? In Weideman, A./ Smieja, B. (eds.) *Empowerment Through Language and Education*. Frankfurt a.M.: Lang, 111–126.

———— / Hilgendorf, Suzanne K. (2006b) Language policies in the context of German higher education. *Language Policy* 5 (3): 267–293.

Ernst, E./ Resch, K. L. (1994) Reviewer bias: a blinded experimental study. *Journal of Laboratory and Clinical Medicine* 124: 178–182.

Esslinger, Dieter (1985) Deutsche Regierungsschulen im Wechsel der Zeit. In Becker, Klaus (ed.) *Vom Schutzgebiet bis Namibia*. Windhoek: Interessengemeinschaft deutschsprachiger Südwester, 102–109.

———— (1990) Das Fach Deutsch als Muttersprache im südlichen Afrika. *Der Deutschunterricht im Südlichen Afrika* 21 (1): 51–58.

———— (2002) Anpassung und Beharrung. Deutsche Regierungsschulen in Namibia. In Hess/ Becker, 490–504.

Ethnologue. Languages of the World. Grimes, Barbara F. (ed.) (1984/ 2000/ 2005/ 2009). 10th, 14th, 15th and 16th editions, Dallas/ TX: Wycliffe Bible Translation.

Eurobarometer Spezial 243 (2006) Europäische Kommission (ed.) *Die Europäer und ihre Sprachen*. (www.ec.europa.eu/public_opinion/archives/ebs/ebs_243_de.pdf)

Eurobarometer Spezial 386 (2012) Europäische Kommission (ed.) *Die europäischen Bürger und ihre Sprachen*. (www.ec.europa.eu/public_opinion/archives/ebs/ebs_386_de.pdf)

Eurobarometre 54 Special (2001) *Les europeens et le langues*. La Direction Générale de l'Education et de la Culture. [Brüssel]. (ec.europa.eu/public_opinion/archives/ebs/ebs_147_en.pdf)

Euromosaic (1996) *The Production and Reproduction of the Minority Language Groups in the European Union*. Erstellt für die EU-Kommission von Nelde, Peter/ Strubell, Miquel/ Williams, Glyn. Luxemburg: Office for Official Publications of the European Commission.

Europäische Kommission (2002) *Der Konferenzdolmetscherdienst und die Erweiterung. Eine Strategie für den SCIC im Hinblick auf das Jahr 2004*. Mitteilung von Herrn Kinnock. Brüssel, SCIC-2001-00007-01-00-DE-TRA-00 (FR).

Europäischer Rat (ed.) (2002) Entschließung des Rates vom 14. Februar 2002 zur Förderung der Sprachenvielfalt und des Erwerbs von Sprachkenntnissen im Rahmen der Umsetzung der Ziele des Europäischen Jahres der Sprachen 2001. *Amtsblatt der Europäischen Gemeinschaft* C 50/ 1 vom 23.2.2002.

Europäisches Parlament (ed.) (1982) *Bericht im Namen des Ausschusses für Geschäftsordnung und Petitionen über die Mehrsprachigkeit der Europäischen Gemeinschaft*. Sitzungsdokument 1–306/ 82 vom 1. Juni 1982.

Europäisches Parlament (ed.) (2001) Entschließung des Europäischen Parlaments vom 13. Dezember 2001 zu den regionalen und weniger verbreiteten europäischen Sprachen. *Amtsblatt der Europäischen Union* C 177/ 334 vom 25.7.2002.

Europäisches Parlament (2004a) *Code of Conduct on Multilingualism*. Brüssel: Europäisches Parlament, E 338.978/ BUR.

Europäisches Parlament (2004b) *Translation and Edition. Parliamentary Documents-Questions and Answers*. Brüssel: Directorate-General-Translation and Edition.

Europarat (2011) *Europäische Charta der Regional- und Minderheitensprachen: Anwendung der Charta in Polen*. (www.ostdeutsches-forum.net/EUFV/PDF/Uebersetzung-Bericht-Europarat.pdf)

European Parliament (ed.) (2001) *Lesser-Used Languages in States Applying for EU Membership (Cyprus, Czech Republic, Estonia, Hungary, Poland and Slovenia* (EBLUL Brochure).

Eurydice (1989) *Teaching of Languages in the European Community: Statistics* (Working Document, March 1989). Brüssel: Eurydice.

Eurydice (2005/ 2008) *Schlüsselzahlen zum Sprachenlernen an den Schulen in Europa*. Ausgabe 2005/ Ausgabe 2008. Brüssel: Eurydice.

Extra, Guus (2008) Immigrant languages in multilingual Europe: comparative perspectives. In Ammon/ Haarmann, Vol. 1, 489–518.

Eysenck, Hans-Jürgen (1980) A comment on the Traxel – Lienert discussion regarding publication in English by German psychologists. *Psychologische Beiträge* 22: 372–376.

Fabricius-Hansen, Cathrine (2000) Deutsch als Wissenschaftssprache in Skandinavien. In Debus/ Kollmann/ Pörksen, 177–193.

Fadeeva, Galina (2011) Lehnwörter aus dem Deutschen im Russischen. In Ammon/ Kemper, 255–271.

Falkenburg, Brigitte (1999) Sprache und Anschauung in der modernen Physik. In Wiegand, 89118.

Fan, Jieping/ Li, Luan [richtiger Name: Li, Yuan] (2007) Studien zum Motivwandel des Deutschlernens chinesischer Studierender. In Ammon/ Reinbothe/ Zhu, 194–209.

Fandrych, Christian/ Hufeisen, Brigitte (2010) Die Situation von Deutsch außerhalb des deutschsprachigen Raums. In Krumm/ Fandrych/ Hufeisen/ Riemer, Vol. 1, 34–43.

———— / Sedlaczek, Betina (2012) *"I need German in my life". Eine empirische Studie zur Sprachsituation in englischsprachigen Studiengängen in Deutschland*. Tübingen: Stauffenburg.

Fase, Willem/ Jaspaert, Koen/ Kroon, Sjaak (eds.) (1992) *Maintenance and Loss of Minority Languages*. Amsterdam/ Philadelphia: Benjamins.

———— / ———— / ———— (eds.) (1995) *The State of Minority Languages. International Pespectives on Survival and Decline*. Lisse: Sweets & Zeitlinger.

Fasold, Ralph (1984) *The Sociolinguistics of Society*. Oxford: Basil Blackwell.

Fearns, Anneliese (1999) Curricula für fach- und berufssprachlich orientierte Wirtschaftsdeutschkurse. *Materialien Deutsch als Fremdsprache* 52: 240–254.

Feddersen, Jan (2002) *Ein Lied kann eine Brücke sein*. Hamburg: Hoffmann und Campe.

Fehlen, Fernand (2009) *BaleineBis: une enquête sur un marché linguistique multilingue en B profonde mutation. Luxemburgs Sprachenmarkt im Wandel*. Luxemburg: SESOPI Centre Intercommunautaire.

Feld, Stacy Amity (1998) Languages and the globalization of the economic market: the regulation of languages as a barrier to free trade. *Vanderbilt Journal of Transnational Law* 31: 155–201.

Fenyvesi, Anna (1998) Linguistic minorities in Hungary. In Bratt Paulston/ Peckham, 135–159.

Ferguson, Charles (1959) Diglossia. *Word* 15: 325–340.

———— (1966) National sociolinguistic profile formulas. In Bright, W. (ed.) *Sociolinguistics. Proceedings of the UCLA Sociolinguistic Conference, 1964*. The Hague/ Paris: Mouton, 309–324.

Ferguson, Gibson (2007) The global spread of English, scientific communication and ESP: questions of equity, access and domain loss. *Ibérica* 13 (1): 7–38.

———— / Perez-Llantada, Carmen/ Plo, Ramón (2011) English as a language of international scientific publication: a study of attitudes. *World Englishes* 30 (1): 41–59.

Fernberger, Samuel W. (1917) On the number of articles of psychological interest published in the different languages. *American Journal of Psychology* 28: 141–150.

———— (1926) On the number of articles of psychological interest published in the different languages: 1916–1925. *American Journal of Psychology* 37: 578–580.

———— (1936) On the number of articles of psychological interest published in the different languages: *American Journal of Psychology* 48: 680–684.

———— (1946) On the number of articles of psychological interest published in the different languages: 1936–1945. *American Journal of Psychology* 59: 284–290.

———— (1956) On the number of articles of psychological interest published in the different languages: 1946–1955. *American Journal of Psychology* 63: 304–309.

Fettes, Mark (2003a) Interlingualism: a world-centric approach to language policy and planning. In Tonkin/ Reagan.

———— (2003b) The geostrategies of interlingualism. In Maurais/ Morris, 37–46.

Fidrmuc, Jan/ Ginsburgh, Victor (2004) Languages in the EU: the quest for equality and its cost. *CEPR (Centre for Economic Policy Research) Discussion Paper Series* Nr. 4795. (www.cepr.org/ pubs/ dps/ DP4795.asp)

———— / ———— (2006) Languages in the European Union: the quest for equality and its cost. *European Economic Review* 51 (6): 1351–1369.

Fiedler, Sabine (2010) The English-as-a-lingua-franca-approach: linguistic fair play? *Language Problems and Language Planning* 34 (3): 201–221.

Finger, Bernd (2000) *Sprachenwahl in der grenzüberschreitenden Kommunikation zwischen Südbaden und dem Elsass: Wer spricht am Oberrhein in welcher Sprache wann zu wem?* Unpublished article in the subject of German in the context of an academic examination for grammar school teaching in Baden-Württemberg. Albert-Ludwigs-Universität Freiburg: Institut für deutsche Sprache und ältere Literatur.

Finison, L. J./ Whittemore, C. L. (1975) Linguistic isolation of American social psychology. A comparative study of journal citations. *American Psychology* 30: 513–516.

Finkelmann, Paul (1993) The war on German language and culture, 1917–1925. In Schröder, H.-J. (ed.) *Confrontation and Cooperation. Germany and the United States in the Era of World War I, 1900–1924*. Vol. 2. Providence: Berg, 177–205. Finkenstaedt, Thomas/ Schröder, Konrad (1990) *Sprachschranken statt Zollschranken? Grundlegung einer Fremdsprachenpolitik für das Europa von morgen.* Essen: Stifterverband für die Deutsche Wissenschaft.

Finzen, Asmus (1998) Der Impact-Factor: Die Veränderung der Wissenschaftskultur durch die Quantifizierung wissenschaftlicher Leistung. *Medizinische Welt* 49: 128–134.

Fischel, Alfred (1910) *Das Österreichische Sprachenrecht.* 2nd expanded edition, Brünn: Irrgang.

Fischer, Lars/ Minks, Karl-Heinz (2010) *Die internationale Positionierung der Geisteswissenschaften in Deutschland.* Hannover: HIS Hochschul-Informations-System (Kurzfassung von Behrens/ Fischer/ Minks/ Rösler 2010).

Fischer, Rudolf-Josef (2006) "Englisch kann doch jeder" – eine Erhebung unter deutschen Muttersprachlern. In Gehling, Thomas et al. (eds.) *Einblicke in Sprache. Festschrift für Clemens-Peter Herbermann zum 65. Geburtstag.* Berlin: Logos, 133–152.

Der Fischer Weltalmanach '88/ '90/ 2007/ 2009/ 2013 (1987/ 1989/ 2006/ 2008/ 2012). Frankfurt a.M.: Fischer Taschenbuch Verlag.

Fishman, Joshua A. (1964) Language maintenance and language shift as a field of inquiry. *Linguistics* 9: 32–70.

———— (1965) Who speaks what language to whom and when? *La Linguistique* 2: 67–88.

———— (1966) Language maintenance in a supra-ethnic age: summary and conclusion. In Fishman/ Nahirny et al. 1966, 392–411.

———— (1967) Bilingualism with and without diglossia; diglossia with and without bilingualism. *Journal of Social Issues* 23 (2): 29–38.

———— (1968) *Readings in the Sociology of Language.* The Hague, Paris: Mouton.

———— (1972a) *Language and Nationalism: Two Integrative Essays.* Rowley, MA: Newbury House.

———— (1972b) Domains and the relationship between micro- and macro-sociolinguistics. In Gumperz, J./ Hymes, D. (eds.) *Directions in Sociolinguistics.* New York: Holt, Rinehart & Winston, 435–453.

———— (ed.) (1974) *Advances in Language Planning.* The Hague/ Paris: Mouton.

———— (1977a) Knowing, using and liking English as an additional language. In Fishman/ Cooper/ Conrad, 302–326.

———— (1977b) English in the context of international societal bilingualism. In Fishman/ Cooper/ Conrad, 329–335.

———— (1982) Sociology of English as an additional language. In Kachru, 15–22.

———— (1991a) *Reversing Language Shift. Theoretical and Empirical Foundations of Assistance to Threatened Languages.* Clevedon/ Philadelphia/ Adelaide: Multilingual Matters.

———— (1991b) Three dilemmas of organized efforts to reverse language shift. In Ammon/ Hellinger, 285–293.

———— (1994) "English only" in Europe? Some suggestions from an American perspective. In *Sociolinguistica* 8, 65–72.

———— (ed.) (2001a) *Can Threatened Languages Be Saved?* Clevedon: Multilingual Matters.

———— (2001b) Why is it so hard to save threatened languages? In Fishman 2001a, 1–22.

—— (2001c) From theory to practice (and vice versa). In Fishman 2001a, 451–483.

—— (2010) Sociolinguistics: language and ethnic identity in context. In Fishman/ García, xxii–xxxv.

—— / Conrad, A. W./ Rubal-Lopez, A. (eds.) (1996) *Post-Imperial English: Status Change in Former British and American Colonies, 1940–1990*. Berlin: Mouton.

—— / Cooper, Robert L./ Conrad, Andrew W. (1977) *The Spread of English: The Sociology of English as an Additional Language*. Rowley, MA.: Newbury House.

—— / —— /Rosenbaum, Yehudit (1977) English around the World. In Fishman/ Cooper/ Conrad, 77107.

—— / García, Ophelia (eds.) (2010) *Handbook of Language and Ethnic Identity*. Vol. I: *Disciplinary and Regional Perspectives*. 2nd ed. Oxford/ New York: Oxford University Press.

—— / Hayden G./ Warshauer, Mary E. (1966) The non-English and the ethnic group press, 19191960. In Fishman/ Nahirni et al. 1966, 51–74.

—— / Hofman, John E. (1966) Mother tongue and nativity in the American population. In Fishman/ Nahirni et al. 1966, 34–50.

—— / Nahirny, Vladimir C. (1966a) The ethnic group school and mother tongue maintenance. In Fishman/ Nahirni et al. 1966, 92–126.

—— / —— (1966b) Organizational and leadership interest in language maintenance. In Fishman/ Nahirni et al. 1966, 156–205.

—— / —— / Hoffman, John E./ Hayden, Robert G. (eds.) (1966) *Language Loyalty in the United States*. London/ The Hague: Mouton.

—— / —— / —— / —— et al. (1966) *Language Loyalty in the United States. The Maintenance and Perpetuation of Non-English Mother Tongues by American Ethnic and Religious Groups*. London/ The Hague/ Paris: Mouton.

Flaitz, Jeffra (1988) *The Ideology of English. French Perceptions of English as a World Language*. Berlin/ New York/ Amsterdam: de Gruyter.

Flasch, Kurt (2005) Zur Verdrängung der deutschen Sprache aus den Wirtschaftswissenschaften in Deutschland. In Pörksen, 30–34.

Flood, L. John/ Swales, Martin (2000) Die Förderung der Auslandsgermanistik: Großbritannien als Beispiel. In Alter (2000a), 152–163.

Flowerdew, John (1999) Problems of writing for scholarly publication in English: the case of Hong Kong. *Journal of Language Writing* 8 (3): 243–264.

—— (2000) Discourse community, legitimate peripheral participation, and the nonnative-Englishspeaking scholar. *TESOL Quarterly* 34: 127–150.

—— (2001) Attitudes of journal editors to nonnative speaker contributions. *Tesol Quarterly* 35 (1): 121–151.

—— (2007) The non-Anglophone scholar on the periphery scholarly publication. *AILA Review* 20: 14–28.

—— / Peacock, Matthew (2001) Issues in EAP: a preliminary perspective. In Flowerdew, J./ Peacock, M (eds.) *Research Perspectives on English for Academic Purposes*. Cambridge: Cambridge University Press, 8–24.

Fluck, Hans-Rüdiger (1985) Deutsch als Fachsprache in der Volksrepublik China. Vermittlung und Anwendung. *Zielsprache Deutsch* 16 (1): 9–16.

—— (2007) Deutsch als Fachfremdsprache (ca. 1920–2004) [in China!]. In Ammon/ Reinbothe/ Zhu, 163–193.

—— / Saarbeck, Ursula/ Zhu, Jianhua/ Zimmer, Thomas (1996) *Deutsch als Fach- und Fremdsprache in Ost- und Zentralasien. Situationen, Sprachbeschreibungen, didaktische Konzepte*. Heidelberg: Groos.

Flynn, John E. (1951) *A History of Biological Abstracts*. Philadelphia/ PE: Biological Abstracts (Unpublished working paper).

Fodor, Ference/ Peluau, Sandrine (2003) Language geostrategy in Eastern and Central Europe: assessment and perspectives. In Maurais/ Morris, 85–98.

Fögen, Thorsten (2000) *Patrii sermonis egestas. Einstellungen lateinischer Autoren zu ihrer Muttersprache. Ein Beitrag zum Sprachbewußtsein in der römischen Antike*. München/ Leipzig: Saur.

Földes, Csaba (1995) Chancen der dialektophonen Methode in der Spracherziehung zwischen Muttersprache und Zweitsprache. *Zielsprache Deutsch* 26 (3): 156–164.

—— (2000a) Was ist die deutsche Sprache wert? Fakten und Potenzen. *Wirkendes Wort* 50: 275296.

—— (2000b) Deutsch als Wissenschaftssprache im östlichen Mitteleuropa. In Debus/ Kollmann/ Pörksen, 193–209.

——— (2001a) Deutsch in Ostmittel-, Ost- Nordost- und Südosteuropa als eine Herausforderung für die Sprachenpolitik. *Deutsche Sprache* 29: 349–369.

——— (2001b) Die deutsche Sprache in Ostmittel-, Ost und Südosteuropa: gestern, heute und morgen? *Germanistische Mitteilungen* 53: 65–83.

——— (2002) Deutsch und Englisch: Ein Sprachnotstand? Befunde und Anmerkungen aus einer ostmitteleuropäischen Perspektive. In Hoberg (2002a), 341–367.

——— (2004a) Perspektiven einer "Anrainer-Germanistik": Überlegungen zum Standort des Faches *deutsche Sprache und Literatur* in Ungarn. *Jahrbuch für Internationale Germanistik* 35 (2): 15–24.

——— (2004b) Deutsch als Europasprache aus ungarischer Sicht. In Lohse, 109–128.

——— (2005) *Kontaktdeutsch. Zur Theorie eines Varietätentyps unter transkulturellen Bedingungen der Mehrsprachigkeit.* Tübingen: Narr.

Forschungsstandbericht Deutsch als Muttersprache im nichtdeutschsprachigen Ausland (July 1988) Im Auftrag des Auswärtigen Amts vorgelegt vom Institut für deutsche Sprache. Mannheim: Institut für deutsche Sprache.

Fort, Marron C. (2001) Das Saterfriesische. In Munske, 409–422.

Fortschritte der Physik (1845–1918). Braunschweig: Vieweg [continued as *Physikalische Berichte*].

Foschi Albert, Marina (2005) "Andere Länder, andere Sitten". Germanistik in Italien und ihr Verhältnis zur Inlandsgermanistik. *Deutsche Sprache* 33: 169–181.

——— / Hepp, Mariane (2010) Deutsch in Italien. In Krumm/ Fandrych/ Hufeisen/ Riemer, Vol. 2, 1693–1697.

Fotos, John T. (1957) *Introductory Reading in Chemical and Technical German; ed. for Rapid Reading With a Summary of Reading Difficulties, a Chemical German Frequency List and Progressive Page Vocabularies and Notes.* New York: Wiley.

Frank, Anne (1947) *Het Achterhuis. Dagboekbrieven 12 Juni 1942–1 August 1944.* Amsterdam/ Antwerpen: Contact.

Frank, Helmar (1983) Europäische Sprachpolitik: Aufgaben, Lösungsangebote und Schwierigkeiten. *Politik und Zeitgeschichte* 12: 26–29.

Franke, Viktor (1937a) Bericht über die Stellung des Deutschen im fremdsprachlichen Unterricht der Kulturländer der Erde. *Deutsche Volkserziehung* 4: 132–139.

——— (1937b) *L'enseignement des langues vivantes. D'après les données fournies par les Ministères de l'instruction publique.* Genf: Bureau International d'Education.

Frankfurter Buchmesse (2013) *Buch und Buchhandel in Zahlen 2012.* (www.buchmesse.de/images/fbm/dokumente-ua-pdfs/2013/buchmarkt_deutschland_buch_und_buchhandel_2012_deutsch.pdf_37215.pd f)

Fränzel, Walter (1938) Statistische Übersicht über den fremdsprachlichen Unterricht in Europa. In Thierfelder, 185–210.

——— (1939) Die lebenden Sprachen im Sprachunterricht der Welt. *Internationale Zeitschrift für Erziehung* 8 (2): 104–128.

Freeman, Robert B. (1976) Psychologie auf deutsch? *Börsenblatt für den deutschen Buchhandel* 32 (74): 1369f.

Frese, Michael (1990) Einfluß der deutschen Arbeits- und Organisationspsychologie im englischsprachigen Bereich: Ein Diskussionsbeitrag zur Zitationshäufigkeit. *Zeitschrift für Arbeits- und Organisationspsychologie* 34 (3): 155–158.

Freudenstein, Reinhold/ Beneke, Jürgen/ Pönisch, Helmut (eds.) *Language Incorporated. Teaching Foreign Languages in Industry.* Oxford/Ismaning: Pergamon/ Hueber.

Friedbichler, Michael/ Friedbichler, Ingrid/ Türp, Jens C. (2008) Wissenschaftliche Fachkommunikation im Zeitalter der Globalisierung. Trends, Herausforderungen und Lösungsansätze für die Zahnmedizin im deutschsprachigen Raum. *Deutsche Zahnärztliche Zeitschrift* 63 (12): 792–803/ *Schweizer Monatsschrift für Zahnmedizin* 118 (12): 1193–1203.

Friese, Eberhard (1990) Kontinuität und Wandel. Deutsch-japanische Kultur- und Wissenschaftsbeziehungen nach dem Ersten Weltkrieg. In Vierhaus/ vom Brocke, 801834.

Frietman, J./ Buis, Th./ Van Broekhoven, S./ Busse, G. (2001) *Bedarf an Fremdsprachenkenntnissen in niederländischen und deutschen Unternehmen im deutschniederländischen Grenzgebiet. Kurzbericht einer im Auftrag der EURES-Euregio RheinWaal & euregio rhein-maas-nord durchgeführten Studie.* Nijmegen: ITS. (www.euregio.org/intabox/medienarchive/publikationen/eurtaal_d.pdf)

Fröschle, Hartmut (ed.) (1979a) *Die Deutschen in Lateinamerika. Schicksal und Leistung.* Tübingen/ Basel: Erdmann.

——— (1979b) Zeittafel [Die Deutschen in Brasilien]. In Fröschle 1979a, 295–300.

———— / Hoyer, Hans (1979) Die Deutschen in Uruguay. In Fröschle, 742–766.

———— / Ritter, Alexander (eds.) (in preparation) *Bibliographie zur deutschen Sprache und deutschsprachigen Literatur im Ausland (1945 ff)* (Auslandsdeutsche Literatur der Gegenwart, 15). Hildesheim: Olms.

Funk, Hermann (2009) Berufsorientierter Fremdsprachenunterricht – erweiterte Anforderungsprofile in der Ausbildung von Lehrkräften. In Barkowski/ Demmig/ Funk/ Würz, 135–147.

———— (2010) Berufsorientierter Fremdsprachenunterricht. In Krumm/ Fandrych/ Hufeisen/ Riemer, Vol. 2, 1145–1151.

Furaschowa/ Kletschko (2010) Deutsch in Belarus. In Krumm/ Fandrych/ Hufeisen/ Riemer, Vol. 2, 1615–1619.

Furman, Nelly/ Goldberg, David/ Lusin, Natalia (2010) *Enrollments in Languages Other Than English in United States Institutions of Higher Education, Fall 2009*. O.O.: The Modern Language Association of America, Web Publication. (www.mla.org/pdf/2009_enrollment_survey.pdf)

Gabanyi, Anneli U. (1988) Die Deutschen in Rumänien. *Aus Politik und Zeitgeschichte* 50: 2839.

Gadeanu, Sorin (1998) *Sprache auf der Suche. Zur Identitätsfrage des Deutschen in Rumänien am Beispiel der Temeswarer Stadtsprache*. Regensburg: S. Roderer.

Gadet, Françoise (2008) Immigrant languages in France. In Ammon/ Haarmann, Vol. 1, 459–469.

Gage, William W. (1986) The world balance of languages. In Fishman, J. A. et al. (eds.) *The Fergusonian Impact*. Berlin/ New York/ Amsterdam: Mouton de Gruyter, 371–383.

Gahler, Michael (2004) Die Rolle der deutschen Sprache in der Zukunft der EU aus der Sicht eines Mitglieds des Europäischen Parlaments. In Lohse, 32–42.

Gal, Susan (1988) The political economy of code choice. In Heller, M. (ed.) *Codeswitching. Anthropological and Sociolinguistic Perspectives*. Berlin/ New York/ Amsterdam: Mouton de Gruyter, 245–264.

———— (1996) Language shift. In Goebl/ Nelde/ Zdeněk/ Wölck, 586–593.

Galle, Helmut (2002) "Germanistik" in Lateinamerika: Kulturwissenschaft als Perspektive? Kritische Bestandsaufnahme und Diskussion alternativer Konzepte. In Deutscher Akademischer Austauschdienst, 213–234.

Ganeshan, Vridhagiri (1990) German Studies in Indien: Möglichkeiten und Grenzen. Zur zentralen Bedeutung eines peripheren Faches. In Althof, 187–194.

Gardner, Robert C. (2001) Integrative motivation and second language acquisition. In Dörnyei, Z./ Schmidt, R. (eds.) *Motivation and Second Language Acquisition*. Honolulu: University of Hawai Press, 1–19.

———— / Lambert, Wallace E. (1959) Motivational variables in second-language acquisition. *Canadian Journal of Psychology* 13 (4): 266–272.

———— / ———— (1972) *Attitudes and Motivation in Second-Language Teaching*. Rowley: Newbury House.

———— / MacIntyre, Peter D. (1991) An instrumental motivation in language study. *Studies in Second Language Acquisition* 13: 57–72.

Gardt, Andreas (2000a) Sprachnationalismus zwischen 1850 und 1945. In Gardt (2000b), 247273.

———— (ed.) (2000b) *Nation und Sprache: die Diskussion ihres Verhältnisses in Geschichte und Gegenwart*. Berlin/ New York: de Gruyter.

———— (2004) Nation. In Ammon/ Dittmar/ Mattheier/ Trudgill, 369–377.

———— / Hüppauf, Bernd (eds.) (2004) *Globalization and the Future of German. With a Select Bibliography*. Berlin/ New York: Mouton de Gruyter.

Garfield, Eugene (1972) Citation analysis as a tool in journal evaluation. *Science* 178: 471–479.

———— (1976a) Journal citation studies 23: French journals. What they cite and what cites them. *Current Contents* 19 (4): 5–10.

———— (1976b) Journal citation studies 25: German journals. What they cite and vice versa. *Current Contents* 19 (18): 5–11.

———— (1977a) *Essays of an Information Scientist*. Volume 1, 1962–1973; Volume 2, 1974–1976. Philadelphia: Institute for Scientific Information.

———— [1974] (1977b) Let's erect a new Tower of Babel! In Garfield (1977a), Vol. 2, 172–174.

———— [1976] (1977c) Journal citation studies. 25. German journals. What they cite and vice versa. In Garfield (1977a). Vol. 2, 467–473.

———— (1979) *Citation Indexing – Its Theory and Application in Science, Technology, and Humanities*. New York: Wiley-Interscience.

———— / Welljams-Dorof, Alfred (1990) Language use in international research. A citation analysis. *Annals of the American Academy of Political and Social Science* 511: 10–24. [Reprinted as "The language of science revisited – English (only) spoken here. Introduction to language use in international research. A citation analysis." *Current Contents* 31 (July): 3–17].

Garrett, Peter (2005) Attitude measurements. In Ammon/ Dittmar/ Mattheier/ Trudgill, 12511260.

———/ Coupland, N./ Williams, A. (2003) *Investigating Language Attitudes: Social Meanings of Dialect, Ethnicity and Performance.* Cardiff: University of Wales Press.

Garrison, Fielding H. [1913] (1924) *An Introduction to the History of Medicine.* 4th edition, Philadelphia/ London: Saunders.

Gauger, Hans-Martin (1991) Auszug der Wissenschaften aus dem Deutschen? *Merkur* 45 (7): 582–594.

——— (2000) Warum nicht Englisch? In Debus/ Kollmann/ Pörksen, 19–45.

Gauler, Gabriele/ Treter, Clemens (2007) "Brücke nach Deutschland" – Das Goethe-Institut in China (1976–2006). In Ammon/ Reinbothe/ Zhu, 291–300.

Gauß, Karl-Markus (2005) *Die versprengten Deutschen. Unterwegs in Litauen, durch die Zips und am Schwarzen Meer.* Wien: Zsolnay.

Gawlitta, K./ Vilmar, F. (eds.) (2002) *"Deutsch nix wichtig?" Engagement für die deutsche Sprache ("German unimportant?" Commitment for the German Language).* Paderborn: vIFB.

Gazzola, Michele (2006a) Managing multilingualism in the European Union: language policy evaluation for the European Parliament. *Language Policy* 5 (4): 393–417.

——— (2006b) La gestione del multilinguismo nell'Unione europea. In Carli, Augusto (ed.) *Le sfide della politica linguistica di oggi. Frau la valorizzazione multilinguismo migratorio locale e le istanze del plurilinguismo europeo.* Mailand: Franco Angeli, 17–117.

———/ Grin, François (2007) Assessing efficiency and fairness in multilingual communication: Towards a general analytical framework. *AILA Review* 20: 87–106.

Gebhardt (1988) *Handbuch der deutschen Geschichte,* 22 Vols. 9th edition, München: DTV.

Gehler, Michael (2008) *Tirol im 20. Jahrhundert. Vom Kronland zur Europaregion.* Innsbruck/ Wien: Tyrolia/ Bozen: Athesia.

Gehnen, Marianne (1991) Die Arbeitssprachen in der Kommission der Europäischen Gemeinschaften unter besonderer Berücksichtigung des Französischen. Eine Fragebogenerhebung in den Generaldirektionen, konzipiert von Hartmut Kleineidam (1990) *Sociolinguistica* 5: 51–63.

Geiger-Jaillet, Anemone (2004) Zweisprachiger Unterricht in einem einsprachigen Land – bilinguales Lehren und Lernen in Frankreich, Schwerpunkt Elsass. In Bonnet, A./ Breidbach, S. (eds.) *Didaktiken im Dialog. Konzepte des Lehrens und Wege des Lernens im bilingualen Sachfachunterricht.* Frankfurt a.M.: Lang, 47–61.

——— (ed.) (2010) *Lehren und Lernen in deutschsprachigen Grenzregionen.* Bern: Lang.

Gellert-Novak, Anne (1993) Europäische Sprachenpolitik und Euroregionen: Ergebnisse einer Befragung zur Stellung der englischen und deutschen Sprache in Grenzgebieten. Tübingen: Narr.

——— (1994) Die Rolle der englischen Sprache in Euroregionen. *Sociolinguistica* 8, 123–135.

Gellner, Ernest (1983) *Nations and Nationalism.* Ithaka: Cornell University Press.

Genscher, Hans-Dietrich (1990) Prinzipien auswärtiger Kulturpolitik. *Jahrbuch Deutsch als Fremdsprache* 16: 293–301.

Georgas, Helen/ Cullars, John (2006) A citation study of the characteristics of the linguistics literature. *College and Research Libraries* 66 (6): 496–515.

Gerbore, Pietro (1964) *Formen und Stile der Diplomatie.* Reinbek bei Hamburg: Rowohlt.

Gerhards, Jürgen (1993) Westeuropäische Integration und die Schwierigkeiten der Entstehung einer europäischen Öffentlichkeit. *Zeitschrift für Soziologie* 22 (2): 96–110.

——— (2010) *Mehrsprachigkeit im vereinten Europa. Transnationales sprachliches Kapital als Ressource in einer globalisierten Welt.* Wiesbaden: VS-Verlag für Sozialwissenschaften.

Gerner, Zsuzsanna (2006) Identität – soziales Netzwerk – nationale Stereotypen. Zur Identitätsbildung und Identitätsforschung in den deutschen Sprachinseln in Ungarn. In Berend/ Knipf-Komlósi, 149–173.

Gerok, Wolfgang (2000) Deutsch als Wissenschaftssprache in der Medizin. In Debus/ Kollmann/ Pörksen, 229–239.

Gerrand, Peter (2008) Estimating linguistic diversity on the Internet: a taxonomy to avoid pitfalls and paradoxes. *Journal of Computer-Mediated Communication* 12 (4): article 8. (www.jcmc.indiana.edu/vol12/issue4/gerrand)

Gerschner, Robert (2011) Das Österreichische Kulturforum in Russland. In Ammon/ Kemper, 344–346.

Gerwald, Josef M. (1995) Auftrag des Auslandsrundfunks. In Mahle, 95–105.

Geschäfte statt Goethe (1980) Das internationale Interesse an der deutschen Sprache verändert sich. *DAAD Letter* 3: 8–10.

Gesche, Katja (2006) *Kultur als Instrument der Außenpolitik totalitärer Staaten. Das Deutsche Ausland-Institut 1933–1945.* Köln: Böhlau.

Gesellschaft für deutsche Sprache/ Institut für deutsche Sprache (eds.) (1999) *Förderung der Sprachkultur in Deutschland. Eine Bestandsaufnahme.* Wiesbaden: Gesellschaft für deutsche Sprache/ Institut für Deutsche Sprache.

Gester, Silke (2011) *Quo vasis, DaF? Betrachtungen zu Deutsch als Fremdsprache in der Tschechischen Republik.* Zlín: VeRBum.

Gethmann, Carl F. (2011) Die Sprache der Wissenschaft. In Berlin-Brandenburgische Akademie der Wissenschaften 2011, 57–63.

Geyer, Klaus (2005) Betriebliche Sprachplanung im Kontext innerer und äußerer Mehrsprachigkeit – am Beispiel der deutschen Großwerft. In Braun/ Kohn, 79–87.

Gibbs, W. Wayt (2002) Saving dying languages. *Scientific American* 287 (2): 78–86.

Giersberg, Dagmar (2002) *Deutsch unterrichten weltweit: Ein Handbuch für alle, die im Ausland Deutsch unterrichten wollen.* Bielefeld: Bertelsmann.

Gilbert, Glenn G. (ed.) (1971) *The German Language in America: A Symposium.* Austin/ London: University of Texas Press.

—— (1981) French and German: a comparative study. In Ferguson, C. A./ Heath, S. B. (eds.) *Language in the USA.* Cambridge: Cambridge University Press, 257–272. Giles, H. (ed.) (1977) *Language, Ethnicity and Intergroup Relations.* London: Academic Press.

—— / Bourhis, Richard Y./ Taylor, Donald M. (1977) Toward a theory of language in ethnic relations. In Giles, Howard (ed.) *Language Ethnicity and Intergroup Relations.* London: Academic Press, 307–348.

—— / Taylor, Donald M./ Bourhis, Richard Y. (1973) Toward a theory of interpersonal accommodation through language: some Canadian data. *Language in Society* 2: 177–192. Gill, Saran Kaur (2004) Medium of instruction policy in higher education in Malaysia: nationalism versus internationalisation. In Toffleson/ Tsui, 135–152.

—— (2007) Shift in language policy in Malaysia: unravelling reasons for change, conflict and compromise in nother-tongue education. *AILA Review* 20: 106–123.

Gilles, Peter (2009) Luxemburgisch in der Mehrsprachigkeit: Soziolinguistik und Sprachkontakt. In Elmentaler, 185–199.

—— / Moulin, Claudine (2009) Die soziale Praxis der Mehrsprachigkeit in Luxemburg. In Willems, H. et al. (eds.) *Handbuch der sozialen und erzieherischen Arbeit in Luxemburg.* Luxemburg: Saint Paul, 183–195.

—— / Seela, Sebastian/ Sieburg, Heinz/ Wagner, Melanie (2010) Sprachen und Identitäten. In IPSE – Identités Politiques Sociétés Espace (ed.) *Doing Identity in Luxemburg. Subjektive Aneignungen – Institutionelle Zuschreibungen – soziokulturelle Milieus.* Bielefeld: Transcript, 63–104.

Gilson, Miriam/ Zubrzycki, Jerzy (1967) *The Foreign-Language Press in Australia 1848–1964.* Canberra: Australian National University Press.

Ginsburgh, Victor et al. (2005) Disenfranchisement in linguistically diverse societies. The case of the European Union. *Journal of the European Economic Association* 3: 946–965.

—— / Weber, Shlomo (2005) Language disenfranchisement in the European Union. *Journal of Common Market Studies* 43: 273–286.

—— / —— (2011) *How Many Languages Do We Need? The Economics of Linguistic Diversity.* Princeton/ Oxford: Princeton University Press.

von Gizycki, Rainald (1973) Centre and periphery in the international scientific community: Germany, France and Great Britain in the 19th century. *Minerva* 11: 474–494.

Glazer, Nathan (1966) The process and problems of language maintenance: an integrative view. In Fishman/ Nahirni et al. 1966, 358–368.

Global Internet Statistics (By Language) (2003) Technical Report Global Reach (ed.). (www.glreach.com/globstats/)

Gloger, Axel (1999) Do you speak Internet? Die zunehmende Kommunikation per Netz verändert die deutsche Sprache. Ein Vorschlag: Englisch wird hier zu Lande zweite AmtsAmtssprache. *Die Welt* 21. Dez.1999: WW3.

Główny Urząd Statystyczny/ Central Statististical Office (2012) *Oświata o wychowanie wroku szkolnym 2011/2012/ Education in 2011/2012.* Warszawa/ Warsaw.

Gloy, Klaus (1975) *Sprachnormen I. Linguistische und soziologische Analysen.* Stuttgart-Bad Cannstatt: Frommann/ Holzboog.

Glück, Helmut (1979) *Die preußisch-polnische Sprachenpolitik: Eine Studie zur Theorie und Methodologie der Forschung über Sprachenpolitik, Sprachbewußtsein und Sozialgeschichte am Beispiel der preußisch-deutschen Politik gegenüber der polnischen Minderheit vor 1914.* Hamburg: Buske.

———— (1986/ 1987) Die deutsche Sprache in der Welt I (II). Ein Bericht über die (zur) Sprachpolitik der Wende. *Zeitschrift für Sprachwissenschaft* 5 (1): 138–147 und 6 (2): 249–258.

———— (1992) Die internationale Stellung des deutschen Sprache auf dem europäischen Arbeitsmarkt. In Kramer/ Weiß, 47–75.

———— (ed.) [1993] (2010) *Metzler Lexikon Sprache.* 4th edition, Stuttgart/ Weimar: Metzler.

———— (1994) Sprachpolitik ist Kulturpolitik. *Zeitschrift für Kulturaustausch* 44 (4): 522–528.

———— (2002) *Deutsch als Fremdsprache in Europa vom Mittelalter bis zur Barockzeit.* Berlin/ New York: de Gruyter.– (2013) *Die Fremdsprache Deutsch im Zeitalter der Aufklärung, der Klassik und der Romantik. Grundzüge der deutschen Sprachgeschichte in Europa.* Wiesbaden: Harrassowitz.

———— / Wigger, Arnd (1979) Kategoriale und begriffliche Probleme der Forschung über Sprach(en)politik. *Osnabrücker Beiträge zur Sprachtheorie* 12: 6–18.

Gnutzmann, Claus (ed.) (2008a) *English in Academia. Catalyst or Barrier?* Tübingen: Narr.

———— (2008b) Fighting or Fostering the Dominance of English in Academic Communication? In Gnutzmann (2008a), 73–91.

Gnutzmann, Claus/ Lipski-Buchholz, Kathrin (2008) Englischsprachige Studiengänge: Was können sie leisten, was geht verloren? In Gnutzmann (2008a), 147–168.

Goebl, Hans (1984) *Dialektometrische Studien. Anhand italoromanischer, rätoromanischer und galloromanischer Sprachmaterialien aus AIS und ALF.* 3 Vols. Tübingen: Niemeyer.

———— (1989) Quelque remarques relatives auch concepts ,Abstand' et ,Ausbau' de Heinz Kloss. In Ammon 1989d, 278–290.

———— (1997) Die altösterreichische Sprachenvielfalt und -politik als Modellfall von heute und morgen. In Rinaldi, U./ Rindler-Schjerve, R./ Metzeltin, M. (eds.) *Sprache und Politik. Die Politik der Donaumonarchie und ihre Aktualität.* Wien: Italienisches Kulturinstitut in Wien/ Institut für Romanistik der Universität Wien, 103–121 + Karten und Figuren am Buchanfang.

———— (1999) Die Sprachensituation in der Donaumonarchie. In Ohnheiser, I./ Kienpointner, M./ Kalb, H. (eds.) *Sprachen in Europa. Sprachsituation und Sprachpolitik in europäischen Ländern.* Innsbruck: Institut für Sprachwissenschaft der Universität, 33–59.

———— (2010) *English only* – ein Aufschrei. In Schröder, H./ Bock, U. (eds.) *Semiotische Weltmodelle. Mediendiskurse in den Kulturwissenschaften. Festschrift für Eckhard Höfner zum 65. Geburtstag.* Berlin: LIT-Verlag, 189–214.

———— / Nelde, Peter/ Starý, Zdeněk/ Wölck, Wolfgang (eds.) (1996/ 1997) *Kontaktlinguistik. Ein internationales Handbuch zeitgenössischer Forschung.* Vol. 1/ 2. Berlin/ New York: de Gruyter.

Goethe-Institut (1988) *Leitlinien für die Arbeit des Goethe-Instituts im Ausland.* München: Goethe-Institut.

———— (2000) *Deutsch als Fremdsprache. Zahlen im Überblick.* München: Goethe-Institut.

———— (ed.) (2001) *Murnau, Manila, Minsk. 50 Jahre Goethe-Institut.* München: Beck.

———— (2011) *Das Goethe-Institut fördert deutsche Minderheiten in Mitteleuropa, Osteuropa und Zentralasien.* [München]: Goethe-Institut. (www.goethe.de/ deutsche-minderheiten)

Goethe-Institut Prag (ed.) (2001) *Deutsch in der Tschechischen Republik.* Prag: Goethe-Institut Prag.

Goffman, Erving [engl. 1959] (2003) *Wir alle spielen Theater. Die Selbstdarstellung im Alltag.* München: Piper.

Goltschnigg, Dietmar/ Schwob, Anton (2004) *Zukunftschancen der deutschen Sprache in Mittel-, Südost- und Osteuropa.* Wien: Edition Praesens.

Gooskens, Charlotte (2007) The contribution of linguistic factors to the intelligibility of closely related languages. *Journal of Multilingual and Multicultural Development* 28 (6): 445–467.

———— / Heringa, Wilbert (2004) The position of Frisian in the Germanic language area. In D. Gilbers/ M. Schreuder/ N. Knevels (eds.) *On the Boundaries of Phonology and Phonetics.* Groningen: University of Groningen, 61–87.

Goossens, Jan (1971) *Was ist Deutsch – und wie verhält es sich zum Niederländischen?* Bad Honnef: Kulturabteilung der Kgl. Niederländischen Botschaft, Bonn.

———— (1973) Niederdeutsche Sprache –Versuch einer Definition. In Goossens, J. (ed.) *Niederdeutsch, Vol. 1: Sprache.* Neumünster: Wachholtz, 9–27.

———— (1977) *Deutsche Dialektologie* (Sammlung Göschen 2205). Berlin/ New York: de Gruyter.

Gordin, Michael D. (2012) Translating textbooks: Russian, German and the language of chemistry. *Isis* 103: 88–98.

———— (2015) *Scientific Babel.* Chicago/ London: The University of Chicago Press.

Gore, James H. [1891] (1893) *A German Science Reader.* 2nd rev. ed. Boston: D.C. Heath.

Görlach, Manfred (1984) Weltsprache Englisch – eine neue Disziplin? *Studium Linguistik* 15: 1035.

———— (2001) *A Dictionary of European Anglicisms. A Usage Dictionary of Anglicisms in Sixteen European Languages*. Oxford: Oxford University Press.

———— (2002a) *An Annotated Bibliography of European Anglicisms*. Oxford: Oxford University Press.

———— (ed.) (2002b) *English in Europe*. Oxford: Oxford University Press.

Gorter, Durk (1987) Surveys of the Frisian language situation: some considerations of research methods on language maintenance and language shift. *International Journal of the Sociology of Language* 68: 41–56.

———— (2001) A Frisian update of reversing language shift. In Fishman 2001a, 215–233.

———— (2008) Frisian (West Frisian, North Frisian, Sater Frisian). In Ammon/ Haarmann, Vol. 1, 335348.

von Gostomski, Christian B. (2008) *Türkische, griechische, italienische und polnische Personen sowie Personen aus den Nachfolgestaaten des ehemaligen Jugoslawien in Deutschland. Erste Ergebnisse der Repräsentativbefragung "Ausgewählte Migranten in Deutschland 2006/2007"*. Nürnberg: Bundesamt für Migration und Flüchtlinge.

———— (2010) *Basisbericht: Berichtsband. Repräsentativbefragung "Ausgewählte Migranten in Deutschland 2006/2007". Zur Situation der fünf größten in Deutschland lebenden Ausländergruppen*. Nürnberg: Bundesamt für Migration und Flüchtlinge.

Gote, James H. [1891] (1893) *A German Science Reader*. 2nd revised edition. Boston: D. C. Heath.

Göttert, Karl-Heinz (2010) *Deutsch. Biographie einer Sprache*. Berlin: Ullstein.

———— (2013) *Abschied von Mutter Sprache. Deutsch in Zeiten der Globalisierung*. Frankfurt a.M.: Fischer.

Gottzmann, Carola L. (1984) Dokumentation Ägypten. Germanistik und Deutsch als Fremdsprache im Hochschulbereich. *Jahrbuch Deutsch als Fremdsprache* 10: 293–306.

Goudailler, Jean-Pierre (ed.) (1987) *Aspekte des Lëtzebuergeschen*. Hamburg: Buske.

Gould, Robert/ Riordan, Tanya (2010) Learning modern foreign languages in England and Wales. *Sociolinguistica* 24: 204–219.

Graddol, David [1997] (2000) *The Future of English*. London: British Council.

———— (1999) The decline of the native speaker. In Graddol/ Meinhof, 57–68.

———— (2006) *English Next. Why Global English May Mean the End of 'English as a Foreign Language'*. Plymouth: The British Council.

———— / Meinhof, Ulrike H. (eds.) (1999) *English in a Changing World. AILA Review* 13.

Gräfin Strachwitz, Helga (2002) Deutschland und das südliche Afrika – Ist Namibia für Deutschland heute noch relevant? *Namibia Magazin* 3: 10–12.

Gramstad, Sigve (1997) The European charter for regional or minority languages. In Røyneland, 91–97.

Gregoire, G./ Derderian, F./ Le Lorier, J. (1995) Selecting the language of the publications included in a meta-analysis: is there a Tower of Babel bias? *Journal of Clinical Epidemiology* 48 (1): 159–163.

Grenier, Gilles/ Vaillancourt, François (1983) An economic perspective on learning a second language. *Journal of Multilingual and Multicultural Development* 4: 471–483.

Grenoble, Lenore A./ Whaley, Lindsay J. (1998a) *Endangered Languages. Language Loss and Community Response*. Cambridge: Cambridge University Press.

———— / ———— (1998b) Towards a typology of language endangerment. In Grenoble/ Whaley (1998a): 2254. Gretschel, Hans-Volker (1994) Deutsch als Fremdsprache im postkolonialen unabhängigen Namibia. Bestandsaufnahme und Zukunftsperspektiven *Info DaF* 21 (6): 632–644.

———— (1995) The status and use of the German language in independent Namibia: Can German survive the transition? In Pütz, 299–312.

Greule, Albrecht (1999) Sprachloyalität – Sprachkultur – Sprachattraktivität. Warum noch Deutsch lernen? *Informationen Deutsch als Fremdsprache* 26 (5): 423–431.

———— (2002) Deutsch am Scheideweg: National- oder Internationalsprache? Neue Aspekte der Sprachkultivierung. In Hoberg (2002a), 54–66.

———— / Janich, Nina (2002) Sprachkulturen im Vergleich: Konsequenzen für Sprachenpolitik und internationale Wirtschaftskommunikation. *Forost-Arbeitspapier* Nr. 7. München: Forost.

Grice, H. P. ([1975] 1989) Logic and conversation. In Grice, H. P. (ed.) *Studies in the Way of Words*. Cambridge, MA: Harvard University Press, 22–40.

Grigat, Felix (2007) Deutsch als Wissenschaftssprache. Die Position des deutschen Hochschulverbandes. In Roggausch/ Giersberg, 9–22.

Griggs, David/ Rulon, Phillip J. (1953) *International Language of Aviation: Instrument Flight*. Cambridge: Educational Research Corporation.

Grillo, R. D. (1989) *Dominant Languages: Language and Hierarchy in Britain and France*. Cambridge: Cambridge University Press.

Grimes, Barbara F. (ed.) (1984/ 2000/ 2005) *Ethnologue: Languages of the World*. 10./ 11./ 12 edition, Dallas/ TX: Wycliffe Bible Translation.

Grimm, Dieter (1995) *Braucht Europa eine Verfassung?* München: Carl-Friedrich-von SiemensStiftung.

Grimm, Jacob [1846] (1884/1966) Über den Werth der ungenauen Wissenschaften. In Grimm, J. *Kleinere Schriften*, Vol. 7. Berlin/ Nachdruck Hildesheim: Olms 1966, 563–566.

———— [1848] (1868) *Geschichte der deutschen Sprache*. Leipzig: Hirzel.

———— / Grimm, Wilhelm (1854) *Deutsches Wörterbuch*. Erster Band. Leipzig: Hirzel.

Grin, François (1992) Towards a threshold theory of minority language survival. *Kyklos* 45: 6997. Wieder abgedr. In Lamberton, D. (ed.) (2002) *The Economics of Language*. Cheltenham: Edward Elgar, 49–76.

———— (1999a) Market forces, languages spread and linguistic diversity. In Kontra, M. et al. (eds.) *Language: A Right and a Resource*. Budapest: Central European University Press, 169–186.

———— (1999b) *Compétences et récompenses. La valeur des langues en suisse.* Fribourg: Editions Universitaires Fribourg.

———— (2000) The economics of English as a global language. In Kam, H. W./ Ward, C. (dir.) *Language in the Global Context*. Singapore: SEAMEO Regional Language Centre, Series No. 41, 284–303.

———— (2001) English as economic value: facts and fallacies. *World Englishes* 20 (1): 65–78.

———— (2004a) On the costs of linguistic diversity. In Van Parijs, Ph. (ed.) *Cultural Diversity and Economic Solidarity*. Bruxelles: De Boeck-Université, 189–202.

———— (2004b) Coûts et justice linguistique dans l'élargissement de l'Union européenne. *Panoramiques* 69: 97–104.

———— / Hexel, Dagmar/ Schwob, Irène (2006) *L'anglais pour tous au Cycle d'orientation: Le projet "Gecko".* Genf: Service de la recherche en éducation.

———— / Moring, T. (2002) *Support for Minority Languages in Europe. Final Report to European Commission Contract No 2000–1288/001–001 EDU-MLCEV.*

———— / Vaillancourt, François (1997) The economics of multilingualism: overview of the literature and analytical framework. In Grabe, W. (ed.) *Multilingualism and Multilingual Communities*. Cambridge: Cambridge University Press.

Gross, Alfredo (2001) *Hunsrücker Mundart in Brasilien. Dialektgedichte und Schriften in Deutscher und Portugiesischer Sprache*. Porto Alegre: Própria.

Gross, Feliks (1998) *The Civic and the Tribal State: The State, Ethnicity, and the Multiethnic State*. Westport, CT: Greenwood.

Gross, P. L. K./ Gross, E. M. (1927) College libraries and chemical education. *Science* 66: 385–389.

Grossmann, Robert (1999) *Main basse sur ma langue. Mini Sproch heisst Frejheit*. Strasbourg: Éditions La Nuée Bleue/ DNA.

Grote, Georg (2005) Vielsprachigkeit in Südtirol. Modell für Europa oder Kapitulation vor der Geschichte? *Acta Germanica. Jahrbuch des Germanistenverbandes im südlichen Afrika* 33: 6980.

———— (2009) *I bin a Südtiroler. Kollektive Identität zwischen Nation und Region im 20. Jahrhundert*. Bozen: Athesia.

Grözinger, Gerd/ Matiaske, Wenzel (2008) Bi-national oder inter-national? Wie misst man die Internationalität eines Studiengangs? *Forschung & Lehre* 15: 316f.

Gruber, Alfed (ed.) (1989) *Nachrichten aus Südtirol. Deutschsprachige Literatur in Italien*. Hildesheim, New York: Olms.

Grucza, Franciszek (1995) Zur Geschichte und Bedeutung der deutschen Sprache in Mitteleuropa. In Popp, 717–727.

———— (2001) Deutschunterricht und Germanistikstudium in Polen. In Helbig/ Götze/ Henrici/ Krumm, Vol. 2: 1528–1543.

———— (2010) Deutsch in Polen. In Krumm/ Fandrych/ Hufeisen/ Riemer, Vol. 2, 1761–1766.

———— (2014) Deutsche Sprache in Polen – Geschichte, Gegenwart, Zukunft. In Grucza, S./ Wierzbicka, M./ Alnajjar, J./ Bąk, P. (eds.) *Polnisch-deutsche Unternehmens-kommunikation. Ansätze zu ihrer linguistischen Erforschung*. Frankfurt/M.: Lang, 9–31.

———— et al. (1999) Expertise zur Situation des Deutschunterrichts und der Zusammenarbeit mit den Mittlerorganisationen in Polen. In Krumm, 114–152.

Grundmann, Siegfried (1965) Der Boykott der deutschen Wissenschaft nach dem ersten Weltkrieg. *Wissenschaftliche Zeitschrift der Technischen Universität Dresden* 14 (3): 799806.

Grypdonck, A. (1982) Language barriers and scientific communication. In Goetschalckx, J./ Rolling, L. (eds.) *Lexicography in the Electronic Age*. Amsterdam, 115–125.

———— (ed.) (1985) *Nederlands als taal van de wetenschap*. Utrecht/ Antwerpen: Aula.

Guardiano, Cristina/ Favilla, M. Elena/ Calaresu, Emilia (2007) Stereotypes about English as the language of science. *AILA Review* 20: 28–53.

Guardiolo, E./ Banos, J. E. (1993) Presence of abstracts of non-English journals indexed in MEDLINE (1981–1990). *Bulletin of the Medical Library Association* 81 (3): 320–322.

Guder, Andreas (2005) Chinesisch und der Europäische Referenzrahmen. Einige Beobachtungen zur Erreichbarkeit fremdsprachlicher Kompetenz(en) im Chinesischen. *Chun* 20: 63–78.

Gühring, Barbara (2002) Die Namibia Wissenschaftliche Gesellschaft. In Hess/ Becker, 248251.

Guilherme, Manuela (2007) English as a global language and education for cosmopolitan citizenship. *Language and Intercultural Communication* 7 (1): 72–90.

Gündisch, Konrad (1998) *Siebenbürgen und die Siebenbürger Sachsen*. München: Langen Müller.

Gunnarsson, Britt-Louise (2001) Swedish, English, French or German – the language situation at Swedish universities. In Ammon, 287–316.

Guseynova, Innara (2011) Der Germanisten- und Deutschlehrerverband Russlands. In Ammon/ Kemper, 382–388.

Ha, Su-Guen (2003) Zum Bedarf von Kenntnissen der deutschen Sprache und Kultur in Korea auch in Zukunft. In Ammon/ Chong, 397–404.

Haarburger, Werner (1974) *Science German S. S. I.* 2 Vols. 3rd. ed. Glen Waverley. VIC: Artemis Educational Materials.

Haarmann, Harald [1972] (1973a) *Soziologie der kleinen Sprachen Europas, Vol. 1: Dokumentation*. 2nd revised edition, Hamburg: Buske.

————— (1973b) *Grundfragen der Sprachenregelung in den Staaten der Europäischen Gemeinschaft*. Hamburg: Stiftung Europa-Kolleg.

————— (1974) Sprachpolitische Organisationsfragen der Europäischen Gemeinschaft. Hamburg: Stiftung Europa-Kolleg.

————— (1984a) Sprachplanung und Prestigeplanung. *Europa Ethnica* 41 (2): 81–89.

————— (1984b) The role of German in modern Japanese mass media: aspects of ethnocultural stereotypes and prestige functions of language in Japanese society. *Hitotsubashi Journal of Social Studies* 16 (1): 31–41.

————— (1986) *Language in Ethnicity: A View of Basic Ecological Relations*. Berlin/ New York: Mouton de Gruyter.

————— (1988) Sprachen- und Sprachpolitik. In Ammon/ Dittmar/ Mattheier, 1660–1678.

————— (1989) *Symbolic Values of Foreign Language Use. From the Japanese Case to a General Sociolinguistic Perspective*. Berlin/ New York: de Gruyter.

————— (1990) Language planning in the light of a general theory of language: a methodological framework. *International Journal of the Sociology of Language* 86: 103–126.

————— (1992) Measures to increase the importance of Russian within and outside the Soviet Union – A case of covert language spread policy. *International Journal of the Sociology of Language* 95: 109–129.

————— (1993) *Die Sprachenwelt Europas: Geschichte und Zukunft der Sprachnationen zwischen Atlantik und Ural*. Darmstadt: Wissenschaftliche Buchgesellschaft.

————— (1994) Symbolische Internationalisierung in Japan und die Rolle des Deutschen. In Ammon 1994d, 117–143.

————— (2001a) *Die Kleinsprachen der Welt – Existenzbedrohung und Überlebenschancen. Eine umfassende Dokumentation*. Frankfurt a.M.: Lang.

————— (2001b) *Babylonische Welt. Geschichte und Zukunft der Sprachen*. Frankfurt a.M./ New York: Campus.

————— (2002a) *Sprachenalmanach. Zahlen und Fakten zu allen Sprachen der Welt*. Frankfurt a.M./ New York: Campus.

————— (2002b) Sprachenvielfalt im Globalisierungsprozess. In Hoberg (2002a), 9–29.

————— (2004) Abstandsprache – Ausbausprache. In Ammon/ Dittmar/ Mattheier/ Trudgill, 238–249.

————— (2005a) Linguistic barriers between speech communities and language choice in international contacts. In Ammon/ Dittmar/ Mattheier/ Trudgill, 1521–1535.

————— (2005b) Roofless dialects. In Ammon/ Dittmar/ Mattheier/ Trudgill, 1545–1551.

————— (2005c) The politics of language spread. In Ammon/ Dittmar/ Mattheier/ Trudgill, 1653–1666.

————— unter Mitarb. von Anna-Liisa V. Haarmann (1974) *Sprachpolitische Organisationsfragen der Europäischen Gemeinschaft* (Schriftenreihe der Europäischen Integration 13). Hamburg: Sasse.

————— / Holman, Eugene (2001) The impact of English as a language of science in Finland and its role for the transition to network society. In Ammon, 229–260.

Haas, Walter (2006) 172a. Die Schweiz/ Switzerland. In Ammon/ Dittmar/ Mattheier/ Trudgill 2004–2006, 1772–1787.

Haataja, Kim (2010) Deutsch in Finnland. In Krumm/ Fandrych/ Hufeisen/ Riemer, Vol. 2, 16541658.

Haberland, Hartmut (1990) Whose English, nobody's business. *Journal of Pragmatics* 13: 927938.

———— (2013) Englisch als "Welt"-Sprache im Hightech-Kapitalismus. *Das Argument* 55 (6): 830–839.

Habermas, Jürgen [1962] (1990) *Strukturwandel der Öffentlichkeit. Untersuchungen zu einer Kategorie der bürgerlichen Gesellschaft.* New edition, Frankfurt a.M.: Suhrkamp.

———— (1995) Remarks on Dieter Grimm's "Does Europe Need a Constitution?" *European Law Journal* 1 (3): 303–307.

———— (1998a) *Die postnationale Konstellation. Politische Essays.* Frankfurt a.M.: Suhrkamp.

———— (1998b) Was ist ein Volk? Zum politischen Selbstverständnis der Geisteswissenschaften im Vormärz. In Habermas (1998a), 13–46.

———— (2001/2006) *Zeit der Übergänge.* Frankfurt a.M.: Suhrkamp/ *Time of Transitions.* Cambridge, MA: MIT Press.

Haensch, Günther (1975) *Wörterbuch der internationalen Beziehungen und der Politik.* 2nd edition, München: Hueber.

Hagège, Claude [frz. 1992] (1996) *Welche Sprache für Europa? Verständigung in der Vielfalt.* Frankfurt a.M./ New York: Campus.

———— (2006) *Combat pour le Français. Au nom de la diversité des langues et des cultures.* Paris: Odile Jacob.

Hagen, Stephen (1986) German – the first foreign language of Northern English industry. In Brown, 23–26.

———— (ed.) (1988) *Languages in British Business: An Analysis of Current Needs.* Newcastle-upon-Tyne: Polytechnic Products/ Centre for Information on Language Teaching and Research.

———— (ed.) (1999) *Business Communication Across Borders. A Study of Language Use and Practice in European Companies.* London: CILT.

———— (2010) Mapping successful language use in international business: how, when and where do European companies achieve success? In Stickel, 23–34.

Hägi, Sara/ Scharloth, Joachim (2005) Ist Standarddeutsch für Deutschschweizer eine Fremdsprache? *Linguistik online* 24 (3):1–26. (www.linguistikonline.de/24_05/haegiScharloth.)

Hahn, Karola (2004) *Die Internationalisierung der deutschen Hochschulen. Kontexte, Kernprozesse, Konzepte und Strategien.* Wiesbaden: Verlag für Sozialwissenschaften.

Hall, C. Michael/ Page, Stephen J. [1999] (2002) *The Geography of Tourism and Recreation. Environment, Place and Space.* 2nd edition, London/ New York: Routledge.

Haller, Martin/ Hepp, Hermann/ Reinold, Emil [1998] (1999) Tötet der "Impact-Factor" die deutsche Sprache? *Der Chirurg BDC* 38 (2): 39–41.

Hamel, Rainer E. (2003a) Regional blocs as a barrier against English hegemony? The Language Policy of Mercosur in South America. In Maurais/ Morris, 111–142.

———— (2003b) *El español como lengua de las ciencias frente a la globalización del inglés. Diagnóstico y propuestas de acción para una política latinoamericana del lenguaje en el campo de las ciencias y la educación superior* [Spanish as a Language of Science in the Face of the Globalization of English. Diagnosis and Proposals for a Latin American Policy for Language in the Field of Sciences and Higher Education]. México: UAM. (www.atriumlinguarum. org/contenido/Esp%C3%B1vsEng.pdf)

———— (2005) El español en el campo de las ciencas: propuestas para una política del lenguaje [The Spanish Language in the Field of Sciences: Proposals for a Language Policy]. In Centro de Estudios Lingüísticos y Literarios (ed.) *Congreso Internacional sobre Lenguas Neolatinas en la Comunicatión Especializada* [International Congress on Neolatin Languages in Specialized Communication] México: Agence Intergouvernementale de la Francophonie, El Colegio de México, Unión Latina.

———— (2006a) The development of language empires. In Ammon/ Dittmar/ Mattheier/ Trudgill, 2240–2257.

———— (2006b) Spanish in science and higher education: perspectives for a plurilingual language policy in the Spanish speaking world. *Current Issues in Language Planning* 7 (1): 44–60.

———— (2007) The dominance of English in the international scientific periodical literature and the future of language use in science. *AILA Review* 20: 53–72.

Hamm-Brücher, Hildegard (1980) *Kulturbeziehungen weltweit. Ein Werkstattbericht zur Auswärtigen Kulturpolitik.* München: Hanser.

Handbuch des Deutschtums im Auslande [1904] (1906) 2nd edition, Berlin: Reimer.

Handelskammer Hamburg (ed.) (June 1989) *Konsulats- und Mustervorschriften.* 28th edition, Hamburg: Carl H. Dieckmann.

Handelskammer Hamburg (ed.) (2005) *Export-Nachschlagewerk "K und M". Konsulats- und Mustervorschriften.* 36th edition, Hamburg: Dieckmann.

Hannequart, Jean-Michel (2013) L'enseignement de l'allemand en France. Bilan et perspectives. *Document – Revue du dialogue franco-allemand* 4.

Hanuljaková, Helena (2009) Zukunftsvisionen Deutsch als Fremdsprache aus der Perspektive des Internationalen Deutschlehrerverbands (IDV). In Barkowski/ Demmig/ Funk/ Würz, 165–178.

Hardt, Michael/ Negri, Antonio (2000) *Empire*. Cambridge, MA/ London: Harvard University Press.

Harmon, David (1996) The status of the world's languages as reported by the *Ethnologue*. *Southwest Journal of Linguistics* 14 (1–2): 1–28.

Harmstorf, Ian/ Cigler, Michael (1985) *The Germans in Australia*. Melbourne: AE Press.

Harnisch, Rüdiger (1996) Das Elsass. In Hinderling/ Eichinger, 413–457.

Harnisch, Thomas (1999) *Chinesische Studierende in Deutschland. Geschichte und Wirkung ihrer Studienaufenthalte in den Jahren von 1860 bis 1945*. Hamburg: Institut für Asienkunde.

——— (2000) Militärische Ausbildung und Universitätsausbildung – Chinesisches Deutschlandstudium vor dem Ersten Weltkrieg. In Ch. Kaderas/ M. Hong (eds.) *120 Jahre chinesische Studierende an deutschen Hochschulen*. Bonn: Deutscher Akademischer Austauschdienst, 19–44.

Harry, Werner (1988) *Deutsche Schulen im Ausland*. Berlin: Westkreuz-Verlag.

Hartig, Falk (2009) Mit Konfuzius ins 21. Jahrhundert – Chinas Auswärtige Kulturpolitik. In Maaß (2009a), 401–410.

——— (2014) Konfuzius sagt: Klasse statt Masse. *Kulturaustausch* (2): 61.

Hartley, James et al. (2007) Lost in translation: contributions of editors to the meanings of text. *Journal of Information Science* XX (X): 1–15.

Hartman, John D. (1967) PH.D. language requirements modified. *Science* 155: 626.

Hartmann, Reinhard (ed.) (1996) *The English Language in Europe*. Oxford: Intellect.

Hartweg, Frédéric (1981) Sprachkontakt und Sprachkonflikt im Elsaß. In Meid/ Heller, 97–113.

——— (1983) Tendenzen in der Domänenverteilung zwischen Dialekt und nicht-deutscher Standardsprache am Beispiel des Elsaß. In Besch, W./ Knoop, U./ Putschke, W./ Wiegand, H. E. (eds.) *Dialektologie*, Vol. 2. Berlin/ New York: de Gruyter, 1428–1443.

——— (1988) L'alsacien. Un dialecte allemand tabou. In *Vingt-cinq communautés linguistiques de la France*. Tome premier: *Langues régionales et langues non territorialisées*. Paris: Éditions L'Harmattan, 33–86.

——— (1997) Das Elsaß: Stein des Anstoßes und Prüfstein der deutsch-französischen Beziehungen. In Picht, R./ Hoffmann-Martinot, V./ Lasserre, R./ Theiner, P. (eds.) *Fremde Freunde. Deutsche und Franzosen vor dem 21. Jahrhundert*. München/ Zürich: Piper, 62–84.

Hartwig, Stefan (2001) *Deutschsprachige Medien im Ausland – fremdsprachige Medien in Deutschland*. Münster: LIT Verlag.

Harwood, Hake/ Giles, Howard/ Bourhis, Richard Y. (1994) The genesis of vitality theory: historical patterns and discoursal dimensions. *International Journal of the Sociology of Language* 108: 167–206.

Haselhuber, Jakob (1991) Erste Ergebnisse einer empirischen Untersuchung zur Sprachsituation in der EG-Kommission. *Sociolinguistica* 5: 37–50.

——— (2012) *Mehrsprachigkeit in der Europäischen Union. Eine Analyse der EU-Sprachenpolitik, mit besonderem Fokus auf Deutschland. Umfassende Dokumentation und Perspektiven für die Zukunft*. Frankfurt a.M.: Lang.

Haslinger, Peter/ Janich, Nina (eds.) (2005) Sprache der Politik – Politik mit Sprache. *Forost Arbeitspapier* Nr. 29. München: Forost.

Haße, Wolfgang (2002) Englisch versus Deutsch in der Medizin. Thesen, Realitäten, Gegenworte. In Ehlich, K. (ed.) *Mehrsprachige Wissenschaft – europäische Perspektiven. Eine Konferenz im Europäischen Jahr der Sprachen*. München. (www. euro-sprachenjahr.de/hasse.pdf.)

——— / Fischer, Rudolf J. (2003) Ärzteschaft gegen Anglisierung der Medizin. *Deutsche Medizinische Wochenschrift* 128: 1338–1341.

——— / Fischer, Rudolf J. (2010) Zitierverhalten deutscher Autoren in "Der Chirurg". Publizieren unter der Dominanz des Impact-Faktors. *Der Chirurg* (4): 361–363.

——— et al. (2007) Wissenschaft ist mehrsprachig – auch in der Chirurgie. *Chirurgische Allgemeine Zeitung für Klinik und Praxis* 8 (5): 255–260. Haszpra, Otto (2004) The price of a common language. *Begegnungen*, Series of Europa Institut Budapest 22: 215–222.

Hattenhauer, Hans (2000) Zur Zukunft des Deutschen als Sprache der Rechtswissenschaft. In Debus/ Kollmann/ Pörksen, 255–273.

Hattesen, Anni B./ Haagen, Kiil (1979) Deutsch als Fremdsprache in Dänemark. *Germanistische Mitteilungen* 10: 75–83.

Haubrichs, Wolfgang (1996) Der Krieg der Professoren. Sprachhistorische und sprachpolitische Argumentation in der Auseinandersetzung um Elsaß-Lothringen zwischen 1870 und 1918. In Marti, 213–250.

Hauenschild, Christa (2004) Maschinelle Übersetzung – die gegenwärtige Situation. In Kittel, H. et al. (eds.) *Übersetzung/ Translation/ Tradiction. Ein internationales Handbuch zur Übersetzungsforschung/* . . .,Vol. 1. Berlin/ NewYork: de Gruyter, 756–766.

Haug, Sonja (2008) *Sprachliche Integration von Migranten in Deutschland* (Working Paper 14). O. O. [Nürnberg]: Bundesamt für Migration und Flüchtlinge.

Haugen, Einar (1966) Linguistics and language planning. In Bright, 50–71.

———— (1972a) *The Ecology of Language*. Standford, CA: Stanford University Press.

———— (1972b) *Language in Ethnicity: A View of Basic Ecological Relations*. Berlin/ New York: Mouton de Gruyter.

———— (1987) Language planning. In Ammon/ Dittmar/ Mattheier, 626–637.

Hauschildt, Jürgen/ Vollstedt, Marina (2002) Unternehmenssprachen oder Company Language? Zur Einführung einer einheitlichen Sprache in global tätigen Unternehmen. *Zeitschrift Führung und Organisation*. 71 (3): 173–183.

Häusler, Maja (1998) *Zur Geschichte des Deutschunterrichts in Kroatien seit dem 18. Jahrhundert*. Frankfurt a.M.: Lang.

Hausmann, Hartmut (2001) Deutsch als Amtssprache? Bislang scheiterte es am Geldmangel im Europarat. *Das Parlament* vom 11.5.2001: 17.

Haut Conseil de la Francophonie présidé par le Président de la République Française (1986) *Rapport sur l'état de la francophonie dans le monde*. Paris: La Documentation Française.

Havemann, Frank (2009) *Einführung in die Bibliometrie*. Berlin: Gesellschaft für Wissenschaftsforschung.

Hawking, Stephen [English 2001] (2001) *Das Universum in der Nussschale*. [Hamburg:] Hoffmann und Campe.

Hayakawa, Tōzō (1994) Die Gesellschaft zur Förderung der Germanistik, Tokio, und die einheitliche Deutschprüfung für ganz Japan. In Ammon 1994d, 295–299.

He, Yun (2013) *Die Auswirkungen der englischsprachigen Studiengänge in Deutschland auf das Deutschlernen in China*. Frankfurt a.M.: Lang.

Heckhausen, Heinz (1986) Dissemination psychologischer Forschung: Internationalisierung, Europäisierung und gemeinsprachliche Rückvermittlung. In Kalverkämper/ Weinrich, 33–37.

Heckmann, Friedrich (1997) Ethnos – eine imaginierte oder reale Gruppe? Über Ethnizität als soziologische Kategorie. In Hettlage, F./ Deger, P./ Wagner, S. (eds.) *Kollektive Identität in Krisen. Ethnizität in Region, Nation, Europa*. Opladen: Westdeutscher Verlag, 46–55.

Heide, Walther (ed.) (1935) *Handbuch der deutschsprachigen Zeitungen im Ausland*. Berlin/ Leipzig: de Gruyter.

Heine, Bernd (1979) *Sprache, Gesellschaft und Kommunikation in Afrika*. München/ London: Weltforum Verlag.

Heinemann, Manfred (ed.) (2000) *Fakten und Zahlen zum DAAD. Personen, Programme und Projekte – ein Rundblick*. Bonn: Deutscher Akademischer Austauschdienst (DAAD).

Heintze, Hans-Joachim (ed.) (1998) *Moderner Minderheitenschutz. Rechtliche oder politische Absicherung?* Bonn: Dietz.

Heise, Eloá/ Aron, Irene (2002) Germanistik in Brasilien: analyse einer Krise. In Deutscher Akademischer Austauschdienst, 53–67.

Helbig, Gerhard/ Götze, Lutz/ Henrici, Gert/ Krumm, Hans-Jürgen (eds.) (2001) *Deutsch als Fremdsprache. Ein internationales Handbuch*. 2 Halbbände. Berlin/ New York: de Gruyter.

Hellmann, Friedrich W. (ed.) (2000) *Mit dem DAAD in die Welt. Ausländer und Deutsche erzählen von ihren Erlebnissen – ein Lesebuch*. Bonn: Deutscher Akademischer Austauschdienst (DAAD).

Hellmann, Jochen/ Pätzold, Mathias (2005) Internationale Studiengänge: Wer braucht so etwas? Überlegungen zu einem Trend, der sich fortsetzen wird. In Motz (2005a), 17–29.

Hemblenne, Bernard (1992) Les prolèmes du siège et du linguistique des Communautés européennes (1950–1967). In Heyen, E. V. (ed.) *Die Anfänge der Verwaltung der Europäischen Gemeinschaft*. Baden-Baden: Nomos, 107–143.

Hempel, Carl G. (1952) *Fundamentals of Concept Formation in Empirical Science*. Chicago: The University Press.

Henkes, André (2005) Die deutsche Sprache als Rechtssprache im belgischen Gerichtswesen im Allgemeinen, und am belgischen Kassationshof im Besonderen – kritische Darstellung des Seins und Werdens eines Grundrechts. In Stangherlin, 163–214.

Henn-Memmesheimer, Beate/ Bahlo, Christine/ Eggers, Ernst/ Mkhitaryan, Samvel (2012) Zur Dynamik eines Sprachbildes: Nachhaltig. In Hansen-Kokorus, R./ Henn-Memmesheimer, B./ Seybert, G. (eds.) *Sprachbilder und kulturelle Kontexte*. St. Ingbert: Röhrig, 159–186.

Henning, Eckart (1998) Auslandsbeziehungen der Kaiser-Wilhelm-/ Max-Planck-Gesellschaft im Überblick (1911–1998). In Vom Bruch, R./ Henning, E. (eds.) *Wissenschaftsfördernde Institutionen im Deutschland des 20. Jahrhunderts.* Berlin: MPG-Archiv, 95–113.

Héraud, Guy (1981) La Communauté Éuropéenne et la question linguistique. *Revue d'integration européenne* 5: 5–28.

——— (1989) Deutsch als Umgangs- und Muttersprache in der Europäischen Gemeinschaft. Synthesebericht. In Kern, 19–122.

Herbillon, Michael (2003) *Rapport d'information sur la diversité linguistique dans l'Union européenne.* Document N° 902, Délégation de l'Assemblée nationale pour l'Union européenne.

Herbst, Thomas/ Heath, David/ Dedering, Hans-Martin (1980) *Grimm's Grandchildren. Current Topics in German Linguistics.* London/ New York: Longman.

Herde, Dieter/ Royce, David (1989) *Vertrag in der Tasche.* London: Edward Arnold.

Herder, Johann G. (1772) *Abhandlung über den Ursprung der Sprache welche den von der Königl. Academie der Wissenschaften für das Jahr 1770 gesezten Preis erhalten hat.* Berlin: Christian Friedrich Voß.

Herfarth, Ch./ Schürmann, G. (1996) Deutsche klinische Zeitschriften und der Impact Faktor. *Chirurg* 67 (4): 267–299.

Herma-Herrle, Benita (2002) Radio hör'n. Der deutsche Dienst der NBC. In Hess/ Becker, 63–66.

Hermand, Jost (1999) Zur Situation der deutschen Sprache und Literatur in den USA. *Jahrbuch Deutsch als Fremdsprache* 25: 327–337.

Hermann, Armin (2000) Das goldene Zeitalter der Physik. In Debus/ Kollmann/ Pörksen, 209227.

——— / et al. (1978) *Deutsche Nobelpreisträger. Deutsche Beiträge zur Natur- und Geisteswissenschaft am Beispiel der Nobelpreisverleihungen für Frieden, Literatur, Medizin, Physik und Chemie.* München: Moos.

Hermann, Elke (2011) Englischzwang kein Spaß. *Forschung & Lehre* 18: 610.

Hermanns, Fritz (1991) Adieu Fremdwort! *Sprachreport* (1): 7 f.

Hernig, Marcus (2005) *Deutsch als Fremdsprache. Eine Einführung.* Wiesbaden: VS Verlag für Sozialwissenschaften.

——— (2007) Die Politik der deutschsprachigen Länder zur Förderung der deutschen Sprache in China. In Ammon/ Reinbothe/ Zhu, 261–268.

——— (2010) Deutsch in China. In Krumm/ Fandrych/ Hufeisen/ Riemer, Vol. 2, 1637–1642.

——— / Zhu, Jianhua (2004) Deutsch als Fremdsprache und Germanistik in China. Eine Entwicklung in Phasen. *Jahrbuch für Internationale Germanistik* 35 (2): 35–52.

Herrera, Antonio J. (1999) Language bias discredits the peer-review system. *Nature* 397: 467.

Herreras, José Carlos (2002) Quelle(s) langue(s)pour l'Union Européenne. In Weydt, H. (ed.) *Langue – communauté – signification. Approches en linguistique fonctionnelle.* Frankfurt a.M.: Lang, 34–39.

Herta, Angelika/ Jung, Martin (eds.) (2011) *Vom Rand ins Zentrum. Die deutsche Minderheit in Bukarest.* Berlin: Frank & Timme.

Hess, Hans-Werner (1992) *"Die Kunst des Drachentötens": Zur Situation von Deutsch als Fremdsprache in der Volksrepublik China.* München: Iudicium.

——— (2001) Deutschunterricht und Gemanistikstudium in China. In Helbig/ Götze/ Henrici/ Krumm, Vol. 2: 1579–1586.

——— (2007) Die Chancen des Deutschen neben dem Englischen in der Zukunft der Globalisierung. In Ammon/ Reinbothe./ Zhu, 322–353.

Heß (=Hess), Klaus A. (1993) Ein Goethe-Institut für Namibia! Interview mit I. E. SchimmingChase, Botschafterin von Namibia. Teil 2. *Namibia Magazin* 4: 10f.

Hess, Klaus A./ Becker, Klaus J. (eds.) (2002) *Vom Schutzgebiet bis Namibia 2000.* Göttingen/ Windhoek: Klaus Hess Verlag.

Hesse, Helmut (2000) Deutsch als Wissenschaftssprache aus der Sicht eines Nationalökonomen. In Debus/ Kollmann/ Pörksen, 277–281.

Hessky, Regina (1995) Die Rolle der großen Verkehrssprachen in Ostmitteleuropa am Beispiel Ungarn. In Wodak/ de Cillia, 63–74.

Hess-Lüttich, Ernest W. B./ Colliander, Peter/ Reuter, Ewald (eds.) (2009) *Wie kann man vom ,Deutschen' leben? Zur Praxisrelevanz der interkulturellen Germanistik.* Frankfurt a.M.: Lang.

Heublein, Ulrich/ Richter, Johanna/ Schmelzer, Robert/ Sommer, Dieter (2012) *Die Entwicklung der Schwund- und Studienabbruchquoten an den deutschen Hochschulen. Statistische Berechnungen auf der Basis des Absolventenjahrgangs 2010.* Hannover: HIS HochschulInformations-System GmbH.

Hewings, Martin (2006) English language standards in academic articles: attitudes of peer reviewers. *Revista Canaria de Estudios Ingleses* 53: 47–63.

Hexelschneider, Erhard (1980) Internationale Kulturbeziehungen und Deutsch als Fremdsprache. *Deutsch als Fremdsprache* 17 (3): 133–138.

———— (1981) 30 Jahre Ausländerstudium in der DDR – 25 Jahre Herder-Institut der Karl-MarxUniversität. *Deutsch als Fremdsprache* 18 (4): 193–199.

———— (1986) 30 Jahre Deutsch als Fremdsprache in der DDR – 30 Jahre Herder-Institut an der Karl-Marx-Universität. *Wissenschaftliche Zeitschrift der Karl-Marx-Universität Leipzig, Gesellschaftswissenschaftliche Reihe* 35 (1): 4–6.

———— / Wenzel, Johannes (1987) Deutsch als Fremdsprache an den Universitäten, Hoch- und Fachschulen der Deutschen Demokratischen Republik. In Sturm (1987a), 173–189.

Heyne, Jürgen (1978) Bilingualism and language maintenance among German speaking immigrants in Brazil. *Sociolinguistics*: 93–106.

Hilberg, Wolfgang (2000a) Die babylonische Sprachverwirrung wird ein Ende finden – durch Technik und nicht durch das Diktat einer Einheitssprache! In Debus/ Kollmann/ Pörksen, 299–308.

———— (2000b) Hat Deutsch als Wissenschaftssprache wirklich keine Zukunft? Internationale Kommunikation mit Hilfe intelligenter Textmaschinen. *Forschung & Lehre* 7 (12): 628–630.

———— (2008) *Sprache und Denken in neuronalen Netzen.* [Groß-Bieberau]: Sprache und Technik.

Hilgendorf, Suzanne K. (2001) *Language Contact, Convergence, and Attitudes: The Case of English in Germany.* Unpubl. PhD dissertation: University of Illinois, Urbana-Champaign.

———— (2005) "Brain gain statt [instead of] brain drain": the role of English in German education. *World Englishes* 24 (1): 53–67.

———— (2007) English in Germany: contact, spread and attitudes. *World Englishes* 26 (2): 131–148.

———— (2010) English and the global market: the language's impact in the German business domain. In Kelly-Holmes, H./ Mautner, G. (eds.) *Language and the Market.* New York: Palgrave Macmillan, 68–80.

———— (2013) Transnational media and the use of English: the case of cinema and motion picture titling practices in Germany. *Sociolinguistica* 27: 167–186.

Hilpold, Peter (2001) *Modernes Minderheitenrecht.* Wien: Manz/ Baden-Baden: Nomos/ Zürich: Schulthess.

———— (ed.) (2009) *Minderheitenschutz in Italien.* Wien: Braumüller.

Hinderdael, Michael/ Nelde, Peter (1996) Deutschbelgien. In Hinderling/ Eichiger, 459–478.

Hinderling, Robert (ed.) (1986) *Europäische Sprachminderheiten im Vergleich. Deutsch und andere Sprachen* (Deutsche Sprache in Europa und Übersee, 11). Wiesbaden: Steiner.

———— / Eichinger, Ludwig M. (eds.) (1996) *Handbuch der mitteleuropäischen Sprachminderheiten.* Tübingen: Narr.

Hirataka, Fumiya (1992) Language spread policy of Japan. In Ammon/ Kleineidam, 93–108.

———— (1994) Die Hintergründe der Verdrängung von Deutsch und Französisch durch Englisch aus japanischen Schulen nach 1945. In Ammon 1994d, 195–205.

———— (2007) Plurilingualismus im Fremdsprachenunterricht und Chancen des Deutschunterrichts in Japan. *Neue Beiträge zur Germanistik* 6 (2): 103–114.

Historical Abstracts, 1775–1945 (1955–1970). Santa Barbara, CA: Clio [continued as *Modern History Abstracts, 1775–1914* und *Twentieth Century Abstracts*].

Historical Abstracts on Disc 19–47 (1973ff.). Expand. Ed. Santa Barbara, CA: ABC-Clio/ Delaware Technologies.

Hoberg, Rudolf (ed.) (2002a) *Deutsch – Englisch – Europäisch. Impulse für eine neue Sprachpolitik.* Mannheim: Dudenverlag.

———— (2002b) English rules the World. Was wird aus Deutsch? In Hoberg (2002a), 171–183.

———— (2002c) Zur Stellung der deutschen Sprache in der Welt und in Europa. In Deutscher Akademischer Austauschdienst, 15–22.

———— (2004) English rules the world. What will become of German? In Gardt/ Hüppauf, 85–97.

———— (2012) Was wird aus Deutsch angesichts der Dominanz von Englisch? *Der Sprachdienst* 56 (1): 19–25.

———— (2013) Anglizismen und Sprachloyalität. Anmerkungen zu einem Beitrag von Horst Haider Munske. *Sprachreport* 29 (4): 2–5.

———— / Eichhoff-Cyrus, Karin M./ Schulz, Rüdiger (eds.) (2008) *Wie denken die Deutschen über ihre Muttersprache und über Fremdsprachen? Eine repräsentative Umfrage der Gesellschaft für deutsche Sprache.* In Zusammenarbeit mit dem Deutschen Sprachrat, durchgeführt vom Institut für Demoskopie Allensbach. Wiesbaden: Gesellschaft für deutsche Sprache.

Hobsbawm, Eric J. (1996) Are all tongues equal? Language, culture and national identity. In Barker, P. (ed.) *Living as Equals.* Oxford: Oxford University Press, 85–98.

Hoch, Paul/ Platt, Jennifer (1993) Migration and denationalization of science. In Crawford/ Shinn/ Sörlin, 133–152.

Hodges, Harry B. (1880) *A Course in Scientific German.* Boston: Ginn and Heath.

Hoekstra, Jarich F. (2001) Standard West Frisian. In Munske, 83–98.

Hoeren, Thomas (2003) Rechtliche Fragen der Einführung einer Hörfunkquote zu Gunsten neuer, deutschsprachiger Musiktitel. *Zeitschrift für Informations-, Telekommunikations- und Medienrecht* 8: 1–28 (separat auch München: Beck).

Hoffmann, Fernand (1979) *Sprachen in Luxemburg: Sprachwissenschaftliche und literaturhistorische Beschreibung einer Triglossie-Situation* (Deutsche Sprache in Europa und Übersee, 6). Wiesbaden: Steiner.

——— (1981) *Zwischenland: Dialektologische, mundartphilologische und mundartliterarische Grenzgänge.* Hildesheim/ New York: Olms.

——— (1987a) Spoo und die Folgen. Kritische Anmerkungen zum Sprachengesetz von 1984. *Galerie. Revue culturelle et pédagogique* 1.

——— (1987b) Pragmatik und Soziologie des Lëtzebuergeschen. Ein Versuch kommunikativer Sprachwissenschaft. In Goudaillier, 9–194.

——— (1987c) Lëtzebuergsch: Mundart und Nationalsprache. Sprachpolitische und sprachensoziologische Überlegungen zum luxemburgischen Triglossie-Problem und zum Sprachgesetz von 1984. In Brücher, W./ Franke, P. R. (eds.) *Probleme von Grenzregionen.* Saarbrücken: Philosophische Fakultät der Universität, 49–65.

——— (1988a) Luxemburg. In Ammon/ Dittmar/ Mattheier, 1334–1340.

——— (1988b) Zur Lage der deutschsprachigen Literatur in Luxemburg. *Rheinische Vierteljahresblätter* 52: 210–220.

——— (1989) Sprachen in Luxemburg. Unter besonderer Berücksichtigung der Situation nach 1945. *Jahrbuch für Internationale Germanistik* 20 (1): 45–62.

Hoffmann, Hellmut (2000) Politik der Bundesregierung Deutschlands zur Förderung der deutschen Sprache im Ausland. In Ammon 2000c, 61–71.

Hoffmann, Hilmar (ed.) (2000) *Deutsch global. Neue Medien – Herausforderungen für die Deutsche Sprache?* Köln: DuMont.

Hoffmann, Rolf (2009) In diplomatischer Mission – Die Außenkulturpolitik der USA. In Maaß (2009a), 359–368.

Hofman, John E. (1966) Mother tongue retentiveness in ethnic parishes. In Fishman/ Nahirni et al. 1966, 127–155.

Hofmann, Eberhard (2002) Ein Blick auf die Medien. In Hess/ Becker, 63–66. Hoheisel, Reinhard (2003) Notwendigkeit der EU-Organe – Amtssprachen, Arbeitssprachen, Osterweiterung. In Wills, W. (ed.) *Die Zukunft der internationalen Kommunikation in Europa (2000–2020).* Tübingen: Narr, 79–88.

——— (2004) Die Rolle der deutschen Sprache in der Zukunft der EU aus der Sicht der Europäischen Union. In Lohse, 73–84.

Höhmann, Beate (2011) *Sprachplanung und Spracherhalt innerhalb einer pommerischen Sprachgemeinschaft. Eine soziolinguistische Studie in Espírito Santo/ Brasilien.* Frankfurt a.M.: Lang.

Höhne, Günter (2000) Deutsch als Wissenschaftssprache in den Ingenieurwissenschaften. Zur Situation in der ehemaligen DDR und in Osteuropa. In Debus/ Kollmann/ Pörksen, 247255.

Höhne, Steffen/ Nekula, Marek (eds.) (1997) *Sprache, Wirtschaft, Kultur. Deutsche und Tschechen in Interaktion.* München: Iudicum.

Homans, George [1957] (1991) *The Human Group.* London: Routledge & Kegan Paul.

Honda, Yoshisaburo (1994) Motive für die Wahl von Deutsch als Fremdsprache und von Germanistik bei Studentinnen und Studenten. In Ammon 1994d, 275–283.

Honemann, Volker (2003) Usbekistan – Deutschland. Oder: wollen wir die Zukunft unserer Sprache und unserer Literatur weiterhin gefährden? *Zeitschrift für Literatur und Linguistik* 130: 134–136.

Hong, Myung-Soon/ Hong, Kyeong-Tae (2003) Die Bedeutung von Deutsch und anderen Fremdsprachen in der koreanischen Philosophie. In Ammon/ Chong, 57–70.

Honnef-Becker, Irmgard (2006) *Interkulturalität als neue Perspektive der Deutschdidaktik.* Nordhausen: Traugott Bautz.

——— /Kühn, Peter (eds.) (2004) *Über Grenzen. Literaturen in Luxemburg.* Esch/ Alzette: éditions phi.

Hopf, Henning (2011) Die Lage der Wissenschaftssprache Deutsch in der Chemie. In Wieland/ Glück/ Pretscher, 95–108.

Hornberger, Nancy H./ Pütz, Martin (eds.) (2006) *Language Loyalty, Language Planning and Language Revitalization. Recent Writings and Reflections.* Clevedon/ Buffalo/ Toronto: Multilingual Matters.

Horner, Kristine/ Weber, Jean J. (2008) The language situation in Luxemburg. *Current Issues in Language Planning* 9 (1): 69–128.

Horvath, Barbara M. (1981) Community languages in the schools: linguistic and cultural dilemmas. In Garner, 37–53.

Hostetler, John A. [1963] (2008) *Amish Society.* 4th edition, London: The Johns Hopkins University Press.

———— (1974) *Hutterite Society.* Baltimore/ London: The Johns Hopkins University Press.

House, Juliane (2002a) Maintenance and convergence in covert translation English-German. In Hassel, H. et al. (eds.) *Information Structure in a Cross-Linguistic Perspective.* Amsterdam: Rodopi, 199–213.

———— (2002b) Englisch als lingua franca – eine Bedrohung für die europäische Mehrsprachigkeit? In Barkowski, H/ Faistauer, R. (ed.) *Deutsch als fremde Sprache unter fremden Sprachen.* Tübingen: Stauffenburg, 62–73.

———— (2003a) English as a lingua franca: a threat to multilingualism? *Journal of Sociolinguistics* 7 (4): 556–578.

———— (2003b) English as a lingua franca and its influence on discourse norms in other languages. In James, G./ Anderson, G. (eds.) *Translation Today.* Clevedon: Multilingual Matters, 168180.

Huang, Chongling (2011) Motivationsforschung zu den neuen Germanistikstudenten in China. *Nouveaux Cahier d'allemend* 29 (1): 1–14.

Huber, Bettina J. (1992) Characteristics of foreign language requirements at US colleges and universities: findings from the MLA's 1987–89 survey of foreign language programs. *ADFL-Bulletin* 24 (1/ Fall): 8–16.

Huck, Dominique (1995a) Deutsch: Weder Mutter- noch Fremdsprache. Zum Erwerb des deutschen Standards bei elsässischen mundartsprechenden Grundschulkindern: soziolinguistische, linguistische und didaktische Fragen. *Germanistische Mitteilungen* 42: 83–102.

———— (1995b) L'enseignement bilingue à l'ecole préélémentaire et élémentaire: genèse, état des lieux et problèmes. In Bonnot, J.-F. (ed.) *Parole régionales, normes, variétés linguistiques et contexte social.* Strasbourg: Press universitaire, 113–137.

———— (1999) Les dialectes en Alsace – l'allemand standard. In Huck, D./ Laugel, A./ Laugner, M. (eds.) *L'eleve dialectophone en Alsace et se langues. L'enseignement de l'allemand aux enfants dialectophone a l'ecole primaire. De la description contrastive dialectes/ allemand à une approche methodologique. Manuel à usage de maîtres.* Strasbourg: Oberlin, 15–17.

———— (2007) Deutsch als Fremd-, Nachbar- und Regionalsprache im Elsass: Konsens und Konflikt. In Valentin, J.-M./ Silhouette, M. (eds.) *Akten des XI. Internationalen Germanistenkongresses Paris 2005 "Germanistik im Konflikt der Kulturen",* Vol. 3. Bern: Lang, 83–87.

———— / Bothorel-Witz, Arlette/ Geiger-Jaillet, Anemone (2007) L'Alsace et ses langues. Eléments de description d'une situation sociolinguistique en zone frontalière. In Abel/ Stuflesser/ Voltmer, 13–101.

Hudson, Manley O. (1932) Languages used in treaties. *The American Journal of International Law* 26: 368–372.

Huebener, Theodore (1961) *Why Johnny Should Learn Foreign Languages.* Philadelphia/ New York: Chilton.

Hufeisen, Britta/ Sorger, Brigitte (2010) Die internationale Institutionalisierung von Deutsch als Zweit- und Fremdsprache. In Krumm/ Fandrych/ Hufeisen/ Riemer, Vol. 1, 166–172.

Huffines, Marion L. (1980) Pennsylvania German: maintenance and shift. In *International Journal of the Sociology of Language* 25: 43–57.

———— (1986) Bemühungen um die Spracherhaltung bei deutschen Einwanderern und ihren Nachkommen in den USA. In Trommler, 253–262.

———— (1989) Convergence and language death: the case of Pennsylvania German. In Enninger/ Raith/ Wandt, 17–28.

———— (1994) Directionality of language influence: the case of Pennsylvania German and English. In Berend/ Mattheier, 47–58.

Hüllen, Werner (1992) Identifikationssprachen und Kommunikationssprachen. *Zeitschrift für germanistische Linguistik* 20: 298–317.

———— (2005) *Kleine Geschichte des Fremdsprachenlernens.* Berlin: Erich Schmidt.

———— (2007) The presence of English in Germany. *Zeitschrift für Fremdsprachenforschung* 18 (1): 326.

von Humboldt, Wilhelm [1809/1810] (1964) Berichte, Anträge, Denkschriften aus der Sektion für Kultus und Unterricht. In W. von Humboldt *Schriften zur Politik und zum Bildungswesen* (Werke in fünf Bänden, 4). Darmstadt: Wissenschaftliche Buchgesellschaft, 1–301.

Hume, David [1748] (2008) *An Enquiry Concerning Human Understanding.* Oxford: Oxford University Press.

Huneke, Hans-Werner/ Steinig, Wolfgang [1997] (2003) *Deutsch als Fremdsprache. Eine Einführung.* 3rd revised edition, Berlin: Erich Schmidt.

Hutchins, W. J./ Pargeter, L. J./ Saunders, W. L. (1971) *The Language Barrier: a Study in Depth of the Place of Foreign Language Materials in the Research Activity of the Academic Community*. Sheffield: University of Sheffield, Postgraduate School of Librarianship and Information Science.

Hutterer, Claus J. (1991) Die deutsche Volksgruppe in Ungarn. In Hutterer, C. J. (ed.) *Aufsätze zur deutschen Dialektologie*. Budapest: Tankönyvkiadó, 345–379.

Hyldgaard-Jensen, Karl (1987) Die Rolle der Deutschlehrerverbände bei der Verbreitung der deutschen Sprache. In Sturm (1987a), 223–228.

—— / Schmöe, Friedrich (eds.) (1982) *Der Bedarf der Gesellschaft an Fremdsprachenkenntnissen*. Kopenhagen: Reitzels.

Hyltenstam, Kenneth/ Stroud, Christopher (1996) Language maintenance. In Goebl/ Nelde/ Zdeněk/ Wölck, 567–578.

Ide, Sachiko (1982) Japanese sociolinguistics: politeness and women's language. *Lingua* 57: 357–385.

Ilg, Karl (1979) Situation und Leistung des Deutschtums in Brasilien nach dem 2. Weltkrieg. In Fröschle, 257–295. Ilse, Viktoria (2011) *Wirtschaftsdeutsch in Ungarn – Position, Bedarf und Perspektiven. Die Vermittlung von Wirtschaftsdeutsch im DaF-Unterricht in Ungarn*. München: Iudicium.

Imperialistische Sprachpolitik in den 70er und zu Beginn der 80er Jahre (1983) Ausgewählte Beiträge (Reihe Gesellschaftswissenschaften). Leipzig: Karl-Marx-Universität.

Industrie- und Handelskammer Nord Westfalen (2011) *Unternehmermangel. Demografischer Wandel in Nord-Westfalen*. (www.ihk-nordwestfalen.de/fileadmin/medien/02_Wirtschaft/00_Standortpolitik/Analysen_Positi onen/medien/Unternehmermangel_2011_150dpi.pdf)

Inoue, Fumio (2001) English as a language of science in Japan. From corpus planning to status planning. In Ammon, 447–469.

—— (2007) Changing economic values of German and Japanese. In Coulmas, 95–113.

Institut für Deutsche Sprache (ed.) [2001] (2004) *Germanistik und Deutschunterricht in 15 Ländern*. 2nd edition, Mannheim: Institut für Deutsche Sprache.

—— (ed.) (2008) *Germanistik und Deutschunterricht in 11 Ländern*. Mannheim: Institut für Deutsche Sprache.

Instituto Cervantes (ed.) (2013) *El Español: Una Lengua viva* (Informe 13). Departemento de Comunicación Digital, Instituto Cervantes.

Interessengemeinschaft Deutschsprachiger Südwester (ed.) (1980) *Die Bemühungen um die deutsche Sprache von 1920 bis 1980 in SWA/ Namibia*. 2nd edition, Windhoek.

International Bibliography of Historical Science (1926ff.). Oxford: University Press/ New York: Wilson.

International Bibliography of the Social Science: Sociology (1951ff.); *Economics* (1952 ff.); *Political Science* (1953 ff.); *Social and Cultural Anthropology* (1955ff.). London: Tavistock/ Chicago: Aldine.

Ipsen, Knut (1997) Minderheitenschutz auf reziproker Basis – die deutsch-dänische Lösung. In H.-J. Heintze (ed.) *Selbstbestimmungsrecht der Völker – Herausforderung der Staatenwelt*. Bonn: Dietz, 327–341.

Isajiw, W. W. (1990) Ethnic identity retention. In Breton, R. et al. (eds.) *Ethnic Identity and Equality: Varieties of Experience in a Canadian City*. Toronto: University of Toronto Press, 36–38.

Ising, Erika (1987) Nationalsprache/ Nationalitätensprache. In Ammon/ Dittmar/ Mattheier, 335–344.

Israel, Jonathan I. (1995) *The Dutch Republic: Its Rise, Greatness, and Fall 1477–1806*. Oxford: Clarendon Press.

Itoi, Toru (1994) Die Oberschulen mit Deutsch als Fremdsprache. In Ammon 1994d, 207–220.

Jacobi, Arno (1979) Keine Lust zur Erlernung der deutschen Sprache? Beobachtungen in SüdBrasilien. Pouca vontade de aprender a lingua alema? Observaçoes no sul do Brasil. *Deutsch-brasilianische Hefte* 18: 382–385.

Jäger, Andreas/ Jasny, Sabine (2007) Zur Lage der Germanistik in Australien. *Info DaF* 34 (5): 472–486.

Jakob, Gerhard (1987) *Deutschsprachige Gruppen am Rande und außerhalb des geschlossenen deutschen Sprachgebiets. Eine bibliographische Dokumentation von Literatur zum Thema 'Sprache' aus der Zeit nach 1945 (Stand Mai 1987)*. Mannheim: Institut für deutsche Sprache.

James, Charles J./ Tschirner, Erwin (2001) Deutschunterricht und Gemanistikstudium in den USA. In Helbig/ Götze/ Henrici/ Krumm, Vol. 2: 1424–1430.

Janich, Nina (2004) *Die bewusste Entscheidung. Eine handlungsorientierte Theorie der Sprachkultur*. Tübingen: Narr.

Jansen, Christian/ Nensa, Christoph (2004) *Exzellenz weltweit – Die Alexander von HumboldtStiftung zwischen Wissenschaftsförderung und auswärtiger Kulturpolitik (1953–2003)*. Köln: DuMont.

Jansen, Louise/ Schmidt, Gabriele (2011) Das Auf und Ab im Deutschstudium: Gründe für die Aufnahme und den Abbruch eines Deutschstudiums in Australien. *Deutsch als Fremdsprache* 48 (3): 166–172.

Jäntti, Ahti (2002) Deutsche Sprache in Finnland. In Deutsch-Finnische Gesellschaft/ Poser, Burkhart E. et al. (eds.) *50 Jahre Deutsch-Finnische Gesellschaft E. V. Festschrift zur Jubiläumsfeier in München 2002*. Berlin: Atelier Schwarz.

Japan Foundation (2008) *Survery Report on Japanese-Language Education abroad 2006: Present Condition of Overseas Japanese-Language Education. Summary.* Tokyo: The Japan Foundation.

Japanische Gesellschaft für Germanistik (in Kooperation mit Goethe-Institut Tokyo) (20th May 2013) *Zur Lage von Deutschunterricht und Deutschlernenden in Japan*. O. O.: Verlagsverband für Deutsch-Lehrbücher (Unterstützung Hueber Verlag). (www.jgg.jp/modules/neues/index.php?page=article&storyid=1192)

Jarausch, Konrad (1991) Universität und Hochschule. In Berg, Ch. (ed.) *Handbuch der deutschen Bildungsgeschichte.* Vol. 4: *1870–1918. Von der Reichsgründung bis zum Ende des Ersten Weltkriegs.* München: Beck, 313–345.

Jaschek, Stephan (1977) Deutsch als Sprache der Vereinten Nationen. *Vereinte Nationen* 1: 1824.

Jaworska, Sylvia (2009) The German language in Poland: the eternal foe and the wars on words. In Carl/ Stevenson, 51–72.

Jenkins, Jennifer (1997) *English as a Lingua Franca: Attitude und Identity.* Oxford: Oxford University Press.

―――― (2003) *World English: A Resource Book for Students.* London/ New York: Routledge.

―――― (2007) *English as a Lingua Franca: Attitude and Identity.* New York: Oxford University Press.

Jenniges, Hubert (2001) *Hinter ostbelgischen Kulissen. Stationen auf dem Weg zur Autonomie des deutschen Sprachgebiets in Belgien (1968–1972).* Eupen: Grenz-Echo Verlag.

Jensen, Stefanie (2001) *Ausländerstudium in Deutschland. Die Attraktivität deutscher Hochschulen für ausländische Studierende.* Wiesbaden: Deutscher Universitäts-Verlag.

Jernudd, Björn H. (1987) World languages in radio broadcasting and as official languages. In Laycock, D. C./ Winter, W. (eds.) *A World of Language.* Canberra: The Australian National University, 297–308.

―――― / Shaw, Willard D. (1979) *World Languages of Wider Communication in the Media and Higher Education.* Honolulu: East-West Center.

Jespersen, Otto (1926/ 1933) *Growth and Structure of the English Language.* 5th and 7th edition, Leipzig: Teubner.

Jezierzanska-Frindik, Krystyna (2000) *EU-Sprachen als Konferenzsprachen – Deutsch als Konferenzsprache in Österreich.* FASK, Johannes Gutenberg-Universität Mainz in Germersheim, Degree dissertation.

Johnson, Marc L./ Doucet, Paule (2006) *A Sharper View: Evaluating the Vitality of Official Language Communities.* Ottawa: Office of the Commissionar of Official Languages in Canada.

Johnson-Weiner, Karen M. (1992) Group identity and language maintenance: the survival of Pennsylvania German in Old Order communities. In Burridge, K./ Enninger W. (eds.) *Diachronic Studies on the Language of the Anabaptists.* Bochum: Brockmeyer, 26–42.

―――― (1999) Educating in English to maintain Pennsylvania German: the old order Parochial school in the service of cultural survival. In Ostler, 31–37.

Jones, Eric (2000) The case of a shared world language. In Casson, M./ Godley, A. (eds.) *Cultural Factors in Economic Growth.* Berlin: Springer, 210–235.

Jordan, Peter (1998) Romania. In Bratt Paulston/ Peckham, 184–223.

Jung, Matthias/ Krumm, Hans-Jürgen/ Wicke, Rainer E. (2010) Institutionen und Verbände für Deutsch als Zweit- und Fremdsprache in Deutschland. In Krumm/ Fandrych/ Hufeisen/ Riemer, Vol. 1, 144–153.

Junge, Hergen/ Tötemeyer, Gerhard/ Zappen-Thomson, Marianne (eds.) (1993) *The Identity and Role of the German-Speaking Community in Namibia.* Windhoek: Namibisch-Deutsche Stiftung für kulturelle Zusammenarbeit.

Jurgensen, Manfred (ed.) (1995) *German-Australian Cultural Relations Since 1945.* Bern: Lang.

―――― / Corkhill, Allen (eds.) (1988) *The German Presence in Queensland.* Brisbane: Department of German, University of Queensland.

Kachru, Braj B. (ed.) (1982) *The Other Tongue. English Across Cultures.* Urbana, IL: University of Illinois Press.

―――― (1986) *The Alchemy of English: The Spread, Functions and Models of Non-Native Englishes.* Oxford: Pergamon.

Kaderas, Christoph/ Meng, Hong (eds.) (2000) *120 Jahre chinesische Studierende an deutschen Hochschulen.* Bonn: DAAD.

Kaestner, Uwe (2003) Deutschland und Brasilien – strategische Partner. In Kaufmann/ Lenhard Bredemeier/ Volkmann, 17–36.

Kahane, Henry/ Kahane, Renée (1976) Lingua franca: the story of a term. *Romance Philology* 30 (1): 25–41.

―――― / ―――― (1979) Decline and survival of Western prestige languages. *Language* 55 (1): 183–198.

Kakinuma, Yoshitaka (1994) Die japanische Medizin im Übergang von Deutsch zu Englisch. In Ammon 1994d, 35–48.

Kalensky, Claudia (2009) *Kompliziert – Komplizierter – Wissenschaftsdeutsch? Kulturelle Prägung von wissenschaftlichen Arbeiten: eine Analyse von österreichischen Seminararbeiten und englischen Essays.* Degree dissertation, Universität Wien. (www.othes.univie.ac.at/4468/1/2009-04-16_0200541.pdf)

Kallenborn, Gerald (1997) *Das Sprachenproblem bei Vertragsabschlüssen mit ausländischen Verbrauchern. Eine analytische Untersuchung zur Frage des Bestehens besonderer Aufklärungspflichten gegenüber dem sprachunkundigen Verbraucher unter Berücksichtigung des EG-Rechts und des Internationalen Privatrechts.* Dissertation Rostock.

Kaltenborn, Karl-Franz/ Kuhn, Klaus (2003) Der Impact-Faktor als Parameter zur Evaluation von Forscherinnen/ Forschern und Forschung. *Klinische Neuroradiologie* (4): 173–193.

Kalverkämper, Hartwig/ Weinrich, Harald (eds.) (1986) *Deutsch als Wissenschaftssprache. 25. Konstanzer Literaturgespräch.* Tübingen: Narr.

Kamusella, Tomasz (2009) *The Politics of Language and Nationalism in Modern Central Europe.* Basingstoke/ New York: Palgrave Macmillan.

Kang, Chang-Uh (2003) Deutschkurse in Hörfunk und Fernsehen. In Ammon/ Chong, 285–296.

Kangro, Ilze (2010) Deutsch in Lettland. In Krumm/ Fandrych/ Hufeisen/ Riemer, Vol. 2, 17251728.

Kaplan, Robert B. (2001) English – the accidental language of science? In Ammon, 3–26.

Karger, Thomas (1986) Englisch als Wissenschaftssprache im Spiegel der Publikationsgeschichte. In Kalverkämper/ Weinrich, 48–52.

Karim, Karim H. (ed.) (2003a) *The Media of Diaspora.* Oxford: Routledge.

――― (2003b) Mapping diasporic mediascapes. In Karim (2003a), 1–17.

Kathe, Steffen R. (2005) *Kulturpolitik um jeden Preis. Die Geschichte des Goethe-Instituts von 1951 bis 1990.* München: Martin Meidenbauer.

Katz, Bernard S. (1989) *Nobel Laureates in Economic Sciences. A Bibliographical Dictionary.* New York/ London: Garland.

Kaufmann, Göz (1997) *Varietätendynamik in Sprachkontaktsituationen: Attitüden und Sprachverhalten rußlanddeutscher Mennoniten in Mexiko und den USA.* Frankfurt a. M.: Lang.

――― (2003) Deutsch und Germanistik in Brasilien. *Jahrbuch für Internationale Germanistik* 35 (1): 29–39.

――― (2004) Eine Gruppe – Zwei Geschichten – Drei Sprachen: Rußlanddeutsche Mennoniten in Brasilien und Paraguay. *Zeitschrift für Dialektologie und Linguistik* 71 (3): 257–306.

――― (2006) Language maintenance and reversing language shift. In Ammon/ Dittmar/ Mattheier/ Trudgill, 2431–2442.

――― / Bredemeier, Maria L./ Volkmann, Walter (eds.) (2003) *V Brasilianischer Deutschlehrerkongress, II Deutschlehrerkongress des MERCOSUL. Tagungsband.* Porto Alegre: UNISINOS.

Kaufmann, Stefanie (1994) Die Förderung von Deutsch als Fremdsprache durch das GoetheInstitut in Japan. In Ammon, 285–294.

Kausen, Ernst (2013) Amtssprachen aller Staaten nach Kontinenten (accessible at: http://homepages.fh-giessen.de/kausen/klassifikationen/Nationalsprachen.doc)

Kawamura, Yoko (2009) Eigenes Konzept: Die Auswärtige Kulturpolitik Japans. In Maaß (2009a), 387–399.

Kawashima, Atsuo (1994) Die Lehnwörter aus dem Deutschen im Japanischen. In Ammon (1994d), 183–191.

Keel, William D. (2003) Patterns of shift in Midwestern German speech islands. In Keel/ Mattheier, 303–321.

――― / Mattheier, Klaus J. (2003) *German Language Varieties Worldwide: Internal and External Perspectives/ Deutsche Sprachinseln weltweit: Interne und externe Perspektiven.* Frankfurt a.M.: Lang.

Keidel, Hannemor (2002) Der internationale Film- und Videomarkt. In Leonhard et al., 2666–2676.

Keim, Lucrecia (2010) Deutsch in Spanien. In Krumm/ Fandrych/ Hufeisen/ Riemer, Vol. 2, 18011804.

Kellermann, Hermann (ed.) (1915) *Der Krieg der Geister. Eine Auslese deutscher und ausländischer Stimmen zum Weltkriege 1914.* Dresden: Duncker.

Kellermeier-Rehbein, Birte (in print) Varietäten der deutschen Sprache im postkolonialen Namibia. In Stolz, Th./ Warnke, I. H./ Schmidt-Brücken, D. (eds.) *Studienbuch Sprache und Kolonialismus.* Berlin/ Boston: de Gruyter.

Kelletat, Andreas F. (2001a) *Deutschland: Finnland 6:0. Saksa: Suomi 6:0* (Deutsche Studien 4). Tampere: University of Tampere.

――― (2001b) Vom Deutschen leben. Beitrag zum DAAD-Lektorensommertreffen im August 2000 in Bonn: Wie viel Deutsch braucht die Welt? Zur aktuellen Diskussion um eine zeitgemäße Sprachenpolitik. *Jahrbuch Deutsch als Fremdsprache* 27: 424–431.

――― (2004a) Ohrenschmaus? Dolmetschen in den Organen der Europäischen Union nach der Osterweiterung. *Jahrbuch Deutsch als Fremdsprache* 30: 213–226.

——— (2004b) Konferenzdolmetschen in den Organen der Europäischen Union nach der Osterweiterung. In Forstner, M./ Lee-Jahnke, H. (eds.) *Internationales CIUTI-Forum. Marktorientierte Translationsausbildung.* Frankfurt/Main: Peter Lang, 135–152.

Kellsey, Charlene/ Knievel, Jennifer E. (2004) Global English in the humanities? A longitudinal citation study of foreign-language use by humanities scholars. *College & Research Libraries* 65: 194–204.

Kelz, Heinrich P. (1990) Deutsch als Fremdsprache in Europa. Bestandsaufnahme und Perspektiven. *Info DaF* 17 (4): 361–367.

——— (ed.) (2002) *Die sprachliche Zukunft Europas. Mehrsprachigkeit und Sprachenpolitik.* BadenBaden: Nomos.

Kemper, Dirk (2011) Deutsche Literaturwissenschaft in Russland. In Ammon/ Kemper, 187–199.

Kerekes, Gábor (2010) Goethe, Golf, Adolf und die Toten Hosen. Das Bild der Ungarn von Deutschland und den Deutschen. In Kostrzewa/ Rada/ Knipf-Komlósi, 147–179.

Kern, Rudolf (ed.) (1983) *Deutsch als Fremdsprache in Belgien* (Cahiers de l'Institute des langues vivantes, 31). Löwen: Peeter.

——— (1986) Zum Fremdsprachenbedarf der Wirtschaft in Belgien. *Germanistische Mitteilungen* 23: 41–47.

——— (ed.) (1989) *Deutsch als Umgangs- und Muttersprache in der Europäischen Gemeinschaft. Akten des Europäischen Symposiums in Eupen vom 26. bis 29. März 1987.* Brüssel: Selbstverlag des Belgischen Komitees des Europäischen Büros für Sprachminderheiten.

——— (1999a) *Europäische Sprach- und Minderheitsinitiativen und Deutsch als Kontaktsprache in Mittel- und Osteuropa.* Bradean-Ebinger, N./ Dávid, G. C. (eds.) Budapest: Universität für Wirtschaftswissenschaften, Lehrstuhl Deutsch.

——— (1999b) Ungarndeutsche Identität in europäischer Dimension. Ergebnisse einer Symposienreihe (1995). In Kern (1999a), 217–267.

——— (2005) Es steht nicht gut um die deutsche Sprache: Eine kritische Rückschau. In Van Leewen, 219–254.

Keul, A./ Gigerenzer, G./ Stroebe, W. (1993) Wie international ist die Psychologie in Deutschland, Österreich und der Schweiz? Eine SSCI-Analyse. *Psychologische Rundschau* 44: 259–269.

Kevles, Daniel J. (1971) "Into hostile political camps": the reorganization of International Science in World War I. *ISIS* 62 (211): 47–60.

Khaleeva, Irina (2011) Geleitwort. In Ammon/ Kemper, 13–19.

Khattab, Aleya (2010) Deutsch in Ägypten. In Krumm/ Fandrych/ Hufeisen/ Riemer, Vol. 2, 1602–1606.

Kibbee, Douglas A. (2003) Language policy and linguistic theory. In Maurais/ Morris, 47–57.

Kießling, Friedrich (2005) Täter repräsentieren: Willy Brandts Kniefall in Warschau: Überlegungen zum Zusammenhang von Bundesdeutscher Außenrepräsentation und der Erinnerung an den Nationalsozialismus. In Paulmann, J. (ed.) *Auswärtige Repräsentation. Deutsche Kulturdiplomatie nach 1945.* Köln, Weimar, Wien: Böhlau, 205–224.

Kiliari, Angeliki (2005) Die deutsche Sprache in Griechenland. *Jahrbuch für Internationale Germanistik* 36 (1): 13–23.

Kim, Hiyoul (2005) Fremdsprachenbedarf in der koreanischen Gesellschaft und Wirtschaft. In Van Leewen, 329–346.

Kim, Hyeong-Duk (2003) Sprachwahl koreanischer Betriebe in Kontakten mit deutschsprachigen Ländern. In Ammon/ Chong, 109–118.

Kim, Ok-Seon (2003) Sprachwahl zwischen Deutschen und Koreanern in der innerbetrieblichen Kommunikation deutscher Firmen in Korea. In Ammon/ Chong, 119–134.

——— (2010) Deutsch in Korea. In Krumm/ Fandrych/ Hufeisen/ Riemer, Vol. 2, 1713–1716.

Kim, Soon-Im (2003) Deutsch und andere Sprachen in der koreanischen Jurispudenz. In Ammon/ Chong, 43–56.

King, David (2004) The scientific impact of nations. *Nature* 430: 311–316.

Kirchner, Frank (ed.) (2006) *World Guide to Scientific Associations and Learned Societies.* München: K. G. Saur.

Kirkby, Mary-Ann (2007) *I am Hutterite.* Winnipeg: Polka Dot Press.

Kittel, Manfred/ Pešek, Jiri/ Tuma, Oldrich (ed.) (2006) *Deutschsprachige Minderheiten 1945.* Ein europäischer Vergleich. München: Oldenbourg Wissenschaftsverlag.

Klapheck, Eva-Maria (2004) *Die Sprachenwahl beim Eurovision Song Contest und ihre Auswirkungen und Konsequenzen. Untersuchung zum Zeitraum 1999–2004.* Unpublished Masters dissertation, Universität Duisburg-Essen.

Klassen, Peter P. (1988) *Die Mennoniten in Paraguay.* Vol. 1: *Reich Gottes und Reich dieser Welt.* Bolanden-Wierhof: Mennonitischer Geschichtsverein.

—— (1995) *Die russlanddeutschen Mennoniten in Brasilien*. Bd 1: *Witmarsum am Alto Rio und Auhagen auf dem Stoltz-Plateau in Santa Catarina*. Bolanden-Weierhof: Mennonitischer Geschichtsverein.

—— (1998) *Die russlanddeutschen Mennoniten in Brasilien*. Bd 2: *Siedlungen, Gruppen und Gemeinden in der Zerstreuung*. Bolanden-Weierhof: Mennonitischer Geschichtsverein.

Klaube, Manfred (1994) Emigration und Migration in den beiden Landkreisen in Westsibirien. *Osteuropa* 44: 74–89.

—— (1997) Fünf Jahre Deutscher Nationaler Rayon. Halbstadt in Westsibirien (1991–1996). *Osteuropa* 47: 373–389.

Klein, Gabriella (1984) Tendenzen der Sprachpolitik des italienischen Faschismus und des Nationalsozialismus in Deutschland. *Zeitschrift für Sprachwissenschaft* 3 (1): 100–113.

Klein Gunnewiek, Lisanne/ Herrlitz, Wolfgang (2010) Deutsch in den Niederlanden. In Krumm/ Fandrych/ Hufeisen/ Riemer, Vol. 2, 1747–1753.

Klein, Pierre (2007) *Langues d'Alsace – et pourquoi les Alsaciens renoncent-ils à leur bilinguisme? Sprachen des Elsass – und warum verzichten die Elsässer auf ihre Zweisprachigkeit?* [Hagenau:] Collection "L'alsatique bilingue"/ Editions Nord Alsace.

Klein, Mars (1995) Partizipierend – aber bedacht auf Abgrenzung. Über das Luxemburger Verhältnis zum deutschsprachigen Kulturraum. *allmende* 44: 9–100.

Klein, Stefan (2007) Dümmer auf Englisch. Die Verödung der Wissenschaftssprache schreitet voran. *FAZ* 06.07.2007. *Forschung & Lehre* 14: 538f.

Klein, Wolfgang (1974) *Variation in der Sprache. Ein Verfahren zu ihrer Beschreibung*. Kronberg, TS: Scriptor.

—— (1985) Über Ansehen und Wirkung der deutschen Sprachwissenschaft heute. *Linguistische Berichte* 100: 511–520.

—— (2000) Das Ende vor Augen: Deutsch als Wissenschaftssprache im 20. Jahrhundert (Versuch einer Zusammenfassung). In Debus/ Kollmann/ Pörksen, 287–293.

Kleineidam, Hartmut (1992) Politique de diffusion linguistique et francophonie: l'action linguistique menée par la France. *International Journal of the Sociology of Language* 95: 11–31.

Kleinz, Norbert (1984) *Deutsche Sprache im Kontakt in Südwestafrika. Der heutige Gebrauch der Sprachen Deutsch, Afrikaans und Englisch in Namibia*. Stuttgart/ Wiesbaden: Steiner.

Klemperer, Victor [1947] (1966) *Notizbuch eines Philologen*. [Berlin: Aufbau Verlag] Darmstadt: Joseph Melzer.

Klinner, Jörg (2012) NAM – Namibische Besonderheiten des Deutschen in Sprachgebrauch und Sprachlandschaft. In *Sprachenvielfalt in Namibia*, 68–74.

Kloss, Heinz (1927) Spracherhaltung. *Archiv für Politik und Geschichte*: 8: 456–462.

—— (1935) *Fremdniederlassungen – Streudeutschtum*. Berlin: Volk und Reich.

—— (1952) *Die Entwicklung neuer germanischer Kultursprachen von 1800–1950*. München: Pohl.

—— (1966) German-American language maintenance efforts. In Fishman, 206–252.

—— (1969a) *Research Possibilities on Group Bilingualism: a Report*. Montreal, Québec: CIRB/ ICRB Université Laval.

—— (1969b) *Grundfragen der Ethnopolitik im 20. Jahrhundert*. Wien: Braumüller.

—— (1971) German as an immigrant, indigenous, foreign, and second language in the United States. In Gilbert, 106–127.

—— (1972) Der multilinguale Staat. In Veiter, T. (ed.) *System eines internationalen Volksgruppenrechts, 2. Teil* Wien/ Stuttgart: Braumüller, 189–221.

—— (1973) Vier Verlierer: Verluste der dänischen, der niederländischen, der jüdischen und der deutschen Sprachgemeinschaft in jüngerer Zeit. In *Linguistische Studien III, Festgabe für Paul Grebe zum 65. Geburtstag*. Düsseldorf: Schwann, 28–39.

—— (bearb.) (1974a) *Deutsch in der Begegnung mit anderen Sprachen: im Fremdsprachenwettbewerb, als Muttersprache in Übersee, als Bildungsbarriere für Gastarbeiter*. Tübingen: Narr.

—— (1974b) Die den internationalen Rang einer Sprache bestimmenden Faktoren. Ein Versuch. In Kloss 1974a, 7–77.

—— (1976a) Über "Diglossie". *Deutsche Sprache* 4: 313–323.

—— (1976b) Abstandsprachen und Ausbausprachen. In Göschel, J./ Nail, N./ Van der Elst, G. (eds.) *Zur Theorie des Dialekts. Aufsätze aus 100 Jahren Forschung mit biographischen Anmer.Anmerkungen zu den Autoren*. Wiesbaden: Steiner: 301–322.

—— (1977) Der sprachenrechtliche Rahmen. In Auburger/ Kloss/ Rupp, 53–57.

—— [1952] (1978) *Die Entwicklung neuer germanischer Kultursprachen seit 1800*. 2nd edition Düsseldorf: Schwann.

—— (1980) Deutsche Sprache außerhalb des geschlossenen deutschen Sprachgebiets. In Althaus, H. P./ Henne, H./ Wiegand, H. E. (eds.) *Lexikon der Germanistischen Linguistik*. 2nd edition Tübingen: Niemeyer, 537–546.

—— (1984) Stellungnahme zum Aufsatz von Harro Schweizer (. . .) *Zeitschrift für Sprachwissenschaft* 3 (1): 135–138.

—— (ed.) (1985a) *Deutsch als Muttersprache in den Vereinigten Staaten, Teil II: Regionale und funktionale Aspekte*. Wiesbaden: Steiner.

—— (1985b) Die Stellung des deutschen Elements in den Abstammungs- und Sprachenzählungen der Jahre 1969–1980. In Kloss 1985a, 259–274.

—— (1986) Der Stand der in Luxemburg gesprochenen Sprache beim Jahresende 1984. *Germanistische Mitteilungen* 24: 83–94.

Kloss, Günther (1989) Bedarf und Probleme aus britischer Sicht. *Jahrbuch Deutsch als Fremdsprache* 15: 211–224.

Knapp, Karlfried (1984) Zum allgemein-linguistischen Interesse an der Weltsprache Englisch. *Studium Linguistik* 15: 1–9.

—— (1989) Why just English? – Warum nicht Deutsch? Soziolinguistische Aspekte und einige offene Forschungsfragen in der Diskussion um Englisch als Wissenschaftssprache. *GALBulletin* 10: 44–55.

—— (2002) The fading out of the non-native speaker. Native speaker dominance in lingua-francasituations. In Knapp, K./ Meierkord, C. (eds.) *Lingua franca Communication*. Frankfurt a.M.: Lang, 217–244.

Knecht, R. J. (1994) *Renaissance Warrior and Patron: The Reign of Francis I*. Cambridge/ New York: Cambridge University Press.

Kneip, Matthias (1999) *Die deutsche Sprache in Oberschlesien. Untersuchungen zur politischen Rolle der deutschen Sprache als Minderheitensprache in den Jahren 1921–1998*. Dortmund: Forschungsstelle Ost-Mitteleuropa.

Knipf-Komlósi, Elisabeth (1988) Muttersprachunterricht und Fremdsprachenunterricht. Lage und Tendenzen des Deutschunterrichts bei den Ungarndeutschen. In Ritter, A. (ed.) *Kolloquium zum Deutschunterricht und Unterricht in deutscher Sprache bei den deutschen Bevölkerungsgruppen im Ausland*. Flensburg: Institut für Regionale Forschung und Information, 183–194.

—— (2001) Dialekt "out" – Standardsprache "in". Zur Varietätenwahl im Sprachgebrauch der deutschen Minderheit in Ungarn. In Egger, K./ Lanthaler, F. (eds.) *Die deutsche Sprache in Südtirol. Einheitssprache und regionale Vielfalt*. Wien/ Bozen: Folio, 99–115.

—— (2003) Sprachwahl und kommunikative Handlungsformen der deutschen Minderheit in Ungarn. In Keel/ Mattheier, 269–281.

—— (2006) Sprachliche Muster bei Sprachinselsprechern am Beispiel der Ungarndeutschen. In Berend/ Knipf-Komlósi, 39–56.

—— (2008) Ungarn. In Eichinger/ Plewnia/ Riehl, 265–327.

Knorr, Andreas/ Arndt, Andreas (2003) *Wal-Mart in Deutschland. Eine verfehlte Internationalisierungsstrategie*. Bremen: Institut für Weltwirtschaft und Internationales Management Universität Bremen.

Knöß, Klaus (1986) Germanistik und Deutschdidaktik in der Türkei. *Info DaF* 13 (3): 230–241.

Koch, Eszter (2007) *Ungarn als Standort für deutsche Unternehmen*. Budapest. (www.elib.kkf.hu/edip/ D_13333.pdf)

Koch, Peter/ Oesterreicher, Wulf (1985) Sprache der Nähe – Sprache der Distanz. Mündlichkeit und Schriftlichkeit im Spannungsfeld von Sprachtheorie und Sprachgeschichte. *Romanistisches Jahrbuch* 36: 15–43.

Koch, Walter (1996) Deutsche Sprachinseln in Südbrasilien. Möglichkeiten und Probleme ihrer Untersuchung. In Radtke, E./ Thun, H. (eds.) *Neue Wege der romanischen Geolinguistik. Akten des Symposiums zur empirischen Dialektologie (21.-24.10.1991)*. Kiel: Westensee Verlag, 307–321.

Koch-Hillebrecht, Manfred (1977) *Das Deutschenbild. Gegenwart, Geschichte, Psychologie*. München: Beck.

Kocka, Jürgen (2005) Nutzen und Nachteil von Ein- und Mehrsprachigkeit. In Nies, 147–151. Kohlauf, Gisela/ Maintz, Michael (2001) Deutsch in Indonesien: Ein Länderbericht. *InfoDaF* 28 (4): 375–396.

Kohlross, Christian/ Mittelmann, Hanni (eds.) (2011) *Auf den Spuren der Schrift. Israelische Perspektiven einer internationalen Germanistik*. Berlin/ Boston: de Gruyter.

Kohnemann, Michel (1986) *Nachrichten aus Ostbelgien. Deutsche Literatur in Belgien*. Hildesheim/ New York: Olms.

Kollmann, Franz G. (2000) Deutsch als Wissenschaftssprache im zwanzigsten Jahrhundert – eine Einführung. In Debus/ Kollmann/ Pörksen, 11–19.

Kommission der Europäischen Gemeinschaft (ed.) (1988) *Der Sprachunterricht in der Europäischen Gemeinschaft*. Brüssel: Eurydice – Europäische Informationsstelle.

Komus, Ayelt/ Wauch, Franziska (2008) *Wikimanagement. Was Unternehmen von Social Software und Web 2.0 lernen können.* München: Oldenbourg.

Kong, Deming (2007) Die Hochschulen mit dem Fach Germanistik [in China!]. In Ammon/ Reinbothe/ Zhu, 123–140.

Königs, Frank G. (2002) Curriculare Innovationen in fremdsprachlichen Studiengängen. In Deutscher Akademischer Austauschdienst, 293–406.

Konrad, H. (2003) Entwurf einer "europäischen Sprachenordnung". In Baumgarten, Nicole et al. (eds.) *Übersetzen, Interkulturelle Kommunikation, Spracherwerb und Sprachvermittlung – das Leben mit mehreren Sprachen. Festschrift für Juliane House zum 60. Geburtstag. Zeitschrift für Interkulturellen Fremdsprachenunterricht [Online]* 8 (2/3): 157–175.

Kontra, Míklos (1996) Hungary. In Goebl/ Nelde/ Starý/ Wölck, 1708–1723.

———— / Bartha, Csilla (2010) Foreign language education in Hungary: concerns and controversies. *Sociolinguistica* 24: 61–84.

Koprivica, Lara (2010) *Die Einstellung deutscher Wissenschaftler zu Englisch als vorrangige internationale Wissenschaftssprache.* Unpublished master's dissertation in the humanities, Universität Duisburg-Essen.

Korhonen, Jarmo (2007) Deutsche Sprache und Germanistik in Finnland. *Jahrbuch für Internationale Germanistik* 39 (2): 61–72.

———— (2008) Finnland. In Institut für Deutsche Sprache, 15–22.

———— / Nikula, Henrik (2004) In Institut für Deutsche Sprache, 15–20.

Korkisch, Friedrich (1978) Amts- und Gerichtssprache. In Veiter, T. (ed.) *System eines internationalen Volksgruppenrechts.* Wien: Braumüller, 128–147.

Kostrova, Olga (2011) Der Deutschunterricht an privaten Sprachschulen in Russland. In Ammon/ Kemper, 234–243.

Kostrzewa, Frank (2009) Die Bedeutung der deutschen Sprache in Korea. *Der Sprachdienst* 53 (3–4): 90–96.

———— / Rada, Roberta V. unter Mitarbeit von Knipf-Komlósi, Elisabeth (eds.) (2010) *Deutsch als Fremd- und Minderheitensprache in Ungarn. Historische Entwicklung, aktuelle Tendenzen und Zukunftsperspektiven.* Hohengehren/ Baltmannsweiler: Schneider.

Kotzian, Ortfried (2005) *Die Umsiedler. Die Deutschen aus West-Wolhynien, Galizien, der Bukowina, Bessarabien, der Dobrudscha und in der Karpatenukraine.* München: Langen Müller.

Kourilová, M (1998) Communicative characteristics of reviews of scientific paper written by nonnative users of English. *Endocrine Regulations* 32: 107–114.

Kraas-Schneider, Frauke (1989) *Bevölkerungsgruppen und Minoritäten. Handbuch der ethnischen, sprachlichen und religiösen Bevölkerungsgruppen der Welt.* Wiesbaden/ Stuttgart: Steiner.

Kraemer, Jordan (2014) Friend or Freund: social media and transnational connections in Berlin. *Human – Computer Interaction* 29 (1): 53–77. (www.dx.doi.org/_10_1080/_07370024.2013.823821)

Kramer, Johannes (1981) *Deutsch und Italienisch in Südtirol.* Heidelberg: Winter.

———— (1984) *Zweisprachigkeit in den Beneluxländern.* Hamburg: Buske.

———— (1986) Gewollte Dreisprachigkeit Französisch – Deutsch – Luxemburgisch. In Hinderling, 229249.

Kramer, Wolfgang/ Weiß, Reinhold (eds.) (1992) *Fremdsprachen in der Wirtschaft. Ein Beitrag zu interkultureller Kompetenz.* Köln: Institut der deutschen Wirtschaft.

Krämer, Walter (2011) Die deutsche Sprache in den Wirtschaftswissenschaften. In Wieland/ Glück/ Pretscher, 85–94.

Krappmann, Lothar (2004) Identität. In Ammon, U. et al., 405–411.

Krasteva, Hristina (2007) *Die Macher der "Visitenkarte Deutschlands" Deutsche Welle. Eine qualitative Studie zum Selbstverständnis von DW-Journalisten.* Magister-Arbeit an der sozialwiss. Fakultät der LMU München. (www.epub.ub.unimuenchen.de/1987/1/MA_Krasteva_Hristina.pdf) Außerdem (2008) Saarbrücken: VDM Verlag Dr. Müller.

Kraus, Peter A. (2000) Political unity and linguistic diversity in Europe. *Archives Européennes de Sociologie* 41: 138–163.

———— (2004) *Europäische Öffentlichkeit und Sprachpolitik.* Frankfurt: Campus.

———— (2008) *A Union of Diversity. Language, Identity and Polity-Building in Europe.* Cambridge, UK: Cambridge University Press.

Kremnitz, Georg (2004) Diglossie – Polyglossie. In Ammon/ Dittmar/ Mattheier/ Trudgill, 158164.

Kretschmer, Bernhard (ed.) (2007) *Rechts- als Geisteswissenschaft.* Hamburg: Dr. Kovač.

Kretzenbacher, Heinz L. (2006) Deutsche Sprache und Germanistik in Australien – ein paar vorsichtig-subjektive Perspektiven. *Jahrbuch für Internationale Germanistik* 38 (2): 11–33.

———— (2010) Deutsch in Australien. In Krumm/ Fandrych/ Hufeisen/ Riemer, Vol. 2, 1611–1615.

——— (2011) German Studies in Australia: a statistical overview, 1995–2010. *German as a Foreign Language (GEL)* (2): 40–54.

——— / Weinrich, Harald (eds.) (1995) *Linguistik der Wissenschaftssprache.* Berlin: de Gruyter.

Kreutzberger, Margarethe/ Springer, Dieter (2002) Die Arbeitsgemeinschaft der Deutschen Schulvereine. In Hess/ Becker, 327–335.

Kriekhaus, Stefan (2005) Die Entwicklung der universitären Grossbetriebe (Berlin, München, Leipzig) vom Kaiserreich bis zum Beginn des Zweiten Weltkriegs. In Schwinges, 227–245.

Krindac, Aleksej (1997) Der Deutsche Nationale Rayon heute. Eine soziologische Untersuchung. *Forschungen zur Geschichte und Kultur der Rußlanddeutschen* 7: 118–133.

Kroll, Frank-Lothar (2003) *Kultur, Bildung und Wissenschaft im 20. Jahrhundert* (Enyklopädie Deutscher Geschichte, 65). München: Oldenbourg.

Kroner, Michael (1998) *Ringen um nationale Selbstbehauptung. Die Siebenbürger Sachsen im ungarischen und rumänischen Staatsverband.* Nürnberg: Schobert.

Kroon, Sjaak/ Sturm, Jan (1994) Das nationale Selbstverständnis im Unterricht der Nationalsprache: der Fall der Niederlande. In Gogolin, I. (ed.) *Das nationale Selbstverständnis der Bildung.* Münster/ New York: Waxmann, 161–192.

Krumm, Hans-Jürgen (ed.) (1998) *Die Sprachen unserer Nachbarn – unsere Sprachen.* Wien: eviva.

——— (1999) *Sprachen – Brücken über Grenzen. Deutsch als Fremdsprache in Mittel- und Osteuropa. Dokumentation der Wiener Konferenz 17. – 21.1998.* Wien: eviva.

——— (2000a) Europäische Mehrsprachigkeit. In Riemer, C. (ed.) *Kognitive Aspekte des Lehrens und Lernens von Fremdsprachen.* Tübingen: Narr, 26–37.

——— (2000b) Einsprachigkeit ist heilbar. *Deutsch lernen* 25 (2): 99–111.

——— (2002) Fremdsprachenunterricht im Europa des 21. Jahrhunderts und die Rolle, die Deutsch als Fremdsprache dabei spielt und spielen sollte. *Materialien Deutsch als Fremdsprache* 65: 89–109.

——— (2003) Deutsch im Konzert der Sprachen – Die Rolle der deutschen Sprache in Konzepten europäischer Mehrsprachigkeit. In Krumm, H.-J. (ed.) *Sprachenvielfalt. Babylonische Sprachverwirrung oder Mehrsprachigkeit als Chance?* Innsbruck: StudienVerlag, 165–180.

——— (2004) Die Zukunft der deutschen Sprache nach der Erweiterung der Europäischen Union. *Jahrbuch Deutsch als Fremdsprache* 30: 163–181.

——— (2008) Die Förderung der Muttersprachen von MigrantInnen als Bestandteil einer glaubwürdigen Mehrsprachigkeitspolitik in Österreich. *ÖDaF-Mitteilungen* 24 (2): 7–15.

——— (2011) Mehrsprachigkeit und Identität in Sprachenbiographien von Migrantinnen und Migranten. *Jahrbuch Deutsch als Fremdsprache* 36: 55–77.

——— / Fandrych, Christian/ Hufeisen, Britta/ Riemer, Claudia (eds.) (2010) *Deutsch als Fremd- und Zweitsprache. Ein internationales Handbuch.* 2 Halbbde. Berlin/ New York: de Gruyter Mouton.

Kruse, Jan (2012) *Das Barcelona-Prinzip. Die Dreisprachigkeit aller Europäer als sprachenpolitisches Ziel der EU.* Frankfurt a.M.: Lang.

——— (2013) "I do not understand the EU-Vorlage." Folgen der sprachenpolitischen Praxis in den Institutionen der EU für den deutschen Bundestag – Ergebnisse einer quantitativen Untersuchung. In Schneider-Wiejowski/ Kellermeier-Rehbein/ Haselhuber, 309–323.

——— / Ammon, Ulrich (2012) Language competence and language choice within EU institutions and their effects on national legislative authorities. In Berthoud, A.-C./ Grin, F./ Lüdi, G. (eds.) *Exploring the Dynamics of Multilingualism. The DYLAN Project.* Amsterdam: John Benjamins, 157–177.

Kryuchkova, Tatjana (2001) English as a language of science in Russia. In Ammon, 405–423.

Kube, Sigrid/ Kotze, Carol (2002) Chronik (compiled by Kube until 1984; by Kotze from 1985). In Hess/ Becker, 257–319.

Kuhn, Thomas S. [1979] (1993) Metaphor in science. In Ortony, A. (ed.) *Metaphor and Thought.* 2nd edition Cambridge: Cambridge University Press, 533–542.

Kuntze, Lisa (2002) Die Evangelisch-Lutherische Kirke in Namibia. In Hess/ Becker, 192–201.

Küppers, Almut/ Quetz, Jürgen (eds.) (2006) *Motivation Revisited.* Berlin: LIT-Verlag.

Küppers, Günter/ Weingarten, Peter/ Ulitzka, Norbert (1982) *Die Nobelpreise in Physik und Chemie, 1901–1929. Materialien zum Nominierungsprozeß.* Bielefeld: Kleine.

Kürten, Markus A. (2004) *Die Bedeutung der deutschen Sprache im Recht der Europäischen Union.* Berlin: Duncker & Humblot.

Kuruyazızı, Nilüfer (2004) Die deutsche akademische Emigration von 1933 und ihre Rolle bei der Neugründung der Universität Istanbul sowie bei der Gründung der Germanistik. In Durzak/ Kuruyazızı, 253–266.

Kurz, Gunde (2000) Studienbegleitender und studienintegrierter DaF-Unterricht in internationalen Studiengängen. *InfoDaF* 27 (6): 584–597.Kußler, Rainer (2001) Deutschunterricht und Gemanistiks-tudium in Südafrika. In Helbig/ Götze/ Henrici/ Krumm, Vol. 2: 1609–1619.

Kusterer, Hermann (1980) Das Sprachenproblem in den Europäischen Gemeinschaften. Ein Plädoyer für Pragmatik. *Europa-Archiv* 35 (22): 693–698.

Kutschker, Michael/ Kirsch, Werner (1979) *Industriegütermarketing und Einkauf in Europa. Deutschlandstudie.* München: Kirsch.

Kvam, Sigmund (2003) Wirtschaftsdeutsch in Norwegen. Eine Bestandsaufnahme. In Reuter/ Piitulainen, 71–89.

Kwon, Oh-Hyung (2003) Motive für die Wahl von Deutsch als Unterrichts- und Studienfach bei Ober-schülern und Studierenden. In Ammon/ Chong, 255–272.

Kymlicka, Will (1999) Citizenship in an era of globalization: comment on held. In Shapiro, I./ Hacker-Cordón, C. (eds.) *Democracy's Edges.* Cambridge: Cambridge University Press, 112–126.

Labrie, Normand (1993) *La construction linguistique de la Communauté Européenne.* Paris: Champion.

Ladin, Wolfgang (1980) Deutsch in Ostfrankreich. Die derzeitige Verbreitung des elsässischen Dialekts. *Germanistische Mitteilungen* 12: 43–57.

————— (1982) *Der Elsässische Dialekt – museumsreif? Analyse einer Umfrage.* Strasbourg: Salde.

Lahr-Kurten, Matthias (2012) *Deutsch sprechen in Frankreich. Praktiken der Förderung der deutschen Sprache im französischen Bildungssystem.* Bielefeld: transcript-verlag.

Lainio, Sirkka-Liisa (2003) Geschäftskorrespondenz im Wandel – gegenwärtige Tendenzen bei den deutsch-finnischen Handelskontakten. In Reuter/ Piitulainen, 187–196.

Laitenberger, Volkhard (1976) *Akademischer Austausch und auswärtige Kulturpolitik. Der Deutsche Akademische Austauschdienst (DAAD) 1923–1945.* Göttingen/ Frankfurt a.M./ Zürich: Musterschmidt.

————— (2000) Der DAAD von seinen Anfängen bis 1945. In Alter (2000a), 20–49.

Laitin, David D. (1993) The game theory of language regimes. *International Political Science Review* 14: 227–239.

————— (1997) The cultural identities of a European state. *Politics & Society* 25: 277–302.

Lakoff, George/ Johnson, Mark (1980) *Metaphors We Live By.* Chicago/ London: The University of Chicago Press.

La Madeleine, Bonnie L. (2007) Lost in translation. *Nature* 445: 454f.

Lammert, Norbert (2006) Politik und Sprache. Eröffnungsrede am 23. November 2006. *Der Sprachdienst* 50 (6): 169–177.

Lämmert, Eberhard (2000) Der DAAD – Wegbereiter für eine weltoffene Germanistik. In Alter (2000a), 130–151.

Landa, Laura (2006) Academic language barriers and language freedom. *Current Issues in Language Planning* 7 (1): 61–81.

Landry, Rodrigue/ Bourghis, Richard (1997) Linguistic landscape and ethnolinguistic vitality: An empiri-cal study. *Journal of Language and Social Psychology* 16 (1): 23–49.

Langdon-Neuner, Elise (2007) Let them write English. *Revista do Colégio Brasileiro de Cirurgiões* 34 (4): 272–276.

Langé, Gisella/ Scifo, Rita M. (eds.) (2012) *Perche studiare il tedesco? Dossier informativo* 2. (www.istruzione. lombardia.gov.it/materiali/protlo832_12dossier-tedesco.pdf)

Längin, Bernd (1996) *Gottes letzte Inseln. Wie die Hutterer und Amischen leben.* Augsburg: Pattloch.

Langner, Michael (2010) Entwicklungen von Deutsch als Fremd- und Zweitsprache in der Schweiz. In Krumm/ Fandrych/ Hufeisen/ Riemer, Vol. 1, 80–88.

Langwasser, Silke (2008) Die Old Order Amish. Eine Glaubensgemeinschaft zwischen Beharrlichkeit und Entwicklung. Marburg: Tectum.

Lanthaler, Franz (1990) Dialekt und Zweisprachigkeit in Südtirol. In Lanthaler, F. (ed.) *Mehr als eine Sprache – Più di una lingua. Zu einer Sprachstrategie für Südtirol.* Meran: Alpha & Beta, 57–81. Reprinted in Lanthaler (2012a), 25–49.

————— (1996) Varietäten des Deutschen in Südtirol. In Stickel, G. (ed.) *Varietäten des Deutschen. Regional-und Umgangssprachen.* Berlin/ New York: de Gruyter, 364–383. Reprinted in Lanthaler (2012a), 69–91.

————— (2012a) *Texte zu Sprache und Schule in Südtirol (1974–2012).* Meran/ Lauben: Edizioni alphabeta Verlag.

————— (2012b) Zur Standardvariation des Deutschen am Beispiel Südtirol. In Lanthaler (2012a), 165191.

————— (2012c) Die deutsche Standardsprache in Südtirol und ihre Rolle in der Schule. In Lanthaler (2012a), 405–425.

Laponce, J[ean]. A. (1987a) Language and communication: the rise of the monolingual state. In Cioffi-Revilla/ Merrit/ Zinnes, 183–207.

———— (1987b) *Languages and Their Territories.* Toronto/ Buffalo/ London: University of Toronto Press.

———— (1996) Who is at the center of the world? Comparing the mental maps of American, Canadian, French, and Polish students. In *Naród – wladza – społeczeństwo* [Nation – Macht – Gesellschaft]. Warschau: Scholar, 77–100.

Large, J. A. (1983) *The Foreign-Language Barrier: Problems in Scientific Communication.* London: Andre Deutsch.

———— (1989) Science and the foreign-language barrier. In Coleman, H. (ed.) *Working With Language.* Berlin/ New York: de Gruyter, 169–192.

Lasagabaster, David (2004) Attitude. In Ammon/ Dittmar/ Mattheier/ Trudgill, 399–404.

Lasatowicz, Maria K./ Weger, Tobias (2008) Polen. In Eichinger/ Plewnia/ Riehl, 145–169.

Laurien, Ingrid (2006) Das Fach Deutsch an Universitäten im "Neuen Südafrika" – Eine Laborsituation für Europa. *Info DaF* 33 (5): 438–445. Lăzărescu/ Lazarescu, Ioan (2005) Stellenangebote in der "Allgemeinen Deutschen Zeitung für Rumänien" aus pragmalinguistischer und sprachpolitischer Sicht. In Lenk, H. E./ Chesterman, A. (eds.) *Pressetextsorten im Vergleich – Contrasting Text Types in the Press.* Hildesheim/ Zürich/ New York: Olms, 243–260.

———— (2006) Ein deutsch-rumänisches Austriazismenwörterbuch – cui bono? In Wolff, D. (ed.) *Mehrsprachige Individuen – vielsprachige Gesellschaften.* Frankfurt a.M.: Lang, 223235.

———— (2011) Rumäniendeutsche sprachliche Besonderheiten. In Katelhön, P./ Settinieri, J. (eds.) *Wortschatz, Wörterbücher und L2-Erwerb.* Wien: Praesens, 11–26.

———— (2013): Rumäniendeutsch – eine eigenständige, jedoch besondere Varietät der deutschen Sprache. In Schneider-Wiejowski/ Kellermeier-Rehbein/ Haselhuber, 371–391.

Leal, Barry/ Bettoni, Camilla/ Malcolm, Ian (1991) *Widening our Horizons: Report of the Review of the Teaching of Modern Languages in Higher Education.* Vol. 1. Canberra: Australian Government Publishing Service.

Lee, Won-Kyung (2007) Deutsch als Fremdsprachen in privaten Sprachschulen Koreas. In Ammon/ Chong, 361–368.

Van Leewen, Eva C. (ed.) *Sprachenlernen als Investition in die Zukunft. Wirkungskreise eines Sprachlernzentrums. Festschrift für Heinrich P. Kelz zum 65. Geburtstag.* Tübingen: Narr.

Le Guen, M. A. (2002) *La pratique et la transmission de l'alsacien en Alsace, rapport de stage maîtrise MASS, année 2001–2002.* Direction régionale de l'INSEE, Alsace.

Lehto, Olli (1998) *Mathematics Without Borders. A History of the International Mathematical Union.* New York: Springer.

Leibniz, Gottfried W. [1679] (1967) *Ermahnung an die Deutschen* [von] *Deutscher Sprachpflege.* Darmstadt: Wissenschaftliche Buchgesellschaft.

———— (1877) [1697/ 1717] *Unvorgreiffliche Gedancken, betreffend die Ausübung und Verbesserung der Teutschen Sprache.* In *Leibniz und Schottelius. Die unvorgreiflichen Gedanken.* Schmarsow, A. (ed.). Straßburg/ London: Trübner, 44–92.

Lemmer, Björn/ Middeke, Martin (2008) Geschichte einer wissenschaftlichen Publikation – nur noch englische Zitate erwünscht. *Deutsche Medizinische Wochenschrift* 133: 1.

Lenaerts, Gilberte (2001) A failure to comply with the EU language policy: a study of the council archives. *Multilingua* 20 (3): 221–244.

Leonhard, Joachim F. (2002) Deutsch in einem vielsprachigen Europa. In Hoberg (2002a), 6773.

———— / Ludwig, Hans-Werner/ Schwarze, Dietrich/ Straßner, Erich (eds.) (2002) *Medienwissenschaft: ein Handbuch zur Entwicklung von Medien und Kommunikationsformen.* Teilband 3. Berlin/ New York: de Gruyter.

Le Page, Robert B./ Tabouret-Keller, Andrée (1985) *Acts of Identity: Creole-based Approaches to Language and Ethnicity.* Cambridge: Cambridge University Press.

Lesch, Phoebe (2002) Die Sprache der Wirtschaft. Analyse der EU-Programme zur Förderung von Vielsprachigkeit und Sprachindustrie. In Weydt, 66–72.

Leutner, Hans (1989) Rio de Janeiro. In Roeloffs, 96–104.

Lévy, Paul (1950/ 1952) *La Langue Allemande en France, 2 vols. I: Des origines à 1830, II: De 1830 à nos jours.* Lyon/ Paris: IAC.

Li, Liudmila (2014) *Die Problematik der sprachlichen Integration von ImmigrantInnen. Unter Berücksichtigung des staatlich geforderten Sprachniveaus B1 (GER) Verbesserungsvorschläge auf Grundlage der empirischen Untersuchung in Berlin-Moabit.* Frankfurt a.M.: Lang.

Lie, Kwang-Sook (2003) Überblick über die Geschichte des Deutschlernens und des Lernens anderer Fremdsprachen. In Ammon/ Chong, 213–228.

Lieberson, Stanley (1980) Procedures for improving sociolinguistic surveys of language maintenance and language shift. *International Journal of the Sociology of Language* 25: 11–27.

————— (1981) *Language Diversity and Language Contact*. Stanford: Stanford University Press.

————— (1982) Forces affecting language spread: some basic propositions. In Cooper, 37–62.

————— (1987) Language barriers between different speech communities/ international problems of communication. In Ammon/ Mattheier/ Dittmar, 744–749.

Liebert, Wolf-Andreas (1997) Interaktion und Kognition. Die Herausbildung metaphorischer Denkmodelle in Gesprächen zwischen Wissenschaftlern und Wissenschaftsjournalisten. In Biere/ Liebert, 180–209.

Lienert, Gustav A. (1977) Über Werner Traxel: Internationalität und Provinzialismus, zur Frage: Sollten Psychologen in Englisch publizieren? *Psychologische Beiträge* 19: 487–492.

Limbach, Jutta (ed.) (2007) *Ausgewanderte Wörter*. Ismaning: Hueber.

————— (2008) *Hat Deutsch eine Zukunft? Unsere Sprache in der globalisierten Welt*. München: Beck.

Lins, Ulrich (1988) *Die gefährliche Sprache. Die Verfolgung der Esperantisten unter Hitler und Stalin*. Gerlingen: Bleicher.

Lipp, Reinhard (2012) Sprachenvielfalt an der Deutschen Höheren Privatschule (DHPS) – Herausforderung für den Unterricht? In *Sprachenvielfalt in Namibia*, 81–88.

Lippert, Herbert (1978) Rückzug der deutschen Sprache aus der Medizin? Die Sprachen medizinischer Zeitschriftentitel der letzten 100 Jahre. *Medizinische Klinik* 73 (14): 487496.

————— (1979) Schlußwort. *Medizinische Klinik* 74 (11): 409–411.

————— (1986) Englisch – neue Wissenschaftssprache der Medizin. In Kalverkämper/ Weinrich, 38–44.

Lipps, Susanne/ Breda, Oliver [2009] (2012) *Mallorca*. 2nd updated edition, Ostfildern: DuMont.

Lo Bianco, Joseph (1987) *National Policy on Languages*. Canberra: Australian Government Publishing Service.

Lochtman, Katja/Lutjeharms, Madeline (2004) Attitüden zu Fremdsprachen und zum Fremdsprachenlernen. In Börner, W./ Vogel, K. (eds.) *Emotion und Kognition im Fremdsprachenunterricht*. Tübingen: Narr, 173–189.

Locquin, Marcel V. (1989) *Situation de la language française dans les périodiques scientifiques et techniques en 1988*. Paris: Commissariat général de la langue française.

Loehr, Kerstin (1998) *Mehrsprachigkeitsprobleme in der Europäischen Union: eine empirische und theoretische Analyse aus sprachwissenschaftlicher Perspektive*. Frankfurt a.M.: Lang.

Löffelholz, Konrad/ Trendelenburg, Ulrich [2006] (2008) *Verfolgte deutschsprachige Pharmakologen 1933–1945*. 2nd edition, Frechen: Dr. Schrör.

Löffler, Heinrich [1985] (2010) *Germanistische Soziolinguistik*. 4th edition, Berlin: Schmidt.

Lohner, Walter F. W./ Nollendorfs, Valters (eds.) (1976) *German Studies in the United States. Assessment and Outlook*. Madison: University of Wisconsin Press.

Lohse, Christian (ed.) (2004) *Die deutsche Sprache in der Europäischen Union. Rolle und Chancen aus rechts- und sprachwissenschaftlicher Sicht*. Baden-Baden: Nomos.

Lötscher, Andreas (1983) *Schweizerdeutsch. Geschichte, Dialekte, Gebrauch*. Frauenfeld/ Stuttgart: Huber.

Louden, Mark L. (2003) Minority language 'maintenance by inertia': Pennsylvania German among nonsectarian speakers. In Androutsopoulos/ Ziegler, 121–137.

————— (2006a) Pennsylvania German in the 21st century. In Berend/ Knipf-Komlósi, 89–107.

————— (2006b) Patterns of language maintenance in German American language islands. In Thornburg, L./ Fuller, J. (eds.) *Studies in Contact Linguistics: Essays in Honor of Glenn G. Gilbert*. New York: Lang, 127–146.

————— / Lovik, Tom (2008) Vereinigte Staaten von Amerika. In Institut für Deutsche Sprache, 75–80.

Louttit, C. M. (1957) The use of foreign languages by psychologists, chemists and physicists. *American Journal of Psychology* 70: 315.

Lovik, Thomas (2004a) Deutsch in den USA: Beschreibung und Beurteilung einer kritischen Lage. *Jahrbuch für Internationale Germanistik* 35 (1): 25–27.

————— (2004b) Vereinigte Staaten von Amerika. In Institut für Deutsche Sprache, 95–100.

Lowenberg, Peter H. (ed.) (1988) *Language Spread and Language Policy. Issues, Implications and Case Studies*. Washington D. C.: Georgetown University Press.

Van der Lubbe, Fredericka (2007) *Martin Aedler and the "High Dutch Minerva". The First German Grammar for the English*. Frankfurt a.M.: Lang.

Lüdi, Georges (2001) Vielfältige mehrsprachige Repertoires für alle Bürger Europas. Leitgedanken für ein europäisches "Gesamtsprachenkonzept". In de Bot, 59–77.

————— (2013) Ist Englisch als lingua franca eine Bedrohung für Deutsch und andere Nationalsprachen? In Schneider-Wiejowski/ Kellermeier-Rehbein/ Haselhuber, 275–292.

Lüsebrink, Claire (1986) Möglichkeiten und Grenzen des rechtlichen Schutzes von Sprachminderheiten am Beispiel Südtirol/ Burgenland. In Hinderling, 57–81.

Lutjeharms, Madeline (2007) Mehrsprachigkeit und Spracherwerb aus Brüsseler Sicht. *Muttersprache* 117 (2): 110–124.

Lutzmann, Eva/ Schneider, Gerald (2009) Global Players – Die Auswärtige Kulturpolitik Frankreichs, Großbritanniens, Italiens, Portugals und Spaniens. In Maaß (2009a); 369385.

Lützeler, Paul M. (1990) Literaturwissenschaft – German Studies – Interkulturelle Germanistik. Zur "Krise" des Fachs Deutsch in den USA. *Mitteilungen des Deutschen Germanistenverbandes* 37 (1): 31–37.

Luxemburger Wörterbuch (1950–1975/1977). 4 Bände und 1 Ergänzungsband. Luxemburg: Linden.

Lyovin, Anatole V. (1997) *An Introduction to the Languages of the World.* New York/ Oxford: Oxford University Press.

Maaß, Kurt-Jürgen (ed.) [2005] (2009a) *Kultur und Außenpolitik. Handbuch für Studium und Praxis.* 2nd completely revised and expanded edition, Baden-Baden: Nomos.

—— (2009b) Überblick: Ziele und Instrumente der Auswärtigen Kulturpolitik. In Maaß (2009a), 2532.

—— (2009c) Das deutsche Modell – Die Mittlerorganisationen. In Maaß (2009a), 269–280.

—— (2013) *Werbung, Werte, Wettbewerb. Wohin steuert die Auswärtige Kulturpolitik? Abschiedsvorlesung am 24. April 2013 an der Universität Tübingen.* Stuttgart: Institut für Auslandsbeziehungen.

MacCallum, T. W./ Taylor, Stephen (1938) *The Nobel Prize-Winners and the Nobel Foundation 1901–1937.* Zürich: Central European Times.

Mackey, William F. (1976) *Bilinguisme et contact des langues.* Paris: Klincksieck.

—— (1989) Determining the status and function of languages in multilingual societies. In Ammon 1989d, 3–20.

—— (2003) Forecasting the fate of languages. In Maurais/ Morris, 64–81.

—— (2005) Bilingualism and multilingualism. In Ammon/ Dittmar/ Mattheier/ Trudgill, 1483–1495.

Mackiewicz, Maciej (2013) Deutschschüler und ihre Motivation im Spiegel der Evaluation der "Deutsch-Wagen-Tour" in Polen. *Info DaF* 40 (1): 23–36.

—— (2014) *Interkulturelle Motivation im Fremdsprachenunterricht. Eine komparative Studie zu Deutsch als Fremdsprache in Polen und den USA.* Frankfurt a.M.: Lang.

Maddison, Angus (2007) *Contours of the World Economy, 1–2030 AD. Essays in Macro-Economic History.* Oxford: Oxford University Press.

Madl, Benedikt L. (2001) *Chinas Auslandsstudium: der Brain-Drain und die Stellung Europas. Zur Politik sino-europäischen Bildungsaustausches sowie eine Analyse der Länderpräfe Länderpräferenzen von Studierenden der Universität Peking.* Wien: Lang.

Magill, Frank N. (1991) *Survey of Social Science. Economics Series.* 5 vols. Pasadena, CA/ Englewood Cliffs, NJ: Salem.

Maher, John [C.] (1986) The development of English as an international language of medicine. *Applied Linguistics* 7: 206–218.

—— (1989) Language use and preference in Japanese medical communication. In Coleman, 299-315.

—— (2007) Remains of the day: language orphans and the decline of German as a medical lingua franca in Japan. In: Coulmas, 141–153.

Maher, Moustafa (2008) Die ägyptische Germanistik zwischen historischem Momentum und Suche nach neuen Perspektiven. *Kairoer Germanistische Studien* 17: 3–17.

Mahle, Walter A. (ed.) (1995) *Deutschland in der internationalen Kommunikation.* Konstanz: Ölschläger.

Mahlmann, Carl/ Zombik, Peter (2002) Der internationale Markt für Musikproduktionen. In Leonhard et al., 2677–2689.

Mahmoud, Youssef (1987) Cost-benefit analysis and language planning in the United Nations. In Tonkin/ Johnson-Weiner, 33–44.

Mai, Richard (1939) Leben und Wirken des Reichsverbandes für die katholischen Auslandsdeutschen. In Büttner, 20–62.

Maier-Leibnitz, Heinz (1986) Should everything be published in English? *Minerva* 24 (2/ 3): 244–247.

Mair, Christian (ed.) (2003) *The Politics of English as a World Language. New Horizons in Postcolonial Culture Studies.* Amsterdam: Rodopi.

Maitz, Péter/ Sándor, Klára (2009) Changes in the linguistic marketplace: the case of German in Hungary. In Carl/ Stevenson, 149–164.

Maiworm, Friedhelm/ Wächter, Bernd (2002) *English-Language-Taught Degree Programmes in European Higher Education: Trends and Success Factors.* Bonn: Lemmens.

———— / ———— (2003) *Englischsprachige Studiengänge in Europa. Merkmale, Impulse, Erfolgsfaktoren.* Essen: Stifterverband für die Deutsche Wissenschaft.

———— / ———— (2008) *English-Taught Programmes in European Higher Education. The Picture in 2007.* Bonn: Lemmens.

Majoub, N. (1995) Der hässliche Deutsche und die deutsche Sprache. Beeinflußt das Deutschlandbild die Einstellung zum Deutschen als Fremdsprache? *Germanistische Mitteilungen* 42: 65–82.

Majtanova, Miroslava (2015) *Die Rolle der deutschen Sprache für die Gruppenidentität von Deutschen im Ausland. Am Beispiel des Vereinslebens in Kuala Lumpur.* Frankfurt a.M.: Lang.

Malicka, Agnieszka (2001) Der Schutz der deutschen Minderheit in der Republik Polen. In Manssen, G./ Banaszak, B. (eds.) *Minderheitenschutz in Mittel- und Osteuropa.* Frankfurt a.M.: Lang, 227–236.

von Maltzan, Carlotta (2009) Sprachenpolitik und die Rolle der Fremdsprachen (Deutsch) in Südafrika. *Stellenbosch papers in linguistics Plus* 38 (Sonderausgabe: *Mehrsprachigkeit und Sprachenpolitik in Südafrika/ Multilingualism and language policies in Africa*): 205214.

———— (2010) Deutsch in Südafrika. In Krumm/ Fandrych/ Hufeisen/ Riemer, Vol. 2, 1805–1808.

Mamadouh, Virginie (1995) *De talen in het Europees parlement* (Amsterdamse SociaalGeographische Studies 52). Amsterdam: Instituut voor Sociale Geographie, Universiteit van Amsterdam.

Manherz, Karl (1998) *Die Ungarndeutschen.* Budapest: Útmutató.

Manz, Viviane (2002) *Sprachenvielfalt und europäische Integration. Sprachenrecht im Spannungsfeld von Wirtschaft, Politik und Kultur.* Zürich: Schulthess Juristische Medien.

Mari, Isidor/ Strubell, Miquel (2002) *The Linguistic Regime of the European Union: Prospects in the Face of Enlargement.* Europa Diversa. (www.europadiversa.org/ eng/ grup_activitats.html)

Markl, Hubert (1986) *Die Spitzenforschung spricht englisch. Deutsch als Wissenschaftssprache.* In Kalverkämper/ Weinrich, 20–25; wiederabgedr. in BerlinBrandenburgische Akademie der Wissenschaften 2011, 147–152.

———— (2002) R&D in Europe: Uniting forces, moving ahead. In Teich, A. H./ Nelson, S. D./ Lita, S. J. (eds.) *AAAS Science and Technology Policy Yearbook 2002.* Washington: AAAS, 387–397.

Markowitsch, Hans J. (1996) Warum englisch veröffentlichen? Kommentar zu Montada, Becker, Schoepflin und Baltes: "Die internationale Rezeption der deutschsprachigen Psychologie". *Psychologische Rundschau* 47: 34–37.

Marschan, R./ Welch, D./ Welch, L. (1997) Language – The forgotten factor in multinational management. *European Management Journal* 15.5: 591–598.

Martens, Charles de/ Geffcken, Friedrich Heinrich [1832] (1866) *Le guide diplomatique, précis des droits et des fonctions des agents diplomatiques et consulaires.* 5th edition Paris/ Leipzig: Heideloff & Campé/ Brockhaus.

Martin, Werner (ed.) (1985) *Verzeichnis der Nobelpreisträger 1901–1984. Mit Preisbegründungen, Kurzkommentaren, literarischen Werkbibliographien und einer Biographie Alfred Nobels.* München.

Martynova, Olga (2010) *Sprachwahl in der deutsch-russischen Unternehmenskommunikation.* Frankfurt a.M.: Lang.

———— (2011) Die deutsche Sprache in russischen Unternehmen und in Unternehmen aus deutschsprachigen Ländern in Russland. In Ammon/ Kemper, 293–300.

Marx, Wolfgang (1989) Bemerkungen zum Sprachenstreit in der deutschen Psychologie. *Psychologische Beiträge* 40: 89–92.

Mast, Claudia (2002) *Unternehmenskommunikation.* Stuttgart: Lucius & Lucius. *Mathematical Reviews* (1940ff.). Providence, RI: American Mathematical Society.

MathSci Disc (1940–1979) (1980–1987) (1988–1992) (1993–1996). *Reviews and Citations of the World's Research Literature in Mathematics and Related Areas, Compiled from the MathSci Online Database Subtitles, "Mathematical Reviews" and "Current Mathematical Publications".* [Providence, RI]: American Mathematical Society/ Silver Platter International.

Mattheier, Klaus (1980) *Pragmatik und Soziologie der Dialekte.* Heidelberg: Quelle & Meyer.

———— (1994) Theorie der Sprachinsel. Voraussetzungen und Strukturierungen. In Berend/ Mattheier, 333–348.

———— (1996) Methoden der Sprachinselforschung. In Goebl/ Nelde/ Starý/ Wölck, 812–819.

———— (2003) Sprachinseltod: Überlegungen zur Entwicklungsdynamik von Sprachinseln. In Keel, William D./ Mattheier, 13–31.

Matthews, Janice R./ Bowen, John M./ Matthews, Robert W. (1996) *Successful Scientific Writing: A Step-by-Step Guide for the Biological and Medical Sciences.* Cambridge: Cambride University Press.

Mattusch, Hans-Jürgen (1999) *Vielsprachigkeit: Fluch oder Segen für die Menschheit? Zu Fragen einer europäischen und globalen Fremdsprachenpolitik.* Frankfurt a.M.: Lang. Maurais, Jacques (2003) Towards a new linguistic world order. In Maurais/ Morris, 13–36.

———— / Morris, Michael A. (eds.) (2003) *Languages in a Globalising World*. Cambridge: Cambridge University Press.

Mauranen, Anna (2003) Academic English as lingua franca – a corpus approach. *TESOL Quarterly* 37: 513–527.

De Mauro, Tullio / Vedovelli, Massimo (1994) La diffusione dell'italiano nel mondo: problemi istituzionali e sociolinguistici. In Ammon 1994e, 25–39.

Mayer, Franz C. / Palmowski, Jan (2004) European identities and the EU – the ties that bind the peoples of Europe. *Journal of Common Market Studies* 24 (3): 573–598.

Mayer, Ruth (2005) *Diaspora. Eine kritische Begriffsbestimmung*. Bielefeld: Transcript.

McArthur, Marilyn (1990) *Zum Identitätswandel der Siebenbürger Sachsen. Eine kulturanthropologische Studie*. Köln / Wien: Böhlau.

McCallen, Brian (1989) *English: A World Commodity. The International Market for Training in English as a Foreign Language*. London: The Economist Intelligence Unit Ltd.

McConnell, Grant D. (1996) A model of language development and vitality. *Indian Journal of Applied Linguistics* 22 (1): 33–48.

———— (2003) Towards a scientific geostrategy for English. In Maurais / Morris, 298–312.

McCrum, Robert (2010) *Globish: How the English Language Became the World's Language*. New York / London: Norton.

McGrail, M. R. / Rickard, C. M. / Jones, R. (2006) Publish or perish: a systematic review of interventions to increase academic publication rates. *Higher Education Research and Development* 25.1: 19–35.

McGuiness-King, Kristina (2004) Die Situation von Deutsch als Fremdsprache und Germanistik in Neuseeland: Ein Fach unter Druck. *Jahrbuch für Internationale Germanistik* 36 (1): 2338.

———— (2005) Geschichte, Gegenwart und Zukunft einer Fremdsprache unter Druck: Deutsch als Fremdsprache und Germanistik in Neuseeland. In Van Leewen, 347–365.

McPhail, Thomas L. [2002] (2007) *Global Communication. Theories, Stakeholders, and Trends*. Malden, USA: Blackwell.

Medgyes, Peter / Kaplan, Robert B. (1992) Discourse in a foreign language: the example of Hungarian scholars. *International Journal of the Sociology of Language* 98: 67–100.

Medgyes, Péter / László, Mónika (2001) The foreign language competence of Hungarian scholars: ten years later. In Ammon, 261–286.

Medline (1966ff.) Washington, DC: National Library Medicine.

Mehlich, Diane et al. (2003) Nationale Sprachenpolitik und europäische Integration. *ForostArbeitspapier* Nr. 18. München: Forost.

Meier, Marcus (2008) *Die Schwarzenauer Neutäufer. Genese einer Gemeindebildung zwischen Pietismus und Täufertum*. Göttingen: Vandenhoeck & Ruprecht.

Meierkord, Christiane (1996) *Englisch als Medium der interkulturellen Kommunikation. Untersuchungen zum non-native- / non-native-speaker-Diskurs*. Frankfurt a.M.: Lang.

Meinecke, Friedrich [1907] (1969) *Weltbürgertum und Nationalstaat* (Friedrich Meinecke Werke, 5). München: Oldenbourg.

Meitzner, Andreas (2012) Zum Konzept Auswärtiger Kulturpolitik des Auswärtigen Amtes. In Drews, 121–129.

Melika, Georg (1994) Spracherhaltung und Sprachwechsel bei der deutschen Minderheit von Transkarpatien. In Berend / Mattheier, 289–301.

Melkerne, Sean / Graham, Anne M. (2011, May) *Labour Market Intelligence on Languages and Intercultural Skills in Higher Education. Shaping the Modern Future*. England o.O.: (UCML) University Council of Modern Languages. Mendieta, Eduardo / Phillipson, Robert / Skutnabb-Kangas, Tove (2006) English in the geopolitics of knowledge. *Revista Canaria de Estudios Ingleses* 53: 15–27.

Meneghini, R. / Packer, A. L. (2007) Is there science beyond English? *Embo Reports* 8: 112–116. Menkhaus, Heinrich (2001) Global German Player. Deutsch in deutschkapitalisierten Unternehmen in Japan. *Deutschunterricht in Japan* 6: 123–139.

Meng, Hong (2005) *Das Auslandsstudium von Chinesen in Deutschland (1861–2001). Ein Beispiel internationaler Studentenmobilität im Rahmen der chinesischen Modernisierung*. Frankfurt a. M.: Lang.

Mennonitisches Lexikon (1913–1967), 5 Bde, in zum Teil mehreren Lieferungen. Unterschiedliche Erscheinungsorte und Verlage.

Di Meola, Claudio / Tonelli, Livia (2008) Italien. In Institut für Deutsche Sprache, 39–45.

Merker, Stefanie (2006) *Deutsch im Europarat – Ablehnung als Amtssprache und deren Folgen*. Unpublished master's dissertation, Universität Duisburg-Essen.

Merz, Hans P. (1987) *Personalpolitik japanischer Unternehmen in der Bundesrepublik Deutschland. Arbeitsbeziehungen und Manpower-Integration als Problem Transnationaler Unternehmen.* Berlin: Schiller.

Mettewie, Laurence/ Van Mensel, Luc (2009) Multilingualism at all costs: language use and language needs in business in Brussels. *Sociolinguistica* 23: 131–149.

Metz, Paul (1990) Bibliometrics: Library use and citation studies. In Lynch, M. J. (ed.) *Academic Libraries: Research Perspectives.* Chicago: ALA, 147–148.

Meyer, Hans J. (2004) Global English – A New lingua franca or a New Imperial Culture? In Gardt/ Hüppauf, 65–84.

Meyer, Kurt – mit einem Beitrag von Hans Bickel (2006) *Schweizer Wörterbuch. So sagen wir in der Schweiz.* Frauenfeld/ Stuttgart/ Wien: Huber.

Michels, Eckard (2004) Deutsch als Weltsprache? Franz Thierfelder, the Deutsche Akademie in Munich and the promotion of the German language abroad, 1923–1945. *German History* 22 (2): 206–228.

——— (2005) *Von der Deutschen Akademie zum Goethe-Institut. Sprach- und auswärtige Kulturpolitik 1923–1960.* München: Oldenbourg.

Michels, Stefan (1989) *Status und Funktion des Deutschen als Fachsprache der Chemie.* Unpublished master's dissertation, Universität-GH-Duisburg.

——— (1991) Recent changes in the status of German as a language of chemistry. In Ammon/Hellinger, 408–420.

Miessen, Werner et al. (1986) *Bibliographie zu Geschichte, Sprache und Literatur der deutschsprachigen Gemeinschaft Belgiens 1945–1983.* Brüssel: Belgische Bibliographiekommission.

Mikhalchenko, Vida I./ Trushkova, Yulia (2003) Russian in the Modern World. In Maurais/ Morris, 260–290.

Milian-Massana, Antoni (1995) Le régime linguistiques de l'Union Européenne: Le régime des institutions et l'incidence du droit communautaire sur la mosaïque linguistique européenne. *Rivista di dritto europeo* 35: 485 ff.

Millar, Sharon/ Jensen, Astrid (2009) Language choice and management in Danish multilingual countries: the role of common sense. *Sociolinguistica* 23: 86–103.

Milroy, Lesley (1980) *Language and Social Networks.* London: Wiley-Blackwell.

Mindadse, Iwa/ Bakuradze, Anna (2010) Deutsch in Georgien. In Krumm/ Fandrych/ Hufeisen/ Riemer, Vol. 2, 1664–1667.

Mittelstaedt, Peter (1999) Sprache und Wirklichkeit in der Quantenphysik. In Wiegand, 64–88.

Mocanu, Delia/ Baronchelli, Andrea/ Perra, Nicola/ Bruno, Gonçalves/ Vespignan, Alessandro (2012) *The Twitter of Babel: Mapping World Languages through Microblogging Platforms.* (www.arxiv.org/pdf/1212.5238v1.pdf)

Mocikat, Ralph (2006) *Die Anglisierung der Wissenschaftssprache am Beispiel der Biomedizin* eine kritische Stellungnahme. (www.adawis.de) (www.adawis.de/admin/upload/navigation/data/Spr-M2.pdf)

——— (2007) Ein Plädoyer für die Vielfalt. Die Wissenschaftssprache am Beispiel der Biomedizin. *Forschung & Lehre* 14: 90–92.

——— (2009) Die Diktatur der Zitatenindizes: Folgen für die Wissenskultur. *GAIA* 18 (2): 100–103.

——— (2010) Fertigwissen in der Einheitssprache. Was hat die "Bologna-Reform" mit Wissenschaftssprache zu tun? *Forschung & Lehre* 17: 652f.

Moelleken, Wolfgang W. (1987) Die rußlanddeutschen Mennoniten in Kanada und Mexiko: Sprachliche Entwicklung und diglossische Situation. *Zeitschrift für Dialektologie und Linguistik* 54 (2): 145–183.

Mohr, Annette/ Schneider, Ulrike (1994) Die Situation der deutschen Sprache in internationalen Organisationen. *Info DaF* 21 (6): 612–631.

Mohr-Sobkowiak, Saskia (2005) *Deutsch als Fremdsprache und Germanistik in Indien. Zur interkulturellen Unterrichtsmethodik im Literaturunterricht und dem Deutschlandbild indischer Schüler und Studenten. Dokumentation und Perspektiven.* Unpublished dissertation, Universität Karlsruhe.

Möller, Joachim/ Nekula, Marek (ed.) (2002) *Wirtschaft und Kommunikation. Beiträge zu den deutsch-tschechischen Wirtschaftsbeziehungen.* München: Iudicum.

Mommsen, Wolfgang J. (2002) *Die Urkatastrophe Deutschlands. Der Erste Weltkrieg 1914–1918.* Stuttgart: Klett-Cotta.

Montada, L[eo] (1985) Retrieving German psychological literature: services available to U.S. psychologists. *American Psychologist* 40: 14–18.

——— (1993) Deutsch als Wissenschaftssprache. In Montada, L. (ed.) *Bericht über den 38. Kongreß der Deutschen Gesellschaft für Psychologie 1992 in Trier.* Vol. 2. Göttingen: Hogrefe, 828830.

—— et al. (1995) Die internationale Rezeption der deutschsprachigen Psychologie. *Psychologische Rundschau* 46: 186–199.

—— / Schoepflin, Urs/ Baltes, Paul B. (1996) Erwiderung auf die Kommentare von Hans Markowitsch, Fritz Strack und Dieter Wolke. *Psychologische Rundschau* 47: 40f.

Montgomery, Scott L. (2013) *Does Science Need a Global Language? English and the Future of Research*. Chicago/ London: The University of Chicago Press.

Moraldo, Sandro M. (2003) Zur Entwicklung der deutschen Sprache und der Germanistik in Italien. *Jahrbuch für Internationale Germanistik* 35 (1): 13–18.

—— (ed.) (2008) *Sprachkontakt und Mehrsprachigkeit. Zur Anglizismendiskussion in Deutschland, Österreich, der Schweiz und Italien*. Heidelberg: Winter.

—— (2009) Hat Deutsch in Italien eine Zukunft? Die ‚questione linguistica' zwischen theoretischer Einsicht und praktischer Umsetzung. *Muttersprache* 119: 112–125.

—— (2010) Die Fremdsprachen an den Schulen Italiens im Kontext einer europäischen Bildungspolitik. *Sociolinguistica* 24: 134–152.

—— (2013) Die deutsche Sprache im Kontext der italienischen Sprachenpolitik. In Schneider Wiejowski/ Kellermeier-Rehbein/ Haselhuber, 391–409.

Moretti, Bruno/ Pandolfi, Elena M./ Casoni, Matteo (eds.) (2011) *Vitalità di una lingua minoritaria: Aspetti e proposte metodologiche/ Vitality of a Minority Language: Aspects and Methodological Issues*. Bellinzona: Osservatorio Linguistico della Svizzera Italiana.

Morgen, Daniel (2003) IV – Langue régionale d'alsace et des pays mosellans. *Bulletin officiel, hors-série* (Ministère éducation nationale) 2, 19 juin.

—— (2004) Die Sprachensituation im Elsass und das bilinguale Angebot in den Schulen im Elsass und am Oberrhein. (www.eurac/edu/en/research/institutes/ multilingualism/Documents/ Thematic_Forum_3_PDF. pdf.)

—— (2006) L'école et le recul du dialecte en alsace. *Nouveau Cahier d'allemand* 24 (4): 381–394.

—— (2007) L'école et le recul du dialecte (2). *Nouveau Cahier d'allemand* 25 (1): 63–78.

Mori, Isamu (1994) Die Bedeutung des Deutschen für die juristischen Fakultäten in Japan: Nachlassen des Einflusses deutschen Rechts? In Ammon 1994d, 49–62.

Morita, Emi (1989) *Sprachenwahl der Japaner in Düsseldorf*. Unpublished degree paper, Universität-GH-Duisburg/ Dokkyo-Universität, Tokyo.

Motz, Markus (2000) *Ausländische Studierende in Internationalen Studiengängen. Motivation, Sprachverwendung und sprachliche Bedürfnisse*. Bochum: AKS Verlag.

—— (ed.) (2005a) *Englisch oder Deutsch in Internationalen Studiengängen?* Frankfurt a. M.: Lang.

—— (2005b) Internationalisierung der Hochschulen und Deutsch als Fremdsprache. In Motz 2005a, 131–152.

Much, Thomas O. (2008) *Die Einführung von Englisch als Unternehmenssprache bei deutschen Firmen*. Unpublished essay for teaching qualification, Sekundarstufe II, Germanistik/ Linguistik, Universität Duisburg-Essen.

Mühleisen, Susanne (2003) Towards global diglossia? The cultural politics of English in the sciences and the humanities. In Mair, 107–118.

Mühlhäusler, Peter (1977) Bemerkungen zum Pidgin Deutsch von Neuguinea. In Molony/ Zobl/ Stölting, 58–70.

—— (1979) Bemerkungen zur Geschichte und zum linguistischen Stellenwert des Pidgindeutsch. In Auburger/ Kloss, 59–87.

—— (1980) German as a contact language in the Pacific. *Michigan Germanic Studies* 6: 163–189.

Muhr, Rudolf (1997) Die Auslandskulturpolitik Österreichs und Deutschlands – ein Vergleich. In Institut für Auslandsbeziehungen (ed.) *Sprachenpolitik in Europa – Sprachenpolitik für Europa* (Materialien zum internationalen Kulturaustausch 36). Stuttgart: Institut für Auslandsbeziehungen, 98–105.

Muljačić, Zarko (1989) Über den Begriff *Dachsprache*. In Ammon 1989d, 256–277.

Mulkerne, Sean/ Graham, Anne M. (May 2011) *Shaping the Future*. UK: England & Wales O.O.: University Council of Modern Languages.

Muller, Karis (2002) Language competition in European community institutions. In Liddicoat, A./ Muller, K. (eds.) *Perspectives on Europe: Language Issues and Language Planning in Europe*. Melbourne: Language Australia, 41–61.

Müller, Márta (2010a) Die Situation des Deutschunterrichts in Ungarn. In Kostrzewa/ Rada/ Knipf-Komlósi, 74–95.

———— (2010b) Die Situation des Schulwesens für die deutsche Minderheit in Ungarn.Vom Kindergarten bis zur Schule. In Kostrzewa/ Rada/ Knipf-Komlósi, 96–117.

———— (2012) Formen und Nutzen des ungarndeutschen Minderheitenunterrichts. In Kerekes, G./Müller, M. (eds.) *Traditionspflege und Erneuerung. Perspektiven der deutschen Nationalität in Ungarn im 21. Jahrhundert*. Budapest: Ad Librum, 99–116.

Muller, Siegfried H. (1964) *The World's Living Languages. Basic Facts of Their Structure, Kinship, Location and Number of Speakers*. NewYork: F. Ungar.

Munske, Horst H. (ed.) (2001) in Zusammenarbeit mit Århammar, Nils et al. *Handbuch des Friesischen / Handbook of Frisian Studies*. Tübingen: Niemeyer.

Müntzel, Uta/ Tiittula, Liisa (1995) *Saksan kieli. Suomalais-Saksalaisessa kaupassa. Saksankielisen viestinnän tarvetutkimus. Deutsch im finnisch-deutschen Handel. Eine Bedarfsanalyse*. Helsinki: Helsinki School of Economics and Business Administration.

Murakami, Junichi (1989) Die Rolle der deutschen Sprache für die japanische Rechtswissenschaft. In Bauer 1989b, 59–62.

Murray, Heather/ Dingwall, Silvia (2001) The dominance of English at European universities: Switzerland and Sweden compared. In Ammon, 85–112.

———— / Wegmüller, Ursula/ Kan, Fayaz A. (2000) *Englisch in der Schweiz. Forschungsbericht*. (www.sbf. admin.ch/htm/dokumentation/publikationen/Bildung/english-d.pdf.)

Muylle, Koen (2005) La représentation de la Communauté germanophone au sein des institutions fédérales: entre la logique de la participation et celle de la protection d'une minorité. In Stangherlin, 245–286.

Myhill, John (1999) Identity, territoriality and minority language survival. *Journal of Multilingual and Multicultural Development* 20 (1): 34–50.

Nahir, M[oshe] (1984) Language planning goals: a classification. *Language Problems and Language Planning* 8: 294–327.

von Nahmen, Carsten (2001) *Deutschsprachige Medien in Namibia: vom Windhoeker Anzeiger zum Deutschen Hörfunkprogramm der Namibian Broadcasting Corporation, 1898–1998*.Windhoek: Namibia Wissenschaftliche Gesellschaft.

Najdič, Larissa (1997) *Deutsche Bauern bei St. Petersburg-Leningrad. Dialekte – Brauchtum – Folklore*. Stuttgart: Steiner.

Naka, Naoichi (1994) Die Anfänge der Germanistik in Japan. In Ammon 1994d, 237–248.

Nakajima,Yuji (1994) Die derzeitige Lage der Germanistik in Japan. In Ammon 1994d, 249–258.

Nakayama, Shigeru (1981) *Teikoku daigaku no Tanjou* [Birth of the Imperial University]. 3rd edition,Tokyo: Chuokoronsha.

Naranchimeg, Kh./ Ganchimeg, D. (2007) Die Bedeutung der deutschen Sprache für die Mongolei. *Jahrbuch für Internationale Germanistik* 39 (2): 73–76.

Nass, Klaus O. (1999) Man spricht (auch) Deutsch . . . Zum Gebrauch von Amts- und Arbeitssprachen auf informellen Ratssitzungen der Europäischen Union. *Europäische Zeitung* 9: 1.

A National Language Policy (1984) Report by the Senate Standing Committee on Education and the Arts. Canberra: Australian Government Publishing Service.

Naumann, Hans-Peter/ Müller, Silvia (eds.) (2000) *Hochdeutsch in Skandinavien. Internationales Symposium, Zürich, 14. – 16. Mai 1998*. Tübingen/ Basel: Francke.

Navarro, Fernando A. (1996a) Englisch oder Deutsch? Die Sprache der Medizin aufgrund der in der Deutschen Medizinischen Wochenschrift erschienenen Literaturangaben (1920 bis 1995). *Deutsche Medizinische Wochenschrift* 121: 1561–1566.

———— (1996b) Die Sprache der Medizin in Österreich (1920–1995). *Wiener klinische Wochenschrift* 108: 362–369.

———— (1997) Die Sprache der Medizin in der Schweiz von 1920 bis 1995. *Schweizerische Medizinische Wochenschrift* 127: 1565–1573.

Neff, Jacquy (2001) Deutsch als Konferenzsprache in den Ländern der Europäischen Union. In Kelletat, A. F. (ed.) *Dolmetschen*. Frankfurt/Main: Peter Lang, 121–143.

———— (2007) *Deutsch als Konferenzsprache in der Europäischen Union. Eine dolmetschwissenschaftliche Untersuchung*. Hamburg:Verlag Dr. Kovač.

Neffe, Jürgen [2005] (2005) *Einstein. Eine Biographie*. 4th edition, Reinbek bei Hamburg: Rowohlt.

Neidhardt, Friedhelm (1994) Jenseits des Palavers. Funktionen politischer Öffentlichkeit. In Wunden, W. (ed.) *Öffentlichkeit und Kommunikationskultur*. Hamburg/ Stuttgart: Steinkopf, 19–30.

Neill, Stephen [1964] (1974) *Geschichte der christlichen Mission*. Erlangen:Verlag der ev.-luth. Mission.

Neisser, Ulric (1984) Interpreting Harry Bahrick's discovery: what confers immunity against forgetting? *Journal of Experimental Psychology: General* 11 (1): 32–35.

Nekula, Marek (1997) Germanismen in der tschechischen Presse und Werbung. Die Einstellung gegenüber den Deutschen. In Höhne/ Nekula, 89–97.

—— (2001) Der tschechisch-deutsche Bilinguismus. In Koschmal, W./ Nekula, M./ Rogall, J. (eds.) *Deutsche und Tschechen. Geschichte – Kultur – Politik.* München: Beck, 208–217.

—— (2002) Kommunikationsführung in deutsch-tschechischen Firmen. In Möller/ Nekula, 65–83.

—— (2004) Deutsch als Europasprache aus tschechischer Sicht. In Lohse, 129–144.

—— / Marx, Christoph/ Šichová, Katerina (2009) Sprachsituation in Unternehmen mit ausländischer Beteiligung in der Tschechischen Republik. *Sociolinguistica* 23: 53–85.

—— / Nekvapil, Jiří/ Šichová, Kateřina (2005a) Sprachen in deutsch-tschechischen, österreichisch-tschechischen und schweizerisch- tschechischen Unternehmen: Ein Beitrag zur Wirtschaftskommunikation in der Tschechischen Republik. *Sociolinguistica* 19. Tübingen: Niemeyer, 128–143.

—— / —— —— (2005b) Sprachen in multinationalen Unternehmen auf dem Gebiet der Tschechischen Republik. *Forost-Arbeitspapier* Nr. 31. München: Forost.

—— / Šichová, Kateřina (2004) Was sind Fremdsprachen wert? [Jakou hodnotu mají cizí jazyky?] In Fröhlich, S./ Scheider, B./ Nový, I. (ed.) *Unternehmenskultur & Unternehmenserfolg.* Vol. 1. Praha: Bundesverband deutscher Unternehmer in der Tschechischen Republik, Goethe Institut, Vysoká škola ekonomická, 238–267.

Nekvapil, Jiří (1997a) Tschechien. In Goebl/ Nelde/ Starý/ Wölck, 1641–1649.

—— (1997b) Die kommunikative Überwindung der tschechisch-deutschen ethnischen Polarisation. Deutsche Kollegen, Expatriates und andere soziale Kategorien im Automobilwerk Škoda. In Höhne/ Nekula, 127–144.

—— (2000) On non-self-evident relationships between language and ethnicity: how Germans do not speak German, and Czechs do not speak Czech. *Multilingua* 19: 37–53.

—— (2003a) Language biographies and the analysis of language situations: on the life of the German community in the Czech Republic. *International Journal of the Sociology of Language* 162: 63–83.

—— (2003b) On the role of the languages of adjacent states and the languages of ethnic minorities in multilingual Europe: the case of the Czech Republic. In Besters-Dilger, J. et al. (eds.) *Mehrsprachigkeit in der erweiterten Europäischen Union/ Multilingualism in the Enlarged European Union/ Multilingualisme dans l'Union Europeénne élargie.* Klagenfurt: Drava Verlag, 76–94.

—— / Nekula, Marek (2006) On language management in multinational companies in the Czech Republic. *Current Issues in Language Planning* 7 (2–3): 307–327.

—— / Neustupný, J[iří] V. (1998) Linguistic communities in the Czech Republic. In Bratt Paulston/ Peckham, 116–133.

—— / Sherman, Tamah (2009) Czech, German and English: finding their place in multilingual companies in the Czech Republic. In Carl/ Stevenson, 122–148.

Nelde, Peter H. (1975) Zur Situation des Deutschen in der Welt. *Germanistische Mitteilungen* 2: 33–43.

—— (1979a) *Volkssprache und Kultursprache. Die gegenwärtige Lage des sprachlichen Übergangsgebietes im deutsch-belgisch-luxemburgischen Grenzraum.* Wiesbaden: Steiner.

—— (ed.) (1979b) *Deutsch als Muttersprache in Belgien. Forschungsberichte zur Gegenwartslage* (Deutsche Sprache in Europa und Übersee, 5). Wiesbaden: Steiner.

—— (1979c) The Present Position of German Among World Languages. *Deutsch-Kanadisches Jahrbuch* 5: 5–12.

—— (1981) Deutsch in der Welt? *Germanistische Mitteilungen* 13: 89–92.

—— (1984) Deutsche Minderheiten und ihre Sprache in Europa. *Language Problems and Language Planning* 8: 1–20.

—— (1986a) Deutsch als Minderheitssprache – Vergleichbarkeit von Sprachkontakten. In Hinderling, 251–273.

—— (1986b) Research on language conflict. In Ammon/ Dittmar/ Mattheier/ Trudgill, 1346–1352.

—— (ed.) (1987) *Wortatlas der deutschen Umgangssprache in Belgien.* Bern/ Stuttgart: Francke.

—— (ed.) (1990) *Deutsch als Muttersprache in Ungarn* (Deutsche Sprache in Europa und Übersee, 13). Stuttgart: Steiner.

—— (2000) Bilingualism among ethnic Germans in Hungary. In Wolff, 125–133.

—— / Vandermeeren, S[onja]/ Wölck W[olfgang] (1991) *Interkulturelle Mehrsprachigkeit. Eine kontaktlinguistische Umfrage in Fünfkirchen* (Plurilingua, 11). Bonn: Dümmler.

Nerrière, Jean-Paul (2004) *Parlez Globish.* Paris: Eyrolles.

Van Ness, Silke (1989) *Changes in an Obsolescing Language. Pennsylvania German in West Virginia.* Tübingen: Narr.

Nettelbeck, Colin et al. (2008) *Beginners' LOTE (Languages Other than English) in Australian Universities: An Audit Survey and Analysis. Report to the Council of the Australian Academy of the Humanities.* Canberra: Australian Academy of the Humanities.

Nettelbeck, Joachim (2000) Deutsch in internationalen Wissenschaftseinrichtungen. In Debus/ Kollmann/ Pörksen, 105–125.

Netzwerk Deutsch (2010) *Statistische Erhebungen 2010. Die deutsche Sprache in der Welt.* München: Goethe-Institut. (www.daad.de/de/download/broschuere_netzwerk_deutsch/DeutschlernerzahlenNetzw erk_Tabelle_2010.pdf.)

———— / von Buddenbrock, Carolin/ Schneider, Gisela/ Makowski, Matthias/ Toledo, Heike (eds.) (2010) *Die deutsche Sprache in der Welt 2010.* München: QS2M Werbeagentur.

Neuland, Eva (2004) Politik für die deutsche Sprache? Aufgaben für Forschung, Lehre, Unterricht. In Goltschnigg, Dietmar/ Schwob, Anton (eds.) *Zukunftschancen der deutschen Sprache in Mittel-, Südost- und Osteuropa. Grazer Humboldtkolleg 2002.* Wien: Edition Praesens, 51–65.

Neusius, Boris (ed.) (2005) Sprache und Kultur Südosteuropas. *Forost-Arbeitspapier* Nr. 26. München: Forost.

Neustupný, J[iří] V./ Nekvapil, Jiří (2003) Language management in the Czech Republic. *Current Issues in Language Planning* 4 (3/ 4): 181–366.

Newton, Gerald (1987) The German language in Luxembourg. In Russ, C./ Volkmar, C. (eds.) *Sprache und Gesellschaft in deutschsprachigen Ländern.* München: Goethe-Institut, 153179.

Nickl, Milutin M. (2007) Transnationales Deutsch als Lingua franca und Internetsprache/ Transnational German in Crosslinguistic Transfer and as an Internet Language. *Tamkang Studies of Foreign Languages and Literatures* (TSFLL) 10: 1–32.

———— (2008) Transnationales Deutsch in der Hochschulpolitik Ostasiens. Beispiel Taiwan/Republik China: zur Internationalisierung und Optimierung der German and Communication Studies. *PAC-Korrespondenz* 80: 57–98.

Niehaus-Lohberg, Erika/ Herrlitz, Wolfgang (1999) Verständigung zwischen Niederländern und Deutschen: Ein Beitrag zur Analyse der interkulturellen Kommunikation zwischen Unternehmen. In Bungarten 1999b, 139–161.

Nielsen, Martin (2003) Internationale Wirtschaftskommunikation auf Deutsch: Forschung und Lehre in Dänemark – eine Bestandsaufnahme. In Reuter/ Piitulainen, 103–124.

Niere, Renate (1977) *Die Entwicklung der Diskussion über Deutsch als Fremdsprache (DaF) beim Goethe-Institut von 1932 bis heute.* Unpublished degree paper, Philipps-Universität Marburg/L.

Nies, Fritz (ed.) (2005) *Europa denkt mehrsprachig. L'Europe pense en plusieurs langues.* Tübingen: Narr.

Nikula, Tarja/ Pöyhönen, Sari/ Huhta, Ari/ Hildén, Raili (2010) When MT+2 is not enough: Tensions within foreign language education in Finland. *Sociolinguistica* 24: 25–42.

Nitschak, Horst (2002) Deutschsprachige Kulturwissenschaften in Lateinamerika: Chancen und Perspektiven. In Deutscher Akademischer Austauschdienst, 235–245.

Nollendorfs, Valters/ Markgraf, Karl F. (eds.) (1986) *Directory of German Departments, German Studies Faculties and Programs in the United States 1985.* 2nd edition, Bonn: Deutscher Akademischer Austauschdienst.

Noro, Kayoko (1994) Deutsch als Fremdsprache in privaten Sprachschulen. In Ammon 1994d, 311–326.

Nunberg, Geoffrey (2002) Will the internet always speak English? In Lamberton, 301–304. (Originally published in *The American Prospect* 2000).

Nye, Joseph S. (1990a) Soft Power. *Foreign Policy* 80 (3): 153–171.

———— (1990b) *Bound to Lead: The Changing Nature of American Power.* New York: Basic Books.

———— (2004) *Soft Power. The Means to Success in World Politics.* New York: PublicAffairs.

Nyhlén, Lars-Olof (2004) Die Stellung der deutschen Sprache und der Germanistik in Schweden. *Jahrbuch für Internationale Germanistik* 35 (2): 25–31.

Nylenna, Magne/ Riis, Povl/ Karlsson, Yngve (1994) Multiple blinded reviews of the same two manuscripts. Effects of referee characteristics and publication language. *The Journal of American Medical Association* 272 (2): 149–151.

Oberacker, Karl H. (1979) Die Deutschen in Brasilien. In Fröschle, 169–257.

Oberreuter, Heinrich/ Krull, Wilhelm/ Meyer, Hans J./ Ehlich, Konrad (eds.) (2012) *Deutsch in der Wissenschaft. Ein politischer und wissenschaftlicher Diskurs.* München: Olzog.

O'Connor, John K. [2007] (2010) *The Eurovision Contest. The Official History.* 3rd edition, United Kingdom: Carlton Books.

O'Driscoll, Jim (2001a) A face model of language choice. *Multilingua* 20 (3): 245–268.

———— (2001b) Hiding your difference: how non-global languages are being marginalised in everyday interaction. *Journal of Multilingual & Multicultural Development* 22 (6): 475–490.

Ogden, C[harles] K. (1934) *The System of Basic English.* New York: Harcourt, Brace.

Ogechi, Nathan O. (2003) On language rights in Kenya. *Nordic Journal of African Studies* 12 (3): 277–295.

Ögmundarson, Ólafur (2002) *Deutsch, eine internationale Handelssprache. Die Kommunikation zwischen deutschen und isländischen Firmen.* Unpublished final-year BA essay, Reykjavík: Islands Universität.

Oh, Tschong-Cha (2003) Koreanische Vereine und Interessenverbände zur Förderung von Deutsch und Germanistik. In Ammon/ Chong, 371–382.

O'Halloran, Edel (2001) *Ist Mode englisch? Französische und englische Einflüsse auf die deutsche Mode- und Gemeinsprache im 20 Jahrhundert.* Frankfurt a.M.: Lang.

Okamoto, Kaori (1991) *Deutschkenntnisse der japanischen Frauen in Düsseldorf.* Unpublished seminar article, Universität-GH-Duisburg in 1990/ 91.

Oksaar, Els/ Skudlik, Sabine/ von Stackelberg, Jürgen (1988) *Gerechtfertigte Vielfalt. Zur Sprache in den Geisteswissenschaften.* Darmstadt: Luchterhand.

Oliveira, Paulo S. (2002) Lokale Antworten auf globale Fragen. In Deutscher Akademischer Austauschdienst, 107–127.

Ollila, Tytti/ Partanen, Heli (2004) *"In Vielfalt geeint": Sprachliche Vielfalt und die Stellung der deutschen Sprache in der Europäischen Union.* Pro-Gradua-Arbeit Deutsche Sprache und Kultur. Institut für moderne und klassische Sprachen, Universität Jyväskalä. (www.jyx.jyu.fi/dspace/bitstream/ . . . / URN_NBN_fi_jyu-200525.pdf.)

Olschki, Leonardo (1919) *Die Literatur der Technik und der Angewandten Wissenschaften vom Mittelalter bis zur Renaissance* (Geschichte der neusprachlichen Wissenschaftlichen Literatur, Vol. 1). Heidelberg: Winter.

———— (1922) *Bildung und Wissenschaft im Zeitalter der Renaissance in Italien* (Geschichte der neusprachlichen Wissenschaftlichen Literatur, Vol. 2). Leipzig/ Firenze/ Roma/ Genève: Olschki [self-published].

———— (1927) *Galilei und seine Zeit* (Geschichte der neusprachlichen Wissenschaftlichen Literatur, Vol. 3). Niemeyer: Halle.

Oppermann, Thomas (2001) Das Sprachregime der Europäischen Union – reformbedürftig? *Zeitschrift für Europarechtliche Studien (ZEuS)* 4: 1 ff.

ORE/ Ośrodek Rozwoju Edukacji (July 2013) Powszechność nauczania języków obcych w roku szkolnym 2011/2012. Warszawa.

Ó Riagáin, Dónall (1997) Unity in diversity: language policies in the New Europe. In Røyneland, 173–187.

Orlowski, Hubert (1988) Die Deutscholympiade in Polen. *Jahrbuch Deutsch als Fremdsprache* 13: 409–414.

Ortmanns, Karl-Peter (1993) *Deutsch in Großbritannien. Die Entwicklung von Deutsch als Fremdsprache von den Anfängen bis 1980.* Stuttgart: Steiner.

Ortner, Brigitte/ von Ruckteschell, Katharina (2010) Sprachenpolitische Konzepte und Institutionen zur Förderung der deutschen Sprache in nichtdeutschsprachigen Ländern. In Krumm/ Fandrych/ Hufeisen/ Riemer, Vol. 1, 133–143.

Ortony, Andrew [1979] (2006) *Metaphor and Thought.* 2nd edition, Cambridge: Cambridge University Press.

Oschlies, Wolf (1982) Deutsche Sprache in Polen wieder gefragt. 200.000 Schüler lernen Deutsch als fakultative Westsprache. *Globus* 14: 36–37.

Österreichisches Wörterbuch [1951] (2012) *Auf der Grundlage des amtlichen Regelwerks.* 42. Edition published on behalf of the Bundesministerium für Unterricht, Kunst und Kultur. Wien: Österreichischer Bundesverlag Schulbuch.

Ostler, Nicholas (ed.) (1999) *Endangered Languages and Education.* Bath: Foundation for Endangered Languages.

———— (2005) *Empires of the World: A Language History of the World.* London: Harper Collins.

Ostrower, Alexander (1965) *Language, Law and Diplomacy*, 2 Vols. Philadelphia: University of Pennsylvania Press.

Otto, Claude (2013) Ortsnamen als Hoheitszeichen. Sprachkonflikt und toponymischer Wechsel im Elsass. *Sprachspiegel* 57 (1): 11–19.

Oud-de Glas, Maria (1982) *Foreign Language Needs: A Survey of Research.* Nijmegen: Institute for Applied Sociology.

———— (1983a) Foreign language needs: a survey of needs. In Van Els/ Oud-de-Glas, 19–34.

———— (1983b) Foreign language needs in the Netherlands. In Van Els/ Oud-de Glas, 151–170.

———— (1993) Languages in the Netherlands. A study of supply and demand. In Ager, D./ Muyskens, G./ Wright, S. (eds.) *Language Education for Intercultural Communication.* Clevedon: Multilingual Matters, 115–129.

Ozil, Şeyda (2004) Stand und Perspektiven der Germanistik in der Türkei. In Durzak/ Kuruyazızı, 267–277.

Pabst, Klaus (1979) Politische Geschichte des deutschen Sprachgebiets in Ostbelgien bis 1944. In Nelde (1979b), 10–38.

—— (1997) Französisch in Verwaltung und Schule des linken Rheinufers 1792/94 bis 1814. In Spillner, B. (ed.) *Französische Sprache in Deutschland im Zeitalter der Französischen Revolution.* Frankfurt a. M.: Lang, 133–154.

Pahl, Gerhard (2000) Deutsch als Wissenschaftssprache in den Ingenieurwissenschaften. Das Verhältnis zum angloamerikanischen Sprachraum. In Debus/ Kollmann/ Pörksen, 239247.

Pakir, Anne (2004) Medium-of-instruction policy in Singapore. In Tollefßen/ Tsui, 117–133.

Pan, Christoph (2006) Die Minderheitenrechte in Frankreich. In Pan/ Pfeil, 169–187.

—— / Pfeil, Beate S. (eds.) [2002] (2006) *Minderheitenrechte in Europa* (Handbuch der europäischen Volksgruppen, Vol. 2). 2nd revised edition, Wien/ New York: Springer.

Panzer, Baldur (1987a) Deutsche Sprachentscheidungen im politischen Umfeld der Vereinten Nationen. *Muttersprache* 97 (1/ 2): 42–51.

—— (1987b) Vereinte Nationen: Dreisprachigkeitsliste Vereinte Nationen Englisch-FranzösischDeutsch. *Vereinte Nationen* 4: 150–151.

—— (1997a) Sprachenkarte von Polen. In Goebl/ Nelde/ Starý/ Wölck, 2037–2039. Paqué, Ruprecht (1980) Sprachen und Sprachendienste der Vereinten Nationen. *Vereinte Nationen* 5: 165–171.

—— (1997b) Vielsprachigkeit, Mehrsprachigkeit, Einsprachigkeit: Zu den Sprachen der Vereinten Nationen und zur Resolution 50/ 11 der Generalversammlung über "Multilingualism". *Vereinte Nationen* 45: 61–68.

Van Parijs, Philippe (2001a) Linguistic justice. *Politics, Philosophy & Economics* 1: 59–74.

—— (2001b) Le rez-de-chaussée du monde. Sur les implications socio-économiques de la mondialisation linguistique. In Delcourt, J./ Woot, Ph. de (eds.) *Les défis de la globalisation. Babel ou Pentecôte?* Louvain-la-Neuve: Presses universitaires de Louvain, 479–500.

—— (2004a) Europe's linguistic challenge. *Archives Européennes de Sociologie,* XLV (1): 113–154.

—— (2004b) L'anglais lingua franca de l'Union européenne: impératif de solidarité, injustice distributive, source d'injustice, facteur de déclin? *Économie publique* 15 (2): 13–32.

—— (2007a) Tackling the Anglophones' free ride: fair linguistic cooperation with a global lingua franca. *AILA Review* 20: 72–87.

—— (2007b) Linguistic diversity as curse and as by-product. In Arzoz, X. (ed.) Respecting Linguistic Diversity in the European Union. Amsterdam: Benjamins, 17–46.

—— (2011) *Linguistic Justice – For Europe and For the World.* New York: Oxford University Press.

Patten, A. (2001) Political theory and language policy. *Political Theory* 29: 691–715.

—— / Kymlicka, W. (2003) Introduction: language rights and political theory: context, issues, and approaches. In Kymlicka, W./ Patten, A. (eds.) *Language Rights and Political Theory.* New York: Oxford University Press, 1–51.

Pavlychko, Oksana (2010) Deutsch in der Ukraine. In Krumm/ Fandrych/ Hufeisen/ Riemer, Vol. 2, 1823–1827.

Pazi, Margarita (ed.) (1979) *Nachrichten aus Israel. Deutschsprachige Literatur in Israel.* Hildesheim: Olms.

Pearl, Stephen B. (1996) Changes in the pattern of language use in the United Nations. In Müller, K. E. (ed.) *Language Status in the Post-Cold-War Era.* Lanham, MD: University Press of America, 29–42.

Pedersen, Karen Margrethe (1996) Die deutsche Minderheit in Dänemark und die dänische Minderheit in Deutschland. In Hinderling/ Eichinger, 31–59.

—— (2000) A national minority with a transethnic identity – the German minority in Denmark. In Wolff, 15–28.

—— (2005) Languages and identities in the national minorities in the Danish German border region and in the Bonn-Copenhagen declarations. In Kühl, J./ Weller, M. (eds.) *Minority Policy in Action: The Bonn-Copenhagen Declarations in a European Context 1955.* Flensburg: European Centre for Minority Issues, 91–139.

Pei, Mario (1958) *One Language for the World.* New York: Devin-Adair.

—— (1966) *Glossary of Linguistic Terminoloy.* Garden City, NY: Anchor Books.

Pelech, William (2002) Charting the interpersonal underworld: The application of cluster analysis to the study of interpersonal coordination in small groups. *Currents: New Scholarship in the Human Services* (1): 1.

Penner, Horst (1972) *Weltweite Bruderschaft. Ein mennonitisches Geschichtsbuch.* 3rd edition, Karlsruhe: Mennonitischer Geschichtsverein.

Pennycook, A. (1994) *The Cultural Politics of of English as International Language.* Harlow: Longman.

Pentlin, Susan L. (1977) *Effect of the Third Reich on the Teaching of German in the United States: A Historical Study*. Diss. University of Kansas, Microfiche.

Perfilowa, Galina (2011) Deutsch als fremdsprachliches Schulfach in Russland. In Ammon/ Kemper, 138–158.

Perlman-Balme, Michaela (2000) *Prüfung Wirtschaftsdeutsch International. Handbuch, Prüfungsziele, Testbeschreibung*. München: Goethe-Institut.

Perlmutter, Howard V. (1969) The tortuous evolution of the multilingual corporation. *Columbia Journal of World Business* Jan./ Feb.: 9–18.

Peter, Karl A. (1987) *The Dynamics of Hutterite Society. An Analytical Approach*. Edmonton: University of Alberta Press.

Petereit, Katja/ Spielmanns-Rome, Elke (2010) Sprecht Deutsch mit uns!" *Forschung & Lehre* 17: 172f.

Petersen, Carl et al. (eds.) (1933) *Handwörterbuch des Grenz- und Auslandsdeutschtums*, 2 Vols. Breslau: Hirt.

Petersen, Karen (1993) *Zur Situation des Deutschen als Fremdsprache im multikulturellen Australien*. Frankfurt a. M.: Lang.

Petit, Jean (1993) *L'Alsace à la reconquête de son bilinguisme*. Nancy: SALDE.

————— (1997) Français – allemand. In Goebl/ Nelde/ Starý/ Wölck, 1222–1240.

Petry, Uwe (2004) Deutsche Sprachpolitik in der Europäischen Union. In Lohse, 43–50.

Philipp, Andrea M./ Koch, Iring (2011) Babylonische Zeitkosten? Vom Wechsel der Sprache in der wissenschaftlichen Kommunikation. *Forschung & Lehre* 18: 54f.

Philippi, Paul (2009) Zur Erhaltung autochthoner Minderheiten unter Diasporabedingungen am Beispiel der deutschen Minderheit in Rumänien. *Europäisches Journal für Minderheitenfragen* 2 (1): 32–38.

Phillips, Francis C. [1913, 1915] (1924) *Chemical German. An Introduction to the Study of German Chemical Literature, Including Rules of Nomenclature, Exercises for Practice and a Collection of Extracts from the Writings of German Chemists and Other Scientists and a Vocabulary of German Chemical Terms and Others Used in Technical Literature*. 2nd ed. Eston, PA: The Chemical Publishing Company.

Phillipson, Robert (1990) *English Language Teaching and Imperialism*. Tronninge: Transcultura.

————— (1992) *Linguistic Imperialism*. Oxford: Oxford University Press.

————— (2000) Angelsächsische Sprachförderungspolitik. In Ammon 2000c, 121–133.

————— (2003) *English-only Europe? Challenging Language Policy*. London: Routledge.

————— (2006a) Colonization and decolonization. In Ammon/ Dittmar/ Mattheier/ Trudgill, 2233–2239.

————— (2006b) Language spread. In Ammon/ Dittmar/ Mattheier/ Trudgill, 2299–2307.

————— (2006c) English: a cuckoo in the European higher education nest of language? *Euroepean Journal of English Studies* 10 (1): 13–32.

————— / Skutnabb-Kangas, Tove (1994) English, panacea or pandemic. In *Sociolinguistica* 8: 73–87.

————— / ————— (1999) Englishisation: one dimension of globalization. In Graddol/ Meinhof, 19–36.

The Philosopher's Index 1940 – March 1997 (on Disc) (1997), Bowling Green, OH: Philosopher's Information Center.

Physics Abstracts (Science Abstracts Series A). (1898ff.) Piscataway, NJ: Institute of Electrical Engineers.

Physics Briefs (1978–1994). Karlsruhe: Fachinformationszentrum.

Physikalische Berichte (1920–1978) Braunschweig: Vieweg (continued as *Fortschritte der Physik*].

Picot, Arnold (1993) Transaktionskosten. In Wittmann, W. et al. (ed.) *Handwörterbuch der Betriebswirtschaft*. Teilband 3. Stuttgart: Schäfer-Posche, 4194–4204.

Pieper, Frauke (2000) *Der deutsche Auslandsrundfunk. Historische Entwicklung, verfassungsrechtliche Stellung, Funktionsbereich, Organisation und Finanzierung*. München: Beck.

de Pietro, Jean-François (1994) Une variable négligée: les attitudes. Représentations culturelles de l'Allemagne et apprentissage de l'allemand. *Education et recherche* 16 (1): 89–111.

Pigeroth-Piroth, Isabella/ Fehlen, Fernand (2005) *Les langues dans les offres d'emploi du Luxemburger Wort 1984–2004*. Luxemburg: Université du Luxemburg.

Pinker, Steven [2011, engl.] (2013) *Gewalt. Eine neue Geschichte der Menschheit*. Frankfurt a. M.: Fischer.

Piron, Claude (2001) L'europe trilingue: un espoir realiste? In Chaudenson, 93–102.

Pistor, Hans-Henning (ed.) (1997) *Hochschulstandort Deutschland. Sind die deutschen Hochschulen international wettbewerbsfähig?* Essen: Stifterverband für die deutsche Wissenschaft.

Plessner, Helmuth (1974) *Die verspätete Nation*. Frankfurt a. M.: Suhrkamp.

Plewnia, Albrecht/ Weger, Tobias (2008) Slowakei. In Eichinger/ Plewnia/ Riehl, 243–264.

Plutzar, Verena (2010) Zuwanderung und Sprachenpolitik der deutschsprachigen Länder. In Krumm/ Fandrych/ Hufeisen/ Riemer, Vol. 1, 107–123.

Pogarell, Reiner (2007) *Warum sollen Dänen Deutsch lernen, studieren und sprechen?* Aalborg/ Paderborn: IFB Verlag.

Pogorelskaja, Swetlana W. (2009a) Teil der neuen Strategie – Die Nichtregierungsorgisationen. In Maaß (2009a), 281–291.

—— (2009b) Im Ausland einmalig – Die politischen Stiftungen. In Maaß (2009a), 293–304.

Polat, Tülin (2004) Die wissenschaftliche Deutschlehrerausbildung in der Türkei: Ein Garant für das Deutsche? In Durzak/ Kuruyazızı, 317–334.

—— / Tapan, Nilüfer (2003) Neustrukturierungen im Prozess der Deutschlehrerausbildung in der Türkei. In Neuner, G. (ed.) *Internationales Qualitätsnetz: Deutsch als Fremdsprache. Tagungsdokumentation 2002.* Kassel: kassel university press, 53–66.

von Polenz, Peter (1994–2000) *Deutsche Sprachgeschichte vom Spätmittelalter bis zur Gegenwart* (1994) Bd 2: *17. und 18. Jahrhundert*; (1999) Vol. 3: *19. und 20 Jahrhundert*; (2000) Vol. 1: *Einführung, Grundbegriffe, 14.-16. Jahrhundert.* Berlin/ New York: de Gruyter.

Ponti, Donatella (2001) Deutschunterricht und Gemanistikstudium in Italien. In Helbig/ Götze/ Henrici/ Krumm, Vol. 2: 1509–1515.

Pool, Jonathan (1991) The world language problem. *Rationality and Society* 3 (1): 78–105.

—— (1996) Optimal language regimes for the European Union. *International Journal of the Sociology of Language* 121: 159–179.

—— (2010) Panlingual globalization. In Coupland, 142–161.

Popp, Heidrun (1995) *Deutsch als Fremdsprache. An den Quellen eines Faches. Festschrift für Gerhard Helbig zum 65. Geburtstag.* München: Iudicium.

Popper, Karl. R. (1975) The logic of scientific discovery. *Journal of Symbolic Logic* 40 (3). See also: https:// de.wikipedia.org/wiki/Karl_Popper.

Pörksen, Uwe (1983) Der Übergang vom Gelehrtenlatein zur deutschen Wissenschaftssprache. Zur frühen deutschen Fachliteratur und Fachsprache in den naturwissenschaftlichen und mathematischen Fächern (ca. 1500–1800). *Zeitschrift für Literaturwissenschaft und Linguistik* 13 (51/52): 227–258.

—— (1986) *Deutsche Naturwissenschaftssprachen. Historische und kritische Studien.* Tübingen: Narr.

—— (1989) The transition from Latin to German in the natural sciences and its consequences. In Coulmas, F. (ed.) *Language Adaption.* Cambridge, London: Cambridge University Press, 127–134.

—— (ed.) (2005) *Die Wissenschaft spricht Englisch? Versuch einer Standortbestimmung.* O.O.: Wallstein.

Posner, Roland (1991a) Society, civilization, mentality: prolegomena to a language policy for Europe. In Coulmas, 121–137.

—— (1991b) Der polyglotte Dialog. Ein Humanistengespräch über Kommunikation im mehrsprachigen Europa. *Sprachreport* (3): 6–10.

—— (1992): Maximen der Sprachverwendung im europäischen Kulturverbund. *Sprachreport* 2–3: 4f.

Povejšil, Jaromír (1997) Tschechisch – Deutsch. In Goebl/ Nelde/ Starý/ Wölck, 1656–1662.

Prah, Kwesi K. (2004) Harmonizing and standardizing African languages for scientific and technological development: the CASAS experience. In Kristinsson, A. P./ Kristmannsson, G. (eds.) *Málstefna/ Language Planning.* Reykjavík: Íslensk málnefnd, 179–195.

Praxenthaler, Martin (2000) Förderung von Deutsch durch die DDR. In Ammon 2000c, 51–60.

—— (2002) *Die Sprachenverbreitungspolitik der DDR. Die deutsche Sprache als Mittel sozialistischer auswärtiger Kulturpolitik.* Frankfurt a. M.: Lang.

Prebersen, Nina K./ Larsen, Sven/ Abelsen, Birgit (2003) I'm not a typical tourist: German tourists' self-perception, activities, and motives. *Journal of Travel Research*: 416–420.

Presse- und Informationsamt der Stadt Wuppertal et al. (ed.) (1984) *Deutschsprachige Medien in aller Welt. Katalog zur Ausstellung in Wuppertal vom 14. bis 27. September 1984.* Wuppertal.

Priegnitz, Frauke (2007) *Die Motivation ausländischer Studierender für den Hochschulstandort Deutschland.* Unpublished master's dissertation, Universität Hamburg.

—— (2015) *Internationale Absolventen im Spannungsfeld zwischen englischsprachigem Studium und landessprachigem Umfeld. Eine Untersuchung am Beispiel der Studienstandorte Deutschland und Dänemark.* Frankfurt a. M.: Lang.

Projektgruppe Spracheinstellungen [2009] (2011) *Aktuelle Spracheinstellungen in Deutschland. Erste Ergebnisse einer bundesweiten Repräsentativumfrage.* 2nd edition, Mannheim: Institut für Deutsche Sprache and University of Mannheim.

Prokop, Manfred (2005) Deutsch als Fremdsprache (DaF) an kanadischen Schulen und Hochschulen. *Jahrbuch für Internationale Germanistik* 37 (1): 63–82.

Prucha, Jan (1983) Foreign language needs in Czechoslovakia: situation and theory. In Van Els/ Oud-de Glas, 171–184.

Publishing Translations in Europe (2010) *Trends 1990–2005.* Aberystwyth University, Wales, UK: Mercator Institute for Media, Languages and Culture.

Pumberger, Klaus (1997) Deutsch-tschechische Kommunikation in Joint ventures. Ein Erfahrungsbericht. In Höhne/ Nekula, 89–97.

Pütz, Joe (2001) *Das grosse Dickschenärie.* Windhoek: Peters Antiques.

Pütz, Martin (1991) "Südwesterdeutsch" in Namibia: Sprachpolitik, Sprachplanung und Spracherhalt. *Linguistische Berichte* 136: 455–476.

——— (1992) The present and future maintenance of German in the context of Namibia's official language policy. *Multilingua* 11 (3): 293–323.

——— (ed.) (1995) *Discrimination through Language in Africa? Perspectives on the Namibian Experience.* Berlin/ New York: de Gruyter.

——— (2004) Sprachrepertoire. In Ammon/ Dittmar/ Mattheier/ Trudgill, 226–231.

——— (2007) The dynamics of language policy in Namibia: a view from cognitive sociolinguistics. In Van der Walt, Ch. (ed.) *Living Through Languages: An African Tribute to René Dirven.* Stellenbosch: SUN Press, 91–113.

Quell, Carsten (1997) Language choice in multilingual institutions. A case study at the European Commission with particular reference to the role of English, French, and German as working languages. *Multilingua* 16 (1): 57–76.

Quetz, Jürgen (2002) Der gemeinsame europäische Referenzrahmen: Ein Schatzkästlein mit Perlen, aber auch mit Kreuzen und Ketten. In Bausch, K.-R. (ed.) *Der Gemeinsame europäische Referenzrahmen für Sprachen in der Diskussion.* Tübingen: Narr, 145–155.

——— (2010) Auf dem Wege zur fremdsprachlichen Monokultur? Fremdsprachen an den Schulen der Bundesrepublik Deutschland. *Sociolinguistica* 24: 170–186.

——— / Karin Vogt (2009) Nationale Bildungsstandards für die Erste Fremdsprache: Sprachenpolitik auf unsicherer Basis. Antwort auf das Positionspapier der DGFF *Zeitschrift für Fremdsprachenforschung* 20 (1): 61–87.

Raasch, Albert (1997) *Sprachenpolitik Deutsch als Fremdsprache. Länderberichte zur internationalen Diskussion.* Amsterdam/ Atlanta, GA: Rodopi.

——— (2002) *L'Europe, les frontiers et les langues.* Strasbourg: Conseil de l'Europe.

——— / Cuny, Marie-Laure/ Bühler, Peter/ Magar, Christoph (eds.) (1992) *Schwerpunktthema: "Nachbarsprachen in Europa". Kurzfassungen der Kongreßbeiträge der 23. Jahrestagung der Gesellschaft für Angewandte Linguistik (GAL).* Saarbrücken: Universität des Saarlandes.

Rabiazamaholy, Harisoa Tiana (2002) Zukunftsperspektive der deutschen Sprache und der Germanistik im Senegal. *Jahrbuch für Internationale Germanistik* 34 (1): 49–59.

Radtschenko, Oleg (2011a) Die Berufschancen von Russinnen und Russen mit Deutschkenntnissen. In Ammon/ Kemper, 287–292.

——— (2011b) Die Alexander von Humboldt-Stiftung in Russland. In Ammon/ Kemper, 375–381.

Raith, Joachim (1991) Diachronic and synchronic aspects of status change: the case of the Old Order Amish and related groups. In Ammon/ Hellinger, 457–483.

——— (2004) Sprachgemeinschaft – Kommunikationsgemeinschaft. In Ammon/ Dittmar/ Mattheier/ Trudgill, 146–158.

Rajan, Rekha Kamath (2001) Deutschunterricht und Germanistikstudium in Indien. In Helbig/ Götze/ Henrici/ Krumm, Vol. 2, 1570–1575.

——— (2010) Deutsch in Indien. In Krumm/ Fandrych/ Hufeisen/ Riemer, Vol. 2, 1680–1685.

Rash, Felicity (1998) *The German Language in Switzerland. Multilingualism, Diglossia and Variation.* Bern: Lang.

Rat der deutschen Kulturgemeinschaft (ed.) (1978) *Unser Rat. Eine Information des Rates der deutschen Kulturgemeinschaft.* Eupen.

Rat der Deutschsprachigen Gemeinschaft (1989) *Die Deutschsprachige Gemeinschaft nach der Verfassungsreform von 1983.* Eupen (Drucksache des Rates).

Rau, Arnold (1986) Deutschlehrerausbildung in Ägypten. *Jahrbuch Deutsch als Fremdsprache* 12: 326–335.

Ray, Punya S. (1963) *Language Standardization.* The Hague: Mouton.

Reershemius, Gertrud (2010) Deutsch in Großbritannien. In Krumm/ Fandrych/ Hufeisen/ Riemer, Vol. 2, 1674–1680.

Regler, Beate (2005) *Deutsch-chinesische Studienprogramme: Analyse und Empfehlungen* (Beiträge zur Hochschulpolitik 8). Bonn: Hochschulrektorenkonferenz.

Reich, Hans H. (2008) Immigrantensprachen in Deutschland. In Ammon/ Haarmann, Vol. 1, 519532.

Rein, Kurt (1977) *Religiöse Minderheiten als Sprachgemeinschaftsmodelle. Deutsche Sprachinseln täuferischen Ursprungs in den Vereingten Staaten von Amerika.* Wiesbaden: Steiner.

———— (1979) Deutsche Minderheiten täuferischen Ursprungs im Mittelwesten der USA. In Auburger/ Kloss/ Rupp, 173–189.

———— (1984) Soziokulturelle und sprachliche Wandlungen bei den Hutterern – Beobachtungen anlässlich eines neuerlichen Besuches. In Wiesinger, P. (ed.) *Beiträge zur bairischen und ostfränkischen Dialektologie.* Göppingen: Kümmerle, 249–266.

———— (1997) Rumänisch – Deutsch. In Goebl/ Nelde/ Starý/ Wölck, 1470–1477.

———— (1999) Diglossie und Bilingualismus bei den Deutschen in Rumänien und Ungarn sowie den GUS-Staaten. In Stehl, T. (ed.) *Dialektgenerationen, Dialektfunktionen, Sprachwandel.* TüTübingen: Narr, 37–53.

Reinbothe, Roswitha (1992) *Kulturexport und Wirtschaftsmacht: Deutsche Schulen in China vor dem ersten Weltkrieg.* Frankfurt a.M.: Verlag für Interkulturelle Kommunikation.

———— (2000) Verbreitung der deutschen Sprache in Kaiserreich und Weimarer Republik. In Ammon 2000c, 31–41.

———— (2006) *Deutsch als internationale Wissenschaftssprache und der Boykott nach dem Ersten Weltkrieg.* Frankfurt a.M.: Lang.

———— (2007a) Deutsche Schulen in China vor dem Ersten Weltkrieg. In Ammon/ Reinbothe/ Zhu, 2740.

———— (2007b) Deutsche Hochschulgründung in China vor dem Ersten Weltkrieg. In Ammon/ Reinbothe/ Zhu, 41–53.

———— (2007c) Die deutsche Sprache in chinesischen und deutschen Bildungseinrichtungen in China nach dem Ersten Weltkrieg. In Ammon/ Reinbothe/ Zhu, 68–81.

———— (2011) Geschichte des Deutschen als Wissenschaftssprache im 20 Jahrhundert. In Eins/ Glück/ Pretscher, 49–66.

———— (2013) *Mehrsprachigkeit auf internationalen Kongressen.* Unpublished research report for the Volkswagen Foundation. Reference number II/83034.

Reinhardt, Kurt (1979) Stellungnahme zu H. Lippert: Rückzug der deutschen Sprache aus der Medizin? *Medizinische Klinik* 74 (11): 408f.

Reinhöfer, Nicolle (2009) *Untersuchungen zur Wissenschaftssprache und zum Publikationsverhalten in zahnmedizinischen Zeitschriften von 1970 bis 2005.* Unpublished dissertation in dental medicine, Friedrich-Schiller-Universität Jena.

Der Rektor der Karl-Marx-Universität Leipzig (ed.) (1987) *30 Jahre Herder-Institut der Karl-MarxUniversität Leipzig. Reden anläßlich des Festaktes am 20. Juni 1986.* Leipzig: Karl-MarxUniversität.

Remme, Karl/ Esch, Margarete (1927) *Die französische Kulturpropaganda. Auf der Grundlage französischen Quellenmaterials und eigener Beobachtungen im Ausland.* Berlin: Preussische Druckerei- und Verlags A.G.

Renan, Ernest (1882) [see: https://en.wikipedia.org/wiki/What_Is_a_Nation%3F].

Report of the Committee on an International Auxiliary Language accepted by the Council at Toronto, December 29, 1921 (1922) *Science* 60 (1416), February 17.

A Report to the President from the President's Commission on Foreign Language and International Studies (1979) *Strength Through Wisdom – A Critique of US Capability and Background Papers and Studies,* 2 Vols. Washington D.C.: Government Printing Office.

Reuter, Ewald/ Piitulainen, Marja-Lena (eds.) (2003) *Internationale Wirtschaftskommunikation auf Deutsch. Die deutsche Sprache im Handel zwischen den nordischen und den deutschsprachigen Ländern.* Frankfurt a.M.: Lang.

———— / Minkkinen, Eila (2001) Interkulturelle Wirtschaftskommunikation zwischen Finnland und den deutschsprachigen Ländern. Bestandsaufnahme, Probleme, Lösungen. In Reuter/ Piitulainen, 27–49.

Ricento, Thomas (ed.) (2006) *An Introduction to Language Policy. Theory and Method.* Oxford: Blackwell.

Richards, J. A. (1943) *Basic English and its Uses.* London: Kegan Paul.

Rickert, Heinrich (1899) *Kulturwissenschaft und Naturwissenschaft.* Freiburg: Mohr:

Riedmann, Gerhard (1984) Literatur eines Grenzlandes im Übergang. Überlegungen zur zeitgenössischen deutschsprachigen Literatur in Südtirol. In Ritter, 65–84.

Riehl, Claudia M. (2000) Nationale und regionale Identität: Das Beispiel der deutschsprachigen Minderheit in Südtirol. In Haslinger, P. (ed.) *Identitäten und Alteritäten.* Würzburg: Ergon, 143–153.

———— (2004) *Sprachkontaktforschung. Eine Einführung.* Tübingen: Narr.

———— (2008) Die deutschen Sprachgebiete in Mittel- und Osteuropa. In Eichinger/ Plewnia/ Riehl, 116.

Riemer, Claudia (2010) Motivierung. In Krumm/ Fandrych/ Hufeisen/ Riemer, Vol. 2, 1152–1157.

—— (2011) Warum Deutsch (noch) gelernt wird – Motivationsforschung und Deutsch als Fremdsprache. In Barkowski/ Demmig/ Funk/ Würz, 327–340.

—— / Schlak, Torsten (eds.) (2004) *Der Faktor Motivation in der Fremdsprachenforschung.* Darmstadt: Sprachenzentrum der Technischen Universität.

Rindler-Schjerve, Rosita (1998) Codeswitching as an indicator for language shift? Evidence from Sardinian – Italian bilingualism. In Jacobson, R. (ed.) *Codeswitching Worldwide.* Berlin/ New York: Mouton de Gruyter, 221–241.

Risager, Karen (2000) Bedeutet Sprachverbreitung immer auch Kulturverbreitung? In Ammon 2000c, 9–18.

Risse, Stephanie/ Roll, Heike (1997) Haben rußlanddeutsche Sprache und Kultur eine Zukunft? Zur Lage der deutschen Minderheiten in den Nachfolgestaaten der Sowjetunion. In Erfurt, J./ Redder, A. (eds.) *Spracherwerb in Minderheitensituationen. OBST* 54: 192–217.

Ritter, Alexander (ed.) (1984) *Kolloquium zur Sprache und Sprachpflege der deutschen Bevölkerungsgruppen im Ausland. Referate und Auswahlbibliographie.* Flensburg: Institut für Regionale Forschung und Information.

—— (1986) Deutschunterricht und Spracherhalt im Ausland. Notierungen zu einem besorgniserregenden Kapitel deutscher Unterrichts- und Sprachgeschichte. *Deutsche Studien* 24 (94): 155–164.

Ritter, Ernst (1976) *Das Deutsche Ausland-Institut in Stuttgart 1917–1945. Ein Beispiel deutscher Volkstumsarbeit zwischen den Weltkriegen.* Wiesbaden: Steiner.

Robbins, Anthony/ Freeman, Phyllis (2007) AuthorAID: developmental editing assistance for researchers in developing countries. *European Scinece Editing* 33 (1): 9–10.

Robertson, Roland (1992) *Globalization. Social Theory and Global Culture.* London: Sage.

—— (1995) Globalization: time-space and heterogeneity-homogeneity. In: Featherstone, M./ Lash, S./ Robertson R. *Global Modernities.* London: Sage, 25–44.

Robinson, H[arry] (1976) *A Geography of Tourism.* London: Macdonald and Evans.

Rocco, Goranka (2010) *Deutsch und Deutschlandbild an einer italienischen Universität. Eine Untersuchung zu den Spracheinstellungen der Studierenden.* Roma: ARACNE.

—— (2014) Sprachlernmotivation, aktuelle und zukünftige Rolle des Deutschen im Vergleich zu anderen Sprachen. Eine Längsschnittstudie zu den Spracheinstellungen der italienischen Studierenden. *Deutsche Sprache* 42 (2): 168–184.

Roche, Jörg (1989) *Xenolekte. Struktur und Variation im Deutsch gegenüber Ausländern.* Berlin/ New York: de Gruyter.

Rode, Rudolf (2008) Deutsch an südafrikanischen Schulen. Eine Bestandsaufnahme. *eDUSA* 3 (2): 26–29. (www.sagv.org.za/publ_dusa.htm)

Roemen, Rob (1998) Amtssprache(n) der EU: English wäre der Favorit. In: *EUmagazin* (172): 3436.

Roggausch, Werner (1996) *Als Lektor im Ausland. Das Lektorenprogramm des DAAD. Zielsetzungen und Verfahren.* Bonn: Deutscher Akademischer Austauschdienst.

—— / Giersberg, Dagmar (eds.) (2007) *Deutsch als Wissenschaftssprache* (Sektion III "Wissenschaft ist mehrsprachig" im Rahmen des Festivals "Die Macht der Sprache, Berlin 15./16. Juni 2007). Bonn: Deutscher Akademischer Austauschdienst.

Rogler, Beate (2005) *Deutsch-chinesische Studienprogramme. Analyse und Empfehlungen* (Beiträge zur Hochschulpolitik 8/2005). Bonn: Hochschulrektorenkonferenz.

Rohkohl, Kai (1993) *Die plautdietsche Sprachinsel Fernheim/ Chaco (Paraguay). Dokumentation des Sprachverhaltens einer russlanddeutschen Mennonitenkolonie.* Marburg: Elwert.

Rokoszova, Jolanta (1997) Poland. In Goebl/ Nelde/ Starý/ Wölck, 1583–1594.

Römer, Christof/ Schöpper-Grabe, Sigrid/ Wegner, Anne/ Weiß, Reinhold (2004) *Bilateraler Fremdsprachenbedarf in Deutschland und Frankreich. Eine Bestandsaufnahme in Großunternehmen.* Abschlussbericht. Köln: Institut der deutschen Wirtschaft Köln. 13.04.2006. (www.iwkoeln.de/default.aspx?p=cont&i=1 8779&n=Informationen210&m=p ub&f=1&b=Informationen)

Rønhof, Charlotte (2010) Linguistic conditions in Danish industries. In Stickel, 61–66.

Rönnefarth, Helmut K.G./ Euler, Heinrich (1958/ 1959/ 1963) *Konferenzen und Verträge: Vertrags-Ploetz,* Teil II. 3. Band: *Neuere Zeit, 1492–1914*; Band 4A: *Neueste Zeit, 1914–1959*; Band 4B: *Neueste Zeit, 1959–1963.* Würzburg: Ploetz.

Röper, Horst (2002a) Der internationale Zeitungs- und Zeitschriftenmarkt. In Leonhard et al., 2661–2665.

—— (2002b) Die internationale Medienverflechtung. In Leonhard et al., 2694–2698.

Rosenberg, Artur (1953) Frankreichs Kampf um unsere Sprache. Keine hundert Menschen konnten ein deutsches Buch lesen. *Die Zeit* (12) 19.03. (www.zeit.de/1953/12/frankreichs-kampf-um-unsere-sprache)

Rosenberg, Peter (1994) Varietätenkontakt und Varietätenausgleich bei den Rußlanddeutschen: Orientierungen für eine moderne Sprachinselforschung. In Berend/ Mattheier, 123164.

――― (2003a) Comparative speech island research: some results from studies in Russia and Brazil. In Keel/ Mattheier, 199–238.

――― (2003b) Vergleichende Sprachinselforschung. Sprachwandel in deutschen Sprachinseln in Rußland und Brasilien. In Harden, T./ Hentschel, E. (eds.) *Particulae particularum. Festschrift zum 60. Geburtstag von Harald Weydt*. Tübingen: Stauffenburg, 273–323.

――― / Weydt, Harald (1992) Sprache und Identität: Neues zur Sprache der Deutschen in der Sowjetunion. In Eisfeld, A/ Meissner, B./ Neubauer, H. (eds.) Die Russlanddeutschen – Gestern und heute. Köln: Markus, 217–238.

Rosensträter, Heinrich (1985) *Deutschsprachige Belgier. Geschichte und Gegenwart der deutschen Sprachgruppe in Belgien*, 3 Vols. Aachen: self-published.

Rosenthal, Erwin T. (1980) Rahmenbedingungen einer fremdsprachlichen Germanistik. Ein Situationsbild am Beispiel Brasiliens. *Fremdsprache Deutsch*: 300–313.

Rösler, Dietmar (2001) Deutschunterricht und Germanistikstudium in Großbritannien. In Helbig/ Götze/ Henrici/ Krumm, Vol. 2: 1464–1471.

Ross, Andreas (2003) *Europäische Einheit in babylonischer Vielfalt. Die Reform des Sprachenregimes der Europäischen Union im Spannungsfeld von Demokratie und Effizienz*. Frankfurt a. M.: Lang.

Ross, Sherman/ Shilling, Charles W. (1966) Language requirements for the Ph.D. *Science* 153: 1595.

Ross, Werner (1967) Die Stellung der deutschen Sprache in der Welt. In Wiese, B. v./ Henns, R. (eds.) *Nationalismus in Germanistik und Dichtung*. Berlin: Schmidt, 219–227.

――― (1969) Ist Deutsch noch eine Weltsprache? In Triesch, M. (ed.) *Probleme des Deutschen als Fremdsprache*. München: Hueber, 15–23.

――― (1972) *Deutsch in der Konkurrenz der Weltsprachen*. München: Hueber.

――― (1987) Wettkampf der Sprachen. Zur Rolle des Deutschen in der Welt. In Sturm, 101–107.

Rossbach, Udo (1980) *Die auswärtige Kulturpolitik der Bundesrepublik Deutschland: Grundlagen, Ziele, Aufgaben. Eine Titelsammlung. Stand: Ende 1979*. Stuttgart: Institut für Auslandsbeziehungen.

Rossner, Mike/ Van Epps, Heather/ Hill, Emma (2007) Show me the data. *The Journal of Experimental Medicine* 204 (13): 3052–3053.

Roth, G. (1989) Anmerkungen zu den "Bemerkungen zum Sprachenstreit in der deutschen Psychologie" von Wolfgang Marx. *Psychologische Beiträge* 40: 94–96.

Rottleuthner, Hubert (1973) *Rechtswissenschaft als Sozialwissenschaft*. Frankfurt a.M.: Fischer Taschenbuch Verlag.

Roudybush, Franklin (1972) *Diplomatic Language*. Basel: Satz + Repro AG.

Rowley, Anthony (1996) Die Sprachinseln der Fersentaler und Zimbern. In Hinderling/ Eichinger, 263–285.

Røyneland, Unn (ed.) (1997) *Language Contact and Language Conflict*. Volda: University of Oslo.

von Ruckteschell, Katharina (2007) Goethe in Europa. Das Institut und seine Sprachenpolitik in der EU. *Muttersprache* 117 (2): 145–154.

Ruecker-Guitelmacher, Katrin (2009) *Le triangle Paris – Bonn – Londres et le processus d'adhésion britannique au marché commun 1969–1973. Quel rôle pour le trilatéral au sein du multilatéral?* Unpublished dissertation from the Institut d'Etudes Politique de Paris/ PhilippsUniversität Marburg.

Rudolf, Walter (1972) *Die Sprache in der Diplomatie und internationalen Verträgen*. Frankfurt a.M.: Athenäum.

Ruhlen, Merritt (1987) *A Guide to the World's Languages*, Vol. 1: *Classifications*. London: Edward Arnold.

Rupp, Heinz (1983) Deutsch in der Schweiz. In Reiffenstein, I. et al. (eds.) *Tendenzen, Formen und Strukturen der deutschen Standardsprache nach 1945*. Marburg: Elwert, 29–39.

Rustow, Dankwart A. (1968) Language, modernization, and nationhood – an attempt at typology. In Fishman, J. A./ Ferguson, A./ Das Gupta, J. (eds.) *Language Problems of Developing Nations*. New York: Wiley, 87–105.

Rüttgers, Jürgen (1997) Studienstandort Deutschland attraktiver gestalten. Immer weniger ausländische Studenten in Deutschland. *Forschung & Lehre* 4: 182–184.

Saari, Mirja (2000) Die Stellung des Hochdeutschen in der finnischen Kulturtradition. In Naumann/ Müller, 155–167.

Sadmon, Zeev W. (1994) *Die Gründung des Technions in Haifa im Lichte deutscher Politik 19071920*. München: Saur.

Said, Edward W. (1978) *Orientalism*. London: Routledge & Kegan Paul.

Sakaguchi, Alicja (1987) Welthilfssprache. In Ammon/ Dittmar/ Mattheier, 365–370.

———— (1989) Towards a clarification of the function and status of international planned languages. In Ammon 1989d, 399–440.

Salager-Meyer, Françoise (2008) Scientific publishing in developing countries: challenges for the future. *Journal of English for Academic Purposes* 7: 121–132.

Salzmann, Oswald (1913) *Das vereinfachte Deutsch: Die Sprache aller Völker.* Leipzig: Salzmann.

Sambe, Shinichi (2013) Abweichende Gründe und Motivationen zum hochschulischen Lernen der deutschen Sprache als "Kultursprache" – Studierende lernen anders als Schüler. Vor-trag bei Podiums-diskussion der Internationalen Deutschlehrertagung in Bozen, August 2013. (www.idt-2013.it/DE/PROGRAMM/PODIEN/P5.html)

Sánchez, Aquilino (1992) Política de difusión del español. In Ammon/ Kleineidam, 51–69.

Sandelin, Bo/ Sarafoglou, Nikias (2004) Language and scientific publication statistics. *Language Problems and Language Planning* 28: 1–10.

Sanders, A. F. (1989) Some Comments on Marx' "Bemerkungen zum Sprachenstreit in der deutschen Psychologie." *Psychologische Beiträge* 40: 93–94.

Sanders, Willi (1974) Deutsch, Niederdeutsch, Niederländisch. In Goossens, 1–22.

Sandrock, Otto (1999) Die deutsche Sprache und das internationale Recht: Fakten und Konsequenzen. In Hübner, U./ Ebke, W. (eds.) *Festschrift für Bernhard Großfeld zum 65. Geburtstag.* Heidelberg: Verlag Recht und Wirtschaft, 971–995.

Sano, H. (2002) A survey of English as the universalizing language of chemistry: the world's lingua franca of Science. *English Today* 18: 45–49.

de Santis, Mark/ Hauber, Eric/ Pearce, Thomas L. (1972) Foreign language requirements for foreign language students in Anatomy. *Journal of Medical Education* 47: 297–301.

Sartingen, Kathrin (2001) Deutschunterricht und Germanistikstudium in Brasilien. In Helbig/ Götze/ Henrici/ Krumm, Vol. 2: 1445–1449.

Sasalatti, Shrishail (1978) Zum Deutschunterricht in Indien. *Indo-German* 2: 30–37.

———— (1990) Deutsch als Fremdsprache in Indien. Einige Grundüberlegungen. *Info DaF* 17 (31): 259270.

Sasse, Hans-Jürgen (1992) Theory of language death. In Brenzinger, 7–30.

Sauer, Christoph (1989) Nazi-Deutsch für Niederländer. Das Konzept der NS-Sprachpolitik in der ,Deutschen Zeitung in den Niederlanden' 1940–1945. In Ehlich. 237–288.

Sauer, Martina (2012) *Zusammenfassung der Ergebnisse der 12. Mehrthemenbefragung [Oktober] 2011.* Universität Duisburg-Essen: Stiftung Zentrum für Türkeistudien und Integrationsforschung. (www.zfti.de)

Savedra, Mônica M. G./ Höhmann, Beate (2013) Das plurizentrische Deutsch in Brasilien und die regionale Kooffizialisierung eines ostniederdeutschen Dialekts. In SchneiderWiejowski/ Kellermeier-Rehbein/ Haselhuber, 411–425.

Savory, Theodore H. (1953) *The Language of Science. Its Growth, Character and Usage.* London: Deutsch.

Scaff, Lawrence A. (2011) *Max Weber in America.* Princeton, NJ: Princeton University Press.

Schabus, Wilfried (1994) Beobachtungen zu Sprachkontakt, Varietätenausgleich, Sprachloyalität und Sprachwechsel in Pozuzo (Peru) und bei den "Landlern" in Siebenbürgen. In Berend/ Mattheier, 221–262.

Schallenberg, Wolfgang (1987) Die Rolle der deutschen Sprache in der Auslandskulturpolitik Österreichs. In Sturm (1987a), 191–196.

———— (2007) Beten, Arbeiten, Forschen und Erleben bei den Hutterern in Kanada. In Ahamer, J./ Lechleitner, G. (eds.) *Um-Feld-Forschung. Erfahrungen – Erlebnisse – Ergebnisse.* Wien: Verlag der Österreichischen Akademie der Wissenschaften, 63–77.

Scharpf, Fritz (1999) *Regieren in Europa. Effektiv und demokratisch?* Frankfurt a.M.: Campus.

Scheibe, Hubertus (1975) Der Deutsche Akademische Austauschdienst 1950 bis 1975. *DAADForum* 7: 33–111.

Scheller, Hanspeter K. (2006) *Die Europäische Zentralbank – Geschichte, Rolle und Aufgaben* (übs. aus dem Englischen). 2nd edition, Frankfurt a.M.: Europäische Zentralbank.

Scheuringer, Hermann (2008) Deutsche Sprachkultur in Bukarest. In Nekula, M./ Bauer, V./ Greule, A. (eds.) *Deutsch in multilingualen Stadtzentren Mittel- und Osteuropas. Um die Jahrhundertwende vom 19. zum 20. Jahrhundert.* Wien: Praesens, 125–137.

Schiewe, Jürgen (1991) Wissenschaftssprachen an der Albert-Ludwigs-Universität Freiburg. *Freiburger Universitätsblätter* 113: 17–51.

———— (1996) *Sprachwechsel – Funktionswandel – Austausch der Denkstile. Die Universität Freiburg zwischen Latein und Deutsch.* Tübingen: Niemeyer.

———— (2000) Von Latein zu Deutsch, von Deutsch zu Englisch. Gründe und Folgen des Wechsels von Wissenschaftssprachen. In Debus/ Kollmann/ Pörksen, 81–105.

Schiffman, Harold (1987) Losing the battle for balanced bilingualism: the German-American case. *Language Problems and Language Planning* 11: 67–81.

——— (2009) Augusto Carli and Ulrich Ammon: linguistic inequality in scientific communication today (AILA Review, Vol. 20) [. . .] 2007 [. . .]. *Language Policy* 8: 303–305.

Schirbel, Sandra et al. (2005) *Report: Deutsche Sprache in niederländischen Unternehmen*. Deutsche Botschaft Den Haag u.a (eds.). Den Haag: Deutsch-Niederländische Handelskammer, Europe Calling/ HHS – Group 25.01.

Schirokich, Valerij (2008) Die russlanddeutsche Minderheit in Baschkirien. In Eichinger/ Plewnia/ Riehl, 71–81.

Schlemmer, Johann A. [1815] (1998) Soll es eine allgemeine europäische Verhandlungssprache geben? *Die slawischen Sprachen* 58: 101–117.

Schlobinski, Peter (ed.) *Von *hdl* bis *cul8r*. Sprache und Kommunikation in den Neuen Medien*. Mannheim: Dudenverlag.

Schlosser, Horst D. (1990) *Die deutsche Sprache in der DDR zwischen Stalinismus und Demokratie. Historische, politische und kommunikative Bedingungen*. Köln: Verlag Wissenschaft und Politik.

Schloßmacher, Michael (1994a) Die Arbeitssprachen in den Organen der europäischen Gemeinschaft. Methoden und Ergebnisse einer empirischen Untersuchung. *Sociolinguistica* 8: 101–122.

——— [1994b] (1997) *Die Amtssprachen in den Organen der Europäischen Gemeinschaft. Status und Funktion.* 2nd edition, Frankfurt a.M.: Lang.

Schmale, Günter (2007a) "Sprechen Sie Deutsch? – No, thank you . . ." – Zur Lage von Deutsch als Fremdsprache in Frankreich. *Muttersprache* 117 (3): 216–237.

——— (2007b) Ist Deutsch als Fremdsprache in Frankreich noch zu retten? In Béhar, Pierre/ Lartillot, Françoise/ Puschner, Uwe (eds.) *Médiation et Conviction. Hommage à Michel Grunewald*. Paris: L'Harmattan, 117–189.

Schmid, Monika S. (2011) *Language Attrition*. Cambridge: Cambridge University Press.

Schmid, Stefan/ Daniel, Andrea (2006) *Measuring Board Internationalization. Towards a More Holistic Approach.* Working Paper 21. ESCP-EAP. Berlin: Europäische Wirtschaftshochschule.

Schmidlin, Regula (2011) *Die Vielfalt des Deutschen: Standard und Variation. Gebrauch, Einschätzung und Kodifizierung einer plurizentrischen Sprache.* Berlin/ Boston: de Gruyter.

Schmidt, Gabriele (1998) Zur Situation der deutschen Sprache in australischen Hochschulen. *Info DaF* 25 (4): 470–476.

——— (2011) *Motives for Studying German in Australia*. Frankfurt a. M.: Lang.

Schmidt, Hansgünther (2007a) Der Deutsche Akademische Austauschdienst (DAAD) in China. In Ammon/ Reinbothe/ Zhu, 226–276.

——— (2007b) Die deutsche Sprache in China – weitere Förderer. In Ammon/ Reinbothe/ Zhu, 301308.

Schmidt, Helmut (2008) *Außer Dienst. Eine Bilanz*. München: Siedler.

Schmidt, Ulla (2012) Deutschland als Partner in Europa und in der Welt – eine Kritik des AKBPKonzepts 2011 des Auswärtigen Amtes. In Drews, 131–136.

Schmidt-Rohr, Georg (1932) *Die Sprache als Bildnerin der Völker. Eine Wesens- und Lebenskunde der Volkstümer.* Jena: Eugen Diederichs.

——— (1933) *Mutter Sprache. Vom Amt der Sprache bei der Volkwerdung.* 2nd revised edition by Schmidt-Rohr 1932. Jena: Eugen Diederichs.

Schmitt, Marco (1995) Why Study German? *Deutschunterricht im Südlichen Afrika (DUSA)* 26: 54–56.

Schmitz, Ulrich (2004) *Sprache in modernen Medien. Einführung in Tatsachen und Theorien, Themen und Thesen.* Berlin: E. Schmidt.

Schneider, Axel (2000) *Die auswärtige Sprachpolitik der Bundesrepublik Deutschland. Eine Untersuchung zur Förderung der deutschen Sprache in Mittel- und Osteuropa, in der Sowjetunion und in der GUS 1982 bis 1995.* Bamberg: Collibri.

Schneider, Gisela (2012) Die Förderung der Mehrsprachigkeit in den Wissenschaften durch den Deutschen Akademischen Austauschdienst (DAAD). In Oberreuter/ Krull/ Meyer/ Ehlich, 245–250.

Schneider, Günther/ Clalüna, Monika (eds.) (2003) *Mehr Sprache – mehrsprachig mit Deutsch. Didaktische und politische Perspektiven.* München: Iudicium.

Schneider, Marion (1989) Lernen in der Bundesrepublik Deutschland. Methoden und Erfahrungen aus den Carl Duisberg Centren. *Jahrbuch Deutsch als Fremdsprache* 15: 150–174.

Schneider, Wolf (2008) *Speak German – Warum Deutsch manchmal wirklich besser ist.* Reinbeck: Rowohlt.

Schneider-Mizony, Odile (2002) Deutsch als Fremdsprache und Germanistik in Frankreich. *Jahrbuch für Internationale Germanistik* 34 (1): 19–25.

———— (2008) Deutsch als Fremdsprache in Frankreich im Jahr 2006. *Jahrbuch für Internationale Germanistik* 39 (2): 19–35.

———— (2010) Politique de l'enseignement des vivantes dans la France du IIIe millénaire. *Sociolinguistica* 24: 187–203.

Schneider-Wiejowski, Karina/ Ammon, Ulrich (2013) Deutschlandismus, Germani(zi)smus, Teutonismus. Wie sollen die spezifischen Sprachformen Deutschlands heißen? *Muttersprache* 123: 48–65.

———— / Kellermeier-Rehbein, Birte/ Haselhuber, Jakob (eds.) (2013) *Vielfalt, Variation und Stellung der deutschen Sprache*. Berlin/ Boston: de Gruyter.

Schoepflin, Urs (1989) Bibliometrische Erfahrungen mit Datenbanken – Bericht zum Projekt "Rezeption deutschsprachiger Psychologie und Soziologie in den USA". In Deutsche Gesellschaft für Dokumentation (ed.) *40 Jahre DGD – Perspektive Information*. Frankfurt a. M.: Deutsche Gesellschaft für Dokumentation, 132–150.

Scholten, Dirk (2000a) *Sprachverbreitung des nationalsozialistischen Deutschlands*. Frankfurt a. M.: Lang.

———— (2000b) Aufnötigung und Vorenthaltung von Deutsch in der NS-Zeit. In Ammon 2000c, 43–49.

Scholtz-Knobloch, Till (2002) *Die deutsche Minderheit in Oberschlesien – Selbstreflexion und politisch-soziale Situation unter besonderer Berücksichtigung des so genannten "Oppelner Schlesiens" (Westoberschlesiens)*. Görlitz: Senfkorn-Verlag.

Schönbach, Klaus/ Knobloch, Silvia (1994) *Die Hörerinnen und Hörer des Deutschen Programms der Deutschen Welle. Wissenschaftliches Gutachten für die Deutsche Welle*. Hannover: Forschungsgruppe Medien, Programm, Publikum.

———— / ———— (1995) Die Deutsche Welle und ihr Publikum: eine Bestandsaufnahme der Funktionen des Deutschsprachigen Programms. In Mahle, 183–191.

Schönrock, Kim Laura/ Krath, Stefany (2014) Wie funktioniert die deutsche Auslandsschularbeit? *Begegnung* 35 (2): 6–9.

Schopenhauer, Johanna [1831] (1930) *Ausflug an den Niederrhein und nach Belgien im Jahr 1828*. In zwei Teilen. Erster Teil. Leipzig: F. A. Brockhaus.

Schöpper-Grabe, Sigrid (2009) Betrieblicher Fremdsprachenbedarf im deutschsprachigen Raum. *Sociolinguistica* 23: 15–162.

———— (2000) *Go global – Fremdsprachen als Standortvorteil*. Köln: Deutscher Instituts-Verlag.

———— / Weiß, Reinhold (1998) *Vorsprung durch Fremdsprachentraining. Ergebnisse einer Unternehmensbefragung*. Köln: Deutscher Instituts-Verlag.

Schreiner, Patrick (2006a) Staat und Sprache in Europa. Nationalstaatliche Einsprachigkeit und die Mehrsprachenpolitik der Europäischen Union. Frankfurt a.M.: Lang.

———— (2006b) Deutsch im Konzert europäischer Sprachen. Über die Sprachenpolitik der EU und die Situation der deutschen Sprache auf europäischer Ebene. *Der Sprachdienst* 50 (4–5): 4151.

Schriftsteller-Lexikon der Siebenbürger Deutschen ([1868, Vol. 1] 2012) Harald Roth (ed.) Vol. 10: Buchstaben Q–R bis Sch. Wien/ Köln/ Weimar: Böhlau.

Schröder, Konrad (1981) Eine Sprache für Europa? *Wort und Sprache. Beiträge zu Problemen der Lexikographie und Sprachpraxis*. Veröffentlicht zum 125-jährigen Bestehen des Langenscheidt-Verlags. [Berlin et al.], 62–69.

———— / Macht, Konrad (1983) *Wieviele Sprachen für Europa? Fremdsprachenunterricht, Fremdsprachenlernen und europäische Sprachenvielfalt im Urteil von Studierenden des Grundstudiums in Deutschland, Belgien und Finnland*. Augsburg: Universität.

Schröder-Gudehus, Brigitte (1966) *Deutsche Wissenschaft und internationale Zusammenarbeit 1914–1928. Ein Beitrag zum Studium kultureller Beziehungen in politischen Krisenzeiten*. Genève: Dumaret & Golay.

Schroeder-Gudehus [=Schröder-Gudehus], Brigitte (1972) Challenge to transnational loyalties: international scientific organizations after the First World War. *Science Studies* 3: 93–118.

———— (1973) Challenge to transnational loyalties: international scientific organizations after the First World War. *Science Studies* 3: 93–118.

———— (1990) Internationale Wissenschaftsbeziehungen und auswärtige Kulturpolitik 1919–1933. Vom Boykott und Gegen-Boykott zu ihrer Wiederaufnahme. In Vierhaus/ Brocke, 858–885.

Schübel-Pfister, Isabel (2004) *Sprache und Gemeinschaftsrecht: die Auslegung der mehrsprachig verbindlichen Rechtstexte durch den Europäischen Gerichtshof*. Berlin: Duncker & Humblot.

Schulz, Gisela (1975) Die Entstehung des Deutschen Akademischen Austauschdienstes und seine Entwicklung bis 1945. *DAAD-Forum* 7: 11–32.

Schümer, Dieter (1979) Franz Thierfelder und Deutsch für Ausländer: Kontinuität und Neuorientierung seit 1932. In Simon, G. (ed.) *Sprachwissenschaft und politisches Engagement*. Weinheim/ Basel: Beltz, 207–229.

Schwabl, Wilhelm (1986) Spitzenforschung auf Englisch – aus verlegerischer Sicht. In Kalverkämper/ Weinrich, 45–47.

Schwartzkopff, Christa (1987) *Deutsch als Muttersprache in den Vereinigten Staaten, Teil III: German Americans. Die sprachliche Assimilation der Deutschen in Wisconsin.* Wiesbaden: Steiner.

Schwarzenbach, Rudolf (1969) *Die Stellung der Mundart in der deutschsprachigen Schweiz. Studien zum Sprachgebrauch der Gegenwart.* Frauenfeld: Huber.

Schweizer Tourismus-Verband (2012) *Schweizer Tourismus in Zahlen 2011. Struktur und Branchendaten.* Bern. Länggass. (www. swisstourfed.ch)

Schwörer, E[mil] (1916) *Kolonial-Deutsch. Vorschläge einer künftigen deutschen Kolonialsprache in systematisch-grammatischer Darstellung und Begründung.* Diessen vor München: Huber.

Science Citation Index (SCI) (1961ff.). Institute for Scientific Information/ Thomson Reuters.

Scott, James B. (1924) *Le français, langue diplomatique moderne. Etude critique de conciliation internationale.* Paris: Pedone.

Seewann, Gerhard (1994) Towards a typology of minorities – The Germans in Hungary. *Regio. A Review of Minority and Ethnic Studies,* 103–113.

——— (2012) *Geschichte der Deutschen in Ungarn.* Vol. 1: *Vom Frühmittelalter bis 1860,* Vol. 2: *1860–2006.* Marburg: Herder-Institut.

Seidlhofer, Barbara (2005a) Englisch als Lingua Franca und seine Rolle in der internationalen Wissensvermittlung. Ein Aufruf zur Selbstbehauptung. In Braun/ Kohn, 27–45.

——— (2005b) Language variation and change: the case of English as a lingua franca. In Dzinbalska-Kotaczyk, K./ Przedlacka, J. (eds.) *English Pronunciation Models: A Changing Scene.* Bern: Lang, 59–75.

——— (2011) *Understanding English as a Lingua Franca.* Oxford: Oxford University Press.

Sekiguchi, Ichiro (1994) Deutsch als Fremdsprache in Fernseh- und Rundfunkkursen. In Ammon 1994d, 301–309.

Sekretariat des Gerichtshofs unter der Autorität des Obersten Kontrollrats (ed.) (1948) *Der Prozeß gegen die Hauptkriegsverbrecher vor dem internationalen Militärgerichtshof Nürnberg.*

Selten, Reinhard/ Pool, Jonathan (1991) The distribution of foreign language skills as a game equilibrium. In Selten, R. (ed.) *Game Equilibrium Models,* Vol. 4: *Social and Political Interaction.* Berlin: Springer, 64–87.

Sennitt, Andrew G. (ed.) [1979] (1989) *World Radio TV Handbook.* New York: Billboard.

——— / *Volume 66–2012* (2011) Gilbert, Sean (international ed.). Oxford: WRTH Publications.

——— / *Volume 68–2014* (2013) Gilbert, Sean (international ed.). Oxford: WRTH Publications.

Serke, Jürgen (1984) *Das neue Exil. Die verbannten Dichter.* Frankfurt a.M.: Fischer.

——— (1987) *Böhmische Dörfer. Wanderungen durch eine verlassene literarische Landschaft.* Wien/ Frankfurt a.M.: Zsolnaj.

Sewann, Georg (1992) *Ungarndeutsche und Ethnopolitik. Ausgewählte Aufsätze.* Budapest.

Shannon, Thomas [1989] (1996) *An Introduction to the World-System Perspective.* Boulder, CO: Westview Press.

Sheehy, Eugene P. (1976) *Guide to Reference Books,* 9th edition. Chicago: American Library Association.

——— [1976] [1980] (1982) *[Guide Reference Books. 9th. ed. Second Supplement.* Chicago: American Library Association.

Sheng, Wenting (in print) *Sprachförderungspolitik Deutschlands, Großbritanniens und Chinas im Vergleich.* Frankfurt a.M.: Lang.

Shenton, Herbert N./ Sapir, Edward/ Jespersen, Otto (1931) *International Communication. A Symposium on the Language Problem.* London: Kegan Paul/ Trench/ Trubner.

——— (1933) *Cosmopolitan Conversation. The Language Problems of International Conferences.* New York: Columbia University Press.

Sheppard, Oden E. (1935) The Chemistry Student Still needs a Reading Knowledge of German. *Journal of Chemical Education* 12: 472 f.

Shimokawa, Yutaka (1994) Die japanische Hochschulpolitik in jüngerer Zeit und ihr Auswirkungen auf das Fremdsprachenstudium in Japan. In Ammon 1994d, 259–274.

Shinohara, Seiei (2000) Kriegsende in Deutschland und kein Entkommen. In Hellmann, 47–49.

Shohamy, Elana/ Gorter, Durk (eds.) (2009) *Linguistic Landscape. Expanding the Scenery.* New York/ London: Routledge.

Šichová, Kateřina (2008) Zur Stellung der deutschen Sprache in der tschechischen Wirtschaft. Überlegungen zum Thema anhand der Situation in einer bestimmten Gruppe von Unternehmen in Tschechien. *Acta Universitatis Carolinae – Studia Territorialia* 14: 221–240.

Sick, Bastian (2013) *Wir braten Sie gern. Ein Bilderbuch aus dem Irrgarten der deutschen Sprache.* Köln: Kiepenheuer & Witsch.

Siebert, Peter/ Sitta, Horst (1984) Schweizerdeutsch zwischen Dialekt und Sprache. *Kwartalnik Neofilologiczny* 1984: 4–40.

Siemens, Heinrich (2012) *Plautdietsch: Grammatik, Geschichte, Perspektiven.* Bonn: Tweeback.

Sigaux, Gilbert (1966) *History of Tourism.* Genf: Edito-Service/ London: Leisure Arts.

Siguan, Marisa (2007) Die deutsche Sprache in Spanien. *Jahrbuch für Internationale Germanistik* 39 (2): 51–60.

Siguan, Miguel (1996) *L'Europe des langues.* Sprimont: Mardaga.

——— (2001) [Spanish/ French 1996] *Die Sprachen im vereinten Europa.* Tübingen: Stauffenburg.

Van der Sijs, Nicoline/ Willemyns, Roland (2009) *Het verhaal van het Nederlands. Een geschiedenis van twaalf eeuwen.* Amsterdam: Uitgeverij Bert Bakker.

da Silva, Jaime F./ Klein Gunnewick, Lisanne (1992) Portuguese and Brazilian efforts to spread Portuguese. In Ammon/ Kleineidam, 71–92.

Simon, Gerd (ed.) (1979a) *Sprachwissenschaft und politisches Engagement. Zur Problem- und Sozialgeschichte einiger sprachtheoretischer, sprachdidaktischer und sprachpflegerischer Ansätze in der Germanistik des 19. und 20. Jahrhunderts.* Weinheim/ Basel: Beltz.

——— (1979b) Materialien über den ‚Widerstand' in der deutschen Sprachwissenschaft des Dritten Reichs: Der Fall Georg Schmidt-Rohr. In Simon (1979a), 153–206.

Sinclair, John/ Cunningham, Stuart (2000) Go with the flow: diasporas and the media. *Television & New Media* 1: 11–31.

Skudlik, Sabine (1988) Die Kinder Babylons. In Oksaar/ Skudlik/ von Stackelberg, 73–129.

——— (1990) *Sprachen in den Wissenschaften. Deutsch und Englisch in der internationalen Kommunikation.* Tübingen: Narr.

——— (1992) The status of German as a language of science and the importance of the English language for German-speaking scientists. In Ammon/ Hellinger, 391–407.

Skutnabb-Kangas, Tove/ Phillipson, Robert (1989) "Mother tongue": the theoretical and sociological construction of a concept. In Ammon 1989d, 450–477.

——— / Pillipson, Robert/ Rannut, Mart (eds.) (1995) *Linguistic Human Rights. Overcoming Linguistic Discrimination.* Berlin/ New York: de Gruyter.

——— (2000) *Linguistic Genocide in Education – or Worldwide Diversity and Human Rights?* Mahwah, NJ: Erlbaum.

Small, Henry/ Garfield Eugene (1997) The geography of science: disciplinary and national mappings. In *Index to Scientific Review 1996. Second Semiannual.* Philadelphia, PA: Institute for Scientific Information, 27–38.

Smith, Adam [1776] (2003) *The Wealth of Nations. Introduction by Alan B. Krueger.* New York: Bantam Dell.

Smith, R. L. (1981) On provincialism and one-language psychology. *Psychologische Beiträge* 23: 293–302.

Smolicz, Jerzy J. (1980a) Language as a core value of culture. *Journal of Applied Linguistics* 11: 1–13.

——— (1980b) Minority languages as core values of ethnic cultures. In Fase/ Jaspaert/ Kroon, 277305.

——— (1981) Core values and cultural identity. *Ethnic and Racial Studies* 4: 75–90.

Social Science Citation Index (SSCI) (1972ff.). Institute for Scientific Information/ Thomson Reuters.

Society of Native English-Speaking SENSE. Tony Cunningham. 9. April 2006. (www.sense-online.nl)

SocioFile (1974ff.). San Diego, CA: Sociological Abstracts/ Silver Platter International.

Sociological Abstracts (1952ff.) New York: Sociological Abstracts.

Soethe, Paulo (2002) Brasilianischer Kanon, germanistische Lupe: ein gemeinsamer Nenner im Auge. In Deutscher Akademischer Austauschdienst, 275–282.

——— (2010) Deutsch in Brasilien. In Krumm/ Fandrych/ Hufeisen/ Riemer, Vol. 2, 1624–1627.

——— / Weininger, M. (2009) Interkulturelle Zusammenarbeit im akademischen Bereich – Geschichtsbewusstsein, Multidiziplinarität und Reziprozität als Rezept für erfolgreiche Projekte. In Hess-Lüttich/ Colliander/ Reuter, 361–376.

de Solla Price, Derek J. (1967) Nations can publish or perish. *Science and Technology* 70: 8490.

——— (1970) Citation measures of hard science, soft science, technology, and nonscience. In Nelson, C. E./ Pollock, D. K. (eds.) *Communication Among Scientists and Engineers.* Lexington, MS: Heath Lexington Books, 3–22.

——— [engl. 1963] (1974) *Little Science, Big Science. Von der Studierstube zur Großforschung.* Frankfurt a. M.: Suhrkamp.

——— [1963] (1986) *Little Science, Big Science . . . and Beyond.* New York: Columbia University Press.

Soltau, Anja (2008a) Englisch als Lingua Franca in der wissenschaftlichen Lehre: Charakteristika und Herausforderungen englischsprachiger Masterstudiengänge in Deutschland. Diss. Univ. Hamburg. (www.sub.uni-hamburg.de/opus/volltexte/2008/3602)

———— (2008b) Englischsprachige Masterprogramme in Deutschland: Qualitätssicherung in der akademischen Lingua-franca-Kommunikation am Beispiel von sprachlichen Zulassungskriterien. In Schumann, A/ Knapp, A. (eds.) *Mehrsprachigkeit und Multikulturalität im Studium*. Frankfurt a.M: Lang, 155–169.

Song, Kyung-An (2003) Über die Schwierigkeiten des Deutschen als Fremdsprache für Koreaner. In Ammon/ Chong, 317–334.

Song, Ludong (2007) Die Schulen mit dem Fach Deutsch als Fremdsprache [in China! ET AL.]. In Ammon/ Reinbothe/ Zhu, 113–122.

Sorger, Brigitte (2010) Institutionen und Verbände für Deutsch als Zweit- und Fremdsprache in Österreich. In Krumm/ Fandrych/ Hufeisen/ Riemer, Vol. 1, 153–160.

———— (2012) *Der Internationale Deutschlehrerverband und seine Sprachenpolitik. Ein Beitrag zur Fachgeschichte von Deutsch als Fremdsprache*. Innsbruck: Studienverlag.

Späth, Lothar (1990) Künftige Aufgaben der auswärtigen Kulturpolitik. *Jahrbuch Deutsch als Fremdsprache* 16: 311–328.

Spitzley, Thomas (2003) Identität und Orientierung. In Petrus, K. (ed.) *On Human Persons*. Frankfurt a.M./ London: Ontos, 195–214.

Spolsky, Bernard (2004) *Language Policy*. Cambridge: Cambridge University Press.

———— (2009) *Language Management*. Cambridge: Cambridge University Press.

———— / Shohamy, Elana (1999) *The Languages of Israel. Policy, Ideology and Practise*. Clevedon: Multilingual Matters.

Sprachatlas (1979) Der Bundesminister des Auswärtigen informiert. Material für die Presse Nr. 2043 B/ 79. 05.09. 1979.

Sprachenvielfalt in Namibia. Brücken und Schranken (2012) *Perspektiven 2012. Aktuelle Beiträge zu Kirche, Gesellschaft und Zeitgeschehen*. Windhoek. *Die Staaten der Erde*, 2 Vols. (1983). Düsseldorf/ Wien: Econ.

von Stackelberg, Jürgen (1988) Die Mehrsprachigkeit der Geisteswissenschaften. In Oksaar/ Skudlik/ von Stackelberg, 131–201.

StADaF (Ständige Arbeitsgruppe Deutsch als Fremdsprache) (2005) *Deutsch als Fremdsprache weltweit. Datenerhebung 2005*. Berlin: Auswärtiges Amt.

Staël, Madame de [1818] (1968) *De l'Allemagne*. 2. Vols. Paris: Garnier-Flammarion.

Stangherlin, Katrin/ Bruell, Christoph (2005) *La communaute germanophone de Belgique*. Bruxelles: La Charte.

Stark, Franz (1993) *Faszination Deutsch. Wiederentdeckung einer Sprache für Europa*. München: Langen Müller.

———— (2000a) Ansätze zur Verbreitung der deutschen Sprache seit der Reichsgründung. In Ammon 2000c, 19–30.

———— (2000b) Sprachförderung und Außenpolitik. Kritik der Politik der Bundesregierung. In Ammon 2000c, 93–102.

———— (2000c) Wenig Deutsch am Fernsehschirm. Beobachtungen und Überlegungen eines Auslandsreporters. In Hoffmann, 279–294.

———— (2002) *Deutsch in Europa. Geschichte seiner Stellung und Ausstrahlung*. Sankt Augustin: Asgar.

———— (2004) Sprache – "Sanftes Machtinstrument" im globalen Wettbewerb. Ohne selbstbewusstere Sprachenpolitik gerät Deutschland immer mehr ins Hintertreffen. *Jahrbuch Deutsch als Fremdsprache* 30: 141–162.

Statistisches Bundesamt (2006) *Tourismus. Tourismus in Zahlen*. Wiesbaden: Statistisches Bundesamt. (www.destatis.de/DE/Publikationen/Thematisch/BinnenhandelGastgewerbeTourismus/Tourismus/TourismusinZahlen1021500057004.pdf?__blob=publicationFile)

———— (2013) *Binnenhandel, Gastgewerbe, Tourismus. August 2013*. Fachserie 6, Reihe 7.1. Wiesbaden: Statistisches Bundesamt.

Statistisches Bundesamt Wiesbaden (ed.) (1983) *Urlaubs- und Erholungsreisen 1981/ 82 (Ergebnisse des Mikrozensus April 1981 – März 1982)*. Stuttgart/ Mainz: Kohlhammer.

———— (ed.) (1988) *Urlaubs- und Erholungsreisen 1985/86 (Ergebnisse des Mikrozensus Mai 1985 – April 1986*. Stuttgart/ Mainz: Kohlhammer.

Steere, W. C. et al. (1976) *Biological Abstracts/ BIOSIS. The First Fifty Years. The Evolution of a Major Science Information Service*. New York: Plenum.

Steffen, Joachim (2006) Vereinzelte Sprachinseln oder Archipel? Die Mennonitenkolonien in Belize im englisch-spanischen Sprachkontakt. Band 1: *Textband*; Band 2: *Kartenband*. Kiel: Westensee-Verlag.

———— / Altenhofen, Cléo V. (2014) Spracharchipele des Deutschen in Amerika: Dynamik der Sprachvernetzungen im mehrsprachigen Raum. *Dialektologie und Linguistik.*

Steinecke, Albrecht (2006) *Tourismus. Eine geographische Einführung.* Braunschweig: Bildungshaus Schulbuchverlage Westermann.

———— (2013) *Destinationsmanagement.* Konstanz/ München: UVK Verlagsgesellschaft.

Steinke, Klaus (1979) Die sprachliche Situation der deutschen Minderheit in Rumänien. In Ureland, 183–203.

———— (1997) Sprachenkarte von Rumänien und Bulgarien. In Goebl/ Nelde/ Starý/ Wölck, 20272029.

Stekeler-Weithofer, Pirmin (2011) Die Bedeutung der eigenen Sprache für das Denken. Zur Lage des Deutschen in der Philosophie. In Wieland/ Glück/ Pretscher, 73–84.

Stenestad, Elva (1986) Der Deutschunterricht vor und nach 1945. *Grenzfriedenshefte* 2: 99–110.

Stephens, Meic (1978) Linguistic Minorities in Western Europe. Dyfed: Gomer.

Stern, Gug/ Rudowski, Victor A. (1968) Ph. Ds Nobel Prize winners, and the foreign-language requirement. *Modern Journal* 52 (7 Nov.): 431–435.

Sternberger, Dolf/ Storz Gerhard/ Süskind, W[ilhelm] E. (1957) *Aus dem Wörterbuch des Unmenschen.* Hamburg: Claassen.

Stevenson, Patrick (2000a) The ethnolinguistic vitality of German-speaking communities in Central Europe. In Wolff, 109–124.

———— (2000b) The multilingual market place: German as a Hungarian language. In Hogan-Brun, G. (ed.) *National Varieties of German Outside Germany.* Frankfurt a.M.: Lang, 243–258.

———— / Carl, Jenny (2010) *Language and Social Change in Central Europe. Discourses on Policy, Identity and the German Language.* Edinburgh: Edinburgh University Press.

Stewart, William A. (1962) An outline of linguistic typology for describing multilingualism. In Rice, F. A. (ed.) *Study of the Role of Second Languages in Asia, Africa and Latin America.* Washington, DC: Center for Applied Linguistics, 15–25.

Stickel, Gerhard (1987) Was halten Sie vom heutigen Deutsch? – Ergebnisse einer Zeitungsumfrage. In Wimmer, R. (ed.) *Sprachtheorie. Der Sprachbegriff in Wissenschaft und Alltag.* Düsseldorf/ Bielefeld: Schwann/ Cornelsen-Velhagen und Klasing, 280–317.

———— (2000) Deutsch als Wissenschaftssprache an außeruniversitären Forschungseinrichtungen. In Debus/ Kollmann/ Pörksen, 125–142.

———— (2002) Eigene und fremde Sprachen im vielsprachigen Europa. In Ehlich, K./ Schubert, V. (eds.) *Sprachen und Sprachenpolitik in Europa.* Tübingen: Stauffenburg, 15–32.

———— (ed.) (2003) *Deutsch von außen.* Berlin/ New York: de Gruyter.

———— (2007a) Deutsche und europäische sprachliche Interessen. *Muttersprache* 117 (2): 134–144.

———— (2007b) Das Europa der Sprachen – Motive und Erfahrungen der Europäischen Sprachenföderation EFNIL. In Blanke/ Scharnhorst, 21–47.

———— (ed.) (2009a) *National and European Language Policies. Contributions to the Annual Conference 2007 of EFNIL in Riga.* Frankfurt a.M.: Lang.

———— (2009b) Unvorgreifliche Erwägungen zum heutigen und zum künftigen Deutsch. In Liebert, W.-A./ Schwinn, H. (eds.) *Mit Bezug auf Sprache. Festschrift für Rainer Wimmer.* Tübingen: Narr, 381–400.

———— (ed.) (2010) *Language Use in Business and Commerce in Europe. Contributions to the Annual Conference 2008 of EFNIL in Lisbon.* Frankfurt a.M.: Lang.

———— (2012) Spekulationen zur Zukunft des Deutschen im europäischen Kontext. In Moraldo, S. M. (ed.) *Sprachenpolitik und Rechtssprache. Methodische Ansätze und Einzelanalysen.* Frankfurt a.M.: Lang, 11–28.

Stolerman I. P./ Stenius, K. (2008) The language barrier and institutional provincialism in science. *Drug and Alcohol Dependence* 92: 3–8.

Strack, Fritz (1996) What's new! Kommentar zu Montada, Becker, Schoepflin und Baltes: "Die internationale Rezeption der deutschsprachigen Psychologie". *Psychologische Rundschau* 47: 37f.

Streidt, Cornelia (2006) *Les langues au Parlement Européen. L'usage des langues officielles par les eurodéputés.* Aachen: Shaker.

Stricker, Gerd (2000) Ethnic Germans in Russia and the former Soviet Union. In Wolff, 165–179.

Strobel, Thomas/ Hoberg, Rudolf/ Vogt, Eberhard (2009) Die Rolle der deutschen Sprache in der mittelständischen Wirtschaft. Eine Trendumfrage der Gesellschaft für deutsche Sprache (GfdS) in Zusammenarbeit mit dem Bundesverband mittelständische Wirtschaft (BVMW) und mit Unterstützung des Deutschen Sprachrats. *Der Sprachdienst* 52 (6): 173186.

Stroh, Wilfried (2007) *Latein ist tot, es lebe Latein! Kleine Geschichte einer großen Sprache.* München: List.

Strubell, Miquel (1997) How to preserve and strengthen minority languages. In Røyneland, 159173.

———— (2001) Some aspects of a sociolinguistic perspective to language planning. In de Bot/ Kroon/ Nelde/ Van de Velde, 91–106.

Stuckenschmidt, Dierck (1989) Quantitäten und Qualität: Anmerkungen zur japanischen Germanistik aus statistischer Sicht. In Brenn/ Dillmann, 13–19.

Sturm, Dietrich (ed.) (1987a) *Deutsch als Fremdsprache weltweit.* München: Hueber.

———— (1987b) Deutsch als Fremdsprache im Ausland. In Sturm (1987a), 11–26.

Sugitani, Masako (2001) Deutschunterricht und Germanistikstudium in Japan. In Helbig/ Götze/ Henrici/ Krumm, Vol. 2, 1586–1594.

———— (2010) Deutsch in Japan. In Krumm/ Fandrych/ Hufeisen/ Riemer, Vol. 2., 1698–1701.

Süllwold, Fritz (1980) Wissenschaftssprache und Originalität. *Psychologische Beiträge* 22: 191203.

Sundhausen, Holm (1992) Deutsche in Rumänien. In Bade, K. (ed.) *Deutsche im Ausland – Fremde in Deutschland. Migration in Geschichte und Gegenwart.* München: Beck, 36–53.

Sverrisdóttir, Oddný G. (1993) The evolving European language system: a theory of communication potential and language competition. *International Political Science Review* 14: 241–255.

———— (1998) The European language constellation. In Bos, N./ Chenal, O./ Van Beugen, A. (eds.) *Report of the Conference "Which Languages for Europe"?* Oegstgeest (Niederlande): OudPoelgeest Conference Centre, 13–23.

———— (2001a) *Words of the World. The Global Language System.* Cambridge: Polity Press.

———— (2001b) English in the social sciences. In Ammon, 71–83.

———— (2003) Wirtschaftsdeutsch in Island. Eine Bestandsaufnahme. In Reuter/ Piitulainen, 91–101.

———— (2005) Zukunftsperspektiven von Deutsch als Fremdsprache in Island. *Jahrbuch für Internationale Germanistik* 36 (1): 39–46. de Swaan, Abram (1993) The emergent world language system: an introduction. *International Political Science Review* 14: 219–226.

de Swaan, Abram (2001) *Words of the World. The Global Language System.* Cambridge: Polity Press.

Swadesh, Morris (1955) Towards greater accuracy in lexicostatistic dating. *International Journal of American Linguistics* 21: 121–137.

———— (1972) What is glottochronology? In Swadesh, M. *The Origin and Diversification of Languages.* London: Routledge & Kegan Paul, 271–284.

Swales, John M. (1985) English language papers and author's first language: preliminary explorations. *Scientometrics* 8 (1/2): 91–101.

———— (1990) *Genre Analysis: English in Academic and Research Settings.* Cambridge: Cambridge University Press.

———— (1997) English as "Tyrannosaurus Rex". *World Englishes* 16.3: 373–382.

———— (2004) *Research Genres.* Cambridge: Cambridge University Press.

Szöllösi-Janze, Margit/ Freitäger, Andreas (2005) *"Doktorgrad entzogen!" Aberkennungen akademischer Titel an der Universität Köln – 1933–1945* Nümbrecht: Kirsch-Verlag.

Tabory, Mala (1980) *Multilingualism in International Law and Institutions.* Alphen aan den Rijn/ Rockville, MA: Sijthoff & Noordhoff.

Tabouret-Keller, Andreé (1986) Social factors of language maintenance and language shift: a methodological approach based on European and African examples. In Fishman, J. A./ Ferguson, C./ Das Gupty, J. (eds.) *Language Problems of Developing Countries.* New York: Wiley, 107–118.

———— / Luckel, Frédéric (1981) Maintien de l'alsacien et l'adoption du français. Éléments de la situation linguistique en milieu rural en Alsace. *Langages* 61: 39–62.

Tajfel, Henri (1974) Social identity and intergroup behaviour. *Social Science Information* 13: 6593.

———— (ed.) (1978) *Social Groups: Studies in the Social Psychology of Intergroup Relations.* London: Academic Press.

Takahashi, Hideaki (2002) Perspektiven des Faches Deutsch als Fremdsprache (DaF) und der Germanistik in Japan. *Jahrbuch für Internationale Germanistik* 34 (1): 33–41.

Tang, Dai et al. (2013) *A Tale of Two Languages: Strategic Self-Disclosure via Language Selection on Facebook.* Ithaca NY. (www.dl.acm.org/citation.cfm?id=1958824.1958884&coll=DL&dl=GUIDE&CFID=2676613 63&CFTOKEN=33283622)

Tapan, Nilüfer (1996) Zum Stand des Faches Deutsch in der Türkei. Karlsruher *pädagogische beiträge* 38: 67–76.

———— (2001) Deutschunterricht und Gemanistikstudium in der Türkei. In Helbig/ Götze/ Henrici/ Krumm, Vol. 2: 1565–1570.

———— (2002) Zukunftsperspektiven der deutschen Sprache und der Germanistik in der Türkei. *Jahrbuch für Internationale Germanistik* 34 (1): 27–32.

—— (2004) Überlegungen zur Realisierung eines mehrsprachigen Ausbildungskonzepts im türkischen Schulwesen. In Durzak/ Kuruyazici, 303–316.

—— (2010) Deutsch in der Türkei. In Krumm/ Fandrych/ Hufeisen/ Riemer, Vol. 2, 1817–1823.

Tardy, C. (2004) The role of English in scientific communication: lingua franca or Tyrannosaurus Rex? *Journal of English for Academic Purpose* 3: 247–269.

Taschner, Rudolf (2013) *Die Zahl, die aus der Kälte kam. Wenn Mathematik zum Abenteuer wird.* München: Hanser.

Tatlock, Lynne (2010) USA: German in the changing landscape of postsecondary education. *Die Unterrichtspraxis/ Teaching German* 43: 11–21.

Tavernier, Paul (1988) Le statut juridique de la langue française dans les organisations de la famille des Nations Unies. In Ministère des affaires étrangères (ed.) *Le Français dans les organisations internationales.* Paris: Centre de conférences internationales, 12–17.

Taylor, Brian (2013) Zwei deutsche Lesekurse für Wissenschaftler an einer australischen Universität: Entwicklungsgeschichtliches und Methodisches. In Schneider-Wiejowski/ Kellermeier-Rehbein/ Haselhuber, 459–475.

Tesnière, L[ucien] (1928) Statistique des langues de l'Europe. In Meillet, A. (ed.) *Les langues dans l'Europe Nouvelle.* 2nd edition, Paris, 293–473.

Thackray, Arnold et al. (1985) *Chemistry in America 1876–1976. Historical Indicators.* Dordrecht/ Boston/ Lancaster: Reidel.

Theiner, Peter (2009) Bahn frei für Visionen – Die Stiftungen. In Maaß (2009a), 305–313.

Thielmann, Winfried (2009) *Deutsche und englische Wissenschaftssprache im Vergleich. Hinführen – Verknüpfen – Benennen.* Heidelberg: Synchron Wissenschaftsverlag der Autoren.

—— (2010) Dreamliner in Richtung Scholastik. Über die Anglifizierung der europäischen Wissenschaft. *Forschung & Lehre* 17: 813–815.

Thierfelder, Franz (1928) (1929) (1930) (1931a) Deutsch im Unterricht fremder Völker I/ II/ III/ IV. *Deutsche Akademie, Mitteilungen:* 1015–1055/ 4–48/ 215–265/ 338–364.

—— (1931) Geistige Grundlagen kultureller Auslandsarbeit. *Süddeutsche Monatshefte* 4: 229.

—— (1933) Deutsch im Unterricht fremder Völker. *Mitteilungen der Akademie zur wissenschaftlichen Erforschung und Pflege des Deutschtums* 8 (3): 298–324.

—— (1935) Zehn Jahre Deutsche Akademie 1925–1935. *Mitteilungen der Akademie zur wissenschaftlichen Erforschung und Pflege des Deutschtums* 2: 180.

—— (1936) Deutsch als Weltsprache. *Mitteilungen der Akademie zur wissenschaftlichen Erforschung und Pflege des Deutschtums* 11 (1): 5–69.

—— (1938) *Deutsch als Weltsprache,* Vol. 1: *Die Grundlagen der deutschen Sprachgeltung in Europa.* Berlin: Kurzeja.

—— (1941) *Sprachpolitik und Rundfunk.* Berlin: Decker.

—— [1952] (1956a) Deutsche Sprache im Ausland. In Stammler, W. (ed.) *Deutsche Philologie im Aufriß.* 2nd edition, Berlin: Schmidt, 1398–1479.

—— (1956b) *Die deutsche Sprache im Ausland,* Vol. 1: *Der Völkerverkehr als sprachliche Aufgabe.* Hamburg/ Berlin/ Bonn: Decker.

—— (1957) *Die deutsche Sprache im Ausland,* Vol. 2: *Die Verbreitung der deutschen Sprache in der Welt.* Hamburg/ Berlin/ Bonn: Decker.

Thimme, Christian (2001) Deutschunterricht und Germanistikstudium in Frankreich. In Helbig/ Götze/ Henrici/ Krumm, Vol. 2: 1502–1508.

—— (2004) Ausländerstudium und Betreuung ausländischer Studierender in Deutschland. In Deutscher Akademischer Austauschdienst (2004a).

—— (2006) *Bildungsexport in der Praxis: Deutsche Studienangebote im Ausland.* Stand: März 2006. (www.gate-germany.de/downloads/dossier_thimme-export.pfd.)

Thode, Bettina (2011) *Español e inglés en el discurso científico. Los biólogos españoles ante la dominacia del inglés.* Unpublished master's dissertation in Spanish Universität Duisburg Essen.

Thomson Reuters (2011) *The Thomson Reuters Impact Factor.* (www.thomsonreuterscom/products_services/science/free/essays/impact_factor/) Tinsley, Teresa (February 2013) *Language: The State of the Nation. Demand and Supply of Language Skills in the UK.* UK: England O.O.: British Academy for the Humanities and Social Sciences.

Tišerova, Pavla (2008) Tschechien. In Eichinger/ Plewnia/ Riehl, 171–242.

Titkova, Olga (2011) Deutschlernen als Zusatzqualifikation in Russland. In Ammon/ Kemper, 200–211.

Tollefson, James W./ Tsui, Ami B. M. (eds.) (2004) *Medium of Instruction Policies. Which Agenda? Whose Agenda?* Mahwah, NJ: Lorence Erlbaum.

Tonkin, Humphrey (1996) Language equality at the United Nations: an achievable dream. In Müller, K. E. (ed.) *Language Status in the Post-Cold War Era.* (Papers of the Center for Research and Documentation on World Language Problems 4). Lanham, MD: University Press of America, 141–148.

———— (2011) Language and the ingenuity gap in science. *Critical Inquiry in Language Studies* 8 (1): 105–116.

———— / Reagan, Timothy (eds.) (2003) *Language in the Twenty-First Century.* Amsterdam/ Philadelphia: Benjamins.

Torgay, Sema (1996) *Die Stellung von Deutsch und anderen Fremdsprachen im Tourismus in der Türkei.* Unpublished master's dissertation, Gerhard-Merator-Universität Duisburg.

Tornquist, Ingrid M. (1997) *"Dos hon ich von meiner Mama" – zu Sprache und ethischen Konzepten unter Deutschstämmigen in Rio Grande do Sul.* Umeå: Department of German.

Totaro-Genevois, Mariella (2005) *Cultural and Linguistic Policy Abroad. The Italian Experience.* Clevedon/ Buffalo/ Toronto: Multilingual Matters.

Trabant, Jürgen (2003) *Mithridates im Paradies. Kleine Geschichte des Sprachdenkens.* München: Beck.

———— (2007) Die gebellte Sprache. *FAZ* 28.09 2007: 40.

———— (2008) *Was ist Sprache?* München: Beck.

———— (2011) Einführende Bemerkungen. In Berlin-Brandenburgische Akademie der Wissenschaften 2011, 13–20.

———— (2014) *Globalesisch oder was? Ein Plädoyer für Europas Sprachen.* München: Beck.

Traxel, Werner (1975) Internationalität oder Provinzialismus? Über die Bedeutung der deutschen Sprache für deutschsprachige Psychologen. *Psychologische Beiträge* 17 (1975): 584–594.

———— (1979) ‚Publish or Perish!' – auf deutsch oder auf englisch? *Psychologische Beiträge* 21 (1979): 62–77.

Tressmann, Ismael (2006) *Dicionário Enciclopédico Pomerano Português/ Pomerisch Portugijsisch Wöirbauk.* Santa Maria de Jetibá (Brasilien): Eigenverlag des Autors (ISBN 8588909–49–9).

Trommler, Frank (1986) *Amerika und die Deutschen. Bestandsaufnahme einer 300jährigen Geschichte.* Opladen: Westdeutscher Verlag.

———— (ed.) (1989) *Germanistik in den USA. Neue Entwicklungen und Methoden.* Opladen: Westdeutscher Verlag.

Troshina, Natalia N. (2004) Zur Stellung der deutschen Sprache und der Germanistik in Rußland. *Jahrbuch für Internationale Germanistik* 35 (2): 31–34.

———— (2010) Deutsch in Russland. In Krumm/ Fandrych/ Hufeisen/ Riemer, Vol. 2, 1775–1781.

———— (2011) Betrieblicher Deutschunterricht in Russland. In Ammon/ Kemper, 225–233.

———— (2013) Nachfrage nach Deutschkenntnissen im heutigen Russland. In Schneider-Wiejowski/ Kellermeier-Rehbein/ Haselhuber, 477–488.

Truchot, Claude (1990) *L'anglais dans le monde contemporain.* Paris: Le Robert.

———— (1994a) La France, l'anglais, le français et l'Europe. *Sociolinguistica* 8: 15–25.

———— (1994b) The spread of English in Europe. *Journal of European Studies* 24 (2): 141–151.

———— (2001) The languages of science in France: public debate and language policies. In Ammon, 319–328.

———— (2002) *Key Aspects of the Use of English in Europe/ L'anglaise en Europe: repères.* Strasbourg: Conseil de l'Europe.

———— (2003) Languages and supranationality in Europe: the linguistic influence of the European Union. In Maurais/ Morris, 99–110.

Truckbrodt, Andrea/ Kretzenbacher, Heinz L. (2001) Deutschunterricht und Gemanistikstudium in Australien. In Helbig/ Götze/ Henrici/ Krumm, Vol. 2: 1651–1658.

Trudgill, Peter (1990) [Rezension von] Ammon, Ulrich/ Dittmar, Norbert/ Mattheier, Klaus J. (eds.) (1987/ 88) *Sociolinguistics/ Soziolinguistik* Berlin/ New York: de Gruyter. *Sociolinguistica* 4: 191–195.

———— (2001) Weltsprache Englisch. In Watts/ Murray, 27–34.

Tsunoda, Minoru (1983) Les langues internationales dans les publications scientifiques et techniques. *Sophia Linguistica* 13: 144–155.

Türp, J. C./ Schulte, J. M./ Antes, G. (2002) Nearly half of dental randomized controlled trials published in German are not included in Medline. *European Journal of Oral Sciences* 110: 405–411.

Twentieth Century Abstracts (1971ff.). Santa Barbara, CA: Clio [continuation of *Historical Abstracts* 1775–1945].

Tyroller, Hans (1986) Trennung und Integration der Sprachgruppen in Südtirol. In Hinderling, 18–36.

Ueda, Koji (1989) Die Geschichte der Vermittlung des Deutschen in Japan. In Bauer 1989b, 2635.

———— / Takai, Takamichi (1994) Zum Verhältnis des Studienumfangs zur Verwendbarkeit von Deutschkenntnissen in Japan. In Ammon 1994d, 327–337.

Ueda, Yasunari (1997) Japan. In Raasch, 50–54.

Uhl, Hans-Peter (O.J.) *Ehegattennachzug – Sprachkenntnisse vor Einreise.* (www.uhlcsu.de/cm/upload/4_0808-Uhl-Ehegattennachzug.pdf)

Ulijn, J. M./ Gorter, T. R. (1989) Language, culture and technical-commercial negotiating. In Coleman, 479–506.

Ülkü, Vural in coll. with Schwerger, Maren/ Seidler, Lilly (2004) Türkei. In Institut für Deutsche Sprache, 81–86.

Ullmann's Encyclopedia of Industrial Chemistry [deutsch 1914–1922] (1996) 5th, completely rev. ed. Weinheim: VCH Verlagsgesellschaft.

Ulrich's International Periodicals Directory. A Classified Guide to Current Periodicals, Foreign and Domestic (1932ff.) New York/ London: Bowker.

Ulrich's International Periodicals Directory (1982) *A Bowker Serials Bibliography.* New York/ London.

Umborg, Viktoria (2003) Internationale Wirtschaftskommunikation in estnischen Unternehmen. In Reuter/ Piitulainen, 125–142.

UNESCO (ed.) (1953) *The Use of Vernacular Languages in Education.* Paris: UNESCO.

———— (ed.) [1971] [1974] [1980] [1981] (1988) *Statistical Yearbook/ Annuaire Statistique.* Paris: UNESCO.

———— Ad Hoc Expert Group in Endangered Languages (2003) *Language Vitality and Endangerment. Document submitted to the International Expert Meeting on UNESCO Programme Safeguarding of Endangered Languages, 10–12 March 2003.* Paris: UNESCO.

von Ungern-Sternberg, Jürgen/ von Ungern-Sternberg, Wolfgang (1996) *Der Aufruf ‚An die Kulturwelt!'. Das Manifest der 93 und die Anfänge der Kriegspropaganda im Ersten Weltkrieg. Mit einer Dokumentation.* Stuttgart: Steiner.

Union der deutschen Akademien der Wissenschaften, Sächsische Akademie der Wissenschaften zu Leipzig (ed.) (1999) *"Werkzeug Sprache". Sprachpolitik Sprachfähigkeit, Sprache und Macht.* 3. Symposion der deutschen Akademien der Wissenschaften. Hildesheim/ Zürich/ New York: Olms.

Unser, Günther (2004) *Die UNO. Aufgaben – Strukturen – Politik.* 7th edition, München: Deutscher Taschenbuch Verlag.

UNWTO Tourism Highlights (2011) O.O.: World Tourism Organisation. (www.mkt.unwto.org/sites/all/files/docpdf/unwtohighlights11enhr_3.pdf)

———— (2013) O.O.: World Tourism Organisation. (www.dtxtq4w60xqpw.cloudfront.net/sites/all/ files/pdf/unwto_highlights13_en_lr_0.pdf)

Urban, Thomas [1993] (2000) *Deutsche in Polen. Geschichte und Gegenwart einer Minderheit.* 4th revised edition, München: Beck.

Vaagland, Erling (2005) Deutsch in Norwegen – Geschichte und Gegenwart. *Jahrbuch für Internationale Germanistik* 37 (1): 83–87.

Vaillancourt, François (ed.) (1985) *Économie et langue.* Québec: Éditeur Officiel du Québec.

Vanden Boer, Anneleen (2008) Die deutschsprachigen Minderheiten in Belgien. *Der Sprachdienst* 52 (6): 245–252.

Vandenbroucke, J. P. (1989) On not Being Born a Native Speaker of English. *BMJ [British Medical Journal]* 298: 1461 f.

Vandermeeren, Sonja (1998) *Der Fremdsprachenbedarf europäischer Unternehmen unter besonderer Berücksichtigung des Deutschen. Eine empirische Untersuchung in Deutschland, Frankreich, den Niederlanden, Portugal und Ungarn.* Waldsteinberg: Heidrun Popp.

———— (1999) Fremdsprachengebrauch in europäischen Unternehmen: Sprachwahlstrategien. *Wirtschaftsdeutsch International* 1: 120–131.

———— (2003) German language needs in Danish companies. *Hermes* 31: 1–29.

———— (2005) Research on language attitudes. In Ammon/ Dittmar/ Mattheier/ Trudgill, 1318–1331.

de Varennes, Fernand (1996) *Language, Minorities and Human Rights.* The Hague/ Boston/ London: Martinus Nijhoff.

Vasconcelos, Sonia M. R. et al. (2008) Researchers' writing competence: a bottleneck in the Latin-American science? *Embo reports* 9: 700–702.

Vassileva, Irena (2005) Englisch und Deutsch als Sprachen internationaler Konferenzdiskussionen. In Van Leewen, 389–404.

Vater, Heinz (2000) *Begriff* statt *Wort* – ein terminologischer Wirrwarr. *Sprachreport* (4): 10–13.

Veiter, Theodor (1970) *Das Recht der Volksgruppen und Sprachminderheiten in Österreich. Mit einer ethnosoziologischen Grundlegung und einem Anhang (Materialien).* Wien/ Stuttgart: Braumüller.

Verdoodt, Albert (1968) *Zweisprachige Nachbarn. Die deutschen Hochsprach- und Mundartgruppen in Ost-Belgien, dem Elsaß, Ost-Lothringen und Luxemburg.* Wien/ Stuttgart: Braumüller.

———— / Sente, Agnes (1983) Interest Shown by Secondary School Pupils in Modern Languages and Adult Language Needs in Belgium. In Van Els/ Oud-de Glas, 263–283.

Verein für das Deutschtum im Ausland (ed.) (1984) *Leitfaden der deutschsprachigen Presse im Ausland.* Berlin/ Bonn: Westkreuz-Verlag.

Verordnung Nr. 1 zur Regelung der Sprachenfrage für die Europäische Wirtschaftsgemeinschaft (1958) *Amtsblatt der Europäischen Gemeinschaften* 385/ 58. 6.10.1958.

Verstraete-Hansen, Lisbeth (2008) *Hvad skal vi met sprog? Holdninger til fremmedsprog i danske virksomheder i et uddannelsespolitisk perspektiv.* Kopenhagen: Institut for Internationale Kultur- og Kommunikationsstudier Handelshøjskolen i København/ Copenhagen Business School.

———— (2010) En route vers le tout-anglais? Pratique et répresentations des langues étrangères dans les entreprises danoises. In Stickel, 67–77.

Vertrag von Lissabon (2008) Published by the Bundeszentrale für politische Bildung. Bonn 2010. (www.bpb.de.)

Viereck, Wolfgang (1996) English in Europe: its nativisation and use as a lingua franca, with special reference to German-speaking countries. In Hartmann, 16–23.

Vierhaus, Rudolf/ vom Brocke, Bernhard (eds.) (1990) *Forschung im Spannungsfeld von Politik und Gesellschaft. Geschichte und Struktur der Kaiser-Wilhelm-/ Max-Planck-Gesellschaft.* Stuttgart: Deutsche Verlags-Anstalt.

Vikør, Lars (2004) Lingua franca and international language/ Verkehrssprache und Internationale Sprache. In Ammon/ Dittmar/ Mattheier/ Trudgill, 328–335.

Vogel, Wanda (2005) L'emploi de la langue allemande en matière administrative et devant la section d'administration du Conseil d'Etat. In Stangherlin, 117–162.

Voigt, Werner (1999) Die Zukunft des Deutschen und anderer Sprachen in Europa. *Terminologie et traduction* 14 (2): 186–257.

Volgger, Ruth M. (2008) *Über den Gebrauch der deutschen Sprache bei öffentlichen Dienstleistungen in Südtirol. Theorie und praktische Anwendung.* Innsbruck/ Wien/ Bozen: StudienVerlag.

Vollstedt, Marina (2002) *Sprachenplanung in der internen Kommunikation internationaler Unternehmen. Studien zur Umstellung der Unternehmenssprache auf das Englische.* Hildesheim: Olms.

———— (2005) "Deutsch ist keine Sprache, mit der man auftreten kann!" – Sprachwahl in mittelständischen Betrieben. In Van Leewen, 255–273.

Volpers, Helmut (2002) Der internationale Buchmarkt. In Leonhard et al., 2649–2660.

Voltmer, Leonhard/ Lanthaler, Franz/ Abel, Andrea/ Oberhammer, Margit (2007) Insights into the linguistic situation of South Tyrol. In Abel/ Stuflesser/ Voltmer, 197–258.

Volz, Walter (1994) Englisch als einzige Arbeitssprache in den Organen der europäischen Gemeinschaft? Vorzüge und Nachteile aus der Sicht eines Insiders. *Sociolinguistica* 8: 88100.

Voronina, Galina (2011) Motive der Wahl von Deutsch an Schule und Hochschule [in Russland]. In Ammon/ Kemper, 275–286.

Voslamber, Dietrich (2006) Gedanken zur institutionellen Mehrsprachigkeit. Vorschläge für eine Verbesserung des Sprachenregimes in den Institutionen der Europäischen Union. *grkg/ Humankybernetik* 47 (1) (Akademia Libroservo/ IfK).

de Vries, John (1992) Language maintenance and shift. Problems of measurement. In Fase/ Jaspaert/ Kroon, 211–222.

———— (2005) Language Censuses. In Ammon/ Dittmar/ Mattheier/ Trudgill, 1104–1116.

Wächter, Bernd/ Maiworm, Friedhelm (2008) *English-Taught Programmes in European Higher Edudation. The Picture in 2007.* Bonn: Lemmens.

Wagener, Hans (2012) *Untergräbt Deutschland selbst die internationale Stellung der deutschen Sprache durch die Förderung von Englisch?* Frankfurt a.M.: Lang.

Wagener, Peter (2003) Wozu noch Deutsch? Funktionen und Funktionsverluste des Deutschen in Wisconsin. In Keel, William D./ Mattheier, Klaus J., 137–150.

Wagner, Ernst (1990) *Geschichte der Siebenbürger Sachsen. Ein Überblick.* 6th edition, Thaur bei Innsbruck: Wort-und-Welt-Verlag.

Wagner, Richard (2000) Ethnic Germans in Romania. In Wolff, 135–142.

Wagner, Udo-Peter (2002) Zur Geschichte des Fremdsprachenunterrichts in Rumänien im XX. Jahrhundert unter besonderer Berücksichtigung des Deutschunterrichts. In Lechner, E. (ed.) *Formen und Funktionen des Fremdsprachenunterrichts im Europa des 20. Jahrhunderts.* Frankfurt a.M.: Lang, 419–450.

Waibel, Jens (2010) *Die deutschen Auslandsschulen – Materialien zur Außenpolitik des Dritten Reiches* (Dissertation an der Kulturwissenschaftlichen Fakultät der Europa-Universität Viadrina Frankfurt (Oder). Frankfurt (Oder): Universitätsbibliothek der Europa-Universität Viadrina. (www.d-nb.info/1027453414/34)

Waite, Jeffrey (1992) *Aoteareo: Speaking for Ourselves. A Discussion on the Development of a New Zealand Languages Policy.* (A report commissioned by the Ministry of Education). Wellington.

Wahl, Ulrich (2005) Internationalisierung der Hochschulen – ein Deutschproblem. In Motz (2005a), 31–37.

Walker, Alastair G. H. (1983) Nordfriesisch – ein deutscher Dialekt? *Zeitschrift für Dialektologie und Linguistik* 50: 145–160.

———— (2001) Extent and position of North Frisian. In Munske, 263–284.

———— (2009) Friesisch, Hochdeutsch und die Sprachenvielfalt in Nordfriesland. In Elmentaler, 1529.

———— / Wilts, Ommo (2001) Die Verschriftung des Nordfriesischen. In Munske, 284–304.

Wallerstein, Immanuel (1974) *The Modern World System: Capitalist Agriculture and the Origins of the European World-economy in the sixteenth Century.* San Fransisco: Academic Press.

———— (1980) *The Capitalist World-Economy.* Cambridge: Cambridge University Press.

———— (1983) *Historical Capitalism.* London: Verso.

———— (1998) *One World, Many Worlds.* New York: Lyenne Rienner.

———— (2004) *World-Systems Analysis: An Introduction.* Durham/ London: Duke University Press.

———— (2005) El idioma del mundo académico [Languages in the Academic World]. *International Sociological Association Bulletin* 67–68: 1–8.

Wang, Jingping (2007) Die Rolle der deutschen Sprache in Unternehmen aus deutschsprachigen Ländern in China. In Ammon/ Reinbothe/ Zhu, 223–230.

Warkentin, Jakob (1998) *Die Deutschsprachigen Siedlerschulen in Paraguay im Spannungsfeld staatlicher Kultur- und Entwicklungspolitik.* Münster: Waxmann.

Warrs, Wendy A. (1988) *Chemical Structures: The International Language of Chemistry.* Berlin/ Heidelberg: Springer.

Warshauer, Mary E. (1966) Foreign language broadcasting. In Fishman/ Nahirni et al. 1966, 7591.

Wassertheurer, Peter (2003) Die Bildungs- und Kulturarbeit der deutschen Minderheit in Tschechien. In Bachmaier, P. (ed.) *Nationalstaat oder multikulturelle Gesellschaft? Die Minderheitenpolitik in Mittel-, Ost- und Südosteuropa im Bereich des Bildungswesens 1945–2002.* Frankfurt a.M.: Lang, 25–40.

Watanabe, Manabu (1994) Die deutsche Sprache im Restaurant-, Hotel- und Tourismuswesen in Japan. In Ammon 1994d, 163–172.

———— (2004) Wusstest du, dass weltweit an allen Ecken Sprachen jammen? Über Anglisierung und Internationalisierung im Deutschen. *Aspekt* 37 (Rikkyo-Universität): 71–90.

Watanabe, Osamu (1989) Internationalisierung und die zweite Fremdsprache. In Bauer 1989b, 44–55.

Watts, Richard/ Murray, Heather (eds.) (2001) *Die fünfte Landessprache? Englisch in der Schweiz.* Bern: Akademische Kommission Universität Bern.

Weber, Peter J. (2004) Bildungspolitik und Sprachenpluralismus in der Europäischen Union. *Bildung und Erziehung* 57 (1): 5–25.

———— (2006) Spreche global, kommuniziere lokal – Perspektiven der Mehrsprachigkeit in der Europäischen Union. In Fischer, R. (ed.) *Herausforderungen der Sprachenvielfalt in der Europäischen Union.* Baden-Baden: Nomos, 81–93.

———— (2009) *Kampf der Sprachen. Die Europäische Union vor der sprachlichen Zerreißprobe.* Hamburg: Krämer.

Weber, Max [1922] (1972) *Wirtschaft und Gesellschaft. Grundriß der Verstehenden Soziologie.* Tübingen: Mohr.

Weck, Udo H./ Glaue, Dieter (2002) Über den Tourismus im Sonnenland. In Hess/ Becker, 374383.

Wedell, George/ Henley, Olivia (2002) International media markets: television-production. In Leonhard et al., 2690–2693.

Weerkamp, Wouter/ Carter, Simon/ Tsagias, Manos (2013) *How People Use Twitter in Different Languages.* University of Amsterdam. (www.websci11.org/fileadmin/websci/Posters/90_paper.pdf.)

Wehrmann, Günter (1988) Förderung der deutschen Sprache. Über eine Aufgabe der auswärtigen Kulturpolitik. In Ritter, 19–26.

Wei, Yuqing (2007) Kommunikation zwischen China und den deutschsprachigen Ländern – auf Chinesisch, Deutsch oder Englisch? In Ammon/ Reinbothe/ Zhu, 231–237.

Weinberg, Alvin M. (1961) Impact of Large-Scale Science on the United States. *Science* 134 (3473): 161–164.

Weindling, Paul (1996) The League of Nations and international medical communication in Europe between the First and Second World Wars. In Chartier/ Corsi, 209–219.

Weingart, Peter (1989) Ist der Sprachenstreit ein Streit um die Sprache? *Psychologische Rundschau* 40: 96–98.

Weinreich, Max [1946] (1999) *Hitler's Professors. The Part of Scholarship in Germany's Crimes Against the Jewish People.* New Haven/ London: Yale University Press.

Weinreich, Uriel [1953] (1974) *Languages in Contact. Findings and Problems.* The Hague/ Paris: Mouton.

Weinrich, Harald (1980) Forschungsaufgaben des Faches Deutsch als Fremdsprache. In Wierlacher, A. (ed.) *Fremdsprache Deutsch*, Vol. 1. München, 29–46.

———— (1981) Fremdsprachen in der Bundesrepublik Deutschland und Deutsch als Fremdsprache. *Der deutsche Lehrer im Ausland* 28: 61–75.

———— (1984) Die Zukunft der deutschen Sprache. In *Vorträge gehalten auf der Joachim-Jungius Gesellschaft der Wissenschaften. Hamburg, am 4. und 5. November 1983* (Veröffentlichungen der Joachim-Jungius-Gesellschaft der Wissenschaften Hamburg, 51). [Göttingen], 83–108.

———— (1985a) *Wege der Sprachkultur.* Stuttgart: Deutsche Verlagsanstalt.

———— (1985b) Sprache und Wissenschaft. *Merkur* 39 (6): 496–506.

———— (1986) Sprache und Wissenschaft. In Kalverkämper/ Weinrich, 183–193.

———— (2000/2001) Deutsch in Linguafrancaland. In Deutsche Welle Kommunikation, 7–16/ *Akademie-Journal* (2): 6–9.

Weirich, Dieter (2000) "Familie Baumann" oder "Deutsch – Warum nicht?" – Die Deutsche Welle als globales Klassenzimmer. In Deutsche Welle Kommunikation, 17–22.

Weiss, Gerhard W. (1987) Bemerkungen zur gegenwärtigen Lage des Deutschunterrichts in den Vereinigten Staaten. In Sturm (1987a), 47–56.

Weiß, Reinhold (1992) Fremdsprachen in der Wirtschaft: Bedarf und Qualifizierung. In Kramer/ Weiß, 77–177.

Weitzel, Wilhelm/ Nöckler, Herbert C./ Crüsemann-Brockmann, Rolf (2002) Die deutsche Privatschule. In Hess/ Becker, 202–211.

Welz, Dieter (1986) Deutsch als Fremdsprache im südlichen Afrika. Ein historisch-kritischer Blick auf das Selbstverständnis des Faches. *Info DaF* 13 (2): 161–177.

Wendt, Heinz F. [1961] (1987) *Fischer Lexikon Sprachen.* Frankfurt a.M.: Fischer.

Wentenschuh, Walter G. (1995) *Namibia und seine Deutschen. Geschichte und Gegenwart der deutschen Sprachgruppe im Südwesten Afrikas.* Göttingen: Klaus Hess Verlag.

Werlen, Iwar (1989) *Sprache, Mensch und Welt, Geschichte und Bedeutung des Prinzips der sprachlichen Relativität.* Darmstadt: Wissenschaftliche Buchgesellschaft.

———— (2002) *Sprachliche Relativität. Eine problemorientierte Einführung.* Tübingen/ Basel: Francke.

———— (2004) Domäne. In Ammon/ Mattheier/ Dittmar/ Trudgill, 335–340.

———— (2005) Linguistische Relativität. In Ammon/ Dittmar/ Mattheier/ Trudgill, 1426–1435.

Werner, Wolfgang (2005) *Assimilation von Migranten in den Arbeitsmarkt.* Wirtschaftswissenschaftliche Seminararbeit FU Berlin. (Hinweis Ingrid Gogolin – www.diw.de/sixcms/detail.php/43143)

Westerwelle Consulting & Media AG (ed.) (2001) *Studie "Fremdsprachen im Job". Im Auftrag des Stern "Campus & Karriere".* Hamburg: Westerwelle Consulting & Media AG.

Weydt, Harald (2004) Offener Brief zu Volker Honemann: "Usbekistan – Deutschland. Oder: wollen wir die Zukunft unserer Sprache und unserer Literatur weiterhin gefährden?" *Zeitschrift für Literatur und Linguistik* 134: 124–128.

White, Paul (1987) Geographic aspects of minority language situations in Italy. In Williams, C. H. (ed.) *Linguistic Minorities: Societies and Territories.* Clevedon, UK: Multilingual Matters, 44–65.

Whorf, Benjamin L. (1941) The relation of habitual thought and behavior to language. In Spier, L. et al. (eds.) *Language, Culture, and Personality: Essays in Memory of Edward Sapir.* Menasha: Sapir Memorial Publication Fund, 75–93.

Whorter, John H. (2014) *The Language Hoax. Why the World Looks the Same in Any Language.* Oxford: Oxford University Press.

Wickler, Wolfgang (1986) Englisch als deutsche Wissenschaftssprache. In Kalverkämper/ Weinrich, 26–31.

Wickström, Bengt-Arne (2005) Can bilingualism be dynamically stable? A simple model of language choice. *Rationality and Society* 17 (1): 81–115.

Wiegand, Herbert E. (ed.) (1999) *Sprache und Sprachen in den Wissenschaften. Geschichte und Gegenwart.* Berlin/ New York: de Gruyter.

Wiegrefe, Klaus/ Pieper, Dietmar (2007) *Die Erfindung der Deutschen. Wie wir wurden was wir sind.* München: Deutsche Verlags-Anstalt.

Wierlacher, Alois (ed.) (1987) *Perspektiven und Verfahren interkultureller Germanistik.* München: Iudicium.

Wiese, Ingrid (2006) Zur Situation des Deutschen als Wissenschaftssprache in der Medizin. In Ehlich/ Heller, 275–295.

Wiesinger, Peter (1980) Deutsche Sprachinseln. In Althaus, H. P./ Henne, H./ Wiegand, H. E. (eds.) *Lexikon der Germanistischen Linguistik.* 2nd completely revised edition, Tübingen: Niemeyer, 491–500.

——— (1983a) Die Einteilung der deutschen Dialekte. In Besch/ Knoop/ Putschke/ Wiegand, 807899.

——— (1983b) Deutsche Dialektgebiete außerhalb des deutschen Sprachgebiets. In Besch/ Knoop/ Putschke/ Wiegand, 900–929.

von Wieterheim, Anton/ Grellmann, Volker (2002) Im Jagdrevier zwischen Kalahari und Namib. In Hess/ Becker, 297–407.

Wiggen, Geirr (1995a) Norway in the 1990s: a sociolinguistic profile. *International Journal of the Sociology of Language* 115: 47–83.

——— (1995b) Les llengües de l'ensenyament a Noruega: lleis i regulacions. *Els Lingüistics a la nova Europa.* Barcelona: Ciemen/ Editorial Mediterrània, 73–96.

Wiktorowicz, Józef (1997) Polnisch – Deutsch. In Goebl/ Nelde/ Starý/ Wölck, 1594–1600.

Wild, Katharina (1985) Sprachliche Situation und Sprachpflege. Zur Sprache der deutschen Volksgruppe in Ungarn. In Ritter, A. (ed.) *Kolloquium zur Sprache und Sprachpflege der deutschen Volksgruppen im Ausland.* Flensburg: Institut für Regionale Forschung und Information, 169–184.

——— (1992) Deutschunterricht und Spracherhalt bei den Ungarndeutschen. *Suevia Pannonica. Archiv der Deutschen aus Ungarn* 10 (20): 5–15.

Wildgen, Wolfgang (2005) Sprachkontaktforschung. In Ammon/ Dittmar/ Mattheier/ Trudgill, 1332–1345.

Wilhelm, Peter (1983) *The Nobel Prize.* London: Springwood.

Wilkie, John R. (1978) Altes und Neues in der britischen Germanistik. *In Brinkmann/ Ezawa/ Hackert,* 127–141.

Willemyns, Roland (2001) English in linguistic research in Belgium. In Ammon, 329–342.

——— (2013) *Dutch. Biography of a Language.* New York: Oxford University Press.

Williams, Colin H. (1991a) *Linguistic Minorities, Society and Territory.* Clevedon: Multilingual Matters.

——— (1991b) *The Cultural Rights of Minorities: Recognition and Implementation.* Stafford: Staffordshire University Dep. of Geography and Recreation Studies.

Williams, Donald R. (2011) Multiple language usage and earnings in Western Europe. *International Journal of Manpower* 32: 372–393.

Wilson, David (2002) *The Englishisation of Academe: A Finnish Perspective.* Jyväskylä: Jyväskylä Yliopiston Kiliekeskus.

Wiltsey, Robert G. (1972) *Doctoral Use of Foreign Languages: A Survey.* 2 Parts. Princeton, NJ: Educational Testing Service.

Wiltz, Ommo (2001) Die Verschriftung des Nordfriesischen. In Munske, 305–313.

Wimmer, Rainer (1984) Wenn einer eine Reise tut . . . Zu Harro Schweizers Reisebericht "Deutsche Sprache unter der Apartheid." *Zeitschrift für Sprachwissenschaft* 3 (1): 129–134.

Wimmer, Roger (2005) Der internationale Schutz kultureller und sprachlicher Minderheiten: Die deutschsprachigen Belgier als nationale Minderheit im Sinne des "Rahmenabkommens des Europarates zum Schutz nationaler Minderheiten". In Stangherlin, 65–92.

Windelband, Wilhelm [1894] (1904) *Geschichte und Naturwissenschaft.* 3rd unaltered edition, Straßburg: Heitz und Mündel.

Wingen, Vibeke (2000) Die Ausgrenzung des Deutschen in Dänemark im 19. Jahrhundert. In Naumann/ Müller, 143–155.

Winkler, Wilhelm (1927) *Statistisches Handbuch des gesamten Deutschtums.* Berlin: Verlag Deutsche Rundschau.

Winkmann, G[ünter]/ Schlutius, S[ylvia]/ Schweim, H[arald] G. (2002a) Publikationssprachen der Impact-Factor-Zeitschriften und medizinischer Literaturdatenbanken. *Deutsche Medizinische Wochenschrift* 127 (4): 131–137.

——— / ——— / ——— (2002b) Wie häufig werden deutschsprachige Medizinzeitschriften in der englischsprachigen Literatur zitiert? *Deutsche Medizinische Wochenschrift* 127: 138–143.

Winter, Martin (2007) Wir sind uns recht peinlich. *Süddeutsche Zeitung* 136: I.

Wirth, Karoline (2010) *Der Verein Deutsche Sprache. Hintergrund, Entstehung, Arbeit und Organisation eines deutschen Sprachvereins.* Bamberg: University of Bamberg Press. (www.opus-bayern.de/uni-bamberg)

Wissenschaftsrat (2006) *Empfehlungen zur Entwicklung und Förderung der Geisteswissenschaften in Deutschland.* (www.wissenschaftsrat.de/download/archiv/7068-06.pdf.)

Withe, J. (1967) *History of Tourism.* London: Leisure Art.

Witte, Barthold C. (1983) Die Stellung des Deutschen als Fremdsprache in Europa. *Deutsch als Fremdsprache in Belgien*: 19–30.

——— (1984) *Förderung der deutschen Sprache als Ziel auswärtiger Kulturpolitik*. München: Hueber.

——— (1985a) Fernsehen ohne Grenze. Schwerpunkte auswärtiger Kulturpolitik: Deutsche Sprache – Medienpolitik. *Auslandskurier* 25 (2).

——— (1985b) Die deutsche Sprache im In- und Ausland. *Auslandskurier* 26 (3): 11–15.

——— (1985c) Förderung der deutschen Sprache als Ziel auswärtiger Kulturpolitik. *Auslandskurier* 26 (3): 110–113.

——— (1987) Was ist mit der deutschen Sprache los? *FAZ* vom 8.7.1987: 7.

——— (1989) Kulturaustausch und internationale Beziehungen der Bundesrepublik Deutschland nach vierzig Jahren. *Jahrbuch Deutsch als Fremdsprache 1989* 15: 67–78.

——— interviewed by Akalin, Oguz (1985) Verstärkte Werbung für die deutsche Sprache im Ausland. *Bildung und Wissenschaft* 5/ 6: 3–7.

de Witte, Bruno (2004) Language law of the European Union: protecting or eroding linguistic diversity? In Smith, R. C. (ed.) *Culture and European Union Law*. Oxford: Oxford University Press.

Wodak, Ruth/ de Cillia, Rudolf (eds.) (2006) *Sprachenpolitik in Mittel- und Osteuropa*. Wien: Passagen Verlag.

Wöhe, Günter/ Döring, Ulrich (2013) *Einführung in die Allgemeine Betriebswirtschaftslehre*. 25th revised and updated edition, München: Franz Vahlen.

Wohlan, Martina (2014) *Das diplomatische Protokoll im Wandel*. Tübingen: Mohr Siebeck.

Wohlmann, Rainer (1983) *Mikrozensus 1980 und Reiseanalyse 1980. Ein methodischer Vergleich*. Starnberg: Studienkreis für Tourismus.

Wölck, Wolfgang (1976) Community profiles: an alternative to linguistic informant selection. *International Journal of the Sociology of Language* 9: 43–57.

Wolf, Bernhard (2002) Die Katholische Kirche in Namibia. In Hess/ Becker, 149–153.

Wolff, Hans (1959) Intelligibility and inter-ethnic studies. *Anthropological Linguistics* 1 (3): 3441.

Wolff, Stefan (2000) *German Minorities in Europe: Ethnic Identity and Cultural Belonging*. New York: Berghahn.

——— (2001) German expellee organizations between "Homeland" and "At Home": a case study of the politics of belonging. *Refuge* 20 (1): 52–65.

Wolke, Dieter (1996) Psychologen publizieren nicht nur in psychologischen Zeitschriften. Kommentar zu Montada, Becker, Schoepflin und Baltes: "Die internationale Rezeption der deutschsprachigen Psychologie". *Psychologische Rundschau* 47: 38f.

Wollin, Lars (2000) Aus deutscher Feder. Die Stellung des Deutschen in moderner schwedischer Belletristik. In Naumann/ Müller, 235–251.

Worbs, Andreas (1993a) Der Sprachgebrauch im Wirtschaftssektor Namibias. Ergebnisse einer Umfrage. *Nambia Magazin* (1): 17–19.

——— (1993b) *Ergebnis einer Umfrage zum Sprachgebrauch im Wirtschaftssektor. Der Deutschunterricht im Südlichen Afrika* (24) 2: 41–49.

World Almanac and Book of Facts 1999/ 2004. McGaveran Jr., W. A. (ed.). New York: World Almanac Books.

World Tourism Organization (WTO) (ed.) (1988) *Yearbook of Tourism Statistics*, 2 Vols. Madrid: World Tourism Organization.

Worton, Michael (1971) *Explanation and Understanding*. Ithaca, NY: Cornell University Press. – (2009) *Review of Modern Foreign Languages Provision in Higher Education im England*. (www.hefce.ac.uk/pubs/year/2009/200941/) von Wright, Georg H. (1963): *Norm and Action. A Logical Enquiry*. London: Routledge and Kegan Paul.

Wright, Sue (2000) *Community and Communication. The Role of Language in Nation State Building and European Integration*. Clevedon: Multilingual Matters.

——— (2004) *Language Policy and Language Planning: From Nationalism to Globalisation*. New York: Palgrave.

——— (2009) The elephant in the room: language in the European Union. *European Journal of Language Policy* 1 (2): 93–120.

——— (2013) Why isn't EU language policy working? In Schneider-Wiejowski/ Kellermeier-Rehbein/ Haselhuber, 259–273.

Woronenkowa, Galina F. (2011) Deutschsprachige Medien in Russland. Geschichte und Gegenwart. In Ammon/ Kemper, 255–271.

Wren, George R. (1966) Ph. Ds need high hurdles. *Science* 154: 962.

Wu, Huiping (2005) *Das Sprachenregime der Institutionen der Europäischen Union zwischen Grundsatz und Effizienz. Eine neue Sichtweise in der institutionellen Sprachenfrage Europas*. Frankfurt a.M.: Lang.

Xavier de Oliveira/ Paulo S. (1997) Brasilien. In Raasch, 23–26.

Yamaji, Asahiko (1994) Das Studium von Deutsch als Fremdsprache an den Hochschulen. In Ammon 1994d, 221–235.

Yamashita, Hitoshi (1994) Der Anteil von Deutsch in japanischen Übersetzungsbüros und in größeren Betrieben. In Ammon 1994d, 83–102.

Yang, Do-Wong (2003) Deutsch als Fremdsprache an den heutigen koreanischen Hochschulen. In Ammon/ Chong, 273–284.

Yoder, Don S. (1980) Palatine, Hessian, Dutchman: three images of the German in America. In Buffington, Albert F. (ed.) *Ebbes fer Alle-Ebber – Ebbes fer Dich: Something for Everyone – Something for you.* Breinigsville, PA: Pennsylvania German Society, 105–129.

—— (1986) Die Pennsylvania-Deutschen. Eine dreihundertjährige Identitätskrise. In Trommler, 6588.

Zabel, Hermann (ed.) [2001] (2003) *Denglisch, nein danke! Zur inflationären Verwendung von Anglizismen und Amerikanismen in der deutschen Gegenwartssprache.* Paderborn: IFB Verlag.

—— (ed.) (2006) Unter Mitarbeit von Disselnkötter, Andreas/ Wellinghoff, Sandra. *Stimmen aus Jerusalem. Zur deutschen Sprache und Literatur in Palästina/ Israel.* Berlin: LIT.

Zabrocki, Ludwig (1978) Das technische Zeitalter und die deutsche Sprache in Polen. In Brinkmann/ Ezawa/ Hackert, 177–190.

Zappen-Thomson, Marianne (2002a) Deutsch in Namibia hat viele Facetten. Deutsch als Fremdsprache (DaF). In Hess/ Becker, 321–326.

—— (2002b) Der Deutschunterricht in Namibia kann sich sehen lassen. *Namibia Magazin* 4: 17f.

—— (2012) Muttersprache, Fremdsprache – Übersicht über den Fachbereich Deutsch an der Universität Namibia. In *Sprachenvielfalt in Namibia*, 75–80.

Zechlin, Walter (1960) *Die Welt der Diplomatie.* 2nd edition, Frankfurt a.M./ Bonn: Athenäum.

Zeevaert, Ludger (2007) Rezeptive Mehrsprachigkeit am Beispiel der Zusammenarbeit der skandinavischen Hochschulen. In Kameyama, S./ Meyer, B. (eds.) *Mehrsprachigkeit am Arbeitsplatz.* Frankfurt a.M.: Lang: 87–107.

Zellweger, Rudolf (1987) Deutsch als Fremdsprache in der Schweiz. In Sturm (1987a), 197–206.

Zentralblatt für Bakteriologie (1902–1979). Stuttgart/ New York: Fischer [various titles, different departments] [continued as *Journal of Microbiology* – with various titles].

Zentralblatt für Mathematik und ihre Grenzgebiete/ Mathematics Abstracts (1931ff.) Published by the Heidelberger Akademie der Wissenschaften/ Fachinformationszentrum Karlsruhe. Berlin/ Heidelberg: Springer.

Zentralblatt für Zoologie, allgemeine und experimentelle Biologie (1894–1918). Leipzig: Teubner [1894–1911 *Zoologisches Zentralblatt*].

Zhao, Jin (1999) Wirtschaftsdeutsch in China: Eine Umfrage unter möglichen Arbeitgebern für Germanistikabsolventen. In *Info DaF* 26 (6): 582–600.

Zhu, Jianhua (2000) Überlegungen zur interlingualen und interkulturellen Fachkommunikation Chinesisch-Deutsch. In: *Arbeiten zur Interkulturellen Kommunikation Chinesisch-Deutsch.* Shanghai: Verlag der Tongji-Universität.

—— (2007) "Hochschuldeutsch" – Deutsch als Anwendungsfach an Hochschulen und Universitäten [in China!]. In Ammon/ Reinbothe/ Zhu, 141–152.

—— (2009) Entwicklung vom Deutschen als Anwendungsfach in China seit 2000. In Fan, Jieping/ Li, Yuan (eds.) *Deutsch als Fremdsprache aus internationaler Perspektive – Neuere Trends und Tendenzen.* München: iudicium, 426–433.

Zhu, Xiaoan (2007) Die Berufschancen von Chinesinnen und Chinesen mit Deutschkenntnissen. In Ammon/ Reinbothe/ Zhu, 210–222.

Zich, František (2001) *The Bearers of Development of the Cross-Border Community on Czech-German Border.* Praha: Institute of Sociology, Academy of Sciences of the Czech Republic.

Ziegler, Arne (1996) *Deutsche Sprache in Brasilien. Untersuchungen zum Sprachwandel und zum Sprachgebrauch der deutschstämmigen Brasilianer in Rio Grande do Sul.* Essen: Die blaue Eule.

Ziegler, Jürgen (1994) Die deutsche Sprache im japanischem Musikleben. In Ammon 1994d, 6368.

Zimmer, Dieter E. (1997) *Deutsch und anders. Die Sprache im Modernisierungsfieber.* Reinbek bei Hamburg: Rowohlt.

Zimmermann, Mosche/ Hotam, Yotam (eds.) (2005) *Zweimal Heimat. Die Jeckes zwischen Mitteleuropa und Nahost.* Frankfurt a.M.: Beerenverlag.

Zingel, Wolfgang-Peter (2002) Indien zwischen Analphabetismus und Software-Entwicklung. In Schucher, G. (ed.) *Asien und das Internet.* Hamburg: Institut für Asienkunde, 63–69.

Zoological Record (1864ff.) Philadelphia, PA: BIOSIS.

Zoologischer Bericht (1922–1943/44) Jena: Fischer.

INDEX

The following index entries are intended primarily as keywords which also occur in the text. In some cases, they are also descriptors summarising parts of the text. German and German-speaking have not been included as separate entries but only in combination with other expressions.